THE OXFORD HANDBOOK OF

AFRICAN AMERICAN LANGUAGE

THE OXFORD HANDBOOK OF

AFRICAN AMERICAN LANGUAGE

Edited by

SONJA LANEHART

OXFORD

UNIVERSITY PRESS

Oxford University Press is a department of the University of
Oxford. It furthers the University's objective of excellence in research,
scholarship, and education by publishing worldwide.

Oxford   New York

Auckland   Cape Town   Dar es Salaam   Hong Kong   Karachi
Kuala Lumpur   Madrid   Melbourne   Mexico City   Nairobi
New Delhi   Shanghai   Taipei   Toronto

With offices in

Argentina   Austria   Brazil   Chile   Czech Republic   France   Greece
Guatemala   Hungary   Italy   Japan   Poland   Portugal   Singapore
South Korea   Switzerland   Thailand   Turkey   Ukraine   Vietnam

Oxford is a registered trademark of Oxford University Press
in the UK and certain other countries.

Published in the United States of America by
Oxford University Press
198 Madison Avenue, New York, NY 10016

© Oxford University Press 2015

Cataloging-in-Publication data is on file at the Library of Congress
ISBN 978-0-19-979539-0

3 5 7 9 8 6 4 2
Printed in the United States of America
on acid-free paper

Contents

PART I ORIGINS AND HISTORICAL PERSPECTIVES

PART III STRUCTURE AND DESCRIPTION

PART IV CHILD LANGUAGE ACQUISITION AND DEVELOPMENT

PART VII LANGUAGE AND IDENTITY

LIST OF FIGURES

LIST OF TABLES

Acknowledgments

THE *Oxford Handbook of African American Language* (affectionately named *OHAAL*) has truly been a labor of love and commitment to highlight and further research on language use in the African American community. Such a massive project could not have been possible without the generous contributions of many who committed to this task. First, thanks to Oxford University Press Linguistics Editor, Brian Hurley, for initiating this huge project in 2008, and his successor, Hallie Stebbins, for taking over so effectively in 2013.

Second, thanks go to the authors who contributed their time and talents, especially those authors who were able to heed the suggestion to co-author with an emerging scholar in the field.

Next, thanks go to the external reviewers who graciously responded to invitations to critique and provide feedback for whole sections of *OHAAL*, sometimes on short notice when a chapter trickled in later than expected and turnaround time was short: Drs. Erik Thomas, Gillian Sankoff, and Walt Wolfram, the MVPs who came through especially in a pinch, as well as Drs. Brandi Newkirk-Turner, Julie Sweetland, Marcyliena Morgan, Rodney Hopson, and two ad hoc reviewers who asked to remain anonymous. Their feedback to authors was crucial for the quality of the chapters and sections—though, of course, their feedback is not responsible for any shortcomings.

Of course, thanks go to funding provided by the University of Texas at San Antonio (UTSA) Brackenridge Endowed Chair in Literature and the Humanities and the Office of the Dean of the College of Liberal and Fine Arts. Their funding resulted in the opportunity to hire a copy-editor and indexer, as well as research assistants. Speaking of which, special thanks go to the personal copy-editor and indexer hired, Lamont Antieau, who was patient, so very patient when the project went over the deadline, and to the UTSA research assistants, Krystin Piña Bankston and Ayesha Malik. Research assistant does not truly grasp all that they have meant to the successful completion of this project. Krystin communicated with authors and editors with a smile and kind voice to keep this project—and Dr. Lanehart—on track before leaving UTSA for another institution. Fortunately, Krystin's work ethic was restored with the hiring of Ayesha Malik, whose enthusiasm and professionalism are beyond impressive.

Last, but not least, gratitude goes to family, friends, and colleagues for their endurance and sustenance throughout this journey. To God be the glory, honor, and praise for reminding us daily that He will never give us more than we can bear.

S.L.

ABOUT THE EDITOR

SONJA LANEHART is Professor and Brackenridge Endowed Chair in Literature and the Humanities at the University of Texas at San Antonio. Her research includes language and uses of literacy in African American communities, language and identity using Critical Race Theory, and educational implications and applications of sociolinguistic research. Her publications include *Sociocultural and Historical Contexts of African American English* (2001), *Sista, Speak! Black Women Kinfolk Talk about Language and Literacy* (2002), and *African American Women's Language: Discourse, Education, and Identity* (2009).

LIST OF CONTRIBUTORS

H. SAMY ALIM is Professor of Education and, by courtesy, Anthropology and Linguistics at Stanford University where he directs the Center for Race, Ethnicity, and Language. His research explores styleshifting, the use of language in local and global Hip Hop communities, the politics of language and identity, and the complex relationships between language, race, power, and education. His most recent books include *Articulate While Black: Barack Obama, Language, and Race in the U.S.* (Oxford, 2012, with Geneva Smitherman) and *Global Linguistic Flows: Hip Hop Culture(s), Youth Identities, and the Politics of Language* (Routledge, 2009, with Awad Ibrahim and Alastair Pennycook).

KATE T. ANDERSON is Assistant Professor in the Mary Lou Fulton Teachers College at Arizona State University. Her interdisciplinary research draws from sociolinguistics, anthropology of education, and literacies studies. Her main research interests center on ideologies of language, literacies, and learning as they relate to opportunity and equity in learning environments, broadly defined. Kate uses discourse analysis, ethnography, and other qualitative methods to study the ways that language, interaction, and taken for granted assumptions about how we speak, learn, and categorize others shape our everyday realities as well as our sociohistorical moment.

GUY BAILEY is Founding President of the University of Texas-Rio Grande Valley and has served as President and Provost at several other universities. He maintains an active research agenda focused on the synchronic approach to language change, on approaches to time in dialectology and sociolinguistics, on the effects of methods on results, and on the speech of African Americans and Southerners.

BETTINA BAKER is Associate Professor of Reading at Flagler College in Saint Augustine, Florida. With William Labov, she has developed and tested programs for raising literacy levels in low-income schools in Philadelphia, Atlanta and throughout California. As Senior Director of Assessment and Curriculum at Chester Community Charter School, her efforts with low-income children include the development of curricula which achieved adequate yearly progress consistently. In Florida, she has partnered with low-income schools to enhance the knowledge and practices of pre-service teachers while serving struggling readers.

JOHN BAUGH is Margaret Bush Wilson Professor in Arts and Sciences at Washington University in St. Louis and Professor Emeritus of Education and Linguistics at Stanford University. He uses linguistic research to promote advances in equal opportunity in the fields of education, employment, medicine, and the law. His studies of linguistic profiling are included in the national science exhibit created by the American Anthropological Association titled, "Race: Are We So Different?" He has published several books related to the African American linguistic experience and has served as a consultant for the PBS documentaries: "The Story of English" and "Do You Speak American?"

ROBERT BAYLEY is Professor of Linguistics at the University of California, Davis. He has conducted research on variation in English, Spanish, Chinese, ASL, and Italian Sign Language as well as ethnographic studies of US Latino communities. His recent book-length publications include *Sociolinguistic Variation: Theories, Methods, and Applications* (edited with Ceil Lucas, 2007), *The Hidden Treasure of Black ASL: Its History and Structure* (with Carolyn McCaskill, Ceil Lucas, and Joseph Hill, 2011), *The Oxford Handbook of Sociolinguistics* (edited with Richard Cameron and Ceil Lucas, 2013), and the five-volume collection, *Language Variation and Change* (edited with Richard Cameron, 2015).

RENÉE A. BLAKE is Associate Professor in the Departments of Linguistics and Social & Cultural Analysis at New York University. Her research examines language contact, race, ethnicity, and class with a focus on African American English, Caribbean Creole English, and New York City English. Her work has been published in journals including *Language in Society, Language and Education, Journal of English Linguistics, Language, Variation and Change*, and *English Today*. She has served as a consultant to many programs and organizations including Disney and the Ford Foundation. She developed two web-based linguistic sites: "Word. The Online Journal on African American English" (http://www.africanamericanenglish.com) and "Voices of New York" (http://www.nyu.edu/classes/blake.map2005).

JENNIFER BLOOMQUIST is Associate Professor of Linguistics and the coordinator of the Africana Studies Program at Gettysburg College. Her work has been published in *First Language, Journal of Pragmatics, Multilingua*, and *American Speech*. Her most recent article, "The Dirty Third: Contributions of Southern Hip Hop to the Study of African American English" (with Isaac Hancock) appears in *The Southern Journal of Linguistics*, Spring 2013. Her research focuses on African American Englishes in the regional context and she is currently at work on a project on the representation of African American English and its role in the construction of ethnicity in children's animated films.

ERICA BRITT is Assistant Professor of Sociolinguistics at the University of Michigan-Flint. Her research focuses on the use of African American Language in public domains and her areas of interest include style shifting, language ideology, and identity performance.

TAMARA BUTLER is Assistant Professor at Michigan State University in the Department of English. She teaches English Education and African American and African Studies courses. Her research focuses on youth activism, social justice, and learning through critical community engagements.

TEMPII B. CHAMPION is Associate Professor of Communication Sciences and Disorders at Long Island University Brooklyn Campus. Her current interests include assessment of African American children's vocabulary, mother-child interactions, and narrative language development. She has published a book on African American children's narration, *Understanding Storytelling among African American Children: A Journey from Africa to America* (2003).

PATRICIA CUKOR-AVILA is Associate Professor at the University of North Texas. Her primary research focuses on linguistic variation and change, specifically in African American Vernacular English (AAVE). Her longitudinal panel study (1988-present) of AAVE in a rural Texas community has provided much of the data for publications concerning approaches to sociolinguistic fieldwork, transmission and diffusion, as well as documenting innovations in African American English. Patricia also researches linguistic stereotyping and accent discrimination. She is currently conducting cross-disciplinary research, incorporating the analytical methods of variation studies into traditional perceptual dialectology research through the use of a GIS and R, to map dialect perceptions and attitudes about perceived dialect regions.

CHARLES E. DEBOSE is Professor Emeritus in the Department of English at California State University, East Bay. His scholarly interests include sociolinguistics, pidgin-creole studies, language varieties of the African Diaspora, language planning, and African American religion. His recent publications include *The Sociology of African American Language: A Language Planning Perspective* (2005); "The Ebonics Phenomenon, Language Planning and the Hegemony of Standard English," in *Talkin Black: Language, Education and Social Change* (Alim and Baugh, eds., 2006), and "Church Lady Talk: African American Women's Language and the Church," in *African American Women's Language: Discourse, Education and Identity* (Lanehart, ed., 2009).

EVANGELOS EVANGELOU is Lecturer in Statistics at the University of Bath. His research is in methodology for estimation and prediction for spatial and spatial-temporal models, spatial sampling design, and Bayesian computational methods.

SABRIYA FISHER is a PhD candidate at the University of Pennsylvania, advised by Gillian Sankoff and William Labov. Her master's thesis (Université de Lyon, 2011) focused on copula variation in Guyanais French Creole. Her research interests include variation in Creoles and African American English, syntactic change, language contact, and fieldwork.

JAMILA GILLENWATERS is Program Coordinator for the Academic English Mastery Program—a national model for serving Standard English Learners. She has over a decade of experience in education as a teacher, administrator, and adjunct professor at the University of Southern California. Her research focuses on equitable learning opportunities for culturally and linguistically diverse students in urban communities, specializing in culturally and linguistically responsive pedagogy.

SHELOME GOODEN is Associate Professor of Linguistics at the University of Pittsburgh, and currently serves as Department Chair. Her research focuses primarily on the prosodic classification and intonational phonology of Caribbean Creole languages. She has published more generally on Afro-American varieties on phonological and phonetic properties of reduplication, stress, and intonation in Jamaican Creole, prosody in Trinidadian Creole, language and identity and intonation in African American English, and tense-aspect variation in Belizean Creole. Her most recent publication, "Aspects of the Intonational Phonology of Jamaican Creole," appears in *Prosodic Typology II: The Phonology of Intonation and Phrasing*, edited by Sun-Ah Jun (Oxford University Press, 2014).

LISA J. GREEN is Professor of Linguistics and Director of the Center for the Study of African American Language at the University of Massachusetts Amherst. Green's research is on the syntax of African American English (AAE). In moving away from the traditional approach of studying isolated features of AAE that differ maximally from constructions in the standard and mainstream varieties of English, she considers systems in the AAE grammar, such as the systems of tense/aspect marking and negation. Her work on child AAE addresses questions about optionality and variation in language development. Green is the author of *African American English: A Linguistic Introduction* (Cambridge University Press) and *Language and the African American Child* (Cambridge University Press).

RANDALL HENDRICK is Professor of Linguistics at the University of North Carolina at Chapel Hill. His research focuses on syntactic theory. That work currently targets the syntax-semantics interface and computational theories of the interaction between memory and language.

JOSEPH HILL is Assistant Professor in the Specialized Education Services department at the University of North Carolina at Greensboro. His research interests are sociohistorical and sociolinguistic aspects of African-American variety of American Sign Language and attitudes and ideologies about signing varieties in the American Deaf community. His contributions include *The Hidden Treasure of Black ASL: Its History and Structure* (2011), which he co-authored with Carolyn McCaskill, Ceil Lucas, and Robert Bayley, and *Language Attitudes in the American Deaf Community* (2012).

SHARROKY HOLLIE is Executive Director of the Center for Culturally Responsive Teaching and Learning, a not-for-profit organization dedicated to building culturally responsive communities across the country. He is an assistant professor in teacher education for the California State University and co-founder of the Culture and Language Academy of Success laboratory school. His research primarily focuses on culturally and linguistically responsive instructional practices for K–12 teachers and effective professional development.

RAMONDA HORTON, PhD, CCC-SLP is Associate Professor in the School of Communication Sciences and Disorders at Florida State University. Her research is concerned with the development and assessment of language in children from culturally and linguistically diverse backgrounds. Research publications have focused on the relationships between language performance, culture, African American English, and socioeconomic status.

DAVID E. KIRKLAND is Associate Professor of English and Urban Education at New York University and bestselling author, activist, cultural critic, educator, and researcher. His transdisciplinary scholarship examines the intersections of language, race, and gender in the lives of urban youth. Kirkland has spent the last decade analyzing material and linguistic artifacts of groups of urban American youth and has expertise in critical literary, linguistic, and ethnographic research methods. He has received many awards for his groundbreaking work, including a 2011 NAEd Spencer Postdoctoral Fellowship and a 2009 Ford Foundation Postdoctoral Fellowship Award, among many others. He is well published, and has authored, co-authored, edited, or co-edited five books, including the TC Press bestseller, *A Search Past Silence: The Literacy of Black Males*, and the newly released, *Students Right to Their Own Language*, a critical sourcebook published by Bedford/St. Martin's Press. He can be reached by email at: dk64@nyu.edu.

MARY E. KOHN is Assistant Professor at Kansas State University. Her interests include language and ethnicity, regional variation, and language variation across adolescence. Her work has recently appeared in *Language Variation and Change* and the *Journal of the Acoustical Society of America*. Her monograph on language variation across adolescence in AAL is forthcoming through *Publications of the American Dialect Society*.

WILLIAM A. KRETZSCHMAR, JR. is Harry and Jane Willson Professor in Humanities at the University of Georgia. He also has appointments at the University of Glasgow and the University of Oulu. He is Editor of the American Linguistic Atlas Project, the oldest and largest national research project to survey how people speak differently across the country, which has led to his preparation of American pronunciations for the online *Oxford English Dictionary*. He also maintains a community-language field site in Roswell, GA. He has been influential in development of digital methods for analysis and presentation of language variation, including application of complexity science.

WILLIAM LABOV is Professor of Linguistics at the University of Pennsylvania. He has carried out research on African American English in New York City and Philadelphia, With Bettina Baker, he has developed and tested programs for raising literacy levels in low-income schools in Philadelphia, Atlanta, and Southern California. He is a senior author of *Portals to Reading*, an Intervention Program for Grades 3–8 (Houghton-Mifflin-Harcourt).

CEIL LUCAS is Professor of Linguistics, Emerita at Gallaudet University, where she has taught since 1982. She was raised in Guatemala City and Rome, Italy. She is a sociolinguist with broad interests in the structure and use of sign languages. She has co-authored and edited many articles and books, including *The Linguistics of American Sign Language*, 5th ed. (with Clayton Valli, Kristin Mulrooney, and Miako Villanueva,

2010) and *The Hidden Treasure of Black ASL: Its History and Structure* (co-authored with Carolyn McCaskill, Robert Bayley, and Joseph Hill).

AYESHA M. MALIK is a dual-major undergraduate in Political Science and Anthropology at the University of Texas at San Antonio. She attributes her love of linguistics to her family, William Ziller, and Dr. Sonja Lanehart and she would like to thank them in supporting her throughout the process of working on *OHAAL*. Her research interests center on the intersectionality of language, culture, identity, and religion, particularly in examining the relationship between Hip Hop Nation Language and Islam, as well as the Hindi-Urdu language controversy in the respective histories, religions, and politics of India and Pakistan. She is also interested in researching linguistic identity in her community of Alief, Texas.

ALLYSSA MCCABE, is Professor of Psychology at University of Massachusetts Lowell. She studies how narrative develops with age, how parents and teachers can facilitate narrative development, and cultural differences in narration. She is coauthor of a theoretical approach to early literacy called the Comprehensive Language Approach, which looks at ways that various strands of oral and written language affect each other in acquiring full literacy. She has published a book, *Chameleon Readers: Teaching Children to Appreciate All Kinds of Good Stories* (1996).

CAROLYN MCCASKILL is Professor in the ASL and Deaf Studies Department at Gallaudet University and has taught in that department since 1996. She attended the Alabama School for the Negro Deaf in Talladega and was in the first integrated class in 1968 at the Alabama School for the Deaf. She received her M.A. degree in Counseling with the Deaf, B.A. in Psychology and PhD in Administration and Supervision from Gallaudet University. Carolyn has conducted numerous seminars and workshops related to Black Deaf people.

MONIQUE T. MILLS, is Assistant Professor in the Department of Speech and Hearing Science at The Ohio State University. Dr. Mills is an affiliate faculty of the Institute for Population Research. Her research explores the social, cognitive, and linguistic resources that school-age African American English-speaking children draw upon to narrate. She teaches courses in language acquisition, multicultural aspects of communication and its disorders, and language disorders of later childhood.

SIMANIQUE MOODY is Assistant Professor at Leiden University. She teaches in the Leiden University Centre for Linguistics and the Bachelor of International Studies program. Simanique is a sociolinguist and a creolist whose current research examines regional variation in African American English and Gullah/Geechee and the historical relationship between these two varieties. Her other scholarly interests include language contact, language variation, language change, language and ethnicity, and language and culture.

MARCYLIENA MORGAN is Professor in the Department of African and African American Studies at Harvard University and the Executive Director of the Hiphop Archive. She received her PhD from the Graduate School of Education at the University of

Pennsylvania. Her research interests include: urban speech communities; the African Diaspora; language, culture, and identity; discourse strategies; verbal performance; Hip Hop language and culture; and language and education. Marcyliena Morgan has conducted field research on the African Diaspora, identity and language in the United States, England, and the Caribbean. She has received major grants from the Ford Foundation and the Centers for Disease Control and Prevention (CDC). She is the author of many publications that focus on youth, gender, language, culture, identity, sociolinguistics, discourse, and interaction, including *Language, Discourse and Power in African American Culture* (Cambridge University Press, 2002), *The Real Hiphop—Battling for Knowledge, Power, and Respect in the Underground* (Duke University Press, 2008), and *Speech Communities: Key Topics in Linguistic Anthropology* (Cambridge University Press, 2014).

SALIKOKO S. MUFWENE is Frank J. McLoraine Distinguished Service Professor of Linguistics and the College at the University of Chicago, where he also serves as Professor on the Committee on Evolutionary Biology and on the Committee on the Conceptual and Historical Studies of Science. His current research is on language evolution, including the indigenization of English and other colonial European languages worldwide. He is the author of *The Ecology of Language Evolution* (Cambridge University Press, 2001), *Créoles, écologie sociale, évolution linguistique* (l'Harmattan, 2005), and *Language Evolution: Contact, Competition and Change* (Continuum Press, 2008); and the (co-)editor of *Africanisms in Afro-American Language Varieties* (UGA Press, 1993) and *African American English: Structure, History and Use* (Routledge, 1998). He edits the book series *Cambridge Approaches to Language Contact*.

BRANDI L. NEWKIRK-TURNER, PHD, CCC-SLP is Assistant Professor in the Department of Communicative Disorders at Jackson State University. Her current research examines language acquisition in the context of dialect variation and multicultural issues that are relevant to the speech-language assessment of nonmainstream dialect speakers, with a particular emphasis on AAE-speaking children.

LUIZA NEWLIN-ŁUKOWICZ is a PhD candidate in the Linguistics Department at New York University. She holds an M.A. in English Linguistics from Eastern Michigan University and an M.A. in English Philology from Adam Mickiewicz University. Her research employs socio-phonetic methodologies to investigate how social and cognitive factors determine the outcomes of language contact and the diffusion of regional variation. She has studied how minority groups, such as African Americans, Caribbean Americans, and Polish Americans, utilize linguistic variation to project complex ethno-racial identities. Building on this work, her current research integrates acoustic methods, formal approaches to linguistics, and social theory to investigate how White ethnics use language to construct their identities in multicultural contexts.

JANNA B. OETTING is Professor in the Department of Communication Sciences and Disorders and the Interdisciplinary Program in Linguistics at Louisiana State University. Her research and teaching interests are in child language acquisition and child language disorders within the context of different dialects of English. She also conducts research and teaches on topics related to the effects of poverty on children's acquisition of language, language testing, and language services for children from low-income families.

JAMES BRAXTON PETERSON is Director of Africana Studies and Associate Professor of English at Lehigh University. His first book, *The Hip Hop Underground and African American Culture*, was published by Palgrave Macmillan Press (2014). He is also the founder of Hip Hop Scholars, LLC, an association of Hip Hop generational scholars dedicated to researching and developing the cultural and educational potential of Hip Hop, urban, and youth cultures. Peterson is a regular blogger for the Huffington Post, a contributor to TheGrio.com, and he has written opinion pieces for OkayAfrica.com, BET.com, and The Daily Beast. He is currently an MSNBC contributor and has appeared on MSNBC, Al-Jazeera, CNN, HLN, Fox News, CBS, ABC News, ESPN, and other networks as an expert on race, politics, and popular culture.

JACQUELYN RAHMAN is Associate Professor of Linguistics at Miami University. Her research focuses primarily on topics related to linguistic expressions of social consciousness. She has written about the origin and perpetuation of epithets and slurs, as they emerge from ideologies. Publications in that area include a formal analysis of the history and use of the N-word in the African American community. Further publications address linguistic practices and attitudes of the African American middle class and African American pop culture as social commentary. More broadly, Rahman has written about historic stereotyped representations of various racial and ethnic groups in the media.

HOWARD RAMBSY II is Associate Professor of English at Southern Illinois University Edwardsville, where he teaches courses on American and African American literature. He has written articles and curated mixed media exhibits focusing on literary history, poetry, and the intersections of race and technology.

JOHN R. RICKFORD is J. E. Wallace Sterling Professor of Linguistics and the Humanities at Stanford University, and President (2015) of the Linguistic Society of America. His main interest is the study of language variation and change in relation to linguistic and social constraints (like ethnicity, social class) and style, and using linguistics to address educational, legal, and other challenges confronting vernacular speakers. His data come primarily from US Englishes, especially African American Vernacular English, and English-based creoles, including his native Guyanese Creole. The author of many articles, he is (co-) author or (co-) editor of several books, including *Dimensions of a Creole Continuum; African American Vernacular English; Spoken Soul: The Story of Black English* (winner of an American Book Award); *Style and Sociolinguistic Variation; Language in the USA: Themes for the 21st Century; Language, Culture and Caribbean Identity;* and *African American, Creole, and Other Vernacular Englishes in Education.* For more information, visit http://www.johnrickford.com.

TYSON L. ROSE is Director of the Upward Bound Program and graduate student at the University of Massachusetts, Amherst. Tyson is a lecturer and facilitator who has taught numerous courses and workshops which focus on: social justice, critical pedagogy, critical theory, and Hip Hop-based educational practices. Tyson's research and practice interests include critical, social justice Hip Hop pedagogy, and social justice-based educational leadership and organizational development. In addition Tyson is one of the original members and organizers of 3rd EyE Unlimited, a Hip Hop-based youth advocacy, activist, and community organization and is a member of the Julius Ford/Harriet Tubman Healthy Living Community, an organization dedicated to fostering social justice and healthy, vibrant communities through critical thinking, leadership development, self-expression, cultural exchange, and environmental sustainability.

EDGAR W. SCHNEIDER is Chair and Professor of English Linguistics at the University of Regensburg, Germany. In his dissertation (published as *American Earlier Black English*, University of Alabama Press, 1989) he analyzed the WPA ex-slave narratives, and he has continued to investigate diachronically relevant sources of African American and other dialects, next to his more recent research specialization in "World Englishes." He has published and lectured on all continents on topics in the dialectology, sociolinguistics, and history of English and its varieties. He edited the scholarly journal *English World-Wide* for many years and has written and edited about twenty books, including *Handbook of Varieties of English* (Mouton, 2004, 2008), *Postcolonial English* (Cambridge University Press, 2007), and *English around the World* (Cambridge University Press, 2011).

CARA SHOUSTERMAN is a PhD candidate in the Department of Linguistics at New York University. She began her linguistic studies with a B.A. from McGill University in Montreal, Quebec. Her work on African American English and West Indian American English has appeared in *English Today* and the *Journal of English Linguistics*. Her research interests are centered on variation and change in American English, and the ways in which language interacts with ethnicity. Her dissertation "Speaking English in Spanish Harlem: Language Change in Puerto Rican English" is a sociolinguistic study of New York-born Puerto Ricans affiliated with a neighborhood community center in East Harlem, New York, which explores how community change is reflected in language. She is a regular contributor to 'Word. The Online Journal on African American English' (http://www.africanamericanenglish.com).

JOHN VICTOR SINGLER is Professor of Linguistics at New York University. He holds an M.A. and PhD in linguistics from UCLA and an M.A. in African Area Studies from the University of London (SOAS). His ties to Liberia date to 1969, when he began his teaching career in Greenville, Sinoe County. Grants from the NSF, NEH, and Fulbright have supported his study of English in Liberia. His linguistic interests span language contact, variationist sociolinguistics, phonology, pidgins and creoles, the history of African American English, African languages, endangered languages, and language in New York City. He is the author of *An Introduction to Liberian English*. With Silvia Kouwenberg, he co-edited *The Handbook of Pidgin and Creole Studies*.

WALTER SISTRUNK is a visiting professor of English at the College of Staten Island City University of New York and research associate at the Center for the Study of

African American Language and the Language Acquisition Lab at the University of Massachusetts. He has a PhD in African American and African Studies from Michigan State University. His research interests are syntax, syntactic variation, and language acquisition. Currently, Walter is investigating the acquisition of relative clauses in African American English, and the correlation between the absence of relative pronouns in relative clauses and its correlation with the occurrence of other structures in African American English such as vacuous movement, resumptive pronouns, and the absence of X-trace effects. In the area of language and culture, Walter is interested in women's use of language in Hip Hop and Dancehall, the linguistic origins of rap, and language contact.

RICHARD L. SMITH is Mark L. Reed III Distinguished Professor of Statistics and Professor of Biostatistics in the University of North Carolina, Chapel Hill, and Director of the Statistical and Applied Mathematical Sciences Institute. His research is in environmental statistics and associated areas of methodological research such as spatial statistics, time series analysis, and extreme value theory, with applications including climate change and the health effects of air pollution. His honors include Fellow of the American Statistical Association and the Institute of Mathematical Statistics, Elected Member of the International Statistical Institute, and the Guy Medal in Silver of the Royal Statistical Society.

GENEVA SMITHERMAN is University Distinguished Professor Emerita of English and Executive Committee member of African American and African Studies at Michigan State University (MSU). A pioneering scholar-activist in Sociolinguistics and Black Studies, Smitherman was a member of the first faculty in "Afro-American Studies" at Harvard University, and she helped create Black Studies programs at Wayne State University and MSU. She was the chief expert witness and advocate for the children in *King v. Ann Arbor* (the "Black English" Federal court case). Since 1972, she has worked on the Conference on College Composition and Communication's "Students' Right to Their Own Language" and related language policy issues. She is internationally known and has received several awards for her research, which includes language policy and planning in South Africa, challenging myths about African American Language, and advocating for the language rights of marginalized communities around the globe. She has authored and edited/co-edited fifteen books and monographs and more than 125 articles, essays, and published opinion pieces. Dr. Smitherman's latest book, *Articulate While Black: Barack Obama, Language and Race in the U.S.*, is co-authored with Dr. H. Samy Alim.

ARTHUR K. SPEARS is Presidential Professor at The City University of New York (CUNY). He is a member of the Linguistics and Anthropology Programs at the CUNY Graduate Center and chair of the Anthropology Department at The City College. His research spans linguistic anthropology, sociolinguistics, pidgins/creoles and language contact, grammatical analysis, race and ethnicity, education, and ideology. The languages he specializes in are African American English and Haitian Creole, along with other French-related creole languages. Prof. Spears is the founder and first editor of *Transforming Anthropology*, a journal of the American Anthropological Association and is a former president of the Society for Pidgin and Creole Linguistics. His latest book is *Languages and Dialects in the U.S.: Focus on Diversity and Linguistics* (co-editor, 2014).

IDA J. STOCKMAN, PHD, CCC-SLP, is a speech-language pathologist and Professor Emerita at Michigan State University (MSU). Her scholarly work helped to change the framework from a deficit to difference approach to investigating the language of young African American children in research, teaching, and professional credentialing practices. This work is included among more than 200 scholarly contributions inclusive of refereed and invited journal publications, book chapters, and conference/workshop presentations. An MSU Distinguished Faculty awardee in 1996, Stockman is also a Fellow of the American Speech, Language and Hearing Association and a recipient of its Honors in 2006.

J. MICHAEL TERRY is Associate Professor of Linguistics at the University of North Carolina at Chapel Hill. His research focuses on semantic theory. That work currently targets the semantics of tense and aspect in dialects of American English with particular emphasis on African American English.

ERIK R. THOMAS is a Professor at North Carolina State University. His research interests lie in sociophonetics, the overlap of language variation and phonetics. He has published widely on minority dialects, including the language of African Americans, and is currently working on a project on Mexican American English. He is also interested in ways that sociophonetic research can be expanded to encompass cognitive and neurolinguistic approaches.

K. C. NAT TURNER is Associate Professor of Teacher Education and Curriculum Studies at the University of Massachusetts, Amherst. Currently he is head of the concentration of Language, Literacy and Culture and coordinates programs in Bilingual, ESL, Multicultural and Reading & Writing. Dr. Turner's socially engaged scholarship and courses span the areas of language and literacy practices of culturally and linguistically diverse urban adolescents (particularly African Americans) in school and non-school settings; racial justice/reparations in education; Hip Hop culture and studies of emergent technologies in community/school/university collaborations. In addition, Dr. Turner has served as faculty advisor for Student Bridges a student-initiated outreach program connecting UMass students with community-based organizations, schools and tutoring-mentoring, college awareness and policy initiatives.

GERARD VAN HERK is Canada Research Chair in Regional Language and Oral Text at Memorial University of Newfoundland. His research generally involves quantitative analysis of morphological and syntactic variables (question formation, past temporal reference, the simple present, negation) in varieties of English (African American, Barbadian, Québec, and especially Newfoundland). He is interested in questions of identity, local-ness, salience, and gender performance. He has published or presented about 100 papers on sociolinguistic topics. He is also interested in the teaching of Linguistics, including how to integrate primary research into the undergraduate classroom. He is the author of *What is Sociolinguistics?* (2012) and the co-editor of *Data Collection in Sociolinguistics* (2013).

JANNEKE VAN HOFWEGEN is a PhD candidate in linguistics at Stanford University. A sociolinguist primarily, she focuses her research on ethnic and world varieties of English. At Stanford, she is a contributing member of the Voices of California research team, where she documents and analyzes sociophonetic variation in the as-yet understudied California inland (non-urban) dialect region, with particular attention paid to minority ethnic and LGBT communities. In addition to her work at Stanford, she is an associate on the North Carolina Language and Life Project (NCLLP), where she studies morphosyntactic variation in African American English from a one-of-a-kind longitudinal sample of African American children, as well as sociophonetic variation in both African American and Chicano Englishes.

JAMES A. WALKER is Associate Professor of Linguistics at York University (Toronto). An expert in variationist sociolinguistics, his research interests include phonology, morphology, syntax, language contact, pidgins and creoles, and ethnicity.

JULIE A. WASHINGTON is Professor in the Department of Educational Psychology and Special Education's Communication Sciences and Disorders program. Dr. Washington is an affiliate faculty of the Research on the Challenges of Acquiring Language and Literacy initiative and the Urban Child Study Center at Georgia State University.

TRACEY L. WELDON is Associate Professor in the English Department and the Linguistics Program at the University of South Carolina. She is a quantitative sociolinguist, specializing in language variation, with a particular focus on Gullah and other African American Language varieties. Weldon is currently writing a book on Middle-Class African American English.

JESSICA WHITE-SUSTAÍTA received her PhD in Linguistics from The University of Texas at Austin in 2012 and is currently an instructor of English as a Second Language at the Texas Intensive English Program in Austin. Her research focuses on both formal and social properties of individual and cross-linguistic variation and change among closely related systems in North America and the Caribbean, with a concentration on African American English, New Orleans varieties, and English-based creoles.

BRIANA WHITESIDE is a graduate PhD student at the University of Alabama Tuscaloosa. Her research interests include Black feminism, science fiction, and representations of Black women in popular culture. She has produced research and writing on Octavia Butler, The Black Panther Party, and natural hair. She earned her B.A. in English at Tougaloo College in Mississippi and her M.A. in English at Southern Illinois University Edwardsville.

ROSE WILKERSON is Lecturer at the University of California at Berkeley. She holds a PhD in Linguistics with a specialization in African American English. Her areas of research are the speech of single black mothers in the Mississippi Delta and the representation of US ethnic dialects in video games. Dr. Wilkerson has had nearly a decade of teaching courses on US minority languages and has taught at different academic institutions, such as University of California at Berkeley, Indiana University at Bloomington, Williams College, and Washington University in St. Louis.

DONALD WINFORD is Professor of Linguistics at The Ohio State University. He did his undergraduate degree in English at King's College, University of London and his PhD in Linguistics at the University of York, England. His teaching and research interests are in creole linguistics, variationist sociolinguistics, contact linguistics, and African-American English. He is the author of *Predication in Caribbean English Creoles* (1993) and *An Introduction to Contact Linguistics* (2003). He has been editor of the *Journal of Pidgin and Creole Languages* since August 2001.

WALT WOLFRAM is William C. Friday Distinguished University Professor at North Carolina State University, where he also directs the North Carolina Language and Life Project. He has pioneered research on social and ethnic dialects of American English since the 1960s, including early research on the descriptive status of African American Language in the urban North and later work on its regional distribution in the rural South. His current research focus is on the development of AAE during the early lifespan, based on a unique longitudinal database that spans twenty years.

TOYA A. WYATT, is Professor in the Department of Human Communication Studies, Communicative Disorders program at California State University, Fullerton. Dr. Wyatt's primary areas of teaching and research focus on the language development and clinical speech and language assessment of children from African American English dialect and bilingual backgrounds. She is the author of several publications dealing with speech-language assessment of children and adults from culturally and linguistically diverse populations. She has also served as an associate editor and an editorial and test bias review consultant for Communication Sciences and Disorders professional journals and test development companies.

THE OXFORD HANDBOOK OF

AFRICAN AMERICAN LANGUAGE

LANGUAGE USE IN AFRICAN AMERICAN COMMUNITIES

An Introduction

SONJA LANEHART AND AYESHA M. MALIK

1 INTRODUCTION

RESEARCH on language use in African American communities began as early as 1920 with a few preliminary investigations into the variety, known then as "Negro non-standard English" (Krapp 1924, 1925), followed later by Lorenzo Dow Turner's influential work, *Africanisms in the Gullah Dialect* (1949). However, research did not truly escalate until the 1960s and 1970s with the work of linguists such as Robbins Burling (1973), Joey L. Dillard (1972, 1977), Ralph Fasold (1972), William Labov and colleagues (1968, 1972), Geneva Smitherman (1977), William Stewart (1967), and Walt Wolfram (1969). As the body of work developed, three very broad categories emerged: linguistic structure and description, origins and development, and language use and attitudes—especially in education.

Since the 1996–97 Ebonics controversy, the number of books about language use in African American communities has grown significantly to meet the demand for information. There are now publications that not only address the Ebonics controversy (see Baugh 2000; Perry and Delpit 1998) and related areas such as classroom pedagogy (Charity Hudley and Mallinson 2011, 2014; Gilyard 2011), education and literacy (Kinloch 2011; Kirkland 2013; Richardson 2003; Young et al. 2014), and education and policy (Alim and Baugh 2007; DeBose 2005), but also publications that provide new insights into past research (see Baugh 1999; Green 2002; Lanehart 2001; Mufwene et al. 1998; Rickford 1999; Rickford and Rickford 2000; Smitherman 2000). The conversation has broadened to include new arenas and understudied areas such as Hip Hop language and culture (Alim 2004, 2006; Morgan 2002, 2009; Richardson

2006; Smitherman 2006), African American Women's Language (Houston and Davis 2001; Jacobs-Huey 2006; Lanehart 2002, 2009), child language acquisition and development (Green 2011), multimedia (Banks 2011; Bloomquist, forthcoming), regional variation (Wolfram and Thomas 2002), and Critical Race Theory (Alim and Smitherman 2012).

Research on language use in African American communities has also been a fruitful area of inquiry in related fields such as education, anthropology, sociology, communication, and popular culture. Not only have questions about its validity and characterization in relation to what to call it and what it is been both politically and ideologically fraught—and continue to be so today (for a more complete discussion, see Smitherman 1977 and Mufwene 2001)—but there also have been other issues: How is it a distinct, rule-governed, systematic linguistic system? What is its origin and history and how does it continue to evolve? How do speakers acquire it? How do speakers use it as a source of identity? What is its relevance? How can linguistic description of the variety be extended to real-world issues in education, society, and language policy and planning?

The goal of the *Oxford Handbook of African American Language (OHAAL)* is to provide readers with a wide range of analyses of both traditional and contemporary work on language use in African American communities in a broad collective. *OHAAL* offers a survey of language and its uses in African American communities from a wide range of contexts. It is a handbook of research on *African American Language (AAL)* and, as such, it provides a variety of scholarly perspectives that may not align with each other—as is indicative of most scholarly research. The chapters in this book "interact" with one another, as contributors frequently refer the reader to further elaboration on related issues within the book. Contributors connecting their research to other chapters in various parts of the *Handbook* creates dialogue about AAL, thus supporting the need for collaborative thinking about the issues in AAL research. This interconnectedness between chapters affirms the idea that the body of AAL research is living and continuously growing. Research on AAL should not be considered stagnant, as new areas of study constantly emerge. As such, *OHAAL*'s goal is also to showcase and celebrate this body of work. Though *OHAAL* does not and cannot include every area of research, it is meant to provide suggestions for future work on lesser-studied areas (e.g., variation/heterogeneity in regional, social, and ethnic communities) by highlighting a need for collaborative perspectives and innovative thinking while reasserting the need for better research and communication in areas thought to be "resolved."

As a handbook for the field, the chapters were aimed at a broad readership in general; however, some chapters with a narrower focus on language structure and description may be better suited for an audience with a background in linguistics whereas other chapters and sections more focused on language use (e.g., education) are more accessible and provide the reader with the range of complexity of research.

2 WHAT SHOULD WE CALL IT AND WHAT DOES IT MEAN?

From the mid to late 1960s, the initial period of heightened interest in language use in African American communities, to the present, many different labels have been used to refer to AAL, and the label has often been related to the social climate (see Baugh 1991 and Smitherman 1991). To some extent, the labels have been used to link the variety to those who speak it. For example, when African Americans were referred to as *Negroes*, AAL was called *Negro English* or *Negro dialect*. As such, the labels have changed over the years, spanning a range from *Negro*, to *Black*, to *African American English*. (For a roughly chronological list of terminology used in linguistic descriptions over the years, see Wolfram, this volume.) Because of the various labels for AAL and the varied definitions (see Mufwene 2001 on defining language use in African American communities), we asked contributors to provide their own labels and definition for what they mean when they refer to language in African American communities. The reader will notice similarities and differences in labels and definitions. Some contributors use *African American English (AAE)* or *African American Vernacular English (AAVE)*, some use *African American Language (AAL)* and *African American Vernacular Language (AAVL)*, and some use a variety of other terms. Furthermore, some definitions refer more broadly to ways of speaking among some African Americans, and others refer to more narrow components of grammar used by those who are members of homogeneous speech communities. The point is that each contributor does not assume we all mean the same thing.

2.1 Why We Use AAL

As is clear from the title of *OHAAL*, we have chosen to use the term *African American Language* to refer to all variations of language use in African American communities, recognizing that there are many variations within the umbrella term, which includes Gullah and AAVL (or English for those who prefer that term) as well as varieties that reflect differences in age/generation, sex, gender, sexuality, social and socioeconomic class, region, education, religion, and other affiliations and identities that intersect with one's ethnicity/race and nationality. Our preference to use AAL, as opposed to AAE, is to bypass some of the problematic implications of "English" within the socioculture and history of African slave descendants in the United States and the contested connections of their language variety to the motherland and colonization and encompass rhetorical and pragmatic strategies that might not be associated with English. In other words, the use of the term AAL is more neutral and, therefore, less marked.

Regardless of which term researchers use—AAE or AAL, AAVE or AAVL—they all refer to a language variety that has systematic phonological (system of sounds), morphological (system of structure of words and relationship among words), syntactic (system of sentence structure), semantic (system of meaning), and lexical (structural organization of vocabulary items and other information) patterns. So, when speakers know AAL, they know a system of sounds, word and sentence structure, meaning and structural organization of vocabulary items, and other linguistic and metalinguistic information about their language, such as pragmatic rules and the social function of AAL. Indeed, the linguistic variety also has a slang component for specialized words and phrases that might be more closely associated with the language of popular culture and used by speakers of a certain age group—but not exclusively. However, AAE is not slang. "Broken English," "bad English," and the like will not work as labels for language use in African American communities because they do not characterize the variety of those who speak AAL, or any variety. Such labels only serve to diminish the language and its speakers.

2.2 A Note on Ebonics

The term "Ebonics," which was coined by Robert Williams in 1973, but which received considerable attention in 1997 during the Oakland School Board case, has been left off the list of labels of AAL listed above, as Williams intended the term to cover the multitude of languages spoken by Black people not just in the United States but also those spoken throughout the African Diaspora, for example. In the introduction to *Ebonics: The True Language of Black Folks* (1975), Williams defined Ebonics as:

> "the linguistic and paralinguistic features which on a concentric continuum represents the communicative competence of the West African, Caribbean, and United States slave descendant of African origin. It includes the various idioms, patois, argots, idiolects, and social dialects of [B]lack people," especially those who have been forced to adapt to colonial circumstances. Ebonics derives its form from ebony (black) and phonics (sound, the study of sound) and refers to the study of the language of Black people in all its cultural uniqueness. (vi)

The view of Williams and other Black scholars included in the 1973 conference was that the language of Black people had its roots in Niger-Congo languages of Africa, not in Indo-European languages. However, during the Oakland School Board controversy, the media and general public adopted the term "Ebonics," using it interchangeably with the labels accepted by linguists, thus not using the terms as it was intended.

Further explaining the term, Smith (1998) notes that "when the term *Ebonics* was coined it was not as a mere synonym for the more commonly used appellation Black English" (55). He points out that a number of scholars

> have consistently maintained that in the hybridization process, it was the grammar of Niger-Congo African languages that was dominant and that the extensive word borrowing from the English stock does not make Ebonics a dialect of English. In fact,

they argue, because it is an African Language System, it is improper to apply terminology that has been devised to describe the grammar of English to describe African
American linguistic structures. (55–56)

In commenting on the misuse of the term "Ebonics," Smith explains:

> In sum, Ebonics is not a dialect of English. The term Ebonics and other Afrocentric
> appellations such as Pan African Language and African Language Systems all refer
> to the linguistic continuity of Africa in Black America. Eurocentric scholars use the
> term Ebonics as a synonym for 'Black English.' In so doing, they reveal an ignorance
> of the origin and meaning of the terms Ebonics that is so profound that their confu-
> sion is pathetic. (57)

Smith cautions against (over-)emphasizing English similarities and overlooking or
de-emphasizing the African structure of AAE, and his points are well taken. The ongoing research on the origin of AAL is evidence that those working in this area are not
oblivious to claims about African and creole contributions. The precise nature of the
relationship between AAL and African languages and creoles is a topic of continued
investigation. In addition to appropriate naming and delineation, scholars continue to
engage in rigorous research that presents accurate descriptions and that provide further
insight into the origins of language in African American communities.

3 Organizational Overview and Description

The nearly fifty chapters of *OHAAL* are organized into seven parts. The seven sections of
OHAAL start with history and structure, which includes Part I: "Origins and Historical
Perspectives," Part II: "Lects and Variation," and Part III: "Structure and Description."
Part IV: "Child Language Acquisition and Development" transitions to the sections of
OHAAL that address language use: Part V: "Education," Part VI: "Language in Society,"
and Part VII: "Language and Identity."

3.1 Origins and Historical Perspectives

Part I: "Origins and Historical Perspectives" focuses on historical accounts of the origins and development of AAL, which is one of the most hotly debated issues in the field.
Viewpoints about the historical origins of AAL are directly related to some accounts
of the structure of AAL and variable constructions. In examining the origins of AAL,
linguists have approached the historical origins of AAL from different angles, including considerations of Anglicist origins espoused by dialectologists and variationists

(Labov et al. 1968; Labov 1972; Poplack 2000; Poplack and Tagliamonte 2001; Schneider 1989), creolist origins (Rickford 1998, 1999; Weldon 2003, 2007), substratist connections (Dalby 1972; DeBose and Faraclas 1993; Dunn 1976), and ecological and restructuralist factors (Mufwene 2000; Winford 1998). Proponents of monolithic origins hypotheses (e.g., Anglicist, creolist, and substratist) have compared morphosyntactic and syntactic features in creoles (Rickford 1998), early varieties of English (Poplack 2000; Poplack and Tagliamonte 2001), and (to a limited extent) African languages to those in AAL as a means of determining the origins, development, and classification of AAL (DeBose and Faraclas 1993). Restructuralist and ecological theorists have also considered factors such as social dynamics and contact effects (Mufwene 2000; Winford 1997, 1998) in explaining the evolution of AAL.

Part I not only addresses traditional monolithic views about the origins of AAL, but also includes authors who approach theorizing about the history and development of the variety from different perspectives. It begins with Gerard Van Herk's discussion of Anglicist perspectives in which he postulates that the distinctive features of AAL originate from early nonstandard dialects of English that have since disappeared. Though modern "monolithic" interpretations of origins are less inflexible than traditional positions (in which historical or counterevidence was dismissed as marginal or non-representative), Van Herk states that the origins debate is still very heated with strong personalities, claims, and counterclaims.

In chapter 2, John Rickford suggests a modern take on the early creolist origins view, which was fairly inflexible. While early creolist positions believed that AAL evolved from a widespread creole, Rickford's creolist position disavows the possibility of a widespread creole and instead asserts that AAL was influenced by the importation of creole features from Caribbean slaves. Rickford investigates the sociohistory of African slave descendants, differences from English dialects, and similarities to the surrounding creoles of slaves.

Following discussions on the Anglicist and creolist origins perspectives, Salikoko Mufwene, in chapter 3, argues that the development of the language of most African slaves and their descendants, as well as Gullah, were influenced most by local ecological factors, establishing that neither variety evolved uniformly. According to Mufwene, this differential language evolution was the product of variance in the population structures and comparative histories. Additionally, he considers the role that racial segregation during Jim Crow played in the evolution and variation of AAL.

In chapter 4, Donald Winford takes a non-monolithic creolist perspective that underscores the way in which second language acquisition and settler principles influenced the development of AAL. He discusses the importation of African slaves in colonial America and their contact with English-speaking settlers and suggests that this contact allowed for the conditions in which Africans could acquire a dialect similar to the English-speaking settlers. Winford suggests the need for future research in studying sociohistoric patterns of interaction between Scotch-Irish and other English-speaking settlers with Africans and reciprocal influence of Southern White vernaculars.

In chapter 5, John Singler discusses the sociohistory and language of the African Americans who left the slavery of the United States for presumed freedom in Liberia and Sinoe County. In doing so, he raises questions about the continued similarities between the language of the Liberian and Sinoe County Settlers and that of the African Americans who remained in the United States, considering the ecological and political constraints for both, and the incorporation of local languages the Settlers are in contact with. He addresses the internal and external linguistic change factors of the Settlers' English in the nearly two centuries since the beginning of their time in their resettled African context.

In chapter 6, Edgar Schneider takes a slightly different approach, surveying different text types and sources that document early AAL. He discusses the contribution of textual evidence—which is dependent on the kinds of texts available, their quality, and their representativeness—in investigating the origins and development of AAL. Having examined the Works Progress Administration (WPA) ex-slave narratives, ex-slave recordings, Hoodoo transcripts, studies of diaspora varieties, a corpus of letters by semi-literate writers, and transcripts of early blues lyrics, Schneider calls attention to the heterogeneity of AAL and the need for further research in AAL variation.

Part I concludes with chapter 7 by Walt Wolfram and Mary Kohn, providing a transition from sociohistoric origin to variation, while highlighting the forces of temporality and regionality in the development of AAL and dispelling the myth of a homogenous AAL based on early studies that focused on basilectal features. Wolfram and Kohn assert that regionality deserves attention in variationist research if we are to understand the trajectory of AAL development. This thought sets the stage for Part II, which includes descriptions of variation across the United States.

3.2 Lects and Variation

Part II: "Lects and Variation" considers AAL in frameworks of general linguistic description and current linguistic theory. Research presented in Part II builds on features that have been commonly associated with AAL and expands the geographical range of work on AAL—heretofore limited to the southeastern United States and urban centers in the north. Chapters in Part II include ongoing research by linguists who focus on long established AAL regional centers, such as Tracey Weldon and Simanique Moody on Gullah, William Labov and Sabriya Fisher in Philadelphia, William Kretzschmar, Jr. in Atlanta and surrounding suburban areas, Walter Edwards in Detroit, and Renée Blake, Cara Shousterman, and Luiza Newlin-Łukowicz in New York City. The section also includes understudied areas, with research on the Mississippi Delta by Rose Wilkerson, rural Texas by Patricia Cukor-Avila and Guy Bailey, and central and western Pennsylvania by Jennifer Bloomquist and Shelome Gooden, as well as an overview by John Rickford on the important work that has been done in California. Additionally, Joseph Hill, Carolyn McCaskill, Robert Bayley, and Ceil Lucas examine Black American Sign Language (ASL). The section concludes with Walt Wolfram's discussion of the influence of regionality and temporality in AAL variation. The authors in Part II present ways that AAL speakers interact with other local and regional dialect speakers, and they also address the contribution of settlement history, community development, and identity (both individual and collective) to language use by AAL speakers in those areas.

Part II begins with a sociohistorical overview of Gullah by Tracey Weldon and Simanique Moody in chapter 8. Weldon and Moody assert that Gullah emerged as a creole variety in the context of the slave trade and, as a result, is a regional variety of AAL used in coastal Georgia and South Carolina.

In chapter 9, Patricia Cukor-Avila and Guy Bailey draw our attention to the incongruity between the origins of AAL (i.e., rural areas of southern and southeastern United States) and where most of the research on AAL has been conducted (i.e., urban environments in the northern United States). They examine how rural AAL influences urban AAL and vice versa by surveying the speech of residents in the small, rural town of Springville, Texas. Cukor-Avila and Bailey show how older features are either obsolete or disappearing, as well as how urban innovations have made their way into rural speech.

Rural AAL is further explored in chapter 10 with Rose Wilkerson's research on copula absence and r-lessness in language use by women in Coahoma County in the Mississippi Delta. In addition to her focus on women, her research is unique in its location. Wilkerson provides a rich overview of the sociohistory and culture of the Mississippi Delta, as well as current political and social issues in the region.

Still in the South, but moving to a metropolitan area, in chapter 11, William Kretzschmar, Jr. surveys African American voices in Atlanta, Georgia. Kretzschmar focuses on a model of complex systems (as opposed to closed and separate) and the frequencies of linguistic features in different communities, adding that we do violence to the study of variation if we view communities too separate from one another.

Shifting from the language in the South to the North in chapter 12, Jennifer Bloomquist and Shelome Gooden investigate phonological, lexical, and syntactic variation in AAL in (urban) Pittsburgh and the (rural) Lower Susquehanna Valley. Bloomquist and Gooden draw attention to the fact that AAL is evolving because of distinct regional ecologies that simultaneously include and disregard the participation and history of African Americans. The authors also highlight views of identity held by local African Americans, as well as beliefs White locals have about what the "true" identity of a regional speaker is, which often does not include African Americans. The authors provide an intricate case study of what Smitherman (1977) calls the "push-pull syndrome" and what W. E. B. Du Bois ([1903] 1994) calls "double consciousness."

In chapter 13, William Labov and Sabriya Fisher compare and contrast White mainstream Philadelphia phonology to Philadelphian AAL vowel systems. While the study of large urban speech communities such as Philadelphia began with an emphasis on linguistic differentiation, they find that social stratification is a better standard by which to examine language variation. And contrary to some research, but in line with the previous chapter by Bloomquist and Gooden, Labov and Fisher examine how African

Americans in Philadelphia exert a regional identity that is similar to and different from local White Philadelphians (again, push-pull/double consciousness).

Next, in chapter 14, Renée Blake, Cara Shousterman, and Luiza Newlin-Łukowicz present sociolinguistic work in an early site in AAL research: New York City. West Indian immigration to the Big Apple caused a shift in the ethnic landscape and subsequently, a linguistic shift in AAL. Even though New York City has been studied extensively, the authors recognize a need to study language variation and change in regional centers of Black populations where the rate of ethnic demographic change over time contributes to complex identities that, inevitably, relate to complex linguistic practices.

In chapter 15, John Rickford takes us to the West Coast with a focus on the rich history of research on AAL in California. Rickford notes the importance of this research area through his discussion of California's role in studies of African American child language, social class variability, identity, perception, and style-shifting, as well as the Oakland Ebonics Controversy.

In chapter 16, Joseph Hill, Carolyn McCaskill, Robert Bayley, and Ceil Lucas introduce us to the distinct use of ASL by Blacks, which they define as a variety of AAL. Hill, McCaskill, Bayley, and Lucas examine linguistic and discourse features of Black ASL in the South, identifying handedness, location of the sign, size of the signing space, the use of repetition, lexical differences, and the incorporation of spoken AAL, while examining the historical factors that contributed to the development and rich distinctiveness of Black ASL.

While the authors of chapters 8 through 16 acknowledge that there are certain linguistic features shared across varieties of AAL, they present ways in which local regional dialects have shaped varieties of AAL in different parts of the country and suggest the ways in which settlement history, community development, and identity (both individual and collective) contribute to language variation and use by AAL speakers in those areas. Hence, AAL may appear homogeneous when African Americans are not included in linguistic research of local or regional use by Whites when, in fact, AAL is simultaneously local and not local; in other words, AAL is heterogeneous, just as its speakers are.

Walt Wolfram provides a fitting end to Part II in chapter 17 by explaining the ways in which the myth of a supraregional AAL has hindered variationist work and the potential implications of such work. He argues that regional dialects have been mistakenly analyzed as White varieties, despite the presence and influence of African Americans in these regions (as shown in the previous chapters in Part II).

3.3 Structure and Description

Some early descriptions of AAL were motivated by questions about its legitimacy and the extent to which it was different from Mainstream American English (MAE). One approach to describing AAL was to highlight surface features that were maximally different from morphological, phonological, and syntactic structures in MAE. However, some early approaches moved away from listing superficial features of AAL and expanded descriptions of the linguistic variety that took into consideration patterns of grammar and rules and principles for generating grammatical structures. The tense/aspect system has been the topic of some of the earliest descriptions of AAL, in which there have been goals to explain the relation between meaning and structure of constructions that convey information about times and events. Current research has built on this work in presenting more articulated structure to account for tense/aspect properties as well as other properties of the AAL grammar. Also, research on AAL has continued to address questions about the sound patterns of AAE ranging from segments of sounds to sound patterns extending over utterances, such as intonation. Current research in these areas of AAL has also begun to include experimental approaches.

Part III: "Structure and Description" considers syntactic, semantic, and phonological properties of AAL in frameworks of general linguistic description and current linguistic theory. Contributors build on the tradition of studying AAL linguistic features while moving to a consideration of AAL linguistic systems, including investigations into interfaces, such as syntax and semantics by Lisa Green and Walter Sistrunk, syntax and phonology by James Walker, tense-modality-aspect systems by Charles DeBose, and understudied areas in segmental phonology by Erik Thomas and Guy Bailey and prosody by Erik Thomas.

First, in chapter 18, Lisa Green and Walter Sistrunk, in presenting an overview of syntactic and semantic properties of certain areas of the grammar of AAL, discuss topics such as the system of tense and aspect marking and the complementizer system. In the section on tense/aspect marking, they discuss meaning associated with preverbal markers syntactic placement, restriction on selection, and morphological properties. In addition, Green and Sistrunk present case studies of embedded question and negation structures in illustrating properties of complex clauses in AAL.

In chapter 19, Charles DeBose highlights generalizations about constructions that convey meaning about tense-mood-aspect in AAL. The goal is to account for constructions, including those in which there is no overt marking that might contribute to tense-aspect meaning. In the overview, DeBose discusses different predicate types and their combination with other structures to give a tense-aspect interpretation.

In chapter 20, James Walker examines the distribution of overt and zero forms of the copula and verbal –s from the angle of prosodic structure of the constructions in which these morphological markers occur in two diaspora varieties that are considered to be representative of early AAL. Walker makes a case for considering the influence of prosodic structure, in addition to grammatical and phonological conditioning, on different morphological forms.

In chapter 21, Erik Thomas and Guy Bailey examine segmental phonological features, such as consonant cluster simplification and deletion, r-lessness, interdental fricative mutations, final /d/ devoicing, vocalic mergers, and glide weakening and bring together research on vowel and consonant sounds from the late 1960s to the present. They explain that over the last twenty-five years, acoustic work has played a major role in the study of segmental phonology.

Lastly, in chapter 22, Erik Thomas provides insight on prosodic properties that have been argued to characterize AAL, with emphasis on prosodic features that might distinguish it from European American English. The chapter also articulates that although prosody is difficult to study and little research has been conducted on AAL prosody, some researchers have duplicated findings related to suprasegmental properties of AAL

3.4 Child Language Acquisition and Development

Part IV: "Child Language Acquisition and Development" considers the growing body of research on the language acquisition and development of children in AAL speech communities. The chapters included here provide an overview of different approaches to research and topics in child language in AAL-speaking communities and poses questions about the acquisition path of development of structures used by children in these speech communities. Questions related to patterns in child AAL before age 4, developmental AAL and variable structures that are part of the AAL grammar, and rhetorical strategies used in child narratives are raised in this section.

Part IV begins with chapter 23 by Brandi Newkirk-Turner, RaMonda Horton, and Ida Stockman, who acknowledge that studies of language acquisition in the past excluded AAL-speaking children, especially younger children. In reviewing research on developmental AAL prior to age 4, the authors underscore the apparent gaps in the literature that result from lack of research on language patterns in children in this age group.

In chapter 24, Janneke Van Hofwegen continues this study of development of language by examining a corpus of evidence spanning eleven years from pre-kindergarten to mid-adolescence (ages 4 to 15) in about seventy African American children. This longitudinal study shows consistent patterns of AAL usage, style-shifting, and vowel development.

In chapter 25, Lisa Green and Jessica White-Sustaíta focus on the syntactic and morphosyntactic structures of the language of 3- to 7-year-old children to understand their language acquisition and development in AAL speech communities, especially ways of distinguishing developmental patterns from variation and optionality in developmental stages from variation in the grammar.

In chapter 26, Tempii Champion and Allyssa McCabe present child language development and narrative production in children from ages 3 to 11. They explain that narratives serve as part of the rich cultural tradition of storytelling in African American communities, and as children develop them, their story grammar elements, grammatical structures, and cohesion devices evolve.

In chapter 27, Janna Oetting presents research on the similarities and differences between AAL and southern White English in 4- to 6-year-olds in rural southeastern Louisiana. The differences in Oetting's research are enumerated by children's production (and the pragmatic functions) of non-mainstream grammatical structures.

Part IV ends with Toya Wyatt's attention to the link between the over-representation of African American children in special education programs and language use.

African American and minority students who do not speak MAE are disproportionately affected by assessment-based judgments about speech and language therapy, as well as being labeled as "intellectually challenged." Wyatt provides innumerable ways clinicians can identify dialect from language disorders to minimize misdiagnosis and inaccurate special education referrals, in order to establish best practice with current law.

The information about the properties and patterns of language development of school-aged children and assessment-related issues addressed in Part IV have practical application in some of the types of educational contexts addressed in Part V, which begins our exploration of AAL research as it relates to language use.

3.5 Education

Despite the research on the linguistic structure of AAL, the variety is still disparaged as substandard, low-prestige, "ghetto" English in a number of political and intellectual centers in the United States. There have been seemingly cyclical debates about its value and "place" in schools and society. Part V: "Education" focuses on one of the long-standing areas of AAL research application due to the social, political, and policy implications involved in the education of AAL-speaking children. Part V expands educational models to the community, which ultimately impact the lives of AAL speakers in the classroom and in larger institutional contexts.

In chapter 29, Geneva Smitherman provides a historical view of AAL and education controversies, which includes deficit research, the "Black English Case" (*Martin Luther King et al. v. Ann Arbor*), and the Oakland Ebonics controversy.

In chapter 30, Monique Mills and Julie Washington focus on the divide between the home language of AAL and target school language (mainstream American English) through an analysis of code-switching and academic performance.

In chapter 31, Sharroky Hollie, Tamara Butler, and Jamila Gillenwaters provide a close examination of AAL in the classroom and a critique of current language teaching pedagogies and policies. They argue for the effectiveness of culturally responsive pedagogy and the need for professional development based on language affirmation—all inspired by the work of Noma LeMoine. They offer concrete strategies to build validating educational spaces.

The theme of academic performance and pedagogical models continues with the work of K. C. Nat Turner and Tyson Rose in chapter 32. They discuss their support of the incorporation of Hip Hop in education and explicate their concept of multiliteracies, which they believe could contribute to students' academic and psychological success in the classroom.

In chapter 33, William Labov and Bettina Baker analyze four morphosyntactic structures of AAL in the context of raising the levels of reading achievement in AAL-speaking African American elementary schoolchildren. They assert that instruction in the use of verbal and possessive –s (rather than plural –s) aimed toward AAL-speaking students and teachers' familiarity with other widespread features of AAL can have significant success in increasing reading comprehension (lexically and arithmetically).

In chapter 34, J. Michael Terry, Randall Hendrick, Evangelos Evangelou, and Richard Smith measure the effect of language on academic performance through standardized testing. They identify specific structural divergences of AAL from Standard Classroom English (SCE) and suggest ways in which the two varieties are at odds within the assessment paradigm. They attempt to identify the problems generated by teaching and testing in SCE for the AAL-speaking child and adolescent, finding that, if linguistic sources of interference were removed from tests, the average student would correctly answer questions presented to them in an assessment that uses SCE.

In chapter 35, John Baugh concludes Part V with a discussion on language planning and policies in regard to bidialectalism and the controversy surrounding AAL institutionally. He argues for more research on bridging the linguistic and cultural gap between the home and school; increasing teachers' familiarity with AAL that may affect literacy and proficiency with Standard English; and creating a language-affirming environment that may encourage the formation of legal statutes and policy measures.

3.6 Language in Society

Part VI: "Language in Society" includes theoretical, empirical, and multimethods research that situates language use in African American communities and American society in general. In chapter 36, Charles DeBose discusses AAL in the social and cultural institution that is "The Black Church." DeBose defines African American Church Language (AACL) as a subvariety of AAL that is used in sacred contexts and is associated with certain linguistic practices. DeBose elaborates on the linguistic aspects of the spiritual and secular range of AACL and other language practices associated with AAL in a spiritual context.

In chapter 37, James Peterson discusses AAL in literature by analyzing orthographical representations of AAL. He outlines the history of orthography in African American novels that are indicative of racial attitudes. Peterson notes that, orally and orthographically, Black voices are best represented by Black voices, suggesting that adjustments toward literary dialect should be made to represent Black linguistic subjectivity.

In chapter 38, Howard Rambsy and Briana Whiteside explain how Black poetry corresponds with spoken practices in AAL. They explore the usage of distinct lexical and verbal practices in the presentation of ideas in poetry. For them, Black poetry is a repository for AAL; AAL is a way for Black poets to express ideas.

In chapter 39, Jacquelyn Rahman examines AAL employed by Black female comedians in a male-dominated context fraught with sexism and harassment. Rahman showcases African American female comedians who use AAL generally but also employ specific strategies that are associated with African American Women's Language (AAWL) as a means of establishing a connection with their predominantly female audiences.

In chapter 40, Jennifer Bloomquist discusses her research on the construction of Blackness through the voicing of African American characters in children's animated film. She demonstrates how representations framed by linguistic manipulations denoting ethnicity reflect historic social and political attitudes about race in general and Blackness in particular. Bloomquist emphasizes that the construction of ethnicity through physical, linguistic, and behavioral representations by animators demands scrutiny because of the impact of these films on children's interpretation of race and themselves.

Part VI ends with chapter 41, John Baugh's research on the pervasiveness and implications of linguistic profiling and bigotry. He presents evidence of racially motivated linguistic discrimination in real-world contexts, such as housing inequity, legal bias, and harassment in employment, and the need for linguistic and legal vigilance as well as judicial and racial equity.

3.7 Language and Identity

Part VII: "Language and Identity" discusses connections between language and identity. It begins in chapter 42 with Kate Anderson's research on ideologies, beliefs, and attitudes, which outlines three complementary linguistic approaches between the socialized construction of race and language: sociophonetic, ethnographic, and discursive methodologies. The analysis is based on data from both Black and White participants' views of AAL and their ability to accurately identify African Americans, as gathered by different types of methodologies, and their implications and impact on research results and our understanding of language attitudes and beliefs.

In chapter 43, Arthur Spears discusses distinctively Black grammatical features associated with what he identifies as Standard AAL. Spears introduces African American Standard English (AASE) as a group of varieties of AAL with distinctively Black grammatical features, all of which are considered standard and are not stigmatized. Spears argues that AASE is a product of racial subordination in which AAL was regimented by external norms, but distinctive linguistic behaviors remained. Internal norms, however, established stigma toward certain vernacular language features and, subsequently, a socioeconomic hierarchy of language use. Thus, Spears notes that AASE serves a role as a form of cultural capital.

In chapter 44, Erica Britt and Tracey Weldon present their research on linguistic behavior in African American middle-class communities, which is very much connected to the previous chapter by Spears. Though the bulk of research on AAL has focused on working-class and urban African Americans, Britt and Weldon examine the sociohistoric contexts of the emergence of the African American middle class, as well as usage patterns, variation, and perceptions of AAL among middle-class African Americans. They also draw attention to the high levels of internal variation and internal and external pressures (e.g., audience composition, perception of self, expression or suppression of ethnic orientation) that may affect linguistic choice.

In the next two chapters, Part VII moves its focus to gendered uses of AAL. In chapter 45, Marcyliena Morgan discusses research on African American women's AAL use and the construction of AAWL. Traditionally, AAL research rendered the speech of African American women indistinguishable from men's language simply by incorporating female data into the description of the speech community. Morgan untangles past research and examines the language of African American women as their own community, apart from Black men and White women.

In chapter 46, David Kirkland examines Black Masculine Language and explores its role in identity construction, as a form of resistance and as posture of power. In his analysis, Kirkland refers to the use of Hip Hop Nation Language (HHNL), which is presented in the following chapter.

In chapter 47, Alim discusses his concept of HHNL and how it reflects and expands on AAL use. He shows how HHNL can be used to subvert dominant language, identity, and power. He also enumerates the tenets of HHNL while analyzing variation within it.

Part VII concludes with chapter 48 by Sonja Lanehart in her explication of the concept of identity and how identity has functioned in AAL communities. She begins with a discussion of difficult terms related to language and identity and the interconnected attitudes, beliefs, practices, and ideologies surrounding AAL by African Americans about African Americans and by White Americans about African Americans—all of which contributes to contradictions and conundrums around AAL. As the concluding chapter for OHAAL, it provides an opportunity for reflecting on research on AAL from the perspective of those in AAL communities and their love-hate relationship with their own language—and themselves.

4 CONCLUSION

OHAAL was carefully crafted to explicate various aspects of research in AAL. However, simply presenting this research in book form is not the "end of it"—we must continue to push the boundaries of linguistic research in African American communities to fully understand the place of AAL in our history, communities, social and cultural institutions, and our own identities.

While it is arguably still the most studied language variety in the Americas, there are areas that remain neglected in much of AAL research. There has been too little regard or recognition that language use in African American communities includes all demographics. For example, while there have been a number of studies that examine adolescent and working-class language use, there has been very little attention paid to child language acquisition as well as variation with respect to class (e.g., middle class and upper class), sex (e.g., African American women), gender (feminine, transgender), age/generation (e.g., children and the elderly), sexuality (e.g., lesbian, gay, bisexual), and religion (e.g., Muslim features for followers of Islam, since the default is usually Christianity). The notion that the most authentic AAL is merely a language restricted to inner-city male teenagers or that it is supraregional has informed linguistic approaches so consistently and for so long that the expansion of contemporary research models, demographic, and communities seems glacial.

Work that includes a broader demographic would provide linguists with a more comprehensive understanding of language use in African American communities. These limitations have been further compounded by the methodological restrictions of the variationist paradigm that has categorized much of the work previously done on AAL. Part of the problem has been the slow evolution of incorporating multimethod, multidisciplinary, interdisciplinary, and allied areas of research, collaborative studies, and applications of research to address complex social, political, and educational issues. As we develop more complex questions surrounding complex dynamics of language, culture, and society, we require more collaborative research that is equally complex to apply to multifaceted social, theoretical, and praxis issues. We hope *OHAAL* has helped to show this and move the conversation forward.

REFERENCES

Alim, H. Samy. 2004. *You Know My Steez: An Ethnographic and Sociolinguistic Study of Styleshifting in a Black American Speech Community*. Publications of the American Dialect Society 89. Durham, NC: Duke University Press.

———. 2006. *Roc the Mic: The Language of Hip Hop Culture*. New York: Routledge.

Alim, H. Samy, and John Baugh, eds. 2007. *Talkin Black Talk: Language, Education, and Social Change*. New York: Teachers College Press.

Alim, H. Samy, and Geneva Smitherman. 2012. *Articulate while Black: Barack Obama, Language, and Race in the U.S.* Oxford: Oxford University Press.

Banks, Adam J. 2011. *Digital Griots: African American Rhetoric in a Multimedia Age*. Carbondale: Southern Illinois University Press.

Baugh, John. 1991. "The Politicization of Changing Terms of Self-Reference among American Slave Descendants." *American Speech* 66 (2): 133–46.

———. 1999. *Out of the Mouths of Slaves: African American Language and Educational Malpractice*. Austin: University of Texas Press.

———. 2000. *Beyond Ebonics: Linguistic Pride and Racial Prejudice*. Oxford: Oxford University Press.

Bloomquist, Jennifer. Forthcoming. *From Dumbo to Donkey: Linguistic Minstrelsy in Children's Animated Film*. Oxford: Oxford University Press.

Burling, Robbins. 1973. *English in Black and White*. New York: Hold, Rinehart, and Winston.

Charity Hudley, Anne H., and Christine Mallinson. 2011. *Understanding English Language Variation in U.S. Schools*. New York: Teachers College Press.

———. 2014. *We Do Language: English Language Variation in the Secondary English Classroom*. New York: Teachers College Press.

Dalby, David. 1972. "The African Element in American English." In *Rappin and Stylin Out: Communication in Urban Black America*, edited by Thomas Kochman, 170–86. Urbana: University of Illinois Press.

DeBose, Charles. 2005. *The Sociology of African American Language: A Language Planning Perspective*. New York: Palgrave MacMillan.

DeBose, Charles, and Nicolas Faraclas. 1993. "An Africanist Approach to the Linguistic Study of Black English: Getting to the Roots of Tense-Aspect-Modality and Copula Systems in Afro-American." In *Africanisms in Afro-American Language Varieties*, edited by Salikoko S. Mufwene, 364–87. Athens: University of Georgia Press.

Dillard, Joey L. 1972. *Black English: Its History and Usage in the United States*. New York: Vintage House.

———. 1977. *Lexicon of Black English*. New York: Seabury.

Du Bois, W. E. B. [1903] 1994. *The Souls of Black Folk*. Mineola, NY: Dover.

Dunn, Ernest F. 1976. "Black-Southern White Dialect Controversy." In *Black English: A Seminar*, edited by Deborah S. Harrison and Tom Trabasso, 105–22. Hillsdale, NJ: Lawrence Erlbaum.

Fasold, Ralph W. 1972. *Tense Marking in Black English*. Arlington, VA: Center for Applied Linguistics.

Gilyard, Keith. 2011. *True to the Language Game: African American Discourse, Cultural Politics, and Pedagogy*. London: Routledge.

Green, Lisa. 2002. *African American English: A Linguistic Introduction*. Cambridge: Cambridge University Press.

———. 2011. *Language and the African American Child*. New York: Cambridge University Press.

Houston, Marsha, and Olga Davis. 2001. *Centering Ourselves: African American Feminist and Womanist Studies of Discourse*. Cresskill, NJ: Hampton.

Jacobs-Huey, Lanita. 2006. *From the Kitchen to the Parlor: Language and Becoming in African American Women's Hair Care*. Oxford: Oxford University Press.

Kinloch, Valerie, ed. 2011. *Urban Literacies: Critical Perspectives on Language, Learning, and Community*. New York: Teachers College Press.

Kirkland, David E. 2013. *A Search Past Silence: The Literacy of Young Black Men*. New York: Teachers College Press.

Krapp, George P. 1924. "The English of the Negro." *American Mercury* 2 (5): 190–95.

———. 1925. *The English Language in America*. Vol. 1. Washington, DC: The Century Co., for the Modern Language Association of America

Labov, William. 1972. *Language in the Inner City: Studies in the Black English Vernacular*. Philadelphia: University of Pennsylvania Press.

Labov, William, Paul Cohen, Clarence Robbins, and John Lewis. 1968. *A Study of Non-Standard English of Negro and Puerto Rican Speakers in New York City*. 2 vols. Philadelphia: US Regional Survey.

Lanehart, Sonja L., ed. 2001. *Sociocultural and Historical Contexts of African American English*. Amsterdam: John Benjamins.

———. 2002. *Sista, Speak! Black Women Kinfolk Talk about Language and Literacy*. Austin: University of Texas Press.

———, ed. 2009. *African American Women's Language: Discourse, Education, and Identity*. Newcastle upon Tyne: Cambridge Scholars.

Morgan, Marcyliena. 2002. *Language, Discourse, and Power in African American Culture*. New York: Cambridge University Press.

———. 2009. *The Real Hiphop: Battling for Knowledge, Power, and Respect in the LA Underground*. Durham, NC: Duke University Press.

Mufwene, Salikoko. 2000. "Some Sociohistorical Inferences about the Development of African American English." In *The English History of African American English*, edited by Shana Poplack, 233–63. Malden, MA: Blackwell.

————. 2001. "What is African American English?" In *Sociocultural and Historical Contexts of African American English*, edited by Sonja L. Lanehart, 21–51. Amsterdam: John Benjamins.

Mufwene, Salikoko S., John R. Rickford, Guy Bailey, and John Baugh, eds. 1998. *African-American English: Structure, History and Use*. London: Routledge.

Perry, Theresa, and Lisa D. Delpit, eds. 1998. *The Real Ebonics Debate: Power, Language, and the Education of African-American Children*. Boston: Beacon.

Poplack, Shana, ed. 2000. *The English History of African American English*. New York: Blackwell.

Poplack, Shana, and Sali Tagliamonte. 2001. *African American English in the Diaspora*. Malden, MA: Blackwell.

Richardson, Elaine. 2003. *African American Literacies*. London and New York: Routledge.

————. 2006. *Hiphop Literacies*. London and New York: Routledge.

Rickford, John. 1998. "The Creole Origin of African American Vernacular English: Evidence from Copula Absence." In *African-American English: Structure, History, and Use*, edited by Salikoko S. Mufwene, John R. Rickford, Guy Bailey, and John Baugh, 154–200. London: Routledge,

————. 1999. *African American Vernacular English: Features, Evolution, Educational Implications*. Malden, MA: Blackwell.

Rickford, John R., and Russell J. Rickford. 2000. *Spoken Soul: The Story of Black English*. New York: John Wiley and Sons.

Schneider, Edgar. 1989. *American Earlier Black English*. Tuscaloosa: University of Alabama Press.

Smith, Ernie. 1998. "What Is Black English? What is Ebonics?" In *The Real Ebonics Debate: Power, Language, and the Education of African-American Children*, edited by Theresa Perry and Lisa Delpit, 49–58. Boston, MA: Beacon.

Smitherman, Geneva. 1977. *Talkin and Testifyin: The Language of Black America*. Boston, MA: Houghton Mifflin.

————. 1991. " 'What Is Africa to Me?': Language, Ideology, and African American." *American Speech* 66 (2): 115–32.

————. 2000. *Talkin that Talk: Language, Culture, and Education in African America*. London and New York: Routledge.

————. 2006. *Word from the Mother: Language and African Americans*. London: Routledge.

Stewart, William. 1967. "Sociolinguistic Factors in the History of American Negro Dialects." *Florida Foreign Language Reporter* 5: 1–7.

Turner, Lorenzo Dow. 1949. *Africanisms in the Gullah Dialect*. Ann Arbor: University of Michigan Press.

Weldon, Tracey. 2003. "Copula Variability in Gullah." *Language Variation and Change* 15 (1): 37–72.

————. 2007. "Gullah Negation: A Variable Analysis." *American Speech* 82 (4): 341–66.

Williams, Robert, ed. 1975. *Ebonics: The True Language of Black Folks*. St. Louis, MO: The Institute of Black Studies.

Winford, Donald. 1997. "On the Origins of African American Vernacular English—A Creolist Perspective. Part I: The Sociohistorical Background." *Diachronica* 14: 305–44.

————. 1998. "On the Origins of African American Vernacular English—A Creolist Perspective. Part II: Linguistic Features." *Diachronica* 15: 1–55.

Wolfram, Walt. 1969. A *Sociolinguistic Description of Detroit Negro Speech*. Washington, DC: Center for Applied Linguistics.

Wolfram, Walt, and Erik Thomas. 2002. *The Development of African American English*. Oxford: Blackwell Publishers.

Young, Vershawn Ashanti, Rusty Barrett, Y'Shanda Young-Rivera, and Kim Brian Lovejoy. 2014. *Other People's English: Code-Meshing, Code-Switching, and African American Literacy*. New York: Teachers College Press.

PART I

ORIGINS AND HISTORICAL PERSPECTIVES

CHAPTER 1

....

THE ENGLISH ORIGINS
HYPOTHESIS

....

GERARD VAN HERK

1.1 INTRODUCTION

ONE prominent perspective on the origins of contemporary African American English (AAE),[1] recently most closely associated with the *Ottawa School* (see Poplack 1999; Poplack and Tagliamonte 2001), is that the distinctive features of AAE were transmitted largely intact from earlier nonstandard varieties of English.[2] The English Origins Hypothesis (EOH) assumes that the English component of AAE has become obscured over time, as the variety has undergone its own internally driven change, and the relevant linguistic features have disappeared from other varieties, especially from the Standard American English (SAE) that researchers sometimes (inappropriately) use as a point of comparison. This hypothesis is thus consonant with the *divergence hypothesis* laid out in Labov and Harris (1986), albeit not dependent on *continuing* divergence.

Among the features that distinguish contemporary AAE from SAE, but not from other historical or regional varieties of English, we note consonant cluster reduction; g-droppin'; interdental stopping or fronting; r-lessness; l-vocalization; mergers of pin/pen, ar/or, and aj/oj; lax vowel shifting; associative *and them*; locative *at*; negative concord; *ain't*; *for to*; existential *it*; irregular or bare past tense forms; preterite/participle variation; verbal s-marking; habitual *be(es)* and *steady*; and perhaps remote perfect *bin* and habitual *da/do*. There are also AAE features that may result from the extension of dialect rules to new contexts; these include non-inverted questions and the zero copula. In some cases, it is the presence of a feature that distinguishes AAE; in others, it is radical differences in frequency of use.

Of course, it is not good science to note surface similarities and assume influence, especially if we indulge in the *cafeteria principle* of choosing some features from one comparison variety and some from another, without considering histories of contact and the mechanics of linguistic diffusion. (I address this issue below.) We must also consider the fact that some of the relevant comparison varieties have been in such long-standing contact with AAE that it has become difficult to determine the direction of influence. This is especially problematic in that direction of influence is central to the discourses of language identity, ethnicity, and contact that form the backdrop to any research on AAE (Winford 2003).

1.2 BACKGROUND

The current instantiation of the EOH, sometimes referred to as *the new Anglicists* or *neo-Anglicist hypothesis*, responds to strong claims from the mid-1960s and later that AAE's distinct features represent retentions from an earlier, less SAE-like stage of the language (possibly creole, creoloid, creole-influenced, or African-influenced, or resulting from universal processes of language change or acquisition) (Bailey 1965; Dillard 1972; Bickerton 1977; Holm 1984; Winford 1997, 1998; Rickford 1998; Sutcliffe 1999; Singler 2007). *Earlier* English-origins work, though, is more firmly situated in the debate over the relationships between Black and White vernaculars in the American South (McDavid and McDavid 1951). That debate occurred against a social background of racist discourses of taint and influence, sparked in part by northerners dismissing White southern language and culture as Black-influenced or hybrid (Bonfiglio 2002). In that social context, claiming that all linguistic influence flows from White to Black varieties (Krapp 1924; McDavid and McDavid 1951, 12) effectively acts as an assertion of White cultural purity. The *non*-Anglicist hypotheses, then, historically occupy the moral high ground, and it is likely that this framing of the debate continues to affect responses to the newer EOH (see, especially, Winford 2003).

The strongest non-Anglicist claims, such as those of Bailey (1965), Stewart (1967), and Dillard (1972), posit a widespread full creole across large areas of the American South, with decreolization not occurring until after the Civil War and the end of slavery. This hypothesis contrasts contemporary AAE with SAE and attributes differences to AAE's creole roots. The strong version is also found in early work by Bickerton (1971), which also shifts the focus of AAE origins research away from phonological differences and toward morphology and syntax. It is this strong version that is often the point of contention for EOH proponents. From the early 1980s onward, we see papers that directly challenge non-Anglicist claims, one variable at a time.

1.3 CURRENT VERSION

There are clear methodological preferences associated with most scholars working in the EOH framework. Most work is part of the variationist paradigm (Labov 1966, 1972), in which large data sets are investigated quantitatively to seek correlations between the choice of linguistic variant and a range of possible social and linguistic conditioning factors. EOH work adapts variationist methodology to the comparative method of historical linguistics (or vice versa) (Poplack and Tagliamonte 2001; Tagliamonte 2002, 2006). This approach goes beyond noting the simple occurrence of a feature, or its rates of use, to examine and compare the linguistic constraints on the choice of variants across multiple data sets. If constraints on use—things like subject or adverbial type, verb class, or frequency—are shared in data from multiple communities, we argue that these represent shared underlying grammars in the communities in question, and we propose a linguistic boundary between those communities and others that do not share such a hierarchy of constraints. Central to this approach is the concept of *diagnosticity*—the need to focus on variables that behave differently in the different potential donor varieties, so that there are unambiguous ways to determine how researched varieties are patterning.

Another similarity with historical linguists is the desire to seek out the earliest available instantiations of the comparison varieties of interest (an approach taken by many researchers with varying perspectives on the AAE origins debate). Rather than comparing contemporary AAE and SAE, we find communities or data sets that can be taken to represent an earlier stage of the language. These include *diaspora communities*, places where the descendants of earlier African American settlers have lived in linguistic isolation and are postulated to have maintained traditional varieties (Poplack and Sankoff 1987; Singler 1989; Poplack and Tagliamonte 1991). Additionally, research has been conducted on recordings or transcriptions of interviews with elderly ex-slaves, conducted largely in the 1930s (Schneider 1989; Bailey, Maynor, and Cukor-Avila 1991; Kautzsch 2002), on letters by semi-literate authors (Montgomery, Fuller, and DeMarse 1993; Montgomery 1999; Kautzsch 2000; Van Herk and Poplack 2003), on blues lyrics (Miethaner 2005), and more. Ideally, multiple sources are accessed, so that similar findings from different places or sources of data can be taken as stronger evidence of a single earlier linguistic system that each community would have maintained across generations.

A third defining characteristic of much recent EOH work is the focus on morphosyntactic variables, rather than phonology or discourse. This in large part reflects the privileging of those domains in linguistics and in the origins debate, but it is also methodologically driven, in that morphosyntax seems to have remained stable across the generations more than phonology has. As morphosyntactic variables occur less frequently than phonetic or phonological variables, this work requires large data sets—major sociolinguistic interview collections, or corpora built from large archival holdings.

1.4 SOME VARIABLES

In this section, I briefly describe a few studies that suggest an English origin for some features of (earlier) African American English. (I sometimes use simplified terms and concepts in the interest of space.)

1.4.1 Verb Morphology

Bare past tense verb forms (as in *jump* for *jumped*) superficially resemble creole bare verbs. But a creole-like system might be expected to restrict marking to anterior contexts (Bickerton 1975), which diaspora varieties do not (Tagliamonte 1991; Poplack and Tagliamonte 2001). Instead, bare weak verbs are phonologically conditioned, while bare strong verbs are restricted to a tiny lexical set, identical to that found in nineteenth-century AAE letters (Van Herk and Poplack 2003) and contemporary California AAE (Rickford 1999). Perfect marking also follows English rules (Tagliamonte 1997; Van Herk 2008).

S-marked present tense verbs (as in *I jumps*) are far more frequent in earlier AAE than in the contemporary variety. In diaspora varieties and earlier letters, they are conditioned by subject type and adjacency (Montgomery et al. 1993; Montgomery 1999; Poplack and Tagliamonte 2001; Walker 2001; Van Herk and Walker 2005), as in northern British dialects. This constraint is weak or nonexistent in some early AAE varieties (Singler 1999; Van Herk and Walker 2005), as well as in some putative donor varieties (Clarke 1997). S-marking is also conditioned by habituality, but the diagnosticity of this constraint is unclear.

1.4.2 Auxiliary Inversion in Questions

Question auxiliary inversion (*Where can he go?* versus *Where he can go?*) is highly variable in both contemporary and diaspora AAE (DeBose 1996). My own work with diaspora data (Van Herk 2000) suggests that this variation is highly constrained (by negation, question type, and auxiliary type) in a pattern very similar to constraints on main verb non-inversion in Early Modern English (Ellegard 1953; Kroch 1989). I argue that the extension of such constraints to auxiliaries represents a dialect-driven restructuring that occurred in much earlier AAE. Melnick and Rickford (2010) have recently noted similar constraints in Caribbean creoles, arguing that the patterned constraints that I observed may be more universal.

1.4.3 Negation

Negation illustrates particularly well a story arc of research on early AAE morphosyntax. First, several papers propose that contemporary AAE negation reflects an earlier, more creole stage (Winford 1992; DeBose 1994; Weldon 1994), especially in the frequent use of negative concord (*we ain't got no money*) and reduced number of negation markers (*don't* for *doesn't*, *ain't* for *didn't*). Howe (1997) and Howe and Walker (1999) find these forms at lower rates in diaspora and ex-slave data, which suggests that their current frequency is a more recent development. They also demonstrate that much earlier variation shares conditioning with English dialects (e.g., verbal constraints on *ain't* and negative postposing), to the extent that overviews such as Winford (1998, 104) attribute the feature to a superstrate (i.e., English) origin, with possible creole reinforcement. A few years later, AAE negation is seen as so "thoroughly English" that choosing to study it (inferentially, to the neglect of other features) is described as "selective and one-sided, conveniently ignoring" non-English aspects of AAE grammar (Winford 2003, 26).

1.4.4 Relative Markers

Dillard (1972) notes that subject zero and *what* relative clause markers (*he got a gun what/Ø sound like a bee*) are shared by contemporary AAE and creoles, but Tottie and Harvie (1999) point out that such forms are also widespread in English dialects. Their quantitative analysis of diaspora and Ex-Slave Recordings (ESR) data finds wide variation but general constraints similar to those described for English dialects. Recent work by Rickford (2010) finds these constraints operative in Barbadian (Creole) English, as well as in Dorset English. Rickford argues that the constraint hierarchy might be universal; however, it is equally likely, given settlement patterns, that all the New World varieties studied have retained the English system exemplified by Dorset.

In each case described here, researchers have found strong similarities between the linguistic conditioning of variables in diverse instantiations of earlier AAE and in dialects of English that are sociohistorically likely to have been available as a model for the earliest generations of AAE speakers. Quantitative analyses of historical or traditional AAE have also argued for a dialect origin for such AAE features as plural marking, *was/were* variation, and zero copula, or have argued that the presence of features such as habitual *be* and preterit *had* in the contemporary variety might be more recent innovations or diffusions (Cukor-Avila and Bailey 1995; Poplack, Tagliamonte, and Eze 1999; Tagliamonte and Smith 1999; Walker 1999). Some features that are sometimes seen as distinctly AAE, such as associative *and them* and habitual *steady* (Labov et al. 1968; Baugh 1984) are also robust in Newfoundland English, a variety that shares English input dialects with AAE and Caribbean creoles (Childs and Van Herk 2008), and these features require future quantitative analysis.

1.5 CRITIQUES AND RESPONSES

The strong version of the EOH reflected in Poplack (1999) and Poplack and Tagliamonte (2001) has been challenged in the years since publication (see Rickford 2006; Singler 2007). Here, I enumerate and evaluate some critiques of the EOH.

Representativity: The data sources used by EOH researchers—diaspora communities, ex-slave recordings—are sometimes claimed to represent "marginal" (Singler 1999) AAE communities or the formal end of informants' continua, although such critiques are themselves disputed (Poplack and Tagliamonte 2001; Van Herk 2009).

Representativity should be less of an issue when studies investigate the *constraints* on use of identifiable and variable AAE features. There may be variations in *rates* of use of these features across African American communities or across speaker styles, but it is less likely that such situations would result in a completely different linguistic system (or rule set) that happens to include all the same features. Individual features, of course, may follow different rules in different places (for nineteenth-century regional differences, see Schneider 1989; Van Herk and Walker 2005; or Van Herk, forthcoming). In those situations, researchers must limit the claimed generalizability of their findings.

Cafeteria principle/feature picking: In any comparative enterprise, it is possible to create an appearance of similarity by carefully choosing the points of comparison from the full menu of available diagnostic features. *Pace* Winford (2003), this seems not to be the case for existing EOH studies. Rather, the choice of variables has largely been reactive, testing claims made by others for the non-English history of a variable. EOH researchers also tend to choose variables that lend themselves to multivariate analysis (i.e., those that are frequently occurring, with robust variation and discrete identifiable variants and constraints).

Strength of claims: The AAE origins debate attracts strong personalities with strong opinions, resulting in strong claims and counterclaims; the same is true of debate over the nature and origins of creole languages (see McWhorter 1998; DeGraff 2001). Research on earlier stages of any vernacular language is hampered by less than ideal data and gaps in documentation. It is unlikely that smoking-gun evidence for any feature will surface, but we do seem to be finding more and more data sources. Perhaps future analyses of such sources will encourage more nuanced claims. Perhaps not.

Points of comparison: Many EOH studies discover the linguistic constraints on an earlier AAE feature, then compare them to potentially diagnostic constraints derived from the literature on dialects and creoles to determine likely origins. Sometimes, the choice of relevant comparison variety is questioned; some creoles may not be typical of Atlantic creoles in general, and some dialect varieties may have been in contact with AAE, so that the direction of influence is uncertain. Sometimes the descriptions of comparison varieties are contested (for creoles, see the critiques of Bickerton [1975] by Muysken [1981] and Winford [1992]) and, thus, so are EOH comparisons based on them. Still, as Poplack and Tagliamonte (2001, 208–9) point out, the comparative method requires a quantitative point of comparison, and critics will need to find or supply quantitative data that satisfies them. We will also need to reconsider what we mean by diagnosticity, as some dialect constraints are found to be shared by creoles (Rickford 2010) and as the very idea of distinctively creole linguistic characteristics is challenged (DeGraff 2001; Mufwene 2001).

1.6 CONCLUSION: HYBRID POSITIONS

Some strong early statements of AAE's origins—or descriptions of those statements by writers who disagree with them—allow little room for compromise or complexity. *Early*

AAE was a full-on creole (or it wasn't creole at all); creole features were everywhere (or only in Gullah regions); AAE's distinct features were generated by a completely different underlying grammar (or they result from perfect transmission of dialect features). By necessity, such strong positions must dismiss historical or linguistic counterevidence as marginal or non-representative, rather than integrate it into a hybrid viewpoint. In this section, I suggest a few ways that different data and hypotheses can coexist.

An obvious point of agreement concerns the historicity of AAE, a claim that unfortunately has to be made repeatedly. No matter where the distinct features of the contemporary variety originate, they are part of a system with a long history. Even fairly obscure lexical items like *mother wit* 'common sense' are found in letters from the eighteenth century (Van Herk 1998), and shibboleths like *ax* (for *ask*) are shared with Caribbean creoles and earlier English.

It is unfortunate for hybrid positions that AAE origins research has focused so heavily on morphosyntax, as this aspect of grammar seems the most likely to be transmitted from input dialect varieties. But we can find dialect roots for many morphosyntactic features of AAE (see, for example, the list in Winford [1998]) without rejecting possible influence from other sources—creole, African, or universal. Some input variants may have survived because they mapped easily onto substrate systems. Some input systems may have been heavily adapted when adopted. For example, my non-inverted question findings (Van Herk 2000) imply a restructuring of the system during its extension to auxiliaries, and such restructuring is consistent with some sort of second language acquisition (SLA) process, as proposed by Winford (1997). Some contemporary features may reflect the application of AAE phonological rules to dialect input. For example, the use of *ain't* for *didn't* (*he ain't go*) may have originally developed as dialect/standard *didn't* underwent the deletion of/d/in flapping contexts after stressed pronouns (also found in AAE *I 'o' know* for *I don't know*) (Van Herk 2003). And some non-morphosyntactic domains of AAE—phonology, pragmatics, discourse—may contain robust examples of non-English retentions (see, for example, Rickford and Rickford [1976] on *suck-teeth* and *cut-eye*).

A hybrid position also needs to consider regional variation in AAE (for contemporary work, see Yaeger-Dror and Thomas [2010]). Gullah influences may have spread farther inland at some point (Kautzsch and Schneider 2000), and creole-like or SLA varieties may have existed in situations where isolation or African-origin population ratios encouraged them. Even within the larger African American population, different ethnic ratios may have led to different weighting of dialect and possibly non-dialect constraints on variant choice, as described in Van Herk and Walker (2005) or Van Herk (forthcoming). There is also some evidence that features that are rare in the input to diaspora communities can persist for many generations. For example, *due* for *owe* (as in *he dues me five dollars*) is infrequent in nineteenth-century Liberian letters and is still infrequent in twentieth-century Liberian Settler English (Singler, pers. comm.), and I have (infrequently) heard Gullah-like constructions such as *dem here!* (for *they're here*) in North Preston, a Nova Scotian diaspora enclave with some South Carolina settlement history. Regional variation would also have led to dialect contact situations during the

Great Migration of the early twentieth century, so that what may have started as minority regionally restricted variants could have later been adopted and disseminated as markers of southern or African American identity in urban areas (Wolfram 2004).

This last scenario might mean that some features of contemporary AAE (e.g., habitual *be*) have creole or other non-dialect origins, without being evidence of a widespread earlier creole. Of course, such a proposal would be highly unsatisfactory for adherents of *any* strong position in the origins debate!

NOTES

1. From among the names available for the variety, I chose African American English (AAE) because it is widely recognized and covers past and present instantiations of the variety, and because I am focusing here on AAE's putative English-ness.
2. A number of researchers have presented work that partially or fully supports an EOH perspective for one or another variable; here, I focus on the work from Ottawa, as it is the most clearly developed EOH research enterprise.

REFERENCES

Bailey, Beryl. 1965. "A New Perspective in American Negro Dialectology." *Language Sciences* 9: 20–21.

Bailey, Guy, Natalie Maynor, and Patricia Cukor-Avila. 1991. *The Emergence of Black English: Texts and Commentary*. Amsterdam: John Benjamins.

Baugh, John. 1984. "Steady: Progressive Aspect in Black Vernacular English." *American Speech* 59 (1): 3–12.

Bickerton, Derek. 1971. "Inherent Variability and Variable Rules." *Foundations of Language* 7: 457–92.

———. 1975. *Dynamics of a Creole System*. Cambridge: Cambridge University.

———. 1977. "Pidginization and Creolization: Language Acquisition and Language Universals." In *Pidgin and Creole Linguistics*, edited by Albert Valdman, 49–69. Bloomington: Indiana University Press.

———. 1980. "Decreolization and the Creole Continuum." In *Theoretical Orientations in Creole Studies*, edited by A. Valdman and A. Highfield, 109–27. New York: Academic.

Bonfiglio, Thomas Paul. 2002. *Race and the Rise of Standard American*. Berlin: Mouton de Gruyter.

Childs, Becky, and Gerard Van Herk. 2008. "A Linguistic Time Machine: What Newfoundland Can Tell Us about Earlier Southern English and African American English." Paper presented at Southeastern Conference on Linguistics 75, Knoxville, Tennessee, April 3–5.

Clarke, Sandra. 1997. "English Verbal -s Revisited: The Evidence from Newfoundland." *American Speech* 72 (3): 227–59.

Cukor-Avila, Patricia, and Guy Bailey. 1995. "Grammaticalization in AAVE." In *Proceedings of the Twenty-First Annual Meeting of the Berkeley Linguistics Society (BLS 21)*, edited by Jocelyn Ahlers, Leela Bilmes, Joshua Guenter, Barbara Kaiser, and Ju Namkung, 401–13. Berkeley: Dept. of Linguistics, University of California.

DeBose, Charles E. 1994. "A Note on Ain't vs. Didn't Negation in African American Vernacular." *Journal of Pidgin and Creole Languages* 9 (1): 127–30.

———. 1996. "Question Formation in Samaná English." Paper presented at NWAV 25, Las Vegas, Nevada, October 19–21.

DeGraff, Michel. 2001. "On the Origin of Creoles: A Cartesian Critique of Neo-Darwinian Linguistics." *Linguistic Typology* 5 (2–3): 213–310.

Dillard, J. L. 1972. *Black English: Its History and Usage in the United States.* New York: Random House.

Ellegard, A. 1953. *The Auxiliary* Do: *The Establishment and Regulation of Its Use in English.* Gothenburg Studies in English. Stockholm: Almqvist and Wikwell.

Holm, John. 1984. "Variation of the Copula in Black English and Its Creole Kin." *American Speech* 59 (4): 291–309.

Howe, Darin M. 1997. "Negation and the History of African American English." *Language Variation and Change* 9: 267–94.

Howe, Darin, and James A. Walker. 1999. "Negation and the Creole-Origins Hypothesis: Evidence from Early African American English." In *The English History of African American English*, edited by Shana Poplack, 109–40. Oxford: Blackwell.

Kautzsch, Alexander. 2000. "Liberian Letters and Virginian Narratives: Negation Patterns in Two New Sources of Earlier African American English." *American Speech* 75 (1): 34–53.

———. 2002. *The Historical Evolution of Earlier African American English: An Empirical Comparison of Early Sources.* Berlin: Mouton de Gruyter.

Kautzsch, Alexander, and Edgar W. Schneider. 2000. "Differential Creolization: Some Evidence from Earlier African American Vernacular English in South Carolina." In *Degrees of Restructuring in Creole Languages*, edited by Ingrid Neumann-Holzschuh and Edgar W. Schneider, 247–74. Amsterdam: John Benjamins.

Krapp, George P. 1924. "The English of the Negro." *American Mercury* 2 (5): 192–93.

Kroch, Anthony S. 1989. "Reflexes of Grammar in Patterns of Language Change." *Language Variation and Change* 1: 199–244.

Labov, William. 1966. *The Social Stratification of English in New York City.* Washington, DC: Center for Applied Linguistics.

———. 1972. *Sociolinguistic Patterns.* Philadelphia: University of Pennsylvania Press.

Labov, William, Paul Cohen, Clarence Robins, and John Lewis. 1968. *A Study of the Non-Standard English of Negro and Puerto Rican Speakers in New York City.* U.S. Office of Education Final Report, Research Project 3288.

Labov, William, and Wendell A. Harris. 1986. "De Facto Segregation of Black and White Vernaculars." In *Diversity and Diachrony*, edited by David Sankoff, 1–24. Philadelphia: John Benjamins.

McDavid, Raven I., Jr., and Virginia G. McDavid. 1951. "The Relationship of the Speech of American Negroes to the Speech of Whites." *American Speech* 26: 3–17.

McWhorter, John H. 1998. "Identifying the Creole Prototype: Vindicating a Typological Class." *Language* 74 (4): 788–818.

Melnick, Robin, and John R. Rickford. 2010. "A Variationist Approach to Question Inversion in Caribbean and American Englishes." Paper presented at New Ways of Analyzing Variation 39, San Antonio, Texas, November 5.

Miethaner, Ulrich. 2005. *I Can Look through Muddy Water: Analyzing Earlier African American English in Blues Lyrics.* Frankfurt: Peter Lang.

Montgomery, Michael B. 1999. "Eighteenth-Century Sierra Leone English: Another Exported Variety of African American English." *English World Wide* 10 (3): 227–78.

Montgomery, Michael B., Janet M. Fuller, and Sharon DeMarse. 1993. "'The Black Men has Wives and Sweet Harts [and Third Person Plural -s] jest like the White Men': Evidence for Verbal -s from Written Documents on 19th-Century African American Speech." *Language Variation and Change* 5 (3): 335–57.

Mufwene, Salikoko S. 2001. *The Ecology of Language Evolution.* Cambridge: Cambridge University Press.

Muysken, Pieter. 1981. "Creole Tense/Mood/Aspect Systems: The Unmarked Case?" In *Generative Studies on Creole Languages,* edited by Pieter Muysken, 181–99. Dordrecht: Foris.

Poplack, Shana, ed. 1999. *The English History of African American English.* Oxford: Blackwell.

Poplack, Shana, and David Sankoff. 1987. "The Philadelphia Story in the Spanish Caribbean." *American Speech* 62: 291–314.

Poplack, Shana, and Sali Tagliamonte. 1991. "African American English in the Diaspora: The Case of Old-Line Nova Scotians." *Language Variation and Change* 3 (3): 301–39.

———. 2001. *African American English in the Diaspora.* Oxford: Blackwell.

Poplack, Shana, Sali Tagliamonte, and Ejike Eze. 1999. "Reconstructing the Source of Early African American English Plural Marking: A Comparative Study of English and Creole." In *The English History of African American English,* edited by Shana Poplack, 73–108. Oxford: Blackwell.

Rickford, John R. 1998. "The Creole Origins of African-American Vernacular English: Evidence from Copula Absence." In *African American English: Structure, History, and Use,* edited by Salikoko Mufwene, John R. Rickford, Guy Bailey, and John Baugh, 154–200. London: Routledge.

———. 1999. *African American Vernacular English.* Oxford: Blackwell.

———. 2006. "Down for the Count? The Creole Origins Hypothesis of AAVE at the Hands of the Ottawa Circle, and their Supporters." *Journal of Pidgin and Creole Languages* 21 (1): 97–155.

———. 2010. "Relativizer Omission in Anglophone Caribbean Creoles, Appalachian, and African American Vernacular English [AAVE], and its Theoretical Implications." In *Language from a Cognitive Perspective: Grammar, Usage and Processing,* edited by Emily M. Bender and Jennifer E. Arnold, 139–60. Stanford, CA: CSLI.

Rickford, John R., and Angela E. Rickford. 1976. "Cut-Eye and Suck-Teeth: African Words and Gestures in New World Guise." *Journal of American Folklore* 89: 294–309.

Schneider, Edgar W. 1989. *American Earlier Black English: Morphological and Syntactic Variables.* Tuscaloosa: University of Alabama Press.

Singler, John V. 1989. "Plural Marking in Liberian Settler English, 1820–1980." *American Speech* 64: 4–64.

———. 1999. "Passing Verbal -s from Northern British Vernacular to the Liberian Settler English of Sinoe: Transfer interrupted!" Paper presented at Methods X, St. John's, Newfoundland, August 1–6.

———. 2007. "Samaná and Sinoe, Part I: Stalking the Vernacular." *Journal of Pidgin and Creole Languages* 22 (1): 123–48.

Stewart, William A. 1967. "Sociolinguistic Factors in the History of American Negro Dialects." *The Florida FL Reporter* 5 (2): 11–26.

Sutcliffe, David. 1999. "Creole in the Ex-Slave Recordings and Other Complementary Sources." *Journal of Pidgin and Creole Languages* 14 (2): 351–57.

Tagliamonte, Sali. 1991. "A Matter of Time: Past Temporal Verbal Structures in Samaná and the Ex-Slave Recordings." PhD diss., University of Ottawa.

———. 1997. "Obsolescence in the English Perfect? Evidence from Samaná English." *American Speech* 72 (1): 33–68.

———. 2002. "Comparative Sociolinguistics." In *The Handbook of Language Variation and Change*, edited by J. K. Chambers, Peter Trudgill, and Natalie Schilling-Estes, 729–63. Oxford: Blackwell.

———. 2006. *Analysing Sociolinguistic Variation*. Cambridge: Cambridge University Press.

Tagliamonte, Sali, and Jennifer Smith. 1999. "Old Was, New Ecology: Viewing English through the Sociolinguistic Filter." In *The English History of African American English*, edited by Shana Poplack, 141–74. Oxford: Blackwell.

Tottie, Gunnel, and Dawn Harvie. 1999. "It's All Relative: Relativization Strategies in Early African American English." In *The English History of African American English*, edited by Shana Poplack, 198–232. Oxford: Blackwell.

Van Herk, Gerard. 1998. "Don't Know Much about History: Letting the Data Set the Agenda in the Origins-of-AAVE Debate." Paper presented at New Ways of Analyzing Variation, Athens, Georgia, October 1–4.

———. 2000. "The Question Question: Inversion in Early African American English." In *The English History of African American Vernacular English*, edited by Shana Poplack, 175–97. Oxford: Blackwell.

———. 2003. "Prosodic and Lenition Effects on AAVE Morphosyntax." Paper presented at the Montreal-Ottawa-Toronto Phonology Workshop, Toronto, Ontario, March 12–14.

———. 2008. "Letter Perfect: The Present Perfect in Early African American Correspondence." *English World-Wide* 29 (1): 45–69.

———. 2009. "Variation and Validation in Early African American English Corpora." Southeastern Conference on Linguistics 76, New Orleans, Louisiana, April 8–10.

———. Forthcoming. "Regional Variation in 19th-Century African American English." In *Language Variety in the South: Historical and Contemporary Perspectives*, edited by Michael D. Picone and Catherine Evans Davies, 380–410. Tuscaloosa: University of Alabama Press.

Van Herk, Gerard, and Shana Poplack. 2003. "Rewriting the Past: Bare Verbs in the Ottawa Repository of Early African American Correspondence." *Journal of Pidgin and Creole Languages* 18 (2): 231–66.

Van Herk, Gerard, and James A. Walker. 2005. "S Marks the Spot? Regional Variation and Early African American Correspondence." *Language Variation and Change* 17 (2): 113–31.

Walker, James A. 1999. "Rephrasing the Copula: Contraction and Zero in Early African American English." In *The English History of African American English*, edited by Shana Poplack, 35–72. Oxford: Blackwell.

———. 2001. "Using the Past to Explain the Present: Tense and Temporal Reference in Early African American English." *Language Variation and Change* 13 (1): 1–35.

Weldon, Tracey. 1994. "Variability in Negation in African American Vernacular English." *Language Variation and Change* 6 (3): 359–97.

Winford, Donald. 1992. "Back to the Past: The BEV/Creole Connection Revisited." *Language Variation and Change* 4: 311–57.

———. 1997. "On the Origins of African American Vernacular English—A Creolist Perspective, Part I: The Sociohistorical Background." *Diachronica* 14: 304–44.

———. 1998. "On the Origins of African American Vernacular English—A Creolist Perspective, Part II: The Features." *Diachronica* 15: 99–154.

———. 2003. "Ideologies of Language and Socially Realistic Linguistics." In *Black Linguistics: Language, Society, and Politics in Africa and the Americas*, edited by S. Makoni, Geneva Smitherman, Anthea Ball, and Arthur Spears, 21–39. London: Routledge.

Wolfram, Walt. 2004. "The Grammar of Urban African American Vernacular English." In *Handbook of Varieties of English*, edited by Bernd Kortmann and Edgar Schneider, 111–32. Berlin: Mouton de Gruyter.

Yaeger-Dror, Malcah, and Erik R. Thomas, eds. 2010. *African American English Speakers and their Participation in Local Sound Changes: A Comparative Study*. Durham, NC: Duke University Press.

CHAPTER 2

··

THE CREOLE ORIGINS
HYPOTHESIS

··

JOHN R. RICKFORD

2.1 INTRODUCTION

In a rarely cited introduction[1] to a reprint of his two classic creolist articles (Stewart 1967, 1968), Stewart (1970) noted that a "disagreement" had surfaced among participants at a Conference on Social Dialects and Language Learning held in Bloomington, Indiana, in summer 1964:[2]

> Beryl L. Bailey and the author took the position that *American Negro dialects probably derived from a creolized form of English, once spoken on American plantations by Negro slaves and seemingly related to creolized forms of English which are still spoken by Negroes in Jamaica and other parts of the Caribbean.* Bailey and the author held the opinion that, although most American Negro dialects have now merged enough with white speech to preclude their still being considered truly creole dialects, the apparent survival of some creole features in many of them was a likely explanation of their more unique (vis-à-vis white speech) structural characteristics. . . . [But] some of the participants had already come to a quite different set of conclusions. . . . In their view, *there never was any pidgin or creole stage through which the English spoken by early American Negro slaves might have passed. Instead, the acquisition of colonial English by Negro slaves on the early North American plantations was believed to have been both rapid and successful, so that within one or two generations American Negro speech evidenced the same inventory of structural features as white speech.* (1970, 352; emphasis added)

This is probably the earliest documented evidence we have of a creolist/Anglicist controversy among linguists about the origins of African American Vernacular English (AAVE),[3] with their respective positions summarized in the italicized parts of Stewart's quotation.

Fifty years later, the "disagreement" or "controversy" continues, but it has evolved, to some extent. For one thing, no current "creolist" favors the view expressed by Stewart (1967) and Dillard (1972) that there was a widespread full creole across large areas of the American South. Even in the writings of the early creolists (see Dillard 1972, 86, 98), there is some acknowledgment that there was variation in AAVE by social group, region, and century, and this is much more so in the work of later creolists like Winford (1998) and myself (see Rickford 1997, 1998), who tend to speak of creole "influences" rather than a widespread full-on creole. Moreover, no creolists worth their salt could deny English influences, since creole varieties invariably include considerable influence from their lexically derived source languages—obvious enough in the vocabulary of Caribbean English creoles, for instance, but also, to varying extents, in their phonology and grammar.

The issue has usually been whether features must be attributed *only* to English dialects (when reasonable African or creole substrate sources were also available—see discussion in Rickford and Rickford 2000, 147-57), or whether *all* possibility of creolist influence must be denied. That seemed to be the position of the earliest "Anglicists" or "dialectologists," as summarized in the preceding quotation from Stewart (1970). That, however, is not the position of Schneider, Van Herk, Winford, or Mufwene, as expressed in their chapters in this volume, who all call for hybrid or compromise positions of some sort. Even Mufwene, who is most skeptical about creole origins hypotheses for African American vernacular varieties other than Gullah, states in his conclusion that "regarding the emergence of AAVE, the evidence appears to speak against *some* creole origins" (emphasis added). To the earlier anti-creolists who would deny *all* possibility of creole influence, I would respond that if we find at least *one* feature in AAVE that *cannot* be attributed to English but only or most likely to creole origins or influence, the creolist hypothesis is sustained. As Armin Schwegler put it (2001, 2014), if we find a car on the moon, we can be (almost) certain that a human being brought it there.

In several publications (Rickford 1977, 1997, 1998; Rickford and Rickford 2000), I have laid out the kinds of evidence that are potentially relevant to this controversy. Table 2.1 lists the six main types I currently consider most important.

Table 2.1 Types of Evidence Relevant to the Creole Origins Hypothesis

1 Sociohistorical conditions (suitable for pidginization and/or creolization)
2 Historical attestations (literary texts, ex-slave narratives and recordings)
3 Diaspora recordings (Samaná, Liberian Settler English, African Nova Scotian English)
4 Creole similarities (between AAVE and Caribbean creoles, Gullah, Hawaiian, etc.)
5 African language similarities (between AAVE and West African varieties)
6 English dialect differences (between AAVE and British/White American dialects)

In this chapter, I will discuss in turn evidence of type 1 (sociohistorical conditions), 6 (English dialect differences), and 4 (creole similarities). I will focus on auxiliary and copula absence as I did in Rickford (1998), because it is one of the most distinctive and extensively researched features of AAVE. But I will draw on relevant work published since then, too, including Morgan (1998), Weldon (2003a, b), and Sharma and Rickford (2009). And I will also respond to relevant observations in other chapters dealing with the AAVE origins issue in this volume.

2.2 SOCIOHISTORICAL CONDITIONS

In general, in considering whether sociohistorical conditions favored prior creolization, we have to distinguish between conditions for the *development* of a creole on US soil and conditions for the *importation* of a creole (developed elsewhere) into the United States. In the thirteen original colonies (1607–1776) conditions for the *development* of a homegrown creole were extremely poor in the New England and middle colonies, where the proportion of Africans or their descendants to the total population in each territory was low (3 percent to 7 percent in 1750). But the conditions were more favorable in the southern colonies, especially in Virginia and South Carolina, where the Black percentages by 1850 were much higher (e.g., 43.9 percent in Virginia and 60.9 percent in South Carolina). Indeed, on some of the islands and along the coast of South Carolina, those percentages were as high as 79 to 93 percent, and these proportions undoubtedly facilitated the emergence in this region of Gullah, whose creole status is not in question. Even Georgia, which was only 19.2 percent Black in 1750, had become 48 percent Black by 1776, and 76 to 77 percent Black in coastal counties like Liberty and Chatham by 1790 (Wood 1975; Smith 1985; Franklin and Moss 1988, 61). Since nearly 90 percent of all Blacks in the United States were concentrated in the South from the mid-eighteenth century until they migrated north and west from the early twentieth century to the mid-1970s (Wilkerson 2010), *it is southern colonies and states that are most significant when the conditions for prior creolization on US soil are considered* (Rickford 1997, 318). And although the 40 to 60 percent Black population percentages in Virginia and South Carolina in 1750 do not quite match the 80 percent substrate language minimum for pidgin-creole genesis that Bickerton (1981, 4) had proposed, lower percentages (e.g., 35 percent in Haiti twenty-five years after its founding, and 51 percent in Martinique) have been associated with the formation of creoles elsewhere (Williams 1985, 31; Singler 1995, 210–11; Parkvall 2000). In short, the percentage of Blacks and Whites (or more generally, of second language learners to first or target language speakers) is not the only relevant demographic or contact consideration, as Singler (2008) and others have noted.

Conditions for the *importation* of a creole were much stronger both in the middle colonies and the South, as I have noted elsewhere (Rickford 1997), especially in the all-important founder populations, which, as Mufwene (1996) has suggested, can have a lasting influence on the language situation of an emerging colony. In New York, from 1701 to 1765, almost three times more slaves were imported from the West Indies (3,324) than directly from Africa (1,201), and most of the West Indian imports were from Jamaica, Antigua, and Barbados (Medford et al. 2009).[4]

In South Carolina, this was also the case in the first twenty-five years of its founding (1670–1695; Wood 1975, 130). This was also the case in Georgia in the intensive mid- to late-eighteenth-century period in which its slave population increased (Smith 1985, 94) and in the Virginia/Maryland region known as the Chesapeake:

> Until the mid-1670s, when slaves were shipped directly from Africa, most of the Chesapeake's blacks came from Barbados and other Caribbean colonies or from the Dutch colony of New Netherland (which the English conquered in 1664 and renamed New York). (Davis 1986, 8)

> The origins of the earliest black immigrants to the Chesapeake and [South Carolina] Low Country were similar. Most came, not directly from Africa, but from the West Indies. Some might have only recently arrived in the islands from their homeland, and a few were probably born in the Caribbean, but most were seasoned slaves—acclimatized to the New World environment and somewhat conversant with the ways of whites. (Morgan 1998, 2–3)

Slaves imported to the British North American colonies from Caribbean colonies with larger Black populations, on bigger plantations, were very likely to be speaking a creole, rather than the nonstandard (but closer to standard English) dialects that indentured servants and other Whites from the British Isles brought to the New World. By 1690, Blacks in Jamaica constituted 75 percent of the population, thirty-five years after the colony was settled (Williams 1985, 31), and it is likely that its distinctive pidgin/creole-like English had already begun to jell (Cassidy and Le Page 1967, xli–xlii; Cassidy 1986). The creole speech of Barbados, where Blacks were about 70 percent of the population by 1684 (Winford 2000, 220), was never as basilectal or nonstandard as the creole speech of Jamaica, although Rickford (1992), Rickford and Handler (1995), and Fields (1995) show that it has had a vibrant mesolectal English creole for some time. Cassidy and Le Page (2002, xl), noting that St. Kitts, Nevis, and Barbados "had been settled since the 1620s," believed that "by the 1650's the patterns of Creole speech in these islands were already formed."

Note that Cassidy and Le Page's statement runs contrary to the skepticism expressed by Mufwene (2004, 308) about whether creole vernaculars (basilects) were already in place at the time when slave importation from Barbados to North America was the most significant, namely in the late seventeenth and early to mid-eighteenth centuries. Also challenging that skepticism is the speech of Tituba, the Amerindian slave from Barbados who testified at the Salem Witch Trials of 1692 in Massachusetts. Her speech is creole-like in displaying a clear zero copula:[5]

He tell me he Ø God. (1692 testimony of Tituba: Breslaw 1996, 195)

Although occasional instances of zero copula have been reported in the British Isles, it is not a regular feature of British English, as it is, for instance, of Caribbean Anglophone creoles or of fluently spoken AAVE.

Mufwene has argued (in 2000 and in his chapter in this volume) that AAVE did not emerge as a separate variety in the United States until after the post–Civil War period of Jim Crow segregation of the late nineteenth and twentieth centuries, and the Great Migration that began in the late nineteenth and early twentieth centuries. He argues that AAVE emerged in the settings of tobacco and cotton plantations, which became racially segregated only after the abolition of slavery in the 1860s. And he suggests (in his chapter in this volume) that

> AAVE and WASE [White American Southern English] have common origins. They appear to have been one and the same regional variety until Jim Crow was introduced in the late nineteenth century and triggered the Great Migration of African Americans out of the South. AAVE was invented as a separate ethnolect in the North, where most White Americans were then getting their first exposure to American Southern English.

However, Virginia, like other southern states (and some northern ones too), was the source of court decisions, and then slave laws in the late seventeenth and early eighteenth centuries that increasingly differentiated Black servants and slaves from (indentured) White servants (Schwartz 2010).[6] In 1640, for instance, two runaway White servants were ordered by the court in Virginia to serve an additional four years, because only the labor of the servant was owned, not the person. But the third runaway, a Black servant named John Punch, was ordered to serve for the time of his natural life. In statutes passed in 1669 and 1670, often based on the Barbados slave code of 1661, the Virginia House of Assembly made it clear that "bondage for life" had become the accepted rule for the Negro (Foner 1975, 193). And in 1705, Virginia consolidated its various regulations concerning Black slaves into a single slave code. As Foner (1975, 194–95) noted:

> The 1705 code ... consolidated previous repressive laws designed to keep the Negroes under control. Such laws had declared assemblies among slaves illegal, prohibited them from carrying any weapons, and forbade them from leaving plantations without the written permission of their masters. But the 1705 code also increased punishments for slaves by providing that for petty offenses slaves were to be whipped, maimed, or branded. . . . With the enactment of the 1705 code Virginia now had a fully developed system of chattel slavery by which Black men and women were reduced to a status of abject degradation as complete as anywhere in the world.

Similar laws were passed in Maryland, the Carolinas, and Georgia in the seventeenth and eighteenth centuries, and they regulated virtually EVERY aspect of slaves' lives, including their ability to go off their plantation (forbidden, except with a ticket from their master or overseer), or congregate in large numbers, carry clubs or arms, or strike a

White person (also forbidden). Also any White person was authorized to apprehend any Negro who could not give a satisfactory account of himself (Foner 1975, 220-23).

One might argue that these repressive laws did not have the same separating effect as the segregation laws of the late nineteenth century, but they *did* restrict the movements, lives, and fortunes of Blacks, and they probably fostered a sense of distinct identity sufficient to promote the emergence of a distinct Black ethnolect (as one style or code among others slaves might have possessed) long before the Jim Crow laws of the nineteenth century. As Wood (1975, 187–88) has noted, speaking about South Carolina as a whole rather than just the Sea Islands or coastal areas:

> The slaves had serious reservations of their own about the acquisition of English. Proficiency could be a means of advancement, but standard English could not, and never would, provide so simple a key to upward mobility for Blacks as it did for White newcomers. And if knowledge of good English could occasionally be used to advantage, as in eavesdropping or newspaper reading, bad English was discovered to be an equally effective weapon. *To cultivate a dialect few Whites could understand and to be able to adopt a stance of incomprehension toward their master's speech proved effectual elements of resistance.* Such things considered, colonial slaves could not have felt the same eagerness to acquire the dominant language that seized voluntary immigrants in later times. (emphasis added)

Moreover, despite Mufwene's assumptions that the language and culture of Blacks and Whites were similar or identical ("one and the same") in the seventeenth, eighteenth, and early nineteenth centuries (the Blacks having acculturated successfully to White norms in homestead and similar contexts), it is striking that many respected historians, often drawing on contemporary sources, paint a different picture. For instance, Peter Wood, a leading South Carolina historian cited by both Mufwene and Winford (in their contributions to this volume and elsewhere), referred in his classic *Black Majority* book to the distinctiveness of the Black South Carolina dialect (again, not just referring to Gullah), which would have been reinforced by the fact that "after the first generation ... most new Negroes learned the local language not from Englishmen, but from other slaves" (1975, 187). And Allan Kulikoff (1986, 351), a leading Chesapeake historian also cited by Mufwene and Winford, reports that late-eighteenth-century observers also referred to Black cultural practices as distinctive and different from those of Whites:

> White observers agreed that the music, dance and religiosity of Black slaves [in the Chesapeake] differed remarkably from those of whites. . . . The practice of a distinctive culture within their own quarters gave them some small power over their own lives and destinies.

Indeed, Kulikoff himself (1986, 327–28) suggests that a creole emerged in the region:

> A new creole language may have emerged in the Chesapeake region combining the vocabulary of several African languages common among the immigrants, African linguistic structures, and the few English words needed for communication with the master.

Morgan (1998, 565) feels in general that "in the Chesapeake, Africans seem to have mastered English rather more quickly than in the Lowcountry."[7] But he too points to "instances of mutual unintelligibility between whites and blacks and of distinctive black speech patterns . . . in the Chesapeake region" (1998, 572).

In sum, sociohistorical conditions for the development of a creole on US soil were stronger in the South than anywhere else, but considering this is where 90 percent of the Black population in the United States lived until the start of the twentieth century (Bailey and Maynor 1987, 466, citing Hamilton 1972, and other sources), the geographical restriction is not significant. Moreover, the conditions for the importation of creole English from the Caribbean, in the founding period up until the end of the eighteenth century, and to some extent thereafter, are very strong. Finally, the evidence of contemporary observers and some attested speech, both suggest that Blacks and Whites differed both linguistically and culturally in at least some regions, rather than exhibiting the homogeneity with White speech that others seem to have assumed.

2.3 COPULA ABSENCE: DIFFERENCE FROM BRITISH DIALECT

Whatever distinctive grammatical features of AAVE might have come from British dialects—and there are several good candidates (Schneider 1989 and this volume; Winford 1998; Van Herk, this volume)—copula absence is not likely to have been one of them. Poplack (2000, 20), introducing her edited collection on the *English* history of African American English, conceded as much: "zero copula is perhaps the only variant studied in this volume which cannot be identified as a legacy of English." Wolfram (1974, 522) found no evidence of this feature in a search of the available records of British varieties either, and as far as I know, it does not show up in transplanted varieties like Australian or New Zealand English.

Martin and Tagliamonte (1999) do report scattered British historical attestations from Visser (1970) and other sources, some contemporary examples from Scots English (the latter all involving existential constructions before __NP, as in, "There Ø a big tree at the gate," from Macaulay 1991, 59) and others from Wheatley Hill in Durham, England. But the frequencies of zero copula in the contemporary Wheatley Hill corpus are low (zero *is* + *are* = 13 percent; zero *is* = 2 percent; zero *are* = 25 percent), much lower than in contemporary AAVE, and there is no evidence that they exhibit the same patterning by following grammatical environment for which AAVE is famous.

As far as White American dialects are concerned, in general, they do not display copula absence, especially outside of the South (e.g., in New York and California, see Labov 1969; McElhinny 1993, respectively). Several southern varieties—e.g., in Mississippi (Wolfram 1974); Alabama (Feagin 1979); and Texas (Bailey and Maynor 1985; Cukor-Avila and Bailey, this volume)—do show copula absence, especially with *are*. But apart from the fact that the effect of following grammatical environment is not always as finely differentiated as it is in AAVE (see Rickford 1998, 187–89), it is very likely that the southern White copula absence pattern represents AAVE influence rather than the other way around, as suggested by Wolfram (1974, 524). It is certainly striking that outside of the South, where most African Americans lived until the start of the twentieth century, copula absence is not found among White Americans.

2.4 COPULA ABSENCE: SIMILARITIES WITH CREOLES

Absence of copula and auxiliary *is* and *are*, as in examples (1)–(5) below, is the most extensively studied feature of AAVE and the one that was first given a quantitative, variationist analysis (Labov 1969). It is also the feature whose parallels with creole varieties led to the first formulations of the creole hypothesis (Bailey 1965; Stewart 1969) and the one that has been invoked in many subsequent formulations (Bickerton 1971; Holm 1976, 1984; Baugh 1980; Edwards 1980; Rickford and Blake 1990; Rickford 1998; Sharma and Rickford 2009, among others):[8]

(1) __Noun Phrase: She Ø the first one started us off. (35, S. Carolina)
(2) __Adj: He Ø fast in everything he do. (16, Jets, Harlem, NY)
(3) __Locative: We Ø on tape (16, Chicago)
(4) __Verb + *ing*: . . . he Ø gettin' cripple up from arthritis (48, N. Carolina)
(5) __ *gon(na)*. Verb: He Ø gon try to get up. (12, T-Birds, Harlem, NY)

The relative frequency with which the AAVE copula[9] is absent in these and similar examples is systematically conditioned by various grammatical and phonological factors, but the one that often emerges as the strongest constraint, and the one that shows the most consistent parallels with creole varieties, is the following grammatical environment. The copula is LEAST likely to be absent before a following noun phrase, and MOST likely to be absent before a following *gon(na)*, with the other following environments ordered in as in (6):

(6) __Noun Phrase < __Locative < __Adjective < __Verb + *ing* < __*gonna* Verb

Although this ordering is not strictly attested in every quantitative study of AAVE copula absence (the relative positions of locative and adjective show the greatest fluctuation), it is followed with amazing consistency, as shown in figure 2.1 (from Sharma and Rickford 2009, 63, based on eight AAVE data sets) and its very high average Spearman coefficient (.93) and Cronbach alpha (.969) measures.[10]

Moreover, a very similar patterning is found in copula absence in mesolectal varieties of creole English,[11] as shown in figure 2.2 (from Sharma and Rickford 2009, 64, based on seven data sets from Jamaica, Barbados, Trinidad, and Hawaii) and *its* high average Spearman coefficient (.84) and Cronbach alpha (.951) measures.

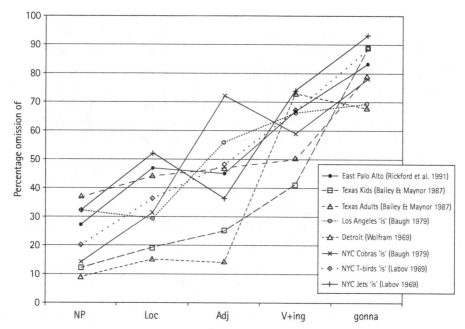

FIGURE 2.1 Copula absence in contemporary AAVE (from Sharma and Rickford 2009, 64, based on table 6.16 in Rickford 1998, 190).

Notes: Average R_S (correspondence to AAVE order): .93 (p < .05, nearly perfect correlation); Cronbach's α (internal consistency): 0.969.

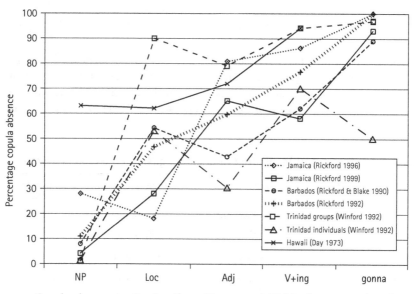

FIGURE 2.2 Copula absence in Creoles (from Sharma and Rickford 2009, 64, based on table 6.16 in Rickford 1998, 190).

Notes: Average R_S (correspondence to AAVE order): .84 (very strong correlation); Cronbach's α (internal consistency): 0.951.

It was these striking similarities, and the fact that they could not be attributed to descent from British or any other English varieties (remember that English makes no similar distinction in the form or frequency of the copula depending on its following grammatical environment), that led many linguists to link the AAVE pattern to possible creole influence. James Sledd is quoted in Labov (1982, 198) as referring to this parallelism between AAVE and the creoles as the first serious evidence for the creole hypothesis. And Winford (1992, 49), after a detailed comparison of copula absence in AAVE and Trinidadian Creole English, concluded that, "in view of the startling similarity of all these patterns of use, there would appear to be little reason to reject the view that the BEV [= AAVE] copula system owes its origin to a process of decreolization similar to that observable in the creole continua of the Caribbean." He went on to provide the model of decreolization for Caribbean English creole copula systems shown in table 2.2.

This model incorporates several of the elements present in earlier attempts to explain the relative frequency of copula absence in AAVE and/or Caribbean mesolectal creoles by reference to decreolization. For instance, the basilectal or deep creole pre-NP copula form *a* (as in *shii a di liida* "She is the leader") is replaced by invariant *is* and later by inflected *be*, rather than zero, as a way of accounting for the fact that this environment almost always shows the lowest rate of zero. By contrast, basilectal preverbal *a* (in progressives and the future) is replaced by zero in the lower mesolect and does not begin to show variable insertion of *be* until the upper mesolect, consonant with the synchronic finding that these environments are always the most favorable to copula absence in AAVE and the Caribbean Creoles.

However, Winford (1998), faced with objections from Poplack and Sankoff (1987) and Mufwene (1992) to the assumption that a model like that in table 2.2 applied also to the development of copula absence in AAVE, formulated a somewhat different hypothesis:

> My present position is that the copula pattern of AAVE is best explained as the result of imperfect second language learning, with transfer from creolized or restructured varieties playing a significant role. . . . On the one hand, many Africans must have acquired a close approximation to the superstrate copula system from the earliest

Table 2.2 Decreolization Model for Caribbean English Creole Copula Systems

	Basilect	Lower mesolect	Upper mesolect	Acrolect
__Noun Phrase	*a*	→ Invariant *is*	→ *is*/forms of *be*	→ Inflected *be*
__Adjective	Ø	→ Ø	→ Ø/forms of *be*	→ Inflected *be*
__Locative	*de*	→ Ø	→ Ø/forms of *be*	→ Inflected *be*
__Progressive	*a* Verb	→ Ø Verb + in	→ (*be*) Verb + in	→ *be* Verb + in
__Future	*a go* Verb	→ Ø *goin* Verb	→ (*be*) *goin to* V	→ *be goin to* V

Source: Winford 1992, 34.

stages of contact. Other groups of Africans speaking African languages, and later, creole or other forms of restructured English in which copula absence was common, shifted toward these established forms of AAVE, introducing further changes due to imperfect learning. This manifested itself in simplification (loss) of copula forms as well as substratum transfer. The latter is most clearly manifested in the patterns of copula absence according to following grammatical environment which AAVE shares to a large extent with creoles like Barbadian and its relative, Gullah. (1992, 111)

In response to this, note first that Winford still attributes some responsibility for the current patterns of AAVE copula absence to creole or restructured English influence, and with this I would concur. On the other hand, the suggestion that the AAVE patterns could be partly attributed to general patterns of simplification in second language acquisition was not supported by Sharma and Rickford's (2009) examination of several studies of the acquisition of English by speakers of other languages, including some (see Mesthrie 1992) originally referred to by Winford himself. As table 2.3 indicates, the relative frequency of copula absence in those studies is very different from the pattern consistently found in AAVE and the creoles.

Note, in particular, the high frequency of zero copula before NPs in South African Indian English and the low frequency of zero copula before V-*ing* in the Singapore English of Chinese and Malay L1 speakers.

But what is the explanation for the consistent pattern of copula absence by following grammatical environment found in the Caribbean English Creole mesolects and AAVE? The traditional explanation, for example, in Stewart (1969), is that these differences in *frequencies* reflect differences in the *forms* of the copula required for different predicates in the creole basilect (the latter ultimately going back to differences in copula forms in ancestral African varieties[12]) and in the *order* and *way* these forms change in the process of decreolization. For instance, Stewart (1969), building on Bailey's (1965, 175) observation that Jamaican Creole distinguished between "zero before adjectives, an obligatory *a* before nominals, and a *de* which is often deleted before locatives," noted that a similar distinction obtained in earlier, basilectal Gullah and thus argued that a hypothetical process of decreolization could explain the modern distribution of copula absence in mesolectal Gullah as well as AAVE. Rickford (1998, 173) summarizes Stewart's argument as follows:[13]

> Earlier recorded forms of Gullah showed *da* as an obligatory copula both before predicate nominals (parallel to *a* in JC [Jamaican Creole]), and before unmarked verbs, so that *Dem da fish* meant both "They are fish" and "They are fishing" (p. 244). However, *da* + V then decreolized to Ø *Ving*, while *da* + NP was retained for equation, and later relexified to *iz* + NP. Subsequently, as Stewart went on to argue (although not in precisely these terms), *iz* was variably introduced in _V+*ing* environments, and zero was variably introduced in _NP environments. But the fact that zero was diachronically introduced in continuative verbal (_V+*ing*) environments earlier than it was in nominal (_NP) environments explained why copula absence was today more common in the verbal than in the nominal environments, both in mesolectal Gullah and—if the same decreolizing process were assumed—in AAVE.

Table 2.3 Frequency of Copula Absence by Following Environment in Creoles, AAVE, and Various Studies of the Acquisition of English by Speakers of Other Languages

Data set		Ordering of predicate contexts (lowest to highest rate of zero copula)								
A	AAVE	NP	<	Loc	<	Adj	<	V-*ing*	<	*gonna*
B	Creole	NP	<	Loc	<	Adj	<	V-*ing*	<	*gonna*
C	Indian English (Indo-Aryan LIs)	*gonna*	<	Adj	<	NP	<	Loc	<	V-*ing*
D	South African Indian English (Mesthrie 1992, Indo-Aryan L1s)	Loc.	<	Adj	<	NP			<	V-*ing*
E	South African Indian English (Mesthrie 1992, Dravidian L1s)	Loc	<	Adj	<	V-*ing*			<	NP
F	Singapore English (Platt 1979, Malay-medium)	V-*ing*	≈	NP	<	Adj			<	Loc
G	Singapore English (Platt 1979, Chinese-medium)	V-*ing*	≈	NP	≈	LOC			<	Adj
H	Singapore English (Platt 1979, English-medium)	Loc	≈	NP	<	V-*ing*			<	Adj
I	Singapore English (Ho 1986, Chinese L1)	Loc	≈	NP	<	Adj			≈	V-*ing*
J	Spanish Learner of English (Butterworth and Hatch 1978)	NP	≈	Adj	≈	LOC			<	V-*ing*
K	Spanish Learners of English (Shapira 1978)					PredP			<	V-*ing*

Source: From Sharma and Rickford 2009, table 4, 76.

Interestingly enough, Stewart had no synchronic quantitative evidence that copula absence by following grammatical environment in mesolectal Gullah followed the general Caribbean/AAVE pattern in AAVE. That would not come until Weldon (2003a, b).

The preceding explanation for the parallelisms between mesolectal English creoles and AAVE has not been without its challenges, discussed and responded to in Winford (1992, 48–49; 1998, 111) and Rickford (1998, 179–85). Space will not allow me to repeat the discussion, but to the extent that there is relevant new data or argumentation, I will mention it here.

For instance, in response to Mufwene's (1992) query about why AAVE showed higher rates of copula absence before NP than Caribbean creole mesolects generally do (contrast figure 2.1 above with figure 2.2), there is now the evidence of Weldon (2003a, 66; 2003b, 182) that mesolectal Gullah shows higher copula absence rates before __NP (27 percent for *is*-absence, 30 to 56 percent for *are*-absence) than does Trinidadian (1 percent) or Jamaican (3 percent), as tabulated in Rickford (1998, 190). And since Gullah is geographically and historically closer to AAVE than the Caribbean varieties, that is perhaps the more relevant comparison. But this finding allows us to note that the pre-NP copula absence rates for some other creole Englishes are also high (JC in DeCamp's 1960 texts: 28 percent; Hawaiian 63 percent), and to make the general variationist point (cf. Poplack 2002, 14, on rates versus conditioning) that it is not the absolute levels of copula absence that matter, but their relative levels compared with other following grammatical environments. In both the Gullah and the other seemingly "aberrant" cases, the "high" pre-NP rates are generally lower than the rates before __Adj, __Ving, and __gon.

Weldon (2003a) is also revealing with respect to another detraction that Mufwene (1992) and others have raised: Shouldn't __Adj copula absence be consistently higher than __Loc, if adjectives never require a copula in the creole basilect, while locatives do (*de*)? Rickford et al. (1991, 121) had already shown that while the "high __Adj" pattern was generally followed in AAVE, the __Loc and __Adj predicates were more likely to be reversed than any other two adjacent predicates in the following grammatical hierarchy for copula absence. To this, Rickford (1998) added the observation that the "high Adj" pattern was more likely to be followed in creole mesolects that were closer to or surrounded by deep basilects (like Jamaican) than those that were not (like Barbadian and Trinidadian). The "mesolectal to upper mesolectal system" that Weldon (2003a, 68) analyzes in Gullah corroborates this analysis, since it is more similar to Barbadian and Trinidadian in showing higher copula absence before __Loc than __Adj (55 percent versus 41 percent, respectively, for *is* absence; 75 percent versus 56 percent, respectively, for post vocalic *are* absence).[14] This may lend some support to decreolizing models like those in Singler (1991) and Winford (1992, see table 2.3 above) in which the pre-locative creole copula (*de*) goes to zero before *be* forms variably come in, blurring or wiping out the basilectal distinction between pre-adjectival and pre-locative predicates.

Turning now to the distinction between copula environments and auxiliary environments in the strict sense (see note 6)—the most robust part of the hierarchy of copula absence by predicate or following grammatical environment, and a pattern that is also found in *some* cases of L1 or L2 acquisition (D, I, J, K in table 2.3 above)—Sharma and Rickford (2009, 84–85) have proposed an explanation:

> This may be attributed in part to the perceived redundancy, on the part of the learner, in using an auxiliary with a verbal predicate. Auxiliary uses of *be* with V-*ing* and *gon(na)* involve verbal content or inflection . . . at a minimum of two points in the

clause—the auxiliary and the progressive verb—whereas copula sentences with non-verbal predicates require morphological inflection at only one point. . . . This perception of redundancy can explain high rates of auxiliary *be* omission insofar as speakers perceive progressive and *gon(na)* future predicates as bearing sufficient marking of verbal features, while non-verbal predicates require an overt bearer of verbal information in the form of a copula.[15]

2.5 CONCLUSION

In closing, I must emphasize the tremendous need for new research, both synchronic, on present-day AAVE use in areas that have been studied minimally if at all, and on sociohistory. Research on *synchronic linguistic variation* in the use of the copula and other features by African Americans and Whites is badly needed, especially in the vast areas of the South that have not been covered by others, for example, Cukor-Avila (1999), Weldon (2003a, b), and Wolfram (this volume), as well as by Wolfram and his colleagues and students (Wolfram and Thomas 2002). Kautzsch and Schneider (2000), for instance, using ex-slave narrative data from different regions of South Carolina with varying densities of Black populations, have suggested that there were varying degrees of "creolization" in those regions, as represented in the number and kinds of "creole" features in the kinds of AAVE attested there. This innovative diachronic research now needs to be accompanied by good synchronic, present-day sociolinguistic, variationist research in the various regions of South Carolina. And we need comparable research in Florida, Mississippi, Tennessee, Virginia, and other areas of the South that have been the site of few if any community studies.

We also additionally need new *sociohistorical research* on language, culture, and the interactions of Blacks (and Whites) in America, from the seventeenth century to the present, colony by colony, state by state, and at the level of counties and plantations and homesteads at which linguistic interactions and acculturations take place. Among linguists, Dillard, Mufwene, Winford, and I, inter alia, have made helpful initial forays into this area, but much more remains to be done.

We all agree, I think, that variations by region and time period in demographic and ecological conditions, attitudes, and source language inputs would have influenced the kinds of English that African, Caribbean, and African American peoples developed in colonial and post-independent America. Given such variation, some Blacks would indeed have come to approximate the speech of indentured and other immigrant Whites closely, but others would *not* have, retaining substrate African or creole languages for a while, and leaving their influences in the distinctive English they spoke and bequeathed to subsequent generations. We also agree that the South—especially colonial Virginia and Maryland, Georgia, and North and South Carolina—should be the primary focus of future research and that documentary evidence is almost nonexistent for the seventeenth century, better (but still limited) for the eighteenth century, and best for the nineteenth and twentieth centuries.

Mufwene and Winford are both more sanguine about the extent to which Black speech was influenced by White speech than I am,[16] but Winford seems more open to acknowledging creole influences on AAVE than Mufwene is. I support Winford's closing observation (in this volume) that "it is high time we recognize that the different positions [Anglicist and creolist] complement each other, and that together, they offer the most comprehensive view of AAVE origins." What I would resist (cf. Rickford 2006, 99) is a return to the pre-Herskovits (1941) position that the acquisition of English language and culture in America by Black people was influenced only or overwhelmingly by the models they encountered from Whites, with little or no impact from the languages they brought with them from Africa and the Caribbean or without adaptations on American soil. Some Anglicists seem to have held such positions, but none of those representing the Anglicist position in this volume, including Mufwene, Schneider, and Van Herk do.

I also believe that we should not treat absence of evidence as evidence of absence (i.e., in relation to the absence of linguistic records in the seventeenth century), and, remembering how *late* in the evolution of AAVE are the periods they represent, that we should not dwell excessively on Hoodoo records, ex-slave narratives, and other texts from the twentieth century (or at best the late nineteenth century). While there *are* difficulties in using literary and other attestations from earlier periods (pointed out by Schneider and others in this volume), there are strategies for dealing with those difficulties (cf. Rickford 1986; Schneider 2002; and others), and we simply cannot afford to differ from all other historical linguists by dismissing them out of hand. I am confident that there *is* more sociolinguistically relevant evidence in the historical archives and historiography of colonial America—including commentary on and attestations of Black "English," than linguists have yet discovered or used. I hope future researchers prove me right, and that, in mining it, they take our discussion of the earliest roots of AAVE considerably further than we have been able to so far.

Two aspects of Black language use in earlier periods strike me as particularly in need of further research. One is the extent to which Black slaves and freedmen had *repertoires of styles or varieties* between which they could switch, much as most African Americans do today (hence Winford's definition of AAVE in this volume—adopted by me [see note 2], as referring to the variety spoken in informal contexts). So much of what we have written and said about their speech in earlier times implies that Blacks had only one variety so that if they were able to develop a pattern closer to White speech, we assume that they did not simultaneously have access to a more distinctly "Black" style as well. But Morgan (1998, 575), whose work I find extremely revealing, suggests otherwise:

> Although significant differences existed between these two regional speech communities, slaves in the Chesapeake and Lowcountry used language in similar ways. In both regions, slaves switched between different varieties of language, employed words in artful and inventive ways, and pronounced words in similar fashion.
>
> Slaves employed varieties of language in different contexts. They switched registers within the same language and switched codes—that is, between languages. . . .

That many slaves, particularly in the Chesapeake, spoke an English that whites could readily understand cannot, therefore, preclude the possibility that they spoke a creole among themselves. In short, the languages both Chesapeake and Lowcountry slaves spoke among themselves might have been far more alike than the ones they spoke to whites.

Another is the way in which *convergence* between various African American speech styles (regional, African versus creole, and so on) came about. Morgan (1998, 670-71) attributes cultural convergence among different regional Black traditions to the mixing of peoples on the frontier, as people moved south and west, for example, to the Natchez District east of the Mississippi River, and to trans-Appalachian territories like Tennessee and Kentucky. He also sees the rise of King Cotton in the nineteenth century as a major innovative and converging force. The role of the internal slave trade by which slaves were moved from the Chesapeake into upcountry Georgia and eastern Texas is yet another lacuna in study of the origins of AAVE that requires new sociolinguistic research.

Notes

1. I am grateful to my former co-author Jerome Handler (Rickford and Handler 1994), currently at the Virginia Foundation for the Humanities, for very helpful feedback on the sociohistorical section of this chapter, and to the editors of this volume for their comments and suggestions. Since I have not always heeded their wise counsel, they should not be held responsible for any errors or infelicities that remain.
2. For historiographers, the papers from that conference appeared in Shuy (1965), but Stewart noted (1970, 351) that the origins debate "does not appear in the published papers from that conference." He also notes that the disagreement surfaced in discussion following a paper by Beryl Bailey. Of course, as Rickford (1998, 154) notes, others had raised the possibility of a pidgin or creole origin for African American vernacular speech even earlier, including the aptly named Wise (1933).
3. Like Winford (this volume), I use the term *African American Vernacular English* to refer to the nonstandard (or vernacular) forms of English used by African Americans in casual everyday conversation. The "Vernacular" qualification is necessary to distinguish these vernacular varieties from the full range of English varieties—including standard varieties—used by African Americans ("African American English"). Rickford and Rickford use Brown's (1968) term *Spoken Soul* for AAVE. I am sympathetic to the innovative use of "African American Language" by the editors of this volume and others, which may help to overcome the negative associations some people have when they think of the variety discussed in this volume as a "dialect" of English rather than as a "language" in its own right. But "African American Language" might also include at least the creole forms of French spoken in Louisiana, and in the broader sense of "American," other forms of French, Spanish, Portuguese, Dutch, and Coromanti spoken by descendants of African peoples in the Caribbean, Central, and South America. "AAVE," by convention, restricts our focus to the distinctive varieties of English spoken in African America (in the United States) and acknowledges that the bulk of AAVE's lexicon is from English.

4. These totals were calculated from the year by year list of African imports into New York, 1701–65, in table 3 in Medford et al. (2009, 45, who cite Donnan 1969 as their source). From table 5, Medford et al. (2009, 47, citing Donnan 1969, 3:462–511), it appears that 900 of the Caribbean imports to New York were from Jamaica, 334 from Antigua, and 183 from Barbados. Other territories do not even come close.

5. Mufwene himself (2000, 239) says that "it is true that CANDY and Tituba, two slaves recently imported from Barbados by the time of the Salem Witch Trials in Massachusetts in 1692, spoke creole/pidgin-like idiolects (Cassidy 1986)." So he does not seem to be disputing the creole-like nature of the features they exemplify. But he goes on to say, "However, we do not know for sure that these were not interlanguages nor how representative they were of Barbadian slaves in general."

6. For some of the main laws, accompanied by statistics about the growth of the Black population in Virginia, see: http://www.history.org/history/teaching/slavelaw.cfm. Many of Virginia's slave laws like those of South Carolina, were modeled on the slave codes of Barbados. Mufwene (in this volume) does note the institutionalization of racial segregation in South Carolina in 1720, but he does not appear to recognize it in other southern states until the late nineteenth century.

7. The core colony of the Chesapeake, as discussed by Morgan (1998, xvii), is Virginia, but the region also includes "Maryland and northern North Carolina." The core colony of Morgan's (ibid.) "Low Country" is South Carolina, but this region also includes "Georgia, East Florida, and southern North Carolina."

8. In tribute to Labov (1969), the first quantitative study of the AAVE copula, these illustrative examples are all from that source (716–17). The age and geographical location of the speakers who provided his examples are indicated in parentheses.

9. Strictly speaking, the term "copula absence" should only be used of examples (1)–(3), where the predicates are noun phrases, locatives, and adjectives, and the term "auxiliary absence" should be used for examples (4) and (5), where the predicates are verbs. However, there is a long tradition of referring to both copula and auxiliary is/are absence broadly as copula absence or zero copula, with the finer distinction only being made where necessary.

10. As Sharma and Rickford (2009, 61) explain: "The Spearman rank-order correlation coefficient (Spearman's rho, R_S) is a common nonparametric measure of the strength and direction of correspondence between two sets of ranked data (Siegel and Castellan 1988). ... Cronbach's alpha (Cronbach 1951; Miller 1995) ... [is] a statistic used to judge the reliability of tests by quantifying the extent to which they provide the same results on repeated trials." The Spearman coefficients below figures 2.1 and 2.2 measure the extent to which the data depicted there match the order of following grammatical environments depicted in (6).

11. In creole continua, like those found in the Anglophone Caribbean, the *basilect* refers to the deepest, furthest from standard English variety (sometimes an idealization, as in Bailey 1966), the *acrolect* to the variety closest to standard English, and the *mesolects* to varieties in between (DeCamp 1971; Rickford 1987). For example, in Guyana: *e a go* (basilect), *(h)e Ø goin* (mesolect), *he is going* (acrolect).

12. For instance, as Holm (1984, 297) noted, the Yoruba copula system distinguishes between predicative adjectives ("a subclass of verbs which require no copula"); locatives (which take "*wà*" [with stylistic variant *ḿbe*]); and noun phrases (which take either *jẹ́* or *se*). So, speakers of Yoruba, and perhaps other African languages acquiring English in the

New World, would have been sensitive to differences in predicate type or following grammatical environment in a way that speakers of English (which makes no distinctions in
form by following grammatical environment) would not have been. Incidentally, we need
research on the other main (West and Central) African languages that Black indentured
servants and slaves coming to the United States and the Anglophone Caribbean brought
with them, and we also need more research on quantitative variability in copula use in
West African English, along the lines pioneered by John Singler.

13. It may be helpful to refer to table 2.2 when reading this, although table 2.2 represents Winford's
slightly different assumptions about decreolizing developments, in a different locale.

14. Note that Weldon's (2003a, 60) 109 post-vocalic plural/second person singular variants
include 3 tokens of *'s*.

15. To illustrate the point: "He *is* a man" involves verbal content or inflection at only one point
(*is*), while "He *is* walk*ing*" involves verbal content or inflection at two points (*is*, *-ing*).

16. Even where a vernacular feature, for example, *th*-stopping or consonant cluster simplification, could have British dialect sources, I continue to wonder (cf. discussion in Rickford
and Rickford 2000, 147ff.) why it MUST be attributed to British sources when it could
equally have come from African and/or creole substrates.

REFERENCES

Bailey, Beryl Loftman. 1965. "Toward a New Perspective in Negro English Dialectology."
    American Speech 40 (3): 171–77.
———. 1966. *Jamaican Creole Syntax*. Cambridge: Cambridge University Press.
Bailey, Guy, and Natalie Maynor. 1985. "The Present Tense of *be* in White Folk Speech of the
    Southern United States." *English World-Wide* 6: 199–216.
———. 1987. "Decreolization?" *Language in Society* 16 (4): 449–73.
Baugh, John. 1980. "A Re-Examination of the Black English Copula." In *Locating Language in
    Time and Space*, edited by William Labov, 83–106. New York: Academic Press.
Bickerton, Derek. 1971. "Inherent Variability and Variable Rules." *Foundations of Language*
    7: 457–92.
———. 1981. *Roots of Language*. Ann Arbor, MI: Karoma.
Breslaw, Elaine G. 1996. *Tituba, Reluctant Witch of Salem*. New York: New York University.
Brown, Claude. 1968. "The Language of Soul." *Esquire*, April.
Cassidy, Frederic G. 1986. "Barbadian Creole—Possibility and Probability." *American Speech*
    61: 195–205.
Cassidy, Frederic G., and R. B. Le Page. 1967. *Dictionary of Jamaican English*.
    Cambridge: Cambridge University Press.
Cronbach, L. J. 1951. "Coefficient Alpha and the Internal Structure of Tests." *Psychometrika*
    16: 297–334.
Cukor-Avila, Patricia. 1999. "Stativity and Copula Absence in AAVE." *Journal of English
    Linguistics* 27: 341–55.
Davis, David Brion. 1986. *Slavery in the Colonial Chesapeake*. Williamsburg, VA: The Colonial
    Williamsburg Foundation.
DeCamp, David. 1960. *Four Jamaican Creole Texts with Introductions, Phonemic Transcriptions,
    and Glosses*. In *Jamaican Creole (=Creole Language Studies 1)*, edited by Robert B. Le Page
    and David DeCamp, 128–79. London: Macmillan.

————. 1971. "Toward a Generative Analysis of a Post-Creole Continuum." In *Pidginization and Creolization of Languages*, edited by Dell Hymes, 349–70. Cambridge: Cambridge University Press.

Dillard, J. L. 1972. *Black English: Its History and Usage in the United States.* New York: Random House.

Donnan, Elizabeth, ed. 1969. *Documents Illustrative of the History of the Slave Trade to America.* 3 vols. New York: Octagon Books.

Edwards, Walter F. 1980. "Varieties of English in Guyana: Some Comparisons with BEV." *Linguistics* 18: 289–309.

Feagin, Crawford. 1979. *Variation and Change in Alabama English.* Washington, DC: Georgetown University Press.

Fields, Linda. 1995. "Early Bajan: Creole or Non-Creole?" In *The Early Stages of Creolization*, edited by Jacques Arends, 89–111. Amsterdam: John Benjamins.

Foner, Philip S. 1975. *From Africa to the Emergence of the Cotton Kingdom.* Vol. 1 of *History of Black Americans.* Westport, CT: Greenwood.

Franklin, John Hope, and Alfred A. Moss, Jr. 1988. *From Slavery to Freedom: A History of Negro Americans.* 6th ed. New York: Alfred A. Knopf.

Hamilton, H. 1972. "The Negro Leaves the South." In *Population Growth and the Complex Society*, edited by H. M. Hughes, 79–90. Boston: Allyn and Bacon.

Herskovits, Melville J. 1941. *The Myth of the Negro Past.* New York: Harper and Brothers.

Holm, John. 1976. "Copula Variability on the Afro-American Continuum." In *Conference Preprints, First Annual Meeting of the Society for Caribbean Linguistics*, compiled by George Cave. Turkeyen: University of Guyana Press.

————. 1984. "Variability of the Copula in Black English and its Creole Kin." *American Speech* 59: 291–309.

Kautzsch, Alexander, and Edgar W. Schneider. 2000. "Differential Creolization: Some Evidence from Earlier African American Vernacular English in South Carolina." In *Degrees of Restructuring in Creole Languages*, edited by Ingrid Neumann-Holzschuh and Edgar W. Schneider, 247–74. Amsterdam: John Benjamins

Kulikoff, Allan. 1986. *Tobacco and Slaves: The Development of Southern Cultures in the Chesapeake, 1680–1800.* Chapel Hill: University of North Carolina Press (for the Institute of Early American History and Culture, Williamsburg, Virginia).

Labov, William. 1969. "Contraction, Deletion, and Inherent Variability of the English Copula." *Language* 45: 725–62.

————. 1982. "Objectivity and Commitment in Linguistic Science: The Case of the Black English Trial in Ann Arbor." *Language in Society* 11: 165–201.

Macaulay, Ron K. S. 1991. *Locating Dialect in Discourse: The Language of Honest Men and Bonnie Lasses in Ayr.* Oxford: Oxford University Press.

Martin, Danielle, and Sali Tagliamonte. 1999. "'Oh, it Beautiful!' Copula Variability in Britain." Paper presented at the annual conference on New Ways of Analyzing Variation, Toronto, Canada, October 14–17.

McElhinny, Bonnie. 1993. "Copula and Auxiliary Contraction in the Speech of White Americans." *American Speech* 68: 371–99.

Medford, Edna Greene, Emilyn L. Brown, Selvyn H. H. Carrington, Linda Heywood, and John Thornton. 2009. "Eighteenth-Century Procurement of African Laborers for New York." In *Historical Perspectives of the African Burial Ground: New York Blacks and the Diaspora*, edited by Edna Greene Medford, 43–49. Washington, DC: Howard University in association with the United States General Services Administration (available online).

Mesthrie, Rajend. 1992. *English in Language Shift: The History, Structure and Sociolinguistics of South African Indian English.* Cambridge: Cambridge University Press.

Miller, M. B. 1995. "Coefficient Alpha: A Basic Introduction from the Perspectives of Classical Test Theory and Structural Equation Modeling." *Structural Equation Modeling* 2: 255–73.

Morgan, Phillip D. 1998. *Slave Counterpoint: Black Culture in the Eighteenth-Century Chesapeake and Lowcountry.* Chapel Hill: University of North Carolina Press, for the Omohundro Institute of Early American History and Culture, Williamsburg, Virginia.

Mufwene, Salikoko. 1992. "Ideology and Facts on African American Vernacular English." *Pragmatics* 2 (2): 141–66.

———. 1996. "The Founder Principle in Creole Genesis." *Diachronica* 13: 83–134.

———. 2000. "Some Sociohistorical Inferences about the Development of African-American English." In *The English History of African American English*, edited by Shana Poplack, 233–63. Oxford: Blackwell.

———. 2004. Review of *The Historical Evolution of Earlier African American English: An Empirical Comparison of Early Sources*, by Alexander Kautzsch. *English World-Wide* 25: 305–11.

Parkvall, Mikael. 2000. "Reassessing the Role of Demographics in Language Restructuring." In *Degrees of Restructuring in Creole Languages*, edited by Ingid Neumann-Holzschuh and Edgar W. Schneider, 185–213. Amsterdam: John Benjamins.

Poplack, Shana. 2000. "Introduction." In *The English History of African American English*, edited by Shana Poplack, 1–32. Malden, MA: Blackwell.

Poplack, Shana, and David Sankoff. 1987. "The Philadelphia Story in the Spanish Caribbean." *American Speech* 62: 291–314.

Rickford, John R. 1977. "The Question of Prior Creolization in Black English." In *Pidgin and Creole Linguistics*, edited by Albert Valdman, 190–221. Bloomington: Indiana University Press.

———. 1986. "Short Note [on the Significance and Use of Documentary Pidgin-Creole Texts]." *Journal of Pidgin and Creole Languages* 1: 159–63.

———. 1987. *Dimensions of a Creole Continuum.* Stanford, CA: Stanford University Press.

———. 1992. "The Creole Residue in Barbados." In *Old English and New: Studies in Language and Linguistics in Honor of Frederic G. Cassidy*, edited by Joan H. Hall, Nick Doane, and Dirck Kingler, 183–201. New York: Garland.

———. 1997. "Prior Creolization of AAVE? Sociohistorical and Textual Evidence from the 17th and 18th Centuries." *Journal of Sociolinguistics* 1: 315–36.

———. 1998. "The Creole Origins of African-American Vernacular English: Evidence from Copula Absence." In *African-American English: Structure, History and Use*, edited by Salikoko S. Mufwene, John R. Rickford, Guy Bailey, and John Baugh, 154–200. London: Routledge.

———. 2006. "Down for the Count? The Creole Origins Hypothesis of AAVE at the Hands of the Ottawa Circle, and their Supporters." *Journal of Pidgin and Creole Languages* 21: 97–155.

Rickford, John R., Arnetha Ball, Renee Blake, Raina Jackson, and Nomi Martin. 1991. "Rappin on the Copula Coffin: Theoretical and Methodological Issues in the Analysis of Copula Variation in African American Vernacular English." *Language Variation and Change* 3: 103–32.

Rickford, John R., and Renee Blake. 1990. "Copula Contraction and Absence in Barbadian English, Samaná English and Vernacular Black English." In *Proceedings of the Sixteenth Annual Meeting of the Berkeley Linguistics Society*, 16–19 February 1990, edited by Kira Hall,

Jean-Pierre Koenig, Michael Meacham, Sondra Reinman, and Laurel A. Sutton, 257–68. Berkeley, CA: Berkeley Linguistics Society.

Rickford, John R., and Jerome S. Handler. 1994. "Textual Evidence on the Nature of Early Barbadian Speech, 1676–1835." *Journal of Pidgin and Creole Languages* 9: 221–55.

Rickford, John R., and Russell J. Rickford. 2000. *Spoken Soul: The Story of Black English.* New York: Wiley.

Schneider, Edgar W. 1989. *American Earlier Black English: Morphological and Syntactic Variables.* Tuscaloosa: University of Alabama Press.

———. 2002. "Investigating Variation and Change in Written Documents." In *The Handbook of Language Variation and Change*, edited by J. K. Chambers, Peter Trudgill, and Natalie Schilling-Estes, 67–96. Malden, MA: Blackwell.

Schwartz, Philip J. 2010. *Slave Laws in Virginia.* Athens: University of Georgia Press.

Schwegler, Armin. 2001. "On the (African) Origins of Palenquero Subject Pronouns." Paper presented at the annual meeting of the Society for Pidgin and Creole Languages, Washington, DC, January 5–6.

———. 2014. "Portuguese Remnants in the Afro-Hispanic Diaspora." In *Portuguese/Spanish Interfaces: Diachrony, Synchrony, and Contact*, edited by Ana M. Carvalho and Patricia Amaral, 403–41. Amsterdam and Philadelphia: John Benjamins.

Sharma, Devyani, and John R. Rickford. 2009. "AAVE/Creole Copula Absence: A Critique of the Imperfect Learning Hypothesis." *Journal of Pidgin and Creole Languages* 24 (1): 53–90.

Shuy, Roger W., ed. 1965. *Social Dialects and Language Learning.* Champaign, IL: National Council of Teachers of English.

Siegel, Sidney, and N. John Castellan, Jr. 1988. *Nonparametric Statistics for the Behavioral Sciences.* 2nd ed. New York: McGraw-Hill.

Singler, John. 1991. "Copula Variation in Liberian Settler English and American Black English." In *Verb Phrase Patterns in Black English and Creoles*, edited by Walter F. Edwards and Donald Winford, 129–64. Detroit, MI: Wayne State University Press.

———. 1995. "The Demographics of Creole Genesis in the Caribbean: A Comparison of Martinique and Haiti." In *The Early Stages of Creolization*, edited by Jacques Arends, 203–32. Amsterdam: John Benjamins.

———. 2008. "The Sociohistorical Context of Creole Genesis." In *The Handbook of Pidgin and Creole Studies*, edited by Silvia Kouwenberg and John Singler, 332–58. Malden, MA: Wiley-Blackwell.

Smith, Julia Floyd. 1985. *Slavery and Rice Culture in Low Country Georgia, 1750–1860.* Knoxville: University of Tennessee Press.

Stewart, William A. 1967. "Sociolinguistic Factors in the History of American Negro Dialects." *Florida FL Reporter* 5: 11.

———. 1968. "Continuity and Change in American Negro Dialects." *Florida FL Reporter* 6: 3–4, 14–16, 18.

———. 1969. "Historical and Structural Bases for the Recognition of Negro Dialect." In *Georgetown University Round Table on Languages and Linguistics 1969*, edited by James E. Alatis, 239–47. Washington, DC: Georgetown University Press.

———. 1970. (Includes 1967 and 1968 papers.) "Toward a History of American Negro Dialect." In *Language and Poverty*, edited by Frederick Williams, 351–79. Chicago: Markham.

Visser, F. T. 1970. *An Historical Syntax of the English Language.* Leiden: E. J. Brill.

Weldon, Tracey L. 2003a. "Copula Variability in Gullah." *Language Variation and Change* 15: 37–72.

————. 2003b. "Revisiting the Creolist Hypothesis: Copula Variability in Gullah and Southern Rural AAVE." *American Speech* 78: 171–91.

Wilkerson, Isabel. 2010. *The Warmth of Other Suns: The Epic Story of America's Great Migration*. New York: Random House.

Williams, Jeffery P. 1985. "Preliminaries to the Study of the Dialects of White West Indian English. *Nieuwe West-Indische Gids* 59: 27–44.

Winford, Donald. 1992. "Another Look at the Copula in Black English and Caribbean Creoles." *American Speech* 67: 21–60.

————. 1998. "On the Origins of African American Vernacular English—A Creolist Perspective. Part 2: Linguistic Features." *Diachronica* 15: 99–154.

————. 2000. "'Intermediate' Creoles and Degrees of Change in Creole Formation: The Case of Bajan." In *Degrees of Restructuring in Creole Languages*, edited by Ingrid Neumann-Holzschuh and Edgar W. Schneider, 215–46. Amsterdam: John Benjamins.

Wise, Claude Merton. 1933. "Negro Dialect." *Quarterly Journal of Speech* 19: 523–28.

Wolfram, Walt. 1974. "The Relationship of White Southern Speech to Vernacular Black English." *Language* 50 (3): 498–527.

Wolfram, Walt, and Erik R. Thomas. 2002. *The Development of African American English*. Oxford, UK: Blackwell.

Wood, Peter H. 1975. *Black Majority: Negroes in Colonial South Carolina from 1670 through the Stono Rebellion*. New York: Norton.

CHAPTER 3

THE EMERGENCE OF AFRICAN AMERICAN ENGLISH

Monogenetic or Polygenetic? With or Without "Decreolization"? Under How Much Substrate Influence?

SALIKOKO S. MUFWENE

3.1 INTRODUCTION

I use *African American English* (AAE) in this chapter as a convenient umbrella term that facilitates discussing together common aspects of both Gullah (the creole spoken in coastal South Carolina and Georgia) and African American Vernacular English (AAVE, the non-creole variety spoken elsewhere in the United States). This is not to suggest that both varieties evolved from a common (creole) ancestor. Rather, I argue that colonial English did not evolve uniformly among (descendants of) Africans in the United States, owing largely to differences between, on the one hand, rice fields and, on the other, cotton and tobacco plantations as contact ecologies. My approach fits within "comparative history" (Diamond and Robinson 2010); it focuses on ecological factors that account for this differential evolution. The ecological approach helps articulate clearly the historical evidence for treating both AAVE and Gullah as sister offspring of English in the United States, while suggesting a critical interpretation of Labov's (1972) claim that AAVE is homogeneous across the country, albeit with a non-monolithic, variable system (Mufwene 1992; Labov 1998).

One of the central questions of the debate on the emergence of AAE concerns the nature and extent of the contributions of languages to its system. I submit that the Africans definitely shaped the varieties now associated with their descendants in the New World by selecting from within English those features that were congruent with those of some of the languages they had spoken in Africa (Corne 1999), by modifying the characteristics of some of the English options they selected, or by introducing new features (identified as "apports" by Allsopp 1977; see also Mufwene 2001a, b). The question remains: Which answer is plausible for which features?

We must bear in mind that the rice fields and the tobacco and cotton plantations generated different population structures, with the latter becoming racially segregated only after the abolition of slavery in the mid-nineteenth century. Owing to the significant "Black majority" (Wood 1974) in the rice fields area, the slaves were already segregated in the early eighteenth century, which fostered Gullah's structural divergence from colonial English in the American Southeast. The smaller size of the tobacco and cotton plantations, on which the slaves were generally a minority, and the late institutionalization of Jim Crow appear to have been less favorable to (extensive) substrate influence. Indeed, AAVE and Gullah do not diverge to the same extent from White American Southern English (WASE), nor does Gullah diverge from the construct "English" to the same extent as Caribbean English creoles (CECs). Along with Schneider (1995) and Bailey and Thomas (1998), I argue that in fact AAVE and WASE have common origins. They appear to have been one and the same regional variety until Jim Crow was introduced in the late nineteenth century and triggered the Great Migration of African Americans out of the South. AAVE was invented as a separate ethnolect in the North, where most White Americans were then getting their first exposure to American Southern English.

3.2 TOBACCO, COTTON, RICE, AND THE DIFFERENTIAL EVOLUTION OF ENGLISH IN THE UNITED STATES

The colonies of Virginia, very central to the emergence of AAVE, and of South Carolina, critical to the emergence of Gullah, did not start at the same time. The former was founded in 1607 directly from England, while the latter started as a "second-generation colony" (Chaudenson 1992, 2001), settled from Barbados in 1670. Neither settlement evolved overnight into a major slave colony, owing to lack of capital to invest in the plantation industry from the start.[1]

The first Africans, twenty-three acquired from a Dutch frigate, arrived in Virginia in 1619 and had the status of indentured servants, entitled to buy their freedom within a few years. They and the other Africans imported later worked typically as domestic servants in the homes of the wealthiest colonists (Tate 1965). The population then was not yet racially segregated, though, to be sure, the Africans were not treated as equal. Still, they had full exposure to the vernacular of the colonists, thanks to regular interactions with them, although, like anybody learning a language naturalistically, they must have started with interlanguages, which need not be confused with a pidgin as a communal variety.[2] According to Tate (1965), it would not be until about 1675 that the Africans became slaves, which is about the time the industrial cultivation of tobacco would develop and the African population started growing rapidly, owing to increased importations, for work on the plantations.

Although, Virginia had the most numerous slave population in the eighteenth century (Rickford 1997), it was actually also the most densely populated colony, totaling 53,184 Europeans and 19,800 Africans in 1750 and 288,200 Europeans versus 105,500 Africans in 1790. Perkins (1988) and Fischer (1989) estimate that, on average, the Black population in the Chesapeake hardly exceeded 38 percent of the total colonial population by the end of the eighteenth century. AuCoin (2002) points out that there were a couple of coastal counties (in the swamps) where the Black population reached about 60 percent, but this was not the regular pattern. Although, according to Rickford (1997), most of the slaves lived in the coastal area,[3] the large tobacco plantations, on which only 29 percent of the African population (according to his source) lived, developed inland. According to Kulikoff (1986),

> By the early 1780s, more than two-fifths of the slaves who resided in eight piedmont counties organized before 1760 lived on plantations with twenty or more other slaves. In contrast, more than two-fifths of the slaves of the frontier piedmont counties organized after 1760 still lived on small units of ten or fewer during the early 1780s. (337–39)

> Only one third of the slaves along the Potomac lived on farms of more than twenty slaves. In Virginia, both James City and York counties were more than 60 percent enslaved in the 1780s. Most of the large plantations in these counties were located in upper Yorkhampton Parish, where more than half the slaves lived on quarters larger than twenty slaves. Only one third to one fourth lived on big quarters in the rest of the counties. (342)

The tobacco plantations apparently claimed less than half the slave population, a demographic distribution that suggests non-uniform evolution of English across the African population, as some interacted more frequently with the European colonists than others.[4] On average a tobacco plantation appears to have had only twenty to thirty slaves, integrated with the indentured servants, in sharp contrast with a sugar-cane plantation in Jamaica, which exceeded one hundred slaves segregated from the European colonists. Thus, the Virginia population structure did not favor the emergence of a Creole slaves' English that was distinct from that of the locally born White population.

Another important factor is that in the eighteenth century, the Virginian slave population grew as much by importation as by birth, with the locally born slaves sometimes constituting no less than 40 percent of the relevant population when importations were at their peak (Kulikoff 1986, 335). This entailed more continuity from the pre–eighteenth-century English the Virginians had developed. As argued by DeGraff (1999), Creole slaves were critical agents of feature selection in the emergence of creoles and undoubtedly other varieties now associated with descendants of slaves. They determined by their speech varieties, which would be targeted by the Bozal (African-born) slaves, what particular substrate influences were more likely to become permanent in the emergent colonial vernaculars.

The Virginia colony thus conjures up a setting very similar to that of colonial Brazil, with its numerous small sugarcane plantations, where no distinct language variety associated exclusively with the slaves emerged. Quoting H. Jones ([1724] 1956), Kulikoff (1986, 317) reports that "slaves born in Virginia 'talk good English, and affect our language, habits, and customs.'" Likewise, Brasch (1981) reports advertisements in local newspapers about runaway slaves of the time that correlate "good English" with being born or having lived long in Virginia and "poor, bad," or "unintelligible" English with recent arrivals from Africa. Virginia is critical to understanding the evolution of English in the United States because it provided the founder slave population for second-generation colonies such as North Carolina, which would develop on its model rather than on that of South Carolina. The northern colonies had very few slaves, 2 to 4 percent of the total colonial population within which they were integrated, though not with equal social status, as noted above.

It is especially noteworthy that the Virginia colony started before that of Barbados (founded in 1627). At the peak of the slave trade during the eighteenth century, American planters imported the overwhelming majority of their slaves straight from Africa. These were brought to them by New England merchants, whose ships could sail in a shorter time, straight from West Africa to Virginia and South Carolina, making the acquisition of slaves less expensive for Americans. During the eighteenth century, only 10 percent of the enslaved Africans were imported from the Caribbean (Rawley 1991).

Equally significant is the fact that the Virginia colony started a little over half a century earlier than South Carolina. Even if a creole had developed at the onset of the latter colony, it could hardly have influenced the evolution of English among the African slaves in Virginia, not only because it started later but also because the South Carolinians then interacted more regularly with Barbadians than with Virginians. Actually, it would also have taken substantial migrations of South Carolina slaves to Virginia for the latter's slave population to change their own way of speaking. No such migration volume has been reported in the history of both colonies.

South Carolina itself evolved only gradually into a lucrative plantation colony. Although the first settlement from Barbados in 1670 included some slaves, they were a negligible proportion absorbed by the White population looking for alternative lands and resources, which they could not afford in the colony of origin.[5] Initially they engaged in fur trade and animal husbandry, including cattle ranching and swine raising. According to Edgar (1998, 133), 1,000 out of South Carolina's slave population of 1,800 in 1708 were engaged in this economic activity. Even though rice cultivation had started already by 1700 and the slave population was then equal to that of the White population (Wood 1974), the figures indicate that, perhaps owing to insufficient capital, the fields must have still been very small and/or very few in number. As a matter of fact, rice cultivation, begun in the 1690s (Edgar 1998, 140), still competed with the production of indigo, wood, and naval stores. We cannot be surprised that historical records do not mention any Gullah yet, because the dominant homestead socioeconomic conditions did not foster the emergence of a separate English variety among the African slaves (Mufwene 1997a, b, 2000, 2001b).

Racial segregation was institutionalized in South Carolina in 1720 (Wood 1974), the year the slave population doubled that of the White population: 21,600 to 9,800 by 1730 (Wood 1989). The rice-cultivation industry was then booming again, after slumping in about 1712 (Edgar 1998, 138), and was turning the colony into the most prosperous one in English North America. The Black population would remain double that of the White population until about 1750: 40,600 to 20,000 (Wood 1989). It was only around 1760 that the White population started growing faster than the slave population: 57,900 slaves to 38,000 Whites, and it would become the majority by 1790: 108,900 slaves to 140,200 Whites, a proportion that would not be eclipsed again.

The above demographics raise the question of what made the emergence of Gullah possible at all, as the disparities in population size do not appear comparable to those reported for colonies such as Jamaica or Guyana. The answer lies in the population structure: most of the slave population in the eighteenth century was concentrated on the coast (Turner 1949; Wood 1974), where rice cultivation was developing and where the Africans constituted the overwhelming majority, at the ratio of nine to one. Another question that arises is: Why did Gullah not diverge from its lexifier to the same extent as Guyanese or Jamaican Creole? Part of the answer lies in the rate of population growth and population replacement (Mufwene 2001b): It was apparently slower in South Carolina than in Jamaica and Guyana, though future research may shed more light on this issue. By the time race segregation was institutionalized in 1720, there may have been a relatively large proportion of English-speaking Creole slaves who would serve as model speakers to the Bozal slaves. African linguistic influence would thus work its way only slowly to modify the colonial vernacular into Gullah, which probably would not become noticeably distinct until the late eighteenth or early nineteenth century. The earliest attestations available are in William Gilmore Simms's *The Wigwam and the Cabin* (1845).[6]

We must also bear in mind Rickford's (1985) comparison of two speakers, White and African American, on Daufuskie Island, South Carolina, which highlights both differences and similarities between them that are generally consistent with observations about other former plantation colonies. White and Black Jamaicans sound more like each other than like their counterparts in North America, just like a traditional White Southerner sounds more like an African American Southerner than like a White New Englander or Midwesterner. If these observations about coastal South Carolina are correct, the two Daufuskie Island speakers must overall sound more like each other than like their hinterland counterparts. Southern English does not include the varieties that developed in coastal South Carolina and Georgia!

The other ecological explanation for why Gullah is less divergent from the construct "English" is to be found in population structure again. While Caribbean sugar cane plantations often grew into huge estates in the eighteenth century, as successful planters bought their neighbors out of business (Dunn 1972), South Carolina planters structured their rice fields more on the model of Brazilian sugarcane estates.[7] According to Edgar (1998, 142):

> South Carolina planters seemed to have settled on 30 to 50 slaves as the ideal size for a working plantation. Large land and slave owners broke up their holdings into

smaller production units. Ralph Izard Jr., for instance, owned 342 slaves. There were 10 slaves at his Charleston town house and 69 at Burton. The remaining 263 were divided among five working plantations. Thomas Elliot of St. Andrews Parish had two plantations and evenly divided his 104 slaves between them. John Ainslie of St. George's Dorchester, who raised thoroughbreds as well as rice, had 134 slaves at his residence, Windsor Hill and working plantations in St. Paul's (51 slaves) and St. Matthew's (30 slaves).

So, if the number of slaves per plantation in South Carolina was not significantly different from that in Virginia, how did Gullah not develop in Virginia, or why did the coastal South Carolina slaves develop Gullah but not something closer to AAVE? In Virginia, the interior of South Carolina and Georgia, and everywhere else where tobacco or cotton became the main industrial crop, the slaves were in the minority and race segregation would start only in the late nineteenth century. In coastal South Carolina and Georgia, they were the overwhelming majority and did not socialize with Whites, even if they met in the work place. Segregated life left a lot of room for substrate influence to prevail, although the nature of this remains to be determined.

There is also a modern observation that bears on the above hypothesis: in South Carolina as in Georgia, there is a geographical continuum from Gullah on the coast to AAVE in the hinterlands, which may reflect variation in the kinds of settlements and the composition of the populations that inhabited them (Mufwene 2001a). The marshes and mosquitoes are the classic explanations for the small population of Whites on the coast during the colonial period and indeed for the frequent absenteeism of some planters during the summer months. The interior was more hospitable and attractive to indentured servants, who constituted 50 to 75 percent of the southern White population (Kulikoff 1986). According to Kulikoff (1991, 202), "as many as four fifths of all colonists, including their families, servants, and slaves, were farmers."

The position emerging here naturally challenges the claim by, for instance, Morgan (1993) that AAE developed as a "counterlanguage" intended to prevent White masters and overseers from understanding much of what its creators and practitioners said. This ignores or downplays the linguistic influence of the White indentured servants that the field hands interacted regularly with, especially during the homestead phase, although they did not socialize together during the plantation phase.[8] It does not explain why there are so many structural similarities between AAE and WASE and, ignoring prosodic features, various nonstandard English varieties in North America and the United Kingdom (Poplack and Tagliamonte 2001). The "decreolization" hypothesis, disputed below as inconsistent with the colonial history, cannot be invoked to account for the similarities. Nor can the Black-nanny theory (invented by British travelers), according to which the linguistic similarities between Blacks and Whites in the American South were due to White children being looked after by Black nannies. Only 5 to 10 percent of Whites, mostly on the coast, could afford Black nannies (Coleman 1978). We are left with what follows from the history articulated above.

The above remarks do not entail that African Americans could not have developed counterlanguages to confuse their masters and overseers. However, in the spirit of Halliday (1976), such varieties must have been parasitic developments from vernacular English and Gullah varieties that had already emerged naturalistically, just like professional jargons, for instance. They should not be confused with the vernaculars that emerged as the Africans were forced by the circumstances of their new places of residence to shift to English for communication not only with those who had enslaved them but also among themselves. It must indeed be informative to compare how English evolved among them with how it did among other relocated populations that appropriated English for usage among themselves, such as the Amish, although the latter had not come to North America in bondage and did not shift languages under identical communicative pressures.

3.3 DOCUMENTARY EVIDENCE

3.3.1 Indirect Documentation

The earliest characterizations of African slaves' English are to be found in ads posted in local papers for the recapture of runaway slaves during the second half of the eighteenth century (Brasch 1981). The quotations below suggest that their competence varied from one speaker to another, corresponding largely to whether they were locally born or African born, and, in the latter case, how long they had lived in the colony:

(1) a. Ran away . . . the following negroe's viz. Sambo, a small, thin visaged Fellow, about 30 years of age, speaks *English* so as to be understood . . . Aron . . . can't even speak *English* . . . Berwick . . . can't speak English. They have been in above 8 months in the country. *Virginia Gazette*, August 24, 1751, p. 3.

   b. . . . as he was imported very young he speaks very good English. *Virginia Gazette*, Dec. 12, 1755, p. 4.

   c. . . . speaks plain for an *African* born, but avoids looking in the face of them he is speaking to as much as possible. *Rind's Virginia Gazette*, August 8, 1788, p. 3.

Stewart (1968) and Rickford (1980, 179) comment that, in characterizing the Africans' competence in English as "good," "tolerable," or "proper," the Europeans may have been lowering their standards. I think that these comments overrate the socioeconomic origins of the overseers who published these ads. Based on Lalla and D'Costa (1990), the kinds of English spoken in some of the plantation mansions, especially those where the masters married down in the lower class, was not particularly standard. English among the average Whites was itself predominantly nonstandard and of variable acceptability relative to native British standard norms, bearing also in mind that some of the indentured servants were not from England. Some of those coming from Ireland may have learned English alongside the African slaves in the colonies.[9] Variation in the competence of the overseers is made more evident in Schneider and Montgomery (2001), even if we focus on the grammatical properties of some of the letters and ignore spelling inaccuracies in the examples below. The features include the zero copula, considered as "creole" in, especially, Rickford's (1998, 2006) and Sutcliffe's (1998) discussions:

(2) a. and we [Ø] Not half Ready [Doyal 3]
   b. Henry arrive here on yesterday [Meadow 19] (No tense marking!)[10]
   c. tooke Seven day to cut [Carter 70] (No number marking with a numeral)

More evidence can be found in *Tarheel Talk* (Eliason 1956), which includes correspondence by various colonists that exhibits many of the same features associated with creoles and AAVE.

3.3.2 Direct Colonial Documentation

Additional supportive evidence lies in the court transcripts of the Salem Witch Trials (1692), in which, incidentally, the speech of an African slave other than the often-cited Candy, in the name of Mary Black, shows no divergence at all from the English of the European colonists, some of whom actually exhibit the same kinds of features now associated with either English creoles or AAVE, as shown below:[11]

(3) a. she choake him (Deliverance Hobbs: no tense marker, or no person/number marking)
   b. Where was you then? (D. Hobbs's prosecutor: no Subject-Verb agreement)
   c. you are become a tormentor (D. Hobbs's prosecutor: auxiliary *be* instead of *have*)
   d. Where be those images, at your house? (D. Hobbs's prosecutor: "invariant *be*")
   e. we eate nothing but drunk (Mary Lacy: *eat* for *ate* and *drunk* for *drank*)
   f. how maney year (M. Lacy's prosecutor: no plural marker with a quantifier)
   g. you say ye Mother was hurt this Spring at e Village (M. Lacy's prosecutor: Gullah-like uses of possessive *ye* 'your' and *e* 'his/her')

Interested readers can find many more examples from the court transcripts, which are available at http://salem.lib.virginia.edu/texts/tei/BoySalCombined. The point of citing all these examples is to underscore Mufwene's (2000 et seq.) position that one must also ask oneself whether the so-called "creole features" originated exclusively in languages other than the European lexifier. The question must be addressed because it is not evident that CECs or Gullah emerged before AAVE (see below).

Negative attitudes already in place toward non-Whites during the early eighteenth century dispute Stewart's and Rickford's lowering-of-standards hypothesis. There simply were slaves who spoke varieties acceptable to Whites. This does not entail that all slaves in the seventeenth and eighteenth centuries spoke English natively or fluently, only that they need not have spoken creole(-like) varieties, even those that were African born. The Creole slaves on the tobacco and cotton plantations probably spoke like the locally born Whites. I am well aware of the inhumane conditions of slavery and of the abusive mistreatments of the slaves, but I also believe that slavery did not incapacitate the language-learning ability of slaves in immersion, as it were (Mufwene 2005). Nor should we ignore the important numerical size of White indentured servants in these plantation colonies, who were not necessarily native English speakers. They are the ones who then interacted regularly with the slaves and who, being the majority labor force, perhaps contributed as much to the emergence of earlier American Southern English (probably also the ancestor of AAVE) as the Africans did.

3.3.3 First Indirect Postcolonial Evidence

An important body of indirect[12] evidence has been identified in offshoot varieties spoken in Samaná, in the Dominican Republic (see DeBose 1983), in Liberia (see Singler 1989, 1997), and in Nova Scotia (Poplack and Tagliamonte 2001), all identified by the latter authors as "Diaspora varieties." The premise in invoking features of these varieties as evidence of what AAVE must have been like in the nineteenth century is that they have remained conservative. Thus, they might provide the missing links that have not materialized in the historical documentary evidence. (For difficulties regarding this assumption, see especially Singler 2007a.)

We must indeed speak of the "relevant varieties," because the populations did not emigrate from the same places in the United States. According to DeBose (1983, 49), "the original settlers [in Samaná] were reportedly from Philadelphia, or a nearby location such as Baltimore or New Jersey." Singler (2007b) adds to these places Boston, New York, and North Carolina. With the exception of the latter, they are all places outside the plantation colonies where, on average, the slaves constituted a tiny demographic proportion of at most 2 percent (Pennsylvania) per state in 1861 (McPherson 1991, 184),[13] and where overall they were not residentially segregated (Nash 1988, 169, cited by Singler 2007b, 324). To be sure, some of the Samaná settlers originated in southern states, although they were a small minority (Singler 2007b, this volume). The heterogeneity of places of origin thus underscores the need to consider the post-emigration evolution that took place in Samaná (Singler 2007b), as the settlers must undoubtedly have created a new local norm, in a process not unlike the koinéization of metropolitan English varieties earlier in North America.

If AAVE spread from the American Southeast to the rest of the United States with the Great Migration of the early twentieth century (see below), then, based on the information available on the settlers' places of origins, Samaná English and similar Diaspora varieties must reflect a working-class American English that has changed in the homeland since some time in the nineteenth century. It need not reflect a creole ancestor of AAVE, contrary to DeBose's (1983) conclusion. Regardless of whether or not the data collected by DeBose and other students of Samaná English are truly vernacular (Singler 2007a), the features discussed by DeBose and other proponents of the "Decreolization Hypothesis" need not be characterized as exclusive creole peculiarities. They may represent homologous overgeneralizations after the institutionalization of race segregation in the relevant Anglophone territories, and, in the case of Samaná English, after geographical separation from its Anglophone homeland.

Thus, while the zero copula has survived in CECs and AAE, there is only partial evidence of it in White nonstandard English. Non-rhoticity appears to have been one of the variants in the United States. Rhoticity has been reported to be a late development, probably of the twentieth century, among White southerners. Subject-verb disagreement and consonant cluster simplification are still well attested in some White American nonstandard English varieties and elsewhere. On the other hand, features such as negation with *ain't, you is,* and *I'm never been* are not part of CECs' basilectal structural repertoires. Nor is the apparent reanalysis of the fusion of the contracted copula with the subject pronoun in constructions such as *I'm, dat's, it's,* or *what's* into a monomorphemic variant of the subject pronoun when they are followed by a nonverbal predicate (as in *that's nice* = PRONOUN + ZERO COPULA + PREDICATE ADJECTIVE). It is not evident why these particular structural peculiarities are invoked to argue for a creole ancestry of AAVE.

It is thus not surprising that, as they focused on a different subset of Samaná English features or on different aspects of some of the same features, Poplack and Sankoff (1987) drew a different conclusion, connecting Samaná to White nonstandard English. The bottom line is that, because the feature pools of the different communities share some of the features, similarities of all kinds are likely to emerge on the family resemblance model.

However, because some of the same languages contributed features (even if only by congruence) to English ethnolects associated today with descendants of Africans in the Caribbean, the Bahamas, and the United States, one should not be surprised by similarities in the particular structural features the ethnolects exhibit. Nonetheless, there is always the ultimate question of where the so-called "creole features" themselves originated. Some of them need not have (exclusive) African substrate origins, for instance, usage of bare nouns for generic reference, of periphrastic markers to pluralize nouns and to specify TENSE and ASPECT for verbs, of *no/na* or a variant of *ain't* to negate the verb, and of some form of the complementizer *for* to introduce non-factive clausal complements (infinitival complement clauses in English). Most of these strategies reflect partial congruence between the lexifier and <u>some</u> substrate languages, for instance, the use of *done* to mark PERFECT and *say* in creoles to introduce complement clauses that would be introduced by *that* in English.[14]

Although we can certainly not deny the determinative influence of *some* substrate languages in the selection of *say* for the role of complementizer even for verbs other than *verba dicendi,* we must also bear in mind that the emergence of creoles need not boil down to the simple substitution of African substrate features for those of the relevant European language (Mufwene 2010). The process was a complex one, indeed one that does not exclude the restructuring processes that have produced the structural divergence of many other varieties not identified as creoles. Since variation among creoles may reflect variation in the numerical presence of different ethnolinguistic groups and in the time of their arrival in the colony, we need not rush to the "Decreolization Hypothesis" to account for differences between AAVE and its creole kin. African slaves could learn a European language like anybody else under similar social interaction conditions, notwithstanding inter-individual variation in language learning skills. There is thus no particular reason to ignore the cross-plantation variation articulated above (regarding population structure, demographic size, rate and pattern of population growth, and timing of race segregation) and to invoke "decreolization" to account for cross- and intra-colony variation.

3.3.4 Second Indirect Postcolonial Evidence

The other kind of diachronic evidence often adduced to bear on this debate is from the "Ex-Slave Narratives," though they should not be interpreted to reflect faithfully how the former slaves or their descendants actually spoke, as the transcripts were usually edited (Dillard 2000).[15] The basic assumption in the use of these narratives is that which is associated with apparent-time data in discussions of language change (see Labov 1994; Bailey 2002), viz., the speech of older generations is assumed to be more conservative than that of younger generations and must reflect the state of the language at the time they developed their competence. Reality suggests, however, that speakers also adjust to various changes in their lifetime and preserve only part of their youth's features. We should not ignore the adjustments that the "narrators" may have made to the outsiders who interviewed them, nor the particular ways the speech samples may have been edited (Dillard 1972, 2000; Montgomery 1991). However, this does not mean that the slave narratives are useless. The significance of these texts lies especially in revealing what particular features were then associated with AAE at the time the stories were transcribed (Mufwene 2004).

The narratives that have been discussed the most are those analyzed by German linguists, especially Schneider (1989), Ewers (1995), and Kautzsch (2002). Their unanimous conclusion is that "earlier Black English" (aka AAVE from the nineteenth century) was not more creole-like than it is today. They argue that the evidence supports the English-origins Hypothesis of the evolution of AAVE (i.e., that the particular features examined can generally be traced back to English nonstandard dialects). This conclusion suggests that the relevant similarities between AAVE and CECs are not proof that AAVE inherited putatively "creole features" from the latter, or a Gullah-like ancestor, or even a more remote ancestor common to all of them, but rather that all of them evolved in homologous ways from the restructuring of local nonstandard English koinés. This hypothesis does not at all exclude the influence of some substrate African languages either in determining the selection of the features or influencing how they were restructured, causing the divergence from White American English varieties.

Thus, one may also argue that Gullah and CECs themselves are among new non-standard English vernaculars, regardless of whether they are characterized as "creoles"

(Mufwene 2009). They are those vernaculars whose structures happen to have diverged farther away from their colonial koiné ancestors than AAVE and perhaps also the restructured vernaculars spoken primarily by descendants of Europeans, although this speculation is based on no systematic comparison.

3.3.5 Third Indirect Postcolonial Evidence

The "Ex-Slave Recordings" fall in a separate category of their own, constituting the most dependable indirect diachronic evidence there is for AAE. The most relevant issue other than reliance on apparent time alone is that we do not know to what extent the speakers' grammar was affected by the interaction with the fieldworker, an outsider. There are enough nonstandard features in the recordings to conclude that the features were part of the speakers' natural vernaculars. My own comparison of present-day Gullah with the speech of Mr. Wallace Quarterman recorded in the 1930s led me to conclude in Mufwene (1991, 1994) that Gullah has not at all changed in the direction of the acrolect and, thus, has not "decreolized" since the early twentieth century. In Mufwene (1991, 216), I observed:

> It is also difficult to determine how much of WQ's speech was the result of his interaction with the non-Geechee community (in the militia and in Savannah) since the Civil War and how much was part of his behavior since childhood. After all, there is so much variation today in Gullah communities, even among those whose experience outside the communities is very limited. At the same time, the Gullah which is the closest to the basilect is not restricted to the elderly, nor to those who have not moved outside their communities, nor to those without schooling. For instance, some of the most stereotypical Gullah, the closest to the putative basilect, is heard from Geechees who hold a college degree or have returned from the city but are emotionally attached to the language, seeing it as part of their identity. Since WQ accepted to be interviewed by various field workers (as evidenced by the samples discussed here), it is quite possible that he was not ashamed of his speech and, needing to be integrated back into the Geechee community, did not let his experience affect his speech. The samples we now have may be close to the way he normally spoke with other Geechees. Although this is pure speculation, it is part of the justification for the comparison undertaken here, in the absence of a more reliable corpus.

The particular Ex-Slave Recordings of interviewees in East and Southeast Texas that Sutcliffe (1998) examined, respectively, Billy McCrea and Laura Smalley, display occasional uses of "creole features" consisting especially of uses of the continuative marker *duh* [də]; the locative verb/copula *deh* [dɛː]; the Gullah-like [ʌ] pronunciation of English first person singular pronoun *I*; the Gullah-like gender-neutral objective third person singular pronoun *um* [ʌm]; and the associative post-nominal plural *dem*. Accepting uncritically Joel Chandler Harris's (1880) representation of "Gullah" in *Uncle Remus*, which is at variance with native-like representations in authors such as William Gilmore Simms, Charles Jones, Ambrose Gonzales, and Albert Stoddard,[16] Sutcliffe concludes that Gullah, presumably its basilect, must have been widespread in the American South and that AAVE must reflect "decreolization" qua debasilectaliza- tion from it. The passages from *Uncle Remus* quoted by Sutcliffe include non-Gullah features such as: (1) *sez Brer Fox sezee*; (2) *I'm des in time fer ter wake 'im up* (made more bizarre by the suggestion of rhoticity, though Troike [2010] says that this is only to indi- cate an r-less pronunciation of the schwa in the South!); (3) *I done hood/year*['hear'?], and the complementizer *for-to* [fə-tə].

Similar non-Gullah features also occur in Troike's (2010) citations from Harris's *Daddy Jack*, in which he claims to represent Gullah accurately: *Da' lilly gal is bin tek dem t'ing*; stereotypical/caricatural additions of a paragogic vowel at the end of some words (*'E no kin bite-a you, me killa-a you dead, B'er Rabitt tell-a too big tale*); *no kin* (instead of *kyaan* or *kiin* or *kehn* 'can't'); *'e gwan fer bite-a me* . . . (instead of *E/He gwine bite me*); *Da mek we is kin* 'that makes us kin'; *'T is-a bin hu't* (instead of *I'/He bin (a) hurt*); and *Dey is bin lif one Màn* (instead of *(deh) bin a man* or *A man live/liß yah/deh*) "there lived a man." Although, to be sure, there are normal features of Gullah and CECs in Harris's representations, he appears to have caricatured the variety to meet his sentiment that this ethnolect is "the negro dialect in its most primitive state" (*Daddy Jack*, xxxii–xxxiii, quoted by Troike 2010, 293). Wasn't Gullah once believed by some White Americans in the early twentieth century to be the worst English spoken anywhere in the world? In his writings, Harris managed to construct a Black dialect that is ultimately more distant from the basilect than Ambrose Gonzales's exaggeration in *The Black Border* (1922), jus- tifying Pederson's (1985) observation that "the artistic license that Harris took in making tales works of literature rendered them problematic as valid historical representations of early AAVE [or indeed Gullah] syntax" (paraphrased by Troike 2010, 288).[17]

We are undoubtedly all guilty, to variable extents, of interpreting data in ways more compatible with the position we prefer, even when reality calls for more research or a more cautious disposition. Nonetheless, the economic history of the American Southeast casts doubt on claims of a generalized Gullah-like English that would have developed among African Americans in the region. Interestingly, William Gilmore Simms, the first to represent Gullah in writing, had to migrate from Mississippi to South Carolina to encounter the variety, much like Joel Chandler Harris, who relocated tem- porarily from hinterland Georgia, to get acquainted with Gullah in coastal Georgia.

On the other hand, Sutcliffe appears justified in invoking the speech of the East and Southeast Texas ex-slaves to highlight the fact that features traditionally associated with Gullah need not be its exclusive trademark. To the extent that they are modifications of colonial nonstandard English, they could surface at any place where the ecology of language contact favored them. Nonetheless, we should not overlook the fact that Texas was annexed to the United States in 1845, after the abolition of the slave trade; its slaves came from former English colonies. Some may have originated from coastal South Carolina, North Carolina, and Virginia (Long 1995). Some of those who origi- nated in coastal South Carolina may have kept some Gullah(-like) features and perhaps transmitted them to some of their offspring. Thus, one need not invoke a generalized

Gullah-like ancestor of AAE spoken all over the cotton, tobacco, and rice plantation states in the nineteenth century to account for the presence of "creole features" in the speech of some of the speakers in the Ex-Slave Recordings. The evidence in support of this position should definitely not be drawn from writers whose primary goal was to demonstrate the "quaint"-ness and "primitive state" of the "negro dialect."

3.3.6 More Direct Colonial Evidence

We will re-examine some of the transcripts from the Salem Witch Trials in this section. These trials took place in Massachusetts in 1692 and 1693, when, the presence of African slaves in the colony was negligible. Three slaves were indicted, one most likely a Native American woman, called Tituba, and the other two, African women called Mary Black and Candy (Ray 2009). Only the Native American was tried; the Africans were not and were eventually cleared of the charges (Ray 2009). Both Tituba and Candy had been brought from the Caribbean and were accused of practicing witchcraft. Because their speech patterns allegedly diverged from those of the White colonists, some creolists have claimed that they spoke either a pidgin or creole, although they could in fact have been characterized as speaking interlanguages. Note that, except perhaps in Barbados and to some extent Suriname, no large plantations employing over one hundred slaves segregated from the European colonists had developed yet by this time, owing to the lack of capital, as explained by Dunn (1972) in the case of Jamaica and by Edgar (1998) in the case of South Carolina. No particular West African Pidgin English had emerged yet in Africa (Mufwene 2014), *pace* Dillard (1972 et seq.). Based on historical sources cited by Mufwene (2014), the slave trade (then also organized on the model of today's capitalist global ventures) and the colonization of Africa until the early twentieth century relied heavily on intermediaries, who also served as interpreters. This corroborates in part Naro's (1978, 1988) argument against the claim that a Portuguese pidgin was used in the trade. The slaves may not have spoken any pidgin during the Middle Passage and probably started learning English or whatever plantation language by immersion, after landing, thus first producing individual interlanguages until they developed some competence in it.[18]

The Europeans then traded with Native Americans in the latters' trade languages, for instance, Delaware Pidgin and the Mobilian Jargon in North America, as well as Lingua Geral in Brazil and Quechua in Southwestern South America. Although Tituba allegedly came from Barbados, it is not clear how long she had lived there, as she had been bought in mainland Latin America. As for Candy, she appears to have just transited briefly in the Caribbean before being brought to Massachusetts. She refers to both the country where she was born and Barbados in her answers to the prosecutor. Because the Caribbean, in the seventeenth-century colonial context, did not provide the kind of ecology where a pidgin would have emerged, we need not assume that both Tituba and Candy would have learned a pidgin there. Although pidgins and interlanguages have similar features, they should not be confused. As explained above, a pidgin is a (stable) communal variety, whereas an interlanguage is an individual speaker's transitional variety toward the acquisition of a target language.

Not much is reported of Candy's and Mary Black's testimonies. The following three utterances of Mary Black's do not sound particularly pidgin or creole: "I hurt no body," "I do not know," and "No, I pin my neck cloth." It's not evident that Candy's divergent utterances need be characterized as creole or pidgin either: "Candy no witch in her country," "Candy's mother no witch," "Candy no witch, [in] Barbados," and "Mistress bring book and pen and ink, make Candy write in it." Candy's speech also includes some features that are not expected in pidgin or creole English, viz., the possessive inflection in *Candy's mother* and the possessive pronoun in *her country*.

The most striking things in the limited speech sample are the zero copula, the absence of a determiner before *Mistress*, and the fact that Candy talks about herself in a child-like manner, as if she was speaking about somebody else. So, Candy's speech is not as creole as Cassidy (1986) claims; these very few utterances do not provide any particular evidence for putative creole origins of AAE. There is nothing particularly striking in Mary Black's examination either. She appears to have spoken the same kind of (nonstandard) English as the White colonists. Both Mary Black's and Candy's materials can be used to argue, after Chaudenson (1992, 2001) and Mufwene (2001b), that AAE, like the related creoles, evolved by basilectalization away from the closer approximations of the lexifier spoken by the slaves of the homestead phase.

3.3.7 Revisiting the Ex-Slave Narratives and Recordings

Rickford (2006) has reassessed the particular ways in which the contributors to Poplack (2000) have interpreted the Ex-Slave Narratives and Recordings, questioning their common conclusion that the origins of the relevant features of AAVE lie in colonial English. Although he acknowledges that colonial nonstandard English varieties have contributed features to AAVE, he still argues that the evidence is not sufficient for giving up the creole-origins hypothesis. He points out in a number of cases that at least some of the contributors could have drawn different conclusions if they had considered different bodies of data.

Note, however, that when it comes to language evolution, no two corpora that have not been collected from exactly the same speakers and/or the same communities will support exactly the same conclusions. Regarding linguistic phenomena that can be explained accurately only by adducing various relevant factors or constraints, I wonder whether different communities can be expected to be equally sensitive to all of them or to weight them in identical ways. Such variation alone can account for differences in the kinds of findings and conclusions questioned by Rickford about the studies.

My motto is that evolution is always local, even if general cross-community patterns obtain that apply regionally or cross-regionally. It is thus normal for evolutionary differences, minor or substantial, to obtain between any two communities. CECs themselves differ from each other in one respect or another. For instance, not every CEC uses *doz* for HABITUAL or the durative combination *de a* + V for "busy V–*ing*" in English, features which are attested in Guyanese Creole (GC) but not in Jamaican Creole. Gullah has only the variant *duhz*, pronounced [dəz], like in British Southwestern dialects and in Newfoundland's English, and with a similar HABITUAL function.

Rickford (2006) also highlights the extent of variation across the AAE Diaspora varieties and in different bodies of Ex-Slave Recordings and Ex-Slave Narratives, which proponents of the English-Origins or Creole-Origins hypotheses have perused in whichever way is compatible with their respective positions. The situation is somewhat reminiscent of the half-empty versus half-full bottle dilemma. We thus must depend on which account is more compatible with the external history of the phenomenon, which I attempted in Part 2. *Pace* Baker's (1997) hypothesis that the slaves deliberately produced their "medi[a] of interethnic communication," this population did not have the luxury of planning for a common language in the way that, say, the founders of Israel did in planning Israeli Hebrew. Even in the latter case, things did not proceed as planned; in the main, Israeli Hebrew still evolved naturalistically, resembling its biblical ancestor only remotely.

Part of the problem in the controversy about the emergence of AAVE arises from a failure to make a useful distinction between ORIGINS and EVOLUTION. In their strongest forms, both the Anglicist and Creole-Origins Hypotheses have been articulated as if the Africans either retained English the way it was spoken by the lower-class Europeans that they interacted with (Krapp 1924) or, as a group, they first developed a pidgin and then a creole which would later decreolize into AAVE. Even studies such as Schneider (1989) and subsequent studies by other Anglicists that focus on specific features suffer from suggesting that the features were retained unmodified in the new language variety, leaving the critical reader to wonder indeed how differences between AAVE and other English dialects, traditional or (post)colonial, can be explained.

To begin with, the English features did not all originate in the same dialect, which conjures up competition and selection in the colonial pool of the English features themselves. As the statistics show, although the features discussed in this controversy are variable, they have higher frequencies in AAVE than in other, White American or British English, dialects. In some cases, such as with negative inversion and copula absence, the grammatical rules are not the same anymore. Thus, like its creole kin, AAVE was produced by the African slaves and undoubtedly bears influence from African substrate languages. However, the question remains of what kind of influence this is. When did it take effect, given part of AAVE's common genesis with WASE? Which specific African languages prevailed for which features? Or could it be that AAVE's peculiarities were already part of tobacco and cotton plantation English before Jim Crow and either White southerners lost them or African Americans amplified them? These open questions must be addressed in future research.

Again, I do not consider the English origins of AAVE's features to be mutually exclusive with substrate influence, which must have played a role in shaping AAVE's grammar, like those of its creole kin, as different from that/those of the lexifier. However, divergence from the target structures alone is not evidence of substrate influence. Mere differences in details of the restructuring process qua feature recombination (Mufwene 2001b), even without substrate influence (compare, for instance, St. Helena and Falkland Englishes), would account for the divergence. While Rickford (1998, 2006) is correct in highlighting incontrovertible structural similarities between AAVE and CECs, the question remains open of whether these had already emerged by the time AAVE or tobacco and cotton plantation English was emerging. Colonial history militates for direct critical influence from African languages and for parallel homologous evolution with CECs, leaving still open the question of the specific ways in which African substrate influence operated.

Take, for instance, the *be + V–in'* construction, which is usually characterized inaccurately as a HABITUAL marker. I find the characterization inaccurate because there is a useful distinction in AAVE between the two utterances in (4):

(4) a. *James be tellin' funny jokes every time I see him.*
     b. *James tells funny jokes.*

Only (4b) is an unmarked expression of HABITUAL; (4a) describes a repeated transient state of affairs, presented as in process at the reference time. The grammatical distinction also highlights the difference between *Pat be sick all the time*, which may also be a put on, and *Pat sick all the time*. As pointed out by Green (1998, 2002), this *be* is an aspectual marker, different from the copula *be*, which is why it is negated differently, with *don't*. On the other hand, although it appears that Africans speaking languages that have a distinct HABITUAL marker would want to have this meaning expressed by a specialized form or construction in English, too (the case of *doz/duhz* in Guyanese Creole and Gullah), I am not aware of a particular Black African language that makes the kind of distinction articulated in AAVE, one that is in fact not attested in CECs either. Could African substrate influence have simply favored the selection from the feature pool of a distinction that is also attested in Irish English (Rickford 1986) but not have introduced it? Why selection operated this way for AAVE (perhaps also forging its meaning in a unique way?) but not for CECs is a question that can be answered largely with a more informed understanding of their respective ecologies of contact.

Actually, this divergent evolution is not an isolated incident. AAE in general has evolved some characteristics that are not attested in (most) CECs that have nothing to do with decreolization. For instance, Gullah has a schwa [ə] and a bilabial fricative [ß] in variance with [v] and [w], as in [ßɛri ßɛl] "very well" and [ßɛks] "vexed, angry." The latter is produced as [bɛks] in Jamaican Creole. Both [ß] and [ə] are not (commonly) attested in Black African languages. Likewise, Gullah expresses the habitual with [dəz], but only Guyanese Creole has [dɔz] to my knowledge. African substrate influence is very likely in the present case, though the marker *does* [dəz] is attested in some British English dialects and was selected also with the same function in Newfoundland English. It remains that CECs other than Guyanese have not selected it. Such facts, in addition to the considerations articulated in the next section, cast as much doubt on the Creole-Origins account of the emergence of AAVE as on the strong English-Origins Hypothesis.

3.4 WHAT ELSE UNDERMINES THE CREOLE-ORIGINS ACCOUNT OF THE EMERGENCE OF AAVE?

Some proponents of the Creole-Origins Hypothesis (see Dillard 1972 et seq.; McWhorter 2000) claim that the initial stages of every contact setting between Europeans and Africans either in Africa or in the New World produced a pidgin, which under favorable conditions would evolve into a creole. An important problem is that incipient pidgins are associated with sporadic contacts, with the relevant populations retaining their heritage languages as the vernaculars of their intra-ethnic interactions. Neither the homesteads that preceded the plantations nor the plantation settings of the New World provided these ecological conditions that would have favored the emergence of a pidgin, lest one confuses the individual speakers' interlanguages with pidgins as communal varieties. The other alternative, favored by McWhorter (2000), heeding Dillard's (1972) invocation of a West African Pidgin English, is that the pidgin(s) must have emerged on the African coast.

The relevant citations from Dillard (1972) are scant and date from the early eighteenth century, about a century later than the first effective settlement of Virginia in 1607, or the arrival of the first African in 1619, or the settlement of Barbados in 1627. Dillard's evidence is closer to nonstandard English than to a pidgin and no more convincing than Candy's testimony at the Salem Witch Trials. Although Hancock (1986) also invokes the existence of a Guinea Coast Creole English, which would have fed into the emergence of New World creoles, this may have been restricted to the mixed households of the European lançados and used perhaps also by the grumetes who served as their go-betweens in the trade with the African interior. The emergence of a creole in this setting seems dubious to me, though the English they spoke must have indigenized under the influence of the local languages spoken by the grumetes and the female partners of the lançados. However, I believe, like Berlin (1998), that a number of African Creoles or Mulattoes on both sides of the Atlantic commanded enough English (or any other European language) to act as power-brokers in the Euro-African trade for various commodities, including slaves (see below).

It has also been pointed out that until the eighteenth century, or the nineteenth century according to Huber (1999), Portuguese, rather than any other European language, served as the trade lingua franca along the African coast and all the way to Southeast Asia (Ostler 2005).[19] This suggests that the ancestor of Nigerian and Cameroon Pidgin English may have emerged relatively late in colonial history[20] and apparently later than the probable emergence of some CECs either in the late seventeenth century or in the early eighteenth century (Mufwene 2014). There is now also mounting evidence that earlier trade between Europeans and non-Europeans depended more on interpreters than on unmediated interactions. These typically slighted agents of colonization are often identified in historical accounts as "linguists" (Fortbath 1977; Samarin 1982, 1989; Reader 1997; Northrup 2002; Fayer 2003; Lawrance, Osborn, and Roberts 2006). I surmise that it is only after trade intensified and there was a shortage of interpreters that less and less competent speakers of the European language were hired and the European trade languages spread, undergoing substantial restructuring. By then, CECs may have started to develop already without the African pidgin input.

English pidgins appear to be the outcomes of the gradual basilectalization of English from the closer approximations thereof spoken by the interpreters, either Africans (from royal courts) who were sent to England to learn the language before the trade started in earnest, or Europeans left behind as gages against the Africans taken to Europe, or lançados/"factors" and their children (Mufwene 2014).

The development of plantations from homesteads, on which the Africans were minorities and integrated, did *not* favor prior pidginization. Creoles emerged after the formation of large plantations, in a protracted process that depended on slow accumulation of capital (Dunn 1972) and involved gradual basilectalization. No wonder one has to wait until the early nineteenth century to see any documented evidence of CECs or Gullah.

Both Dillard (1972) and Alleyne (1980) were correct in arguing that creole continua date from the earliest phases of settlement colonization. Though they associated this phenomenon with the stratification of slaves on the plantations (e.g., house slaves versus field hands), we may infer from Dunn (1972) that this phenomenon was due partly also to the fact that until the end of the seventeenth century, most of the slaves lived on farms, where the population size and ratios did not foster residential segregation and the emergence of different ethnolects spoken only by the slaves. Another contributing factor usually ignored is inter-individual variation in learning skills; populations may indeed vary in their proportions of skilled versus less-skilled learners. In the United States, the late institutionalization of segregation and the subsequent divergence of AAVE as an ethnolect separate from the White American variety of the former tobacco and cotton plantation English are not consistent with claims of decreolization (Mufwene 1994).

If Rickford (2006) is right in arguing that the evidence for the English-Origins Hypothesis account of the emergence of AAVE is weak, weaker is even that for the Creole-Origins Hypothesis. My conclusion is for parallel, concurrent evolution of all colonial varieties, subject to local ecological conditions of population contacts, including the local population structure, not barring cross-territorial crossovers, which Rickford is well justified in pointing out. We should focus not just on similarities that obtain on the family resemblance model, but also on differences between CECs and AAE and between varieties within the two major groups. Rickford is also justified in underscoring the role of substrate influence, naturally expected in varieties that were shaped in the New World predominantly by Africans or their descendants, though it is a totally different ball game to articulate what the nature of the influence is.

3.5 CONCLUSION

Regarding the emergence of AAVE, the evidence appears to speak against some creole origins. Nor is it accurate to suggest the variety is just a conservative legacy of colonial nonstandard English. However, like any colonial offspring of English, including CECs and Gullah, AAVE selected materials for its grammar from English itself, albeit its nonstandard varieties, which were the actual targets for the African slaves. Much of the grammar came in fact with its vocabulary, as the model speakers used it. The grammatical features were recombined, thanks to competition and selection in the contact feature pool, under the influence of substrate languages into the new emergent variety. The documentary evidence shows that the modifications were less extensive in AAVE than in Gullah and CECs, though one may also argue that they were relatively less extensive in Gullah than in CECs. Under this scenario, no decreolization need be invoked for AAE, though some explanations are still needed for why, based on Rickford and Handler (2004), debasilectalization appears to have affected Bajan. This shows again that all evolution is local and the same trajectory need not be replicated elsewhere, despite similarities.

The colonial and postcolonial history of the United States suggests polygenesis for Gullah and AAVE as two distinct varieties of AAE, notwithstanding the geographical continuum between them as one travels from the coast inlands. Qualitative structural analyses to date suggest more substrate influence on Gullah than on AAVE. For instance, unlike the latter, the former has serial verb constructions; uses *say* and *fuh* as complementizers; does not systematically distinguish between possessive and subjective pronouns; uses the objective forms *me, him,* and *dem* as subjects and the subjective *we* as object; and has a relative tense system. This is not to say that the features originated as such from African substrate languages, only that one can recognize the role of structural congruence in the selection of these features into Gullah's grammar. This differential evolution is consistent with the fact that the Africans constituted an overwhelming majority of the colonial population on the coasts of South Carolina and Georgia, where they were segregated from the European population about a century and a half earlier than their counterparts inland. In the same vein, the rice fields represented a different kind of contact ecology from those of the Caribbean, which accounts for evolutionary differences between Gullah and CECs, despite structural similarities between them.

Finally, the expansion of cotton cultivation in the eighteenth century, especially after the invention of the cotton gin in 1793, fostered the relocation of slaves from some plantation states, where forms of (the ancestor of) AAE must have already emerged, to others. Thus, we need not assume that a Gullah-like offspring of Colonial English was spoken all over the plantation South. Some of its features may have been spread to some new plantations of the nineteenth century. And, of course, the Great Migration appears to have spread (the ancestor of) AAVE before Jim Crow to other parts of the United States.

Notes

1. Every plantation settlement colony appears to have evolved gradually, from a homestead phase, during which capital had to be raised and the physical infrastructure had to be built. Dunn (1972) explains that in the case of Jamaica most English colonists either remained on small farms or worked for pirates, who had helped the Royal Navy win Jamaica over from Spain in 1655. The first handful of plantations did not emerge before the late seventeenth and early eighteenth centuries. The big difference from one colony to another lay in the duration of the homestead phase, which was shorter for second-generation colonies. The tobacco industry was in place in Virginia only by the late seventeenth century, whereas rice cultivation in South Carolina would not stabilize until the early eighteenth century. It would take less time in Georgia, settled in part from South Carolina.

2. Rickford (2006) objects that the distinction I make between the Africans going through interlanguages and speaking pidgins is like splitting hairs. No, because pidgins are communal varieties associated with sporadic contacts between those who brought the trade language with them and people who still speak their heritage vernaculars for intra-group communication but use the other party's language only for the purposes of their encounters, typically trade. This was not the situation that the early African captives in Virginia and other New World colonies were in. Interlanguages, on the other hand, are associated with the gradual nature of L2 acquisition as experienced by individual speakers, who may not even interact with other learners of the same language in this variety (as in the case of immigrant workers in Europe and the United States). They are considered as the transition to some level of stabilized competence in the target language. History actually suggests that Plag's (2008, 2009) hypothesis that pidgins are the outcomes of learners' interlanguages is mistaken (Mufwene 2010; Aboh 2015), as pidgins are more likely to have emerged by basilectalization, just like creoles (Chaudenson 1992, 2001; Mufwene 2001b) and perhaps also concurrently with, if not later than, the latter (Mufwene 2014).

3. After listening to a sample Gullah recording I played at a public lecture at the University of Georgia in the late 1980s, a Virginian colleague observed that traditional coastal Black Virginians speak with a similar accent. Although this may prove that isolation, rather than just the rice fields, contributed to the emergence of Gullah, nobody else to my knowledge has made a similar comment.

4. There are indeed other factors that complicate this plausible scenario and show how difficult it is for us to know the full story. Notwithstanding variation in language learning skills among the Africans, what kind of competence one developed also depended on whether or not the Europeans one interacted (more) regularly with were native or fluent speakers, as indentured servants were not all English and did not necessarily have acceptable levels of fluency.

5. Barbados, the point from which other, mostly Caribbean territories were colonized, was getting overcrowded, with its land becoming too expensive for many colonists since the mid-seventeenth century. The new, second-generation colonies included Jamaica and Suriname in the second half of the seventeenth century, Guyana in the late eighteenth century (acquired officially in 1814), and Trinidad in 1797.

6. In earlier work, I incorrectly gave the reference as *The Book of My Lady* (1833). There is no Gullah to be found there. There are several editions of *The Wigwam and the Cabin*; not all of them include the relevant parts: "The lazy crow. A story of the cornfield" and "Caloya: or, the loves of the driver."

7. Brazil launched sugar cane cultivation a century earlier than the Caribbean, produced more sugar than the Caribbean colonies until the eighteenth century, and had far more slaves than the latter. However, it did not produce a creole. The reason is that its population structure with small farms of thirty to forty slaves, with the planters sharing distilleries (Schwartz 1985), did not favor the emergence of a separate variety of Portuguese among the slaves, who remained integrated (Mufwene 2008).

8. Note that Jim Crow, which imposed race-based residential segregation in the former tobacco and cotton plantation colonies, was institutionalized only after the abolition of slavery. The former indentured servants had then lost the peculiarity of being the only people in bondage that were guaranteed freedom at the end of a specified term. One must wonder why this institution was set in place just at this time, if socialization across race boundaries had not been taking place and had not been accepted or tolerated until that late in the nineteenth century. The advantages Jim Crow conferred to Whites could still be implemented even without residential segregation, just like slavery had been institutionalized earlier without residential segregation. The only colonies that had institutionalized race segregation earlier were South Carolina and Georgia, presumably on the coast, where the rice fields were developed and the Africans were the overwhelming majority.

9. The settlement colonization of Ireland by England was just intensifying in the early to mid-seventeenth century, especially under the rule of Oliver Cromwell. It would take until the late nineteenth century before English became a widespread vernacular in Ireland, thanks to the textile industry (Corrigan 2010; Mufwene 2012).

10. The comments between the parentheses have been added by the present author.

11. I identify the speakers and the relevant grammatical features between the parentheses. Many more have been omitted in order to shorten this chapter.

12. The evidence in the following sections are framed as "indirect" because it is only inferred as characteristic of a particular earlier period, although it was obtained much later in the relevant history.

13. In the state of New York, most of the slaves were concentrated around New York City: 25 percent of the combined population of Kings, Queens, Richmond, New York, and Worchester counties (Harper 2003). It is not clear whether they lived in segregated communities of their own and spoke a then identifiable Black ethnolect distinct from White (nonstandard) varieties.

14. I have underscored "some" because the substrate languages in contact with English were not typologically identical. The speakers contributing to the emergence of AAE need not all have done the same thing. It is not evident which particular speakers exerted the most critical influence where and when (Mufwene 2010). On the other hand, typological diversity among the African languages may in itself have weakened the extent of possible substrate influence (Mufwene 2008).

15. Manipulations of data by the field workers or the editors may actually have worked in two ways, exaggerating the differences or reducing them, depending on the manipulator.

16. Joel Chandler Harris was born in Eatonton, Georgia, at least 150 miles inland, and relocated to Savannah, Georgia at the age of about 17, to work for the *Savannah Morning News*. He married a local Savannah woman and would move to Atlanta in 1876 (ten to eleven years later), to work for the *Atlanta Constitution*, where he started publishing the stories that would be republished together as *Uncle Remus* in 1880. In his own Introduction, Harris states that he wanted to capture the "quaint"-ness of the "the speech of the negro" (1880). He also notes, contrary to Troike (2010), "the difference between the dialect of the

cotton plantations [where no Gullah was spoken], as used by Uncle Remus, and the lingo in vogue on the rice plantations and the Sea Islands of the South Atlantic States" (8). Harris also claims that the variety he represents is no longer spoken.

Harris's ideology is similar to that of Ambrose Gonzales's early twentieth-century representations of Gullah, made more different from present-day basilectal Gullah, whose statistical distribution of "creole features" is more similar to his late nineteenth-century representations of the same language variety (Mille 1990). Gonzales's declared intention was also to capture the same "quaint"-ness that interested Whites wanted to hear. Harris claims that his representation of cotton plantation AAE is more accurate than that of the "minstrel stage" (4) but he also endorses "Mrs. Stowe's wonderful defense of slavery as it existed in the South" (4), as he would undoubtedly espouse Gonzales's invocation of the "mental inferiority" of the African slaves and their alleged inability to acquire the European language. How can one not wonder whether Harris had not produced a cotton plantation variety of his imagination after having experienced Gullah in the Savannah area?

17. Although Troike appears to be aware of these problems, he prefers to forgive Harris and the like with the comment that "this stereotypification is a usual characteristic of literary representations." This is certainly a good reason for not taking the renditions at face value.

18. This conclusion is consistent with the European colonists' comments on the variable speech of runaway slaves published by Brasch (1981), discussed above.

19. The English, the French, and the Dutch joined the Portuguese and Spaniards in the colonial venture only in the early seventeenth century, a century and a half after the former two. Portugal had then established the monopoly of trade east of the Atlantic Ocean and in the Indian Ocean. Though the newcomers would confiscate the majority of Portuguese colonies, it would take longer before Portuguese would be replaced by other languages as the lingua franca of trade or diplomacy.

20. English was introduced to Cameroon, then a German colony, in 1847 (1845 according to Wikipedia 6/28/2012), by Baptist missionaries. While the Germans banned usage of English from their official institutions, they retained it for communication with the natives (Todd 1982, cited by Anchimbe 2006), which may have helped spread the new indigenized/pidginized variety as a lingua franca.

REFERENCES

Aboh, Enoch. 2015. *The Emergence of Hybrid Grammars: Language Contact and Change.* Cambridge: Cambridge University Press.

Alleyne, Mervyn C. 1980. *Comparative Afro-American: An Historical-Comparative Study of English-Based Afro-American Dialects of the New World.* Ann Arbor, MI: Karoma.

Allsopp, Richard. 1977. "Africanisms in the Idioms of Caribbean English." In *Language and Linguistics Problems in Africa*, edited by Paul F. Kotey and Haig Der-Houssikian, 429–41. Columbia, SC: Hornbeam.

AuCoin, Michelle M. 2002. "The Sociohistorical and Linguistic Development of African American English in Virginia and South Carolina." PhD diss., University of Chicago.

Bailey, Guy. 2002. "Real and Apparent Time." In *The Handbook of Language Variation and Change*, edited by J. K. Chambers, Peter Trudgill, and Natalie Schilling-Estes, 312–31. Malden, MA: Blackwell.

Bailey, Guy, and Erik Thomas. 1998. "Some Aspects of African-American Vernacular English Phonology." In *African American English: Structure, History, and Use*, edited by Salikoko S. Mufwene, John R. Rickford, Guy Bailey, and John Baugh, 85–109. London: Routledge.

Baker, Philip. 1997. "Directionality in Pidginization and Creolization." In *The Structure and Status of Pidgins and Creoles*, edited by Arthur K. Spears and Donald Winford, 91–109. Amsterdam: John Benjamins.

Berlin, Ira. 1998. *Many Thousands Gone: The First Two Centuries of Slavery in North America*. Cambridge, MA: Harvard University Press.

Brasch, Walter M. 1981. *Black English and the Mass Media*. New York: University Press of America.

Cassidy, Frederic G. 1986. "Barbadian Creole: Possibility and Probability." *American Speech* 61 (3): 195–205.

Chaudenson, Robert. 1992. *Des îles, des hommes, des langues: Essais sur la créolisation linguistique et culturelle*. Paris: L'Harmattan.

———. 2001. *Creolization of Language and Culture*. London: Routledge.

Coleman, Kenneth. 1978. *Georgia History in Outline*. Revised ed. Athens: University of Georgia Press.

Corne, Chris. 1999. *From French to Creole: The Development of New Vernaculars in the French Colonial World*. London: University of Westminster.

Corrigan, Karen P. 2010. *Irish English*. Vol. 1, *Northern Ireland*. Edinburgh: Edinburgh University.

DeBose, Charles E. 1983. "Samana English: A Dialect that Time Forgot." In *Proceedings of the Ninth Annual Meeting of the Berkeley Linguistics Society*, edited by Amy Dahlstrom et al., 47–53. Berkeley, CA: BLS.

DeGraff, Michel. 1999. "Creolization, Language Change, and Language Acquisition: A Prolegomenon." In *Language Creation and Language Change: Creolization, Diachrony, and Development*, edited by Michel DeGraff, 1–46. Cambridge, MA: MIT Press.

Diamond, Jared, and James A. Robinson, eds. 2010. *Natural Experiments of History*. Cambridge, MA: Harvard University Press.

Dillard, J. L. 1972. *Black English: Its History and Usage in the United States*. New York: Random House, Vintage Books.

———. 2000. "The Evidence for Pidgin/Creolization in Early American English." In *Creolization in the Americas*, edited by David Buisseret, Daniel H. Usner, Jr., Mary L. Galvin, Richard Cullen Rath, and J. L. Dillard, 131–45. College Station: Texas A & M University Press.

Dunn, Richard S. 1972. *Sugar and Slaves: The Rise of the Planter Class in the English West Indies, 1624–1713*. Chapel Hill: University of North Carolina Press.

Edgar, Walter. 1998. *South Carolina: A History*. Columbia: University of South Carolina Press.

Eliason, Norman E. 1956. *Tarheel Talk: An Historical Study of the English Language in North Carolina to 1860*. New York: Octagon Books.

Ewers, Traute. 1995. *The Origin of American Black English: Be-Forms in the Hoodoo Texts*. Berlin: Mouton de Gruyter.

Fayer, Joan. 2003. "African Interpreters in the Atlantic Slave Trade." *Anthropological Linguistics* 45: 281–95.

Fischer, David Hackett. 1989. *Albion's Seed: Four British Folkways in America*. New York: Oxford University Press.

Fortbath, Peter. 1977. *The River Congo: The Discovery, Exploration, and Exploitation of the World's Most Dramatic River*. Boston: Houghton Mifflin.

Gonzales, Ambrose. 1922. *The Black Border: Gullah Stories of the Carolina Coast (with a Glossary)*. Columbia, SC: The State Company.

Green, Lisa. 1998. "Aspect and Predicate Phrases in African-American Vernacular English." In *African-American English: Structure, History and Use*, edited by Salikoko S. Mufwene, John R. Rickford, Guy Bailey, and John Baugh, 37–68. London: Routledge.

———. 2002. *African American English: A Linguistic Introduction*. Cambridge: Cambridge University Press.

Halliday, M. A. K. 1976. "Anti-Languages." *American Anthropologist* 78: 570–84.

Hancock, Ian. 1986. "The Domestic Hypothesis, Diffusion and Componentiality: An Account of Atlantic Anglophone Creole Origins." In *Substrata versus Universals in Creole Genesis: Papers from the Amsterdam Creole Workshop*, edited by Pieter Muysken and Norval Smith, 71–102.

Harper, Douglas. 2003. *Slavery in the North*. http://www.slavenorth.com/author.htm.

Harris, Joel Chandler. 1880. *Uncle Remus, His Songs and Sayings: The Folklore of the Old Plantation*. New York: Appleton.

Huber, Magnus. 1999. "Atlantic Creoles and the Lower Guinea Coast: A Case against AfroGenesis." In *Spreading the Word: The Issue of Diffusion among the Atlantic Creoles*, edited by M. Huber and M. Parkvall, 81–110. London: University of Westminster Press.

Jones, H. [1724] 1956. *The Present State of Virginia: From Whence is Inferred a Short View of Maryland and North Carolina*, edited by Richard L. Morton. Reprint, Chapel Hill: University of North Carolina Press.

Kautzsch, Alexander. 2002. *The Historical Evolution of Earlier African American English: An Empirical Comparison of Early Sources*. Berlin: Mouton de Gruyter.

Krapp, George Philip. 1924. "The English of the Negro." *The American Mercury* 2: 190–95.

Kulikoff, Allan. 1986. *Tobacco and Slaves: The Development of Southern Cultures in the Chesapeake, 1680–1800*. Chapel Hill: University of North Carolina Press.

———. 1991. "Colonial Economy." In *The Reader's Companion to American History*, edited by Eric Foner and John A. Garraty, 201–3. Boston: Houghton Mifflin.

Labov, William. 1972. *Language in the Inner City*. Philadelphia: University of Pennsylvania.

———. 1994. *Principles of Linguistic Change: Internal Factors*. Oxford, UK: Blackwell.

———. 1998. "Co-Existent Systems in African-American Vernacular English." In *African-American English: Structure, History, and Use*, edited by Salikoko S. Mufwene, John R. Rickford, Guy Bailey, and John Baugh, 110–53. London: Routledge.

Lalla, Barbara, and Jean D'Costa. 1990. *Language in Exile: Three Hundred Years of Jamaican Creole*. Tuscaloosa: University of Alabama Press.

Lawrance, Benjamin N., Emily Lynn Osborn, and Richard L. Roberts, eds. 2006. *Intermediaries, Interpreters, and Clerks: African Employees in the Making of Colonial Africa (Africa and the Diaspora)*. Madison: University of Wisconsin Press.

Long, John H. 1995. "The Cotton Kingdom Expands: The Movement of African Americans in the South, 1830–60." In *The Settling of North America: The Atlas of the Great Migrations into North America from the Ice Age to the Present*, edited by Helen Hornbeck Tanner, 92–93. New York: Macmillan.

McPherson, James M. 1991. "Civil War: Causes and Results." In *The Reader's Companion to American History*, edited by Eric Foner and John A. Garraty, 182–85. Boston: Houghton Mifflin.

McWhorter, John H. 2000. "Strange Bedfellows[:] Recovering the Origins of Black English." Review of *The English History of African American English*, edited by Shana Poplack. *Diachronica* 17: 389–432.

Mille, Katherine. 1990. "A Historical Analysis of Tense-Mood-Aspect in Gullah Creole: A Case of Stable Variation." PhD diss., University of South Carolina.

Montgomery, Michael. 1991. "The Linguistic Value of the Ex-Slave Recordings." In *The Emergence of Black English: Text and Commentary*, edited by Guy Bailey, Natalie Maynor, and Patricia Cukor-Avila, 173–89. Amsterdam: John Benjamins.

Morgan, Marcyliena. 1993. "The Africanness of Counterlanguage among Afro-Americans." In *Africanisms in Afro-American Language Varieties*, edited by Salikoko S. Mufwene, 423–35. Athens: University of Georgia Press.

Mufwene, Salikoko S. 1991. "Is Gullah Decreolizing? A Comparison of a Speech Sample of the 1930's with a Speech Sample of the 1980's." In *The Emergence of Black English*, edited by Guy Bailey, Patricia Cukor-Avila, and Natalie Maynor, 213–30. Amsterdam: John Benjamins

——. 1992. "Why Grammars Are not Monolithic." In *The Joy of Grammar: A Festschrift in Honor of James D. McCawley*, edited by Diane Brentari, Gary N. Larson, and Lynn A. MacLeod, 225–50. Amsterdam: John Benjamins.

——. 1994. "On Decreolization: The Case of Gullah." In *Language and the Social Construction of Identity in Creole Situations*, edited by Marcyliena Morgan, 63–99. Los Angeles: UCLA Center for African-American Studies.

——. 1997a. "Jargons, Pidgins, Creoles, and Koinés: What Are They?" In *The Structure and Status of Pidgins and Creoles*, edited by Arthur K. Spears and Donald Winford, 35–70. Amsterdam: John Benjamins.

——. 1997b. "Gullah's Development: Myths and Sociohistorical Evidence." In *Language Variety in the South Revisited*, edited by Cynthia Bernstein, Robin Sabino, and Tom Nunally, 113–22. Tuscaloosa: University of Alabama Press.

——. 2000. "Some Sociohistorical Inferences about the Development of African-American English." In *The English History of African American English*, edited by Shana Poplack, 233–63. Malden, MA: Blackwell.

——. 2001a. "African-American English." In *The Cambridge History of the English Language*. Vol. 6, *History of American English*, edited by John Algeo, 291–324. Cambridge: Cambridge University Press.

——. 2001b. *The Ecology of Language Evolution*. Cambridge: Cambridge University.

——. 2004. Review of *The Historical Evolution of Earlier African American English: An Empirical Comparison of Early Sources*, by Alexander Kautzsch. *English World-Wide* 25: 305–11.

——. 2005. *Créoles, écologie sociale, évolution linguistique*. Paris: L'Harmattan.

——. 2008. *Language Evolution: Contact, Competition and Change*. London: Continuum.

——. 2009. "Some Offspring of Colonial English are Creole." In *Vernacular Universals vs. Contact-Induced Language Change*, edited by Juhani Klemola, Markku Filppula, and Heli Paulasto, 280–303. London: Routledge.

——. 2010. "SLA and the Emergence of Creoles." *Studies in Second Language Acquisition* 32: 1–42.

——. 2012. "Driving Forces in English Contact Linguistics." In *English as a Contact Language*, edited by Daniel Schreier and Marianne Hundt, 204–21. Cambridge: Cambridge University Press.

——. 2014. "Globalisation économique mondiale des XVIIe–XVIIIe siècles, émergence des créoles, et vitalité langagière." In *Langues créoles, mondialisation, éducation*, edited by Arnaud Carpooran. Vacoas, Mauritius: Editions le Printemps.

Naro, Anthony J. 1978. "A Study on the Origins of Pidginization." *Language* 54: 314–47.

————. 1988. A Reply to "Pidgin Origins Reconsidered" by Morris Goodman. *Journal of Pidgin and Creole Languages* 3: 95–102.

Nash, Gary B. 1988. *Forging Freedom: The Formation of Philadelphia's Black Community, 1720–1840*. Cambridge, MA: Harvard University Press.

Northrup, David. 2002. *Africa's Discovery of Europe, 1450–1850*. Oxford: Oxford University Press.

Ostler, Nichos. 2005. *Empires of the Word: A Language History of the World*. New York: Harper Collins.

Pederson, Lee. 1985. "Language in the Uncle Remus Tales." *Modern Philology* 82: 292–98.

Perkins, Edwin J. 1988. *The Economy of Colonial America*. New York: Columbia University Press.

Plag, Iingo. 2008. "Creoles as Interlanguages: Syntactic Structures." *Journal of Pidgin and Creole Languages* 23: 307–28.

————. 2009. "Creoles as Interlanguages: Phonology." *Journal of Pidgin and Creole Languages* 24: 119–38.

Poplack, Shana, ed. 2000. *The English History of African American English*. Malden, MA: Blackwell.

Poplack, Shana, and David Sankoff. 1987. "The Philadelphia Story in the Spanish Caribbean." *American Speech* 62: 291–314.

Poplack, Shana, and Sali Tagliamonte. 2001. *African American English in the Diaspora*. Malden, MA: Blackwell.

Rawley, James A. 1991. "Slave Trade." In *The Reader's Companion to American History*, edited by Eric Foner and John A. Garraty, 994–95. Boston: Houghton Mifflin.

Ray, Benjamin. 2009. "'Candy No Witch': Two African Slaves Caught up in the Salem Witch Trials of 1692." April 2, 2009. http://news.clas.virginia.edu/woodson/x15296.xml.

Reader, John. 1997. *Africa: Biography of a Continent*. New York: Alfred Knopf.

Rickford, John R. 1980. "Analyzing Variation in Creole Languages." In *Theoretical Orientations in Creole Studies*, edited by Albert Valdman and Arnold Highfield, 165–84. New York: Academic.

————. 1985. "Ethnicity as a Sociolinguistic Boundary." *American Speech* 60: 99–125.

————. 1986. "Social Contact and Linguistic Diffusion: Hiberno-English and New World Black English." *Language* 62: 245–89.

————. 1997. "Prior Creolization of AAVE? Sociohistorical and Textual Evidence from the 17th and 18th Centuries." *Journal of Sociolinguistics* 1: 315–36.

————. 1998. "The Creole Origins of African-American Vernacular English: Evidence from Copular Absence." In *African-American English: Structure, History, and Use*, edited by Salikoko S. Mufwene, John R. Rickford, Guy Bailey, and John Baugh, 154–200. London: Routledge.

————. 2006. "Down for the Count? The Creole Origins Hypothesis of AAVE at the Hands of the Ottawa Circle and Their Supporters." Review article. *Journal of Pidgin and Creole Languages* 21: 97–155.

Rickford, John R., and Jerome S. Handler. 1994. "Textual Evidence on the Nature of Early Barbadian Speech, 1676–1835." *Journal of Pidgin and Creole Languages* 9 (2): 221–55.

Samarin, William J. 1982. "Goals, Roles, and Language Skills in Colonizing Central Equatorial Africa." *Anthropological Linguistics* 24: 410–22.

————. 1989. *The Black Man's Burden: African Colonial Labor on the Congo and Ubangi Rivers, 1880–1900*. Boulder, CO: Westview.

Schneider, Edgar W. 1989. *American Early Black English*. Berlin: Mouton de Gruyter.

———. 1995. "Verbal -s Inflection in 'Early' American Black English." In *Linguistic Change under Contact Conditions*, edited by Jacek Fisiak, 315–26. Berlin: Mouton de Gruyter.

Schneider, Edgar W., and Michael B. Montgomery. 2001. "On the Trail of Early Nonstandard Grammar: An Electronic Corpus of Southern U.S. Antebellum Overseers' Letters." *American Speech* 76 (4): 388–410.

Schwartz, Stuart B. 1985. *Sugar Plantations in the Formation of Brazilian Society: Bahia, 1550–1835.* Cambridge: Cambridge University Press.

Simms, William Gilmore. 1845. *The Wigwam and the Cabin.* New York: Wiley and Putnam.

Singler, John V. 1989. "Plural Marking in Liberian Settler English, 1820–1980." *American Speech* 64: 40–64.

———. 1997. "The Configuration of Liberia's Englishes." *World Englishes* 16: 205–31.

———. 2007a. "Samaná and Sinoe, Part 1: Stalking the Vernacular." Column. *Journal of Pidgin and Creole Languages* 22: 123–48.

———. 2007b. "Samaná and Sinoe, Part 2: Provenance." *Journal of Pidgin and Creole Languages* 22: 309–46.

Stewart, William. 1968. "Continuity and Change in American Negro Dialects." *The Florida FL Reporter* 6. Also in *Perspectives on Black English*, edited by J. L. Dillard, 233–47. The Hague: Mouton.

Sutcliffe, David. 1998. "Gone with the Wind? Evidence for 19th Century African American Speech." *Links and Letters* 5: 127–45.

Tate, Thad W. 1965. *The Negro in Eighteenth-Century Williamsburg.* Williamsburg, VA: The Colonial Williamsburg Foundation.

Todd, Loreto. 1982. *Varieties of English around the World T1: Cameroon.* Heidelberg: Julius Groos.

Troike, Rudoph C. 2010. "Assessing the Authenticity of Joel Chandler Harris's Use of Gullah." *American Speech* 85: 287–314.

Turner, Lorenzo Dow. 1949. *Africanisms in the Gullah Dialect.* Chicago: University of Chicago Press.

Wood, Peter H. 1974. *The Black Majority: Negroes in Colonial South Carolina from 1670 through the Stono Rebellion.* New York: Alfred Knopf.

———. 1989. "The Changing Population of the Colonial South: An Overview by Race and Region, 1685–1790." In *Powhatan's Mantle: Indians in the Colonial Southeast*, edited by Peter H. Wood, Gregory A. Waselkov, and M. Thomas Hatley, 35–103. Lincoln: University of Nebraska Press.

CHAPTER 4

....

THE ORIGINS OF
AFRICAN AMERICAN
VERNACULAR ENGLISH
Beginnings

....

DONALD WINFORD

4.1 THE EMERGENCE OF AAVE

DISCUSSION of the varieties of English used by African Americans inevitably faces issues of definition concerning the scope of reference of the labels used to describe these varieties. I use the term *African American English* to refer to all forms of English employed by African Americans, though I do not include Gullah among them.[1] I follow the general linguistic practice of using the term *African American Vernacular English* (AAVE) to refer to the nonstandard varieties used by African Americans as their everyday vernacular, and this chapter is concerned with the origins and early history of these forms of English. These forms differ in various ways from region to region, and across social groups based on age, social class, and other characteristics. In general, however, AAVE constitutes a relatively uniform set of varieties that share the vast majority of their grammar and vocabulary. The history of this dialect and its variations is closely bound to the history of Southern White American Vernacular English (SWAVE), itself a mosaic of varieties that vary by region and across social groups in the southern United States. The roots of both AAVE and SWAVE were established during the first century of the British colonization of America, in the Chesapeake Bay area (Virginia and Maryland), and in the Carolinas. Understanding the sociohistorical background to the settlement of the southern colonies is therefore a vital first step toward understanding the origins of both AAVE and SWAVE. They both had their origins in the British settler dialects introduced into the South during the colonial period (between 1607 and 1776) but continued to evolve and to influence each other over time. Henceforth, my focus will be on AAVE alone. A complete picture of its origins would require investigation of the developments that took place in both Black and White Southern speech during the nineteenth and twentieth centuries, but that is beyond the scope of this chapter.

The question of AAVE origins has long been a subject of intense debate, particularly between the adherents of the "dialectologist" and "creolist" hypotheses (for fuller discussion, see Van Herk, this volume; Rickford, this volume). There seems to be consensus among most scholars today that AAVE, like SWAVE, is in fact in direct line of descent from earlier British dialects. But there is still disagreement about possible creole or African influence on the structure of AAVE. As we will see, the sociohistorical facts provide no evidence for the view that AAVE was once a creole. Rather, as Schneider (1989), Mufwene (1994, 2000), and others have argued, the conditions in the upper southern colonies, particularly Virginia, Maryland, and North Carolina, were favorable for many, if not most, Africans to acquire close approximations to the settler dialects. These were, in fact, the earliest forms of AAVE. The situation in the other early colonies, South Carolina and Georgia, were quite different, particularly in the coastal areas, where the plantation economy created conditions that were favorable to the emergence of a creole, Gullah. At the same time, even in these colonies, many African Americans also acquired the local forms of English, and it seems reasonable to assume that there was a linguistic continuum in these colonies. The varieties of AAVE in this area of the South must have been influenced to varying degrees by Gullah. At the same time, early AAVE was subject to influence from African languages and creolized varieties of English that were part of the linguistic picture in the South at different points from the seventeenth century onward.

To support claims about AAVE origins, one can appeal to various kinds of evidence, both sociohistorical and linguistic. My focus here is on the former type of evidence, which directly addresses the sociohistorical contexts in which early AAVE emerged. This will provide some idea of the British settler dialects that were the sources of AAVE structure, but it falls far short of reconstructing these early forms of English, or early AAVE itself. Previous work by scholars such as Schneider (1989) and the contributors to Poplack (2000) has shed some light on the British sources and possible inputs to AAVE, but much more needs to be done if we are to meet the strict standards of historical reconstruction. One of the greatest obstacles to this task is the fact that we have practically no records of the earliest forms of AAVE as spoken in the seventeenth and eighteenth centuries. Our most extensive records date from the nineteenth century, in the form of the ex-slave narratives, the Hoodoo texts, and data from diaspora varieties (Bailey, Maynor, and Cukor-Avila 1991; Poplack 2000; Schneider, this volume.) But even these data have generated much controversy about the origins or sources of particular features, how old or recent they are, and so on. The extent to which they are representative of seventeenth- or, even, eighteenth-century AAVE is still a matter of conjecture. This means that our attempts at reconstructing the nature of the earliest forms of AAVE must rely on inferences we can make primarily on the basis of sociohistorical and demographic data, and partly on the basis of brief and fleeting comments made by observers during the time in question.

It is now a matter of consensus that the earliest forms of AAVE emerged in the southern American colonies, permanent settlement of which began with Virginia in 1607, then Maryland in 1634, continuing with the Carolinas and later, Georgia. The two main foci of early settlement were the Chesapeake Bay area—coastal Virginia and Maryland—and the coastal areas of South Carolina, first settled in 1670. These two areas were characterized by very different kinds of demographic ratios and patterns of contact between Blacks and Whites, leading to very different linguistic outcomes. As Wood (1989, 38) informs us, the vast majority of the southern population, both White and Black, was located in Virginia and the Carolinas during the seventeenth and eighteenth centuries. Virginia's population numbered 153,900 out of a combined total of 222,100 for the three colonies in 1730 (Wood 1989, 38). The more than seventy-two thousand Blacks and Whites outside of Virginia were heavily concentrated along the coastal areas of the Carolinas, with Blacks significantly outnumbering Whites in South Carolina. Thus, it was clearly the demographics of these southern colonies that were central to the development of AAVE in the seventeenth to eighteenth centuries. In the following sections, I discuss the early history of settlement and the resulting contact situations that emerged in the Chesapeake Bay area and in the Carolinas during the colonial period. I will touch on the relative proportions of the various groups in contact, over time, in each situation; the codes of social interaction regulating the statuses and relationships of the groups; and the types of community settings in which they interacted (Mintz 1971, 481). Differences in each of these conditions affected the linguistic outcomes of the contact in specific ways.

4.2 The Chesapeake Colonies: Virginia and Maryland

I follow Kulikoff's (1979, 528) division of the social history of the Chesapeake region into five distinct periods between 1607 and 1800. However, I adjust it somewhat to conform to the three stages of the development of the African American community in the Chesapeake, as proposed in Kulikoff (1978, 229). The first period covers 1607 to 1650, when the Chesapeake colonies were struggling to establish themselves and Blacks were a tiny element of the population. The second period spans roughly 1651–1680, a period of rapid expansion of tobacco cultivation, when Blacks were outnumbered by White servants and arguably had the opportunity to learn their dialects. The third covers 1681–1740, a period that witnessed heavy importation of African slaves from the Caribbean and Africa, and a more natural increase of the population, as plantations grew in number and size. The fourth period runs from 1741–1800, a time during which immigration declined, there was greater natural increase of the Black population, and plantation sizes increased.

4.2.1 1607–1650

Virginia was the first of the American colonies to be successfully settled, in 1607. According to Cheyney (1907), roughly 300 settlers arrived from England between

1607 and 1609; 1,500 between 1609 and 1618; and an additional 3,570 between 1618 and 1631. It is generally accepted that the first Africans arrived in 1619, numbering around 20 and brought by a Dutch man-of-war, the captain of which sold them to the governor and cape merchant for supplies (Vaughan 1972, 470). The 1624 census recorded a total population of 1,227, including 487 servants and only 23 Blacks (Smith 1947, 328). By 1649, the population was estimated at around fifteen thousand (Craven 1971, 26), and in 1650, according to Kulikoff (1978, 229), Blacks constituted only 3 percent (1,700) of the (non–Native American) population.

Maryland was established in 1634 by between 132 and 148 settlers (mostly indentured servants) arriving from London on two ships, the Ark and the Dove (Menard 1985, 30–31). By 1642, the population had grown to between 340 to 390 persons (Menard 1985, 40). According to Wright (1921, 13) slavery began in the first decade of Maryland's history; slaves were mentioned in two acts of the provincial assembly in 1638–39, and in 1642 the governor became owner of a gang of slaves. The real growth of Maryland's population began in the 1650s, with the expansion of tobacco cultivation. This was accompanied by an increase in immigration, including planters and other free persons, servants, and some slaves.

We know practically nothing about the status of the Blacks who came to the Chesapeake before 1650. According to Vaughan (1972, 470), some came as servants, some from England, and some were free and had slaves themselves, but most appear to have been held as servile laborers. The twenty-three Blacks (twelve men and eleven women) listed in the 1625 Virginia census are described simply as "negroes" and as widely distributed across the colony (471). Over the next two decades, Blacks continued to enter Virginia at the rate of two or three per year (476). The figures from the 1625 census suggest that they were vastly outnumbered by White servants (Vaughan 1972). The fact that they were such a small minority and entered Virginia in very small numbers per year during the first half of seventeenth century suggests that they had the opportunity to adapt to the language and customs of the White settlers, particularly servants, with whom they were most in contact. There is also evidence that the Blacks who entered the Chesapeake from 1630 until around 1675 came predominantly from the West Indies, particularly Barbados, and many were likely to have already learned some English (Breen 1973, 6; Menard 1998, 217).

4.2.2 1651–1680

The period from 1651–1680 was one of greater stability, when settlements became well established in both Virginia and Maryland (Kulikoff 1979, 530). As Kulikoff (ibid.) points out, "the years from 1650–1680 have been aptly dubbed the 'age of the small planter'. . . . [when] the adult children of planters and some freed servants . . . lived comfortably as landowners." Immigration to the Chesapeake increased greatly, and the vast majority of these new arrivals came as indentured servants. According to Menard (1985, 117), "70 percent of the colonists who came to Maryland between 1634 and 1681 arrived as indentured servants," though he further notes that the percentage may have been as high as 85 percent (ibid.). Craven (1971, 5) also points out that "the vast majority of settlers in seventeenth-century Virginia, perhaps 75 percent or more of them, reached the colony under some form of contract, or indenture." In 1671, Governor Berkeley estimated the total population of Virginia at about forty thousand, of whom some six thousand were servants and two thousand were Black (Smith 1947, 328), though some historians think the estimate is a bit high (Breen 1973, 6). According to Wood's (1989, 38) estimate, by 1685 the total non–Native American population had grown to 40,700, of whom 38,100 were White, and 2,600 were Black.

A similar pattern of development applied to Maryland. Between 1633 and 1680, a total of about twenty-one thousand servants came to the colony to supply badly needed labor for the expanding tobacco farms (Smith 1947, 323). By 1660, the total population was around 12,000, including 1,078 servants (Smith 1947, 324). Most of the servants who had arrived earlier had satisfied the terms of their indentureship and become free persons, and even landowners and owners of servants and slaves themselves (Menard 1998, 230). Menard (1998, 210) informs us that during the period 1674–1679, the ratio of servants to slaves was 3.88 to 1. In 1681, the Black population in Maryland is estimated to have been at around 760, or 4 percent of the total population of approximately nineteen thousand (Menard 1985, 129).

According to Kulikoff (1979, 520), "until around 1680 so few Blacks were forced to come to the Chesapeake colonies that the growth of the White population approximated that of the total population." Menard (1998, 231) also points out that in 1680, "slaves were of slight importance in Chesapeake," making up less than 5 percent of the population. Of particular relevance is the fact that, until the 1670s or so, most of the slaves that were transported to the Chesapeake came from the West Indies, and many may have known some form of English (Kulikoff 1978, 229).

White servants, as well as small farm owners, worked side by side with Blacks in the fields, and many White owners treated Blacks in much the same way as they treated their servants. Other evidence of close association between Blacks and White servants in particular, comes from Breen's (1973) account of Black participation in the servant uprising in Virginia in 1663. Some Blacks, like the White servants, even achieved freedom (Kulikoff 1978, 230). However, Blacks still stood in a relationship of gross inequality and inferiority to Whites. This grew worse after 1660, when strict laws prohibiting interracial sex, unions, and other kinds of contact, were passed, in response to the growth of the Black population and events like Bacon's Rebellion of 1675, in which many Black servants participated.

4.2.3 1681–1740

The period from 1681 to 1740 witnessed another dramatic transformation of the demographics and social landscape of the Chesapeake colonies. Beginning in the 1670s, more Black slaves were imported to work on expanding plantations, and natural increase began to overtake immigration as the major factor in population growth (Craven 1971, 25; Menard 1985, 262). During this period, slavery gradually replaced indentured servitude as the principal form of unfree labor on the Chesapeake tobacco coast (Menard 1985, 244). Slaves would dominate the unfree labor force for the remainder of the colonial period, though there was continued and substantial immigration of servants during the eighteenth century. Contact between slaves and servants continued, though by 1700 both groups were more heavily concentrated in the estates of large planters (Menard 1985, 302). At the same time, many small planters (many of them ex-servants) also owned slaves well into the eighteenth century (Craven 1971, 108 n. 2).

4.2.3.1 *Demographics*

The growth in the Black population had begun in the 1670s. Menard (1998, 216) estimates that the Royal African Company delivered at least five hundred, and possibly as many as one thousand slaves to the Chesapeake between 1674 and 1679. Between 1679 and 1686, seven ships arrived with about 1,450 slaves, and by 1690, Blacks were 15 percent (11,500) of the non–Native American population of Virginia. The percentage of Blacks in the population increased from 25 percent in 1710 to 28 percent in 1740 (Kulikoff 1979, 242). In Maryland, slaves numbered around 5,609 out of a total population of 36,213 in 1704; 7,948 out of 43,742 in 1710; and 8,379 out of 45,733 in 1712 (Menard 1985, 293).

Before 1680, the vast majority of slaves had come from the Caribbean, especially Barbados. Moreover, even though direct supply from Africa began in the 1670s, Menard (1998, 217) points out that shipments of slaves from the West Indies to the Chesapeake probably increased over the last quarter of the seventeenth century, as trade between the tobacco coast and the islands expanded. However, by the 1720s Africa had become the chief source of supply of slaves. Between 1700 and 1740, Virginia imported around forty-three thousand Blacks, of whom roughly thirty-nine thousand were African (Kulikoff 1978, 230).

The second major demographic development in the Chesapeake during this period was the fact that natural increase gradually overtook immigration as the chief cause of population growth (Craven 1971, 25; Menard 1985, 132). As early as 1686, William Fitzhugh, a planter, noted that most of the twenty-nine Black slaves he owned were native to Virginia. There was a significant increase in native-born slaves after 1720, which continued into the eighteenth century (Kulikoff 1979, 532). According to Menard (1985, 282), "it seems likely that by 1730 most slaves were Maryland-born, although among adults Africans may still have predominated." The same applied to Virginia. By the 1740s locally born slaves dominated the Black population of the Chesapeake (Kulikoff 1979, 536).

4.2.3.2 *The Language Situation*

As far as their language was concerned, the new African arrivals presented a stark contrast to the Creole slaves. In 1724, Hugh Jones, a Virginia clergyman, commented that "the languages of the new Negroes are various harsh jargons," but added that slaves born in Virginia "talk good English, and affect our language, habit and customs" (Jones 1956,

cited by Kulikoff 1978, 226). By contrast, travelers and clergymen in the eighteenth century frequently observed that African-born slaves did not understand or speak English
well. For instance, the Rev. John Bell of Virginia wrote in 1724 that there were "a great
many Black. . . . infidels that understand not our language nor me theirs." His view was
echoed by the Rev. James Falconer in the same year (Perry 1840, cited in Blassingame
1979, 26). There is also evidence that some form of Africanized English was spoken by
some African-born slaves. As late as 1773, the English traveler J. F. D. Smyth wrote that,
in trying to converse with Virginia slaves, he could not "understand all of them, as great
numbers, being Africans, are incapable of acquiring our language, and at best imperfectly
if at all; many of the others speak a mixed dialect between the Guinea and the English"
(Smyth 1773, cited in Blassingame 1979, 26). But these forms of English could not survive,
given the low numbers of Africans who spoke like that, and their dispersal throughout
the locally born Black population. Also, younger Africans appeared to have acquired
English more easily, as might be expected. A native of Maryland reported in 1822 that a
group of African boys "have been three months only among the English and they now
speak it better than most of the Blacks in these southern states" (Staudenraus 1956, 149,
cited in Blassingame 1979, 25). We can assume then that most slaves in seventeenth- and
eighteenth-century Virginia acquired English rather successfully, particularly as children. However, it seems clear that the forms of English spoken by Blacks in this period
were quite variable, based on factors such as their language background, the age of acquisition, the particular target varieties they were exposed to, whether these were spoken
by Blacks or Whites, and their language learning abilities. In his account of descriptions
of runaway slaves in the southern colonies during the eighteenth century, Read (1939)
establishes five categories of slaves based on their command of English: newly arrived
African slaves who knew no English; slaves described as speaking "broken," "bad," or
"indifferent" English; slaves who spoke "tolerable" or "pretty good" English within two
to three years after landing; slaves from the Caribbean who are described as speaking
good to very good English; and finally slaves born in the American colonies, who are uniformly described as speaking good English. Read (1939, 258) concludes that:

> The present study shows that during colonial times there were Negroes in all stages
> of proficiency in their knowledge of English; a constant stratum of recently arrived
> ones without any English; those who were learning English during their first years in
> the new country, and a group who had learned successfully. The Negroes born in this
> country invariably used, according to these records, good English.

Various factors promoted the acculturation of Black slaves during the late seventeenth to mid-eighteenth centuries. First, Blacks comprised a minority of the population, never exceeding 15 percent up to 1700, and rising to around 40 percent by the
end of the eighteenth century (Wood 1989, 38). Second, there was frequent interaction between Blacks and White settlers, including small planters and servants in particular, as they worked together in the fields on the plantations. Third, most planters
owned few slaves, by contrast with the large slave holdings in the Caribbean and South

Carolina. Fourth, there was a high rate of natural increase within the slave population. Mullin (1994, 19) points out that the tidewater tobacco planters commanded the only self-producing slave population in the hemisphere, and after 1740 they were no longer as active in the slave market as they had been. Moreover, slave owners encouraged their slaves to form monogamous families that would add slave children to their possessions. Such children no doubt played an important role in the acquisition and consolidation of English among the slave population. This was true even on large plantations owned by the gentry. For instance, according to Kulikoff (1978, 244), "a native born slave on Robert Carter's plantation in 1733 usually lived in a family composed of husband, wife and children, whereas new Negroes were placed in sex-segregated barracks, and seasoned immigrants often lived in conjugal units without children." Also, even though the large numbers of Africans imported during this period may have used highly divergent forms of English, conditions did not favor the conventionalization of these varieties. The new arrivals were dispersed among the Creole population or sent to small and remote satellite plantations, called "quarters" (Mullin 1994, 19). For instance, nearly two-thirds of the recently imported African slaves on Robert Carter's plantation lived "with numerous native adults and children, and White overseers resided at almost every quarter" (Kulikoff 1978, 243). This meant that the new arrivals had the opportunity to interact with Whites as well as Creole slaves who already spoke English. We might speculate that the African-born slaves had some influence on the emerging forms of AAVE.

Finally we should not overlook the important role played by religion in the acculturation of Blacks. A statement by the Virginia House of Burgesses in 1699 points out that "Negroes borne in this Country are generally baptized and brought up in the Christian religion, but for Negroes imported hither" among other reasons, "the variety and strangeness of their languages ... renders it impossible to attain any Progress in their Conversion" (Menard 1985, 417 n. 75, citing Kennedy and McIlwaine "Journals," 1695–1702, 174). All of these factors, among others, favored the acquisition and consolidation of forms of Black speech more or less closely modeled on those of White and Black speakers of English with whom they were in greatest contact.

4.2.4 1741–1790

The third phase of the history of African Americans in the Chesapeake colonies, from 1741 to 1790, coincided with the settlement of the piedmont areas. This period saw a huge increase in the area's population, brought about by c ontinuing natural increase among the White and Black population, as well as continuing immigration of settlers and servants. There was a large influx of Scotch-Irish and, to a lesser extent, German immigrants who began to move down the Valley of Virginia and settle the backcountry after 1730. Their numbers rose especially in the 1730s and early 1740s with the second and third waves of the great migration of Scotch-Irish from Ulster (Leyburn 1962, 203). By 1745, the total population of Virginia had grown to about 234,200, of whom 148,300 were White, 85,300 were Black, and 600 were Native American (Wood 1989, 38). By 1775, the total had grown to 466,200, of whom 196,300 were White, 130,900 were Black, and 300 were Native American (ibid.) Maryland's population grew to around 149,973 in 1755, of whom 107,209 were White and 42,764 were Black (Smith 1947, 332). By the time of the first federal census in 1790, the total population of the Chesapeake colonies was over a million. At this time, according to Menard (1985, 274), "approximately 50 percent more Blacks lived in Maryland and Virginia alone than had immigrated to all of British North America before 1790." By this time too, the Scotch-Irish made up 14 percent of the population of Virginia (Crozier 1984, 315) and were well established in the piedmont areas.

In the course of the eighteenth century, new land suitable for tobacco was cleared in the interior, and the children of poor planters and tenants migrated to the piedmont counties to seek new opportunities (Kulikoff 1979, 528). Eventually, "the frontier moved beyond the mountains into the Shenandoah Valley in the 1730s and 1740s and into West Virginia and Kentucky by the 1760s and 1770s" (Kulikoff 1979, 521). Accompanying this, more foreign-born Blacks moved to the piedmont than to the tidewater during the 1730s to 1740s, and after 1755 every African newcomer was sent to the piedmont (Kulikoff 1978, 259). Many tidewater slaves were also sold to piedmont planters or were forced to accompany their masters to the area (252). From 1790 onward, there was a heavy concentration of slaves in the area. This area also became the dominant focal area of the dialect associated with the piedmont South, which was heavily influenced by Ulster Scots. It follows that the linguistic inputs to this dialect also had some influence on AAVE as spoken in the piedmont areas, thus adding to the spectrum of varieties of Black speech.[2] But the dominant forms of AAVE were probably those that had been brought from the coastal areas by Creole slaves.

4.5 The Linguistic Inputs to the Chesapeake Colonies

What we know about the linguistic inputs to the Chesapeake colonies is sketchy at best, since so little research has been done on the precise origins of the White settlers and slaves who arrived there during the colonial period. The evidence suggests that, during the seventeenth century, most of the White immigrants came from southern England, particularly London and adjacent counties such as Middlesex. Many other settlers in this period came from southwestern England, via the port of Bristol (Smith 1947, 309) or via Liverpool, and some came from northern counties such as Yorkshire (Craven 1971, 35 n. 46, citing Campbell 1959). As Craven (1971, 24) notes, "it seems safe enough to conclude that, although emigrants to Virginia might hail from any county in the kingdom, most of them came either from London or the so-called home counties lying immediately in its neighborhood." Thus, the speech of the Chesapeake Bay area had solid southeastern English roots. Indeed, in 1724, Hugh Jones, describing the situation in Virginia, strongly implies that the speech of the colonists was that of London:

> The Habits, Life, customs, computations, etc. of the Virginians are much the same as about London, which they esteem their home; and for the most part have

contemptible notions of England, and wrong sentiments of Bristol, and the other outports, which they entertain from seeing and hearing the common dealers, sailors, and servants that come from those towns, and the country places in England and Scotland, whose language and manners are strange to them; for the planters, and even the native Negroes generally talk good English without idiom or tone. (Jones, quoted in Morton 1956, 80)

It is particularly instructive that Jones likens the speech of locally born Blacks to that of the settlers from the London area in general. The further suggestion is that this type of speech was seen as the norm against which other forms of dialectal speech were judged. Support for this comes from Read's (1938) account of advertisements for runaway servants in eighteenth-century Virginia and other colonies. The servants include speakers from the West Country, Yorkshire, other parts of northern England such as Lincolnshire, Scotland, and Ireland. Read (1938, 74) points out, "It is noteworthy that, out of the hundreds of such advertisements examined, no mention is made of speakers from the East Anglian or southeastern counties." This suggests that, by the mid-eighteenth century, "the speaking of English dialects and 'broad' English was a noticeable deviation from the general body of American speech. Except for the East Anglians and the southeasterners, those who used the dialects could be identified by them" (Read 1938, 79). Read also notes that "the body of speakers from the west and north is shown to have been considerable, no doubt enough to modify American speech."

The eighteenth century also witnessed migration of more settlers, mostly servants, from all parts of England. The available data suggest that the majority still came from the London area, with the Southwest and North also contributing significant numbers (Smith 1947, 307–31). Many others came from Ireland, and smaller numbers from Scotland and Wales, as well as significant numbers of convicts, most of whom seem to have embarked in London and Bristol (Smith 1947, 329). But, as already noted, the major migration of settlers during the eighteenth century involved the Scotch-Irish from Northern Ireland, who migrated to the piedmont of Virginia and the Carolinas, not to the coastal areas where the vast majority of African Americans were to be found (Montgomery 2001, 119). However, the eventual movement of planters and their slaves to the piedmont areas throughout the eighteenth century led to contact between Scotch-Irish dialects and the evolving forms of English that had emerged among both Blacks and Whites east of the mountains. It is generally accepted that Scotch-Irish had a profound influence on Appalachian English and significant influence on Southern American English in general, both Black and White (Montgomery 1991, 2004). The precise nature of Scotch-Irish influence on Black forms of speech in the eighteenth century and later is still a topic for further research.

It also seems reasonable to assume that varieties of English introduced by servants and slaves from the Caribbean in the seventeenth to eighteenth centuries, and African languages that were introduced, particularly in the eighteenth century, must have had some influence on the varieties of English spoken by African Americans in the Chesapeake colonies. It is, however, impossible to tell how many slaves imported from the Caribbean actually spoke English, or, if they did, what forms of English they spoke. British slave ships often stopped in Caribbean ports before continuing to the American colonies, hence we cannot identify how many slaves were counted as being from the Caribbean when they were in fact from Africa. Klein (1975) claimed that as late as 1710–1718, 53 percent of the slaves transported to Virginia were from the West Indies. But Menard (1998, 219 n. 25) rejects this figure on the grounds that it fails to take into account those slaves that were transported from Africa via the Caribbean. Still, he suggests that around 16.5 percent of slaves brought to Virginia in this period did in fact come from the Caribbean. In addition, there must also have been considerable variation among the forms of English spoken by Blacks in this period. On the one hand, there would have been differences in the degree of proficiency with which they spoke English; on the other, they may have been in contact with various dialects, both social and regional, that served as models for their acquisition of the language. Unfortunately, all of this must remain speculative, since we have no records of the actual forms of English spoken by African Americans during this time.

4.3 NORTH CAROLINA

The Chesapeake Bay area was the hearth from which further settlement spread both inland, to the Piedmont of Virginia, and south to coastal North Carolina. This led to the diffusion of the already established forms of Black and White Virginian speech to these areas. According to Edgar (1998, 1), Virginia settlers eager for land began moving south into what would become North Carolina as early as 1650, migrating from the Chesapeake region into the area of Albemarle Sound (Wood 1989, 43). By 1685, the non-Indian population (Blacks and Whites) stood at roughly 5,900, of whom only 200 were Black. In 1689, the proprietors of Carolina named a separate governor for the region stretching from Albemarle to Cape Fear, establishing North Carolina as a distinct colonial entity. Migration from the north continued, and by 1730 there were 27,300 Whites to 5,500 Blacks (Wood 1989, 38). Many of the latter were not enslaved, having found a refuge in this still obscure colony. As the plantations expanded along the coast, the ratio of Blacks to Whites increased to some extent in the course of the eighteenth century. By 1745, Blacks numbered roughly 14,000, and Whites about 42,700 (ibid.). From the 1740s onward, the population expanded greatly as a result of the continuous migration of White farmers from England and Scotland, Virginia, and Pennsylvania (Wood 1989, 46). As in the case of Virginia, the vast majority of these were Scotch-Irish, continuing their movement down the great valley into the piedmont. According to Leyburn (1962, 213), there were at least 60,000 settlers in the North Carolina backcountry by the time of the Revolutionary War, representing about 36 percent of the total White population of about 160,000. As they had in Virginia, they first established farms rather than plantations, hiring relatively few slaves. Leyburn (1962, 221) points out that in Orange County, for example, more than three-quarters of the property holders owned between 100 and

500 acres of land, and only 5 percent had farms bigger than one thousand acres. The demographics, as well as the community settings of Black-White contact in the coastal and piedmont areas of North Carolina in the eighteenth century, favor the view that Blacks, in general, acquired close approximations to the dialects of the Whites with whom they were in contact and passed these on to newly arrived Blacks. Again, as in Virginia, different linguistic inputs in the lowlands, as distinct from the uplands, may well have made for differences in the forms of English used by Blacks in the two areas of the colony during the eighteenth century. These varieties would later spread with the migration of significant numbers of Blacks and Whites from Virginia and North Carolina into the cotton belt of the Gulf States and also into the western areas of the Upper South, such as Kentucky and Tennessee. The other hearth of settlement that served as a major point of diffusion of Black and White speech into the rest of the South was South Carolina.

4.4 SOUTH CAROLINA

After unsuccessful attempts by a company of Barbadians led by John Vassall to establish a settlement on the Cape Fear River in 1665 (Edgar 1998, 40), the colony of Carolina was finally established in 1670 when the ship *Carolina* made landfall at Bull's Bay, thirty miles south of Charleston (Edgar 1998, 47). According to Edgar (1998, 48), the first group of colonists consisted of about 130 people, most of them English men and women, with a few from Barbados, and a family from Nevis. Over the next twenty years, 54 percent of all White immigrants came from Barbados, with more coming from other British West Indian islands, including Bermuda and the Bahamas. A majority of them were servants, but many were merchants or the sons of planters (ibid.). More than half of the enslaved Blacks brought during this period also came from the Caribbean, especially Barbados, many arriving with their owners. The English Barbadians remained a majority of the White population for the first two decades of settlement, and they shaped the fabric of South Carolina society in many ways. From 1680 onward, two waves of immigration consisting of English dissenters, French Huguenots, Baptists from Massachusetts, and a few Quakers and Irish Catholics added to the mix of colonists (Carver 1987, 125). By 1700, Whites numbered around 3,800 and Blacks around 2,800 (Wood 1989, 46). After 1700, Barbadians made up only a fraction of the colony's English-descended inhabitants. The earlier emphasis on raising cattle, pigs, and sheep soon shifted to rice cultivation, and by 1690 the crop was already bringing wealth to the Carolina lowlands. With the growth of the plantations, the number of slaves imported from Africa and the Caribbean also increased. By 1708, Blacks were in the majority, making up 50.1 percent (4,100) of the population, with Whites making up 49.9 percent (4,080). The Black majority would continue to grow after that, until it made up two-thirds of the population by about 1730, a ratio that persisted until the Civil War (Wood 1989, 38).

The demographics of settlement during the first three decades of the colony's establishment suggest that the forms of English that were introduced included a significant
input of Barbadian English as spoken by servants and slaves. These forms of English
were modeled after southwestern English dialects, in particular, since the vast majority of indentured servants in Barbados came from that part of England (Niles 1980).
Whether Blacks spoke close approximations to the English dialects or a creole variety
is a matter of speculation. Some scholars suggest that, whatever language they brought
with them, Blacks in seventeenth-century South Carolina eventually acquired the dialects of Whites in the colony, since they interacted closely with them in the first few
decades. Wood (1974, 175) quotes a pastor, Rev. Thomas Hassell, who commented in 1713
that locally born Blacks in South Carolina spoke English as well as he did, while African
immigrants had a poor command of the language. Edgar tells us that "during the first
three decades of settlement, the relationship between owner and slave was quite different from what it would become" (1998, 68). For a start, all new arrivals, Black and White,
were pioneers, attempting to tame the South Carolina wilderness. Blacks had great freedom of movement, and they were allowed to travel from plantation to plantation, and
to the Charleston market. They were even allowed to carry weapons, and many of them
were members of the South Carolina militia and participated in the 1702 expedition
against the Spanish in St. Augustine (Edgar 1998, 69). Such circumstances, along with
others, may well have led to African Americans (especially children) acquiring close
approximations to White settler dialects. This picture would change dramatically over
the next fifty years.

The expansion of rice cultivation and the introduction of indigo as a major cash
crop led to increased importation of slaves. From 1712 onward, about 600 slaves were
imported each year (Edgar 1998, 66). The low country became a classic plantation society, with an economic system modeled after that of Barbados. This produced a situation
in which, by 1720, Blacks made up 64.5 percent (11,800) of the population, and Whites
35.5 percent (6,500) (Edgar 1998, 78). The ratio was even higher in the low country where
there was an average of three Blacks for every White by the late eighteenth century. For
example, Blacks made up 79 percent of the population in Goose Creek, and 74 percent
in St. James Santee (Edgar 1998, 69). The first half of the eighteenth century witnessed
growing separation between Blacks and Whites due to growing resistance among the
Black population, which culminated in the Stono Rebellion of 1739. This led to the Slave
Code of 1740, introducing new restrictions on slaves and the importation of slaves from
Africa. Only 1,562 Africans were imported in the 1740s, compared with 12,589 between
1735 and 1740 (Edgar 1998, 76). Until 1740, the majority of Blacks in South Carolina had
been born in Africa, but after that year, Creole slaves became the majority. Still, Edgar
(1998, 70) informs us that African-born Blacks remained a high percentage of the population until the Revolutionary War.

With increasing plantation sizes came decreasing opportunities for Blacks and
Whites to interact with one another. According to Edgar (1998), the geography of the
lowland areas created hundreds of isolated pockets where there were thirty or more
Black slaves and rarely a White. Also, even when Whites were present, they interacted

little with Blacks (ibid.). This would have meant that new arrivals from Africa had to acquire English from seasoned or Creole slaves, as well as from other Africans with a low command of English. In these circumstances, there was great potential for African languages to leave their stamp on the forms of English that slaves spoke. Thus, it was that Gullah was created—the first creole language to survive in the English colonies of America. Exactly how widespread Gullah became during the eighteenth century, and how many Blacks spoke it in addition to other forms of English, remain matters of speculation. It is at least certain that it was far more widespread in the eighteenth and nineteenth centuries than is generally assumed, especially given that the coastal plain made up two-thirds of South Carolina, and plantations continued to spread throughout that area from 1720 onward.

In late-eighteenth-century Charlston, with its diverse and multilingual population, Gullah was heard everywhere, and even some Whites spoke it (Edgar 1998, 166, citing Wood 1974, 169, 314). Indeed, according to Edgar (1998, 202), "low country Whites spoke English with a little lilt that has been characterized as 'high Gullah.'" It seems reasonable to assume that Gullah also influenced the forms of AAVE used by Gullah speakers, as well as other Blacks. By the mid-eighteenth century, the language situation in the low country would have taken the form of a creole continuum within the Black population as part of a broader spectrum encompassing the English varieties used by the elite, Whites of lower status, enslaved Blacks, and free Blacks who were in closer contact with Whites.

Also in the 1750s, a massive migration of Scotch-Irish from southeast Pennsylvania, as well as other migrants from Maryland and Virginia, began. Between 1730 and 1760, the White population grew from about 9,700 to about 39,000 (Wood 1989, 38), most of it in the piedmont area. Beginning in the 1750s, thousands of Scotch-Irish from southeast Pennsylvania, as well as the Chesapeake area, began moving into this area. After the defeat of the Cherokee in 1761, the population of the area expanded even more quickly, and by 1776, according to Leyburn (1962, 213), there were around eighty-three thousand settlers in the South Carolina piedmont who made up about four-fifths of the entire White population of South Carolina. Scotch-Irish constituted the majority of these and continued to represent more than half of the upland population for the rest of the century (Crozier 1984, 315). By 1790, the total population of South Carolina, both Black and White, had grown to 249,400 (Wood 1989, 38). Of these, 56 percent (139,440) were White and 44 percent were Black (ibid.). The White population consisted of three major groups, English, Scots (from both Scotland and Northern Ireland), and Irish, representing 36.7, 32.9, and 11.7 percent of that population, respectively. There were also Germans (5 percent), French (3.9 percent), and others, including Dutch and Swedish settlers (Edgar 1998, 50). The vast majority of the English remained concentrated in the low country, where they made up 80 percent of the White population, while the Scotch-Irish constituted the vast majority of the population of the piedmont area.

Linguistically, there was a wide gulf between the language of the piedmont and that of the coast, reflecting the situations in Virginia and North Carolina to some extent. However, the pattern of settlement was quite different from that of other colonies, and the area was the most heterogeneous of the southern colonies. As in the other colonies, there was a far heavier concentration of Blacks in the coastal areas, resulting in contact between Blacks and settlers of mostly southern English origin, though Blacks far outnumbered Whites in South Carolina. The precise sources of the forms of English used in these areas have not been explored in any detail. In the piedmont areas, there was a much higher ratio of Whites to Blacks and closer contact between the races. We can assume that African Americans in the piedmont areas of South Carolina would also have had good opportunity to acquire the settler dialects of those areas, at least during the earlier periods of settlement. The latter part of the eighteenth century, however, saw an increasing shift toward larger farms in the piedmont areas, leading to greater movement of Blacks from the low country. The planter class of the coastal areas continued to dominate the political, social, and economic affairs of the colony, and eventually the plantation system would more or less submerge the piedmont (Kurath 1972, 51). In the late eighteenth century, while the low country continued to concentrate on rice, the piedmont turned increasingly to cotton cultivation. By 1808, cotton had become the major crop of two-thirds of the state, mostly in the non-coastal areas (Edgar 1998, 270). This was accompanied by large forced relocation of Blacks to the interior and piedmont areas. In 1800, nearly 25 percent of families in the piedmont owned slaves and, by 1820, it had grown to 40 percent (Edgar 1998, 271). By 1860, there were owners of slaves in every district of the state, and there were owners of more than one hundred slaves in every district except Anderson (Edgar 1998, 312). This redistribution of the Black population would have meant that the forms of English that had emerged in the low country would have spread to the uplands, merging with those acquired by slaves from upland settlers, the vast majority of whom were of Scotch-Irish descent. Gullah remained confined mostly to the coastal areas, though we can assume that some Gullah-speaking slaves could be found in the uplands as well. Just as it had in Virginia, the blending of all these forms of English would result in varieties of AAVE that drew on the resources of all available forms of Black and White speech.

4.5 CONCLUSION

The discussion above provides a broad sketch of the sociohistorical contexts in which Africans in colonial America were brought into contact with English-speaking settlers. The demographic evidence provides little support for the view that an English-lexicon creole language was in general use among the Black population of the South during the colonial era and that this creole consequently "decreolized" to become AAVE. Rather, it suggests that conditions were favorable for most Blacks to acquire relatively close approximations of the dialects spoken by White settlers throughout the Atlantic South, with creole formation restricted to the coastal areas of South Carolina, and later Georgia.[3] The varieties of (nonstandard) English acquired by Blacks in this colonial period were the earliest forms of AAVE. These became models for later arrivals from Africa and the Caribbean who spoke African languages, as well as perhaps creole or pidginized forms of English. Early AAVE, therefore, acquired many of its linguistic features from the British English dialects introduced into Virginia and Maryland in the Upper South and into the Carolinas and Georgia in the Lower South, during the course of the seventeenth and eighteenth centuries. And it was influenced by African languages as well as creole varieties, both Caribbean and homegrown, particularly in South Carolina. The distinctive nature of Black speech in this colony began to be noticed quite early. According to Wood (1974, 190), the first recorded use of the term "Black English" appeared in the *South Carolina Gazette* of March 30, 1734.

There can be no doubt that the Chesapeake Bay colonies and coastal Carolina were the primary cradles of the origins of AAVE and the points from which it spread to other colonies and, eventually, to the rest of the South. We can therefore conclude that much of the structural character of AAVE can be traced to the southern English dialects introduced to the coastal areas in the seventeenth and eighteenth centuries. But there were also influences from the upland areas as a result of the Scotch-Irish migrations during the eighteenth century. The expansion of the plantations and movement of Blacks to the piedmont, where they came increasingly into contact with the Whites who had settled there suggests that the Scotch-Irish dialect must have had some degree of influence on AAVE, as it had on SWAVE. There is still need for research on the patterns of contact and interaction both among the Scotch-Irish and other English-speaking settlers and between all of them and Africans, before we can explain fully the circumstances that led to the emergence of both SWAVE and AAVE. We also have to explain how the interaction of all these varieties of settler English and other linguistic inputs resulted in the spectrum of varieties that made up both AAVE and SWAVE in the colonial period.

The spread of AAVE beyond the South Atlantic colonies began in the Chesapeake after the 1730s, as the western frontier extended into what is now West Virginia and Kentucky. Many Chesapeake settlers and slaves also migrated to the Carolinas and Georgia in significant numbers after the mid-1750s (Kulikoff 1979, 539). More research is needed on the influence these migrations may have had on the language of all these areas. Also of crucial importance to the spread of AAVE (and White dialects) were the huge migrations of Whites and Blacks from the Atlantic South to the Gulf States between 1790 and 1860. Kulikoff (1979, 539) describes this as "the most dramatic spatial expansion in all of southern history." During this period, the spread of cotton plantations was accompanied by a massive movement of both Blacks and Whites from the Atlantic South to the Gulf States, as well as by importation of large numbers of new slaves from Africa. According to Kulikoff (1979, 539), "about 609,000 Whites born in Maryland, Virginia and the Carolinas lived in slave states to the south and west in 1850, and at least 835,000 slaves were forced to migrate from the upper South (mostly Maryland, Virginia and the Carolinas) to the lower South (mostly Alabama, Mississippi, Louisiana and Texas) between 1790 and 1860." The details of this population shift and its consequences for the development of both AAVE and

SWAVE have yet to be explored in detail. An important question for future research is how much the forms of language that Blacks created in the Gulf States in the nineteenth century were similar to those that they brought with them from the Atlantic South. It is from this period, the nineteenth century, that we have substantial texts of Black speech, including the ex-slave narratives, the Hoodoo texts, etc., that have been the primary basis for discussions of the origins of AAVE. It stands to reason that these texts represent continuations of the forms of AAVE that originated during the colonial period, though these varieties undoubtedly continued to evolve and change in the Antebellum Era. Finally, the great migrations of African Americans to urban areas in the North and South from the late nineteenth century onward created another set of contact scenarios that influenced the further development of AAVE. Future research on the patterns of this migration is clearly needed for us to establish the mix of linguistic inputs that led to the emergence of distinctive, though still varied, forms of urban AAVE.

Another question that needs to be addressed more fully is the mutual influence between AAVE and SWAVE over the centuries. Carver (1987, 150) points out that evidence for this mutual influence can be found in "(a) the currency of Africanisms in American English and particularly Lower South English, (b) the close historical relationship between southern Blacks and Whites and (c) the coinciding of Black population with the Lower South linguistic region." As he notes, "the Black slaves were, after all, among the first settlers of the Lower South and inevitably contributed many features to its regional character" (149). Other scholars such as Feagin (1979, 266) and Schneider (1989, 37) have presented arguments for the bidirectional effects of southern Black and White speech on each other. Tracing the influence of these varieties on each other is a highly challenging task that scholars have only recently begun to address.

Finally, any attempt to reconstruct the origins of AAVE must also recognize that, while its general character was shaped by British dialectal input, other forces, including input from other languages (African, creole) and internal developments, also contributed to the emergence and evolution of this dialect. Debates over this question have tended to be selective, with researchers, whether Anglicist or creolist, focusing their attention primarily on those features of the dialect that tend to support their own assumptions and positions. It is high time we recognize that the different positions complement each other and that together they offer the most comprehensive view of AAVE origins. Finally, there is a fairly extensive set of AAVE features that has received comparatively little attention in this debate, and we therefore know very little about their origins, whether they be in British dialects, influence from other languages, or internal developments. They include stressed ("remote perfect") *BIN*, "pluperfect" unstressed *been*, aspectual *steady* and *stay*, auxiliary combinations such *done + bin, be + done*, and complementizer *say* (see Winford 1998; Spears 2008). There is need for investigation of these questions and for increased research not only on the early history of AAVE in the seventeenth and eighteenth centuries but also on developments in AAVE from the nineteenth century on.

NOTES

1. At the same time, I recognize that there is a great deal of mixture and interaction between Gullah and AAVE in South Carolina and Georgia, such that the boundaries between the two are difficult to establish precisely.
2. Crozier (1984, 317), citing Bridenbaugh ([1952] 1976, 169), notes that a runaway Black farrier was characterized as speaking "in the Scotch-Irish dialect."
3. This sociohistorical sketch omits many other details about the codes of social interaction between Blacks and Whites that lend further support to the view that Blacks acquired close approximations to White settler speech. A more detailed overview would have to pay attention to the role played by Christian churches, and by the offspring of sexual unions between Blacks and Whites, as well as free Blacks, all of whom had greater degrees of contact with Whites, and some of whom owned slaves. Also relevant is the fact that some slaves had the benefit of education in schools. See Kulikoff (1978) on Black life in eighteenth-century Chesapeake society; Edgar (1998), chapter 9, on Black-White relationships in eighteenth-century South Carolina; and Blassingame (1979), especially chapter 2, on the acculturation of African slaves in the South, in general.

REFERENCES

Bailey, Guy, Natalie Maynor, and Patricia Cukor-Avila, eds. 1991. *The Emergence of Black English*. Amsterdam: John Benjamins.

Blassingame, John W. 1979. *The Slave Community: Plantation Life in the Antebellum South*. Oxford: Oxford University Press.

Breen, T. H. 1973. "A Changing Labor Force and Race Relations in Virginia 1660–1710." *Journal of Social History* 7 (1): 3–25.

Bridenbaugh, Carl. [1952] 1976. *Myths and Realities: Societies of the Colonial South*. Reprint. New York: Atheneum.

Campbell, Mildred. "Social Origins of Some Early Americans." In *Seventeenth-Century America: Essays in Colonial History*, edited by James Morton Smith, 63–89. Chapel Hill: University of North Carolina Press.

Carver, Craig M. 1987. *American Regional Dialects: A Word Geography*. Ann Arbor: University of Michigan Press.

Cheyney, Edward P. 1907. "Some English Conditions Surrounding the Settlement of Virginia." *American Historical Review* 12 (3): 507–28.

Craven, Wesley Frank. 1971. *White, Red, and Black: The Seventeenth-Century Virginian*. Charlottesville: University Press of Virginia.

Crozier, Alan. 1984. "The Scotch Irish Influence on American English." *American Speech* 59: 310–31.

Edgar, Walter. 1998. *South Carolina: A History*. Columbia: University of South Carolina Press.

Feagin, Crawford. 1979. *Variation and Change in Alabama English: A Sociolinguistic Study of the White Community*. Washington, DC: Georgetown University Press.

Jones, Hugh. [1724] 1956. *The Present State of Virginia*. Edited by Richard L. Morton. Reprint. Chapel Hill: University of North Carolina Press.

Kennedy, James Pendleton, and H. R McIlwaine, eds. 1905–1915. *Journals of the House of Burgesses of Virginia [1619–1776]*. 13 vols. Richmond: Virginia State Library.

Klein, Herbert S. 1975. "Slaves and Shipping in Eighteenth-Century Virginia." *Journal of Interdisciplinary History* 5 (3): 383–412.

Kulikoff, Alan. 1978. "The Origins of Afro-American Society in Tidewater Maryland and Virginia, 1700–1790." *William and Mary Quarterly* 35 (2): 226–59.

———. 1979. "The Colonial Chesapeake: Seedbed of Antebellum Southern Culture?" *Journal of Southern History* 14 (4): 513–40.

Kurath, Hans. 1972. "Relics of English Folk Speech in American English." In *Studies in Linguistics in Honor of Raven I. McDavid, Jr.*, edited by Lawrence M. Davis, 367–75. Tuscaloosa: University of Alabama Press.

Leyburn, James G. 1962. *The Scotch-Irish: A Social History.* Chapel Hill: University of North Carolina Press.

Menard, Russell R. 1985. *Economy and Society in Early Colonial Maryland.* New York: Garland.

———. 1998. "From Servants to Slaves: The Transformations of the Chesapeake Labour System." In *The Worlds of Unfree Labour: From Indentured Servitude to Slavery*, edited by Colin A. Palmer, 205–40. Aldershot, UK: Ashgate.

Mintz, Sidney W. 1971. "The Socio-historical Background to Pidginization and Creolization." In *Pidginization and Creolization of Languages*, edited by Dell Hymes, 481–96. Cambridge: Cambridge University Press.

Montgomery, Michael. 1991. "The Roots of Appalachian English: Scotch-Irish or British Southern?" *Journal of the Appalachian Studies Association.* Vol. 3, *Southern Appalachia and the South: A Region within a Region*, 177–91.

———. 2001. "British and American Antecedents of American English." In *Cambridge History of the English Language*, VI: *English in North America*, 86–153. Cambridge: Cambridge University Press.

———. 2004. "Solving Kurath's Puzzle: Establishing the Antecedents of the American Midland Dialect Region." In *Legacies of Colonial English: Studies in Transported Dialects*, edited by Raymond Hickey, 310–25. Cambridge: Cambridge University Press.

Mufwene, Salikoko. 1994. "On Decreolization: The Case of Gullah." In *Language and the Social Construction of Identity in Creole Situations*, edited by Marcyliena Morgan, 63–99. Los Angeles: UCLA Center for African-American Studies.

———. 2000. "Some Sociohistorical Inferences about the Development of African American English." In *The English History of African American English*, edited by Shana Poplack, 233–63. Oxford: Blackwell.

Mullin, Michael. 1994. *Africa in America: Slave Acculturation and Resistance in the American South and the British Caribbean, 1736–1831.* Urbana: University of Illinois Press.

Niles, Norma A. 1980. "Provincial English Dialects and Barbadian English." PhD diss., University of Michigan.

Perry, William Stevens. 1840. *Historical Collections Relating to the American Colonial Church.* Vol. 1—Virginia. Hartford, CT: Church Press Company

Poplack, Shana. ed. 2000. *The English History of African American English.* Oxford: Blackwell.

Read, Allen Walker. 1938. "The Assimilation of the Speech of British Immigrants in Colonial America." *Journal of English and Germanic Philology* 37 (1): 70–79.

———. 1939. "The Speech of Negroes in Colonial America." *Journal of Negro History* 24 (3): 247–58.

Schneider, Edgar W. 1989. *American Earlier Black English.* Tuscaloosa: University of Alabama Press.

Smith, Abbot Emerson. 1947. *Colonists in Bondage: White Servitude and Convict Labor in America 1607–1776*. Chapel Hill, NC: University of North Carolina Press.

Smyth, J. F. D. 1773. "Smyth's Travels in Virginia in 1773." *Virginia Historical Register* 6, April 1853, 84–85.

Spears, Arthur. 2008. "Pidgins/creoles and African American English." In *The Handbook of Pidgin and Creole Studies*, edited by Silvia Kouwenberg and John Victor Singler, 512–42. Malden, MA: Wiley-Blackwell.

Staudenraus, P. J. 1956. "Victims of the African Slave Trade: A Document." *Journal of Negro History* 41: 149.

Vaughan, Alden T. 1972. "Blacks in Virginia—A Note on the First Decade." *William and Mary Quarterly* 29 (3): 469–78.

Winford, Donald. 1998. "On the Origins of African American Vernacular English: A Creolist Perspective, Part II: Linguistic Features." *Diachronica* 15: 99–154.

Wood, Peter H. 1974. *Black Majority: Negroes in Colonial South Carolina from 1670 through the Stono Rebellion*. New York: Alfred A Knopf.

———. 1989. "The Changing Population of the Colonial South: An Overview by Race and Region, 1685–1790." In *Powhatan's Mantle: Indians in Colonial Southeast*, edited by Peter H. Wood, G. A. Waselkov, and M. Thomas Hatley, 35–103. Lincoln: University of Nebraska Press.

Wright, James Martin. 1921. *The Free Negro in Maryland, 1634–1860*. New York: Columbia University.

CHAPTER 5

··

AFRICAN AMERICAN ENGLISH OVER YONDER

The Language of the Liberian Settler Community

··

JOHN VICTOR SINGLER

5.1 INTRODUCTION

In the nineteenth century, sixteen thousand African Americans immigrated to West Africa[1] to what became the sovereign nation of Liberia.[2] Their descendants today form one of Liberia's ethnic groups, and the language of these descendants, Liberian Settler English (LSE), is a source of evidence as to the character of the nineteenth-century African American English (AAE) that the original Settlers brought with them from the United States.[3]

While the contribution of LSE to an understanding of the history of AAE is substantial, the need for caution in interpreting LSE is critical. This is true any time one seeks to draw inferences from a modern variety as to details regarding the character of its nineteenth-century ancestor. The earliest Settlers arrived in Liberia in 1822; thus, the apparatus of internal change has had nearly two centuries in which to operate. Beyond that, LSE has been subject to a range of external linguistic forces.

I base this study on sociolinguistic interviews, the bulk of which were carried out in Liberia in the 1980s. Sixteen of these interviews come from the settlements in Sinoe County, with two others coming from settlements elsewhere along the Liberian coast. While the Sinoe and non-Sinoe data are qualitatively similar, they display quantitative differences that merit examination.

In early work (Singler 1987, 1989), I used Hancock's (1971) term in describing LSE as a "vestigial creole" (i.e., a variety that was first a creole and then was subject to extensive decreolization). As we have come to understand the limitations of what decreolization is likely to achieve, a scenario that has LSE/AAE originating as a full creole (and then undergoing wide-ranging decreolization) becomes insupportable. This is not to say that there are neither creole nor creole-like features in LSE. There clearly are such features. A further point about LSE is its ability to show individual AAE features to be of long standing, including ones that have sometimes been proposed as relatively recent innovations.

5.2 The Provenance of the Settlers

The American Colonization Society (ACS) engineered the Settlers' immigration to West Africa. Founded in December 1816, the ACS had as its ostensible goal the establishment of a colony in West Africa where free African Americans could enjoy the full rights of citizenship, something denied them in the United States. American slaveholders, who saw free African Americans as an ongoing threat to the status quo, embraced the ACS campaign as a mechanism for removing free African Americans. Accordingly, it was slaveholders who provided the bulk of funding for the ACS venture. For their part, most free people of color denounced the ACS's plan from the outset. For example, barely a month after the founding of the ACS, three thousand people—fully one-fourth of Philadelphia's African American population—met to express their vehement opposition to the plan (see Singler 2007b, 333–34).

The ACS began sending African Americans to West Africa in 1820, with the first people settling in Monrovia in what came to be Liberia in January 1822 (see figures 5.1 and 5.2). Over the first two decades, the number of those immigrating was small and fitful, and the mortality rate for Settlers "shockingly high" (Shick 1980, 27). Specifically, in the years from 1820 to 1843, the ACS brought 4,472 African Americans to Liberia, yet at the end of that period, the 1843 census showed the Settler population to be only 2,389

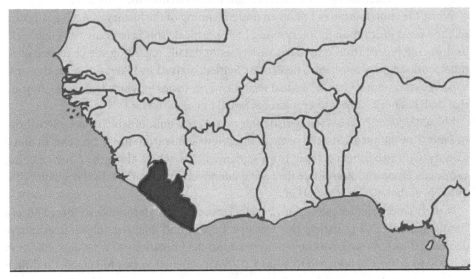

FIGURE 5.1 Map of Liberia, within West Africa. Liberia has an area of approximately 43,000 square miles, making it equivalent in size to the American state of Virginia.

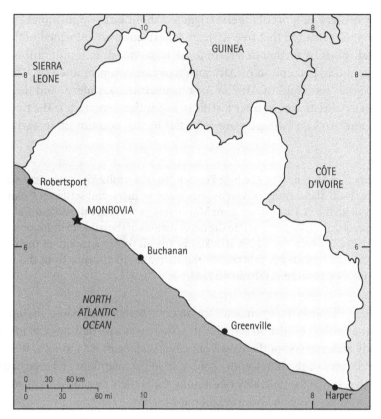

FIGURE 5.2 Map of Liberia with cities. African American immigrants to Liberia settled first in Monrovia (1822) and then in several settlements along the St. Paul River above Monrovia (Montserrado County). Other settlements down the coast were established in and around Buchanan (Grand Bassa County), starting in 1832, and in Greenville (Sinoe County), starting in 1838. These three counties were the founding counties when Liberia declared its independence in 1847. Throughout the nineteenth century, a majority of the immigrants settled in and near Monrovia. The central government started directing immigrants to the newly created settlement of Robertsport (Grand Cape Mount County) in 1856. The Maryland State Colonization Society established its own colony at and near Harper (Maryland in Africa) in 1834; it was absorbed into Liberia as a constituent county in 1857.

(McDaniel 1995, 146). Of those counted in the census, 650 were Settler children born in Liberia. Forty-nine percent of the immigrants had died by the time of the census, and another 12 percent had emigrated from Liberia, with most returning to the United States. Further, of the fatalities, 43 percent had occurred within a year of the individual's arrival in Liberia (McDaniel 1995, 77), with "fever" listed as the cause of death roughly 40 percent of the time. (Presumably, it was malaria—and the Settlers' lack of resistance to it—that brought on the mortal fever.) McDaniel states, "The life tables created for the African American immigrants to Liberia appear to embody the highest mortality ever reliably recorded" (1995, 104).

The slaveowners' support of Liberia triggered abolitionist opposition to the colony, and abolitionists ensured that free African Americans were informed of the Settlers' high mortality rate. A further deterrent to African American immigration to Liberia was the prevailing perception of Africans, a perception promoted by Whites (who would have the "rescuing" of African Americans from "savagery" and the introducing of them to Christianity as utter justification for the slave trade). The twin specters of disease and African barbarity are reflected in this account of an early group of Settlers:

> On the 13th of March, 1825, the brig Hunter, from Norfolk, Va., with sixty-six emigrants arrived. These emigrants were principally farmers, and settled at Caldwell [a settlement up the St. Paul's River from Monrovia], preferring this situation, although an unbroken forest, and exposed to the depredations of the wild Africans, on account of the rich soil. The fever, which attacked nearly all within a month of their arrival in the Colony, was greatly protracted, and increased in violence from the want of proper medical treatment. (Stockwell 1868, 79)

After Liberia declared independence in 1847, a seven-year boost in immigration increased the Settler population significantly. There was a second surge in immigration immediately after the end of the American Civil War, from 1865 to 1872. It seems that, by the middle part of the nineteenth century, medical treatment and care had become more effective. While the mortality rate among the Settlers remained elevated, it was no longer as devastating as it had been at Liberia's outset.

The number of free people immigrating to Liberia was too low for the colony to succeed; consequently, owners sympathetic to colonization emancipated slaves on the condition that they immigrate to Liberia. In fact, of all who immigrated to Liberia prior to the Civil War, approximately 64 percent—more than 7,500 individuals in all—were slaves emancipated on these terms.

Overall, the five coastal states from Maryland south to Georgia provided 70 percent of all those who immigrated, but the timeframe of immigration varied significantly by state. In the first twenty-five years, Virginia provided 35 percent of all immigrants and Maryland 21 percent. These states continued to provide immigrants until the Civil War but then stopped. Georgia only began sending significant numbers with Liberia's post-independence boom but was the leading state from then on. Finally, two-thirds of the immigrants from South Carolina went after the Civil War. African Americans from free states were never numerous, amounting to only 8 percent of the total number of immigrants.

5.2.1 Virginia

The figures that I have cited come from the ACS's publication, *The African Repository and Colonial Journal* (1825–92), especially those cited in table 5.1, and the Society's

Annual Reports. Svend Holsoe has drawn on these and other records to map the Settlers' provenance county by county in the United States. (The maps are available in the Svend Holsoe Collection at Indiana University.) As discussed in Singler (1989), Virginia illustrates the importance of this information. The largest number of emigrants from Virginia came from three areas: Norfolk/Portsmouth, Richmond/ Petersburg, and a string of counties in northern and central Virginia, each of which provided at least one-hundred emigrants. The first two regions were basically non-rural, and the third was a "fringe agricultural" area, where slaveholdings were ordinarily comparatively small (Svend Holsoe, personal communication). This distribution is consonant with Frederic Cassidy's remarks concerning Virginia and Maryland: "In Virginia and Maryland ... slaves were never as separate from the work and general life of their owners as in the South. Plantations or households were much smaller, and the numerical proportion of Blacks to Whites was never as high" (1986, 35).

5.2.2 The Sinoe Settlements

After Monrovia, the Settlers and the ACS established a number of small settlements, with most of them located just up the St. Paul River from Monrovia. In the early 1830s, another set of colonies was established sixty miles southeast of Monrovia in the Bassa region. In 1834, the Maryland State Colonization Society, impatient with the national ACS and acting independently of it, established its own colony at Cape Palmas, 250 miles down the coast from Monrovia. The colony was absorbed as a constituent county into Liberia itself in 1857.

The Mississippi Colonization Society (MCS) followed Maryland in establishing its own colony. Staudenraus (1980, 236) characterizes the MCS as being "composed of wealthy slaveholders in southwestern Mississippi who wished to rid themselves of an infinitesimal free Negro population." In 1838, the MCS established Mississippi in Africa at the mouth of the Sinoe River, 150 miles down the Atlantic coast from Monrovia. However, lawsuits arose in Mississippi that quickly drained the state society of its resources. (The lawsuits involved wills that left one family's plantation and its slaves to the MCS.) By 1840, the society was "nearly defunct" (Sydnor 1933, 215) and, by 1841, the state society transferred administration of its colony to the central government in Monrovia.[4]

Thus, little more than a year after its founding, Mississippi in Africa found itself virtually abandoned. "After 1840, the tiny colony lived in perpetual poverty" (Staudenraus 1980, 236). While the governor of Liberia had accepted the Sinoe colony into Liberia in 1841, he had scant resources at his command and slight inclination to direct what little he had toward Sinoe. If anything, Liberia's independence in 1847 placed the Sinoe settlements at an even greater disadvantage. The further a settlement was from Monrovia, the less support it received.[5] "Distance from the center caused Sinoe problems throughout the nineteenth century" (Sullivan 1978, 165). Apart from that, there was the matter of sheer isolation from other Settlers; the nearest Settler community was ninety miles away in Bassa. The initial Sinoe settlement was Greenville. A port town, it was in a swampy area, and subsequent immigrant groups founded five agricultural settlements a few miles up the Sinoe River from Greenville.

The MCS ultimately prevailed in its lawsuits; over the next decade it arranged for 370 people to be sent to its ex-colony.[6] Of this number, only four were free. The arrival of the last of the Mississippi immigrants coincided with the beginning of the post-independence immigration boom that lasted from 1848 to 1854. Of the two thousand immigrants who were placed in the Sinoe settlements over the years, more than 70 percent of them came during this period, with the largest number (at that time and overall) coming from Georgia. The Sinoe colony may have been established by the MCS (and then left in a basket on the doorstep of the central government in Monrovia), but it was Georgians who immigrated in the largest numbers to Sinoe.

Earlier, I drew on the example provided by Virginia to indicate that by and large the immigrants to Liberia had not come from large plantations. In this, Sinoe was different. Of the 1,713 individuals who immigrated to Sinoe prior to the American Civil War, over one-third (619, 36.1 percent) came from just five plantations.

In table 5.1, I present the state of origin for all those who immigrated to Liberia from the beginning through 1891. In doing so, I separate Sinoe from the rest of Liberia.

Singler (1989, 46 n. 61) adduces evidence to establish the dominance in Liberia of "emigrants from Virginia and states north of it." Of the Sinoe Settlers, only 3.4 percent came from the aggregate of Virginia, the District of Columbia, Maryland, and the free states. This is in sharp contrast to the rest of Liberia, where virtually half the population (48.5 percent) came from these places. The Sinoe Settlers—four-fifths of them—came instead from the Lower South—the five-state swath that extends from South Carolina across to Louisiana. Less than one-quarter of the immigrants to the rest of Liberia came from there.

Relations between the Sinoe Settlers and the indigenous population of the region were hostile and sometimes violent. In 1855, war broke out. Restrictions that the Settlers sought to place on Klao (Kru) trade and opposition to the continuing expansion of the Settler presence motivated the Klao to wage war, carrying out attacks on all five of the upriver settlements. The war lasted for six months, after which, "with the help of European ship captains, the Monrovia government intervened to defeat the attackers" (Sullivan 1978, 208). Although the Settlers suffered fewer casualties from the fighting, the resulting loss of food and shelter in the months following the war had a devastating effect on the community; many died of disease and starvation. The loss of life and property and the deteriorating relationships with their neighbors set the Sinoe community back many years (Sullivan 1978, 208): "The sudden attack and the immense damage were the worst fears of the settlers come true. The attack reinforced a siege mentality of a small group of immigrants in a foreign environment. ... [T]he small band who remained became even more determined to survive and more committed to resist than to cooperate with their Kru neighbors" (Sullivan 1978, 217).

Table 5.1 State of Origin for African American Immigrants to Liberia, Divided into Sinoe and Non-Sinoe, 1820–1891

Sinoe			Rest of Liberia		
Slave States	n	%	Slave States	n	%
Georgia	834	41.0	Virginia	3,719	26.6
Mississippi	401	19.7	North Carolina	2,033	14.6
Tennessee	253	12.4	Maryland	1,725	12.4
South Carolina	195	9.6	Georgia	1,431	10.2
Louisiana	106	5.2	South Carolina	1,179	8.4
Alabama	82	4.0	Tennessee	741	5.3
Kentucky	41	2.0	Kentucky	638	4.6
Virginia	36	1.8	Mississippi	263	1.9
			Arkansas	254	1.8
			Louisiana	210	1.5
Others	53	2.6	Others	559	4.0
	(2,001)	98.4		(12,752)	91.3
Free States	n	%	Free States	n	%
Pennsylvania	13	0.6	Pennsylvania	360	2.6
			New York	302	2.2
Others	19	0.9	Others	549	3.9
	(32)	1.6		(1,211)	8.7
	2,033			13,963	

Note: In calculating figures such as the state-by-state counts of Settlers transported to Liberia by the ACS, I have incorporated the individuals sent by the two state societies.
Sources: American Colonization Society, *Annual Reports*, nos. 50, 55, 61, and 69–76; Maryland State Colonization Society Papers.

5.3 EXTERNAL FORCES OPERATING ON LSE

5.3.1 The External from Within: Gullah

If the Settlers brought AAE with them to Liberia, it is appropriate to weigh the languages with which they came into contact and the possibility of influence from these languages on the Settlers' English. The first language to be considered is one whose speakers were on the immigrants' roll: Gullah.

In all, 203 Settlers immigrated to Liberia from the Sea Islands and the coastal counties adjacent to them. The largest component was the population of the Jacob Wood plantation in McIntosh County, Georgia—155 people were emancipated on condition of immigration to Liberia. The people in this group and thirteen others from the Sea Islands went to Sinoe. Further, "commercially-minded immigrants from Savannah and Charleston" settled in Greenville (Sullivan 1978, 161); these included 101 free emigrants from Savannah and 52 from Charleston.

For present purposes, I assume that those from Charleston and Savannah should be counted as Gullah speakers. In all, then, 23.7 percent of Sinoe's population came from the Gullah-speaking region (8.3 percent from the Sea Island region, and 15.4 percent from Charleston and Savannah). This compares with 2.84 percent for the rest of Liberia (0.25 percent and 2.59 percent, respectively).

Within LSE, with the exception of one Settler community's regional construction calqued from a local language,[7] I have yet to identify any feature that is not shared by all Settler communities. If a grammatical feature is found in LSE today, it is found in every settlement. Within the Settlers' Liberia as a whole, the Sinoe Settlers were few in number, low in status, and lived far from the rest. Thus, it is not plausible to posit a scenario in which a feature began in Sinoe and then spread to the rest of the country. On these grounds, I maintain that there are no features in LSE that obtained in nineteenth-century Gullah but not also in at least some portion of nineteenth-century AAE.

5.3.2 The External from Within: Recaptured Africans

Just as the British Navy delivered to Freetown in Sierra Leone the captives on slave ships seized after Britain abolished the slave trade, so the US Navy delivered *Recaptured Africans* to Monrovia, 5,700 in all. Of this total, 4,700 were delivered there in or around 1860. With the prominent exception of one boatload of Yorùbá speakers taken to Sinoe, the Recaptured Africans usually came from the Congo-Angola region. "Since nearly all of these individuals came from the Congo River area, they were referred to as Congoes" (Dunn and Holsoe 1985, 45).

Like the Settlers, the Recaptured Africans had no local ties in Liberia. "When recaptured Africans came in small numbers, they were often assigned to various families as apprentices, to work for the family, learn English, convert to Christianity, and be absorbed into the community" (Sullivan 1978, 197–98). When they were delivered in large numbers, separate communities were established for them. Absorbed at first into the lower echelons of Settler society, their integration over time has been such that, in 1969, Liebenow remarked, "Today it is difficult to differentiate a Congo from other Americo-Liberians [Settlers]" (27). Moreover, the term *Congo* has come to be used to refer to Settlers more generally. It retains a mildly pejorative cast but is the term used more than any other to refer to Settlers, even by the Settlers themselves.[8]

5.3.3 The Truly External

Throughout their history—certainly from their arrival in 1822 across their unbroken control of the country for more than 150 years and even after the 1980 military coup that ended that control up to the present time—the Settlers have identified themselves as different from the rest of Liberia's population, seeing the maintenance of that difference as necessary for their survival. The Settlers, less than 5 percent of Liberia's population, have based the maintenance of a distinct identity—and have claimed the right to rule—on the basis of their command of English, their Christianity, and their command of western civilization. Of the three, it has arguably been their English that gave them the greatest cachet, as this mid-nineteenth-century oration attests:

> Here, on this coast . . . is an organized community, republican in form and name; a people possessed of Christian institutions and civilized habits, with this one marked peculiarity, that is, that in color, race, and origin, they are identical with the masses around them; and yet speak the refined and cultivated English language.
> —Alexander Crummell, Independence Day Oration, Harper,
> Liberia, July 26, 1860 (Crummell 1862, 9)

This attitude has in turn framed Settler attitudes toward the languages that they encountered upon their arrival, both towards Niger-Congo "dialects" and the pidginized language of the coast.

The specific Niger-Congo languages that would have been present along the Liberian coast in the nineteenth century were the Mande language, Vai and the Kru languages, Dewoin, Bassa, Klao (known in English as *Kru*), and Grebo. However, from the outset, the primary medium of communication between Settlers and non-Settlers would seem to have been based on English, whether the Settlers' own English, West African Pidgin English (the pidgin that had developed out of a trade language along the West African coast during the eighteenth century), or some combination of the two. When the Settlers arrived, the missionary who governed them, Jehudi Ashmun, wrote back to the United States that "very many in all of the maritime tribes, speak a corruption of the English language" (*African Repository*, Nov. 1827, 263).

The modern-day Liberian descendant of West African Pidgin English is a variety that I call *Vernacular Liberian English* (Singler 1997). I have argued that in Liberia (and nowhere else in West Africa), a continuum has emerged, along the lines originally posited by DeCamp (1971), with the difference being that the basilectal end of the Liberian continuum is a pidgin, not a creole. Vernacular Liberian English (VLE) shows broad and deep influence from LSE. For example, alone among West African English-lexifier pidgins and creoles, VLE has as its second person plural pronoun *yall* [yɔ]. The exact timetable of the evolution from pidgin to a full range of varieties along a continuum has never been attempted. For present purposes, I refer to the nineteenth-century variety with which the earliest Settlers were in contact as *pidgin*, and I refer to the modern continuum as *VLE*.[9]

5.4 LSE Grammar

Except for the discussion of coda consonants given below, I do not address LSE phonology in this chapter. The interested reader is referred to Singler (2004a). Rather than attempting a reasonably complete overview of LSE grammar in the space allotted, I instead focus on points of special interest to the issue of the relationship of LSE to AAE. For more detailed discussions of LSE grammar, I refer the reader to the following: Singler (2004b) is a discussion of LSE syntax, with a focus on the verb phrase. Singler (2011) consists of LSE's representation in e-WAVE, the online comparative study of varieties of English (http://www.ewave-atlas.org/languages/37); for individual features, the site is limited to statements as to whether a feature obtains in LSE and, if so, how often. Actual example sentences for these features are found as an appendix to Singler (2012), whose central text is a brief overview of LSE.

5.4.1 A Note on the Data

The foundation for the grammatical description that follows is a set of sociolinguistic interviews. Three interviews done in different Settler communities in 1980 support the Liberian view that the speech of the upriver Sinoe settlements was the most conservative. I returned to Sinoe in 1988–89. Hosea Ellis, himself a Sinoe Settler, conducted most of the thirteen interviews from this period. These interviews are a rich source of data, but they also raise questions about their relationship to the Settler English of the rest of the country. Liberia's civil war and Charles Taylor's reign of tyranny precluded interviews in a "new" Settler community. (During this fourteen-year span, we carried out two interviews with Sinoe Settlers, one in Monrovia, the other in Sinoe. They were with Nancy, Hosea's cousin—whom I had known for many years—and then with Nancy's brother, Joshua. The interview with Joshua came after I had carried out the various quantitative analyses that I report upon here.) Recovery has been slow in Liberia. Interviews in Settler communities other than those in Sinoe may become a possibility, but for now non-Sinoe data comes from the two 1980 interviews from elsewhere, specifically from Robertsport, in Cape Mount, fifty miles up the coast from Monrovia, and Fortsville, in Bassa. Additionally, I have supplemented interview data via elicitation, working with Sinoenian and non-Sinoenian Settlers alike.

5.4.2 Negation

Three aspects of negation seem especially noteworthy: negative contraction, negative concord, and the general lack of negative inversion.

5.4.2.1 *Negative Contraction*

Preverbal negative auxiliary contractions expressing tense and negation—*don't, didn't*, and *ain't*—are subject to reduction to the point of neutralization. When the subject is a pronoun other than *it*, the maximally reduced auxiliary is a nasalized copy of the subject vowel. In the examples below and subsequently, I express the copied vowel orthographically by <n't>. The reduction occurs most commonly when *I* is the subject, especially if it is followed by a word that begins with /n/ such as *know* or *never*, as in (1). However, the reduction also occurs when *I* is subject but a non-nasal element follows (2), and it also occurs with other pronoun subjects (3).

(1) *I n't* [aã] know my pa, leopard kill my pa.
     'I didn't know my father; he was killed by a leopard.'
(2) *I n't* [aã] reach too far o.
     'I didn't go too far [in school].'
(3) *We n't* [wiĩ] use to buy pepper.
     'We didn't use to buy pepper.'

The full forms of the contractions do obtain (examples 4 to 6). However, "full" does not entail the presence of coda consonants as consonants. The sequence of a vowel followed by a coda consequence is realized in (4) to (6) as a nasalized vowel. Thus, the pronunciations are [ẽ], [dõ], and [dedɛ̃].

(4) Ma Esther *ain't come* yet o.
(5) Well, I *don't got* no fish to fry in yall part of thing.
(6) I n't know why I *didn't tell* you to take it off.

In the case of *don't*, there is also the intermediate form *on't* (cf. Rickford 1974).
    The minimal contraction can also occur with non-past forms of *be*; the unreduced form is *not*.

(7) *I n't* [aã] talking about them.
     'I'm not talking about them.'
(8) When they grab you, *you n't* [yuũ] stupid to go home say, "Ma, this woman here beat me."
     'When they [an adult in the community other than one's parents or grandparents] disciplined you because you misbehaved, you weren't so foolish as to go home and tell your mother, "Ma, this woman [in the community] beat me."'

5.4.2.2 *Negative Concord*

Negative concord is routine though not obligatory, with the verb and subsequent indefinite arguments marked for negation. In some instances, the concord extends into a lower clause, as in (9).

(9) I *n't never* hear it burn *nobody* house.
     'I never heard of it [a rat gnawing at the wick of a palm oil lantern] causing a house to burn down.'

Negative concord can also be inserted before definite arguments for the sake of emphasis.

(10)   And my heart *don't* tell me to go to *no* Monrovia.
       '[Even though my sister had been calling and calling for me to come visit her in Monrovia], I just didn't feel like going to that Monrovia place.'

Negative subjects sometimes trigger negation in the verb phrase.

(11)   *No organization* in the church *can't* do without me.
       'There's no organization in the church that can do without me.'

5.4.2.3 *Negative Inversion*

Negative inversion is rare in LSE and does not show up in the corpus. I obtained grammaticality judgments from Edward Railey, a Sinoe Settler. Although there is more going on, the primary determinant of acceptability seems to be the choice of fronted auxiliary, with *ain't* sentences accepted while *can't*, *didn't*, *don't*, and *wasn't* sentences were generally rejected. Thus, Edward accepted (12a) but not (12b).

(12)   a. . . . and *ain't nobody* want to give up that ghost.
       b. *. . . and *don't nobody* want to give up that ghost.
           '. . . and there isn't anybody who just wants to give up and die.'

5.4.3 AAE and LSE

The acceptance of negative inversion—but only in limited ways—represents a phenomenon that recurs. That is, several features that have been proposed as being more recent innovations in AAE obtain in LSE but do so in restricted ways (see Myhill 1995; Singler 1998). Consider stressed *BÍN*, for example (Rickford 1975). In an elicitation session, Hosea Ellis accepted the following sentences and provided the translations for each.

(13)   He BÍN greedy.
       'He has long been known for his greediness.'
(14)   I BÍN receiving certificates.
       'I have been receiving certificates [for outstanding churchwork] for years now.'
(15)   That boy BÍN gone Monrovia.
       'That boy left a long time ago for Monrovia.'

However, he also rejected these sentences as LSE, which are grammatical in AAE.

(16)   Speaker A: Hello, I came to talk to Bruce.Speaker B: *He not here; he BÍN dən gone.
       'He's not here; he left a long time ago.' (Green 1998, 44)
(17)   Speaker A: You gonna quit?
       Speaker B: *I BÍN quit. (Labov 1998, 136)

The unstressed counterparts of (13) to (15) are grammatical in LSE. Hosea was quick to point out the difference between the stressed and unstressed variants, giving a reading for the stressed variants that corresponded to their meaning in AAE. In contrast, the unstressed variants of (16) and (17), as well as similar AAE sentences that I presented him with, are not grammatical in LSE.

Along similar lines, Wolfram (2004, 328) discusses a 'future perfect' use of *be done* and a resultative-conditional use and mentions that Dayton (1996) and Labov (1998) see the second type as a more recent development. LSE has the first type only.

(18)   You *be done crack* you palm nut, palm kernel, everything, then you make you palm butter and set it down.
        '(By that time) you would have cracked all your palm kernels, and then you would make your palm butter [a stew made from palm nut pulp] and set it down.'

With regard to habitual *be*, Wolfram (2004, 322) cites studies that "suggest that it is largely an innovation of the post–World War II era and that the change has spread from an urban locus outward." Habitual *be* + V–*ing* is a feature of LSE, occurring most commonly but not exclusively in the antecedent of a habitual conditional. It can have present reference (19) or past (20).

(19)   But the Kru people now they sing when they *be dancing.*
        'But the Kru now, they sing when they're dancing [the quadrille].'
(20)   . . . we *be dancing* like that-a-there, and you see the girls jump up, the man *be playing* the music box.
        '. . . we'd be dancing like that, and you'd see the girls jump up, and the man would be playing the accordion.'

In Singler (2007a), I suggest as a reliable diagnostic for AAE's congener varieties the *presence* of nonstandard features (as opposed to the *absence* of standard ones, for which several explanations are possible, e.g. "vernacular universals," cf. Chambers 2003, 2004). There I referred to the five overt non-quantitative features that Myhill (1995) posits as potential innovations in African American Vernacular English (AAVE): the use of *ain't* for *didn't*, *be done*, the semi-auxiliary *come* (see Spears 1982), *steady* (see Baugh 1983), and stressed *BÍN*. While acknowledging that LSE has more restricted distribution than AAVE for three of these features, I pointed out that their existence in LSE argued against the idea that they were recent innovations in AAVE.[10] As far as I am aware, these are not features of Southern White Vernacular English. Even with the more restricted domain of some of these features, their existence in LSE attests to their presence in pre–Civil War AAE and argues for the long-standing distinctiveness of that variety.

Nonetheless, given the long period involved and the separation of peoples, it is not surprising that some features have endured on one side and disappeared on the other. For example, the habitual AUX *də* and the copula *sə* have remained in LSE but not in AAE. Furthermore, it is not unexpected that there will be features in AAE that are not found in LSE, arguably because they constitute innovations that took root in AAE after the Settlers had left the United States, for example, *fixin' to* and its reduced variants (*finna, fitna,* among others) (cf. Green 2002), as well as the use of *had* as a preterit (Rickford and Théberge-Rafal 1996). There are innovations on the LSE side as well, most of them recognizable as syntactic borrowings.

5.4.4 The Impact of a Syllable Structure Constraint: NO-CODA

5.4.4.1 *Number Marking*

When an irregular noun is semantically plural, use of the plural form is virtually categorical. As table 5.2 shows, this is true for Sinoe and non-Sinoe Settlers alike.

Both of the doubly marked items occurring in the present corpus, *childrens* and *mens*, are attested in AAE. In contrast to the near categorical presence of irregular nouns, number marking on regular nouns is variable. The fact that number marking is categorical when the form is irregular yet is variable when the form is regular suggests that overt plural marking is a feature of LSE but that phonological forces sometimes block its occurrence on the surface.

Standard English inflectional morphology consists primarily of suffixes (and one clitic, the possessive) consisting of a single coda consonant: plural *–z*, possessive *'s*, third-person singular nonpast verbal *–s*, past tense *–d*, and past participle *–d*. Phonologically conditioned allomorphy and irregular forms (the latter only for the plural, past tense, and past participle) provide morpheme-specific exceptions to the general statement. In addition to these single-consonant morphemes, a lone coda consonant is also relevant grammatically in at least two other ways:

- the contracted form of the non-past copulas *am* and *is* is *'m* and *'z*, respectively, and
- the final consonant distinguishes among the three perfect forms, *have, had,* and *has.*

Table 5.2 Overt Marking of Irregular Nouns

	Overtly marked with standard marking: e.g., *children*		Not overtly marked: *man, woman, foot*		Overtly marked with *–z: fishmans*		Doubly marked: irregular plural plus *–z, childrens* and *mens*		
	n	%	n	%	n	%	n	%	n
Slim (Cape Mount) and Albert (Grand Bassa)	27	96	–		1	4	–		28
15 Sinoe Settlers	311	96	9	3	–		5	1.5	325
Total	338	96	9	3	1	0.3	5	1.4	353

Source: Adapted from Singler 1989, 1994.

5.4.4.2 *The* NO-CODA *Constraint and Its Impact*

One of the universal phonological constraints proposed in Optimality Theory is NO-CODA: "Syllables end with a vowel" (Archangeli 1997, 8). Without going into Optimality Theory, it is possible to see that languages vary as to the strength of NO-CODA. Indeed, in many West African languages, the NO-CODA constraint is inviolable. That is, as the name of the constraint indicates, no syllable in the language has a coda consonant in its output (i.e., on the surface). While NO-CODA is not inviolable in LSE, it is highly ranked. It is powerful enough that coda consonants present in the input frequently do not obtain in the output. If a morpheme consists in its entirety of a coda consonant, in instances where the NO-CODA constraint prevails, then the morpheme is blocked from appearing in the output, as shown in table 5.3.

The question arises as to which other constraints bear on the strength of NO-CODA in LSE. Certainly, there is a sensitivity to attributes of the consonant in question, with a bilabial stop more likely to occur in the output than a velar stop, which is in turn more likely than /l/ (i.e., the final segment in *tip* is more likely to occur on the surface than is the one in *tick*, which in turn is more likely to occur than the final segment in *till*).

Within LSE, tables 5.2 and 5.3 show that, when NO-CODA is not in play (i.e., in the case of irregular plurals), the Sinoe Settlers behave identically with other Settlers. However, when NO-CODA matters, there is a clear difference between Sinoenians and others. The other morphemes show the same pattern as the plural,[11] that is, Sinoe Settlers show a greater dispreference for coda consonants. In an effort to account for this difference, I point to three different factors, with differences in their relative strength accounting for the differences between the Sinoe Settlers and other Settlers: (1) the influence of Niger-Congo languages, (2) the strength of standardizing forces, (3) the American provenance of the Settlers. The relevant Niger-Congo languages spoken in Liberia, as well as the languages of the Recaptured Africans, whether Bantu or Yorùbá, are all strict NO-CODA languages. Strong substratal influence has made coda-consonant absence likewise a salient feature of VLE (Singler 2000), one noticeable to other West Africans. Still, there are coda consonants in VLE, though not as many as in LSE.

Table 5.3 Overt Marking of Regular Nouns

	Overtly marked with standard marking, e.g., *friends*	
	n	%
Slim (Cape Mount)	109/144	76
Albert (Grand Bassa)	179/248	72
15 Sinoe Settlers	917/2,204	42
Total	1,205/2,596	46

Source: Adapted from Singler 1989, 1994.

In sum, Niger-Congo languages, both directly and via VLE, might well push LSE speakers toward NO-CODA. Given that this influence would be found everywhere along the Liberian coast, the question is whether Niger-Congo languages pushed harder in Sinoe than elsewhere and, if so, why. This explanation for differences within LSE between Sinoe and the rest is especially challenging given differences in the degree of integration of Settlers and Niger-Congo-speaking ethnic groups, with integration most complete in Robertsport and most vexed in Sinoe.

The second factor that bears on the degree of coda-consonant absence or presence is the strength of standardizing forces. Within Liberia, the Settlers' claim to superiority on the basis of their superior English (Singler 1977) would seem to make them receptive to standard English. Church and school alike promoted standard English, with the strongest force coming when the two converged (i.e., at mission-run schools). These provided the strongest standardizing pressure because of the more extensive educational training of the missionaries but also because of mission resources (e.g., the missions' ability to provide schools with books). This is not to say that these were the only loci for standardization. There were other schools as well. Nonetheless, it surely matters that Sinoe was the sole Settler area without a missionary presence in the nineteenth century. One basis, then, for the difference regarding coda consonants between Sinoe and elsewhere could well be the absence in Sinoe of a strong force militating for the presence of coda consonants.

As the discussion first of Virginia and then of Sinoe establishes, Settlers came from very different backgrounds, with those settling in Sinoe being the most divergent from the rest. This suggests that the differences that obtain today between Settlers in Sinoe and, say, Cape Mount and Bassa began with differences in the AAE phonology that different immigrants and groups of immigrants brought with them. If we have moved past the idea of nineteenth-century AAE as a monolithic entity, we can consider what the range of differences might be and, for LSE, what the consequences might be.

5.5 CONCLUSION

The present chapter has been built primarily on data from the cluster of settlements in Sinoe County. As indicated above, Sinoe is different from the rest of Liberia in that, while nearly half of the immigrants to the rest of the Liberia came from Virginia, Maryland, the District of Columbia, and free states, a mere 3.4 percent of the immigrants to Sinoe came from these places; instead, it was a five-state swath of the Lower South that provided four-fifths of the immigrants to Sinoe. Moreover, the Sinoe settlements are the ones that have been the most isolated across their history. During Liberia's civil war, the Settlers were at times targeted by some of the warring factions; nonetheless, LSE continues to be spoken, continues to be transmitted, particularly in isolated agricultural settlements. As a climate for research re-emerges, it is the language of these sites that promises to be the most instructive, particularly with regard to the extent to which

LSE shows regional variation, both qualitatively and quantitatively. Research in such settlements—specifically, the more remote of the communities up the St. Paul River from Monrovia and especially Tallah in Grand Cape Mount County and the smaller settlements of Grand Bassa County—has potential bearing on the character and range of the AAE that the Settlers brought to their new home in the nineteenth century. If a more detailed examination of LSE confirms the existing indications that LSE possesses a high degree of similarity all along the Liberian coast, this would lead to the next research question: is that similarity a consequence of fundamental similarity within the AAE that the original emigrants from the United States brought with them (thereby suggesting that regional differences in modern AAE are largely a post–Civil War development; see Wolfram 2007; Wolfram and Kohn, this volume), or are they instead more a consequence of post-arrival koineization? Clearly, there is much to be done.

In the years from 1822 to 1860 and beyond, sixteen thousand African Americans immigrated to West Africa to a colony created for them. The language of the immigrants and their descendants, Liberian Settler English, has now incorporated some local grammatical features not discussed here (two AUXs, an emphatic marker, and the like), some post-immigration forces would seem to have promoted crucial restrictions on coda consonants, and internal change stands always as a potential force. Nevertheless, four thousand miles from the American South, this African American enclave continues to speak the language that their ancestors brought with them 150 years ago and more. As such, when analytical caution is applied, their language speaks to the history of the language that remained in America.

Notes

1. The Rev. D. Hosea Ellis was central to my research on the Liberian Settler English of Sinoe County. His death in 2008 was a great personal loss for me, as well as a professional loss. I here acknowledge four others who provided friendship and guidance until their deaths: the Rev. Emmanuel Hodges, Nora Jones, Missouri Montgomery, and the Rev. Charles Bailey. In recent years, Edward Railey has been a valuable associate. Peter Robert Toe and Comfort Swen Toe facilitated my research in Sinoe. A National Science Foundation grant and a National Endowment for the Humanities summer stipend supported my research. The Over Yonder of my title is a section of the upriver Sinoe settlement of Louisiana that, flattened in Liberia's civil war, is currently under reconstruction.

2. As set out in Singler (1989), 11,819 emigrated from the United States in the period from 1820 to 1860; 2,810 in the years immediately following the US Civil War (1865–72); and 1,367 in the two decades from 1873 to 1891.

3. Those who immigrated to Liberia came from across African America, both geographically and socially. I raise the possibility that there were differences (either social or regional or some combination thereof) regarding the likelihood of pronunciation of coda consonants, and I consider the possibility of Gullah influence on LSE. Beyond these two points, I have not addressed in any more specific way the regional or social provenance in America of these features. Accordingly, in this chapter, I opt for the more neutral term *African American English*.

4. The book *Mississippi in Africa* (2003) by Alan Huffman overstates the Mississippi presence in the consciousness of today's Sinoenians. With the exception of Mississippi Street in Greenville and the Mississippi Inn located on that street, there is no physical reminder of the tie. In the year that I lived in Greenville (1969–70) and in all of my subsequent visits there, I have never heard anyone refer to Greenville or Sinoe as *Mississippi* (*pace* Huffman).

5. The Maryland Settlers were furthest from Monrovia but, at first, were independent of it. Further, they continued to receive support from their benefactors in the American state of Maryland.

6. In using nineteenth-century sources to compile immigration figures, I have been guided by Jo Mary Sullivan's (1978) dissertation. Only when there is specific counterevidence have I departed from Sullivan.

7. The lone regionalism in LSE that I have identified is an equational copula construction of the form *that* NP *with* NP. A calque from the Mande language Vai, it occurs in LSE and VLE in Grand Cape Mount County, the coastal region northwest of Monrovia where Vai is spoken. The example in (i) comes from a young Settler in Robertsport, the county capital of Grand Cape Mount:

    (i) *That* my friend *with* Mr. Singler; *that* not my friend *with* you.
    　　'Mr. Singler's my friend; you're not.'

8. *Settlers* is a scholars' term, though it has come to be used occasionally in formal discourse by Liberian leaders. Likewise, *Americo-Liberian* is an older term whose use is largely limited to formal and academic contexts. The Settlers sometimes call themselves *the Pioneers*, though they do so most often when discussing their nineteenth-century history. To other Liberians, the term *Pioneer* connotes narrow Settler privilege at the expense of Liberia's indigenous majority. It is only in recent years that *Pioneers' Day*, commemorating the landing of the first Settlers in 1822, has ceased to be celebrated as a national holiday on January 7.

9. Within Liberia today, education serves an integrating function. The further a Liberian student goes in school, the more the student sounds likes his or her classmates, whether they are ethnically Settler or indigenous.

10. All five of the features are found in LSE. Apart from the use of *ain't* for *didn't*, they are apparently not features of Samaná English (Singler 2007, 145).

11. Possessives form a limited exception. In the corpus, possessive *'s* only occurs in the speech of teachers (and occurs there less than one-fourth of the time); the only teachers in the corpus are from Sinoe. This seems to be an instance where being in contact with—and being an agent of—standardizing forces trumps Settler geography.

REFERENCES

The African Repository and Colonial Journal. 1825–92.

Archangeli, Diana. 1997. "Optimality Theory: An Introduction to Linguistics in the 1990s." In *Optimality Theory: An Overview*, edited by Diana Archangeli and D. Terence Langendoen, 1–32. Malden, MA: Blackwell.

Baugh, John. 1983. *Black Street Speech*. Austin: University of Texas Press.

Cassidy, Frederic G. 1986. "Some Similarities between Gullah and Caribbean Creoles." In *Language Variety in the South*, edited by Michael B. Montgomery and Guy Bailey, 30–37. Tuscaloosa: University of Alabama.

Chambers, J. K. 2003. *Sociolinguistic Theory: Linguistic Variation and Its Social Significance.* 2nd ed. Oxford: Blackwell.

———. 2004. "Dynamic Typology and Vernacular Universals." In *Dialectology Meets Typology: Dialect Grammar from a Cross-Linguistic Perspective*, edited by Bernd Kortmann, 127–45. Berlin: Mouton de Gruyter.

Crummell, Alexander. 1862. "The English Language in Liberia." In *The Future of Africa.* New York: Charles Scribner.

Dayton, Elizabeth. 1996. "Grammatical Categories of the Verb in African-American Vernacular English." PhD diss., University of Pennsylvania.

DeCamp, David. 1971. "Toward a Generative Analysis of a Post-Creole Speech Community." In *Pidginization and Creolization of Language*, edited by Dell Hymes, 349–70. Cambridge: Cambridge University Press.

Dunn, D. Elwood, and Svend E. Holsoe. 1985. *Historical Dictionary of Liberia.* African Historical Dictionaries, No. 38. Metuchen, NJ: Scarecrow.

Green, Lisa J. 1998. "Aspects and Predicate Phrases in African-American Vernacular English." In *African-American English: Structure, History and Use*, edited by Salikoko S. Mufwene, John R. Rickford, Guy Bailey, and John Baugh, 37–68. London: Routledge.

———. 2002. *African American English: A Linguistic Introduction.* Cambridge: Cambridge University Press.

Hancock, Ian F. 1971. "A Survey of the Pidgins and Creoles of the World." In *Pidginization and Creolization of Language*, edited by Dell Hymes, 509–23. Cambridge: Cambridge University Press.

Holsoe, Svend E. 1977. "Slavery and Economic Response among the Vai (Liberia and Sierra Leone)." In *Slavery in Africa: Historical and Anthropological Perspectives*, edited by S. Miers and I. Kopytoff, 287–303. Madison: University of Wisconsin Press.

Huffman, Alan. 2003. *Mississippi in Africa.* New York: Gotham Books.

Labov, William. 1998. "Co-Existent Systems in African-American Vernacular English." In *African-American English: Structure, History and Use*, edited by Salikoko S. Mufwene, John R. Rickford, Guy Bailey, and John Baugh, 110–53. London: Routledge.

Liebenow, J. Gus. 1969. *Liberia: The Evolution of Privilege.* Ithaca, NY: Cornell University.

McDaniel, Antonio. 1995. *Swing Low, Sweet Chariot: The Mortality Cost of Colonizing Liberia in the Nineteenth Century.* Chicago: University of Chicago.

Myhill, John. 1995. "The Use of Features of Present-Day AAVE in the Ex-Slave Recordings." *American Speech* 70: 115–47.

Rickford, John R. 1974. "The Insights of the Mesolect." In *Pidgin and Creole Linguistics: Current Trends and Prospects*, edited by David DeCamp and Ian F. Hancock, 92–117. Washington, DC: Georgetown University.

———. 1975. "Carrying the New Wave into Syntax: The Case of Black English *Bin*." In *Analyzing Variation in Language*, edited by Ralph Fasold and Roger Shuy, 162–83. Washington, DC: Georgetown University.

Rickford, John R., and Christine Théberge-Rafal. 1996. "Preterit *Had* in the Narratives of African American Preadolescents." *American Speech* 71: 227–54.

Shick, Tom W. 1980. *Behold the Promised Land: A History of Afro American Settler Society in Nineteenth Century Liberia.* Baltimore, MD: Johns Hopkins University.

Singler, John Victor. 1977. "Language in Liberia in the Nineteenth Century: The Settlers' Perspective." *Liberian Studies Journal* 7: 73–85.

———. 1987. "The City, the Mesolect, and Innovation." *Journal of Pidgin and Creole Languages* 2: 119–47.

————. 1989. "Plural Marking in Liberian Settler English, 1820–1980." *American Speech* 64: 40–64.

————. 1997. "The Configuration of Liberia's Englishes." *World Englishes* 16: 205–31.

————. 1998. "What's Not New in AAVE." *American Speech* 73: 227–56.

————. 2000. "Optimality Theory, the Minimal-Word Constraint, and the Historical Sequencing of Substrate Influence in Pidgin/Creole Genesis." In *Current Issues in Pidgin and Creole Linguistics*, edited by John H. McWhorter, 336–51. Amsterdam: John Benjamins.

————. 2004a. "Liberian Settler English: Phonology." In *A Handbook of Varieties of English*, Vol. 1, *Phonology*, edited by Bernd Kortmann, Kate Burridge, Rajend Mesthrie, Edgar W. Schneider, and Clive Upton, 874–84. Berlin: Mouton de Gruyter.

————. 2004b. "The Morphology and Syntax of Liberian Settler English." In *A Handbook of Varieties of English*, Vol. 2, *Morphology and Syntax*, edited by Bernd Kortmann, Kate Burridge, Rajend Mesthrie, Edgar W. Schneider, and Clive Upton, 879–97. Berlin: Mouton de Gruyter.

————. 2007a. "Samaná and Sinoe. Part I: Stalking the Vernacular." *Journal of Pidgin and Creole Languages* 22: 123–48.

————. 2007b. "Samaná and Sinoe, Part II: Provenance." *Journal of Pidgin and Creole Languages* 22: 309–46.

————. 2011. "Liberian Settler English." In *The Electronic World Atlas of Variation in English: Grammar*, edited by Bernd Kortmann and Kerstin Lunkenheimer. Max Planck Digital Library in cooperation with Mouton de Gruyter. http://www.ewave-atlas.org/languages/37.

————. 2012. "Liberian Settler English." In *Mouton World Atlas of Varieties of English*, edited by Bernd Kortmann and Kerstin Lunkenheimer, 358–68. Berlin: Mouton de Gruyter.

Spears, Arthur K. 1982. "The Black English Semi-Auxiliary *Come*." *Language* 58: 850–72.

Staudenraus, P. J. 1980. *The African Colonization Movement, 1816–1865*. New York: Octagon.

Stockwell, G. S. 1868. *The Republic of Liberia: Its Geography, Climate, Soil, and Productions: With a History of its Early Settlement*. New York: A. S. Barnes.

Sullivan, Jo Mary. 1978. "Settlers in Sinoe County, Liberia, and their Relations with the Kru, c. 1835–1920." PhD diss., Boston University.

Sydnor, Charles Sackett. 1933. *Slavery in Mississippi*. New York: D. Appleton-Century.

Wolfram, Walt. 2004. "The Grammar of Urban African American Vernacular English." In *A Handbook of Varieties of English*, Vol. 2, *Morphology and Syntax*, edited by Bernd Kortmann, Kate Burridge, Rajend Mesthrie, Edgar W. Schneider, and Clive Upton, 319–40. Berlin: Mouton de Gruyter.

————. 2007. "Sociolinguistic Folklore in the Study of African American English." *Language and Linguistic Compass* 2: 292–313.

CHAPTER 6

DOCUMENTING THE HISTORY OF AFRICAN AMERICAN VERNACULAR ENGLISH

A Survey and Assessment of Sources and Results

EDGAR W. SCHNEIDER

6.1 INTRODUCTION

IT is close to fifty years now that a debate on the origin of African American Vernacular English (AAVE)[1] has been going on. To date, this issue has not been consensually resolved, even if by now many scholars tend to accept hybrid positions (see Mufwene's and Winford's chapters, this volume), and certainly the discussion is no longer as heated as it once was. In 1965, what came to be known as the *creole origin hypothesis* was voiced for the first time—the idea that the dialect could be traced back to a seventeenth- or eighteenth-century *plantation creole*, implying the presence of substrate traces of African linguistic input in its structure (Bailey 1965, further discussed below). The alternative view, that the characteristic features of the dialect derive from British settler dialects with whom African slaves in those days had close contacts, was then known as the *dialectologists' hypothesis* and became relabeled as the *(neo-)Anglicist position* decades later. The more specific assumptions and claims associated with these positions have been summarized repeatedly (see Bailey 2001, 54–58; Kautzsch 2002, 4–8; Schneider 1989, 16–41).[2]

The issue concerns the diachrony of a covert and low-prestige nonstandard dialect—but here we are faced with the "bad data" problem: such dialects were usually not written down; and if they were, for whatever reason, such manuscripts were much less likely to have been preserved than formal documents. Hence, a primary reason for the debate being allowed to simmer for such a long time has been a far-reaching dearth of reliable evidence. The question has always been: What do we really know about the linguistic properties of earlier forms of AAVE, and from which sources is this knowledge derived? In the beginning of the debate, an honest answer clearly would have been "next to nothing, for lack of original records"; and in the course of time, new phases in the discussion on the roots of AAVE have usually been sparked by scholars having unearthed and analyzed new original evidence. By now, a sizeable body of sources on earlier AAVE has been accumulated, but questions remain as to the reliability and representativeness of some of these records.

As befits a handbook contribution, therefore, the purpose of this chapter is to survey and weigh the evidence available for the issue in question and, on that basis, to assess our knowledge of the subject. I proceed historically, by characterizing the kinds of sources and records that were available to scholarship in different phases of the debate and the results achieved on that basis, respectively. Even if we still do not know reliably how AAVE originated, we have learned a lot, and I intend to show that this learning process has gone hand in hand with the discovery and analysis of new sources and that therefore the nature (and limitations) of the available records determine the substance and also the limits of our knowledge.

6.2 THE EARLY PHASE: THE 1960S AND 1970S

In 1965, Beryl Bailey, a Jamaican creolist, published a seminal paper in which it was suggested for the first time that "the Southern negro 'dialect' differs from other Southern speech because its deep structure is different, having its origin as it undoubtedly does in some Proto-Creole grammatical structure" (1965, 172). The concept of a difference in deep structure reflects the linguistic spirit of the period, the early heyday of Chomsky's generative grammar. It was elaborated on enthusiastically by some writers (see Loflin 1969) but essentially refuted by the results of large-scale sociolinguistic projects of the time, which found only differences in "low-level realization rules, lexical inputs, phonological and late transformational rules" (Labov 1972, 48; similarly Wolfram 1971, 156). But the creole origin idea sparked a lively debate. The thesis was first developed in some articles by the creolist William Stewart (1967) and was then disseminated widely in Dillard (1972). Subsequently, it was generally accepted and found its way, for instance, into Labov's (1982) expert witness statement in *Martin Luther King Junior Elementary School Children et al. v. Ann Arbor School District* (1977).

What was the evidence for these claims then? The surprising answer is: there was very little or next to none, at least when it comes to reliable diachronic sources. Bailey (1965) used only a single text of literary dialect as a source, namely, the speech of "Duke," the narrator of Warren Miller's 1959 novel *The Cool World*. This sample cannot be assumed to record the early phase of AAVE, as it represents literary dialect, rather than natural usage, and contemporary, rather than historical, AAVE. Dillard (1972), in his chapter on history, presents a small number of examples, mostly from stage dialect or travelers' reports. This is interesting material, but it is highly limited in scope and known to be of questionable reliability. Dramatists are known to use dialect for its artistic effects, not for its authenticity. With travelers, we never know how much, in foreign lands, they understood and recorded correctly, so there is a possibility that the speakers who were represented actually came from the Caribbean, rather than from the North American mainland. Thus, most of the support for the creole hypothesis in the early phase came from a small set of surface similarities with Caribbean creole patterns and from extra-linguistic considerations, and the general acceptance of the thesis was fostered by the cultural context of the period of heightened civil rights activism: the desire to identify African roots in African American cultural manifestations. But large-scale textual evidence of what a predecessor of modern AAVE looked like on southern plantations of, say, the eighteenth or nineteenth century was simply lacking.

6.3 New Evidence: The 1980s and 1990s

6.3.1 Written Documentation: The WPA Ex-Slave Narratives

In the 1980s, a voluminous new source that promised to offer a window into AAVE usage of earlier times became available, namely, the so-called *WPA* (Works Projects Administration) ex-slave narratives. The WPA, and also the Federal Writers' Project (FWP) as the branch that was in charge of this project, was a New Deal activity, meant to provide employment to some of the unemployed (and, more specifically, "writers") in the 1930s. In this case, the idea was to carry out and transcribe interviews with African Americans who were old enough to have experienced the days of slavery and to collect their memories as oral history, at that time on the verge of being lost. The "writers" occupied in this project were instructed to record the interviewees' statements verbatim, as closely as possible, so these thousands of records, taken together, constitute a uniquely large and linguistically promising corpus of earlier African American speech. The collection was compiled in the 1930s and 1940s, which makes it historical in any case; however, the common assumption that a speaker's grammar remains fairly stable throughout one's lifetime implies that it offers a diachronic linguistic window into the time when these speakers—then in their eighties, nineties, or even older—acquired their speech (i.e., in the mid- to late nineteenth century). Thousands of such interviews were carried out and recorded on location, submitted to regional headquarters, and, in most cases, delivered to Washington, where they were archived, until George Rawick began to publish them as huge collections of facsimile reproductions of the original transcript sheets (Rawick 1972–79). Here is an example:

(1) I never knowed Sunday from Monday, 'cept on Sunday the white man come and we are called out under the brush arbor, didn' have no work in the fiel' at day, and he stand up 'fore us and preach. . . I knows now it was a Bible.

—(Tishey Taylor, Mo.; Rawick 1972–79, Series 1, 11:343)

The first scholar to discover and analyze these texts was Jeutonne Brewer. In a 1974 University of North Carolina at Chapel Hill dissertation and in several articles, Brewer investigated forms of the verb *to be* in these documents (see also Brewer 1973, 1980). The most comprehensive analysis of the texts is the book by Schneider (1989), which investigates twenty morphosyntactic variables and was preceded by a German dissertation completed in 1981 and two articles published in the United States (1983a, b). It presented data that was in stark contrast with the dominant thinking of the time. Against the creolist view, then widely accepted, which predicted mainly suffix-less verbs and preverbal markers to predominate in earlier stages of AAVE, Schneider (1983a) showed that the historical record was rich in verbal –*s* endings. Schneider (1983b) also argued that a three-verb perfective group consisting of a finite auxiliary *be* or *have* plus *done* before the main verb (as in *I sho is done been wukin'*) provided a missing link with well-documented northern British sources. On the whole, Schneider (1989) found the speech preserved in the FWP ex-slave narratives to be "predominantly determined by its descent from nonstandard British and American English of the colonial period" (277) but also sprinkled with "structures that are unquestionably creole or creole-influenced in character" (278), thus arguing for a recognition of the complex internal variability shaped by varying contact conditions that has characterized AAVE from its beginning.

These studies were widely read and well received (see Wolfram 1990). However, the reliability of the records remained a central question, given the recording conditions: were the interviewers really able and willing to manually record dialect details in the speech of their informants on the spot? Furthermore, as Maynor (1988) showed, some of the texts were edited by regional project directors before being submitted to the Washington headquarters. Schneider (1997) conceded such limitations but defended the basic reliability of the data by testing them for internal consistency and validating them against other sources, such as the recordings to be discussed in the next section (for a discussion of principled problems, see also Schneider 2013). Another consequence, drawn consistently in later investigations of the ex-slave narratives (see Kautzsch 2002) was to use the supplement volumes of Rawick (1972–79) rather than the original series, as these built upon original, unedited versions from regional archives.

In light of the growing interest in the regional and internal variability of AAVE (see Wolfram, this volume) it may be worth noting that the study of these written records already provided a baseline by documenting consistent regional variation between different state records. For example, Schneider (1983a, 1985, and 1989, 231–50) showed in the ex-slave narratives that verbal –*s* endings occur much more frequently in southeastern states with a long-standing colonial history (e.g., North Carolina, South Carolina, and Georgia) than in western states settled later (e.g., Missouri, Arkansas, and Texas); that the pronoun form *us* predominates over *we* in South Carolina, Georgia, Alabama, and Mississippi (but not further to the north and west); and that the remnant third singular pronoun form *hit* (for *it*) is strongly upper southern (predominant in Tennessee and very strong also in North Carolina and Arkansas).

6.3.2 Oral Data: The Library of Congress Recordings

Another highly influential diachronic source that contributed to the issue of the genesis of AAVE being reopened was a small set of oral recordings with ex-slaves carried out at roughly the same time and with a similar inspiration as the collection of the ex-slave narratives, this time by the Archive of Folk Song. An excerpt from the transcription of one of these recordings is cited as (2) below. Guy Bailey discovered them in the Library of Congress, shared them with a select group of scholars, and, in a unique and most useful book design, published transcripts together with scholarly analyses from various perspectives (Bailey, Maynor, and Cukor-Avila 1991).[3] Again, obviously, this was exciting material, mainly for its age—recordings antedating all accessible oral data substantially. This was the first time linguists could actually listen to and investigate AAVE speakers from more than fifty years ago, with language acquisition roots extending deep into the nineteenth century.

> (2) An' when I come back, why I carry it to my master an' give that to him, that'd be all right. But I couldn' jus' walk away like the people does now, you know. It was what they call, we were slaves. We belonged to people.
>
>   (Fountain Hughes, Va., from Bailey et al. 1991, 33)

The surprising finding was that these recordings also show very few if any traces of typically creole language structures. But again, of course, as Rickford (1991) pointed out, possible doubt as to the representativeness of even these audio data remains. It is conceivable, for example, that the recording situation increased the formality of performance, that the speakers chosen were not representative of the majority of African American speakers, notably field hands, of the time in question, or that their speech changed under the impact of wider social contacts after emancipation. Of course, such concerns can be voiced on practically all early sets of data, since none of them was compiled with any notion of sampling strategies or representativeness in mind.

6.3.3 Other New Written Data

The 1990s saw the discovery and first-time analysis of a few more (types of) records thought to be relevant for an understanding of the history of AAVE. One of these was the "Hyatt Hoodoo Recordings," named after John Middleton Hyatt, an Episcopal priest interested in medical folklore, who carried out over 1,600 interviews with (mostly) African American witchcraft practitioners all across the South in the 1930s and 1940s (and produced a few supplements much later); Hyatt then recorded the responses to his interview prompts accurately (originally using an Ediphone with a speaking tube into which he repeated the responses), transcribed them, and published them in several volumes in the 1970s. Hyatt's records are of interest because of their historical significance and sheer magnitude, even if there are also reasons to question their accuracy: it was not the interviewees' words that were recorded directly but only Hyatt's repetitions of them (and the discs with the recordings are lost), and there is no way of assessing any possible impact of Hyatt's interview style and transcription quality on the results.

This material was used for the first time in Ewers (1996), a dissertation that investigated forms of *to be*, including finite agreement patterns, invariant *be* (found to not be restricted to habitual contexts), and (very rare) instances of "remote" preverbal *been*. In summary, Ewers (1996) reports finding "strong evidence against the creole theory" (215) and considers the variety as a whole to be "an independent system" (241). Example (3) offers a sample of this type of record.

> (3) I brough 'em wit me. I didn't bring de lickred. I got lickred medicine at home. An' I ain't scared to take a shake of it an' take a drink of it.
>
> (Va., from Kautzsch 2002, 42)

Another type of source that became influential during this period was letters—"imagined speech" to their writers (Schneider 2013)—relevant as an authentic source provided they contain vernacular language. Michael Montgomery, in particular, has spent some energy to locate and analyze letters by "semi-literate" writers from various origins, including African Americans. Using a corpus of such letters from the mid-nineteenth century, Montgomery, Fuller, and DeMarse (1993) showed effects of the "Northern Subject Rule" on earlier African American English for the first time, which was an important presentation at the *Language Variety in the South* conference at Auburn University in 1993. Bill Labov, in a discussion at the conference, recognized the presentation as convincing proof of strong British dialect lineage. The Northern Subject Rule is a complex and typologically unusual agreement pattern known to have originated in northern British dialects, according to which verbal –*s* endings tend to be used after full noun phrase subjects, but not after subject pronouns (as in *the dogs barks* but *they bark*)—a distribution that is most unlikely to have originated independently in two varieties and, thus, suggests historical continuity through diffusion. It should be noted, however, that vernacularity was not normally typical of the letter-writing genre in the nineteenth century: as Kautzsch (2000) showed, letters written home by "repatriates" to Liberia are relatively formal in style and display only a limited number of nonstandard phenomena.

As a consequence of these insights and considerations, the quality of available written sources rather than their amount became an increasing concern in the study of such materials. Kautzsch (2002) is a model study in that respect and indicative of the level of sophistication that can be achieved. The study explicitly combines data from various sources (selections from ex-slave narratives and recordings, hoodoo transcripts, and letters), but in each case it takes pains to select maximally reliable samples. For example, from Rawick (1972, 1977–79), the author selects only transcripts from the supplement volumes taken from unedited regional archives from just two states where external evidence implies that special care was taken to achieve accurate linguistic representation of what was said in the interview situation. Employing an apparent time methodology, the author builds a timeline by categorizing informants by birth decades, ranging between the 1830s and the 1920s. A detailed investigation of three linguistic variables allows him to document a number of interesting changes in the negation, copula, and relativizer systems. He is able to show, for instance, that the full verb negator function of *ain't* (corresponding to *didn't*), putatively a fairly recent innovation characteristic of modern AAVE (cf. Weldon 1994), can in fact be traced back much further in time, being found in the speech of African Americans born in the 1840s and later in the mid-nineteenth century (Kautzsch 2002, 44–48).

6.4 DIASPORA SPEECH ISLANDS AS LINGUISTIC ARCHEOLOGY: THE 1990S AND 2000S

A new type of linguistic archeology of AAVE began to attract a lot of attention around 1990: Shana Poplack and her research associates in Ottawa discovered and analyzed isolated diaspora communities. The basic idea is simple: groups of dialect speakers who migrate to faraway places, in totally different linguistic environments, establish speech islands that are linguistically conservative and are assumed to be isolated from any possible linguistic changes in the community of origin, thus preserving in their speech a window into the linguistic past, as it were. Again, of course, restrictive considerations apply. Accepting a present-day diaspora dialect as indicative of some earlier origin dialect stage requires the assumptions that: (a) the speech island dialect has indeed been fully isolated from later developments in the original dialect and (b) it has also been free of (relevant) internal linguistic developments. Both assumptions can be defended for good reasons for speech islands but for both assumptions some remaining skepticism is also justified.

The best known and most widely discussed diaspora dialect of AAVE is Samaná English, spoken on the Samaná peninsula of the Dominican Republic by descendants of African Americans from the eastern and southern United States who had settled there in the 1820s. For more than 150 years, these speakers handed down their dialect from one generation to the next, with hardly any outside contacts and in a wholly Spanish-speaking environment. Poplack and Sankoff (1987) were the first to introduce this variety and to defend the assumption of linguistic continuity in isolation. Poplack and Tagliamonte (1991a) presented a sophisticated analysis of verbal –s inflection in Samaná compared to the ex-slave recordings. Largely in line with earlier findings and explicitly "extrapolating from Schneider's (1983[a]) suggestion" (Poplack and Tagliamonte 1991a, 314), the authors find a variable inflectional system that is best explained as having descended from British dialectal input. Their methodological and theoretical approach is more sophisticated, however: while the earlier studies (see Schneider 1983a, 1989) looked at and compared frequencies and rank orders of variants only, Poplack and Tagliamonte (1991a) considered constraint strengths and constraint hierarchies, arguing that these are historically more stable and thus more strongly diagnostic than mere frequencies.

Work along these lines was extended to include two other African American diaspora communities in Nova Scotia, which consisted of descendants of late-eighteenth-century "Black Loyalists" who settled there after the War of Independence and early-nineteenth-century British Black troops who had deserted from the prospect of slavery in the United States. Results were similar, confirming a fundamentally non-creole character of the grammar of these speakers (see Poplack and Tagliamonte 1991b). The contributions in Poplack (2000), which cover a range of grammatical phenomena, as well as the book by Poplack and Tagliamonte (2001), which focuses upon the tense and aspect subsystems, draw together data from all of these oral sources along with analyses of the ex-slave recordings. They find consistent constraint hierarchies across all varieties of earlier AAVE and argue for a long-standing, conservative British origin of earlier AAVE. These volumes thus epitomize what has come to be known as the *neo-Anglicist* position.

This claim has not remained unchallenged, however. Following in Poplack's footsteps, Dawn Hannah carried out fieldwork of her own in Samaná and found "a greater resemblance to West Indian Creoles than previously reported" (Hannah 1997, 343) in the domain of copula absence. Furthermore, she questioned the representativeness of the Samaná migrants for the "majority of African Americans of the time" (341) and suggested that the interviewees of the earlier recordings may have accommodated to the standardizing influence of the speech of the interviewers (346–47). Rickford (2006), in a lengthy review of Poplack (2000), challenges the main thrust of the Anglicists' arguments by questioning the accuracy and relevance of some of their analyses and claims (arguing mostly that many interpretations are not backed by the respective figures). Singler (2007a, b) also challenges Poplack and Tagliamonte's findings, arguing that the Samaná settlers largely stemmed from Philadelphia and other northern cities and had been free African Americans speaking less vernacular styles, so they were not representative of the majority of southern slaves. These conflicting perspectives and pieces of evidence suggest that the Samaná community may also have been internally heterogeneous and that their roots and representativeness need to be contextualized with care and reluctance.

John Singler has published a series of articles in which he investigated various linguistic properties of another diaspora and offspring variety, the English spoken by descendants of African Americans who colonized Liberia, mostly emancipated slaves, roughly between the 1820s and 1870s. Singler (2004) provides a summary that shows this dialect to be much closer to creoles than other sources of earlier AAVE, and Singler (2007a, b) discusses some central sociolinguistic issues in this context, notably the putative vernacularity of the Samaná and Liberia communities based on settlement data. Of course, Singler's Liberian data are an ocean and a century away from nineteenth-century AAVE, so the possibility of later changes and influences from West African Pidgin English forms cannot be excluded.

6.5 NEW PERSPECTIVES: THE 2000S

6.5.1 Semi-Literate Letters as Evidence: OREAAC, COAAL

More recently, two electronic corpora of early letters written by semi-literate African Americans have been compiled in order to open up this type of source to corpus-linguistic, computerized analyses and thus to contribute to a better understanding of the origins of AAVE. Both are large but also heterogeneous, comprising texts that presumably vary in quality.

The Ottawa Repository of Early African American English Correspondence (OREAAC) builds upon more than 400 letters written around the middle of the nineteenth century by African American immigrants to Liberia, drawn from the archives of the American Colonization Society. Van Herk and Poplack (2003), in a paper that also discusses methodological issues at great length, and Van Herk and Walker (2005) used this source to investigate past tense marking and the regional conditioning of verbal inflection, respectively.

Co-directed by the present author, Michael Montgomery, and Lucia Siebers, an electronic corpus of mid-nineteenth-century semi-literate African American letters called COAAL (Corpus of Older African American Letters) is currently being compiled at the University of Regensburg. An example from this corpus is given in (4).

(4) November the 24 1864
    greenville NC
 to you i take my Peen in Heend to wrie
 you a fee linds to let you know How we
 all are all are well witchout my Sallf I
 have been doon ever centies August witch
 my net it is gettig beter so that i am
 up h late i has not been abral to doo
 any thing...
 I have nortieng more
    to rite
  But dis is your Servant
  Sam Perry

Overall, the corpus consists of 1,530 letters by about 900 writers spanning a period from 1763 to 1919 (with the vast majority being from the 1860s, however). About one-third of the letters derive from collections published earlier by historians or on microfilm; two-thirds have been discovered in various southern and eastern archives, in deliberate searches both by Michael Montgomery over a number of years and by Lucia Siebers during an archive tour in 2008. Further details on this corpus and some preliminary results showing, for instance, historical continuity of an old *for to* + infinitive pattern (lost in

present-day AAVE), as well as some degree of variability in verbal and nominal morphology, are available in Schneider (2012).

6.5.2 Blues Lyrics as Evidence: BLUR

Another electronic text collection of a special variety representing earlier AAVE is BLUR,
the corpus of Blues Lyrics compiled at the University of Regensburg. It builds upon transcripts of early country blues recordings mainly from the 1920s to the 1940s, under the
assumption that the lyrics of these performances mirror the African American dialect of
the singers from that period, still largely unspoiled by the influences and demands of the
recording industry. To a great extent, these recordings preserve a large body of authentic
Black dialect from an earlier period, by singers from all across the South and beyond; on
the other hand, constraints are imposed by the nature of song lyrics, which are strongly
influenced by the needs of verse and rhythm structures and restricted pragmatically (by
the monologic song and performance setting) and semantically (by conventional topics
and phrases of blues songs). BLUR consists of 7,341 songs by more than 800 singers from
16 states and is close to 1.5 million words in size. About 10 percent of this corpus is religious, the majority being secular.[4] Miethaner (2005) describes the corpus and its compilation principles in great detail and offers a range of exemplary analyses of a wide range of
nonstandard grammatical features, including, at varying frequencies, traditional dialectal ones (e.g., variable verbal inflection, preverbal *a-*, *for to*, personal datives, etc.), features
considered typical of late-twentieth-century, innovative AAVE (e.g., future perfective *be
done*, continuative *steady*, indignant *come*, and the pattern *call oneself V–ing*) and also, if
relatively rarely, features considered typical of creoles (e.g., lack of verbal and nominal
inflection, or the quotative complementizer *say*). Schneider and Miethaner (2006) document the innovative potential that this corpus has by analyzing a syntactic construction
that is quite common in BLUR but unusual in mainstream English, the complementation
of the verb *start* by *to* plus a verbal *–ing* form (as in *the snow starts to falling*).

6.5.3 Trajectories of Change

As is well known, in the 1980s the so-called *divergence controversy*, suggesting that
some features of recent urban AAVE are becoming more different from comparable
white dialects, sparked a new debate on the evolution of AAVE, focusing more on
twentieth-century developments than on the variety's historical roots (see Bailey and
Maynor 1989; Butters 1989). Strictly speaking, this topic is indirectly related to but
essentially independent from the issues discussed so far, considering recent evidence
that fails to represent the initial stages of the formation of AAVE centuries ago. It is
uncontroversial that there are grammatical differences between earlier and present-day
forms of AAVE (as conceded, for instance, by Poplack and Tagliamonte 2001, 245–50; cf.

Bailey and Maynor 1989; Bailey 2001, 57; Wolfram and Thomas 2002, 28–31), but there is no general agreement on the direction and nature of more recent developments.

Consequently, some recent work has focused on the trajectories of recent changes in the dialect. At least two large-scale and ongoing projects need to be mentioned here. Walt Wolfram and his collaborators at NCSU have continued to contribute important work on what has been happening to AAVE in North Carolina, with a special focus on Hyde County; notably, Wolfram and Thomas (2002) document local and supraregional processes of alignment and vernacular norming within AAVE, showing the attraction and diffusion effect of emerging urban forms of the dialect that have been gaining indexical prestige. Guy Bailey and Patricia Cukor-Avila have provided clear evidence for the model role of young, male, urban African Americans in some ongoing developments and they have also observed and documented changing speech patterns in both rural and adjacent urban communities in east central Texas for decades (Bailey and Cukor-Avila, forthcoming; Cukor-Avila and Bailey, this volume).

6.6 CONCLUSION

What have we learned, essentially, in this review of the growth of scholarly knowledge of the evolution of AAVE? First, to know what we really know, it is important to learn how we have come to know something, that is, to familiarize ourselves with and to be able to assess the evidence—the kinds of textual sources available, their quality, and their representativeness. Second, while the issue of AAVE is probably no longer as loaded as it once was, it is still touchy in some respects because it is associated with ideologies and processes of identity formation. The history of research is also a history of researchers and their subjectivities, and these, in turn, are motivated by changing communal and individual goals and societal spirits. With changing times and continuing additions to our evidence base regarding earlier stages of AAVE, the questions that are being asked and the prevailing answers being offered are also changing. The overall trajectory of this change, of our understanding of the subject matter, has been one toward the recognition of diversity and complexity.

One important point is that AAVE is far from monolithic today, and throughout its history variability has no doubt characterized the dialect—it has always been a composite of several different varieties, varying on regional and social grounds. I suggest that it makes sense to posit at least two major types of varieties. Today's emphasis of scholarship is clearly on a modern AAVE, associated with young, male speakers and artistic expressions like Hip Hop (called "Hip Hop Nation Language" by H. Samy Alim), and characterized by features that include *camouflaged forms* (e.g., *steady, come, call oneself Xing*; e.g., *Ricky be steady steppin' in*;[5] *They come talking that trash about him; They call themselves dancing*); special tense/aspect markers (e.g., *be done*, as in *the chicken be done jumped out of the tub*); the use of *ain't* for full verb negation (corresponding to *didn't/don't*, as in *She ain't do it*); the *had* + past participle pattern for simple past time reference (e.g., *They had went outside*); the absence of verbal inflection in the third person singular (e.g., *She walk; She have money*); habitual "*be + V–ing*" (e.g., *Sometimes they be playing games*); and others. Some of these features may effectively be products of more recent developments. Conversely, in older sources of AAVE we find much stronger evidence of a Conservative, Rural AAVE, indicative of a rural, agricultural, and religious orientation in life and expressed by forms such as rich verbal inflections (e.g., *The dogs barks*); preverbal *a-* (e.g., *She was a-fishin'*); or *for to* (e.g., *I want for to go now*)—some of which have all but disappeared from current AAVE.

The recognition of a mixed origin of AAVE has also been reflected on theoretically, and attempts have been made to investigate the issue empirically. In the 1990s the notion of *semi-creole*, with AAVE repeatedly mentioned as a likely candidate, was popular for a while (Holm 2000). For lack of empirical grounding, it was abandoned subsequently, but the basic idea has remained and has found its expression, for example, in Holm's (2004) concept of *partially restructured vernaculars*, with AAVE as a core representative. Based on historical AAVE data (samples from the ex-slave narratives), Kautzsch and Schneider (2000) document that idiolects from within the state of South Carolina show a cline of decreasing frequencies of creole features (e.g., preverbal *been*; habitual *does*; copula omission; lack of past tense, genitive, or plural suffixes; *ain't* as negator; and others) that correlates with increasing distance from the coast and decreasing African American population proportion in different counties.

Hence, in line with recent developments in contact linguistics, where increasingly the importance of different kinds of contact scenarios and their varying outcomes and degrees of restructuring are recognized (Winford 2003; Neumann-Holzschuh and Schneider 2000), the accumulated evidence suggests that AAVE has always been characterized by internal heterogeneity (see also Wolfram and Kohn, this volume). It has been composed of components drawn from standard English, dialectal English, innovative developments, and creole, to varying proportions, and it is best described by carefully weighing, moderate assessments that recognize the complexity of its contexts and its linguistic evolution (Winford 1997, 1998, this volume).

NOTES

1. I use this term to refer to the dialect spoken by working-class African Americans in interactions with peers, marked by certain distinctive features especially on the grammatical level. Lisa Green, who uses the term *African American English* (AAE), refers to the variety as "an ethnic and social dialect spoken by African Americans who are members of the working class" (2002, 6–7), and her useful discussion of the various labels for this variety in their historical context points out that in contrast to classroom English, it shares many properties with other spoken English varieties. It should be clear that to some extent the notion of AAVE is an abstraction, disregarding internal variability along the rural–urban dimension and generational lines, for instance. It does not include Gullah, which is a different linguistic system spoken in more tightly knit communities among Blacks on the coastal islands of Georgia and South Carolina.

2. It goes without saying but may still be worth pointing out in this context that the discussion revolves around a limited set of linguistic properties of AAVE that are considered

distinct and different from standard English. Of course, a substantial proportion of the features of the dialect are identical and shared with standard English—such as the basic word stock, most of the sounds, and most fundamental grammatical rules (e.g., to name just a few trivial examples: a subject-verb-object basic word order, rules on how to form a transitive clause, a passive, or a relative clause headed by who).

3. These recordings have since been made publicly available on the web by the Library of Congress (see http://memory.loc.gov/ammem/collections/voices/).

4. Regrettably, due to copyright restrictions, neither COAAL nor BLUR can be made publicly available. Both corpora are accessible on location at Regensburg.

5. All examples in this paragraph are taken from Wolfram (2008, 517–24).

References

Bailey, Beryl Loftman. 1965. "Toward a New Perspective in Negro English Dialectology." *American Speech* 40: 171–77.

Bailey, Guy. 2001. "The Relationship between African American Vernacular English and White Vernaculars in the American South: A Sociocultural History and Some Phonological Evidence." In *Sociocultural and Historical Contexts of African American English*, edited by Sonja L. Lanehart, 53–92. Amsterdam: John Benjamins.

Bailey, Guy, and Patricia Cukor-Avila. Forthcoming. *The Development of African American Vernacular English since 1850: The Evolution of a Grammar*. Cambridge: Cambridge University Press.

Bailey, Guy, and Natalie Maynor. 1989. "The Divergence Controversy." *American Speech* 64: 12–39.

Bailey, Guy, Natalie Maynor, and Patricia Cukor-Avila, eds. 1991. *The Emergence of Black English: Text and Commentary*. Amsterdam: Benjamins.

Brewer, Jeutonne. 1973. "Subject Concord of *Be* in Early Black English." *American Speech* 48: 5–21.

———. 1974. "The Verb Be in Early Black English: A Study Based on the WPA Ex-Slave Narratives." PhD diss., University of North Carolina at Chapel Hill.

———. 1980. "The WPA Slave Narratives as Linguistic Data." *Orbis* 29: 30–54.

Butters, Ronald R. 1989. *The Death of Black English: Divergence and Convergence in Black and White Vernaculars*. Frankfurt: Peter Lang.

Dillard, Joe. 1972. *Black English: Its History and Usage in the United States*. New York: Random House.

Ewers, Traute. 1996. *The Origin of American Black English: Be-Forms in the HOODOO Texts*. Berlin: Mouton de Gruyter.

Green, Lisa. 2002. *African American English*. Cambridge: Cambridge University Press.

Hannah, Dawn. 1997. "Copula Absence in Samaná English: Implications for Research on the Linguistic History of African-American English." *American Speech* 72: 339–72.

Holm, John. 2000. "Semi-Creolization: Problems in the Development of Theory." In *Degrees of Restructuring in Creole Languages*, edited by Ingrid Neumann-Holzschuh and Edgar W. Schneider, 19–40. Amsterdam: Benjamins.

———. 2004. *Languages in Contact: The Partial Restructuring of Vernaculars*. Cambridge: Cambridge University Press.

Kautzsch, Alexander. 2000. "Liberian Letters and Virginian Narratives: Negation Patterns in Two New Sources of Earlier African American English." *American Speech* 75: 34–53.

———. 2002. *The Historical Evolution of Earlier African American English: An Empirical Comparison of Early Sources*. Berlin: Mouton de Gruyter.

Kautzsch, Alexander, and Edgar W. Schneider. 2000. "Differential Creolization: Some Evidence from Earlier African American Vernacular English in South Carolina." In *Degrees of Restructuring in Creole Languages*, edited by Ingrid Neumann-Holzschuh and Edgar W. Schneider, 247–74. Amsterdam: Benjamins.

Labov, William. 1972. *Language in the Inner City. Studies in the Black English Vernacular*. Oxford, UK: Blackwell.

———. 1982. "Objectivity and Commitment in Linguistic Science: The Case of the Black English Trial in Ann Arbor." *Language in Society* 11: 165–201.

Loflin, Marvin. 1969. "Negro Nonstandard and Standard English: Same or Different Deep Structure? *Orbis* 18: 74–91.

Maynor, Natalie. 1988. "Written Records of Spoken Language: How Reliable Are They?" In *Methods in Dialectology*, edited by Alan Thomas, 109–20. Philadelphia: Multilingual Matters.

Miethaner, Ulrich. 2005. *"I Can Look through Muddy Water"—Analyzing Earlier African American English in Blues Lyrics (BLUR)*. Frankfurt: Peter Lang.

Montgomery, Michael, Janet M. Fuller, and Sharon DeMarse. 1993. "'The Black Men has Wives and Sweet Harts [and Third Person Plural -s] jest like the White Men': Evidence for Verbal -s from Written Documents on 19th-Century African American Speech." *Language Variation and Change* 5: 335–57.

Neumann-Holzschuh, Ingrid, and Edgar W. Schneider, eds. 2000. *Degrees of Restructuring in Creole Languages*. Amsterdam: Benjamins.

Poplack, Shana, ed. 2000. *The English History of African American English*. Oxford: Blackwell.

Poplack, Shana, and David Sankoff. 1987. "The Philadelphia Story in the Spanish Caribbean." *American Speech* 62: 291–314.

Poplack, Shana, and Sali Tagliamonte. 1991a. "There's No Tense like the Present: Verbal *-s* Inflection in Early Black English. In *The Emergence of Black English: Text and Commentary*, edited by Guy Bailey, Natalie Maynor, and Patricia Cukor-Avila, 275–324. Amsterdam: Benjamins.

———. 1991b. "African American English in the Diaspora: Evidence from Old-Line Nova Scotians." *Language Variation and Change* 3: 301–39.

———. 2001. *African American English in the Diaspora*. Malden, MA: Blackwell.

Rawick, George P. 1972–79. *The American Slave: A Composite Autobiography*. 19 vols. and Supplement. Westport, CT: Greenwood.

Rickford, John. 1991. "Representativeness and Reliability of the Ex-Slave Materials, with Special Reference to Wallace Quarterman's Recording and Transcript. In *The Emergence of Black English: Text and Commentary*, edited by Guy Bailey, Natalie Maynor, and Patricia Cukor-Avila, 191–212. Amsterdam: Benjamins.

———. 2006. "Down for the Count? The Creole Origins Hypothesis of AAVE at the Hands of the Ottawa Circle, and Their Supporters." *Journal of Pidgin and Creole Languages* 21: 97–155.

Schneider, Edgar W. 1983a. "The Origin of the Verbal *-s* in Black English." *American Speech* 58: 99–113.

———. 1983b. "The Diachronic Development of the Black English Perfective Auxiliary Phrase." *Journal of English Linguistics* 16: 55–64.

———. 1985. "Regional Variation in Nineteenth Century Black English in the American South." In *Papers from the 6th International Conference on Historical Linguistics*, edited by Jacek Fisiak, 467–87. Amsterdam and Poznan: John Benjamins and Adam Mickiewicz University.

————. 1989. *American Earlier Black English: Morphological and Syntactic Variables.* Tuscaloosa: University of Alabama Press.

————. 1997. "Earlier Black English Revisited." In *Language Variety in the South Revisited*, edited by Cynthia Bernstein, Thomas Nunally, and Robin Sabino, 35–50. Tuscaloosa: University of Alabama Press.

————. 2012. "Tracking the Evolution of Vernaculars: Corpus Linguistics and Earlier Southern U.S. Englishes." In *Corpus Linguistics and Variation in English: Theory and Description*, edited by Joybrato Mukherjee and Magnus Huber, 185–212. Amsterdam: Rodopi.

————. 2013. "Investigating Historical Variation and Change in Written Documents: New Perspectives." In *Handbook of Language Variation and Change*, 2nd ed., edited by J. K. Chambers and Natalie Schilling, 57–81. Oxford, UK: Blackwell.

Schneider, Edgar W., and Ulrich Miethaner. 2006. "When I Started to Using BLUR: Accounting for Unusual Verb Complementation Patterns in an Electronic Corpus of Earlier African American English." *Journal of English Linguistics* 34: 233–56.

Singler, John Victor. 2004. "Liberian Settler English: Morphology and Syntax." In *A Handbook of Varieties of English*, Vol. 2, *Morphology and Syntax*, edited by Bernd Kortmann et al., 879–97. Berlin: Mouton de Gruyter.

————. 2007a. "Samaná and Sinoe, Part I: Stalking the Vernacular." *Journal of Pidgin and Creole Languages* 22: 123–48.

————. 2007b. "Samaná and Sinoe, Part II: Provenance." *Journal of Pidgin and Creole Languages* 22: 309–46.

Stewart, William A. 1967. "Sociolinguistic Factors in the History of American Negro Dialects." *Florida Foreign Language Reporter* 5 (2): 11, 22, 24, 26, 30.

Van Herk, Gerard, and Shana Poplack. 2003. "Rewriting the Past: Bare Verbs in the Ottawa Repository of Early African American English Correspondence." *Journal of Pidgin and Creole Languages* 18: 231–66.

Van Herk, Gerard, and James A. Walker. 2005. "S Marks the Spot? Regional Variation and Early African American Correspondence." *Language Variation and Change* 17: 113–31.

Weldon, Tracey. 1994. "Variability in Negation in African American Vernacular English." *Language Variation and Change* 6: 359–97.

Winford, Donald. 1997. "On the Origins of African American Vernacular English—A Creolist Perspective. Part 1: The Sociohistorical Background." *Diachronica* 14: 305–44.

————. 1998. "On the Origins of African American Vernacular English—A Creolist Perspective. Part 2: Linguistic Features." *Diachronica* 15: 99–154.

————. 2003. *An Introduction to Contact Linguistics.* Malden, MA: Blackwell.

Wolfram, Walt. 1971. "Black–White Speech Differences." In *Black–White Speech Relationships*, edited by Walt Wolfram and Nona H. Clarke, 139–61. Washington, DC: Center for Applied Linguistics.

————. 1990. "Re-Examining Vernacular Black English." *Language* 66: 121–33.

————. 2008. "Urban African American Vernacular English: Morphology and Syntax." In *Varieties of English 2: The Americas and the Caribbean*, edited by Edgar W. Schneider, 510–33. Berlin: Mouton de Gruyter.

Wolfram, Walt, and Erik R. Thomas. 2002. *The Development of African American English.* Oxford: Blackwell.

CHAPTER 7

REGIONALITY IN THE DEVELOPMENT OF AFRICAN AMERICAN ENGLISH

WALT WOLFRAM AND MARY E. KOHN

7.1 INTRODUCTION

REGIONAL differentiation is one of the primitive factors in dialect differences and a natural starting point in the examination of language variation.[1] As is often the case for African American speech, however, the role of regionality in African American Language (AAL) has turned out to be controversial and open to debate. In fact, Wolfram (see Wolfram 2007, this volume) observes that the role of regional differentiation in AAL has often been misunderstood and misrepresented by sociolinguists, leading to one of the major sociolinguistic myths about AAL—The Homogeneity Myth. According to this myth, there is uniformity in AAL in the United States and in the African diaspora in which regionality is invariably trumped by ethnicity. In racialized, popular culture, it is often assumed that "all Black folks talk the same way," but there is also a more sophisticated version of the homogeneity assumption in which sociolinguists maintain that there is a uniform core in the vernacular speech of African Americans throughout the United States. As William Labov, arguably the most influential voice on AAL over the last half century, put it relatively early in his descriptive account of AAL:

> By the "Black English vernacular" we mean the relatively uniform dialect spoken by the majority of Black youth in most parts of the United States today, especially in the inner city areas of New York, Boston, Detroit, Philadelphia, Washington, Cleveland, Chicago, St. Louis, San Francisco, Los Angeles, and other urban centers. It is also spoken in most rural areas and used in the casual, intimate speech of many adults. (Labov 1972, xiii)

The uniformity hypothesis set forth by Labov and others (Fasold and Wolfram 1970; Wolfram and Fasold 1974) became an assumed sociolinguistic position—and part of the descriptive canon of AAL studies (see Labov 1998; Rickford 1999; Wolfram and Schilling-Estes 2006). Wolfram (2007), however, has suggested that the uniformity position overlooks and dismisses significant aspects of regional variation in AAL; he further contends that this position resulted from biased sampling in earlier AAL studies, authoritative entextualization by sociolinguists, and interpretive ethnocentrism by the influential pioneers of AAL descriptive studies.

Practically all of the formative, early studies of AAL were concentrated on non-southern metropolitan areas, notwithstanding the fact that the roots of contemporary AAL were established in the rural South (see Labov et al. 1968; Wolfram 1969; Legum et al. 1971; Fasold 1972; Labov 1972). In the history of AAL description, these studies set a precedent for the types of structures worthy of description in AAL while establishing an interpretive paradigm about the significance of these structures. The northern, urban context of AAL, however, is hardly representative of the full range of the AAL-speaking populations, particularly those of the rural South, where AAL was nurtured historically in quite localized settings.

Sociolinguists became fixated on a core, basilectal set of distinctive AAL structures, rather than the full range of structures found within and across representative communities, thus, obscuring the role that local dialect communities might play in the development of AAVE. Though linguists and sociolinguists would no doubt maintain that all dialects are of equal interest and value, they are hardly immune from "the exotic language syndrome," where varieties that are structurally and socially most different in terms of the linguist's previous experience would hold heightened descriptive intrigue. Accordingly, there has been a disproportionate descriptive focus in AAL on its most vernacular structures and those shared transregionally.

On a more racially sensitive level, it might be pointed out that the early descriptive studies that established the tradition of AAL inquiry were largely carried out by northern, White (male) linguists who would less likely be attuned to intra- and inter-community variation than those whose dialect sensitivities were developed and experienced within the communities themselves. Sociolinguists are not immune to the biracial socialization of American society that leads to overgeneralization and the "illusion of ethnic homogeneity" (Bonfiglio 2002, 62). Some linguists (see Spears 1999, 2008; Green 2002; Weldon 2004) have explicitly recognized the regional, temporal, and social heterogeneity of AAL, but this has often been trivialized, or even dismissed, in the supraregional assumption that assigns descriptive preference to structural features that are shared by different African American communities.

In this account, we examine the regional voices of AAL by comparing African American communities embedded in different dialect regions, with particular attention paid to the rural South. By considering a more diverse, regionally situated range of African American communities in the South and an age range of speakers to which we can apply the apparent-time assumption, we can see how space and time have played an essential role in the past and present development of AAL—and, perhaps, even project how regionality may play a role in its future development. Current studies of AAL certainly represent a much more diverse set of regional and social demographics than those examined in the early tradition of AAL research, particularly in the rural South (see Bailey 2001; Cukor-Avila 2001; Mallinson and Wolfram 2002; Wolfram and Thomas 2002; Wolfram 2003; Carpenter 2004, 2005; Childs and Mallinson 2004; Childs 2005; Mallinson 2006; Bloomquist 2009; Kohn and Farrington 2011; Yaeger-Dror and Thomas 2010). Furthermore, descriptive studies are now complemented by perceptual studies and experimentation that offer insight into the interaction of regional and ethnic variables in the delimitation of AAL (see Graff, Labov, and Harris 1986; Thomas 2002; Fridland, Bartlett, and Kreuz 2004; Thomas and Reaser 2004; Torbert 2004). Finally, there is an expanding body of ethnographic evidence on regionality, including observations by community participants themselves about the distribution of AAL over time and place (Childs and Mallinson 2006; Mallinson 2006; Wolfram 2007). These increasingly diverse and complementary data sets serve as an empirical foundation for re-examining the role of region in the development and contemporary status of AAL.

7.2 THE REGIONAL ALIGNMENT OF AAL

There are several possible configurations for the regional alignment of African American speech. To begin with, there may be accommodation to the generalized regional cohort variety by African Americans. This kind of accommodation involves sharing regionally distinctive features between African Americans and European Americans, ranging from limited, selective accommodation to widespread sharing that makes the speech of these groups indistinguishable to outsiders. Regional accommodation is not an all-or-nothing phenomenon and may be sensitive to differential social effect and linguistic level of organization. Accordingly, phonological accommodation, particularly vowels, may differ from morphosyntactic or lexical levels of language (Childs and Mallinson 2004, 2006; Childs 2005; Bloomquist 2009). And this accommodation may show differing degrees of alignment, from complete overlap to highly selective, symbolically significant partial accommodation. The accommodation of regional varieties shared by European Americans is clearly recognized within African American communities, as indicated by a prominent African American community leader from the foothills of Appalachia when she notes:

> They'd say, "Say 'honey chil'", because I would always—it's just a part of my language, 'honey child', because I talk just like the people at the foot of the Blue Ridge Mountain, with that kind of twang and that kind of thing, and so that was just a part of me. (quote from 70-year-old female in *Voices of North Carolina* [Hutcheson 2005])

Though such community observations may be couched in nontechnical, popular phrasing, they suggest that regionality is an integral part of experiencing dialect differences by African Americans, as it is with any other group.

By the same token, African Americans may experience language variation within the shared, ethnolinguistic features distinctive to African American communities—the so-called "common core" of AAL structures (Labov 1972; Wolfram and Fasold 1974; Rickford 1999; Green 2002). Some of these differences across diverse African American communities may be qualitative, in which a linguistic structure found in one region is different from another region, and some are quantitative, in that there are systematic differences in the relative frequency with which AAL-exclusive structures are used. Early in the description of AAL, regional differences were recognized such that Wolfram and Fasold (1974, 136) noted that the use of *v* for voiced *th* in medial and final position (e.g., *breave* for *breathe* or *brovuh* for *brother*) is "far more common in Atlantic Coast speech than further inland," a "difference in geographical location." Notwithstanding the long-standing concession of regional variation within AAL, it has generally taken a back seat to the description of features shared by different African American communities. Sociolinguists tend to assign footnote status to regional differences in their descriptions of AAL, but it cannot be assumed that such differences are lost on African American communities. Thus, an African American resident of Durham, North Carolina, who travels widely throughout the state, comments on regional differences within vernacular speech of residents from different areas:

> Inside the African American community, when you go from region to region there're really different voices and sounds. You can tell the difference between an African American who lives in Northeast [North Carolina] 'cause they say "skraight", which is not something you'd hear in Durham, or you'd hear in Winston-Salem, or you'd hear in Fayetteville, but if you hear "skraight" or "skreet", you know exactly where they came from. (quote from a 50- to 60-year-old female in *Voices of North Carolina* [Hutcheson 2005])

In this instance, the commentator is referring to a distinction in the use of a linguistic structure that is found exclusively among African Americans, noting that the structure is much more typical in some rural regions of the state than in urban regions. Differences in urban and rural speech and from region to region, thus, seem to be a natural dimension of recognized differences within and across African American communities.

In many respects, regionality in AAL cannot be separated from past and present language change and from other social factors that influence language variation within AAL. Accordingly, a complex set of intersecting factors needs to be considered in describing change over time and space in African American speech communities. Regionality is just one of these factors, but there is now emerging evidence to conclude that it has and continues to be an essential part of the development of AAL.

7.3 EMPIRICAL EVIDENCE FOR REGIONAL AAL

Our studies of small, rural African American communities in the southeastern United States over the past decade provide an ideal testing ground for the examination of regionality in AAL. To begin with, these communities represent quite disparate regional dialect contexts, ranging from the distinctive Outer Banks dialect of coastal North Carolina (Schilling-Estes and Wolfram 1997; Wolfram, Hazen, and Schilling-Estes 1999) to the dialects of southern Appalachia (Childs and Mallinson 2004; Childs 2005; Mallinson 2006; Wolfram 2013). In figure 7.1, we situate a number of African American communities examined by the North Carolina Language and Life Project (NCLLP) within the broader context of the regional dialects of North Carolina. In the comparison, a couple of African American communities in the Outer Banks region, Hyde County (Wolfram and Thomas 2002; Wolfram 2003) and Roanoke Island (Carpenter 2004, 2005); a community in the coastal plain, Princeville (D'Andrea 2005; Rowe 2005); and two communities in the mountains of Appalachia in the western part of the state, Beech Bottom (Mallinson and Wolfram 2002) and Texana (Childs and Mallinson 2004; Childs 2005; Mallinson 2006) are examined in order to represent distinct regional dialect settings for AAL. We consider a couple of representative consonantal and morphosyntactic variables in this section and devote a separate section to vowels given their prominent role in American English regional variation. The regional locations where we have conducted research in North Carolina are given in figure 7.1.

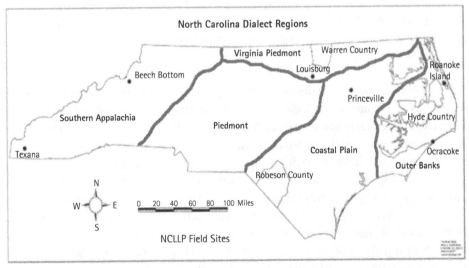

FIGURE 7.1 Regional contexts of AAL described in North Carolina by the staff of North Carolina Language and Life Project (NCLLP).

For comparison, figures for two variables in these disparate settings are given, one for postvocalic r-lessness (figure 7.2), as in the pronunciation of *fear* as *fea'* or *fourteen* as *fou'teen*, and one for the absence of third person singular *–s* inflection (figure 7.3), as in *She go* for *She goes*. Three different African American communities (Hyde County, Roanoke Island, and Princeville) in the eastern part of the state are compared with a neighboring Outer Banks European American English community (Outer Banks EAE), and two African American communities in Appalachia (Texana, Beech Bottom) are compared with a European American Appalachian English variety (Appalachian EAE). For each community, three different age groups of speakers are included in order to give an indication of language change for these features over apparent time. The graphs given here are summaries; more detailed quantitative and statistical analyses are provided in the sources cited above.

First, consider the case of postvocalic r-lessness in figure 7.2. The graph represents the relative frequency of *r* loss in terms of potential cases where *r* might have been vocalized (e.g., *fea'* for *fear*). The different communities of African Americans obviously indicate r-lessness at quite different frequency levels. The two African American Appalachian communities (Texana, Beech Bottom) have little r-lessness, much like the European American Appalachian community with which they are compared. Furthermore, this seems to be a relatively stable pattern, showing little change among the different generational groups. The r-lessness pattern in the communities in

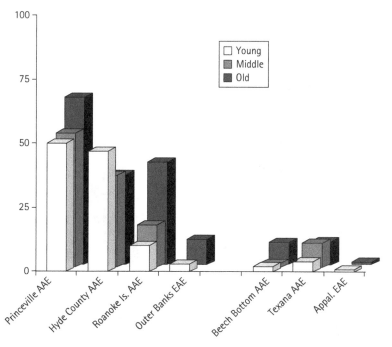

FIGURE 7.2 Comparison of postvocalic r-lessness in regionally situated communities in North Carolina.

eastern North Carolina shows much more variability linked to place and generation. Princeville, situated in the coastal plain region that was historically r-less, shows the highest incidence of r-lessness, while Hyde County and Roanoke Island, situated in a traditionally r-full dialect region, the Outer Banks of North Carolina (Wolfram and Thomas 2002), vary considerably.

We also see differences over apparent time in terms of regional alignment. For example, the Roanoke community, a small community of approximately 150 African Americans (Carpenter 2005) surrounded by the dominant European American community, shows a reduction in the level of r-lessness over time, thus indicating more regional alignment with the local r-full pattern for this variable. At the same time, in Hyde County to the south, a stable population of more than two thousand African Americans comprising 35 percent of the overall population of the county reveals a significant increase in r-lessness among the younger generation of speakers, thus, showing divergence from the regional norm over time.

Now consider figure 7.3, which summarizes the incidence of third person inflection –s absence in structures such as *She like school* or *The dog always like to eat*. The pattern of –s absence is one of the structures considered to be part of the common-core structures of AAL (cf. Labov 1972; Rickford 1999; Green 2002).

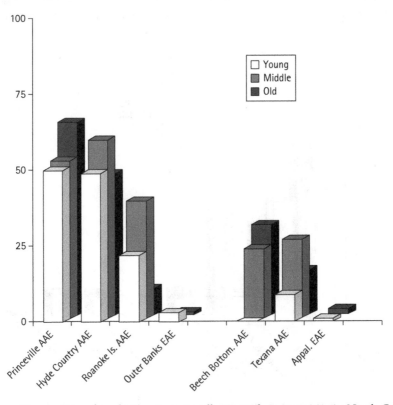

FIGURE 7.3 Comparison of –s absence in regionally situated communities in North Carolina.

Again, we see a significant difference in the relative incidence of –s absence based on locale and generation. The Black Appalachian communities of Texana and Beech Bottom obviously do not share this structural pattern to the same degree with the other African American communities; in fact, they tend to align with the regional white community, a finding confirmed by the examination of southern highland regional traits such as the use of –s on third-person plural forms in *The dogs barks* (Mallinson and Wolfram 2002; Childs and Mallinson 2004) and the use of /ai/ ungliding before voiceless consonants (e.g., *raht* for *right*). As with r-lessness, the communities in coastal North Carolina (Princeville, Hyde County, Roanoke Island) show more internal and external variability for verbal –s absence. Though quantitative, there are significant differences in the frequency levels of –s absence. Thus, we saw that the frequency of third-person singular –s absence ranged from more than 75 percent to less than 5 percent.

Finally, we should note that there are cases in which common-core features and regional features may converge, as in the case of r-lessness. That is, the linguistic trait is characteristic both of AAL and of some adjacent regional European American varieties in which AAL exists. While r-lessness is commonly cited as a core trait of AAL (Labov 1972; Wolfram and Fasold 1974; Rickford 1999; Green 2002), it is obviously affected by regional context. In fact, the re-inspection of some of the early studies of AAL reveals that this was evident in the initial studies of AAL. For example, Labov et al.'s (1968) study of AAL in New York City, a regional r-less context, shows levels of r-lessness that were nearly categorical, whereas Wolfram's study of AAL in Detroit, an r-full area, shows levels between 60–70 percent for working-class African American speakers (Wolfram 1969). The results of such comparisons provide evidence for concluding that AAL may show significant regional and generational variability from community to community, both in terms of its accommodation to the overarching regional dialect and in terms of the distribution of features exclusive to the African American communities within these regional settings.

In addition to our objective studies of regional AAL, there are some recent perceptual experiments to tease out the intersection of ethnicity and regionality in dialect identification (Wolfram and Thomas 2002; Thomas and Reaser 2004; Torbert 2004; Childs and Mallinson 2006). Listeners from outside the region consistently misjudge the ethnic identity of African Americans from Appalachia and the Outer Banks (Wolfram and Thomas 2002; Childs and Mallinson 2006), showing that regionality may trump ethnicity in listener perception of African Americans in some settings. These perceptual studies support the conclusion that regional features can take on primary indexicality (Silverstein 2003) for African Americans, in which speakers are primarily identified as being from the coast or the mountains vis-à-vis being African American. The evidence from speaker identification experiments, along with the cross-generational sociolinguistic analysis of dialect features, supports the contention that both earlier varieties of English spoken by African Americans and contemporary varieties of AAL may indeed be quite regionalized.

In asserting the role of regionality in AAL, we do not mean to say that linguists have categorically denied this dimension of variation. Lisa Green, for example, notes:

> There are regional differences that will distinguish varieties of AAL spoken in the United States. For example, although speakers of AAL in Louisiana and Texas use very similar syntactic patterns, their vowel systems may differ. Speakers of AAL in areas in Pennsylvania also share similar syntactic patterns with speakers in Louisiana and Texas; however, speakers in areas in Pennsylvania are not likely to share some of the patterns that the Louisiana and Texas speakers share with other speakers of southern regions. (2002, 1)

Though Green (2002) acknowledges regionality, this tends to be the exception rather than the rule in AAL descriptions. By the same token, the acknowledgment lacks specific descriptive detail about the nature of regional differences in AAL and thus is a minor qualification. Our empirical inquiry here suggests that region is a more significant variable than has been admitted, and that it cannot be ignored as a factor in describing the variable nature of AAL.

7.4 REGIONAL VOWELS IN AAL

The following comment by an African American teenager illustrates how the implicit linguistic knowledge of community members can supersede the knowledge of academic experts:

> I can tell . . . You from Durham, right? Yeah, I can tell because of the way you talk, boy. You like, "you like to [stədi] (study)."

In less than ten minutes, this teen was able to identify the location of the peer's home, justifying this identification by imitating a distinctive vocalic feature, the raised and fronted version of /ʌ/ found in the speech of several Frank Porter Graham (FPG) participants from Durham, North Carolina (Kohn and Farrington 2011). Until recently, the lack of detailed acoustic studies has left linguists with little empirical evidence to discuss the regional distribution of AAL vowels. Although Labov (1991, 1994, 2001) stated that African Americans resist participation in local sound changes, empirical evidence suggests that this is not always the case, particularly in enclave communities (Mallinson and Wolfram 2002; Wolfram and Thomas 2002; Childs and Mallinson 2004; Childs 2005; Yaeger-Dror and Thomas 2010). Further, participation in local European American sound changes is not the only source for regional differences in AAL vowels. Older regional variants may be retained, or natural diachronic processes can lead to independent vowel innovations.

The lack of vocalic accommodation to the Northern Cities Shift (NCS) has often been a prime source of evidence used to reinforce the homogeneity myth of AAL. A number of research studies indicate that AAL did not participate in regional vowel shifts such as the NCS (Labov 1991, 1994; Gordon 2000). Other studies indicate that some aspects of the Southern Vowel Shift (SVS) (Bailey and Thomas 1998) and other regional changes such as the merger of /a/ and /ɔ/ and /ai/ glide weakening in prevoiceless phonetic contexts were not accommodated in African American communities (Bernstein 1993). Ironically, these observations contrast starkly with the earliest positions held by dialectologists. Some of the earliest researchers who studied AAL vowels, including Kurath and McDavid (1961) and Williamson (1968), assumed that once class and education levels were controlled AAL vowels were identical to the regional vowels of European Americans English (EAE).

Further analysis reveals that both positions are oversimplifications. For example, in an examination of the African American speakers in the *Linguistic Atlas of the Middle and South Atlantic States* (*LAMSAS*), Dorrill (1986) identifies that while AAL was distinct from local EAE, resisting back vowel fronting and retaining monophthongal variants of /e/ and /o/, it also showed similarities including allophonically conditioned /ai/ glide weakening. Similar results emerge from Bailey and Thomas's (1998) analysis of ex-slave recordings which demonstrates shared innovations among European American Southern English (EASE) and AAL including /ai/ glide weakening, the *pin/pen* merger, and several pre-liquid mergers in word pairs such as *still/steal* and *sell/sale*.

In addition to evidence provided by these early studies, the existence of relic forms in some African American speech communities indicates that regional influences impact AAL. The decline of diphthongal schwa (as in *boid* for *bird*) in Louisiana, for example, lagged in AAL compared to other varieties in the region (Strand, Wroblewski, and Good 2010). Evidence from New York City English indicates that even as the distinctive raised /ɔ/ variant, found in words like *coffee* and *dog*, is declining among local European American speakers, young African Americans continue to use this form (Becker 2009; Coggshall and Becker 2010). This feature differentiates New York City AAL from southern varieties of AAL, just as diphthongal schwa is a regionally distinct feature of Louisiana AAL.

Studies of enclave communities in the Appalachian and tidewater regions of North Carolina identify a range of regional vocalic features in local AAL varieties, although the extent of accommodation to regional EAE varies from almost indistinguishable vowel spaces in Beech Bottom, to mixed alignment in the communities of Texana (Childs and Mallinson 2004; Childs 2005); Hyde County (Wolfram and Thomas 2002); Roanoke (Childs, Mallinson, and Carpenter 2010); and Ocracoke (Wolfram, Hazen, and Tamburro 1997). Evidence for accommodation to local varieties includes the fronting of /o/ and /u/ in Hyde, Roanoke, Beech Bottom, and Texana. As AAL typically retains back vowels (Thomas 2007), back-vowel fronting in these enclave communities emerges as a local distinction. Older African Americans in these communities also use local variants of /ai/ gliding (Childs, Mallinson, and Carpenter 2010). Although the regional "hoi toid" diphthong variants are not as common in the speech of younger African Americans, the local /ai/ variant in Beech Bottom shows no signs of dying out across generations. While younger generations in some of these enclave communities appear to orient more toward national AAL norms, some features continue to make local AAL regionally distinct.

Increased interest in regional vocalic distinctions of AAL has resulted in a more extensive sample of cities and rural communities in the northern and southern United States. Like previous work in enclave communities, these studies indicate a range of accommodation to the predominate variety, from almost complete accommodation to only partial alignment.

Fridland (2003a, b) and Fridland and Bartlett (2006) identify a host of SVS features in the AAL of Memphis, Tennessee, including reversal of /eɪ/ and /ɛ/ nuclei, back vowel fronting, and reduced /ai/ glides before voiceless obstruents. Evidence for the SVS in the nuclei of /eɪ/ and /ɛ/ among African Americans has also been found in the suburbs of Atlanta, Georgia (Andres and Votta 2010), and the research triangle in North Carolina (Kohn and Farrington 2011). Looking at front vowels and /ai/ in Statesville, North Carolina, Holt (2011) concludes that, except for duration and trajectory qualities for /ɪ/ and /ɛ/, AAL and the local dialect are statistically indistinguishable. Urban/rural distinctions also contribute to regional variation in AAL, as illustrated in Dodsworth and Kohn's (2009) comparison of the AAL of Raleigh, North Carolina, to that of rural Warren County, North Carolina. Results indicate that SVS patterns are more advanced among rural African Americans than among urban African Americans.

Although the emergence of regional norms may be expected in the southern United States where African Americans and European Americans have lived in biracial communities for centuries, partial accommodation to regional norms may also be found outside of the South. Jones (2003) finds that some middle-class African American females in Lansing, Michigan, are participating in /æ/ raising, in line with the NCS. African Americans with extensive European American contacts in Milwaukee, Wisconsin, were also found to lower the nucleus of /ɛ/, following the NCS (Purnell 2010). Several studies identify back vowel fronting among African Americans in Columbus, Ohio (Thomas [1989] 1993; Durian, Dodsworth, and Schumacher 2010). In Pittsburgh, Pennsylvania, while local African Americans do not participate in the socially salient /au/ monophthongization (as in *dahntahn* for *downtown*), Eberhardt (2008, 2009) presents evidence of low back vowel mergers between /a/ and /ɔ/. As AAL generally maintains this phonemic distinction (Thomas 2007), Eberhardt concludes that this finding indicates alignment with the local variety. Mixed alignment predominates in most analyses of AAL regional vocalic accommodation, with variables such as social contact with European Americans (Purnell 2010), levels of integration in the schools (Deser 1990; Kohn and Farrington 2013), social stratification (Jones 2003), history of race relations, as well as the social salience of the features (Eberhardt 2009), all potentially playing a role.

Regional differences among vowels in AAL also emerge independently of local EAE. For example, pre-rhotic front vowel centralization, commonly depicted orthographically with two RRs, as in *thurr* for *there*, is an iconic St. Louis AAL feature (Blake and Shousterman 2010). Found in Memphis, Tennessee, as well (Pollock and Berni 1996; Hinton and Pollock 2000), this feature appears to have emerged in AAL in the mid-twentieth century.

Unsurprisingly, the extent to which individuals identify with a region may also influence the frequency and extent of local variants in speech. For example, in a resampling study of Detroit, Nguyen (2006) finds voice-conditioned allophony for /ai/ glide weakening (that is, /ai/ glide weakening is strongly favored when the following phonetic context is voiced) in both her data set and in Wolfram's 1969 sample. This contradicts findings from Anderson's (2003) Detroit study where /ai/ glide weakening also appeared in pre-voiceless conditions. Nguyen attributes this difference to regional attitudes as individuals from Anderson's (2003) study indicated a cultural affinity with the South. Fridland (2003b) similarly cites the importance of southern identity in the expansion of /ai/ glide weakening among African Americans in Memphis. One African American female from Hickory, North Carolina, specifically discusses the regional significance of /ai/ glide weakening in pre-voiceless environments:

> When you go anywhere else they automatically know you're from the South . . . and
> we got all the little Ebonics stuff that we be using . . . but I mean like [ɹaːs] ('rice')
> I know I say [ɹaːs] . . . I'm from down here. You gotta accommodate me.

Recent research into regional variations among AAL vowel systems illustrates the important role of regional features in AAL vowels. First, researchers should not assume that a failure of African Americans to participate in local EAE vowel changes indicates a lack of regional differences as a whole. Even as EAE changes, older vowel productions may continue to mark AAL as regionally distinct from other regional varieties of AAL (Coggshall and Becker 2010), and regional differences unique to AAL are also emerging (Blake and Shousterman 2010). Second, AAL is not impervious to regional vowel changes. Selective participation appears to be the norm, rather than the exception. Third, it should be noted that the status of accommodation is dynamic and may change over time. For example, there is now evidence that some African American residents in some northern cities are accommodating to parts of the NCS (Jones 2003; Jones and Preston 2006) and perhaps will show more participation in the future. Similarly, Henderson (1996) found that, although a minority pattern, some middle-class Africans Americans participate in the regionally distinctive Philadelphia short *a* pattern, notwithstanding Graff et al.'s (1986) finding that this vowel has indexical status as a "white vowel." The likelihood of accommodation to regional European American features depends on a host of demographic, social, and psychological factors, potentially including the importance of regional identity to the individual. Explicit community member awareness of regional distinctions indicates that regional vowel variation is an important part of AAL.

7.5 THE INTERACTION OF TIME AND SPACE

The relationship between regionality and temporality in AAL, like any other variety, can be quite complex and interactional. As Rickford (1987, 1999) points out, convergence and divergence between AAL and cohort European American English can take place at different points in time. Research on small, rural southern communities empirically supports the conclusion that there may be different trajectories of change and regional accommodation at different times and in different places. The empirical evidence from apparent-time studies reveals at least three different trajectories of change, as indicated in figures 7.4a–c. These include one (7.4a) that shows strong regional alignment at an earlier period of time and subsequent divergence, one (7.4b) that shows more recent regional alignment, and one that shows a curvilinear trajectory that includes both periods of regional alignment and divergence over time (7.4c). The trajectory lines represent

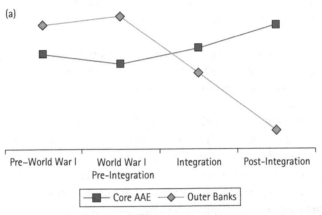

FIGURE 7.4a Regional reduction and AAE intensification: The Hyde County (Eastern NC) trajectory.

Source: Adapted from Wolfram and Thomas 2002, 200.

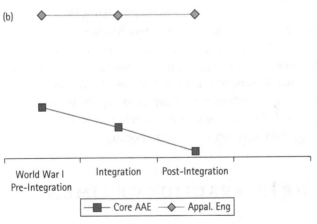

FIGURE 7.4b AAE reduction and regional dialect maintenance: The Beech Bottom trajectory (Appalachian NC).

Source: Mallinson and Wolfram 2002.

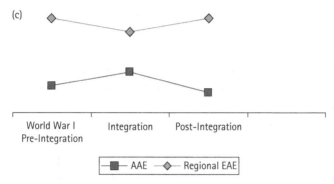

FIGURE 7.4c The curvilinear model: Texana (Appalachian NC)/Roanoke Island (Eastern NC).

an approximation of usage levels for the inventory of features examined, rather than a precise, composite measurement of the actual linguistic features found in analyses such as Wolfram and Thomas (2002), Wolfram (2003), Mallinson and Wolfram (2002), Childs and Mallinson (2004), Carpenter (2004, 2005), D'Andrea (2005), and Rowe (2005). Core AAL refers to features that have traditionally been associated with vernacular varieties of AAL, including inflectional –s absence, copula absence, prevocalic syllable-final cluster reduction, and so forth. Regional varieties used in the comparison (Outer Banks English, Appalachian English, regional European American English) refer to local dialect varieties typically associated with the European American population, though our analysis indicates that this ethnolinguistic demarcation is not completely justified. The labels on the *x* axis refer to different generations of speakers based on significant historical events; these include speakers born before World War I (for Hyde County), those born following World War I but before racial integration of public schools (pre-1960), those who attended school while integration was being implemented (1960–1975), and those who attended school following integration (after 1975).

There are obviously a variety of patterns of regional accommodation and different explanations for the patterns of alignment that emerge over time. For example, the Appalachian African American community in Beech Bottom is a very small, receding community that has been quite removed from other African American communities geographically and socially over the past half-century. Furthermore, the few remaining members of the community self-report mixed ethnicity rather than African American identity, even though the older residents attended a segregated school established for African Americans in the area (Mallinson 2004). Perhaps more importantly, residents show a value orientation that aligns with the surrounding European American culture (Mallinson and Wolfram 2002; Mallinson 2004). In this context, regional convergence seems quite understandable, and speakers are losing remnants of AAL as they more fully accommodate the Appalachian English features of the European American dialect community.

In contrast, Hyde County has a long-term African American community of more than two thousand people that was once highly insulated from outside influences. At present, the younger community members indicate increasing social contact with external African American communities, and many youth reveal a kind of exocentric (i.e., community-external) value orientation that accommodates urban cultural norms (Wolfram and Thomas 2002). In this context, once-entrenched regional dialect features of the Outer Banks dialect from almost three centuries of coexistence between African Americans and European Americans are rapidly receding and linguistic features associated with urban AAL are intensifying.

The cases of Texana and Roanoke Island, which show curvilinear paths of change, are somewhat more complicated by internal social divisions, particularly with respect to external values and norms. Thus, some middle-aged and younger speakers show shifts toward or away from AAL and the neighboring European American variety that correlate with endocentric (i.e., community-internal) and exocentric value orientations (Carpenter 2004, 2005; Childs and Mallinson 2004, 2006; Carpenter and Hilliard 2005; Mallinson 2006). Both of these communities are relatively small but have differential patterns of external contact that provide choices between traditional rural and encroaching urban value orientations.

We have already noted that the early, canonical position on the transregional status of AAL was derived from a northern, urban vernacular sampling bias focused on transplant southern communities from different regions of the South. In fact, at the time of the pioneering studies of AAL in the North, the majority of middle-aged and older speakers in many northern cities were still first-generation southern in-migrants, and it was often difficult to find enough older, lifetime residents in these urban contexts for sociolinguistic interviews (see Labov et al. 1968; Wolfram 1969). The vernacular was clearly aligned with southern dialects, so regionality was obviously in play—just not the regionality of the cohort northern metropolitan norms. In studies over the next couple of decades, it did not appear that African Americans in these northern metropolitan contexts accommodated to cohort vowel norms (Graff et al. 1986). But change over time might take place differently in an urban northern transplant community than in a long-standing small southern rural community, and regional accommodation can change over time as well. We cannot necessarily assume that that lack of local dialect accommodation suggested in Graff et al. (1986) will persist as a norm. Indeed, as indicated in the discussion of vowel alignment, there is emerging evidence that some social groups of African Americans in the North are now accommodating local vowel norms in northern metropolitan areas (Jones 2003; Jones and Preston 2006).

Studies of AAL change in apparent time and real time show that a number of historical, demographic, and social factors need to be considered in explaining different trajectories of change and regional alignment over time. Factors include the regional setting, the size of the community, macro- and micro-sociohistorical events, patterns of contact with adjacent European American communities and with external African American communities, intra-community social divisions, and cultural values and ideologies. The nature of linguistic variables is also a factor; different linguistic variables may follow diverse paths of change based on their linguistic composition and their indexical status within the community.

7.6 CONCLUSION

An authentic understanding of AAL variation can neither overlook nor underestimate the role of region in accounting for differences across AAL communities. Accommodation to overarching regional traits that are shared with cohort European American communities as well as regional differences within the linguistic traits exclusive to the African American communities need to be recognized in AAL dialect differentiation. Furthermore, there are different constellations of these traits that may be involved in the regional and social construction of AAL. Regional alignment is sensitive to time and space in AAL, and it will no doubt continue to shift in the future development of AAL as well. In the descriptive focus on AAL over the past half-century, regionality has not taken its rightful place at the sociolinguistic table; it is time for regionality to receive the same portion as other variables in the study of past, present, and future trends of development in AAL.

NOTE

1. Support from NSF grants BCS-0843865, BCS-0544744, BCS-0236838, and BCS-9910224 for research reported here is gratefully acknowledged. Special thanks to Charlie Farrington and Robin Dodsworth for commenting on a draft of this chapter, as well as the editors of the *Handbook*.

REFERENCES

Anderson, Bridget L. 2003. "An Acoustic Study of Southeastern Michigan Appalachian and African American Southern Migrant Vowel Systems." PhD diss., University of Michigan.

Andres, Claire, and Rachel Votta. 2010. "African American Vernacular English: Vowel Phonology in a Georgia Community." In *African American English Speakers and their Participation in Local Sound Changes: A Comparative Study*, edited by Malcah Yaeger-Dror and Erik R. Thomas, 75–100. Publication of the American Dialect Society. Durham, NC: Duke University Press.

Bailey, Guy. 2001. "The Relationship between African American Vernacular English and White Vernaculars in the American South: A Sociocultural History and Some Phonological Evidence." In *Sociocultural and Historical Contexts of African American English*, edited by Sonja L. Lanehart, 53–92. Philadelphia: John Benjamins.

Bailey, Guy, and Erik R. Thomas. 1998. "Some Aspects of African-American Vernacular English Phonology." In *African American English: Structure, History and Use*, edited by Salikoko S. Mufwene, John Rickford, John Baugh, and Guy Bailey, 85–109. London: Routledge.

Becker, Kara. 2009. "/r/ and the Construction of a Place Identity on New York City's Lower East Side." *Journal of Sociolinguistics* 13 (5): 634–58.

Bernstein, Cynthia. 1993. "Measuring Social Causes of Phonological Variables." *American Speech* 68: 227–40.

Blake, Renée, and Cara Shousterman. 2010. "Diachrony and AAE: St. Louis, Hip-Hop, and Sound Change outside of the Mainstream." *Journal of English Linguistics* 38 (3): 230–47.

Bloomquist, Jennifer. 2009. "Dialect Differences in Central Pennsylvania: Regional Dialect Use and Adaption by African Americans in the Lower Susquehanna Valley." *American Speech* 84: 27–47

Bonfiglio, Thomas P. 2002. *Race and the Rise of Standard American*. Mouton: DeGruyter.

Carpenter, Jeannine. 2004. "The Lost Community of the Outer Banks: African American Speech on Roanoke Island." Master's thesis, North Carolina State University.

———. 2005. "The Invisible Community of the Lost Colony: African American English on Roanoke Island." *American Speech* 80 (2): 27–56.

Carpenter, Jeanine, and Sarah Hilliard. 2004. "Shifting Parameters of Individual and Group Variation: African American English on Roanoke Island." *Journal of English Linguistics* 33 (2): 161–84.

Childs, Rebecca L. 2005. "Investigating the Local Construction of Identity: Sociophonetic Variation in Smoky Mountain African American Speech." PhD diss., University of Georgia.

Childs, Becky, and Christine Mallinson. 2004. "African American English in Appalachia: Dialect Accommodation and Substrate Influence." *English World-Wide* 25 (2): 7–50.

———. 2006. "The Significance of Lexical Items in the Construction of Ethnolinguistic Identity: A Case Study of Adolescent Spoken and Online Language." *American Speech* 81: 3–30.

Childs, Becky, Christine Mallinson, and Jeannine Carpenter. 2010. "Vowel Phonology and Ethnicity in North Carolina." In *African American English Speakers and their Participation in Local Sound Changes: A Comparative Study*, edited by Malcah Yaeger-Dror and Erik R. Thomas, 23–47. Publication of the American Dialect Society 94. Durham, NC: Duke University Press.

Coggshall, Elizabeth, and Kara Becker. 2010. "The Vowel Phonologies of African American and White New York City Residents." In *African American English Speakers and their Participation in Local Sound Changes: A Comparative Study*, edited by Malcah Yaeger-Dror and Erik R. Thomas, 101–28. Publication of the American Dialect Society 94. Durham, NC: Duke University Press.

Cukor-Avila, Patricia. 2001. "Co-Existing Grammars: The Relationship between the Evolution of African American and Southern White Vernacular English in the South." In *Sociocultural and Historical Contexts of African American English*, edited by Sonja L. Lanehart, 93–128. Philadelphia: John Benjamins.

D'Andrea, Kristy D. 2005. "African American English in Princeville, NC: Looking at Dialect Change through the Feature of r-lessness." Paper presented at American Dialect Society Annual Meeting, Oakland, California, January 6–9.

Deser, Toni. 1990. "Dialect Transmission and Variation: An Acoustic Analysis of Vowels in Six Urban Detroit Families." PhD diss., Boston University.

Dodsworth, Robin, and Mary Kohn. 2009. "Urban and Rural African American English Vowels in North Carolina: A Supraregional Shift and Regional Accommodation." Paper presented at New Ways of Analyzing Variation 38, Ottawa, October 22–25.

Dorrill, George T. 1986. *Black and White Speech in the Southern United States: Evidence from the Linguistic Atlas of the Middle and South Atlantic States*. Bamberger Beiträge zur Englischen Sprachwissenschaft 19. New York: Peter Lang.

Durian, David, Robin Dodsworth, and Jennifer Schumacher. 2010. "Convergence in Urban Blue Collar Columbus AAVE and EAE Vowel Systems." In *African American English Speakers and their Participation in Local Sound Changes: A Comparative Study*, edited by Malcah Yaeger-Dror and Erik R. Thomas, 161–90. Publication of the American Dialect Society 94. Durham, NC: Duke University Press.

Eberhardt, Maeve. 2008. "The Low-Back Merger in the Steel City: African American English and Pittsburgh Speech." *American Speech* 83 (3): 284–311.

———. 2009. "Identities and Local Speech in Pittsburgh: A Study of Regional African American English." PhD diss., University of Pittsburgh.

Fasold, Ralph W. 1972. *Tense Marking in Black English: A Linguistic and Social Analysis.* Arlington, VA: Center for Applied Linguistics.

Fasold, Ralph W., and Walt Wolfram. 1970. "Some Linguistic Features of Negro Dialect." In *Teaching Standard English in the Inner City*, edited by Ralph W. Fasold and Roger W. Shuy, 41–86. Washington, DC: Center for Applied Linguistics.

Fridland, Valerie. 2003a. "Network Strength and the Realization of the Southern Vowel Shift among African-Americans in Memphis, TN." *American Speech* 78 (1): 3–30.

———. 2003b. "'Tie, Tied and Tight': The Expansion of /ai/ Monophthongization in African-American and European-American Speech in Memphis, Tennessee." *Journal of Sociolinguistics* 7 (3): 279–98.

Fridland, Valerie, and Kathy Bartlett. 2006. "The Social and Linguistic Conditioning of Back Vowel Fronting across Ethnic Groups in Memphis, Tennessee." *English Language and Linguistics* 10: 1–22.

Fridland, Valerie, Kathryn Bartlett, and Roger Kreuz. 2004. "Do You Hear What I Hear? Experimental Measurement of the Perceptual Salience of Acoustically Manipulated Vowel Variants by Southern Speakers in Memphis, TN." *Language Variation and Change* 16: 1–16.

Gordon, Matthew. 2000. "Phonological Correlates of Ethnic Identity: Evidence of Divergence?" *American Speech.* 75 (2): 115–36.

Graff, David, William Labov, and Wendell A. Harris. 1986. "Testing Listeners' Reactions to Phonological Markers of Ethnic Identity: A New Method for Sociolinguistic Research." In *Diversity and Diachrony*, edited by David Sankoff, 45–58. Philadelphia: John Benjamins.

Green, Lisa J. 2002. *African American English: A Linguistic Introduction*. New York: Cambridge University Press.

Henderson, Anita. 1996. "The Short 'a' Pattern of Philadelphia among African American Speakers." In *(N)WAVES and MEANS: A Selection of Papers from NWAV 24*, edited by Miriam Meyerhoff, 127–40. University of Pennsylvania Working Papers in Linguistics 3.1.

Hinton, Linette N., and Karen E. Pollock. 2000. "Regional Variations in the Phonological Characteristics of African American Vernacular English." *World Englishes* 19 (1): 59–71.

Holt, Yolanda. 2011. "A Cross Generational Dialect Study in Western North Carolina." PhD diss., The Ohio State University.

Hutcheson, Neal, producer. 2005. *Voices of North Carolina*. Raleigh: North Carolina Language and Life Project.

Jones, Jamila. 2003. "African Americans in Lansing and the Northern Cities Vowel Shift." PhD diss., Michigan State University.

Jones, Jamila, and Dennis Preston. 2006. "AAE and Identity: Constructing and Deploying Linguistic Resources." Journal of African Language Learning and Teaching: Festschrift for David Dwyer. Special issue, *Journal of African Language Learning and Teaching*. Available at: https://www.msu.edu/~preston/AAE%20and%20Identity.pdf.

Kohn, Mary, and Charlie Farrington. 2011. "The Socio-Regional Distribution of African American Vowel Systems in Piedmont, North Carolina." Paper presented at NWAV 40: New Ways of Analyzing Language Variation, Washington, DC, October 27–30.

———. 2013. "A Tale of Two Cities: Community Density and African American English Vowels." *Penn Working Papers in Linguistics* 19 (2): 101–10.

Kurath, Hans, and Raven I. McDavid, Jr. 1961. *The Pronunciation of English in the Atlantic States*. Ann Arbor: University of Michigan Press.

Labov, William. 1972. *Language in the Inner City: Studies in the Black English Vernacular*. Philadelphia: University of Pennsylvania Press.

———. 1991. "The Three Dialects of English." In *New Ways of Analyzing Variation*, edited by Penelope Eckert, 1–44. New York: Academic.

———. 1994. *Principles of Linguistic Change: Internal Factors*. Malden, MA: Blackwell.

———. 1998. "Coexistent Systems in African-American Vernacular English." In *African American English: Structure, History and Use*, edited by Salikoko S. Mufwene, John R. Rickford, Guy Bailey, and John Baugh, 110–53. London: Routledge.

———. 2001. *Principles of Linguistic Change: Social Factors*. Malden, MA: Blackwell.

Labov, William, Paul Cohen, Clarence Robins, and John Lewis. 1968. *A Study of the Non-Standard English of Negro and Puerto Rican Speakers in New York City*. Final Report, Research Project 3288. Washington, DC: United States Office of Education.

Legum, Stanley E., Carole Pfaff, Gene Tinnie, and Michael Nichols. 1971. *The Speech of Young Black Children in Los Angeles*. Inglewood, CA: Southwest Regional Laboratory.

Mallinson, Christine. 2004. "The Construction of Ethnolinguistic Groups: A Sociolinguistic Case Study." In *Linguistic Diversity in the South: Changing Codes, Practices and Ideology*, edited by Margaret Bender, 66–79. Athens: University of Georgia Press.

———. 2006. "The Dynamic Construction of Race, Class, and Gender through Linguistic Practic among Women in a Black Appalachian Community." PhD diss., North Carolina State University.

Mallinson, Christine, and Walt Wolfram. 2002. "Dialect Accommodation in a Bi-Ethnic Mountain Enclave Community: More Evidence on the Development of African American Vernacular English." *Language in Society* 31: 743–75.

Nguyen, Jennifer. 2006. "The Changing Social and Linguistic Orientation of the African American Middle Class." PhD diss., University of Michigan.

Pollock, Karen E., and Mary C. Berni. 1996. "Vocalic and Postvocalic /r/ in African American Memphians." Paper presented at New Ways of Analyzing Variation 25, Las Vegas, Nevada, October 19–21.

Purnell, Thomas. 2010. "The Vowel Phonology of Urban Southeastern Wisconsin." In *African American English Speakers and their Participation in Local Sound Changes: A Comparative Study*, edited by Malcah Yaeger-Dror and Erik R. Thomas, 191–217. Publication of the American Dialect Society 94. Durham, NC: Duke University Press.

Rickford, John R. 1987. "Are Black and White Vernaculars Diverging?" *American Speech* 62: 55–62.

———. 1999. *African American Vernacular English: Features, Evolution, and Educational Implications*. Malden, MA: Blackwell.

Rowe, Ryan D. 2005. "The Development of African American English in the Oldest Black Town in America: -S Absence in Princeville, North Carolina." Master's thesis, North Carolina State University.

Schilling-Estes, Natalie, and Walt Wolfram. 1997. "Symbolic Identity and Language Change: A Comparative Analysis of Post-Insular /ay/ and /aw/." *Penn Working Papers in Linguistics* 4: 83–109.

Silverstein, Michael. 2003. "Indexical Order and the Dialectics of Sociolinguistic Life." *Language and Communication* 23: 193–229.

Spears, Arthur K. 1999. "Race and Ideology: An Introduction." In *Race and Ideology: Language, Symbolism, and Popular Culture*, edited by Arthur K. Spears, 11–58. Detroit: Wayne State University Press.

———. 2008. "Pidgins/Creoles and African American English." In *The Handbook of Pidgin and Creole Studies*, edited by Silvia Kouwenberg and John Victor Singler, 512–42. Oxford, UK: Wiley-Blackwell.

Strand, Thea R., Michael Wroblewski, and Mary K. Good. 2010. "Words, Woods, Woyds: Variation and Accommodation in Schwar Realization among African American, White, and Houma Men in Southern Louisiana." *Journal of English Linguistics* 38 (3): 211–29.

Thomas, Erik. [1989] 1993. "Vowel Changes in Columbus, Ohio." *Journal of English Linguistics* 22 (2): 205–15.

———. 2002. "Sociophonetic Applications of Speech Perception Experiments." *American Speech* 77: 115–47.

———. 2007. "Phonological and Phonetic Characteristics of African American Vernacular English." *Language and Linguistics Compass* 1 (5): 450–75.

Thomas, Erik R., and Jeffrey Reaser. 2004. "Delimiting Perceptual Cues for the Ethnic Labeling of African American and European American Voices." *Journal of Sociolinguistics* 8: 54–87.

Torbert, Benjamin. 2004. "Southern Vowels and the Social Construction of Salience." PhD diss., Duke University.

Weldon, Tracey. 2004. "African American English in the Middle Classes: Exploring the other End of the Continuum." Paper presented at NWAV 33: New Ways of Analyzing Language Variation, Ann Arbor, Michigan. September 30–October 3.

Williamson, Juanita V. 1968. *A Phonological and Morphological Study of the Speech of the Negro in Memphis, Tennessee*. Publication of the American Dialect Society 50. Tuscaloosa: University of Alabama Press.

Wolfram, Walt. 1969. *A Sociolinguistic Description of Detroit Negro Speech*. Washington, DC: Center for Applied Linguistics.

———. 2003. "Reexamining the Development of African American English: Evidence from Isolated Communities." *Language* 79: 282–316.

———. 2007. "Sociolinguistic Myths in the Study of African American English." *Linguistic and Language Compass* 2: 292–313.

———. 2013. "African American Speech in Southern Appalachia." In *Talking Appalachian: Voice, Identity, and Community*, edited by Nancy Hayward and Amy Clark, 81–93. Lexington: University of Kentucky Press.

Wolfram, Walt, and Ralph W. Fasold. 1974. *The Study of Social Dialects in the United States*. Englewood Cliffs, NJ: Prentice Hall.

Wolfram, Walt, and Natalie Schilling-Estes. 2006. *American English: Dialects and Variation*. 2nd ed. Malden, MA: Blackwell.

Wolfram, Walt, and Erik R. Thomas, eds. 2002. *The Development of African American English*. Malden, MA: Blackwell.

Yaeger-Dror, Malcah, and Erik Thomas, eds. 2010. *African American English Speakers and their Participation in Local Sound Changes: A Comparative Study*. Publication of the American Dialect Society 94. Durham, NC: Duke University

PART II

LECTS AND VARIATION

CHAPTER 8

THE PLACE OF GULLAH IN THE AFRICAN AMERICAN LINGUISTIC CONTINUUM

TRACEY L. WELDON AND SIMANIQUE MOODY

8.1 INTRODUCTION

GULLAH (also known as *Geechee* or *Sea Island Creole*) is an African American variety spoken primarily along the coast and Sea Islands of South Carolina and Georgia.[1] Early, non-linguistic accounts of Gullah attributed its distinctive features (relative to other varieties of American English) to "intellectual indolence or laziness, physical or mental". (Bennett 1908; see also Gonzales 1922). Such racist, linguistically unfounded myths, were later challenged by dialectologists, who contended that Gullah was an English dialect, whose "grammar and phonology [were] directly descended from the midland and southern English dialects" (Johnson 1930a, 17; see also Crum 1940). Related to this hypothesis, some proposed that it was the "baby talk" or "foreigner talk" of slave masters and the "rustic" speech of poor White indentured servants during the plantation era, which early Gullah speakers approximated in their efforts to learn English (Johnson 1930b, 49).[2] However, it was Lorenzo Dow Turner's seminal work *Africanisms in the Gullah Dialect* (1949) that drew attention to the unique cultural and linguistic heritage of the variety. As observed in Mufwene (2001), Turner's work "[did] not preclude British influence beyond the vocabulary, nor [did] it claim that African linguistic influence was primary" (313). However, several scholars interpreted Turner's work as evidence that "Gullah's system [was] essentially African," thus subscribing to the strongest statement of the African Substrate Hypothesis (Mufwene 2001, 313; see also Dalby 1971; Dunn 1976; Van Sertima 1976.)

A more intermediate perspective, and the most commonly accepted theory today, is that Gullah is a creole (or contact variety) that emerged in the context of the Atlantic slave trade as massive numbers of Africans,[3] many speaking non-mutually intelligible languages, were brought together under extreme conditions that would likely have necessitated the formation of a variety to serve as a common form of communication between them and the English speakers who enslaved them. The resulting variety would have drawn its vocabulary primarily from English, while the grammatical structure and pronunciation would have been heavily influenced by a number of West African languages. From this perspective, Gullah would have emerged under conditions of contact similar to those that led to the formation of creole varieties spoken in the Caribbean (e.g., Jamaica, Trinidad, Barbados, etc.). Grammatical features in modern-day Gullah, such as preverbal tense marking (e.g., *I been work* 'I worked'); pronominal leveling (e.g., *ee* for 'he', 'she', 'it'); and variable absence of the copula, or the verb *be* (e.g., *Anna_the teacher*), as well as African-influenced traditions such as the assigning of "basket" names (or nicknames), are reflective of the linguistic contact that contributed to Gullah's development.

Contention remains, however, over the nature of the relationship between Gullah and other African American language (AAL) varieties. For years, linguists have speculated over whether Gullah represented the remnant of an earlier stage in the development of African American Vernacular English (AAVE).[4] This question dates back to the earliest statements of the Creolist Hypothesis (see Stewart 1967, 1968; Dillard 1972), which postulated that AAVE derived from a widespread plantation creole that underwent a process of decreolization[5] following the breakdown of the plantation system.[6] This position was intended to challenge early statements of the Dialectologist (or Anglicist) Hypothesis, which contended that AAVE derived from British English sources, like other English dialects (see Kurath 1949; McDavid and McDavid 1951). Though some aspects of these positions have changed over the years, the Creolist and Dialectologist Hypotheses remain two of the main competing theories regarding the origins of AAVE.

While most of the attention to this question has been directed at the past, some recent work has also considered the contemporary relationship between Gullah and other AAL varieties. In this chapter, we reflect on theories about Gullah's origins and its role in the emergence and continuing development of AAVE.

8.2 ORIGINS AND SOCIOHISTORICAL DEVELOPMENT

8.2.1 The Sociohistorical Context

In 1627, British colonists settled on the island of Barbados, which, because of its easterly location, became a prime dispersal point for slaves being transported from Africa to other locations (Cassidy 1980; Hancock 1980). These colonists brought with them

African slaves to assist in preparing the island for habitation. The first two years of settlement saw a rapid influx of Whites to the island, with only a small number of African slaves (Wood 1974). But the growth of the sugar industry in Barbados led to an increased demand for slave importations directly from Africa, such that, by 1700, Africans in Barbados outnumbered Europeans five to two (Hancock 1980, 22). This shift in proportions was due not only to an increase in slave importations but also to European migration away from the island during the second half of the seventeenth century, caused by increased competition for land and a number of natural disasters (Wood 1974).

From 1651 to 1670, Europeans left Barbados to set up colonies in Surinam, Jamaica, and Carolina. The Carolina settlement, known as the Charles Town colony, was established in May of 1670 by British colonists, accompanied by a small number of African slaves. For the first thirty to fifty years of this settlement, Africans and Europeans could have interacted regularly with one another on small homestead dwellings, where they participated in farming and trade activity with local Native Americans (Mufwene 1993). During this time, Europeans constituted a majority, with about 800 English to 300 Africans in the colony in 1672 (Wood 1974, 25). The African population increased only gradually during these years, through natural reproduction as well as newcomers who arrived mostly from the West Indies (Mufwene 1993).

In the 1690s, a rice seed from Madagascar was introduced into the swamplands of the Charles Town colony, sparking a booming new rice industry that became the primary source of export for the colony for the next one hundred years.[7] With the introduction of this new industry came the need for an increase in labor, resulting in importations of slaves directly from Africa by the end of the seventeenth century. By 1708, there was a slight Black majority in the colony, with 4,100 Africans and 4,080 Europeans (Mufwene 1993, 10). In 1720, racial segregation was institutionalized, and the number of Africans in the colony had reached a sizeable majority, with 11,828 Africans compared to 6,525 Europeans (10–11).

By 1740, Africans made up about two-thirds of South Carolina's settler population (Joyner 1984, 15).[8] According to Wood (1974, 39), there were 20,000 Whites and 40,600 Blacks in the colony in 1745. During this decade, a second industry, involving the growth and exportation of indigo, was introduced into the colony from the French islands of the Caribbean. The popularity of indigo, used as a dye by clothiers in Great Britain, further contributed to the increase of African slave importations into the colony (Rawley 1981, 309).

The interaction between Blacks and Whites that characterized the first fifty years of settlement was drastically altered by this shift to a plantation economy. House servants still had some amount of contact with Whites. But the majority of slaves were field hands who interacted only with White uneducated small farmers, primarily of Scotch-Irish descent, who worked as overseers (Montgomery and Fuller 1996). And even among the field hands, it was the drivers (i.e., slaves charged with the task of managing the labor gangs and slave quarters) who functioned as the primary liaisons between the overseers and the other slaves (Crum 1940; Clifton 1981).

The threat of malaria and yellow fever in the moist, swampy rice plantations along the Sea Islands also contributed to increasing isolation between Blacks and Whites during these years. While many of the Africans had developed some immunity to these diseases, European planters and their families had no such resistance and were thus forced to leave the plantation sites during the summer and fall months when the diseases were at their peak. As a result, Blacks on the South Carolina rice plantations spent at least half of each year in almost total isolation from Whites, with the exception of a few White overseers, assisted by drivers (Opala 1986).

Living conditions among slaves became much harsher in the transition to the plantation system in South Carolina. Infant and adult mortality rates among Africans increased, and the African population on the plantations grew primarily through slave importations (Rawley 1981; Mufwene 1993). In 1776, Congress voted to discontinue the importation of slaves into any of the thirteen United Colonies. However, in South Carolina, additional labor was needed to support a growing cotton industry, which had developed inland. South Carolina, therefore, reopened the African slave trade in 1803 and continued to engage in the trade until the legal ban of 1808 (Rawley 1981).

In 1732, Georgia was established as the thirteenth and last of the original American colonies. Although slavery was originally prohibited in Georgia, White planters from coastal South Carolina clandestinely moved their enslaved Black labor force to coastal Georgia to expand their rice-based plantations, a practice that continued until the ban on slavery was overturned in 1751 (Nelson 2005). The mid-1700s thus saw the beginning of large-scale importation of enslaved Africans into coastal Georgia via the Caribbean and directly from Africa (Littlefield 1981).

8.2.2 Theories Regarding Gullah's Emergence

Within this general sociohistorical framework, linguists have attempted to reconstruct the course of events that led to the emergence of Gullah. One theory linked the origins of all Atlantic creoles to a sixteenth-century Portuguese-based proto-pidgin that was subsequently relexified by pidgin speakers in contact with other European traders along the coast of West Africa.[9] Thus, a seventeenth-century English-based maritime pidgin, referred to by Stewart (1968) and Dillard (1972) as West African Pidgin English (WAPE), was said to have emerged out of the English trade, as speakers of the English superstrate came into contact with speakers of various West African substrate languages.[10]

Many contend that British slave traders made a practice of separating Africans speaking the same languages, in order to prevent them from communicating with one another and organizing uprisings (see Dillard 1972). Such practices would have contributed to the need for a pidgin to serve as the vehicle of communication both among Africans whose native languages were not mutually intelligible and between Africans and their European overseers.[11] According to Bickerton (1981, 4), the prototypical setting for creole development is one in which superstrate speakers make up no more than 20 percent of the contact population, while the remaining 80 percent consist of a linguistically diverse substrate. In such contexts, the pidgin would likely undergo a process of "nativization" as children adopt the contact variety as their primary means of communication, ultimately resulting in the formation of a full-fledged creole.

While Stewart (1967, 1968) and Dillard (1972) traced the period of creolization to the North American plantations themselves, others argued that the slaves arrived on the plantations already speaking a creole. According to Frederick Cassidy (1980, 1994), it was a seventeenth-century Barbadian creole that served as the predecessor to Gullah, as well as Jamaican Creole and Sranan.[12] Cassidy argued that the three Creoles, despite undergoing separate linguistic developments and/or inputs, exhibited a remarkable number of lexical similarities that could only be explained by this common source. His theory was challenged, however, by Ian Hancock (1980, 22), who questioned the likelihood that a Barbadian creole developed prior to the colonization of Surinam, Jamaica, and Carolina (in 1651, 1655, and 1670, respectively), given that Blacks did not outnumber Whites on the island of Barbados until about 1665.[13]

Instead, Hancock traced the period of creolization back to sixteenth-century Africa, arguing that Gullah (as well as the Caribbean English Creoles) derived from a Guinea Coast Creole English (GCCE) spoken along the Upper Guinea Coast of West Africa (cf. WAPE). Hancock argued that this creole developed during the second half of the sixteenth century, as English-speaking traders settled along the Senegambia littoral, intermarrying with the locals and creating a racially mixed population. The language that emerged from this contact might have been, at first, a "means of local, domestic communication" between the Africans and Europeans (Hancock 1980, 18). However, as trade expanded southward, the creole would have spread to other slaves in the West African depots, reaching the Gulf of Guinea by the mid-seventeenth century (29).

With regard to Gullah, specifically, Hancock (1980) argued that the speech of the first slaves transported from Barbados to Carolina most likely approximated a "metropolitan" variety of English, given the high percentage of native English speakers who could have served as models both in Barbados and in Carolina during the early years. By 1720, however, "Blacks in South Carolina had come to outnumber Whites, the foreign-born to outnumber the native-born, and those from Africa to outnumber those from the Caribbean" (Hancock 1980, 24). It was at this time, Hancock argued, that creolization (or "demetropolitanization") would have begun in South Carolina, with GCCE contributing significantly to its formation, as "creole-speaking slaves were brought in from GCCE-speaking areas of West Africa and came to constitute a majority" (27).[14]

Questioning the plausibility of either GCCE or WAPE playing a determinative role in Gullah's origins, Salikoko Mufwene (1993, 1997) proposed, instead, three phases of development corresponding to three periods of colonization in the Carolina region.[15] Phase One consisted of the first thirty to fifty years of settlement—from 1670 to around 1700 or 1720. Mufwene, like Hancock, maintained that conditions during this phase were not conducive to the creation of a creole and that Africans in the area probably spoke a second language variety of English. The speech of this group of slaves, which included a racially "mixed" population, would have been the "model and lexifier" for the creole that would later develop (Mufwene 1993, 11).

The period from 1720 to 1750 was characterized by the growth of the rice industry, institutionalized segregation, and an African majority on the plantations. It was during this time, Mufwene contends, that the creole would have developed via a process of

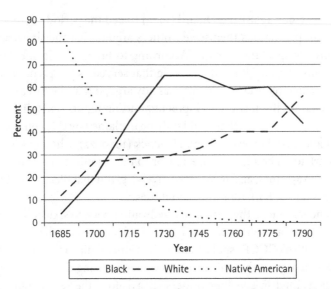

FIGURE 8.1 Estimated population percentages for South Carolina (east of the mountains) from 1685 to 1790.

Source: Adapted from Wood, Waselkov, and Hatley. 1989, 38.

"basilectalization" of the vernaculars spoken during the first phase (cf. Hancock's "demetropolitanization").[16] Between 1745 and 1760, there was a reversal in population growth in favor of the European population, resulting in part from an effort by White colonists to counterbalance the African majority with the importation of European indentured labor (Mufwene 1993, 10). Mufwene, therefore, estimates that the creole emerged by 1750 but continued to develop and stabilize throughout the remainder of the second phase of colonization (roughly from 1750 to 1862). The third phase of colonization began with the abolition of slavery, which was likely marked by some cross-plantation leveling of the creole as interactions among Blacks became more regular (Mufwene 1993, 5).

Figure 8.1 summarizes the demographic statistics for South Carolina during the presumed formative period.

Compared to South Carolina, the demographic statistics for Georgia, shown in figure 8.2, suggest that the independent development of a creole in this area was unlikely.

What these figures fail to show, however, is that most of the White population in Georgia was concentrated inland, while the coast was primarily populated by Blacks, particularly in later years. According to Rickford:

> The Sea Islands and coastal rice-growing regions of Georgia rapidly became similar to those of South Carolina in many respects, including their high proportions of Blacks. By 1790, Blacks constituted 76 percent and 77 percent of the population in coastal Liberty and Chatham counties, respectively. . . . What is more striking than the Sea Island situation is the fact that the combined total of 12,226 Blacks in Liberty

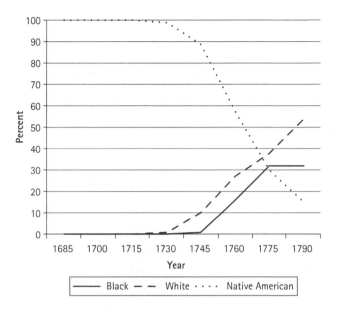

FIGURE 8.2 Estimated population percentages for Creeks/Georgia/Alabama from 1685 to 1790.

Source: Adapted from Wood et al. 1989, 38.

and Chatham counties in 1790 represented 42 percent of the colony's Black population of 29,264 (Smith 1985: 216, Table A-4), suggesting that nearly half of the colony's Blacks in this critical founding period may have been creole speakers. (1997, 327)

There was also a significant amount of creole speech imported into Georgia from South Carolina and the West Indies. According to Hancock (1980), the majority of Blacks in Georgia prior to 1770 were from the Caribbean. Thus, it appears that linguistic input from South Carolina Blacks and others of African descent together with the vernacular English spoken by Whites in this region shaped the development of the varieties of Gullah spoken in coastal Georgia (Turner 1949; Hancock 1980; Cassidy 1980; Rickford 1997; Winford 1997).

8.3 THE RELATIONSHIP BETWEEN GULLAH AND OTHER AAL VARIETIES

8.3.1 Historical Relationship

As noted earlier, speculation about the AAVE-Gullah connection dates back to the earliest statements of the Creolist Hypothesis and the contention that Gullah represented a fairly direct descendant of the creole spoken on the North American plantations, which was preserved by the geographical and social isolation of the Sea Islands. Varieties spoken by African Americans further inland, however, were said to have undergone a process of decreolization under more direct contact with other English varieties. Stewart (1968, 18 n. 26) described AAVE on the South Carolina mainland as a "slightly decreolized" form of Gullah and suggested that by observing the process of decreolization in Gullah, researchers might see a "continuation of the same process which earlier gave rise to the contemporary forms of other American Negro dialects."

According to the *life cycle hypothesis*, first proposed by Robert Hall (1966) and adopted in seminal studies such as DeCamp (1971) and Bickerton (1975), continuum formation resulted from "post-emancipation decreolization" by which a radical creole (i.e., the *basilect*) in contact with a superstrate variety (i.e., the *acrolect*) yielded intermediate *mesolectal* varieties. Both Stewart (1967) and Dillard (1972) acknowledged that the hierarchical division of slaves into house servants and field hands most likely laid the foundation for a linguistic continuum by which house servants would have spoken varieties closer to the English superstrate, while field hands would have spoken more basilectal varieties. They maintained, however, that the process of decreolization that resulted in the emergence of AAVE did not take place until the breakdown of the plantation system, following the end of the Civil War. It was at this time that the continuum would have been fully realized, owing to increased opportunities for African Americans to acquire English, both through education and more regular contact with other English speakers.

> Over the last two centuries, the proportion of American Negroes who speak a perfectly standard variety of English has risen from a small group of privileged house slaves and free Negroes to persons numbering in the hundreds of thousands, and perhaps even millions. Yet there is still a sizable number of American Negroes—undoubtedly larger than the number of standard-speaking Negroes—whose speech may be radically nonstandard. The nonstandard features in the speech of such persons may be due in part to the influence of the nonstandard dialects of Whites with whom they or their ancestors have come in contact, but they also may be due to the survival of creolisms from the older Negro field hand speech of the plantations. (Stewart 1967, 26)

Other researchers have argued that the occupational stratification of the slaves on the plantations would have necessitated the formation of a linguistic continuum from the very beginning of stable contact (see Alleyne 1971, 1980; LePage 1960, 1977). In other words, domestics, who were in close contact with Europeans, would have acquired the regional superstrate (i.e., the acrolect), while field hands, having virtually no personal contact with their European masters, would have developed a more basilectal creole variety. In between these two extremes would have been the more mesolectal varieties spoken by artisans and drivers, who communicated with both domestics and field hands (Alleyne 1980). From this perspective, the continuum would have already been in place on the plantations, and decreolization would simply have involved the shifting of speakers from one level of the continuum to another as they came into greater contact with speakers of different lects. Following emancipation, some mesolectal speakers would have acquired more acrolectal speech, while some basilectal speakers would have acquired mesolectal varieties. Alleyne (1980) described this view of decreolization as follows:

> This speech modification was not so much a mixing of creole forms with standard forms as it was: (1) the rejection of a number of features perceived as being of greatest deviancy from English, and (2) the general adoption by each sector of the population of some of the speech characteristics of the social group above it. This meant first of all a constant erosion of features ... until they became obsolete, residual, or extinct. Secondarily, it meant that the most deviant forms of speech would be represented by fewer and fewer persons, while the intermediate varieties, of highly restricted demographic importance during slavery, now become prominent. (194)

Rickford (1987) supported this view of the continuum, referring to the "constant erosion of features" in the basilect as "qualitative decreolization" and the use of the basilect "by fewer and fewer persons" as "quantitative decreolization." Rickford took issue, however, with Alleyne's contention that basilectal speakers passively adopted the mesolect, arguing instead that intermediate varieties were constantly restructured, with basilectal speakers "actively creating [the mesolects] anew" as they moved toward the acrolect (1987, 34–35).

Going a step further, Winford (1997) proposed that AAVE probably never existed as a creole in and of itself, but instead emerged through a process of language shift as Africans, speaking either a creole or African languages or both transferred features from these varieties into their newly acquired English.[17] Winford's theory took into account the sociohistorical evidence discussed earlier, which cast doubt on the likelihood that US plantations ever met the necessary conditions for creolization (as defined by Bickerton) anywhere other than in the southeast region, where Gullah developed[18] (see also Schneider 1989; Mufwene 1993, 1997; Rickford 1997; Winford 1992).

Similar to Mufwene, Winford argued that Gullah most likely emerged in South Carolina between 1720 and 1775, as conditions in South Carolina prior to this time would have favored Africans learning an approximation to the settler dialects.[19] With the introduction of the creole, the linguistic situation among Africans in South Carolina would have come to resemble a continuum:

> Africans in closer contact with Whites must have continued to learn closer approximations to their dialects. By the mid-eighteenth century, the linguistic situation on the South Carolina coast would have been similar to that in other Caribbean colonies—a creole continuum within the African population, complicated by continuing input from White dialects on the one hand, and the African languages of newly-arrived slaves on the other. (Winford 1997, 315)

Within this framework, Winford saw the period from 1780 to 1860 as one of consolidation and leveling across both creole and dialectal English varieties, as creole-speaking Africans and those speaking approximations to the settler dialects came into contact with one another.

> We can assume that there was a sizeable body of Africans throughout the southern states in this period whose primary vernacular was a creole English, and many of whom shifted over the years to AAVE as their primary vernacular, 'transferring' or preserving in the process certain elements of the creole grammar. I also assume that there was a sizeable body of Africans whose primary vernacular was an earlier form of AAVE which was fashioned after the settler dialects, and which provided the target of the shift. Contact between these groups of Africans on the plantations is likely to have contributed to the development of AAVE. (Winford 1997, 317)

According to Winford (1997), the distinctive features that emerged during this period of contact would have spread to other areas of the country during the post-emancipation period of the nineteenth and twentieth centuries, as increased mobility led to increased contact among African Americans of different regional and social backgrounds.[20]

From this perspective, AAVE would have *preceded* Gullah in its emergence, rather than descending from it, as maintained by early supporters of the Creolist Hypothesis. According to Mufwene:

> Virginia was colonized [in 1607] more than a half century before South Carolina [in 1670] and the first Africans arrived [in Jamestown, Va., in 1619] about half a century before the colonization of the second territory to work in tobacco plantations. Moreover, Gullah, like other creoles, must have developed in the direction of basilectalization. (1991) Since so far it has not been associated with Virginia, one would assume that AAVE, or a variety less different from colonial White varieties of English, is likely to have started earlier. (1993, 8)

This is not to say, however, that creole influence was restricted to South Carolina and Georgia alone. As observed in Rickford (1997), creole speakers (imported primarily from the West Indies) were present during the presumed formative stages of AAVE in most regions of the South and in many northern territories as well.

> Most striking in the historical record is the evidence that slaves brought in from Caribbean colonies where creole English is spoken were the predominant segments of the early Black population in so many American colonies, including Massachusetts, New York, South Carolina, Georgia, Virginia and Maryland in particular. . . . Moreover, if Mufwene (1996), Chaudenson (1992) and others are right about the importance of the early, founding populations, these Caribbean imports may have had an important creolizing influence on the colonies to which they came. (331)

Furthermore, it is argued that in several pockets of North Carolina and Virginia (as in South Carolina and Georgia) some creoles are likely to have emerged alongside AAVE in areas where access to the superstrate was more restricted, thus yielding a continuum of varieties spoken by Africans throughout the South in the seventeenth and eighteenth centuries.

8.3.2 Contemporary Relationship

While growing numbers of scholars have begun to explore linguistic diversity within African American communities, showing that the language of African Americans varies both regionally and socially, much of this work has excluded Gullah. However, Mufwene's (2001) categorization of Gullah as a regional variety of AAVE reframes this discussion, allowing a more accurate picture to emerge with regard to the contemporary relationship between Gullah and other AAL varieties.

In coastal Georgia, for example, Gullah speakers live and work side by side with other African Americans, and intermarriage between members of these groups is common. This long-standing social contact, spanning at least two centuries, has affected the linguistic structure of African American varieties spoken in the region. Although historically, Gullah and AAVE share many linguistic similarities, findings from Moody (2011) reveal that the varieties spoken in southeast Georgia show an even greater degree of linguistic continuity than has previously been documented. Below, we highlight some of the present-day linguistic outcomes of contact between speakers of AAVE and Gullah in coastal Georgia by providing an overview of several grammatical features.[21]

Previous descriptions of Gullah (Cunningham 1970; Nichols 1976; Jones-Jackson 1978, 1983) have reported that speakers do not inflect or mark regular verbs with third person singular *–s* in the present tense (e.g., *she **work** hard* 'she works hard') or with *–ed* in the past tense (e.g., *she **work** hard yesterday* 'she worked hard yesterday'). And temporal properties of situations are marked pre-verbally, rather than directly on the verb (e.g., *she **da** work* 'she is working' or *I **bin** pick 'em* 'I picked them'). In coastal Georgia, however, Gullah speakers in greater contact with speakers of other English varieties show variation in their use of these grammatical constructions depending on the social and/or linguistic context.

While early studies of AAVE revealed near categorical presence of the plural *–s* ending on regular nouns (see Labov et al. 1968; Wolfram 1969), Gullah has been characterized by high rates of plural *–s* absence (or zero plural) (Mufwene 1986; Rickford 1986).[22] Gullah speakers also mark plurality with *dem* (e.g., *sister **dem*** 'sisters', *light **dem*** 'lights') or by using quantifiers with an unmarked noun (e.g., ***plenty** plum* 'plenty of plums', ***three time a day*** 'three times a day'). In coastal Georgia, zero plural is found at higher rates among African American speakers than has been reported for most other regions in the United States, particularly in the speech of people aged 65 and over. In Moody (2011), for example, speakers exhibited rates of plural *–s* absence ranging from 7 to 40 percent, with some showing rates as high as 60–70 percent. Moreover, both AAVE speakers and Gullah speakers alike use *dem* in coastal Georgia to denote plurality (e.g., *people **dem*** 'people').

Finally, while both Gullah and AAVE exhibit copula absence (e.g., *you **in** the way* 'you're in the way', *he **a** nice old man* 'he's a nice old man', *they **gone*** 'they're gone'), the use of zero copula in first person singular environments (e.g., *I **glad** to see you* 'I'm glad to see you' or *I **waitin'** on you* 'I'm waiting on you') is associated primarily with Gullah.

In coastal Georgia, however, AAVE speakers also exhibit *am* absence, as illustrated below:[23]

I the one bought that car	'I'm the one who bought that car'
what *I poseta* do with that	'what am I supposed to do with that?'
the kind of shape *I in*	'the kind of shape I'm in'
I still not satisfied	'I'm still not satisfied.'

Variation in the grammatical structure of the varieties described above reflects a long and varied history of social and linguistic contact among speakers of Gullah and other African American varieties, providing a new perspective on the place of Gullah in the African American linguistic continuum. While contemporary parallels such as those described above likely reflect some aspects of their origins and historical development, present-day contact between speakers of these varieties deserves more attention in the sociolinguistic literature for the insight that it provides into the regional and social diversity of African American varieties.

8.4 CONCLUSION

Assessing the linguistic vitality of Gullah, particularly among younger speakers, should be a key consideration in future studies. For years, linguists and non-linguists alike feared the demise of Gullah, resulting from increased mobility of its speakers and the growth of the tourism industry, both of which disrupted the earlier isolation of more remote Sea Island communities (see Jones-Jackson 1978, 1984). These effects have been compounded by the stigmatization and negative stereotyping of Gullah, which have discouraged many older speakers from passing on the variety to younger generations of speakers. Nevertheless, Gullah remains a significant marker of culture, history, and identity in the communities where it is spoken (see Mufwene 1991b). And there has been a concerted effort in recent years to preserve and promote Gullah language and culture through storytelling, Bible translations, heritage tours, music festivals, and other initiatives. More research is needed to determine the extent to which such factors have impacted the vitality of Gullah, particularly among younger speakers.[24]

Future research might also include attention to less well-documented varieties of Gullah, particularly along the coasts of North Carolina and Florida, to determine the degree to which linguistic uniformity exists across communities. Documenting these varieties will permit comparisons with existing descriptions of Gullah and help determine the extent to which they pattern typologically with varieties spoken in South Carolina and Georgia.

Finally, more research like Moody (2011) is needed to assess the linguistic consequences of sustained contact between Gullah and other AAL varieties. Such research is important not only for the ways in which it informs the current status and trajectory of these varieties but also for the ways in which it can inform our understanding of earlier patterns of contact that helped to situate Gullah on the AAL continuum.

Notes

1. While most linguistic attention has been directed at the use of Gullah in South Carolina, and to a lesser extent Georgia, the variety might have spread as far north as coastal North Carolina and as far south as coastal Florida.
2. The terms "baby talk" and "foreigner talk" refer to the type of simplified speech that is sometimes used by native speakers when addressing speakers of other languages.
3. In this chapter, the terms *African, African American,* and *Black* are all variably used to refer to American slaves and/or slave descendants of African origin. However, some effort is made to use the label that is appropriate for the time period under consideration. See Smitherman (1998, 210–14) for more on "names for the race."
4. We use the term *African American Vernacular English* (AAVE) here to refer to the distinctive, nonstandard varieties of English used by and among many African Americans in the United States.
5. In this context, the term *decreolization* refers to the process by which the plantation creole, described by early proponents of the Creolist Hypothesis as a fairly homogeneous basilectal variety (i.e., far removed from its English lexifier), became more acrolectal (i.e., more English-like) under increased contact with other English dialects. See Rickford (1987) and Mufwene (1991a) for more on the various ways that the term *decreolization* has been used in creole studies.
6. Somewhat related to the Creolist Hypothesis is the African Substrate Hypothesis, mentioned earlier in the text, which posits a more direct historical connection between AAVE and West African languages than the Creolist Hypothesis, which posits this connection through one or more creole intermediaries (See Herskovits [1941] 1958; Turner 1949; Dalby 1971; Dunn 1976; Van Sertima 1976; and Debose and Faraclas 1993).
7. Rice plantations were later extended to the Georgia coast as well, as discussed later in this chapter.
8. While there is no consensus on exactly when the split occurred, the Carolina colony appears to have split into North Carolina and South Carolina sometime between 1690 and 1730 (http://www.carolana.com/Carolina/thesplit.html).
9. The Portuguese held a monopoly on the slave trade along the coast of West Africa until the end of the sixteenth century, when British, French, and later Dutch traders began to challenge the monopoly (Cassidy 1980, 9–10).
10. In situations of contact between speakers of different languages, the term *superstrate* refers to the variety or varieties spoken by those with more power and prestige, while the term *substrate* refers to those with less.
11. Singler (1988, 28), however, cautions that the extent to which Africans speaking the same languages were separated from one another and the effects that were said to have resulted from this practice may have been somewhat overstated.

12. Cassidy's theory derives from the observation, noted earlier, that Carolina, Jamaica, and Surinam were all initially colonized by Barbadian settlers.

13. In response to Hancock's challenge, Cassidy conceded that creolization in Barbados was not likely before 1660 or 1670 but could have taken place in Barbados after this period, as the number of African importations in the area rose to support the needs of the growing sugar industry. It is not certain, however, whether the creole would have developed early enough to have had the formative influence on Sranan, Jamaican Creole, and Gullah posited by Cassidy. See also Rickford and Handler (1994).

14. Noting a number of similarities between Gullah and modern-day Krio, Hancock contends that GCCE was also the ancestor to Krio, spoken today in Sierra Leone.

15. Mufwene derived his model from one presented in Chaudenson (1992) and Baker (1993) for French colonies in the Indian Ocean and the New World. Several parallel observations were made in Winford (1997) with regard to the development of AAVE, to be discussed later in this chapter.

16. As observed in Mufwene (1993, 21 n. 19), the ratios in South Carolina did not appear to have reached the proportions estimated by Bickerton (1981) to have been necessary for creole formation, though they might have been more closely approximated on larger plantations along the coast. Mufwene (1993, 12) also questioned, however, whether Bickerton's numbers were too conservative to account for all instances of creolization that took place. See also Rickford (1997).

17. Winford favored the language shift hypothesis over that of qualitative decreolization as it applied to the history of AAVE, arguing that the latter "assume[d] too much about the speed of change and fail[ed] to take account of all the relevant sociohistorical and linguistic evidence" (1997, 311). A similar observation was made by Edgar Schneider, who noted that if AAVE had indeed developed from a creole origin, "then it would occupy a unique position as the only fully decreolized variety in the Central and North American region" (1989, 39).

18. John Rickford observed that some creole features were, in fact, attested in the New England and Middle colonies of the United States. However, he argued that they were more likely to have been "imported" into these regions from already established creole-speaking communities than to have been "home-grown" (1997, 321).

19. In Winford's (1997, 326) estimation, Gullah would have spread to Georgia during the last few decades of the eighteenth century, as planters and slaves from South Carolina migrated to the Georgia coast.

20. The "Great Black Migration" of southern Blacks moving to northern and western cities in the early to mid-twentieth century is said to have played a significant role in the regional spread of Southern AAVE.

21. For an examination of the AAVE-Gullah connection in the Carolinas, see Weldon (1998, 2003a, and 2003b).

22. At least a couple of studies have reported higher rates of plural –s absence in AAVE. For example, Kessler (1972) reported 19.6 percent –s absence in a socially stratified study of African Americans in Washington, DC. And Rowe (2005) observed 23.9 percent –s absence among the oldest generation in Princeville, North Carolina—a rural African American enclave community. From what is currently known, these findings do not appear to be generalizable to most AAVE varieties.

23. It is possible that some varieties of AAVE spoken in other parts of the United States also permit first person zero copula; however, there is little to no published research documenting such usage.

24. Anecdotally, it has been observed that many younger speakers from the South Carolina low country tend to associate the Gullah label with older varieties, while using Geechee to describe their own cultural and linguistic identities. This phenomenon is particularly noteworthy, given the stigma that has been historically linked to the Geechee label. However, the extent to which this shift in labeling is tied to actual linguistic differences between older and younger speakers remains unknown.

References

Alleyne, Mervyn C. 1971. "Acculturation and the Cultural Matrix of Creolization." In *Pidginization and Creolization of Languages*, edited by Dell Hymes, 169–86. Cambridge: Cambridge University Press.

———. 1980. *Comparative Afro-American: An Historical-Comparative Study of English-Based Afro-American Dialects of the New World*. Ann Arbor, MI: Karoma.

Baker, Peter. 1993. "Assessing the African Contribution to French-based Creoles." In *Africanisms in Afro-American Language Varieties*, edited by Salikoko S. Mufwene, 123–55. Athens: University of Georgia Press.

Bennett, John. 1908. "Gullah: A Negro Patois." *South Atlantic Quarterly* 7: 332–47.

Bickerton, Derek. 1975. *Dynamics of a Creole System*. New York: Cambridge University Press.

———. 1981. *Roots of Language*. Ann Arbor, MI: Karoma.

Cassidy, Frederic G. 1980. "The Place of Gullah." *American Speech* 55 (1): 3–16.

———. 1994. "Gullah and the Caribbean Connection." In *The Crucible of Carolina: Essays in the Development of Gullah Language and Culture*, edited by Michael Montgomery, 16–22. Athens: University of Georgia Press.

Chaudenson, Robert. 1992. *Des îles, des hommes, des langues: Langues créoles—cultures créoles*. Paris: L'Harmattan.

Clifton, James M. 1981. "The Rice Driver: His Role in Slave Management." *South Carolina Historical Magazine* 82 (4): 331–53.

Crum, Mason. 1940. *Gullah: Negro Life in the Carolina Sea Islands*. Durham, NC: Duke University.

Cunningham, Irma Aloyce Ewing. 1970. "A Syntactic Analysis of Sea Island Creole ('Gullah')." PhD diss., University of Michigan.

Dalby, David. 1971. "Communication in Africa and the New World." In *Black–White Speech Relations*, edited by Walt Wolfram and Nona H. Clark, 99–138. Arlington, VA: Center for Applied Linguistics.

Debose, Charles, and Nicholas Faraclas. 1993. "An Africanist Approach to the Linguistic Study of Black English: Getting to the Roots of the Tense-Modality-Aspect and Copula Systems in Afro-American." In *Africanisms in Afro-American Language Varieties*, edited by Salikoko Mufwene and Nancy Condon, 364–87. Athens: University of Georgia Press.

DeCamp, David. 1971. "Toward a Generative Analysis of a Post-Creole Continuum." In *Pidginization and Creolization of Languages: Proceedings of a Conference held at the University of the West Indies, Mona, Jamaica, April 1968*, edited by Dell Hymes, 349–70. Cambridge: Cambridge University Press.

Dillard, Joe L. 1972. *Black English: Its History and Usage in the United States*. New York: Random House.

Dunn, Ernest F. 1976. "The Black-Southern White Dialect Controversy: Who Did What to Whom?" In *Black English: A Seminar*, edited by Deborah S. Harrison and Tom Trabasso, 105–22. Hillsdale, NJ: Lawrence Erlbaum.

Gonzales, Ambrose. 1922. *The Black Border: Gullah Stories of the Carolina Coast*. Columbia, SC: The State Co.

Hall, Robert A., Jr. 1966. *Pidgin and Creole Languages*. Ithaca, NY: Cornell University Press.

Hancock, Ian F. 1980. "Gullah and Barbadian—Origins and Relationships." *American Speech* 55 (1): 17–35.

Herskovits, Melville J. [1941] 1958. *The Myth of the Negro Past*. Reprint. Boston: Beacon.

Johnson, Guy B. 1930a. *Folk Culture on St. Helena Island*. Chapel Hill: University of North Carolina Press.

———. 1930b. "St. Helena Songs and Stories." In *Black Yeomanry: Life on St. Helena Island*, edited by T. J. Woofter, Jr., 48–81. New York: H. Holt.

Jones-Jackson, Patricia Ann. 1978. "The Status of Gullah: An Investigation of Convergent Processes." PhD diss., University of Michigan.

———. 1983. "Contemporary Gullah Speech: Some Persistent Linguistic Features." *Journal of Black Studies* 13 (3): 289–303.

———. 1984. "On Decreolization and Language Death in Gullah." *Language in Society* 13: 351–62.

Joyner, Charles. 1984. *Down by the Riverside*. Chicago: University of Illinois Press.

Kessler, Carolyn. 1972. "Noun Plural Absence." In *Tense Marking in Black English: A Linguistic and Social Analysis*, edited by Ralph Fasold, 223–37. Washington, DC: Center for Applied Linguistics.

Kurath, Hans. 1949. *A Word Geography of the Eastern United States*. Ann Arbor: University of Michigan Press.

Labov, William, Paul Cohen, Clarence Robins, and John Lewis. 1968. *A Study of the Non-Standard English of Negro and Puerto Rican Speakers in New York City*. Report on Cooperative Research Project 3288. Vols. 1 and 2. New York: Columbia University.

LePage, R. B. 1960. *An Historical Introduction to Jamaican Creole. Creole Language Studies 1*. London: Macmillan.

———. 1977. "Processes of Pidginization and Creolization." In *Pidgin and Creole Linguistics*, edited by Albert Valdman, 222–55. Bloomington: Indiana University Press.

Littlefield, Daniel. 1981. *Rice and Slaves: Ethnicity and the Slave Trade in Colonial South Carolina*. Baton Rouge: Louisiana State University Press.

McDavid, Raven I., Jr., and Virginia Glenn McDavid. 1951. "The Relationship of the Speech of the American Negroes to the Speech of Whites." *American Speech* 26: 3–17.

Montgomery, Michael, and Janet Fuller. 1996. "What Was Verbal *-s* in 19th-Century African-American English?" In *Focus on the USA*, edited by Edgar W. Schneider, 211–30. Amsterdam: Benjamins.

Moody, Simanique. 2011. "Language Contact and Regional Variation in African American English: A Study of Southeast Georgia." PhD diss., New York University.

Mufwene, Salikoko. 1986. "Number Delimitation in Gullah." *American Speech* 61 (1): 33–60.

———. 1991a. Review of *Grammatical Relations in a Radical Creole*, by Francis Byrne. *SECOL Review* 13: 200–206.

———. 1991b. "Some Reasons Why Gullah Is Not Dying Yet." *English World-Wide* 12 (2): 215–43.

———. 1993. "Gullah's Development: Myths and Sociohistorical Facts." Revised version of a paper presented at the Language in Society II Conference, Auburn University, April.

——. 1996. "The Founder Principle in Creole Genesis." *Diachronica* 13: 83–134.

——. 1997. "Gullah's Development: Myths and Sociohistorical Evidence." In *Language Variety in the South Revisited*, edited by Cynthia Bernstein, Thomas Nunnally, and Robin Sabino, 113–23. Tuscaloosa: University of Alabama Press.

——. 2001. "African-American English." In *History of American English*. Vol. 6 of *The Cambridge History of the English Language*, edited by John Algeo, 291–324. Cambridge: Cambridge University Press.

Nelson, Megan Kate. 2005. *Trembling Earth: A Cultural History of the Okefenokee Swamp*. Athens: University of Georgia Press.

Nichols, Patricia C. 1976. "Linguistic Change in Gullah: Sex, Age, and Mobility." PhD diss., Stanford University.

Opala, Joseph. 1986. *The Gullah: Rice, Slavery, and the Sierra-Leone American Connection*. Freetown, Sierra Leone: United States Information Service.

Rawley, James A. 1981. *The Transatlantic Slave Trade: A History*. New York: W. W. Norton.

Rickford, John R. 1986. "Some Principles for the Study of Black and White Speech in the South." In *Language Variety in the South*, edited by Michael B. Montgomery and Guy Bailey, 38–62. Tuscaloosa: University of Alabama Press.

——. 1987. *Dimensions of a Creole Continuum: History, Texts, and Linguistic Analysis of Guyanese Creole*. Stanford, CA: Stanford University Press.

——. 1997. "Prior Creolization of AAVE? Sociohistorical and Textual Evidence from the 17th and 18th Centuries." *Journal of Sociolinguistics* 1 (3): 315–36.

Rickford, John R., and Jerome Handler. 1994. "Textual Evidence on the Nature of Early Barbadian Speech, 1676–1835." *Journal of Pidgin and Creole Languages* 9: 221–55.

Rowe, Ryan D. 2005. "The Development of African American English in the Oldest Black Town in America: –s Absence in Princeville, North Carolina." Master's thesis, North Carolina State University.

Schneider, Edgar W. 1989. *American Earlier Black English: Morphological and Syntactic Variables*. Tuscaloosa: University of Alabama Press.

Singler, John. 1988. "The Homogeneity of the Substrate as a Factor in Pidgin/Creole Genesis." *Language* 64 (1): 27–51.

Smith, Julia Floyd. 1985. *Slavery and Rice Culture in Low Country Georgia, 1750–1860*. Knoxville: University of Tennessee Press.

Smitherman, Geneva. 1998. "Word from the Hood: The Lexicon of African-American Vernacular English." In *African American English: Structure, History, and Use*, edited by Salikoko Mufwene, John R. Rickford, Guy Bailey, and John Baugh, 203–25. London: Routledge.

Stewart, William. 1967. "Sociolinguistic Factors in the History of American Negro Dialects." *The Florida FL Reporter* 5 (2): 11, 22, 24, 26, 28.

——. 1968. "Continuity and Change in American Negro Dialects." *The Florida FL Reporter* 6 (1): 3–4, 14–16, 18.

Turner, Lorenzo Dow. 1949. *Africanisms in the Gullah Dialect*. Chicago: University of Chicago.

Van Sertima, Ivan. 1976. "My Gullah Brother and I: Exploration into a Community's Language and Myth through its Oral Tradition." In *Black English: A Seminar*, edited by Deborah S. Harrison and Tom Trabasso, 123–46. Hillsdale, NJ: Lawrence Erlbaum.

Weldon, Tracey. 1998. "Exploring the AAVE-Gullah Connection: A Comparative Study of Copula Variability." PhD diss., Ohio State University.

————. 2003a. "Revisiting the Creolist Hypothesis: Copula Variability in Gullah and Southern Rural AAVE." *American Speech* 78 (2): 171–91.

————. 2003b. "Copula Variability in Gullah." *Language Variation and Change* 15 (1): 37–72.

Winford, Donald. 1992. "Back to the Past: The BEV/Creole Connection Revisited." *Language Variation and Change* 4 (3): 311–57.

————. 1997. "On the Origins of African American Vernacular English: A Creolist Perspective: Part 1: Sociohistorical Background." *Diachronica* 14 (2): 305–44.

Wolfram, Walt. 1969. *A Sociolinguistic Description of Detroit Negro Speech*. Washington, DC: Center for Applied Linguistics.

Wood, Peter H. 1974. *Black Majority: Negroes in Colonial South Carolina from 1670 through the Stono Rebellion*. New York: Knopf.

Wood, Peter H., Gregory Waselkov, and M. Thomas Hatley, eds. 1989. "The Changing Population of the Colonial South: An Overview by Race and Region, 1685–1790." In *Powhatan's Mantle: Indians in the Colonial Southeast*, 35–103. Lincoln: University of Nebraska Press.

CHAPTER 9

RURAL TEXAS AFRICAN AMERICAN VERNACULAR ENGLISH

PATRICIA CUKOR-AVILA AND GUY BAILEY

9.1 INTRODUCTION

FOR many years the prevailing understanding about African American Vernacular English (AAVE) was that it was largely a northern, urban variety spoken primarily by adolescents and young adults under age 30. This was because most of the defining research that described AAVE phonology and syntax was conducted on adolescents in the urban North in the decades following World War II (see Labov et al. 1968 and Labov 1972 in Harlem; Wolfram 1969 in Detroit; Fasold 1972 in Washington, DC). One of the unintended consequences of the early research in the urban North, however, was an ahistorical approach to the study of AAVE since that research ignored the sociocultural context in which AAVE first developed—the rural South. A second unintended consequence was that non-linguists sometimes cited the linguistic features described in the early AAVE studies in support of the deficit hypothesis (cf. Bereiter and Engelmann 1966; Jensen 1969; Deutsch, Katz, and Jensen 1968), comparing those AAVE features to features of "standard" English (i.e., non-Southern, White varieties) and finding the former to be inferior. A third unintended consequence of the early research on adolescents in northern cities was that the results of the research helped skew the debates about the origins of AAVE that preoccupied many researchers and saw them split into two camps: Anglicist or Creolist.[1] Many of the questions about the origins of AAVE have yet to be resolved (cf. Poplack 2000; Rickford 2006), but it is clear that the origins debate must begin with the understanding that for the first 300 years of its history, AAVE was largely spoken in the rural South (cf. Bailey 1987; Bailey and Maynor 1987; Wolfram and Thomas 2002) and was an important part of a complex linguistic matrix there. This chapter thus examines rural AAVE as the variety that must be the focus of

Table 9.1 Historical Contexts for the Development of AAVE in the United States

1. The Colonial Period: 1620–1790
   - Although the first slaves were imported in 1619, large-scale importation came after 1680.
   - Slaves were imported from both Africa and the Caribbean and would have spoken both African and creole languages.
   - Until 1790, slavery in the United States was localized along the East Coast, with two focal areas in the VA Tidewater and SC Low Country.
   - These two focal areas saw the emergence of different kinds of slave societies, with larger plantations and less contact with whites in the Carolina Low Country and smaller plantations and more contact in the Upper South. These areas created two distinct patterns of linguistic contact.
   - A third focal area developed on the large sugar plantations in LA; French was the superstrate language in most of the area.

2. The Emergence of the Cotton Kingdom: 1780–1860*
   - More than half the slaves were imported after 1780; the period between 1790 and 1810 was the most active in the slave trade.
   - The invention of the cotton gin in 1793 was the impetus for the expansion of the slave trade and brought slavery to the interior South.
   - The domestic slave trade expanded rapidly, with perhaps 1,000,000 slaves moved from the East Coast (especially VA and NC) to the interior South.
   - Making the foreign slave trade illegal did not end it, with 13 percent of the slaves imported to the United States coming after that trade was made illegal in 1808.
   - The rapid expansion of slavery into the interior South created a variety of linguistic mixtures, with different varieties of English, African languages, and some creoles spoken in varying proportions.

3. The Expansion of the Cotton Kingdom and the Development of Farm Tenancy: 1880–1940
   - The end of slavery did not eliminate the plantation system of agriculture; the system of farm tenancy replaced slavery.
   - General stores emerged as the primary distributors of credit after 1880; increasingly, they required that virtually all farmland be devoted to cotton.
   - Cotton production extended into marginal lands, into the newly settled areas of OK and TX, and northward into southern VA. By 1930, more than 42,000,000 acres were devoted to cotton, and cotton production was nearly four times as great as in 1860.
   - Between 1880 and 1930, many whites also fell into tenancy; by 1930, 58 percent of white farmers in Texas were tenants.
   - The spread of white tenancy often created contexts in which African Americans and whites were in close contact with one another; this further complicated the linguistic context in which AAVE was developing.

4. Urbanization and the Great Migration: 1910–1970
   - In 1910, 89 percent of all African Americans lived in the South, and some 75 percent still lived in rural areas (with populations less than 2,500).
   - During World War I, African Americans began to migrate to northern cities; the migration expanded dramatically with World War II.
   - Migration from the South followed clear patterns due north except in TX and OK, where migration was to the West.
   - By 1970, 47 percent of all African Americans lived outside the South; 77 percent lived in cities; 34 percent were concentrated in seven cities.
   - Northward migration created new African American communities, often with minimal contact with whites.

---

* The years between 1860 and 1880 represent a period of instability characterized by war, reconstruction, and economic and social experimentation before farm tenancy was adopted.
Source: Adapted from Bailey 2001.

work on the origins debate and as the variety from which urban AAVE developed. In addition, it explores rural AAVE as a variety that more recently has been influenced by urban innovation.

9.2 SOCIOHISTORICAL CONTEXT

Bailey (2001) outlines four key periods in the history of African Americans in the United States that are crucial to understanding the sociohistorical context in which AAVE emerged: (1) the Colonial Period (1619–1790), which saw the establishment of slavery; (2) the Emergence of the Cotton Kingdom (1790–1880), which saw the rapid numeric and geographic expansion of slavery; (3) the Development of Farm Tenancy and the Country Store (1880–1940), which saw the development of a system that preserved the plantation economy but altered relationships among Blacks and Whites; and (4) Urbanization and the Great Migration (1915, but primarily after 1940, to 1980), which saw the movement of the African American population to cities, primarily in the North. To this, a fifth period (after 1980) probably should be added: this period has seen both the reversal of the Great Migration, with African Americans moving from the urban North to the urban South, and also the beginnings of the dispersal of the highly concentrated African American population in inner cities. Table 9.1 provides a brief overview of each of these periods.

A complete understanding of AAVE, its historical development, and its recent trajectory requires an understanding of the relationship between features of that variety and the sociocultural history of African Americans that is rooted in the rural South. Our work suggests that the evolution of AAVE in the rural South can be characterized by three processes—obsolescence, continuity, and innovation—that reflect the demographic events outlined in table 9.1. In what follows, we outline these processes and illustrate them with examples primarily from our research on rural AAVE in Texas,[2] drawing on additional examples from other research when applicable.

9.3 RECESSIVE/OBSOLETE FORMS

Research on Southern enclave varieties (Wolfram 2003) and change over time in the South (Tillery and Bailey 2003; Bailey et al. 1996; Bailey 1997) suggests that a significant number of traditional Southern phonological and grammatical features are now either obsolete or rapidly becoming so. A similar pattern exists for rural AAVE. Table 9.2 provides a list of older AAVE features that are either obsolete or diminishing in contemporary rural AAVE. Note that not all of them are exclusive to AAVE and several (especially some of the phonological features) have received little attention in the literature on AAVE, even though they are potentially crucial to larger issues such as the origins debate.

Table 9.2 Recessive/Obsolete Phonological and Grammatical Features in Rural AAVE

	Features	Examples	Status
1.	Monophthongal /e/ and /o/	day → [de:]; know → [no:]	obsolete
2.	long offglides after /æ/; before vl. fricatives, nasals, and /g/	half → [hæif]; bag → [bæig]	obsolete
3.	vocalization or loss of intersyllabic /r/	hurry → [hʌi]; furrow → [fʌə]	obsolete
4.	vocalization of stressed syllabic /r/	bird → [bɜɪd]; burr → [bɜ]	recessive/obsolete
5.	*for to*	They just wanted somethin' *for to* snack on later.	recessive/obsolete
6.	*a-verb-ing*	We just *a-playin'* aroun'.	recessive
7.	first/second person *–s*	I *tends* to my own business.	recessive
8.	plural verbal *–s*	Copperheads *loves* to be around clay.	recessive
9.	invariant *be* derived from *will/would* deletion	About the middle of nex' month *it be* white as snow. An' man girl *it be thunderin'* an' lightnin' so I'd get so scared I didn' know what to do.	recessive
10.	*would* deletion	They ø make cheese when I was a boy.	recessive
11.	regularized preterites	I *knowed* her when she was a baby.	recessive
12.	*is* for *are*	So many people *is* movin' in.	recessive (except for existentials)

Source: Adapted from Bailey and Thomas 1998; Bailey 2001; and Cukor-Avila 2001.

While many of the grammatical features of rural AAVE that are recessive or obsolete were shared with White Southern vernaculars (cf. Christian, Wolfram, and Dube 1988; Bailey 1997; Tillery and Bailey 2003), the phonological features listed in table 9.2 seem to have been more frequent and more widespread in AAVE. For example, Thomas and Bailey (1998) and Bailey and Thomas (1998, 97) point out that some phonological features documented in early AAVE (but rare in comparable Southern vernaculars) have parallels in Caribbean creoles. Two such features are monophthongal /e/ and /o/, which are present in the speech of former slaves and late nineteenth-century informants (Bailey and Thomas 1998, 97) but disappear by the early twentieth century. Bailey and Thomas (1998) argue that features like monophthongal /e/ and /o/ "reflect a shared heritage" between AAVE, Gullah, and the creoles spoken in Grenada and Guyana, and that this heritage may reveal (at least phonologically) West African roots for AAVE. Both monophthongal /e/ and /o/, however, are now obsolete in AAVE.

Two grammatical features, *for to* and *a*-prefixing, that are iconic in Ozark and Appalachian English (Christian, Wolfram, and Dube 1988; Wolfram and Fasold 1974; Henry 1992) were not documented in urban varieties of AAVE and consequently were assumed not to occur in any variety of AAVE (Wolfram and Fasold 1974). Almost every-one in our Springville sample born before 1965 uses these forms at least occasionally, though, so they clearly occurred in earlier AAVE. We have no evidence of these features in the speech of rural informants born after 1965, however, so both forms are recessive, if not obsolete.

9.3.1 First/Second Singular and Plural Verbal –s

Figures 9.1 illustrate the steady decline over time of three other grammatical features that occurred in both older Black and older White vernaculars in the rural South but are now recessive. In earlier rural AAVE, –s appeared occasionally in first and second singular and third plural as well as variably in third singular. In contemporary rural AAVE, verbal –s in first and second singular and third plural is now almost obsolete, and the frequency of –s in third singular has diminished. Figure 9.1 illustrates the decline of –s in first and second singular and third plural for Springville AAVE speakers. Cukor-Avila (2003, 101–2) summarizes the almost complete loss over time of what was a variable verbal –s in Springville AAVE (for a discussion of third singular –s, see section 9.4.1 below). She describes this as a three-stage process triggered by the weakening of two competing constraints on present tense marking in the nineteenth and early twenti-eth centuries: person/number and NP/PRO.[3] Cukor-Avila (ibid.) suggests that as these

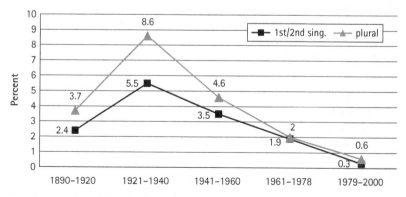

FIGURE 9.1 Percentage of first and second singular and plural verbal –s over time in five cohorts of Springville speakers.

Source: Adapted from table 5.4 in Cukor-Avila 2003, 96.

constraints are lost (Stage II), the use of –s (in all persons) by speakers in the 1920–1940 cohort temporarily increases as they try to sort out its function, as figure 9.1 shows. Examples (1) and (2) illustrate the unsystematic use of –s in connected discourse by an informant born in 1932.

(1) But if one is jealous, you notice every time *you tries* to go somewhere an' come back you're gonna be fussin' at him about somethin', that's gonna make it even worser. That's how I can get along so good so long, you know. I, *I travels* a lot. *I go* a lot. *I see* a lot of people. An' I ain' seen nobody yet that I couldn' talk to. (male/b. 1932)

(2) *I loves* that outside. I would rather be out there an' smell that fresh air. You know it jus', it jus' fun outside. *An' Leons can tell you. He likes* to get out there in them weeds. I'm kin'a like them little kids when *they come* in jus' from the city to the country. They prowlin' all off in them weeds an' things. *I likes that. I loves it.* (male/b. 1932)

As –s loses its association as a marker of present tense (Stage III) its frequency decreases, and by the end of the twentieth century, non-concord –s has almost completely disappeared; as we show in section 4.1, –s in concord environments also declines significantly.

9.3.2 Non-Habitual Invariant *be*

In older rural AAVE, there were two forms of uninflected or invariant *be*: one marked past habituals and occurred primarily as a result of *will/would* deletion,[4] as in example (3), while the other was simply an alternative form of finite *be*, as in example (4). Both occurred occasionally in early White vernaculars in the South.

(3) Mr. Arnold carried his mail all the time an' Mr. Arnold would tell me when he'd leave, *when it be rainin'* like this an' I couldn' work in the field, he'd say, "Harvey, take up a lotta time with my wife at the house." (male/b. 1892)

(4) See the dog wants to get you. That's one thing the dog gon get you. I don' care how long *you be gone,* he wants to get you now. (male/b. 1913)

Over the course of the twentieth century, invariant *be* derived from *will/would* deletion began to decline dramatically (see figure 9.2). Interestingly, the decline in the use of invariant *be* derived from *will/would* deletion paralleled and may be related to the expansion of finite invariant *be*, as detailed in section 9.5.1 below. The decline in the occurrence of *be* derived from *will/would* deletion and the subsequent increase in the occurrence of finite invariant *be* seems to have been the result of a syntactic reanalysis of the latter. Over the course of the twentieth century (and especially after World War II), finite invariant *be* came to be used almost exclusively in habitual contexts, as in

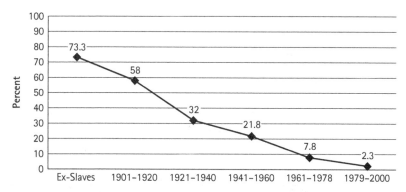

FIGURE 9.2 Percentage of all invariant *be* forms derived from *will/would* deletion over time.

Source: Adapted from Bailey 2007; Cukor-Avila and Bailey 2011.

example (5), perhaps taking on the habituality associated with invariant *be* derived from *will/would* deletion that can be seen in example (3) above (for a detailed discussion of this process, see Bailey and Maynor 1987 and Bailey 2007).

(5) This woman right over there in that house by the church she got two daughters an' they got five kids a piece. An' then she got one daughter got three. An' then she got one daughter got two. *An' all of 'em sometime be over there,* all them gran'children. (fem./b. 1907)

As finite invariant *be* came to be used almost exclusively in habitual contexts, invariant *be* derived from *will/would* deletion began to decline dramatically, although it has never entirely disappeared, as figure 9.2 shows.[5] While invariant *be* derived from *will/would* deletion still appears in rural AAVE, it is recessive.

9.3.3 *Is* for *are*

The status of *are* in AAVE has always been problematic. In earlier varieties, *are* was relatively uncommon, with Ø, *is*, and, to a lesser extent, finite invariant *be* occurring where other varieties have *are* (Bailey and Maynor 1985). In the recordings with former slaves and in older rural speech (Bailey and Maynor 1989), *is* was as frequent as *are* in plural and second singular contexts, with each accounting for about one-fifth of plural and second singular forms, while Ø accounted for a little more than half of the tokens, and finite invariant *be* the remainder. As figure 9.3 shows, the use of plural and second singular *is* in rural AAVE decreased significantly and steadily over the twentieth century. While *is* for *are* is still frequent in existential environments, in non-existential environments it is recessive.

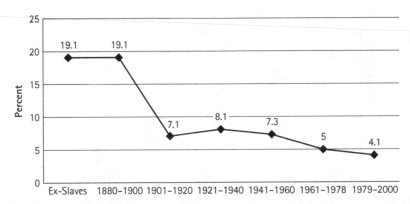

FIGURE 9.3 Decrease of *is* for *are* over time for rural AAVE speakers.

Source: Adapted from Bailey and Maynor 1989; Cukor-Avila 2001.

9.4 Continuous Forms

A number of the characteristic phonological and grammatical features of contemporary rural AAVE have persisted over many years. These "continuous" features are listed in table 9.3. Some of them have a shared history with other English dialects, and in particular with Southern White vernaculars (Bailey 2001; Cukor-Avila 2001). Others, such as reduction of final nasals to vowel nasality, non-recent perfective *been*, or resultative and non-sequential *be done*, are poorly documented in earlier AAVE, and it is unclear if these features have been present in AAVE since its inception or if the constraints on their use have persisted over time. The earliest records of AAVE, however, provide ample evidence for other present-day features like consonant cluster reduction, multiple negation, *ain't*, existential *it*, zero copula, and zero possessive *–s*. What is most noteworthy about some of the features, however, is that while they seem to be features that have persisted over centuries, they have actually undergone internal developments that differentiate their use in younger generations from that in older generations. Two such features are zero third singular verbal *–s* and copula absence.

9.4.1 Zero Third Singular Verbal *–s*

Variable tense marking of present tense verbs (Myhill 1995; Poplack and Tagliamonte 2001) characterized earlier AAVE and remains in contemporary rural AAVE, although the frequency and distribution of *–s* marking has changed over time. Myhill (1995, 128) notes that present tense marking in nineteenth-century AAVE followed "a more or less standard agreement pattern, affected by phonological factors, while modern AAVE has no agreement and phonological factors have no effect." As changes in the constraints

Table 9.3 Continuous Phonological and Grammatical Features in Rural AAVE

	Features	Examples
	Features	Examples
1.	final consonant cluster reduction	cold → [coul]; hand → [hæn]
2.	vocalization of postvocalic /l/	bell → [bɛo]; pool → [puo]
3.	syllable-initial fricative stopping	those → [douz]; these → [diz]
4.	stopping of vl. interdental fricatives	tenth → [tɪnt]; with → [wɪt]
5.	labialization of interdental fricatives	bath → [bæf]; baths → [bævz]
6.	metathesis of final /s/ + stop	ask → [æks]; grasp → [græps]
7.	vocalization of post-vocalic /r/	four → [foə], [fou]; ford → [foəd]
8.	vocalization of unstressed syllabic /r/	father → [fɑðə]; never → [nɛvə]
9.	loss of /r/ after consonants (after θ and in unstressed syllables)	throw → [θou]; professor → [pəfɛsə]
10.	front stressing of initial syllables	police → [poúlis]; Detroit → [dítrɔit]
11.	fricative stopping before nasals	isn't → [ɪdn]; wasn't → [wʌdn]
12.	reduction of final nasal to vowel nasality	man → [mæ̃]
13.	final consonant deletion (esp. affects nasals)	five → fi ___ [faː]; fine → fi [faː]
14.	final stop devoicing	bad → [bæt]
15.	zero plural –s	You want some pea?
16.	zero subj. rel. pronouns	I got some friends ø do that.
17.	have/had deletion	That school ø been there a long time.
18.	non-recent perfective been	I been knowin' her all my life.
19.	be done (resultative)	You might be done met him already.
20.	was for were	They was born and raised right here.
21.	unmarked preterites	They come in here last night.
22.	multiple negation	She don't let 'em go no more.
23.	ain't	Well you ain't too pretty.
24.	existential it	It's a lady, it's a girl, it's a girl that'll bring some by.
25.	perfective done	Before I could get the phone they done hung up.
26.	non-sequential be done	They'll be done burn up.
27.	demonstrative them	When you tell them kids they don't listen.
28.	ain't for didn't	I ain' know what he was talkin' about.
29.	zero possessive –s	She think she everybody mama.
30.	zero third sing. –s	She bring 'em in every mornin'.
31.	copula absence	She ø ready to talk now. / They ø goin' through hard times right now.

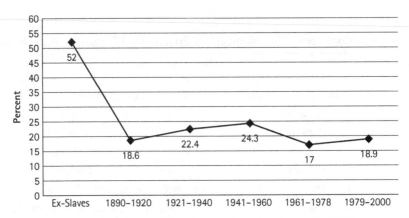

FIGURE 9.4 Percentage of third singular verbal –*s* over time in rural AAVE.

(discussed above) that governed present tense marking weakened and eventually were lost in modern AAVE, the frequency of –*s* in the third singular decreased, just as it did in other present tense contexts (see figure 9.1). While there is still variable tense marking of third singular present tense verbs in contemporary rural AAVE, the frequency of verbal –*s* in this environment has diminished significantly over the past 150 years, as shown in figure 9.4. The history of present tense marking in AAVE suggests that changes in constraints often have quantitative effects. A similar restructuring has affected copula absence over time.

9.4.2 Copula Absence

Both older AAVE and its contemporary descendent use five copula/auxiliary forms—*am, is, are, Ø,* and *be*—but the factors that influence the distribution of the forms have changed over time. In older rural AAVE, the form of the copula was influenced both by its subject and also by its predicate (see figure 9.5). The subject effects reflected the influence of two different English patterns, one of which was driven by the person and number of the subject and the other by the type of subject (NP or PRO). In the person/number system, first person singular is signaled by *am* and all other persons are signaled by *is* or *Ø; are* and *be* occur sporadically as alternative forms, especially in the plural/second singular. The type of subject affects only third person (outside of third person, only pronoun subjects occur). In this system, NP subjects require marked verbs (generally *is*) in both third singular and third plural, while pronoun subjects promote the occurrence of unmarked verbs, or *Ø* in this case.

The predicate effects parallel (but do not necessarily derive from) those in creole languages. In this system, the type of the following predicate influences the form of the copula/auxiliary. Verbal predicates (*gonna* and V+–*ing*) usually take *Ø* as the form of

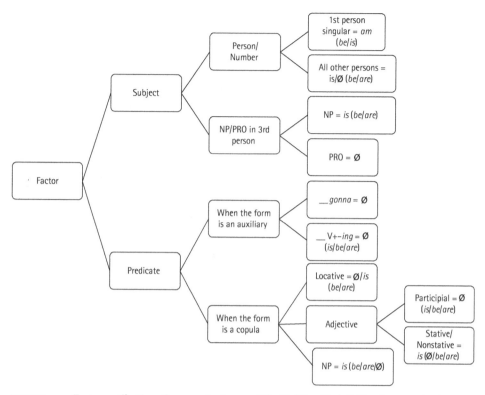

FIGURE 9.5 Factors affecting the copula in pre–World War II AAVE, along with the preferred form in the environment (less frequent forms are in parentheses).

the copula, while NP predicates take *is*. Adjectival and locative predicates take Ø and *is* variably.

Over time this blended copula/auxiliary system was reanalyzed so that after World War II, and especially after 1970, a different set of factors begin to take precedence (see figure 9.6). The predicate effects in older AAVE more-or-less comprise an action versus state system, with those predicates that clearly signal actions taking Ø, and those that clearly signal states taking *is*. Among younger African Americans, this action/state distinction continues to be refined and grammaticalized. As a result, over time, Ø has expanded dramatically before non-stative adjectives, while *is* has come to be preferred before statives (Cukor-Avila 1999). By the 1970s, Ø had become the predominant form before *gonna*, V+–*ing*, participial adjectives, and non-stative adjectives. Before stative adjectives and NPs, *is* was the predominant form and locatives fell somewhere in between. Figure 9.7 illustrates this pattern.

As figure 9.7 suggests, while the zero copula has persisted throughout the history of AAVE, the constraints on its use have changed in subtle but significant ways. The overall effect of the changes in constraints would seem to lead to an increase in the frequency of the zero copula since the contexts in which it occurs have expanded, but the emergence of habitual invariant *be* tends to mitigate against an increase, as shown below.

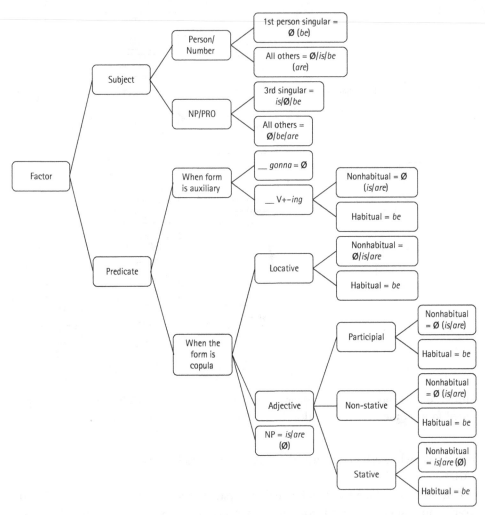

FIGURE 9.6 Factors affecting the copula in post–World War II AAVE, along with the preferred form in the environment (less frequent forms are in parentheses).

9.5 INNOVATIONS

It is important to recognize that while the features listed in table 9.3 occur throughout the history of AAVE, some of them may have changed in subtle ways that research has yet to document fully, as the discussion of the copula above illustrates. Table 9.4 lists innovative features that are widely documented in rural AAVE. They are of three types: (1) ones that were acquired by AAVE speakers in the late nineteenth and early twentieth centuries (e.g., 1 to 8) and for the most part were (and still are) shared with speakers of Southern White vernaculars; (2) grammaticalizations of forms present in older rural AAVE (e.g., 9 and 10) that developed during the course of the twentieth century and

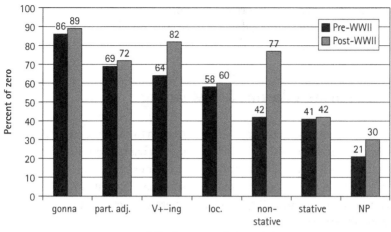

FIGURE 9.7 Comparison of the effects of following grammatical environment on copula absence for pre– and post–World War II speakers.

Source: Cukor-Avila 1999.

Table 9.4 Innovative Phonological and Grammatical Features in Rural AAVE

	Features	Examples	Time period
1.	*yall*	*Yall* don't make any sense.	late nineteenth century
2.	*fixin' to/ fitna*	I'm *fixin' to* fall. / An' they was *fitna* take him to jail.	late nineteenth century
3.	multiple modals	I *might could* help you later today.	late nineteenth/early twentieth century
4.	inceptive *get to/go to*	I *got to* thinkin' about that.	late nineteenth/early twentieth century
5.	merger of /ɛ/ and /ɪ/ before nasals	pen → [pɪn]; Wednesday → [wɪnzdɨ]	late nineteenth/early twentieth century
6.	glide reduction of /ai/ before vd. obstruents and finally	tied → [taːd]; tie → [taː]	late nineteenth/early twentieth century
7.	merger of tense and lax front vowels before /l/	bale → [bɛəɫ]; feel → [fɪəɫ]	late nineteenth/early twentieth century
8.	raising of /æ/ in isolation (i.e., not part of a chain shift)	bag → [bɛg]; pads → [pɛdz]	late nineteenth/early twentieth century
9.	habitual *be* + V+–*ing*	Sometime I *be hearin'* that bus during eighth period.	mid-twentieth century
10.	preterite *had* + past	I *had worked* at Taco Bell today.	mid-twentieth century
11.	quotative *be like*	She was *like*, "You don't have any money?"	early 1990s

are unique to AAVE; and (3) a borrowed form, acquired by young rural AAVE speakers in the late-twentieth century, that has been structurally adapted to AAVE grammar (e.g., 11).

9.5.1 Old Forms Take on New Meaning

Bailey (2007) suggests that grammatical innovations in twentieth-century AAVE are largely a response to grammatical ambiguity (where one form has multiple functions) and have the effect of more closely aligning form and function. For example, in earlier AAVE invariant *be* was used for the entire range of present tense meanings, but gradually *be* has become restricted to habitual contexts (figure 9.8). Furthermore, invariant *be* in early AAVE was used before all predicates roughly equally, but over time its use has become restricted, occurring primarily before V+–*ing* (figure 9.9). Example (6), from a 2002 recording with a Springville informant born in 1982, illustrates invariant *be* in these two contexts.

(6) An' *everybody be hangin' aroun'* McDonald's an' orderin' their food. *Everybody be in there* eatin' an' stuff. . . . 'Cause *it be like people*, you know, mostly *everybody be outside* or if they go eat they come right back outside. (fem./b. 1982)

The reanalysis of the pluperfect in AAVE is also the result of disambiguating form and meaning (Cukor-Avila and Bailey 1995b). In earlier AAVE there were a variety of past tense forms, including unmarked verbs (weak and strong), regularized strong verbs, and past participles for past tense forms. At approximately the same time that unmarked verbs were becoming largely restricted to third singular present tense, speakers began to use the pluperfect, an existing form that was rarely used (Cukor-Avila and Bailey 1995b) as a marker of simple past rather than as a marker of past before past (figure 9.10). This reanalyzed form took the syntactic shape of *had* + past. The following excerpts from two

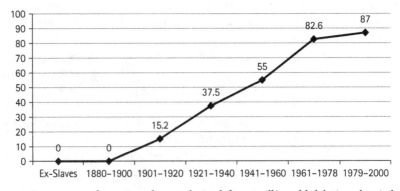

FIGURE 9.8 Percentage of invariant *be* not derived from *will/would* deletion that is habitual.

Source: Adapted from Bailey 2007; Cukor-Avila and Bailey 2011.

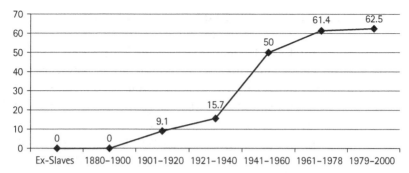

FIGURE 9.9 Percentage of invariant *be* not derived from *will/would* deletion that occurs before V+–*ing*.

Source: Adapted from Bailey 2007; Cukor-Avila and Bailey 2011.

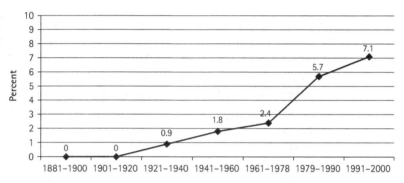

FIGURE 9.10 Expansion of innovative *had* + past (percentage of *had* + past as a simple past out of all past tense forms).

Source: Adapted from Cukor-Avila and Bailey 2011.

Springville young adults illustrate how contemporary rural AAVE speakers[6] use this innovative form both in narrative discourse (7) and for simple past events (8).

(7) So *I had got* his phone number. An' I was bored when *I had got* home. An' it was like three o'clock in the mornin' or somethin' when I got home an' I called him. An' then he was like uh, he was like, "I'm surprised you called," or whatever. I was like, "Why you say that?" He was like, "I don't know. I'm jus' surprised you called," or whatever. An' *we had started talkin'*. An' then um, when I uh, I think Bugger was about two months old when he firs' started goin' aroun', you know. An' uh, *we had went an' stayed* the night at his house with him one night. (fem./b. 1982)

(8) S: I wanted to go to Imperial today. *I had tol'* DW *today.*
V: Ohhh they have big buffets.
S: *I had wanted* that shrimp fried rice they be havin'. (fem./b. 1979)

9.5.2 Structural Adaptation of a Borrowed Form

A third innovation in rural AAVE, and one that clearly has no roots in earlier stages of the vernacular, is the use of quotative *be like* to introduce recreated speech or constructed dialogue, inner thoughts, or non-lexicalized sounds or gestures. Research on quotative *be like* in both Canadian and American English (cf. Tagliamonte and D'Arcy 2007; Ferrara and Bell 1995) suggests that in the last half of the twentieth century speakers began to use this form with increasing frequency, so that by the 1980s, *be like* had replaced *say* as the quotative of choice for speakers born after 1960. This innovative form has also diffused into AAVE. While there are few studies on the use of *be like* for urban AAVE speakers (cf. Sánchez and Charity 1999), Cukor-Avila (2002, 2012) has documented both the diffusion and grammatical adaptation of this form in rural AAVE. Figure 9.11 shows that the crossover, where *be like* begins to replace *say*, does not occur in rural AAVE until the Cohort 5 speakers (born between 1979 and 1990) are in their teens, around the mid-1990s.

Research on the diffusion of quotative *be like* in rural AAVE suggests that this feature first developed in the surrounding urban areas and then subsequently spread into rural AAVE speech communities (Cukor-Avila 2012, 18). Moreover, Cukor-Avila's data further suggest that *be like* did not diffuse structurally intact into the rural vernacular, but rather speakers adapted it into the AAVE copula system by encoding invariant *be* as the predominant form to mark present habitual *be like* quotatives, as in example (9), and by encoding Ø and the inflected forms *am, is, are, was,* and *were* in non-habitual contexts, as in examples (10) and (11).

(9) He's O.K. You be tryin' to talk an' he interrupt you. "I'm talkin' right now." An' *I be like,* "I wanna talk." (fem./b. 1978)

(10) You know Samantha got a little boyfriend. *She like,* "I don' want you talkin' to the boy." (fem./b. 1979)

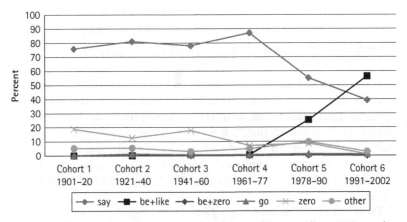

FIGURE 9.11 Distribution of quotatives over six cohorts of Springville AAVE speakers.

Source: Cukor-Avila 2012.

(11) An' like it was scary 'cause this one girl, her friend name Cheyenne, an' she, she was like about ten when we were like friends with her. She was like eleven or twelve. An' then *we were like*, "We gotta drive." An' she can't drive. So we were like on this big ol' ramp an' she's all swervin'. *I'm like*, "Oh my God she's about to kill us." An' we were like swervin' everywhere. An' *I was like*, "OK we should go back down now." (fem./b. 1995)

Thus, innovative quotative *be like* is an example of a borrowed form in rural AAVE that not only has the same range of forms found in the AAVE present tense copula system (*am, is, are,* zero, and *be*) but also has a distribution of these forms in quotative contexts that parallels their distribution in non-quotative contexts.

9.6 CONCLUSION

Rural AAVE exists in a complex historical context. For three centuries, the rural South was the home of most African Americans, and AAVE was rooted there, but the twentieth century saw two remarkable demographic developments (the Great Migration from the South and the Reversal of the Great Migration) that reorganized the African American population in significant ways. These demographic developments correlated with significant linguistic developments in rural AAVE. Many of the older features associated with rural speech have disappeared or are disappearing, while several urban innovations have made their way to the countryside. The end result, however, is not a vernacular that is dying, but one that is dynamic and responsive to cultural change.

NOTES

1. See Bailey (2001, 53–57) for a detailed discussion of the origins debate.
2. The data from Texas come from a longitudinal panel survey comprised primarily of conversational recordings made with residents living in and around the rural community of Springville. See Cukor-Avila (2001) and Cukor-Avila and Bailey (1995a) for a detailed discussion of Springville and its history.
3. The NP/PRO constraint or "Northern subject rule," in which a preceding NP-subject favored the presence of *–s* on third-person plural verbs, was a significant determining factor for present tense marking in earlier English varieties (cf. Bailey, Maynor, and Cukor-Avila 1989; Filppula 1999; Godfrey and Tagliamonte 1999) and for mid- to late-nineteenth-century AAVE and SWVE (Montgomery, Fuller, and DeMarse 1993; Schneider and Montgomery 2001).
4. Deleted *will* also occurs in this environment as in "*They be ready* this winter."
5. As in other vernaculars, deleted past habitual *would* in contemporary rural AAVE has been replaced by the grammaticalized auxiliary *useta*, which is undeletable.
6. Labov et al. (1968) and Rickford and Rafal (1996) report the use of *had* + past or preterit *had* for urban AAVE speakers as well.

REFERENCES

Bailey, Guy. 1987. "Are Black and White Vernaculars Diverging?" Papers from the NWAVE 14 panel discussion. *American Speech* 62: 32–40.

———. 1997. "When Did Southern American English Begin?" In *Englishes around the World 1: Studies in Honour of Manfred Gorlach*, edited by Edgar W. Schneider, 255–75. Philadelphia: John Benjamins.

———. 2001. "The Relationship between African American and White Vernaculars in the American South: A Sociocultural History and some Phonological Evidence." In *Sociocultural and Historical Contexts of African American English*, edited by Sonja Lanehart, 53–92. Philadelphia: John Benjamins.

———. 2007. "Ambiguity and Innovation in the Evolution of African American Vernacular English." Presentation at Studies in the History of the English Language (SHEL-5). University of Georgia, Athens, Georgia.

Bailey, Guy, and Natalie Maynor. 1985. "The Present Tense of *be* in Southern Black Folk Speech." *American Speech* 60: 195–213.

———. 1987. "Decreolization?" *Language in Society* 16: 449–73.

———. 1989. "The Divergence Controversy." *American Speech* 64: 40–68.

Bailey, Guy, Natalie Maynor, and Patricia Cukor-Avila. 1989. "Variation in Subject-Verb Concord in Early Modern English." *Language Variation and Change* 1: 285–301.

Bailey, Guy, and Erik Thomas. 1998. "Some Aspects of African-American Vernacular English Phonology." In *African-American English: Structure, History and Use*, edited by Salikoko S. Mufwene, John R. Rickford, Guy Bailey, and John Baugh, 85–109. New York: Routledge.

Bailey, Guy, Tom Wikle, Jan Tillery, and Lori Sand. 1996. "The Linguistic Consequences of Catastrophic Events: An Example from the American Southwest." In *Sociolinguistic Variation: Data, Theory, and Analysis: Selected Papers from NWAV 23 at Stanford*, edited by Jennifer Arnold, Renée Blake, and Brad Davidson, 435–51. Stanford, CA: Center for the Study of Language and Information, Stanford University.

Bereiter, Carl, and Siegfried Engelmann. 1966. *Teaching Disadvantaged Children in the Pre-School*. Englewood Cliffs, NJ: Prentice Hall.

Christian, Donna, Walt Wolfram, and Nanjo Dube. 1988. *Variation and Change in Geographically Isolated Communities: Appalachian English and Ozark English*. PADS 74. Tuscaloosa: University of Alabama Press.

Cukor-Avila, Patricia. 1999. "Stativity and Copula Absence in AAVE: Grammatical Constraints at the Sub-Categorical Level." *Journal of English Linguistics* 27: 341–55.

———. 2001. "Co-Existing Grammars: The Relationship between the Evolution of African American Vernacular English and White Vernacular English in the South." In *Sociocultural and Historical Contexts of African American English*, edited by Sonja Lanehart, 93–127. Philadelphia: John Benjamins.

———. 2002. "'She *say*,' 'she *go*,' 'she *be like*': Verbs of Quotation over Time in African American Vernacular English." *American Speech* 77: 3–31.

———. 2003. "The Complex Grammatical History of African-American Vernaculars in the South." In *English in the Southern United States*, edited by Stephen J. Nagle and Sara L. Sanders, 82–105. Cambridge: Cambridge University Press.

———. 2012. "Some Structural Consequences of Diffusion." *Language in Society* 41: 1–26.

Cukor-Avila, Patricia, and Guy Bailey. 1995a. "An Approach to Sociolinguistic Fieldwork: A Site Study of Rural AAVE in a Texas Community." *English World-Wide*. 16 (2): 159–93.

————. 1995b. "Grammaticalization in AAVE." *Proceedings of the Twenty-First Annual Meeting of the Berkeley Linguistic Society*, edited by Jocelyn Ahlers, Leela Bilmes, Joshua S. Guenter, Barbara A. Kaiser, and Ju Namkung, 401–13. Berkeley: University of California, Department of Linguistics.

Deutsch, Martin, Irwin Katz, and Arthur Jensen, eds. 1968. *Social Class, Race, and Psychological Development.* New York: Holt, Rinehart and Winston.

Fasold, Ralph W. 1972. *Tense Marking in Black English: A Linguistic and Social Analysis.* Arlington, VA: Center for Applied Linguistics.

Ferrara, Kathleen, and Barbara Bell. 1995. "Sociolinguistic Variation and Discourse Function of Constructed Dialogue Introducers: The Case of *be + like*." *American Speech* 70: 265–90.

Filppula, Markku. 1999. *The Grammar of Irish English.* London: Routledge.

Godfrey, Elizabeth, and Sali A. Tagliamonte. "Another Piece for the Verbal –*s* Story: Evidence from Devon in Southwest England." *Language Variation and Change* 11: 87–121.

Henry, Alison. 1992. "Infinitives in a *for-to* Dialect." *Natural Language and Linguistic Theory* 10: 279–301.

Jensen, Arthur. 1969. "How Much Can We Boost IQ and Scholastic Achievement?" *Harvard Educational Review* 39: 1–123.

Labov, William. 1972. *Language in the Inner City.* Philadelphia: University of Pennsylvania Press.

Labov, William, Paul Cohen, Clarence Robins, and John Lewis. 1968. *A Study of the Non-Standard English of Negro and Puerto Rican Speakers in New York City.* Philadelphia: U.S. Regional Survey.

Montgomery, Michael, Janet M. Fuller, and Sharon DeMarse. 1993. "The Black Men Has Wives and Sweet Harts [and Third Person Plural –*s*] Jest Like the White Men: Evidence for Verbal –*s* from Written Documents on Nineteenth-Century African-American Speech." *Language Variation and Change* 5: 335–57.

Myhill, John. 1995. "The Use of Features of Present Day AAVE in the Ex-Slave Recordings." *American Speech* 70: 115–47.

Poplack, Shana, ed. 2000. *The English History of African American English.* Malden, MA: Blackwell.

Poplack, Shana, and Sali Tagliamonte. 2001. *African American English in the Diaspora: Tense and Aspect.* Oxford: Blackwell.

Rickford, John R. 2006. "Down for the Count? The Creole Origins Hypothesis of AAVE at the Hands of the Ottawa Circle, and their Supporters." *Journal of Pidgin and Creole Languages* 21: 97–154.

Rickford, John R., and Christine Théberge Rafal. 2006. "Preterit *had* in the Narratives of African American Adolescents." *American Speech* 71: 227–54.

Sánchez, Tara, and Anne Charity. 1999. "Use of *be like* and other Verbs of Quotation in a Predominantly African-American Community." Paper presented at New Ways of Analyzing Variation in English (NWAVE 28), Toronto, Ontario.

Schneider, Edgar, and Michael Montgomery. 2001. "On the Trail of Early Nonstandard Grammar: An Electronic Corpus of Southern U.S. Antebellum Overseers' Letters." *American Speech* 76: 388–410.

Tagliamonte, Sali, and Alexandra D'Arcy. 2007. "Frequency and Variation in the Community Grammar: Tracking a New Change through the Generations." *Language Variation and Change* 19: 199–217.

Thomas, Erik R., and Guy Bailey. 1998. "Parallels between Vowel Subsystems of African American Vernacular English and Caribbean Creoles." *Journal of Pidgin and Creole Languages* 13: 267–96.

Tillery, Jan, and Guy Bailey. 2003. Urbanization and the Evolution of Southern American English." In *English in the Southern United States*, edited by Stephen J. Nagle and Sara L. Sanders, 159–72. Cambridge: Cambridge University Press.

Wolfram, Walt. 1969. *A Sociolinguistic Description of Detroit Negro Speech*. Washington, DC: Center for Applied Linguistics.

———. 2003. "Enclave Dialect Communities in the South." In *English in the Southern United States*, edited by Stephen J. Nagle and Sara L. Sanders, 141–58. Cambridge: Cambridge University Press.

Wolfram, Walt, and Ralph Fasold. 1974. *The Study of Social Dialects in American English*. Englewood Cliffs, NJ: Prentice-Hall.

Wolfram, Walt, and Erik R. Thomas. 2002. *The Development of African American English*. Oxford: Blackwell.

CHAPTER 10

AFRICAN AMERICAN ENGLISH IN THE MISSISSIPPI DELTA

A Case Study of Copula Absence and r-Lessness in the Speech of African American Women in Coahoma County

ROSE WILKERSON

10.1 INTRODUCTION

COAHOMA COUNTY AAE,[1] located in the Mississippi Delta, has a linguistic unique-ness that is not found in other contemporary AAE varieties. Throughout its history, the Mississippi Delta has experienced migrations of people both within and outside of the state of Mississippi for over a hundred years. It has also been predominantly African American since the 1850s. We believe that these factors have contributed to the develop-ment of a unique regional AAE variety. The intent of this chapter is to analyze the speech of twenty-one African American women in Coahoma County, Mississippi. The geographic focus is on two towns, Clarksdale, which is the county seat and is both demographically and racially mixed, and Jonestown, a predominantly African American town. Subjects from other less-populated, rural areas are also included in the analysis. The present study points out how Coahoma County AAE differs from other contemporary AAE varieties.

Many of the chapters in this volume, including those on Gullah by Weldon and Moody, rural Texas AAE by Cukor-Avila and Bailey, and AAE in North Carolina by Wolfram and Kohn, provide a discussion of the historical and regional development of these lan-guage varieties. Delta AAE as a distinct regional variety has been influenced by settlers from neighboring states (Tennessee, Kentucky, and Alabama) and also southeastern states (the Carolinas and Georgia) from the 1820s to the 1860s (Cobb 1992, 8). The Delta's his-tory does not end there. There were also two large migrations of African Americans into the Mississippi Delta region. The first occurred in the 1880s, a period of time in which the railway provided the main transportation into the region.[2] During this time, most of the incoming African Americans came from other parts of Mississippi (Cobb 1992, 83). The second migration occurred in the early 1900s, with the advent of World War I, when approximately 100,000 African Americans left the Delta; however, thousands more entered the region, which increased the African American population by 17 percent between 1910 and 1920. Many African Americans also came from eastern Mississippi, as well as Kansas[3] (Cobb 1992, 115). This history of migration into the region helps to provide an explanation for the Delta being a unique linguistic area. This distinction is also supported by many of the regional maps in the *Linguistic Atlas of the Gulf States* (Pederson et al. 1986).[4]

In this chapter, I present data from Wilkerson's (2008) quantitative analysis on copula absence and r-lessness, two prominent features of Coahoma County AAE. The data come from a sociological study that included recorded interviews of single African American mothers in Coahoma County (Dill 1988). The results of the current quantitative study show (1) a connection between Coahoma County AAE and older, diasporic AAE varieties and English-based Caribbean creoles through the analysis of copula absence; (2) statistical differences in the production of the two features based on the subject's township; and (3) that the educational level of the subject and of their parent(s) also plays a role in the production of both features.

We begin the study by presenting geographic information about the Delta and Coahoma County and continuing with a discussion of previous AAE studies situated in the Mississippi Delta. We continue by presenting the data and the subjects, as well as a description of copula absence and r-lessness explaining why it is important to analyze these features in AAE speech. Towards the end of the chapter, I discuss the results of the quantitative analysis followed by our conclusion.

10.2 GEOGRAPHY OF THE MISSISSIPPI DELTA

The Mississippi Delta is located in the northwest part of the state of Mississippi between the Mississippi and Yazoo Rivers, and it comprises seventeen counties. This region is commonly referred to as the *Delta* by the residents of the state of Mississippi. The Mississippi Delta River lies to the west of the Delta region,[5] and the Yazoo River forms its eastern border. The Delta runs as far north as Memphis, Tennessee, and as far south as Vicksburg, Mississippi. The area has some of the world's most fertile soil, which is ideal for agriculture both currently and historically, due to thousands of years of annual flooding; it is approximately 7,100 square miles (Cobb 1992, 3) and comprises 4,000,000 acres of rich soil.

Coahoma County is located in the northwest part of the Delta on the banks of the Mississippi River. It was one of the first counties established in the Delta's history due to its easy access to the river. Coahoma County is approximately 75 miles south of Memphis, 184 miles north of Jackson, and hundreds of miles from other major southern cities (e.g., Birmingham, Nashville, and Dallas). A little over three-quarters of the land in the Delta is used for agricultural purposes, including the growing of cotton, rice, soybeans, sorghum, and wheat. There are six incorporated communities in Coahoma County: Clarksdale,[6] Coahoma, Friars Point, Jonestown, Lyon, and Lula. Clarksdale is the largest and most populated town in the county. At the time the data were collected, African Americans in Coahoma County made up 64.5 percent of the total population, which is shown in table 10.1.

Small, predominantly African American towns in the Delta were originally the living quarters of the African American labor force that worked on nearby plantations or farms. For example, Jonestown originally serviced a local farm up until the 1970s, when the landowners abandoned their farmland without telling the Jonestown residents, who had no other economic resources. Mound Bayou, another predominantly African American town, was founded as an independent African American community by former slaves (Cobb 1992) and thus was not set up as many of the other predominantly African American towns in the Delta were. Many of these towns were relatively isolated, and their residents had to travel several miles, usually by foot, in order to get to a larger town for staple food items and services not provided by the local farm.[7]

Before White colonists settled into the region in the mid-1800s, the Delta was a swampy and forested area. Delta plantation landowners came from as close as Tennessee and as far away as the Carolinas. In order to cultivate Delta land for agriculture, a huge labor force was required to clear, drain, and cultivate the land as "quickly and extensively as possible" (Cobb 1992, 21). African American labor was essential to this process and required a large number of slaves, establishing a predominance of slaves very early in the Delta's history. The large African American labor force was a contributing factor to slaves outnumbering Whites five to one by 1850 (Cobb 1992, 8). Other conditions that called for a large slave population were cleanups after annual flooding (e.g., draining the water, cleaning up debris and dead carcasses); the creation and maintenance of a flood-control levee system; and a very high child mortality rate among the slave

Table 10.1 1990 Racial Demographics of Clarksdale, Jonestown, and Coahoma County

Race	Clarksdale	Jonestown	Coahoma county
White	7,406	74	11,001 (34.7%)
African American	12,195	1,392	20,454 (64.5%)
American Indian, Eskimo, or Aleut	15	1	20 (.06%)
Asian or Pacific Islander	88	0	112 (.35%)
Other Race	13	0	78 (.24%)
Total	19,717	1,467	31,665[a]

[a] The total numbers of Clarksdale and Jonestown do not make up the total population of Coahoma County since there are other towns within the county.
Source: US Census Bureau, online.

population, as an estimated one-quarter of the slave children never made it to adulthood (Cobb 1992, 21–22). Because of the slave labor and the region's rich soil, Delta landowners enjoyed a very lucrative cotton industry in the early 1900s that lasted for decades.

With the high demand for labor in the Delta came a predominance of African Americans, who outnumbered the White population and then grew exponentially as the need for African American labor increased, especially with the boom of the cotton agriculture in the region. Thus, while the Delta began as a distinct region geographically, it also distinguished itself demographically as well. The African American population has remained over 60 percent of the total population throughout the Delta's history. Its geographic isolation, agricultural significance, and well-established socioeconomic caste-like system help to make the region a valuable area for linguistic research.

10.3 Previous Research on AAE in the Mississippi Delta

There have been several studies on African American speech in the Mississippi Delta. The earliest linguistic studies focused on the similarities and differences between African American and White southern speech. These studies were conducted by Wolfram (1971, 1974)[8] and Vaughn-Cooke (1976, 1986). While Wolfram (1971, 1974) analyzed habitual *be*, copula absence (for White speakers only), verbal –s marking, possessive –s, and consonant cluster reduction (CCR), Vaughn-Cooke (1976, 1986) analyzed the process of resyllabification in unstressed initial syllables. These studies are reflective of a period of time in AAE sociolinguistics research when distinguishing White and African American speech was important to the field.

Walton et al. (1990) conducted research on African American and White speech in a prison population at the state penitentiary in Parchman, which is located in the Delta. The study's goal was to distinguish dialectal features versus communicative disorders in order to provide proper rehabilitation services to prisoners. These authors analyzed nine features: final stop devoicing, distributive *be*, remote aspect *been*, the plural –s marker, third singular present tense marker –s, possessive –s, CCR, copula absence, and *is/are* auxiliary absence.

The Delta as a linguistic region was also a part of a fifteen-year research project on southern American English called the Linguistic Atlas of the Gulf States (LAGS) by Pederson et al. (1986). LAGS used a 104-page questionnaire to collect linguistic data from over 1,100 subjects in the Gulf states of Florida, Georgia, Tennessee, Alabama, Mississippi, Louisiana, Arkansas, and Texas, resulting in approximately 5,300 hours of recorded speech. African American and White speakers made up the subjects of this significant research study.

The mid-1990s to early 2000 marked a time that focused on rhotic variation (e.g., r-lessness and r-retention). Lambert (1995), Hinton and Pollock (2000), Weaver (2000), and Fletcher (2002) studied rhotic variation among children and female adult AAE speakers with a focus on the presence or absence of /r/ to the phonetic quality of /r/ using word elicitation tasks. Lambert's (1995) study, which focused on Mississippi and eastern Louisiana, examined the changes that had taken place in the retention of /r/ in the South using data from LAGS. Hinton and Pollock (2000) analyzed the vocalic and postvocalic /r/ of African Americans in Davenport, Iowa.[9] Weaver (2000) presented an acoustic description of the vocalic and postvocalic /r/ of child and adult speakers in the Mid-South region within one-hundred miles of Memphis. Fletcher's (2002) rhotic study examines the speech of 3- and 5-year-old AAE speakers and their primary caregivers (all female) from Memphis and Shelby County in Tennessee.

Lastly, Wilkerson's (2008) quantitative analysis on copula absence and r-lessness is the most recent sociolinguistic study conducted on Delta AAE,[10] and the highlights of this particular work are featured in the current chapter. Thus, (1) the study differs from other studies in that it analyzes social factors (i.e., education and township), which influence the production of copula absence and r-lessness; and (2) it is one of the most recent sociolinguistic studies on Delta AAE.

10.4 DATA AND SUBJECTS

10.4.1 The Data

The data come from a two-year sociological study that examined "the relationship between gender, race, family structure, and poverty within the context of Southern rural political economies" in the Mid-South (Dill 1988, 1). This comprehensive study is based on in-depth recorded interviews that are approximately an hour and a half long, approximately 37.5 hours of AAE speech. Twenty-five African American single mothers living in Coahoma County, the largest data source of Dill's (1988) study, were interviewed. The interview questions provided insight on the subject's family background, education, health care, food and diet, family income and its distribution, employment and public aid and welfare, local politics, community organizations, and race relations. Some of the interviews were conducted one-on-one, while others had one or two family members present during the interview. Dill's (1988) research team[11] was a multi-race and mixed-gender team, which allowed them to gain access and information about their subjects, especially in reference to sensitive topics relating to racial relations.

The early 1990s was an important period of time for the analysis of AAE speech in the region because it preceded the arrival of the gambling casinos in the Delta area. The subjects in the current study rarely traveled outside of the Delta, especially those that resided in predominantly African American towns that were several miles in distance from the county seat, Clarksdale. Many of the single mothers in places like Jonestown had to walk a total of twenty-four miles to do their main grocery shopping in Clarksdale (Jonestown had a small store that did not contain staple food items). With the arrival of the gambling casinos in the mid-1990s came a new public transportation system and paved roads, which were set up for local tourism and for easy access for workers. Prior to the arrival of casinos, African Americans in small towns like Jonestown did little traveling within the Delta area, making the pre-casino time period essential in studying AAE.

10.4.2 The Subjects

Twenty-one subjects are included in the present linguistic study; half of the subjects fall within the range of 18 to 25 years of age and the other half, 26 to 31 years. One subject who was 38 years old was interviewed as well. Seven of the female subjects were raised in Jonestown and another seven in Clarksdale in Coahoma County. Six of the subjects were raised in another rural town either within or outside of Coahoma County and one subject's specific town is unknown, although it is known that she was raised in Marshall County.[12]

At the time the data were collected, job employment opportunities for African American women were severely limited, especially in Coahoma County. African American women in rural communities in the Delta often have seasonal jobs, such as catfish farming (Dill 1990). These types of jobs as well as government welfare were their primary source of income. Those jobs that were available were low-level, low-skilled, minimum-wage jobs that were most often located far away from their communities (Dill 1990). Single mothers with these types of jobs had to spend most of their income earnings on transportation costs alone. The women's ability to work was based upon having a support system (i.e., extended family, for basic needs, such as childcare). With regard to the quality of life, rural residents found accessible health care and child care largely unavailable. Rural children were vulnerable to being left behind educationally and their families were more likely than their urban counterparts to live in substandard housing even though they spent a larger share of their income on housing (Dill 1999).

Most of the subjects were from predominantly African American rural towns in Coahoma County or from a nearby county within the Delta. At the time of the interviews, all of the subjects lived in either Jonestown or Clarksdale. Although two-thirds of the subjects lived in either of these two towns, six of them were raised in other rural areas within and outside of Coahoma County, but within the Delta. These towns are the following: Belzoni (Humphreys County), Shaw (Bolivar County), and Mound Bayou (Coahoma County). With the exception of Belzoni, Shaw and Mound Bayou are the only predominantly African American towns. Table 10.2 shows the demographic data in 1990 at the time of the recordings.

The subjects all had varied levels of education. Some of the subjects had a high school degree or GED,[13] and others had one to two years of a college level of education. Most of the subjects with a college level of education were students at Coahoma Community College, which provided special educational programs for single mothers. As far as the educational level of the parents who raised the subjects is concerned, we find that most of them had an elementary or secondary level of education. And, in one case, one parent had a college level of education.

Table 10.2 1990 Racial Demographics of other Rural Towns Outside of Coahoma County

Race	Belzoni, MS (Humphreys County)	Shaw, MS (Bolivar County)	Mound Bayou, MS (Bolivar County)
White	1,108	377	6
African American	1,405	1,970	2,213
American Indian, Eskimo, or Aleut	4	0	1
Asian or Pacific Islander	19	2	2
Other Race	0	0	0
Total	2,536	2,349	2,222

Source: US Census Bureau, online.

10.5 THE PRESENT STUDY: COPULA ABSENCE AND r-LESSNESS

The current study is a variation study of two prominent grammatical features in Coahoma County AAE. A variation study is a quantitative analysis which allows linguists to identify and/or generalize the relationships between language use and social factors (i.e., different ethnic, regional, and social varieties of a language as well as different circumstances of language use). That is to say that a variation study helps us to understand how copula absence and r-lessness is used among African American single mothers who have been raised in different areas within the Delta and who have different educational backgrounds. Below is a description of each grammatical feature and its importance in AAE quantitative study. A description of the education and township variables follows.

10.5.1 Copula Absence

Copula absence, the absence of *is* and *are* in a present tense sentence, is one of the best studied features in quantitative AAE research. It has sparked many a discussion and several research studies on the origins of AAE, that is, whether AAE derived from an earlier plantation creole resembling an English-based Caribbean creole or an earlier White American English or British dialect spoken in the early colonial period (Fasold et al. 1987; Wolfram 1987; Winford 1997, 1998; Rickford 1998; Poplack 1999). Copula absence "sets AAVE apart from all other American dialects" (Rickford et al. 1991; Rickford 1999, 61) in that the absent copula is a unique feature of AAE occurring at high rates of frequency among the lower socioeconomic classes (Wolfram 1969). Analyzing copula absence[14] in Coahoma County AAE helps us to understand its linguistic uniqueness and allows us to compare it with other AAE varieties in the United States.

Previous copula variation studies, more specifically Labov (1972) and Rickford et al. (1991) have determined the constraints or grammatical environments in which copula absence is used: subject of sentence, following grammatical environment, preceding phonological environment, and following phonological environment. Copula absence in Coahoma County AAE shares many similarities with other AAE varieties; one example is the following grammatical conditions that favor copula absence. The results in Wilkerson (2008) quantitative research show that Coahoma County AAE speakers delete the copula before *gonna* at a very high occurrence of deletion similar to other AAE varieties with Verb+–*ing* taking second place. What sets Coahoma County apart from other AAE varieties is the subject of sentence, which is the main discussion on copula absence in the current study.

10.5.2 *r*-lessness

r-lessness has also been a widely studied phonological feature, especially in American dialectology, due to its long standing as a feature in the southern and northeastern regions of the United States[15] and its recent change in use among White southern speakers. Older generational African American and White speakers of English in the South tend to vocalize /r/ in certain phonological contexts: syllabic /r/ as in *father*/faðə/ and non-syllabic coda /r/ as in *card*/kad/. In the examples just cited, the /r/ is vocalized or deleted; this is referred to as r-lessness.[16] Another aspect of the current study is how the use of r-lessness varies by the educational level of the speakers (and parents) and their township.

10.5.3 Education and Township Variables

There are three social variables that are used in the current quantitative analysis: subject's educational level, parent's educational level, and township of subject. These three variables represent the social factors that distinguish the speakers from each other. The subject's education variable refers to the educational level achieved by the subject. There are three variants: secondary level, vocational level, and college level. The secondary educational level refers to the subject spending a couple of years in high school, or receiving their diploma or GED. The college variant refers to those subjects who have had some years of college education.[17] The vocational variant refers to subjects who were trained as nurse's or teacher's assistants. It also refers to those who have had some job training aimed at upgrading work skills through the Job Corps organization.

The second social variable is parent's educational level. The variants are elementary, secondary, college, and unknown. The elementary variant refers to an elementary school level of education of a subject's primary parent.[18] The secondary and college variants have already been described above. Six subjects did not know the educational level of their parents and for them the variable is identified as unknown.

The third social variable, township, represents the town in which the subject lived for the first fifteen years of their life. A couple of the subjects moved to their township at the age of 5, but the rest were raised in their township from birth. At this point, it is important to remember that at the time of the recorded interviews the subjects lived either in Jonestown or Clarksdale. The variants for the township variable are Clarksdale, Jonestown, other rural towns,[19] and unknown. About a third of the subjects were born and raised in Jonestown, another third in Clarksdale, and the last third in other rural towns in the Delta.

10.6 THE RESULTS

To analyze the data, a variable rule software program, GoldVarb 3.0, was used to provide a statistical analysis; this is a program that analyzes social and linguistic variation, and is commonly used to analyze copula absence and r-lessness (Rand and Sankoff 1990). For each variant, the probability values (*p*-value) that are higher than 0.5 favor r-lessness; the further above 0.5, the more strongly it is favored. Probability values below 0.5 disfavor it; the further below 0.5, the more strongly it is disfavored. The tables will present the *p*-value of each variant, its percentage rate (percent), and the number of deleted copulas counted (N) with the total number of copulas counted (Total).

10.6.1 Subject of Sentence for Copula Absence

The *subject of sentence* variable, taken from Rickford et al.'s (1991) study, consists of three variants: personal pronouns (*you, he, she, we, they*), other pronouns (e.g., *there, everybody*), and NP or noun phrase (e.g., *my mother, the landlord*). Examples of the variants are the following: "*You* crazy!" where the italicized is the personal pronoun that precedes the absent copula; "*My mother* forty years old" shows the use of a noun phrase (NP); "*Everybody* out dancing" shows the use of another pronoun.[20] The total number of copula tokens is 1,928. On average, there are approximately one-hundred tokens per subject. In table 10.3, I present the results for the subject of sentence of copula absence only.

For the *subject of sentence* variable, the noun phrase (.820) has a very strong effect on copula absence while the personal pronoun (.465) has a relatively weak effect. AAE varieties

Table 10.3 Probability Analysis for Subject of Sentence

Subject of sentence	Absent Copula		
	p-value	%	N/Total
Noun phrase	.820	58.7	88/150
Other pronoun	.501	25	35/140
Personal pronoun	.465	41	671/1,638

Input: 0.370; Log likelihood: −758.010; Significance: 0.024.

show that personal pronouns as subjects consistently favor copula absence more strongly than NPs; however, the Coahoma County AAE data seem to show the reverse. In his study, Rickford (1998) states that there is not much parallelism between creoles and AAVE when it comes to the effect of subject of a sentence on copula absence. He goes on to say, "the relation between an NP and a personal pronoun subject is absolutely regular in AAVE: the latter favors copula absence more than the former does, by substantial margins (20 to 40 percent). By contrast, in three of the creole sets ... the ordering is reversed, with a nominal subject [or NP] favoring copula absence more than a pronoun subject" (Rickford 1998, 183–84). Rickford (1998) adds that the diasporic AAE of Samaná and Nova Scotia also show that copula absence is strongly favored by the NP subject. The percentages that Rickford (1998) refers to are presented in table 10.4 below, which shows the *p*-value and percentage differences between creoles, AAVE, and other AAE varieties in the diaspora.

Table 10.4 Preceding Grammatical Environment of Creoles, AAVE, and Diaspora AAE

AAE varieties and Caribbean Creole languages	NP__	Personal pro__	Other pro__
Coahoma County AAE	.820 (58.7%)	.465 (41%)	.501 (25%)
Caribbean Creoles			
Barbadian, 1980s data (Rickford and Blake 1990, 267)	.84	.19	.45
Barbadian, 1991 data (Rickford 1992, 192)	.48	.52	–
Jamaican (Rickford 1996, 369)	.70	.60	.23
Trinidadian group sessions (Winford 1992, 34)[a]	.42/.46	.49/.60/.64	.39
Diaspora Recordings			
Liberian Settler English, Albert and Slim (Singler 1991, 145)[b]	.43/.89	.24/.51/.51	.22/–/.63
Samaná (Poplack and Sankoff 1987, 307)[b]	.81	.06/.28/.90	.06/.43/.53
ANSE (Poplack and Tagliamonte 1991, 321)[b]	.89	.16/.52/.91	.29/–/.37
Urban AAVE			
AAVE, NYC Thunderbirds, zero *is* (Labov 1972, 84)[c]	12%/42%	51%/60%	–
AAVE, NYC Cobras, zero *is* (Labov 1972, 84)[c]	18%/42%	51%/60%	–
AAVE, Detroit WC (Wolfram 1969, 170)[d]	30%/18%	63%/41%	–
AAVE, East Palo Alto (Rickford et al. 1991)	.42/(.54)	.62/(.51)	.46/(.44)
Rural AAE			
Texana, NC (Childs and Mallinson 2004, 36)	.53	.49	–
Hyde County, NC (Wolfram and Thomas 2002)	.43	.56	–

[a] Figures in first column represent Singular NP/Plural NP; second column figures are 1s *I*, 3s *he* & *she*, and 3p forms *we, you,* and *they,* respectively.
[b] Personal Pro figures = 1s *I*, 3s *he* and *she,* and 3p forms *we, you,* and *they,* respectively.
[c] First figure represents single style; second figure is for group style.
[d] First figure represents the lower working class; second figure the upper working class.
Source: Adapted from Rickford 1998, 184, table 6.13, with the addition of Delta AAE and rural AAE data results.

In table 10.4, with the results of the current study at the top of the table for easy comparison, we see that Coahoma County AAE has more similarity to English-based Caribbean creoles (i.e., Barbadian and Jamaican creoles) and diaspora recordings, that is, Liberian Settler English, Samaná, and African Nova Scotia English (ANSE), which are reported to reflect much older forms of AAE (early nineteenth century). This is quite different from what is found in urban AAE data, where according to table 10.4, the NP in East Palo Alto AAE has a neutral (.54) or disfavorable (.42) effect on copula absence.[21] When comparing percentages of Coahoma County AAE with New York and Detroit AAE varieties, we see that the former has a much higher percentage rate of deletion after an NP than the latter. In the rural AAE studies, Texana AAE shows that the NP-subject (.53) favors the deleted copula more than the pronoun (.49), even though this variable was not chosen as significant (Childs and Mallinson 2004, 36) and the difference between the two is not that great. With Hyde County AAE, the personal pronoun (.56) favors the deleted copula more strongly than the subject NP (.43) and the variable is significant (Wolfram and Thomas 2002).

What these comparisons show is that copula absence in Coahoma County AAE appears to have a similar pattern to creoles and older diasporic AAE varieties for the subject of sentence than with other contemporary AAE varieties, be they urban or rural. This pattern is unusual and an explanation for why this occurs is not completely known at this time. Linguistic analysis of other AAE features and a deeper look into the history of the Delta[22] would be necessary to determine the possible connections between diasporic AAE varieties and Caribbean creole languages. It is possible that urban AAE has undergone linguistic change due to the influence of local non-AAE varieties, and possibly the influence of educational system in urban areas.

10.6.2 Variation in Production of Copula Absence and r-lessness by Education and Township

Social variables (i.e., *education* and *township*) also have an effect on copula absence as they do with r-lessness. The results for this part of the analysis are presented in table 10.5. For the subject's education, we see that the college-educated subjects have a higher *p*-value of copula absence (.561) and r-lessness (.523) than the other educational levels for both features. In fact, the college level subjects favor copula absence and r-lessness, whereas the secondary (.456 for copula absence and .499 for r-lessness) and vocational level (.326 for copula absence and .376 for r-lessness) do not. The higher the educational level of the subject, the higher the occurrence of copula absence and r-lessness.

For the *parent's education* variable, we see under copula absence the unknown (.677) and elementary (.646) variants strongly favor copula absence. There is a similar pattern in r-lessness as well; elementary (.596) and unknown (.583) favor r-lessness while the secondary level has a neutral effect (.505) and college level disfavors r-lessness (.334). Overall the *parent's education* variable seems to suggest that subjects who had parents with an elementary level of education tend to have higher occurrences of copula absence

Table 10.5 Education and Township Results of Copula Absence and r–Lessness

Social variables	Copula absence			r-lessness		
	p-value	%	N/Total	p-value	%	N/Total
Subject's Education						
College	.561	50.8	475/935	.523	67.6	1,148/1,698
Secondary	.456	32.8	294/896	.499	56.8	744/1,310
Vocational	.326	25.8	25/97	.376	45.9	139/303
Parent's Education						
Unknown	.677	60.3	412/683	.583	69.9	595/851
Elementary	.646	40.0	52/130	.596	63.1	245/388
Secondary	.438	32.6	242/742	.505	55.9	784/1,403
College	.256	23.6	88/373	.334	60.8	407/669
Township of Subject						
Other rural towns	.675	52.6	193/367	.493	64.7	651/1,006
Jonestown	.611	52.1	462/886	.697	72.7	784/1,079
Unknown	.290	34.5	19/55	.436	50.0	69/138
Clarksdale	.269	19.4	120/620	.318	48.4	527/1,088

and r-lessness. In other words, the lower the educational level of the parent, the higher the occurrence of copula absence and r-lessness in the speech of the subject.

For the *township of subject* variable, other rural towns (.675) and Jonestown (.611) variants strongly favor copula absence, which means a higher production of copula absence. For r-lessness, we see that Jonestown (.697) not only has the highest p-value but it also strongly favors copula absence whereas the other rural towns (.493) and Clarksdale do not. These results highlight significant differences between the smaller, predominant African American towns, especially Jonestown, and Clarksdale.

10.7 CONCLUSION

What we can conclude about copula absence for Coahoma County AAE is that structurally it functions in some ways like other urban and rural AAE varieties, but, in fact, is quite different. The NP subject highly favors copula absence; in other contemporary AAE varieties it is the personal pronoun subject that favors copula absence. This pattern shows some similarity with diasporic AAE varieties (an earlier form of AAE) and English-based creole languages in the Caribbean. A more in-depth look at the history of the Delta and other analyses of more linguistic features will help to determine why this pattern exists.

The overall pattern that is seen in the results for the social variables, *education* and *township*, is that they play a strong role in the production of both features. The *subject's education* variable showed that college level subjects had higher occurrences of copula absence and r-lessness than their secondary and elementary level counterparts.

Typically, one would think that the higher the educational level, the more r-ful the subject would be in speech (Schönweitz 2001); a similar assumption can be made about copula absence. However, in the case of r-lessness it is possible that the subjects are imitating a Southern, educated speech or perhaps an upper-class, "prestigious" Southern speech, which is typically an r-less variety (Feagin 1997). One could also say that the high occurrences of r-lessness and copula absence are the AAE norm in the smaller, predominantly African American towns. This represents a high comfort level that the college-level subjects have with their speech. The Clarksdale subjects with lower p-values for both features may reflect social pressures to minimize the use of AAE features because of more frequent interaction with Whites in their town.

Also, we see that subjects with parents who have only an elementary level of education have high occurrences of r-lessness and copula absence, which indicates that the lower the educational level of the parent the higher the occurrence of both features. One thing to note is that the present study does not show that there is a direct influence of parent's speech on the subject's speech; however, there is an overall pattern indicating that the educational level of the parent does play a role in the production of each feature.

For the *township* variable, we see that there appears to be a difference between Clarksdale, which is racially mixed, and predominantly African American towns like Jonestown. Since we know that r-lessness in the South was influenced by AAE varieties (Feagin 1997), we can state that Jonestown and the other rural towns have higher occurrences of r-lessness and copula absence, most likely due to the racial demographics of these towns. It was previously stated that with the exception of Mound Bayou, most of the predominantly African American towns in the Delta were originally the living quarters of the labor force (or slaves historically) that serviced a local plantation. The racial demographics help to explain the differences found in the high production of the features analyzed in both communities. However, it must be pointed out that although Jonestown residents attended an elementary school in their own town, their middle and high school years were spent with Clarksdale residents. In fact, those particular schools were located in Clarksdale. In other words, those two communities are not as isolated from each other as originally thought, yet the differences in the production of the two features are quite clear.

In conclusion, Coahoma County AAE's copula absence shows a grammatical pattern that is similar to older nineteenth-century varieties. The results of the present study also show that there are strong differences in the production of copula absence and r-lessness when comparing predominant African American towns (i.e., Jonestown) and a racially mixed town (i.e., Clarksdale). Even though the towns are not as isolated from one another, they do have different production rates of each feature.

For future directions of the current study, it would be important to include other AAE features (Rickford 1998) to learn more about the connection between Coahoma County AAE and early nineteenth-century AAE speech, including a variation analysis of features such as consonant cluster reduction, lack of nominal plural –s, lack of possessive marker ('s), habitual *be*, /ai/ glide weakening, and the verbal third person –s would provide a fuller picture of its linguistic structure and perhaps help us to discover more about its origins.

Changing the setting of the interviews would also be important to have a better representation of AAE data. The way in which the data were collected in the present study works well for a sociological study on rural single mothers; however, for a linguistic analysis this set up is not as productive for capturing more casual speech patterns. Peer groups (Labov 1972; Filardo 1996), with different interlocutors and locales or settings (Rickford and McNair-Knox 1994; Bailey 1997), in public places frequented by locals (Cukor-Avila 1995), and perhaps even by telephone (Bailey 1997) are the best ways of collecting natural linguistic data. A non-traditional (ethnographic) interview process would probably also increase the number of tokens making a larger data set of informal speech.

The Delta region appears not only to be rich in soil, but rich in language and language use. It is possible that learning more about its connections with early nineteenth-century AAE varieties still yet to be determined may be able to help us learn more about the origins of this unique AAE regional variety. The current study offers a foundation for more extensive research on this linguistically rich region of the United States and the hope is that this work inspires others to continue AAE sociolinguistic research on the Mississippi Delta.

Notes

1. African American English (AAE) is a language variety spoken by African Americans who are the direct descendants of US slaves. It has structural similarities with the English language family, but maintains its distinction with grammatical features that are unique to this speech form. AAE is considered by this scholar to be a part of the African American Language family, which includes all languages spoken by African Americans, (i.e., Louisiana Creole, Gullah, and all regional, urban, rural varieties of AAE).

2. The railway had boosted the economy of the Delta by opening the agriculture to the nation's greatest markets, allowing railway stations at each plantation and cotton gin, increasing land values, and helping new industries to be created (e.g., timber).

3. World War I created an African American migration out of the Delta as well due to the halt of the cotton industry.

4. Many, not all, of the *LAGS* maps indicate that the distinctiveness in the Delta region is located in the central area of the region as opposed to the entire Delta area that I discuss later in this chapter.

5. For this chapter, when using the term *the Delta*, I am specifically referring to the Mississippi Delta.

6. Clarksdale is known for its famous crossroads of highways 49 and 61 where, according to a local legend, Robert Johnson (a bluesman of the early 1900s) "sold his soul to the devil" to become a famous bluesman.

7. When the welfare system was established in the 1970s, the money was given to White landowners to distribute to Blacks needing government assistance (Cobb 1992). This perpetuated Black economic dependency on White landowners, which is seen throughout the history of the Delta region.

8. Wolfram (1971) was conducted in Holmes County, which is located in the Mississippi Delta; however, his 1974 study is in Franklin County, which is not in the Delta, but nearby.

9. Hinton and Pollock (2000) state that more than likely their Iowan African American subjects migrated from the Delta region based on historical migration patterns after World War I.

10. This statement is based upon a recent library database search on AAE sociolinguistic studies at the time the current chapter was written.
11. The Coahoma County interviews were conducted by two African American female professors and one African American female graduate student from Memphis State University.
12. Marshall County is located just outside of the Delta. This subject is different from the others because she did not have any of her formative school years in the Delta. While I will not separate out this subject, her production rates for both features are similar to Clarksdale residents, but with a copula absence pattern that is noticeably different.
13. The General Equivalency Diploma (GED) is similar to a high school diploma except that it is typically earned by passing a high school equivalency exam.
14. The focus of the results in the current study is on the absent (or deleted) copula only.
15. *r*-lessness is also a feature found in the traditional New England dialect as well. The fact that the New England dialect and some Southern English varieties share r-lessness reflects a common geographic origin of the White settlers within the British Isles. But within the Southern context, r-lessness was no doubt reinforced by the r-less nature of the speech of many of the African slaves and their descendants (Feagin 1997).
16. Studies have shown that r-lessness is disappearing among younger White speakers in the South (Feagin 1997; Bailey and Thomas 1998; Schönweitz 2001; Childs and Mallinson 2004). *r*-lessness in southern speech has traditionally been one of the ways in which one could distinguish southern speech from northern speech. It appears now that there is a change taking place in what used to be a prominent feature of Southern English. Since these changes are occurring among White speakers, then it is important to investigate r-lessness in specific AAE communities in the South.
17. Many of the subjects attended Coahoma County Community College. None of the subjects had graduated at the time of the interview.
18. Parent is defined as someone who raised the subject from childhood (i.e., a mother, a stepparent, or a grandparent). When a subject has two parents, the highest educational level of either parent was selected as the appropriate variant.
19. Other rural towns refer to Belzoni, Shaw, and Mound Bayou that are Delta towns, but are not located in Coahoma County.
20. The copula forms that are excluded from the current study are presented in detail in Wilkerson (2008). We refer you to that research study for more information.
21. Even the Labov Deletion values for East Palo Alto AAE show that the personal pronoun (.51) has a neutral effect on copula deletion (Rickford et al. 1991, 75).
22. In-depth research into the history of the Delta requires more localized research in the Delta counties.

References

Bailey, Guy. 1997. "Southern American English: A Prospective." In *Language Variety in the South Revisited*, edited by Cynthia Bernstein, Thomas Nunnally, and Robin Sabino, 21–32. London: University of Alabama Press.
Bailey, Guy, and Erik Thomas. 1998. "Some Aspects of African-American Vernacular English Phonology." In *African-American English: Structure, History and Use*, edited by Salikoko Mufwene, John R. Rickford, Guy Bailey, and John Baugh, 85–109. New York: Routledge.

Childs, Becky, and Christine Mallinson. 2004. "African American English in Appalachia." *English World-Wide* 25 (1): 27–50.

Cobb, James. 1992. *The Most Southern Place on Earth: The Mississippi Delta and the Roots of Regional Identity*. New York: Oxford University Press.

Cukor-Avila, Patricia. 1995. "The Evolution of AAVE in a Rural Texas Community: An Ethnolinguistic Study." PhD diss., University of Michigan.

Dill, Bonnie T. 1988. "Female Headed Households in the Rural Mid-South." Unpublished project description. Center for Research on Women. Memphis State University.

———. 1990. "Single Mother Families in the Rural and Mid-South: Data Analysis." Unpublished project notes. Center for Research on Women. Memphis State University.

———. 1999. "Notes on Poverty in the Rural U.S. and the Implications for Children, Families, and Communities." College Park: University of Maryland.

Fasold, Ralph W., William Labov, Faye Boyd Vaughn-Cooke, Guy Bailey, Walt Wolfram, Arthur Spears, and John Rickford. 1987. "Are Black and White Vernaculars Diverging?" Papers from the NWAVE 14 Panel Discussion. *American Speech* 62: 3–80.

Feagin, Crawford. 1997. "The African Contribution to Southern States English." In *Language Variety in the South Revisited*, edited by Cynthia Bernstein, Thomas Nunnally, and Robin Sabino, 123–39. London: University of Alabama Press.

Filardo, Emily K. 1996. "Gender Patterns in African American and White Adolescents' Social Interactions in Same-Race, Mixed-Gender Groups." *Journal of Personality and Social Psychology* 71 (1): 71–82.

Fletcher, Deborah Golden. 2002. "Variation in the Production of Vocalic and Postvocalic /r/ in Three- and Five-year-olds and Their Caregivers Who Speak African American Vernacular English." PhD diss., University of Memphis.

Hinton, Linette N., and Karen E. Pollock. 2000. "Regional Variations in the Phonological Characteristics of African American Vernacular English." *World Englishes* 1 (1): 59–71.

Labov, William. 1972. *Language in the Inner City: Studies in the Black English Vernacular*. Philadelphia: University of Pennsylvania Press.

Lambert, S. K. 1995. "The R-full Truth of the Matter: An Analysis of the Construction of /r/ in Mississippi and Eastern Louisiana." Master's thesis, University of Memphis.

Pederson, Lee, McDaniel, Susan Leas, Bailey, Guy, and Marvin Bassett, eds. *Linguistic Atlas of the Gulf States*. Athens: University of Georgia Press.

Poplack, Shana, ed. 1999. *The English History of African American English*. Oxford: Blackwell.

Poplack, Shana, and David Sankoff. 1987. "The Philadelphia Story in the Spanish Caribbean." *American Speech* 62: 291–314.

Poplack, Shana, and Sali Tagliamonte. 1991. "African American English in the Diaspora: Evidence from Old-line Nova Scotians." *Language Variation and Change* 3: 301–39.

Rand, David, and David Sankoff. 1990. "Goldvarb 2.1: A Variable Rule Application for the Macintosh." Montreal: Centre de Recherches Mathematiques, University of Montreal. Version 2. http://www.crm.umontreal.ca/~sankoff/GoldVarb_Eng.html.

Rickford, John R. 1992. "The Creole Residue in Barbados." In Old English and New: Studies in Honor of Frederic G. Cassidy, edited by Joan H. Hall, Nick Doane, and Dick Ringler, 183–201. New York and London: Garland.

———. 1996. "Copula Variability in Jamaican Creole and African American Vernacular English: A Reanalysis of DeCamp's Texts." In Towards a Social Science of Language, Vol. 1: Variation and Change in Language and Society, edited by Gregory R. Guy, Crawford

Feagin, Deborah Schiffrin, and John Baugh, 357–72. Amsterdam and Philadelphia: John Benjamins.

———. 1998. "The Creole Origins of AAVE." In *African-American English: Structure, History, and Use*, edited by Salikoko S. Mufwene, John R. Rickford, Guy Bailey, and John Baugh, 154–200. London: Routledge.

———. 1999. *African American Vernacular English: Features, Evolution, Educational Implications*. Oxford: Blackwell.

Rickford, John R., and Renée Blake. 1990. "Copula Contraction and Absence in Barbadian English, Samaná English, and Vernacular Black English." In *Proceedings of the Sixteenth Annual Meeting of the Berkeley Linguistics Society, 16–19 February 1990*, edited by Kira Hall, Jean-Pierre Koenig, Michael Meacham, Sondra Reinman, and Laurel A. Sutton, 257–68. Berkeley, CA: Berkeley Linguistics Society.

Rickford, John R., Arnetha Ball, Renee Blake, Raina Jackson, and Nomi Martin. 1991. "Rappin' on the Copula Coffin: Theoretical and Methodological Issues in the Analysis of Copula Variation in African American Vernacular English." *Language Variation and Change* 3 (1): 103–32.

Rickford, John R., and Faye McNair-Knox. 1994. "Addressee- and Topic-Influenced Style Shift: A Quantitative Sociolinguistic Study." In *Perspectives on Register: Situating Register Variation within Sociolinguistics*, edited by Douglas Biber and Edward Finegan, 235–76. Oxford: Oxford University Press.

Schönweitz, Thomas. 2001. "Gender and Postvocalic /r/ in the American South: A Detailed Socioregional Analysis." *American Speech* 76 (3): 259–85.

Singler, John. 1991. "Copula Variation in Liberian Settler English and American Black English." In *Verb Phrase Patterns in Black English and Creoles*, edited by Walter F. Edwards and Donald Winford, 129–64. Detroit: Wayne State University Press.

Vaughn-Cooke, Anna Fay. 1976. "The Implementation of a Phonological Change: The Case of Resyllabification in Black English." PhD diss., Georgetown University.

Vaughn-Cooke, Fay Boyd. 1986. "The Challenge of Assessing the Language of Nonmainstream Speakers." In *Treatment of Communication Disorders in Culturally and Linguistically Diverse Populations*, edited by O. Taylor, 23–48. San Diego, CA: College-Hill.

Walton, Julie H., Peggy McCardle, Thomas A. Crowe, and Bruce E. Wilson. 1980. "Black English in a Mississippi Prison Population." *Journal of Speech and Hearing Disorders* 55 (2): 206–16.

Weaver, Rebecca Ann. 2000. "Acoustic Features of /r/ variations in African American Vernacular English Speaking Children and Adults in the Midsouth." PhD diss., University of Memphis.

Wilkerson, Rose. 2008. "Talkin' Country: African American English of Black Women in the Mississippi Delta." PhD diss., Indiana University.

Winford, Donald. 1992. "Another Look at the Copula in Black English and Caribbean Creoles." *American Speech* 67 (1): 21–60.

———. 1997. "On the Origins of African American Vernacular English—A Creolist Perspective, Part I: The Sociohistorical Background." *Diachronica* 14: 304–44.

———. 1998. "On the Origins of African American Vernacular English—A Creolist Perspective, Part II: The Features." *Diachronica* 15: 99–154.

Wolfram, Walt. 1969. *A Sociolinguistic Description of Detroit Negro Speech*. Washington, DC: Center for Applied Linguistics.

———. 1971. *Black–White Speech Relationships*. Vol. 7. Center for Applied Linguistics, 1971.

————. 1974. "The Relationship of White Southern Speech to Vernacular Black English." *Language* 50 (3): 498–527.

————. 1987. "On the Divergence of Vernacular Black English." *American Speech* 62: 40–48.

Wolfram, Walt, and Erik R. Thomas. 2002. *The Development of African American English.* Oxford: Blackwell.

....

CHAPTER 11

AFRICAN AMERICAN VOICES IN ATLANTA

....

WILLIAM A. KRETZSCHMAR, JR.

11.1 INTRODUCTION

ATLANTA is known as "the center of the New South," and even the abbreviation of its name, ATL, has resonance in popular speech of the region; *ATL* made the title for a 2006 feature film. There is no doubt that Atlanta holds a central position in national African American culture. We need only consider the Hip Hop music scene to know the truth of this, as thoroughly documented by Joycelyn Wilson (2008). Still, when you look closely at survey evidence regarding the vowels of African American speakers in Atlanta, it is hard to tell that they speak with one voice. African Americans in Atlanta and surroundings show highly variable vowel production that does not match traditional accounts of the vowels of African American English (AAE; defined for this essay as the real speech of people in the United States who have ancestry from any of the native populations of sub-Saharan Africa). Moreover, we know that speakers from the historic African American community in Roswell, a town just north of Atlanta, also differ from our expectations. The resolution of this apparent paradox lies in a new way of understanding what we take to be language varieties: complex systems. This chapter will discuss the vowels of African Americans from both Atlanta and from Roswell, especially in comparison with the vowels of non–African Americans.

11.2 PREVIOUS RESEARCH ON AFRICAN AMERICAN ENGLISH IN ATLANTA

Let's begin with historical data collected in Atlanta for the Linguistic Atlas project (http://www.lap.uga.edu; all data discussed and presented here is available on the website). Tables 11.1 through 11.9 show both the White and the African American speakers, each table for the vowel used in a single word.

Interviews from earlier dates represent information collected from the South Atlantic portion of the *Linguistic Atlas of the Middle and South Atlantic States* (*LAMSAS*); interviews from the 1960s and 1970s were collected for the *Linguistic Atlas of the Gulf States* (*LAGS*). *LAMSAS* interviews were transcribed in the field (in the time before field recording) and the fine phonetic transcriptions presented here show the single words and short phrases so transcribed as modified to remove material not relevant to the focus here on stressed vowels. Only forty-one African Americans were interviewed for *LAMSAS*, not a full quota given the extent of the project, but these forty-one interviews constitute some of the best available evidence on the history of AAE from the 1930s and 1940s. Unfortunately, no *LAMSAS* interviews with African Americans were conducted in Atlanta, but there are some in Clarke (GA34), Walton (GA35), and Rockdale (GA36) counties nearby in North Georgia, in the same topographical region as Atlanta but in rural instead of urban locations. *LAGS* interviews were tape recorded in the field and transcribed later; full audio recordings from the interviews are now available on the Atlas website. Transcriptions for *LAMSAS* and *LAGS* are by Raven McDavid (earlier interviews) and by Lee Pederson (later interviews), whose transcription practices are highly calibrated but not exactly the same (for details of transcription practices, see Kretzschmar et al. 1993). *LAGS* interviewed African Americans in proportion with

Table 11.1 Atlas Data from Atlanta: *three*

Speaker	Item	Pron	Date	Type	Sex	Age	Race
GA37A	three	θri·j	1947	I	M	95	W
GA37B	three	θri·	1947	II	M	75	W
GA37C	three	θri	1970	II	F	45	W
GA37D!	three	θri·	1968	III	M	59	W
GA37D!	three	θri·{iʌ}	1968	III	M	59	W
GA37E!	three	θri·	1970	III	F	53	W
GA37E!	three	θri·{iʌ}	1970	III	F	53	W
GA37G!	three	θri·j	1947	III	M	51	W
GA37H!	three	θri·{j}	1947	III	M	73	W
GA37I!	three	θri	1968	III	F	59	W
GA37I!	three	θri·	1968	III	F	59	W
GA37I!	three	θri·{iʌ}	1968	III	F	59	W
GA37M!	three	θri·{iʌ}	1968	III	M	55	B
GA37M!	three	θriv·{iʌ}	1968	III	M	55	B
GA37N	three	θri·	1971	I	F	82	B
GA37N	three	θri·{iʌ}	1971	I	F	82	B

Table 11.2 Atlas Data from Atlanta: *six*

Speaker	Item	Pron	Date	Type	Sex	Age	Race
GA37A	six	sɪʌks	1947	I	M	95	W
GA37B	six	sɪʌks	1947	II	M	75	W
GA37C	six	sɪks	1970	II	F	45	W
GA37C	six	sɪʌks	1970	II	F	45	W
GA37D!	six	sɪ·{ɪ-}ks	1968	III	M	59	W
GA37D!	six	sɪks	1968	III	M	59	W
GA37D!	six	sɪʌks	1968	III	M	59	W
GA37E!	six	sɪʌks	1970	III	F	53	W
GA37G!	six	sɪʌks	1947	III	M	51	W
GA37H!	six	sɪʌks	1947	III	M	73	W
GA37I!	six	sɪks	1968	III	F	59	W
GA37M!	six	sɪks	1968	III	M	55	B
GA37M!	six	sɪʌks	1968	III	M	55	B
GA37N	six	sɪks	1971	I	F	82	B

Table 11.3 Atlas Data from Atlanta: *eight*

Speaker	Item	Pron	Date	Type	Sex	Age	Race
GA37A	eight	e·ɪ>t	1947	I	M	95	W
GA37B	eight	e·ɪ-<t	1947	II	M	75	W
GA37C	eight	eɪ-ʌt	1970	II	F	45	W
GA37D!	eight	e{ɪ-}t	1968	III	M	59	W
GA37D!	eight	eɪ-t	1968	III	M	59	W
GA37D!	eight	eɪ̃t	1968	III	M	59	W
GA37E!	eight	eʌɪ-t	1970	III	F	53	W
GA37F!	eight	e·{ɪ-}t	1947	III	F	84	W
GA37G!	eight	e·{ɪ-}t	1947	III	M	51	W
GA37H!	eight	e·ɪt	1947	III	M	73	W
GA37H!	eight	e·ɪ-t	1947	III	M	73	W
GA37I!	eight	e·{ɪ-}t	1968	III	F	59	W
GA37I!	eight	eɪ-t	1968	III	F	59	W
GA37M!	eight	eɪ-t	1968	III	M	55	B
GA37N	eight	e·{ɪ-}t	1971	I	F	82	B
GA37N	eight	eɪ-t	1971	I	F	82	B

Table 11.4 Atlas Data from Atlanta: *ten*

Speaker	Item	Pron	Date	Type	Sex	Age	Race
GA37A	ten	tɛʌ·{ə}n	1947	I	M	95	W
GA37A	ten	tɪ{ə}n	1947	I	M	95	W
GA37B	ten	tɪv{ə}n	1947	II	M	75	W
GA37C	ten	tɪ·{ɪ·}n	1970	II	F	45	W
GA37C	ten	tɪn	1970	II	F	45	W
GA37D!	ten	tɪ·n	1968	III	M	59	W
GA37E!	ten	tɪ·n	1970	III	F	53	W
GA37G!	ten	tɪʌ{ɪ·}n	1947	III	M	51	W
GA37H!	ten	tɛʌ{ə}n	1947	III	M	73	W
GA37I!	ten	tɛ·n	1968	III	F	59	W
GA37I!	ten	tɛʌn	1968	III	F	59	W
GA37M!	ten	tɛʌ·{ə}n	1968	III	M	55	B
GA37N	ten	tɪv·{ə}n	1971	I	F	82	B

Table 11.5 Atlas Data from Atlanta: *half*

Speaker	Item	Pron	Date	Type	Sex	Age	Race
GA37A	half past seven	hæ{ɛ}f	1947	I	M	95	W
GA37B	half past seven	hæ{ɛ}f	1947	II	M	75	W
GA37D!	half past	hæʌ{ɛ}f	1968	III	M	59	W
GA37D!	half after	hæʌ{ɛ}f	1968	III	M	59	W
GA37E!	half past eleven	hæ{ɛ}f	1970	III	F	53	W
GA37G!	half past seven	hæ·{ɛ}f	1947	III	M	51	W
GA37H!	half past seven	hæ{ɛ}f	1947	III	M	73	W
GA37H!	half past seven	hæ{ɛ}f	1947	III	M	73	W
no AfAm responses							

White speakers all across the Gulf States in a quota sample, so besides the two African Americans interviewed in Atlanta itself, it will be possible to find numerous other African American speakers from the 1960s and 1970s for comparison. There is some missing data in the tables, notably the lack of evidence for African American /æ/. The tables give the date of the interview, and the sex, age, and race of the speaker; the "Type" classification encodes the relative education and social connections of the speaker, where Type I is little educated and socially restricted, Type II is moderately educated (most often high school) and socially involved, and Type III is highly educated (most

Table 11.6 Atlas Data from Atlanta: *two*

Speaker	Item	Pron	Date	Type	Sex	Age	Race
GA37A	two	tu-·w	1947	I	M	95	W
GA37B	two	tu-·	1947	II	M	75	W
GA37B	two	tu-<·	1947	II	M	75	W
GA37C	two	tu-·	1970	II	F	45	W
GA37D!	two	tu-·	1968	III	M	59	W
GA37D!	two	tu-·{u-ʌ}	1968	III	M	59	W
GA37D!	two	tu-	1968	III	M	59	W
GA37E!	two	tu-{u-ʌ}	1970	III	F	53	W
GA37E!	two	tu-<{u-ʌ}	1970	III	F	53	W
GA37F!	two	tu-·	1947	III	F	84	W
GA37G!	two	tju-<·w̥	1947	III	M	51	W
GA37G!	two	tu-	1947	III	M	51	W
GA37H!	two	tu-·	1947	III	M	73	W
GA37H!	two	tu-<·	1947	III	M	73	W
GA37I!	two	tu-	1968	III	F	59	W
GA37I!	two	tu<uʌ<	1968	III	F	59	W
GA37I!	two	tu-{u-ʌ}	1968	III	F	59	W
GA37M!	two	tu<·	1968	III	M	55	B
GA37N	two	tu-·	1971	I	F	82	B
GA37N	two	tu-<	1971	I	F	82	B
GA37N	two	tu-{u-ʌ}	1971	I	F	82	B

Table 11.7 Atlas Data from Atlanta: *good*

Speaker	Item	Pron	Date	Type	Sex	Age	Race
GA37A	good morning	gʊ<d	1947	I	M	95	W
GA37B	good morning	gʊ<d	1947	II	M	75	W
GA37C	good morning	gʊ<d	1970	II	F	45	W
GA37D!	good morning	gʊ<d	1968	III	M	59	W
GA37D!	good morning	gʊ<d	1968	III	M	59	W
GA37E!	good morning	gʊ->d	1970	III	F	53	W
GA37G!	good morning	gʊ<d	1947	III	M	51	W
GA37H!	good morning	gʊ<d	1947	III	M	73	W
GA37I!	good morning	gʊ<d	1968	III	F	59	W
GA37M!	good morning	gʊ̈d	1968	III	M	55	B
GA37N	good morning	gʊd	1971	I	F	82	B
GA37N	good morning	gʊd	1971	I	F	82	B

Table 11.8 Atlas Data from Atlanta: *sofa*

Speaker	Item	Pron	Date	Type	Sex	Age	Race
GA37B	sofas	so<·ʊ<	1947	II	M	75	W
GA37C	sofa	so<ʊ<	1970	II	F	45	W
GA37D!	sofa	soʊ-	1968	III	M	59	W
GA37E!	sofa	so<ʊ<	1970	III	F	53	W
GA37F!	sofa	so<·ʊ<	1947	III	F	84	W
GA37G!	sofa	so<·ʊ<	1947	III	M	51	W
GA37H!	sofa	soʌ<·ʊ<	1947	III	M	73	W
GA37I!	sofa	soʊ<	1968	III	F	59	W
GA37M!	sofa	so<ʊ<	1968	III	M	55	B

Table 11.9 Atlas Data from Atlanta: *one*

Speaker	Item	Pron	Date	Type	Sex	Age	Race
GA37A	one	wɣv{ə}n	1947	I	M	95	W
GA37A	one	wɣvn	1947	I	M	95	W
GA37B	one	wɣvn	1947	II	M	75	W
GA37C	one	wʌʌ<·{ə}n	1970	II	F	45	W
GA37C	one	wʌʌn	1970	II	F	45	W
GA37D!	one	wʌʌ<·n	1968	III	M	59	W
GA37D!	one	wʌʌn	1968	III	M	59	W
GA37D!	one	wʌʌ<n	1968	III	M	59	W
GA37E!	one	wʌʌ{ə}n	1970	III	F	53	W
GA37E!	one	wʌʌ<·{ə}n	1970	III	F	53	W
GA37E!	one	wʌʌn	1970	III	F	53	W
GA37G!	one	wɣv{ə}n	1947	III	M	51	W
GA37H!	one	wɣvn	1947	III	M	73	W
GA37I!	one	wʌʌ<{ə}n	1968	III	F	59	W
GA37I!	one	wʌʌ<n	1968	III	F	59	W
GA37M!	one	wʌʌ·{ə}n	1968	III	M	55	B
GA37M!	one	wʌʌ<·n	1968	III	M	55	B
GA37M!	one	wʌʌn	1968	III	M	55	B
GA37N	one	wʌʌ<·{ə}n	1971	I	F	82	B

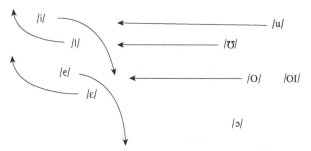

FIGURE 11.1 The "Southern Shift" (as represented in Bailey and Thomas 1998).

often college) and highly involved socially. The choice of words is constrained by which items have digital phonetic transcriptions for *LAMSAS*, which means that some words (notably *half* and *ten*) may not be representative of the entire class of words for the vowel.

Our expectations for African American vowels in Atlanta, and elsewhere, have been established by Guy Bailey and Erik Thomas. Bailey and Thomas have called phonology "the neglected step child of research on African American vernacular English" (1998, 85). While Bailey and Thomas (1998) list and assess realizations of consonants and consonant clusters commonly attributed to African American speakers, which constitutes the bulk of what the literature reports, they also claim that "the vowel system may be a more important locus for addressing some of the fundamental questions about the history of AAVE and its relation to other American dialects" (1998, 92). Bailey and Thomas (1998) cite Labov's regional framework of vowel shifts underway in America—the *Northern Cities Shift*, the *Southern Shift* (as illustrated graphically in figure 11.1), and *Western Merger* (Labov, Ash, and Boberg 2006)—and show that African American speakers are not participating in them.

Thus, the bottom line for Bailey and Thomas (1998, 106):

> Although some of the earlier AAVE features that most clearly tie AAVE to its creole relatives have disappeared (e.g., monophthongal /e/ and /o/), other features (e.g., non-front onsets of /au/ and fully back vowels) persevere. . . . During the last quarter of the nineteenth century and first decades of the twentieth century, a number of innovations emerged in AAVE. Some of these are shared with Southern [W]hite vernaculars (e.g., glide shortening in /ai/ before voiced obstruents and a series of conditioned vowel mergers), while others (e.g. the raising of /æ/) appear only in AAVE. AAVE does not share more recent innovations that developed in Southern [W]hite vernaculars (e.g. the radical reorganization of vowel space ["Southern Shift"] which began to emerge around the turn of the century). The changes in [W]hite vernaculars serve to accentuate and widen differences that already existed between these vernaculars and AAVE.

This account suggests that, even without grammatical, lexical, or consonantal cues, the vowels can create an impression of a separate AAE because the vowel system for African Americans is simply different from any of the regional non–African American vowel systems.

As for what the tables actually show, in no case is it possible to say that the two African American speakers have distinctly different vowels from the White speakers in Atlanta. Indeed, the overall impression of the fine phonetics is that Atlanta speakers, both Black and White, are quite variable in how they pronounced their vowels, and the same speakers sometimes pronounced the same word in different ways. Some of the differences are small, consisting of shift signs and other minor or weakly realized variants (the segments in curly braces). Nonetheless, the differences were there to be heard and recorded by the highly trained and experienced Atlas transcribers. For the African American speakers and most of the White speakers from Atlanta (namely, those from *LAGS*), it is now possible to listen to the interview itself, to verify for oneself the impressions of the transcribers. As for the specific points raised by Bailey and Thomas (1998), in Atlas evidence for Atlanta neither the African Americans nor the White speakers show changes in /i, ɪ, ei/ characteristic of the Southern Shift, and both groups do show some raising of /ɛ/. While we unfortunately lack Atlas evidence for African American /æ/, all of the White speakers show some tendency toward raising, which Bailey and Thomas (1998) suggested was restricted to African Americans. As for the suggestion by Bailey and Thomas (1998) that African Americans retain fully back back vowels, in the Atlas evidence we see that both African American speakers front /u/ to some extent, just like the White speakers (the "-" diacritic indicates a degree of centralization); one of the African Americans, GA37M!, also fronts /ʊ, ou/. These facts do not make Bailey and Thomas (1998) wrong, but they do highlight the difference between a broad generalization such as the one they made and the facts on the ground in any given locality. Atlanta has its own historical characteristics, which sometimes agree with the big picture and sometimes disagree—and of course the Atlas sample of only two African American speakers from Atlanta is not sufficient to get a broad sense of the speech overall in the Black community there.[1]

11.3 ATLANTA SURVEY

We achieved a better picture of speech in Atlanta with survey research carried out beginning in 2002.[2] As part of this project, we conducted a random-sample survey of Fulton County and DeKalb County, the two most populous counties of the Atlanta metropolitan area, with a total population of approximately 1.5 million people according to the 2000 census (http://www.census.gov). Then, we created parallel samples based on three binary variables: race (African American versus non–African American), sex (female versus male), and occupational type (blue collar versus white collar). Because of housing patterns in Atlanta, we ended up with the African American speakers all in the southern part of the survey area and the non–African Americans in the northern part.

Table 11.10 shows the speakers in the sample as we drew it. All the subjects were primary English speakers, adults aged 18 years or older, and ideally lifelong residents. We followed current standard methods for randomized field research to draw the sample,

Table 11.10 Speakers in the Atlanta Survey

Code	Sex	Race	OccType	Age
A01Mw	M	AfAm	White	48
A02Mw	M	AfAm	White	35
A03Mb	M	AfAm	Blue	50
A04Mb	M	AfAm	Blue	38
A05Mb	M	AfAm	Blue	33
A01Fb	F	AfAm	Blue	25
A02Fb	F	AfAm	Blue	43
A03Fw	F	AfAm	White	38
A04Fw	F	AfAm	White	20
A05Fw	F	AfAm	White	24
NA01Mw	M	Non-AfAm	White	43
NA02Mw	M	Non-AfAm	White	28
NA03Mw	M	Non-AfAm	White	84
NA01Fb	F	Non-AfAm	Blue	?45
NA02Fb	F	Non-AfAm	Blue	54
NA03Fw	F	Non-AfAm	White	33
NA04Fw	F	Non-AfAm	White	69
NA05Fb	F	Non-AfAm	Blue	?38

using a random telephone list to qualify potential speakers before in-person interviews. When our quotas were mostly full, in the end we were not able to find two non–African American male blue-collar speakers. As it happens, all of the non–African Americans in our small sample are Caucasians, although our sampling plan would have admitted Hispanic or Asian or other ethnic speakers.

The data presented here comes from a fixed-format elicitation task in which the speakers were asked to say particular words for us. For elicitation cues, we used the word set developed by Hagiwara so that we would stay as close as possible to the practice of speech scientists (Hagiwara 1997; see also Hillenbrand et al. 1995):

beat/teak/heed	boot/duke/hoot
bit/tick/hid	put/took/hood
bate/take/hate	boat/toke/Hode
bet/tech/head	bought/tock/hod**
bat/tack/had	but/tuck/hut

**mixed class of /ɑ/ and /ɔ/ words.

Unfortunately, we realized in the middle of the work that Hagiwara's cues are deficient in the low-back vowels /ɑ/ as in *cot* and /ɔ/ as in *bought*. This set of cues also does not include diphthongs, paired vowels such as /aɪ/ in *eye*. We also encountered another problem: that some African American speakers either resisted or otherwise had trouble with the task, while non–African American speakers did not (Osiapem 2005). On the whole, however, the task was easy and effective for most speakers.

Acoustic analysis of the fixed-format data was carried out by Mi-Ran Kim (Kim, Kong, and Kretzschmar 2005). *Acoustic analysis* involves computer study of the waveforms of speech sounds. Results are commonly reported by speech scientists and sociolinguists as frequency values on F1/F2 plots, on which two different measurements from the waveform are plotted against each other on a chart arranged to correspond to the way that linguists talk about vowel sounds (high/low, front/back). Tokens were analyzed by Kim from the spectrographic and waveform display of the TF32 program implemented in CSpeech SP (Milenkovic and Read 2000). Formant frequency measures were made from the Fourier transform spectrum. For monophthongs, the F1 and F2 were measured in the center of the segment that showed steady state formants. For vowels that occurred in diphthongs, formant frequencies were taken 35 ms from the onset of the vowel. I report here the mean F1/F2 scores for nine tokens of each vowel per speaker (but not /ɑ/ in *cot* and /ɔ/ in *bought* or diphthongs, as above). In order to help evaluate the Atlanta data, I present it in comparison to the national means compiled by Kent and Read (2002). Also, in order to simplify comparison of vowels between different groups and different speakers, I report differences between vowels as *steps*, so that, for example, one might say that in Atlanta, as we shall see, African American male speakers tend to pronounce the /ae/ vowel two steps higher than the Kent and Read value.[3]

The Kent and Read means that we use as a reference point are national and thus will not show the effects of any of the contemporary regional shift patterns claimed by Labov, such as the Southern Shift (see Labov and Ash 1997). Following Bailey and Thomas (1998), we might expect to see evidence that the African Americans mostly have vowels relatively close to the *unshifted* Kent and Read means, while we might expect to see evidence that the non–African American speakers have *shifted* vowels. In particular, the Southern Shift should have us look for fronted /u/ as in *boot*, /ʊ/ as in *put*, and /ou/ as in *boat* from non–African American speakers while African American speakers should have *fully back vowels*. We should also observe the reversal in height of the tense and lax mid and high front vowels (/ɪ/ as in *bit* higher than /i/ as in *beat*; /ɛ/ as in *bet* higher than /ei/ as in *bait*) in non–African American speakers affected by the Southern Shift. For such speakers, many listeners might hear *still meal* when the speakers said *steel mill*. African American speakers should retain the unreversed Kent and Read positions so that people would hear *steel mill* when they said it.

In fact, the situation in Atlanta is more complicated than the popular generalization has it. The mean F1/F2 values for African American speakers do not remain unshifted from the Kent and Read means. We see that /æ/ as in *bat* is two steps higher than the

Kent and Read mean for the male speakers (figure 11.2), as Bailey and Thomas (1998) suggested, and that the back vowels are all fully back, again as they suggested.

However, /ɛ/ and /ei/ have reversed positions as might be expected from speakers with the Southern Shift, although /ɪ/ and /i/ have not reversed positions. The F1/F2 means for the African American women in our survey (figure 11.3) show the same basic pattern for these vowels, high /æ/, fully back high-back vowels, and reversal of /ɛ/ and /ei/ but not /ɪ/ and /i/.

AfM	3200	3000	2800	2600	2400	2200	2000	1800	1600	1400	1200	1000	800	600	F2
200															
250															
300					i□i■										
350							I■				u□u■				
400							I□				ʊ■				
450						ei□ɛ■					ʊ□				
500								ei■			ou□	ou■			
550								ɛ□æ■		ʌ■					
600											ʌ□				
650								æ□							
700															
750															
800															
850															
900															
950															
F1															
	Kent & Read mean vowel scores for F1/F2							□ male							
	Atlanta survey mean vowel scores, AfAm							■ male							

FIGURE 11.2 Atlanta African American male vowel means versus Kent and Read national means.

AfF	3200	3000	2800	2600	2400	2200	2000	1800	1600	1400	1200	1000	800	600	F2
200															
250															
300															
350			io												
400			i●							uo					
450				I●	Io						u●				
500				eio					ʊ●	ʊo					
550					ɛ●					ouo					
600															
650					ei●										
700					æ●	ɛo			ʌ●		ou●				
750									ʌo						
800															
850						æo									
900															
950															
F1															
	Kent & Read mean vowel scores for F1/F2							○ female							
	Atlanta survey mean vowel scores, AfAm							● female							

FIGURE 11.3 Atlanta African American female vowel means versus Kent and Read national means.

If anything, the women's vowels are more different from the Kent and Read means than the men's vowels, with /æ, ɛ, ei/ fully three steps away from the national means when only /æ, ɛ/ are as much as two steps different for the men. In addition, the women show a distinctly lower mean for /ou/, again three steps, a difference that is not implicated in any of the regional shifts. Part of this difference from the men comes from the broader vowel space of women speakers, something we expect from the difference between sexes. However, this result does not match the Bailey and Thomas (1998) generalization that African Americans' vowels are not participating in regional shifts and thus must be near the national means. Several of the Atlanta African Americans' vowel means are quite different from the national means, and while Atlanta African Americans do not show all the characteristics of the Southern Shift, they do have the reversal of /ɛ/ and /ei/ as claimed for the Southern Shifters.

Our non-African Americans in Atlanta also fail to match the national generalizations. The male speakers approximate the national means for all of our vowels except for /ɪ, ei/, which are two steps lower than the national means. However, the high front tense and lax vowels are not reversed in position, and there is no fronting of the high and mid back vowels, so that the men show no sign of the Southern Shift. The non-African American women have means two steps lower for /ɪ, ei/, still without reversal of the high front tense and lax vowels, just like the men. The women do have /u/ fronted by two steps, the only characteristic anything like the Southern Shift among the non-African Americans, but the other back vowels are well back; /o/ is lowered by two steps, which parallels the situation for the African American women. It is clearly the case that the common generalization of shifted non-African Americans versus unshifted African American speakers simply does not work in Atlanta. The African American speakers show one characteristic of the shift, reversal of /ɛ/ and /ei/, and the non-African American women show one other, fronting of /u/ when compared to the national mean. Our women speakers appear to have greater differences from the national means overall than the men, but there are differences for every category of speakers.

To introduce one final dimension of the Atlanta data, we have also surveyed speakers from Roswell, Georgia, a city just north of Atlanta (see Kretzschmar et al. 2007; Roswell interviews are available at http://www.lap.uga.edu). The site of Roswell was in Cherokee territory, and in 1839, after the Native Americans were expelled in the *Trail of Tears*, the Roswell settlement was founded with a textile mill on the Chattahoochee River. The coastal Georgians who built the town made homes for themselves, cottages and apartments for mill workers, and dwellings for slaves not much different from those of the mill workers. Eventually, the historic African American population formed its own neighborhood within the community, Groveway, which today thrives as a center for African American culture in the northern section of the Atlanta metro area. Groveway has two megachurches that serve African American interests to anchor an African American population that has now spread out across Roswell, as Roswell itself has spread from its original town square and mill to cover an area of 39 square miles.

Our survey of Roswell speakers began in 2002 when the local Convention and Visitors Bureau invited us (the present author, Sonja Lanehart, and Bridget Anderson) to conduct language and life interviews there, in preparation for the sesquicentennial celebration of the official incorporation of the town in 1854. We talked to community icons of the oldest living generation, both Black and White, and then extended our coverage to their children's and grandchildren's generation. We used guided conversational interviews for this purpose, including, for most speakers, a fixed-format elicitation task like the one we pioneered in the Atlanta survey. I report here front vowel means from two pairs of African American speakers, men and women from the oldest and youngest generations, derived from work by graduate assistants, Claire Andres (who carried out the acoustic phonetic measurements) and Rachel Votta.

Figures 11.4 and 11.5 add the Roswell front vowel means to those from figures 11.2 and 11.3, the Kent and Read national means and the Atlanta African American means.

The acoustic phonetic measurements were carried out slightly differently, which accounts for some of the separation between the Roswell plots and the Atlanta plots. However, the relationship between the two pairs of vowels implicated in the Southern Shift, /i, ɪ/ and /ei, ɛ/, shows that the Roswell African American speakers are different from those in the Atlanta survey. Both the men and the women in Atlanta showed mean values of /i, ɪ/ that were closer together than the Kent and Read national means, perhaps a suggestion of the Southern Shift, and reversal of the positions of /ei, ɛ/ from the Kent and Read means, definitely like the Southern Shift. For Roswell African Americans, however, /i, ɪ/ are well separated and /ei, ɛ/ remain unreversed, which is more like the status of these vowels for Atlanta White speakers. We are not talking about a highly mobile suburban population in Roswell (African Americans like that

AfM	3200	3000	2800	2600	2400	2200	2000	1800	1600	1400	1200	1000	800	600	F2
200															
250						i♦									
300						i□i■									
350							I■	I♦							
400							I□		ei♦						
450							ei□ε■		ε♦						
500							ei■								
550							ε□								
600															
650															
700															
750															
800															
850															
900															
950															
F1															
	Kent & Read mean vowel scores for F1/F2							□ male							
	Atlanta survey mean vowel scores, AfAm							■ male							
	Roswell survey mean vowel scores, AfAm							♦ male							

FIGURE 11.4 Roswell African American male front vowel means versus Atlanta means.

AfF	3200	3000	2800	2600	2400	2200	2000	1800	1600	1400	1200	1000	800	600	F2
200															
250			i♦												
300															
350		io													
400		i●		ei♦		I♦									
450				I●	Io										
500				eio			ε♦								
550				ε●											
600															
650				ei●											
700						εo									
750															
800															
850															
900															
950															
F1															
	Kent & Read mean vowel scores for F1/F2							o female							
	Atlanta survey mean vowel scores, AfAm							● female							
	Roswell survey mean vowel scores, AfAm							♦ female							

FIGURE 11.5 Roswell African American female front vowel means versus Atlanta means.

do live in Roswell, but we have not interviewed them), but instead about people affiliated with the long-standing Groveway community, so we cannot explain these Roswell vowels on those grounds. Instead, we can cite work by Walt Wolfram and his students on small North Carolina localities, among them Hyde County, Texana, Princeville, and Roanoke Island (Wolfram and Thomas 2002; Childs and Mallinson 2004; Rowe and Kendall 2004; Hilliard and Carpenter 2004; Childs 2005). These studies have found Black speech and White speech in each place to be much more comparable than expected. Local social dynamics such as literacy and occupation appear to account for the differences or, as Childs (2005) demonstrates, even smaller communities of practice. One of the younger Roswell African American speakers reported that, when students were bused to schools in different parts of the county (Roswell and Atlanta are both in Fulton County):

> they were bringing kids from south county, up to north county schools, and I just remember those kids just thinking they were like so bad, you know, "We're so tough," you know, "We'll whoop you all up here in Roswell," you know, "You all are up here with the [W]hite folks and" you know, "you guys. . .". It's like they almost tried to make it seem like we weren't [B]lack enough because we lived in Roswell and they were from like College Park and East Point or something like that. (Kretzschmar et al. 2006)

Stories like this one confirm that, as much as we often want to consider Atlanta as one big, central cultural entity, people from different parts of the county live different lives, Black speakers and White speakers alike, and it shows in their different voices.

11.4 Discussion

None of this evidence of variation in speech by African Americans in Atlanta actually undercuts the status of a national African American cultural pattern including language, or of Atlanta as a cultural center within it. Traditional models for languages and language varieties have emphasized rule systems that made varieties appear to be more closed and separate than they are. A new model, complex systems (Kretzschmar 2009, 2010), instead focuses on the frequencies with which pronunciations, words, and other linguistic features are used in different communities. The essential process of all complex systems can be summed up in just a few principles: (1) random interaction of large numbers of components, (2) continuing activity in the system, (3) exchange of information with feedback, (4) reinforcement of behaviors, and (5) emergence of stable patterns without central control. Complex systems were originally described and are still used in the physical and biological sciences (see Prigogine and Stengers 1984; Gould 2003; Hawking and Mlodinow 2010). Complex systems in speech consist of randomly interacting variant realizations of linguistic features as deployed by human agents, speakers. Human agents can choose how to deploy linguistic variants, and our implicit comparison of the use of different components by different speakers and writers contributes to the operation of feedback and reinforcement. The order that emerges in speech is simply the configuration of components used at different frequencies, whether particular words, pronunciations, or constructions, that comes to occur in the local communities, regional and social, and in the occasions for speech and writing, text types and registers, in which we actually communicate.

An important aspect of complex systems of all kinds, and the one that explains the variation in Atlanta vowels, is that such systems are scale-free, that is, order emerges at all levels of scale simultaneously. For any size community we care to consider, there will be some features that occur a great deal, and many features that hardly ever occur. This means that practically no features are the exclusive property of any community, but instead that differences between communities occur as differences in the frequency of use of the features. So, White speakers and Black speakers can share a great many features, and we can note that African Americans considered at the top, national level of scale use some features much more frequently than other communities of speakers. At the same time, the usage of African Americans in Atlanta does not have to go along with the national pattern point for point, but instead is likely to have some differences from it. And the same is true in the "north county" and the "south county" in Atlanta, as our younger Black speaker from Roswell put it in the passage cited above, where the African American kids tend to act and to sound a little different. As this speaker went on to say, "And, once we got past that, I mean, it was fine. But there was a little tension there at first, you know, between the south county students and the north county students that grew up here in Roswell" (Kretzschmar et al. 2006). We cannot help but notice the differences, but such differences in frequency of use of linguistic features, or other cultural activities, does not prevent us from still being part of local, regional, and national communities, all at the same time.

11.5 Conclusion

As the evidence from Atlanta shows clearly, we do violence to the facts if we try to make our communities too separate from each other. The complex systems model allows explicitly for what we actually find in and around Atlanta: scale-free patterns in vowel usage that vary in frequency, not categorically. The Atlas evidence shows that, historically, the possible pronunciations of individual vowels in Atlanta are largely shared by African Americans and non–African Americans. The Atlanta survey shows the same thing but also indicates that we can describe trends in the evidence that mark the operation of complex systems and identify how communities may differ in large terms, even while they can share all of the components individually. The Roswell evidence, both from vowels and from the accounts of residents, shows that such trends can vary across the city but that the differences need not keep people apart in the end. We can all "get past that" when we recognize that our local communities all contribute to our larger sense of cultural identity.

Notes

1. The term *Black* is used alongside the term *African American* in this essay, since both terms are current in both the community and the literature about this variety of speech.
2. The present author and Sonja Lanehart, the PIs, are grateful for funding from NSF grant SBR-0233448 for the survey.
3. We selected these 50 × 200 Hz intervals because they represent a rough indication of the standard deviations we often found between tokens from individual speakers, and between speakers in the group means. The actual mean values for individuals or groups are put into the closest grid box. Thus, sometimes two different values appear in the same grid box, and they may actually vary by nearly 50 Hz in F1 and 200 Hz in F2; values reported in adjoining boxes may actually vary by as little as 5 or 10 Hz, but may also vary by up to nearly 100 Hz in F1 and 400 Hz in F2. The *steps* are thus merely a useful heuristic for assessing whether particular values are similar or different; selection of a different size interval would affect the assessment.

References

ATL. 2006. Directed by Chris Robinson. Hollywood: Warner Brothers.

Bailey, Guy, and Erik Thomas. 1998. "Some Aspects of AAVE Phonology." In *African American English: Structure, History, and Use*, edited by Salikoko Mufwene, John Rickford, Guy Bailey, and John Baugh, 85–109. London: Routledge.

Childs, Rebecca. 2005. "Investigating the Local Construction of Identity: Sociophonetic Variation in Smoky Mountain African American Women's Speech." PhD diss., University of Georgia.

Childs, Rebecca, and Christine Mallinson. 2004. "African American English in Appalachia: Dialect Accommodation and Substrate Influence." *English World Wide* 25: 27–50.

Gould, Stephen Jay. 2003. *The Hedgehog, the Fox, and the Magister's Pox: Mending the Gap between Science and the Humanities.* New York: Three Rivers.

Hagiwara, R. 1997. "Dialect Variation and Formant Frequency: The American English Vowels Revisited." *Journal of the Acoustical Society of America* 102: 655–58.

Hawking, Stephen, and Leonard Mlodinow. 2010. *The Grand Design.* New York: Bantam.

Hillenbrand, James, Laura A. Getty, Michael J. Clark, and Kimberlee Wheeler. 1995. "Acoustic Characteristics of American English Vowels." *Journal of the Acoustical Society of America* 97: 3099–111.

Hilliard, Sarah, and Jeanine Carpenter. 2004. "Vocalic Alignment of Roanoke 'Oisland.'" Paper presented at the SECOL conference. Tuscaloosa, Alabama: University of Alabama, April 15–17.

Kent, R., and C. Read. 2002. *Acoustic Analysis of Speech.* 2nd ed. New York: Delmar.

Kim, Mi-Ran, Nicole Kong, and William A. Kretzschmar Jr. 2005. "Vowel Formant Characteristics from the Atlanta Survey Project." Paper presented at ADS/LSA 2005, Oakland, California, January 6–8.

Kretzschmar, William A., Jr. 2009. *The Linguistics of Speech.* Cambridge: Cambridge University Press.

———. 2010. "Language Variation and Complex Systems." *American Speech* 85: 263–86.

Kretzschmar, William A., Jr., Claire Andres, Rachel Votta, and Sasha Johnson. 2006. *Roswell Voices, Phase 2.* Roswell: Roswell Folk and Heritage Bureau. Pamphlet and CD.

Kretzschmar, William A., Jr., Sonja Lanehart, Bridget Anderson, and Becky Childs. 2007. "The Relevance of Community Language Studies to HEL: The View from Roswell." In *Managing Chaos: Strategies for Identifying Change in English,* edited by Christopher Cain and Geoffrey Russom, Studies in the History of the English Language, 3, 173–86. Berlin: Mouton de Gruyter.

Kretzschmar, William A., Jr., Virginia G. McDavid, Theodore K. Lerud, and Ellen Johnson. 1993. *Handbook of the Linguistic Atlas of the Middle and South Atlantic States.* Chicago: University of Chicago Press.

Labov, William, and Sharon Ash. 1997. "Understanding Birmingham." In *Language Variety in the South Revisited,* edited by Cynthia Bernstein, Thomas Nunnally, and Robin Sabino, 508–73. Tuscaloosa: University of Alabama Press.

Labov, William, Charles Boberg, and Sherry Ash. 2006. *Atlas of North American English: Phonetics, Phonology and Sound Change.* Berlin: Mouton de Gruyter.

Milenkovic, Paul, and Charles Read. 2000. *CSpeechSP.* Software and manual. Madison: University of Wisconsin, Dept. of Electrical and Computer Engineering, Dept. of Linguistics.

Osiapem, Iyabo. 2005. "Fixed-Format Elicitation in the Atlanta Survey Project." Paper presented at ADS/LSA 2005, Oakland, California, January 6–8.

Prigogine, Ilya, and Isabelle Stengers. 1984. *Order Out of Chaos.* New York: Bantam.

Rowe, Ryan, and Tyler Kendall. 2004. "Regional and Social Diversity in the Development of Rural Southern AAE: The Case of Princeville." Paper presented at SECOL. Tuscaloosa: University of Alabama, April 15–17.

Wilson, Joycelyn. 2008. "Outkast'd and Claimin' True: The Language of Schooling and Education in the Southern Hip-Hop Community of Practice." PhD diss., University of Georgia.

Wolfram, Walt, and Erik Thomas. 2002. *The Development of African American English.* Oxford: Blackwell.

CHAPTER 12

AFRICAN AMERICAN LANGUAGE IN PITTSBURGH AND THE LOWER SUSQUEHANNA VALLEY

JENNIFER BLOOMQUIST AND SHELOME GOODEN

12.1 INTRODUCTION

IT is now reasonably well accepted that African American Language (AAL) is not a monolithic dialect and that sociocultural attributes of local ecologies contribute to the variety spoken in each locale; still AAL shows distinctiveness from regional White vernaculars. This chapter reviews the literature on variation in the North Midland, in particular, Pittsburgh and the south central region of Pennsylvania, which is known as the Lower Susquehanna Valley (LSV). We focus on phonological/phonetic, lexical, and, to a lesser extent, syntactic variation. The discussion is weighted toward Pittsburgh AAL rather than LSV, since there is much more research on that variety. We present information on African American presence in earlier periods in both areas and discuss implications for influence on the contemporary AAL spoken in each area. Finally, we also present a sociophonetic analysis of vowel variation in the LSV and compare the results with Pittsburgh AAL.

Discussions in this chapter are couched in a broader framework of language contact that views linguistic outcomes of contact as conditioned largely by sociocultural factors.[1] We take the position that ecology is part-psychological and part-sociological (Haugen 1972; Mufwene 2000), a perspective that is consistent with current sociolinguistic inquiry into the role of identity and identity construction and social meaning in language use (Silverstein 2003). Speakers' language attitudes and perspectives toward local communities help to shape the ecology in which AAL exists and is used. Thus, an approach that embraces the vital role of ecological factors in shaping linguistic variation offers more nuanced explanations of observed patterns. This underscores our perspective that an explanation of AAL language variation in terms of accommodation or resistance to local White vernacular norms is a complex issue and not a binary choice (see Mallinson and Wolfram 2002; Purnell and Yaeger-Dror 2010; Yaeger-Dror and Thomas 2010; Yaeger-Dror and Purnell 2010).

We use the term *AAL*[2] to describe the varieties spoken by descendants of southern Blacks, while acknowledging that the data we describe is certainly not representative of all Americans of African descent. We should be clear that existing descriptions of AAL in Pittsburgh and the LSV do not address ethnic diversity within the African American community. Thus, linguistic variation due to ethnolinguistic diversity has not been investigated (as we suspect is the case for many varieties of AAL in the United States), but see Blake et al. (this volume) for views on New York City.

12.2 LOCAL VARIETIES AND ETHNOLINGUISTIC VARIATION

12.2.1 Situating Ideologies of AAL and Ethnolects in Research

In reviewing works on AAL (as well as other varieties spoken by people of color in the United States), it becomes apparent that determining accommodation is skewed toward the speech of local Whites. In fact, Yaeger-Dror and Thomas (2010, 1) identify speakers of the predominant vernacular English spoken in different locales as non–African American. At the same time, they are careful to note that non–African Americans who speak these local varieties are not necessarily all of European descent. Notwithstanding this, we ought to start asking instead which speakers (regardless of race/ethnicity) are a part of creating/recreating local speech.

The sociolinguistic enterprise, grounded by years of research, has left us with the current "common sense" knowledge of what to expect regarding the role of ethnicity in sociolinguistic variation. (Early) research has shown that ethnicity is important for maintaining linguistic boundaries or the use/nonuse of and adaptation to ongoing sound change (Labov 1966). Hoffman and Walker (2010) note that, in the United States, ethnicity is not fully explored as it is very often simply equated with race, and studies look at variation in terms of Black and White or Brown. Researchers ask respondents: "How do Black people or White people sound?" Hoffman and Walker (2010) argue that this is a strong—and perhaps faulty (our view)—interpretation of ethnolect, which predicts that all members of the group share the same linguistic behavior but are different from other populations. They suggest instead a combination of both etic and emic approaches to ethnic categorization of speakers in sociolinguistic research. In fact, ethnic groups are not static, and speakers' identities might shift due to social context (Fought 2006).

Following their perspective, another way to think of dominant local varieties is in terms of the "founder principle" (Mufwene 2001), by which the founding populations establish the speech patterns adopted[3] by later arrivals. Enslaved Africans and later Southern African Americans would therefore be situated to adapt varieties spoken by founder groups in northern areas. The pool of linguistic features available to them (see Mufwene 2008, this volume) could have already been in existence or be introduced by the first generation of migrants. Bloomquist (2009a) notes that communities of African Americans were in the LSV from before 1800, and Brown and Holland (1994) indicate that Pittsburgh had a "large long-standing" African American community from the 1800s, with one of these, namely, Arthursville,[4] the lower section of today's Hill district, being firmly established by 1820. The effect these speakers[5] may have had on contemporary varieties of AAL is still not clear. The small number of enslaved Africans likely learned local varieties (Chaudenson 1992; Rickford 1997), but the communities that formed later were just as likely to result in the restructuring of local features or the retention of substrate properties (Winford 1997; Weldon and Moody, this volume).

A weaker view of ethnolects is that they differentiate speakers who wish to convey ethnic group membership by (optionally) using substrate features. In their Canadian study, Hoffman and Walker (2010) provide empirical support for the idea that different ethnic groups have different degrees of ethnic orientation. They suggest also that "visible" minorities might accommodate less than less-visible minorities. Very importantly, they argue that ethnolinguistic variation (in a multiethnic community) has less to do with non-accommodation to the majority language than with the way speakers actively construct and express ethnic identity. If we are to accept their hypothesis, then investigations on identity construction ought to be a necessary part of discussions on linguistic variation in AAL.

12.2.2 Urban Bias

Some long-standing views on AAL were based on empirical research on *urban* working-class varieties. Although we no longer adhere to the idea of widespread ethnic homogeneity of AAL (Wolfram, this volume), some vestiges of this idea linger, when we delineate core AAL features as those described in these earlier city-based studies. Although the influence of urban centers on rural areas (due to outmigration, for example) cannot be overlooked (Wolfram and Thomas 2002; Wolfram 2004), Tillery, Bailey, and Wikle (2004) suggest that the epicenter for change is not always urban centers. The fact is that the linguistic ecology of urban centers is quite different from that of rural locations, and so the linguistic implication for AAL will be different in each (see Rickford 1997, 1999; Cukor-Avila and Bailey, this volume; Wolfram, this volume). Tillery et al. (2004) note that significant changes in the migration patterns across the United States have even bigger linguistic consequences. Urban populations grew from 50 percent in 1920 to 75 percent in 1990, and by 2000, 80.3 percent of Americans resided in metropolises[6] versus roughly the same percentage residing in rural areas in 1860. Wolfram (2004, 113) argues that the social environment created in these cities as a result of this migration fostered the maintenance of ethnolinguistic differences. A large part of this is the continued de facto segregation of African American populations in these urban centers.

12.2.3 What Does It Mean to Be Black and Local?

Eberhardt (2008) identifies Pittsburgh as "a place where there is a close connection between local identity and local speech." This view is well supported by the work of Johnstone, Bhasin, and Wittkofski (2002) and Johnstone and Kiesling (2008), whose results are based on the speech of White speakers, and it is well documented that the term "Pittsburgher," by and large/almost exclusively refers to someone White who uses and recognizes the features of the variety. As noted in earlier work (Gooden and Eberhardt 2006, 2007), this is problematic when it comes to native-born African Americans in Pittsburgh.[7] The fact is that African Americans in Pittsburgh connect Pittsburghese with White speech. If we continue to equate Pittsburghese with local speech, then the speech of African Americans is effectively excluded. This should cause us to rethink what we mean by locals or local speech.

In the LSV, African Americans in Bloomquist's (2009a) surveys do identify as locals, but they also all acknowledge that local Whites sound different than local African Americans. We speculate that this might be part of the desire to distance themselves from "country Whites" and perceptions of "country-ness" in general. We may also need to step away from linguistic features that have been heavily studied, are readily recognizable, or that have been commodified and instead look at the dialects of the area more broadly[8] and clearly delineate what we mean by Pittsburgh or LSV AAL, while acknowledging that these intersect at some point with the broader dialects of their local areas.

Hazen (2000) suggests that what is local is intertwined with *cultural identity*, the sociolinguistic factor that involves how speakers view themselves in relation to their local and larger regional communities, that is, the degree of orientation to the local community, which may include linguistic and non-linguistic factors. It is possible that African Americans in Pittsburgh buy into the non-linguistic markers of local identity like the city's sports teams but not the linguistic variants that are indexed with or enregistered with "Whiteness." So, it may be necessary to reexamine sociocultural explanations of linguistic variation in Pittsburgh AAL in these terms, as it is clear that African Americans have a different cultural orientation toward the city, or what is local, than Whites have (Gooden and Eberhardt 2007; Gooden 2009; Eberhardt 2012). In comparison, African Americans in the LSV partially share cultural orientation with Whites.

12.3 EARLY SETTLEMENT IN THE NORTH MIDLAND REGION

Descriptions of linguistic variation in early Pittsburgh and the LSV might not accurately reflect the speech of African Americans, since early researchers tended not to investigate or include their speech. Even now, the bulk of the published work on Pittsburgh speech, for example, is based on the speech of Whites (see Gagnon 1999; McElhinny 1993, 1999; Johnstone et al. 2002; Johnstone, Andrus, and Danielson 2006; Johnstone and Kiesling 2008). In more recent work, however, Eberhardt (2008 et seq.) provides a detailed sociophonetic study of the vowel systems of African American and White speakers from several Pittsburgh neighborhoods.

The ecology in early (pre- and post-emancipation) Pittsburgh and the LSV and its potential impact on the speech of African Americans is a complex issue. Both areas had small numbers of enslaved Africans and had their fair share of diverse groups of migrants, both African American and White.

The first mention of enslaved Africans in the parts of the Dutch and Swedish colonies that later became incorporated into Pennsylvania was around 1644, but there may have been slaves in the area as early as 1633 or 1639 (Trotter and Smith 2010). After 1780,[9] Blacks born in Pittsburgh were "free,"[10] an attractive and motivating factor for migrant African Americans to reside in Pittsburgh. In fact, Glasco (2009) reports that roughly half of the freedom papers filed in Pittsburgh around that time were from southern Blacks. The larger influx of enslaved Africans began in 1684 with 150 persons, and by 1780, 1,140 enslaved Africans were reported in Westmoreland (which includes what is now Pittsburgh), Washington, Allegheny, and Fayette counties (State of Pennsylvania records). Only sixty-four enslaved Africans were reported in 1840 for Pennsylvania, but a total of forty-eight thousand African Americans for the state, representing the largest concentration of African Americans in any northern state. The demographic changes also represented a shift from a majority enslaved population in 1780 to a majority free people in 1840,[11] and with this came the development of free rather than enslaved African American communities. Dickerson (1981) noted that the first Black church formed in Western Pennsylvania did so in Pittsburgh in 1822, when the Black population was only 185 (Brown and Holland 1994) and there were at least six other Black churches by 1868,[12] many partially funded by Pittsburgh steel mill owners as incentives to their African American workers. It is likely that the speech of migrant African Americans, who became part of these growing communities, was somewhat different from that of rural southerners, since in the pre–World War II era, migrants were twice as likely to be educated than not (Bodnar, Simon, and Weber 1983; Vigdor 2002). Still, adapting to local speech might not have been altogether straightforward. White speakers in Pittsburgh around the 1900s were ethnically and linguistically diverse, due to the influx of European migrants (Bodnar et al. 1983), and during this time frame, native and immigrant Whites together outnumbered African Americans.

The LSV area was originally settled by several groups, including Palatinate Germans who immigrated to the United States during the early eighteenth century and the Scotch-Irish who began arriving around 1720 (Carver 1987). Ethnically, the region has remained solidly Pennsylvania German with over 42 percent of current European American residents claiming German ancestry (US Census 2010). Aside from the German American population, there are also substantial Pennsylvania German-speaking Amish and Mennonite communities throughout the region's countryside, especially in Lancaster County. Although most of the region is largely rural and agriculture is the largest industry, the LSV also features three moderately sized cities—Harrisburg, Lancaster, and York—which grew as a result of the steel and railroad industries. Yet currently, only 8.6 percent of the total population (African American and otherwise) resides in the cities. In addition to the German and Irish urban populations established in the late 1700s and the small African American population in place before 1800, during the Great Migration of 1916, these cities also drew large numbers of African American migrants from the South. Today most of the LSV's African American residents remain in the cities, but there are several rural African American communities in the area as well. We can expect that this fact may contribute to differences in LSV and AAL usage (see Bloomquist 2009a, b).

African Americans still make up a relatively small percentage of the LSV total population (in the US 2010 census, Adams County reported 1.2 percent of the population as African American and 3.7 percent in York), which may be one of the reasons why, historically, African Americans have been almost completely ignored by dialectologists. Despite their low numbers, the African American residents in the LSV live in long-established communities, and some are the descendants of a cultural presence that predates the Civil War. Between 1820 and 1850, both Gettysburg and York had very small African American communities (e.g., there were roughly three-hundred African American residents of Adams County and between four hundred and seven hundred in York). By 1900, however, due to communal migrations largely from Bamberg County, South Carolina, the York African American population had more than doubled to 1,675, and by 1960 it had reached 5,300, while that of Adams County remained relatively constant with only 330 African American residents even by 1960 (University of Virginia Geospatial and Statistical Data Center). The use, nonuse, and adaptation of the LSV dialect by African Americans native to the region reflect important details about broader issues concerning contact between African Americans and European Americans in the LSV. Their contact also provides valuable insight into the development of AAL in central Pennsylvania, from which we may draw parallels to the development of the variety in other such socially isolated communities (Mallinson and Wolfram 2002).

The numbers alone or contact by itself are not sufficiently explanatory, as linguistic outcomes of contact are conditioned by a variety of sociocultural factors. The fact that African Americans experienced social distancing enhanced the possibility that they did not right away adopt the speech of the resident Whites. Bodnar et al. (1983) document that the paths to "urbanization" for these migrant groups in Pittsburgh during the Great Migration era were strongly differentiated along racial and ethnic lines. They argue that although both African Americans and Whites worked in the steel mills and sometimes lived in similar locations, their economic outcomes and engagement with the city were very different. If the sound changes that are currently observed in Pittsburgh began later in the speech of African Americans, then it is reasonable that it might be complete only in the speech of White Pittsburghers. Factors affecting the observed linguistic features in Pittsburgh AAL are now compounded by issues of ecology as noted above, which continue to reinforce social distancing between African Americans and Whites in Pittsburgh today (see Washington 2010; Eberhardt 2012). African Americans are the second-largest ethnic group in Pittsburgh (US Census 2010), approximately 26 percent of the entire population, and as Eberhardt (2012) notes, reside in a city with the highest index of segregation in the country. In the LSV, the rural–urban divide reinforces social distancing.

12.4 CONTEMPORARY LANGUAGE VARIATION

Contemporary variation in Pittsburgh and LSV AAL is captured by vowel variation and a few lexical items and syntactic constructions, which are described below. As Wolfram (this volume) notes, however, a language variety is much more than a list of linguistic features, and other aspects of language such as discourse, conversational style, semantics (see Washington 2010), and prosody (Thomas and Carter 2006; Thomas 2007; Gooden 2009 on Pittsburgh) are very likely to be just as important in delineating a dialect for listeners.

12.4.1 Phonological Features in the Lower Susquehanna Valley

Due to the substantial Pennsylvania German-speaking communities in the LSV, historically, the area has been of particular interest to linguists, and, as a result, there has been a great deal of information published on the region's rural European American speakers. The LSV dialect has been described as a Midland dialect of the eastern Pennsylvania type and shows substantial Philadelphia influence as a result of migration routes from Philadelphia to Pittsburgh (Kurath and McDavid 1961; Carver 1987; Salvucci 1997). Past work on the LSV dialect has focused on the Pennsylvania German influence on the lexical, grammatical, and phonological patterns, with the bulk of the work focusing on lexical and grammatical features. However, in their 1961 survey of the pronunciation of English in the eastern United States, Kurath and McDavid (1961) describe some of the most prominent phonological features that characterize the LSV dialect as follows:

(1) /ɑ/ ≠ /ɔ/ in words like *cot* and *caught*
(2) Centralized or fronted /ou/ → /ɛu/ in words like *toe* or *though*

(3) [r] insertion: "wash" as *warsh*[13]

(4) /aɪ/ monophthongization before liquids in words like *bile*

Phonological data collected by the TELSUR project at the University of Pennsylvania confirms the first two of these features, as well as the regional /ɪ/ ~ /ɛ/ distinction before nasals as in *pin/pen* (Labov, Ash, and Boberg 2006). Other regional phonological variants include a vowel merger before tautosyllabic [l], as in *pool/pull/pole*, and /aʊ/ monophthongization before liquids (e.g., in *howl*). Further research is needed to determine the extent to which the remaining features are found in modern LSV speech, and if there are new features that have contributed to regional pronunciations due to contact with speakers from neighboring dialect regions.

12.4.2 Phonological Features in Pittsburgh

> This city is not Midwestern. It's not East Coast. It's just Pittsburgh.
>
> (O'Neill 2009)

O'Neill's characterization of Pittsburgh perhaps reflects the city being uniquely situated in the geolinguistic landscape and with Pittsburgh AAL representing a microcosm within that area. Pittsburgh is also in the North Midland dialect region, but it is perhaps more appropriately comparable to the northern West Virginia[14] region (Hankey 1972; McElhinny 1999). The city has been identified as the epicenter or locus of several vowel changes, or is uniquely situated in linguistic change in other ways. Labov, Ash, and Boberg (2006), for example, identify the city as following more diverse principles of language change than other areas involved in vowel chain shifts. Johnson (1971) describes the western Pennsylvania dialect as having Pittsburgh as its focal point.

Hankey (1965) is one of the earliest general reports on the presence of /aɪ/ monophthongization in western Pennsylvania, as in the case of *tire* merged with *tar*. This was reported earlier in Kurath and McDavid's (1961) survey in the speech of a "cultured" informant from Pittsburgh. They identify Pittsburgh as the location of the northernmost point for this feature. In Hankey's (1965) view, this feature is perhaps what led Kurath and McDavid to characterize the dialect area as "a blend of Pennsylvania and Southern features, graded from north to south" (1961, 18–19). The occurrence of /aɪ/ monophthongization was noted as particularly prevalent before liquids, and voiced phones more generally, with a glide-like realization [aᵋ] or [ɑᵋ] before /n/. These variants were reported in Pittsburgh in the 1930s and 1940s in Kurath and McDavid (1961). Variable /aɪ/ monophthongization then is very likely a long-standing feature of Pittsburgh speech (McElhinny 1991). This would have reinforced the retention of /aɪ/ monophthongization in the speech of southern African Americans and encouraged its occurrence in contemporary AAL Midland varieties. In such a scenario, it is difficult to argue for a pure transfer effect on sound changes, but there are other explanations. Sound changes may occur because sounds that are not socially meaningful receive less attention and so become susceptible to pronunciation innovations. Weinreich (1953) identifies areas of congruence as precisely the areas where learners make errors, which often precipitate sound changes. Van Coetsem (1988), on the other hand, argues that changes are more likely to occur in cases where there are differences between systems.

Of interest is that another long-standing feature, /aʊ/ monophthongization, is realized as /a:/ before /l/, just like the /aɪ/ monophthongization process, so that homophony is created in words like *file* and *fowl* [fa:l] (McElhinny 1991). McElhinny notes that there is no monophthongization of /aʊ/ in the speech of African Americans in Pittsburgh. Gooden and Eberhardt (2006, 2007), however, found that /aʊ/ monophthongization was in fact present in Pittsburgh AAL but at lower rates than in the speech of Whites. Further, the study argued that African Americans in Pittsburgh identify "Pittsburghese" as reflective of the speech of White speakers (see discussion in Eberhardt 2009a, 2012). Their results were based only on impressionistic analyses, although the method aided comparison with earlier studies (Johnstone et al. 2002; Johnstone et al. 2006). Eberhardt (2008, 2009a, 2009b, 2010) offered more rigorous sociophonetic analyses providing empirical support for these earlier results.

Johnson (1971) is perhaps the first sociophonetic study on the western Pennsylvania dialect, appearing in the first volume of the *Journal of the International Phonetic Association* (*JIPA*). Johnson identifies the *cot-caught* merger as a *salient* feature of western Pennsylvania speech and argues that speakers might be differentiated based on whether they have a raised vowel (younger than twenty or born around 1950, as estimated from the publication date) or not (older speakers). McDavid's (1952) report suggests that the merger was in place since the 1950s. Labov (1991) describes this merger as radiating outwards from Pittsburgh (along with Boston). However, whereas the merger is reported throughout the western United States (see Labov, Ash, and Boberg 2006), the phonetic realizations are different from that in Pittsburgh and the merged vowel is more often realized with the more fronted, unrounded vowel. Gooden and Eberhardt (2006, 2007) reported that AAL speakers have a lower probability of merging *cot/caught*. Eberhardt (2008) found that 74 percent of Pittsburgh AAL speakers had the merger, with variable patterns of distinction in *cot/caught* and *pond/pawned* variables in word list data for older African Americans. Two other speakers were shown to manipulate F_1—vowel height (25-year-old male) or duration (41-year-old female) to create some difference between the sounds, showing that several aspects of vowel properties may need to be considered in deciphering how or by what means speakers create distinctions for hearers. Eberhardt (2008) argues, based on absence of the merger from the speech of older informants, that the *cot-caught* merger in Pittsburgh AAL was not fully complete in the first part of the twentieth century, despite its reported early presence in the speech of Whites (297).

McElhinny's (1999) variationist analysis focuses on speech of White Pittsburghers, but she also mentions quantitative differences in the use of l-vocalization by African Americans (40 percent) and Whites (30 percent) (see note 10). Other reported features of Pittsburgh AAL are the laxing of /i/ before /l/ (Hankey 1972; McElhinny 1999). Although Johnson (1971) identified the neutralization of /u/ and /ʊ/ before /l/ as a feature of Pittsburgh speech, some twenty-eight years later McElhinny (1999) reported that this was not a sociolinguistic feature in Pittsburgh AAL.[15]

12.4.3 Lexical and Syntactic Features

Child, please! Troutman (2001) describes what she terms "culturally toned diminutives" as terms of endearment or an expression of familiarity. These are roughly equivalent to Standard American English (SAE) affixes like *–let, –ling, –ette*. Troutman argues that while White (female) Americans consistently reject terms like *girl* as reinforcements of White hegemonic masculine dominance, the term is freely used among (female) African Americans and is devoid of negative denotations and connotations in in-group—but *not* out-group use. A demonstration of this in-group versus out-group use was observed between HBO talk show host Bill Maher (White) and Dr. Melissa Harris-Perry (African American and then professor at Tulane University) on June 2011.[16] In this exchange, Maher attempts to use *girl* as an expression of familiarity, but Harris-Perry rejects this usage and proceeds to correct Maher publicly by saying "grown woman" in response. In doing so, Harris-Perry invokes the dominant pejorative usage of the word and explicitly positions herself as an adult who should not be referred to as a child.

Washington's (2010) study on semantic variation in Pittsburgh AAL provides empirical evidence that the use of culturally toned diminutives is widespread. Not only have many words with formerly pejorative meanings been generally reclaimed among African Americans, but the reported differences in usage are also very clearly linked to perceptions of racial inequality in the city. Collectively, AAL speakers in Pittsburgh use these words to establish solidarity and bridge social distance between strangers (cf. van Dijk, Ting-Toomey, and Troutman 1997). In more recent work, Washington (2012) provided a quantitative analysis of the use of the N-word in Pittsburgh AAL. These results preliminarily indicate that younger speakers are more likely to have a positive connotation associated with a final *a*-spelling or pronunciation of the word (i.e., *nigga* [nɪgə]), while older speakers are more likely to have a negative connotation of the *er*-spelling or pronunciation of the word (i.e., *nigger* [nɪgər]).

There is some evidence of iconic Pittsburgh terms such as *nebby* 'nosey,' *redd up* 'to clean/tidy up,' and *slippy* 'slippery,' being used by African Americans in Pittsburgh (Gooden and Eberhardt 2007). Some of these terms are also present in AAL in the LSV where the regional lexicon includes a number of German borrowings such as *smear case (schmierkas, schmierkäse)* for 'cottage cheese,' *fastnacht* (similar to a doughnut), and *thick milk* (milk soured to the point of thickening), modeled on *dickemilich*. Other local words and expressions include those determined to be of Scotch-Irish origin, such as *redd up*, which we have noted also occurs in Pittsburgh (Reed 1949; Shields 1985; Carver 1990; Salvucci 1991).

The discussion of syntactic features of Pittsburgh AAL is limited here to broad descriptions, since there are no systematic studies of syntactic or morphosyntactic variation. Sternglass (1974) reported quantitative but no qualitative differences in grammatical structures in the academic writing of African American and White students in

Pittsburgh, with invariant *be* being the only exception. In the LSV, AAL speakers use or recognize region-specific grammatical patterns that feature nonstandard word order that have also been attributed to German influence, as in *"it wonders me"* or *"throw the cow over the fence some hay."* Another prominent regional grammatical feature, which has also been reported in Pittsburgh, and which has been determined to be the result of Scotch-Irish influence (Crozier 1984; Montgomery 1989), is the deletion of *to* + auxiliary after *needs/wants/likes* as in the following:

(5) The house needs/doesn't need Ø painted.
    SAE: 'The house does (not) need to be painted'; or
    'The house does (not) need painting'; or
    'The house does (not) need to be painted.'
(6) The baby wants/doesn't want Ø picked up.
    SAE: 'The baby does not want to be picked up.'
(7) That cat likes/doesn't like Ø brushed.
    SAE: 'That cat does (not) like to be brushed'; or
    'That cat does (not) like being brushed.'

While several researchers have contributed to our understanding of the way in which *needs/wants/likes* functions in the region (Murray, Frazer, and Simon 1996; Frazer 2000; Ash 2006), it is a feature that has been attributed almost entirely to European American residents. As is the case with the local phonological and lexical variants, we believe this grammatical pattern is possibly used by certain segments of African American populations in Pennsylvania as well, which future research would need to confirm.

12.5 VOWEL VARIATION IN THE LSV—DATA ANALYSIS AND DISCUSSION

Foulkes and Docherty (2006) and Foulkes, Scobbie, and Watt (2012) argue that objects of sociophonetic variation studies must at least be socially meaningful; otherwise, we are not really reporting on meaningful (socio)linguistic variation. We believe speech perception is a critical component in discussing what is socially meaningful to speakers. In this regard, although Bloomquist (2009a) and Eberhardt (2010) report some perception results, by and large the Pittsburgh and LSV studies have yet to include more rigorous perception studies.[17] Perception studies are an important complement to discussions on the metalinguistic discussions about language and language use (see Eberhardt 2012 on Pittsburgh). We therefore present LSV vowel plots on an ERB scale to better reflect speaker perceptions of $F_1 F_2$ differences.

A comprehensive analysis of the vowel systems of Pittsburgh and LSV African Americans is beyond the scope of this chapter. We present here an acoustic analysis of vowel variation in the LSV focusing on choice items in word list data. Since vowel quality changes due to situational context, the first production (as in a word list) is likely to be clearer than subsequent productions. The implication is that vowels that are less clear tend to be reduced, meaning that there is a deviation from its position in the vowel space, as opposed to its more clear citation form counterpart. In sociolinguistic studies, by employing word lists to elicit the speaker's most careful speech, observed vowel mergers in the word list can be then treated as illustrative of what is possible more generally.

The vowels discussed here are some of the most prominent phonological features characterizing both LSV and Pittsburgh AAL. That is, they include /aɪ/ monophthongization, /aʊ/ monophthongization, and merging of *pool* and *pull, cot* and *caught*, and *pill* and *peel*.

12.5.1 Vowel Variation Method

The data reported below are from four women and four men who were part of a larger study (Bloomquist 2009a). All participants self-identified as African Americans and were native-born lifelong residents of the LSV. They ranged in ages from 25 to 48 at the time of the recordings.[18] Speakers answered questions in loosely structured interviews about their personal histories, living in the LSV, and attitudes pertaining to the dialect, and they also read a story and a minimal-pair word list. The word list yielded a variety of words with target vowels occurring before voiced stops, nasals, laterals, voiceless consonants, and word finally in stressed positions (e.g., *feel/fill, pin/pen, shade/bait/day, bide/bite, caught/cot, hock/hawk, sighted/sided*). Attempts were made to ensure the comfort of participants to encourage natural pronunciations.[19]

The words were digitized at a sampling rate of 44.1 kHz. All data were analyzed acoustically in Praat (Boersma and Weenink 2010) by a phonetically trained speech and hearing researcher. The data were crosschecked by the independent researcher and by the second author following the initial coding. The frequencies of the first (F_1) and second formants (F_2) were measured for each vowel. Vowel onset and offset were marked at points when both F_1 and F_2 ceased transition into and out of the vowel, respectively; otherwise, the latest point of inflection where the amplitude was high was marked. F_1 and F_2 measurements were taken at 20 percent, 50 percent, and 80 percent of the duration between onset and offset and were facilitated by a formant extraction script in Praat. Vowels traditionally designated as monophthongs, as in *bid* and *bad*, were plotted using the midpoint measurement (see figure 12.1). Vowels traditionally designated as diphthongs, *bite, bide*, were plotted so that the nucleus and off-glide of the vowels (shown as arrows in figure 12.1) would be captured (DiPaolo, Yaeger-Dror, and Wassink 2010). Some word classes had as many as seventeen tokens and occasionally speakers skipped over a word so that there were no tokens. Words with only one token were omitted.

Following Hawkins and Midgley (2005), F_1 and F_2 Hz values were converted[20] to an auditory scale, Equivalent Rectangular Bandwidth (ERB), using the formula 21.4 $*$ log(10) [0.00437 $* f + 1$] (Moore 1997), where f is frequency (Hz). The purpose of this psycho-acoustic scale is to provide steps that correspond to equal perceptual intervals between frequencies (see figure 12.1). The ERB scale used in figure 12.1(b) effectively

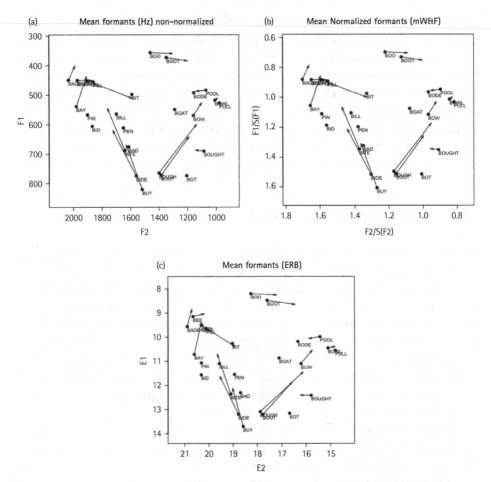

FIGURE 12.1 Mean frequencies (Hz: (a); normalized: (b); ERB: (c)) of the first (F_1) and sec-ond (F_2) formants for all speakers in the sample.

expands the F_1 and compresses F_2 dimensions relative to one another, the result of which is that the distributions for phones shown are slightly more distinct than in the linear Hz scale used in figure 12.1(a). In figure 12.1(b), for example, the BEE vowel is clearly differ-entiated from the BADE/BAIT and the PEEL/PILL sets.

Finally, the raw Hz formant values were normalized using the modified Watt and Fabricius method,[21] as this has been shown to be one of the best methods for sociopho-netic purposes (Fabricius 2008; Flynn and Foulkes 2011; Watt and Fabricius 2011). Notice though that the normalization plot in figure 12.1(b) again masks the difference between BADE/BAIT and PEEL/PILL, hence we refer to the ERB values for the rest of the analysis.

12.5.2 Vowel Variation Results

A visual inspection of the vowel plots shows that *peel* and *pill* are closer to each other than they are to *bit* or *bee*. This apparent merger is similar to that reported for Pittsburgh AAL and other AAL varieties. A Welch 2-sample t-test[22] of ERB values for F_1 ($p = 0.7215$) and F_2 ($p = 0.7296$) at the midpoint confirms that there are no significant differences between these vowel categories. Not surprisingly, *pin* and *pen* are differentiated in the vowel space, as has been previously reported (Labov, Ash, and Boberg 2006). However, these vowel categories are merged in Pittsburgh AAL (Eberhardt 2010). At the back of the vowel space, *pool* and *pull* appear to be separated, as is the case for Pittsburgh AAL (ibid.). Taken together, the lack of merger before /l/ might be taken as a feature of North Midland AAL. Figure 12.1(c) also shows that the /aɪ/ glides are strong in the contexts considered, before voiced and voiceless obstruents and in open syllables, though there is some difference in the onset of the glides. In contrast, Pittsburgh AAL speakers produced weakened or monophthongal glides. This is not surprising since monophthongization is predicted to occur preceding /l/ and the word list data lacked these contexts. Eberhardt (ibid.) reports that in Pittsburgh AAL there is very little gliding in this prelateral context. Similarly, /aʊ/ is consistently produced as a diphthong, as is the case for Pittsburgh AAL. Noticeably absent in these data is the *cot-caught* merger, which has been shown to be pervasive in Pittsburgh AAL.

12.6 CONCLUSIONS

These data confirm the contemporary thesis that varieties of AAL are not only evolving in ways that are different from the varieties spoken by neighboring Whites but also that AAL is continuing to be shaped by the distinct regional ecologies and sociocultural and sociohistorical contexts in which they exist as well. In the LSV results, the absence of the *pin-pen* merger points to language behavior unexpected for "typical" AAL speakers, but the lack of the *cot-caught* merger suggests that, in some ways, LSV African Americans do not sound like "typical" (i.e., European American) LSV speakers either. These findings confirm previous analyses in which LSV African Americans have been found to perform in linguistically hybrid regional and ethnic ways that reveal their joint identities as "local" and African American.

The participants in Bloomquist (2009a) reported uniformly that out-of-town AAL speakers characterized their LSV AAL as "country" or "White," while also acknowledging that local African Americans and Whites speak differently. Some of this can be seen in LSV African Americans' rejection of particular lexical items used by Whites (such as *redd up* and *outen the lights*), but these same speakers use regional syntactic structures (deletion of *to* + auxiliary after *needs/wants/likes*, etc.) that most clearly identify them as LSV speakers. From the data reported here, it is not clear which sound features are indexed with "local" and "White" for LSV AAL speakers who seem to want to identify as both "authentically Black" and local. Many of them point out that their speech is preferable to that heard in nearby AAL communities such as Baltimore, where "people don't speak as clearly" or "don't sound as proper" as African Americans in the LSV (Bloomquist 2009a). This is different from Pittsburgh, where AAL speakers are concerned with differentiating themselves from Whites and where sounding "local" is equated with "Whiteness."

NOTES

1. While we do not address all of these issues, we want to make it clear that sociocultural factors include geographic and demographic distributions, race, ethnicity, as well as different social functions of language use and ideological factors (Weinreich 1953; Labov 2001, 2010).
2. Although the linguistic literature has moved beyond focusing on gang-oriented/youth subculture/inner-city "hood" views of AAL, some "complicated" perspectives still exist, part of the issue being that race is still a critical part of the discussion on AAL.
3. Of course, speakers need not adopt founder varieties outright, but instead, over time, help to recreate/restructure the existing variety.
4. Also known as Prospect Hill in the late eighteenth century.
5. Weldon and Moody (this volume) review research showing that the speech of southern African Americans most likely involved a continuum of varieties and that, in many areas, conditions were ripe for creolized Englishes to emerge and thereby influence emerging AAL varieties. In some cases, Creole English speakers are likely to have been imported to these northern areas.
6. Urban centers with more than 250,000 people, some over 5 million.
7. This is something that Gooden noticed almost immediately when she began interacting with African Americans upon her move to Pittsburgh in 2003, and what sparked interest in this issue in the first place.
8. Daniel Stuchel (2014) argues that whereas some speakers outside the city of Pittsburgh use the same features readily identified as Pittsburghese, they do not grow up using that term to refer to their speech.
9. Passing of the Gradual Abolition Act.
10. Blacks born into "freedom" had to serve another twelve years as indentured laborers.
11. In 1833, Pittsburgh's first Antislavery Society was formed in the home of a prominent Black entrepreneur.
12. In this history of Black churches in Pittsburgh, Brown and Holland (1994) identify the period 1840–1917 as the Church of the Old Pittsburghers and 1917–1950 as the rise of the industrial Migrants' Church (61).
13. While /r/ in warsh is lexically constrained in other parts of Appalachia, in the LSV, /r/ insertion occurs also in expressions like Oh my go(r)sh! The environment is clearly limited, but there appears to be enough evidence to suggest that this is a phonological feature that could be productive if there were a wider range of potential occurrences.
14. The area was involved in a constant dispute between Pennsylvania and West Virginia. For example, in 1776, Virginia created what it called the District of West Augusta, which included three counties and also included Pittsburgh. In 1779, the Mason-Dixon Line was extended and Pittsburgh was declared to be part of Westmoreland County, being fifty miles removed from the border.
15. Labov, Ash, and Boberg (2006) found this merger to be general in White Pittsburgh speech.
16. http://castroller.com/podcasts/RealTimeWith/2357865. Real Time with Bill Maher, Episode 215 (aired June 3, 2011).
17. See, for example, research on American dialects by Clopper and Pisoni (2004), Clopper and Bradlow (2008), Kendall and Fridland (2012), among many others.

18. Some recordings were not included in the analysis due to poor sound quality or heavy background noise.

19. The Pittsburgh data were collected using similar techniques, with interviews done by either an African American or a White interviewer, as part of the Pittsburgh Speech and Society project (see Eberhardt 2008, 2009, 2010, for details). It might be of interest to see whether there are effects of interlocutor on the Pittsburgh data. Scanlon and Wassink (2010), for example, report that on average there were significant differences in the starting F_1 of /aɪ/ vowel production of their Seattle speaker across all contexts when the interlocutor was African American.

20. Conversion of the Hertz values was done using the convert.erb function in the vowels package (1.2) for R (Kendall and Thomas 2012).

21. This was done using the norm.wattfabricius function in the vowels package (1.2) for R (Kendall and Thomas 2012).

22. We acknowledge that these apparent mergers/non-mergers may need to be confirmed by checking whether other cues like formant trajectory information and duration is used to distinguish these vowels (MacLeod, Stoel-Gammon, and Wassink 2009). Other tests such as spectral overlap assessment could test the relative contributions of spectral and duration information on differentiating between vowel categories (DiPaolo et al. 2010).

References

Ash, Sharon. 2006. "The North American Midland as a Dialect Area." In *Language Variation and Change in the American Midland: A New Look at "Heartland" English,* edited by Thomas E. Murray and Beth Lee Simon, 33–56. Amsterdam: John Benjamins.

Bloomquist, Jennifer. 2009a. "Dialect Differences in Central Pennsylvania: Regional Dialect Use and Adaptation by African Americans in the Lower Susquehanna Valley." *American Speech* 84: 27–47.

———. 2009b. "'People Say I Speak Proper, but Girl, I'm Ghetto!' Regional Dialect Use and Adaptation by African American Women in Pennsylvania's Lower Susquehanna Valley." In *African American Women's Language,* edited by Sonja Lanehart, 165–83. Cambridge: Cambridge Scholars.

Bodnar, John, Roger Simon, and Michael P. Weber. 1983. *Lives of Their Own: Blacks, Italians, and Poles in Pittsburgh, 1900–1960.* Champaign: University of Illinois Press.

Boersma, Paul, and David Weenink. 2010. *Praat: Doing Phonetics by Computer* [Computer program]. Version 5.1.41, retrieved from http://www.praat.org/.

Brown, Eliza Smith, and Daniel Holland. 1994. *African American Historic Sites Survey of Allegheny County.* Harrisburg, PA: Diane.

Carver, Craig. 1987. *American Regional Dialects: A Word Geography.* Ann Arbor: University of Michigan Press.

Chaudenson, Robert. 1992. *Des îles, des hommes, des langues: Langues creoles, cultures Creoles.* Paris: L'Harmattan.

Clopper, Cynthia G., and Ann R. Bradlow. 2008. "Perception of Dialect Variation in Noise: Intelligibility and Classification." *Language and Speech* 51: 175–98.

Clopper, Cynthia G., and David B. Pisoni. 2004. "Some Acoustic Cues for the Perceptual Categorization of American English Regional Dialects." *Journal of Phonetics* 32: 111–40.

Crozier, Alan. 1984. "The Scotch-Irish Influence on American English." *American Speech* 59 (4): 310–31.

Dickerson, Dennis C. 1981. "The Black Church in Industrializing Western Pennsylvania, 1870–1950." *Western Pennsylvania History* 64: 329–44.

DiPaolo Marianna, Malcah Yaeger-Dror, and Alicia Beckford Wassink. 2010. "Analyzing Vowels." In *Sociophonetics: A Student's Guide*, edited by Marianna DiPaolo and Malcah Yaeger-Dror, 87–106. London: Routledge.

Eberhardt, Maeve. 2008. "The Low-Back Merger in the Steel City: African American English in Pittsburgh." *American Speech* 83: 284–311.

———. 2009a. "Identities and Local Speech in Pittsburgh: A Study of Regional African American English." PhD diss., University of Pittsburgh.

———. 2009b. "African American and White Vowel Systems in Pittsburgh." *Publication of the American Dialect Society* 94: 129–57.

———. 2010. "African American and White Vowel Systems in Pittsburgh." In *African American Speakers and Their Participation in Local Sound Changes: A Comparative Study*, edited by Malcah Yaeger-Dror and Erik Thomas, Publication of the American Dialect Society 94, 129–57. Durham, NC: Duke University Press.

———. 2012. "Enregisterment of Pittsburghese and the Local African American Community." *Language and Communication* 32: 358–71.

Fabricius, Anne. 2008. "Vowel Normalization in Sociophonetics: When, Why, How?" Paper presented at Sociolinguistics Circle, Copenhagen University, September 16.

Flynn, Nicholas, and Paul Foulkes. 2011. "Comparing Vowel Formant Normalization Methods." *Online Proceedings of ICPHS XVII*, 683–86.

Fought, Carmen. 2006. *Language and Ethnicity*. New York: Cambridge University Press.

Foulkes, Paul, and Gerard Docherty. 2006. "The Social Life of Phonetics and Phonology." *Journal of Phonetics* 34: 409–38.

Foulkes, Paul, James M. Scobbie, and Dominic Watt. 2012. "Sociophonetics." In *The Handbook of Phonetic Sciences*, 2nd ed., edited by William J. Hardcastle, John Laver, and Fiona E. Gibbon, 703–54. New York: John Wiley & Sons.

Frazer, Timothy. 2000. "Are Rural Dialects Endangered Like Island Dialects?" *American Speech* 75: 347–49.

Gagnon, Christina. 1999. "Language Attitudes in Pittsburgh: 'Pittsburghese' vs. Standard English." Master's thesis, University of Pittsburgh.

Glasco, Laurence. 2009. *Free at Last?: Slavery in Pittsburgh in the 18th and 19th Centuries*. http://www.library.pitt.edu/freeatlast/papers_listing.html. Office of Public Affairs, University of Pittsburgh.

Gooden, Shelome. 2009. "Authentically Black, Bona Fide Pittsburgher: A First Look at Intonation in African American Women's Language in Pittsburgh." In *African American Women's Language: Discourse, Education and Identity*, edited by Sonja Lanehart, 142–64. Newcastle upon Tyne, UK: Cambridge Scholars.

Gooden, Shelome, and Maeve Eberhardt. 2006. "Local Identity and Ethnicity in Pittsburgh AAVE." Paper presented at New Ways of Analyzing Variation 35, Columbus, Ohio, November 9–12.

———. 2007. "Local Identity and Ethnicity in Pittsburgh AAVE." *University of Pennsylvania Working Papers in Linguistics. Selected Papers from NWAV 35*, 81–94.

Hankey, Clyde T. 1965. "'Tiger,' 'Tagger' and [aɪ] in Western Pennsylvania." *American Speech* 40: 226–29.

——. 1972. "Notes on West Penn-Ohio Phonology." In *Studies in Linguistics in Honor of Raven I. McDavid Jr*, edited by Lawrence M. Davis, 49–61. Tuscaloosa: University of Alabama Press.

Haugen, Einar. 1972. *The Ecology of Language*. Stanford, CA: Stanford University Press.

Hawkins, Sarah, and Jonathan Midgley. 2005. "Formant Frequencies of RP Monophthongs in Four Age Groups of Speakers." *Journal of the International Phonetic Association* 35: 183–99.

Hazen, Kirk. 2000. "Identity and Language Variation in a Rural Community." *Language* 78: 240–57.

Hoffman, Michol, and James Walker. 2010. "Ethnolects and the City." *Language Variation and Change* 22: 37–67.

Johnson, Bruce Lee. 1971. "The Western Pennsylvania Dialect of American English." *Journal of the International Phonetic Association* 1: 69–73.

Johnstone, Barbara, Jennifer Andrus, and Andrew E. Danielson. 2006. "Mobility, Indexicality, and the Enregisterment of 'Pittsburghese.'" *Journal of English Linguistics* 34: 77–104.

Johnstone, Barbara, Neeta Bhasin, and Denise Wittkofski. 2002. "'Dahntahn' Pittsburgh: Monophthongal /aw/ and Representations of Localness in Southwestern Pennsylvania." *American Speech* 77: 148–76.

Johnstone, Barbara, and Scott Kiesling. 2008. "Indexicality and Experience: Exploring the Meanings of /aw/-Monophthongization in Pittsburgh." *Journal of Sociolinguistics* 12: 5–33.

Kendall, Tyler, and Valerie Fridland. 2012. "Variation in Perception and Production of Mid Front Vowels in the U.S. Southern Vowel Shift." *Journal of Phonetics* 40: 289–306.

Kendall, Tyler, and Erik R. Thomas. 2012. *Vowels: Vowel Manipulation, Normalization, and Plotting in R. R Package*, Version 1.2. [Software Resource: http://ncslaap.lib.ncsu.edu/tools/norm/].

Kurath, Hans, and Raven I. McDavid. 1961. *The Pronunciation of English in the Atlantic States: Based upon the Collections of the Linguistic Atlas of the Eastern United States*. Ann Arbor: University of Michigan Press.

Labov, William. 1966. *The Social Stratification of English in New York City*. Washington, DC: Center for Applied Linguistics.

——. 1991. "The Three Dialects of English." In *New Ways of Analyzing Sound Change*, edited by Penelope Eckert, 1–44. San Diego, CA: Academic.

——. 2001. *Principles of Linguistic Change*. Vol. 2, *Social Factors*. Oxford: Blackwell.

——. 2010. *Principles of Linguistic Change*. Vol. 3, *Cognitive and Cultural Factors*. Oxford: Blackwell.

Labov, William, Sharon Ash, and Charles Boberg. 2006. *The Atlas of North American English: Phonetics, Phonology and Sound Change*. Berlin: De Gruyter.

MacLeod, A. N., C. Stoel-Gammon, and A. B. Wassink. 2009. "Production of High Vowels in Canadian English and Canadian French: A Comparison of Early Bilingual and Monolingual Speakers." *Journal of Phonetics* 37 (4): 374–87.

Mallinson, Christine, and Walt Wolfram. 2002. "Dialect Accommodation in a Bi-Ethnic Mountain Enclave Community: More Evidence on the Development of African American English." *Language in Society* 31: 743–75.

McDavid, Raven I. 1952. "Some Social Differences in Pronunciation." *Language Learning* 4: 102–16.

McElhinny, Bonnie. 1993. "We All Wear the Blue: Language, Gender and Police Work." PhD diss., Stanford University.

——. 1999. "More on the Third Dialect of English: Linguistic Constraints on the Use of Three Phonological Variables in Pittsburgh." *Language Variation and Change* 11: 171–95.

Montgomery, Michael. 1989. *Exploring the Roots of Appalachian English*. New York: John Benjamins.

Moore, Brian C. J. 1997. "Aspects of Auditory Processing Related to Speech Production." In *The Handbook of Phonetic Sciences*, edited by William J. Hardcastle and John Laver, 539–65. Cambridge, MA: Basil Blackwell.

Mufwene, Salikoko S. 2000. "Language Contact, Evolution, and Death: How Ecology Rolls the Dice." In *Assessing Ethnolinguistic Vitality*, edited by Gloria E. Kindell and M. Paul Lewis, 145–66. Dallas, TX: Summer Institute of Linguistics.

———. 2001. *Ecology of Language Evolution*. Cambridge: Cambridge University.

———. 2008. *Language Evolution: Contact, Competition and Change*. New York: Continuum.

Murray, Thomas E., Timothy C. Frazer, and Beth Lee Simon. 1996. "*Need* + Past Participle in American English." *American Speech* 71 (3): 255–71.

O'Neill, Brian. 2009. *The Paris of Appalachia: Pittsburgh in the Twenty-First Century*. Pittsburgh, PA: Carnegie Mellon University Press.

Purnell, Thomas C., and Malcah Yaeger-Dror. 2010. "Accommodation to the Locally Dominant Norm: A Special Issue." *American Speech* 85: 115–20.

Reed, Carroll E. 1949. *The Pennsylvania German Dialect Spoken in the Counties of Lehigh and Berks: Phonology and Morphology*. Seattle: University of Washington Press.

Rickford, John R. 1997. "Prior Creolization of African American Vernacular English? Sociohistorical and Textual Evidence from the 17th and 18th Centuries." *Journal of Sociolinguistics* 1: 315–36.

———. 1999. *African American Vernacular English*. Malden, MA: Blackwell.

Salvucci, Claudio R. 1991. *Linguistic Geography of Pennsylvania*. Available: http://www.evol-pub.com/Americandialects/PennaDialMap.html.

———. 1997. *A Dictionary of Pennsylvanianisms*. Southampton, PA: Evolution.

Scanlon, Michael, and Alicia Beckford Wassink. 2010. "African American English in Urban Seattle: Accommodation and Intraspeaker Variation in the Pacific Northwest." *American Speech* 85: 205–24.

Shields, Kenneth, Jr. 1985. "Germanisms in Pennsylvania English: An Update." *American Speech* 60: 228–37.

Silverstein, M. 2003. "Indexical Order and the Dialectics of Sociolinguistic Life." *Language and Communication* 23: 193–229.

State of Pennsylvania. *Black History in Pennsylvania: Slavery and Resistance 1644 to 1865*. http://www.phmc.state.pa.us/bhp/blackhistory/slavery-and-resistance-1644-to-1865.pdf.

Sternglass, Marilyn S. 1974. "Close Similarities in Dialect Features of Black and White College Students in Remedial Composition Classes." *TESOL Quarterly* 8 (3): 271–83.

Stuchel, Daniel. 2014. "Pittsburgh Dialect Study: Opinions and Performances of Non-Native Speakers." Office of Undergraduate Research Grant Proposal. University of Pittsburgh.

Thomas, Erik R. 2002. "Sociophonetic Applications of Speech Perception Experiments." *American Speech* 77: 115–47.

Thomas, Erik R., and Phillip M. Carter. 2006. "Prosodic Rhythm and African American English." *English World-Wide* 27: 331–55.

Tillery, Jan, Guy Bailey, and Tom Wikle. 2004. "Demographic Change and American Dialectology in the Twenty-First Century." *American Speech* 79: 227–49.

Trotter, Joe, and Eric Ledell Smith. 2010. *African Americans in Pennsylvania: Shifting Historical Perspectives*. University Park: Pennsylvania State Press.

Troutman, Denise. 2001. "African American Women: Talking that Talk." In *Sociocultural and Historical Contexts of African American English*, edited by Sonja Lanehart, 211–38. Amsterdam: John Benjamins.

US Census Bureau. 2010. "State and County Quickfacts: Pennsylvania." University of Virginia Geospatial and Statistical Data Center. http://quickfacts.census.gov/qfd/states/42000.html.

Van Coetsem, Frans. 1988. *Loan Phonology and the Two Transfer Types in Language Contact*. Vol. 27. Walter de Gruyter.

van Dijk, Teun A., Stella Ting-Toomey, and Denise Troutman. 1997. "Discourse, Ethnicity, Culture and Racism." In *Discourse as Social Interaction*, edited by Teun A. van Dijk, 144–80. Thousand Oaks, CA: Sage.

Vigdor, Jacob L. 2002. "The Pursuit of Opportunity: Explaining Selective Black Migration." *Journal of Urban Economics* 51: 391–417.

Washington, Adrienne Ronee. 2010. "Bad Words Gone Good: Semantic Reanalysis in African American English." Master's thesis, University of Pittsburgh.

———. 2012. "Language Attitudes towards the Use of NiggER and NiggA among Whites and Blacks." PhD comprehensive paper, University of Pittsburgh.

Watt, Dominic, and Anne H. Fabricius. 2011. "A Measure of Variable Planar Locations Anchored on the Centroid of the Vowel Space: A Sociophonetic Research Tool." *Proceedings of the 17th International Congress of Phonetic Sciences*, 2102–5.

Weinreich, Uriel. 1953. *Languages in Contact: Findings and Problems*. New York: Mouton.

Winford, Donald. 1997. "On the Origins of African American Vernacular English: A Creolist Perspective. Part 1: Sociohistorical Background." *Diachronica* 14: 305–44.

Wolfram, Walt. 2004. "The Grammar of Urban African American Vernacular English." In *Handbook of Varieties of English*, edited by Bernd Kortmann and Edgar Schneider, 111–32. Berlin: Mouton de Gruyter.

Wolfram, Walt, and Erik R. Thomas. 2002. *The Development of African American English*. Oxford: Blackwell.

Yaeger-Dror, Malcah, and Thomas Purnell. 2010. "Accommodative Tendencies in Multidialect Communication." *Journal of English Linguistics* 38: 187–289.

Yaeger-Dror, Malcah, and Erik R. Thomas. 2010. *African American English Speakers and Their Participation in Local Sound Changes: A Comparative Study*. Publication of the American Dialect Society 94. Durham, NC: Duke University Press.

CHAPTER 13

....

AFRICAN AMERICAN PHONOLOGY IN A PHILADELPHIA COMMUNITY

....

WILLIAM LABOV AND SABRIYA FISHER

13.1 LINGUISTIC CHANGE IN NORTH AMERICA

....

THIS is a study of the relation of mainstream Philadelphia phonology to the vowel systems of the African American community in that city.[1] It adds another chapter to the effort to distinguish between two types of language learning: the nearly error-free transmission from parent to child and the less accurate diffusion across the adult population (Labov 2007).

Recent studies of linguistic change in North America show that it flows in two different directions. On the one hand, the White mainstream dialects have invested in radically different vowel systems. The *Atlas of North American English* (Labov, Ash, and Boberg 2006) finds steadily increasing regional differentiation (Inland North, Canada, the Middle Atlantic States, western Pennsylvania), a calm maintenance of traditional patterns (Eastern New England, New York City, North Central, the Midland), or a slowly receding regional generalization (the South). Several moderate-sized cities have abandoned their local configurations but have replaced them with neighboring regional patterns—Charleston (Baranowski 2007), Cincinnati (Boberg and Strassel 2000), and St. Louis (Labov 2007).

We find a very different situation when we turn to African American Vernacular English (AAVE). This dialect has undergone rapid grammatical evolution on a national scale with no detectable regional differentiation. Remarkably similar findings have appeared in studies of morphosyntactic features (absence of verbal –s, absence of possessive attributive –s, presence of plural –s, variable deletion of copula and auxiliary) in cities throughout the country (New York: Labov et al. 1968; Washington, DC: Fasold 1972; Detroit: Wolfram 1969; San Francisco Bay area: Mitchell-Kernan 1969; Philadelphia: Cofer 1972; Labov and Harris 1986; Los Angeles: Baugh 1983). Newly incrementing elements of the tense and aspect system (habitual *be*, preterite *had*) have appeared simultaneously in widely separated cities across the United States (Cukor-Avila and Bailey 1996; Labov et al. 1968; Rickford et al. 1991).

Given this uniformity, nine AAVE researchers were able to jointly issue a summary statement describing the common features that educators would have to take into account (Labov 2013, appendix). This national distribution appears to be largely a product of the twentieth century, the outcome of the Great Migration of African Americans from the South to northern cities beginning in 1914 (Cukor-Avila and Bailey 1996).

A somewhat different situation has begun to emerge from studies of AAVE phonology, where considerable regional differentiation is to be found. The summary statement describes several common phonological features (*th-* fronting; merger of /i/ and /e/ before nasals; /l/ vocalization), but one feature was reported as "regional": the vocalization of /r/. Studies of AAVE in /r/-less New York City found that adolescent African American speakers had 98–100 percent vocalization, considerably exceeding the White pattern (Labov et al. 1968, 1:99–106) while in /r/-pronouncing Philadelphia, the highest level of /r/-vocalization reached by core speakers of AAVE was 71 percent (Myhill 1988). The general pattern shows an influence of the surrounding /r/-pronouncing mainstream dialect on an originally /r/-less AAVE. Yet, the most striking regional feature of AAVE is an increase in the influence of coda /r/ on the vowel: the St. Louis realization of front vowels /ihr/ and /ehr/ as mid-central [ɝ] (made nationally famous by the Hip Hop artists Chingy in "Right Thurr" and Nelly in "Hot in Herre"). Blake and Shousterman (2010) track the development of this sound change within African American English in St. Louis and East St. Louis and trace its origins to Memphis.

In contrast, most other reports of regional differences in AAVE phonology show an approximation to the surrounding regional pattern of the White community. In Pittsburgh, Gooden and Eberhardt (2007) examined the use of well-known features of the vowel system by local African American speakers. African Americans showed 7 percent of monophthongal /aw/ as in "dahntahn," compared to 21 percent for Whites. The low back merger was represented by the backing and rounding of /o/ in *cot, Don*, etc.; here, Whites presented 52 percent but African Americans only 22 percent. In Milwaukee, Purnell (2008) demonstrated that local African Americans shifted their vowel systems measurably in the direction of the White dialect in interaction with White speakers of that dialect. In Michigan, Evans et al. (2006) found that minority ethnic groups exhibit vowel shifting in the direction of the Northern Cities Shift. For African Americans, Jamila Jones's (2003) study showed a partial reflection of the Northern Cities Shift (figure 13.1): short-*a* has moved up to approximate the height of short-*e* but does not go beyond it. This diagram may reflect a general tendency in African American phonology that will also emerge from the present study of African American phonology in Philadelphia.

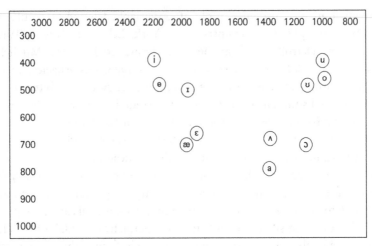

FIGURE 13.1 The African American vowel system in Detroit (Jones 2003), with short-*a* approximating the position of short-*e*.

13.2 AFRICAN AMERICAN PHONOLOGY IN PHILADELPHIA

The studies of African American phonology cited above show a regional effect: a measurable influence of the surrounding White dialect on the phonetic parameters of African American speech. A more complete comparison of local African American and White phonology can be obtained from the Philadelphia Neighborhood Corpus (PNC) by means of the Forced Alignment and Vowel Extraction (FAVE) computational analysis of vowel systems. Labov, Rosenfelder, and Fruehwald (2013; hereinafter LRF) traced one-hundred years of sound change in the speech of 264 White adults in the PNC. LRF (2013) focused entirely on mainstream Whites, who comprise less than half of the Philadelphia total population of 1.55 million.[2] Among the Whites of Irish, Italian, Jewish, Polish, Greek, and other European backgrounds, there is little difference in the use of Philadelphia phonology (Labov 2001, 245–50). But African Americans are a different story. This study examines the vowel systems of thirty-six African American speakers in that corpus to determine how much they participate in the ongoing changes and the degree to which they conform to the traditional phonological pattern of the local White mainstream.

African American speakers in PNC are drawn from two sources:

1. Twelve were from the project of the 1980s on "The Influence of Urban Minorities on Linguistic Change" (Ash and Myhill 1986; Graff, Labov, and Harris 1986; Labov and Harris 1986). They show the most characteristic forms of the African American vernacular, as defined by Baugh (1983): African Americans who live

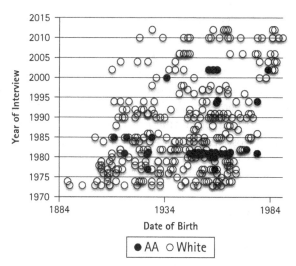

FIGURE 13.2 Philadelphia Neighborhood Corpus subjects analyzed for the current study by race, date of birth, and year of interview.

with, work with, and speak with other African Americans primarily. Speakers were recorded in intimate exchange with well-known interlocutors, where linguistic variables reach their most categorical form.

2. The other twenty-four speakers were drawn from the neighborhood studies of LING560, The Study of the Speech Community, as with most of the PNC interviews. These were people living in racially mixed neighborhoods—Frankford, Port Richmond, Mount Airy, and West Philadelphia—where they had considerable interaction with White and Hispanic neighbors.

Figure 13.2 shows the distribution of the thirty-six African American speakers by date of birth and year of interview against the main body of White speakers in the PNC. African Americans are not as evenly distributed as one would like, but year of interview ranges from 1977 to 2002 and date of birth from 1910 to 1983; they are evenly divided among men and women.

13.3 PARTICIPATION OF AFRICAN AMERICANS IN PHILADELPHIA SOUND CHANGES

LRF (2013) reported two Philadelphia sound changes that progressed in a linear fashion across the century: (eyC),[3] the raising along the front diagonal of /ey/ before a consonant in *made, pain*, etc. and (ayo), the centralization of /ay/ before voiceless

consonants in *right, wife,* etc.[4] The entire White community participated in this raising, with women and college graduates slightly ahead in the most recent decades.
Neither of these are salient variables: (eyC) has never been cited in public as a feature of
Philadelphia English and (ayo) rarely is. Figure 13.3 compares the mean values of these
two variables for Whites and African Americans by date of birth. The dashed lines are
the locally weighted regressions for the White majority and the solid lines for African
Americans.[5] The majority of African Americans lag behind the White majority, though
one outlier born in 1979 closes the gap. The (ayo) graph registers centralization as lowering of F1. Some tendency to follow the White majority appears among older speakers,
but among younger speakers, only the same African American outlier approximates the
White trend.

LRF (2013) found unexpected reversals in the development of back upgliding vowels
/aw, ow, uw/ in the White mainstream, which had shown a steady pattern of increased
fronting in the 1970s. The reversal began with speakers born in the 1950s; though it
appears at the same time in four variables, there is at present no explanation as to why it
occurred at this time.[6] LRF (2013) points out that the variables that are reversed are those
that are also found in southern dialects, while those that continue in the same direction are found in northern dialects. It is also true that the two sets differ in the degree
of salience in the speech community. The strongly fronted forms of the back upgliding
vowels show a certain degree of social awareness for Whites, as demonstrated in subjective reaction experiments (Labov 2001, 208–22).

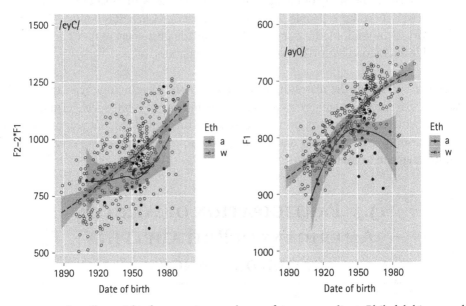

FIGURE 13.3 Locally weighted regression analyses of two nonsalient Philadelphia sound
changes by date of birth and race.

Grey area = 95% confidence intervals.

a: African American, N = 36. w: white, N = 330.

Figure 13.4 shows that the reversal is not to be found in our African American sub-group. African Americans do not echo the mainstream rise and fall pattern for (aw) in *south, out, down*, etc., nor for checked (owC), in *road, goat, phone*, etc. Their movement, if any, appears to be in the opposite direction.

The opposing shifts in the realization of (aw) and (ow) take on greater significance in the light of the experimental results of Graff, Labov, and Harris (1986). Sentences spo-ken by African Americans with characteristic back forms of /aw/ and /ow/ were resyn-thesized with fronted nuclei characteristic of White speakers.[7] These were incorporated into a matched guise experiment in which White, African American, and Hispanic participants were asked to say whether the speakers were Black or White. The results showed that the controlled fronting of these vowels effectively converted judgments from Black to White for the great majority of judges.[8]

A third pattern in the White mainstream dialects was found by LRF (2013) for the most salient sound changes, which remained at a high level for the first part of the century but showed a general decline in the second half. These are (æh), the product of raising and fronting along the front diagonal of a subset of short-*a* defined by intricate phonological, lexical, and grammatical conditions, and (oh), the corresponding back ingliding vowel in *talk, lost, saw*, etc. In the self-report tests of the 1970s, upper-mid forms of (æh) were most often the subject of overt comment such as, "Unfortunately, it's South Philly slang, not the best pronunciation," and (æh) showed the greatest disparity between self-report and

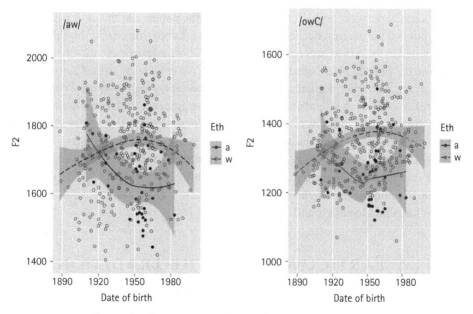

FIGURE 13.4 Locally weighted regression analyses of two back upgliding Philadelphia sound changes in Philadelphia by date of birth and race. /aw/ (in *south, out, down*) and /owC/ (in *road, goat, phone*).

a = African American, w = White. Grey area = 95% confidence intervals.

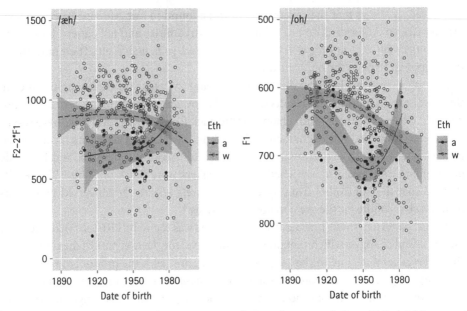

FIGURE 13.5 Locally weighted regression analyses of two ingliding Philadelphia sound changes in Philadelphia by date of birth and race. /æh/ (in *man, bath, mad*) and /oh/ (in *water, talk, off*).

a = African American, w = White. Grey area = 95% confidence intervals.

actual use (Labov 2001, 203). In matched guise tests, upper-mid forms of (æh) such as [e:ə] produced the greatest decline in job suitability (Labov 2001, 213). Though (oh) was not included in these field experiments, it is the topic of increasing mention in public discourse on the Philadelphia dialect as the stereotype *water* with a high back vowel [wuɾɚ].

Figure 13.5 presents the corresponding locally weighted regressions by date of birth and race for these most salient variables. There is no evidence of African Americans following the pattern of the White community; on the contrary, African Americans follow the inverse pattern, moving *toward* the traditional stigmatized target rather than away from it. The number of younger speakers born in the 1980s is too small to produce a reliable result, as the enlarged gray areas representing 95 percent confidence intervals indicate. But none of these figures show African Americans participating in the pattern of the White Philadelphia sound changes.

13.4 Participation in the Traditional Short-*a* Split

The phonetic path of the tense /æh/ class is a relatively superficial measure of African American participation in Philadelphia phonology. To obtain a more precise indication of the participation of African Americans in the system of Philadelphia phonology, we must consider the structural conditions that define the Philadelphia split between lax and tense short-*a* (Ferguson 1975; Labov 1989). The core set of conditions that require tense vowels are given as (1).

(1) in syllables closed with front nasals and voiceless fricatives /m, n, f, s, θ/: *ham, hand, past, half, bath,* etc.
     and in open syllables before inflectional suffixes: *planning, passes,* etc.
     and before /d/ in three affective adjectives *mad, bad, glad*
     but not in irregular verbs *ran, swam, began*
     and not in function words *am, an, and, can*
     and not in polysyllabic words with zero codas: *aspirin, athletic,* etc.
     and not in learned words *alas, haft,* etc.

The main focus of our examination is on the extent to which the African American speakers integrate these conditions into their phonology. Table 13.1 shows an early answer to this question in Henderson (1996), a study of the short-*a* split among thirty middle-class African Americans in West Philadelphia. Closed syllables before nasals are close to categorically tense, but short-*a* before voiceless fricatives shows only 69 percent tense and the lexical set of three words before /d/ is only 83 percent tense as compared to the 99.6 percent for Whites found in the 1970s (Labov 1989). Even more striking is the fact that the traditionally lax set before intervocalic nasals is tense almost half the time. As a whole, this pattern corresponds to the characterization projected at the outset: African American communities approximate the phonology of the surrounding northern city.

We can now use the locally weighted regression technique to display the phonetic contrast between the traditionally defined tense and lax classes in Philadelphia across the century. Figure 13.6a displays the contrast by date of birth of the mean values of tense /æh/ versus lax /æ/ for the White mainstream population of the PNC. The two distributions are widely disjunct, although the distance appears to be diminishing in

Table 13.1 Percent Tensing of Short-*a* for Thirty African Americans in West Philadelphia

	Examples	% Tense
Normally tense		
Nasals	*can, ham*	95
Voiceless fricatives	*half, glass, bath*	69
	mad, bad, glad	83
Normally lax		
Intervocalic nasals	*hammer, banana*	43
Irregular verbs	*ran, swam began*	71

Source: Henderson 1996.

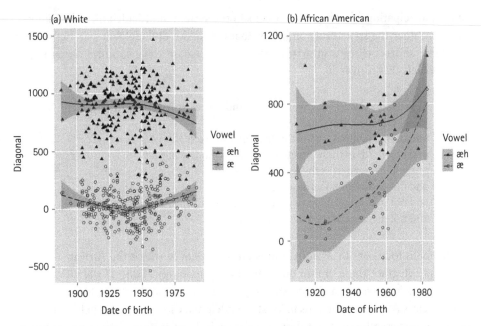

FIGURE 13.6 Locally weighted regression analyses of tense and lax short-*a* classes in Philadelphia by date of birth for Whites and African Americans.

Gray area = 95% confidence areas.

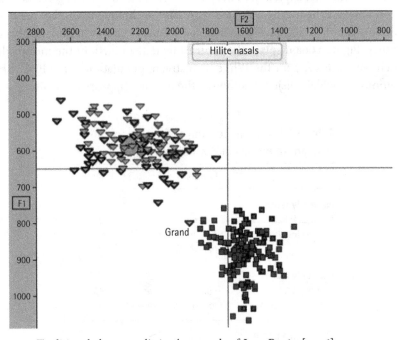

FIGURE 13.7 Traditional short-*a* split in the speech of Jean B., 60 [2006].

recent decades as the tense class becomes slightly lower. LRF (2013) showed that this reduction is primarily the result of younger speakers with higher education switching to the nasal system in which vowels are tensed before all and only nasal consonants. In contrast, the diagram for African Americans in figure 13.6b shows that the distinction has practically disappeared as a consequence of the opposite upward movement for the lax class. The broad overlap of the gray 95 percent confidence areas indicates that there is no significant difference between /æh/ and /æ/.

To illustrate the disjunct character of the traditional opposition in the White community, figure 13.7 shows the FAVE analysis of tense and lax short-*a* for PNC participant Jean B., a 60-year-old working-class woman interviewed by Josef Fruehwald in 2006. The downward pointing triangles represent the traditionally tense class. Words with nasal codas are highlighted, displaying no substantial differences from the unhighlighted tokens before voiceless fricatives. One instance of the tense class—*grand*—approaches the lax class, a phonetic effect of coarticulation of the initial obstruent-liquid cluster that has been frequently noted (Labov, Ash, and Boberg 2006).

13.5 Measures of Bimodality

One useful index of this disjunct character is Ashman's *D* in (2)—a measure of bimodality expressed by the absolute difference of the means divided by the square root of the average of the two standard deviations (Ashman, Bird, and Zepf 1994; Gnedin 2010).

$$D \equiv \frac{\left|\mu_1 - \mu_2\right|}{\left|\left(\sigma_1^2 + \sigma_2^2\right)/2\right|^{1/2}} \tag{2}$$

The value of *D* for distance along the front diagonal in figure 13.7 is 3.439. For a clear separation like that of Jean B., bimodality ranges between 3 and 4.

Figure 13.8 displays the distribution of this bimodality measure for all PNC speakers with more than seven tokens of /æh/, including 293 Whites and 33 African American speakers. The range is from close to 0.02 to 7.91. It is evident that the black columns are heavily concentrated in the lower end of the distribution.

From this diagram, it would appear that the African American speakers have absorbed the short-*a* system of one particular subtype of the White mainstream pattern, presumably the people they are in closest contact with. But this proves to be an understatement of the differences. The Whites with low bimodality are actually those found by LRF (2013) to have switched abruptly from the traditional split short-*a* system to the nasal system, in which all short-*a* before nasal consonants are fronted and raised along the front diagonal and all others are retained in low front position (Labov, Ash, and Boberg 2006, 174–75). This shift to the nasal system is most characteristic of college students in nationally oriented universities and high school students oriented in that direction.

Figure 13.9 shows the two aspects of this conversion from the traditional Philadelphia system in the speech of a Penn freshman who graduated from an elite high school in Philadelphia. The left-hand figure shows the redistribution of traditionally tense vowels represented by downward triangles. All tokens before front nasals in closed syllables—highlighted here—are retained in upper-mid position, with one exception, a token of the word *man*. All tokens before voiceless fricatives—not highlighted here—are found in low-front position. The right-hand figure shows the redistribution of tradition-ally lax vowels. Those before nasals are tensed: intervocalic (*hammer, Danny, Miami*) and velar (*angry*, with one exception).

The same measure of bimodality, Ashman's *D*, can be used to express the extent to which a speaker has converted to the nasal short-*a* system. Figure 13.10 shows bimodality for the traditional system on the horizontal axis and bimodality for the

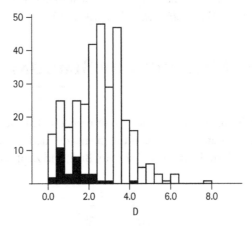

FIGURE 13.8 Distribution of bimodality values of Ashman's D for /æh/ versus /æ/ for PNC speakers with more than 7 tokens of /æh/.

Black = African American (n = 33), white = White (n = 293).

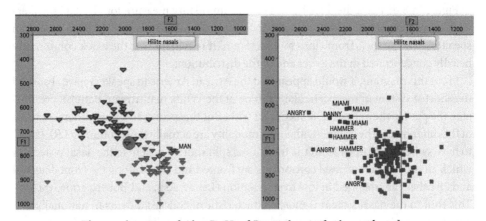

FIGURE 13.9 The nasal system of Alex P., U. of Pennsylvania freshman [2012].

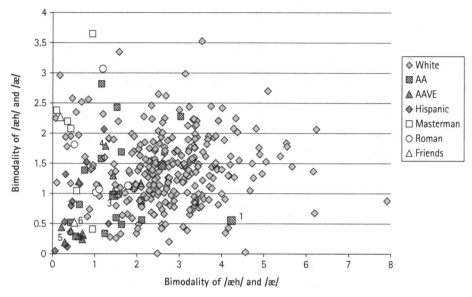

FIGURE 13.10 Bimodality measured by Ashman's D for the traditional Philadelphia system (x-axis) against bimodality of innovative nasal system (y-axis) for White mainstream speakers, African Americans, Hispanics, and graduates of three Philadelphia high schools.

Table 13.2 Mixed Models Regression Analysis of Bimodality (/æh/ versus /æ/) for PNC

Ethnicity (1.8e-11)	
White	1.027
African American	−0.356
Hispanic	−0.671
Date of birth (1.04e-05)	−0.012
Sex (.0352)	
Female	0.127
Male	−0.127

N = 293. Random factor Speaker.

nasal system on the vertical axis. The speakers are divided into seven types. The White majority is indicated by gray diamonds. African Americans are divided into two groups as described earlier. Hatched squares indicate speakers drawn from the LING560 studies of mixed neighborhoods (AA), while hatched triangles designate speakers in the 1986 studies of African American networks in North Philadelphia (AAVE). Vertically striped diamonds indicate the fifteen Hispanics who are included here, from LING560 studies of largely mixed neighborhoods. The open symbols show college students from three Philadelphia high schools who lead in the development of the nasal system.

One difference between African Americans and Whites in figure 13.10 is evident from distribution on the horizontal axis: 203 out of 293 Whites have values greater than 2.5, but this is true for only 3 of the 33 African Americans. The fifteen Hispanic speakers in the PNC are even more clearly grouped to the left. Table 13.2 shows the results of a mixed-models regression analysis of these data. Fixed factors ethnicity, date of birth, and sex are significant in that order. In the ethnicity group, Hispanics are even further distanced from the traditional short-*a* system than African Americans are.

13.6 OUTLIERS

A great deal can be learned from an examination of the small number of African American outliers in figure 13.10. One is the speaker indicated by the AA square located at 4.23, 0.55, labeled with the number 1. This is Gloria S., interviewed in 1981 at the age of 60. Her family was among the first African Americans to move into the White neighborhood of South Philadelphia some fifty years earlier.[9] She expresses herself with a precise and carefully articulated style of speech, using none of the grammatical features of AAVE. Her bimodality values indicate her close adherence to the traditional Philadelphia system of short-*a*.

> (3) So then maybe you've made a new recipe or you've discovered something in another field that might make you famous for life. You can't tell. But try. You keep on going until life stops in one form or another, because we all know we're going to die one day. But just because you're old or just because you're sick, just because you're handicapped, you're supposed to not keep trying and keep doing? And I think the more you do, the more you're able to do. I really do.

Much lower in the use of Philadelphia phonology is seen in the placement on figure 13.10 of two close friends in the integrated Mount Airy neighborhood, interviewed together in their early twenties in 1980. They are located by two other AA squares: Jerome, labeled 2 at 2.59, 1.46, and Burt, labeled 3 at 1.45, 0.97. The two friends disagreed about the extent of integration and every other aspect of Black/White relations, with Jerome taking the most positive view.

> (4) Fine, because one reason is, Mount Airy was, you know, always had Black and White. I mean, y'know the Whites, if they moved, they didn't move too far. I mean it wasn't bad, it was still a good neighborhood, it was a neighborhood that never went deep under, y'know, like poverty or despair or whatever. I don't know. . .

Burt's view of racial relations in the area was more negative. Typically.

> (5) I lived among White people all my life. Don't hate 'em. I don't *like* some of 'em, but I don't hate 'em. Y'know. It was like uh . . . color doesn't bother me. But when

you walk up in Chestnut Hill, honest to God, if you walk on one side of the street, you get a weird look every time you wanna go. .... And people can say that it doesn't bother them, but it's bullshit if they say that. Because just somebody jus' looking at you *weird*, like you're a criminal.

The difference in outlook on race relations is reflected in the two friends' use of Philadelphia phonology, which is immediately evident on listening. Jerome sounds very much like a White Philadelphian; Burt does not. Figure 13.11 makes this comparison, first showing how Jerome has a clearer separation of tense and lax short-*a* than Burt does. The lower two diagrams add the mean values for the back upgliding vowels (aw) and (ow).

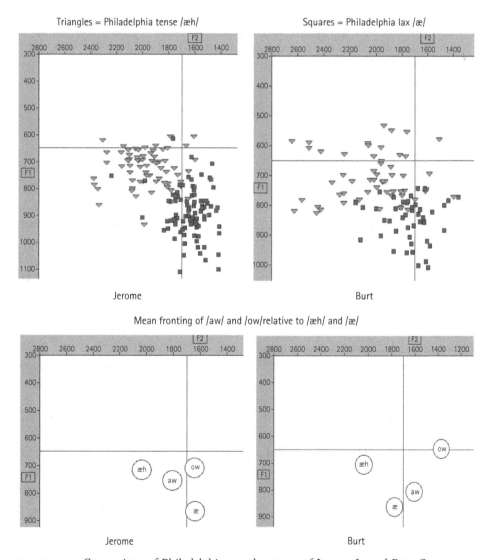

FIGURE 13.11 Comparison of Philadelphia vowel systems of Jerome L. and Burt C.

Jerome's system shows a fronted and raised nucleus for (aw), while Burt's (aw) is well back of center. Jerome has strongly fronted (ow), but for Burt, (ow) is a back vowel.

In figure 13.10, the AAVE speakers indicated by hatched triangles include some speakers who had extensive interaction with Whites political activists, confidence men, and musicians in addition to those with minimal contact with Whites. The outlier labeled 4 at 1.26, 1.79 in figure 13.10 shows a strong shift toward the nasal system. The speaker is Steve P, a musician interviewed in 1981, when he was 28 years old. His profession involved him in continual interaction with people of different ethnic and linguistic backgrounds. At the time of the interview, he was about to travel to Germany, where he had a number of jobs lined up. At one point in the interview, he underlined the advantages of being a Black man surrounded by Whites:

(6) I figure, man, I have to leave town to make it. Because, you know, well I been–
    I been told it's very nice over there for people of my color. You know? Plus, uh,
    I heard the blacker, the better.

13.7 INLIERS

To a certain degree, figure 13.10 shows the approximation of African Americans to the surrounding White system that was found in the review of the previous literature. The reverse aspect appears in the concentration of minority speakers in the lower left of figure 13.10. No Whites are to be found in the region bounded by 1 on the horizontal axis and .5 on the vertical axis.[10] A prototypical speaker in this region is Jackie C., identified with the black triangle labeled 5 at 0.21,0.44. Her short-*a* data are shown in figure 13.12 . They display an effective merger of tense and lax categories. The phonetic character of that merger involves a general raising of all short-*a* words but avoids the strongly fronted domain of the White mainstream tensed style. The contrast between short /e/ and short /æ/ is small in the F1/F2 dimensions, enhanced by a small difference in mean duration (87 msec versus 105 msec).

The phonetic pattern found among the speakers in the lower left corner of figure 13.10 resembles the pattern reported by Jones in Michigan in figure 13.2. The raising of short-*a* to a non-peripheral, lower-mid vowel may be a general characteristic of dialects that reject the peripheral raising of the White community. A similar pattern has been noted among Hispanic speakers in New York City.

Jackie C. is a prototypical speaker of the AAVE community in several respects. The following extract from her speech shows many characteristic features of AAVE, including *had* as a simple past marker, *axe* for *ask*, and negative concord. Her relatively lax, merged short-*a* vowels are found in *grandmother, axe, back*, and *smack*.

(7) Yeah, I remember when I f– when, one time I took her over to the house and my *grand*mother was tellin' me, wa– I shouldn't be bringin' people over her house. She was arguin' with *Pam* then and, when I had brung the baby home, The first day I brung the baby home, and *Pam* came over, and *Pam* just went to the, um, to the crib and just looked at the baby.

And my *grand*ma was fussin' at her sayin' "You might carry all kinds of germs," you know, she was lookin' at her, bus'in' on an everything, [Yeah?] and—yeah, you can *axe* her for herself! She was bustin' on an' tellin' us the way you sh– ain't got no business bein' around that baby, that baby just got home! I don't want that baby catchin' no germs." She ain't say nuttin'. But then I told *Pam*, I said "*Pam*, you know what, you should say something smart right *back* to her." Then that's when my aunt *smacked* me, 'cause my aunt was sittin' right there. Said, "Don't go *back* talkin' *back* to your *grand*mother." No, my aunt don't like my *grand*mother. But yet, she don't like me talkin' smart to her either.

In addition to the phonology and grammar of AAVE, Jackie displays an immersion in the speech events characteristic of the AAVE community: *busting, back talking*, and *talking smart*. At this stage in her life, Jackie C. is prototypical of the core younger speakers of AAVE. In terms of language and in terms of social interaction, she is an inlier as

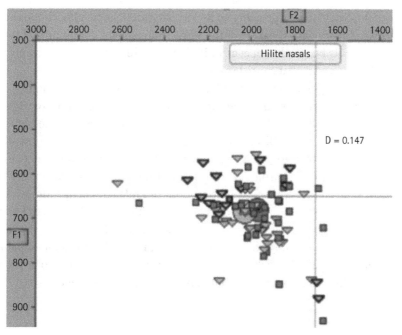

FIGURE 13.12 Short-*a* in the vowel system of Jackie C. Triangles = Philadelphia tense /æh/; squares = Philadelphia lax /æ/.

opposed to the outliers Gloria S. and Steve P. Instead of the tendency to approximate the

Table 13.3 Indices of Dominance for Five Ethnic Groups in Philadelphia from 1850 to 1970

	1850	1880	1930	1940	1950	1960	1970
Black	11	12	35	45	56	72	74
Irish		34	8			5	3
German	25	11			5	3	
Italian		38			23	21	
Polish		20			9	8	

Source: From Hershberg et al. 1981, table 8.

surrounding system that we projected from earlier work, her short-*a* pattern shows no influence of the White mainstream system that surrounds her North Philadelphia speech community.

13.7.1 Residential Segregation

The limited sharing of linguistic patterns is a logical consequence of the residential seg-regation of the city. Children growing up in African American neighborhoods have lim-ited personal contact with speakers of the White mainstream community. Table 13.3 is from the 1981 study by Hershberg et al. of Philadelphia history, showing the proportion of a person's census tract that consists of the same group.

Over a century, segregation of Blacks has steadily increased, while the figures for oth-ers have steadily declined. In *American Apartheid*, Massey and Denton (1993) point out that America has achieved a higher degree of residential segregation than South Africa ever did. The extent to which Blacks live in neighborhoods that are predominantly Black jumped from 27.3 in 1930 to 75.6 in 1970 in Philadelphia, and similar increases were found in Atlanta, Boston, Detroit, Los Angeles, and San Francisco (Massey and Denton 1993, table 3.4). Even in the mixed neighborhoods of Philadelphia like Mount Airy and Port Richmond, most African Americans grow up without any daily interchange with White speakers, and contact is primarily diffuse across adult lines. Given what we know about adult language-learning abilities, it is not surprising that the short-*a* patterns of most African American Philadelphians does not even approximate the complex pattern of the White mainstream community, but makes only passing reference to it.

13.8 MEASURES OF THE
DEGREE OF CONTACT

The effect of contact across speech communities can be assessed more clearly by measures of the extent of contact for individual speakers. Ash and Myhill (1986) found a correlation between contact with the White community and decreased use of both grammatical and phonological variants of AAVE among African Americans in Philadelphia. Twenty-two African American and three Puerto Rican speakers were assigned contact indices (0–16, 0 = no contact, 16 = high contact) based on sociolinguistic interviews in which speakers were asked about the racial composition and degree of integration of their neighborhoods and social networks throughout their lives. Four phonological and four morphosyntactic variables of AAVE were analyzed from spontaneous speech. Results for three of the phonological and all four morphosyntactic variables can be seen in figures 13.13 and 13.14.

The findings show a strong negative correlation between degree of contact with the White community and use of AAVE features by African American Philadelphians. The contrast is sharpest for the morphosyntactic variables, specifically for third-person singular –s deletion, where two separate groups emerge: those with little contact with the White community and majority African American social networks (contact = ≤ 8) and those with higher contact with the White community and multi-ethnic or majority White social networks (contact = > 8).

To further illustrate the impact communication across racial lines has on linguistic behavior, the short-a systems of twelve of the original and eight additional speakers from the UMLC[11] studies were reexamined with the indices assigned by Ash and Myhill (1986). Figure 13.15 shows the bimodality measures for the twenty speakers. Again, degree of participation in the Philadelphia short-a system is illustrated by position on the x-axis, while degree of participation in the nasal system is shown by position on the y-axis. Speakers with the neutralized system are concentrated in the lower-left corner.

Pam, labeled in figure 13.15, shows the lowest bimodality score for both the Philadelphia and the nasal short-a systems (0.04, 0.27), reflecting the neutralized short-a pattern. She is a 17-year-old female from North Philadelphia with a contact score of 4. Her social network includes Jackie C., the prototypical speaker discussed above (contact = 4). She simply answers "no" to questions about having White friends. Along with other low contact speakers in figure 13.13, her speech displays a predominance of AAVE grammatical features including negative concord, preterit ain't, habitual be, copula deletion, and third person singular –s deletion.

(8)   I had one, but I don't have none now.
(9)   Yeah, sh– no, she ain't ask me. I'll tell her right off the bat.
(10) And they old ladies be tryin' to talk to like a Black friend, they get jealous, tell
      them this and tell them that.

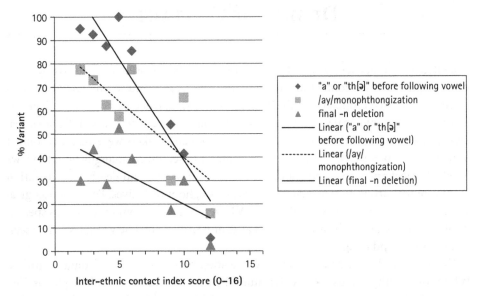

FIGURE 13.13 AAVE variants of phonological variables for Black speakers by degree of inter-ethnic contact (x-axis).

Source: Ash and Myhill 1986.

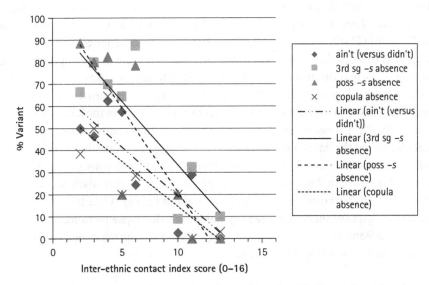

FIGURE 13.14 AAVE variants of grammatical variables for Black speakers by degree of inter-ethnic contact (x-axis).

Source: Ash and Myhill 1986.

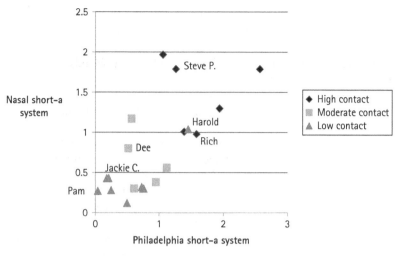

FIGURE 13.15 Bimodality of /aeh/ and /ae/ for twenty African American speakers.

(11) 'Cause too much stuff happen for me down there.

In contrast, Rich (contact = 12) has a relatively high bimodality for both short-*a* systems (1.58, 0.98), in line with his extensive contact with the local White community. This places him closer to speakers with a sharper split between tense and lax short-*a* tokens like Steve P., the musician shifting toward the nasal system discussed above. Rich is a 20-year-old driver and the son of a prominent community activist. His family was one of the first African American families to move to the now mixed neighborhood of Germantown. Rich's speech shows close to no grammatical features of AAVE.[12]

(12) This is – uh, this block and all, used to be all White. We were the first Black ones to move in on this block. So everybody that we were playin' with right here, they were White. Most, you know, then other kids started comin' around, Black kids. Yeah, so playin' with them too.

A more illuminating description of Rich's degree of contact with the White community comes from an interview with his sister Dee (also labeled in figure 13.15).

(13) Interviewer: [Your mother] told me that her kids have more White friends than Black friends. Is that true?
Dee: They do … Aaron, yeah, and Aaron and Rich, their friends. . . . They be around there, sittin' around there drinkin' beer, playin' cards. They go to Atlantic City together, take different little trips, to the mountains, hikin', fishin', no tellin' whatever else they do.

It is interesting to find that Dee has a bimodality score of 0.52, 0.8, reflecting moderate contact with the White community. Despite early contact, Dee's orientation toward the

African American community and the Muslim community, in particular, is evident in the remainder of her interview. Her use of AAVE grammatical features is also prevalent.

(14)   Interviewer: How come you don't have a lot [of White friends]?
       Dee: Cause they don't turn me on (laughs).
       Interviewer: They don't turn you on?
       Dee: You know, they alright. I don't know. I just, you know, we never got together.
       Interviewer: Yeah, but you meet 'em through your brothers and sisters.
       Dee: And that's it. It be 'hi' and 'goodbye.' I be on my way to work or from work either pickin' my son up, you know. That's all.
       Interviewer: Your mom also said that when your father passed away you had as many White people at the funeral as Blacks. So evidently he had a lot of White friends too, right?
       Dee: Yeah, well, I guess so. You know, he knew a lot of White – I didn't think it was a lot. You know, like his boss and his foreman, you know. They were White, you know, and couple of other people, you know. But, and people in the neighborhood he liked and...
       Interviewer: Alright, so, would you approve of your kid growin' up and marryin' someone White?
       . . .
       Dee: Well, I would rather him be with his people, you know, yeah.

These two siblings thus illustrate the impact of intimate contact with speakers of other dialects as an influence on linguistic behavior.

One speaker, Harold, has a low contact index of 3 but scores relatively high for bimodality for both short-a systems (1.45, 1.04). Harold is a shoe repairman aged 29 years who grew up in North Philadelphia. He did not finish the last two years of high school and spent five years in prison before returning to North Philly. He has also worked as a cook (possibly while in prison). Harold is included in the core network along with Jackie C. and Pam, so it is unclear why he patterns with speakers with higher contact indices. His interview, unfortunately, does not shed light on his history of contact except for a brief mention that his childhood neighborhood was predominantly Black. Furthermore, Harold uses a sizeable number of AAVE grammatical variants throughout his interview. Harold is a mixed type, an exception to the generalization that communication across racial lines is a strong determinant of African American participation in the speech patterns of the White community.

13.9 CONCLUSION

The study of large urban speech communities began with a focus on linguistic differentiation, but as the regularity of social stratification emerged, it gradually became apparent that these cities were united by common patterns of style shifting, reflecting a common set of norms. It also appeared that there was a common structural base for that shifting, with a common definition of the linguistic variables involved. To a surprising extent, these great cities turned out to be geographically uniform, and the local designations such as "Brooklynese" or "South Philadelphia" were actually labels for social class patterns of speech. But that uniformity stops short at racial lines, where we find very different patterns for Blacks and Whites.

African Americans in this city are Philadelphian in many ways. They eat cheese steaks and hoagies, call out "Yo," and walk on the *pavement*. Some linguistic features spread easily across racial lines, in both directions. Previous studies have shown that a moderate level of cross-racial contact leads to a high incidence of mainstream morphosyntactic features in the speech of African Americans. This study examines the treatment of the traditional Philadelphia split of the short-*a* category in the African American community. It finds a categorical absence of the distinction between tense and lax /æ/ for the majority who grow up with minimal contact with speakers of other dialects. It also shows that moderate levels of cross-racial contact leads to only a limited importation of the traditional Philadelphia short-*a* system. This is consistent with other findings (Labov 2007) that individual features of a linguistic system may readily diffuse across the adult population but that systems at a higher level of linguistic organization do not.

NOTES

1. The work reported here was supported in part by NSF grant 921643: Automatic alignment and analysis of linguistic change, and in part by NSF grant 1251437: The impact of higher education on local phonology.
2. As of the 2010 census (http://quickfacts.census.gov/qfd/states/42/42101.html), Philadelphia was 48.6 percent White, 43.7 percent African American, 11.7 percent Hispanic or Latino, and 5.7 percent Asian.
3. The parenthesis notation indicates a linguistic variable, as distinguished from a linguistic category indicated by the virgule//notation.
4. Fruehwald (2013) shows that (eyC) is defined more precisely as /ey/ followed by a [+ consonant] feature (/l/ is not included) across morpheme boundaries (*daze* and *dayz* are both included). (ayo) is defined on the voicing of the underlying coda so that the pronunciation of the words *writer* and *rider* are distinct, and this opacity has led to lexical diffusion (*spider*, *Snyder*, and *tiger* are frequently included).
5. For (eyC), the vertical axis registers movement along the front diagonal, defined as $F2 - 2 * F1$.
6. Parallel reversal is found for (aw), checked (owC), free (owF), and (Kuw) before non-coronals.
7. As for example, converting [noʊ daʊt əbaʊɹt] to [nəʊ dæʊt əbæʊɹt].
8. The experiment also included questions about how much contact the speaker had with African Americans, which showed parallel results.
9. A detailed account of the stoning of their house by White neighbors is analyzed in chapter 3 of Labov (2013), with quotations from Gloria S. that illustrate her ideological and cultural views.

10. The white triangle labeled 6 is an African American college student who graduated from Friends Select High School.

11. UMLC is an abbreviation for the NSF-funded research project 8023306: "The Influence of Urban Minorities on Linguistic Change," 1981–1984.

12. Some nonstandard features like negative concord ("I don't give nobody that chance") and participle leveling ("But I'd went up there") can be found in Rich's speech.

REFERENCES

Ash, Sharon, and John Myhill. 1986. "Linguistic Correlates of Inter-Ethnic Contact." In *Diversity and Diachrony*, edited by David Sankoff, 33–44. Amsterdam: John Benjamins.

Ashman, Keith M., Christina M. Bird, and Steven E. Zepf. 1994. "Detecting Bimodality in Astronomical Datasets." *Astronomical Journal* 108: 2348–61.

Baranowski, Maciej. 2007. *Phonological Variation and Change in the Dialect of Charleston, South Carolina*. Publication of the American Dialect Society 92. Durham, NC: Duke University Press.

Baugh, John. 1983. *Black Street Speech: Its History, Structure and Survival*. Austin: University of Texas Press.

Blake, Renée, and Cara Shousterman. 2010. "Diachrony and AAE: St. Louis, Hip-Hop, and Sound Change Outside of the Mainstream." *Journal of English Linguistics* 38: 230ff.

Boberg, Charles, and Stephanie M. Strassel. 2000. "Short-*a* in Cincinnati: A Change in Progress." *Journal of English Linguistics* 28: 108–26.

Cofer, Thomas. 1972. "Linguistic Variability in a Philadelphia Speech Community." PhD diss., University of Pennsylvania.

Cukor-Avila, Patricia, and Guy Bailey. 1996. "The Spread of the Urban AAVE: A Case Study." In *Sociolinguistic Variation: Data, Theory and Analysis*, edited by Jennifer Arnold, Renee Blake, and Brag Davidson. Stanford, CA: CSLI.

Evans, Betsy E., Rika Ito, Jamila Jones, and Dennis R. Preston. 2006. "How to Get to Be One Kind of Midwesterner: Accommodation to the Northern Cities Chain Shift." In *Language Variation and Change in the American Midland: A New Look at Heartland English*, edited by Thomas E. Murray and Beth Lee Simon, 179–97. Amsterdam: John Benjamins.

Fasold, Ralph W. 1972. *Tense Marking in Black English*. Washington, DC: Center for Applied Linguistics.

Ferguson, Charles A. 1975. " 'Short a' in Philadelphia English." In *Studies in Linguistics in Honor of George L. Trager*, edited by M. Estellie Smith, 259–74. The Hague: Mouton.

Fruehwald, Josef. 2013. "The Phonological Influence on Phonetic Change." PhD diss., University of Pennsylvania.

Gnedin, O. 2010. "Quantifying Bimodality." Available at http://www.astro.lsa.umich.edu/~ognedin/gmm/gmm_user_guide.pdf.

Gooden, Shelome, and Maeve Eberhardt. 2007. "Local Identity and Ethnicity in Pittsburgh AA." *University of Pennsylvania Working Papers in Linguistics* 13: 81–94.

Graff, David, William Labov, and Wendell Harris. 1986. "Testing Listeners' Reactions to Phonological Markers." In *Diversity and Diachrony*, edited by David Sankoff, 45–58. Amsterdam: John Benjamins.

Henderson, Anita. 1996. "The Short-*a* Pattern of Philadelphia among African American Speakers." *Penn Working Papers in Linguistics* 3: 127–40.

Hershberg, Theodore, Alan N. Burstein, Eugene P. Ericksen, Stephanie Greenberg, and William L. Yancey. 1981. "A Tale of Three Cities: Blacks and Immigrants in Philadelphia: 1850–1880, 1930, and 1970." In *Philadelphia: Work, Space, Family, and Group Experience in the Nineteenth Century: Essays toward an Interdisciplinary History of the City*, edited by Theodore Hershberg, 461–95. New York: Oxford University Press.

Jones, Jamila. 2003. "African Americans and the Northern Cities Vowel Shift: Language Contact and Accommodation." PhD diss., Michigan State University.

Labov, William. 1989. "The Exact Description of the Speech Community: Short-*a* in Philadelphia." In *Language Change and Variation*, edited by Ralph Fasold and Deborah Schiffrin, 1–57. Washington, DC: Georgetown University Press.

———. 2001. *Principles of Linguistic Change*. Vol. 2, *Social Factors*. Oxford: Blackwell.

———. 2007. "Transmission and Diffusion." *Language* 83: 344–87.

———. 2013. *Dialect Diversity in America: The Politics of Language Change*. Charlottesville: University of Virginia Press.

Labov, William, Sharon Ash, and Charles Boberg. 2006. *Atlas of North American English: Phonology and Sound Change*. Berlin: Mouton de Gruyter.

Labov, William, Paul Cohen, Clarence Robins, and John Lewis. 1968. *A Study of the Non-Standard English of Negro and Puerto Rican Speakers in New York City*. Cooperative Research Report 3288. Vols. 1 and 2. Vol. 1: ERIC ED 028423; Vol. 2: ERIC ED 028424. Available at http://www.eric.ed.gov.

Labov, William, and Wendell A. Harris. 1986. "De Facto Segregation of Black and White Vernaculars." In *Diversity and Diachrony*, edited by David Sankoff, 1–24. Philadelphia: John Benjamins.

Labov, William, Ingrid Rosenfelder, and Josef Fruehwald. 2013. "100 Years of Sound Change in Philadelphia: Linear Incrementation, Reversal and Re-Analysis." *Language* 89: 30–66.

Massey, Douglas S., and Nancy A. Denton. 1993. *American Apartheid: Segregation and the Making of the Underclass*. Cambridge, MA: Harvard University Press.

Mitchell-Kernan, Claudia. 1969. *Language Behavior in a Black Urban Community*. Monographs of the Language-Behavior Research Laboratory No. 2. Berkeley: University of California.

Myhill, John. 1988. "Postvocalic /r/ as an Index of Integration into the BEV Speech Community." *American Speech* 63: 203–13.

Purnell, Thomas. 2008. "AAE in Milwaukee: Contact at a Vowel Shift Frontier." Paper presented at the Annual Meeting of the Linguistic Society of America, Chicago, Illinois, January 3–6. To appear in a volume edited by Malcah Yaeger-Dror and Erik Thomas.

Rickford, John R., Arnetha Ball, Renee Blake, Raina Jackson, and Nomi Martin. 1991. "Rappin on the Copula Coffin: Theoretical and Methodological Issues in the Analysis of Copula Variation in African American Vernacular English." *Language Variation and Change* 3: 103–32.

Wolfram, Walt. 1969. *A Sociolinguistic Description of Detroit Negro Speech*. Arlington, VA: Center for Applied Linguistics.

CHAPTER 14

AFRICAN AMERICAN LANGUAGE IN NEW YORK CITY

RENÉE BLAKE, CARA SHOUSTERMAN, AND LUIZA NEWLIN-ŁUKOWICZ

> It is safe to say that the language of New York City is better known to the people of the United States as a whole than the language of any other single city.
>
> (Labov 1966, 18)

14.1 INTRODUCTION

NEW YORK CITY is characterized by a diverse population that contains a mix of long-standing residents, more recent immigrants, and transient younger people for whom New York is only a short-term home. Even with such a diverse population of speakers from various linguistic backgrounds, features of the New York City accent are pervasive enough to be found in dialects throughout the city that transgress ethnic and class boundaries and are well-known to people outside of New York on a national level as well as internationally. Thus, African American Language (AAL)[1] in New York City contains both shared features, that is, features that are found cross-regionally as well as features unique to this region and surrounding areas. What is clear about New York City as a whole is that it is a valuable site for examining linguistic exchanges between different groups living in contact. In this chapter, we examine the English of two groups of Black New Yorkers who are often grouped together racially, socially, and linguistically: second-generation West Indian Americans (SGWAs) of West Indian-born parentage and African Americans of US-born parentage.[2] In previous work, Blake and Shousterman (2010) investigated r-pronunciation in New York City for these two groups of Black New Yorkers. It was found that both groups show higher rates of r-lessness than what has been found previously for New York City's Black community and also that there is a significant difference between the two groups, such that SGWAs are more r-ful than African Americans. In this chapter, we highlight not only the findings for r-pronunciation for these groups but also for BOUGHT raising and the pronunciation of the vowel in the word class BOAT. We begin with an overview of the studies of AAL in New York City over the last fifty years. This is followed by a discussion of the diversity of New York City's Black communities, with a focus on African Americans and SGWAs. Finally, a case study is presented to exemplify linguistic variation within New York City's Black communities and to outline the implications of this diversity for methodologies of racial categorization in sociolinguistic studies as well as for the study of AAL more generally.

14.2 AFRICAN AMERICAN LANGUAGE VARIATION IN NEW YORK CITY OVER A HALF CENTURY (1966–PRESENT DAY)

New York City has long been an important site in the field of African American Language studies and sociolinguistics more generally (see table 14.1 for a summary of studies and features examined). To begin, it provides the setting for two of Labov's seminal works, *The Social Stratification of English in New York City* (Labov 1966), which includes his famous department store study, and *Language in the Inner City* (Labov 1972), which includes the critical piece "The Logic of Nonstandard English." These studies sampled speakers from two very different neighborhoods in New York City, the Lower East Side and Harlem. Although *Social Stratification* focused largely on White speakers of European ancestry, Labov (1966) also reported on data collected from eleven Black New Yorkers,[3] thus providing initial insight into New York City AAL in the mid-twentieth century. He found that many Black speakers living on the Lower East Side were producing well-known New York City English variables, such as raised /ɔ/ for words in the BOUGHT class (e.g., pronouncing the words *coffee* as "cawfee" [kɔ̝fi] and *talk* as "tawk" [tɔ̝k]), and the short-a split (e.g., pronouncing words such as *bad* with a raised /æ/ to sound like "beahd" [bɛːˀd]). However, these speakers did not show much change in usage as conversational style shifted (e.g., from casual speech to reading a word list), nor did they show much variation according to socioeconomic class, unlike White New Yorkers.[4] Thus, Labov (1966) argued that Black New Yorkers formed a separate speech community from the canonical White New Yorkers, as the two groups of speakers appeared to not share the same social evaluations of these variables. In her 2010 dissertation, Becker surveyed speakers on the Lower East Side from multiple ethnic groups, nearly fifty years after Labov's original study. She found that African Americans living on the contemporary Lower East Side continued to raise BOUGHT across all age groups, with younger speakers having the highest /ɔ/s.[5] Further, she finds that while

Table 14.1 Major Features Examined in Studies of New York City AAL

	/r/	/θ/ /ð/	t,d	/ɔ/	short-a	Back vowel fronting	/aɪ/ and /ɔɪ/	PIN-PEN	FEEL-FILL	FAIL-FELL	FULL-FOOL	Negation	Copula
Labov 1966	✓	✓	✓	✓	✓								✓
Labov 1972	✓		✓									✓	✓
Wolfram 1974		✓	✓									✓	
Cutler 1999	✓						✓	✓			✓		
Labov, Ash, and Boberg 2006		✓						✓	✓	✓			
Coggshall and Becker 2010				✓			✓	✓	✓				
Becker 2010				✓	✓	✓							
Mather 2012	✓					✓							
Newman 2014	✓	✓	✓		✓	✓							

some older African Americans have the short-a split, younger African Americans typically have a nasal tensing system (e.g., raising the vowel in words like *band* but not in words like *bad*).

Labov's (1966) department store study included 38 Black speakers out of a sample of 264 speakers who worked at New York City department stores. Labov (1966) found that the majority of Black workers were employed at the stores on the lower end of the price and fashion scale, S. Klein and Macy's, as opposed to the higher end store, Saks Fifth Avenue (Saks), which highlighted the racial and economic segregation that was present in the city at the time. In order to determine rates of r-fulness, Labov (1966) asked workers where certain items were located, with the goal of eliciting the response *fourth floor*. He found that in general Black workers were much less r-ful than White workers in the same stores, so that the phrase *fourth floor* was more likely to be pronounced as "fou'th flo" [fɔθ flɔ]. Further, Black workers followed the same pattern of social stratification as White workers; that is, S. Klein workers were less r-ful than workers at the mid-range store Macy's, who were less r-ful than workers at Saks. Mather (2012) recreated Labov's department store study five decades later and found that a significant difference between Black and White workers persists, such that Black workers are much less r-ful than White workers, and that this difference continues to be socially stratified according to the store's prestiged.

In 1972, Labov presented a detailed sociolinguistic analysis of New York City AAL in *Language in the Inner City*. A synthesis of years of research beginning in 1965, the aim of this work was to address the failure of New York City's schools to teach Black youths adequate literacy skills. It was based on research completed for two major projects by the Office of Education, Cooperative Research Projects 3091 and 3288 (Labov, Cohen and Robins 1965; Labov et al. 1968). Although the aforementioned projects included both male and female speakers from a range of ages and socioeconomic classes, *Language in the Inner City* (1972) focused on a group of speakers who were most at-risk for reading failure: Black male adolescents and pre-adolescents living in south-central Harlem. At the time Labov began to investigate Black literacy, little research had been done on the linguistic variety spoken by the Black community. The popular ideology surrounding this dialect (which tends to persist even today) was that it was slang, or simply "bad" or broken English. Labov was among the first researchers to argue for the systematicity of AAL. One of the outcomes of this work was a better understanding of the differences between the vernacular language of Black inner-city residents as a legitimate linguistic variety in its own right and the standard English of the classroom. This work also marked the beginning of what would become decades of research on AAL within the field of linguistics. In *Language in the Inner City*, Labov (1972) operationalized aspects of the AAL grammar system by explaining the rules for copula absence (e.g., "He good" versus "He's good") and negative concord (e.g., "I ain't seen no dog" versus "I haven't seen any dog"), in order to highlight the complexity of AAL grammar. He also explored verbal games that were popular with these young men like the "dozens" (ritual insults), arguing that the high level of linguistic skill needed for these games was evidence that problems with reading were not the result of cognitive deficiency.

Although an updated study of AAL in central Harlem has not yet taken place, there are other noteworthy studies of AAL in New York City more generally, which provide insight into Black New Yorkers' participation in sound changes and linguistic mergers found throughout the United States. Coggshall and Becker (2010) provided an acoustic analysis of the complete vowel systems of African American and White speakers from across a range of New York City neighborhoods and boroughs.[6] They found that although African Americans in New York City do not have many of the AAL features that are commonly found in the American South, such as the PIN-PEN merger (/ɛ/ is pronounced /ɪ/ before a nasal consonant) and FILL-FEEL merger (/i/ is pronounced /ɪ/ before /l/), they do retain /aɪ/ and /ɔɪ/ monophthongization (words such as *bide* and *boy* are pronounced "bahd" [baːd] and "boh" [bɔː], respectively). Like Becker (2010), Coggshall and Becker (2010) find that African Americans of all ages are raising /ɔ/ but for the most part do not appear to be using the NYC English short-a system. Although it is focused primarily on the speech of White New Yorkers, *The Atlas of North American English* (Labov, Ash, and Boberg 2006) also provided data from three Black New Yorkers (299). Although we know very little about their individual sociodemographic profiles, it is confirmed by the *Atlas* that these three speakers were producing high rates of r-vocalization, and have mergers for the word classes FILL-FEEL and FULL-FOOL (pronounced [ful]), which are mergers not typically found in White New York City English. Two of the three speakers are also merged for PIN-PEN. In a volume that thoroughly details the range of work conducted on New York City English as a whole, Newman (2014) includes his analysis of the speech of four adolescent Black New Yorkers (two African Americans and two West Indian Americans), as part of an investigation of language use among speakers of various ethnicities from Brooklyn and Queens. Newman found that all four Black speakers had raised /ɔ/, but were differentiated from other ethnic groups by showing a merger in the acoustic space among words from the NORTH class (e.g., *fourth, more*) and words from the BOUGHT class. In line with previous work on AAL in New York City, these speakers showed little evidence of a short-a split (with the majority opting instead for a nasal tensing system), limited fronting of back vowels, some use of /aɪ/ monophthongization, and very low rates of r-fulness (with one speaker being categorically r-less).

Finally, there are a number of studies of AAL in New York City that focus on groups of New Yorkers who do not identify as African American per se, yet appear to use features of AAL. Wolfram (1974) focused on contact between Puerto Rican English and AAL in East Harlem, New York City. He found that AAL exerted a strong influence on Puerto Rican English at both the phonological and syntactic levels. For example, when looking at the pronunciation of morpheme-final *th* [θ], all of the Puerto Rican speakers favored the *f* variant (*mouth* pronounced "mouf" [maʊf]) that is found in AAL cross-regionally over the more Spanish-influenced /s/ pronunciation [maʊs]. Further, Puerto Ricans who had extensive African American contacts showed higher rates of /f/ realization than those whose contacts were mainly other Puerto Ricans.[7] Zentella (1981) corroborated this finding, noting that in East Harlem some ten years later many of the young Puerto Rican males in her sample who had extensive African American contacts spoke AAL in a way that was auditorily indistinguishable from their African American cohorts. Shousterman (2014) finds that many Puerto Ricans in East Harlem today continue to use features of AAL in combination with Spanish substrate features, like syllable-timed rhythm. In another study, Cutler (1999) focused on Mike, a young White adolescent from Yorkville (a relatively affluent neighborhood on New York City's Upper East Side) who participated in Hip Hop culture and consistently employed features of AAL. She found that while Mike had acquired many of the superficial phonological and lexical features of AAL, he did not display the canonical features of the AAL syntactic system.

14.3 ETHNIC DIVERSITY IN NEW YORK CITY'S BLACK POPULATION

According to the 2010 Census, 26 percent of New Yorkers identify as Black or African American. What this figure masks, however, is the rich ethnic diversity that makes up New York City's Black community, and the histories of migration and immigration that bring together Black speakers from various cultural and linguistic backgrounds. African Americans and West Indians have similar migration histories to New York City, although on different scales. New York City's African American population underwent a substantial increase from the beginning of the twentieth century lasting through the early 1970s. During this period, African Americans participated in two Great Migrations (one during the industrialization period from 1910 to 1930, and one after the Great Depression from 1940 to 1970) in which more than six million people moved from the rural southern United States to the North, Midwest, and West (Jolly 2006; Reich 2006; Taylor 2002). Manhattan's expanding population during this time forced many African Americans out of the downtown neighborhoods they first resided in to neighborhoods further uptown, away from city life as it was known then. This northeastern movement eventually led to the establishment of Harlem as the capital of Black life in New York City.

West Indians generally had three waves of immigration to the United States. The first wave took place from 1900 to 1930, in which it was estimated that there were 200,000 foreign-born predominantly male workers from the West Indies living in the United States. Dodson (2007) notes that in 1900, New York City had a population of 60,000 people of African descent, which ballooned to more than 350,000 by 1930, representing the largest grouping of people of African descent in the nation. According to Dodson, "a significant percentage had immigrated from Africa and the Caribbean to come to New York during this period [Harlem Renaissance]. . . . Each of them aligned with African descended peoples from the United States and other parts of the African Diaspora for social, political, cultural and at times familial purposes" (2007, 5).[8] He further notes that while, at times, "frictions, jealousies, resentments … and conflicts" arose between various groups, new transformations and integrations were also happening that transcended ethnic boundaries, and cultural and class lines, many of which could be seen in movements such as the Harlem Renaissance. Later, he argues that this remains the case today for Black ethnics in New York City.

The second wave of West Indian immigration to the United States, between 1930 and 1965, was the smallest wave, and due to quota restrictions and the effects of the Great Depression, West Indian immigrants to the country never numbered more than 3,000 in any one year during this time. The third wave started in 1965 with the passing of the Immigration and Nationality Act and continues to the present day (Kasinitz 1992). The passing of the Immigration and Nationality Act led to large increases in immigration not just from the Caribbean but also from Latin America and Asia, which reshaped New York City's ethnic and racial composition (City of New York 2004, 41). By 1967 there were half a million Caribbean immigrants residing in the United States. At the beginning of the twenty-first century, New York City had one of the largest populations of West Indians outside of the Caribbean (Foner 2001). According to Foner (2001), when the second generation is combined with the immigrant population, two-fifths of New York City's Black population can trace their heritage to the West Indies. Thus, we argue that an investigation of African American Language in New York City is incomplete unless we also consider the contribution of West Indians to the linguistic landscape of the city.

14.4 BLACK NEW YORK SPEECH: A COMPARISON

Assimilationist models for immigration would have West Indians becoming virtually African American by the second generation. However, sociological research challenges these models by showing that the children of Black West Indian immigrants are adept at switching their identities between those couched within larger American society and those couched within the English-speaking communities from which their parents arrived (Waters 1999). Here, we present a summary of the results of several smaller studies on two groups of Black New Yorkers: second generation West Indian Americans (SGWAs) and native-born African Americans (see Blake and Shousterman 2010; Blake et al. 2012).

The complexity of race, culture, and ethnicity for SGWAs is evident in our interviews, as this group typically does not self-identify as African American only, but makes reference to their West Indian ancestry. Being native-born and Black, one might expect that they would identify as African American, and indeed others may see them this way. Instead, speakers from this population tend to use labels such as "West Indian slash half African American," or "Jamerican." This corresponds to the observation of Kasinitz et al. (2008) that "second generation young people may see themselves as very 'American' compared to their immigrant parents and yet still feel and seem very much like for-eigners compared to the children of natives" (15). What is also evident for SGWAs is the racial link that they have with African Americans who are their "clearest reference group" (Kasinitz et al. 2008, 16), and the group with whom they are most likely to inter-act in school, at work, and in their neighborhoods.

We present on two groups of Black New Yorkers' use of three linguistic variables—postvocalic /r/ production in words like *floor*, the raising of the BOUGHT word class, and the realization of the vowel in the BOAT word class—that have come to be associated with either New York City, African American, or Creole English speech. An examina-tion of these variables can shed light on the ways in which Black New Yorkers make use of linguistic features in creating their social identities.

Recent studies have shown that /r/ varies regionally in African American Language. In dialects that do vocalize /r/, a historical /r/ in syllable coda position is deleted or realized vocally as schwa. *r*-fulness is the prestige form in both New York City and the Caribbean.[9] BOUGHT raising is a well-known feature of New York City speech, often parodied in the media, for example, on the Saturday Night Live series "Coffee Talk with Linda Richman." This feature clearly indexes New York City speech, and while it has stereotypically been associated with White speakers of New York City English, numer-ous studies have shown that it appears robustly in New York City African American Language as well (see section 14.2).[10] BOUGHT raising is a unique feature of AAL spoken in New York City and the surrounding areas and is not found cross-regionally in AAL.

The vowel in the BOAT word class has distinctive realizations in American English versus various dialects of Creole English, which gives it geographical, and in some cases, stylistic distinctiveness. As shown in figure 14.1, for West Indian speakers of English, both Creole English and Caribbean Colloquial English, the BOAT vowel has a markedly different pronunciation from the general American English variant [1], which typically starts back with a glide offset that is out- and up-gliding (the arrow above /ɔʊ/ indicates the direction of the glide). The Caribbean Colloquial English realization of BOAT tends to start back with little or no glide [2], while the BOAT vowel in Creole English starts high and glides downward [3].

In the current study, we analyze linguistic data from eight young men and women in their twenties to early thirties. They are equally divided by gender and ethnicity (SGWA or African American), and they are all of similar socioeconomic backgrounds—lower

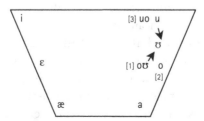

FIGURE 14.1 Schematic representation of the different realizations of BOAT.

middle class. They are members of the social and familial networks of two undergraduate students at New York University who were hired and trained to conduct sociolinguistic interviews. The interviewers are Black women who are in their early twenties and from New York and who identify as West Indian American or African American. All of the speakers interviewed were born and raised in New York City and live in various neighborhoods in Manhattan, Brooklyn, Queens, and the Bronx. The SGWAs in the sample have parents born in Jamaica or St. Thomas.[11] All of the SGWAs have some competency in the English-lexifier Caribbean Creole spoken by their parents, in addition to dialects of American English, meaning they can consciously codeswitch between these varieties.

14.4.1 The Linguistic Variables

14.4.1.1 /r/-production

/r/ vocalization, colloquially referred to as "dropping your /r/s," and also as r-lessness by linguists, is the pronunciation of words like *guard, sore,* or *court* in which the /r/ is realized as a short vocalic segment (hence, "vocalized").[12] As a result, *guard* will often sound like *god, sore* like *saw,* and *court* like *caught.* This phenomenon only affects postvocalic /r/ (following a vowel) such that /r/ is retained in words like *road* or *fret.* /r/ vocalization is often mentioned as a characteristic feature of the phonology of AAL (e.g., Green 2002; Rickford 1999; Wolfram and Schilling-Estes 1998). Indeed, many studies have found that African Americans do vocalize /r/ (see, e.g., Labov 1966, 1972, for New York City; Wolfram 1969, for Detroit; Wolfram 2003a, Wolfram and Thomas 2002, for North Carolina), although to varying degrees (Wolfram 2003b). /r/ vocalization is also associated with most English-lexifier Creoles in the Caribbean, with the exception of Barbadian Creole English (Bajan) where constricted /r/ (r-fulness) occurs in all syllabic positions (Roberts 1988). This particular variable is then expected to be present in the linguistic repertoire of both African Americans and West Indian Americans in the United States, particularly those living in New York City, where /r/ vocalization has traditionally been treated as a dialect feature (Babbitt 1896; Labov 1966). The social evaluation of its variants (vocalized /r/ and constricted /r/) is also likely to be similar for the two groups of speakers, as constricted /r/ is the overtly prestigious form both in New York City and the Caribbean.[13] In New York City, vocalized /r/ is stigmatized for its associations with the lower classes (Labov 1966), and in the Caribbean, it reflects basilectal usage (Wells 1982).

Blake and Shousterman (2010) found quantitative differences in postvocalic /r/ vocalization in the speech of African Americans and second generation West Indian Americans. The data were analyzed using GoldVarb x (Sankoff, Tagliamonte, and Smith 2005), a statistical program that measures the strength of an independent variable by providing a number between 0 and 1, which represents a weight or probability for the conditioning factor. A factor weight less than .5 shows a disfavoring effect, whereas a factor weight greater than .5 shows a favoring effect (.5 is considered neutral). The statistical analysis revealed that /r/ realization was influenced by a host of linguistic factors, including the position of /r/ within a word, the word class of /r/-containing tokens, following phonological environment, and lexical stress (for detailed results, see Blake and Shousterman 2010). In addition, overall rates of r-fulness varied for individual speakers. Some of them produced constricted postvocalic /r/ rather infrequently (17 percent of the time), while others realized constricted /r/ nearly categorically (up to 85 percent of the time). Ethnicity was found to account for some of the between-speaker variation, as statistically significant differences were observed between the SGWAs and African Americans. As seen in table 14.2, SGWAs slightly favored the retention of postvocalic /r/ (with a factor weight of .55), while African Americans slightly disfavored it (with a factor weight of .45). Higher rates of /r/ retention among SGWAs may be tied to notions of class and prestige, as they were in Labov's (1966) department store study, and may be further elevated by the prestigious status of /r/ in the Caribbean (Wells 1982). Specifically, these speakers may be producing postvocalic /r/ to create or maintain a higher social class identity.

14.4.1.2 BOUGHT *Raising*

BOUGHT raising refers to realizations of the vowel in words like *bought, coffee,* or *dog* that involve a raised position of the tongue. Raised BOUGHT is diphthongal, meaning that the tongue position for the first part of the vowel is higher than for the second part (the glide). We analyzed BOUGHT raising in the speech of the same two groups of speakers whose /r/ productions were studied in Blake and Shousterman (2010). BOUGHT tokens were measured in Praat (Boersma and Weenink 2014), a program for acoustic analysis. Since raised BOUGHT tends to be diphthongal, measurements were taken at two points: (1) at approximately 30 ms into the vowel, and (2) at approximately 30 ms before the vowel offset (end of the vowel). Speaker means were normalized using NORM,[14] a web-based vowel normalization and plotting suite (Thomas and Kendall 2007), and are illustrated in figure 14.2.

Figure 14.2 demonstrates that all speakers have the characteristic New York City raised BOUGHT, with normalized mean F1s that are less than 700 Hz (the cut-off point for BOUGHT raising as defined by Labov, Ash, and Boberg [2006] in *The Atlas of North American English*). The glides, the second part of the vowel, produced by almost all

Table 14.2 Effect of Ethnicity on Retention of Constricted Postvocalic /r/

Ethnicity	Factor weight	Frequency (%)	N	
Caribbean American	.55	49	1,225	
African American	.45	40	1,101	
Total N			2,326	
Overall Frequency (%)				45
Corrected Mean				.445
Log Likelihood				−1433.374

Source: Adapted from Blake and Shousterman 2010.

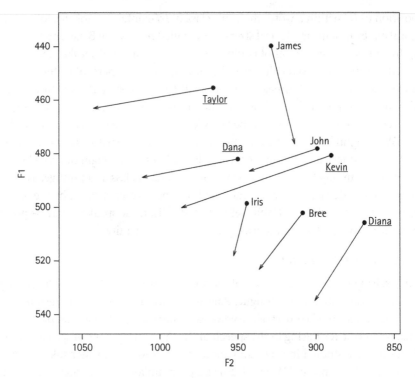

FIGURE 14.2 Normalized means for BOUGHT realizations, by speaker (SGWAs are underlined).

speakers are down- and in-gliding, as indicated by the direction of the arrows in figure 14.2. Some individual differences do exist, however. For example, one African American speaker, James, produces glides that are down- and out-gliding rather than in-gliding.

A further examination of speaker means for BOUGHT indicates that subtle differences exist between the SGWAs (Dana, Diana, Kevin, and Taylor) and African Americans (Bree, Iris, James, and John), with the SGWAs (underlined in figure 14.2) producing glides that show more dramatic formant changes (reflecting changes in tongue position) than African Americans. These changes are illustrated in figure 14.2 by the length of glides: the longer the glide, the more substantial the change in either the first or second formant (corresponding to tongue height and backness, respectively).[15] For example, Kevin, who is a SGWA, produces tokens of BOUGHT that start with a mean F2 value of 890 Hz and end with a mean value of approximately 990 Hz, yielding a change of 100 Hz in F2. As lower second formant values indicate a more back tongue position, the increase in F2 for the second part of the vowel signifies that the vowel has moved toward the front of the vowel space. On the other hand, the tokens of BOUGHT produced by Iris or Bree, who are both African American, show little movement on the F2 dimension (20–40 Hz). This suggests that BOUGHT remains relatively back for these speakers.[16] Similar glide differences were visually observed in Coggshall and Becker (2010), where White New Yorkers manifested more glide movement than Black New Yorkers.

14.4.1.3 *Realization of* BOAT

In the previous section, we showed that African Americans and second generation West Indian Americans display subtle differences in the production of /r/ and BOUGHT, two sociolinguistic variables that are also present in the broader New York City dialect area. Vowel measurements for BOAT, similarly to BOUGHT, were taken at the vowel onset and offset. Mean formant values per speaker are presented in figure 14.3.

The results for BOAT show that all speakers have the typical New York City BOAT that is backed, with a vowel offset that is out- and up-gliding, as illustrated by the direction of arrows in figure 14.3. However, the vowels produced by these two groups differ in terms of vowel height. Specifically, SGWAs typically produce BOAT with a higher tongue position, which correlates with lower values on the F1 dimension. A typical American English BOAT will begin with the tongue in mid position (and a higher F1) and end with a high tongue position (and a lower F1), tracing the trajectory from /ɔ/ to /ʊ/ in the vowel space (see figure 14.1). This is indeed what is observed for Iris and Bree, who are African American, and whose mean F1 values for BOAT are relatively high. The fact that African Americans, on average, show a higher F1 than SGWAs (underlined in figure 14.3) when producing BOAT suggests that SGWAs may be producing words in the BOAT class with a monophthongal variant, similar to what one might find in Caribbean Creole English varieties, as monophthongal realizations show very little change in F1.

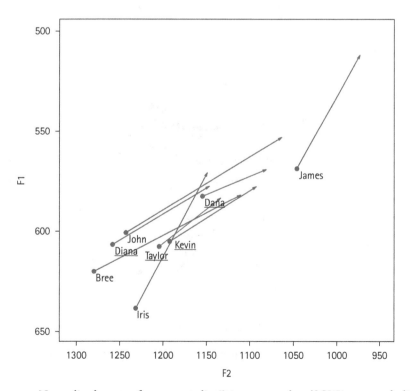

FIGURE 14.3 Normalized means for BOAT realizations per speaker (SGWAs are underlined).

14.5 DISCUSSION

The findings for /r/, BOUGHT, and BOAT in this study provide evidence that Black New Yorkers are using linguistic resources available to them to do identity work on multiple levels (see Le Page and Tabouret-Keller 1985). Place identity is particularly salient, as speakers' linguistic choices and practices seem linked to a representation of New York (see Myers 2006). r-fulness is on the rise in New York City English, and it is a variable to which both Black ethnic groups are attuned. Relatively higher rates for West Indian Americans may be tied to notions of class and prestige as well. Raised BOUGHT also suggests place identity for both groups, as well as ethnic differentiation evidenced by subtle qualitative differences in the realization of its off-glide. The pronunciation of BOAT may indicate linguistic differentiation along the lines of ethnicity, as SGWAs tend to realize BOAT tokens with higher F1 values, which may be indicative of monophthongization, similar to the Caribbean Creole English variant. For West Indian Americans, these linguistic differences combined may be an expression along the lines of "I'm a Black New Yorker, who is somewhere in between African American and West Indian."

Perhaps no one exemplifies this identity better than DD, a 20-year-old SGWA of Grenadian parentage, who was a part of a group interview with students in a Caribbean

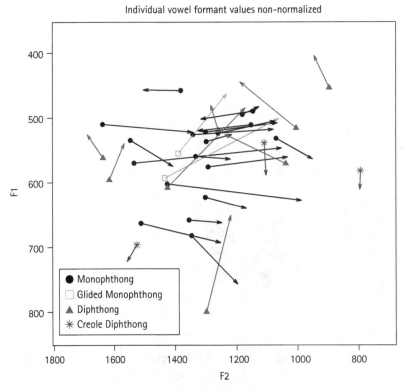

FIGURE 14.4 DD's realizations of BOAT.

Students Association meeting at an American university. DD was not included in the analysis presented here, as her interview took place at an earlier time and under different circumstances. It is instructive to consider her realization of BOAT at a micro-level, as it provides a clearer picture of the type of intra-speaker variation that can take place for speakers with complex ethnic and regional identities. Excerpts of DD's speech were taken from a transcript of a meeting of a Caribbean Students organization, where people join to engage in "being Caribbean" along the lines of cultural practices, interests, and language.

Overall, while DD appeared to behave similarly to the SGWAs examined earlier, we perceived variations that warranted further inquiry. DD's BOAT mean is similar to a New York City BOAT that is backed, with a vowel offset that is out- and up-gliding. However, when all of her BOAT vowels are plotted individually, as shown in figure 14.4, we see that DD seems to have a range of realizations including monophthongs with little change in F1 (the majority of which seem to be like the Colloquial Creole English realization), and diphthongs representing New York as well as the Creole English realizations. What the vowel plot does not show is that DD also appeared to sound slightly different depending on topic. For example in excerpt 1, shown in the Appendix, DD juxtaposes herself to her Grenadian-born family members while introducing herself to group members. In contrast, in excerpt 2, she asserts a Caribbean identity. When we compare the frequencies of the three variables in the two excerpts, as shown in figure 14.5, it appears that while she is

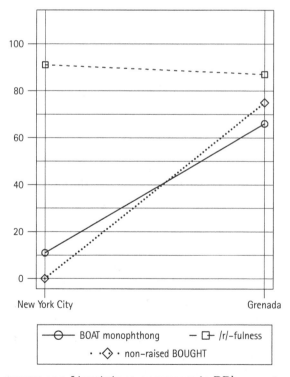

FIGURE 14.5 Linguistic co-occurrence in DD's excerpts.

quite r-ful in both excerpts, her BOUGHT and BOAT may be co-occurring or interdependent, such that high rates of BOAT monophthongization (no change in F1) occur with higher rates of unraised BOUGHT.

14.6 CONCLUSION

While our study is limited in terms of the number of individuals included, it is suggestive of the need to acknowledge often-missed complexities and negotiations across ethnic spaces. Just as African American Language is complex and varied, so too is the social category "African American." The linguistic behavior of second-generation West Indian Americans and their African American counterparts calls attention to the ways in which individuals and communities of speakers can use and manipulate language, consciously and unconsciously, as a resource to mark their identification. Clearly, more work is needed to have a more comprehensive picture of the English(es) spoken by Black people in New York City. It is our hope that this work contributes to that direction. As researchers continue to study and describe African American Language, and contribute to the ever-growing body of research on race as a social variable in language behavior, they will also need to consider the role of ethnicity, beyond the categories "Black" or "African American." We believe that examining ethnic variation within the Black community has important implications not just for the study of AAL in New York, but for studies of African American Language more generally.

APPENDIX

Excerpt 1

My entire family is from Grenada. My mother's from Carriacou in Grenada and my father is from the larger island of – and he's from St. Georges which is the capital. And I was born here and – which is interesting cause I'm the oldest American-born on my mom's side so that's always an interesting dynamic cause they sometimes exclude me.

Excerpt 2

Actually, no, the only reason much like you it was like you know everyone kind of ostracized you because you weren't quite African American? And you know it wasn't being called "coconut," but they did tell me go back to Grenada, and I was like but I wasn't born there! I mean and that happened through junior high and stuff like that 'cause I went to predominantly white school. So first they had to negotiate the idea that I was black, and then the second idea that I was Caribbean. And I kept talking about it and talking about it and that just bothered all hell out of them. And then when I got to high school I met some other Caribbean students who had the exact same situation. Their parents thought that upward mobility meant sending them to a predominantly white school, Catholic school so they all had that same identity of being called, you know trying – being called sellouts and then having their African American friends and their West Indian friends like you know, disgusted with them so we all kind of merged off of that and we found pride in that and we started participating in DC carnival so that really helped it.

NOTES

1. In this chapter, we refer to African American English as African American Language (AAL), in line with the editors of this volume. In doing so, no claims are made about the origins or development of this language variety. Moreover, we argue that this term is broad enough to capture the variety of African American dialects that form as a result of contact within Black communities.

2. We use the term *African American* to refer to speakers who identify as being descended from enslaved Africans in the United States. The term *West Indian* generally indicates individuals descended from the Caribbean community (CARICOM) nations that are former British colonies or overseas territories. We use the term *Black* as an umbrella term for speakers who trace their ancestry to any part of the African Diaspora, including (but not limited to) those who identify as African American, West Indian, or being of Continental African descent.

3. As Labov (1966) did not address the ethnicity of the Black speakers in his studies, it is presumed that they were African Americans of US-born parentage, although this has not been confirmed.

4. In the New York City short-a system, /æ/ is generally raised when it is in a non-initial position and when it precedes a voiced stop, a voiceless fricative, or a non-velar nasal. Hence, there is a contrast between the raised /æ/ in *bag, half,* and *hand,* and the non-raised /æ/ in *absent, back, halve,* and *hang.* The short-a system also exhibits a number of lexical exceptions, such as *avenue, after,* and *ask,* all of which are word-initial and raised. For more detail, see Labov (1966) or Becker (2010).

5. Here, we use Becker's (2010) reference to African American, the more recent reference for Black Americans (cf. Smitherman 1999).

6. The majority of African Americans sampled here were from the Bronx. In addition, one speaker was from Brooklyn, and one was from the Lower East Side.

7. We explicitly say African American and not Black, as many Puerto Ricans identify racially as Black, but differentiate themselves from Black New Yorkers who do not have Latino ancestry.

8. Continental African migration to the United States is a more recent phenomenon. In 2007, 11 percent of the total population of African immigrants to the United States, or approximately 152,000 resided in New York, making it the most populated host state in the United States (Terrazas 2009).

9. In this section containing the linguistic analysis, we use the term *Caribbean* as opposed to *West Indies* when referring to a geographic area or related dialect, to correctly reflect the terminology of the languages/dialects spoken. Thus, West Indians in the Caribbean speak dialects of Creole English and Caribbean Colloquial English, for example.

10. Black New Yorkers are not the only non-White group in New York City who have this feature, as raised /ɔ/ is also found in the English spoken by New York City's Chinese Americans (Wong 2007) and Latinos (Slomanson and Newman 2004).

11. Although St. Thomas is a district of the United States Virgin Islands, it is located in the Caribbean Sea and its residents identify as West Indian.

12. r-lessness indicates no [r] present with no assumption of an underlying /r/.

13. Forms carrying overt prestige are recognized by speakers as being more standard or aesthetically more pleasing. Forms associated with covert prestige are also evaluated positively within community, but this evaluation is never explicit or conveyed outside of the community of speakers (Baugh 1999; Trudgill 1972).

14. We use the Labov ANAE speaker extrinsic method through NORM.

15. Lip rounding also plays a role in formant changes, such that formants typically decrease as lips are rounded.

16. A t-test revealed that this difference is statistically significant, with SGWAs showing a greater difference in F2 from the first point of measurement to the second ($M = 79$ Hz, $SD = 32$), when compared to African Americans ($M = 19$ Hz, $SD = 30$), $t(6) = 2.73, p < .05$, two-tailed.

References

Babbitt, Eugene H. 1896. "The English of the Lower Classes in New York City and Vicinity." *Dialect Notes* 1: 457–64.

Baugh, John. 1999. *Out of the Mouths of Slaves: African American Language and Educational Malpractice*. Austin: University of Texas Press.

Becker, Kara. 2010. "Social Conflict and Social Practice on the Lower East Side: A Study of Regional Dialect Features in New York City English." PhD diss., New York University.

Blake, Renée, and Cara Shousterman. 2010. "Second Generation West Indian Americans and English in New York City." *English Today* 26 (3): 35–43.

Blake, Renée, Cara Shousterman, Luiza Newlin-Łukowicz, and Lindsay Kelley. 2012. "Linguistic and Ethnic Diversity in Black New York." Paper presented at the Sociolinguistics Symposium (SS) 19, Berlin, Germany.

Boersma, Paul, and David Weenink. 2014. "Praat: Doing Phonetics by Computer" [Computer Program]. Version 5.3.77, http://www.praat.org.

City of New York. 2004. *Newest New Yorkers 2000: Immigrant New York in the New Millenium*. New York: New York Department of City Planning and Population Division.

Coggshall, Elizabeth L., and Kara Becker. 2010. "A Vowel Comparison of African American and White New York City Residents." In *AAE Speakers and Their Participation in Local Sound Changes: A Comparative Study*, edited by Malcah Yaeger-Dror and Erik R. Thomas, Publication of the American Dialect Society 94, 101–28. Durham, NC: Duke University Press.

Cutler, Cecelia A. 1999. "Yorkville Crossing: White Teens, Hip Hop, and African American English." *Journal of Sociolinguistics* 3 (4): 428–42.

Dodson, Howard. 2007. "What's at Stake: Redefining African American, 6.3." *Logos* 6. Available at http://www.logosjournal.com/issue_6.3/dodson.htm.

Foner, Nancy. 2001. *Islands in the City: West Indian Migration to New York*. Berkeley: University of California Press.

Green, Lisa J. 2002. *African American English*. Cambridge: Cambridge University Press.

Jolly, Kenneth S. 2006. *Black Liberation in the Midwest: The Struggle in St. Louis, Missouri, 1964–1970*. New York: Taylor & Francis.

Kasinitz, Philip. 1992. *Caribbean New York: Black Immigrants and the Politics of Race*. Ithaca, NY: Cornell University Press.

Kasinitz, Philip, John H. Mollenkopf, Mary C. Waters, and Jennifer Holdaway. 2008. *Inheriting the City: The Children of Immigrants Come of Age*. New York: Russell Sage Foundation.

Labov, William. 1966. *The Social Stratification of English in New York City*. Washington, DC: Center for Applied Linguistics.

———. 1972. *Language in the Inner City*. Philadelphia: University of Pennsylvania Press.

Labov, William, Sharon Ash, and Charles Boberg. 2006. *The Atlas of North American English: Phonetics, Phonology, and Sound Change*. New York: Mouton de Gruyter.

Labov, William, Paul Cohen, and Clarence Robins. 1965. *A Preliminary Study of the Structure of English Used by Negro and Puerto Rican Speakers in New York City*. Final report. Cooperative Research Project 3091.

Labov, William, Paul Cohen, Clarence Robins, and John Lewis. 1968. "A Study of the Non-Standard English of Negro and Puerto Rican Speakers in New York City." In *Cooperative Research Report 3288 (1 and 2)*. New York: Columbia University. (Reprinted by U.S. Regional Survey, 204 North 35th Street, Philadelphia, PA 19104).

Le Page, Robert B., and Andrée Tabouret-Keller. 1985. *Acts of Identity*. Cambridge: Cambridge University Press.

Mather, Patrick-André. 2012. "The Social Stratification of /R/ in New York City: Labov's Department Store Study Revisited." *Journal of English Linguistics* 40 (4): 338–56.

Myers, Greg. 2006. "'Where Are You from?' Identifying Place." *Journal of Sociolinguistics* 10: 320–43.

Newman, Michael. 2014. *New York City English*. Berlin: Mouton De Gruyter.

Reich, Steven A. 2006. *Encyclopedia of the Great Black Migration*. Westport, CT: Greenwood Press.

Rickford, John R. 1999. *African American Vernacular English: Features, Evolution, Educational Implications*. Language in Society 26. Malden and Oxford: Blackwell.

Roberts, Peter A. 1988. *West Indians and Their Language*. Cambridge: Cambridge University Press.

Sankoff, David, Sali A. Tagliamonte, and Eric Smith. 2005. *Goldvarb X: A Variable Rule Application for Macintosh and Windows*. University of Toronto: Department of Linguistics.

Shousterman, Cara. 2014. "Speaking English in Spanish Harlem: The Role of Rhythm." *University of Pennsylvania Working Papers in Linguistics* 20 (2). Available at http://repository.upenn.edu/pwpl/vol20/iss2/18.

Slomanson, Peter, and Michael Newman. 2004. "Peer Group Identification and Variation in New York Latino English Laterals." *English Worldwide* 25: 199–216.

Smitherman, Geneva. 1999. *Talkin that Talk: Language, Culture and Education in African America*. London: Routledge.

Taylor, Monique M. 2002. *Harlem between Heaven and Hell*. Minneapolis: University of Minnesota Press.

Terrazas, Aaron. 2009. *African Immigrants in the United States*. Available from http://www.migrationinformation.org/USfocus/display.cfm?id=719.

Thomas, Erik R., and Tyler Kendall. 2007. "NORM: The Vowel Normalization and Plotting Suite." http://ncslaap.lib.ncsu.edu/tools/norm.

Trudgill, Peter. 1972. "Sex, Covert Prestige and Linguistic Change in the Urban British English of Norwich." *Language in Society* 1: 179–95.

Waters, Mary C. 1999. *Black Identities: West Indian Immigrant Dreams and American Realities.* Cambridge, MA: Harvard University Press.

Wells, John C. 1982. *Accents of English.* Vol. 2, *The British Isles.* Cambridge: Cambridge University Press.

Wolfram, Walt. 1969. *A Sociolinguistic Description of Detroit Negro Speech.* Washington, DC: Center for Applied Linguistics.

———. 1974. *Sociolinguistic Aspects of Assimilation: Puerto Rican English in New York City.* Arlington, VA: Center for Applied Linguistics.

———. 2003a. "Reexamining the Development of African American English: Evidence from Isolated Communities." *Language* 79: 282–316.

———. 2003b. "Sociolinguistic Folklore in the Study of African American English." *Language and Linguistics Compass* 1: 1–22.

Wolfram, Walt, and Natalie Schilling-Estes. 1998. *American English: Dialects and Variation.* Language in Society 25. Malden, MA: Blackwell.

Wolfram, Walt, and Erik R. Thomas. 2002. *The Development of African American English.* Malden, MA: Blackwell.

Wong, Amy. 2007. "Two Vernacular Features in the English of Four American-Born Chinese." *University of Pennsylvania Working Papers in Linguistics* 13 (2): 217–30.

Zentella, Ana Celia. 1981. "'Hablamos Los Dos. We Speak Both': Growing up Bilingual in El Barrio." PhD diss., University of Pennsylvania.

CHAPTER 15

....

AFRICAN AMERICAN VERNACULAR ENGLISH IN CALIFORNIA

Over Four Decades of Vibrant Variationist Research

....

JOHN R. RICKFORD

15.1 INTRODUCTION

....

AFRICAN AMERICANS account for only 6.6 percent of the population of California, about half as much as African Americans do in the United States overall (13.1 percent), about a fifth of what they do in Mississippi (37.4 percent), and less than a seventh of what they do in Washington, DC (hereinafter DC) (50.1 percent).[1] Given its relatively small proportion of African Americans, one might wonder why California merits its own chapter in this Handbook. One answer is that this is because California is the most highly populated US state; 6.6 percent represents a huge number of African Americans (2,507,992), considerably more, for instance, than African Americans in Mississippi (1,116,932) or DC (317,346). A better answer, from the perspective of lects and variation, is that African American Vernacular English (AAVE) in California has been the focus of vibrant ethnographic and/or (socio)linguistic study since the years of the earliest community studies in New York City (NYC), Detroit, and DC, and this tradition continues to this day.[2] Moreover, California was the site of the 1996-1997 Oakland Ebonics controversy—the biggest public controversy to date concerning the use of AAVE in US schools—although educational research is outside the purview of this chapter (see, instead, Part V, this volume). Another distinctive feature of variationist scholarship on AAVE in California is how much of it has been done by African Americans, perhaps more than in any other state.[3] Labov (1982, 165) has emphasized the contributions to the study of AAVE made by "the entrance of [B]lack linguists into the field"; these are especially evident in work done in California.

15.2 SOCIOLINGUISTIC COMMUNITY STUDIES OF THE 1970S

The earliest study in this category is Legum et al's (1971) 172-page report on *The Speech of Young Black Children in Los Angeles*. Closely modeled in feature coverage on Labov et al's (1968) Harlem study, it was listed by Wolfram (1974, 498), along with Labov et al. (1968), Wolfram (1969), and Fasold (1972), as one of the four earliest major studies of "northern" urban Black speech. Because I discuss this report extensively in Rickford (2014), I will only highlight some of its significant features here. First, it was the earliest study of the speech of young Black children (kindergarten to third grade) in the United States, complementing an earlier acquisition study of Black preschoolers (ages 4–5) in the San Francisco Bay Area (Henrie 1969). Legum et al. (1971) also confirmed the findings of Labov et al. (1968) that the simplification of word-final consonant clusters ending in *t* or *d* was much more frequent in words with mono-morphemic clusters like *past* (64 percent in Los Angeles, hereinafter LA) than in words like *passed* where it represented the past tense (32 percent). The LA study also confirmed Wolfram's (1969) finding that *are*-deletion (50/61, or 82 percent, across all age groups in LA) was much more common than *is*-deletion (79/272, or 29 percent). Finally, the LA children used invariant habitual *be* (e.g., "When I *be* appetizing, it *be* a picture on") much more frequently in third grade (47 examples) than in kindergarten (4 examples), anticipating subsequent evidence (Craig and Washington 2006; Van Hofwegen and Wolfram 2010) that some vernacular features occur more often as children progress from kindergarten to higher grades.

In 1971, another study of AAVE in California was published—Claudia Mitchell-Kernan's ethnographic study in a low-income West Oakland community. Herself African American, Mitchell-Kernan spent years observing language use and attitudes in her African American neighborhood, and her ethnography is well-known for its insightful analyses of *signifying, marking,* and *loud-talking* (see also Mitchell-Kernan 1972). Less familiar are its quantitative studies of present-tense copula absence and auxiliary *have* absence in the speech of two young African American women, Rita (23) and Esther (26). Both were born out of state but "spent the major portion of their lives in the San Francisco Bay Area" (Mitchell-Kernan 1971, 19). Their combined recorded data is not extensive (two hours total), but the copula absence data are presented in detail in her Appendix I, allowing us to reanalyze it to take into account "don't count" cases and other conventions established by later research (see Rickford et al. 1991; Blake 1997).[4] Thus reanalyzed, the data on *is* + *are* absence nicely confirm the evidence of other features (see table 15.1) that Rita is more vernacular than Esther.[5]

Mitchell-Kernan relates this difference between the two women to the fact that they represent different "socio-cultural strands." Rita earns "below poverty level" and her "interaction network was almost exclusively intra-community." Esther's earnings were closer to middle class and her networks were broader, involving interactions both inside

Table 15.1 Contrast between Rita and Esther's Use of Canonical AAVE Features

Speaker	Ø is + are p = .0297*	Invariant habitual be or be₂	Exis. i's (versus there) p = .004*	Ø third sg. –s
Rita	43% (52/120)	16	100% (8/8)	60% (46/77)
Esther	27% (19/71)	0	30% (3/10)	0% (no n's)

*Significance by Fischer's exact test; significance cannot be calculated for other columns.
Source: Constructed from data in Mitchell-Kernan 1971, ch. 2 and appendix I.

and outside the community, many with professionals (1971, 20–21). Almost ten years before Milroy's (1980) book on language and social networks, Mitchell-Kernan's insights on this subject are quite striking.

The combined copula absence data from Rita and Esther also confirmed the evidence of other studies that *are*-deletion (39/70, or 56 percent) is more frequent ($p < .0001$) than *is*-deletion (32/121, or 26 percent); that pronoun subjects are more favorable ($p = .0042$) to *is/are* deletion (61/148, or 41 percent) than NP [noun phrase] subjects (10/52, or 19 percent); and that there was a relatively consistent hierarchy ($p = .0009$) of following grammatical environments, with __NP (11/35, or 20 percent) and __Loc (3/16, or 19 percent) least favorable to copula absence; __V-ing (26/40, or 65 percent) and __gonna (12/19, or 63 percent) most favorable; and __Adj in between (19/56, or 34 percent).[6] Together with Legum et al. (1971), Mitchell-Kernan's (1971) California study reinforced the early evidence of Labov et al. (1968) from NYC and Wolfram (1969) from Detroit that AAVE was grammatically similar nationwide. The most likely explanation for this similarity is the common origins of AAVE in the North and West via the Great Migration from the South of the early twentieth century.

The next quantitative community study in California, this time incorporating the variable rule framework of Labov et al. (1968) and Cedergren and Sankoff (1974), was Baugh's (1979) dissertation study of style-shifting in the Black community in Pacoima, greater Los Angeles (see also Baugh 1983). Baugh's fieldwork methods were ethnographic, like Mitchell-Kernan's, involving local residence and work as a lifeguard at a community pool over several summers, but his recorded database was much bigger (eighty-eight hours). At its core were nine primary participants, six men and three women, aged 21 to 54. Innovatively, he distinguished four speech event types or styles (1979, 23) based on interlocutors' familiarity and their ability to speak AAVE: *Type 1, Familiar/Vernacular,* represents interactions between familiars who speak AAVE; *Type 2, Unfamiliar/Vernacular,* represents events in which participants share AAVE but are not well known to each other; *Type 3, Familiar/Nonvernacular,* represents events involving participants who know each other but do not share AAVE; and *Type 4, Unfamiliar/Nonvernacular,* represents events where participants neither know each other nor speak AAVE.

Baugh (1979, 1983) examined many variables, including *be done*, stressed *BIN*, aspectual marking with *steady* (identified as a distinctive AAVE feature for the first time), multiple negation, *is*-absence, *are*-absence, final *t/d* deletion, post-vocalic *r*-deletion, and absence of third person singular *-s*, possessive *-s*, and plural *-s*. His study confirms and extends our knowledge of the internal constraints on these variables provided by earlier studies, but only the last four features in this list (bolded in table 15.2) showed significant variable rule probability distinctions among his four situational styles.[7] Baugh (1979, 1983) suggested that variables like *is*-absence are primarily constrained by their complex internal constraints.

A fourth California community study of the 1970s (presented out of order because it differs in kind from the others and provides a better geographical link with those in the next section) was Hoover's (1978) survey of attitudes toward "Black English" among sixty-four African American parents of first and sixth graders in East Palo Alto (near Stanford University) and sixteen similar parents in Oakland. Although this was not a study of AAVE usage, it is worth noting in Part II of this book because it consolidated the notion of standard Black English (see Spears, this volume) as a variety with standard English grammar but "Black" pronunciation (cf. Taylor 1971, and see Spears, this volume) and revealed a more complex and positive set of attitudes toward the Black varieties than had previously been reported.[8] As Hoover concluded:

> it should be remembered that 85 percent of Black parents interviewed accepted one level of Black English (standard) in all contexts and accepted the vernacular level in many contexts dependent on situation, topic, and person spoken to. This is certainly not the picture of a group rejecting itself. (Hoover 1978, 85)

A final "community" study worth mentioning is Folb's (1980) study of teenage slang in Los Angeles, based on fieldwork done between 1968 and 1976.[9] The book is valuable, not only for the 2,500 slang terms (i.e., fleeting, popular vocabulary among particular groups) the author collected, listed in a thirty-four-page glossary at the end, but also for its analysis by subcategory (e.g., Name Terms, Male Female Interaction, Drugs) in the six preceding chapters. Also striking are the extensive quotes the author provides from her recordings of African American teenagers, in which the vernacular of the time shines through:

Table 15.2 Varbrul Probabilities, by Style, for Five of Baugh's (1979) AAVE Variables

Variable Styles	Ø Is	Ø Post–vocalic *r*–	Ø third sg. *–s*	Ø Possessive *–s*	Ø Plural *–s*
Type 1	.514	.626	.601	.635	.621
Type 2	.489	.489	.443	.421	.488
Type 3	.472	.491	.538	.704	.549
Type 4	.472	.393	.417	.249	.345

Like d'name of d'game down here it be runnin' down some fine lines. Like you talkin' to some young lady, tryin' to catch. Else you be blowin' on d' brother hard, fast and heavy. (Folb 1980, 90)

15.3 EAST PALO ALTO NEIGHBORHOOD STUDIES [EPANS] IN THE 1980S TO 1990S AND BEYOND

In the mid-1980s, assisted by Faye McNair-Knox and several Stanford students, I began recording African American (and some of the few White) residents of the low-income, primarily African American, Latino/a, and Pacific Islander East Palo Alto community adjacent to Stanford and Palo Alto. Eventually, the database from this East Palo Alto Neighborhood Study (EPANS) included recordings from more than eighty men and women, of all ages, and portions of it were used in a variety of studies in the 1980s to 1990s and beyond.

Stanford graduate or undergraduate students pioneered several EPANS projects. For instance, Théberge (1988) first noted the existence of preterit *had* (as in *I had slipped and fell* instead of *I slipped and fell*) in the narratives of 12-year-old, sixth-grade students with whom she had been working in East Palo Alto. In an NWAV conference presentation on this feature, Rickford and Théberge Rafal (1996) provided a detailed analysis of the semantics and discourse significance of the form, noting that it often marked or foreshadowed a narrative or evaluation peak. Drawing on EPANS data from older teenagers and adults, and other studies (see Labov et al. 1968 and Cukor-Avila 1995), we concluded that while preterit *had* was sharply age-graded in East Palo Alto, it might represent change in progress in AAVE elsewhere beginning in narrative orientation clauses and spreading from there to "complicating action clauses and even to single event and unsequenced listings outside of narratives" (Rickford and Théberge Rafal 1996, 247).

The late Keith Denning, using EPANS data from seventeen speakers, eleven Black and six White, showed that younger Black speakers were converging with White speakers in using "higher, fronter realizations of the final /i/ in words like *happy*" (Denning 1989, 145), rather than the lower, laxer, and backer realizations (more southern like) characteristic of their parents and grandparents. His acoustic phonetic evidence challenged the then new and controversial claim (cf. Bailey and Maynor 1989) that AAVE was diverging from White Vernacular American Englishes and showed that convergence and divergence (in grammatical features like invariant *be*) could coexist. This point was reinforced by Rickford (1992), who, using a small cross-section of old, middle, and young speakers in the EPANS corpus, reported that divergence from the norms of standard and vernacular White American Englishes was evident in much higher uses of invariant habitual *be* and zero copula among East Palo Alto teenagers but that stability or convergence was evident in other features, like plural and past tense marking. Rickford (1992) also attributed the divergence between old and young East Palo Alto speakers to differences in their respective attitudes to Black (versus White) identity and culture but emphasized that we needed further research to explain why particular features diverged and others did not.

Richardson (1991; now Fought) drew on data from three White and twelve Black speakers in the EPANS corpus to investigate variability in the expression of habitual aspect in the present and the past, beginning with the semantics rather than the forms. She found that, contrary to popular stereotype, the African American speakers did not just depend on invariant *be* for present tense habituals (as in *we be cracking up*, used in 27 percent of the 668 combined present-tense tokens from Foxy Boston and Tinky Gates). The African American speakers also used other strategies, like the simple present verb (as in *we crack up*, used 63 percent of the time) and zero copula (as in *we Ø cracking up*, used 4 percent of the time). This range of strategies made them appear similar to Whites in the area, but Richardson showed that there was still a significant difference between Black and White strategies for marking habituality in the present and the past, and she noted other interesting findings, such as co-occurrence between habitual verb forms and frequency adverbials.

Finally, in terms of student-initiated research, Blake (1997) drew on 842 "count" tokens and 1,636 "don't count" tokens from six African American speakers in the EPANS corpus to provide a thorough review of the diverse decisions made by linguists studying zero copula in AAVE about what to include and exclude in defining the envelope of variation. She ended with clear recommendations for subsequent research, including the suggestion that WIT tokens (*Wha's*, *I's*, and *Tha's*) should be excluded, and negative forms, including *ain't*, should be included. Some of McWhorter's (1998) discussion of AAVE was also based on EPANS and his own California research.

Rickford et al. (1991) drew on 1,424 present tense copula "count" tokens from thirty or more speakers in the EPANS corpus to address two significant unresolved theoretical and methodological issues in the study of AAVE zero copula: (1) Whether *is*-contraction and deletion should be tabulated and analyzed separately from that of *are* (recall that Labov et al. [1968] studied only *is*), and (2) whether the different methods used by researchers to compute copula contraction and deletion significantly influenced the results. With respect to (1), Rickford et al. concluded that *is* and *are* should be studied together, facilitating one statement of the very similar conditioning both forms displayed. With respect to (2), they concluded that the different computation methods, which they dubbed "Labov Contraction and Deletion," "Straight Contraction and Deletion," and "Romaine Contraction,"[10] made a tremendous difference in the results. For transparency, neutrality, and other reasons, Rickford et al. (1991) recommended that researchers follow the "Straight Contraction and Deletion" method. They also found a hierarchy of following grammatical and subject constraints that strikingly matched the reports of earlier researchers in other communities and a strong apparent time effect (e.g., factor weights of .23, .42, and .82 for old, middle, and young groups, respectively, for Straight Deletion of *is* + *are*) that could be attributed either to change in progress or age-grading.

Rickford and McNair-Knox (1994) drew on four different recordings with EPANS teenager Foxy Boston to investigate some of Bell's (1984) hypotheses about style as audience design, as part of a larger interest in reviving the study of style-shifting in sociolinguistics. The pivotal data came from two interviews with Foxy in 1990 and 1991, one with the African American mother (Faye) of a teenage acquaintance from East Palo Alto (Roberta), with Roberta and two other African American neighborhood teenagers as minor participants, the other from a one-on-one interview with an unfamiliar White graduate student (Beth). For three of the five linguistic variables investigated (see table 15.3), Foxy showed significant variation between the two interviews, using the vernacular variants significantly more often with the familiar Black interviewer.

Had we had only one of these interviews as our data point (the norm in sociolinguistics), our impression of Foxy's competence and of teenage usage in East Palo Alto would have been dramatically different.

The authors also used Foxy's data to assess several of Bell's (1984) hypotheses about stylistic variation. For instance Foxy's style-shifting by addressee is bigger than by topic, as Bell (1984, 178ff.) predicted, but only if we restrict ourselves to cells with a minimum of thirty tokens, as Guy (1980, 26) had recommended. And among three possibilities raised by Bell (1984, 167), Foxy seems to be responding to her interlocutors' personal characteristics (e.g., race and familiarity) rather than the general level of their speech or their frequencies for specific linguistic variables.

Table 15.3 Significant Contrasts (χ^2, $p < .001$) between Foxy's Interviews III and IV (1990, 1991)

Variable	Foxy III (1990, familiar Afr. Am. interviewer)	Foxy IV (1991, unfamiliar Eur. Am. interviewer)
Ø third sg. –s	73% (83/114)	36% (45/124)*
Ø Copula is/are	70% (197/283)	40% (70/176)*
Invariant habitual be	385 (= 241 per hr)	97 (= 78 per hr)*

* The difference between the Foxy IV and Foxy III relative frequencies for each feature is statistically significant, by chi-square test, $p < .001$.
Source: Adapted from Rickford and McNair-Knox 1994, table 10.1, 247.

Table 15.4 Tinky and Foxy's Teenager versus Adult Use of Vernacular Features

Variable	TINKY GATES Age 15, 1987	Age 35, 2006	FOXY BOSTON Age 13, 1986	Age 34, 2008
Invariant be	50 (25 per hour)	10 (3 per hour)	146 (97 per hour)	27 (10 per hour)
Ø third sg. –s	96% (56)	57% (201)	97% (69)	23% (109)
Ø is + are	81% (256)	54% (464)	90% (154)	35% (376)

Source: Adapted from Rickford and Price 2013, table 4, 154.

The most recent publication to draw substantially on the EPANS corpus was Rickford and Price (2013), which benefited from re-interviews with Tinky Gates and Foxy Boston done by RaShida Knox (aka "Roberta") in 2006 and 2008, when they were about twenty years older than in their first teenage interview. As table 15.4 shows, both women showed significantly lower usage rates of key AAVE features as adults.

However, despite the complicating factor of stylistic variability (which led them to recommend that studies of change in real time utilize at least three data points rather than two), the authors conclude that the contrasts in table 15.4 represent stable age-grading rather than generational change (cf. Sankoff and Blondeau 2007).

15.4 OTHER VARIATIONIST STUDIES FROM THE 1990S AND 2000S

Other studies of AAVE in California conducted around the turn of this century extend our understanding of issues raised in the EPANS and earlier community studies, and/or provide new insights. DeBose (1992) wrote an interesting non-quantitative study of code-shifting by one of the ten speakers from Oakland ("P") that he recorded for the innovative study of AAVE grammar in DeBose and Faraclas (1993).[11] P, a college graduate and a balanced bilingual in AAVE and standard American English (SAE), was born in South Carolina but was "raised, from an early age, in the San Francisco/Oakland Bay area" (DeBose 1992, 161). DeBose (1992) discusses several striking instances of P's code-switching between SAE and AAVE, explaining them in terms of addressee characteristics and other factors. DeBose's larger point is that AAVE is "frequently spoken by middle-class persons" (1992, 165). He relates this in turn to "the fact that many educated, middle-class African Americans begin their lives in predominantly Black urban ghettoes or rural southern communities where BE [Black English] is the normal medium of everyday communication." Other aspects of DeBose's research on AAVE in California are reflected in his 2005 work.

In 1987, John Baugh re-recorded four African American males—Jojo, Russell, Leon, and Carlos—whom he had first recorded as teenagers for his 1976 dissertation study in Pacoima, Los Angeles. Baugh (1996), comparing their adult and teenage usage, is one of the first (panel) studies of change in AAVE in real time. But like Rickford and Price (2013), Baugh concludes that the variation exhibited by his subjects represents age-grading. Jojo, Russell, and Leon display sharp reductions in vernacular usage as adults, but Baugh attributes this to the demands of their adult middle-class jobs and their ethnically and economically diverse networks. Carlos, by contrast, is in prison, and retains a level of vernacular usage that is more highly valued in his interactional milieu.

Chappel (1999), an unpublished study of variation in AAVE by class and age in Oakland, California, is worth citing because there has been no quantitative study of social class variation in AAVE since Wolfram's (1969) study of Detroit. (See related discussion by Spears, this volume.) Chappel indeed set out to replicate Wolfram's study, using a modified Education and Occupation scale to place twelve females she interviewed (each for about two hours) into two socioeconomic status groups: Lower Middle (LM) and Lower Working (LW). The interviewees came from four families, representing three generations: Adolescents (11–16 years old), their mothers (33–41 years old), and their grandmothers (56–76 years old). As table 15.5 shows, copula absence and consonant cluster reduction by social class in Oakland were remarkably similar to what Wolfram (1969) found in Detroit. The most striking difference was in the lower copula absence rate for LW in Oakland (38.3 percent), which was closer to that of Wolfram's (1969) *Upper* Working class group in Detroit (37.3 percent).[12] Additionally, Chappel (1999) discussed systematic quantitative variation by age group and several internal linguistic constraints on both variables.

The most substantive variationist study of AAVE in this category is Alim's (2004) study of AAVE in "Sunnyside," a community contiguous with East Palo Alto, in the San Francisco Bay Area. Alim's book is innovative in many respects, but especially in its theoretical and empirical discussion of style-shifting. Among other things, he provides analyses of the use of five grammatical AAVE features in the speech of four 17-year-old Black Sunnyside Hip Hop fans, each recorded talking to eight Stanford students who differed in race, gender, and Hip Hop knowledge. Drawing on Varbrul results, Alim provides considerable information about linguistic constraints on his most frequent variables, but his most fascinating data involve social and stylistic constraints. Table 15.6, for instance, shows how dramatically the teens vary stylistically by interlocutor,

Table 15.5 Zero Copula and Consonant Cluster Reduction in Oakland AAVE in 1999, Compared with Detroit AAVE Thirty Years Earlier

Variable	Zero copula		Consonant cluster reduction	
Social class	Lower middle	Lower working	Lower middle	Lower working
Oakland 1999	10.9% (1,204)	38.3% (1,261)	72.4% (2,948)	83.6% (2,428)
Detroit 1969	10.9% (n.d.)	56.9% (n.d.)	65.9% (n.d.)	84.2% (n.d.)

Source: Chappel 1999; Wolfram 1969 (n.d. = no data on sample size available).

Table 15.6 Percentage Ø *is/are* and Third Person Singular *–s* by Four Black Sunnyside Teens According to Familiarity and Race of their Interlocutors

Interlocutor variable	Unfamiliar whites	Unfamiliar blacks	Familiar black peers
Ø Copula *is/are*	11% (718)	37% (819)	80% (235)
Ø third sg. *–s*	19% (394)	40% (540)	85% (61)

Source: Alim 2004, 154, 170.

Table 15.7 AAVE Feature Use by Black Sunnysidaz (Varbrul Factor Weights for Ø
is/are and Third Person Singular −*s*, Ns for *be*), by Interlocutor Characteristics

Interlocutor	Race		Gender		Hip hop knowledge	
Variable	Black	White	Male	Female	Yes	No
Ø *is/are*	.716	.259	.638	.325	.619	.350
Ø third sg. −*s*	.658	.289	.631	.323	.615	.373
Invariant *be*	56	16	43	29	52	20

Source: Alim 2004, 146, 164, 178.

across a range of 67 to 69 percentage points—about twice as much as that exhibited by
Foxy in table 15.3.

The high vernacular values (80–85 percent) exhibited by the Sunnysidaz with familiar
Black peers also provided key evidence for Rickford and Price's (2013) argument that
AAVE teenage norms for copula and third singular −*s* absence had not changed fundamentally since the 1980s and that the diminution in Foxy and Tinky's vernacular use
in 2006–2008 (table 15.4) represented age-grading. Table 15.7 shows that while interlocutor's race remains the primary social constraint, gender and Hip Hop Knowledge
(a variable not previously considered in variationist analyses) are significant too. The
implications for our field methods and theorizing are enormous.

15.5 New AAVE Features and Analyses from California

Several new AAVE forms or analyses made their debut in the literature from research
done in California. For instance, future perfective *be done* (e.g., "They *be done* spent my
money before I even get a chance to look at it") (151) and aspectual marking with *steady*
(e.g., "Ricky Bell *be steady* steppin' in them number nines") (165) were first discussed in
Baugh's (1979) dissertation on Pacoima. Spears's (1982) *Language* article on the *come* of
indignation, as in "He *come* walking in here like he owned the damn place," drew on data
from "participant observation in San Francisco and Oakland," especially "in a hair-care
establishment where lively, uninhibited speech prevails" (852). Théberge (1988) provided the earliest discussions of preterit *had*, as in "I was on my way to school and I *had*
slipped and fell" (Rickford and Théberge Rafal 1996, 229) based on data from East Palo
Alto. And East Palo Alto was also the source of invariant *be₃*, as in "The Clovers *be* the
baddest ones around here" (Alim 2004, 184). Although there is "some semantic overlap
between *be₂* and *be₃*," the latter only occurs before noun phrases and has situational and
semantic restrictions not shared by the former (ibid., 189–90).

In terms of new analyses, Sells, Rickford, and Wasow (1996), drawing in part on intro-spection and usage data from East Palo Alto residents, provided a unified Optimality Theoretic analysis of Negative Inversion, as in "Ain't nothin' happenin'" and "Can't nobody beat em" (examples from Labov et al. 1968, 350, 367) as an alternative to the dual analysis of this construction in the latter work. Similarly, Bender (2001, 2005), drawing in part on experimental evidence from speakers in the San Francisco Bay Area, argued that AAVE variation in copula absence is syntactic rather than phonological (contra Labov 1969), and that its social meaning is modulated by internal constraints. Two other experimental studies conducted in Stanford, California, involving reactions to AAVE versus non-AAVE features (consonant cluster reduction and/or *th*-fronting) are Staum Casasanto (2009) and King and Sumner (2014).

15.6 Use of AAVE by Asian, Mexican, Pacific Islander, and White Youth

One interesting aspect of sociolinguistic variation in California is the use of AAVE fea-tures—lexical, grammatical, and phonological—by youth from a variety of ethnic back-grounds, usually in school, and as a marker of youth or Hip Hop identity. Kuwahara (1998) was one of the first to study this, focusing on ten adolescents (10 to 12 years old) from Cambodian, Chinese, Mien, Thai, Vietnamese, and Mexican backgrounds as they moved from elementary to middle school in "Cooltown," in the San Francisco Bay Area. Along with detailed ethnographic discussion of each adolescent's background, school performance, and language use, she provides quantitative analysis of their usage of various grammatical and lexical features of AAVE. Bucholtz (2011) looks at the youth identity styles of White high schoolers in a multi-ethnic urban high school in the San Francisco Bay Area too, but a significant component of this involves their use of AAVE features.[13] Paris's (2011) study of African American, Latino/a, and Pacific Islander youth at South Vista High School is also set in the San Francisco Bay Area, but closer to East Palo Alto. In addition to discussing variation in each group's use of grammatical and lex-ical features, he examines the positive/negative attitudes of the African American youth to the use of AAVE resources—including non-racialized deployment of the N-word—by Latino/a and Pacific Islander youth. Finally, Igoudin (2013) explores the everyday use of AAVE by three Asian American girls in a Southern California high school "as a means to enrich their social personae" (61).

15.7 CONCLUSION

Over the past four decades, California has been and continues to be the site of vibrant research on variability in AAVE, much of it by African American researchers. The earliest work (Legum et al. 1971; Mitchell-Kernan 1971; Baugh 1979) provided *confirmation* for generalizations emerging from New York City and Detroit research about internal *constraints* on consonant cluster simplification, zero copula, and other variables, and about the *relative* grammatical *uniformity* of AAVE nationwide. Research in California also produced one of the first book-length discussions of the AAVE *lexicon* (Folb 1980), and two of the earliest studies on AAVE of *young children* (preschoolers and K-third graders) (Henrie 1989 and Legum et al. 1971, respectively). A distinctive feature of California AAVE research, throughout, has been the frequency with which *ethnographic* methods have been employed (see, among others, Mitchell-Kernan 1971; Baugh 1979; Alim 2004; Paris 2011). The focus in many of the California studies (see Baugh 1979; DeBose 1992; Rickford and McNair-Knox 1994; Alim 2004) on a deeper understanding of *stylistic* variation in AAVE—often using innovative approaches—is also striking. *Attitudes* towards AAVE and other varieties, and the role of the vernacular in social *identity*—factors that often influence use by community insiders and outsiders—also received attention in California studies, for instance, in the work of Hoover (1978); Ogbu (1999); Kortenhoven (2008); Bucholtz (2011); Paris (2011); and Igoudin (2013).

Variation studies of AAVE in California have also been important in revealing *new distinctive forms* (e.g., *steady* in Baugh 1979; *come* of indignation in Spears 1982; and preterit *had* in Théberge 1988; Rickford and Théberge Rafal 1996), or in providing *new analyses* of already known features (e.g., invariant *be* and other habitual markers in Richardson 1991; negative inversion in Sells et al. 1996; and copula absence in Bender 2005). California research is also valuable for its *theoretical and methodological contributions to the quantitative study* of zero copula (Rickford et al. 1991; Blake 1997), and to larger issues like the *divergence controversy* (Denning 1989; Rickford 1992), variation by *social class and age* (Rickford et al. 1991; Chappel 1999), and *age-grading versus generational change* in panel studies (Baugh 1996; Rickford and Price 2013). Finally, California has been the site of innovative *experimental and/or processing studies* of AAVE (Staum Casasanto 2009; King and Sumner 2014), a trend likely to grow stronger in future research.

In these and other respects, the contribution of California research to our larger understanding of variability in AAVE has been substantial and significant, and it shows every sign of continuing.[14]

NOTES

1. US Census Bureau Data from http://quickfacts.census.gov/qfd/states/06000.html for 2012. These statistics are for "Black or African American alone"; if people representing "Two or More Races" were included (3.6 percent in California in 2012; somewhat less in

other states cited), the percentage of "African Americans" would be higher. But the comparison of California to the other states would be essentially the same.

2. By African American Vernacular English (AAVE), I mean the vernacular or nonstandard varieties used by African Americans, as distinct from African American English (AAE), a continuum of English-based varieties spoken by African Americans that would include African American Standard English (see Rickford 1999, xxi; Spears, this volume).

3. The list, for California, includes, alphabetically: H. Alim, A. Ball, J. Baugh, R. Blake, C. DeBose, M. Hoover, R. Jackson, S. King, L. Luster, N. Martin, F. McNair-Knox, J. McWhorter, C. Mitchell-Kernan, J. Ogbu, D. Paris, A. Piestrup, M. Price, A. Rickford, J. Rickford, and A. Spears. If work on AAVE in education or the Ebonics issue were included, the list would increase substantially. My apologies to anyone inadvertently omitted.

4. Among the reanalyses required on the basis of their categorical or indeterminate behavior (see Rickford et al. 1991; Blake 1997) were the discounting of tokens with *It* and *That* subjects, tokens in clause final position, and tokens involving embedded sentences, negatives, and questions.

5. Mitchell-Kernan (1971, 27–28) had also found this to be true of *is–are* absence as calculated by her methods (Rita, 27 percent; Esther, 13 percent), but her deletion rates were lower because she included the very common but categorical *i's* and *tha's* tokens.

6. Significance probabilities here as in table 15.2 were calculated by me using Fischer's exact test. In terms of following grammatical environments, it is noteworthy that Mitchell-Kernan, like Wolfram (1969), separated adjectives and locatives. In studying copula absence, Labov et al. (1968) had calculated __Adj/Loc together, but as Holm (1976, 1984), Baugh (1979, 1980), and Rickford (1998) showed, separating the two environments was important to arguments for the AAVE creole origins hypothesis.

7. Factors with probabilities over .5 favor rule application; those under .5 disfavor it, and those at or very close to .5 make little difference. Baugh (1979) also found an interesting percentage differentiation for multiple negation by style (from 61 percent to 28 percent, p. 162) but had no corresponding variable rule results (that would allow him to control for multivariate effects).

8. Luster (1992) and Ogbu (1999), both ethnographic studies in the San Francisco Bay Area by Black researchers, also reported more complex attitudes toward AAVE and Standard English than Stewart (1970)—singled out by Hoover (1978, 73, 78)—and some other researchers had assumed.

9. Folb's book includes a long and generally praiseworthy foreword by Claudia Mitchell-Kernan and received a positive review from Baugh (1981).

10. With F = Full Forms, C = Contractions, and D = deletions, the formulae for Straight Contraction is C/F + C + D, for Straight Deletion D/F + C + D, for Labov Contraction C + D/F + C + D, for Labov Deletion D/C + D, and for Romaine Contraction C/F + C. As shown in Rickford et al.'s (1991) table 2, given a data set of ten Full forms, ten contractions and ten deletions, computed "Contraction" rates could vary from 33 percent (Straight), to 50 percent (Romaine) or 67 percent (Labov), and computed "Deletion" rates could range from 33 percent (Straight) to 50 percent (Labov).

11. "Innovative" because they describe the AAVE Tense-Modality-Aspect system on its own terms and not in contrast with English, more like Green (2002). They do, however, compare it to Nigerian languages to highlight possible Africanist sources.

12. Wolfram's (1969) results (which did not include Ns) are from Fig. 6, p. 60, and Fig 47, p. 169. Chappel's (1999) results are calculated from class and age group data in Figures 4-1-4-3, pp. 31–34, and Fig. 5-1, p. 46.

13. Compare Bucholtz (2004) with respect to AAVE use by two Laotian teenage girls in the same high school.

14. Ongoing research includes work on the linguistic effects of Moving to Opportunity by African American and Latina/o speakers in Los Angeles, compared with their counterparts in other US cities (Rickford and Ludwig 2013), and research on African American speakers in the Voices of California corpus (Merced, Redding, and Bakersfield) at Stanford.

References

Alim, H. Samy. 2004. *You Know My Steez: An Ethnographic and Sociolinguistic Study of Styleshifting in a Black American Speech Community*. Publication of the American Dialect Society, No. 89. Durham, NC: Duke University Press.

Bailey, Guy, and Natalie Maynor. 1989. "The Divergence Controversy." *American Speech* 64 (1): 12–39.

Baugh, John. 1979. "Linguistic Style-Shifting in Black English." PhD diss., University of Pennsylvania.

———. 1980. "A Re-Examination of the Black English Copula." In *Locating Language in Time and Space*, edited by William Labov, 83–106. New York: Academic.

———. 1981. Review of *Runnin Down Some Lines: The Language and Culture of Black Teenagers*, by Edith A. Folb. *Language in Society* 10: 461–63.

———. 1983. *Black Street Speech: Its History, Structure and Survival*. Austin: University of Texas Press.

———. 1996. "Dimensions of the Theory of Econolinguistics." In *A Social Science of Language: Papers in Honor of William Labov*, edited by Gregory R. Guy and William Labov, 397–419. Philadelphia, PA: John Benjamins.

Bell, Allan. 1984. "Language Style as Audience Design." *Language in Society* 13: 145–204.

Bender, Emily M. 2001. "Syntactic Variation and Linguistic Competence: The Case of AAVE Copula Absence." PhD diss., Stanford University. Available at: http://faculty.washington.edu/ebender/dissertation/.

———. 2005. "On the Boundaries of Linguistic Competence: Matched-Guise Experiments as Evidence of Knowledge of Grammar." *Lingua* 115 (11): 1579–98.

Blake, Renée A. 1997. "Defining the Envelope of Linguistic Variation: The Case of 'Don't Count' Forms in the Copula Analysis of African American Vernacular English." *Language Variation and Change* 9: 57–79.

Bucholtz, Mary. 2004. "Styles and Stereotypes: The Linguistic Negotiation of Identity among Laotian American Youth. *Pragmatics* 14 (2/3): 127–47.

———. 2011. *White Kids: Language, Race, and Styles of Youth Identity*. Cambridge: Cambridge University Press.

Cedergren, Henrietta, and David Sankoff. 1974. "Variable Rules: Performance as a Statistical Reflection of Competence." *Language* 50: 333–55.

Chappel, Catherine A. 1999. "Variation by Class and Age among Oakland Females." Master's thesis, Stanford University.

Craig, Holly K., and Julie A. Washington. 2006. *Malik Goes to School: Examining the Language Skills of African American Students from Preschool–5th Grade*. Mahwah, NJ: Lawrence Erlbaum.

Cukor-Avila, Patricia. 1995. "The Evolution of AAVE in a Rural Texas Community: An Ethnolinguistic Study." PhD diss., University of Michigan.

DeBose, Charles E. 1992. "Codeswitching: Black English and Standard English in the African American Linguistic Repertoire." *Journal of Multilingual and Multicultural Development* 13: 157–67.

———. 2005. *The Sociology of African American Language: A Language Planning Perspective*. New York: Palgrave Macmillan.

DeBose, Charles E., and Nicholas Faraclas. 1993. "An Africanist Approach to the Linguistic Study of Black English: Getting to the Roots of the Tense-Aspect-Modality and Copula Systems in Afro-American." In *Africanisms in Afro-American Language Varieties*, edited by Salikoko Mufwene, 364–87. Athens: University of Georgia Press.

Denning, Keith. 1989. "Convergence with Divergence: A Sound Change in Vernacular Black English." *Language Variation and Change* 1: 145–67.

Fasold, Ralph. 1972. *Tense Marking in Black English: A Linguistic and Social Analysis*. Washington, DC: Center for Applied Linguistics.

Folb, Edith A. 1980. *Runnin Down Some Lines: The Language and Culture of Black Teenagers*. Cambridge, MA: Harvard University Press.

Green, Lisa J. 2002. *African American English: A Linguistic Introduction*. Cambridge: Cambridge University Press.

Guy, Gregory R. 1980. "Variation in the Group and the Individual: The Case of Final Stop Deletion." In *Locating Language in Time and Space*, edited by William Labov, 1–36. New York: Academic.

Henrie, Samuel N. 1969. "A Study of Verb Phrases Used by Five Year Old Nonstandard Negro English Speaking Children." PhD diss., University of California, Berkeley.

Holm, John. 1976. "Copula Variability on the Afro-American Continuum." Paper presented at the inaugural conference of the Society for Caribbean Linguistics, Guyana.

———. 1984. "Variability of the Copula in Black English and its Creole Kin." *American Speech* 59 (4): 291–309.

Hoover, Mary Rhodes. 1978. "Community Attitudes toward Black English." *Language in Society* 7 (1): 65–87.

Igoudin, A. Lane. 2013. "Asian American Girls Who Speak African American English: A Subcultural Language Identity." In *Multilingual Identities: New Global Perspectives*, edited by Inke du Bois and Nicole Baumgarten, 51–65. Frankfurt: Peter Lang.

King, Sharese, and Meghan Sumner. 2014. "Voices and Variants: Effects of Voice on the Form-Based Processing of Words with Different Phonological Variants." In *Proceedings of the 36th Annual Conference of the Cognitive Science Society*, edited by P. Bello, M. Guarini, M. McShane, and B. Scassellati. Quebec City, Canada: Cognitive Science Society.

Kortenhoven, Andrea. 2008. "You Don't Know like I Know: Identity Construction in Black Women's Church Testimonies." Paper presented at the African American Women's Language (AAWL) Conference, San Antonio, Texas. March 7–8.

Kuwahara, Yuri Lea. 1998. "Interactions of Identity: Inner-City Immigrant and Refugee Youths, Language Use, and Schooling." PhD diss., Stanford University.

Labov, William. 1969. "Contraction, Deletion and Inherent Variability of the English Copula." *Language* 45 (4): 715–62.

———. 1982. "Objectivity and Commitment in Linguistic Science: The Case of the Black English Trial in Ann Arbor." *Language in Society* 11: 165–201.

Labov, William, Paul Cohen, Clarence Robins, and John Lewis. 1968. *A Study of the Non-Standard English of Negro and Puerto-Rican Speakers in New York City*. Final Report, Research Project No. 3288. Vols. 1 and 2. Philadelphia, PA: U.S. Office of Education, U.S. Regional Survey.

Legum, Stanley E., Carol Pfaff, Gene Tinnie, and Michael Nicholas. 1971. *The Speech of Young Black Children in Los Angeles*. Technical Report, 33. Inglewood, CA: Southwest Regional Laboratory.

Luster, Laura. 1992. "Schooling, Survival, and Struggles: Black Women and the GED." PhD diss., Stanford University.

McWhorter, John. 1998. *The Word on the Street: Fact and Fable about American English*. New York: Plenum.

Milroy, Lesley. 1980. *Language and Social Networks*. Oxford: Basil Blackwell.

Mitchell-Kernan, Claudia. 1971. *Language Behavior in a Black Urban Community*. Monographs of the Language-Behavior Research Laboratory, 2. University of California, Berkeley.

———. 1972. "Signifyin and Marking: Two Afro-American Speech Acts. In *Directions in Sociolinguistics*, edited by John J. Gumperz and Dell Hymes, 161–79. New York: Holt, Rinehart and Winston.

Ogbu, John U. 1999. "Beyond Language: Ebonics, Proper English, and Identity in a Black American Speech Community." *American Educational Research Journal* 36 (2): 147–84.

Paris, Django. 2011. *Language across Difference; Ethnicity, Communication, and Youth Identities in Changing Urban Schools*. Cambridge: Cambridge University Press.

Richardson, Carmen. 1991. "Habitual Structures among Blacks and Whites in the 1990s." *American Speech* 66 (3): 292–302.

Rickford, John R. 1992. "Grammatical Variation and Divergence in Vernacular Black English." In *Internal and External Factors in Syntactic Change*, edited by Marinel Gerritsen and Dieter Stein, 174–200. Berlin: Mouton.

———. 1998. "The Creole Origins of African American Vernacular English: Evidence from Copula Absence." In *African American English: Structure, History and Use*, edited by Salikoko S. Mufwene, John R. Rickford, Guy Bailey, and John Baugh, 154–200. London: Routledge.

———. 2014. "An Early Study of the Speech of Young Black Children in California: Why It Matters." *American Speech* 89 (2): 121–42.

Rickford, John R., Arnetha Ball, Renée Blake, Raina Jackson, and Nomi Martin. 1991. "Rappin on the Copula Coffin: Theoretical and Methodological Issues in the Analysis of Copula Variation in African American Vernacular English." *Language Variation and Change* 3: 103–32.

Rickford, John R., and Jens Ludwig. 2013. "Neighborhood Moves and Sociolinguistic Mobility in Five American Cities." Paper presented at the annual meeting of the Linguistic Society of America, Boston, Massachusetts, January 3–6.

Rickford, John R., and Faye McNair-Knox. 1994. "Addressee- and Topic-Influenced Style Shift: A Quantitative Sociolinguistic Study." In *Sociolinguistic Perspectives on Register*, edited by Douglas Biber and Edward Finegan, 235–76. New York: Oxford University Press.

Rickford, John R., and Mackenzie Price. 2013. "Girlz II Women: Age-Grading, Language Change and Stylistic Variation." *Journal of Sociolinguistics* 17 (2): 143–79.

Rickford, John R., and Christine Théberge Rafal. 1996. "Preterite *had* + *V-ed* in the Narratives of African American Preadolescents." *American Speech* 71: 227–54.

Sankoff, Gillian, and Hélène Blondeau. 2007. "Longitudinal Change across the Lifespan: /r/ in Montreal French." *Language* 83: 560–88.

Sells, Peter, John R. Rickford, and Thomas Wasow. 1996. "An Optimality Theoretic Approach to Variation in Negative Inversion in AAVE." *Natural Language and Linguistic Theory* 14 (3): 591–627.

Spears, Arthur K. 1982. "The Black English Semi-Auxiliary *come*." *Language* 58 (4): 850–72.

Staum Casasanto, Laura. 2009. "What Do Listeners Know about Sociolinguistic Variation?" *University of Pennsylvania Working Papers in Linguistics* 15 (2): 40–49.

Stewart, William A. 1970. "Sociopolitical Issues in the Linguistic Treatment of Negro Dialect." In *20th Annual Round Table on Languages and Linguistics*, edited by James Alatis, 215–23. Washington, DC: Center for Applied Linguistics.

Taylor, Orlando. 1971. "Response to Social Dialects and the Field of Speech. In *Sociolinguistics: A Cross Disciplinary Perspective*. Washington, DC: Center for Applied Linguistics.

Théberge, Christine. 1988. "Some Sixth Grade Rappers, Readers and Writers." Senior honors essay, Stanford University.

Van Hofwegen, Janneke, and Walt Wolfram. 2010. "Coming of Age in African American English: A Longitudinal Study." *Journal of Sociolinguistics* 14 (4): 427–55.

Wolfram, Walt. 1969. *A Sociolinguistic Description of Detroit Negro Speech*. Washington, DC: Center for Applied Linguistics.

———. 1974. "The Relationship of White Southern Speech to Vernacular Black English." *Language* 50 (3): 498–527.

CHAPTER 16

....

THE BLACK ASL
(AMERICAN SIGN
LANGUAGE) PROJECT

An Overview

....

JOSEPH HILL, CAROLYN MCCASKILL, ROBERT BAYLEY, AND CEIL LUCAS

16.1 INTRODUCTION

....

THIS chapter describes the geographical and social factors that fostered the development of Black American Sign Language (hereinafter, Black ASL) and outlines the phonological, morphological, syntactic, and discourse features that make Black ASL recognizable as a distinct variety of ASL. Because there has been relatively little research on Black ASL until very recently, the chapter is based on findings from the Black ASL project that the authors undertook from 2007 to 2011 (McCaskill et al. 2011). As Rickford states in his discussion of African American English (AAE),[1] "all languages, if they have enough speakers, have dialects—regional or social varieties that develop when people are separated by geographic or social barriers" (1999, 320). The geographical and social factors that create these barriers include settlement patterns, migration, topographic features, language contact, economic status, social stratification, social interaction (e.g., social practices, speech communities), and group and individual identity (Wolfram and Schilling-Estes 2006).

The same geographic and social factors that promote the formation of spoken language varieties were also involved in the formation of Black ASL. Not surprisingly, Black deaf people were affected both by the same racial discrimination of the era that affected Black hearing people and by the same social isolation and marginalization due to race that contributed to the development and maintenance of AAE. Racial discrimination was also present in local, state, and regional organizations in the Deaf[2] community. For example, the National Association of the Deaf (NAD) was founded in 1880. At first the association welcomed Black Deaf Americans. However, at its Cleveland conference in 1925, the NAD revoked the membership of the Black members, changing the bylaws to prohibit Black Deaf membership (Burch 2002; Tabak 2006).

The effects of desegregation on the public education of Black Americans have received a great deal of attention in the literature; however, very little attention has focused on the effects of desegregation on Black Deaf and hard-of-hearing Americans. Aramburo (1989) and Hairston and Smith (1983) demonstrated that for more than a century and a half, White Deaf children had been educated in state-funded residential schools and Black Deaf children, especially those in the southern states, had been relegated to segregated residential schools that were also funded by the states. Seventeen states with public school systems (see table 16.1) required White Deaf and Black Deaf students to be taught separately, and, in some cases, the laws required that only Black teachers could teach Black students (Doctor 1948).

The sociohistorical reality characterized by geographically and socially isolated residential schools led to the development of a distinct variety of ASL, especially in the

Table 16.1 Black and White Deaf Schools: Founding and Desegregation

State	White school established	Black school/ department established	Desegregation	Years between establishment of Black and White schools	Years between establishment of Black schools and desegregation
DC, KDES	1857	1857 (dept.)	1958	0	101
N. Carolina	1845	1868–1869	1967	24	98
Maryland	1868	1872	1959	4	84
Tennessee	1845	1881 (dept.)	1965	36	84
Georgia	1846	1882	1965	36	83
Mississippi	1854	1882 (dept.)	1965	28	83
S. Carolina	1849	1883 (dept.)	1966	34	83
Kentucky	1823	1884 (dept.)	1954–60	61	70
Florida	1885	1885	1965	0	80
Texas	1857	1887	1965	30	78
Arkansas	1850/1867	1887	1967	37	80
Alabama	1858	1892	1968	34	76
Missouri	1861	1888 (dept.)	1954	37	66
Kansas	1861	1888 (dept.)	1954	27	66
Virginia	1839	1909	1965 (2 schools)	70	56
Oklahoma	1898	1909, dept	1962	11	53
Louisiana	1852	1938	1978	86	40
W. Virginia	1870	1926	1956	56	30

Source: McCaskill et al. 2011, 20.

South. Hairston and Smith state that there is "a Black way of signing used by Black deaf people in their own cultural milieu—among families and friends, in social gatherings, and in deaf clubs" (1983, 55). Tabak (2006), based on his research on Black Deaf Texans, remarks that the differences between Black and White signing include lexical items, the size of signing space, and voiceless mouthing. Burch and Joyner (2007) also report on the difference in the signing at a formerly segregated school in Raleigh, North Carolina. Thus, reports acknowledge the existence of Black ASL, but they are based on anecdotes and observations rather than systematic linguistic research.

Despite the limitations of early studies, in the last five decades, researchers who have noticed the differences between Black and White signing in the South have presented some data to support the claim that they are two separate dialects with distinct features. For example, in an appendix to the 1965 *Dictionary of American Sign Language* (DASL), co-authored with William Stokoe and Dorothy Casterline, Carl Croneberg suggests that these differences arose as a consequence of the segregation of Southern deaf schools. Based on responses to a 134-item signed vocabulary list, Croneberg reports "a radical dialect difference between the signs" of a young Black woman from North Carolina and those of White signers living in the same city (1965, 315). Except for Lucas, Bayley, and Valli (2001), earlier studies of Black ASL dealing with specific linguistic features are mostly small in scale. These include work on phonology (Woodward, Erting, and Oliver 1976; Woodward and DeSantis 1977); lexical variation (Aramburo 1989; Guggenheim 1993; Lucas et al. 2001); language attitudes (Lewis, Palmer, and Williams 1995); and parallels between Black ASL and AAE language styles (Lewis 1998). Clearly, the study of Black ASL lacks the breadth and depth of the extensive research on AAE. For instance, the early phonological studies in the 1970s relied on self-report data and small numbers of participants, and most of the other studies focused on lexical variation. For this reason, our large-scale project on Black ASL included a greater number of participants than previous work and analyzed linguistic features from levels other that phonology and the lexicon. Moreover, in contrast to some of the earlier studies, the Black ASL project was based on data derived from video recordings of actual signing.

Researchers from the Black ASL project collected data in six of the seventeen states that had formerly segregated schools. These research sites were in Talladega, Alabama; Little Rock, Arkansas; New Orleans, Louisiana; Raleigh, North Carolina; Houston, Texas; and Hampton, Virginia. Sites were selected to represent a broad range, geographically as well as in the dates when schools were founded and when they were integrated. The signers at each of the six sites were identified and recruited by contact persons, who were similar to the *brokers* described by Milroy, that is, individuals who "have contacts with large numbers of individuals" in the community (1987, 70). Although we used the techniques of the sociolinguistic interview developed by Labov (1972, 1984), we needed to be careful with ASL users' sensitivity to an interviewer's audiological status (i.e., hearing or deaf) and ethnicity (i.e., Black or White). This sensitivity may be manifested by rapid switching from ASL to *Signed English* (a manual code for English) or *Contact Signing* (an outcome of the contact between ASL and English characterized by core features from both languages and continuous voiceless mouthing) to accommodate the perceived communication style (Hill 2012) of interlocutors based on their audiological status (Lucas and Valli 1992) and ethnicity (Rickford and McNair-Knox 1994). The sensitivity to an interviewer's presence and social characteristic is related to the Observer's Paradox, as described by Labov (1972). For this study, Black signers were recorded with no White researchers present and interviewed by a Black Deaf interviewer in an attempt to minimize the effect of the Observer's Paradox.

Participants at each of the six sites include members of the local Black Deaf community, selected to represent two general age groups: "55 and over" and "35 and under." Because Deaf families are traditionally held in high esteem in the community, attempts were made to recruit their members as participants. Of the total number of participants for whom we have demographic data, nine are from Deaf families. The older participants, all of whom had attended segregated schools, related the history of the schools during segregation and provided a basis for contrast with the younger signers, who had attended integrated schools. Seventy-six signers were interviewed and filmed in four settings. Because research has shown that different genres, that is, *narrative* or *conversation*, may result in significant differences in use of variable linguistic forms (Bayley, Lucas, and Rose 2000; Jia and Bayley 2002; Travis 2007), we collected data representing a number of different genres: thirty to forty minutes of free conversation among signers without researchers present; thirty- to forty-minute interviews with Black Deaf interviewers; and ten to twenty minutes of lexical elicitation with cue cards for specific signs. The Black ASL database also includes a sampling of twenty conference attendees filmed at the 2007 National Black Deaf Advocates (NBDA) conference. These signers did not participate in formal interviews but engaged in casual conversations and told narratives in the course of the conversations. (See table 16.2 for more information.)

Table 16.2 Participant Characteristics

	35 years and younger		55 years and older		
	Female	Male	Female	Male	Total
Alabama	2	4	5	3	14
Arkansas	3	3	5	6	17
Louisiana	1	4	4	2	11
North Carolina	3	4	4	3	14
Texas	2	1	3	2	8
Virginia	2	3	4	3	12
NBDA	0	0	14	6	20
Total	13	19	39	25	96

Source: McCaskill et al. 2011, 53.

16.2 Linguistic Features

The main challenge in the Black ASL project was to identify and to analyze the specific linguistic features that might make up a distinct variety of Black ASL and to compare the use of the features in the production of Black and White signers. We chose eight features for analysis, in the areas of phonology, lexicon, syntax and discourse, and language contact. Although there may well be other areas where Black and White ASL varieties differ, these eight features were most striking in the available data. Phonological data were subjected to multivariate analysis with GoldVarb, the most commonly used program for quantitative analysis in sociolinguistics (Bayley 2013; Tagliamonte 2006). Data related to the other linguistic features were quantified and described in terms of frequency.

16.2.1 Phonology

We examined three phonological variables: the handedness of ASL signs that can be produced with one or two hands, the location of signs that are usually produced on the forehead but sometimes produced at a lower level, and the size of the signing space. All three variables have been explored in previous studies of ASL (Aramburo 1989; Lewis et al. 1995; Lucas et al. 2007; Lucas, Bayley, and Valli 2001; Lucas et al. 2002; Mauk and Tyrone 2008) and, in the case of the lowering of signs, in Australian and New Zealand Sign Languages as well (Schembri et al. 2009).

16.2.1.1 *Handedness*

Some two-handed signs can be produced with only one hand without detracting from their meaning, while producing other two-handed signs with only one hand may cause misunderstanding. For example, the ASL sign DEER[3] can be produced with one or two hands, since both variants refer to the same creature. In contrast, the sign ROUGH requires two hands to make sense. Battison (1978) observes that signers' choices between one-handed and two-handed variants are constrained by two morpheme structure conditions: the Symmetry Condition and the Dominance Condition. Battison states:

> the Symmetry Condition holds that if both hands move independently during a given two-handed sign (as opposed to one or both being static), then the specifications for handshape and movement must be identical. . . . The Dominance Condition is an implicational statement that works from the other direction. For those signs which have *non-identical* handshapes, one hand must remain static, while the other, usually the dominant one, executes the movement. (1974, 5–6)

Two-handed signs that permit the deletion of one hand were the focus of analysis in the Black ASL Project. The two-handed versions are the citation, or dictionary, forms that can be found in ASL dictionaries and are therefore considered standard or conservative variants.

Results of multivariate analysis show that Black Deaf signers' choices between one-handed and two-handed variants of target signs are systematic and constrained by both linguistic and social factors (see table 16.3 and figure 16.1). Significant linguistic constraints include the handedness of the preceding and following signs and contact with the face or body. That is, if the preceding or following sign is produced with two hands, the two-handed variant is more likely to be chosen. However, if the preceding or following sign is produced with one hand, signers tend to choose the one-handed variant. In addition, contact of the target sign with the face or body favors the one-handed form, although this constraint is not as strong as the preceding and following environment. As for the social factors, only age (and, by implication, the type of school attended) had a significant effect. Older signers, who attended segregated schools, were more likely to use the two-handed variants. Younger signers, who attended school after integration, were more likely to use the one-handed variant, but in each case, the younger Black signers used fewer one-handed variants than the younger White signers, who used the one-handed variant in 60 percent of the tokens. In terms of region, White signers used a higher percentage of one-handed signs than Black signers in the same region. Based on the frequent use of two-handed variants, Black signers exhibited their preference for this particular form, which is considered standard in ASL. Figure 16.1 summarizes the results from four studies of this variable.

16.2.1.2 *Location*

The location at which a sign is produced is one of the parameters that characterize signs. The signs of the class of which KNOW is a typical example share features of location and hand placement. In citation form, signs of this class are produced at the forehead or temple. In addition to KNOW, examples include verbs of perception and thinking (e.g., BELIEVE, DECIDE), nouns (e.g., DEER, FATHER), prepositions (i.e., FOR), and interrogatives (e.g., WHY). Figure 16.2 shows the citation and lowered variants of the sign TEACHER. Signs produced at the forehead can be lowered; the lowering is systematic

Table 16.3 Two–Handed versus One–Handed Signs (Application Value = One–Handed)

Factor group	Factor	N	Percentage 1 hand	Weight	Range
Following sign	1 handed	256	45.3	.598	
	Pause	288	33.0	.492	
	2 handed	274	26.6	.416	.182
Preceding sign	Pause or 1 handed	565	49.6	.554	
	2 handed	253	23.7	.381	.173
Contact	Contact	286	44.8	.603	
	No contact	532	29.3	.444	.159
Age	35 and younger	349	39.5	.552	
	55 and older	469	31.1	.461	.091
Total	Input	818	34.7	.336	

Note: Log likelihood = –497.783, chi-square/cell–0.0963.
Source: McCaskill et al. 2011, 83.

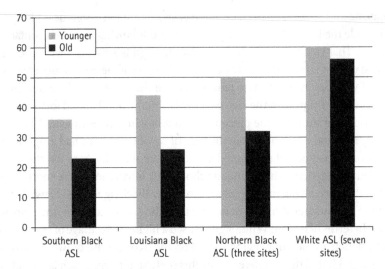

FIGURE 16.1 One-handed versus two-handed signs: comparison of results for Southern Black ASL, Louisiana Black ASL, Northern Black ASL, and White ASL (percentage one-handed).

> *Notes:* The Southern Black ASL data are from McCaskill et al. (2011). The Louisiana Black ASL results are from Bayley and Lucas (in press). The Northern Black ASL results are from signers in California, Massachusetts, and Missouri who participated in the study reported in Lucas, Bayley, and Valli (2001). The White ASL results are from signers in California, Kansas, Louisiana, Maryland, Massachusetts, Virginia, and Washington State are from Lucas et al. (2007).

> *Source:* McCaskill et al. 2011, 85.

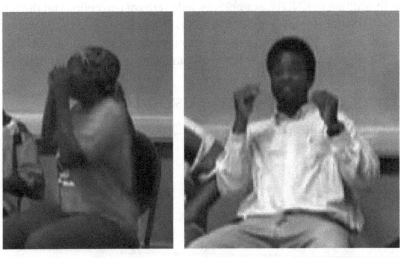

FIGURE 16.2 ASL sign, TEACHER, in citation (right) and lowered (left) form.

> *Source:* McCaskill et al. 2011, 87.

and subject to complex linguistic and social constraints as demonstrated in the studies of sign languages in the United States, Australia, and New Zealand (Frishberg 1975; Lucas, Bayley, and Valli 2001; Lucas et al. 2002; Schembri et al. 2009).

With respect to linguistic constraints, the results (see table 16.4) show that the grammatical category (e.g., compound, noun, proposition/interrogative, adjective/adverb,

Table 16.4 Location: Linguistic Constraints (Application Value = –cf, Lowered Variant)

Factor group	Factor	N	Percentage	Weight	Range
Grammatical category	Compound	47	48.9	.716	
	Noun	111	39.6	.602	
	Preposition/ interrog.	107	35.3	.582	
	Adjective/adverb	60	21.7	.464	
	Verb	552	25.0	.448	.268
Preceding contact	Body, contact	150	29.3	.562	
	Body, no contact	419	27.7	.505	
	Head, contact	106	26.4	.492	
	Head, no contact	54	22.2	.379	.183
Total	Input	877	29.2	.260	

Notes: Log likelihood = –496.154, chi-square/cell = 0.9314.
Source: McCaskill et al. 2011, 93.

and verb, in that order) is a major constraint, a result that parallels earlier work among Black and White signers reported in Lucas, Bayley, and Valli (2001). Whether the preceding sign contacts the head or the body also significantly affects the observed variation. When the preceding sign contacts the body, a signer is more likely to choose the lowered variant. When the preceding sign is at the level of the head with no contact, a signer is less likely to choose the lowered variant (see figure 16.2). Signs where the preceding sign has no contact with the body or contact with the head cover the great majority of tokens that we examined and constitute nearly neutral reference points.

Social factors also significantly affected Black and White signers' choices between the citation and the lowered variants. Region significantly affected the signers' choice of variants, with Texans favoring the lowered variants, Arkansans and Louisianans disfavoring the lowered variants, and signers in other states having intermediate values. Age also significantly affected the choice between the two variants in the expected direction. Younger Black signers, who attended school after integration, were more likely to select a lowered form than older Black signers, who had attended segregated schools. Overall, Black signers produced fewer lowered, or non-citation, variants than the White signers reported on in Lucas, Bayley, and Valli (2001) (see table 16.5).

16.2.1.3 *Size of the Signing Space*

One of the anecdotal observations about Black ASL is that it uses a larger signing space, that is, signs extend beyond the usual signing space that covers the area from the top of the head to the waist, from shoulder to shoulder, and a foot in front of the signer. For the Black ASL Project, researchers collected videos of free narratives and cartoon retellings

Table 16.5 Location: Social Constraints (Application Value = −cf, Lowered Variant)

Factor group	Factor	N	Percentage	Weight	Range
State	Texas	140	43.6	.650	
	Alabama, North Carolina, Virginia	454	28.6	.529	
	Arkansas, Louisiana	283	23.0	.405	.245
Age	35 and younger	390	36.4	.587	
	55 and older	487	23.4	.430	.157
Total	Input	877	29.2	.260	

Note: Log likelihood = −496.154, chi-square/cell = 0.9314.
Source: McCaskill et al. 2011, 95.

created by both Black and White signers and, for the video of each signer, superimposed a grid covering the area of signing space. The EUDICO Linguistic Annotator (ELAN) system was used to code the unmarked (i.e., normal signing area) and marked (i.e., extending beyond the usual signing area) spaces on the grid. Linguistic analysis focused on the grammatical category of the sign (noun, adjective/adverb verb [plain, depiction, locative, and indicating], grammatical function sign). Verb types had to be analyzed separately because the dynamic verbs (depiction, locative, and indicating), for example, THROW-BALL and YOU-GIVE-ME, may exploit more signing space than do plain verbs (verbs whose structure provides no indication of person), for example, THINK and HUNGRY (Padden 1988). The relative intensity of the production of a sign, with noticeable tension in the arms, the torso possibly leaning forward, and signing with furrowed eyebrows and a direct gaze at the co-interlocutor, was also coded.

Results of multivariate analysis showed that the order of factors in the grammatical function factor group was similar for Black and White signers (see figure 16.3). Also, the intensity factor group showed similar results for both Black and White signers. Intensity proved to be the first-order constraint in all of the analyses. As hypothesized, signs produced with indications of greater intensity were more likely to extend beyond the usual signing space.

Turning to social factors, both Black and White signers produced most of the 2,247 signs coded within the usual signing space, but Black signers produced a higher percentage of the variants that exceeded the unmarked signing space (see table 16.6). As for gender, in both Black and White groups, women are less likely to use a larger signing space than men. Although older Black signers produced a slightly higher percentage of marked variants, the difference between the older and the younger Black groups was not greater than what could be attributed to chance. However, for the White signers, the difference was highly significant, with 28.5 percent of the marked variants produced by older White signers in contrast to 40 percent of the marked variants produced by the younger White signers. It appears that younger White signers may be signing more like Black signers than like the older White signers, a finding that parallels recent research among hearing adolescents in the United States (see Bucholtz 1999) (see figure 16.4).

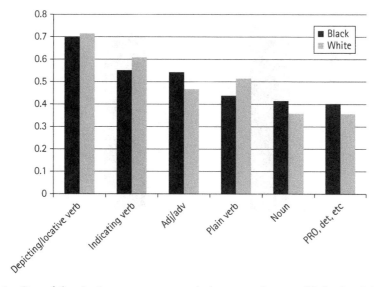

FIGURE 16.3 Size of the signing space: grammatical category by race (Varbrul weights, application value, beyond the unmarked space).

Source: McCaskill et al. 2011, 101.

Table 16.6 Size of the Signing Space: Distribution of Variants by Race

Variant	Black		White		Total	
	N	%	*N*	%	*N*	%
Unmarked	671	58.5	724	65.8	1395	62.1
A foot away from the side of the body	322	28.1	268	24.4	590	26.3
More than a foot away from the side of the body	87	7.6	49	4.5	136	6.1
Above the top of the head	43	3.7	36	3.3	79	3.5
Below the waist	24	2.1	23	2.1	47	2.1

Source: McCaskill et al. 2011, 100.

16.2.2 Syntax and Discourse

In examining Black ASL syntax and discourse, we focus on the use of repetition and the use of constructed action and constructed dialogue.

16.2.2.1 *Repetition*

Repetition refers to the complete repetition of a single sign or a phrase by one signer within one turn. The use of repetition in ASL and other sign languages has been

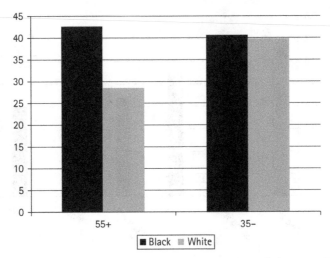

FIGURE 16.4 Size of the signing space by race (percentage beyond the unmarked space).

Source: McCaskill et al. 2011, 105.

discussed by other researchers, mainly in the context of Chomskyan analyses of WH-movement. Petronio and Lillo-Martin (1997) mention "a very commonly found type of ASL WH-question, in which a WH-element is found both sentence initially and sentence finally," for example, "WHO LIKE NANCY WHO" (26). However, in the Black ASL project, we found evidence that repetition can also serve a pragmatic function, with the repetitions usually consisting of declarative statements rather than questions, for example, "HATE ATLANTA, HATE ATLANTA, PRO.1 HATE ATLANTA." Moreover, frequent use of repetition is a feature that distinguishes Black signers, especially older signers, from White signers. This is an interesting change in the Black population, with more repetition among the older signers than among the younger signers. This repetition may have been a feature in earlier White ASL that has diminished over generations.

16.2.2.2 *Discourse Constructions*

A variety of studies have examined constructed action (CA) and constructed dialogue (CD), commonly referred to as "taking a role." As Metzger (1995) explains, CA and CD are the ways that signers take a role by using "their body, head and eye gaze to report the actions, thoughts, words and expressions of characters within a discourse" (256). Dudis (2004) has also examined this phenomenon with a focus on real-space blends and of body partitioning, whereby "different parts of [a] signer's body [are] projected as separate visible real-space elements into their respective blends" (225). There is some indication from previous research that Black signers may use more CA and CD than White signers (Metzger and Mather 2004). Therefore, in the Black ASL Project, we examined free narratives and cartoon retellings to see if indeed there was a difference between Black and White signers in the use of these two features. Results indicated that there were no striking differences in the number of units of CA and CD, individually or in combination, produced by White and Black signers in the cartoon narratives (see figures 16.5 and 16.6). However, in the free narratives, older signers, both Black and White, used simple narrative more than did the younger signers. Older White signers supplied more units of CA than older Black signers, while the narratives of older Black signers had more instances of CD. Due to the extent of individual variation in the data, we can only conclude that this is an area that merits further investigation.

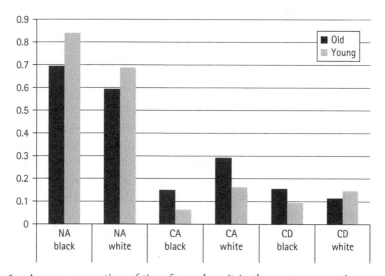

FIGURE 16.5 Average proportion of time for each unit in the cartoon narratives.

Note: NA, no constructed action (CA) or dialogue (CD).

Source: McCaskill et al. 2011: 124.

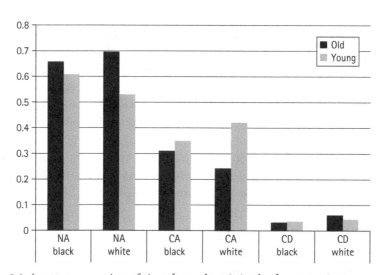

FIGURE 16.6 Average proportion of time for each unit in the free narratives.

Note: NA, no constructed action (CA) or dialogue (CD).

Source: McCaskill et al. 2011, 125.

16.3 LANGUAGE CONTACT

Given the fact that most Black Deaf people, like all other Deaf people, are usually born to hearing families and can hardly avoid contact with the variety of the language of the hearing majority, contact between spoken English, particularly AAE, and Black ASL, is an area of investigation that promises interesting results. The Black ASL project focused on two features: the use of voiceless mouthing and the incorporation of AAE into the signing of Deaf Black signers.

16.3.1 Mouthing

The general claim is that Black signers use mouthing less than White signers (Tabak 2006). Voiceless mouthing has been extensively examined in the sign language research literature, but the subjects in the studies are mostly European signers living in European countries who use a variety of sign languages (Boyes Braem and Sutton-Spence 2001). In studying mouthing in sign languages, an important distinction must be made about two kinds of voiceless mouthing: *mouthing* (i.e., events that are derived from the spoken language) and *mouth gestures* (i.e., events that are part of the sign language and have no relation to the spoken language). For example, in ASL, the former can be illustrated with the mouth configuration *f-sh*, which might accompany the sign FINISH. This mouthing might be more complete, such that a signer might silently mouth a whole English word. A good example of a mouth gesture, on the other hand, would be the voiceless mouth configuration *pah* that accompanies the sign glossed as FINALLY or AT LAST. This configuration is indigenous to the sign language and has no relation to any English word. Our focus here is the mouthing of English words.

As other researchers have found with voiceless mouthing (Boyes Braem and Sutton-Spence 2001), we also found that among Black ASL signers, nouns were the most frequently mouthed, followed by plain verbs and predicates, phrases, and finally adjectives and adverbs (see table 16.7). Also, the data for the Black ASL project contain a number of phrases mouthed by young Black signers. Overall, older Black signers mouth markedly less than young Black signers and White signers in both age groups. In the younger Black group, there is also a gender effect. Young women tended to mouth continuously, while men tended to mouth intermittently. However, the results come from a small sample of a large corpus and are therefore necessarily tentative. As in the case of CA and CD, mouthing is an area in need of further investigation.

16.3.2 Incorporation of AAE

Generally, sign languages are in contact with spoken languages in respective communities, so it is natural for sign languages to incorporate some elements from spoken

Table 16.7 Mouthing by Grammatical Class/Function, Race, Age, and Gender

Signer	Noun	Adj/adv	Verb/ predicate	WH	Function word	Phrase	Token response	Total
OBM	22	8	13	3	0	0	0	46
OBF	11	6	25	3	4	0	0	49
YBM	24	11	15	1	0	13	0	64
YBF	6	9	3	1	4	16	0	39
Subtotal	63	34	56	8	8	29	0	198
OWM	3	0	2	0	1	0	0	6
OWF	*	*	*	*	*	*	*	*
YWM	6	0	1	0	2	8	0	17
YWF	*	*	*	*	*	*	*	*
Subtotal	9	0	3	0	3	8	0	23
Total	72	34	59	8	11	37	0	221

Notes: OBM = old, Black, male; OBF = old, Black, female, OWM = old, White, male, OWF = old, White, female, YBM = young, Black, male, YBF = young, Black, female, YWM = young, White, male, YWF = young, White, female, * = no data.
Source: McCaskill et al. 2011, 130.

languages (e.g., words, phrases, syntactic structure, mouthing, and discourse markers). Since Black signers have been part of the Black community in which some members use AAE, the extent to which AAE is incorporated into Black ASL deserves special attention.

In response to the interview questions, "Do you think that Black signing is different from White signing?" and "Do Black people sign differently than White people?" many more younger participants in the Black ASL project provided examples that were indicative of AAE than did older signers, who gave the examples of the signs they used in school. This makes sense because with the advances in technology and the increased attendance of younger signers in mainstream schools, the younger signers have had much more exposure to the use of AAE through movies and the media of various kinds as well as their personal contact with AAE speakers.

One example is the phrase *stop trippin'*, which appears in Black ASL as "TRIP (head) FINISH" with TRIP signed on the head. TRIP (head) is similar to TRIP with a crooked V handshape; the location is produced on the forehead to signify the mental meaning. The phrases "STUPID FOOL" and "GIRL, PLEASE" were also offered by the signers. In addition, younger participants demonstrated their perception of Black signing style by shifting their bodies markedly to one side, exaggerating the movement and expanding the size of the signing space. For example, the sign WHASSUP?

was produced in Black signing style with a slow upward movement and a larger use of space. Another example is a lexicalized fingerspelling of the English word *dang*, #DANG.[4] One signer produced it at the waist level, well below the usual fingerspelling area in front of the shoulder, and moved her body forward for emphasis as she was signing. Finally, in a discussion with the interviewer about Black signs, the participants signed and discussed the Black version of MY BAD, an S handshape with the palm down contacting the upper side of the chest with repeated movement, similar to QUALIFIED. One participant contrasted this with how White signers might sign it, that is, the sign MY and the sign BAD in sequence, as opposed to the separate lexical item shown by the Black signers. Figures 16.6 through 16.9 show a number of borrowings from AAE. Figures 16.7a and 16.7b illustrate two versions of TRIPPING. Figures 16.8 and 16.9 illustrate WHASSUP and GIRL PLEASE, while Figures 16.10(a) and 16.10(b) show MY BAD.

FIGURE 16.7(a) TRIPPING, forehead with movement out.

FIGURE 16.7(b) TRIPPING, forehead, short repeated movement, no movement out.

FIGURE 16.8 WHASSUP?

FIGURE 16.9 GIRL PLEASE.

16.3.3 Lexicon

Users of Black ASL recognize differences between Black signing and White signing and Black signers do incorporate lexical items, phrases, and gestures from AAE into their signing. In the data for the Black ASL project, we also observed lexical variation that the participants spontaneously produced or discussed during the free conversation part of the filming. We also observed lexical variation in the signs the participants produced in response to the interview questions about the difference in signs between Black and White signers, signs that are no longer used, and unique regional signs. It must be noted

FIGURE 16.10(a) MY BAD (male).

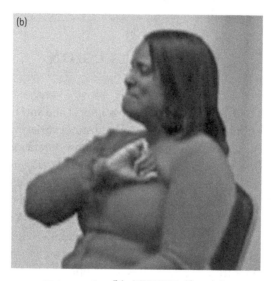

FIGURE 16.10(b) MY BAD (female).

this is not a systematic comparison of the signs used by Black signers and White signers because the signs reported in the study may also be regional variants used by signers of all races. Nevertheless, Black signers perceived the signs they provided and discussed as part of Black ASL.

In response to the questions or during the free conversations, the older signers often produced signs in the noun and predicate categories that were different from those used at the White school, for example, MOVIE, CORNBREAD, STORE, BLACK, WHITE, FLIRT, and STEAL. They also produced older signs and compared them with newer signs. In contrast, the younger Black signers did not produce the signs used by the older signers. Rather, they either produced the signs used in their own regions or lexical items and phrases adopted from AAE. This suggests that old signs have fallen out of use.

In addition to the study of the lexicon, we examined signs studied earlier by Woodward, Erting, and Oliver (1976), who compared Black and White signers to observe a change in a subset of signs (including MOVIE, RABBIT, LEMON, COLOR, PEACH, and PEANUT) that could be either produced on the face or on the hands. Woodward et al. found that Black signers used more of the hand variants than White signers, who tended to favor face variants. In the Black ASL Project, we used cue cards to elicit the subset of signs from the participants and looked at the frequency of face and hand variants in their *first* responses. Nearly all of the younger and older signers produced the face variants of COLOR and LEMON, which differs from earlier results. Some older signers still produced the hand variants of PEACH and PEANUT, but younger signers did not. The older face variant of MOVIE was still used by half of the older signers, but younger signers used the hand variant. Most signers produced the hand variant of RABBIT. As for AFRICA, most younger signers produced the hand variant and most older signers produced the face variant. Results such as these suggest that lexical change is ongoing.

16.4 CONCLUSION

Research carried out to date has linked the geographical and social isolation of residential schools in the South to the development of a distinct variety of ASL, characterized by, among other things, more two-handed signs, more forehead level signs, a larger signing space, more repetition, possibly more constructed dialogue, less mouthing, and lexical differences. However, there are also Black Deaf communities outside of the South whose signing has distinctive features. This fact indicates a need to expand the pool of signers to make the data available for comparison. Also, as with any language or language variety, other features are doubtless worthy of analysis. One example we can give is prosody in signing. We have observed that Black Deaf signers move their heads and torsos in ways that differ from White signers. In addition, the rate of signing appears to differ as well.

In the course of researching Black ASL and presenting the results to the public, we have become aware of different issues that need to be addressed. These issues include the current geographical and social factors that maintain Black ASL, the number of Black Deaf families and their primary means of communication, the geographical and social factors in the history of Black ASL in different regions of the United States outside of the South, variation of AAE forms in Black ASL in different Black Deaf communities, the register of Black ASL used in specific settings with different interlocutors, the perceptions of and attitudes toward Black ASL expressed by Black Deaf signers and other signers, and the borrowing of Black ASL forms into mainstream ASL. Finally, we suggest that work on Black ASL has implications that extend beyond research on sign languages. First, because residential schools for the Deaf have long been instrumental in transmitting ASL and Deaf culture, research on Black ASL requires a close examination of an understudied aspect of African American history, the education of Deaf African Americans in the South both before and after segregation. Second, in the case of a number of the variables examined here, for example, the location of signs such as KNOW or the use of two-handed variants of signs that can also be produced with one hand, Black ASL, particularly as used by older signers, is closer to the standard variety taught in ASL classes and codified in ASL dictionaries than the ASL of many White communities. Thus, Black ASL directly contradicts deficit models of African American Language. Of course, there are more implications than these, but the important thing is that we know that Black ASL is a distinct variety of ASL, and it is truly a treasure to uncover. It deserves to be acknowledged, researched, and shared.

NOTES

1. The terms used to describe the English dialect spoken informally by many African Americans in homes, communities, churches, etc. have varied considerably over the years, from *Black English Vernacular* to *African American Vernacular English* to *African American English*. We have chosen to follow the contemporary usage of scholars such as Green (2011) and Charity Hudley and Mallinson (2011) and used the term *African American English* to refer to this dialect, which is characterized by phonological, grammatical, and lexical features that are distinct from those of Standard American English.
2. The use of uppercase *Deaf* indicates cultural deafness, as opposed to the strictly audiological condition indicated by lowercase *deaf*. Both uses are conventional in the literature on deafness.
3. By convention, ASL signs are written in capital letters. Thus, DEER refers to the ASL sign, not to the corresponding English word.
4. The symbol # used with an ASL gloss represents a lexicalized fingerspelling; a fingerspelled word behaves more like a single sign rather than individual signs representing each letter.

REFERENCES

Aramburo, Anthony. 1989. "Sociolinguistic Aspects of the Black Deaf Community." *The Sociolinguistics of the Deaf Community*, edited by Ceil Lucas, 103–22. New York: Academic.

Battison, Robbin. 1974. "Phonological Deletion in American Sign Language." *Sign Language Studies* 5: 1–19.

———. 1978. *Lexical Borrowing in American Sign Language*. Silver Spring, MD: Linstok.

Bayley, Robert. 2013. "The Quantitative Paradigm." *The Handbook of Language Variation and Change*, 2nd ed., edited by Jack K. Chambers and Natalie Schilling, 85–107. Malden, MA: Wiley-Blackwell.

Bayley, Robert, and Ceil Lucas. In press. "Phonological Variation in Louisiana ASL: An Exploratory Study." *New Perspectives on Language Variety in the South: Historical and Contemporary Approaches*, edited by Michael Picone and Catherine Evans Davies. Tuscaloosa: University of Alabama Press.

Bayley, Robert, Ceil Lucas, and Mary Rose. 2000. "Variation in American Sign Language: The Case of DEAF." *Journal of Sociolinguistics* 4: 81–107.

Boyes Braem, Penny, and Rachel Sutton-Spence, eds. *The Hands Are the Head of the Mouth.* Hamburg: Signum-Verlag, 2001.

Bucholtz, Mary. 1999. "'You Da Man': Narrating the Racial Other in the Production of White Masculinity." *Journal of Sociolinguistics* 3: 443–60.

Burch, Susan. 2002. *Signs of Resistance: American Deaf Cultural History 1900–1942.* New York: New York University Press.

Burch, Susan, and Hannah Joyner. 2007. *Unspeakable: The Story of Junius Wilson.* Chapel Hill: University of North Carolina Press.

Charity Hudley, Anne H., and Christine Mallinson. 2011. *Understanding English Language Variation in U.S. Schools.* New York: Teachers College Press.

Croneberg, Carl G. 1965. "Appendix D: Sign Language Dialects." *A Dictionary of American Sign Language,* edited by William C. Stokoe, Dorothy C. Casterline, and Carl G. Croneberg, 313–19. Silver Spring, MD: Linstok.

Doctor, Powrie V. 1948. "Deaf Negroes Get a Break in Education." *The Silent Worker,* 45–50.

Dudis, Paul. 2004. "Body Partitioning and Real-Space Blends." *Cognitive Linguistics* 15: 223–38.

Frishberg, Nancy. 1975. "Arbitrariness and Iconicity: Historical Change in American Sign Language." *Language* 51: 696–719.

Green, Lisa J. 2011. *Language and the African American Child.* Cambridge: Cambridge University Press.

Guggenheim, Laurie. 1993. "Ethnic Variation in ASL: The Signing of African Americans and How It Is Influenced by Topic." *Communication Forum,* edited by Elizabeth Winston, 51–76. Washington, DC: School of Communication, Gallaudet University.

Hairston, Ernest, and Linwood Smith. 1983. *Black and Deaf in America: Are We That Different?* Silver Spring, MD: TJ Publishers.

Hill, Joseph. 2012. *Language Attitudes in the American Deaf Community.* Washington, DC: Gallaudet University Press.

Jia, Li, and Robert Bayley. 2002. "Null Pronoun Variation in Mandarin Chinese." *University of Pennsylvania Working Papers in Linguistics* 8 (3): 103–16.

Labov, William. 1972. *Sociolinguistic Patterns.* Philadelphia: University of Pennsylvania Press.

———. 1984. "Field Methods of the Project on Language Variation and Change." *Language in Use: Readings in Sociolinguistics,* edited by John Baugh and Joel Sherzer, 28–53. Englewood Cliffs, NJ: Prentice Hall.

Lewis, John. 1998. "Ebonics in American Sign Language: Stylistic Variation in African American Signers." *Deaf Studies V: Toward 2000: Unity and Diversity* Conference proceedings, April 17–20, 1997, edited by C. Carroll, 229–40. Washington, DC: College for Continuing Education, Gallaudet University.

Lewis, John, Carrie Palmer, and Leandra Williams. 1995. "Existence of and Attitudes toward Black Variations of Sign Language." *Communication Forum* 1995, edited by Laura Byers, Jessica Chaiken, and Monica Mueller, 17–48. Washington, DC: School of Communication, Gallaudet University.

Lucas, Ceil, Robert Bayley, Ruth Reed, and Alyssa Wulf. 2001. "Lexical Variation in African American and White Signing." *American Speech* 76: 339–60.

Lucas, Ceil, Robert Bayley, Mary Rose, and Alyssa Wulf. 2002. "Location Variation in American Sign Language." *Sign Language Studies* 2: 407–40.

Lucas, Ceil, Robert Bayley, and Clayton Valli. 2001. *Sociolinguistic Variation in American Sign Language*. Washington, DC: Gallaudet University Press.

Lucas, Ceil, Amber Goeke, Rebecca Briesacher, and Robert Bayley. 2007. "Variation in ASL: 2 Hands or 1?" Paper presented at the Conference on New Ways of Analyzing Variation 36, Philadelphia, Pennsylvania, October 11–14.

Lucas, Ceil, and Clayton Valli. 1992. *Language Contact in the American Deaf Community*. Washington, DC: Gallaudet University Press.

Mauk, Claude E., and Martha E. Tyrone. 2008. "Sign Lowering as Phonetic Reduction in American Sign Language." *International Seminar on Speech Production 2008: Proceedings*, edited by Rudolph Sock, Susanne Fuchs, and Yves Laprie, 185–88. Strasbourg: INRIA.

McCaskill, Carolyn, Ceil Lucas, Robert Bayley, and Joseph Hill. 2011. *The Hidden Treasure of Black ASL: Its History and Structure*. Washington, DC: Gallaudet University Press, 2011.

Metzger, Melanie. 1995. "Constructed Dialogue and Constructed Action in American Sign Language." *Sociolinguistics in Deaf Communities*, edited by Ceil Lucas, 255–71. Washington, DC: Gallaudet University Press.

Metzger, Melanie, and Susan Mather. 2004. "Constructed Dialogue and Constructed Action in Conversational Narratives in ASL." Poster presented at the Conference on Theoretical Issues in Sign Language Research (TISLR 8), Barcelona, September 30–October 2.

Milroy, Lesley. 1987. *Language and Social Networks*. 2nd ed. Oxford: Blackwell.

Padden, Carol. 1988. *The Interaction of Morphology and Syntax in American Sign Language*. New York: Garland.

Petronio, Karen, and Diane Lillo-Martin. 1997. "WH-movement and the Position of SPEC-CP: Evidence from American Sign Language." *Language* 73: 18–57.

Rickford, John R. 1999. *African American Vernacular English: Features, Evolution, Educational Implications*. Oxford: Blackwell.

Rickford, John R., and Faye McNair-Knox. 1994. "Addressee- and Topic-influenced Style Shift: A Quantitative Sociolinguistic Study." *Sociolinguistic Perspectives on Register*, edited by Douglas Biber and Edward Finegan, 235–76. New York: Oxford University Press.

Schembri, Adam, David McKee, Rachel McKee, Sara Pivac, Trevor Johnston, and Della Goswell. 2009. "Phonological Variation and Change in Australian and New Zealand Sign Languages: The Location Variable." *Language Variation and Change* 21: 193–231.

Tabak, John. 2006. *Significant Gestures: A History of American Sign Language*. Westport, CT: Praeger.

Tagliamonte, Sali A. 2006. *Analysing Sociolinguistic Variation*. New York: Cambridge University Press.

Travis, Catherine. 2007. "Genre Effects on Subject Expression in Spanish: Priming in Narrative and Conversation." *Language Variation and Change* 19: 101–33.

Wolfram, Walt, and Natalie Schilling-Estes. 2006. *American English: Dialects and Variation*. 2nd ed. Oxford: Blackwell.

Woodward, James, and Susan DeSantis. 1977. "Two to One It Happens: Dynamic Phonology in Two Sign Languages." *Sign Language Studies* 17: 329–46.

Woodward, James, Carol Erting, and Susana Oliver. 1976. "Facing and Hand(l)ing Variation in American Sign Language." *Sign Language Studies* 10: 43–52.

CHAPTER 17

THE SOCIOLINGUISTIC CONSTRUCTION OF AFRICAN AMERICAN LANGUAGE

WALT WOLFRAM

17.1 INTRODUCTION

IN one of the earliest television detective series, *Dragnet*, Officer Joe Friday, played by actor Jack Webb, popularized a couple of quotes that endured far longer than the series.[1] At the beginning of each episode, he would say, "My name is Friday—I'm a cop," and in each show he would question citizens by declaring, "All we want are the facts" or "Just the facts, ma'am." One might extend these dictums to sociolinguists who claim, "My name is X, I'm a sociolinguist, and I just report the facts." In reality, of course, *facts, data,* and *evidence* are socially constructed notions within linguistics, as they are in other fields of scientific inquiry, and the appeal to facts and data in the construction of a theory of language has been controversial for decades (Harder 2003). Some scientists prefer not to talk about "facts" because it is difficult to tell what is a fact and what isn't, and physicist Sean Carroll (2009) observes that "one might go so far as to argue that what counts as a 'fact' depends on one's theoretical framework."

The extensive description of African American Language (AAL) over the past half-century has led to a fairly well-established tradition of study and a particular set of sociolinguistic axioms; in fact, there now appears to be a sociolinguistic AAL canon (Wolfram 2011). A small, select set of descriptive works is routinely cited as primary sources for the description of AAL, beginning with some of the early structural descriptions within the variationist framework (see Labov et al. 1968; Wolfram 1969; Fasold 1972; Labov 1972) and progressing to current descriptions (see Baugh 1983; Rickford 1999; Green 2002). Of course, many earlier descriptive works (see Mitchell-Kernan 1969; Houston 1969; Legum et al. 1971) could just as well have been referenced as the works now considered to be the "landmark" descriptions. The extent to which sociolinguistics has reified a small set of primary descriptive studies was exemplified by a recent encounter with a graduate student whom I directed to one of the earlier works on AAL not usually referenced in current studies. After examining the description, he asked me why it hadn't been brought to his attention earlier. My immediate quip "Because it's not in the canon!" may have been more indicative and symbolic of a tradition of reification than I recognized at the time. Perhaps more important, my response may have unwittingly exposed an ideological stance on *how* AAL is defined, *what* is described, and *the way* it is presented.

In other presentations (Wolfram 2007, 2011), I have attempted to set forth some of the assumptions, approaches, and conclusions about the "facts" of AAL that have been filtered through an interpretive sociolinguistic lens. In fact, I have claimed (Wolfram 2007) that scholars have unwittingly participated in the creation of a type of sociolinguistic folklore about the nature of AAL, going so far as to refer to these as *sociolinguistic myths*. In making such a claim, I do not intend to be disrespectful of the substantive contributions sociolinguists have made to the description and understanding of AAL or to attribute misrepresentation and intentional deceit. And, I also confess that this discussion includes self-criticism. At the same time, critical scrutiny and reflexivity is an appropriate and productive exercise that should lead the study of AAL to a more informed, inclusive, and expansive direction as this variety continues to occupy its showcase research status in the field of sociolinguistics (Schneider 1996; Rickford et al. 2013).

17.2 SOCIOLINGUISTS AS IDEOLOGUES

Sociolinguists are well aware of the ideologies that frame vernacular varieties in popular culture. In fact, most sociolinguists who study AAL have spent considerable time and energy attempting to debunk widespread, erroneous assumptions and beliefs about this variety. Linguists have spoken as a forceful, unanimous voice against the application of the *principle of linguistic subordination* (Lippi-Green 2012) in popular culture and mainstream society. At the same time, it must be understood that linguists are not ideologically neutral; in fact, Johnson (2001, 606) notes that linguists "like all other interested social actors—are 'ideological brokers' bidding for authoritative entextualization, that is, trying to influence those readings of language debates which will eventually emerge as dominant." Milroy (2001, 624) observes that "claims that stand in opposition to popular ideologies will be recognized and interpreted by the public as ideological." Sociolinguists naturally justify their ideologies on the basis of rigorous, specialized expertise in the analysis of language as a kind of scientific inquiry. In this capacity, linguists have rendered an important professional and public service to counter the public folklore about AAL. But it must also be recognized that sociolinguists are not exempt from the interpretation of "facts" in a way that reflects their predisposition, social background, and experience. The selection and the framing of facts for the presentation and description of AAL may privilege some kinds of data and observations over others, and accordingly create a socially constructed description of the variety. The goal of this discussion is to scrutinize and question some of the descriptive "facts" that seem to have become canonized as the sociolinguistic stance on AAL.

I have suggested elsewhere (Wolfram 2007) that historical circumstance, professional entextualization, and ethnographic dissociation have led to some unwarranted claims about the status of AAL and that some of our current sociolinguistic axioms do not stand up to critical scrutiny. The pioneering descriptive studies of AAL launched in the 1960s concentrated on non-Southern, working-class urban areas despite the fact that the roots of contemporary AAL were established in the rural South. The restricted regional, demographic, and class focus set a precedent for describing and interpreting a number of facts about the sociolinguistic status of AAL, including the types of structures to be described and how they should be framed. These studies made an essential and significant contribution to our understanding of AAL, but they also reified a set of axioms about AAL that privileged certain speakers from particular social backgrounds and regions, leading to a kind of sociolinguistic nostalgia for the authentic vernacular speaker (Bucholtz 2003)—the most basilectal speaker. Though there have been some more recent efforts to counter this trend (Weldon 2004, forthcoming, this volume; Linnes 1998; Spears and Hinton 2010; Spears, this volume), the vernacular fixation has continued to the present.

As noted, sociolinguists have spent a lot of time countering public folklore and myths about the nature of AAL. Given the popular misunderstanding of the nature of language differences and the popular ideology that frames the interpretation of AAL, linguists have also become dismissive of public commentary about the status of AAL. But, in the process, they may have also developed a socialized immunity to alternative observations from within the community itself. The linguist-knows-best attitude thus may have ended up depriving sociolinguists of ethnographically valid observations about the status of AAL in time and place. Many of my early presentations on AAL to racially mixed or predominantly Black audiences were met with objections by African Americans about a definition of AAL that seemed dismissive of their experienced social and regional variation within the African American population. In retrospect, my disregard for such comments reflected a kind of ethnographic dissociation and academic elitism that deprived some ensuing sociolinguistic studies of potentially insightful observations variation within AAL.

It is time to reconsider critically some of our assumptions and conclusions about AAL that have been accepted as sociolinguistic truth. In the following sections, I consider—and challenge—some of the entrenched positions that have evolved since the emergence of AAL as the quintessential ethnic variety of American English. For convenience, these are discussed under major headings that include (1) definition; (2) structure; (3) change; and (4) variation.

17.3 DEFINITION

The varied labels AAL has been assigned over the last half-century are no doubt indicative of the controversy and ambiguity that has followed this variety. Among the labels since the 1960s in rough chronological order are Negro Dialect, Nonstandard Negro English, Black English, Vernacular Black English, Afro-American English, Ebonics,

African American (Vernacular) English, and African American Language. Labeling practices, of course, tend to fall in line with terminological trends evolving within the larger community (Rickford 1999, xxi) and are often a proxy for deeper sociopolitical and sociocultural issues and changing self-definitional tendencies (Smitherman 1991). At the same time, defining a linguistic variety is not simply a matter of terminological fashion, having consequences for its linguistic objectification, determining parameters of the speech community, and indexing social attributes of speakers—as well as emotive responses to the language variety. Some sociolinguists, for example, prefer not to use the term *Ebonics* because it "tends to evoke strong emotional reactions and has unfortunately given license to racist parodies of various types in recent years" (Wolfram and Schilling-Estes 2006, 211). As Spears and Hinton (2010, 5) note, "The Ebonics Controversy was a prime example of attitudes toward a group of people channeled through remarks about its language." Fasold (2000, 2001), on the other hand, defends the use of the variant *Ebonic* as a legitimate term for a linguistic entity constituting a language (cf. *Arabic, Icelandic, Aramaic,* and so on).

Most of the influential, early descriptions of AAL focused on the linguistic structure that distinguished it from idealized Mainstream American English (MAE) as well as from other dialects of English, with secondary reference to the social groups most likely to exhibit these structural traits. Thus, Fasold and Wolfram (1970, 42) observed that the distinctiveness of AAL "lies in the fact that it has a number of pronunciation and grammatical features that are not shared by other dialects."

The developing tradition of AAL description naturally has consequences for the social construction of AAL that has evolved over the decades. For example, these structural descriptions emphasize the uniformity of AAL vis-à-vis its variation in regional and social space. Labov (1972), thus, observes that it is "the relatively uniform dialect spoken by the majority of black young in most parts of the United States today. . . . It is also spoken in most rural areas and used in the casual, intimate speech of many adults" (xiii). One of the conclusions that emerged from the first wave of AAL descriptive studies was the observation that a common set of structural features represents the vernacular speech of African Americans. These features include a set of canonical morphosyntactic structures such as invariant *be* with a *habitual* denotation (e.g., They always *be* playing); the absence of copula and auxiliary *be* (e.g., She _ nice; she _ playing ball); verbal –*s* (e.g., She *play*_ ball); possessive –*s* (e.g., The *man*_ hat); and plural –*s* (e.g., Three *dog*_), as well as phonological structures such as syllable-coda prevocalic consonant cluster reduction (e.g., *Wes'* Africa); labialization of non-initial interdental fricatives (e.g., *baf* for *bath*); and postvocalic r-lessness (e.g., *fea'* for *fear*). The structurally based definition also privileged language structure in terms of phonology and morphosyntax when, in fact, there is no a priori reason that these levels of language index ethnolinguistic repertoire over discourse, narrative, and even lexical items (Smitherman 1977, 2001; Morgan 2002).

The apparent transregional distribution of a shared set of features in AAL seemed exceptional to sociolinguists familiar with regionally situated varieties of European American English, and the structural homogeneity of AAL rapidly became an assumed sociolinguistic axiom. Though empirical research does support a set of shared vernacular AAL structural features cross-regionally, further studies have also revealed considerable variability in the use of features that correlate with an array of social, regional, situational, and psychosocial factors. Even within the set of shared features that may unite AAL, there is great variability on an intra- and inter-community level that was overlooked or understated in "the illusion of homogeneity" (Bonfiglio 2002, 62).

The structural focus on the basilectal structures also has led to a restricted social definition of AAL, confining it to working-class, urban youth—the social and age group where the use of vernacular structures seemed to be the most extensive (see Van Hofwegen and Wolfram 2010). But that cohort is just one of the social groups within the speech community of African Americans who employ resources from an ethnolinguistic repertoire (Benor 2010). Furthermore, there is a continuum of use in terms of the structures that correlates with multifarious social, situational, and personal characteristics. The bias toward idealized vernacular structures clearly impeded the development of a more inclusive, representative definition of an ethnolinguistic speech community.

Finally, we should mention the controversy over the status of AAL as a dialect or language. Linguists are well aware of the fact that the difference between "dialect" and "language" is not definable by a set of structural properties or lack of intelligibility, but by the "the conviction that the linguistic system in question is a symbol of nationalist or ethnic identity" (Fasold 2000, 149). By the same token, dialect is, at best, used as a neutral term and, at worst, used to refer to a kind of deficient or "corrupted" English, a variety with little to no nationalistic capital (Wolfram and Schilling-Estes 2006, 3). Fasold (2001, 2) argues that the notion of 'a language' "is PURELY a social construct and that linguistic criteria play no role whatsoever"; instead, the role linguistic factors play is an epiphenomenon. In this context, there is less to gain from referring to AAL as a dialect (i.e., African American English) rather than a language, though there is still no consensus on the most felicitous term. For this discussion, it is more important to see how the ad hoc, traditional ways of defining AAL as a set of vernacular features distinct from MAE have unwittingly led to assumptions of homogeneity and vernacularity that do not reflect the sociolinguistic reality of the African American language community.

17.4 STRUCTURE

As noted above, it is commonly assumed that the vernacular core of AAL comprises an array of distinctive structural features that sets it apart from cohort European American vernacular varieties. The ordained list of features is primarily grammatical—the so-called *distinctively Black grammatical features* (DBGF)—and has routinely been cited as the foundational linguistic core of AAL. But even within grammar, there is a selection process that includes some structures while ignoring others. More subtle structures, so-called *camouflaged forms* that appear on the surface to be very much like those in other dialects of English but turn out, upon closer inspection, to have uses or meanings that are unique, have often been overlooked. Spears (1982) describes the case of *indignant come*, in which *come* in a construction with an *-ing* verb (e.g., She *come act-ing* like she was real mad) functions as a kind of auxiliary verb indicating annoyance or indignation on the part of the speaker. A different type of camouflaging (Wolfram 1994) is found in sentences such as *Walt call(s) himself dancing*, in which the counter-factual meaning of a shared MAE and AAL construction obscures the fact that AAL extends its verb complementation subcategorization rules to include V-*ing* construc-tions, unlike cohort European American varieties.

It should be noted further that the conventional reduction of AAL to an inventory of grammatical or phonological structures (see Fasold and Wolfram 1970; Rickford 1999) ignores the integrated, structural system of AAL. Syntacticians such as Green (2004) and Terry (2004), however, describe AAL in terms of its overall system of tense and aspect, and Labov (1998) demonstrates that its TMA (tense-mood-aspect) system needs to be described as a cohesive aspectual system rather than as an inventory of unre-lated grammatical markers. By the same token, Thomas (2007) describes the vowel sys-tem of AAL in terms of systematic shift within a subsystem of vowels rather than as a set of unrelated vowel differences.

Though the TMA system of AAL may be the site of its greatest structural divergence from other varieties of English, this does not mean that it carries the most socioethnic cap-ital, as is often assumed in most sociolinguistic descriptions. In fact, research on percep-tual cues (Graff, Labov, and Harris 1986; Thomas 2002; Thomas and Reaser 2004; Thomas 2007; Thomas and Bailey, this volume) suggests that ordinary listeners may be paying just as much, if not more, attention to other components of the AAL system as they are to mor-phosyntax in categorizing speakers ethnically. Phonetic cues that include vowel produc-tion and prosody may be just as important as morphosyntax for those who do not view language in terms of levels or components of organization. The myopic focus on structural morphosyntactic detail has also sometimes marginalized the essential role of discourse, conversational style, lexicon, and even narrative and poetics. As a number of language scholars (see Smitherman 1977; Morgan 2002; Lanehart 2002) have now pointed out, the distinctive attributes of AAL extend far beyond a set of grammatical patterns. We cannot simply assume that the levels of differentiation that emerge from our structural preoccu-pation on particular components of the AAL system are shared by ordinary listeners who make ethnic judgments based on speech as a routine part of their everyday interaction.

The focus on the most basilectal, vernacular grammar of AAL has another repercus-sion. It excludes a significant portion of the African American community, namely, those who are ethnically indexed but do not use vernacular structures as a regular part of their repertoire. As defined by Spears and Hinton (2010, 3), AAL (or in his nomenclature, "African American English") should refer to one language that unites many regional and social varieties of English used by African Americans. Among those varieties are African American Standard English, which is largely devoid of socially stigmatized grammatical features, though its speakers use some non-stigmatized, camouflaged syn-tactic forms (Spears 1982; Baugh 1984; Wolfram 1994) and bear some non-stigmatized phonological and phonetic traits (Farrington 2011), along with conversational and dis-course markers that index them ethnically.

17.5 VARIATION

AAL is highly variable, though it has sometimes been cast as a relatively uniform variety following Bonfiglio's "illusion of ethnic homogeneity" (2002, 62). Variation in terms of the basilect-acrolect continuum, regionality (see Wolfram and Kohn, this volume), social stratification, setting, and other sociopsychological factors can be extensive on an intra- and inter-speaker level. It may be highly variable over the lifespan as well (Van Hofwegen and Wolfram 2010; Rickford and Price 2013; Van Hofwegen, this volume).

Early in the study of AAL, it was noted that "social status is the single most important variable correlating with linguistic differences" and that "linguistic differentiation correlates more consistently with differences on the education and occupation scales than with the residency scales" (Wolfram 1969, 214). There is a corresponding assumption among sociolinguists that vernacular AAL is not spoken by middle-class African Americans so that there is a fairly straightforward social dichotomy in the use of vernacular AAL (Weldon 2004) and an idealized distinction between standard and vernacular AAL (see Spears 1999, this volume; Weldon 2004, this volume). The results of Weldon's (2004) study of language use by an accomplished group of nationally prominent African Americans is an important empirical step in examining a more representative spectrum of language variation by African Americans across social strata and in different social settings. Weldon's study exposes spurious dichotomies, including the nominal distinction between standard and vernacular African American English; it also raises questions about the role of personal presentation in public, including the extent of stylistic shift, performative code-switching, and the persistence of vernacular variants in the speech of some prominent African Americans in more formal public settings with mainstream, public audiences.

Kendall and Wolfram (2009) departs from the kinds of objective socioeconomic status indices traditionally applied in investigations of social stratification (see Wolfram 1969). Instead, they focus on a broadly defined linguistic marketplace in the Bourdieuian sense (1991), comparing the speech of recognized African American community leaders in their public speech at town meetings, during radio interviews, and at other public events with their speech during sociolinguistic interviews and in other informal interactional contexts. It also compares the speech of community leaders with the norms for their age and gender cohorts from the community. The case study of two community leaders in rural North Carolina, one the mayor of the oldest town established by Blacks in the United States, Princeville, North Carolina, and one a county commissioner from Roanoke Island, a long-standing Outer Banks Black community surrounded by a European American population, reveals dramatic differences in their speech despite their educational and residency similarities. Despite their comparable social positions and status—both female speakers have attained college degrees and post-baccalaureate education, and live in analogous types of residences within their respective communities—their use of vernacular forms differs dramatically. The Princeville mayor uses vernacular forms robustly, while the Roanoke Island commissioner rarely does. Furthermore, the speech of these leaders does not necessarily conform to age and gender norms within their respective communities. The Princeville mayor, for example, is among the most vernacular speakers in her age and gender cohort and the Roanoke Island commissioner is among the least in her age-sex cohort. Part of the difference between them may be related to their local leadership roles and principal public constituencies. In Princeville, the mayor's primary service community is centered on the local citizens of a near-exclusive Black municipality. The historical values of Princeville are largely endocentric, and most of the public speaking still occurs within the local, largely autonomous community setting. In fact, it might be hypothesized that the mayor's vernacularity helps her establish solidarity with local community members in Princeville. For sure, it does not exclude her from serving in public office and community leadership roles.

By contrast, the Roanoke Island commissioner's constituency is largely external to the local Black community, a small community of about 150 residents surrounded by the predominantly European American community. The commissioner, a pioneering leader in a dominant White social order for decades now, could not win any elected office without a significant White vote, whereas there is no White vote to speak of in Princeville. The use of vernacular forms by respective community leaders has more to do with differential contexts, social order, community organization, and public constituencies than with traditional socioeconomic indices such as education or residency. The investigation further indicates that a host of community, contextual, social, and personal factors has to be taken into account in understanding the use of vernacular forms and in explaining the public and non-public speech of the community leaders and other speakers. The relative autonomy of the community, the primary marketplace, different social affiliations and divisions within the community, personal background and history, and socialized demands in public presentation all seem to be factors in understanding the use of local vernacular and mainstream standard variants by such speakers.

A variety of contextual factors enter into the explanation of variation in AAL but some have received a lot more attention than others. We have already discussed the regional dimension of AAL (see Wolfram and Kohn, this volume) often being overlooked or minimized despite its obvious relevance for understanding variation in AAL. While the capacity to shift styles is an integral, fundamental dimension of language variation, the description and explanation of style have challenged variation studies since their inception (Labov 1966; Eckert and Rickford 2001; Coupland 2007), but defining style operationally in sociolinguistic research has also proven to be a methodological and analytical challenge. Meanwhile, stylistic variation has taken on heightened significance in the study of AAL. Theoretically, the range of variation exhibited by AAL speakers and the role of stylistic variation within a unitary system vis-à-vis code-switching between distinct but overlapping systems have become significant in understanding the relationship between AAL and MAE (see Labov 1998; Rickford and Price 2013). On a practical level, the role of style has now become an issue in predicting academic achievement, since some researchers have established correlations between stylistic capability and general academic skills such as reading achievement (Charity, Scarborough, and

Griffin 2004; Craig et al. 2009). Given the significance of stylistic variation in terms of social interaction (Schilling-Estes 2002), personal presentation (Coupland 2007), and academic performance (Charity, Scarborough, and Griffin 2004; Craig et al. 2009), it is somewhat surprising that so little research in AAL has actually explored this phenomenon at various stages in the lifespan.

Popular and educational discussions of style shifting sometimes assume that African Americans show greater stylistic versatility than speakers from other communities and that code-switching between an acrolectal and basilectal version of AAL is commonplace, but this is an assumption without adequate empirical verification. Kendall and Wolfram's (2009) case study in rural North Carolina does not support the assumption that speakers shift their use of vernacular forms significantly in public speeches vis-à-vis sociolinguistic interviews or in casual conversation. Rickford's (2013) case studies, on the other hand, document some noteworthy differences in stylistic variation at different stages for speakers in adulthood, and Weldon's (forthcoming) self-study shows substantive shifts in her speech based on interlocutor and setting. At the same time, there is no substantive evidence for a discrete acrolectal-basilectal code-switching. Rather, it appears that speakers use a matrix variety within a standard-vernacular continuum and vary a subset of features in different speech situations in stylistic manipulation (Myers-Scotton 2002).

A systematic study of over one-hundred African American students followed longitudinally (Wolfram et al., 2013) again supports the contention that variation in style based on context or task does not qualify as discrete code-switching between autonomous linguistic systems, contrary to popular opinion. Data from Renn (Renn 2007, 2010; Renn and Terry 2009) provide the first large-scale, longitudinal study of stylistic variation during the early lifespan, considering stylistic data at three temporal points: from speakers in first and second grade, from speakers in sixth grade, and from speakers in eighth grade. The data for 'informal' speech at the earliest stage were taken from child–mother interactions, whereas the data for formal speech were taken from an interview with an unfamiliar stranger in which children were asked to describe pictures and to engage in narrative elicitation tasks. The sixth- and eighth-grade data were taken from peer protocol tasks designed to create both formal and informal peer situations. Each pair of students performed formal tasks such as a planned mock speech directed toward parents of children who would be entering their school in the fall, and these were compared with informal speech such as a free-talk period in which the subjects ate a snack without an examiner present. The quantitative analysis indicated that the majority of the speakers did not engage in a significant amount of shifting in first grade and that they acquired sensitivity to style shifting as they moved toward sixth grade with no significance between sixth and eighth grade on a group level, though individual speakers showed significant variation. This examination also confirmed, to some extent, that speakers at this stage tend to have a matrix variety in the acrolect-basilect continuum that is sensitive to contextual setting and task rather than code-switching between different systems. The notion of code-switching between AAL and MAE based on dialectal parallel with code-switching between discrete languages remains popular among educators who desire to encourage MAE in educational settings while accepting vernacular AAL at home and in the neighborhood, but a discrete version of this dichotomy still awaits empirical verification. Thus, it appears that some stylistic variation may be assigned symbolic switching significance, but the identification of the features that index such emblematic switching remains a question that has received little to no attention.

17.6 CHANGE

Change in the past and present development of AAL is an integral part of its constructed status. The origin of AAL has been in dispute for decades, fluctuating between extremes of an exclusive Anglican founder hypothesis to a foundational proto-creole hypothesis. Given the dispute, it is somewhat ironic that sociolinguistics has now gone through several declared "consensus" positions regarding its development—from the Anglicist position of the 1950s, to the Creolist position of the 1970s, to the Neo-Anglicist divergence position of the 1990s. As reported in Wolfram and Kohn (this volume), research in diverse, rural Southern communities suggests that an assumption of common origin and change in AAL is unwarranted. We have documented at least three different trajectories of change in AAL communities, one in line with the divergence hypothesis (see Labov and Bailey, in Fasold et al. 1987), one that supports the convergence hypothesis (Vaughn-Cooke, in Fasold et al. 1987; Mallinson and Wolfram 2002), and one that shows a curvilinear trajectory that includes periods of convergence and divergence over time (Rickford, in Fasold et al. 1987, 1999). A number of historical, demographic, and social factors must be taken into account in any attempt to explain the origin and trajectories of change in AAL. Population demographics and sociohistorical circumstances of African Americans in North America and in the antebellum South were radically different (Rickford 1997, 1999), a fact often ignored in studies of the origin of AAL in North America. But the vast demographic differences in diverse regions and communities and the varying sociohistorical circumstances (Rickford 1997) suggest that there has been extensive variation in the speech of African Americans from the earliest importation of slaves—for reasons that range from simple population demographics to complex interactional differences. The sociohistorical reality thus counters the unilateral representation of AAL in the public media and in many of the accounts of origin and early developments of AAL presented by sociolinguists as well. Given the diversity of demographics alone, Rickford (1999) can reasonably conclude that the early origins of AAL extended from small, isolated pockets of speakers who learned varieties of their European American masters relative early and quickly to those on large plantations who may have maintained a creole-like variety. In other words, the extremes of the Anglicist and Creolist hypothesis may well have been represented in early AAL, notwithstanding the adamant, unilateral stances taken by different proponents in the debate on its origin and early development in North America. Accordingly, it seems as important to recognize diversity in earlier AAL as it is to recognize the contemporary diversity of AAL as a dynamic collection of social and regional varieties subsumed under the convenient label of AAL.

Change over the lifespan of African American speakers has also been subjected to a presumed status in AAL. Following Labov (1965), the commonsense assumption is that speakers will be most vernacular during their late adolescence because of peer influence, although others (Stewart 1968; Craig and Washington 2006) have maintained that preschool, early childhood is the period of optimal vernacular use because this period is most unaffected by the imposition of MAE educational norms. Both of these explanations, however, were offered without the benefit of longitudinal studies. The unique longitudinal study of more than sixty African Americans through the first twenty years of language and life (Van Hofwegen and Wolfram 2010; Van Hofwegen, this volume) reveals that there may actually be several different trajectories of change over the early lifespan. The most common pattern, in fact, is a roller coaster pattern that was not predicted in any of the accounts of the optimal vernacular period. The only shared pattern among the speakers is the minimal vernacular period that occurs between first and fourth grade. We thus see that counterintuitive sociolinguistic reality may confront commonsense assumptions once again—not only in popular culture but in the academy's construction of AAL change over the lifespan of African American speakers.

17.7 CONCLUSION

As a byproduct of the rich and productive tradition of research on AAL studies, a constructed reality has been nurtured in the sociolinguistic academy. In many respects, this was inadvertent and unavoidable given the understanding that facts are never isolated from theory and social circumstance. In the current approach to AAL, sociolinguists have been preoccupied with some aspects of the speech of African Americans while excluding other dimensions, and our ideological stance has privileged some kinds of data and evidence over others, leading to questionable interpretations of sociolinguistic reality. More critical scrutiny of how we have defined and described this variety and its speakers can only profit sociolinguistic inquiry as a whole and the study of AAL in particular. It is time to reconsider, revise, expand, and move forward in our understanding how AAL lives in the African American population and in American society through its speakers.

NOTE

1. Support from NSF grants BCS-0843865, BCS-0544744, BCS-0236838, and BCS-9910224 for research reported here is gratefully acknowledged. Special thanks to Charles Farrington and Mary Kohn for commenting on a draft of this chapter, as well as the editors of the handbook.

References

Baugh, John. 1983. *Black Street Speech: Its History, Structure, and Survival.* Austin: University of Texas Press.

———. 1984. "Steady: Progressive Aspect in Black Vernacular English." *American Speech* 59: 3–12.

Benor, Sarah Bunin. 2010. "Ethnolinguistic Repertoire: Shifting the Analytic Focus in Language and Ethnicity." *Journal of Sociolinguistics* 14: 151–83.

Bonfiglio, Thomas P. 2002. *Race and the Rise of Standard American English.* Mouton: DeGruyter.

Bourdieu, Pierre. 1991. *Language and Symbolic Power.* Cambridge, MA: Harvard University Press.

Bucholtz, Mary. 2003. "Sociolinguistic Nostalgia and the Authentication of Identity." *Journal of Sociolinguistics* 7: 398–416.

Carroll, Sean. 2009. "Data on 'Facts' and Facts on 'Data.'" Cosmic Variance (blog), October 14. http://blogs.discovermagazine.com/cosmicvariance/2009/10/14/data-on-facts-and-facts-on-data.

Charity, Anne, Hollis Scarborough, and Darion Griffin. 2004. "Familiarity with 'School English' in Low SES-African-American Children and its Relation to Early Reading Achievement." *Child Development* 75: 1–17.

Coupland, Nikolas. 2007. *Style, Language Variation, and Identity.* Cambridge: Cambridge University Press.

Craig, Holly K., and Julie A. Washington. 2006. *Malik Goes to School: Examining the Language Skills of African American Students from Preschool-5th Grade.* Mahwah, NJ: Lawrence Erlbaum.

Craig, Holly K., L. Zhang, S. Hensel, and E. Quinn. 2009. "African American English-speaking Students: An Examination of the Relationship between Dialect Shifting and Reading Outcomes." *Journal of Speech, Language, and Hearing Research* 52: 839–55.

Eckert, Penelope, and John R. Rickford, eds. 2001. *Style and Sociolinguistic Variation.* Cambridge: Cambridge University Press.

Farrington, Charles R. 2011. "Devoicing in African American English: A Longitudinal and Apparent Time Analysis." Capstone Project. Raleigh: North Carolina State University.

Fasold, Ralph W. 1972. *Tense Marking in Black English: A Linguistic and Social Analysis.* Arlington: Center for Applied Linguistics.

———. 2000. "Ebonic Need not be English." *AAA-Arbeiten aus Anglistik und Amerikanistik* 25: 149–60.

———. 2001. "A Subtle Linguistic Science: The Social Construction of 'a Language.'" Washington, DC: Georgetown University. Unpublished ms.

Fasold, Ralph W., William Labov, Fay Boyd Vaughn-Cooke, Guy Bailey, Walt Wolfram, Arthur K. Spears, and John R. Rickford. 1987. "Are Black and White Vernaculars Diverging?" Papers from the NWAV-XIV panel discussion. Special issue of *American Speech* 62 (1): 3–80.

Fasold, Ralph W., and Walt Wolfram. 1970. "Some Linguistic Features of Negro Dialect." In *Teaching Standard English in the Inner City*, edited by Ralph W. Fasold and Roger W. Shuy, 41–86. Washington, DC: Center for Applied Linguistics.

Graff, David, William Labov, and Wendell A. Harris. 1986. "Testing Listeners' Reactions to Phonological Markers of Ethnic Identity: A New Method for Sociolinguistic Research." In *Diversity and Diachrony*, edited by David Sankoff, 45–58. Philadelphia: John Benjamins.

Green, Lisa J. 2002. *African American English: A Linguistic Introduction*. New York: Cambridge University Press.

———. 2004. "African American Vernacular English." In *Language in the USA: Themes for the Twenty-First Century*, edited by Edward Finegan and John R. Rickford, 76–91. Cambridge: Cambridge University Press.

Harder, Peter. 2003. "The Status of Linguistic Facts: Rethinking the Relation between Cognition, Social Institution and Utterance from a Functional Point of View." *Mind & Language* 18: 52–76.

Houston, Susan H. 1969. "A Sociolinguistic Consideration of the Black English of Children in Northern Florida." *Language* 45: 599–607.

Johnson, Sally. 2001. "Who's Misunderstanding Whom? Sociolinguistics, Public Debate, and the Media." *Journal of Sociolinguistics* 5: 591–610.

Kendall, Tyler, and Walt Wolfram. 2009. "Local and External Language Standards in African American English." *Journal of English Linguistics* 37: 5–30.

Labov, William. 1965. "Stages in the Acquisition of Standard English." In *Social Dialects and Language Learning*, edited by Roger W. Shuy, 77–103. Champaign, IL: National Council of Teachers of English.

———. 1966. *The Social Stratification of English in New York City*. Washington, DC: The Center for Applied Linguistics.

———. 1969. "Contraction, Deletion, and Inherent Variability of the English Copula." *Language* 45: 715–62.

———. 1972. *Language in the Inner City: Studies in the Black English Vernacular*. Philadelphia: University of Pennsylvania Press.

———. 1998. "Coexistent Systems in African-American Vernacular English." In *African American English: Structure, History and Use*, edited by Salikoko S. Mufwene, John R. Rickford, Guy Bailey, and John Baugh, 110–53. London: Routledge.

Labov, William, Paul Cohen, Clarence Robins, and John Lewis. 1968. *A Study of the Non-Standard English of Negro and Puerto Rican Speakers in New York City*. Washington, DC: United States Office of Education Final Report, Research Project 3288.

Lanehart, Sonja L. 2002. *Sista, Speak!: Black Women Kinfolk Talk about Language and Literacy*. Austin: University of Texas Press.

Legum, Stanley E., Carole Pfaff, Gene Tinny, and Michael Nicholas. 1971. *The Speech of Young Black Children in Los Angeles*. Los Angeles: Southwest Regional Laboratory for Research and Development, Technical Report 33. 01.

Linnes, Kathleen. 1998. "Middle-Class AAVE versus Middle-class Bilingualism: Contrasting Speech Communities." *American Speech* 73: 339–67.

Lippi-Green, Rosina. 2012. *English with an Accent: Language, Ideology, and Discrimination in the United States*. 2nd ed. London: Routledge.

Mallinson, Christine, and Walt Wolfram. 2002. "Dialect Accommodation in a Bi-ethnic Mountain Enclave Community: More Evidence on the Development of African American Vernacular English." *Language in Society* 31: 743–75.

Mitchell-Kernan, Claudia. 1969. *Language Behavior in a Black Urban Community*. Berkeley: Language Behavior Laboratory, University of California.

Milroy, James. 2001. "Language Ideologies and the Consequences of Standardization." *Journal of Sociolinguistics* 5: 530–55.

Morgan, Marcyliena. 2002. *Language, Discourse, and Power in African American Culture*. Cambridge: Cambridge University Press.

Myers-Scotton, Carol. 2002. *Contact Linguistics: Bilingual Encounters and Grammatical Outcomes*. Oxford: Oxford University Press.

Renn, Jennifer. 2007. "Measuring Style Shift: A Quantitative Analysis of African American English." Master's thesis, University of North Carolina.

———. 2010. "Acquiring Style: The Development of Dialect Shifting among African American Children." PhD diss., University of North Carolina at Chapel Hill.

Renn, Jennifer, and J. Michael Terry. 2009. "Operationalizing Style: Quantifying Style Shift in the Speech of African American Adolescents." *American Speech* 84: 367–90.

Rickford, John R. 1997. "Prior Creolization in African American English? Sociohistorical and Textual Evidence from the 17th and 18th Century." *Journal of Sociolinguistics* 1: 315–36.

Rickford, John R. 1999. *African American Vernacular English: Features, Evolution and Educational Implications*. Malden, MA: Blackwell.

Rickford, John R., and Mackenzie Price. 2013. "Girlz II Women: Age-Grading, Language Change, and Stylistic Variation." *Journal of Sociolinguistics* 17: 143–79.

Rickford, John R., Julie Sweetland, Angela Rickford, and Thomas Grano. 2012. *An Annotated Bibliography of African American, Creoles, and Other English Vernacular Varieties*. Champaign-Urbana: NCTE and Routledge/Taylor Francis.

Schilling-Estes, Natalie. 2002. "Investigating Stylistic Variation." In *The Handbook of Language Variation and Change*, edited by J. K. Chambers, Peter Trudgill, and Natalie Schilling-Estes, 375–401. Malden: Blackwell.

Schneider, Edgar. 1996. *Focus on the USA*. Philadelphia: John Benjamins.

Smitherman, Geneva. 1977. *Talkin' and Testifyin': The Language of Black America*. Boston: Houghton Mifflin.

———. 1991. "What is Africa to Me? Language Ideology and *African American*." *American Speech* 66: 115–32.

———. 2001. *Black Talk: Words and Phrases from the Hood to the Amen Corner*. Boston: Houghton Mifflin.

Spears, Arthur K. 1982. "The Black English Semi-Auxiliary *come*." *Language* 58 (4): 850–72.

———. 1999. "Race and Ideology: An Introduction." In *Race and Ideology: Language, Symbolism, and Popular Culture*, edited by Arthur K. Spears, 11–58. Detroit: Wayne State University Press.

Spears, Arthur K., and Leanne Hinton. 2010. "Language and Speakers: An Introduction to African American English and Native American Languages." *Transforming Anthropology* 18: 3–14.

Stewart, William A. 1968. "Continuity and Change in American Negro Dialects." *The Florida FL Reporter* 6: 14–16, 18, 30.

Terry, J. Michael. 2004. "On the Articulation of Aspectual Meaning in African American English." PhD diss., University of Massachusetts Amherst.

Thomas, Erik R. 2002. "Sociophonetic Applications of Speech Perception Experiments." *American Speech* 77: 115–47.

———. 2007. "Phonological and Phonetic Characteristics of AAVE." *Language and Linguistics Compass* 1: 450–75.

Thomas, Erik R., and Jeffrey Reaser. 2004. "Delimiting Perceptual Cues for the Ethnic Labeling of African American and European American Voices." *Journal of Sociolinguistics* 8: 54–87.

Van Hofwegen, Janneke, and Walt Wolfram. 2010. "Coming of Age in African American English: A Longitudinal Study." *Journal of Sociolinguistics* 14: 27–52.

Weldon, Tracey. 2004. "African American English in the Middle Classes: Exploring the Other End of the Continuum." Paper presented at New Ways of Analyzing Variation 33, Ann Arbor, Michigan, September 30–October 3.

Weldon, Tracey. Forthcoming. *Middle-Class African American English.* Cambridge: Cambridge University Press.

Wolfram, Walt. 1969. *A Sociolinguistic Description of Detroit Negro Speech.* Washington, DC: Center for Applied Linguistics.

———. 1994. "On the Sociolinguistic Significance of Obscure Dialect Structures: NP$_i$ *call* NP$_i$ V-*ing* in African American Vernacular English." *American Speech* 69: 339–60.

———. 2007. "Sociolinguistic Myths in the Study of African American English." *Linguistic and Language Compass* 2: 292–313.

———. 2011. "The African American English Canon in Sociolinguistics." In *Contours of English and English Language Studies*, edited by Michael Adams and Anne Curzan, 34–52. Ann Arbor: University of Michigan Press.

Wolfram, Walt, and Natalie Schilling-Estes. 2006. *American English: Dialects and Variation.* 2nd ed. Malden, MA: Blackwell.

Wolfram, Walt, and Erik R. Thomas. 2002. *The Development of African American English.* Malden: Blackwell.

Wolfram, Walt, Janneke Van Hofwegen, Jenn Renn, and Mary Kohn. 2013. "The Progression of African American English in Childhood and Adolescence: A Longitudinal Study." Unpublished manuscript.

PART III

STRUCTURE AND DESCRIPTION

CHAPTER 18

SYNTAX AND SEMANTICS IN AFRICAN AMERICAN ENGLISH

LISA J. GREEN AND WALTER SISTRUNK

18.1 INTRODUCTION

QUESTIONS about the status of African American English (AAE) as a dialect or language and about the extent to which it is different from other varieties of English, including Standard American English (SAE), have guided research on the linguistic variety in different areas. For instance, in an effort to show that AAE was both different from SAE and yet systematic, linguists isolated the features of the linguistic variety that were maximally different from structures and constructions in SAE and provided general descriptions of them. The emphasis on proving that AAE was indeed a separate dialect has significantly influenced the way the linguistic variety has been described and the types of questions that continue to drive research on it. In some cases, the description of AAE was presented from historical perspectives, such that the features of AAE that were purported to be maximally different from SAE were argued to be closely linked to other sources such as creoles or African languages. The maximally different features were also compared to General American English (GAE) given that they were in some sense similar to constructions in other English varieties except that they were either represented by a "missing" morpheme, such as the copula or auxiliary *be*, or they were represented as including an "extra" morpheme or marker, such as a negative element, that might have been used in earlier versions of English but that were no longer acceptable in modern-day English. (See chapters in Part I, "Origins and Historical Perspectives," for an overview of the relation between AAE and other linguistic systems; see also the chapter by Charles DeBose in Part III, which takes an Africanist approach to the tense/aspect system of AAE.)

This chapter presents an overview of some syntactic and semantic patterns in certain areas of the AAE grammar. AAE can be defined in a number of ways, such as: a variety spoken by a certain group of people; a variety characterized by certain features that distinguish it from other varieties of English; a variety that might be said to have been formed by two distinct components (as in Labov's 1998 dual components approach). One component could be said to contribute all of the similarities that AAE shares with GAE, and the other component might be said to contribute all of the differences that distinguish AAE from other nonstandard American English varieties and make it stand out as a unique variety.

In this chapter, the characterization of AAE that will be assumed is one that highlights the systematic patterns within the linguistic variety. Here, AAE is characterized as a linguistic variety spoken natively by some, not all, African Americans (and some non-African Americans) in AAE-speaking communities in the United States and that has set syntactic, semantic, morphological, phonological, lexical, and pragmatic patterns. The first point to note about this characterization of AAE is that it is somewhat narrow in that it refers to native speakers. In acquiring AAE as their first language, speakers will pass through the same type of developmental stages in acquiring systems of sound, morphology, sentence structure (syntax), and meaning patterns (semantics) that speakers of other speech communities experience. The latter systems, sentence structure and meaning, will be the topic of this chapter. It is obvious that some non-native speakers of the variety use different structures of AAE with native competency, but the focus here is on the overall AAE system of speaking, not just the use of some constructions used in isolated instances by some speakers.

18.2 SYNTAX, SEMANTICS, AND AAE IN THE EARLY PERIOD

The early descriptions of syntactic and semantic patterns in AAE (see Dillard 1975; Labov 1972; Labov et al. 1968) provided incredible insight into the linguistic system. The report in Labov et al. (1968) is an extensive overview of structures in AAE in comparison to those in SAE. Some of these structures are also discussed in Labov (1972), along with educational and social issues. In Labov et al. (1968) and Labov (1972), the differences between SAE and AAE were characterized as differences in surface structure brought about by low-level rules that apply in AAE. For instance, the copula may not be pronounced superficially in AAE because some phonological rule that applies in AAE, but not in SAE, can delete it (e.g., *He's tall* → *He tall*). The claim is that in other respects or at deeper levels, AAE and SAE are very similar, if not identical.

Two chapters in Dillard's (1975) book, *Perspectives on Black English*, offered an alternative account to characterizing AAE as a variety that differed only superficially from SAE. In that text, both Fickett (1975) and Loflin (1975) argued that AAE differed from SAE in the grammar beyond superficial differences reflected in the surface structure. These studies presented analyses of AAE syntax from the viewpoint of transformational grammar, in which the researchers proposed rules that were designed to generate AAE surface forms. For instance, Loflin (1972, 1975) proposed an auxiliary structure to account for the pattern of co-occurrence of auxiliaries in matrix clauses and embedded clauses. He noted that one pattern was the occurrence of a perfective auxiliary in the matrix clause and a generic auxiliary in the embedded clause, which accounted for sentences such as the following from Loflin (1975, 71):

(1) *Ey say dey be countin up you' food, man, see how much you ha'.*

One of the co-occurrence restrictions that Loflin proposed is a case in which a generic verb form in the matrix clause occurred with an atemporal verb in the embedded clause, as instantiated in sentence (1) by the verb form *say* (generic) and aspectual *be* (atemporal). The claim was that the co-occurrence restrictions postulated for the relative clauses were independently motivated by the restrictions needed in other parts of the AAE grammar.

Fickett (1975) also addressed the verb system in AAE with particular focus on the uses of negative elements *ain't*, *not*, and *don't* from the perspective of tenses. In that study, AAE was analyzed as distinguishing the following categories:

(2) a. Negation in present *not singing*
     b. Negation in inceptive *ain't singing, don't sing*
     c. Negation in recent *done sung*
     d. Negation in imminent *ain't sung*
     e. Negation in post-imminent *she ain't gonna sing*

Fickett's conclusion about AAE was that, "because it has a system of tenses which indicate degrees of pastness and degrees of futurity, it can talk about how long ago things didn't happen, or how far ahead they aren't going to happen" (1975, 90). Fickett's (1975) is one of the earliest studies to offer an account for the grammatical structure of AAE beyond superficial morphosyntactic differences that distinguished the variety from SAE and that also considered the contrastive stress patterns and meaning associated with negative elements. Loflin's (1972, 1975) and Fickett's (1975) research placed considerable emphasis on the syntactic structure of AAE either by formulating rules that generated the correct order of auxiliaries in matrix and embedded clauses or combination of negative auxiliary and main verb. However, both studies also made important contributions to the semantics of AAE, especially in light of the type of meaning that can be expressed by auxiliary and other verbal elements. Researchers took a syntax-semantics approach in descriptions and analysis of structures in AAE. For instance, Loflin (1972) proposed a habituative category in the grammar of AAE as a means of accounting for the recurring activity expressed in some sentences.

Work such as that in Loflin (1972, 1975) and Fickett (1975) served to show that beyond looking at the surface structure of constructions, it was important to consider meaning conveyed by those constructions, which could provide more insight into the deep meaning and structure in AAE. One basic, but important, observation that researchers such as Loflin and Fickett made was that it was not always possible to construe the meaning just by considering surface forms. Although research on the syntax and semantics of AAE has been limited, over the years a number of studies in these areas have been conducted. For instance, syntactic and semantic properties of the AAE auxiliary system were addressed in Green (1993, 1998, and 2000). Martin (1992) presented an overview and analysis of syntactic and semantic properties of negation in AAE as well as in other varieties of American English. Terry's research (2004, 2005, and 2006) focuses primarily on meaning associated with tense/aspect constructions in AAE, but it also addresses important properties of sentence structure.

18.3 FROM FEATURES TO PATTERNS

Putting the previous research on AAE into perspective, we find that although it is probably the most commonly studied variety of American English, some areas of the linguistic system have not received much attention. Erik Thomas (this volume) underscored this point in reference to the limited amount of research that has been conducted on intonation and related topics in AAE. A similar observation can be made about syntactic and semantic analyses of constructions in AAE. Syntactic and semantic properties of AAE that are different from those in SAE have been identified as features, and general descriptions of them have been presented, also. Consider, for instance, the properties that have been argued to define AAE and reported in features lists, such as that in Rickford (1999). He includes a list of what he labels "Distinctive Phonological (Pronunciation) Features of AAVE [African American Vernacular English]" in table 1.1 (4–5) and "Distinctive Grammatical (Morphological and Syntactic) Features of AAVE" in table 1.2 (6–9) (Rickford 1999). In Rickford's (1999) table 1.2, he provides the following subcategories:

19. Preverbal markers of tense, mood, and aspect (19a–19m, 6–7)
20. Other aspects of verbal tense marking (20a–20f, 7)
21. Nouns and pronouns (21a–21g, 7–8)
22. Negation (22a–22d, 8)
23. Questions (23a and b, 8)
24. Existential and locative constructions (24a–c, 8–9)
25. Complementizer/quotative *say* (25a, 9)

Rickford's (1999) is the only features list that we have seen that provides a general description of each feature and subcategorizes the grammatical features into components such as preverbal markers and other aspects of verbal tense marking. Configuring the features list in this fashion is quite useful, and the approach makes it possible to begin to characterize the patterns of language use of AAE and to show that it is a system.

For instance, aspectual *be* or invariant *be* (which indicates habituality of some eventuality) and *done* (which indicates the resultant state of an event expressed by a verb) are generally included on AAE features lists, but very little—if any—information is given about their meaning and distribution, and the environments in which they occur. (These markers will be discussed in the following section.) Furthermore, the lists do not give any sense of the relationship between these markers and their roles in the grammar of AAE. Fully aware of the shortcoming of features lists, and, at the same time, aware of the necessity of conveying what are taken to be "distinctive features" of AAE, Rickford (1999) notes at the beginning of the descriptive list:

> Although it is impossible in a chapter of this length to add all the qualifying details about each feature which one would like to (but see the accompanying footnotes and references), two general comments should be made, one about the frequency with which these features occur among African American speakers, and the other about their distinctiveness vis-à-vis the colloquial or vernacular English of other Americans. (4, 9)

In addressing these two issues, Rickford (1999) comments on the extent to which some of these features are produced (or provides mean percentages of use in recordings with twelve speakers from each class) by speakers who are categorized as lower working class, upper working class, lower middle class, and upper middle class. The summarizing view is that younger lower- and working-class speakers use selected features more in urban settings and in informal contexts most often, but the frequency rates vary from feature to feature (Rickford 1999, 9–11).

Although many of the properties associated with AAE and that are different from structures in SAE have been identified, only a few constructions and properties have been subjected to syntactic and semantic analysis or linguistic description that includes information about linguistic environments in which the constructions are used or constraints on their distribution and meaning. Syntactic and semantic analyses of constructions in AAE have been cast in particular theoretical frameworks, such as the principles and parameters theory, optimality theory, or head-driven phrase structure grammar. From the features in Rickford's (1999) list of grammatical features, we find that syntactic and semantic analyses of preverbal markers of tense, mood, and aspect have been conducted. These markers include *be, done*, and stressed *BIN*, as well as markers *steady* and *come*. Take, for example, Charles DeBose's discussion in this volume (which is based on DeBose and Faraclas 1993), in which the goal is to identify constructions and grammatical structures in the verbal system of AAE. Analyses of preverbal markers are also presented in Fasold (1972), Green (1993, 1998, and 2000), and Terry (2004, 2005, and 2006), in which one goal is to convey the type of meaning the markers contribute to structures in which they occur. Descriptions of these markers are useful in contributing to our understanding of the possible superficial and "deep" differences between AAE and other varieties of English, and they also provide some insight into what speakers know when they know AAE. For instance, information about the subtle meanings of these markers, the environments in which they occur in sentences, the restrictions on their occurrence, and the way they combine with other elements in sentences helps to make clear what it is speakers must know to use the markers grammatically. Other topics, such as negation and questions in AAE, have been analyzed from syntactic and semantic angles and presented in theoretical frameworks.

18.4 APPROACHES TO THE STRUCTURE AND MEANING OF CONSTRUCTIONS IN AAE

The early work and progression of research by Fasold (1972), Fickett (1975), and Loflin (1975) on the structure and meaning of particular constructions in AAE help to explain why syntactic and semantic research in certain areas of the AAE grammar is further along (e.g., properties of tense/aspect markers) than research in other areas (e.g., intonation). Both the claim that AAE was substantially different from SAE and that verbal markers played a major role in the AAE grammar fueled interest in the AAE verbal system, which led to more research in that area. In addition, there has been interest in claims that AAE shares properties of negation with some other varieties of English (see Martin 1992). Finally, complex sentences, such as those in which one sentence is embedded within another sentence, have been addressed in the literature in more recent studies (see Green 2014; Martin and Wolfram 1998). In such research on these embedded sentences, emphasis has been placed on the obligatory or optional occurrence of the element, such as the complementizer (e.g., *that, if*) or auxiliary (e.g., *do*), that introduces the embedded sentence.

18.4.1 On the Verbal System of AAE: Time and Events

The phrase *verbal system* is used here to refer to the system of conveying information about the way events progress as well as the system of expressing the beginning, progression, or completion of events from the perspective of time. The markers that are considered in this system of talking about events are preverbal markers and inflectional endings that occur on verbs. Preverbal markers aspectual *be*, remote past *BIN*, and unstressed *done* (represented here as *dǝn*) are considered. It is the case that research on *BIN* and *dǝn* has waned during certain phases of research on AAE, but discussions about aspectual *be* have remained steady over the years. Descriptive analyses of *BIN* were presented in Labov (1972), Rickford (1973, 1975), Green (1993, 1998), and Dayton (1996), noting that the stress or pitch accent is a distinguishing feature of the remote past marker and that *BIN* combines with certain predicate types to indicate that part or all of the event expressed by the predicate is in the distant past. The marker *dǝn* has received less attention in the literature, quite possibly because of its superficial resemblance to the marker *done* that occurs in varieties of American English spoken in the southern

United States. Descriptions of the marker are presented in Green (1993), Winford (1993), Dayton (1996), Edwards (2001), Terry (2004, 2005, and 2006), and these studies raise questions about whether the marker indicates a stative meaning of the event expressed by the predicate.

Aspectual *be*, which has also been referred to as invariant *be*, habitual *be*, and *be2* by Labov et al. 1968, indicates that an eventuality recurs. Early research reported in Labov et al. (1968), Dillard (1972), and Fasold (1972) has certainly informed more current research on markers, such as Bailey and Maynor (1987), Myhill (1988, 1991), Green (1993, 2000, 2007), and Dayton (1996).

At least four important questions (among others) should be addressed in a discussion about the syntactic and semantic properties of the markers *be, BIN,* and *dən*:

1. What meaning is associated with the markers and how is that meaning expressed in connection with other predicates in the sentence?
2. What is the syntactic placement of the markers, and with what other elements do the markers combine to form larger phrases in sentences?
3. Do the markers select predicates that bear certain morphological marking?
4. What are the restrictions on the occurrence of the markers?

Consider the following sentences in (3) to (5) where the markers occur from the perspective of the four questions above. (The sentences in single quotes are paraphrases of the sentences that contain the aspectual markers.)

(3) a. Mrs. Marple be singing in that classroom.
       'Mrs. Marple generally sings/is generally singing in that classroom.'
    b. Mrs. Marple don't be singing in that classroom.
       'Mrs. Marple is not generally singing/does not generally sing in that classroom.'
    c. Mrs. Marple be in that classroom/quiet/the leader.
       'Mrs. Marple is generally in that classroom/quiet/the leader.'
(4) a. Mrs. Marple BIN singing in that classroom.
       'Mrs. Marple has been singing in that classroom for a long time.'
    b. Mrs. Marple ain't BIN singing in that classroom.
       'Mrs. Marple has not been singing in that classroom for a long time.'
    c. Mrs. Marple BIN singing in that classroom on Thursdays.
       'For a long time, Mrs. Marple has had the habit of singing in that classroom on Thursdays.'
    d. Mrs. Marple BIN in that classroom/quiet/the leader.
       'Mrs. Marple has been in that classroom/quiet/the leader for a long time.'
    e. Mrs. Marple BIN sung in that classroom.
       'Mrs. Marple sang in that classroom a long time ago.'
(5) a. Mrs. Marple dən sung in that classroom.
       'Mrs. Marple has already sung in that classroom.'
    b. Mrs. Marple ain't dən sung in that classroom.
       'Mrs. Marple has not already sung in that classroom.'

The marker aspectual *be* (be_{asp}) indicates that an eventuality recurs, even in cases in which it occurs in passive contexts.[1] One way to capture the semantic interpretation of be_{asp} is by way of the feature [habitual], such that the feature applies to the eventuality expressed by the predicate. The remote past *BIN* situates some part (or all) of an eventuality in the distant past. It refers to a long period that extends from some point in the past to the moment of the utterance. The eventualities to which *BIN* applies start at some point in the far past and continue throughout the long period until the moment of the utterance, or they start and end in the distant past, as in the case of the BIN sung event in (4c), in which the singing event ended in the remote past. The marker *dən* indicates that the eventuality is in the state of having ended or in its resultant state.

All of the markers precede verb forms with either *–ing* or PAST morphology, and the markers *be* and *BIN* also precede non-verbal predicates, such as prepositional phrases, adjectives, and nouns. It should also be noted that aspectual *be* can precede verbs with PAST morphology, as in the following utterance produced by ex-slave Laura Smalley in an interview in 1941, which is available at http://memory.loc.gov/cgi-bin/query/ S?ammem/afcesnbib:@field(AUTHOR+@od1(Smalley,+Laura+) on the Library of Congress's website, *Voices from the Days of Slavery*: "If I can get it together, I don' want to sing it if I cain get it together. Sometime you know that way I get 'em wrong and they be sung wrong." In general, when aspectual *be* occurs with verbs that take PAST morphology, the reading is passive. For instance, Laura Smalley's sentence can be paraphrased as "... and they are generally sung wrong."

The negative sentences (3b, 4b, and 5b) provide crucial information about the syntactic placement of the aspectual markers: They occur in a position lower than auxiliaries such as *do(n't)* and *ain't*. The auxiliary serves an important role in aspectual constructions although it is separable from the aspectual marker construction. For instance, if the aspectual marker construction is elided or simply omitted, the auxiliary remains:

(6) a. Mrs. Marple BIN singing in that classroom, and Mr. Whipple have ~~BIN singing in that classroom~~, too. (i.e., Mrs. Marple BIN singing in that classroom, and Mr. Whipple have, too.)

b. *Mrs. Marple BIN singing in that classroom, and Mr. Whipple have BIN ~~singing in that classroom~~, too.

Ellipsis can apply to the aspectual marker plus the following verb phrase (e.g., "*BIN* singing in that classroom"), with the auxiliary *have* standing in for the elided material. The auxiliary and the aspectual marker construction are separable. On the other hand, as indicated by the asterisk (*) preceding the ungrammatical sentence in (6b), the aspectual marker cannot remain while the verb phrase is elided. It, too, must be deleted. The auxiliary *have* is definitely connected to the *BIN* aspectual marker phrase and shares some features with it. However, the auxiliary *have* must be in a syntactic phrase that excludes the aspectual marker because it can be split from it, which is what is shown in the grammatical (6a).

Of course, a syntactic and semantic analysis of the markers should also address the co-occurrence restrictions on the markers, so that it is clear which other elements can occur with the markers. The elements might be other aspectual markers, predicate phrases, and adverbs (or adverbial phrases). Along similar lines, it is important to consider the types of elements that can occur in subject position, especially in the case of be_{asp}. For instance, different meanings can be conveyed with definite *the dog* (7a), indefinite *a dog* (7b), and bare plural *dogs* (7c) subjects in be_{asp} constructions.

(7) a. The dog be barking.
    b. A dog be barking.
    c. Dogs be barking.

In each case (7a to c), there are occasions of barking. Compare (7b) to simple present tense sentences with indefinite subjects, such as in "a dog bark," which also occur in AAE.[2] The first reading of this present tense sentence is one in which "a dog" refers to members of the class of dogs. As such, "a dog bark" makes a general or generic statement about dogs. That is, members of the class of dogs have the general property that they bark. On the other hand, the most salient reading of "a dog be barking" (7b), which also has an indefinite subject, is that on different occasions a certain dog is generally barking or generally barks.

These restrictions can also be addressed from the perspective of the types of features that can co-occur. The features [habitual] and [resultant state] can occur, as indicated by the combination of $be_{[+habitual]}$ $dən_{[+resultant\ state]}$ (e.g., *Mrs. Marple be dən sung in the classroom by the time the students get there.* 'Mrs. Marple has generally already sung in the classroom by the time the students get there'). However, in the case of [habitual] and [remote past], it is possible to convey both meanings, but only one aspectual marker (*BIN*) is allowed to do so. That is, *BIN singing* in *Mrs. Marple BIN singing in that classroom for one hour* has both remote past and habitual meanings, such that for a long time, Mrs. Marple has had the habit of singing in that classroom for one hour at a time. The adverbial *for one hour* cannot modify *BIN* or the long period, but it can modify the length of each singing event that occurs on occasion, that is the habitual singing events. It seems as if the meaning of [habitual] + [remote past] should be able to be expressed by *be BIN*, as in **Mrs. Marple be BIN singing in the classroom*, but the sentence is ungrammatical. There is some syntactic clash between *be* and *BIN* that prevents them from co-occurring.

Many questions remain to be asked and answered about aspectual constructions. Some very important questions about the tense/aspect system of AAE are raised and addressed in Terry's (2004, 2005, and 2006) semantic work on perfect, perfective, and *dən* constructions. One of Terry's (2004) central claims in his formal semantics account is that "the source of perfect (or completive) aspect in both simple V-*ed* and preverbal *done* sentences is –*ed*, and that the role of *done* is to introduce stativity, which … makes preverbal *done* sentences more like SAE *have* constructions than their simple V-*ed* counterparts" (224). Terry's semantic work on *dən* is also very important in that it provides some insight into the relation between morphological marking (e.g., *–ed*) and tense and aspect. As he points out, the *dən* constructions are present tense; the role of the morphological marking (i.e., *–ed*) that occurs on verbs in *dən* constructions is to introduce precedence (Terry 2005, 225). In this way, it gives information that one time precedes another. Take, for instance, *dən jumped*. Simply put, the time of the jumping eventuality precedes the time about which the jumping event is asserted. Terry (2004, 2005, 2006) brings together empirical data and theoretical claims about tense and aspect to explore the semantics of the perfect and perfective. On a broader level, in his research of AAE, Terry (2004) maintains that the tense and aspect systems of AAE and SAE are pretty much the same in that the same tense and aspectual meaning is available in both varieties. The difference is in the morphological structure.

Further work along the line of Terry's would be useful in exploring other types of tense and aspect relations in AAE. For instance, auxiliaries (e.g., *do* and *have*) can occur with aspectual markers, but they differ in the property of expressing past tense. For example, *do* cannot be inflected for past tense in aspectual *be* constructions, but *have* can be in *dən* constructions:

(8) a. *Bruce did be running.
    b. Bruce had *dən* sung.

The meaning (past habitual) that is expressed by the ungrammatical sentence in (8a) makes sense, but in order to express it grammatically, speakers of AAE would have to say "Bruce used to run" certainly not "*Bruce did be running." The *dən* construction can also be used in past contexts. In the case of the *dən* construction, both the meaning and the combination of *had + dən* are felicitous.

Another area that should be considered in the tense and aspect system of AAE is the relationship between markers and morphological endings. For instance, both the auxiliary *be* (e.g., *is*) as in *Mrs. Marple is dancing/Mrs. Marple dancing* and be_{asp} occur with verbs carrying *–ing* morphology. What is the relationship between *is*/$\emptyset_{auxiliary\ be}$ and *–ing* and be_{asp} and *–ing*? This is one question that can be taken up in future research on tense and aspect in AAE.

18.4.2 Syntactic and Semantic Properties of Complex Sentences

Two types of complex sentences that will be addressed in this section are those that are formed with embedded question constructions and negation constructions. Words such as *whether* and *if* can introduce clauses that convey questions:

(9) a. I wonder [whether the game gon start late].
        'I wonder whether the game is going to start late.'
    b. I wonder [if the game gon start late].

The matrix verb *wonder*, which has question properties, takes interrogative clauses that are introduced by *if* and *whether*. Compare *wonder* to the verb *say*, which selects a declarative clause:

(10)   He said [that the game was gon start late].

Auxiliaries can also introduce embedded interrogative clauses that are similar to those in (9):

(11)   a.   I wonder [if Mrs. Marple be singing in class.]
            'I wonder if Mrs. Marple is generally singing/generally sings.'
       b.   I wonder [do Mrs. Marple be singing in class].
       c.   *I wonder [that Mrs. Marple be singing in class].
       d.   *I wonder [if do Mrs. Marple be singing in class].
       e.   *I wonder [__ Mrs. Marple be singing in class].

The sentences in (11a and b), which have the same meaning, are grammatical with either a complementizer (e.g., *if*) or auxiliary (e.g., *do*) in the initial clause position. The sentences in (11 c to e) are ungrammatical: (11c) is ruled out because the complementizer *that* introduces declarative clauses, not interrogative clauses; *wonder* requires an interrogative clause. The sentence in (11d) is ungrammatical because either the complementizer *if* or the auxiliary *do* can occur in the clause initial position; they cannot both occur at the same time because there is a slot for only one. Finally, the sentence in (11e) is ruled out because the initial position is empty. Neither a complementizer nor an auxiliary is present.

The sentences in (11) provide information about the structure of embedded clauses in AAE as well as about the selectional properties of the verbs associated with these clauses. In short, the clause initial position must be filled with an overt element in embedded clauses, and the type of element that occurs has semantic properties that match those of the matrix verb. Indirect questions embedded under question verbs such as *wonder* are introduced by a [Question] complementizer (*whether* or *if*) or by an auxiliary. The sentences in (11) also help to reveal an important difference between matrix questions and embedded questions in AAE. Matrix questions in AAE can be rendered with an initial inverted auxiliary or without one:

(12)   a.   Do Mrs. Marple be singing in class?
            'Is Mrs. Marple generally singing in class?'/Does Mrs. Marple generally sing in class?
       b.   Mrs. Marple be singing in class?

Both questions are genuine yes/no questions and have the same meaning. The sentence in (12b) differs from that in (12a) in that it does not have an overt auxiliary. The sentence in (12b) is produced with question intonation (see the chapter by Erik Thomas in Part III for a discussion of AAE intonation.). As it turns out, although more research is needed in this area, prosodic properties or intonational properties are sufficient to signal that the sentence is a question. Furthermore, the sentence is grammatical without an overt auxiliary. On the other hand, the embedded question in (11e) is unacceptable because it does not have an overt element in the clause initial position. Here we see that matrix questions and embedded questions in AAE differ in the requirement to have an overt element in the clause initial position. One question is whether the restriction is a structural one, related to syntactic requirements, or a semantic one, related to selection or interpretation.

Sistrunk (2012) discusses AAE relative clause structures in which the relative marker is zero, or there is no overt *that* or *who* introducing the clause, such as __ *prepared the meal* in (13):

(13) The man [__prepared the meal] is a chef.
      'The man that prepared the meal is a chef.'

In his analysis of these constructions, Sistrunk (2012) makes a number of important observations. One is that these relative clauses are produced with a specific intonation (46). More research needs to be conducted on intonation and relative clauses, but it should be noted that the same type of relation between yes/no questions without overt initial auxiliaries such as those in (12b) and special question prosody might also hold between zero relative clauses and the relative clause prosody.

The final type of complex construction that will be discussed in this section is embedded negation. One of the properties of the negation system in AAE is concord or agreement, as represented by the following illustration:

(14) <NEG, Neg$_{Agr}$, Neg$_{Agr}$, Neg$_{Agr}$ . . .>

The illustration in (14) represents negative concord as a type of agreement such that a negative element (NEG) triggers negative agreement with subsequent negative elements, which are represented as Neg$_{Agr}$. By agreement, it is meant that the Neg$_{Agr}$ elements do not add any additional negative force; they are negative in agreement with NEG. The illustration captures negative agreement within a string, which might also extend across a clause boundary.

(15) a. I ain't gon buy nothing for no classes now.
          NEG   Neg$_{Agr}$ Neg$_{Agr}$
          'I am not going to buy anything for any classes now.'
      b. I didn't know $_{CLAUSE\ BOUNDARY}$[that Bruce was eating no apple].
          NEG   Neg$_{Agr}$
          'I did not know that Bruce was eating an apple.'

The sentences in (15) show that negative concord is not restricted to a single clause; the concord or agreement can extend into another clause. In (15b), NEG crosses the clause boundary to form a concord relation with *no apple* in the lower clause, so the reading of *no apple* is 'an apple', as indicated in the paraphrase.

Negative concord is also a property of declarative negative auxiliary inversion (NAI) sentences, which are characterized by an initial negated auxiliary followed by an indefinite noun, as in the sentence in (16). The initial negative elements (*didn't* and *nobody*) form a concord relationship, such as that represented in (14):

(16)   Didn't nobody find out about the test until yesterday.
         'Not a single person found out about the test until yesterday.'

A number of analyses of these NAI constructions in AAE and in other varieties of English have been set forth in the literature (see Feagin 1979; Foreman 1999; Green 2014; Labov 1972; Labov et al. 1968; Martin 1992; Parrott 2000; Sells, Rickford, and Wasow 1996; Weldon 1994; White-Sustaíta 2010; Wolfram and Christian 1976). In Green (2014), the claim is that the structural position of the negated auxiliary (e.g., *didn't*) preceding the negative indefinite noun (e.g., *nobody*)—in initial position of the clause—signals an absolute negation reading that could be interpreted along the lines of 'not a single person/thing' (see the discussion of NAI in Green and White-Sustaíta, this volume).

Many of the analyses of NAI constructions have been concerned with the structural position of the negated auxiliary and indefinite noun in matrix clauses, but these constructions can also occur in embedded contexts:

(17)   a.   She didn't say CLAUSE BOUNDARY[that didn't nobody want to ride the bus].
          b.   They don't know [(that) can't nobody ride the bus].
          c.   They don't know [if can't nobody ride the bus].

In (17a) and (17b) the embedded NAI clause is introduced by *that*, and in (17c) by *if*. Note the different interpretations of the embedded clauses in (17b) and (17c). In (17b) the meaning is something along the lines of not knowing the fact that not a single person can ride the bus, and (17c) indicates something along the lines of not knowing the answer to the question of whether or not a single person can ride the bus. Another important difference is that the complementizer *that* in (17b) is optional, but *if* in (17c) is obligatory, so it must occur in the sentence. In comparing (17c) to the embedded question in (11a), we see that embedded declarative NAI constructions and regular declarative sentences can be embedded under a question complementizer, but note an important difference: The sequence *if*... AUXILIARY (e.g., **if do*) cannot occur when *do* introduces an interrogative clause, as in (11d), but the sequence of *if* ... AUXILIARY (e.g., *if can't*) as in (17c) can occur felicitously in embedded NAI constructions.

18.5 CONCLUSION

Syntactic and semantic properties in some areas of the grammar of AAE, such as the tense and aspect system, have a longer history of research than in other areas. The research has helped to reveal important patterns about co-occurrence restrictions and the distribution of verbal markers. In addition, it has also contributed to our understanding of the types of meaning that aspectual elements and morphological elements contribute to constructions.

In moving forward with research on syntactic and semantic properties of complex clauses in AAE, we continue to raise questions about the complementizer system and strategies for introducing embedded clauses. One element in the complementizer system of AAE that has been included in some general descriptions, but that has not been addressed in current work on AAE embedded constructions, is quotative *say*. It would be interesting to explore *say* in current frameworks as a means of determining how it fits into the AAE complementizer system and complex clauses. Moving away from features lists and building on earlier research, we take a syntactic and semantic approach in describing properties of systems of language use in AAE. Questions are raised about general patterns of language use and general restrictions on constructions in different components of the grammar.

NOTES

1. The term *eventuality* is used here as a cover term for events and states, which are characterized as holding. Aspectual markers occur with both predicates that indicate events and those that indicate states, such as adjectives (e.g., tall) and stative verbs (e.g., know).
2. *–s* is not generally marked on verbs in third person singular contexts.

REFERENCES

Bailey, Guy, and Natalie Maynor. 1987. "Decreolization?" *Language and Society* 16: 449–73.

Dayton, Elizabeth. 1996. "Grammatical Categories of the Verb in African American Vernacular English." PhD diss., University of Pennsylvania, Philadelphia.

DeBose, Charles, and Nicholas Faraclas. 1993. "An Africanist Approach to the Linguistic Study of Black English: Getting to the Roots of Tense-Aspect-Modality and Copula Systems in Afro-American." In *Africanisms in Afro-American Language Varieties*, edited by Salikoko S. Mufwene, 364–87. Athens: University of Georgia Press.

Dillard, Joey L. 1972. *Black English: Its History and Usage in the United States*. New York: Random House.

———. 1975. *Perspectives on Black English*. The Hague, Netherlands: Mouton de Gruyter.

Edwards, Walter. 2001. "Aspectual *Dən* in African American Vernacular English in Detroit." *Journal of Sociolinguistics* 5: 413–27.

Fasold, Ralph. 1972. *Tense Marking in Black English*. Arlington, VA: Center for Applied Linguistics.

Feagin, Crawford. 1979. *Variation and Language Change: A Sociolinguistic Study of the White Community*. Washington, DC: Georgetown University Press.

Fickett, Joan. 1975. "*Ain't*, not, and *Don't* in Black English." In *Perspectives on Black English*, edited by Joey L. Dillard, 86–90. The Hague, Netherlands: Mouton de Gruyter.

Foreman, John. 1999. "Syntax of Negative Inversion in Non-Standard English." In *Proceedings of the Seventeenth West Coast Conference on Formal Linguistics*, edited by Kimar Shahin, Susan Blake, and Eun Sook Kim. Stanford, CA: CSLI.

Green, Lisa. 1993. "Topics in African American English: The Verb System Analysis." PhD diss., University of Massachusetts Amherst.

——. 1998. "Remote Past and States in African American English," *American Speech* 73: 115–138.

——. 2000. "Aspectual *Be*-type Constructions and Coercion in African American English." *Natural Language Semantics* 8: 1–25.

——. 2007. "NPs in Aspectual *Be* Constructions in African American English." In *Noun Phrases in Creole Languages: A Multi-faceted Approach*, edited by Marlyse Baptista and Jacqueline Gueron, 403–20. Philadelphia: John Benjamins.

——. 2014. "Force, Focus, and Negation in African American English." In *Micro-Syntactic Variation in North American English*, edited by Raffaella Zanuttini and Laurence R. Horn, 115–42. New York: Oxford University Press.

Labov, William. 1972. *Language in the Inner City: Studies in the Black English Vernacular*. Philadelphia: University of Pennsylvania Press.

Labov, William, Paul Cohen, Clarence Robins, and John Lewis. 1968. *A Study of Nonstandard English of Negro and Puerto Rican Speakers in New York City*. USOE final report, research project no. 3288.

Loflin, Marvin. 1972. "Black American English: Independent Motivation for the Auxiliary Hypothesis." Technical Report No. 2, Institute for the Study of Urban Linguistics, University of Wisconsin, Milwaukee.

——. 1975. "Black American English and Syntactic Dialectology." In *Perspectives on Black English*, edited by Joey L. Dillard, 65–73. The Hague, Netherlands: Mouton de Gruyter.

Martin, Stefan E. 1992. "Topics in the Syntax of Nonstandard English." PhD diss., University of Maryland, College Park.

Martin, Stefan, and Walt Wolfram. 1998. "The Sentence in African-American Vernacular English." In *African-American English: Structure, History, and Use*, edited by Salikoko S. Mufwene, John R. Rickford, Guy Bailey, and John Baugh, 11–36. New York: Routledge.

Myhill, John. 1988. "The Rise of *Be* as an Aspect Marker in Black English." *American Speech* 63: 304–25.

——. 1991. "The Use of Invariant *Be* with Verbal Predicates in BEV." In *Verb Phrase Patterns in Black English and Creole*, edited by Walter Edwards and Donald Winford, 101–13. Detroit, MI: Wayne State University Press.

Parrott, Jeffrey K. 2000. "Negative Inversion in African American Vernacular English: A Case of Optional Movement." In *Proceedings of the 28th Western Conference on Linguistics, Vol. 11 (WECOL 1999)*, edited by Nancy Mae Antrim, Grant Goodall, Martha Schulte-Nafeh, and Vida Samiian. Fresno: California State University, Department of Linguistics.

Rickford, John R. 1973. "Been in Black English." University of Pennsylvania, unpublished ms.

——. 1975. "Carrying the New Wave into Syntax: The Case of Black English *Been*." In *Variation in the Form and Use of Language*, edited by Ralph W. Fasold, 98–119. Washington, DC: Georgetown University Press.

——. 1999. *African American Vernacular English: Features, Evolution, Educational Implications*. Malden, MA: Blackwell.

Sells, Peter, John Rickford, and Thomas Wasow. 1996. "An Optimality Approach to Variation in Negative Inversion in AAVE." *Natural Language and Linguistic Theory* 14: 591–627.

Sistrunk, Walter. 2012. "The Syntax of Zero in African American Relative Clauses." PhD diss., Michigan State University.

Terry, J. Michael. 2004. "On the Articulation of Aspect in African American English." PhD diss., University of Massachusetts, Amherst.

———. 2005. "The Past Perfective and Present Perfect in African-American English." In *Perspectives on Aspect*, edited by Henk Verkuyl, Henriette de Swart, and Angeliek van Hout, 217–32. Dordrecht: Springer.

———. 2006. "A Present Perfect Puzzle for African-American English." In *Proceedings of NELS 36*, edited by Christopher Davis, Amy Rose Deal, and Youri Zabbal, 559–618. Amherst, MA: GLSA.

Weldon, Tracey. 1994. "Another Look at Negative Inversion in African-American English: An HPSG Account." Unpublished ms. Ohio State University.

White-Sustaíta, Jessica. 2010. "Reconsidering the Syntax of Non-Canonical Negative Inversion." *English Language and Linguistics* 14: 429–55.

Winford, Donald. 1993. *Predication in Caribbean English Creoles*. Amsterdam: John Benjamins.

Wolfram, Walt, and Donna Christian. 1976. *Appalachian Speech*. Arlington, VA: Center for Applied Linguistics.

CHAPTER 19

THE SYSTEMATIC MARKING OF TENSE, MODALITY, AND ASPECT IN AFRICAN AMERICAN LANGUAGE

CHARLES E. DEBOSE

19.1 INTRODUCTION

THIS chapter offers a systematic account of tense, modality, and aspect (TMA) marking in African American Language (AAL). Throughout the discussion, it is taken for granted that AAL differs little from other varieties of American English (AE) in such basic ways as the internal structure of noun, adjective, and prepositional phrases, and their occurrence in the constituent structure of sentences. What is most distinctive about the grammar of AAL is the manner in which tense, modality, and aspect is expressed.

For the sake of the present discussion, *tense* refers to the part of the meaning of a sentence that expresses the time of a predicated event with reference to the time at which the sentence is spoken. The time of the events predicated by sentences (1) to (4) is understood by an AAL listener to be simultaneous with the act of speaking, that is, the present, even though it is not overtly marked as such.

(1) *She my sister.*
    'She is my sister.'
(2) *He tall and skinny.*
    'He is tall and skinny.'
(3) *They at home.*
    'They are at home.'
(4) *We havin a party.*
    'We are having a party.'

In sentence (5), the predicated event is understood as occurring before the time of the speech act, and commonly referred to as past tense. Furthermore, the meaning of past tense is overtly marked by the occurrence of *was*, before the phrase *at home*.

(5) *They was at home.*
     'They were at home.'

The grammar of AAL also allows for the overt marking of future tense: either by the marker *gon* (pronounced /gõ/), occurring before a predicate phrase, as in (6) and (7), or by the auxiliary *will*, as in (8).

(6) *We gon have a party.*
(7) *We gon be at home.*
(8) *They will be at the office.*

Modality, for present purposes, may be thought of as the part of the meaning of a sentence that expresses a degree of doubt or uncertainty about the truth of a predicated event, or makes its truth contingent upon circumstances. In sentence (9), for example, the speaker expresses doubt. In sentence (10), s/he makes the ability to fix the car contingent upon the hearer leaving it overnight.

(9) *I might can fix the car.*
(10) *If you can leave the car overnight, I can fix it.*

Modality is often marked in AAL sentences by modal auxiliaries that differ little from their Standard English (SE) equivalents: words such as *should, might,* and *can*. Some AAL modals, such as *kin* (can) and *kaint* (can't) have distinctive pronunciations and occur in distinctive combinations with negative words such as in sentence (11).

(11) *It aint no way he kin fix that car overnight.*

Aspect refers to how a predicated event is viewed as ongoing or completed at a particular point in time, or recurring in a manner expressed by adverbial forms like *usually* and *on occasion*. The event predicated by sentence (12) is ongoing at the time of the speech act. The aspect of similar SE structures is commonly referred to as *progressive* or *continuous*.

(12) *He walkin around the lake.*

Sentences (13) to (15) exemplify *completive aspect*. They have in common an ambiguity with respect to past tense and what is commonly referred to as present perfect aspect. Sentence (13), for example, in different contexts could mean either 'I forgot my hat' or 'I have forgotten my hat.'

(13) *I forgot my hat.* 'I forgot/have forgotten my hat.'
(14) *I done forgot my hat.* 'I forgot/have forgotten my hat.'
(15) *I cook a mess of greens.* 'I cooked/have cooked a bunch of greens.'

Sentences (13) to (15) also illustrate two distinctive features of AAL syntax: the variable occurrence of a completive aspect marker, *done* before past or past participle forms of irregular English verbs like *forget*, and the variable absence of the suffix *–ed* on regular verbs like *cook*. The status of the past participle in all varieties of AE is complicated by its similarity to past tense forms. The aspect of the SE sentence *I have cooked a bunch of greens* is commonly referred to as *perfect*.

The word *been* occurs in AAL in two contrasting ways referred to as unstressed *been* and stressed *BIN*. Unstressed *been* is treated in the following discussion as a marker of *durative* aspect that differs little from *been* in other varieties of AE, as in sentence (16). The stressed form, represented by all capital letters, situates the beginning of a predicated event in the remote past, as in (17).

(16)   *He been at home.*
       'He has been at home.'
(17)   *He BIN at home.*
       'He has been at home for a long time.'

Sentences (18) and (19) exemplify habitual aspect.

(18)   *We be at home.*
       'We are at home at particular times.'
(19)   *We usually be at home.*
       'We are usually at home.'

The event predicated by sentence (18) is understood as recurring at particular times in the experience of the speaker. An AAL listener understands that the speaker is not talking about the present time, whether or not it is specified by an adverbial expression such as in (19).

The use of *be* directly following the subject of a sentence as a marker of habitual aspect is commonly referred to as *invariant be*. It is one of a small number of AAL features that have been the focus of seminal research by leading scholars. Another is the variable absence of the present tense copula/auxiliary forms *is* and *are* in sentences like (1) to (5) above. Existing research on those and other AAL TMA features is discussed in the following section.

19.2 EXISTING RESEARCH

Existing studies of AAL have been conducted by scholars interested in its relevance to theoretical claims and controversies in particular areas of study, as much as, if not more so than description of the variety as a linguistic system in its own right. Some of the earliest studies are by scholars of pidgin and creole languages, who use certain AAL features as evidence in support of a theory of the origin of AAL known as the *Creolist Hypothesis* (Stewart 1966; Dillard 1971; Rickford, this volume). Ensuing discussion of the pros and cons of the Creolist Hypothesis includes debate of the extent to which AAL differs from other varieties of AE in its underlying structure.

Other early studies by linguists specializing in the study of language variation and change, and known as variationists, take issue with the view that AAL differs from SE in its underlying structure, arguing instead that surface differences reflect the application of variable rules to an inherently variable system shared by speakers of AAL and SE. Labov uses variation in empirical samples of AAL data in support of his claim of the existence of a variable rule that under different circumstances produces full, contracted, and deleted forms of the copula (1969).

Labov's account of AAL copula variation is part of a general claim that differences between AAL and SE are the consequence of "low-level rules" and/or minor additions to the rules of SE. Typical arguments in support of the low-level rules view allude to selected phonological features to account for the variable absence of morphological features such as the verb suffix /d/. Fasold (1969) accounts for the AAL feature commonly known as *habitual be* in a way that supports the low-level rules argument by postulating the existence of an invariant *be*, labeled *be₂*, which coexists with the inflected *be₁* common to all varieties of AE.

DeBose (1977) calls attention to linguists who have clear intuitions of a stable linguistic system underlying a continuum of variation in empirical data samples of their native languages and insists that an adequate theory of language should not only hold researchers accountable to empirical data but also the grammaticality judgments of native speakers. He cites the work of Jamaican linguist Beryl Bailey who offers a formal description of her native language in the book *Jamaican Creole Syntax: A Transformational Approach* (Bailey 1965).

DeBose and Faraclas (1993) offer an "Africanist account" of the AAL TMA system, which attributes its distinctiveness to the survival of a system of TMA marking common to languages of West Africa, referred to as a *lexical stativity parameter* (LSP), in which verbs are not inflected; rather, TMA values are assigned to syntactic predicates based on the extent to which a predicated event is interpreted semantically as an action or as a state (Mufwene 1983; Faraclas 1987, 1988).

Table 19.1 summarizes similarities and differences between the TMA systems of Nigerian Pidgin (NP), Gullah, and present-day AAL. It is noteworthy that cognates of English *go, done,* and *been* function in NP and Gullah systems to mark future time, completive aspect, and anterior aspect, respectively. Table 19.1 implies that the anterior aspect category survives in AAL but is marked by cognates of the English auxiliaries *was* and *had*. The inclusion of *been* as an AAL anterior marker is in recognition of the fact that it survives in archaic varieties of AAL such as Samaná English (DeBose 1983, 1988).

Green (1998) accounts for the internal structure of AAL using an X-bar model of AAL syntax to make the case that the TMA system has a unique category of words referred to as "aspect markers" that coexist with auxiliaries found in other varieties of AE. She shows that auxiliaries such as *was* may switch positions with the subject in questions and "host" the negation marker *not* in grammatical sentences, whereas aspect markers such as *done* and habitual *be* lack such properties, as illustrated by the following examples:

> *Was they ready when you got there?*
> *They wadn ready when I got there.*
> *She done went home.*
> ** done she went home?*
> **She done not went.*
> *We be having a good time.*
> **Be yall havin a good time?*

Green also discusses the above-mentioned stressed *BIN* feature and makes the case for classifying it as an aspect marker.

Labov (1998) revisits earlier claims regarding the extent to which AAL participates in a single inherently variable system of AE and develops the idea of "coexistent systems," one of which accounts for the distinctive TMA features of AAL. Labov mentions the work of two scholars who might be seen as symbolizing the two coexistent systems: Beryl Bailey, who was a fellow graduate student with Labov at Columbia University, and Elizabeth Dayton, who completed her dissertation on "the tense and aspect system of AAVE [African American Vernacular English]" (1996, 110) under Labov's supervision, using empirical samples of AAL. Bailey (1965), by contrast, uses examples selected from a novel entitled *The Cool World* as a source for describing patterns in the selection of "the negative markers *don't* and *ain't*" in a manner that has proven to be highly accurate. Labov comments on Bailey's "first paper on the topic, 'A new perspective on American Negro dialectology,'" noting that "her insights into the nature of the dialect were motivated in part by her reaction against the dialectological view of AAVE as a collection of mistakes and deviations from Standard English" (Labov 1998, 111). Recent work on AAL reflects a growing diversity of perspectives on the subject including formal methods of linguistic analysis.

Table 19.1 TMA Systems in Nigerian Pidgin, Gullah, and AAL

	Nigerian Pidgin	Gullah	African American Language
Completive	don	Done	done, –ed, –EN
Non-completive	de	də	do, –s, –in
Anterior	bin	Been	was
			had
			been
Future	go	Gwine	gõ

Terry (2004) contributes to the study of AAL aspect marking as it informs ongoing study of perfect aspect from a cross-linguistic perspective focused on questions posed by the ambiguity of AAL sentences such as "The frog done jumped."

Walker (this volume) calls attention to the need for more study of phonological constraints on the occurrence of selected features of AAL TMA marking and applies a theory of prosodic phonology to empirical data of variation in the copula and the third person singular suffix –s in archaic varieties of AAL spoken in Nova Scotia and the Samaná Peninsula of the Dominican Republic.

DeBose (2005), in a chapter entitled, "The Grammar: We Be Following Rules," offers "a succinct overview of what an *autonomous grammar* of [AAL] would look like," that is, a description of the variety in terms of its internal structure without reference to other language varieties to which it may be related historically or at the present time. The challenge of such an approach is to describe features such as the variable occurrence of the copula and tense-marking suffixes with reference to a system of rules that generate sentences that are grammatically acceptable to native speakers and prioritize systematic description of the language as a whole as opposed to studying isolated features. Such is the approach taken in the following sections focused on key elements of the AAL TMA system.

19.3 ELEMENTS OF THE AAL TMA SYSTEM

In the following pages, an informal account is offered of words and phrases that play a key role in the interpretation of TMA in AAL sentences. A working hypothesis is that the following TMA values are encoded into AAL utterances either through overt markers, default values assigned to unmarked predicates by the LSP, or through innovative features that have come into the language as a result of contact with other varieties of AE over time (DeBose and Faraclas 1993):

- non-completive aspect/present tense
- completive aspect/past tense
- future tense
- habitual aspect/present tense
- anterior aspect
- remote anterior aspect
- durative aspect.

The above-mentioned innovative features include present participle (V + –*in*) and past participle (V + –*ed*) forms, which, unlike similar SE participles, may occur directly following the subject with no preceding form of the auxiliaries *be* or *have*. These include the above-mentioned invariant *be* and stressed *BIN* features, and the use of positive and negative forms of selected auxiliaries for sentence negation and anterior aspect marking. Those and other innovative features are explained in detail in the following pages.

19.3.1 Constituent Structure of Sentences

At the highest level of structure, sentences consist of a basic sentence and an auxiliary that may optionally occur before the subject, between the subject and the predicate, or not at all. Auxiliaries play a key role in sentence negation, anterior aspect marking, and other ways discussed below.

A detailed account of the role of different types of predicate phrases in the TMA system is developed in the next section on the constituent structure of basic sentences followed by sections on verb suffixes, selectional restriction, auxiliaries, patterns of complementation, and TMA markers in that order.

19.3.2 Constituent Structure of Basic Sentences

A basic AAL sentence consists of a subject followed directly by one or another of four types of predicate phrases. Each type of predicate has a default TMA interpretation in the absence of overt markers or context clues to the contrary, and these pattern alike with respect to restrictions on their co-occurrence with selected negation and anterior aspect markers, as well as with special variants of the subject pronouns *I, it, that*, and *what* (DeBose and Faraclas 1993).

19.3.3 Type I Predicates

Type I predicates (table 19.2) have a default non-completive aspect/present tense interpretation consistent with the value assigned to stative predicates by the LSP. Inclusion of present participle phrases in the Type I category is supported by the fact that they pattern similarly to other Type I predicates in a number of ways discussed in detail below.

Table 19.2 Type I Predicates

Phrase type	Examples
Nominal complement of the subject (NP)	*He my son*
Adjectival complement of the subject (PA)	*She smart*
Locative complement of the subject (LOC)	*They at home*
Present participle (V + in)	*We walkin*

19.3.4 Type II Predicates

Table 19.3 displays examples of phrases that qualify as Type II predicates. The frequent absence of the *–ed* suffix in AAL data, even in environments where it is rarely absent in other varieties, such as at the end of an utterance or in the environment of a following vowel, is adequately accounted for in this model by a default completive aspect/past tense interpretation that Type II predicates derive from the LSP. They are redundantly marked as such in either of the following ways:

- by attachment of the *–ed* suffix to the base form of a SE regular verb;
- by selection of the past tense or past participle form of a SE irregular verb; or
- by selection of the completive aspect marker *done*.

For some AAL speakers, a sentence like (20) is ungrammatical, and for that reason the above-mentioned options for a Type II predicate do not include selection of the base form of an irregular verb.

(20) *I done eat a lotta rice.*

Speakers who have trouble accepting the grammaticality of sentence (20) might assign a default habitual aspect/present tense interpretation to a sentence like (21) in which the predicate is the base form of an irregular verb, whether or not the *–s* suffix is attached as in sentence (22).

(21) *I eat a lotta rice.*
'I habitually eat lots of rice.'
(22) *I eats a lotta rice.*
'I habitually eat lots of rice.'

The predicates of sentences (21) and (22) are instances of Type III predicates (table 19.4), which, like Type II predicates, are non-stative.

Type III predicates, contrary to the default completive aspect/past tense interpretation assigned to non-stative predicates by the LSP, are marked for non-completive, habitual aspect and illustrate tense in one of the following ways:

- by selection of the base form of an irregular verb;
- by attachment of the *–s* suffix to the base form of a verb (regular or irregular); or, in the case of an unmarked regular verb,
- by context.

Type IV predicates (table 19.5), headed by stative verbs, are assigned a default non-completive aspect/present tense interpretation by the LSP. A relatively small group of AAL verbs are stative and include linking verbs such as *seem, feel, look, taste* as well as verbs of thinking, saying, and knowing.

Table 19.3 Type II Predicates

Phrase type: (done) v (–ed)	Examples
Unmarked regular verb	*I cook a lotta rice*
Regular verb with –ed attached	*I cooked a lotta rice*
Done + regular verb	*I done cook a lotta rice*
Irregular past tense or past participle form	*I ate a lotta rice*

Table 19.4 Type III Predicates

Phrase type: V [–stative] (–s)	Examples
Unmarked regular verb	*I cook a lotta rice*
Regular verb with –s attached	*I cooks a lotta rice*
Base form of irregular verb	*I eat a lotta rice*
Base form of irregular verb with -s attached	*I eats a lotta rice*

Table 19.5 Type IV Predicates

Phrase type: V [+ stative] (–s)	Examples
Unmarked regular verb	*It taste good*
Regular verb with –s attached	*It tastes good*
Base form of irregular verb	*I know Im right*
Base form of irregular verb with –s attached	*I knows Im right*

It is interesting to note that the examples in table 19.5 are ambiguous with respect to whether or not the predicated event occurs at the present time, as in (23), or habitually, as in (24).

(23) *I feel tired now.*
(24) *I often feel tired.*

To the extent that habitual aspect is subsumed under the general heading of non-completive aspect, but not always explicitly marked, it has implications for the invariant *be* feature, which is discussed further below after the following discussion of the status of verb suffixes in the AAL TMA system.

19.3.5 Verb Suffixes

This section summarizes some points made thus far about the role of verb suffixes in the AAL system. The following comment by DeBose and Faraclas suggests that in general it is at best a marginal role. "Verb forms similar to the English infinitive, simple present, simple past, and past participle frequently occur in [AAL], but such variation does not play a primary role in the tense-mood-aspect interpretation of [AAL] sentences" (1993, 368). It was noted above that the *–in* suffix of present participle predicates is best treated as a derivational affix and that the variable occurrence of the *–ed* suffix attached to the base form of regular verbs in Type II predicates redundantly marks the completive aspect/past tense interpretation assigned to such predicates by the LSP, and to that extent plays a marginal role at best. The *–ed* suffix is also used, however, to assign anterior aspect to a Type IV predicate that has a default non-completive/present aspect/tense interpretation, as in sentence (25).

(25) *It tasted good.*

Explanation of the difference between the role of the *–ed* suffix in Types II and IV predicates is facilitated by positing an abstract feature [+/– verb] that is present in predicate Types III and IV and absent from Types I and II. Given that assumption, a general rule for attaching *–ed* to a predicate would indicate that it overrides the default non-completive aspect/present tense interpretation of a [+stative/+ verb] and marks the predicated event for anterior aspect. Attachment of the same suffix to a [–stative/–verb] predicate, however, redundantly marks it for the completive aspect/past tense interpretation assigned by the LSP.

The reality of an abstract [+/– verb] feature in the linguistic competence of AAL speakers is supported by evidence of selectional restrictions that coincide with predicate types discussed in the next section.

19.3.6 Selectional Restrictions

A number of rules of AAL grammar specify the selection of one or another of a set of alternatives in the environment of selected predicate types, or more abstractly, different combinations of the features [+/– verb] and [+/– stative]. A case in point is the selection of the special pronouns *im, its, thats,* and *whats,* which co-occur with Type I [–verb/+stative] predicates. Other selectional restrictions involve the auxiliaries *aint* and *dont*. The rule for selection of one or the other is discussed in detail in the next section, which also discusses selection of the auxiliaries *was* and *had*.

19.3.7 Auxiliaries

In this section, the point is developed that AAL auxiliaries are related paradigmatically in a manner highlighted in table 19.6, in which the auxiliaries listed are grouped into pairs of affirmative and negative forms of each word.

Table 19.6 highlights the rule for selecting *aint* or *don't* based on the value of a predicate for the feature [+/– verb]; i.e., select *aint* with [–verb] predicates as in sentences (26) and (27), otherwise select *don't*. The grammaticality of the Type II predicate of (27),

Table 19.6 Auxiliaries

Co-occurs with	Question/ affirmation	Negation
[–verb]	is	aint
[–verb/+stative/+anterior	was	wadn
[–verb/–stative/+anterior]	had	hatn
[+verb]	do	don't
+verb/+stative/+anterior	did	ditn

as well as the Type I predicate of (26) supports the general applicability of the rule to [–verb] predicates.

(26) Type I: *She aint at home.*
'She is not at home.'
(27) Type II: *He aint cook no rice.*
'He didn't cook any rice.'

Table 19.6 also highlights the role of auxiliaries in the overt marking of sentences for anterior aspect. The auxiliary *was* functions to mark Type I sentences like (28) that have a default present tense interpretation as occurring at a point in time before the present, as illustrated in (29).

(28) *She at home*
(29) *She was at home*

The auxiliary *had* is selected to mark a Type II sentence such as (30), which has a default completive aspect/past tense interpretation for anterior aspect, for example (31).

(30) *They done went home.*
'They went/have gone home.'
(31) *They had done went home.*
'They had gone home.'

The anterior markers *was* and *had*, like all auxiliaries, have negative forms and occur alternately in sentence initial position in questions. Sentence (32) exemplifies use of the negative form *wadn* to mark a negative yes/no question with a Type I predicate for anterior aspect. Sentence (33) illustrates the use of *hatn* to negate a Type II predicate while simultaneously marking it for anterior aspect.

(32) *Wadn you gon drive?*
'Weren't you going to drive?'
(33) *We hatn finish.*
'We hadn't finished.'

19.4 TMA Markers and Patterns of Complementation

In the following discussion, the term *TMA marker* is used for forms that are an integral part of the AAL predicate phrase. The markers *gon, done, be*, and *been* were tentatively defined above as markers of future tense, completive aspect, habitual aspect, and durative aspect, respectively. The search for more definitive definitions is facilitated by information summarized in the following paragraphs about each marker with reference to patterns of complementation.

The term *complement* as used here is a phrase structure that is required to complete a sentence constituent in a way that satisfies speaker intuitions of grammaticality. The ungrammaticality of sentence (34) and acceptability of sentence (35) supports the conclusion that *done* accepts a Type II predicate such as *went to the store* as a complement, whereas *gon* does not.

(34) *They gon went to the store.*
(35) *They done went to the store.*

The grammaticality of sentences (36) and (37) support the rule that *gon* does accept [+verb] complements such as *take* and *be*.

(36) *We gon take a break.*
(37) *We gon be at home.*

The marker *done*, as noted above, occurs variably in a Type II predicate to redundantly mark it for completive aspect/past tense and may be complemented by a Type II predicate or the durative marker *been*. It is treated as a subtype of Type II predicate based on its co-occurrence with the auxiliary *had* in sentences marked for anterior aspect and with regular variants of the subject pronouns *I, it, that*, and *what*.

The marker *gon* is treated as a subtype of the Type I predicate based on its co-occurrence with the negative auxiliary *aint*, the anterior marker *was*, and special subject pronouns. As noted above, it takes [+verb] complements, including the marker *be*. When *gon* is used to mark a [–verb] predicate for future time, *be* is inserted between gon and the predicate phrase to satisfy the requirement of a [+verb] complement, as in sentence (38).

(38) *You gon be done forgot.*
       'You are going to have forgotten.'

The inclusion of *gon* as a subtype of the Type I predicate is relevant to the so-called copula absence issue insofar as the phrase types include all of the post-copula environments specified in previous studies except the negative marker *not*. It has been noted that while all [−verb] predicates accept *aint* negation, as illustrated by sentences (39)–(42), Type I predicates but not Type II predicates are also grammatical when negated by *not* (DeBose 2005, 201).

(39) Type I: *They aint at home*
(40) Type II: *He aint cook no rice*
(41) Type I: *They not at home*
(42) Type II: * *He not cook no rice*

When the classification of *gon* as a Type I predicate and the co-occurrence of such predicates with *not* are taken into account, the copula absence feature is adequately accounted for as an intrinsic feature of the AAL system without reference to rules of a different system from which it deviates.

The marker *be* qualifies as a subtype of the Type IV predicate insofar as it accepts [+stative] Type I predicates as complements and patterns with [+verb] predicates in accepting *dont* negation. A point worth noting about the characterization of *be* in previous studies as a marker of habitual aspect is that unmarked Type I predicates are ambiguous with respect to whether or not a predicated event takes place habitually or at the present time. As such, sentences like (43) and (44) are synonymous.

(43) *We usually at Grandma's.*
(44) *We usually be at Grandma's.*

The marker *be* functions in such cases to overtly mark a Type I or Type II *done* predicate for habitual aspect.

Evidence presented thus far supports the continued operation of an innovative version of the LSP in present-day AAL, insofar as preverbal markers similar to those of the archaic system survive in the markers *gon* and *done* (see table 19.1 above).

The marker *been*, in its unstressed form, patterns similarly with Type I predicates to the extent that it takes *aint* negation and accepts unmarked Type I predicates as complements. As such, it is treated here as a subcategory of Type I predicates that assigns durative aspect to a predicated event, as in sentence (45).

(45) *We been at Grandma's all morning.*

The marker known as stressed *BIN* differs in notable ways from unstressed *been*. Unlike unstressed *been*, which is restricted to [−verb/+stative] predicates, stressed *BIN* also occurs before predicate Types II and IV as in the following sentences.

(46) Type II: *We BIN ate breakfast!*
(47) Type IV: *I BIN know her name!*

An adequate account of the stressed *BIN* feature is difficult without reference to a conversational context such as the following:

Speaker A: *Y'all done ate breakfast?*
Speaker B: *We BIN done ate breakfast!*

Prospects for future research on stressed *BIN* and other questions considered in this article are briefly discussed in the conclusion.

19.5 CONCLUSION

The foregoing informal account of the TMA system of AAL responds to the need for description of the variety as an autonomous linguistic system in a way that highlights its systematic and rule-governed nature and effectively counters erroneous beliefs about it as failed attempts to speak SE.

A clear case has been made for the existence of four major predicate types based on different combinations of the features [+/− verb] and [+/− stative] that, when directly juxtaposed to a noun phrase subject, result in sentences that satisfy native speaker intuitions of grammaticality. Type I [−verb/+stative] predicates are shown to account for the so-called copula absence feature when the future marker *gon* is included based on evidence that it patterns like unmarked Type I predicates in such features as *aint* negation, acceptance of special pronouns, and anterior marking by *was*. The negative marker *not* is shown to pattern similarly in sentences in which it substitutes for *aint*. In a like manner, the habitual *be* feature is accounted for by evidence that predicates headed by the marker *be* are subtypes of the unmarked Type IV predicate that take Type I predicate phrases as complements.

The findings presented in this chapter strongly support the claim of DeBose and Faraclas (1993) that the LSP continues to play a major role in the marking of TMA in present-day AAL. The quote above about the frequent occurrence of *"verb forms similar to the English infinitive, simple present, simple past, and past participle"* that *"[do] not play a primary role in the tense-mood-aspect interpretation of [AAL] sentences"* calls attention to a dynamic tension between an archaic system in which TMA is based on the LSP and a superstrate system in which grammatical tense plays a prominent role.

While it is true that residual elements of the superstrate system "do not play a primary role," some of them play noteworthy roles that can point the way to fruitful future studies. A case in point is the verb suffix *–s*. Although it does not play the role in AAL of a third person singular present tense inflection, it has an innovative role in overtly marking the AAL [+verb] feature and applies to all lexical items thusly marked, including *be*, as in the African American saying "It bees dat way sometime" (Smitherman 1977).

Future research can also benefit from continued study of the so-called stressed *BIN* feature. It was noted above that cognates of English *been* function in archaic African diaspora varieties to mark anterior aspect, while present-day varieties of AAL mark anterior aspect with the auxiliaries *was/wudn* or *had/hatn*, depending on whether the predicate is Type I or Type II. Such comparative evidence suggests that stressed *BIN* is an innovative feature of the AAL system representing change motivated by the above-mentioned tension between the LSP and the SE grammatical tense system.

The time may be ripe for revisiting representations of African diaspora varieties as diachronic continua and/or mesolectal variation among speakers of a single variety implicationally ordered along points of a speech continuum (DeCamp 1971; Alleyne 1980; Rickford 1974). Descriptions of the grammatical structure of AAL and other African diaspora varieties by native speaker linguists (Bailey 1965; DeBose 1977; Green 2002) can play a valuable role in such research by describing native speaker intuitions of the idealized system at the opposite extreme of such continua from the acrolectal system. Such descriptions support the most hoped for outcome of this study: that the sentences listed as examples are consistent with rules that AAL speakers know and follow. While the account is informal, it is hopefully sufficiently precise to make the point to teachers of AAL-speaking students that when they talk that way,

They dont be messin up;
they be following rules.

REFERENCES

Alleyne, Mervyn C. 1980. *Comparative Afro-American: An Historical-Comparative Study of English-Based Afro-American Dialects of the New World*. Ann Arbor, MI: Karoma.

Bailey, Beryl L. 1965. "Toward a New Perspective in American Negro Dialectology." *American Speech* 40: 171–77.

Dayton, Elizabeth. 1996. "Grammatical Categories of the Verb in African-American Vernacular English." PhD diss., University of Pennsylvania.

DeBose, Charles E. 1977. "The Status of Native Speaker Intuitions in a Polylectal Grammar." *Proceedings of the Third Annual Meeting of the Berkeley Linguistics Society*, 465–74. Berkeley Linguistics Society.

———. 1983. "Samaná English: A Dialect that Time Forgot." *Proceedings of the Ninth Annual Meeting of the Berkeley Linguistic Society*, 47–53.

———. 1988. "*be* in Samaná English." Society for Caribbean Linguistics, Occasional Paper No. 21. St. Augustine, Trinidad.

———. 2005. *The Sociology of African American Language: A Language Planning Perspective*. Hampshire, UK: Palgrave Macmillan.

DeBose, Charles E., and Nicolas Faraclas. 1993. "An Africanist Approach to the Linguistic Study of Black English: Getting to the Roots of the Tense-Aspect-Modality and Copula Systems." In *Africanisms in Afro-American Language Varieties*, edited by Salikoko Mufwene, 364–87. Athens: University of Georgia Press.

DeCamp, David 1971. "Towards a Generative Analysis of a Post-Creole Continuum." In *Pidginization and Creolization of Languages*, edited by Dell Hymes, 349–70. London: Cambridge University Press.

Dillard, J. L. 1971. "The Creolist and the Study of Negro Non-Standard Dialects in the Continental United States." In *Pidginization and Creolization of Languages*, edited by Dell Hymes, 393–408. London: Cambridge University Press.

Faraclas, Nicolas. 1987. "Creolization and the Tense Aspect Modality System of Nigerian Pidgin." *Journal of African Languages and Linguistics* 9: 45–59.

———. 1988. "Nigerian Pidgin and the Languages of Southern Nigeria." *Journal of Pidgin and Creole Languages* 3: 177–97.

Fasold, Ralph W. 1969. "Tense and the Form *be* in Black English." *Language* 45: 763–76.

Green, Lisa. 1998. "Aspect and Predicate Phrases in African American Vernacular English." In *African American English: Structure, History and Use*, edited by Salikoko Mufwene, John Rickford, Guy Bailey, and John Baugh, 37–68. New York: Routledge.

———. 2002. *African American English: A Linguistic Introduction*. Cambridge: Cambridge University Press.

Labov, William. 1969. "Contraction, Deletion, and Inherent Variability of the English Copula." *Language* 45: 715–62.

———. 1998. "Coexistent Systems in African American Vernacular English." In *African American English: Structure, History and Use*, edited by Salikoko Mufwene, John Rickford, Guy Bailey, and John Baugh, 110–53. New York: Routledge.

Mufwene, Salikoko. 1983. *Some Observations of the Verb in Black English Vernacular*. Austin: Afro and Afro-American Studies and Research Center, University of Texas at Austin.

Rickford, John R. 1974. "The Insights of the Mesolect." In *Pidgins and Creoles: Current Trends and Prospects*, edited by David DeCamp and Ian Hancock, 92–117. Washington, DC: Georgetown University Press.

Smitherman, Geneva. 1977. *Talkin and Testifyin: The Language of Black America*. Boston: Houghton Mifflin.

Stewart, William A. 1966. "Social Dialect." In *Research Planning Conference on Language Development in Disadvantaged Children*, edited by Joan Gussow and Beryl L. Bailey. New York: Yeshiva University.

Terry, Jules Michael Eugene. 2004. "On the Articulation of Aspectual Meaning in African-American English." PhD diss., University of Massachusetts Amherst.

CHAPTER 20

....

ON THE SYNTAX-PROSODY INTERFACE IN AFRICAN AMERICAN ENGLISH

....

JAMES A. WALKER

20.1 INTRODUCTION

....

PERHAPS no other variety of English has received as much attention over the last forty years as African American English (AAE),[1] although most of this attention has focused on a relatively small set of grammatical features (see Green 2002) implicated in the debate over the origins of AAE (see Poplack 2000; Wolfram and Thomas 2002). While some attention has been paid to its phonological features—for example, consonantal variables, such as t/d-deletion and postvocalic r-deletion, figured in the first studies of AAE (see Fasold 1972; Labov et al. 1968; Wolfram 1969), and there is a growing body of studies examining vowel systems (see Fridland 2003; Hinton and Pollock 2000; Kohn and Farrington 2013)—the suprasegmental features of AAE, that is, features above the level of consonants and vowels, such as stress, intonation, rhythm, and prosody, have received much less attention. This lack of attention may be due to the inherent methodological difficulties in studying such features (see Thomas, this volume), but it is surprising in light of the evidence that prosody in spoken language serves to provide clues to the listener about how to parse or interpret the syntactic phrasing or information structure of the sentence (see Cooper and Paccia-Cooper 1980), the relative prominence of grammatical features in the study of AAE, and the implication of phonological factors in conditioning variation in the occurrence of grammatical features (see Labov 1969).

In this chapter, I begin by defining what I mean by *prosody* and outlining a theory of prosodic phonology that has been developed to address questions about the interface between syntax and phonology. Using the variationist method, I examine the variable occurrence of two grammatical features in two African diaspora varieties considered to be representative of Early AAE and their conditioning by grammatical, phonological, and prosodic factors. Although prosodic structure can be shown to be significant for one of these features, it plays no role in conditioning the occurrence of the other feature. I suggest that the differences in the significance of prosodic factors stems from differences in the morphological status of the two variables.

20.2 Prosody and Its Interface with Syntax

The term *prosody* is used to refer to a number of suprasegmental features of language: the relative prominence of syllables within a word or phrase (*stress*); the height and range of the fundamental frequency of speech (*pitch, tone*, and *intonation*); rate of speech and the relative duration of syllables (*timing*); and the tendency for phonological rules or processes to occur within particular domains, such as the syllable, the word, and the phrase (*prosodic phonology*). In this chapter, I focus on the last approach (for an overview of other approaches, see Thomas, this volume).

Beginning in the mid-1980s (Nespor and Vogel 1986; Selkirk 1984), a theory of prosodic phonology was developed that concerns itself with the question of the interface between phonology and syntax. This approach, which has been developed in subsequent work (see Inkelas and Zec 1995; Ladd 1986; Selkirk 1995, 2011; Wagner and Watson 2010; Zec and Inkelas 1990), assumes that the linguistic system consists of a phonological component and a syntactic component, each of which has its own structures and properties. The theory addresses the question of what information each component makes available to the other. Specifically, it asks the question: What information from the syntactic component is available to the phonological component?

This theory conceives of prosodic structure as a hierarchy of levels or domains within which different phonological rules or processes apply. A simplified version of the prosodic hierarchy is shown in (1), with the levels relevant to the analysis presented in this chapter in boldface. The *prosodic word* (ω) and the *phonological phrase* (φ) lie above the level of the syllable (the phonological/prosodic unit that carries pitch and length, and is used for calculating word stress) and below that of the (sentence-level) *intonation phrase*.

(1)

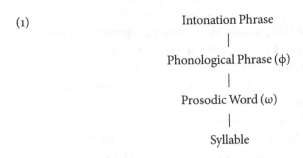

Intonation Phrase

|

Phonological Phrase (φ)

|

Prosodic Word (ω)

|

Syllable

These prosodic domains are obviously analogous to the syntactic objects *word* and *phrase*, but they are not identical. Although it is a matter of some disagreement exactly how syntactic constituents are mapped to prosodic domains (see Selkirk 1986, 1995, 1996, 2011; Truckenbrodt 1995, 1996), all approaches agree that the syntactic objects word and phrase are *mirrored* in prosodic structure, but that prosodic mapping distinguishes between lexical and functional syntactic categories: lexical (or content) categories such as noun (N), verb (V), and adjective/adverb (A) and their corresponding phrases (NP, VP, AP) serve to define prosodic domains, while functional categories such as determiner (Det), preposition (P), and auxiliary verb (Aux) are invisible to prosodic mapping. An example of this mapping is shown in (2), where (2a) is the syntactic structure and (2b) is the prosodic structure. Each lexical category (N, V) corresponds to a prosodic word, and each lexical phrase (NP, VP) corresponds to a phonological phrase, while the functional determiner *the* does not map to its own prosodic word but is included in the following prosodic domain.[2]

(2) *The dog licked the man.*
   a. [[The]$_{Det}$ [dog]$_N$]$_{NP}$ [[licked]$_V$ [[[the]$_{Det}$ [man]$_N$]$_{NP}$]$_{VP.}$
   b. ((The dog)$_\omega$)$_\varphi$ ((licked)$_\omega$ (the man)$_\omega$)$_\varphi$

Note that the second NP in (2b) does not form its own phonological phrase. A further assumption of prosodic phonology is that prosodic domains are not only constructed on the basis of syntactic constituents but also obey a requirement for phonological phrases to consist of two prosodic words wherever possible (Inkelas and Zec 1995, 544). This requirement means that prosodic structure differs depending on whether syntactic phrases are *light* (that is, consisting of one prosodic word) or *heavy* (consisting of two prosodic words). The figures in (3) show two possible prosodic mappings of the syntactic phrase XP, headed by the lexical word X and containing another syntactic phrase YP. If YP is light (consisting of a single lexical word Y), X and Y form a single phonological phrase. If YP is heavy (consisting of two lexical words, Z and Y), YP is mapped to a phonological phrase, and the remaining lexical word X forms its own phonological phrase (Zec and Inkelas 1990).

(3)

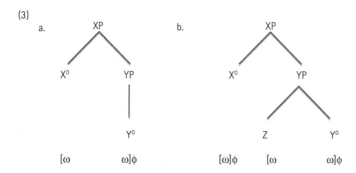

The interaction of the requirements of prosodic mapping accounts for some of the differences between syntactic and prosodic structure. In the remainder of this chapter, I will explore the consequences of this theory of prosodic phonology and its application to AAE.

20.3 THE SYNTAX-PROSODY INTERFACE AND LINGUISTIC VARIATION IN AAE

As mentioned above, the suprasegmental features of AAE have received relatively little attention. Existing research on prosody in AAE has tended to focus on those aspects of prosody dealing with stress, timing, and pitch. For example, many speakers of AAE put the primary stress of a two-syllable word on the first syllable where other speakers would stress the final syllable (e.g., *pólice* rather than *políce*). Timing differentiates languages between those like (Standard) English that keep the time between stressed syllables roughly equal regardless of the number of intervening syllables (*stress-timed*) and those like Spanish in which each syllable receives equal duration (*syllable-timed*). Thomas (this volume) provides some evidence that, in contrast with mainstream varieties of English, at least some varieties of AAE may be characterized as syllable-timed. Pitch or intonation received attention early in the study of AAE. Loman (1975) noted the use of falsetto (uncharacteristically high-pitched speech) in certain registers of AAE, and Tarone (1973) noted that speakers of AAE seem to have wider ranges of pitch than do speakers of other varieties of English. Tarone's observations have received confirmation from more recent research by Jun and Foreman (1996), who found greater pitch variation for AAE speakers in declarative utterances and higher final boundary tones in yes/no questions (see also Smith 2011). Furthermore, Smith (2012) found that the slope of the pitch of the final syllable increased in the absence of any syntactic cues that the sentence was a question. This last finding underlines the interaction of syntactic structure and prosody in AAE.

Unfortunately, outside of my own research (Walker 2000a, 2000b, 2001; cf. Sweetland, Rickford, and Hsu 2006, cited in Rickford 2006), there is no work on AAE that I am aware of that makes use of the theory of prosodic phonology outlined in the previous section. This lack of comparable research in other varieties of AAE limits the ability to generalize the results in this chapter more widely, but it does offer possible alternative explanations for the findings of other research.

In the remainder of this chapter, I will illustrate the application of the theory of prosodic phonology outlined above to two variable grammatical features of AAE: contraction and omission of the third person singular verb *be* (the *copula*) and the use of the third person singular verbal suffix –s. Although these features have different grammatical functions, they both involve alternation in the use of a single sound (/s/), with the same set of allophones: [s] after voiceless sounds, [z] after voiced sounds, and [əz] after sibilants.

In the analyses that follow, I adopt the variationist method (see Walker 2010) to examine the factors of the linguistic context that condition the different realizations of linguistic features to express the same meaning. Instead of elucidating the meaning of individual examples, I look for quantitative patterns of association between the different realizations and the potential conditioning factors. Because the variation may be conditioned by multiple factors simultaneously, I make use of the multiple regression feature of GoldVarb (Sankoff, Tagliamonte, and Smith 2012) to determine the statistical significance of factors in conditioning the variation and to assign numerical values to the relative contribution of each factor when all factors are considered simultaneously.

The data used in these analyses, which were taken from a much larger data set that was originally assembled to study the entire system of present temporal reference (Walker 2000b), come from two spoken-language corpora considered to be representative of Early AAE: Samaná English (SamE), spoken in a community on the Samaná Peninsula of the Dominican Republic founded by African Americans in the early nineteenth century (Poplack and Sankoff 1987); and African Nova Scotian English (ANSE), also spoken by the descendants of African Americans, who settled remote parts of Nova Scotia in the late eighteenth and early nineteenth centuries (Poplack and Tagliamonte 1991, 2001).[3]

20.3.1 Contracted and Zero Copula

The copula[4] is probably the most studied feature of AAE, but its origins and the factors conditioning its variability remain controversial. All varieties of English show variability between *full* and *contracted* forms of the copula (4a), but a *zero variant* (4b) occurs only in certain varieties, such as English-based creoles and AAE (and, to a lesser extent, in some Southern White vernacular varieties; see Feagin 1979; Wolfram 1974).

(4) a. The way the world's going, I don't think half of them believe in the God. (Nova Scotian English 101/1A:350) … The way the world *is* going and the way people is acting, I don't know, it don't seem like half of them believe in any God. (Nova Scotian English 101/1A:358)[5]

   b. So, hey, this *is* my home, home where- this Ø where I was born. (ANSE/008:150)

Contraction can be viewed as a form of phonological simplification, since it reduces the number of syllables in a word (see Labov 1969, 727), though it also complicates the phonology by creating clusters of consonants. The zero variant, which has figured prominently in the debate over the origins and development of AAE, has variously been interpreted as an extension of contraction that further simplifies phonological structure by reducing consonant clusters (Labov 1969; Poplack and Sankoff 1987; Poplack and Tagliamonte 1991), as evidence of a prior creole (Baugh 1980; Holm 1984), and subsequent decreolization (Singler 1991; Winford 1992), or as the relic of second language acquisition (Winford 1998).

In this chapter, I am not so much concerned with the possible origins of zero copula as I am with whether prosodic structure plays a role in conditioning its occurrence. From the corpora discussed above, I took a representative sample of present-tense declarative sentences with nonverbal predicates, in which *be* was used or could have been used. In addition to noting whether the copula occurred in its full, contracted, or zero form, I coded every token for a series of factor groups representing hypotheses about the linguistic constraints on variability: the number and grammatical person of the subject (third person singular, third person plural, other); the preceding and following phonological context (vowel or consonant); the type of subject (pronoun or NP); and the following grammatical category (future *going to/gonna*, present participle with *–ing*, adjective phrase, prepositional phrase, noun phrase, or adverbial phrase). For the purposes of the analysis presented here, I examine the results for third person singular contexts only, and I will not examine the results for the grammatical factor groups (type of subject and following grammatical category), in order to focus on the effects of the phonological and prosodic context.

Since the copula, as an auxiliary verb, is not a lexical word, it does not map to its own prosodic word, and its prosodic position is determined by the syntactic context in which it occurs. As shown in (5), the syntactic position of the full copula is included in the following prosodic domain (Inkelas and Zec 1993, 218). However, the contracted form *'s* is considered a *clitic* (Inkelas 1989; Inkelas and Zec 1993, 243), a phonologically weak form that cannot stand on its own, which contains its own set of requirements. In English, clitics generally attach to the preceding word, as shown in (6b).

(5) [(The white)$_\omega$ (dog)$_\omega$]$_\varphi$ [(ız running)$_\omega$]$_\varphi$

(6) a.   [(The white)$_\omega$ (dog)$_\omega$]$_\varphi$ ['z (running)$_\omega$]$_\varphi$

  b.   [(The white)$_\omega$ (dog'z)$_\omega$]$_\varphi$ [(running)$_\omega$]$_\varphi$

Recall that the prosodic structure of the sentence depends on whether the subject and predicate are light or heavy. These considerations lead to two types of prosodic sentence structure, as listed in (7) with illustrative examples: one that consists of a single phonological phrase, and one that consists of two phonological phrases. The crucial difference between these two sentence types is the presence of a φ-boundary between the copula and the subject, which may be interpreted as deterring the attachment of the contracted clitic to the preceding word.

(7) I: SINGLE φ (NO INTERVENING φ BOUNDARY)

  Clitic Subject

  [(subject)$_{cl}$ *COP* (predicate)$_\omega$]$_\varphi$

  a.   [(They)$_{cl}$ Ø (the same)$_\omega$]$_\varphi$ (ANSE/008:137)

  [(subject)$_{cl}$ *COP* (predicate)$_\omega$ (predicate)$_\omega$]$_\varphi$

  b.   Well, [(they)$_{cl}$ *'re* (all)$_\omega$ (living)$_\omega$]$_\varphi$ (ANSE/043:60)

  Light Subject + Light Predicate

  [(subject)$_\omega$ *COP* (predicate)$_\omega$]$_\varphi$

  c.   [(Some)$_\omega$ *are* (younger)$_\omega$]$_\varphi$ (SamE/008:296)

II: TWO φS (INTERVENING φ BOUNDARY)

Light Subject + Heavy Predicate
[(subject)ω]$_φ$ [*COP* (predicate)$_ω$ (predicate)$_ω$]$_φ$
d. [(Her twin)ω]$_φ$ [*is* (over)$_ω$ (in Sunnyville)$_ω$]$_φ$ (ANSE/053:533)

Heavy Subject
[(subject)$_ω$ (subject)$_ω$]$_φ$ [*COP* (predicate)$_ω$]$_φ$
e. [(*This*)$_ω$ (one)$_ω$]$_φ$ [*is* (easy)$_ω$]$_φ$ (ANSE/015:864)
[(subject)$_ω$ (subject)$_ω$]$_φ$ [*COP* (predicate)$_ω$ (predicate)$_ω$]$_φ$
f. [(Number)$_ω$ (nine)$_ω$]$_φ$ [*is* (over)$_ω$ (there)$_ω$]$_φ$ (SamE/002:538)

Table 20.1 shows the results of a multivariate analysis of contracted and zero copula for the two varieties of AAE.[6] Note the strong effect of the preceding segment, with vowels favoring contraction and consonants disfavoring. More interestingly, we see a consistent effect of the prosodic sentence structure in both varieties, with an intervening φ-boundary disfavoring contraction. Exactly the opposite pattern is seen for zero copula: preceding consonant, following consonant, and an intervening φ-boundary all favor zero.

In summary, both contracted and zero copula are conditioned by segmental-phonological and prosodic-phonological factors: contraction is deterred by a preceding consonant and an intervening φ boundary, while these contexts are conducive to zero copula. These results provide some evidence for the interpretation that contraction is a

Table 20.1 Prosodic and Phonological Factors Contributing to the Occurrence of Contracted and Zero *is* in Early African American English

	Contracted		Zero	
	ANSE	SamE	ANSE	SamE
Total N	309	464	215	274
Input	.750	.597	.307	.186
Preceding Phonological Environment				
Vowel/[r]	.67	.70	.44	.46
Consonant	.27	.15	.65	.80
Range	*40*	*55*	*21*	*34*
Sentential Prosodic Structure				
No φ boundary	.53	.60	.45	.47
φ boundary	.46	.21	.60	.77
Range	*7*	*39*	*15*	*30*
Following Phonological Environment				
Vowel	[.51]	.61	.31	.21
Consonant	[.50]	.45	.58	.70
Range		*16*	*27*	*49*

[ ] = not selected as significant.

strategy for reducing phonological complexity, but they also suggest that the zero copula is an additional means of reducing phonological complexity in contexts where contraction is disfavored.

20.3.2 Verbal –s

In standard English, the verbal affix –s marks agreement with a third person singular subject. Along with English-based creoles and nonstandard white varieties of English, AAE variably affixes verbal –s in contexts across the person-number paradigm, as shown in (8a), as well as omitting it in third person singular contexts (8b). The occurrence of verbal –s, which, like the zero copula, has figured in the debate over the origins of AAE, has variously been characterized as a random hypercorrection (see Labov et al. 1968, 165), as the legacy of nonstandard British English systems of subject-verb agreement (see Poplack and Tagliamonte 1989; Schneider 1983), or as the relic of a prior creole aspectual marker (see Brewer 1986; Pitts 1981).

(8) a.   And I *works* just like it was way back in the days. I still *go* on, *carry* on.
(ANSE/002:146)
b.   She only *get* in the car and she *goes* right to her work.   (SamE/005:394)

As with the copula, I am not concerned here with the origins of variability in verbal –s, but rather with its possible conditioning by prosodic structure. In a study of Reading (UK) English, Cheshire and Ouhalla (1997) argued that verbal –s indicates the prosodic integration of the verb and its complement. Under Hayes's (1984) model, syntactic structures are organized into discourse-informational units and constituents are designated as informationally autonomous or non-autonomous with respect to other constituents. Non-autonomous constituents are *integrated* and treated as a single prosodic unit. NP objects are normally integrated with the verb, but heavy complements (whether NPs or clauses) are not integrated. According to this view, verbal –s in Reading English marks the syntactic and prosodic integration of a verb and its complement. These predictions were tested in nonstandard varieties of English in Devonshire (UK) (Godfrey and Tagliamonte 1998)[7] and Newfoundland (Canada) (Clarke 2001), although the results proved to be inconsistent in supporting Cheshire and Ouhalla's argument. However, it remains unclear whether the observed effects reflect prosodic or grammatical conditioning.

Cheshire and Ouhalla's explanation bears obvious similarities to that offered for the copula in the preceding section: that /s/ is conditioned by the presence of prosodic boundaries. We might ask, then, whether /s/ is conditioned similarly by prosodic structure across different grammatical functions (copula or verbal affix). In an unpublished conference presentation, Poplack and Tagliamonte (1993) attempted to address this question by examining /s/ in ANSE in all its guises (copula, verbal affix, plural marker, and possessive affix, as well as monomorphemically), although they found that the grammatical and phonological effects were much more significant than prosodic boundaries. However, because they focused on the intonational phrase as the unit of prosodic analysis, they may have overlooked the phonological-phrase-level effects that were shown to be significant for the copula in the preceding section.

From the two AAE corpora discussed above, I took a representative sample of present-tense verb forms eligible for variable –s-marking. In addition to noting whether each verb was bare or marked with –s, I coded for a number of factors found to condition verbal –s in previous studies: the type of subject, the grammatical person and number of the subject, and the preceding phonological segment. Additionally, I coded the verbal complement as one of four types: (i) finite clauses containing a tensed verb (with or without a complementizer) (9a); (ii) non-finite clauses, including infinitivals (9b), small clauses (9c), and participial clauses (9d); (iii) non-clausal complements, including pronominal (9e) and nominal objects (9f) as well as prepositional phrases (9g); and (iv) verbs with no complement (9h).

(9) a. I *suppose* [you'll pass your Christmas home with your family].   (SamE/014:518)
     b. I *deserve* [to be up a little higher].   (ANSE/002:184)
     c. John *want* [him to retire now].   (ANSE/062:159)
     d. So, sometime you *see* [it looking bright].   (SamE/001:1250)
     e. The quiet room, we *call* [it].   (ANSE/040:599)
     f. Some *speaks* [the English] and some *speaks* [the Spanish].   (SamE/014:430)
     g. The inside box with the coffin what *sits* [down in the grave].   (ANSE/015:904)
     h. Now I *remember* [ ].   (SamE/021:1010)

Since the effect of the verbal complement might be related not only to the *presence* of a complement, but also to its heaviness, the prosodic structure of the sentence may play a role. If the complement is light (10a), it is prosodically incorporated with the verb, which is φ–internal. If the complement is heavy (10bi–ii), it forms its own φ, and the verb is φ-final. The remaining tokens were classed as φ-final (10biii).

(10) a. *φ-Internal*
          i.   Iodine or whatever you *call* it]_φ.   (ANSE/030:1178)
          ii. My children *speaks* English]_φ.   (SamE/006:438)
          iii. Every time, it *come* there]_φ.   (ANSE/039:1148)
          iv. Because he uh, he *depend* from 'Merican]_φ.   (SamE/002:218)
          v.   I *think* I did]_φ.   (ANSE/057:102)
      b. *φ-Final*
          i.   People *gets*]_φ [all kind of family allowance]_φ.   (ANSE/009:230)
          ii. I *think*]_φ [the bullet passed]_φ.   (SamE/016:171)
          iii. Every time somebody I know *die*]_φ.   (ANSE/053:1252)

Table 20.2 shows the results of the multivariate analysis for each community, divided between third person singular and other persons to test for separate effects

Table 20.2 Factors Contributing to the Occurrence of Verbal −*s*
in Three Varieties of Early African American English, by
Grammatical Person

	ANSE		SamE	
Total N	345	1,667	406	1,261
Input	.555	.033	.515	.205
	3rd sg.	non 3rd sg.	3rd sg.	non 3rd sg.
Type of Subject				
Pronoun	.57	.48	[.53]	.49
NP	.45	.86	[.41]	.68
Range	*13*	*38*		*19*
Sentential Aspect				
Habitual	[.46]	.70	[.53]	.54
Non-Habitual	[.58]	.32	[.44]	.40
Range		*38*		*14*
Preceding Segment				
Sibilant	[.21]	[.43]	.83	[.59]
Other Consonant	[.51]	[.54]	.44	[.51]
Vowel	[.52]	[.45]	.60	[.49]
Ra nge			*39*	
Type of Complement				
Finite Clause	[.29]	[.36]	.30	.27
Infinitival Clause	[.38]	[.45]	.16	.52
Non-Clausal	[.53]	[.58]	.57	.52
No Complement	[.50]	[.50]	.40	.62
Range			*41*	*35*
Prosodic Position				
φ-Internal	[.49]	[.49]	[.48]	[.51]
φ-Final	[.51]	[.51]	[.53]	[.49]

according to grammatical person. Note that the subject type effects are consistent across varieties, with pronominal subjects favoring −*s* in third person singular contexts, and NP subjects favoring in non-third contexts. The effect of sentential aspect is similarly consistent, with habituals favoring in non-third singular, while phonological effects are inconsistent. The following constituent is selected as significant only in SamE, where the direction of effect differs according to grammatical person: in third singular, non-clausal complements favor −*s*; whereas in non-third singular, verbs with no complement favor −*s*. The only consistent result, which largely holds across grammatical persons (and even when not selected as significant, as in ANSE), is that clausal complements, especially finite clauses, disfavor −*s*.

Contrary to the hypothesis of prosodic conditioning, prosodic position was not selected as significant in either variety, regardless of grammatical person. Moreover, the direction of effect is inconsistent, sometimes favoring –s, sometimes disfavoring. Thus, it appears that prosodic structure plays no role in conditioning the variable occurrence of verbal –s in these varieties.

20.4 DISCUSSION

The analyses presented above show quite different results for the effects of prosody on two variable grammatical features in AAE that involve the same segmental content. The contracted copula is favored in phonological-phrase-internal contexts and disfavored across phrase boundaries, while the zero copula is favored in contexts where contraction is disfavored. In contrast, verbal –s shows no significant effects that can be attributed to phonological phrasing.

Given the similarities in the segmental content of these two variables, and the fact that the theory and coding of prosodic phonology for the two analyses were identical, how can we explain the disparity between the significance of prosodic effects? An obvious explanation involves the morphological status of the two forms. Work in morphological theory has provided evidence that clitics and affixes differ in their selectional properties, the linguistic structures they attach to, and the component of the language in which that attachment takes place (Zwicky and Pullum 1983). Since the contracted copula is a clitic, a prosodically weak element that requires a host, it attaches to the preceding phonological word. In contrast, verbal –s is a grammatical affix, which, despite the fact that its phonologically conditioned allophony resembles that of the copula, attaches to a verb stem in the syntactic component. Thus, we can view the different effects of prosodic structure in conditioning the variability of the copula and verbal –s as a consequence of their different morphological statuses.

20.5 CONCLUSION

In this chapter, I have focused on a little-studied aspect of AAE, the interface between syntax and prosody. Making use of an approach to prosodic phonology that views prosodic structure as a hierarchy of domains that are mapped from (but not identical to) syntactic structure, I have used different prosodic configurations as factor groups in variationist analyses of the variable occurrence of contracted and zero copula and verbal –s in two varieties considered to be representative of Early AAE.

The crucial distinction in the prosodic conditioning of the copula is the presence of a φ-boundary, which deters the resyllabification necessary for contraction. The zero copula makes available another option in contexts where contraction is disfavored. Thus, we may view both contraction and zero copula as strategies for avoiding phonological and prosodic complexity. Prompted by Cheshire and Ouhalla's (1997) observation that the type of verbal complement conditions the occurrence of verbal –s, I extended the analysis of prosodic structure, which proved significant in conditioning copula variation to the occurrence of verbal –s. However, not only was the prosodic factor group not selected as significant, but the direction of effect was not consistent across or within varieties of AAE. I suggested that the disparity in the significance of prosodic structure for two grammatical variables that share the same segmental content can be explained by the different morphophonological status of the two forms: the copula as a clitic and verbal –s as an affix.

The analyses presented in this chapter demonstrate that prosodic boundaries can provide an additional explanation for the variability of features observed in AAE, though care has to be taken to distinguish the different grammatical and morphophonological properties associated with each form. Obviously, there remains much work to do in this area. Apart from the necessity of extending this analysis to more mainstream varieties of AAE, the analyses presented here represent one interpretation of how prosodic structure might be operationalized. The syntax-prosody interface thus represents an area of research ripe for exploration.

Notes

1. In this chapter, I use the term *African American English* to refer to the range of English(-based) varieties spoken by (the descendants of) Americans of African descent (for a discussion of the uses of this term, see Mufwene 2001).
2. The prosodic domain in which the functional element is included (ω or φ) is a matter of disagreement (see Selkirk 1995). For the purpose of clarity, I have simplified the representation.
3. For details on the speakers included in the corpora and how the data were collected, see Poplack and Sankoff (1987) for SamE and Poplack and Tagliamonte (1991, 2001) for ANSE.
4. In this chapter I use the term *copula* to refer to the use of *be* as both an auxiliary and a true copula, though I differentiate the two uses where appropriate.
5. Examples are taken verbatim from recorded sociolinguistic interviews and are identified by corpus, speaker number, and line number in the transcription. Corpora include African Nova Scotian English (ANSE; Poplack and Tagliamonte 1991); Samaná English (SamE; Poplack and Sankoff 1987); and Nova Scotian English, the vernacular English spoken by European-origin residents of Guysborough and Halifax, Nova Scotia (see Poplack and Tagliamonte 1991, 2001).
6. Multivariate analysis was conducted using the binomial stepup/stepdown procedure incorporated in GoldVarb X (Sankoff, Tagliamonte, and Smith 2012). In tables 20.1 and 20.2, the decimal numbers represent the individual contribution of each factor (factor weight) to the relevant variant (contracted and zero copula in table 20.1; verbal –s in table 20.2) when all factors are considered together. Factor weights above .5 are said to favor, those below .5 to disfavor. The input value indicates the overall probability of the occurrence of the variant, and the range value indicates the relative strength of each significant factor group within each multivariate analysis.
7. The results I present here are taken from a prepublication version of Godfrey and Tagliamonte (1999). I gratefully acknowledge permission from Sali Tagliamonte to cite this version here.

REFERENCES

Baugh, John. 1980. "A Reexamination of the Black English Copula." In *Locating Language in Time and Space*, edited by William Labov, 83–106. New York: Academic.

Brewer, Jeutonne. 1986. "Durative Marker or Hypercorrection? The Case of –*s* in the WPA Ex-Slave Narratives." In *Language Variety in the South: Perspectives in Black and White*, edited by Michael B. Montgomery and Guy Bailey, 131–48. Tuscaloosa: University of Alabama.

Cheshire, Jenny, and Jamal Ouhalla. 1997. "Grammatical Constraints on Variation." Paper presented at the Language Variation Workshop, University of Reading, April 3–5.

Clarke, Sandra. 2001. "Back to the Roots—Again. Type of Subject and the Issue of Historical Provenance in the Verbal –*s* Debate." Paper presented at New Ways of Analyzing Variation 30, Raleigh, North Carolina, October 11–14.

Cooper, William E., and Jeanne Paccia-Cooper. 1980. *Syntax and Speech*. Boston: Harvard University.

Fasold, Ralph. 1972. *Tense Marking in Black English: A Linguistic and Social Analysis*. Washington, DC: Center for Applied Linguistics.

Feagin, Crawford. 1979. *Variation and Change in Alabama English: A Sociolinguistic Study of the White Community*. Washington, DC: Georgetown University.

Fridland, Valerie. 2003. "Network Strength and the Realization of the Southern Shift among African Americans in Memphis, Tennessee." *American Speech* 78: 3–30.

Godfrey, Elizabeth, and Sali Tagliamonte. 1998. "Another Piece for the Verbal –*s* Story: Evidence from Devon in Southwest England." Unpublished ms., University of York.

———. 1999. "Another Piece for the Verbal –s Story: Evidence from Devon in Southwest England." *Language Variation and Change* 11: 87–121.

Green, Lisa. 2002. *African American English: A Linguistic Introduction*. Cambridge: Cambridge University.

Hayes, Bruce. 1984. "The Phonology of Rhythm in English." *Linguistic Inquiry* 13: 227–76.

Hinton, Linette N., and Karen E. Pollock. 2000. "Regional Variations in the Phonological Characteristics of African American Vernacular English." *World Englishes* 19 (1): 59–71.

Holm, John. 1984. "Variability of the Copula in Black English and Its Creole Kin." *American Speech* 59: 291–309.

Inkelas, Sharon. 1989. "Prosodic Constituency in the Lexicon." Ph.D. diss., Stanford University. [Published in 1990, New York: Garland Publishing.]

Inkelas, Sharon, and Draga Zec. 1993. "Auxiliary Reduction without Empty Categories: A Prosodic Account." *Working Papers of the Cornell Phonetics Laboratory* 8: 205–53.

———. 1995. "Syntax-Phonology Interface." In *The Handbook of Phonological Theory*, edited by John A. Goldsmith, 543–49. Oxford: Blackwell.

Jun, Sun-Ah, and Christina Foreman. 1996. "Boundary Tones and Focus Realization in African-American English Intonation." 3rd Joint Meeting of the Acoustical Society of America and the Acoustical Society of Japan. Honolulu, Hawaii, December.

Kohn, Mary, and Charlie Farrington. 2013. "A Tale of Two Cities: Community Density and African American English Vowels." *University of Pennsylvania Working Papers in Linguistics* 19 (2): 101–10.

Labov, William. 1969. "Contraction, Deletion, and Inherent Variability of the English Copula." *Language* 45: 715–62.

————. 1972. *Language in the Inner City: Studies in the Black English Vernacular*. Philadelphia: University of Pennsylvania.

Labov, William, Paul Cohen, Clarence Robins, and John Lewis. 1968. *A Study of the Non-Standard English of Negro and Puerto Rican Speakers in New York City*. Co-operative Research Report 3288, Vol. I. Philadelphia: U.S. Regional Survey.

Ladd, D. R. 1986. "Intonational Phrasing: The Case for Recursive Prosodic Structure. *Phonology Yearbook* 3: 311–40.

Loman, Bengt. 1975. "Prosodic Patterns in a Negro American Dialect." In *Style and Text: Studies Presented to Nils Erik Enkvist*, edited by Håkan Ringbom, Alfhild Ingberg, Ralf Norrman, Kurt Nyholm, Rolf Westman, and Kay Wikberg, 219–42. Stockholm: Språkförlaget Skriptor AB.

Mufwene, Salikoko. 2001. "What is African American English?" In *Sociocultural and Historical Contexts of African American English*, edited by Sonja L. Lanehart, 21–51. Amsterdam: John Benjamins.

Nespor, Marina, and Irene Vogel. 1986. *Prosodic Phonology*. Dordrecht: Foris.

Pitts, William. 1981. "Beyond Hypercorrection: The Use of Emphatic *-z* in BEV." *Chicago Linguistic Society* 17: 303–10.

Poplack, Shana, ed. 2000. *The English History of African American English*. Oxford: Blackwell.

Poplack, Shana, and David Sankoff. 1987. "The Philadelphia Story in the Spanish Caribbean." *American Speech* 64: 291–314.

Poplack, Shana, and Sali Tagliamonte. 1989. "There's No Tense like the Present: Verbal *-s* Inflection in Early Black English." *Language Variation and Change* 1: 47–84.

————. 1991. "African American English in the Diaspora: The Case of Old-Line Nova Scotians." *Language Variation and Change* 3: 301–39.

————. 1993. " 'They Talks with Grammar, with *-s*': Phono-Prosodic vs. Grammatical Influences on Word-Final *-s* Variability in African Nova Scotian English." Paper presented at New Ways of Analyzing Variation 22, University of Ottawa, October 14–17.

————. 2001. *African American English in the Diaspora: Tense and Aspect*. Oxford: Blackwell.

Rickford, John R. 1996. "Copula Variability in Jamaican Creole and African American Vernacular English: A Reanalysis of DeCamp's Texts." In *Towards a Social Science of Language*, Vol. 1, *Variation and Change in Language and Society*, edited by Gregory R. Guy, Crawford Feagin, Deborah Schiffrin, and John Baugh, 357–72. Amsterdam and Philadelphia: Benjamins.

————. 1998. "The Creole Origins of African-American Vernacular English: Evidence from Copula Absence." In *African-American English: Structure, History, and Use*, edited by Salikoko S. Mufwene, John R. Rickford, Guy Bailey, and John Baugh, 154–200. London: Routledge.

————. 2006. "Down for the Count? The Creole Origins Hypothesis of AAVE at the Hands of the Ottawa Circle, and Their Supporters." *Journal of Pidgin and Creole Languages* 21 (1): 97–155.

Sankoff, David, Sali Tagliamonte, and Eric Smith. 2012. *GoldVarb X: A Multivariate Analysis Application*. Department of Mathematics, University of Ottawa and Department of Linguistics, University of Toronto.

Schneider, Edgar W. 1983. "The Origin of the Verbal *-s* in Black English." *American Speech* 58: 99–113.

Selkirk, Elisabeth. 1984. *Phonology and Syntax: The Relation between Sound and Structure*. Cambridge, MA: MIT Press.

———. 1986. "On Derived Domains in Sentence Phonology." *Phonology* 3: 371–405.

———. 1995. "Sentence Prosody: Intonation, Stress, and Phrasing." In *The Handbook of Phonological Theory*, edited by John A. Goldsmith, 550–59. Oxford: Blackwell.

———. 1996. "The Prosodic Structure of Function Words." In *Signal to Syntax: Prosodic Bootstrapping from Speech to Grammar in Early Acquisition*, edited by James L. Morgan and Katherine Demuth, 187–214. Mahwah, NJ: Lawrence Erlbaum.

———. 2011. "The Syntax-Phonology Interface." In *The Handbook of Phonological Theory*, 2nd ed., edited by John Goldsmith, Jason Riggle, and Alan Yu, 435–84. Oxford: Wiley Blackwell.

Singler, John V. 1991a. "Copula Variation in Liberian Settler English and American Black English. In *Phrase Patterns in Black English and Creole*, edited by Walter F. Edwards and Donald Winford, 129–64. Detroit, MI: Wayne State University Press.

Smith, Cybelle. 2011. "The Intonational Phonology of Yes–No Questions in African American Vernacular English." New Ways of Analyzing Variation 40, Georgetown University, Washington, DC, October 27–30.

———. 2012. "Intonational Cues to Interrogative Intent in African American English." Annual Meeting of the Linguistic Society of America, Portland, Oregon, January 5–8.

Sweetland, Julie, John R. Rickford, and Joy Hsu. 2000. "Prosodic Conditioning of the Copula: A Second Opinion." Paper presented at New Ways of Analyzing Variation 29, Michigan State University, October 5–8.

Tarone, Elaine E. 1973. "Aspects of Intonation in Black English." *American Speech* 48: 29–36.

Truckenbrodt, Hubert. 1995. "Phonological Phrases: Their Relation to Syntax, Focus and Prominence." PhD diss., MIT.

———. 1999. "On the Relation between Syntactic Phrases and Phonological Phrases." *Linguistic Inquiry* 30: 219–56.

Wagner, Michael, and Duane G. Watson. 2010. "Experimental and Theoretical Advances in Prosody: A Review. *Language and Cognitive Processes* 25: 905–45.

Walker, James A. 2000a. "Present Accounted for: Prosody and Aspect in Early African American English." PhD diss., University of Ottawa.

———. 2000b. "Rephrasing the Copula: Contraction and Zero in Early African American English." In *The English History of African American English*, edited by Shana Poplack, 35–72. Oxford: Blackwell.

———. 2001. "Before You Say *-s*: Grammatical and Prosodic Constraints in Early African American English." Paper presented at New Ways of Analyzing Variation 30, North Carolina State University, Raleigh, North Carolina, October 11–14.

———. 2010. *Variation in Linguistic Systems*. London: Routledge.

Winford, Donald. 1992. "Another Look at the Copula in Black English and Caribbean Creoles." *American Speech* 67: 21–60.

———. 1998. "On the Origins of African American Vernacular English—A Creolist Perspective, Part II: Linguistic Features." *Diachronica* 15: 99–154.

Wolfram, Walt. 1969. *A Sociolinguistic Description of Detroit Negro Speech*. Washington, DC: Center for Applied Linguistics.

———. 1974. "The Relationship of White Southern Speech to Vernacular Black English." *Language* 50 (3): 498–527.

Wolfram, Walt, and Erik Thomas. 2002. *The Development of African American English*. Oxford: Blackwell.

Zec, Draga, and Sharon Inkelas. 1990. "Prosodically Constrained Syntax." In *The Phonology-Syntax Connection*, edited by Sharon Inkelas and Draga Zec, 365–78. Chicago: University of Chicago.

Zwicky, Arnold, and Geoffrey K. Pullum. 1983. "Cliticization vs. Inflection: English *n't*." *Language* 59: 502–13.

CHAPTER 21

....

SEGMENTAL PHONOLOGY
OF AFRICAN AMERICAN
ENGLISH

....

ERIK R. THOMAS AND GUY BAILEY

21.1 INTRODUCTION

....

LINGUISTS over the last half-century have produced a massive body of research on the morphosyntactic properties of African American English (AAE)—or at least on those morphosyntactic properties thought to be defining features of the AAE vernacular. By *AAE*, we mean any kind of speech that can be audibly distinguished as African American, including both middle-class and working-class varieties. Nevertheless, the body of research focused on the segmental phonology of AAE is relatively small. Several factors account for this discrepancy. First, features of segmental phonology do not typically provide the kinds of absolute distinctions favored in textbook descriptions of AAE. While most of the AAE segmental variables that have been described occur at least to some extent in other varieties of English, the most prominent morphosyntactic features (e.g., invariant habitual *be*, zero copula in the third singular, and verbal –*s* absence) are either exclusive to AAE or quite limited in other varieties, and at least one such variable (zero copula) has parallels in Caribbean Anglophone creoles. Second, many earlier studies of AAE focused on consonants because they did not have easy access to equipment required for the acoustic analysis necessary to analyze vowel differences most accurately. As we point out below, though, many of the most revealing features of AAE are in fact vocalic. Finally, historical questions, whether they involve the origins of African American Vernacular English (AAVE) or its later trajectory, have been a primary concern of much of the research on AAE. Many researchers have assumed that the unique (or nearly unique) morphosyntactic variables of AAE provide the best venue for addressing historical questions about that variety. However, as we contend here, vowel features may actually provide a richer mechanism for addressing these historical questions.

The fact that the body of research on the segmental phonology of AAE is smaller than that on morphosyntax does not mean that there is no important work on segmental phonology, though. In fact, just the opposite is true. Linguistic atlases and other research using the methods of dialect geography began collecting phonetic evidence from African American subjects as early as the 1930s, and the work of early sociolinguists incorporated important analyses of features such as consonant cluster reduction and r-lessness. That work even identified a few segmental features (e.g., the shift of /str/, as in *street*, to /skr/) that may be unique to AAE, although the distributions of these features have not been studied widely enough to allow for definitive conclusions. It is the research based on the acoustic analysis of vowel features, however, that has made the greatest contribution to our understanding of AAE segmental phonology. Most acoustic work on AAE has been conducted over the last twenty-five years. It not only fills out the sketchy picture of AAE segmental phonology that early work on consonants had provided, but it also offers highly nuanced insights into the relationships among AAE and other American English varieties. We hope to show here what is known about AAE segmental phonology based on existing research, including both the degree of diversity within AAE and, when possible, how the center of gravity for AAE differs from that of White varieties.

21.2 SEGMENTAL PHONOLOGY

21.2.1 Consonants

Among consonantal features, the three variables that have been the subject of the most intensive analysis are consonant cluster simplification, as in [pʰæs] for *past* or *passed*; r-lessness, as in [foə] for *four*; and the use of either coronal stops or labiodental fricatives in place of historical interdental fricatives, as in [dæt] for *that* or [bouf] for *both*. All of these variants also occur in other varieties of English to some degree, but they are apparently more frequent and widespread in AAE. As we point out below, several lesser studied variables also appear to be salient in AAE.

The simplification of word-final consonant clusters, which typically involves the loss of the final stop in a cluster of two consonants (as in *cold* → *col'*) and the penultimate consonant in a cluster of three consonants (as in *fists* → *fis:*), is often viewed as a signature variable in quantitative sociolinguistics because it is easily quantifiable, it lends itself to the logistic regression included in the widely used Varbrul or GoldVarb statistical packages, and the factors that influence simplification are well known. Among the factors that most affect consonant cluster simplification are the type of syllable in which the cluster occurs, the type of cluster involved, and the linguistic environment that follows the cluster. Simplification is more frequent in unstressed than stressed syllables. The other two factors are more complex. Figures 21.1 and 21.2 summarize the cluster types and the following environments. As figure 21.1 indicates, clusters may be homorganic

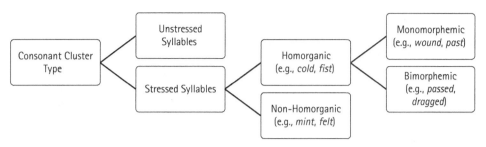

FIGURE 21.1 Consonant clusters by syllable type and cluster type.

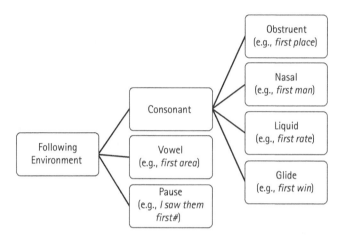

FIGURE 21.2 Following environments affecting consonant cluster simplification.

(i.e., both consonants have the same voicing, as in *cold* and *fist*) or non-homorganic (as in *mint* and *felt*). Simplification is more frequent in homorganic than non-homorganic clusters. Homorganic clusters may be either monomorphemic (i.e., they are part of a single morpheme, as in *wound* and *bust*) or bimorphemic (i.e., the second consonant represents a separate morpheme such as the past tense, as in *bussed* and *stunned*). Simplification is more frequent in monomorphemic than bimorphemic clusters.

As figure 21.2 shows, clusters can be followed by words that begin with consonants (as in *first place*) or vowels (as in *first area*), or by pauses (which may or may not correspond to phrase boundaries, as in *I saw it first*). In all varieties of English, simplification is more frequent before words that begin with consonants than those that begin with vowels, but the effect of a following pause varies from one variety to another. The type of consonant that follows also makes a difference: simplification is most frequent before obstruents, then nasals and liquids, and then glides. The effects of the following environment can be summarized in terms of the *sonority hierarchy*: the less sonorous the following sound, the more likely consonant cluster simplification will occur.

Numerous sociolinguistic studies and descriptions have described consonant cluster simplification in AAE (Labov et al. 1968; Wolfram 1969; Fasold and Wolfram 1970; Labov 1972; Baugh 1983; Ash and Myhill 1986; Butters and Nix 1986; Miller 1986; Gordon

2000; Wolfram and Thomas 2002). These studies suggest that while the order of the constraints on consonant cluster simplification is generally the same for all groups, simplification is more frequent in AAE than in other varieties of English and is especially more frequent before vowels and pauses and in bimorphemic clusters. Wolfram and Thomas (2002, 134) also note that in AAE deletion becomes more common as the first member of the cluster moves up the sonority hierarchy of stop (as in *duct*); sibilant (*list*); /l/ (*fold*); and nasal (*wind*).

One other circumstance also deserves mention. The presence of such forms as ['nɛsəz] for *nests* suggests that some African Americans may lack the affected stop entirely. Compare this with the more common plural formation in AAE, made with prolonged [s], as in [nɛsː].

The second most commonly studied consonantal variable, r-lessness or non-rhoticity, actually involves not only the absence of non-syllabic /r/ in final, preconsonantal, and sometimes intervocalic positions (as in *store*, *stored*, and *story*, respectively) but also a vocalic feature: the use of non-rhoticized vowels where other varieties have rhoticized ones in both stressed and unstressed syllabics (as in *bird* and *butter*, respectively). Figure 21.3 summarizes these environments. As with consonant cluster simplification, the environment significantly affects the extent of r-lessness. R-lessness has always been less common in intervocalic and stressed syllabic environments than in non-syllabic or unstressed syllabic ones.

Although historically r-lessness occurred in White varieties in the Lower South, it is most often associated with AAE, and for good reason: r-lessness is characteristic not only of most traditional varieties of AAE in the South but also of many non-southern AAE varieties.[1] Moreover, in communities where both Blacks and Whites are (or were) r-less, African Americans are (or were) usually r-less in a greater range of environments

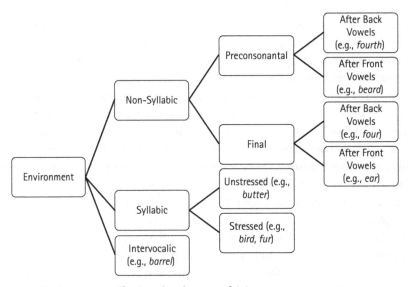

FIGURE 21.3 Environments affecting the absence of /r/.

(e.g., in intervocalic and stressed syllabic environments) and have a higher frequency of r-less forms in all environments. These tendencies have been found repeatedly both in the South (see Williamson 1968; Anshen 1970, as compared with Levine and Crockett 1966; Foley 1972; Pederson et al. 1986–1992; Bernstein 1993; Wolfram and Thomas 2002), and in several cities outside the South (see Labov et al. 1968; Wolfram 1969; Baugh 1983; Myhill 1988; Edwards 1997). R-lessness has declined precipitously among Whites in the South (see Levine and Crockett 1966; Feagin 1990; McNair 2005), but its decline among African Americans in these same environments and elsewhere has been much slower, though the decline is clearly evident in intervocalic and vocalic environments. It is most likely declining in all environments among middle-class African Americans every-where, including the South. Previous research has also shown that social constraints exert a strong influence on r-lessness in AAE in some places. Wolfram (1969) showed that in Detroit r-lessness decreases as social class rises and speaking style becomes more formal, while Myhill (1988) found that in Philadelphia r-lessness declined as contact with Whites increased. Finally, in spite of the general historical r-lessness of AAE, there have been reports of a few communities in which AAE shows little or no r-lessness. These are usually non-Southern communities in which the African American popu-lation is relatively small (Thomas 1989/1993; Hinton and Pollock 2000) or in parts of the South (such as Appalachia) with historically small African American populations (Mallinson and Wolfram 2002; Childs and Mallinson 2004).

The phonetic constraints on r-lessness are remarkably consistent across vari-ous African American communities (and also among Whites). The most likely con-text for r-lessness is in unstressed syllables, as in *better, entertain*, and *survive*, and the next most likely is syllable coda /r/, whether followed by a consonant or a pause, as in *stored* and *store*. Syllable coda /r/ is also affected to some extent by the vowel that pre-cedes it, with r-lessness more likely after a back vowel (*store*) than after a front vowel (*stair*). Stressed syllabic /r/, as in *first* and *sir*, is much less likely to exhibit r-lessness than either unstressed syllabic or syllable coda /r/. Most African Americans today are r-ful in stressed syllabic contexts, but Thomas (2001) reports that in the past AAE was largely r-less even there. In the region from South Carolina to eastern Texas, the variant [əi] occurred in checked position, as in *first* [fəis(t)], in both AAE and White variet-ies (Kurath and McDavid 1961; Pederson et al. 1986-1992). This variant is now highly recessive, although some older African Americans still preserve it (Wroblewski, Strand, and DuBois 2010). Intervocalic r-lessness in such words as *sorry* ['sɑ.i] is less common than r-lessness in any other context, but it can occur in more vernacular (and especially older vernacular) varieties of AAE. Finally, one other feature sometimes associated with r-lessness deserves comment: "linking /r/," the realization of a word-final /r/ when the next word begins with a vowel (e.g., in *store on*) in many r-less varieties, is frequently absent in AAE, just as it was in old-fashioned southern White varieties.

The English interdental fricatives, /θ/ and /ð/, are subject to various processes in non-standard varieties. In AAE, especially its more vernacular varieties, at least two pro-cesses can affect /θ/ and /ð/ (Rickford 1999, 4). One is stopping, in which /θ/ appears as a voiceless dental or alveolar stop and /ð/ as a voiced dental or alveolar stop. Stop variants are most common in syllable onsets, as in *three* [tʰɹi] and *that* [dæt]. Affricates representing intermediate forms between fricatives and stops ([tθ], [dð]) also occur sporadically in syllable onsets. Stops can occasionally appear in other environments, as in *worth* [wˈɪt] and *further* [ˈfɪɹdə]. The second process is the realization of /θ/ and /ð/ as the labiodental fricatives, [f] and [v], respectively. These variants seem to be restricted in AAE to syllable codas, as in *south* [saɔf], to intervocalic position, as in *brother* [ˈbɹʌvə], and before /r/, as in *three* [fɹi] (Fasold and Wolfram 1970, 50–51). In addition to these, two other processes may also affect /ð/: it may be assimilated to a preceding consonant, as in *stop that* [ˈstɑˌpːæʔt], or it can be deleted altogether in intervocalic contexts (e.g., *other* [ʌː]). Sociolinguistic studies that have analyzed /θ/ and /ð/ in AAE (Labov et al. 1968; Wolfram 1969; Butters and Nix 1986) have found that /ð/ is affected more often than /θ/ and that the incidence of the nonstandard variants is lower among higher social classes, women, and African Americans with more contact with Whites. Pederson et al. (1986–1992) found the nonstandard variants among both Blacks and Whites in the Gulf states, but with a greater incidence among African Americans: 35 percent of African Americans but only 11 percent of Whites had [d]~[t] in *with*.

Researchers have noted a variety of other consonantal aspects of AAE, including deletions, shifts, and metathesis. Perhaps the most important deletion is the loss of a final nasal in words like *on* [ɔ̃], leaving nasalization of the preceding vowel as the only remaining trace of the nasal consonant. Bailey (2001, 76) calls nasal deletion "apparently unique to AAVE," while Ash and Myhill (1986) found that the incidence of nasal deletion among African Americans in Philadelphia was inversely correlated with an individual's contact with Whites. Another deletion is that of /l/ before labials, as in *help* [hɛp], and its old-fashioned preterit, *holp* [houp]. This process is basically an extension of the loss of laterals before dorsals and labials that occurred several hundred years ago in such words as *yolk, half,* and *salve,* and it also occurs in other vernaculars in the southern United States. The deletion of /l/ can likewise occur syllable-finally, as in *full* [fʊ] (Labov et al. 1968). Two environments disfavor the deletion of final /l/: (1) a following vowel, as in *full of,* and (2) a preceding front vowel, as in *feel*. A much more recent deletion process is the loss of /j/ in /Cju/ (C = consonant) sequences. This loss is widespread both in AAE and in other American varieties after coronals, as in *dune* and *new*. However, in some AAE vernaculars, the process is extended to other contexts, as in *beautiful* [ˈbuɾəfʊ] (Bailey and Thomas 1998; Bailey 2001). Finally, /r/ may be deleted sometimes in syllable-onset clusters (usually in unstressed syllables, such as the first syllable of *prescription*) and in /θr/ clusters, as in *through* (Rickford 1999, 4; Hinton and Pollock 2000).

A frequently mentioned consonant shift in AAE is the mutation of /str/ to /skr/, as in *street* [skɹit]. It has been reported in numerous studies (Fasold and Wolfram 1970; Labov 1972, 20; Wolfram and Fasold 1974, 144; Dandy 1991; Bailey and Thomas 1998; Rickford 1999; Bailey 2001; Green 2002, 122–23; Wolfram and Thomas 2002, 131), but to our knowledge it has never been analyzed quantitatively. As a result, its social, regional, and lexical distributions are unknown. A second shift involves the /ʃr/ cluster, as in *shrink* and *shrug*. Both in AAE and in southern White varieties, [sɹ] frequently occurs for /ʃr/ in words like *shrimp*, but several other variants are more closely associated with

AAE. These include the variants [ʃw] and [sw], which were used in *shrimp* by 19 percent of the African American subjects in Pederson et al. (1986–1992) but by only 1 percent of the other subjects. Alicia Beckford Wassink (personal communication, n.d.) suggests, additionally, that [skɹ] may also occur sometimes in words such as *shrimp* in AAE, and Sonja Lanehart (personal communication, n.d.) attests that [skɹ] occurs in Louisiana AAE. A third consonant shift involves the use of voiceless for voiced stops. In words that have syllable-final /d/, as in *good*, the stop may be devoiced to [t] or even [ʔ]. While southern Whites may exhibit this devoicing in unstressed syllables, as in *salad*, devoicing in stressed syllables is largely restricted to AAE (Fasold and Wolfram 1970, 53–54).[2] Although this feature has long been a part of AAE, studies such as Nguyen (2006) and Farrington (2012) have documented its vitality and persistence in AAE today. Fasold and Wolfram (1970, 54) indicate that deletion of /d/ in this context is also possible. Finally, two other consonant shifts should be mentioned here as well. First, syllable-coda /l/ is subject not only to deletion, as described earlier, but also to vocalization. Vocalization to a back, rounded vowel, as in *feel* [fio], is common both in AAE and other American varieties, but vocalization to schwa, as in [fiə], is for the most part a feature of AAE. Second, Pollock (2001) reports a shift of /Cj/, as in *cute*, to [Cɹ], for some African Americans, at least in the Memphis area.

One additional consonant process frequently ascribed to AAE is the putative metathesis of /sk/ to /ks/ in *ask*, so that it is produced as [æks]. Although this pronunciation is a stereotype of vernacular forms of AAE, Pederson et al. (1986–92) document its presence in older White vernaculars. The persistence of the /ks/ pronunciation in *ask* in White folk dialects of both England and the United States to the present day suggests that it is most likely a continuation of Old English *acsian*. Fasold and Wolfram (1970), however, reported that other words, such as *grasp* [gɹæps], may sometimes show metathesis, too.

21.2.2 Vowels

Much of the work on AAE consonants has focused on social differences among African Americans (such as social class and gender) and on what makes AAE as a whole distinctive and different from other varieties. In contrast, analyses of vowels have been more likely to explore how AAE is changing with respect to White varieties. Two issues addressed by vocalic studies are the *Divergence/Convergence Controversy* and the *Uniformity Controversy*. The first of these concerns whether vernacular AAE is becoming more like White vernaculars, becoming less like them, or maintaining a steady degree of separation. The Uniformity Controversy has to do with how much regional differentiation exists in AAE, whether AAE is characterized by nationwide (i.e., non-regional) norms, and whether the geographical variation that does exist in AAE is independent of geographical variation in White varieties. As can be seen in what follows, the solutions to these controversies are far from straightforward. We do not wish to depict AAE either as having a distinctive vowel configuration or as being best viewed in relation to White varieties: we leave it to readers to make up their own minds.

21.2.2.1 *The Southern Heritage*

The extant evidence on earlier Black and White varieties suggests that the AAE vowel system has always differed to some extent from that of White vernaculars. Dorrill (1986) used data from the *Linguistic Atlas of the Middle and South Atlantic States* (*LAMSAS*), whose subjects were almost all born in the nineteenth century, to pair Black and White subjects in the communities covered by *LAMSAS*. Although both ethnicities showed some monophthongal tense vowels, Dorrill found that, in most communities, African Americans were more likely to show monophthongal /e/, /o/, /i/, /u/, and /ɔ/ (as in *bait, boat, beet, boot*, and *bought*, respectively) than Whites. Thomas and Bailey (1998) corroborated this finding with acoustic analyses of recordings made with former slaves in the 1930s and 1940s. Thomas (2001) shows that monophthongal /e/ and /o/ have largely disappeared in present-day AAE, though they persist in southern Louisiana (Wroblewski et al. 2010) and possibly the Gullah area. Nevertheless, considerable variation remains within AAE for /ɔ/.

AAE also shares features with southern White vernaculars, however. Two vowel variants that are frequently associated with both AAE and Southern European American English (SEAE) are the weakening of the glide of /ai/ in words such as *side* and the merger of /ɪ/ and /ɛ/ before nasals, as in *pin* and *pen*. Glide weakening occurs to varying degrees and in various configurations in both Black and White speech. The weakening may result in a short glide, as in [aæ],[3] or it may produce genuine monophthongization, usually [aː]. It is most common before /l/ and /r/, as in *tile* and *tire* (Myhill 1988; Tillery et al. 2003), though some middle-class African Americans hypercorrect the glide weakening in these contexts, producing forms such as [tʰajɹ]. The often weakly stressed pronominals *I* and *my* are also particularly subject to glide weakening. Perhaps the most common configuration for glide weakening is for forms with the weakened glide to occur in all contexts except before voiceless obstruents, as in *sight*. This configuration is widespread in AAE and was long the prestige norm among southern Whites as well. Another configuration is for glide weakening to occur in all contexts, including before voiceless consonants. This configuration occurs primarily among Whites and is most frequent in parts of the South, such as the southern Appalachians and central and western Texas, that traditionally had relatively small African American populations. Pederson et al. (1986–1992) show glide weakening in *right* for 25 percent of Whites but only 8 percent of Blacks in the Gulf states. Bernstein (1993) found glide weakening in *night* to be far more prevalent in Texas among Whites than among African Americans. The vowel plots in Thomas (2001) corroborate this tendency.

African Americans have often carried glide weakening outside the South (Ash and Myhill 1986; Myhill 1986; Deser 1990; Edwards 1997; Gordon 2000). Among African Americans in Detroit, Deser (1990) correlated greater degrees of glide weakening with southern (as opposed to northern) identification, while Edwards (1997) found that glide weakening declined with increasing social class. Purnell (2010) discovered that glide weakening among African Americans in Milwaukee declined as contacts with Whites increased. African Americans outside the South usually exhibit the configuration that disfavors weakening before voiceless obstruents (Coggshall and Becker 2010; Eberhardt 2010; Purnell 2010). However, Anderson (2002) reported that glide weakening before voiceless obstruents was increasing among African Americans in Detroit, ostensibly from contact with Appalachian Whites. In Appalachia itself, small communities of African Americans also exhibit glide weakening of /ai/ in all contexts (Mallinson and Wolfram 2002; Childs and Mallinson 2004; Childs, Mallinson, and Carpenter 2010). Andres and Votta (2010) found some glide weakening before voiceless obstruents among African Americans in a suburb of Atlanta.

Although less frequently studied, the same kind of glide weakening that affects /ai/ also affects /oi/. Before /l/, as in *boil*, /oi/ may be monophthongized. In other contexts, the sound is often described as monophthongal, but analyses in Thomas (2001) show that the process actually involves lowering of the glide. Hence, *boy* may be realized in AAE, especially in older AAE, as [boɛ]. As with /ai/, glide weakening is shared with southern White varieties, and particularly with older ones.

Another feature that occurs widely in both AAE and southern White speech is the conditioned merger of /ɪ/, as in *pin*, with /ɛ/, as in *pen*. This merger has long been a hallmark of southern varieties, both Black and White (for a history of this merger, see Brown 1991), and African Americans carried this merger with them to areas outside the South where the regional vernaculars do not usually exhibit it (Labov et al. 1968, 119-20; Thomas 1989/1993; Edwards 1997; Gordon 2000; Labov, Ash, and Boberg 2006; Eberhardt 2010). However, Coggshall and Becker (2010) found that African Americans in New York City are losing the merger.

The mergers of certain vowels before /l/ have also been reported for AAE. Gordon (2000) cites the /il/–/ɪl/ (as in *feel* and *fill*); /el/–/ɛl/ (*fail, fell*); and /ul/–/ʊl/ (*fool, full*) mergers as characteristic of AAE in northwestern Indiana. Tillery, Bailey, and Wikle (2004) indicate that Blacks and Whites in Texas share the first two of these but that the third is more frequent among Whites. Further research is needed to determine how widespread pre-/l/ mergers are in AAE and other varieties.

21.2.2.2 *Resistance to Back Vowel Fronting*

While the features just described represent shared features between AAE and various southern varieties, a slowness to adopt the frontward shifts of certain vowels has

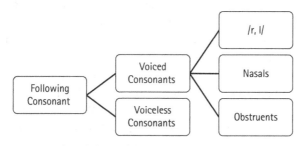

FIGURE 21.4 Environments for glide weakening of /ai/.

often been cited as a feature that differentiates AAE from other varieties. The oldest of these shifts involves the fronting of the nucleus of /au/ in words like *how* so that the diphthong is produced as [æɔ] or something similar. Records from both *LAMSAS* (Dorrill 1986) and the *Linguistic Atlas of the Gulf States* (Pederson et al. 1986–1992) show nuclear fronting to be more common among White than Black subjects. In Pederson et al., 41 percent of White subjects had [æo] in *cow*, while only 18 percent of the African Americans did. Using random sample data from *A Phonological Survey of Texas*, Bernstein (1993) found nuclear fronting in *thousand* much more often among Whites than African Americans in Texas. Thomas (2001) and Labov et al. (2006) report similar patterns.

The glide of /au/ also shows some differentiation. Its glide may be weakened or lost, and some evidence suggests that glide weakening of /au/ is more common among African Americans than among Whites in the South. Wolfram and Thomas (2002) found that younger African Americans in Hyde County, North Carolina, showed increasing amounts of glide weakening. Pederson et al. (1986–1992) documented glide weakening in *plow* for 25 percent of African Americans but only 15 percent of Whites among their Gulf states subjects; strikingly, the incidence of this feature among Whites was highest in eastern and middle Tennessee, regions with relatively low densities of African Americans. However, in Pittsburgh, where glide weakening of /au/ is an iconic feature of the local White vernacular, Eberhardt (2010) found that African Americans avoid it (see Gooden and Bloomquist, this volume).

The other fronting processes involve /o/, as in *toe*, /ʊ/, as in *took*, and /u/, as in *too*. For example, non-fronted forms of /o/ would be [ou], [oː], and [ɔu], while fronted forms would include such variants as [əu] and [ɜʉ]. Fronting of these vowels has spread widely in White vernaculars and has been viewed as a component of the *Southern Shift*, a series of vowel mutations affecting White vernaculars in the South. Several studies have examined the participation of African Americans in these shifts, but the results are complicated and difficult to interpret because of discrepancies in the samples obtained and differences in the historical role of fronting in local vernaculars. In general, it seems that African Americans do eventually adopt some fronting of back vowels. However, they are at least a generation or two behind Whites in a given community and may ultimately show less extreme fronting. Thomas (1989) found a stark difference for /o/ between younger African Americans and Whites in Wilmington, North Carolina, while Thomas and Coggshall (2006/2007), using a combined sample from three North Carolina counties, found significant differences for both the nucleus and glide of /o/, the former for young speakers and the latter for both old and young subjects. Thomas (2001) noted a general resistance by African Americans to /o/- and /u/-fronting across the South.

Other studies have found much subtler differences. In Memphis, Tennessee, Fridland (2003) and Fridland and Bartlett (2006) found that both ethnic groups show considerable fronting of /u/ and mild fronting of /o/, with Whites holding only a moderate lead in each shift. African Americans led slightly in fronting of /ʊ/. Kohn (2013), a longitudinal study of African American children from the area of Durham/Chapel Hill, North Carolina, found a great deal of /u/-fronting after coronals (e.g., *too*), but far less

/o/-fronting. In Hyde County, North Carolina, where fronting of both the nucleus and glide of /o/ is a traditional feature of the dialect, Wolfram and Thomas (2002) found it robust among both groups, though Whites fronted the glide more. Columbus, Ohio, and Pittsburgh, Pennsylvania, are two other communities in which fronting of /o/ and /u/ has a long history. In Columbus, Thomas (1989/1993) found fronting (or centralization) of both vowels among both ethnicities, but to a greater degree among Whites—except before /l/, where African Americans showed some fronting and Whites categorically avoided it. A subsequent study in Columbus by Durian, Dodsworth, and Schumacher (2010) corroborated the finding of general /u/-fronting among African Americans. They also determined that /o/-fronting had increased among African Americans. Eberhardt (2010) showed that some African Americans in Pittsburgh have adopted fronting of /o/ and /u/.

21.2.2.3 *Shifts of Front Vowels*

Shifts involving front vowels likewise include complicated interactions between AAE and local White vernaculars. A number of studies have examined AAE /æ/, as in *bat*, in northern communities that feature the raising and diphthongization of /æ/ to [ɛæ] in the local White variety. Deser (1990) found greater /æ/ raising among those Detroit African Americans who identified with the North instead of the South, while Gordon (2000) found little raising of /æ/ at all among African Americans in northwestern Indiana. Two studies that examined AAE /æ/ in communities where the local White vernaculars exhibit a split of /æ/ into raised and unraised allophones also yielded mixed results. Henderson (1996) found that African Americans in Philadelphia had partially adopted the local /æ/ pattern but did not follow it categorically, while Coggshall and Becker (2010) discovered that in New York City, older and middle-aged Africans had accommodated somewhat to the local pattern there, but young African Americans had abandoned it entirely. They found, however, that younger Whites were also abandoning the local pattern. In the South, the raising of /æ/ without the corresponding diphthongization characteristic of /æ/-raising in White vernaculars, yielding something close to [ɛ], has emerged as a distinctive AAE feature (Thomas and Bailey 1998; Kohn 2013). Vowel plots in Thomas (2001) show many African Americans with /æ/ means in the mid range or close to it. While many southern Whites in Thomas (2001) also show mild /æ/-raising, those born after about 1960 are more likely to exhibit lowering of /æ/. No such reversal has appeared yet in southern AAE.

Some recent research on the front vowels of AAE has focused on the penetration of the Southern Shift into AAE. Again, the results are complicated. In the Southern Shift, the front vowels, /i/, as in *beet*, and /e/, as in *bait*, become increasingly diphthongal to the point that their nuclei become lower than the nuclei of /ɪ/ and /ɛ/, respectively. Fridland (2003) and Thomas (1989/1993) found significant lowering of the /e/ nucleus among African Americans in Memphis, Tennessee, and Columbus, Ohio, respectively. The lowering of /e/ has completely different consequences in Memphis and Columbus, in the first case making AAE more like the White vernaculars of the region and in the second making it less like them. Andres and Votta (2010) reported that young African

Americans (but not older ones) in a middle-class, mostly White suburb of Atlanta had the /e/ nucleus lower and/or backer than the /ɛ/ nucleus. None of their subjects showed an analogous transposition of /i/ and /ɪ/. Kohn (2013) found that African American children in mostly African American Durham, North Carolina, showed higher /æ/ and /ɛ/ and lower /e/ nuclei than African American children in nearby but mostly White Chapel Hill.

21.2.2.4 *Other Vowel Shifts*

Resistance to the unconditioned merger of /ɑ/, as in *cot*, and /ɔ/, as in *caught*, is another feature that sometimes distinguishes AAE from other varieties. As Labov, Ash, and Boberg (2006) show, this merger is widespread in White vernaculars in many parts of the United States. Using random sample data, Bernstein (1993) found that while the occurrence of unrounded vowels in *lost* and *walk* was expanding among Whites in Texas, it remained rare among African Americans. Outside the South, Thomas (1989/1993) and Durian et al. (2010) found partial resistance to the merger among African Americans in Columbus, Ohio, while Eberhardt (2010) found the merger nearly as pervasive in Pittsburgh AAE as in Pittsburgh White speech.

Durian, Dodsworth, and Schumacher (2010) and Kohn (2013) uncovered another variant that may characterize vernacular AAE: the raising of /ʌ/, as in *cut*.

Finally, two features involving vowels in unstressed syllables deserve mention. Vaughn-Cooke (1986) analyzed vowels in initial unstressed syllables in words such as *ahead* and *electric* and found that they were frequently lost, especially among older African Americans. In addition, she found that the deletion process sometimes extended to consonants in initial unstressed syllables as well (e.g., 'spect for *expect*). Vaughn-Cooke's (1986) research suggested that the deletion of unstressed syllables was declining among younger African Americans, especially when the deletion included consonants. Cukor-Avila (1989) confirmed the processes identified by Vaughn-Cooke (1986) but not their decline over time, finding instead that the deletion of initial unstressed syllables was a case of "stable variation." Denning (1989) analyzed vowels in final unstressed syllables in such words as *happy* and *empty*. He found that AAE maintained the older variant, [ɪ], longer than other varieties and that many older African Americans still have it. Younger African Americans in his sample, however, followed other varieties of English in shifting to [i] in final unstressed syllables.

21.3 CONCLUSION

Although not as well known or as voluminous as research on AAE morphosyntax, work on the segmental phonology of AAE has explored a wide range of consonant and vowel features. As a result, we know a great deal about such matters as constraints on consonant cluster simplification and on r-lessness and the distributions of vocalic stereotypes such as glide-weakened /ai/ and the *pin-pen* merger; we are beginning to understand something of the complexities of AAE vowel systems and their relationships to White vernaculars. Table 21.1, which summarizes data on ethnic variation for a dozen features elicited in *A Phonological Survey of Texas*, illustrates the intricacies of the situation. As table 21.1 shows, during the last decades of the twentieth century, Black and White speech in Texas differed significantly in the use of (1) unrounded vowels in words such as *lost* and *walk* (the *caught-cot* merger); (2) unconstricted variants of postvocalic /r/; (3) glide-weakened variants of /ai/ before voiceless obstruents; and (4) fronted onsets of /au/. In the use of the first two features, Blacks and Whites differed not only from each other but also from Hispanics. In the use of the latter two features, though, African Americans and Hispanics were similar to each other but different from Whites. Blacks and Whites were similar to each other (but different from Hispanics) in their use of lax variants of front vowels before /l/, while Whites and Hispanics were like each other (but unlike African Americans) in their use of lax variants of back vowels before /l/. As the rest of the country becomes more like Texas (and California), such complex ethnic configurations may become the rule rather than the exception (Tillery, Bailey, and Wikle 2004).

Despite the rapidly growing body of work on the segmental phonology of AAE, however, the overall picture remains incomplete and somewhat conflicting. A basic assumption underlying the academic enterprise is that the more research we have on an issue, the more likely we are to reach consensus on it. This has not been the case with

Table 21.1 The Effects of Ethnicity on Some Features of Texas English

Feature	Anglo	African American	Hispanic	PR > F
Significantly different				
unrounded vowel in *lost*	BBB	CCC	AAA	.0001
unrounded vowel in *walk*	BBB	CCC	AAA	.0001
unconstricted /r/ in *forty*	AAA	CCC	BBB	.0001
lax vowel in *field*	BBB	BBB	AAA	.0005
lax vowel in *sale*	BBB	BBB	AAA	.0001
lax vowel in *school*	AAA	BBB	AAA	.0001
monophthongal /ai/ in *night*	AAA	BBB	BBB	.0001
fronted onset in thousand	*AAA*	*BBB*	*BBB*	.0007
Not significantly different				
deletion of /h/ in *Houston*	AAA	AAA	AAA	.0796
intrusive /r/ in *Washington*	AAA	AAA	AAA	.1612
unrounded vowel in *forty*	AAA	AAA	AAA	.1212
/tu/ in *Tuesday*	AAA	AAA	AAA	.1633

Note: Summary of results of the Scheffe Test on data from the 1989 Texas Poll portion of a Phonological Survey of Texas, with contrasting upper case letters indicating significant ethnic differences. Shading highlights shared features.
Source: Tillery, Bailey, and Wikle 2004.

AAE, though: it seems that as more research is conducted on AAE, consensus becomes more elusive. Research on AAE segmental phonology suggests why this is so. Sampling differences (some studies focus on more vernacular varieties, while others include middle-class subjects), different interviewing techniques (conversational, question-naire, or directed task), different time frames (from linguistic atlas informants born pri-marily in the nineteenth and early twentieth centuries to some sociolinguistic survey subjects born much later), and the lack of solid longitudinal data from a given place over many decades make it difficult to reach definitive conclusions about the origins of AAE, its current trajectory, or even its uniformity. This review should not be the final word on AAE segmental phonology, but it is our best provisional assessment for now.

Notes

1. By *South*, we mean states that comprised the Confederacy during the Civil War, though parts of the border states (Missouri, Kentucky, Maryland, and Delaware), where slavery was also legal, could be added.
2. Devoicing of final obstruents may also occur in dialects that have German, other Germanic languages, or Slavic languages as a substrate. Wolfram and Fasold (1970, 53) report that devoicing may affect obstruents besides /d/ in AAE.
3. Weakly gliding /ai/ is often transcribed as [aɛ], but the acoustic analyses in Thomas (2001) and Yaeger-Dror and Thomas (2010) show that [aæ] is a more appropriate transcription. Forms whose glides actually reach a mid front position generally sound as if their glides are strong/full.

References

Anderson, Bridget L. 2002. "Dialect Leveling and /ai/ Monophthongization among African American Detroiters." *Journal of Sociolinguistics* 6: 86–98.

Andres, Claire, and Rachel Votta. 2010. "African American Vernacular English: Vowel Phonology in a Georgia Community." In Yaeger-Dror and Thomas 2010, 75–98.

Anshen, Frank. 1970. "A Sociolinguistic Analysis of a Sound Change." *Language Sciences* 9: 20–21.

Ash, Sharon, and John Myhill. 1986. "Linguistic Correlates of Inter-Ethnic Contact." In *Diversity and Diachrony*, ed. by David Sankoff, 33–44. Amsterdam: John Benjamins.

Bailey, Guy. 2001. "The Relationship between African American and White Vernaculars in the American South." In *Sociocultural and Historical Contexts of African American English*, edited by Sonja L. Lanehart, 53–92. Varieties of English around the World, General Series 27. Amsterdam: John Benjamins.

Bailey, Guy, and Erik Thomas. 1998. "Some Aspects of African-AmericanVernacular English Phonology." In *African American English*, edited by Salikoko S. Mufwene, John Rickford, John Baugh, and Guy Bailey, 85–109. London: Routledge.

Baugh, John. 1983. *Black Street Speech*. Austin: University of Texas.

Bernstein, Cynthia. 1993. "Measuring Social Causes of Phonological Variables." *American Speech* 68: 227–40.

Brown, Vivian. 1991. "Evolution of the Merger of /ɪ/ and /ɛ/ before nasals in Tennessee." *American Speech* 66 (3): 303–15.

Butters, Ronald R., and Ruth A. Nix. 1986. "The English of Blacks in Wilmington, North Carolina." In *Language Variety in the South: Perspectives in Black and White*, edited by Michael B. Montgomery and Guy Bailey, 254–63. Tuscaloosa: University of Alabama.

Childs, Becky, and Christine Mallinson. 2004. "African American English in Appalachia: Dialect Accommodation and Substrate Influence." *English World-Wide* 25: 27–50.

Childs, Becky, Christine Mallinson, and Jeannine Carpenter. 2010. "Vowel Phonology and Ethnicity in North Carolina." In Yaeger-Dror and Thomas 2010, 23–47.

Coggshall, Elizabeth L., and Kara Becker. 2010. "The Vowel Phonologies of African American and White New York City Residents." In Yaeger-Dror and Thomas 2010, 101–28.

Cukor-Avila, Patricia. 1989. "Determining Change in Progress vs. Stable Variation in Two Studies of Black English Vernacular." *SECOL Review* 13: 92–124.

Dandy, Evelyn B. 1991. *Black Communications: Breaking down the Barriers*. Chicago: African American Images.

Denning, Keith. 1989. "Convergence with Divergence: A Sound Change in Vernacular Black English." *Language Variation and Change* 1: 145–67.

Deser, Toni. 1990. "Dialect Transmission and Variation: An Acoustic Analysis of Vowels in Six Urban Detroit Families." PhD diss., Boston University.

Dorrill, George T. 1986. *Black and White Speech in the South: Evidence from the Linguistic Atlas of the Middle and South Atlantic States*. Bamberger Beiträge zur Englische Sprachwissenschaft 19. New York: Peter Lang.

Durian, David, Robin Dodsworth, and Jennifer Schumacher. 2010. "Convergence in Blue Collar Columbus, Ohio African American and White Vowel Systems?" In Yaeger-Dror and Thomas 2010, 161–90.

Eberhardt, Maeve. 2010. "African American and White Vowel Systems in Pittsburgh." In Yaeger-Dror and Thomas 2010, 129–57.

Edwards, Walter F. 1997. "The Variable Persistence of Southern Vernacular Sounds in the Speech of Inner-City Black Detroiters." In *Language Variety in the South Revisited*, edited by Cynthia Bernstein, Thomas Nunnally, and Robin Sabino, 76–86. Tuscaloosa: University of Alabama.

Farrington, Charlie. 2012. "Devoicing in African American English: A Longitudinal and Apparent Time Analysis." Georgetown University Roundtable, Washington, DC, March 10.

Fasold, Ralph W., and Walt Wolfram. 1970. "Some Linguistic Features of Negro Dialect." In *Teaching Standard English in the Inner City*, edited by Ralph Fasold and Roger W. Shuy, 41–86. Washington, DC: Center for Applied Linguistics.

Feagin, Crawford. 1990. "The Dynamics of a Sound Change in Southern States English: From r-less to r-ful in Three Generations." In *Development and Diversity: Linguistic Variation across Time and Space*, edited by Jerold A. Edmondson, Crawford Feagin, and Peter Mühlhäusler, 129–46. Arlington: SIL/University of Texas at Arlington.

Foley, Lawrence M. 1972. *A Phonological and Lexical Study of the Speech of Tuscaloosa County, Alabama*. Publication of the American Dialect Society 58. Tuscaloosa: University of Alabama.

Fridland, Valerie. 2003. "Network Strength and the Realization of the Southern Shift among African Americans in Memphis, Tennessee." *American Speech* 78: 3–30.

Fridland, Valerie, and Kathy Bartlett. 2006. "The Social and Linguistic Conditioning of Back Vowel Fronting across Ethnic Groups in Memphis, Tennessee." *English Language and Linguistics* 10: 1–22.

Gordon, Matthew J. 2000. "Phonological Correlates of Ethnic Identity: Evidence of Divergence?" *American Speech* 75: 115–36.

Green, Lisa J. 2002. *African American English: A Linguistic Introduction.* Cambridge: Cambridge University Press.

Henderson, Anita. 1996. "The Short *a* Pattern of Philadelphia among African American Speakers." *University of Pennsylvania Working Papers in Linguistics* 3: 127–40.

Hinton, Linette N., and Karen E. Pollock. 2000. "Regional Variations in the Phonological Characteristics of African American Vernacular English." *World Englishes* 19: 59–71.

Kohn, Mary. 2013. "Adolescent Ethnolinguistic Stability and Change: A Longitudinal Study." PhD diss., University of North Carolina at Chapel Hill.

Kurath, Hans, and Raven I. McDavid, Jr. 1961. *The Pronunciation of English in the Atlantic States.* Ann Arbor: University of Michigan.

Labov, William. 1972. *Language in the Inner City: Studies in the Black English Vernacular.* Philadelphia: University of Pennsylvania.

Labov, William, Sherry Ash, and Charles Boberg. 2006. *Atlas of North American English: Phonetics, Phonology, and Sound Change.* Berlin: Mouton de Gruyter.

Labov, William, Paul Cohen, Clarence Robins, and John Lewis. 1968. *A Study of the Non-Standard English of Negro and Puerto Rican Speakers in New York City.* Report on Cooperative Research Project 3288. New York: Columbia University.

Levine, Lewis, and Harry J. Crockett, Jr. 1966. "Speech Variations in a Piedmont Community." *Sociological Inquiry* 36: 204–26.

Mallinson, Christine, and Walt Wolfram. 2002. "Dialect Accommodation in a Bi-Ethnic Mountain Enclave Community: More Evidence on the Development of African American English." *Language in Society* 31: 743–75.

McNair, Elizabeth DuPree. 2005. *Mill Villagers and Farmers: Dialect and Economics in a Small Southern Town.* Publication of the American Dialect Society 90. Durham, NC: Duke University.

Miller, Michael I. 1986. "The Greatest Blemish: Plurals in *-sp, -st, -sk.*" In *Language Variety in the South: Perspectives in Black and White,* edited by Michael B. Montgomery and Guy Bailey, 235–53. Tuscaloosa: University of Alabama.

Myhill, John. 1988. "Postvocalic /r/ as an Index of Integration into the BEV Speech Community." *American Speech* 63: 203–13.

Nguyen, Jennifer G. 2006. "The Changing Social and Linguistic Orientation of the African American Middle Class." PhD diss., University of Michigan.

Pederson, Lee A., Susan Leas McDaniel, Guy Bailey, Marvin H. Basset, Carol M. Adams, Caisheng Liao, and Michael B. Montgomery, eds. 1986–1992. *The Linguistic Atlas of the Gulf States.* 7 vols. Athens: University of Georgia Press.

Pollock, Karen E., et al. 2001. "Phonological Features of African American Vernacular English (AAVE)." http://www.rehabmed.ualberta.ca/spa/phonology/features.htm.

Purnell, Thomas C. 2010. "The Vowel Phonology of Urban Southeastern Wisconsin." In Yaeger-Dror and Thomas 2010, 191–217.

Rickford, John R. 1999. *African American English: Features, Evolution, Educational Implications.* Malden, MA: Blackwell.

Thomas, Erik R. 1989. "The Implications of /o/ Fronting in Wilmington, North Carolina." *American Speech* 64: 327–33.

———. 1989/1993. "Vowel Changes in Columbus, Ohio." *Journal of English Linguistics* 22: 205–15.

———. 2001. *An Acoustic Analysis of Vowel Variation in New World English*. Publication of the American Dialect Society 85. Durham, NC: Duke University Press.

Thomas, Erik R., and Guy Bailey. 1998. "Parallels between Vowel Subsystems of African American Vernacular English and Caribbean Creoles." *Journal of Pidgin and Creole Languages* 13: 267–96.

Thomas, Erik R., and Elizabeth L. Coggshall. 2006/2007. "Comparing Phonetic Characteristics of African American and European American Speech." *Linguistica Atlantica* 27–28: 112–16.

Tillery, Jan, Guy Bailey, Claire Andres, Jeff Miller, and Naomi Palow. 2003. "Monophthongal / ai/ in the American South: Evidence from Three Linguistic Surveys." Paper presented at the Southeastern Conference on Linguistics, Washington, DC, April 13.

Tillery, Jan, Guy Bailey, and Tom Wikle. 2004. "Demographic Change and American Dialectology in the 21st Century." *American Speech* 79: 227–49.

Vaughn-Cooke, Fay Boyd. 1986. "Lexical Diffusion: Evidence from a Decreolizing Variety of Black English." In *Language Variety in the South: Perspectives in Black and White*, edited by Michael B. Montgomery and Guy Bailey, 111–30. Tuscaloosa: University of Alabama.

Williamson, Juanita V. 1968. *A Phonological and Morphological Study of the Speech of the Negro in Memphis, Tennessee*. Publication of the American Dialect Society 50. Tuscaloosa: University of Alabama.

Wolfram, Walter A. 1969. *A Sociolinguistic Description of Detroit Negro Speech*. Urban Language Series 5. Washington, DC: Center for Applied Linguistics.

Wolfram, Walt, and Ralph Fasold. 1974. *The Study of Social Dialects in the United States*. Englewood Cliffs, NJ: Prentice Hall.

Wolfram, Walt, and Erik R. Thomas. 2002. *The Development of African American English*. Language in Society. Vol. 31. Oxford: Blackwell.

Wroblewski, Michael, Thea Strand, and Sylvie DuBois. 2010. "Mapping a Dialect 'Mixtury': Vowel Phonology of African American and White Men in Rural Southern Louisiana." In Yaeger-Dror and Thomas 2010, 48–72.

Yaeger-Dror, Malcah, and Erik R. Thomas, eds. 2010. *African American English Speakers and Their Participation in Local Sound Changes: A Comparative Study*. Publication of the American Dialect Society 94. Durham, NC: Duke University Press.

CHAPTER 22

....

PROSODIC FEATURES OF AFRICAN AMERICAN ENGLISH

....

ERIK R. THOMAS

22.1 INTRODUCTION

....

THE prosody of African American English (AAE)[1] shares one frustrating characteristic with the prosody of other varieties of English. That is, it may be quite salient to listeners (see Bezooijen and Gooskens 1999; Foreman 2000; Thomas, Lass, and Carpenter 2010), but it is difficult to study and thus relatively little work has been conducted on it. Here, I use *African American English* (AAE) to mean any kind of English spoken by African Americans that could be identified by American listeners with a greater than chance frequency as African American. An additional difficulty is that because prosody itself encompasses a diverse set of features, including word stress, rhythm and rate of speech, overall fundamental frequency, intonation, and other factors less relevant to AAE, the study of AAE prosody has proceeded in a disjointed fashion.

Nevertheless, techniques have emerged over several decades for studying various aspects of prosody. As methods have appeared, a few researchers have exploited them to investigate AAE prosody. As a result, it is possible to provide a general outline of the prosodic variants that characterize AAE and, in particular, those that make it distinctive. Considerable work remains to be done, though, both in specifying the descriptive details of the variants and in determining how pervasive these variants are among African Americans (e.g., across social class and social network lines). Moreover, regional variation has yet to be worked out: how different are AAE and European American prosody within the South, how much regional variation does AAE prosody exhibit, and do all distinctively African American features of prosody have a southern origin? All of these questions are poorly resolved or have not been addressed at all. Ambitious students should view this situation as an opportunity.

22.2 WORD STRESS

One process that is stereotypically associated with AAE, or at least the speech of older African Americans, is the tendency to place primary stress on the first syllable of words whose standard pronunciations place the primary stress on a later syllable. This process can be observed in words such as *police, united, Detroit*, and *November* (see Fasold and Wolfram 1970; Baugh 1983; Sutcliffe 2003). Baugh (1983) refers to this as "forestressing." The following quotes, uttered by an elderly African American man from a small town in North Carolina, illustrate forestressing:

> In nineteen forty-five, I was drafted. Décember the eighth, nineteen forty-five.
> . . . we got on a troop train and went to Fórt Hood, Texas.
> So I came back home in—uh—Nóvember of fifty-three.
> I thought Maine was sárdines.
> I was díscharged up there.
> I stayed there—stayed there twénty-nine years and six months.
> But that hurricane tore down the screen for the óutdoor théàter.

For *Fort Hood, sardines, twenty-nine*, and *outdoor*, the forestressing represents transposition of primary and secondary stresses.[2] In *December, November*, and *discharged*, forestressing constitutes placing of a primary stress on an initial syllable that is most often unstressed in Standard English. *Theater*, in the last sentence, illustrates a related phenomenon in which a syllable falling after the primary stress is given a secondary stress.

Forestressing occurs among both African Americans and European Americans in the South, as indicated by data from the *Linguistic Atlas of the Gulf States* (Pedersen et al. 1986–92; hereafter LAGS).[3] Table 22.1 shows percentages of forestressing for nine words, based on the tables in volume 6 of LAGS. The percentages of forestressing are broadly

Table 22.1 Percentages of Subjects Showing Forestressing for Nine Words in LAGS

Word	African Americans (%)	European Americans (%)
address	62	46
cigars	53	60
hotel	84	74
Tennessee	66	41
July	56	56
September	19	30
October	33	53
November	31	36
December	55	55

similar for African Americans and European Americans. Forestressing is a feature that, among whites, is concentrated mostly in Southern dialects but, in AAE, is widespread, with the obvious connection that AAE originated in the South. Unfortunately, the percentages do not reflect a complete accounting of the LAGS data except for the word *July* because volume 6 gives tallies only for some forms of each word. For example, for *November*, the transcriptions were coded according to whether there was forestressing or not, whether /r/ in the last syllable was constricted or vocalized, and whether the vowel in the second syllable was [ɛ] or [ɪ], but there are tables for only five of the eight possible combinations of these three variables. Because of these omissions, it is impossible for readers of LAGS to say with certainty whether European American and African American speech differ at all in the LAGS territory for forestressing. Data in LAGS also indicate that forestressing is most prevalent among lower social levels and older subjects, but the tables are not broken down by ethnicity/social level or ethnicity/age group combinations.

22.3 RATE OF SPEECH AND PROSODIC RHYTHM

A number of timing issues can affect how speech is realized and perceived. One is simply the overall speech rate—that is, whether all syllables are prolonged or shortened in duration. Overall rate of speech can vary according to one's emotional state, but it is possible that it varies cross-culturally (see Robb, Maclagan, and Chen 2004; Kendall 2009). In addition, though, syllables can differ in their durations relative to each other, and this factor can result in recognizable differences.

Kendall (2009) compared speech rate and pause durations among African Americans, European Americans, Latinos, and Lumbee Native Americans in conversational speech. Overall, African Americans showed slow mean speech rates, but a mixed-models statistical analysis predicted them to be near the middle. The difference was due to the fact that the African American females in the sample had slow rates, while the African American males were near the middle among all the ethnicity/sex combinations. Many of the females were children, which may have skewed the speech rate values toward slower rates. Kendall's data for pause duration showed that African Americans averaged longer pauses than other ethnic groups, and a mixed-model analysis found the African American ethnicity to be a significant factor, but the model found African American ethnicity to predict shorter pause durations. The discrepancy was due to the greater heterogeneity of the African American sample used as compared with other groups.

The way syllables differ (or do not) in relative duration is called *prosodic rhythm*. In English, stressed syllables are typically much longer than neighboring unstressed syllables, whereas in Spanish, stressed and unstressed syllables do not differ as dramatically in duration. The former situation is called *stress timing* because it was formerly thought that the durations between stresses were more or less the same. The latter situation is called *syllable timing* because each syllable was thought to have roughly the same duration (Abercrombie 1967).

Various quantitative methods have been created in recent years for measuring prosodic rhythm (see Ramus, Nespor, and Mehler 1999; Low, Grabe, and Nolan 2000). Before that time, it had been suggested that AAE differed from European American varieties in rhythm (Spears 1988), though without empirical evidence, and probably not with the specific meaning that prosody specialists associate with *rhythm*. Thus far, the main study of prosodic rhythm in AAE is Thomas and Carter (2006), which used a modified version of the Pairwise Variability Index (nPVI) method of Low et al. (2000). This study, based on speakers from North Carolina, found that contemporary AAE is just as firmly stress-timed as European American English. However, the study also examined the ex-slave recordings, a series of audio recordings of African Americans who had been born as slaves and were thus much older.[4] These recordings are described in Bailey, Maynor, and Cukor-Avila (1991). It turned out that the ex-slaves, with one exception, showed nPVI values in line not with those of contemporary African Americans but with those of Jamaicans and Mexican Americans. That is, the ex-slaves were more syllable-timed than present-day African Americans or European Americans of any vintage. Jamaican is a known creole, and Mexican American English has an obvious non-English substrate. The results suggest, then, that AAE has some non-English influence in its past, though the influence may be directly from contact with West African languages instead of through any earlier creole.

22.4 OVERALL FUNDAMENTAL FREQUENCY

One group of features studied for AAE, overall characteristics of fundamental frequency (F_0) values, straddles the line between prosody and voice quality. Several studies have addressed overall F_0, and the results contradict each other in various ways. One line of research has focused on mean F_0 values. Hollien and Malcik (1962), using a reading passage, found that African American male adolescents showed lower average F_0 than European American male adolescents from other studies. Ducote (1983), whose subjects were older adults, and Wheat and Hudson (1988), whose subjects were 6-year-old boys and girls, also found lower mean F_0 values for African Americans than for comparable European Americans reported in other studies. Two more recent studies conducted by speech pathologists have reported no difference in mean F_0 between African American and European American subjects. Using adult males who were mostly (Walton and Orlikoff 1994) or entirely (Mayo and Grant 1995) young, no statistically significant differences were found in mean F_0. However, their data are from sustained [ɑ] vowels, not from running speech.

Another line of research has examined the distribution of F_0 values. Tarone (1973) noted that African Americans used a wider range of pitch values than European

Americans. She also reported that the wide pitch range was associated with competitive speech acts and that other styles of speech apparently did not show the same property. Similarly, Loman (1975) found falsetto, which certainly broadens the range of F_0 values, to be common in AAE.

F_0 range appeared again in Hudson and Holbrook (1981, 1982). They reported that their African American subjects showed a wider range of F_0 values than their European American subjects. In addition, they found that the range was wider in spontaneous speech than in reading. Moreover, they determined that African Americans showed a greater range of F_0 above their mean modal F_0 value, while European Americans showed the opposite distribution of F_0 values. Jun and Foreman (1996) also found that African Americans use a wider pitch range than European Americans.

In contrast, a few studies have reported that African Americans use a narrower pitch range than other groups. Thomas (1999) reported that European Americans in a rural Texas community showed a greater fall in F_0 than African Americans from the initial pitch accent to the end of an utterance. Cole et al. (2005) presented further evidence of this pattern from North Carolina. They suggested that the pattern of showing an exaggerated degree of declination across an utterance was associated with some European American females in the southern United States. Other European American females lacked it and it did not appear to typify male speech. Using data collected in Los Angeles and South Carolina involving girls playing hopscotch, Goodwin, Goodwin, and Yaeger-Dror (2002) showed that African American girls tended to show a narrower pitch range, often with flat stretches in the F_0 tracks, than Mexican American girls, who were more likely to show decided contours in their F_0 tracks. The Mexican Americans, it might be added, were recorded speaking mainly Spanish.

What can be made of these conflicting reports? The key is probably Tarone's (1973) remark that wide pitch ranges in AAE are associated with competitive speech acts. It would seem that a wide pitch range, including the falsetto that Loman (1975) reported, is a resource that African Americans use only in certain registers, perhaps for effect. It is more common in informal styles and is usually avoided in reading, as Hudson and Holbrook's (1981, 1982) results suggest. Consideration of such register differences is crucial for an accurate understanding of AAE prosody. Thomas's (1999) data, which found a wider pitch range for European Americans, were based on read speech, and the data in Cole et al. (2005) were based on interview-style speech, which leaves little opportunity for the situations that would cue wider pitch ranges. Tarone (1973) and Loman (1975) were based on more informal speech. Only the results from Goodwin et al. (2002) seem to contradict this tendency.

22.5 INTONATION AND TONE

Two speech identification experiments, Foreman (2000) and Thomas et al. (2010), have shown that American listeners can use intonation as a cue to determine whether a speaker is African American or European American. This result implies that there are diagnostic intonational differences between the two groups. Over the past forty years, several studies have examined AAE intonation, as will be discussed below. As these studies have shown, AAE may exhibit distinctive intonational characteristics, but pinpointing just what these characteristics are has been elusive. A number of factors conspire to obfuscate the issue. Over the long span of time during which studies of AAE intonation have taken place, different intonational transcription systems have been in vogue, which makes it hard to compare the findings of different studies. Various studies have examined different factors as well: some have focused on tones at the end of *intonational phrases* (IP), some on tones within phrases, and some on other features. Social factors add to the confusion. My own casual observations suggest that the intonational features that are diagnostically African American are subject to style shifting, social class variation, and, quite likely, regional variation. Many African Americans appear to be adept at emphasizing or ameliorating these features to sound "more Black" or "less Black." Middle-class African Americans apparently use them less than working-class African Americans. Furthermore, these features may be diminished in areas with low concentrations of African Americans compared to regions, especially parts of the South, with higher concentrations.

In spite of the problems in comparability, the various studies of AAE intonation appear to report many of the same phenomena, as is evident once the differences in terminology and methods are cleared away. The recurrence of patterns is striking when one considers the diversity of communities that were studied. Some examined rural Southern communities (Thomas 1999, in Texas; Wolfram and Thomas 2002 and Cole et al. 2005, in North Carolina; Goodwin et al. 2002, in South Carolina; and Green 2002, in Louisiana). Loman (1975) and McLarty (2011) studied urban Southern environments, namely, Washington, DC and Raleigh, North Carolina, respectively. The remainder investigated widely scattered non-Southern urban communities: Tarone (1973) in Seattle; Jun and Foreman (1996) and Foreman (2000) in Los Angeles; and Gooden (2009) in Pittsburgh. In addition, the ex-slave recordings, representing locations across the South, were analyzed by Sutcliffe (2001, 2003) and McLarty (2011).

An IP is the largest unit in intonation. Within an IP, F_0 gradually falls, usually with a few local rises representing pitch accents, and this general fall is called *declination*. A special high or low tone marks the end of an IP. In addition, a pause may optionally follow the IP, and the F_0, having descended because of declination, is reset to a relatively high pitch when the next IP begins. Goodwin et al. (2002, 1627) report that a low rising final tone characterizes declarative statements in some AAE. A number of studies have focused on differences in the final tone for yes/no questions between AAE and European American varieties. European American English ordinarily marks the end of a yes/no question with a high tone. This high tone is commonly preceded by a low pitch accent. However, African Americans show less consistency, often ending yes/no questions with a level (Green 2002) or falling (Tarone 1973) tone. Similarly, Jun and Foreman (1996) find that African Americans are less consistent than European Americans in producing the low pitch accent before the edge tone. Jun and Foreman (1996) also noted some difference in the placement of high final tones: European Americans normally located it on the final syllable, while African Americans tended to locate the high tone at the onset of the final word, after which they produced a fall in F_0.

Within IPs, another consistent finding arises. Loman (1975), based on his earlier field-work in Washington, DC, reported that African Americans produced more primary stresses than European Americans and that they showed a "constant and marked shift" between higher and lower pitches (231, 242). Loman used the now-antiquated transcrip-tional system of Trager and Smith (1951), but "primary stresses" could be interpreted as referring to pitch accents. His report of the "constant and marked shift" between high and low pitches suggests a relatively high incidence of pitch accents by his African American subjects. Analogous findings are reported by Thomas (1999), from southeast-ern Texas, and by Wolfram and Thomas (2002), from eastern North Carolina. McLarty (2011) investigated this phenomenon, analyzing the ex-slave recordings (Bailey, Maynor, and Cukor-Avila 1991) and recordings of modern speakers from Raleigh, North Carolina, using the Tone and Break Index (ToBI) transcription system (Beckman and Hirschberg 1994). He found that African Americans used a greater incidence of the L+H* pitch accent, which is characterized by a rising contour, but not of the H* pitch accent, which is characterized by a generally falling contour. This result explains one aspect of the distinctiveness of AAE intonation: the greater incidence of L+H* pitch accents reflects a tendency of tonal peaks to occur later within syllables for AAE than for European American English. His data also show, however, that African Americans exhibit a greater incidence of pitch accents (of any type) than European Americans. In intonational analyses of English and other languages, pitch accents ordinarily occur with such high frequency only under special circumstances with narrow focus, such as in reciting lists. Jun and Foreman (1996), who also employed ToBI, reported a (prob-ably related) finding that African Americans generally produce more pitch accents after the focus of the sentence. The relatively high rate of L+H* in some forms of AAE, with its use extended to broad-focus instances, opens the possibility that certain varieties of AAE may not distinguish H* from L+H*.

Figures 22.1 and 22.2, featuring two utterances by the same male from a small town in North Carolina who was excerpted earlier, illustrate the "constant and marked shift" that Loman (1975) described.[5] In each sentence, all of the primary stresses have a high tone associated with them, marked by H* in the textgrids. (The first and fourth high tones in figure 22.1 might better be labeled as L+H* because their F_0 tracks show a ris-ing slope within the vowel.) In the first example, the sentence begins with two weakly stressed syllables (*But their*) with low tone, but they are followed by a series of four high tones with low tones in between. The second example has three high tones, all on pri-mary stresses. Both sentences show a low boundary tone, labeled as L-L%, which typifies broad-focus declarative statements.

At least four explanations could be proposed for the pattern observed by Loman and later researchers. One is that lexical stress is realized as a jump in F_0 in AAE. However, not every lexical stress is associated with the high F_0 points. Secondary stresses commonly show low tones, as with the first syllable of *operation* in figure 22.1. Primary stresses often show a low tone when they fall at the end of an IP, as with *days* in figure 22.3. Moreover, primary stresses may show a low tone when they fall between two other closely spaced high tones, as with the stressed syllable of *started* in figure 22.4. The occurrence of low tones on some stressed syllables would appear to disqualify lexical stress as an explanation.

A second explanation, promoted by Sutcliffe (2001, 2003) and Spears (in preparation), would be that AAE is "a tone language (or perhaps post-tone language)" (Sutcliffe 2001, 141). Lexical tone is common in West African languages (e.g., Welmers 1973; Yip 2007).

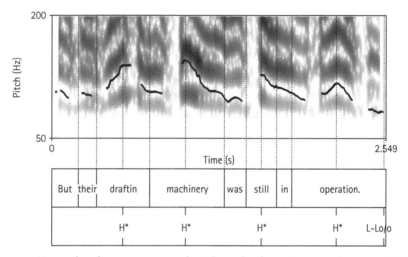

FIGURE 22.1 Narrowband spectrogram and pitch track of an utterance showing a high density of high tones distinct from lower tones in between. In this and subsequent figures, the spectrogram is scaled from 0 to 400 Hz and the pitch track from 50 to 200 Hz.

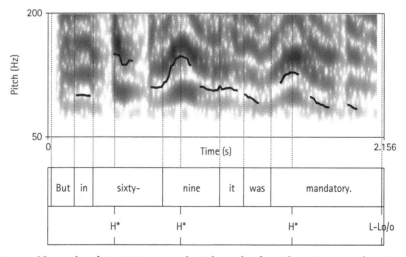

FIGURE 22.2 Narrowband spectrogram and pitch track of another utterance showing a high density of high tones.

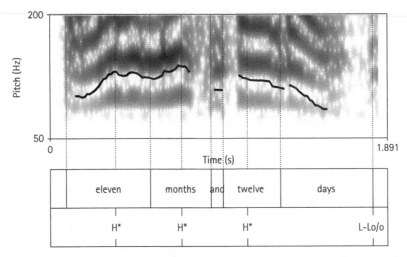

FIGURE 22.3 Narrowband spectrogram and pitch track of an utterance showing a low tone on the final stressed syllable (*days*).

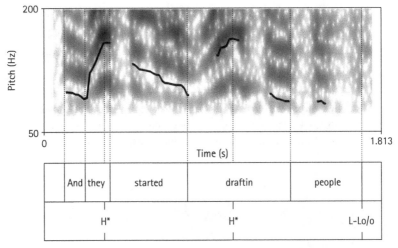

FIGURE 22.4 Narrowband spectrogram and pitch track of an utterance showing a low tone on a non-final syllable with primary stress (in *started*).

A pure lexical tone system requires two things. First, all or nearly all syllables have to be specified for tone. Second, the tones have to be consistent on particular syllables of the same inflectional form of a given word, unless a predictable phonological process acts on a syllable to transform one tone into another. In AAE, however, syllables in particular words can vary as to whether they show high or low tones, and they can do so with no apparent phonological motivation. Figure 22.5 shows an utterance with three instances of the word *hospital*. The stressed syllable of *hospital* shows a low tone in the first and third instances, but a high tone in the second one. Similarly, figures 22.6 and 22.7 show

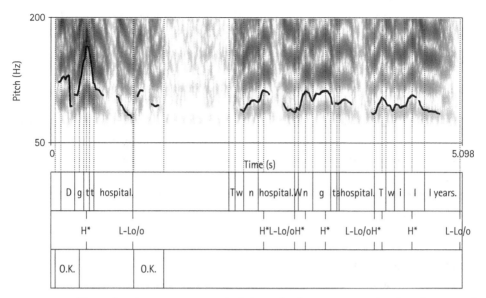

FIGURE 22.5 Narrowband spectrogram and pitch track of an utterance showing the stressed syllable of *hospital* with (second and third instances) and without (first instance) a high pitch accent. For most words, only the first letter is shown. The utterance is "Didn't go to the hospital. There was no hóspital. Was no goin' to a hóspital. That was in later years." The interviewer says "O.K." twice.

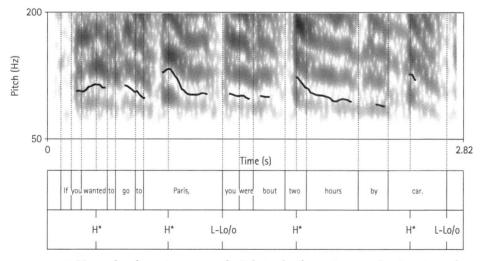

FIGURE 22.6 Narrowband spectrogram and pitch track of an utterance showing stressed *go* with a relatively low tone. The utterance is "If you wanted to go to Paris, you were 'bout two hours by car."

two utterances that contain the word *go*, with an apparent low tone on *go* in figure 22.6 and a high tone on *go* in figure 22.7. This evidence would appear to refute the notion that AAE shows a pure lexical tone system. Sutcliffe (2001, 2003) based his assertions on evidence from the ex-slave recordings, not on contemporary AAE. McLarty (2011) also utilized the ex-slave recordings but found their intonational systems to be similar to those of contemporary African Americans.

There is one other way that AAE could exhibit tone, though. Not all tonal systems are "pure" in that they require all syllables to be specified for tone. In contrast, so-called "lexical pitch-accented" languages such as Japanese and Swedish tonally specify only certain syllables. Sutcliffe (2001, 2003) noted that high tones in the ex-slave recordings ordinarily corresponded to syllables with lexical stress, but he noted certain lexical exceptions, such as *bábý*. Spears (in preparation) argues that this process still holds true for contemporary AAE in a few words, such as low-toned intensifier *bàck* versus tonally unspecified locative *back*: that is, in those words, high or low tones that may not be predicted by lexical stress are specified. This configuration still differs from lexical pitch-accented languages, in which a large fraction of words have at least one syllable with a tonal specification. However, the patterns described by Sutcliffe (2001, 2003) and Spears (forthcoming), if they hold true, could conceivably have originated as a substrate effect from tonal West African languages when Africans encountered the quite different prosodic system of English; Thomason and Kaufman (1988) demonstrate in detail how transfer effects are not always one-to-one. Sutcliffe (2001, 2003) certainly provides a plausible mechanism for such transfer, in that Africans may have identified lexical stresses with high tone and lack of stress with low tone. In that scenario, the lexical exceptions that Sutcliffe reported could represent fossilized relics, in some cases from West African borrowings.

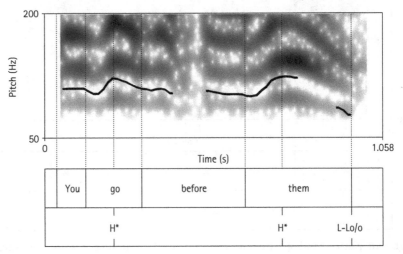

FIGURE 22.7 Narrowband spectrogram and pitch track of an utterance showing stressed *go* with a high tone.

A third explanation would be that AAE exhibits a different inventory of intonational pitch accents from other forms of English. One suggestion is that it features H+L* or perhaps H*+L pitch accents.[6] Such accents would be characterized by a fall in F_0, but unlike for H* pitch accents, the fall would be an integral part of the pitch accent, one that is consistently present. Gooden (2007) posits H+L* for Jamaican Creole, which, of course, is lexically English-based. Gooden (2009) suggests that AAE may have not just L+H* and H*, as European American varieties do, but also H+L* and/or H*+L. This explanation may account for the strong F_0 dynamics before and after tonal peaks. Of course, it does not address the observation that there seem to be too many points of high F_0 (i.e., more pitch accents) in examples such as those shown in figures 22.1 to 22.7. The other suggestion, noted earlier, is that the L+H* pitch accent is extended to broad-focus utterances, possibly eliminating the distinction between H* and L+H*.

One way that intonational systems can show higher densities of pitch accents consistently, however, represents a fourth possible explanation. This possibility, suggested by Cole et al. (2005), is that AAE (or some varieties of it) exhibit *accentual phrases* (AP). Nevertheless, this explanation, like the others, is unsatisfactory, as will be seen below. APs are intonational divisions that are shorter than the IP and *intermediate phrase* (ip) divisions that "Mainstream American English" is considered to have in standard ToBI treatments (see Beckman and Hirschberg 1994). Whereas IPs and ips may have multiple content words, an AP ordinarily contains only one content word, though it can contain more (Jun and Fougeron 2002). Each AP contains a pitch accent, which would explain the high frequency of apparent pitch accents, represented by the points of high F_0, in the AAE examples shown earlier. The AP explanation has a serious problem, however. In AAE, high tones are always linked to lexically stressed syllables, whereas in recognized AP languages, marked tones are not obligatorily associated with lexical stresses. This problem would appear to disqualify the AP explanation.

A few miscellaneous findings emerged from the previous studies. Tarone (1973) reported that African Americans often deleted the word *if* in conditional clauses and marked the conditionality by intonation. In addition, both Jun and Foreman (1996) and Thomas (1999) found that African Americans were more likely than European Americans to produce a high tone at the beginning of a sentence. Cole et al. (2005) suggested that African Americans showed smoother F_0 juncture between syllables, while European Americans were more likely to exhibit abrupt disjuncture. McLarty's (2011) finding that African Americans showed more L+H* pitch accents is compatible with that suggestion in that L+H* shows a lower initial F_0, which would be relatively close to the F_0 of a preceding low-pitched syllable. Nonetheless, what remains is the question of whether there is any unifying principle behind the features that make AAE intonation distinctive.

At this point, we are left without a suitable explanation for all aspects of the AAE intonational pattern. AAE shows differences in the location of tonal peaks within syllables, which current models easily account for. However, AAE also appears to show an unusually high density of pitch accents (though further confirmation of this observation is desirable). Extant models either fail to account for the high incidence of pitch accents or violate other principles of intonational analysis. The questions of whether and how broad and narrow focus are differentiated offer potential avenues for further investigation.

22.6 Conclusion

In spite of prevailing neglect, interest in AAE prosody has generated a small body of research that has yielded important findings. Forestressing, as in *pólice*, is linguistically well-described, but what is lacking is thorough knowledge of its social, generational, and regional distribution within AAE. In contrast, consensus is needed on the linguistic interpretation of AAE intonation, though it seems to be attracting increased attention recently. Variation in overall F_0 could use a good deal of additional attention, largely in clarifying its stylistic and social distribution. For prosodic rhythm, the apparent convergence with European American varieties would tend to discourage much further study, though future work could produce surprises, and this variable offers valuable insights into AAE's past. Finally, analysis of speech rate remains incipient.

Any of these features could contribute to the overriding scholarly controversies about AAE, particularly those relating to its origins, its continuing development relative to European American varieties, and its degree of internal diversity. Prosodic rhythm and intonation are probably the most informative prosodic variables on the origins of AAE. Satisfactory demonstration of a connection between West African tonal systems and AAE intonation would greatly alter the debate on the origins of AAE. At present, such a connection remains conjectural. Intonation, forestressing, and overall F_0 are all relevant to questions about the continuing development of AAE. They all bear directly on whether AAE and European American varieties are converging, diverging, or maintaining a steady distance, and on how much regional and social diversity AAE shows. Moreover, they all contribute to the vitality of AAE. In that regard, it could be fruitful to explore the links between these features and various styles of music, poetry, and public speaking that African Americans have bestowed upon American culture.

Notes

1. I use AAE as a more general term than I use *African American Vernacular English* (AAVE). By AAVE, I mean varieties of AAE with numerous nonstandard features such as copula absence, habitual be, and third-person singular *–s* absence. AAE includes both AAVE and middle-class varieties that largely lack nonstandard features but are still recognizably African American, mostly by subtle phonetic cues, some of which are likely prosodic.

2. In compounds such as *outdoor theater*, it may not be uncommon for Standard English speakers to reverse the stresses in *outdoor*.

3. With which group it originated is a question that I leave for others to determine. By *European American,* I mean Americans whose ancestry is entirely or mostly from Europe, regardless of how many generations have passed since the immigration.
4. The ex-slaves were from states across the South, from Virginia to Texas.
5. I assume that this speaker's patterning reflects a prototypical Southern AAE prosodic system, though it is possible that he represents one end of a continuum and not the center of the continuum.
6. In a lexical pitch-accented language such as Swedish, a particular syllable in a particular word is specified as having a particular pitch accent. In an intonation pitch accent system such as English shows, pitch accents can appear on any stressed syllable in an utterance.

References

Abercrombie, David. 1967. *Elements of General Phonetics.* Edinburgh: Edinburgh University Press.

Bailey, Guy, Natalie Maynor, and Patricia Cukor-Avila. 1991. *The Emergence of Black English: Text and Commentary.* Creole Language Library, vol. 8. Amsterdam and Philadelphia: John Benjamins.

Baugh, John. 1983. *Black Street Speech: Its History, Structure, and Survival.* Austin: University of Texas Press.

Beckman, Mary E., and Julia Hirschberg. 1994. "The ToBI annotation Conventions." Online typescript. http://www.ling.ohio-state.edu/~tobi/ame_tobi/annotation_conventions.html.

Bezooijen, Renée van, and Charlotte Gooskens. 1999. "Identification of Language Varieties: The Contribution of Different Linguistic Levels." *Journal of Language and Social Psychology* 18: 31–48.

Cole, Jennifer, Erik R. Thomas, Erica Britt, and Elizabeth L. Coggshall. 2005. "Intonational Distinctiveness of African American English." Paper presented at conference on New Ways of Analyzing Variation XXXIV, New York, New York, October 20–23.

Ducote, Charlotte Anne. 1983. "A Study of the Reading and Speaking Fundamental Frequency of Aging Black Adults." PhD diss., Louisiana State University.

Fasold, Ralph W., and Walt Wolfram. 1970. "Some Linguistic Features of Negro Dialect." In *Teaching Standard English in the Inner City,* 41–86, edited by Ralph W. Fasold and Roger W. Shuy. Washington, DC: Center for Applied Linguistics.

Foreman, Christina. 2000. "Identification of African-American English from Prosodic Cues." *Texas Linguistic Forum* 43: 57–66.

Gooden, Shelome. 2007. "Intonational Phonology of Jamaican Creole: An Autosegmental Metrical Analysis." Online Proceedings of the ICPhS Satellite Workshop on the Intonational Phonology of Understudied or Fieldwork Languages, Saarbrücken, Germany, July 2007. www.linguistics.ucla.edu/people/jun/Workshop2007ICPhS/WorkshopSchedule.htm.

———. 2009. "Authentically Black, bona fide Pittsburgher: A First Look at Intonation in African American Women's Language in Pittsburgh." In *African American Women's Language: Discourse, Education, and Identity,* edited by Sonja L. Lanehart, 142–64. Newcastle-upon-Tyne, UK: Cambridge Scholars.

Goodwin, Marjorie Harness, Charles Goodwin, and Malcah Yaeger-Dror. 2002. "Multi-Modality in Girls' Game Disputes." *Journal of Pragmatics* 34: 1621–49.

Green, Lisa J. 2002. *African American English: A Linguistic Introduction.* Cambridge: Cambridge University Press.

Hollien, Harry, and Ellen Malcik. 1962. "Adolescent Voice Change in Southern Negro Males." *Speech Monographs* 29: 53–58.

Hudson, Amelia I., and Anthony Holbrook. 1981. "A Study of Reading Fundamental Vocal Frequency of Young Black Adults." *Journal of Speech and Hearing Research* 24: 197–201.

———. 1982. "Fundamental Frequency Characteristics of Young Black Adults: Spontaneous Speaking and Oral Reading." *Journal of Speech and Hearing Research* 25: 25–28.

Jun, Sun-Ah, and Christina Foreman. 1996. "Boundary Tones and Focus Realization in African-American Intonation." Paper presented at the 3rd joint meeting of the Acoustical Society of America and the Acoustical Society of Japan, Honolulu, Hawaii, December 6.

Jun, Sun-Ah, and C. Fougeron. 2002. "Realizations of Accentual Phrase in French Intonation." *Probus* 14: 147–72.

Kendall, Tyler S. 2009. "Speech Rate, Pause, and Linguistic Variation: An Examination through the Sociolinguistic Archive and Analysis Project." PhD diss., Duke University.

Loman, Bengt. 1975. "Prosodic Patterns in a Negro American Dialect." In *Style and Text: Studies Presented to Nils Erik Enkvist,* edited by Håkan Ringbom, Alfhild Ingberg, Ralf Norrman, Kurt Nyholm, Rolf Westman, and Kay Wikberg, 219–42. Stockholm: Språkförlaget Skriptor AB.

Low, Ee Ling, Esther Grabe, and Francis Nolan. 2000. "Quantitative Characterizations of Speech Rhythm: Syllable-Timing in Singapore English." *Language and Speech* 43: 377–401.

Mayo, Robert, and William C. Grant, II. 1995. "Fundamental Frequency, Perturbation, and Vocal Tract Resonance Characteristics of African-American and White American Males." *Echo* 17: 32–38.

McLarty, Jason A. 2011. "An Apparent Time Analysis of Intonation Using Ex-Slaves: Comparing Raleigh, North Carolina AAE and EAE Pitch Accent Types and Frequencies." Master's capstone project, North Carolina State University.

Pederson, Lee A., Susan Leas McDaniel, Guy Bailey, Marvin H. Basset, Carol M. Adams, Caisheng Liao, and Michael B. Montgomery, eds. 1986–1992. *The Linguistic Atlas of the Gulf States.* 7 vols. Athens: University of Georgia Press.

Ramus, Franck, Marina Nespor, and Jacques Mehler. 1999. "Correlates of Linguistic Rhythm in the Speech Signal." *Cognition* 73: 265–92.

Robb, Michael, Margaret Maclagan, and Yang Chen. 2004. "Speaking Rates of American and New Zealand Varieties of English." *Clinical Linguistics and Phonetics* 18: 1–15.

Spears, Arthur K. 1988. "Black American English." In *Anthropology for the Nineties: Introductory Readings,* edited by Johnnetta B. Cole, 96–113. New York: Free Press; London: Collier Macmillan.

———. In preparation. "Tone in African American English (AAE)." Typescript.

Sutcliffe, David. 2001. "The Voice of the Ancestors: New Evidence on 19th-Century Precursors to 20th-Century African American English." In *Sociocultural and Historical Contexts of African American English,* Varieties of English around the World, General Series, vol. 27, edited by Sonja L. Lanehart, 129–68. Amsterdam: John Benjamins.

———. 2003. "African American English Supersegmentals: A Study of Pitch Patterns in the Black English of the United States." In *Phonology and Morphology of Creole Languages,* Linguistische Arbeiten, vol. 478, edited by Ingo Plag, 147–62. Tübingen: Max Niemeyer Verlag.

Tarone, Elaine E. 1973. "Aspects of Intonation in Black English." *American Speech* 48: 29–36.

Thomas, Erik R. 1999. "A First Look at African-American Vernacular English Intonation." Paper presented at the conference on New Ways of Analyzing Variation XXVIII, Toronto, Ontario, October 16.

Thomas, Erik R., and Phillip M. Carter. 2006. "Rhythm and African American English." *English World-Wide* 27: 331–55.

Thomas, Erik R., Norman J. Lass, and Jeannine Carpenter. 2010. "Identification of African American Speech." In *A Reader in Sociophonetics*, Trends in Linguistics: Studies and Monographs 219, edited by Dennis R. Preston and Nancy Niedzielski, 265–85. New York: De Gruyter Mouton.

Thomason, Sarah Grey, and Terrence Kaufman. 1988. *Language Contact, Creolization, and Genetic Linguistics*. Berkeley: University of California Press.

Trager, George L., and Henry Lee Smith. 1951. *An Outline of English Structure*. Norman, OK: Battenburg.

Walton, Julie H., and Robert F. Orlikoff. 1994. "Speaker Race Identification from Acoustic Cues in the Vocal Signal." *Journal of Speech and Hearing Research* 37: 738–45.

Welmers, William E. 1973. *African Language Structures*. Berkeley: University of California Press.

Wheat, Marcia C., and Amelia I. Hudson. 1988. "Spontaneous Speaking Fundamental Frequency of Six-Year-Old Black Children." *Journal of Speech and Hearing Research* 31: 723–25.

Wolfram, Walt, and Erik R. Thomas. 2002. *The Development of African American English: Evidence from an Isolated Community*. Oxford: Blackwell.

Yip, Moira. 2007. "Tone." In *The Cambridge Handbook of Phonology*, edited by Paul de Lacy, 229–51. Cambridge: Cambridge University Press.

PART IV

CHILD
LANGUAGE
ACQUISITION
AND
DEVELOPMENT

CHAPTER 23

LANGUAGE ACQUISITION IN THE AFRICAN AMERICAN CHILD

Prior to Age Four

BRANDI L. NEWKIRK-TURNER,
RAMONDA HORTON, AND IDA J. STOCKMAN

23.1 INTRODUCTION

LANGUAGE acquisition research broadly aims to reveal the evolution of children's understanding and use of language across time and the types of factors (biological, social, cognitive, and linguistic) that influence its learning and change. This chapter reviews language acquisition research on children who acquire African American English (AAE) in the United States. AAE is a native English dialect primarily spoken by African Americans with an indigenous slave history and ancestral ties to Sub-Saharan Africa. AAE has phonological, morphosyntactic, semantic, and pragmatic/discourse features that may or may not contrast with Mainstream American English (MAE).

We recognize that all African Americans do not speak or learn AAE. This chapter samples studies of developing language by African American children who were presumed to do so. It focuses specifically on the acquisition period from birth up to age 4 for two reasons. First, the initial three years of the life span are a critical time period during which the foundation of a language is established. Research on MAE learners shows that within this short window of development, children typically move from pre-intentional communication to the comprehension and production of single words, phrases, and sentences that serve different pragmatic goals (Brown 1973; Bloom and Lahey 1978; Owens 2007). Descriptions of the language used by AAE-speaking African American children would be incomplete without knowledge of the same early developmental period. Research on typically developing language is especially valued at the youngest ages because such information can be used as a model to guide the language and literacy instruction of AAE-speaking African American children as they enter mainstream educational settings. Besides their practical usefulness, developmental outcomes for the youngest learners in different communities (e.g., AAE-speaking African Americans, MAE-speaking African Americans, MAE non-African Americans, and AAE-speaking non-African Americans) can inform theoretical hypotheses about the universal- and group-specific characteristics of language and its acquisition process.

A second reason to focus on African American children prior to age 4 is that their language has not been frequently investigated. In general, African American children were historically excluded from seminal language acquisition research. The participant samples of those investigations concerned with the language development of young English speakers included mostly White children. Their spontaneous talk was sampled frequently, across multiple time points, and in familiar settings (Bloom 1992; Stockman 2007a, 2010). Children with different language patterns and learning experiences were excluded from these developmental studies to reduce the amount of variability likely to influence findings (Bloom 1992; Stockman 2007a). Furthermore, studies that did include African American children often emphasized their differences relative to children who were acquiring MAE. Their differences were often interpreted as a deficit relative to MAE speakers, who were not always comparable on demographic variables (e.g., socioeconomic status) that can influence language learning and use.

Erosion of this *deficit* paradigm for interpreting group differences still did not encourage studies of the youngest AAE learners. Language research on African American children in the eroded deficit paradigm era focused most often on older children. Inspired by sociolinguists, this paradigm shift emphasized the systematic nature of linguistic patterns that differentiated typical mature speakers of AAE and MAE (see Labov 1972; Wolfram 1969). Research in applied fields such as speech-language pathology and educational pedagogy focused on whether the distinctive AAE features used by mature speakers were also used by children and the practical consequences of doing so. These research goals could be met by excluding the youngest African American children, whose spontaneous speech was expected to exhibit few, if any, contrastive AAE-MAE patterns (Cole 1980; Stockman 1986). Therefore, their language was not expected to be useful for addressing practical issues such as how to identify AAE-speaking children or their use of dialect differences during language assessment and intervention practices. Seminal studies on child use of AAE (see Washington and Craig 1994, 2002) described the contrastive AAE-MAE patterns of African American preschoolers but did not explore the developmental pathway to their use prior to age 4.

The premise of this chapter is that from birth onward, African American children who acquire AAE begin learning their whole language system. The AAE language system includes input about its contrastive and noncontrastive patterns relative to other American English dialects (Seymour, Bland-Stewart, and Green 1998). Contrastive features are those that show a difference between AAE and MAE (e.g., third person singular –s, auxiliary *be*, copula *be*, and past tense –*ed*), whereas noncontrastive features are those with no contrast between AAE and MAE (e.g., articles, conjunctions, modals, and locatives). Because the AAE system comprises both types, we should expect evidence for both types of patterns before the age of 4, when mapping the developmental trajectory of the child-to-adult AAE system.

23.2 GOALS OF THE CHAPTER

This chapter (1) reviews the major findings on African American children's language acquisition prior to age 4 and (2) highlights the knowledge gaps and potential areas of future language acquisition research on them. This review will show that African American children who acquire AAE are no exception to the long-standing evidence that children acquire the language system to which they are exposed from a very early age (Heath 1983; Owens 2007). The studies of language form, content, and use that we singled out for the most detailed review in this chapter included (1) children who were typical-developing learners of AAE and (2) descriptions of their spontaneous language sampled in natural settings at two or more ages that included those within the age range of birth to four years. We also included single-age studies with multiple data points within this age range if naturalistic data were used and they supported developmental changes for the same children described in another study. Participant ages were represented in either months or years, as designated by the author/s of the respective studies.

23.3 LANGUAGE FORM: PHONOLOGY, MORPHOLOGY, AND SYNTAX

23.3.1 Phonology

The few studies of African American children's spontaneous speech development show that AAE and MAE contrastive and noncontrastive sound patterns emerge prior to age 4. Bland-Stewart (2003) described the consonant inventories and phonological patterns of eight low-income, 2 year olds. She found that they produced all consonant stops, nasals, glides, and some fricative sounds (e.g., /s/, /f/, /v/, /h/) in various word shapes—with CV and CVC combinations occurring most frequently. On average, 80 percent of the words produced by the children were monosyllabic and 39 percent were closed syllables, which indicated the early presence of word-final consonants (e.g., *bird, rug, purse, book*).

Stockman (2008) identified initial consonants produced spontaneously by 102 African American 3 year olds from low-income homes in cities in the northern and southern United States. Each child met the criteria for accurately producing a minimal core of thirteen word-initial single consonants—/m/, /n/, /p/, /b/, /t/, /d/, /k/, /g/, /w/, /j/, /f/, /s/, /h/—which included all major sound classes; 75 percent of the children also produced the consonants /r/ and /l/. These fifteen consonants were produced in a variety of word shapes that included word-initial consonant clusters—particularly those that combined two consonants such as an obstruent (e.g., /p/, /b/, /t/, /d/, /k/, /g/) plus a sonorant (e.g., /l/, /w/, /r/, /j/), as in the *pl-* of *play* and the *sw-* of *sweet*.

Besides expanding their speech sound repertoire between ages 2 and 3, young AAE learners use phonological processes that are consistent with those described for young typically developing MAE speakers. Such patterns have commonly included cluster reduction (e.g., *cold* as /kol/); stopping of fricatives/affricates (e.g., *chop* as /sɑp/); gliding of liquids (e.g., *lap* as /wæp/, where a liquid becomes a glide); vowelization of /r/ (e.g., *car* as /kɑə/); and the substitution of /d/ for the voiced interdental fricative /ð/ (e.g., *that* as /dæt/) (Bland-Stewart 2003; Horton-Ikard and Weismer 2005).

African American children's speech is attuned to dialect-specific phonological patterns before or by age 3. Although word-final consonant zero-marking is observed among typical AAE and MAE learners early on, it is comparatively more frequent across age for the former group, but only in particular speech conditions. For example, for older speakers of AAE, word-final nasal consonants are variably zero-marked, and the preceding vowel is nasalized (Wolfram 1969, 1991). However, these phenomena may not be easily observed with younger speakers of AAE until they reach a certain age.

Data from the Center for Applied Linguistics (CAL) archives documented the acquisition of word-final nasal consonants, /m/, /n/, and /ŋ/, in a cross-sectional sample of twelve children (four each at 18, 36, and 54 months of age) in Washington, DC (Stockman and Vaughn-Cooke 1982; Wolfram 1986). Wolfram (1986) indicated that 18-month-olds produced few words that could end in final nasal consonants. There was inconsistent and variable nasalization of the final vowel sounds across children and lexical items. Comparatively more words with a potential final nasal consonant were produced by the 36-month-old, and zero-marking patterns were clearly biased by the type of phonetic context and consonant sound produced. Overt production of the final nasal consonant was most favored by contexts in which it was followed by a vowel (e.g., *pan of peas*) as opposed to another consonant or no sound at all (e.g., *pan to cook*). Within these contexts, overt production occurred less often for the word-final /n/, an alveolar, than for /m/ and /ŋ/, which are labial and velar, respectively. These same rule-governed patterns of final nasal consonant zero-marking were observed before 36 months in Wolfram's *longitudinal* analysis of just one participant's use of final nasal consonants between 18 and 36 months.

Children's early sensitivity to the variable AAE rules for overt word-final nasals was also observed in a study of word-final, voiceless stops (i.e., /p/, /t/, and /k/) using the same children in the CAL archives who were studied by Wolfram, as just described. Stockman (2006) showed that at ~36 months of age, word-final /t/, an alveolar stop, was more often deleted than were word-final /p/ and /k/ as labial and velar stops, respectively. Zero-marking of all three final stop consonants occurred more often in phonetic contexts that preceded another consonant than a vowel or no sound at all.

Horton-Ikard and Weismer (2005) described the use of four AAE contrastive phonological patterns in the spontaneous speech of African American 2 and 3 year olds (eleven per age). Besides word-final consonant zero-marking, these patterns included /d/ for /ð/ substitution, word-final cluster reduction, and loss of postvocalic /r/. Only the two patterns, /d/ for /ð/ and word-final cluster reduction, yielded noticeably higher percentages of use at the older rather than younger age. At both ages, all four patterns were used more frequently by AAE-speaking children than by their age-matched, MAE-speaking peers in the same study—an outcome that suggested differential group sensitivity to the sound patterns associated with AAE as early as age 2.

23.3.2 Morphology

This aspect of language includes the grammatical morphemes that have been so frequently studied as a source of differences between AAE and MAE. Studies show developing use of the variable AAE rules for grammatical morphemes before age 4. Steffensen (1974) completed the first longitudinal study of developing AAE-marked morphemes in the spontaneous speech of African American children before age 3. Her study of two children at ages 17 to 26 months included five morphological structures: plural –s, possessive –s, third person singular –s, copula *be*, and auxiliary *be*. Across the sampling period, both groups of children demonstrated zero marked plural –s (e.g., *two ball*) and 3rd person singular –s in almost all contexts. They rarely produced possessive –s, its meaning expressed instead through word order in a noun-noun structure such as *mommy coat, Jackson milk*, and *the girl candy*. But copula *be* was produced more variably than other morphemes in the same developmental period. Steffensen reported that both children imitated overt and zero marked forms of copula *be* around 17 months. Stabilized overt production was evident first in utterance-final position around 21 months and before use in emphatic contexts. By 25 months, the children had increased production of copula *be* contexts. Overt production was variable when the copular verb was positioned medially in a grammatical context but not when it was in the final position.

Most morphological forms described in Steffensen (1974) were among the six included in Horton-Ikard and Weismer's (2005) cross-sectional study of 2- and 3-year-olds: variable copula absence, zero-marked subject/verb agreement, third person singular –s, plural –s, possessive –s, and past tense –ed. Although this study was not designed to explore the variable context rules that may have governed the use of these AAE-marked grammatical morphemes, they were each observed in the speech of 2 to 46 percent of the eleven African American children at age 2.5 years and in 2 to 55 percent of those at 3.5 years. The comparatively smaller percentages (0–37 percent) of the age-matched MAE speakers who used the same forms at each age implied that they already differed from AAE-speaking African American children at age 3.

Newkirk (2010) examined the acquisition of auxiliary *be* and *do* as well as modal auxiliaries (e.g., *can* and *may*) in thirty-six longitudinal language samples of five African American children in the CAL archives who were at different age cross-sections between 18 and 52 months. The analysis revealed that *be, do*, and modal auxiliaries emerged in the children's spontaneous language between 19 and 24 months, and proliferated in frequency of use between 29 and 33 months. Across the developmental period, both *be* and *do* auxiliaries were variably absent, but modal auxiliaries were almost always overtly marked across age. These findings indicate that patterns of contrastive and noncontrastive auxiliary use emerge before age 4.

23.3.3 Syntax

The developing syntactic complexity of young African American children's language production has been investigated in terms of the mean length of utterance (MLU) and the types of sentences used. Regarding utterance length, studies show that at 18 months, their mean length of utterance (MLU) was approximately 1.04–1.3 (Stockman and Vaughn-Cooke 1986; Newkirk 2010). At 24 months, African American children's MLU was near 2.0 (Bland-Stewart 2003; Newkirk 2010). By thirty months, their MLUs had increased to near 3.0 (Newkirk 2010). By 44 months, MLU was approximately 3.6 (Horton-Ikard, Weismer, and Edwards 2005; Newkirk 2010). Figure 23.1 superimposes the average MLU values from cross-sectional studies onto the MLUs of the five children from the longitudinal studies of Stockman and Vaughn-Cooke (1986) and Newkirk (2010), which included the same children. As shown, the MLU of children who acquire AAE increases with age in a linear fashion.

Regarding syntactic structure, studies show that by age 3 African American children acquiring AAE produce syntactic constructions that do not conform to MAE rules (contrastive) as well as those that do (noncontrastive). Data on four children in the CAL archives showed that at 18 months, African American children produce syntactic constructions with verb + complement structure (Stockman 1986). At 30 months, sentences were produced with verb + object + complement (e.g., *Give it to me*) and subject + verb + complement

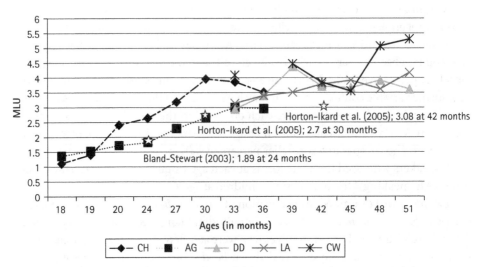

FIGURE 23.1 MLU values of AAE-speaking children across age (18 to 51 months).

structures (e.g., *Mommy make it for me*). By age 3, they most frequently produce sentences with subject + verb + complement structures that were elaborated with either inflectional or non-inflectional grammatical modifiers or both (e.g., *I made it for Daddy*) (Stockman 1996). Newkirk's (2010) study, which was referenced earlier, is likely the first one to describe developmental changes in African American children's use of grammatical auxiliary forms to elaborate sentence structure. In a longitudinal study of five children in the CAL archives, she described their production of auxiliary verbs in syntactic constructions with declarative, interrogative, negative, and elliptical structure. Of these four, simple declaratives and negatives emerged first at or just before age 2, and elliptical constructions emerged last, at or just after age 3.

Children who acquire AAE also produce various forms of complex syntax by age 3. In a cross-sectional study of eighty children at ages 3 and 4, Jackson and Roberts (2001) showed that the number and types of complex forms used increased with age. Of the eighty participants, 91 percent spontaneously produced some type of complex sentence at age 3. The percentages of utterances in a speech sample with at least one of the complex form ranged from 0 to 26 percent, and 6.2 percent of the utterances contained one or more of the ten complex syntactic forms (see Jackson and Roberts 2001). Those with same-subject infinitives (e.g., *I need to go outside*) and clauses conjoined by conjunctions (e.g., *I hit the boy and he ran away*) were the most frequently used types. Emergent use of other complex clauses included *let's/lemme* (e.g., *Let's put her in the sandbox*); non-infinitive wh- clauses (e.g., *Show me where it is*); different-subject infinitives (e.g., *I want you to go*); unmarked infinitives (e.g., *Make it stand up by itself*); noun phrase complements (e.g., *I think I can do it*); wh- infinitive (e.g., *I know how to do that*); and relative clauses (e.g., *It's the one I got*). At age 4, the percentage of utterances with at least one complex syntactic form was as high as 30 percent for some children, and the percentages of utterances with one or more of the ten complex syntactic forms increased to 11.7 percent.

There is evidence for African American children's early use of contrastive AAE syntactic structures. At age 3, some forms of questions conform to contrastive AAE patterns (Green 2011). For example, some questions are produced without auxiliaries (e.g., *What you doing?*). Questions with auxiliaries are often produced without an inverted grammatical subject, as is permissible in AAE (e.g., *You eating dinner?*). Green, Wyatt, and Lopez (2007), Green (2011), and Newkirk (2010) provide a more comprehensive review of contrastive AAE syntactic structures that may be observed prior to age 4.

23.4 LANGUAGE CONTENT: SEMANTICS

The semantic development in African American children learning AAE may not be very different from other groups during the first year of life. Hart and Risley's (1995) longitudinal investigation of language outcomes indicated that for the 17 African American children included in their investigation, the first meaningful words appeared by 12 months regardless of socioeconomic status. This finding was comparable to what was observed for their child participants from White middle- and working-class backgrounds. The African American children's number of words produced also increased with age. Additional studies suggest that before age 4, they also will exhibit word-learning skills and vocabulary diversity that are comparable to SES-matched speakers of other English dialects (Horton-Ikard and Ellis Weismer 2007).

Young African American children make some semantic distinctions that may or may not contrast with MAE language behaviors. Two studies tracked the number and types of global semantic categories used across age: Stockman and Vaughn Cooke's (1986) cross-sectional study of twelve children included four each at 18, 36, and 54 months in the CAL archives; and Blake's (1993) longitudinal study of three children spanned the ages of 17 to 25 months. Both studies adapted Bloom and Lahey's (1978) taxonomy for identifying broad semantic relational meanings such as object actions, states, locations, attributes, and so on. Using productivity criteria of three to five different utterances, both studies showed that the number and type of semantic categories used increased with age.

Stockman and Vaughn-Cooke (1986) revealed that just three to five of the seventeen categories selected met criteria for the four children at 18 months. Two categories, *existence* and *action*, were used by all children. At 36 months, the number of categories used included not only these two categories but also *locative action, state, locative state, negation, possession, attribution, notice*, and so on. But these additional categories only appeared after age 3, when criteria were met for coding such notions as causality, which also underlies the meaning of complex sentences. Blake's (1993) study also revealed that action was among the earliest semantic categories observed at 18 months in addition to locative action and state. The number of categories used increased to fourteen different ones in the last sampling period at 27 months. They encompassed the same major categories identified by Stockman and Vaughn-Cooke (1986) at age 3. Findings from the above two studies revealed that African American children used the same semantic relational categories that had been described for White middle-class and working-class children.

The literature also suggests that African American children's production of global semantic categories increases with age and that each category undergoes some degree of elaboration as language matures. Stockman and Vaughn-Cooke (1992) revealed how the single semantic category of locative action expressions developed longitudinally for a sample of eight African American children (four each at ages 18 and 36 months at the outset) in the CAL archives. Specifically, utterances that refer to the spatial relocation of objects are semantically elaborated by growth in the number and types of locative words used in them. The earliest such expressions (around 17 to 23 months) combined a movement action verb with a preposition or adverb that coded the source or path of movement, as in *go away/out/up/down*. Between ages 23 and 34 months, children increased their use of locative words, as in *go on/in/under*, which coded the destination or goal of the spatial relocation. Between 28 and 36 months, locative word combinations *go out/in, go down/under*, and *go in/on* proliferated in use. These children were learning to talk about the spatial relocation of objects in increasingly more varied and complex ways over time, as has been shown for children learning MAE varieties.

In addition to semantic categories that are noncontrastive with MAE, those with unique or contrastive meanings appear in African American children's early language (Green 2011). One example is the verb *go* used as a copula or stative verb (e.g., *there go the chair*), as it codes the existence of an object in the perceptual field as opposed to its more frequent reference to a movement event (Cole 1980; Horton-Ikard and Weismer 2005; Stockman 2007b).

In a longitudinal study of eleven children at different cross-sections of age between 18 and 72 months, Stockman (2007b) observed the *go* copula form before 24 months of age and that its use was most frequent between 24 and 41 months. Afterwards, its relative frequency of use decreased instead of increasing with age. Stockman argued that the declining use of *go* copula at older ages may reflect the greater tendency to talk more about objects in past and future events as opposed to those present in the perceptual field.

Aspectual *be* is another AAE form that differs semantically from MAE. This is the overtly produced uninflected form of *be*, which indicates that eventualities recur habitually (Green 2002, 2011). Green (2011) documented the production of uninflected *be* in the language of children as young as 3. She gave the following example: In response to the adult speaker's question (*What does he be doing?*), the 3-year-old child responded, *He be bad and fooling with me* (2011, 53). According to Green (2011), the extent to which uninflected *be* is part of this child's grammar as an aspectual marker is not clear from her spontaneous speech. In this example, it could be the case that the child used uninflected *be* in a habitual sense to communicate that her cousin's behavior is bad on occasion and that he teases her from time to time. However, because the aspectual system in AAE has been shown to emerge after age 4, it could be the case that the child's utterance, which contained uninflected *be*, was not intentionally produced as an habitual marker. This example and the questions it raises underscore the importance of the age group that is the focus of this chapter. Data from young African American children's language will provide the opportunity to observe whether they use contrastive semantic features such as aspectual *be* earlier than age 4, and, if so, what might be the developmental path to the intentional use of uninflected *be* as a habitual marker.

23.5 LANGUAGE USE: PRAGMATIC FUNCTIONS AND DISCOURSE

Like other aspects of language, the range of pragmatic functions and discourse forms used over time has been underexplored for children acquiring AAE at age 3 and younger. The few existing studies show that children at this age do express a variety of pragmatic intentions during familiar verbal interactions, and they begin to acquire narrative discourse structure. Bridgeforth (1984) created a taxonomy of 17 pragmatic functions expressed in the spontaneous language of eight African American children (four each at ages 3 and 4.5 years) in the CAL archives. They included five macro functions (informatives, requests and regulators, recycles, imaginatives, and social conventions), each incorporating two or more microfunctions. For example, informatives were differentiated by the reporting of personal facts versus general facts, personal feelings, and so on. All five macrofunctions were evident at age 3, but each one was used more frequently at age 4 with few exceptions. But their relative frequencies of use were ranked in the same order at both ages. The informative function was ranked the highest—comprising 62.18 percent and 75.58 percent of the utterance counts for 3- and 4-year olds, respectively. In the same respect, the category of social conventions was ranked the lowest at 9 and 30 percent. There were age differences in the number and type of microfunctions observed within a macrofunction. For example, the younger group reported personal events more often than did the older group. Conversely, the older group more often reported general facts. Bridgeforth (1984) proposed that African American child speakers of AAE were similar to White MAE speakers, as described in the literature.

Blake (1993) used a different taxonomy modeled after Lois Bloom and her colleagues to track the pragmatic intentions expressed in the spontaneous language of three children ages 18 to 27 months of age. This longitudinal study included eight types of functions: *interpersonal expressive, effective, objective, directive, self-expressive social, self-expressive non-social, attentive,* and *participative.* Blake reported that all eight of them were present in each child's repertoire at 18 months. As age increased, so did the frequency and types of contexts for expressing pragmatic intentions. All three children most frequently used an interpersonal function that allowed them to manage relations with others (e.g., to seek attention and to request objects). She argued for a social-emotional hypothesis to account for the observation that her African American child participants from working-class backgrounds demonstrated a bias toward the use of speech behaviors that served social, rather than cognitive functions. Blake inferred that African American children are likely to be more attuned to the interpersonal aspects of communicative interactions at an early age compared to Caucasian children at the same age (Miller 1981).

Regarding narrative discourse, few studies have investigated its development in typically developing African American children before age 4. Sperry and Sperry (1996) examined emerging use of narrative-like talk in a longitudinal ethnographic study of eight children, ages 24 to 40 months. In 24 half-hours of videotaped conversation, the eight children produced 166 narrative-like event episodes. Among them, most (64 percent) were classified as fictional (i.e., non-real), and 35 percent as temporal (i.e., real but displaced in time or not present). Fictional episodes were more frequently observed at 24 to 30 months than at 32 to 40 months. The differences between fictional and temporal episodes were more pronounced between the ages of 24 and 30 months than between the ages of 32 and 40 months. The authors reported that children showed more heightened interest in fictional episodes than temporal ones. They also provided more relevant and higher rates of new action-oriented information about the topic in fictional than in temporal narratives. These characteristics—relevant information and action-oriented information—made the fictional episodes appear to be more complex than temporal ones.

McGregor (2000) described the emerging use of narrative story elements in a cross-sectional study of fifty-two African American children at ages 3, 4, and 5 years. In their stories generated from a wordless picture book, young African American children demonstrated a variety of discourse behaviors and developmental trends. The 3-year-old children demonstrated the emerging use of characters, feelings, setting, complicating action, dialogue, and codas in their narratives. Production of these elements increased as the children got older.

The complexity of young African American children's oral narratives, as expressed by their use of specific literate forms, is also evident early in development (see Champion and McCabe, this volume; Wyatt, this volume). In a cross-sectional study of sixty-seven children distributed among African American and White children at 3, 4, and 5 years of age, Curenton and Justice (2004) examined the use of the following literate language forms: simple and complex elaborated noun phrases, adverbs, conjunctions, and mental and linguistic verbs. Use of each form increased with age. Developmental increases were greater for the use of conjunctions, mental, and linguistic verbs than for other forms. No racial group differences were observed.

Taken together, these three studies show developing narrative competence among young AAE-speaking children prior to age 4. Their development of narrative types, story elements, and literate language forms is comparable to similarly aged White peers acquiring MAE.

23.6 SUMMARY

Previous language acquisition studies of American English-speaking children historically excluded children who acquire non-mainstream varieties of American English, such as AAE. When studies of African American AAE-speaking children began, they were conducted with the goal of revealing whether the AAE patterns observed in adult AAE speakers were also used by child AAE speakers. Very young AAE speakers were excluded from these early studies due to the assumption that they used few, if any, distinctive AAE patterns. As a result, significantly less is known about the language use and acquisition patterns of AAE speakers prior to age 4.

This chapter presented findings from studies of African American children who were acquiring AAE. We primarily reviewed those that had analyzed spontaneous language at two or more ages using a longitudinal or cross-sectional method of observation. By focusing primarily on studies of developmental change, we acknowledge that this review has obviously excluded some more recent single-age studies that contribute to the whole picture of what African American children know about language early on. We also acknowledge that several of the studies reviewed in this chapter were based on the same few children from the CAL database because of the limited number of studies that have been done using longitudinal data. Nevertheless, the studies we have reviewed, although few in number, have contributed significantly to descriptions of African American children's language development prior to age 4.

23.7 Conclusion

There still remains a critical need for empirical studies on young African American children's language acquisition. Although the studies cited in this chapter were primarily completed in the eroded deficit paradigm era, it is fair to say that much of the existing research described in this review was done years ago. Additional updated research that is attuned to current descriptive and theoretical models of early language learning is necessary for expanding the literature base on developmental pathways to AAE.

The studies reviewed here suggest that young AAE speakers are developing language in a fashion similar to their MAE-speaking peers. They acquire many aspects of form, content, and use of the English language prior to age 4. Children this young simultaneously produce those language behaviors that have been observed across MAE varieties (noncontrastive) and those that appear to be unique (contrastive) to children who are learning AAE.

It should not be surprising that contrastive patterns exist so early in development. After all, children acquire the words to which they are exposed, and that language input is not specified in terms of contrastive or noncontrastive differences with another language dialect. The challenge for future research is to figure out if and how learning an English dialect like AAE may be differentially influenced by ambient language input that includes aspects of both the home language and MAE varieties. There may be a perceptual cost for learning a language in which input is not homogeneous across the various strata of language experience.

Yet, given the comparatively more plentiful research on MAE varieties in the first three years of life coupled with what seems to be less frequent displays of AAE-contrastive patterns at the earliest ages, it may be reasonable to expect African American children to progress through and achieve the same early pre-linguistic developmental milestones as all children learning English. But this assumption needs to be supported by empirical evidence, given the pejorative historical context in which AAE speakers have been viewed. That is, we should not assume that there is no reason to study noncontrastive AAE patterns and their acquisition.

This review also exposes gaps in the research on the development and use of language before age 4 by children who acquire AAE. Very little is known about their development prior to first words. Even the ages at which they use their first word have not been documented across studies. So there is still much to learn about the development of AAE in the first three years of life.

Research is needed on two levels. One level will encourage more detailed description of the basic milestones achieved across time in different geographical locations and social strata as research exposes the heterogeneity among AAE-speaking children. The second level should be concerned with the processes that enable such milestone achievements. What comes to be known must extend beyond the context-neutral word counts based on selected streams of daily experience. Research observations and their interpretation must cater to the context of lived events. What do we know about the pattern of social interaction between African American children and their caregivers and how these patterns may be influenced by the cultural expectations about even the role of talk in everyday experience, as the work of Heath (1983) hinted at more than three decades ago? Virtually no research has focused on the perception of speech by young African American children.

Meeting these challenges should continue to require frameworks that (1) permit the examination of language forms in relation to their meanings or use or both; (2) allow both contrastive and noncontrastive features of AAE to be explored in ways that go beyond description to include explanatory principles that guide the acquisition process; and (3) encourage study of African American children in under-investigated areas of language acquisition such as speech perception. Research that makes progress in these areas should yield a more comprehensive picture of child AAE than that which currently exists.

REFERENCES

Blake, Ira Kincade. 1993. "The Social-Emotional Orientation of Mother–Child Communication in African American Families." *International Journal of Behavioral Development* 16: 443–63.

Bland-Stewart, Linda. 2003. "Phonetic Inventories and Phonological Patterns of African American Two-Year-Olds: A Preliminary Investigation." *Communication Disorders Quarterly* 24: 109–12.

Bloom, Lois. 1992. "Racism in Developmental Research," *Division 7 Newsletter*. American Psychological Association 1–2.

Bloom, Lois, and Margaret Lahey. 1978. *Language Development and Language Disorders*. New York: John Wiley and Sons.

Bridgeforth, Cheri. 1984. "The Identification and Use of Language Functions in the Speech of Three- and Four-and-a-Half-Year-Old Black Children from Working Class Families." PhD diss., Georgetown University.

Brown, Roger. 1973. *A First Language: The Early Stages*. Cambridge, MA: Harvard University.

Cole, Lorraine. 1980. "Developmental Analysis of Social Dialect Features in the Spontaneous Language of Preschool Black Children." PhD diss., Northwestern University.

Curenton, Stephanie M., and Laura M. Justice. 2004. "African American and Caucasian Preschoolers' Use of Decontextualized Language: Literate Language Features in Oral Narratives." *Language, Speech, and Hearing Services in Schools* 35: 240–53.

Green, Lisa. 2002. "A Descriptive Study of African American English: Research in Linguistics and Education." *International Journal of Qualitative Studies in Education* 15: 673–90.

———. 2011. *Language and the African American Child*. New York: Cambridge University.

Green, Lisa, Toya A. Wyatt, and Qiuana Lopez. 2007. "Event Arguments and BE in Child AAE." *University of Pennsylvania Working Papers in Linguistics* 13: 95–108.

Hart, Betty, and Todd Risley. 1995. *Meaningful Differences.* Baltimore, MD: Brookes.

Heath, Shirley Brice. 1983. *Ways with Words: Language, Life, and Work in Communities and Classrooms.* Cambridge: Cambridge University.

Horton-Ikard, RaMonda, and Susan Ellis Weismer. 2005. "Distinguishing African-American English from Developmental Errors in the Language Production of Toddlers." *Applied Psycholinguistics* 26: 601–20.

———. 2007. "A Preliminary Examination of Vocabulary and Word-Learning in African-American Toddlers from Low and Middle SES Homes." *American Journal of Speech-Language Pathology* 16: 381–92.

Horton-Ikard, RaMonda, Susan Ellis Weismer, and Claire Edwards. 2005. "Examining the Use of Standard Language Production Measures in the Language Samples of African-American Toddlers." *Journal of Multilingual Communication Disorders* 3: 169–82.

Jackson, Sandra, and JoAnne Roberts. 2001. "Complex Syntax Production of African American Preschoolers." *Journal of Speech, Language, and Hearing Research* 44: 1083–96.

Labov, William. 1972. *Language in the Inner City: Studies in the Black English Vernacular.* Philadelphia: University of Pennsylvania Press.

McGregor, Karla K. 2000. "The Development and Enhancement of Narrative Skills in a Preschool Classroom: Towards a Solution to Clinician-Client Mismatch." *American Journal of Speech-Language Pathology* 9: 55–71.

Miller, Jon F. 1981. *Assessing Language Production in Children: Experimental Procedures.* Baltimore, MD: University Park Press.

Newkirk, Brandi L. 2010. "The Auxiliary System of Typically Developing Children Acquiring African American English." PhD diss., Louisiana State University.

Owens, Robert E. 2007. *Language Development: An Introduction.* 7th ed. Boston: Allyn and Bacon.

Seymour, Harry N., Linda Bland-Stewart, and Lisa J. Green. 1998. "Difference Versus Deficit in Child African American English." *Language, Speech, and Hearing Services in Schools* 29: 96–108.

Sperry, Linda, and Douglas Sperry. 1996. "Early Development of Narrative Skills." *Cognitive Development* 11: 443–65.

Steffensen, Margaret. 1974. "The Acquisition of Black English." PhD diss., University of Illinois.

Stockman, Ida J. 1986. "The Development of Linguistic Norms for Nonmainstream English Speakers." *ASHA Reports* 16: 101–10.

———. 1996. "The Promises and Pitfalls of Language Sample Analysis as an Assessment Tool for Linguistic Minority Children." *Language, Speech and Hearing Services in Schools* 27: 355–66.

———. 2006. "Alveolar Bias in the Final Consonant Deletion Patterns of African American Children." *Language, Speech and Hearing Services in Schools* 17: 85–95.

———. 2007a. "Acquisition of *Go* Copula Constructions in African American English." Poster presentation at the annual conference of New Ways of Analyzing Variation, Philadelphia, Pennsylvania, October 11–14.

———. 2007b. "Social-Political Influences on Research Practices: Examining Language Acquisition by African American Children." In *Sociolinguistic Variation: Theories, Methods, and Applications,* edited by Robert Bayley and Ceil Lucas, 297–317. Cambridge: Cambridge University.

————. 2008. "Toward Validation of a Minimal Competence Phonetic Core for African American Children." *Journal of Speech, Language, and Hearing Research* 51: 1–19.

————. 2010. "A Review of Developmental and Applied Language Research on African American Children: From a Deficit to Difference Perspective on Dialect Differences." *Language, Speech, and Hearing Services in Schools* 41: 23–28.

Stockman, Ida J., and Faye Vaughn-Cooke. 1982. "A Re-Examination of Research on the Language of Black Children: The Need for a New Framework." *Journal of Education* 164: 157–72.

————. 1986. "Implications of Semantic Category Research for the Language Assessment of Nonstandard Speakers." *Topics in Language Disorders* 6: 15–25.

————. 1992. "Lexical Elaboration in Children's Locative Action Constructions." *Child Development* 63: 1104–125.

Washington, Julie, and Hollie Craig. 1994. "Dialectal Forms during Discourse of Urban, African-American Preschoolers Living in Poverty." *Journal of Speech and Hearing Research* 37: 816–23.

————. 2002. "Morphosyntactic Forms of African-American English Used by Young Children and Their Caregivers." *Applied Psycholinguistics* 23: 209–31.

Wolfram, Walt. 1969. *A Sociolinguistic Study of Detroit Negro Speech*. Washington, DC: Center for Applied Linguistics.

————. 1986. "Structural Variability in Phonological Development: Final Nasals in Vernacular Black English." In *Language Change and Variation*, edited by Ralph W. Fasold and Deborah Schriffrin, 301–32. Amsterdam: John Benjamins.

————. 1991. *Dialects and American English*. Englewood Cliffs, NJ: Prentice Hall.

CHAPTER 24

....

THE DEVELOPMENT OF AFRICAN AMERICAN ENGLISH THROUGH CHILDHOOD AND ADOLESCENCE

....

JANNEKE VAN HOFWEGEN

24.1 INTRODUCTION

....

THIS chapter describes research on the development of African American English (AAE) across the early lifespan, from pre-kindergarten to mid-adolescence. In particular, it highlights evidence from a longitudinal corpus of AAE spanning eleven years in the lives of around seventy African American children.[1] Panel studies chronicling language change in speech communities are notoriously difficult to attain and, to date, there are few such studies on AAE, most notably, Cukor-Avila (1995, 2002), Cukor-Avila and Bailey (2007), Baugh (1996), and Rickford and Price (2013). These studies have shown much about the use of AAE between adolescence and adulthood, including evidence for generational change (Cukor-Avila 1995, 2002; Cukor-Avila and Bailey 2007) and variability across age levels (Baugh 1996; Rickford and Price 2013). The question remains about what patterns of AAE usage are demonstrated in the period prior to adolescence.

AAE here refers to a variety of English spoken by many African Americans in the United States. Like all varieties, it is a rich, diverse linguistic system. It shares many structural similarities with Mainstream American English (MAE), but it also utilizes unique phonological, morphosyntactic, and semantic/pragmatic features as well as variation patterns of its own. As Newkirk-Turner, Horton, and Stockman (this volume) describe, the acquisition of the AAE linguistic system often occurs in contexts of exposure to varying degrees of contrastive and non-contrastive input from other English dialects. Beyond acquisition, AAE speakers use their variety in interactions with and without speakers of other varieties. The character, intensity, and frequency of these interactions may be different for different individuals and at different points in time in the life of the same individual. But, in a multilingual, multidialectal world, speakers are continually gathering resources for variation from both their local community—what Eckert (1997) calls the "home of the vernacular"—and the standard language marketplace (Sankoff and Laberge 1978), to whatever extent they participate in it.

This chapter takes a *developmental perspective* on language change (Eckert 1997), assuming linguistic development to be a lifelong endeavor. "Throughout the life course, speakers have a sense of moving forward … anticipating the next development in their lives and assuming new ways of being—and perhaps new ways of talking" (Eckert 1997, 157). Thus, even after the acquisition phase, linguistic usage can be linked to other arenas of personal development.

One way of conceptualizing a speaker's orientation within a multidialectal context is through a continuum. While not without its shortcomings, as Rickford (1987) explains, a continuum can usefully characterize the relationship between two interrelated dialects and a speaker's relative facility with each or both of them. The language continuum concept has been utilized for AAE, in particular, by Baugh (1983) and Green (2002), though the schematization of it here is more consistent with Rickford's (1987) creole continuum (conceptualized in terms of Labov's [1973] property-item matrices for continuous transition between two categories).[2] Specifically, the properties for this continuum are identifiable morphosyntactic/phonological features that are implicationally shared/not shared at various points along it. A pole on either side indicates a speech style in which the most possible features utilized are part of one variety. For the sake of discussion, these are deemed *optimal* here—optimal in terms of highest concentration of features used (i.e., not *better*). Midrange points indicate a speech style utilizing features of both varieties.

Figure 24.1 (adapted from Green 2011, 32) portrays the MAE-AAE continuum. As it shows, the usage patterns of two speakers of AAE (Speaker 1 and Speaker 2) can each inhabit different spaces and ranges. For example, Speaker 1 is a fairly categorical speaker of AAE and makes little use of MAE features. On the other hand, Speaker 2 has a range extending broadly into the MAE side of the continuum, while also encompassing much of Speaker 1's range. Thus, Speaker 2 has the linguistic resources to style-shift between the two varieties.

FIGURE 24.1 MAE–AAE continuum.

Snapshots of an AAE-speaking child's vernacular usage[3] at different points in her life might place her at different absolute points on the continuum, with potentially different stylistic ranges as well. Would other AAE-speaking children show similar trends? Scholars of AAE have asked these questions over the years, but until now the data necessary to address them have been nonexistent.

24.2 THE FPG LONGITUDINAL DATABASE

Recently, however, a longitudinal database has become available for just this sort of analysis. The database was compiled by researchers at the Frank Porter Graham Child Development Institute (FPG) and was initiated in 1990 with a cohort of eighty-eight African American children recruited at an age of 6 to 12 months and visited yearly thereafter. Seventy-one percent of the children came from families living below federally defined poverty guidelines, and socioeconomic status was monitored for each child over the twenty-year course of the study. After the first year, the cohort was reduced to seventy participants, and sixty-eight of them continue in the study to date.

Through the course of the study, the children provided conversationally based language samples collected at one- or two-year increments and were also administered a battery of additional tests and measures. To ensure naturalness in speech, age-appropriate interlocutors were chosen for each language recording. Thus, earlier recordings (when the children were 24 months to about age 9) included their mothers, while later recordings (from about age 11 to about age 15) included a peer of each child's choosing. The children's peers, brought in at about age 11, were themselves inducted into the study, increasing the sample size to 129. Additional demographic data pertinent to African American youth were also collected for each participant at each data point (Burchinal et al. 2000a; Burchinal et al. 2000b; Burchinal et al. 2006). Altogether, the progressive twenty-year corpus of data on language development and change, along with the host of other social factors and measures collected, have resulted in a unique longitudinal database appropriate for examining the development of AAE across the early lifespan.

24.3 OVERALL PATTERNS IN AAE USAGE: WHEN IS THE OPTIMAL PERIOD?

Many canonical studies of AAE (see Labov et al. 1968; Wolfram 1969; Fasold 1972; Rickford 1999) have raised the question as to when the optimal period of AAE usage emerges. A review of the literature reveals three prevailing theories. The first theory is the *Childhood Basilectal Hypothesis*, which is summarized best in the largely ethnographic work of Stewart (1965) and Dillard (1972). According to this hypothesis, the youngest children utilize the highest concentration of AAE features, in contrast to their elders. According to Dillard and Stewart, child speech has a "comparatively archaic character" (Dillard 1972, 236) (i.e., most basilectal), a position consistent with the Creole Origins Hypothesis of AAE (see Rickford, this volume). To summarize, this position holds that AAE in all of its structures is most robustly evidenced in the earliest years, and gradually recedes through life.

The second theory, one Van Hofwegen and Wolfram (2010) call the *Preschool Optimization Hypothesis*, builds primarily off the work of Craig and Washington (2006) and their colleagues. It is not much different from the first theory in its ultimate conclusion, but it is based upon a different type of data and analysis. Dillard (1972) and Stewart (1965) used ethnographic observation, following children through life in their homes and neighborhoods. Craig and Washington (2006) use recorded language data in a school setting, conducting quantitative analyses on the numbers and types of AAE structures observed. Specifically, they use a *Dialect Density Measure* (DDM) compiled from a list of canonical features of AAE (see Labov et al. 1968; Wolfram 1969; Fasold 1972; Baugh 1983; Rickford 1999)—thirty-three morphosyntactic and nine phonological features. While they admit that this particular array of features may not be wholly adequate in describing the grammar of AAE-speaking children, as the feature list reflects adult AAE (Washington and Craig 2002; Craig et al. 2003)—their extensive DDM study of diachronic change in child AAE has been groundbreaking, and their methods have informed subsequent studies of the development of AAE across the lifespan (see Van Hofwegen and Wolfram 2010).

In their work, Craig, Washington, and colleagues looked at children with ages ranging from preschool through mid-elementary school (ages 3–10) and found "optimal" AAE usage to be in the speech of preschool children. Indeed, once formal schooling commenced, the children markedly declined in AAE usage in Grade One (about age 6) and progressively reduced their AAE usage as they proceeded through early schooling. By Grade Five (about age 10), on average, children used the fewest number of AAE features. Reasons for this reduction, the authors claim, are likely due to "longer systematic exposure to SAE [Standard American English]" (Craig and Washington 2006, 51), reflected in their natural discourse and academic (i.e., reading) performance. Altogether, even though they derive from different methods, the *Childhood Basilectal Hypothesis* and the *Preschool Optimization Hypothesis* both predict higher usage of AAE in the youngest years of childhood, with a reduction in use over the early lifespan as the child has (presumably) more contact with MAE.

A third hypothesis is perhaps the most familiar, as it has served as the basis for much language variation study in the twentieth century. Labov (1965) observed an upsurge in the usage of nonstandard features in African American adolescents and generalizes this surge to speakers of all nonstandard varieties. The prevalent avoidance of standard language in adolescence has been widely substantiated by other sociolinguists working on adolescent language (see Eckert 2004). Specifically regarding AAE, Labov notes, "there is a sub-system of English used by pre-adolescents and adolescent Negro speakers in Northern ghetto areas which is remarkably uniform over the age range 8–17, especially for those who participate fully in the vernacular culture" (Labov et al. 1968, 4). Accordingly, fueled perhaps by this assumption, variationists who have studied AAE have largely focused on early adulthood (see Labov et al. 1968; Baugh 1983; Rickford 1991, 1999), and apparent time analyses of change across the lifespan tend to start at early adulthood (see Wolfram 1969; Fasold 1972).

Despite the numerous studies conducted on AAE over the last decades, tracing the usage of AAE across the lifespan is still quite elusive, primarily because of the complementarity of these hypotheses and the scholars who hold them. Depending on their assumptions, sociolinguists and speech-language pathologists have diverged: sociolinguists have not typically studied AAE variation in the early lifespan; likewise, speech-language pathologists have not typically studied AAE beyond the realm of acquisition. What is more, despite the ubiquity of the apparent-time paradigm, its shortcomings are notable when compared to authentic, real time, longitudinal analysis (Bailey et al. 1991; Bailey 2002).

Using the FPG longitudinal data, Van Hofwegen and Wolfram (2010) put the various optimization hypotheses to the test by analyzing language samples from thirty-two longitudinal participants at six points in their lifespans: 48 months; Grade One (ages 6-7); Grade Four (ages 9-10); Grade Six (ages 11-12); Grade Eight (ages 13-14); and Grade Ten (ages 15-16).[4] Three different analyses were conducted: a token-based DDM; a type-based, differential-structure tabulation; and a traditional variation analysis based on potential versus actual occurrences of salient features. The three methods were triangulated to provide a full picture of variation and to circumvent some common critiques of the DDM.[5] DDM scores were calculated based on a list of forty-one morphosyntactic and three phonological variables (Renn 2007), which were counted for each recording and calculated per "communication unit" (Loban 1976).[6] Thus, in this paradigm, a child's relative AAE usage at a point in time is best understood to be her use of a number of salient AAE features from the DDM per utterance. Figure 24.2 shows the DDM scores for the thirty-two speakers across the six temporal data points.

Even the most cursory of glances at this figure reveals a clear trend. Specifically, the majority of children exhibit a *roller coaster* trajectory of change, whereby they produce the highest levels of AAE usage at the earliest age (48 months) and again in early adolescence (ages 9-10 and 11-12). The curve shows two phases of statistically significant change: the trough in the early years of schooling (ages 5-6 and 9-10) and the peak in early adolescence (ages 11-12 and 13-14). It should be noted that a subset (N = 6) of the speakers exhibited a curvilinear trajectory, with a more gradual upward climb from the early grades.[7] Thus, while optimal periods of AAE usage may vary across speakers, the minimal period for AAE use is more regularly evidenced. Figures 24.3a and 24.3b depict the distribution of the thirty-two speakers in terms of how many speakers exhibited the highest and lowest AAE usage levels, respectively, at each time point. From these figures, it is evident that not a single speaker peaked in Grades One and Four, illustrating the prominence of this early school period for minimal AAE usage.

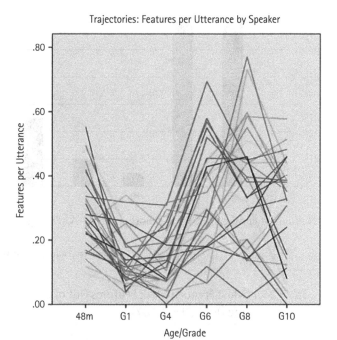

FIGURE 24.2 DDM scores (features per utterance) for thirty-two speakers at six time points.

Source: Van Hofwegen and Wolfram 2010, 437.

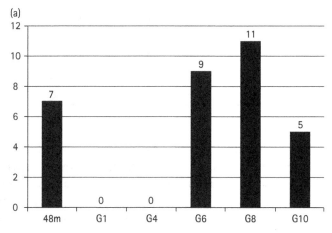

FIGURE 24.3(a) Number of speakers (N = 32) whose optimal AAE usage occurred at each time point.

Source: Van Hofwegen and Wolfram 2010, 438.

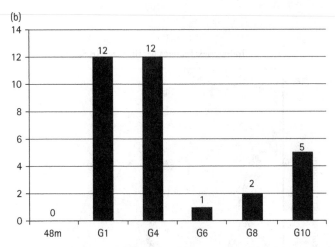

FIGURE 24.3(b) Number of speakers (N = 32) whose minimal AAE usage occurred at each time point.

Source: Van Hofwegen and Wolfram 2010, 438.

Table 24.1 Most Frequent AAE Features Out of all Features in the DDM (N = 4,137)

Most prominent features	N	Percentage of total AAE features in DDM
–ing fronting	1,343	32.5
Copula absence	667	16.1
Auxiliary absence	493	11.9
Third-person singular *–s* absence	265	6.4
Negative concord	132	3.2
Invariant *be*	132	3.2
Ain't (to be)	101	2.4

Speakers and time points with the most AAE usage also utilize the broadest array of AAE features. Table 24.1 shows the distribution of the most frequent AAE features across the sample. While these seven features themselves comprised a majority (76 percent) of all the AAE tokens, statistical analysis reveals their prevalence does not artificially skew results. Linear regression analysis confirms that high DDM scores correlate strongly ($R^2 = .467; p < .001$) with high numbers of different feature types used (see figure 24.4).

Traditional variation analysis (Cedergren and Sankoff 1974; Tagliamonte 2006) was also conducted on three of the features—copula absence, *-ing* fronting, and third-person singular (*-s* absence). For each of these features, actual versus potential counts were tabulated using the parameters set forth in previous variationist work (summarized in

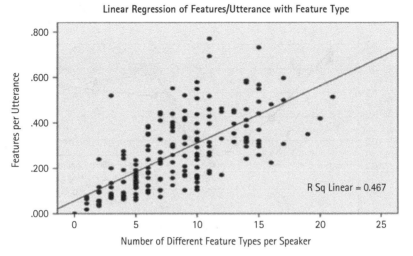

FIGURE 24.4 Linear regression of DDM scores (features per utterance) against number of feature types.

Source: Van Hofwegen and Wolfram 2010, 443.

Rickford 1999, 4, 6–7). With sex, age/grade, and individual speaker as factors, logistic regression (using GoldVarb; Sankoff, Tagliamonte, and Smith 2005) revealed that the *roller coaster* pattern was prevalent for two variables (*-ing* fronting and third-person singular *-s* absence), while the curvilinear pattern was evident for copula absence (see figure 24.5). Factor weights generated via logistic regression plotted across time for all three variables revealed a steep decline from favoring (at 48 months) to disfavoring effects by Grade Four; yet, for copula deletion, this decline was more gradual and the following rise was not as steep as for the other variables. Following Callahan-Price's (2010, 2011) analysis of the acquisition of copula absence for speakers in this data set (aged 24 to 48 months), Van Hofwegen and Wolfram (2010) hypothesize there to be a conflation of sociolinguistic and acquisition effects at 48 months, which is not present to the same degree with the other two features. In contrast to copula absence, invariant *be* (plotted in raw counts[8] in figure 24.6) shows an opposite trajectory, whereby speakers rarely use the feature in early childhood but are prolific with it in adolescence. This finding suggests that a feature such as invariant *be* is likely acquired later than copula.

The triangulation of the DDM, type/token, and variation analyses confirms aspects of the proposed hypotheses for the development of AAE. The two trajectories—*roller coaster* and curvilinear—share in common a dip in the early years of schooling, suggesting that school and the introduction/institutionalization of SAE at these ages is a powerful force controlling even conversational speech. These results mirror Craig and Washington (2006), who likewise find a decrease in overall AAE usage in early schooling. Beyond this, the majority of children in Van Hofwegen and Wolfram (2010) peaked dramatically in early adolescence, suggesting that theories about the overall use of AAE across the lifespan are quite consistent with real time longitudinal data.

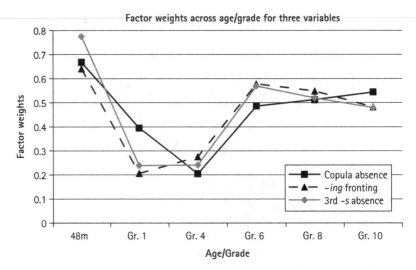

FIGURE 24.5 Factor weights across age/grade for copula absence, –*ing* fronting, and third-person singular –*s* absence.

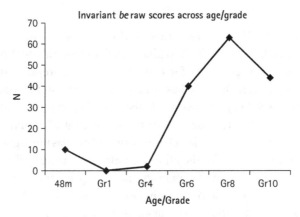

FIGURE 24.6 Invariant *be* raw use by age/grade.

24.4 AAE VOWELS ACROSS THE EARLY LIFESPAN

If the DDM, type/token, and variation analyses are based primarily on canonical morphosyntactic features of AAE, there are also key phonological features of the variety that have quite a bit of productive and perceptual salience (see Rickford 1999; Green 2002; Rahman 2008). Features such as –*ing* fronting and consonant cluster reduction pattern consistently with morphosyntactic counterparts as components in the DDM. Some vocalic features, such as /ay/ monophthongization and *pin-pen* merger, are likewise perceptually salient in the AAE-speaking community (Rahman 2008). And more generally, it has been found that vowels play an essential role in the ethnic perception of the variety (Graff, Labov, and Harris 1986; Torbert 2004; Thomas 2007). However, there are a host of other segmental features unique to AAE that are acquired and used by AAE-speaking children. Vowel distinctions associated with AAE (Thomas 2007) do not seem to be marked in a typological way. An analysis of vowel development across the early lifespan can shed light on which of these sorts of phonological features may or may not develop in line with their morphosyntactic counterparts.

Studies of AAE vowels of adults (cf. Bailey and Thomas 1998; Thomas 2007) are abundant compared to those of vowels in early childhood. In fact, longitudinal studies of AAE vowel development were nonexistent until new work by Kohn, Farrington, and Ethier (2010) and Kohn and Farrington (2011a, 2011b). General research on child vowels and sociolinguistic variation indicates that the vowel systems of children are malleable likely due to sociolinguistic and peer influences, especially when children are exposed to multiple varieties of language (Chambers 1992; Kerswill 1996; Roberts 2002; Smith, Durham, and Fortune 2007). Additionally, even as vowel systems largely stabilize by adolescence (Payne 1980; Roberts 2002), children at the same time can use wide-ranging vocalic variation in stylistic and symbolic ways (Eckert 2000). The question remains whether AAE-speaking children show similar patterns of first malleability and then stability across the early lifespan.

To address this question, Kohn et al. (2010) examined a subset of ten of the speakers from the Van Hofwegen and Wolfram (2010) study, at five of the same time points (Grades One, Four, Six, Eight, and Ten). Altogether, they collected and normalized more than four thousand tokens of BEET, BAT, BAN, BITE/BIDE, BUT, BOT, BOUGHT, BOAT, BOWL, and BOAR vowels, fifty to one hundred tokens per speaker, and ran linear regressions for the vowels' measurements against linguistic internal factors (vowel duration and following place of articulation) and external factors (age/grade and speaker). Regression results supported an unmistakable picture of vocalic stability for these speakers across their lifespans for most of the vowels. Figure 24.7 illustrates this stability by plotting the relative degree of difference from Grade Ten at each grade level.

Figure 24.7 shows relative change as a function of mean Lobanov-normalized scores for the vowels BEET, BAT, BUT, BOT, and BOAT for each speaker. At no time point did any of the ten speakers vary more than 10 percent from their Grade Ten baseline, a statistically insignificant margin. Thus, overall, the vowels for these individuals do not mirror the dramatic trajectories of lifespan change demonstrated for morphosyntactic features. These data support Roberts's (2002) contention that vowel systems are relatively stable once they are established in the grammar, but Kohn et al. (2010) speculate that this vocalic stability is also evidence for a lack of social salience of vocalic variables vis-à-vis morphosyntactic variables in AAE. Aside from very well-known, socially salient vocalic variables (e.g., /ai/-ungliding, *pin-pen* merger), vowels tend to mark more nuanced regional and ethnic variation than do morphosyntactic features. The comparison of vocalic analysis with morphosyntactic analysis in this longitudinal sample suggests that speakers utilize nonvocalic markers more prominently than vowels to mark AAE in early childhood and adolescence.

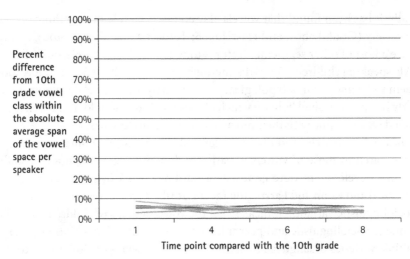

FIGURE 24.7 Percentage of vowel shift difference (for means of five vowel classes: BEET, BAT, BUT, BOT, and BOAT) from Grade Ten for ten speakers.

24.5 THE DEVELOPMENT OF STYLE-SHIFTING ABILITY

Not only are trajectories of morphosyntactic and phonological AAE development important to examine in a longitudinal study such as this one, but the development of stylistic competence is as well. The question remains as to when a child may develop the skills to style-shift in and out of his/her home variety. What factors would contribute to the width of a speaker's range on the MAE–AAE continuum (figure 24.1), and at what point(s) in the lifespan would that range emerge? Discussions and studies of style have been an important component of the study of variation (Labov 1966; Eckert and Rickford 2001; Schilling-Estes 2002; Coupland 2007) but defining style operationally is challenging. Adult AAE speakers often vary their speech stylistically within their own variety or code-switch between AAE and other varieties. The ability to style-shift has been tied to academic achievement (Charity, Scarborough, and Griffin 2004; Craig et al. 2009; Van Hofwegen and Stob 2011, 2012), but no comprehensive analysis of how it develops in young speakers has thus far been conducted. However, the FPG longitudinal corpus provides one interesting avenue through which to do this (see Renn 2007; Renn and Terry 2009).

Renn (2007, 2010) and Renn and Terry (2009) examined stylistic variation at three temporal points: Grades One to Two, Grade Six, and Grade Eight. The stylistic data were gathered via "formal" and "informal" speech settings for each speaker. The informal settings were the same language samples utilized in Van Hofwegen and Wolfram (2010): mother–child interactions at Grade One and peer–peer interactions at Grades Six and Eight. For the formal settings at Grades Six and Eight, speakers were asked to give a speech on a given topic. The younger formal speech data were collected at Grade

Two, in which children were asked—in the presence of an examiner—to describe pictures and engage in narrative elicitation tasks. Altogether, Renn examined 73 children in Grades One to Two; 125 in Grade Six; and 164 in Grade Eight.

Using the DDM developed by Renn (2007) and used by Van Hofwegen and Wolfram (2010), Renn (2010) compared the scores for each child in each context according to a "difference score" (see Craig et al. 2009), which is simply the informal DDM score minus the formal DDM score. To conceptualize style-shifting in terms of a difference score, what matters is the score's relation to zero, not necessarily the absolute score (remember that on the whole, children in Grades One to Two used less AAE than did those in Grades Six and Eight). Renn calculated a difference score for each child at all three age points, which are plotted in Figure 24.8.

As the figure shows, the majority of the Grade Eight children inhabit the positive side of the scale. This means that they exhibit higher DDM scores in informal contexts than in formal contexts, suggesting that they contextually style-shift in the direction of their home variety in more informal contexts and toward a more standard variety in formal contexts. Children in Grades One to Two, on the other hand, are balanced on either side of zero—suggesting that they are either unable or unwilling to style-shift at this age. Grade Six children show the greatest variation in their trajectory—either dipping below their Grades One to Two difference score or rising above it; few Grade Eight children had lower difference scores than they did at Grades One to Two. Figure 24.9 shows box plots for the children at the three time points.

As is evident in the figure, children of all ages style-shift in either direction (i.e., toward AAE or toward MAE), but not always in predictable ways. Grade Six and Grade Eight children had wider ranges (indicated by the vertical lines) than did children in Grades One to Two, suggesting that not only are children at these ages able to style-shift

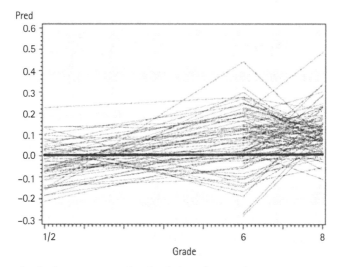

FIGURE 24.8 Individual trajectories of style shifting for Grades One to Two, Grade Six, and Grade Eight, by difference scores.

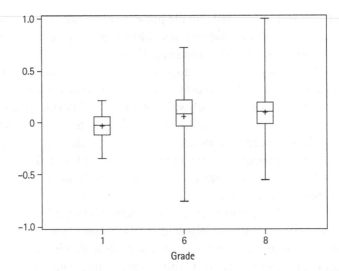

FIGURE 24.9 Median, mean, standard deviation, percentile, and range for difference scores at three time points.

extensively, but many of them are choosing to *not* style-shift in situations where it may otherwise be expected of them. As it is unlikely that these children lose the ability to style-shift as they age, these divergences are likely explained through personal, peer, and external factors. For example, gender is also an important factor in predicting over-all difference: in Renn (2010), girls style-shifted more dramatically than boys. Overall, Renn (2010) statistically substantiated that children improve in style-shifting ability sig-nificantly between Grades One to Two and Grades Six and Eight. This suggests that the ability to style shift is acquired before the middle-school grades.

24.6 Personal and Psychosocial Factors and the Development of AAE

As mentioned above, this longitudinal database is rich not only with language data from children across the lifespan and speech from their mothers and peers as well but also with an array of psychological, social, and academic measures (see Burchinal et al. 2006; Burchinal et al. 2008). Specifically, children's longitudinal speech data were fur-ther examined with respect to similarities/differences with mothers and peers (Van Hofwegen 2011, 2014), academic performance (Renn 2015; Van Hofwegen and Stob 2011, 2012; Terry et al. 2010), and psychosocial factors related to ethnic identity (Renn 2010; Van Hofwegen and Wolfram 2010; Van Hofwegen 2014).

Calculated from Grade One and Grade Four speech samples, each mother's DDM score (AAE features per utterance) was compared to her child's speech at each of the six time points used in Van Hofwegen and Wolfram (2010). Regression analysis found mothers' speech to be significantly predictive of children's speech at all points except in early adolescence (Grades Six and Eight), at which time the children's speech diverged sharply from that of their mothers. In later adolescence (Grade Ten), however, the children veered back into their mothers' ranges, becoming significantly similar to the adult norm again. These results support Eckert's (2000) observation that adolescents often reject standard and/or adult norms. It is noteworthy that by Grade Ten, the trend for nonstandard divergence curbs, perhaps because the children are beginning to feel the effects of the linguistic marketplace. Figure 24.10 shows the mean overall *roller coaster* trajectory for the children across the six time points, plotted against the mothers' mean. At only two time points are the two groups significantly different (Grades Six and Eight).

Not only did mothers' *speech* reliably predict their children's speech at every age except early adolescence, but mothers' *education* also predicted both relative AAE usage and style-shifting ability. Regression analyses conducted by both Van Hofwegen and Wolfram (2010) and Renn (2010) found that mothers' education (in terms of number of years of formal schooling) was a significant predictor of relative AAE usage and style-shifting performance. Namely, children with more educated mothers generally used less AAE and were less likely to style-shift.

Given accommodation theory (see Coupland 1984) and audience design theory (cf. Bell 1984), it could be hypothesized that much of the variation evidenced in the roller coaster or curvilinear trajectories in the longitudinal data are due to the effect of the interlocutor in each speech sample. The interlocutors were mothers at Grades One and Four and peers at Grades Six, Eight, and Ten (interlocutors for the 48-month-olds were examiners), which could perhaps explain the dip in the early grades and the spike in early adolescence. However, this does not explain why children at 48 months used comparatively more AAE or why Grade Ten children used less AAE than they did at Grade

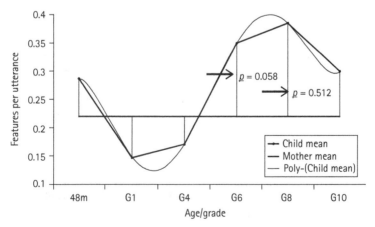

FIGURE 24.10 Mean child DDM (features per utterance) plotted against the mean mother's DDM at six time points, significant differences indicated.

Eight. However, the interlocutor effect is nevertheless an important one and has been examined in a dyadic analysis of the peer–peer speech (Van Hofwegen 2014) in Grades Six, Eight, and Ten.

The dyadic analysis found peer DDM scores to be extremely significantly correlated to each other (i.e., within-dyad factors significantly predicted the overall variance more than between-dyad factors), particularly at Grade Eight. Interestingly, boys and girls exhibited different trajectories of dyadic correlation at the three time points (see Figure 24.11). As the figure shows, girls had significantly similar within-dyad variance at all three time points, whereas boy dyads were weakly significantly similar at Grade Six and not at all so at Grade Ten. One possible explanation for these results is that girls more consistently accommodate to their interlocutor regardless of age and familiarity with them, whereas boys either develop accommodative skill later than girls or are more selective in their use of it.

Much has been written on the relationship between academic performance and AAE use. Connor and Craig (2006) and Craig et al. (2003) studied emerging literacy skills and dialect usage in apparent time, and found that AAE-speaking kids with high meta-linguistic awareness performed better on reading tasks than did others. The FPG longitudinal sample supports that finding. Van Hofwegen and Stob (2011, 2012) analyzed fifty of the longitudinal children and their Broad Reading scores on the Woodcock-Johnson Revised Tests of Achievement (Woodcock and Johnson 1989) at all points in which language samples and reading scores were taken between Grade One and Grade Ten. Regression analyses were conducted to see if AAE use (DDM scores) reliably predicted reading achievement and what that relationship looked like at different points in the lifespan.

Gender proved to be an important predictor for reading success: boys' reading scores were extremely significantly impacted ($p < 0.001$) by their relative AAE usage, whereas girls showed no significant effect at all. A closer look at the distribution of the data

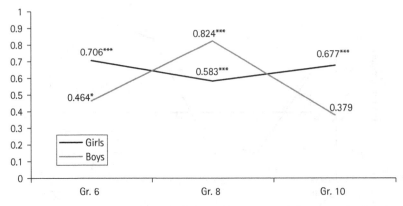

FIGURE 24.11 Intra-class correlation coefficients for girls and boys at Grades Six, Eight, and Ten.

$^*p < 0.05$; $^{**}p < 0.01$; $^{***}p < 0.001$.

indicated that girls with the greatest extremes in AAE use performed best on the Broad Reading test. Boys had an inverse relationship between AAE use and literacy scores.

Renn (forthcoming) and Terry et al. (2010) looked at reading scores and mathematic reasoning scores, respectively, in Grade Three (Renn 2015) and Grades One to Three (Terry et al. 2010). Specifically, Renn (2015) found a correlation between high AAE usage and low performance on Letter-Word ID tasks (which assess the child's ability to discern letters and words), whereas performance on Passage Comprehension and Word Attack tasks (assessing reading comprehension and phonological awareness) had no relationship with AAE use. Terry et al. (2010) found that children whose speech consistently omitted third person singular -*s* had significantly lower scores on the Woodcock Johnson-R Applied Problems subtest, even controlling for mathematic ability (i.e., the WJ-R Calculation score). Both of these studies suggest that AAE-speaking children in the younger grades are particularly vulnerable in their academic achievement, as their home variety may interfere with their abilities to discern what is being asked of them, irrespective of cognitive ability. In all, these longitudinal data support the contention that AAE use can affect academic performance detrimentally, particularly for boys and particularly for younger children.

Finally, another psychosocial aspect explored in the longitudinal database was the relationship between the children's AAE use and components of their ethnic identity. Particularly, demographic and personal details such as the percentage of African Americans in school, number and quality of African American contacts, and number and quality of European American contacts were examined, as well as the child's self-regard score on a racial centrality index (Sellers et al. 1997). None of these ethnic factors proved to be significant predictors of overall AAE usage across the lifespan (Van Hofwegen and Wolfram 2010). However, when considering style-shifting and academic performance, ethnic factors did play an important role. For example, Renn (2010) found that school demographics significantly predicted style-shifting in children, such that those with a larger proportion of African Americans in their school were more likely to style-shift. Children with fewer African American classmates used less AAE in both contexts and therefore shifted less overall. The percentage of African Americans in school also affected Broad Reading scores for girls in the longitudinal sample (higher percentages correlated with lower reading scores) (Van Hofwegen and Stob 2011, 2012).

24.7 CONCLUSION

In all, the longitudinal study on AAE reported here has been able to substantiate with real-time data what has to date only been theorized. Sixty-eight children, recorded at regular intervals from birth to early adulthood, have shown some consistent and regular patterns in their overall relative AAE usage, style-shifting abilities, vowel development, AAE usage vis-à-vis that of their caregivers and their peers, and academic performance.

Largely consistent with both Craig and Washington (2003, 2006) and colleagues' findings, these AAE-speaking children are more likely to start high, but decrease their AAE usage in the early years of primary schooling (Grades One to Four). And, consistent with the observations of Labov, Eckert, and many others, the adolescent stage for these children was markedly divergent from MAE, with wide envelopes of variation. The children also more readily and ably style-shift as they age. Vowels, however, remain largely stable in relative placement throughout the lifespan.

Certainly, the results so far have shown how complex the relationship is between MAE and AAE in the developing speaker. While most children show similar broad patterns of movement within the proposed AAE–MAE continuum (see figure 24.1), these results show that they can differ in absolute placement and range, and that different linguistic levels (i.e., phonological versus morphosyntactic) change in different ways. That said, however, to think about development in terms of both intra- and inter-dialect movement along a continuum is helpful for conceptualizing how most AAE-speaking children navigate their linguistic landscape.

Notes

1. This research was made possible through the support of NSF grants BCS-0843865 and BCS 0544744.
2. Rickford's (1987) creole continuum is mentioned here to demonstrate how the relationship between similar varieties can be productively schematized. This paper is agnostic as to the origins of AAE (i.e., creole or not), hypotheses for which are described in more detail in Part I of this volume.
3. *Vernacular* is used here consistently with Labov's (1972) *vernacular principle*, holding that "the style which is more regular in its structure and in its relation to the evolution of the language is the vernacular, in which the minimum attention is paid to speech" (112).
4. Following Van Hofwegen and Wolfram (2010), this chapter uses school grade levels instead of ages to label temporal data points for the FPG longitudinal speaker sample. These American school grades correspond roughly to the following ages: Grade One (about 6 years old), Grade Four (about 9 years old), Grade Six (about 11 years old); Grade Eight (about 13 years old); and Grade Ten (about 15 years old). The decision to use grades rather than ages is grounded in the original purpose/design of the FPG longitudinal project, a goal of which was to assess the relationship between AAE use and school performance. Given the dynamics of the schooling process, using age at these time points is imprecise, as children may begin school at ages ranging from 4 to 6 or repeat a year at some point along the way.
5. As Green (2011) and others have attested, one concern in using the DDM alone to assess AAE usage is that it may miss nuances in the variation of individual features by taking too much of a bird's-eye view. Wolfram and Van Hofwegen (2012) counter this with three main points: (1) DDM studies have recognized validity in allied fields; (2) their findings parallel those for individual features; and (3) that "language variationists need to consider the sociolinguistic forest as well as the variable trees."
6. Like Craig and Washington (2006), Van Hofwegen and Wolfram (2010) also calculated features per word scores, and they were highly correlated ($p < 0.001$; R = 0.879) with features per utterance scores.

7. A follow-up study using data from fifty subjects (Van Hofwegen and Stob 2011) substantiated the prominence of these two trajectories but found the *rollercoaster* trajectory to be statistically dominant enough in regression analysis to characterize the entire sample.

8. Invariant/habitual/aspectual *be* is a well-studied AAE feature but is notoriously difficult to analyze via traditional variation analysis (i.e., potential versus actual cases). Hence, raw counts are reported here.

References

Bailey, Guy. 2002. "Real and Apparent Time." In *The Handbook of Linguistic Variation and Change*, edited by J. K. Chambers, Peter Trudgill, and Natalie Schilling-Estes, 312–32. Malden, MA: Blackwell.

Bailey, Guy, and Erik Thomas. 1998. "Some Aspects of African-American Vernacular English Phonology." In *African American English*, edited by Salikoko S. Mufwene, John Rickford, John Baugh, and Guy Bailey, 85–109. London: Routledge.

Bailey, Guy, Tom Wikle, Jan Tillery, and Lori Sand. 1991. "The Apparent Time Construct." *Language Variation and Change* 3: 241–64.

Baugh, John. 1983. *Black Street Speech: Its History, Structure, and Survival*. Austin: University of Texas.

———. 1996. "Dimensions of a Theory of Ecolinguistics." In *A Social Science of Language: Papers in Honor of William Labov*, edited by Gregory R. Guy, Crawford Feagin, Deborah Schiffrin, and John Baugh, 397–419. Philadelphia: John Benjamins.

Bell, Allan. 1984. "Language Style as Audience Design." *Language in Society* 13: 145–204.

Burchinal, Margaret R., Joanne E. Roberts, Steven Hooper, and Susan A. Zeisel. 2000a. "Cumulative Risk and Early Cognitive Development: A Comparison of Statistical Risk Models." *Developmental Psychology* 36: 793–807.

Burchinal, Margaret, Joanne E. Roberts, Susan A. Zeisel, E. A. Hennon, and Steven Hooper. 2006. "Social Risk and Protective Child, Parenting, and Child Care Factors in Early Elementary School Years." *Parenting: Science and Practice* 6: 79–113.

Burchinal, Margaret R., Joanne E. Roberts, R. Riggins, Susan A. Zeisel, E. Neebe, and D. Bryant. 2000b. "Relating Quality of Center Childcare to Early Cognitive and Language Development Longitudinally." *Child Development* 71: 339–57.

Burchinal, Margaret, Joanne E. Roberts, Susan A. Zeisel, and S. Rowley. 2008. "Social Risk and Protective Factors for African American Children's Academic Achievement and Adjustment during the Transition to Middle School." *Developmental Psychology* 44: 286–92.

Callahan-Price, Erin. 2010. "Childhood Copula Development in African American English." Paper presented at New Ways of Analyzing Variation 39, San Antonio, Texas. November 4–6.

———. 2011. "Generalized Acquisition Constraints and Dialect-Specific Norms in Child AAE Copula Development." Paper presented at New Ways of Analyzing Variation (NWAV) 40, Washington, DC, October 27–30.

Cedergren, Henrietta, and David Sankoff. 1974. "Variable Rules: Performance as a Statistical Reflection of Competence." *Language* 50: 333–55.

Chambers, Jack K. 1992. "Dialect Acquisition." *Language* 68: 673–705.

Charity, Anne H., Hollis S. Scarborough, and Darion M. Griffin. 2004. "Familiarity with School English in African American Children and its Relation to Early Reading Achievement." *Child Development* 75: 1340–56.

Connor, Carol McDonald, and Holly K. Craig. 2006. "African American Preschoolers' Language, Emergent Literacy Skills, and Use of African American English: A Complex Relation." *Journal of Speech, Language, and Hearing Research* 49: 771–92.

Coupland, Nikolas. 1984. "Accommodation at Work: Some Phonological Data and their Implications." *International Journal of Society and Language* 46: 49–70.

———. 2007. *Style: Language Variation and Identity.* Cambridge: Cambridge University.

Craig, Holly K., C. Thompson, Julie A. Washington, and S. L. Potter. 2003. "Phonological Features of Child African American English." *Journal of Speech, Hearing, and Language Research* 46: 623–35.

Craig, Holly K., and Julie A. Washington. 2006. *Malik Goes to School: Examining the Language Skills of African American Students from Preschool–5th grade.* Mahwah, NJ: Lawrence Erlbaum Associates.

Craig, Holly K., L. Zhang, S. Hensel, and E. Quinn. 2009. "African American English-speaking Students: An Examination of the Relationship between Dialect Shifting and Reading Outcomes." *Journal of Speech, Language, and Hearing Research* 52: 839–55.

Cukor-Avila, Patricia. 1995. "The Evolution of AAVE in a Rural Texas Community: An Ethnolinguistic Study." PhD diss., University of Michigan.

———. 2002. "She Say, She Go, She Be Like: Verbs of Quotation over Time in African American Vernacular English." *American Speech* 77: 3–31.

Cukor-Avila, Patricia, and Guy Bailey. 2007. "Age-grading and Linguistic Diffusion." Paper presented at New Ways of Analyzing Variation 36, Philadelphia, Pennsylvania, October 11–14.

Dillard, J. L. 1972. *Black English: Its History and Usage in the United States.* New York: Random House.

Eckert, Penelope. 1997. "Age as a Sociolinguistic Variable." In *The Handbook of Sociolinguistics,* edited by Florian Coulmas, 151–67. Oxford: Basil Blackwell.

———. 2000. *Linguistic Variation as Social Practice.* Malden, MA: Blackwell.

———. 2004. "Adolescent language." In *Language in the USA: Themes for the 21st Century,* edited by Edward Finegan and John Rickford, 361–74. New York: Cambridge University Press.

Eckert, Penelope, and John R. Rickford, eds. 2001. *Style and Sociolinguistic Variation.* Cambridge: Cambridge University Press.

Fasold, Ralph W. 1972. *Tense Marking in Black English: A Linguistic and Social Analysis.* Arlington, VA: Center for Applied Linguistics.

Graff, David, William Labov, and Wendell A. Harris. 1986. "Testing Listeners' Reactions to Phonological Markers of Ethnic Identity: A New Method for Sociolinguistic Research." In *Diversity and Diachrony,* edited by David Sankoff, 45–58. Philadelphia: John Benjamins.

Green, Lisa J. 2002. *African American English: A Linguistic Introduction.* Cambridge: Cambridge University.

———. 2011. *Language and the African American Child.* Cambridge: Cambridge University Press.

Kerswill, Paul. 1996. "Children, Adolescence, and Language Change." *Language Variation and Change* 8: 177–202.

Kohn, Mary, and Charlie Farrington. 2011a. "Evaluating Acoustic Speaker Normalization Algorithms: Evidence from Longitudinal Child Data." *Journal of the Acoustical Society of America* 131: 2237–48.

———. 2011b. "The Socio-regional Distribution of African American Vowel Systems in Piedmont, North Carolina." Paper presented at New Ways of Analyzing Variation 40, Washington, DC, October 27–30.

Kohn, Mary E., Charles Farrington, and David Ethier. 2010. "A Longitudinal Analysis of the Vowel Spaces in Childhood and Adolescent African American English." Paper presented at New Ways of Analyzing Variation 39, San Antonio, Texas, November 4–6.

Labov, William. 1965. "Stages in the Acquisition of Standard English." In *Social Dialects and Language Learning*, edited by Roger W. Shuy, 77–103. Champaign, Illinois: National Council of Teachers of English.

———. 1966. *The Social Stratification of English in New York City.* Washington, DC: Center for Applied Linguistics.

———. 1972. "Some Principles of Linguistic Methodology." *Language in Society* 11: 165–201.

———. 1973. "The Boundaries of Words and their Meanings." In *New Ways of Analyzing Variation in English*, edited by Charles Bailey and Roger Shuy, 340–73. Washington, DC: Georgetown University Press.

Labov, William, Paul Cohen, Clarence Robins, and John Lewis. 1968. *A Study of the Non-Standard English of Negro and Puerto Rican Speakers in New York City.* 2 vols. Philadelphia: United States Office of Education Final Report, Research Project 3288.

Loban, Walter. 1976. *Language Development: Kindergarten thru Grade Twelve.* Urbana, IL: National Council of Teachers.

Payne, Arvilla. 1980. "Factors Controlling the Acquisition of the Philadelphia Dialect by Out-of-state Children." In *Locating Language in Time and Space*, edited by William Labov, 143–78. New York: Academic.

Rahman, Jacquelyn. 2008. "Middle-Class African Americans: Reactions and Attitudes toward African American English." *American Speech* 83: 141–76.

Renn, Jennifer. 2007. "Measuring Style Shift: A Quantitative Analysis of African American English." Master's thesis, University of North Carolina at Chapel Hill.

———. 2010. "Acquiring Style: The Development of Dialect Shifting among African American Children." PhD diss., University of North Carolina at Chapel Hill.

Renn, Jennifer. 2015. "Investigating the relationship between African American English use and early literacy skills." Paper presented at the American Dialect Society 2015 Annual Meeting, Portland, Oregon, January 8–11.

Renn, Jennifer, and J. Michael Terry. 2009. "Operationalizing Style: Quantifying Style Shift in the Speech of African American Adolescents." *American Speech* 84: 367–90.

Rickford, John R. 1987. *Dimensions of a Creole Continuum.* Stanford, CA: Stanford University.

———. 1991. "Grammatical Variation and Divergence in Vernacular Black English." In *Internal and External Factors in Language Change*, edited by Marinel Gerritsen and Dieter Stein, 175–200. Berlin: Mouton de Gruyter.

———. 1999. *African American Vernacular English: Features, Evolution and Educational Implications.* Malden, MA: Blackwell.

Rickford, John, and Mackenzie Price. 2013. "Girlz II Women: Age-Grading, Language Change and Stylistic Variation." *Journal of Sociolinguistics* 17: 143–79.

Roberts, Julie. 2002. "Child Language Variation." In *The Handbook of Language Variation and Change*, edited by J. K. Chambers, Peter Trudgill, and Natalie Schilling-Estes, 333–48. Malden, MA: Blackwell.

Sankoff, David, and Suzanne Laberge. 1978. "The Linguistic Market and the Statistical Explanation of Variability." In *Linguistic Variation: Models and Methods*, edited by David Sankoff, 239–50. New York: Academic.

Sankoff, David, Sali A. Tagliamonte, and E. Smith. 2005. *GoldVarb X: A Variable Rule Application for Macintosh and Windows.* http://individual.utoronto.ca/tagliamonte/goldvarb.html.

Schilling-Estes, Natalie. 2002. "Investigating Stylistic Variation." In *The Handbook of Linguistic Variation and Change*, edited by J. K. Chambers, Peter Trudgill, and Natalie Schilling-Estes, 375–401. Malden, MA: Blackwell.

Sellers, Robert M., Stephanie A. J. Rowley, Tabbye M. Chavous, J. Nicole Shelton, and Mia A. Smith. 1997. "Multidimensional Inventory of Black Identity: A Preliminary Investigation of Reliability and Construct Validity." *Journal of Personality and Social Psychology* 73: 805–15.

Smith, Jennifer, Mercedes Durham, and Liane Fortune. 2007. "'Mam, My Trousers is Fa'in Doon!': Community, Caregiver, and Child in the Acquisition of Variation in a Scottish Dialect." *Language Variation and Change* 19: 63–99.

Stewart, William A. 1965. "Urban Negro Speech: Sociolinguistic Factors Affecting English Teaching." In *Social Dialects and Language Learning*, edited by Roger W. Shuy, 10–18. Champaign, IL: National Council of Teachers of English.

Tagliamonte, Sali A. 2006. *Analysing Sociolinguistic Variation*. Cambridge: Cambridge University.

Terry, J. Michael, Randall Hendrick, Evangelos Evangelou, and R. L. Smith. 2010. "Variable Dialect Switching among African American Children: Inferences about Working Memory." *Lingua* 120: 2463–75.

Thomas, Erik R. 2007. "Phonological and Phonetic Characteristics of AAVE." *Language and Linguistics Compass* 1: 450–75.

Torbert, Benjamin C. 2004. "Southern Vowels and the Social Construction of Salience." PhD diss., Duke University.

Van Hofwegen, Janneke. 2011. "A Caregiver's Influence on AAE Vernacularity across the Early Lifespan." Paper presented at the Linguistic Society of America 2011 Annual Meeting, Pittsburgh, Pennsylvania, January 6–9.

———. 2014. "Dyadic Analysis: Factors Affecting African American English Usage and Accommodation in Adolescent Peer Dyads." *Language and Communication*. http://dx.doi.org/10.1016/j.langcom.2014.10.004.

Van Hofwegen, Janneke, and Reuben Stob. 2011. "A Longitudinal Analysis of the Relationship between Reading and AAE Vernacularity." Paper presented at New Ways of Analyzing Variation (NWAV) 40, Washington, DC, October 27–30.

———. 2012. "The Gender Gap: How Dialect Usage Affects Reading Outcomes in African American Youth." Paper presented at the Linguistic Society of America 2012 Annual Meeting, Portland, Oregon, January 5–8.

Van Hofwegen, Janneke, and Walt Wolfram. 2010. "Coming of Age in African American English: A Longitudinal Study." *Journal of Sociolinguistics* 14: 27–52.

Washington, Julie A., and Holly K. Craig. 2002. "Morpho-syntactic Forms of African American English Used by Young Children and their Caretakers." *Journal of Applied Psycholinguistics* 23: 209–31.

Wolfram, Walt. 1969. *A Sociolinguistic Description of Detroit Negro Speech*. Washington, DC: Center for Applied Linguistics.

Wolfram, Walt, and Janneke Van Hofwegen. 2012. "Composite Dialect Indexes Confront Variationism: The Case of AAE." Paper presented at New Ways of Analyzing Variation 41, Bloomington, Indiana, October 25–28.

Woodcock, Richard, and Mary Bonner Johnson. 1989. *Woodcock-Johnson Psycho-educational Battery-Revised*. Chicago: Riverside.

CHAPTER 25

DEVELOPMENT OF VARIATION IN CHILD AFRICAN AMERICAN ENGLISH

LISA J. GREEN AND JESSICA WHITE-SUSTAÍTA

25.1 INTRODUCTION

AFRICAN American English (AAE), a linguistic variety spoken natively by some—not all—African Americans (and some non-African Americans) in the United States, has set syntactic, semantic, morphological, phonological, lexical, and pragmatic patterns. Many speakers who live in AAE-speaking communities acquire it as their first variety, and others who have early experiences in more diverse communities and networks may acquire patterns of AAE in varying degrees along with patterns of other varieties, including varieties of Standard American English (SAE).

AAE is often characterized by variability; however, some constructions in the linguistic variety are invariable. The overwhelming majority of research on variation in AAE has been from the perspective of variable rules and related analyses in which frequency and probability of occurrence of variable morphosyntactic forms are considered in relation to social and linguistic conditioning. The general assumption is that the competing morphosyntactic forms are those from AAE and those from SAE, and the choice of one or the other (e.g., either the overt –s, as in *Jack's books*, or the zero form in *Jack books*) is due to a number of linguistic and extralinguistic factors. There is no doubt that some of the variability in the speech of some AAE speakers is due to contact with SAE and non-AAE speakers in their regions. However, not all aspects of children's use of variable AAE patterns are a result of language contact and mixture, especially because children can produce morphosyntactic variants even when there is limited contact with SAE.

This chapter reports some of the research that places considerable emphasis on variation in early stages of AAE child acquisition as part of the developing grammar. Some observations will be made about morphosyntactic variation from the perspective of the genitive marker (–s), and the remaining space will be dedicated to syntactic variation from the perspective of processes associated with questions and negation, which has received less attention in research on child AAE.

25.2 MORPHOSYNTACTIC AND SYNTACTIC VARIATION IN AAE

Research on the development of AAE and its use by young children started in the 1970s, almost ten years after the first major wave of research on AAE. Researchers followed the trend set in previous AAE variation studies; that is, the early child AAE studies concentrated on morphosyntactic features that were associated with adolescent and adult AAE. Often the questions were about the extent to which the developing speakers used AAE variants and SAE variants, that is, the extent to which their language resembled that of adult AAE speakers' language. For instance, the studies considered the use (or non-use, marked as Ø) of –s for plural (e.g., *two dogs/Ø*), possessive (e.g., *daddy's/Ø car*), and third person singular (*He sings/Ø*). Also, full and contracted copula forms in medial and final positions in sentences (e.g., *There is/'s Bob; There Bob is*), and auxiliary *be* absence (e.g., *She Ø running*) in age groups from 1½ to 7 years were considered. Steffensen (1974) reported that third person singular –s inflection emerges rather late, and Reveron (1978) showed that the morpheme is the least frequently produced SAE morpheme from ages 3 to 6 years. The current research on morphosyntactic features in child AAE is still in the traditional variation framework (see Renn 2011; Renn and Terry 2009; Van Hofwegen and Wolfram 2010; see the review of previous research in Newkirk-Turner, Horton, and Stockman, this volume, and the discussion in Van Hofwegen, this volume). On the other hand, work on syntactic variation and early AAE was not a topic that received much attention.

Possessive marking is traditionally analyzed as part of AAE morphosyntactic patterns. Labov et al. (1968) observed that speakers did not produce –s inflection in attributive contexts, as in the examples in (1) (Green 2011, 197–99):

(1) a. He broke Kynosha phone. (Rashanna 3;4) (N.B.: #;# refers to age in years;months)
    b. Now I'm in Miss Savoie class.
    c. They in John car.
    d. Then they went in they mama room and they dump powder on Carl's head.[1] (Nia 5;9)
    e. And then Carl pour some milk in the baby cup. (where *baby cup* refers to the glass that the baby is using).

Labov et al. (1968) also noted that speakers did produce overt possessive marking in absolutive contexts (e.g., *This is my brother's*). The only absolutive constructions reported in Green (2011, 17) are those that refer to a location, such as in example (2):

(2) LJG: Have you ever gone to a birthday party?
     Dawn: Yes ma'm … a girl birthday to my cousin. (5;9)

There is often no overt possessive marking in contexts in which reference is to a location, such as a house, as reflected in Dawn's response in (2), in which *to my cousin* refers 'to my cousin's house.' However, in work on possessive marking and ellipsis, Tracy Conner (pers. comm.) found that adult AAE speakers overwhelmingly produce overt possessive *–s* marking in absolutive contexts, excluding contexts in which the reference is to a location. Conner also reported on data collected in the *Diagnostic Evaluation of Language Variation* (2003) that showed that children are more likely to use overt *–s* marking in absolutive contexts and zero marking in attributive contexts.[2]

Wolfram (1969) noted that *–s* inflection is optional in attributive contexts but that no claims could be made about the marker in other contexts because of lack of data reflecting patterns. The point that Wolfram underscores is that data reflecting absolutive constructions are limited. However, considering work by Labov et al. (1968), we find clear cases illustrating absolutive contexts that show possessive marking in absolutive contexts is more often overt than covert.

Steffensen (1974) reported on morphosyntactic patterns in the language use of family members of children in the 17- to 20-month age range, as a means of getting a picture of caregivers' input that influences children's speech during developmental stages. Steffensen found that marking in attributive contexts was indeed optional in adult patterns of possessive marking, and also some cases of unmarked possessives in absolutive contexts, as in (3) and (4) (Steffensen 1974, 36):

(3) a. Peg: Whose daughter?
     b. Mrs. Lewis: My grandfather.
(4) I met her through another friend, which was a real good friend of my older sister
     …

Steffensen's (1974) is one of the few studies on developing AAE-speaking children younger than four years. In her study of two children, Steffensen (1974) noted that there was only one occurrence of overt *–s* marking (i.e., *Where the bird's eyes?*) (56), which was an instance of imitation produced by a child at 23.1 months. She found that "the psychological reality of the concept of possession as expressed with the noun-noun sequence or an isolated noun is supported by the use of these forms interchangeably with other structures expressing possession that the children had been using in a semantically appropriate way" (59). In addition, she noted that the children in her study were just approaching the age of child SAE speakers who were beginning to produce overt possessive marking. As such, her view was that the children "showed the same development of nominal –Z inflections as children in the [SAE] environment" (61). It has been well established that the language of children younger than 4 years old acquiring AAE is quite similar to the language of children acquiring SAE (and probably other varieties of English). For this reason, it is important to bear in mind that not all patterns that overlap with features associated with AAE are actually indicative of adult AAE; they might be representative of early developmental stages.

If early possessives in AAE look like those in general developmental stages produced by children who speak other varieties of English, what does possessive marking look like in children developing AAE in later stages and at older ages or when children begin to mark inflection? Given that inflectional marking is optional in some contexts in AAE, it is not always clear what to expect in normally developing children and at what age this grammatical optionality should be reflected in the grammar. Another layer of complexity is that optionality is a characteristic of developmental stages (Anderssen, Bentzen, and Westergaard 2010). As such, it can be extremely difficult to tease apart optionality resulting from early development and stable optionality in the grammar of child AAE speakers. Nevertheless, it is important to recognize that AAE-speaking children will also exhibit variation as part of the developmental process, but this point is often overlooked given the focus on comparing optionality in child AAE to that in adult AAE.

Syntactic variation refers to variation at the level of the sentence, such that two similar sentences are taken to express the same meaning, as in *Kerry go to the beach* and *Kerry be going to the beach*, which can both be interpreted as habitual to mean 'Kerry generally goes to the beach.' By five years, developing child AAE speakers begin to produce the habitual sentences above; however, there is no research on the extent to which they use the habitual constructions in the same contexts or continue to use the simple tense construction (*Kerry go to the beach*) after they have begun to acquire the aspectual or habitual *be* construction (*Kerry be going to the beach*). In general, syntactic variation has received little attention in research in sociolinguistics quite possibly because it is not clear that two seemingly related sentences should be seen as variants (Lavandera 1978; Paolillo 2002). Two areas in the development of syntactic variation in AAE that have received some attention are question formation and negation.

25.3 INVERSION: SYNTACTIC VARIATION AND DEVELOPMENT

Inversion in this discussion refers specifically to word order between a subject and auxiliary verbs (e.g., *is, am, was, can, could, would, should*) in a sentence. For instance, in statements in AAE, the subject of the sentence (e.g., *Bruce*) generally precedes the auxiliary verb (e.g., *can*), such as in *Bruce can draw stars*. However, in questions in AAE, the auxiliary verb may precede the subject (*Can Bruce draw stars?*), but it can also follow the subject (*Bruce can draw stars?*). The former question construction, in which the auxiliary precedes the subject, is characterized by inversion. The latter question construction is a non-inversion structure. There is no inverted order of the subject and auxiliary to signal question force in non-inversion questions, but the prosodic properties such as intonation indicate that the sentence is a question.[3] It is certainly the case that, in general, speakers of different varieties can produce non-inversion questions that look like declarative statements. In AAE, these non-inversion questions are true questions that request a *yes* or *no* response. The prosodic properties of these questions might further distinguish AAE from other systems.

Another case of subject-auxiliary inversion in AAE occurs in negated sentences, and, in this case, the auxiliary is negated: *Couldn't nobody draw the green star*. In AAE, related sentences can occur with the non-inversion order, as in *Nobody couldn't draw the green star*. Question inversion and negative inversion are explored from the perspective of language development and variation.

25.3.1 Questions and Inversion

Questions are an important topic in the study of variation in AAE, because AAE questions vary on two levels: 1) morphologically between an expressed and unexpressed auxiliary and, 2) when an auxiliary is expressed, syntactically between subject auxiliary inversion and non-inversion. Thus, there are three main question types in AAE: subject auxiliary inversion (SAI), non-inversion (Non-Inv), and auxiliary-less questions (ØAux). All three types can occur in both *yes/no* (see table 25.1) (Green 2007, 88) and *wh*-questions (see table 25.2) (Green 2007, 89).

Questions like (8) and (9) are subject to two interpretations—one in which the question is an echo question or request for confirmation, and another in which the question is a genuine request for information (i.e., a direct question). The alternations between SAI and Non-Inv and between an overt auxiliary and ØAux are constrained by features such as polarity and auxiliary type (for a full description, see White-Sustaíta 2012).

AAE question variation between SAI, on the one hand, and Non-Inv and ØAux,[4] on the other, is syntactically motivated and represents "true syntactic variation" in the sense of Barbiers (2009)—where true syntactic variation is restricted to variation between constructions that are semantically equivalent (White-Sustaíta 2012). Research on the

---

Table 25.1 *Yes/No* Questions in Adult AAE

(5) Do you want to read my book?	*SAI*
(6) You saw my book?	*ØAux*
'Did you see my book?'	
(7) You can see my book?	*Non-Inv*
'Can you see my book?'	

Table 25.2 *Wh*–Questions in Adult AAE

(8) What did you say?		*SAI*
(9) What he said?		*ØAux*
'What did he say?'		
(10) How she was doing when you saw her?		*Non-Inv*
'How was she doing when you saw her?'		

Table 25.3 *Yes/No* Questions for AAE 3– to 5–Year–Olds

(11) Do this phone go down or up? (J025, 5)	*SAI*
'Does this phone go down or up?'	
(12) You a pour me some juice? (J003, 3;8)	*ØAux*
(where *a* can be taken to be a reduced form of *will, will—>'ll—>a*)	
'Will you pour me some juice?'	

normal developmental patterns of question variation in child AAE is important in distinguishing variation associated with development from variation associated with adult patterns. Such research can also shed light on the nature of the variation (e.g., where variation is located in the grammar and whether variants are acquired as part of the grammar or are "borrowed" from neighboring dialects, such as SAE).

In work on question acquisition in AAE, Green (2007, 2011) reports that speakers between ages 3 and 5 vary among different question forms after they show the ability to produce subject auxiliary inversion. The following examples in tables 25.3 and 25.4 (from Green 2007, 95–96) show variation among SAI, Non-Inv, and ØAux in children 3 to 5 years of age.

This variation is similar to findings for developing speakers of SAE before the age of 5; a crucial difference, however, is that by age 5 SAI becomes the canonical form for SAE speakers. Green (2007) emphasizes that the 5-year-old AAE child speakers in her study continue to use Non-Inv and ØAux with at least as much frequency as they use SAI.

In a comparative study on the question syntax of AAE-speaking children and their SAE-speaking peers, White-Sustaíta (2012) used experimental tasks to elicit *yes/no* and *wh*-questions from twenty-nine AAE-speaking children, ranging in age from 5;2 to 7;7 (mean age = 6;1). One of the goals of this experiment was to determine whether AAE speakers had acquired the question syntax documented in adult AAE by age 5 and to what extent children were acquiring features of SAE question syntax from their peers.

Children were prompted to produce approximately seven questions each. The examples in table 25.5 show each question type produced by a single AAE-speaking child participant during an elicitation task.

Table 25.4 *Wh*–Questions for AAE 3– to 5–Year–Olds

(13) And who this is? (Z091, 4;5)	*Non-Inv*
'And who is this?'	
(14) How she broke her leg? (T127, 5;7)	*ØAux*
'How did she break her leg?'	

Table 25.5 Example Elicitations

Prompt	Response (AAE #001; male, age 5;7)	Question type
Ask the store what they sell.	*What do y'all sell?*	SAI
Ask them where you can get a bike now.	*Where I can get a bike now?*	Non-Inv
Ask them who they sold them to.	*Who you sold them to?*	ØAux

Table 25.6 Mean Proportion Scores and Standard Deviations of AAE Question Type Produced in Elicitation Tasks

SAI		Non-Inv		ØAux	
M	SD	M	SD	M	SD
.55	.31	.14	.11	.33	.25

A total of 194 questions in AAE were collected in the elicitation tasks. Differences according to age among the question types produced in elicitation tasks were analyzed with a series of one-way analyses of covariance (ANCOVAs) by covarying age in months, using the statistical software program SPSS. For each of the three ANCOVAs, the dependent measures were the proportion SAI, ØAux, or Non-Inv responses.[5] The independent measures included the scalar covariant of age in months. The main effect of age was examined.

Table 25.6 lists the mean scores of question form production and their standard deviations. As the table indicates, speakers produced SAI 55 percent of the time on average in contrast to a mean rate of 97 percent for SAE speakers: $F(1, 57) = 49.99, p < .01$. AAE speakers produced Non-Inv in 14 percent of their responses in contrast to 1 percent for SAE speakers: $F(1, 57) = 25.41, p < .01$. Finally, AAE speakers produced ØAux 33 percent of the time, in contrast to 1 percent for SAE speakers: $F(1, 57) = 40.22, p < .01$.

However, these figures are somewhat misleading with regard to production rate of each form for AAE speakers, for these proportions represent a rate of production with respect to all questions included in the elicited data. Yet, as noted above, Non-Inv and

Table 25.7 Frequency of Question Types in Elicited
AAE Questions out of Total Number Where They Are
Licensed in Adult AAE

Question type	SAI	Non-Inv	ØAux
Yes/no	27/35	2/3	6/34
	77%	67%	18%
Wh-questions	84/159	25/64	52/127
	53%	39%	41%
Total	111/194	27/67	58/161
	57%	40%	36%

ØAux have grammatically restricted distributions in adult AAE. Analyzing Non-Inv only in the environments where it can occur in adult AAE reveals that AAE-speaking children produced Non-Inv in 40 percent of the contexts that permitted it. Likewise, analyzing ØAux only in the environments where it can occur in adult AAE reveals that it occurs 36 percent of the time. Table 25.7 lists the scores and percentages for each question form that occurs in the AAE data. None of the children produced Non-Inv or ØAux in contexts in which those forms are unattested in adult AAE—that is, no child produced a form like "What y'all do sell?" (where the *do* is not emphatic but is simply an auxiliary).

The ANCOVAs revealed no significant main effect of age on the rate of production for SAI ($F_{(1,57)}$ = .036 p = .851), Non-Inv ($F_{(1,57)}$ = .361 p = .550), or ØAux ($F_{(1,57)}$ = .142 p = .708). For example, 5-year-olds did not show a greater preference for Non-Inv than 7-year-olds, and older participants were no more likely to produce SAI than younger participants.

Of the 194 tokens in the AAE data, there were just two errors, both auxiliary doubling.

(15) Why *did* y'all *don't* sell bicycles no more?
(16) Why do y'all don't sell bicycles?

The fact that the children do not produce forms in the elicited questions that are unattested or ungrammatical in adult AAE, coupled with the absence of an effect of age on variation among the three types, suggest that AAE speakers have mastered the grammatical constraints of AAE questions and question variation by age 5—participants' use of SAI, ØAux, and Non-Inv by AAE child speakers aligns with adult AAE. These results also show that developing speakers of AAE do not go through a period during which they only use SAI before exhibiting adult-like variation. Developmental variation segues directly into variation associated with the adult variety.

These results bear out Henry's (2002) prediction for the acquisition of syntactic variation. Based on acquisition in Belfast English, Henry (2002) argues that certain types of variation are inherent to the core syntax of a speaker: "If grammars are naturally variable, we would expect variation to appear in the early stages of children's grammars. On the other hand, if grammars were in some sense naturally invariant, then we would expect children to perhaps acquire a single grammar, only later adding another variant for stylistic or sociolinguistic reasons" (278). Grammatical question variation—as opposed to question variation associated with development—is apparent in AAE speakers' earliest grammars, providing further evidence that optionality is an inherent feature of AAE question syntax and is acquired as such.

As noted above, this research on the question syntax of child speakers was carried out alongside research on child speakers of the local variety of SAE. A crucial finding of the study was that the SAE speakers produced SAI questions near-categorically and that, from kindergarten through second grade, there appeared to be no observable influence of the SAE-speakers' question syntax on AAE-speakers' question syntax. Within the elicitation context, SAE speakers produced invariant SAI question syntax and AAE speakers produced question variation that was grammatically aligned with the question variation of adult AAE. This finding provides further support for the point made in the introduction, i.e., that certain types of syntactic variation in AAE are observably inherent to the system, rather than the product of code-switching AAE and SAE forms.

What this study does not reveal is whether question variation in child AAE is pragmatically aligned with question variation in adult AAE. Whereas AAE-speaking children do not appear to use different question types according to pragmatic context (White-Sustaíta 2012), there are no adult studies by which to compare these findings. Thus, further research is necessary to determine how question variation in child AAE may differ from question variation in adult AAE beyond just grammaticality.

Examining question syntax variability in child AAE enriches our understanding of the nature of variability in AAE. The following section turns to negation and negative inversion—another area of AAE grammar that exhibits inherent morphological and syntactic variability and that has received less attention in research on child AAE.

25.3.2 Negation and Inversion

Speakers of AAE, along with speakers of other varieties of SAE and other Englishes, use negative concord, in which two or more negative elements, such as *don't, never,* and *no,* are used to indicate a single negation:

> (17) I *don't never* have *no* problems. (Green 2002, 77)
>   'I don't ever have any problems'

In one of the earliest studies on negation in AAE, Labov (1972) observed that "the first thing that we note in BEV [Black English Vernacular] is the extraordinary proliferation of the negative" (178). He noted that the participants in his study "come close to consistent negative concord," so in a limited number of cases they produce what he referred to as the "standard form" (184), as in the following example:

(18) No, I don't want anybody to die in my family.

Labov characterized sentence (18) as an instance of the speaker's codeswitching from AAE to SAE in a solemn context; instead of using *nobody* to match *don't* in the sentence, the speaker "switched" to *anybody*. In other words, according to Labov, by using *anybody*, the speaker indicated that she was codeswitching and was aware that the form (*anybody*) is in a different system. The conclusion that can be drawn from observations such as Labov's is that deviating from negative concord by using a "standard form" is seen as an instance of variation resulting from a switch from AAE. In their discussion of the expression of negation in sentences, Martin and Wolfram (1998) agree that negative concord is not required by the AAE grammar in all possible contexts. The point is that negative concord occurs with high frequency in AAE, but there is some variation, so instead of using multiple negatives to mark a single negation, speakers might simply use one negative element in a simple sentence, as in *I don't have problems* or *I don't have any problems*. Martin and Wolfram do not take the use of single negation to indicate a switch. Single negation is part of the AAE system, too, so it does not have to be seen solely as the result of a switch to SAE.

For a number of reasons, negative concord is an excellent angle from which to explore developmental patterns in child AAE. It occurs in the negative inversion constructions that will be discussed at the end of the section, and it is also a pattern that occurs in the early language of children developing different varieties of English. For instance, in her work on the acquisition of negation, Bellugi (1967) noted that one of the children in her study from an SAE background already had instances of multiple negatives by the time of an early period of acquisition that is characterized by the introduction of auxiliary verbs and number and tense marking in declarative, negative, and echo sentences, as well as in yes/no questions. In the later periods, Bellugi noted that children seemed to be operating with the rule "apply negative wherever possible in single propositions," in that they marked negation on pronouns, determiners, and adverbs, as well as on auxiliaries (1967, 142–43):

(19) Sarah
    a. No one didn't took it.
    b. Because nobody didn't broke it.
    c. Nothing can't reach it, see.

Henry et al. (1997) reported that children developing Bristol English and Belfast English, which are negative concord varieties, master negative concord around ages 3;3 and 4;6, respectively.

In her study of negation in child AAE, Stokes (1976) referred to negative concord as being unmarked, a general strategy of marking negation in the early stages. She addressed the universality of negative concord by underscoring the fact that in the early stages, there are similarities between negative concord produced by children developing AAE and those developing SAE, but differences are evident in later stages. For instance, older children developing AAE increase the use of negative concord (e.g., *I don't have no dog.*).

Data from spontaneous speech and elicitation tasks reported in Green (2011) are in line with the findings in Stokes (1976), in which it is concluded that negative concord is productive in developing AAE. Examples from children aged 4 to 5 in Green (2011, 120–21) are below:

(20) a. Darnell: And second it didn't have no gas.
      b. LJG: Wait a minute?
      c. Darnell: They didn't have no gas in my bike.

Children used negative concord sentences such as those in (20) in spontaneous speech. They also produced single negation in elicitation tasks, which shows that negative concord is not obligatory; single negation can also be produced in the same contexts in which negative concord can occur as in (21) and (22) (Green 2011, 124).

(21) Don't have training wheels on it.
(22) This one don't have training wheels.

At this developmental stage, concord is productive and overwhelmingly present, but it is not obligatory.

Examples such as the negative concord sentences in child AAE represented in this chapter are, without a doubt, taken to be a clear indication of children's use of negative concord as a pattern of AAE with little, if any, attention paid to developmental patterns, although negative concord is observed in developmental stages across languages. The fact is that, in the early stages, developing AAE-speaking children begin to produce negative concord in the way that children developing other varieties of English do. However, along the acquisition path, developing AAE speakers retain negative concord as part of their grammar and changes in the use may be related to patterns in frequency, as well as syntactic structure.

Coles (1998) and Coles-White, de Villiers, and Roeper (2004) analyzed negative concord in the language of 4- to 7-year-old developing AAE-speaking children to determine the extent to which children allowed a negative element in one part of a sentence to be connected to another negative in another phrase in a sentence. They argued that some structures serve as barriers preventing other negative elements from forming a concord relation. Green (2011) presented data to support the claim that 4- to 5-year-old developing AAE-speaking children do allow a negative to form concord with a following negative that is within a prepositional phrase, as in sentence (23):

(23) Who *didn't get no cookie* with *no rainbow sprinkles* on top? (133)

The children allowed the first two negatives *didn't* and *no* to form concord with the second *no* (in the prepositional phrase *with no rainbow sprinkles on top*); that is, they construed the sentence as meaning 'Who didn't get a cookie with rainbow sprinkles on top?' All of the work of negation is being done by one word: *didn't*. As such, *no* in the prepositional phrase *with no rainbow sprinkles* is not a separate negation; rather, it forms part of the concord with the preceding two negative elements. Further research is certainly needed to determine whether the construal of concord over prepositional boundaries is a developmental stage that changes as children mature.

The data reported from elicitation tasks and in spontaneous speech in works such as Stokes (1976), Coles (1998), Coles et al. (2004), and Green (2011) are extremely helpful in documenting the use of negation and negative marking in the path of development and, to some extent, in comprehension of negation in negative concord. However, the data are limited in providing insight into the pragmatic uses associated with negative concord constructions, which must be taken into consideration in evaluating children's negation structures and the acquisition path of the development of the negation system.

The search for instantiations of adult AAE "features" in child AAE without much consideration of syntactic, semantic, and pragmatic constraints in children's grammar has led to a strong tradition of comparing developmental AAE to adult AAE and making claims about whether developing AAE speakers are already exhibiting the full adult grammar. The approach has not been very insightful in generating and answering questions about the acquisition path of language development or about the nature of variation in developing AAE, which could be different from that in adult AAE.

Although it is clear that developing AAE-speaking children use negative concord in what could also be single negation contexts, there are no claims about the pragmatic contexts in which children use negation. Exploring the pragmatics of negation is important, especially in light of the different ways of emphasizing negation and the different uses of negation in speech situations. One erroneous view about negative concord is that it is used to express emphasis or that it is used pragmatically in speech situations to indicate emphasis. This erroneous view might persist because negative concord seems to be variable. In this way, the instances in which negation is marked at multiple points in the sentence might appear to be a strategy to express emphasis. On the other hand, when the speaker opts for single negation, it could appear that the "simple" form of negation correlates with non-emphasis. Simply put, however, negative concord on its own—no matter how many negative elements occur in the sentence—is not a strategy for emphasizing negation.

One way speakers can emphasize negation in negative concord structures is by placing stress on the negative elements, thereby pronouncing them with more force than is associated with other words in the sentence. The stress, not the negative concord alone, adds emphasis.

Negative modification can also be used to express negation. Labov (1972) discussed the strategy of using *no* to modify the object and add emphasis, as in (24):

(24) a. I think you like that picture.
      b. I don't like *no* picture. 'No, I do not like THAT picture.'

Note that the addition of "no" turns the sentence into a negative concord construction. The use of "no" does not contribute additional negative meaning; it contributes to the emphatic interpretation of the sentence. The emphasis is on not liking the particular picture that is the topic of the conversation. Green (2014) gives an overview of the negative modification strategy that is used to emphasize negation. Consider examples of *nothing* modification:

(25) a. Those people bought that big house.
      b. Those people didn't buy that big house *nothing*.
          'Those people DID NOT buy that big house.'
(26) a. Those people bought that big house.
      b. Those people didn't buy *nothing*.
          'Those people didn't buy THAT BIG HOUSE.'

It is the case that negative modification with "nothing" results in negative concord, and the sentence has two readings, one with emphasis on "did not" and the other with emphasis on "that big house." Such emphatic negation constructions have not been reported in children's speech, so it is not clear when children develop this strategy of distinguishing non-emphatic negative concord structures and emphatic concord constructions and how they begin to use negation in different pragmatic situations.

Another pragmatic strategy that is associated with the expression of negation in AAE is declarative negative auxiliary inversion (NAI). In Green (2014), "Declarative negative auxiliary inversion is characterized by an initial negated auxiliary followed by a negative indefinite DP, which together receive a negative concord interpretation," as in sentence (27):

(27) Don't nobody want to ride the bus.
      'Not a single person wants to ride the bus.'

Previous research on these constructions in AAE (e.g., Labov et al. 1968; Martin 1992; Sells, Rickford, and Wasow 1996; White-Sustaíta 2010) have placed considerable emphasis on the order of the negative elements: the negated auxiliary (e.g., *don't*) followed by an indefinite noun (e.g., *nobody*), especially given that declarative sentences in English generally begin with the subject before the verb. Green (2014) made a more precise observation about NAI than Labov (1972): Green links the meaning of the construction to the order of the negated auxiliary and negative indefinite subject. Labov's observation was that these constructions are "affective" or "emphatic." Further exploration into these constructions led Green (2014) to conclude that speakers use them as a strategy to underscore that the reference is to *absolutely zero* or *nothing/nobody*. In short, the NAI constructions communicate absolute negation, as conveyed in a statement such as "Nobody, I mean not a single person, wants to ride the bus" and can be argued to occur in certain pragmatic situations. Another example, *Didn't no money make it back to the community*, could be used to convey the following: "No money made it back to the community—not a single red cent!"

Given reports in the literature, NAI constructions appear to develop late, or, at least, they rarely occur in the speech of developing AAE speakers. Stokes (1976) reports one case of NAI in her collection of child AAE negation structures, and it is given in (28).

(28) Don't nobody know him. (122)

She observed that the construction was limited in both children's spontaneous production and their responses to elicitation tasks. Green (2011) also observed that children in her study did not produce NAI constructions in their spontaneous speech samples or in their negative elicitation tasks. However, children as young as 3;10 produced non-inversion constructions, in which the negated indefinite noun (e.g., *nobody*) precedes the negated auxiliary (e.g., *can't, didn't*):

(29) a. Nobody can't get in this. (4;11)
      b. Nobody didn't steal it. (3;10)

There are three possible explanations for why developing AAE-speaking children do not produce NAI constructions to the extent that they produce other general negative concord constructions. One explanation is that the NAI constructions are rare in adult AAE, so the input for NAI that children get from the adult community is limited. As a result, the children do not hear the constructions often enough to develop early proficiency in using them and subsequently do not produce them very often. A second explanation is that children do not produce NAI constructions because they are not proficient in the process of inversion, which is required to place the negated auxiliary (e.g., *can't*) in front of the indefinite noun (e.g., *nobody*). These first two explanations can be ruled out relatively quickly. NAI constructions are not rare in AAE, and the continued focus on them in the literature suggests that they are still productive. The second explanation is not really plausible because children have certainly begun the process of inversion in the context of questions, as already explained in this chapter and in other studies (see de Villiers, de Villiers, and Roeper 2011; Green 2011). Their limited production of NAI cannot be attributed to the lack of proficiency with inversion.

The third explanation for the late development of NAI is related to the pragmatic complexity of the construction. That is, the constructions are virtually absent from developmental child language samples because of the pragmatic complexity involved in the use of the structure. The pragmatic complexity explanation accounts for the fact that although children hear these constructions in their speech communities, they are not proficient in producing them because production and comprehension of the NAI structures require knowledge about the meaning of NAI and pragmatic contexts in which the constructions occur felicitously, as well as mastery of a number of syntactic processes. Children's spontaneous speech and responses to elicitation tasks show that these speakers have acquired negative concord as well as inversion of the auxiliary in questions; however, in early development, the children do not seem to put the two syntactic processes together to form NAI constructions. The inversion in NAI does not change the declarative force of the sentence; it has a pragmatic effect of triggering an absolutely zero meaning. In the developmental stage, children seem to be able to handle inversion, the process of producing an auxiliary before a subject, but they do not associate that process with pragmatic meaning of absolutely zero in negative concord structures.

In comparison to processes of producing inversion of the auxiliary in questions, the acquisition of inversion of the auxiliary in NAI is relatively late. Developing AAE-speaking children produce negative constructions in which the negative indefinite noun precedes the negated auxiliary first and must develop NAI constructions later. These two negation constructions are very similar, but the subtle differences in pragmatics may lead to their taking different acquisition paths. In addition, the subtle differences might suggest that the two constructions might not be equal variants, but more research that provides information about the contexts in which they are used is needed to come to a conclusion about their status as equal variants.

25.4 CONCLUSION

The discussion presented here shows that children's acquisition of variation in AAE may depend on a number of factors, such as pragmatic complexity. One reason that children may acquire patterns of question variation between inversion and non-inversion prior to patterns of variation with negative concord and NAI may be because of the pragmatic complexity of the absolutely zero reading of NAI. The two case studies on inversion highlight how different types of variation are subject to different patterns of acquisition based on, for example, pragmatic components of the grammar.

These studies also underscore the importance of research on syntactic variation in child AAE; not only does such research shed light on child AAE and language development, it also contributes insights into the nature of syntactic variation and its acquisition more generally. Questions and negation are especially fruitful areas of research because they exhibit variation at morphological and syntactic levels. Thus, questions and negation provide an opportunity to examine syntactic patterns in addition to just the occurrence or non-occurrence of individual features.

NOTES

1. In producing narratives, children systematically overtly marked Carl with –s in possessive contexts. We are addressing the question about whether proper names are overtly marked more often than common nouns.
2. The Diagnostic Evaluation of Language Variation (DELV) screening and norm-referenced tests are assessment tools designed for American English-speaking children (Seymour et al. 2003). One of the DELV's important advantages is that it will not over-identify non-SAE-speaking children as having speech disorders.

3. Prosodic properties refer to rhythm and stress in speech. See the chapter in this volume by Erik Thomas for a discussion of prosodic properties in AAE.

4. See White-Sustaíta (2012) for the argument that Non-Inv and ØAux in AAE questions are morphological variants of syntactically equivalent forms.

5. See Guy and Bayley (1995) for a similar analytical procedure on relative pronoun realization in English, which also has three possible outcomes (i.e., *that*, *wh*-word, or zero).

REFERENCES

Anderssen, Merete, Kristine Bentzen, and Marit Westergaard. 2010. *Variation in the Input: Studies in the Acquisition of Word Order*. Dordrecht, Netherlands: Springer.

Barbiers, Sjef. 2009. "Locus and Limits of Syntactic Microvariation." *Lingua* 119 (11): 1607–23.

Bellugi, Ursula. 1967. "The Acquisition of the System of Negation in Children's Speech." PhD diss., Harvard University.

Coles, D'Jaris R. 1998. "Barrier Constraints on Negative Concord in African American English." PhD diss., University of Massachusetts Amherst.

Coles-White, D'Jaris, Jill de Villiers, and Tom Roeper. 2004. "The Emergence of Barriers to *Wh*-movement, Negative Concord, and Quantification." In *Proceedings of the 28th Annual Boston University Conference on Language Development*. Vol. 1, edited by Alejan Brugos, Linnea Micciulla, and Christine E. Smith, 98–107. Somerville, MA: Cascadilla.

De Villiers, Jill G., Peter A. de Villiers, and Thomas Roeper. 2011. "*Wh*-questions: Moving beyond the First Phase." *Lingua* 121: 352–66.

Green, Lisa. 2002. *African American English: A Linguistic Introduction*. Cambridge: Cambridge University Press.

———. 2007. "Syntactic Variation." In *Sociolinguistic Variation: Theories, Method, and Application*, edited by Robert Bayley and Ceil Lucas, 76–124. Cambridge: Cambridge University Press.

———. 2011. *Language and the African American Child*. Cambridge: Cambridge University Press.

———. 2014. "Force, Focus, and Negation in African American English." In *Micro-Syntactic Variation in North American English*, edited by Raffaella Zanuttini and Laurence Horn, 115–42. Oxford: Oxford University Press.

Guy, Greg R., and Robert Bayley. 1995. "On the Choice of Relative Pronouns in English." *American Speech* 70 (2): 148–62.

Henry, Alison. 2002. "Variation and Syntactic Theory." In *The Handbook of Language Variation and Change*, edited by Jack K. Chambers, Peter Trudgill, and Natalie Schilling-Estes, 267–82. New York: John Wiley.

Henry, Alison, Rose MacLaren, John Wilson, and Cathy Finlay. 1997. "The Acquisition of Negative Concord in Non-Standard English." In *Proceedings of the 21st Annual Boston University Conference on Language Development*, Vol. 1, edited by Elizabeth Hughes, Mary Hughes, and Annabel Greenhill, 269–80. Somerville, MA: Cascadilla.

Labov, William. 1972. *Language in the Inner City: Studies in the Black English Vernacular*. Philadelphia: University of Pennsylvania Press.

Labov, William, Paul Cohen, Clarence Robins, and John Lewis. 1968. *A Study of the Non-Standard English of Negro and Puerto Rican Speakers in New York City*. 2 vols. Philadelphia: United States Office of Education Final Report, Research Project 3288.

Lavandera, Beatriz. 1978. "Where Does the Sociolinguistic Variable Stop?" *Language in Society* 7: 171–82.

Martin, Stefan, and Walt Wolfram. 1998. "The Sentence in African-American Vernacular English." In *African-American Vernacular English: Structure, History and Use*, edited by Salikoko S. Mufwene, John R. Rickford, Guy Bailey, and John Baugh, 11–36. New York: Routledge.

Paolillo, John C. 2002. *Analyzing Statistical Variation: Statistical Models and Methods*. Stanford, CA: CSLI Publications.

Renn, Jennifer. 2011. "Patterns of Style in the Language of African American Children and Adolescents." In *Proceedings of the 35th Annual Boston University Conference on Language Development*, Vol. 2, edited by Nick Danis, Kate Mesh, and Hyunsuk Sung, 513–25. Somerville, MA: Cascadilla.

Renn, Jennifer, and J. Michael Terry. 2009. "Operationalizing Style: Quantifying Style Shift in the Speech of African American Adolescents." *American Speech* 84: 367–90.

Reveron, Wilhelmina Wright. 1978. "The Acquisition of Four Rules by Black Preschool Children." PhD diss., The Ohio State University.

Sells, Peter, John R. Rickford, and Thomas Wasow. 1996. "An Optimality Approach to Variation in Negative Inversion in AAVE." *Natural Language and Linguistic Theory* 14: 591–627.

Seymour, Harry N., Thomas W. Roeper, and Jill de Villiers, with contributions by Peter de Villiers, 2003. *Development and Diagnostic Evaluation of Language Variation™ Screening Test (DELV™ Screening Test)*, Harcourt Assessments.

Steffensen, Margaret S. 1974. "The Acquisition of Black English." PhD diss., University of Illinois.

Stokes, Nona Hopson. 1976. "A Cross-Sectional Study of the Acquisition of Negation Structures in Black Children." PhD diss., Georgetown University.

Van Hofwegan, Janneke, and Walt Wolfram. 2010. "Coming of Age in African American English: A Longitudinal Study." *Journal of Sociolinguistics* 14: 427–55.

White-Sustaíta, Jessica. 2010. "Reconsidering the Syntax of Non-Canonical Negative Inversion." *English Language and Linguistics* 14: 429–55.

———. 2012. "The Syntax of Questions and Variation in Adult and Child African American English." PhD diss., The University of Texas.

Wolfram, Walt. 1969. *A Sociolinguistic of Detroit Negro Speech*. Washington, DC: Center for Applied Linguistics.

CHAPTER 26

NARRATIVE STRUCTURES OF AFRICAN AMERICAN CHILDREN

Commonalities and Differences

TEMPII B. CHAMPION AND ALLYSSA MCCABE

26.1 INTRODUCTION

NARRATIVES may be defined as the linguistic meeting grounds of culture, cognition, and emotion, and narratives often contain a chronological sequence of events often given in the past tense (McCabe 1991, 1997). Narratives refer to real or fictional past experiences. African American children's narratives are complex, varied, and both reflective of and contributive to African American culture. Labov and Waletsky (1967) were the first researchers to document narration by preadolescent (9- to 13-year-old) and adolescent (14- to 19-year-old) African American boys. They found that African American boys told narratives that began with orientation (see table 26.1 for definitions), gave a series of complicating events that built to a heavily evaluated climax (meaning that the narrator told the listener how strongly they felt about this experience), followed by a series of resolving events, and often ended with a coda that brought discourse from the past to the present. This form is what Peterson and McCabe (1983) termed a classic narrative pattern in their work on the development of narration in European North American (ENA) children. Kernan (1977) investigated personal and fictional narratives of African American girls aged 7 to 14 years and also found that even the youngest participants tended to follow the same classic narrative pattern by beginning with orientation statements.

In contrast to Labov (1972) and Kernan (1977), Michaels (1981, 1988, 1991) argued that African American children tell *topic-associating* narratives during Sharing Time[1] performances for their peers that are very different in form from the kind described by Labov and very different from those of their ENA peers, which are classic narratives

Table 26.1 Elements of High Point Analysis

Orientation: information that describes who, what, when, and where some past experience occurred (e.g., "Last Friday, my sister was playing outside in our back yard.").

Evaluation: statements or words that tell a listener what a narrator thinks about some aspect of an experience (e.g., "My sister is a clutz."). There are many types of evaluation, including negative events, sound effects ("Geeesh"), specific evaluative words (e.g., "clutz"), and repetition. As Gates (1988) defines *signifying* in African American culture, it is a type of narrative repetition, sometimes with a twist.

Some researchers (e.g., Reese et al. 2010) refer to some such information as "descriptors"—adjectives or adverbs that describe objects, characters, or actions (e.g., "ran *quick*"). Other types of evaluation in that study included "qualifiers"—adverbs or adjectives that amplify meaning (e.g., "that chair was *way too* small"). "Internal states" was a third type of evaluation (e.g., *thought, wanted*).

Complicating Action: Specific past tense events in a sequence that build to a high point, a climax (e.g., "She ran and fell down.").

High Point: A cluster of evaluative clauses that define the most important, most emotional point of a narrative (e.g., "She cried and cried.").

Resolution: Specific past tense events that occur in a sequence after the high point (e.g., "My mama put a Band-aid© on her knee.").

Coda: a statement at the end of a narrative that returns the conversation to the present (e.g., "Do you want to sign my cast?" at the end of a narrative about breaking an arm).

Dialogue is a reference to what was said directly and indirectly in the past and has been differentiated from other past nonverbal events by some (e.g., Ely and McCabe 1993; Reese et al. 2010).

Cohesion is an aspect of narration that is often studied in conjunction with the above aspects of High Point Analysis and looks at ways that narrators tend to integrate their narratives. This includes conjunctions and temporal (e.g., *first, next*) and causal (e.g., *because, so*) terms, as well as character introduction (e.g., "my sister).

Source: After Labov 1972; Peterson and McCabe 1983.

that Michaels called *topic-centered*. According to Michaels (1981), topic-centered narratives are "tightly organized, centering on a single clearly identifiable topic and thematic development … characteristically achieved through a linear progression of information" (428), whereas topic-associating narratives are a "discourse consisting of a series of implicitly associated personal anecdotes" (429).

The apparent contradiction in the literature regarding the structure of African American children's narration is due primarily to methodological differences among researchers; specifically, Michaels studied narratives performed for a group of other children and teachers, while other researchers (such as Hyon and Sulzby 1994; Kernan 1977; Labov 1972) studied narratives told to a single adult listener. Most of the rest of the research also looks at narratives told by African American children to single adult listeners. Champion, Seymour, and Camarata (1995) found that the 6- to 10-year-old African American children they studied produced narratives that displayed highly structured narratives in terms of two analyses: *High Point Analysis* and *Story Grammar*. Peterson and McCabe (1983) adapted High Point Analysis from Labov and Waletsky's

(1967) work for studying children's development of narrative structure. As Peterson and McCabe (1983) noted, the most advanced developmental structure is termed classic narrative structure and is a property of the narrative as a whole, with evaluative (meaning, feelings) as well as informative (orientation and action) content registered. Story Grammar (Stein and Glenn 1979) is adapted from an analysis of Russian folktales (Propp 1968) and looks at the extent to which a narrative conforms to a canonical story schema organized around the precipitation and resolution of problems. Champion et al. (1995) found that African American children most frequently produced classic personal narratives consisting of complete and/or complex sequences and that they did so at a rate higher than that of their ENA peers. Similarly, other researchers (Hyon and Sulzby 1994; Gorman et al. 2011) found that the majority of African American children's narratives were topic-centered. Reese et al. (2010) found that narratives told by low-income African American preschoolers were more likely to include descriptors (see table 26.1 for definitions), qualifiers, internal states, temporal and causal terms, character introduction, and dialogue than were narratives told by low-income ENA or Hispanic peers because of the way their mothers encouraged those children to elaborate narration (see also Gardner-Neblett, Pungello, and Iruka 2012, for review). Studies by Champion, Seymour and Camarata (1995), Hester (1996), Champion (1998), Champion et al. (1999), and Bloome et al. (2001) have shown that African American children produce a range of narrative structures depending on their audience, the task, and the prompts they are given.

Not only do researchers find variation in the structure of stories produced by individual African American children on different occasions or when given different tasks, systematic differences have also been documented for various groups of African American children. For example, there are gender and socioeconomic differences in narration among African American children: African American girls tell narratives with more complex propositions than African American boys and African American children from low-income homes tell narratives with more complex propositions than African American children from higher income homes (Mainess, Champion, and McCabe 2002). While girls of various ethnicities are often found to verbally outdo boys (Hyde and Linn 1988), the greater discourse elaboration of the low-income children is counter to the kind of social class (SES) effects found with older lower SES European American girls (e.g., Hemphill 1989). It is worth noting that Vernon-Feagans et al. (2001) also found low-income African American boys to tell the most elaborate narratives. This may reflect African American cultural values regarding elaborate storytelling noted below, cultural values that may be displaced by middle-class, school-based values of succinctness and explicitness; in particular, middle-class African American boys in the Mainess et al. (2002) study tended to be quite terse and extremely explicit in their narration.

Structural differences among African American students from different SES classes reflect profound SES and cultural differences in the kinds of stories valued by a community. Heath (1982, 1983) conducted an ethnographic study of three communities in the South: (a) a working-class African American community; (b) a middle-class community; and (c) a working-class ENA community. Heath's (1982, 1983) studies, like previous studies (Michaels 1981, 1991), observed children prior to beginning school. In each community, children were socialized differently toward literacy. The middle-class children were socialized toward school literacy from an early age. Children were read topic-centered stories and talked to in a way that matched discourse in school settings. That is, children were encouraged to pay attention to books and information derived from books and to answer questions about books. While the working-class ENA children were also read to, their parents did not link the events in books to events in life like their middle-class peers did. African American working-class children interacted socially with adults and children on a continuous basis. Children were not often given books as presents, had to learn how to insert themselves into conversations instead of being invited to participate, and were encouraged to draw analogies (e.g., "What's that like?") but not to name specific features that make two items or events alike. As far as narratives are concerned, once in school, both working-class ENA and African American children encountered notions about truthfulness and language appropriateness in stories that differed from those they were accustomed to at home. The working-class ENA community allowed only concise, factual stories, while the working-class African American community valued narratives that were more creative than factual and more contextualized than decontextualized; African American children expected their listeners to be able to figure out who they were talking about rather than needing to be told. These characteristics of narration in both working-class communities contradicted classroom expectations of elaborate, decontextualized, factual personal narratives, causing both groups of children to experience difficulty in the classroom.

In historical research on narration in African American communities, Zora Neale Hurston (1935, 65, 124) noted that occasions of storytelling are often referred to as putting down "lies," a means of signifying or showing off. Gates (1988, xxiv) expands on this: "signifyin(g) ... *is* repetition and revision, or repetition with a signal difference." As Gates defines it, then, signifying in narration may be considered to be an especially valued type of narrative evaluation in African American culture (see table 26.1). Gee (1985, 1986) underlines ways in which African American narration displays more of an implicit/oral rather than an explicit/literate style of narration, the latter a style in which repetition and other features of talk meant to be heard, rather than read, are prominent.

However, Hester (1996) complicated Gee's depiction of African American children demonstrating an oral style of narration. Hester examined two narratives each of African American fourth-grade students from a database of sixty-one African American children in an urban school setting. There were three different prompting tasks in the original study: having a conversation, retelling an event, and generating a narrative from pictures. Hester (1996) selected narratives about an accident scene and a fight because those topics had been found to evoke the most elaborative narratives in a prior study (Peterson and McCabe 1983). Hester found that African American children displayed flexibility by means of shifting back and forth from oral to literate styles in their narratives and that this was also accompanied in complex ways by code-switching from Standard American English (SAE) features to those typifying African American English (AAE) on the levels of grammar and phonology. Furthermore, shifting style from oral to literate form was task dependent; the story-generation task elicited topic-centered narratives from both children, while the story-retelling task was interpreted in different ways by the two.

Others (Hicks 1991; Hicks and Kanevsky 1992) have also found that African American children occasionally interpret narrative elicitation tasks differently from each other and from their non-African American peers. This is specifically due to some African American children telling topic-associating narratives on some occasions (Michaels 1991). Hicks and Kanevsky (1992) followed the journal writings of one African American first grader over a two-month period and found that he never engaged in topic-associating narration; individuals, as well as groups, should be the focus of further study regarding the intersection of narrative and literacy in their view.

In addition to gender and SES differences, African American children from Caribbean families differ from their peers whose families have resided in the United States for much longer. Children from families who immigrated to the United States from the Dominican Republic (Cuneo, McCabe, and Melzi 2008) are much less likely to tell the kind of classic, complete episodes told by the non-immigrant African American children studied by Champion et al. (1995). Haitian American children, for example, also tell narratives that are quite distinct from those told by African American children and employ devices commonly found in West African oral storytelling defined below (Champion, McCabe, and Colinet 2003).

The deep cultural roots of African American storytelling have been explored by a number of researchers, who provide alternative analyses of topic-associating narratives. Gee (1985, 1986) illuminated a strong poetic pattern of four-line stanzas in some of the performed narratives collected by Michaels. Craddock-Willis and McCabe (1996, 108) found that some of Michaels's narratives exhibited a cyclical pattern quite similar to the one described by Winton Marsalis (1994) for some African American jazz forms: "In ... rondo form ... a theme keeps coming back ... like going away from home and returning." One example of this, taken from Michaels's (1981) corpus, involves a 6-year-old African American boy who begins and ends his Sharing Time narrative with references to Thanksgiving dinner, but in between the two narrates a series of episodes improvising on Thanksgiving themes such as eating and family exchanges.

Champion (2003) prefers the term *performative narratives* to describe Michaels's (1981) topic-associating narratives. She links such a term to characteristics of oral storytelling in West Africa, as delineated by Okpewho (1992). Specifically, Okpewho (1992) notes that oral West African literature is characterized by (1) repetition; (2) parallelism, in which identical words are transposed within the same or adjacent statements; (3) piling and association, or heaping one detail onto another to build the whole narrative to a climax; (4) tonality, or intonation changes throughout the narrative; (5) ideophones, or the use of sound to convey meaning; (6) digression, or departure from the main theme of a narrative to address or comment to a person or object related to the theme of the narrative; (7) imagery, including metaphors; (8) allusion; and (9) symbolism. In Michaels's Sharing Time narratives, as well as in Champion's (2003) own corpus, African American children made frequent use of repetition, parallelism, and digression especially.

26.2 EXAMPLE OF WELL-FORMED NARRATIVES DISPLAYING DIVERSE STRUCTURE

Examples help clarify the contrast between topic-centered and topic-associating narratives, as well as those displaying Africanist features. The following examples are offered in order for readers to understand what well-structured African American narratives look like—their similarities (each of the three is lengthy and engaging) as well as their differences (different analyses are required in order to highlight the different structural forms the children were using). Examples of good narration are offered so that professionals working with African American children can compare their productions to these exemplary ones.

The following is a topic-centered, classic narrative produced by a 10-year-old African American boy (from Champion 2003):

Narrative 1 Topic-Centered, Classic Narrative by a 10-year-old African American boy analyzed using High Point Analysis (O = Orientation, CA = Complicating Action, EHP = Evaluation: High Point, RA = Resolving Action)

01 A: Have you ever had to get stitches?	
02 C: No but my little brother	O
03 C: He, um he was real young	O
04 C: I think he was two years old	O
05 C: An' my mother was drivin'	O
06 C: An' my uncle was in fron' seat	O
07 C: An' me an' my younger cousin dat lives in Baltimore,	O
08 C: She's eight years old	O
09 C: Her name is Whitney	O
10 C: An' my little brother was sittin' next to us	O
11 C: An' we was lookin' aroun'	O
12 C: An' he started playin' with da door	O
13 C: An' the door was unlocked	O
14 C: An' he opened the door an' fell out the car	CA
15 C: An' he was flippin' back	CA
16 C: An' he his head was busted open an' he had to get stitches	CA
17 C: An' me an my cousin Whitney was sittin' in the back o' the car cryin'	CA
18 C: Because he fell out the car	CA
19 C: My mother kep' goin'	CA
20 C: An' he did then my uncle Al said, "Rhonda stop the car"	CA
21 C: because he fell out the car	CA

Contrast the previous narrative, which was tightly focused on a single, dramatic incident, with the following topic-associating, performative narrative of multiple dental experiences produced by an 8-year-old African American girl. It has been analyzed and displayed using Gee's (1985, 1986) stanza analysis, showing a more-or-less regular pattern of about four lines for each subtopic discussed:

Narrative 2 Topic-associating, performative narrative of multiple dental experiences produced by an 8-year-old African American girl

Stanza 1
01 We went to the dentist before
02 and I was gettin' my tooth pulled
03 and the doc, the dentist said, "Oh, it's not gonna hurt."
04 and he was lying to me.

Stanza 2
05 It hurt.
06 It hurted so bad I coulda gone on screamin' even though I think some.
07 (I don't know what it was like.)
08 I was, in my mouth like, I was like, "Oh that hurt!"
09 He said no, it wouldn't hurt.

Stanza 3
10 Cause last time I went to the doctor, I had got this spray.
11 This doctor, he sprayed some spray in my mouth
12 and my tooth appeared in his hand.

Stanza 4
13 He put me to sleep,
14 and then, and then I woke up.
15 He used some pliers to take it out,
16 and I didn't know.

Stanza 5
17 So I had told my, I asked my sister how did, how did the man take (it out).
18 and so she said, "He used some pliers."
19 I said, "Nah, he used that spray."
20 She said, "Nope he used that spray to put you to sleep,
21 and he used the pliers to take it out."

Stanza 6
22 I was, like, "Huh, that's amazin'!"
23 I swear to God I was so amazed that, hum.
24 It was so amazing, right? that I had to look for myself,

Stanza 7
25 and then I asked him too.
26 and he said, "Yes, we, I used some pliers to take out your tooth,
27 and I put you to sleep, an, so you wouldn't know,
28 and that's how I did it."

Stanza 8

29 and I was like, "Ooouuu."

30 and then I seen my sister get her tooth pulled.

31 I was like, "Ooouuu"

32 Cause he had to put her to sleep to, hmm, to take out her tooth.

33 It was the same day she got her tooth pulled,

Stanza 9

34 and I was scared.

35 I was like, "EEEhhhmmm."

36 I had a whole bunch cotton in my mouth, chompin' on it

37 Cause I had to hold it to, hmm, stop my bleeding.

Stanza 10

38 I, one day I was in school.

39 I took out my own tooth.

40 I put some hot water in it the night, the, the night before I went to school.

41 and I was taking a test.

Stanza 11

42 And then it came out right when I was takin', when I finished the test.

43 And my teacher asked me, was it bleeding.

44 I said, "No It's not bleeding,

45 Cause I put some hot water on it."

Stanza 12

46 And so my cousin, he wanted to take out his tooth,

47 and he didn't know what to do,

48 so I told him.

49 "I'm a Pullin' Teeth Expert."

Stanza 13

50 "Pull out your own tooth,

51 but if you need somebody to do it,

52 Call me,

53 and I'll be over."

Note that both the aforementioned narratives by African American children contrast with that told by a 7-year-old Haitian American girl. The child produced it in English (she speaks primarily English but also Creole and a little French, as is typical for Haitian American children). Note that while it would be seen as rather a minimal two-event narrative in High Point Analysis and a descriptive sequence in Story Grammar (the most primitive developmental structure), Gee's (1985, 1986) stanza analysis displays its poetic form and Okpewho's (1992) Africanist analysis recognizes the rich use of repetition (rep), parallelism (par), and detailing (det) of her dress and hair and even the dress and hair of another flower girl:

Narrative 3 Stanza Analysis (Gee 1985, 1986) and Africanist Analysis (Okpewho 1992) of the dress and hair of the flower girl (Repetition = Rep, Parallelism = Par, and Detailing = Det)

Stanza 1

01 And once when I was in this wedding,	
02 I was a flower girl.	
03 And my friend Isadora too was a flower girl	Rep, Par
04 And I was wearing this dress.	
05 Can I show the dress?	Rep

Stanza 2

06 It was a long dress with a ribbon around it.	
07 It was a blue dress.	Rep, Par, Det
08 It was a long dress.	Rep, Par, Det
09 And they stuck something on it.	Det
10 I think it's still there.	
11 And it was a pretty dress.	Rep, Par, Det

Stanza 3

12 And I was sooo lucky	
13 Because there was a flower girl with curly hair	
14 —the same thing as me—	
15 at this other wedding.	

Stanza 4

16 This flower girl—they wore ugly dresses.	
17 They was green.	
18 And my friend said it was ugly dress.	Rep, Det

Stanza 5

19 Their hair was ugly.	Det
20 This girl had, her hair was like this, like that (demonstrates).	Det
22 And it was up	Det
23 And curled up	Rep, Par, Det
24 And curled.	Rep, Par, Det

Stanza 6

25 I, I was like ewww!	
26 I was glad I wasn't that flower girl!	
27 Because, and her hair was like, did she wake up in the morning?	

Stanza 7

28 And these other flower girls their hair was different from my hair.	Rep, Par
29 Cause theirs was curly too,	Rep, Det
30 But it was different.	Rep, Par, Det
31 It was skinny curly.	Rep, Par, Det

Stanza 8

32 But I don't like the dress	
33 And I don't like their hairs,	Rep, Par
34 But I like, but they had this same flower girl from at the wedding.	
35 It wasn't different.	Rep, Par, Det

Stanza 9

36 And the reception: Ghetto superstar.	
37 And I like "Ghetto Superstar"	Rep
38 It goes (singing), "Ghetto superstar, that is what you are."	Rep
39 Yeah, Mya sings it.	Det
40 Maya and Pras from the Fugees.	Det

Stanza 10

41 Can I show you the dress now?	Rep

26.3 AFRICAN AMERICAN NARRATION AND PEER CULTURE

Several studies document a rich involvement of peers in African American storytelling. As we now understand it, Michaels (1991) in effect documented the increased sense of a need to perform by young African American children addressing their narratives primarily to peers during Sharing Time. Goodwin (1982) documents the phenomenon of "instigating," a gossip-dispute activity in which working-class African American girls ages 7 through 13 inform a person that another person talked about her poorly behind her back. Such events sometimes lead to a restructuring of friendships. Similarly, Shuman (1986) looks at story exchanges among African American adolescent girls and finds that they often concern quarreling over who said what to whom, frequently going beyond what actually happened to elaborate blow-by-blow accounts of fights in which actual physical blows were never exchanged, accounts that are sometimes challenged by others who shared the experience and at other times accepted by audiences. Champion (2003) also found these types of narratives by girls in her study.

26.4 NARRATIVE CONTENT

Narrative structure is not the only important topic to consider in giving a full account of African American children's narratives; content of narratives is also worthy of analysis. In a series of articles and papers, Bloome et al. (2001) and Champion et al. (1999)

examined the production of oral and dictated narratives among three different groups of African American preschoolers over a span of four years. In order to collect young children's narratives, Bloome and colleagues developed a storytelling project that was conducted two times a week in a preschool and was designed to elicit children's narratives in a variety of settings and in both spoken and written modes (Champion 2003). Preschool and kindergarten children revealed their current and projected future identities (e.g., as members of their families, schools, community), among other important themes, in their narratives, as in the example below:

Narrative 4 Preschool and kindergarten children's current and projected future identities

---

01 **My mama** and me went to the grocery store to buy ice cream for **my sister.**

02 She had the chicken pox.

03 And then she gave them to me.

04 And then my mama came and I told her my sister dropped me off the bed with her feet.

05 And then **my daddy** said "why don't you sleep up there with her."

06 And I said no because she stinks.

07 She doesn't brush her teeth.

08 And then we went swimming with each other and we saw a shark.

09 And then I took my sister to the part.

10 We played for 20 minutes and

11 Then we went home and to bed.

12 I sleeped up there with my sister

13 Because I told her she could brush her teeth with me.

In addition, this narrative displays the kind of moral-centered theme that Champion (2003) has found in other samples of African American children's narration; here the moral value is being a good sister, which she exemplifies by taking her sister to the park and having her brush her teeth with her.

Another kind of content that has been noted in African American narratives is the relatively abundant inclusion of fantasy even in narratives that purport to be true. This is the central value of African American culture encapsulated in the use of *lies* to refer to stories, as was mentioned above (Hurston 1935). Relative to their Latino and Caucasian peers, African American first- and second-grade children included more fantasy in their retellings of a wordless picture book (Gorman et al. 2011). Having a boring life is no excuse for telling a boring narrative in the African American community (Craddock-Willis and McCabe 1996). At times, this strong cultural preference (Miller et al. 1990) has been documented to be misunderstood by white teachers and peers who criticize African American children for not telling the truth; one graduate student noted that an African American boy who met with such criticism retorted, "Some of the boring parts are true" (Craddock-Willis and McCabe 1996, 102).

26.5 DEVELOPMENT OF NARRATION IN AFRICAN AMERICAN CHILDREN

African American children's narration develops with age, though this has primarily been examined in African American children from low-income (lower SES) backgrounds. McGregor (2000) found that 3-year-olds used significantly fewer settings, complicating actions, and codas than did 4- and 5-year-olds in a story retelling task. Curenton and Justice (2004) found that 3-year-olds used fewer conjunctions than 4- and 5-year-olds and fewer mental and linguistic verbs than did 5-year-olds in a story retelling task, but that there were no differences between African American and ENA peers in any regard. There was a significant increase in length of narrative with age.

Price, Roberts, and Jackson (2006) studied preschool African American children's narrative skills exhibited in a retelling of "The Bus Story" (Renfrew 1991) using Story Grammar Analysis. These researchers included African American children from diverse SES backgrounds. The specific questions for the study were to describe and differentiate story grammar elements at two age levels: 4 and 5 years old. This was a longitudinal study and the research is part of a larger study of children recruited at ages 6 and 12 months. There were a total of sixty-five African American children (thirty-five girls and thirty boys) in this study from nine center-based childcare centers in two small southern cities. The results demonstrated growth in narrative structure of African American children between 4 years and 5 years of age. At age 4, children had fewer elements of story grammar, including introductions, initiating events, attempts to achieve a goal, and endings, although they did include some attempts to solve problems and some elements of endings. At age 5, kindergarten-entry children were using more total story elements.

Horton-Ikard (2009) researched the use of cohesive devices (personal reference, demonstrative reference, conjunctive, and lexical markers) produced by 7-, 8-, and 9-year-old African American English speakers. Participants for this investigation were thirty-three African American children (fifteen girls and eighteen boys). The children attended public schools in middle and upper SES communities in Wisconsin. Their elicitation procedure asked participants to retell a story or movie that they had previously encountered. The prompt used to initiate talk in this context included the following: "What's your favorite movie; tell me about your favorite movie." Counterintuitively, the average total number of t-units[2] decreased with age: Average t-units for 7-year-olds was 116.00; for 9-year-olds 112.00; and for 11-year-olds 108.00. However, the average *number* of t-units may not be the most appropriate measure of complexity. Nelson et al. (2004) argue that mean *length* of t-units (MLTU) is more sensitive to development; MLTU registers the elaboration of independent and dependent clauses in the t-unit. Using the latter, Horton-Ikard (2009) found that MLTU did significantly increase with age: 11-year-olds had significantly longer MLTU than their 7- and 9-year-old peers. Referential adequacy also significantly increased with age. Findings indicated that African American participants used all four forms of cohesive devices at rates comparable to their peers who spoke SAE.

26.6 NARRATION AND LITERACY SKILL

The relationship between African American children's narrative abilities and literacy skills is complicated and to some extent contradictory due to differences in the kinds of narratives examined; as noted above, different tasks elicit different kinds of narratives. On the one hand, consider the results of an important longitudinal study of Head Start children that began when those children were 4 years old and followed them through graduation or dropping out of school (Snow et al. 2007). Working with a sample that was 21 percent African American and 7 percent biracial (with the rest either Latino or ENA), the researchers used a series of pictures to prompt children entering kindergarten to tell a story and found that their ability to do so predicted fourth-, seventh-, and tenth-grade reading comprehension. (Note that African American children were not examined apart from children of other ethnicities in that study.) On the other hand, Vernon-Feagans et al. (2001) review their work looking at low-income Black children's storytelling and literacy. While they found that although African American children's joint construction of a fictional story with an older child—especially low-income African American boys—was often more elaborate and complicated than that of their female and middle-class peers, measures of these superior narrative skills were negatively related to literacy and other school-related and teacher-rating measures. (Note also that these researchers found a positive relationship between narratives skills and literacy for their Caucasian peers.) Vernon-Feagans and her colleagues argue that the aforementioned notable cultural preference for elaborating stories by adding fantasy to them led these African American children to eschew accurately paraphrasing a story just told to them—a story retelling task—in favor of making up a better one themselves—something teachers did not value. In short, African American children's narration advances their performance in literacy tasks when they are asked to tell, rather than to retell, a story.

Hester (2010) looked at the relationship between narratives and reading skills of African American children. She looked at sixty-one fourth-grade African American children, about half of whom spoke AAE and half SAE. The AAE speakers were from low-income, usually urban homes, while the SAE speakers were from middle-income, suburban homes and had college-educated parents. None of the children involved exhibited language impairment. She elicited two narratives from each child that were generated in response to two pictures. Hester analyzed these narratives using Peterson and McCabe's (1983) High Point Analysis. Furthermore, she used the Reading Comprehension subtest of the Wechsler Individual Achievement Test (WIAT; Wechsler 1992) to classify children with reading disability (one–two years below grade level) or children who were reading on age level or up to two years above grade level. Hester (2010) found no effect for dialect (for extensive description of the features of AAE; see Mills and Washington, this volume; Newkirk-Turner, Horton, and Stockman, this volume; Oetting, this volume; van Hofwegen, this volume; Wyatt and Fullerton, this volume), but she did find a significant effect of reading level. Thus, dialect was not found to relate to children's reading difficulty, but narrative ability did. Specifically, African American children with reading difficulty told stories with significantly fewer evaluations, complicating actions, high points, resolutions, and codas than did their African American peers who read on or above age level. Of these components of high point structure, resolution statements were the single best predictor of reading comprehension.

Klecan-Aker and Caraway (1997) studied the relationship between storytelling ability and reading comprehension for eighty middle-class fourth- and sixth-grade African American students with typical development. She asked children to make up a story in response to a picture and analyzed t-units and story grammar components. She used the Iowa Test of Basic Skills (Hieronymous, Hoover, and Lindquist 1986) Reading Subtest grade equivalency score as a measure of reading achievement. She found that children whose narratives were at a higher developmental level had significantly higher reading achievement than their peers with lower narrative skill.

In short, the narrative skill of African American children has been demonstrated to correlate with reading comprehension so long as the narrative task in question is one involving storytelling (Klecan-Aker and Caraway 1997; Snow et al. 2007; Hester 2010), rather than story retelling (Vernon-Feagans et. al 2001). Gardner-Neblett, Pungello, and Iruka (2012) explore the ways in which African American children's narrative skills could be leveraged to bolster their reading comprehension.

26.7 CLINICAL APPLICATIONS

Professionals such as teachers and speech-language clinicians need to be very careful to distinguish cultural differences from cultural deficits, as both misdiagnosing differences as deficits and mistakenly attributing deficits to cultural differences—in effect denying children services that could benefit them—are both unacceptable mistakes that do not serve African American children well. Bliss, Covington, and McCabe (1999) offer a way of summarizing the variations in form of typical and atypical African American narration (see figure 26.1).

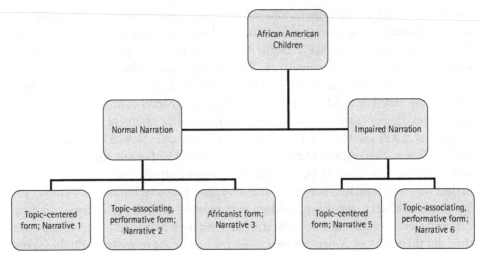

FIGURE 26.1 Possible narrative performances from African American children.

The following narrative is from an African American boy aged 4 years, eight months, diagnosed with Language Impairment and impaired narration:

Narrative 5 African American boy aged 4 years, 8 months, diagnosed with language impairment and impaired narration (A = Adult, C = Child)

01 A: My neighbor had his car stolen last night. He went outside and it was gone. He was really mad. Have you ever had anything stolen?

02 C: Didn't. I was big. I was . . . I was a baby. I didn't want speak.

03 A: Do you know anybody who had something stolen?

04 C: My daddy. Him, my, our car. And him got it back. Him car got stolen and him got it back. Him got it back. It, it was a hole. When him got it back, there was a hole. When him got it back, there was a hole. Him got it back. He took the speakers in their hole. There was a hole for the speakers. Bigger. It was...it was a speaker right here and a speaker right there. And when it got stolen now, him got speakers back. Go through here.

05 A: He put the speakers back?

06 C: No, him got them back. But he didn't put them here.

Although the narrative is topic-centered around the stolen car, there are very few actions (car got stolen from father, father got car back) and mostly repetitive descriptions of a hole. The construction "Him got it back" is not AAE; rather it is also disordered in terms of referencing. And also consider Narrative 6, which is an example of an impaired narrative that is topic-associating in form:

Narrative 6 Topic–associating, impaired narrative of an African American boy aged 4 years, 7 months

01 No . . . when I get some pets, they be, they be using it in our house.

02 Because we be taking them outside and they don't be move because they don't need to move.

03 Ain't no need to use the bathroom though.

04 When they come in there, they use it.

05 We be going outside quickest.

06 We be running outs . . . out the door.

07 We be on the door, and we run out through it.

08 And our pappy in the back, uh, and she, uh, he use it.

09 He got a big cage for all of them.

10 We got lots of dogs.

11 Once when we have five dogs and none ran away.

12 Then we played with them.

13 We brought them some chew toys, and they chew them when they hungry.

14 They get . . . they, we, be seeing they full. That's the end of my story.

This narrative is meaningful (Bliss et al. 1999), and it has elements of chronological structure in the first sequence until "We got lots of dogs," where a topic-associating pattern emerges. Both sections are connected through the thread "dogs," which makes it a topic-associating narrative (Michaels 1981). This narrative has characteristics of AAE with the use of the habitual *be* and double negatives. However, the sentence "We be on the door, and we run through it" appears to not be appropriate in AAE and could be an indicator of SLI, as one SLI characteristic that has been repeatedly noted is problems with verb formation (Paul and Norbury 2012).

A professional seeking to determine whether the narration of an African American child is typical or not should first examine the language the child uses; presence of nonstandard constructions not typical of AAE is a sign of problems. If the professional is not a speaker of AAE, s/he should consult an adult who is. Whether or not such morphosyntactic problems occur, the next step is to determine whether the narrative is topic-centered, performative, or one displaying Africanist features of repetition, parallelism, and detailing, rather than concern for a plotted action sequence. Once professionals know what kind of narrative the child is telling, they can then determine whether it is well-developed in comparison to those of peers or not by comparison to examples given above or from their own sample. More research focusing on African American children is needed in this area to provide professionals with the kind of quantitative norms that would be useful in assessment of such culturally relevant narrative forms as that of personal narration (Champion 2003).

Knowledge about the narration of African American children can influence not only assessment of narration but also therapeutic intervention. For example, McGregor (2000) found not only that preschool AAE speakers can be influenced by the narratives of their peers but that this influence can be harnessed for clinical benefit for African American children with language delay in cases in which clinicians are not from the African American child's cultural background. In another project specifically designed to improve the narrative writing skills of severely remedial third- and fourth-grade African American children, Lee et al. (2004) capitalized on much of what we have reviewed above. They used pictures by the famed African American artist Annie Lee that depicted scenes relevant to African American life (e.g., a Black church, the historical act of jumping the broom) to elicit written narratives. Children were encouraged to work together. Use of African American Discourse Features was appreciated. Lee et al. (2004) present examples and analysis of many of the engaging written stories produced by the children. The authors make the point that typical instruction of "severely remedial students" focuses on surface features of writing (spelling, punctuation) and gives little or no attention to the deep narrative structural level skills promoted by their program, a situation that quite probably ensures that such students remain severely remedial writers.

26.8 CONCLUSION

African American children develop the ability to tell narratives between the ages of 3 and 11 years. This development involves the ability to produce narratives that vary in terms of structure, depending on task and audience. To fully appreciate that structure requires employing diverse narrative analyses. While African American children usually tell classically formed stories, they also occasionally tell performative ones. Not all African American children tell the same kinds of narratives; that is, there are differences among African American children due to gender, socioeconomic class, and culture of origin of their parents. African American children often involve their peers in storytelling. Not only does the structure of narration in this community require commentary, but the typical content of narration does as well. In particular, African American narratives involve relatively frequent inclusion of fantasy even in factual stores, along with mention of children's identities, and presentation of morals (e.g., "I am a good big sister"). Storytelling (though not necessarily retelling) is related to literacy acquisition in African American children, and the information in this chapter may be used in both diagnosis and treatment of African American children who lag behind their peers in this critical ability. Storytelling in the African American community both reflects and contributes to African American culture in myriad deep and meaningful ways.

NOTES

1. Sharing Time is an event in many preschools in which children sit in a circle and listen as, one at a time, each child tells about an important experience they had.
2. "A T-unit was defined as a main clause with all of its subordinate clauses attached to it" (Hunt 1965, 1970, as cited in Horton-Ikard 2009).

REFERENCES

Bliss, Lynn S., Zenara Covington, and Allyssa McCabe. 1999. "Assessing the Narratives of African American Children." *Contemporary Issues in Communication Science and Disorders* 26: 160–67.

Bloome, David, Tempii Champion, Laurie Katz, M. B. Morton, and R. Muldrow. 2001. "Spoken and Written Narrative Development: African American Preschoolers as Storytellers and Storymakers." In *Literacy in African American Communities*, edited by J. L. Harris, A. G. Kamhi, and K. E. Pollock, 45–77. Mahwah, NJ: Lawrence Erlbaum.

Champion, Tempii B. 1998. "Tell Me Somethin' Good: A Description of Narrative Structures among African American Children." *Linguistics and Education* 9 (3): 251–86.

———. 2003. *Understanding Storytelling among African American Children*. Mahwah, NJ: Erlbaum.

Champion, Tempii B., Laurie Katz, Ramona Muldrow, and Rochelle Dail. 1999. "Storytelling and Storymaking in an Urban Preschool Classroom: Building Bridges from Home to School Culture." *Topics in Language Disorders* 19 (3): 52–67.

Champion, Tempii B., Allyssa McCabe, and Yvette D. Colinet. 2003. "The Whole World Could Hear: The Structure of Haitian American Children's Narratives." *Imagination, Cognition, and Personality* 22 (4): 381–400.

Champion, Tempii B., Harry Seymour, and Stephen Camarata. 1995. "Narrative Discourse of African American Children." *Journal of Narrative and Life History* 5 (4): 333–52.

Craddock-Willis, Karen, and Allyssa McCabe. 1996. "Improvising on a Theme: Some African American Traditions." In *Chameleon Readers: Teaching Children to Appreciate all Kinds of Good Stories*, edited by Allyssa McCabe, 98–115. New York: McGraw Hill.

Cuneo, C. Nicholas, Allyssa McCabe, and Gigliana Melzi. 2008. "*Mestizaje*: Afro-Caribbean and Indigenous Costa Rican Children's Narratives and Links with other Traditions." In *Spanish-Language Narration and Literacy: Culture, Cognition, and Emotion*, edited by Allyssa McCabe, Alison L. Bailey, and Gigliana Melzi, 237–72. Cambridge: Cambridge University Press.

Curenton, Stephanie M., and Laura M. Justice. 2004. "African American and Caucasian Preschoolers' Use of Decontextualized Language: Literate Language Features in Oral Narratives." *Language, Speech, and Hearing Services in Schools* 35: 240–53.

Gardner-Neblett, Nicole, Elizabeth P. Pungello, and Iheoma U. Iruka. 2012. "Oral Narrative Skills: Implications for the Reading Development of African American Children." *Child Development Perspectives* 6 (3): 218–24.

Gates, Henry Louis, Jr. 1988. *The Signifying Monkey: A Theory of African-American Literary Criticism*. New York: Oxford University Press.

Gee, James Paul. 1985. "The Narrativization of Experience in the Oral Style." *Journal of Education* 167 (1): 9–35.

———. 1986. "Units in the Production of Narrative Discourse." *Discourse Processes* 9: 391–422.

Goodwin, Marjorie Harness. 1982. "'Instigating': Storytelling as Social Process." *American Ethnologist* 9 (4): 799–816. DOI: 10.1525/ae.1982.9.4.02a00110.

Gorman, Brenda K., Christine E. Fiestas, Elizabeth D. Pena, and Maya Reynolds Clark. 2011. "Creative and Stylistic Devices Employed by Children during a Storybook Narrative Task: A Cross-Cultural Study." *Language, Speech, and Hearing Services in Schools* 423: 167–81.

Heath, Shirley Brice. 1982. "What No Bedtime Story Means: Narrative Skills at Home and School." *Language in Society* 11: 49–76.

———. 1983. *Ways with Words: Language, Life, and Work in Communities and Classrooms.* Cambridge: Cambridge University Press.

Hemphill, Lowry. 1989. "Topic Development, Syntax, and Social Class." *Discourse Processes* 12: 267–86.

Hester, Eva Jackson. 1996. "Narratives of Young African American Children." In *Communication Development and Disorders in African American Children*, edited by A. Kamhi, D. Pollack, and J. Harris, 227–45. Baltimore, MD: Brookes.

———. 2010. "Narrative Correlates of Reading Comprehension in African American Children." *Contemporary Issues in Communication Science and Disorders* 37: 73–85.

Hicks, Deborah. 1991. "Kinds of Narrative Genre: Genre Skills among First Graders from Two Communities." In *Developing Narrative Structure*, edited by Allyssa McCabe and Carole Peterson, 97–124. Hillsdale, NJ: Lawrence Erlbaum.

Hicks, Deborah, and Rhoda Kanevsky. 1992. "Ninja Turtles and Other Superheroes: A Case Study of One Literacy Learner." *Linguistics and Education* 4: 59–105.

Hieronymous, Albert N., H. D. Hoover, and E. F. Lindquist. 1986. *Iowa Tests of Basic Skills* (Form G and H). Chicago: Riverside.

Horton-Ikard, RaMonda. 2009. "Cohesive Adequacy in the Narrative Samples of School-Age Children Who Use African American English." *Language, Speech, and Hearing Services in the Schools* 40: 393–402.

Hurston, Zora Neale. 1935. *Mules and Men.* New York: Harper and Row.

Hyde, Janet Shibley, and Marcia C. Linn. 1988. "Gender Differences in Verbal Ability: A Meta-Analysis." *Psychological Bulletin* 104: 53–69.

Hyon, Sunny, and Elizabeth Sulzby. 1994. "African American Kindergartners' Spoken Narratives: Topic Associating and Topic Centered Styles." *Linguistics and Education* 6: 121–52.

Kernan, Keith. 1977. "Semantic and Expressive Elaboration in Children's Narratives." In *Child Discourse*, edited by Susan Ervin-Tripp and Claudia Mitchell-Kernan, 91–102. New York: Academic.

Klecan-Aker, Joan S., and Teresa H. Caraway. 1997. "A Study of the Relationship of Storytelling Ability and Reading Comprehension in Fourth and Sixth Grade African-American Children." *European Journal of Disorders of Communication* 32: 109–25.

Labov, William. 1972. *Language in the Inner City.* Philadelphia: University of Pennsylvania Press.

Labov, William, and Joshua Waletsky. "Narrative Analysis: Oral Versions of Personal Experience." In *Essays on the Verbal and Visual Arts*, edited by J. Helm, 12–44. Seattle: University of Washington Press.

Lee, Carol D., Ruby Rosenfeld, Ama R. Mendenhall, and Brendesha Tynes. 2004. "Cultural Modeling as a Frame for Narrative Analysis." In *Narrative Analysis: Studying the Development of Individuals in Society*, edited by Colette Daiute and Cynthia Lightfoot, 39–62. Thousand Oaks, CA: Sage.

Mainess, Karen J., Tempii B. Champion, and Allyssa McCabe. 2002. "Telling the Unknown Story: Complex and Explicit Narration by African American Preadolescents—Preliminary Examination of Gender and Socioeconomic Issues." *Linguistics in Education* 13 (2): 151–73.

Marsalis, Winton. 1994. "Remarks." *The Berkshire Eagle* 103: 84, July 22.

McCabe, Allyssa. 1991. "Editorial." *Journal of Narrative and Life History* 1 (1): 1–2.

———. 1997. "Developmental and Cross-Cultural Aspects of Children's Narration." In *Narrative Development: Six Approaches*, edited by Michael Bamberg, 137–74. Hillsdale, NJ: Lawrence Erlbaum.

McGregor, Karla K. 2000. "The Development and Enhancement of Narrative Skills in a Preschool Classroom: Towards a Solution to Clinician–Client Mismatch." *American Journal of Speech-Language Pathology* 9: 55–71.

Michaels, Sarah. 1981. "Sharing Time: Children's Narrative Styles and Differential Access to Literacy." *Language and Society* 10: 423–42.

———. 1988. "Sharing Time." In *Classroom Discourse: The Language of Teaching and Learning*, edited by Courtney Cazden, 7–28. Portsmouth, NH: Heinemann.

———. 1991. "The Dismantling of Narrative." In *Developing Narrative Structure*, edited by Allyssa McCabe and Carole Peterson, 303–52. Hillsdale, NJ: Erlbaum.

Miller, Peggy J., Randolph Potts, Heidi Fung, Lisa Hoogstra, and Judy Mintz. 1990. "Narrative Practices and the Social Construction of Self." *American Ethnologist* 17 (2): 292–311.

Nelson, Nickola W., Christine M. Bahr, Adelia Van Meter, and Kathryn Kinnucan-Welsch. 2004. *The Writing Lab Approach to Language Instruction and Intervention*. Baltimore, MD: Brookes.

Okpewho, Isidore. 1992. *African Oral Literature: Backgrounds, Character, and Continuity*. Bloomington: Indiana University Press.

Paul, Rhea, and Courtenay F. Norbury. 2012. *Language Disorders from Infancy through Adolescence*. 4th ed. St. Louis, MO: Mosby Elsevier.

Peterson, Carole, and Allyssa McCabe. 1983. *Developmental Psycholinguistics: Three Ways of Looking at a Child's Narrative*. New York: Plenum.

Price, Johanna R., Joanne E. Roberts, and Sandra C. Jackson. 2006. "Structural Development of the Fictional Narratives of African American Preschoolers." *Language, Speech, and Hearing Services in Schools* 37: 178–90.

Propp, Vladimir. 1968. *Morphology of the Folktale*. Austin: University of Texas Press.

Reese, Elaine, Diana Leyva, Alison Sparks, and Wendy Grolnick. 2010. "Maternal Elaborative Reminiscing Increases Low-Income Children's Narrative Skills Relative to Dialogic Reading." *Early Education and Development* 21: 318–42. Doi: 10.1080/10409289.2010.481552.

Renfrew, Catherine. 1991. *The Bus Story Language Test: A Test of Continuous Speech*. Oxford: Author.

Shuman, Amy. 1986. *Storytelling Rights: The Uses of Oral and Written Texts by Urban Adolescents*. Cambridge: Cambridge University Press.

Snow, Catherine E., Michelle V., Patton O. Tabors, and Stephanie R. Harris. 2007. *Is Literacy Enough?: Pathways to Academic Success for Adolescents*. Baltimore, MD: Brookes.

Stein, Nancy, and Christine Glenn. 1979. "An Analysis of Story Comprehension in Elementary School Children." In *New Directions in Discourse Processing*, edited by Roy Freedle, 53–120. Norwood, NJ: Ablex.

Vernon-Feagans, Lynne, Carol Scheffner Hammer, Adele Miccio, and Elizabeth Manlove. 2001. "Early Language and Literacy Skills in Low-Income African American and Hispanic Children." In *Handbook of Early Literacy Research*, edited by Susan B. Neuman and David K. Dickinson, 192–210. New York: Guilford.

Wechsler, David. 1992. *Wechsler Individual Achievement Test*. New York: The Psychological Corporation.

CHAPTER 27

SOME SIMILARITIES AND
DIFFERENCES BETWEEN
AFRICAN AMERICAN
ENGLISH AND SOUTHERN
WHITE ENGLISH IN
CHILDREN

JANNA B. OETTING

27.1 INTRODUCTION

THIS chapter highlights some of the similarities and differences between *African American English* (AAE) and *Southern White English* (SWE) documented in our studies of Louisiana children, aged 4 to 6 years. Our training is in child language acquisition and the cross-linguistic study of a clinical condition referred to as *specific language impairment* (SLI). SLI can be defined as an impairment of language in the absence of sensory deficits, general developmental delays or autism, and neurological impairment (Rice 2007; Schwartz 2009). Repeatedly and across many different languages, grammar differences between children with and without SLI have been found to be quantitative rather than qualitative, with the affected structures varying as a function of the type of language (or dialect) being acquired (Leonard 2014). Given this, most of our studies are designed to test the hypothesis that frequency-based grammar differences exist between children with SLI and their same-dialect-speaking, typically developing peers. In this chapter, we present data from studies that pertain to typically developing, child AAE and SWE speakers, with the caveat that our findings are byproducts of studies that were not designed to fully describe child AAE or SWE.

We use the terms *AAE* and *SWE* as labels for the children's dialects because the children produce many of the same nonmainstream grammar forms that have been documented for adults who have been described as speaking AAE or SWE (see Bailey 2001; Bernstein, Nunnally, and Sabino 1997; Cukor-Avila 2001; Montgomery and Bailey 1986; Wolfram 1991; Wolfram and Schilling-Estes 1998). Our working assumption is that child AAE and SWE include surface grammar forms that may or may not be similar to each other or to those produced in mainstream dialects of English such as General American English or British English. We use the following nomenclature to classify AAE- and SWE-speaking children's productions of different types of grammatical forms: overtly marked mainstream forms (e.g., "I *am* walking," as defined as a grammatical form that is produced in adult AAE, SWE, and General American English); overtly marked nonmainstream forms (e.g., "They *was* walking," as defined as a grammar form that is produced in adult AAE or SWE, but not in adult General American English); and nonmainstream zero-marked forms (e.g., "He Ø walking"; as defined as a zero-marked or omitted grammar form that can be zero marked or omitted in adult AAE or SWE but not in adult General American English).

We also use the terms *dialect-specific* to refer to aspects of language use that are specific to a dialect and *dialect-universal* to refer to aspects of use that have been documented across many dialects of English. For example, children's use of relative clause markers presents both dialect-specific and dialect-universal aspects. The rate at which subject and object relative pronouns are zero marked or omitted may be characterized as dialect-specific because different English dialects (including American and British, among others) show different rates of zero marking; whereas the influence of an antecedent's humanness on a speaker's selection of particular types of relative pronouns (*who, that,* Ø, and so on) may be viewed as dialect-universal because an antecedent's humanness has been found to influence the selection of relative pronouns in multiple English dialects.

Most of our AAE data come from children living in one of three rural parishes (Ascension, Assumption, West Baton Rouge) along the Mississippi River in southeastern Louisiana; however, a few of our AAE studies have been completed with children living in the larger metropolitan parish of East Baton Rouge. The SWE data come from children who live in the same rural parishes and attend the same schools as the AAE-speaking rural children. Although we initially used race to classify a child's dialect within our studies, our goal has always been to develop methods by which a child's dialect can be classified independent of race. This goal has led us to classify a child's dialect type (AAE versus SWE versus other) through both perceptual and statistical methods. The perceptual method focuses on multiple aspects of a child's dialect (i.e., phonology, morphosyntax, semantics, paralinguistics), and the statistical method is based on the rate at which a child produces nonmainstream grammar forms. These two methods of dialect classification are completed independently from each other. The former is completed with three highly trained raters within two or three days at the end of a study, whereas the latter involves a large team of student transcribers and coders, begins at the time a language sample is collected, and continues for many months until transcription and coding are deemed reliable.

The perceptual method asks the raters to independently listen to one- to ten-minute audio excerpts of each child's language sample. As they listen, they classify the child's dialect using two Likert scales, one for AAE and another for SWE. The scoring form also allows raters to indicate a dialect that differs from AAE and SWE, such as General American English, Cajun English, or Creole English. During the task, the raters are blind to the age, gender, and race of the children, and excerpts are selected so that they are void of content (e.g., names, skin color) that may bias a rater to select one type of dialect over another.

In a study of ninety-three children, 85 percent of the children's dialects were classified by three raters in the same way when one-minute excerpts were used (Oetting and McDonald 2002). This percentage increased to 97 percent when ten-minute excerpts were used and dialect classification was defined as agreement between two of the three raters. The raters reported that their dialect classifications were heavily tied to the children's use of phonology; however, they also used the children's morphosyntax, paralinguistic features, and vocabulary in 61 percent, 41 percent, and 24 percent of the excerpts, respectively. Other child studies have also found the listener judgment method to lead to high levels of dialect classification consistency (Cottrell et al. 2012; Garrity and Oetting 2010; Horton-Ikard and Weismer 2005; Moland 2011; Oetting and Richardson 2012; Pruitt and Oetting 2009).

The statistical method is based on a child's production of thirty-five or thirty-six nonmainstream grammar forms during an examiner-child language sample of one-hundred to two-hundred utterances. The focus on a speaker's rate of nonmainstream grammar forms is consistent with other child and adult dialect studies (for child, see Horton-Ikard and Weismer 2005; Washington and Craig 1994; for adult, see Dubois and Horvath 1998; Wolfram and Thomas 2002). The samples are collected in a quiet room at each child's school. Once transcribed, the children's nonmainstream grammar forms are coded, counted, and divided by the number of utterances or words analyzed. The data are then subjected to a discriminant function analysis that weights and combines each child's relative frequency of each nonmainstream grammar form for maximum separation of the dialects. Again, in a study of ninety-three children, when a discriminant function included all of the coded nonmainstream grammar forms, 97 percent of the children's dialects were accurately classified as AAE or SWE (Oetting and McDonald 2001). Moreover, when the perceptual, listener judgment method and the statistical, language sample method were compared, the dialect classifications of 90 percent of the children were the same (Oetting and McDonald 2002).

Findings from these studies give us confidence that our AAE and SWE child dialects are perceptually and grammatically distinct. Nevertheless, the findings also show that some (approximately 10 percent) children's dialects are difficult to classify. These dialects need to be further explored. As an example, Oetting and Garrity (2006) compared AAE- and SWE-speaking children whose dialects were perceived as presenting a Cajun or Creole English influence to those whose dialects were not perceived to present this influence. To examine the children's dialects further, the adult literature was used to identify five morphosyntactic and six phonological features that are produced at elevated rates in adult varieties of Cajun and Creole English (Cheramie 1998; Dubois and Horvath 1998, 1999, 2003a, 2003b; Rubrecht 1971; Walton 1994). Although no group differences were observed for morphosyntax, AAE- and SWE-speaking children perceived as presenting some Cajun or Creole English influence within their dialects produced higher rates of the six phonological features than the others, with statistically significant group differences documented for two (i.e., word initial nonaspirated stops involving /p, t, k/ in words such as *pat* and glide weakening in vowels, as in the word *see*). These findings highlight the variability that can exist within various groups of AAE and SWE child speakers in Louisiana and perhaps elsewhere.

When comparing child AAE to child SWE, it is critical to document children's socioeconomic and psycholinguistic profiles to establish group equivalency and to determine the generalizability of a study's findings to other groups of children. Consistent with other studies (e.g., Dollaghan et al. 1999; Hadley and Holt 2006; Redmond, Thompson, and Goldstein 2011; Rice, Wexler, and Hershberger 1998; Schuele and Tolbert 2001), we use maternal education as a proxy for a child's socioeconomic status, collect family history information and hearing screenings, and administer a battery of tests to help rule in or out the presence of childhood language impairment. The battery includes a test of nonverbal intelligence and tests of vocabulary, grammar, and articulation. Table 27.1 presents the psycholinguistic profiles of

Table 27.1 Psycholinguistic Profiles of Typically Developing Children, by Dialect

	AAE	SWE
Age in months	64.98 (9.14)	62.18 (15.11)
Nonverbal IQ[a]	103.90 (8.55)	104.47 (9.09)
PPVT[b]	99.49 (10.42)	103.55 (9.51)
TOLD-P[c]	99.49 (9.82)	102.58 (12.40)
MLU[d]	5.79 (1.20)	5.33 (.83)

[a] Standard score of the *Columbia Mental Maturity Scale* (Burgmeister, Blum, and Lorge 1972) or converted standard score from the *Leiter International Performance Scale–Revised* (Roid and Miller 1998); M = 100; SD = 15.
[b] Standard score on the *Peabody Picture Vocabulary Test-R* (Dunn and Dunn 1981) or *Peabody Picture Vocabulary Test-III* (Dunn and Dunn 1997); M = 100; SD = 15.
[c] Syntactic quotient on the *Test of Language Development-Primary: Revised* (Newcomer and Hammill 1988) or *Test of Language Development-Primary: Third Edition* (Newcomer and Hammill 1997); M = 100; SD = 15.
[d] Mean length of utterance in morphemes as calculated from a language sample.
Source: Data from children studied in Oetting and Newkirk 2008.

ninety-nine typically developing AAE- and SWE-speaking children from Oetting and Newkirk (2008). As confirmed by analyses of variance, the AAE and SWE groups did not differ in their ages or standardized tests scores. Although a group difference was detected in their mean length of utterance (MLU) levels, with the AAE MLU higher than the SWE MLU, the effect size was small (eta^2 = .04). Together, these findings establish group equivalency and allow linguistic differences observed in the data to be attributed to the children's dialects rather than to differences between the children's psycholinguistic abilities.

27.2 Some Similarities between Child AAE and SWE

Group comparison studies are designed to identify differences between groups rather than similarities. Given this, it is with caution that we highlight a few similarities between child AAE and SWE that we have documented. This list should not be considered exhaustive, and it also needs to be considered within the context of the language sampling method, which is experimentally controlled.

The first similarity we have documented between AAE- and SWE-speaking children is the frequency at which contexts for grammatical forms occur within their language samples. For example, Ross, Oetting, and Stapleton (2004) found that AAE- and SWE-speaking children produce similar rates of utterances describing the simple past or preterite in their samples (AAE = 13 percent; SWE = 15 percent). This similarity was documented even though the AAE child speakers produced a greater range of nonmainstream forms to express the simple past than did the child SWE speakers. Also, in Roy, Oetting, and Moland (2013), AAE- and SWE-speaking children were found to produce questions within their samples at similar rates (AAE = 9 percent; SWE = 10 percent). This similarity was documented even though the AAE- and SWE-speaking children produced different rates of yes/no question inversion when the question contained a mainstream overtly marked form of BE. For these types of questions, 79 percent were produced by the AAE-speaking children without inversion (e.g., *He's coming tomorrow?*) and 97 percent were produced by the SWE-speaking children with inversion (e.g., *Is he coming tomorrow?*).

The second similarity we have documented is the near identical inventory of nonmainstream grammar forms that are produced within child AAE and SWE. For example, Oetting and McDonald (2002) found thirty-one of thirty-five different nonmainstream grammar structures to be present in the language samples of both the AAE- and SWE-speaking children. The only structures that were not produced within both dialects were *I'ma* (e.g., *I'ma go*) and preterite *had* + verb (e.g., *Then he had walked to me*), which were produced by the AAE child speakers, and completive *done* (e.g., *I done went fishing*) and existential *it/they* (e.g., *When they's only men*), which were produced by the SWE child speakers. There was also a great deal of overlap in the structures that were produced at high frequencies by the AAE- and SWE-speaking children. In fact, seven of the ten nonmainstream grammar forms that were produced with the greatest frequencies in child AAE were also produced with the greatest frequencies in child SWE. These seven nonmainstream forms (with the percentage of children in each dialect who produced at least one token of each form) included: zero BE (AAE 100 percent; SWE 89 percent); multiple negation (AAE 82 percent; SWE 72 percent); zero regular verbal –s (AAE 100 percent; SWE 70 percent); omission of auxiliary DO (AAE 70 percent; SWE 66 percent); subject-verb non-agreement with DO (AAE 78 percent; SWE 60 percent); subject-verb non-agreement with BE (AAE 85 percent; SWE 58 percent); zero irregular past (AAE 75 percent; SWE 51 percent).[1]

Finally, both child AAE and SWE show evidence of some dialect-universal aspects of their use of grammar even when a grammar structure is shown to have dialect-specific aspects. As an example, and as mentioned earlier, Oetting and Newkirk (2011) examined AAE- and SWE-speaking children's use of relative clause markers. Consistent with child studies of General American English (e.g., Schuele and Nicholls 2000), rates of relative clauses within the samples of the AAE- and SWE-speaking children were rare (less than one per one-hundred utterances or < .002 per one-thousand words). Nevertheless, both child dialect groups produced six different types of relative clause markers (*that, who, which, where, Ø,* and *what*). Of these, the first four are produced within many English dialects, while the last two, Ø in subject relatives (e.g., *Maybe there's a crawfish in there Ø pinched him on the tail*) and the relative clause marker *what* (e.g., *I ain't got a sister what I can fight much*), are dialect-specific, with documented use in AAE and a few other non-mainstream dialects of English (Ball 1996; Green 2002; Guy and Bayley 1995; Sistrunk 2012; Tagliamonte, Smith, and Lawrence 2005; Tottie 1995, 1997; Tottie and Harvie 2000; Tottie and Rey 1997).

Nevertheless, dialect-universal aspects of the AAE- and SWE-speaking children's relative clause markers were documented when we examined the six markers as a function of the marker's syntactic role within the clause and the humanness of the antecedent to which the marker referred. When the marker served as the subject within the clause, rates of Ø were relatively low (AAE = 5 percent; SWE = 6 percent). In contrast, when the marker served as a direct object or object of a preposition within the clause, rates of Ø increased (AAE = 46 percent; SWE = 45 percent). Also, when the antecedent of the relative marker was human, the marker was almost always either *that* or *who* (94 percent for AAE; 90 percent for SWE). In contrast, when the antecedent was non-human, rates of *that* and *who* decreased (67 percent for *that* and 0 percent for *who* for both dialect groups) with rates of Ø increasing (16 percent for AAE; 24 percent for SWE). As demonstrated by these data, the child AAE and SWE dialect groups varied their selection of relative clause markers as a function of the syntactic role of the marker and humanness of the antecedent in ways that have been documented in other English dialects (for studies of other American and British dialects that guided our work, see Guy and Bayley 1995; Tottie 1995, 1997; Tottie and Rey 1997).

27.3 SOME DIFFERENCES BETWEEN
CHILD AAE AND SWE

The most pronounced difference between child AAE and SWE we have documented relates to the frequency or rate at which nonmainstream grammar forms are produced. Rate-based differences are detected when (1) children's language samples are judged holistically with listener judgment tasks; (2) nonmainstream grammar forms are counted using various methods; and (3) children's use of nonmainstream grammar forms are examined within dialect screeners, such as the *Diagnostic Evaluation of Language Variation-Screening Test* (DELV-ST; Seymour, Roeper, and de Villiers 2003). Table 27.2 presents results from these different methods to illustrate rate-based differences between child AAE and SWE. The data for the listener judgments and language sample indices come from ninety-three children studied by Oetting and McDonald (2002), and the data for the DELV-ST come from eighty-two different children studied by Oetting et al. (2011). For each index, we list the mean, standard deviation, and range of values for each dialect.

For the DELV-ST, two measures are reported in the table. The first reflects each group's nonmainstream dialect ranking following the guidelines of the test manual; a one indicates that a child produced a low number of nonmainstream forms on the DELV-ST (less than seven out of a possible fifteen responses) and a three indicates that the child produced a high number (up to fifteen possible responses). The second measure for the DELV-ST reflects each group's percentage of nonmainstream responses out of all score-able responses. This second method follows work by Terry et al. (2010) and Terry et al. (2012), and leads to higher correlations with other measures of children's nonmainstream grammar use than the three-point system. Nevertheless, both DELV-ST measures, like the other measures, show AAE-speaking children producing higher rates of nonmainstream English grammar forms than their SWE-speaking peers.[2]

Dialect differences in the frequency at which children produce nonmainstream grammar forms are also evident when some structures are examined in isolation. For example, Cleveland and Oetting (2013) examined AAE- and SWE-speaking children's nonmainstream zero-marking of verbal –s (e.g., *he play*). For the typically developing children, rates of zero-marking were higher for the AAE than SWE dialect group, and this finding occurred with regular and irregular verbs (regular: AAE = 78 percent versus SWE = 8 percent; irregular: AAE = 78 percent versus SWE 14 percent) and with DO + negation as in *he don't drive* (AAE = 96 percent versus SWE = 42 percent). Other nonmainstream grammar forms that occur in both child dialects but show statistically significant rate-based differences between AAE and SWE include: zero BE, be$_2$, subject-verb non-agreement with BE, zero regular past, multiple negation, indefinite article, zero plural, zero possessive, zero of, and demonstrative (Oetting and McDonald 2001).

A second difference between child AAE and SWE relates to the function that some grammar forms play within the dialects. One of these structures is *had* + verb, as in *had brought, had jumped, had eat,* and *had walk.* In both child AAE and SWE, as well as many other

Table 27.2 Rates of Nonmainstream English
Structures, by Dialect

	AAE	SWE
Listener judgments	5.71	4.11
	(1.04)	(.91)
	3–7	2–6
Language samples[a]		
Percent of utterances with a nonmainstream	29	12
grammar form	(9)	(6)
	10–52	3–35
Rate of nonmainstream forms by	34	13
number of utterances	(12)	(7)
	11–67	3–42
Rate of nonmainstream structure by	7	3
number of words	(2)	(2)
	3–13	1–8
DELV-ST[b]		
Dialect ratings	2.64	1.79
	(.58)	(.89)
	1–3	1–3
Percent of nonmainstream responses	.83	.42
	(.17)	(.30)
	.36–1.00	0–.92

[a] From "Methods for Characterizing Participants' Nonmainstream
Dialect on Child Language Research," by J. B. Oetting and
J. L. McDonald. 2002. *Journal of Speech, Language, and
Hearing Research* 45, 512. Copyright [2002] by the American
Speech-Language Hearing Association. Adapted with permission.
[b] From Oetting et al. 2011.

dialects of English, *had* + verb structures indicate past perfect tense as in *I had glued it by the time she brought me tape.* However, this structure can also be used to express the preterite or simple past tense in AAE. Rickford and Theberge-Rafal (1996) documented this finding in a study of nine California preadolescents. The authors also reported that the preadolescents used this structure as a narrative device, with 96 percent of their preterite *had* + verb structures occurring in the complicating action clauses of their stories. Cukor-Avila (2001) further documented the use of this structure in Texas post–World War II speakers of AAE without finding any tokens of this structure in samples of adults who spoke SWE.

Consistent with these preadolescent and adult studies, Ross, Oetting, and Stapleton (2004) identified eighty-two preterite *had* + verb structures in samples of children who spoke AAE, and none of these structures was found in the SWE samples. Moreover, 90 percent of the AAE-speaking children's preterite *had* + verb structures were found in narratives, and the children who produced these structures presented the longest and most complex narratives within the AAE dialect group. Finally, when the AAE-speaking children produced a preterite *had* + verb structure within a narrative, 80 percent of the time the structure occurred within a complicating action clause. These findings demonstrate a dialect difference between child AAE and SWE in the function of *had* + verb structures, while also showing a great deal of consistency in the function of preterite had + verb structures across studies of child, preadolescent, and adult AAE.

Finally, child AAE and SWE differ from each other in the types of linguistic variables that influence (or do not influence) the use of some grammar forms. For example, using adult AAE studies by Blake (1997) and Rickford et al. (1991) as a guide, Roy, Oetting, and Moland (2013) examined children's mainstream overt marking of BE (e.g., "She's walking") as a function of three linguistic variables: the person, number, and tense of the BE form (*am, is, are, was/were*); the contractibility of the BE form (contractible, uncontractible); and the grammatical function of BE (copular, auxiliary).

As demonstrated in table 27.3, the two child dialects differed in the number and magnitude of the effect that the linguistic variables played on the children's overt marking of BE. For AAE, all three variables affected the children's rates of marking, and rates of marking were lowest for *are* and *is* relative to *am* and *was/were*. Rates of overt marking

Table 27.3 Proportion of Overtly Marked Forms of BE, by Dialect

	AAE	SWE
Person, Number, Tense		
Am	94	96
Is	59	95
Are	27	77
Was/were	96	99
Contractibility		
Contractable	57	93
Uncontractable	77	94
Grammatical Function		
Copular	70	96
Auxiliary	53	87

Source: From "Linguistic Constraints on Children's Overt Marking of BE by Dialect and Age," by J. Roy, J. Oetting, and C. W. Moland. 2013. *Journal of Speech, Language, and Hearing Research* 56, 940. Copyright [2013] by the American Speech-Language-Hearing Association. Adapted with permission.

for *are* were also lower than rates for *is*. For SWE, only two of the linguistic variables, the person, number, and tense of the BE form and the contractibility of the BE form, affected their rates of overt marking, and only *are* was found to be marked at a lower rate than the others. These dialect differences between child AAE and SWE are consistent with dialect differences that have been documented in the adult AAE and SWE literature (Blake 1997; Bailey and Maynor 1985; Cukor-Avila 2001; Hazen 2001; Rickford et al. 1991; Wolfram 1974; Wolfram and Thomas 2002). These dialect differences also differ from what has been reported for children who speak General American English, because by 6 years of age, General American English-speaking children produce high rates of overt marking for all forms of BE and show minimal to no effects for a BE form's contractibility or grammatical function (Rice, Wexler, and Hershberger 1998).

In this chapter, we have highlighted some of the similarities and differences between child AAE and SWE that we have documented in studies of children living in Louisiana. Similarities involve the number of contexts for grammatical forms that AAE- and SWE-speaking children produce within school-based language samples, the types of nonmainstream grammar forms they produce, and the dialect-universal ways in which some linguistic variables (e.g., humanness of a relative marker's antecedent) influence the selection of some grammar forms over others. Differences involve the frequency at which AAE- and SWE-speaking children produce nonmainstream grammar forms, the function that some grammatical structures play within each dialect, and the dialect-specific ways in which some linguistic variables (e.g., the person, number, tense of the BE form) influence the selection of some grammar forms over others.

Additional studies are needed to uncover additional similarities and differences between child AAE, SWE, and other English dialects and to explore the within-group variation that exists within each of these child dialects. Future studies should also examine the emergence of nonmainstream forms in children younger than 4 years (see Newkirk-Turner, Horton-Ikard, and Stockman, this volume), older children's use of nonmainstream forms across age and tasks, and the relation between children's use of nonmainstream forms and their performance on different types of language-literacy tasks (see Van Hofwegen, this volume; Mills and Washington, this volume). In the future, it will also be important for researchers to move beyond studies of children's nonmainstream, grammatical forms. System-based studies such as those by Green (2011) are needed to learn more about the underlying grammars of children's dialects.

Notes

1. The list of high frequency forms for our AAE-speaking children aligns with lists of high frequency forms for other AAE-speaking children who live outside of Louisiana (for some AAE group comparisons, see Oetting and Pruitt 2005; Van Hofwegen and Wolfram 2010).
2. Data in table 27.2 can also be used to show that rates of nonmainstream grammar use by our AAE-speaking children are comparable to rates produced by AAE-speaking children who live outside of Louisiana (for some AAE group comparisons, see Oetting and McDonald 2002; see also Craig and Washington 2004).

REFERENCES

Bailey, Guy. 2001. "The Relationship between African American Vernacular English and White Vernaculars in the American South: A Sociocultural History." In *Sociocultural and Historical Contexts of African American English*, edited by Sonja L. Lanehart, 53–92. Philadelphia, PA: John Benjamins.

Bailey, Guy, and Natalie Maynor. 1985. "The Present Tense of BE in White Folk Speech of the Southern United States." *English World-Wide* 6: 199–216.

Ball, Catherine. 1996. "A Diachronic Study of Relative Markers in Spoken and Written English." *Language Variation and Change* 6: 179–200.

Bernstein, Cynthia, Thomas Nunnally, and Robin Sabino, eds. 1997. *Language Variety in the South Revisited*. Tuscaloosa: University of Alabama Press.

Blake, Renée. 1997. "Defining the Envelope of Linguistic Variation: The Case of 'Don't Count' Forms in the Copula Analysis of African American Vernacular English." *Language Variation and Change* 9: 57–79.

Burgmeister, Bessie, Lucille H. Blum, and Irving Lorge. 1972. *Columbia Mental Maturity Scale*. 3rd ed. New York: The Psychological Corporation.

Cheramie, Deany. 1998. "Cajun Vernacular English and the Influence of Vernacular on Student Writing in South Louisiana." PhD diss., University of Southwestern Louisiana.

Cleveland, Leslie H., and Janna B. Oetting. 2013. "Verbal –*s* Marking by Dialect and Clinical Status." *American Journal of Speech-Language Pathology* 22: 604–14. doi:10.1044/1058-0360(2013/12-0122).

Cottrell, Sunni E., Shavonica Williams, Kathleen Talley, and Valentina Taran. 2012. "Comparing DELV Scores with Listener Judgments of AAE." Paper presented at the convention of the Black Association for Speech-Language and Hearing, Raleigh, North Carolina, April 19–21.

Craig, Holly K., and Julie A. Washington. 2004. "Grade-Related Changes in the Production of African American English." *Journal of Speech, Language, and Hearing Research* 47: 450–63.

Cukor-Avila, Patricia. 2001. "Co-Existing Grammars: The Relationship between the Evolution of African American and White Vernacular English in the South." In *Sociocultural and Historical Contexts of African American English*, edited by Sonja L. Lanehart, 93–128. Philadelphia, PA: John Benjamins.

Dollaghan, Christine A., Thomas F. Campbell, Jack L. Paradise, Heidi M. Feldman, Janine E. Janosky, Dayna N. Pitcairn, and Marcia Kurs-Lasky. 1999. "Maternal Education and Measures of Early Speech and Language." *Journal of Speech, Language, and Hearing Research* 20: 489–501.

Dubois, Sylvie, and Barbara M. Horvath. 1998. "From Accent to Marker in Cajun English: A Study of Dialect Formation in Progress." *English World-Wide* 19: 161–88.

———. 1999. "Let's Tink about Dat: Interdental Fricatives in Cajun English." *Language Variation and Change* 10: 245–61.

———. 2003a. "The English Vernacular of the Creoles of Louisiana." *Language Variation and Change* 15: 255–88.

———. 2003b. "Verbal Morphology in Cajun Vernacular English." *Journal of English Linguistics* 31: 34–59.

Dunn, Lloyd M., and Leota M. Dunn. 1981. *Peabody Picture Vocabulary Test-Revised*. Circle Pines, MN: American Guidance Service.

———. 1997. *Peabody Picture Vocabulary Test-Third Edition*. Circle Pines, MN: American Guidance Service.

Garrity, April W., and Janna B. Oetting. 2010. "Auxiliary BE Production by African American English–Speaking Children with and without Specific Language Impairment." *Journal of Speech, Language, and Hearing Research* 53: 1307–20.

Green, Lisa J. 2002. *African American English: A Linguistic Introduction.* Cambridge: Cambridge University Press.

———. 2011. *Language and the African American Child.* Cambridge: Cambridge University Press.

Guy, Gregory R., and Robert Bayley. 1995. "On the Choice of Relative Pronouns in English." *American Speech* 70: 148–62.

Hadley, Pam A., and Janet K. Holt. 2006. "Individual Differences in the Onset of Tense Marking: A Growth-Curve Analysis." *Journal of Speech, Language, and Hearing Research* 49: 984–1000.

Hazen, Kirk. 2001. *Identity and Ethnicity in the Rural South: A Sociolinguistic View through Past and Present BE.* Durham, NC: Duke University Press.

Horton-Ikard, Ramonda, and Susan Ellis Weismer. 2005. "Distinguishing African-American English from Developmental Errors in the Language Production of Toddlers." *Applied Psycholinguistics* 26: 597–620.

Leonard, Laurence. 2014. *Children with Specific Language Impairment.* 2nd ed. Cambridge, MA: MIT Press.

Moland, Christy W. 2011. "Comparison of the Diagnostic Evaluation of Language Variation-Screening Test (DELVT-ST) to Two Other Screeners for Low-Income Children." PhD diss., Louisiana State University.

Montgomery, Michael, and Guy Bailey, eds. 1986. *Language Variety in the South.* Tuscaloosa: University of Alabama Press.

Newcomer, Phyllis, and Donald Hammill. 1988. *Test of Language Development-Primary: Revised Edition.* Austin, TX: Pro-Ed.

———. 1997. *Test of Language Development-Primary: Third Edition.* Austin, TX: Pro-Ed.

Oetting, Janna B., and April W. Garrity. 2006. "Variation within Dialects: A Case of Cajun/Creole Influence within Child SAAE and SWE." *Journal of Speech, Language, and Hearing Research* 49: 16–26.

Oetting, Janna B., and Janet L. McDonald. 2001. "Nonmainstream Dialect Use and Specific Language Impairment." *Journal of Speech, Language, and Hearing Research* 44: 207–23.

———. 2002. Methods for Characterizing Participants' Nonmainstream Dialect Use in Child Language Research." *Journal of Speech, Language, and Hearing Research* 45: 508–18.

Oetting, Janna B., and Brandi L. Newkirk. 2008. "Subject Relatives by Children with and without SLI across Different Dialects of English." *Clinical Linguistics and Phonetics* 22: 111–25.

———. 2011. "Children's Relative Clause Markers in Two Nonmainstream Dialects of English." *Clinical Linguistics and Phonetics* 25: 725–40.

Oetting, Janna B., Karmen L. Porter, Christy Seidel, Janet McDonald, and Michael Hegarty. 2011. "Evaluation of the DELV-ST for Kindergarteners in the Rural South." Paper presented at the convention of the American Speech-Language-Hearing Association, San Diego, CA.

Oetting, Janna B., and Sonja L. Pruitt. 2005. "Use of Southern African American English across Groups." *International Journal of Multicultural Communication Disorders* 3: 136–44.

Oetting, Janna B., and Jessica Richardson. 2012. "Listener Judgment as a Method for Characterizing Children's Dialect." Paper presented at the convention of the National Black Association of Speech-Language and Hearing, Raleigh, North Carolina, April 19–21.

Pruitt, Sonja L., and Janna B. Oetting. 2009. "Past Tense Marking by African American English-Speaking Children Reared in Poverty." *Journal of Speech, Language, and Hearing Research* 52: 2–15.

Redmond, Sean M., Heather L. Thompson, and Sam Goldstein. 2011. "Psycholinguistic Profiling Differentiates Specific Language Impairment from Typical Development and from Attention Deficit Hyperactivity Disorder." *Journal of Speech, Language, and Hearing Research* 54: 99–117.

Rice, Mabel L. 2007. "Children with Specific Language Impairment: Bridging the Developmental and Genetic Perspectives." In *Handbook of Language Development*, edited by Erika Hoff and Marilyn Shatz, 411–31. Malden, MA: Blackwell.

Rice, Mabel L., Kenneth Wexler, and Scott Hershberger. 1998. "Tense over Time: The Longitudinal Course of Tense Acquisition in Children with Specific Language Impairment. *Journal of Speech, Language and Hearing Research* 41: 1412–31.

Rickford, John R., Arnetha Ball, Renée Blake, Raina Jackson, and Nomi Martin. 1991. "Rappin on the Copula Coffin: Theoretical and Methodological Issues in the Analysis of Copula Variation in African-American Vernacular English." *Language Variation and Change* 3: 103–32.

Rickford, John R., and Christine Theberge-Rafal. 1996. "Preterite *Had* + V-ed in the Narratives of African American Preadolescents." *American Speech* 71: 227–54.

Roid, Gail, and Lucy Miller. 1998. *Leiter International Performance Scale–Revised.* Chicago: Stoelting.

Ross, Sarah H., Janna B. Oetting, and Beth Stapleton. 2004. "Preterite *Had* + Ved: A Developmental Narrative Structure of African American English." *American Speech* 79: 167–93.

Roy, Joseph, Janna B. Oetting, and Christy W. Moland. 2013. "Linguistic Constraints on Children's Overt Marking of BE by Dialect and Age." *Journal of Speech, Language, and Hearing Research* 56: 933–44.

Rubrecht, August W. 1971. "Regional Phonological Variants in Louisiana Speech." PhD diss., University of Florida.

Schuele, C. Melanie, and Lisa Nicholls. 2000. "Subject Relative Clauses: Evidence of Continued Linguistic Vulnerability in Children with Specific Language Impairment." *Clinical Linguistics and Phonetics* 14: 563–85.

Schuele, C. Melanie, and Leslie Tolbert. 2001. "Omissions of Obligatory Relative Markers in Children with Specific Language Impairment." *Clinical Linguistics and Phonetics* 15: 257–74.

Schwartz, Richard G. 2009. *The Handbook of Child Language Disorders.* New York: Psychological Press.

Seymour, Harry N., Thomas Roeper, and Jill de Villiers. 2003. *Diagnostic Evaluation of Language Variation: Screening Test.* San Antonio, TX: The Psychological Corporation.

Sistrunk, Walter. 2012. "The Syntax of Zero in African American Clauses." PhD diss., Michigan State University.

Tagliamonte, Sali, Jennifer Smith, and Helen Lawrence. 2005. "No Taming the Vernacular? Insights from the Relatives in Northern Britain." *Language Variation and Change* 17: 75–112.

Terry, Nicole P., Carol M. Connor, Yaacov Petscher, and Catherine R. Conlin. 2012. "Dialect Variation and Reading: Is Change in Nonmainstream American English Use Related to Reading Achievement in First and Second Grades?" *Journal of Speech, Language, and Hearing Research* 55: 55–69.

Terry, Nicole P., Carol M. Connor, Shurita Thomas-Tate, and Michael Love. 2010. "Examining Relationships among Dialect Variation, Literacy Skills, and School Context in First Grade." *Journal of Speech, Language, and Hearing Research* 53: 126–45.

Tottie, Gunnel. 1995. "The Man Ø I Love: An Analysis of Factors Favouring Zero Relatives in Written British and American English." In *Studies in Anglistics*, edited by Gunnel Melchers and Beatrice Warren, 201–15. Stockholm: Almqvist and Wiksell.

——. 1997. "Overseas Relatives: British-American Differences in Relative Marker Usage." In *Studies in English Language Research and Teaching*, edited by Flor Aarts, Jan Aarts, Inge de Monnink, and Herman Wekker, 153–65. Amsterdam: Rodopi.

Tottie, Gunnel, and Dawn Harvie. 2000. "It's All Relative: Relativization Strategies in Early African American English." In *The English History of African American English*, edited by Shana Poplack, 198–230. Malden, MA: Blackwell.

Tottie, Gunnel, and Michael Rey. 1997. "Relativization Strategies in Earlier African American Vernacular English." *Language Variation and Change* 9: 219–47.

Van Hofwegen, Janneke, and Walt Wolfram. 2010. "Coming of Age in African American English: A Longitudinal Study." *Journal of Sociolinguistics* 14: 427–55.

Walton, Shana. 1994. "Flat Speech and Cajun Ethnic Identity in Terrebonne Parish." PhD diss., Tulane University.

Washington, Julie, and Holly Craig. 1994. "Dialectal Forms during Discourse of Poor, Urban, African American Preschoolers." *Journal of Speech and Hearing Research* 37: 816–23.

Wolfram, Walt. 1974. "The Relationship of White Southern Speech to Vernacular Black English." *Language* 50: 850–72.

——. 1991. *Dialects and American English*. Englewood Cliffs, NJ: Prentice Hall.

Wolfram, Walt, and Natalie Schilling-Estes. 1998. *American English*. Malden, MA: Blackwell.

Wolfram, Walt, and Erik Thomas. 2002. *The Development of African American English*. Malden, MA: Blackwell.

CHAPTER 28

ASSESSING THE LANGUAGE SKILLS OF AFRICAN AMERICAN ENGLISH CHILD SPEAKERS

Current Approaches and Perspectives

TOYA A. WYATT

28.1 INTRODUCTION

THERE are a number of challenges that have historically been associated with the testing of African American students for special education eligibility and placement decisions. The most significant concerns have been raised about the validity of standardized tests that are used to make assessment decisions about African American and other minority students, particularly those who speak a dialect other than Mainstream American English (MAE), which have often resulted in the overrepresentation of African American students identified with a special education label and/or inappropriately placed in certain special education settings. For example, in 1979 a group of African American parents in San Francisco filed a class action lawsuit (*Larry P. v. Riles*) against the state of California (California 2003), charging that the administration of culturally biased standardized IQ tests had resulted in a disproportionate number of African American children being identified as "mentally retarded" (more current terms include *intellectual disability, intellectually challenged, mentally handicapped*). Plaintiffs also challenged the disproportionately higher rate of African American children being placed in classes for the Educable Mentally Retarded (EMR). One of the key points shared during the trial by experts was the fact that, on average, African American students scored one standard deviation (fifteen points) below White students on the standardized IQ tests used to make placement decisions. Another 15 percent of African American children had scores that fell below a two standard deviation cut-off point compared to only 2 percent of the total US population.

Based on the evidence that was presented, the court ruled against the use of standardized IQ tests for determining the eligibility of African American children for placement in EMR classes or their substantial equivalent unless such tests have been validated for the specific purpose of identifying African American children in this setting and have also been reviewed for evidence of racial and cultural bias by the Federal Court of Appeals. To date, the California Department of Education (CDE) has continued to advise against the use of standardized IQ tests with African American students for any type of special education testing because of its potential for misdiagnosis and possible discrimination (Memorandum and Order, p. 10, August 31, 1992). In more recent years, additional evidence of disproportionality in the special education placement of African American and other minority students has been documented through research studies such as those based on an analysis of data obtained by the US Office of Civil Rights between 1990 and 2000. For example, analyses reported by Oswald, Coutinho, and Best (2002) revealed that African American males compared to White females were 3.26 times more likely to be recommended for special education placements. Statistics cited by Fierros and Conroy (2002) revealed that 28 percent of Hispanic and 33 percent of African American special education students were placed in restrictive, substantially separate settings (e.g., special day class settings where they were out of the regular classroom 60 percent of the time) compared to only 16 percent of their White counterparts. Parrish (2002) revealed that the national risk ratio for African American students being labeled as "mentally retarded" to be 2.88 compared to that of White students. This means that African American students were almost three times more likely to receive this label.

This type of data helped to usher in a number of important changes to current special education law (e.g., Individuals with Disabilities and Education Act 2004; hereinafter IDEA 2004) and underscored the importance of previous special education law regulations with regard to the assessment of students being considered for special education services. Under IDEA 2004 regulations:

(a) All assessments and evaluation materials used to assess children "be selected and administered so as not to be discriminatory on a racial or cultural basis." (§ 6.14, (b) (3) (A) (1))

(b) No single criteria is to be used for eligibility decisions. (§ 300.532 (f))

(c) Assessors must use a variety of different tools and strategies to gather relevant functional and developmental information about a child, including information provided by the parent, teacher, and information obtained from classroom-based assessments and observations. (§ 300.532(b), 300.533 (a)(1) (i, ii, iii), 300.535(a)(1))

(d) Professionals must "draw upon information from a variety of different sources including . . . parent input, and teacher recommendations" as well as information about the child's "social or cultural background." (§ 300.306 (c) (1) (i))

(e) Assessments should be done "in the form most likely to yield accurate information about what the child knows and can do academically, developmentally, and functionally." (§ 300.304 c(ii))

(f) The determination of whether or not a child has a specific learning disability "must permit the use of a process based on a child's response to a scientific research-based intervention." (§ 300.8 (c) (10))

IDEA (2004) regulations also mandate that, individual states have "policies and procedures to prevent the inappropriate overidentification or disproportionate representation by race and ethnicity of children with disabilities" including those with "a particular impairment" (34 CFR 300.173). States receiving assistance under Part B of the act must also have procedures for collecting and examining data "to determine if significant disproportionality based on race and ethnicity is occurring" (US Department of Education, Office of Special Education Programs 2007).

These regulations have important implications for SLPs, psychologists, and other educators involved in the special education assessment process for all students, but particularly those such as African American students who have historically been overrepresented in some special education categories and placements. Specifically, SLPs and others involved in the evaluation process must carefully consider the types of assessment procedures and diagnostic criteria that they use to identify children with true language disorder versus those who only display normal language differences. They must also be aware of the inherent biases of certain assessment procedures, as well as current research on the language development of both typically developing and language-impaired AAE child speakers. The same issues that create problems of overrepresentation in some categories and special education placement settings can lead to problems with underrepresentation in other areas, such as determining a child's eligibility for Gifted and Talented Education classes. There can also be the potential for overlooking true disorders within what appears to be normal dialect difference if clinicians are also not sensitive to the dialect-specific and universal markers of disorder across children from different dialect backgrounds.

The purpose of this chapter is to summarize some of the current recommended speech and language assessment practices in the field of speech-language pathology that help to minimize the overrepresentation as well as underrepresentation of African American children who are AAE speakers. Doing so enables professionals to make eligibility decisions that are in compliance with current IDEA 2004 regulations. It also helps to highlight some of the current speech and language research on AAE preschool, school age, and adolescent child speakers that can further enhance clinical decision-making and accurate differential diagnosis of difference versus disorder in AAE child speakers.

28.2 STANDARDIZED SPEECH-LANGUAGE ASSESSMENTS AND TEST BIAS

When a child is assessed to determine or confirm the presence of a speech and/or language disorder, there are a number of different types of assessments that clinicians might use to do so. One is to use a formal standardized test to compare the performance of the child to the performances of clients from similar language and age backgrounds by using pre-established norms and age expectations that rely on test percentiles and age-equivalent scores.

According to Lahey (1988), a language disorder can be defined as "any disruption in the learning or use of one's native language" (21). This definition implies that an accurate language diagnosis can only be made when children are compared to children from similar cultural-linguistic backgrounds. This means that it is very important to select assessments that are developed for use with the child population with whom they are to be used and that the sample of children used for a test are similar in cultural and language background to the child to whom a test is being given.

Historically, standardized speech and language tests used with African American as well as other students have been either exclusively or primarily standardized on children from White, middle-class backgrounds who are MAE speakers. Generally speaking African American students have only made up about 15 percent of the standardization sample. The number of AAE speakers within those samples has rarely been reported and was likely to be fairly small, if it was reported. When a test is primarily standardized on a certain population, it is also typically designed to conform to theories of language development associated with that group. It will also contain test items that are representative of what is considered to be normal for that group. Additionally, it will fail to accommodate some of the normal cultural-linguistic differences that exist in the language and patterns of language use in the groups that are not included or included to a limited degree in the standardization sample. This often results in a number of different forms of test bias with other test-taker groups, including, but not limited to: linguistic bias, situational bias, format bias, and value bias (Taylor and Payne 1983; Vaughn-Cooke 1986; Wyatt 2012).

Linguistic bias occurs whenever tests assess speech sounds or grammatical forms that can be produced differently without adjusting for this difference during scoring. This applies to the interdental fricatives /θ/ and /ð/, which can be produced as /d/, /f/, or /v/ in AAE, depending on the position of the sound in a given word and whether the target sound is voiced or voiceless.

Situational bias occurs whenever there is a mismatch between the communication style of the client and the communication style or expectations of the SLP and that of a child's cultural speech community. In some culturally traditional African American homes and communities, children have been raised to respond to adults only when spoken to and also to be succinct in their responses (providing only that information that is requested).

Children who have been socialized according to these cultural expectations may initiate very little conversation with clinicians and/or use limited language to describe pictured test stimulus items, which can be misinterpreted as a pragmatic or other language deficit by an SLP who is not familiar with this cultural socialization difference.

Format bias occurs whenever clinicians use testing formats or procedures that are less familiar (e.g., known information questions) which, according to the research of Heath (1982), was rarely used by working-class African American adults with their children in one of the communities studied by Heath.

Value bias occurs whenever there is a greater value placed on certain types of responses (those that would be considered correct according to the social norms of one group but not another). This is most likely to occur with questions such as "What should you do when. . . .?" or "What should you do if. . . .?" Children growing up in different cultural communities are likely to respond to this question differently dependent on how they have been socialized to respond to different "What should you do when/if. . . .?" scenarios.

28.3 Minimizing Test Bias

A number of solutions have been recommended for addressing and minimizing possible test bias influences that can occur when assessing the speech and language skills of AAE-speaking students. The following is a summary of some of the most current recommended solutions.

28.3.1 Using Tests that Are Primarily Standardized on AAE Speakers

One obvious solution to the test bias problem is to develop tests primarily normed on AAE speakers. To date, however, there is only one commercially available test that is primarily normed on this population: the *Diagnostic Evaluation of Language Variation* (DELV) is a test that is comprised of two different assessments: *The DELV Screening Test* (DELV-ST) (Seymour, Roeper, and de Villiers 2003b) and the *DELV Norm-Referenced* (DELV-NR) (Seymour, Roeper, and de Villiers 2005). The DELV Screening Test was primarily normed on African American AAE speakers who made up more than 50 percent of the sample. This contrasts with other tests in the field that often fail to report and/or include AAE speakers and in which 15 percent or less of the sample is composed of African American children. While inclusion of a significant number of AAE speakers within the standardization sample increases the viability of this assessment for making an accurate differential assessment of AAE child speakers who are potentially at risk for or identified with a true language impairment, the inclusion of AAE speakers alone is insufficient to overcome potential bias. The DELV-NR was derived from an earlier version of the test, the DELV-Criterion Referenced, that was standardized on a child population with the same demographic profile as the DELV-ST. The screener and the norm-referenced assessment were also both designed to incorporate existing knowledge, research, and theories of developing AAE grammar and phonology in AAE child speakers. In addition, both incorporate principles of universal or non-dialect-specific language development that enables them to be effective in use with AAE as well as MAE speakers. Evidence from initial field testing studies of the DELV screener, for example, revealed similar patterns of test performance by typically developing MAE as well as AAE speakers on Part II of the Screening Test, which was designed to identify possible disorder (Pearson 2004). There was no gap in the performance of MAE and AAE speakers across all age groups. This differs from what is typically seen in other assessments. Additional sampling of eighty typically developing children from four different American English dialect backgrounds (children who spoke Appalachian English, Cajun English, Southern English, or Spanish-influenced English) revealed patterns of responses for three of these groups (all except the Spanish-influenced English group) to those produced by MAE and AAE speakers (Seymour et al. 2003a). Collectively, these findings support the appropriateness of this test for use with speakers from a variety of different American English-speaking backgrounds. It also lends support to the theory that this test assesses universal or shared aspects of language ability across different American English dialect populations, which will be discussed later as another approach for minimizing test bias and misdiagnosis of language impairment in children from differing English dialect backgrounds.

28.3.2 Using Tests that Accommodate Possible Dialect Differences

Some test developers have also attempted to address the issue of possible dialect difference by including reference tables and/or alternative scoring guidelines that accommodate possible dialect differences. Examples include the *PLS-5* which has reference tables for scoring possible dialect variations that can be produced by speakers from a number of different dialect backgrounds on certain test items or subtests. The *Structured Photographic Expressive Language Test: Third Edition* (Dawson, Stout, and Ever 2003) is an example of another standardized language test that includes a reference table for scoring possible AAE differences.

28.3.3 Using Assessments Developed with Test Bias Review Panel Input

Some test developers have also included as part of the pilot test development process the use of test bias review panels made up of professionals and scholars with expertise in the assessment of children from diverse cultural and language backgrounds. The purpose of a test bias review panel is to identify possible forms of test bias within preliminary test items for one or more child language populations and in some cases to provide suggestions for possible modifications to reduce the bias. Tests that include professionally recognized experts on the topic of AAE and/or African American assessment ensure that possible test bias influences are taken into account for AAE child speakers by identifying items where certain speech sounds and/or grammar forms might be produced differently by AAE speakers due to normal versus disorder based influences. Test bias review panels can also review pictures and/or vocabulary to ensure that African American children with differing life experiences from different communities (rural and/or urban) around the country can recognize and/or verbally label pictured items and events, given their social and cultural exposure/experiences.

28.3.4 Using Modified Test Administration and/or Scoring

In the absence of established test administration and scoring adjustments for dialect variations, SLPs can do their own modified scoring by scoring items that would typically be considered incorrect by test and MAE standards, but correct by AAE rule standards. Laing (2003) and Terry et al. (2010) both provide examples of how modified scoring adjusting for possible dialect differences made a difference in testing outcomes for AAE speakers. It is important, however, for clinicians who attempt to do modified scoring on their own to be familiar enough with the rules of AAE to do so. Any types of scoring modifications should be addressed in diagnostic reports summarizing test findings. SLPs also need to recognize that using modified scoring procedures, unless allowable according to the test manual, can further invalidate test outcomes. Caution should be taken in interpreting any scores reported where test modifications were used.

28.3.5 Dynamic Assessment and Process-Dependent Measures

Dynamic assessments that incorporate a test-teach-retest paradigm have also been proposed as an alternative to static knowledge assessment procedures. Peña, and Iglesias (1992) found improvement in the scores of African American and Puerto Rican Head Start preschoolers on a standardized measure of expressive vocabulary before and after a brief twenty-minute mediated learning/intervention. Prior to the intervention, children with and without suspected language disorders performed similarly, often providing descriptions rather than labels to name pictured objects, with scores falling below the mean. After the intervention, the scores of those children determined to be typically developing improved significantly to rise above the mean, while the scores of those determined to be at risk for language impairment changed little.

Process-dependent measures such as incidental word-learning tasks (Campbell et al. 1997) have also been proposed as an alternative to more language knowledge-based measures for assessing the language skills of children with diverse life experiences and language backgrounds because there is less emphasis placed on prior existing world knowledge and more on the process of learning. According to Brackenbury and Pye (2005), the word-learning tasks can be beneficial for assessing the vocabulary skills of children from diverse backgrounds because they minimize the potential influence of factors such as sociocultural history, language differences, and socioeconomic status. There are two subtests ("Fast-mapping: Real verb items" and "Fast-mapping: Novel verb items") on the DELV-NR (Seymour et al. 2005) that require children to use a process-dependent approach to figuring out the correct response to items that contain either nonsense words or words used in an unfamiliar way. This minimizes the potential impact of prior cultural experience for test-takers from MAE as well as non-MAE backgrounds because the items are equally unfamiliar to both language groups and therefore provide a non-biased approach to identifying those children with language processing difficulties.

28.3.6 Supplemental Assessment Measures

28.3.6.1 *Language Sampling*

Language sampling has often been proposed as a strong viable alternative to standardized test assessments for AAE child speakers. Language samples represent more authentic and naturalistic forms of assessment than standardized tests. They also enable clinicians to use existing information and research on AAE dialect features, rules and language structure as well as normative AAE child language data to distinguish difference from disorder in AAE child speakers. A single language sample can also be used to analyze various aspects of language ability (e.g., vocabulary, narrative ability, phonology, grammar). There are also certain language sample analysis measures such as the *Index of Productive Syntax* (*IPSyn*; Scarborough 1990) initially developed for use with MAE speakers that have been found to be appropriate for use with AAE speakers (Oetting et al. 2010). As more research on AAE developmental norms becomes available, the appropriateness of using language sampling with AAE speakers is also likely to improve.

28.3.6.2 *Curriculum-Based and Portfolio Assessments*

Another recommended approach for minimizing test bias is to use a portfolio of curriculum-based work samples and assessments that track a child's progress over time from the initial exposure to that curriculum. Like dynamic assessments, it includes an evaluation of learning over time versus static knowledge at one point in time with pre- and post-test change serving as the basis for making final eligibility decisions and diagnoses.

The use of classroom-based portfolio assessments that include data obtained at the beginning, middle, and end of the year is a key characteristic of RTI, an approach that is increasingly being used in schools to identify children at risk for academic achievement and in need of possible special education services. With information from ongoing assessments through the academic school year, educators can help identify students who are in need of intervention or classroom modification. Educators can also track their response to these interventions over time. This assessment approach can be effective in helping to distinguish child speakers from AAE as well as MAE backgrounds who display classroom academic language weaknesses as a result of limited cultural exposure from those with true disorder. Under the RTI model, children with normal language differences will show normal progress in the acquisition of new classroom language concepts compared to their peers over the course of the school year. Those with true underlying language deficits will continue to struggle in the acquisition of new knowledge or progress at a much slower rate compared to their peers. This model is based on IDEA regulations that emphasize the use of processes based on a "child's response to scientific, research-based intervention" when attempting to determine the presence of a language learning disorder (34 CFR 300.307; 20 U.S.C. 1221e-3; 1401(30); 1414(b)(6)).

28.3.6.3 *Parent Interviews*

Another way to minimize possible test bias is to use parent interview as a key source of assessment data. Using parents as informants enables clinicians to obtain a clear picture of a child's communication difficulties from the perspective of the parents and with respect to established speech-language community norms. Research studies show that parents can actually be fairly accurate in providing an overview of a child's communication concerns (Guiberson, Rodriquez, and Dale 2011). When parents express a concern about their child's language development they are typically comparing them to siblings and other age peers in the child's family and community from similar cultural-linguistic (i.e., dialectical) and sociocultural backgrounds. According to Battle (2000), culturally competent clinicians ask whether or not any differences observed are different enough to make a difference in the ability of the client to communicate effectively in his/her speech community or family (21). Case history interviews serve as one mechanism for accomplishing this. Parent input is also, as discussed earlier, a required part of the assessment process under new IDEA regulations. It also helps to provide information that meets the mandate for an accurate assessment of what a child "knows and can do academically, developmentally, and functionally" (34 CFR 300.304(c)(1)(ii); 20 U.S.C. 1414(b)(3)(A)(ii)). The elicitation of information on how a child's language skills impact on their overall functioning within the home environment is also in line with the International Classification of Functioning, Disability, and Health framework developed by the World Health Organization (2001). This framework places an emphasis on viewing disorder from the perspective of how it impacts an individual's ability to participate in meaningful activities and daily interactions with others in various social and family networks (e.g., immediate family, friends, other care providers, neighbors, community members, and healthcare providers).

When a parent says, for example, that a child's speech is difficult to understand and that he or she often has to ask the child to repeat him/herself, a clinician knows that the child most likely has a true articulation disorder, regardless of dialect exposure. The clinician can then select a set of articulation assessment measures that help to verify these patterns of disorder, taking other possible dialect differences into account.

28.3.6.4 *Additional Sources of Assessment Data*

In addition to the assessment data sources already cited, SLPs should attempt to incorporate as much as possible information from a child's medical and/or health history. For example, reviewing results from recent audiological assessments can provide information about a possible hearing loss that may be contributing to a child's speech or language delays, regardless of dialect status. Reviewing medical records that indicate a series of transient ischemic attacks (TIAs), which are characterized as "mini-strokes," are important when assessing the language learning skills of a child with a diagnosis of sickle cell anemia, a condition that is particularly important to consider when working with African American children because of its prevalence in the community. This type of information helps to support an accurate diagnosis of impairment in spite of language difference.

28.4 Using Assessments that Focus on Language Universals and Non-Dialect Specific Language Abilities

Another way to minimize potential test bias in the formal as well as the informal testing administration, scoring, analysis process is to use standardized as well as informal language assessment measures that assess universal aspects of language development and ability or that enable clinicians to analyze child language assessment data in light of universally based language criteria and expectations that are applicable regardless of dialect background, cultural-linguistic exposure or experience. The following is a summary of findings from recent research studies that help to highlight examples of shared language abilities that can potentially be used as part of the language analysis process to help identify children from both AAE and MAE backgrounds with possible language disorder. Examples of assessments that incorporate the construct of universal language abilities as part of the test's underlying theoretical framework and design are also to be discussed.

28.4.1 AAE Child Research Findings

28.4.1.1 *Zero- to Three-Year-Olds*

Studies involving young African American children have found the language development from birth to 3 years old to be fairly similar to that reported for MAE speakers. For example, all typically developing English as well as other child language speakers begin to babble around 4 to 6 months of age, use communicative gestures around 8 to 10 months of age, say their first words around 10 to 12 months of age, and begin to combine their first two word combinations around 18 to 24 months of age. It is not until around the age of 3 years that children begin to master the culture- or language-specific aspects of the grammar, phonology, vocabulary, narrative, and pragmatic aspects of language use that differences become more noticeable.

Horton-Ikard and Weismer (2005) found that toddlers of 2.5 and 3.5 years of age exposed primarily to AAE in the home did not differ from same age peers exposed primarily to SAE in the home with respect to mean length of utterance in terms of number of words. There were also some similarities in terms of the types of nonstandard grammatical forms produced. These findings suggest that using measures of sentence length that are based on word length can be universally applied to determine whether utterances produced by an AAE child speaker during language sampling are within a normal range of expectation.

Stockman (1996) examined the language skills of children up to 3 years old exposed to AAE in the home and noted that they had acquired the same "minimal core" of consonants as SAE speakers in initial word position by age 3, similar to SAE age peers. This shared set of fifteen sounds (/m/, /n/, /p/, /b/, /t/, /d/, /k/, /g/, /f/, /s/, /h/, /w/, /j/, /l/, /r/) were accurately produced by seven of the typically developing African American children studied by Stockman (1996) but not an eighth child with suspected speech delays.

Stockman (1996) used these findings to propose a "minimal core competency" conceptual framework that she defined as the least amount of linguistic knowledge necessary for a child to be judged as typically developing based on a common shared set of obligatory linguistic features and contexts. Under this framework, all of the sounds identified in her study, with the exception of /l/ and /r/, which were later dropped from the proposed set of shared sounds based on research by Stockman (2008), represent a common core of sounds that children should have acquired by 3 years of age, regardless of dialect background. Stockman discussed the benefits of using this MCC framework for analyzing speech and language sample data to differentiate disorder from difference in AAE child speakers.

Stockman (1996) also identified minimal core language features and characteristics in other language domains that were produced productively by the typically developing children in her study. In the pragmatics domain, this included the following speech act functions that were productively used four or more times: commenting, requesting information, requesting objects/acts, responding to questions, initiating repairs and making repairs on request. The one child with suspected language delay used these functions less often than his typically developing peers. There were nine semantic categories that were productive in the samples of the typically developing children (produced more than one time): existence, state, locative state, action, locative action, specification, possession, time, negation. There were only two that were considered to be productive for the child with suspected delay. These findings corroborated results from an earlier study by Stockman and Vaughn-Cooke (1982) that found that 0- to 3-year-old African American children acquire and code the same range of semantic category meanings and functions as those noted by Bloom and Lahey (1978) and Lahey (1988) for other children. The only difference is that the grammatical code used by the children to express these meanings is likely to differ in the case of those children acquiring AAE (e.g., "This Minnie Mouse" versus "This is Minnie Mouse" to express existence).

In the area of grammar, there was one grammatical form (the present progressive *–ing* marker) that was identified as a minimal core grammatical feature, along with a number of simple and complex sentence constructions determined to be productive in the speech of typically developing subjects. The child with suspected delay produced only one complex sentence but no elaborated simple sentences on present progressive *–ing* inflections.

28.4.1.2 *Preschool and School-Aged Children*

Research on preschool children between the ages of 3 and 5 years and school-age children between the ages of 5 and 11 years have also revealed evidence of universal language behaviors that are also produced by MAE speakers that clinicians can use to identify and distinguish typically versus language disordered children. Oetting and Newkirk (2008) identified difficulties in children's use of subject relative clauses as a universal marker of specific language impairment in preschool and school-age AAE as well as Southern White English (SWE) speakers. Burns et al. (2012) were able to identify four dialect neutral aspects of narrative skills in the areas of narrative cohesion and evaluation that can be used as clinically significant measures for differentiating normal versus disordered development across differing dialects of English.

Research studies such as that of Seymour, Bland-Stewart, and Green (1998) have also been able to document universally shared or non-dialect-specific aspects of language performance that can serve as an important basis for distinguishing difference from disorder. For example, in a study of elementary school-age AAE speakers (ranging in age from 5 to 8) with and without language disorder, Seymour, Bland-Stewart, and Green (1998) identified several non-contrastive features of AAE (features that overlap with and are produced similarly in MAE) that accurately distinguished those children with disorders. These features included: articles, complex sentences, conjunctions, demonstratives, locatives, modals, negatives, verb particles, prepositions, present progressive *–ing*, and pronouns. There were no significant group differences, with the exception of past tense *–ed* in the production of contrastive features (aspects of English grammar that operate differently in AAE versus MAE) such as third-person singular *–s*, auxiliary *be*, copula *be*, plural *–s*, and possessive *–s*. These research findings provide supporting evidence of shared English dialect grammar features that can be used to make a differential diagnosis of disorder in children from both dialect groups.

28.5 TESTS BASED ON LANGUAGE UNIVERSALS AND NON-DIALECT-SPECIFIC LANGUAGE

28.5.1 Assessing Language Universals

In light of previous research findings, SLPs should attempt to select tests that can be reliably used with AAE as well as MAE speakers to assess universally shared aspects of dialect ability. For example, the *Evaluating Acquired Skills in Communication-Third Edition (EASIC-3)* "Expressive I Inventory" (Marcott 2009) contains items that target some of the early developing semantic relations noted by Bloom and Lahey (1978) and Lahey (1988) that have been found to be coded similarly by African American children (Stockman and Vaughn-Cooke 1982). Examples include: expressing noun labels for common objects (equivalent to the concept of existence); non-existence; identifying noun locations (equivalent to the concept of locative state); expressing a desire for recurrence of an object or action; and naming actions. This test also targets language uses such as requests for objects, action, and information, and answering which are also similar to the minimal core language functions identified by Stockman (1996).

The DELV-NR (Seymour et al. 2005), although normed on a standardization population replicating the US demographic profile, is a test that was derived from an earlier criterion-reference measure that was primarily normed on AAE speakers. This test, which is appropriate for use with 4- to 9-year-old English speakers, regardless of dialect background contains a number of subtests that focus on universally shared aspects of language development in older AAE and SAE speakers. Examples include the "Article Item" subtest that focuses on children's ability to use the appropriate article (indefinite *a* or definite *the*) to respond to various *wh*-questions. As indicated in the research of Seymour et al. (1998), articles represent one example of a non-dialect-specific feature that identified AAE children with a disorder just as it can be used with MAE speakers.

Another example is the DELV-NR "Short Narrative" items task that assesses children's ability to retell a narrative using clear character/pronominal referencing, temporal links between events, and the coding of character mental states. Although narratives can vary cross-culturally in structure, organization, and the way in which cohesion is expressed, the aspects assessed by this task, as listed above, represent universal aspects of narrative production documented as being similar in pattern and use across different dialect speakers groups.

28.5.2 Language Analyses that Use Dialect-Specific Criteria

In addition to being knowledgeable about universally shared aspects of language development, clinicians also need to be aware of some of the dialect-specific aspects of language development that need to be taken into account when evaluating standardized or informal language assessment data.

28.5.2.1 *Zero- to Three-Year-Olds*

In the research by Horton-Ikard and Weismer (2005) that was previously described, AAE toddlers were generally similar to their SAE counterparts in the types of nonstandard forms produced, although there were some differences that are most likely associated with emerging dialect exposure influences. One example is the *go* copula that was produced in language samples of AAE child subjects but not SAE subjects. There were seventeen tokens of the *go* copula in the AAE group language sample of 2.5-year-olds but none in the SAE sample. The use of undifferentiated pronoun case was also produced more than twice as much in the AAE samples compared to the SAE samples. These research findings help to highlight important differences that clinicians need to be aware of when analyzing younger AAE child language sample data.

28.5.2.2 *Preschoolers*

When Horton-Ikard and Weismer (2005) compared the language performance of AAE speakers of 2.5 years of age and those 3.5 years of age in their study, they also noted that there was an increase in the use of certain nonstandard English grammatical forms in the language samples of AAE speakers of 2.5 years when compared to older AAE speakers of 3.5 years. Horton-Ikard and Weismer (2005) observed as well significant differences between AAE speakers of 2.5 years versus those of 3.5 years with respect to changes in the dialect density ratio (determined by dividing the number of AAE tokens by the number of words in a child's sample). The calculated dialect density ratio (DDR) was not significantly different between the AAE and SAE groups at 2.5 years, but was so at 3.5 years. These findings support earlier research studies by researchers such as Cole (1980) and Kovac (1980) who noted an increase in the use of dialect-specific forms such as the zero copula with age in preschoolers who were acquiring AAE as their primary dialect.

28.5.2.3 *School-Aged Children*

Dialect differences that distinguish school-aged SAE and AAE speakers have also been noted. Haynes and Moran (1989) who studied typically developing preschool and school-age AAE child speakers in rural east Alabama found that similar to MAE speakers, the use of developmental phonological process patterns decreased systematically with age with the exception of final consonant deletion, which was still evident in the speech of AAE speakers beyond third grade.

Horton-Ikard (2009) studied the narratives of school-aged AAE child speakers and found that although they used the same forms of cohesion in their narratives as SAE speakers (e.g., personal pronouns, demonstratives, conjunctions, lexical repetition), they also used referential forms different from those used by SAE speakers (e.g., undifferentiated pronoun case, appositive pronouns, pronoun extension, regularized reflexive pronouns).

Differences have also been noted with respect to how preschool and school-aged children use and interpret certain English vocabulary items (Champion et al. 2003; McCabe and Champion 2010; Stockman 2000); organize their narratives (Champion 1998, 2003; Gutiérrez-Clellen and Quinn 1993; Hyter and Westby 1996; Taylor and Matsuda 1988); use certain culture-specific speech acts (Wyatt 1999); and comprehend some grammatical forms (Johnson 2010). Dialect use patterns have also been found to have some degree of impact on children's written language skills (Ivy and Masterson 2011).

28.6 Conclusions

This chapter has provided a summary of relevant research on the universal and dialect-specific aspects of AAE child speech and language development that can help provide clinicians with normative data, and evidence-based frameworks for accurately distinguishing disorder from normal development in children at different stages across different aspects of language ability (phonology, morphology/syntax, pragmatics, and semantics). Some of these research findings, frameworks, and recommended best practice assessment principles for assessing non-mainstream American English speakers have been incorporated into tests such as the DELV. These findings and frameworks have also contributed to more accurate analyses of language sample and other non-standardized assessment data which has in turn led to improved clinical decision making. Clinicians are also better prepared to analyze child AAE language ability using other forms of assessment such as language sample analyses. The number of standardized tests and other assessment procedures however, that have incorporated findings from research studies focused on universal as well as dialect-specific aspects of child language development in typically developing or language-impaired AAE child speakers remains small highlighting an area of continued need. Addressing this need is critical for changing a historical past that for too long has failed to produce equitable, fair, accurate, reliable, and appropriate speech-language, as well as other special education assessments for African American students.

References

Battle, Dolores E. 2000. "Becoming a Culturally Competent Clinician." *Special Interest Division 14: Communication Disorders and Sciences in Culturally and Linguistically Diverse Populations* 6: 20–25.

Bloom, Lois, and Margaret Lahey. 1978. *Language Development and Language Disorders.* New York: Macmillan.

Brackenbury, Tim, and Clifton Pye. 2005. "Semantic Deficits in Children with Language Impairments: Issues for Clinical Assessment." *Language, Speech, and Hearing Services in Schools* 36: 5–16.

Burns, Frances A., Peter de Villiers, Barbara Z. Pearson, and Tempii B. Champion. 2012. "Dialect Neutral Indices of Narrative Cohesion and Evaluation." *Language, Speech, and Hearing Services in Schools* 43: 132–52.

California Speech-Language-Hearing Association. 2003. *The Assessment of African-American Children: An Update on Larry P.* January 7. Retrieved from http://www.csha.org/diversitypapers.cfm.

———. n.d. "Practice Guidelines for the Assessment of the African American Child." Retrieved from http://www.csha.org/documents/positionpapers/LarryP.pdf.

Campbell, Thomas, Chris Dollaghan, Herbert Needleman, and Janice Janosky. 1997. "Reducing Bias in Language Assessment: Processing-Dependent Measures." *Journal of Speech, Language, and Hearing Research* 40: 519–25.

Champion, Tempii B. 1998. "'Tell Me Something Good': A Description of Narrative Structures among African American Children." *Linguistics and Education* 9: 251-86.

———. 2003. *Understanding Storytelling among African American Children: A Journey from Africa to America.* Mahwah, NJ: Lawrence Erlbaum.

Champion, Tempii B., Yvette D. Hyter, Allyssa McCabe, and Linda M. Bland-Stewart. 2003. "A Matter of Vocabulary: Performances of Low-Income African American Head Start Children on the Peabody Picture Vocabulary Test-III." *Communication Disorders Quarterly* 24: 121–27.

Cole, Lorraine T. 1980. "A Developmental Analysis of Social Dialect Features in the Spontaneous Language of Preschool Black Children." *Dissertation Abstracts International* 41 (06): 2132B. (University Microfilms No. AAC8026783).

Dawson, Janet I., Connie E. Stout, and Julia A. Eyer. 2003. *Structured Photographic Expressive Language Test: Third Edition.* DeKalb, IL: Janelle.

Fierros, Edward Garcia, and James W. Conroy. 2002. "Double Jeopardy: An Exploration of Restrictiveness and Race in Special Education." In *Racial Inequity in Special Education*, edited by Daniel J. Losen and Gary Orfield, 39–70. Cambridge, MA: Harvard Education.

Guiberson, Mark, Barbara L. Rodriquez, and Phillip S. Dale. 2011. "Classification Accuracy of Brief Parent Report Measures of Language Development in Spanish-Speaking Toddlers." *Language, Speech, and Hearing Research* 42 (4): 536–49.

Gutiérrez-Clellen, Vera F., and Rosemary Quinn. 1993. "Assessing Narratives of Children from Diverse Cultural/Linguistic Groups." *Language, Speech, and Hearing Services in Schools* 24: 2–9.

Haynes, William O., and Michael J. Moran. 1989. "A Cross-Sectional Developmental Study of Final Consonant Production in Southern Black Children from Preschool through Third Grade." *Language, Speech, and Hearing Services in Schools* 20: 400–406.

Heath, Shirley Brice. 1982. "Questioning at Home and at School: A Comparative Study." In *Doing Ethnography of Schooling: Educational Anthropology in Action*, edited by George Spindler, 102–31. New York: Holt, Rinehart, & Winston.

Horton-Ikard, RaMonda. 2009. "Cohesive Adequacy in the Language Samples of School-Age Children Who Use African American English." *Language, Speech, and Hearing Services in Schools* 40: 393–402.

Horton-Ikard, RaMonda, and Susan Ellis Weismer. 2005. "Distinguishing African American English from Developmental Errors in the Language Production of Toddlers." *Applied Psycholinguistics* 26: 597–620.

Hyter, Yvette D., and Carol E. Westby. 1996. "Using Oral Narratives to Assess Communicative Competence." In *Communication Development and Disorders in African American*

Children: Research, Assessment and Intervention, edited by Alan G. Kamhi, Karen E. Pollock, and Joyce L. Harris, 247–75. Baltimore, MD: Paul H. Brookes.

Individuals with Disabilities Education Improvement Act PL 108-446. 2004. Washington, DC: U.S. Department of Education.

Ivy, Lennette J., and Julie J. Masterson. 2011. "A Comparison of Oral and Written English Styles in African American Students at Different Stages of Writing Development." *Language, Speech, and Hearing Services in Schools* 42: 31–40.

Johnson, Valerie E. 2010. "Fast Mapping Verb Meaning from Argument Structure." *Topics in Language Disorders* 30: 103–18.

Kovac, Ceil. 1980. "Children's Acquisition of Variable Features." *Dissertation Abstracts International* 42(02): 687A. (University Microfilms No. AAC8116548).

Lahey, Margaret. 1988. *Language Disorders and Language Development.* New York: Macmillan.

Laing, Sandra P. 2003. "Assessment of Phonology in Preschool African American Vernacular English Speakers Using an Alternate Response Mode." *American Journal of Speech-Language Pathology* 12: 273–81.

Marcott, Anita. 2009. *Evaluating Acquired Skills in Communication, Third Ed.* Austin, TX: Pro-Ed.

McCabe, Allyssa, and Tempii B. Champion. 2010. "A Matter of Vocabulary II: Low-Income African American Children's Performance on the Expressive Vocabulary Test." *Communication Disorders Quarterly* 31: 162–69.

Oetting, Janna B., and Brandi L. Newkirk. 2008. "Subject Relatives by Children with and without SLI across Different Dialects of English." *Clinical Linguistics and Phonetics* 22: 111–25.

Oetting, Janna B., Brandi L. Newkirk, Lekeitha R. Hartfield, Christy G. Wynn, Sonja L. Pruitt, and April W. Garrity. 2010. "Index of Productive Syntax for Children Who Speak African American English." *Language, Speech, Language, and Hearing Services in Schools* 41: 328–39.

Oswald, Donald P., Martha J. Coutinho, and Al M. Best. 2002. "Community and School Predictors of Overrepresentation of Minority Children in Special Education." In *Racial Inequity in Special Education,* edited by Daniel J. Losen and Gary Orfield, 1–14. Cambridge, MA: Harvard Education.

Parrish, Tom. 2002. "Racial Disparities in the Identification, Funding, and Provision of Special Education." In *Racial Inequity in Special Education,* edited by Daniel J. Losen and Gary Orfield, 15–37. Cambridge, MA: Harvard Education Press.

Pearson, Barbara Zurer. 2004. "Theoretical and Empirical Bases for Dialect-Neutral Language Assessment: Contributions from Theoretical and Applied Linguistics to Communication Disorders." *Seminars in Speech and Language* 25: 13–25.

Peña, Elizabeth, and Aquiles Iglesias. 1992. "The Application of Dynamic Methods to Language Assessment: A Nonbiased Procedure." *Journal of Special Education* 26: 269–80.

Scarborough, Hollis S. 1990. "Index of Productive Syntax." *Applied Psycholinguistics* 11: 1–22.

Seymour, Harry N., Linda Bland-Stewart, and Lisa J. Green. 1998. "Difference versus Deficit in Child African American English." *Language, Speech, and Hearing Services in Schools* 29: 96–108.

Seymour, Harry N., Thomas W. Roeper, and Jill de Villiers. 2003a. *Diagnostic Evaluation of Language Variation Criterion Referenced.* San Antonio, TX: The Psychological Corporation.

———. 2003b. Diagnostic Evaluation of Language Variation Screening Test. San Antonio, TX: The Psychological Corporation.

———. 2005. *Diagnostic Evaluation of Language Variation Norm-Referenced.* San Antonio, TX: The Psychological Corporation.

Stockman, Ida J. 1996. "The Promises and Pitfalls of Language Sample Analysis as an Assessment Tool for Linguistic Minority Children." *Language, Speech, and Hearing Services in Schools* 27: 355–66.

———. 2000. "The New Peabody Picture Vocabulary Test-III: An Illusion of Unbiased Assessment." *Language, Speech, and Hearing Services in Schools* 31: 340–53.

———. 2008. "Toward Validation of a Minimal Competence Phonetic Core for African American Children." *Journal of Speech, Language, and Hearing Research* 51: 1244–62.

Stockman, Ida J., and Faye Vaughn-Cooke. 1982. "Semantic Categories in the Language of Working Class Black Children." *Proceedings of the Second International Child Language Conference* 1: 312–27.

Taylor, Orland L., and Mari M. Matsuda. 1988. "Storytelling and Classroom Discrimination." In *Discourse and Discrimination*, edited by Geneva Smitherman and Teun van Dijk, 206–20. Detroit, MI: Wayne State University.

Taylor, Orlando L., and Kay T. Payne. 1983. "Culturally Valid Testing: A Proactive Approach." *Topics in Language Disorders* 3: 8–20.

Terry, J. Michael, Sandra C. Jackson, Evangelos Evangelou, and Richard L. Smith. 2010. "Expressive and Receptive Language Effects of African American English on a Sentence Imitation Task." *Topics in Language Disorders* 30: 119–34.

US Department of Education. n.d. *Statute: Public Law 108-446—108th Congress, An Act.* http://idea.ed.gov/explore/view/p/%2Croot%2Cstatute%2CI%2CB%2C614%2C.

US Department of Education, Special Education and Rehabilitative Services. 2007, July 19. *Archived: A 25-Year History of the IDEA.* http://www2.ed.gov/policy/speced/leg/idea/history.html.

Vaughn-Cooke, Faye. 1986. "The Challenge of Assessing the Language of Nonmainstream Speakers." In *Treatment of Communicative Disorders in Culturally and Linguistically Diverse Populations*, edited by Orlando L. Taylor, 23–48. San Diego, CA: College-Hill.

World Health Organization. 2001. *International Classification of Functioning, Disability and Health: ICF.* Geneva: World Health Organization.

Wyatt, Toya A. 1999. "An Afro-Centered View of Communicative Competence." In *Constructing (In)Competence: Disabling Evaluations in Clinical and Social Interaction*, edited by Dana Kovarsky, Madeline Maxwell, and Judith F. Duchan, 197–221. Mahwah, NJ: Lawrence Erlbaum.

———. 2012. "Assessment of Multicultural and International Clients with Communication Disorders." In *Communication Disorders in Multicultural and International Populations*, 4th ed., edited by Dolores E. Battle, 243–78. St. Louis, MO: Elsevier.

PART V

EDUCATION

....

CHAPTER 29

AFRICAN AMERICAN LANGUAGE AND EDUCATION

History and Controversy in the Twentieth Century

....

GENEVA SMITHERMAN

29.1 INTRODUCTION

....

DURING the centuries of enslavement of Africans in Colonial America, and after 1776, as the United States of America, there was no concern about the language or education of Africans. Education was not essential to the performance of slave labor, and there were laws making it illegal to teach the enslaved to read and write. Then, in the post-Emancipation era, Jim Crow emerged and, with it, the establishment of "separate but equal" education. Hence, the relationship between African American Language and the education of US slave descendants was not addressed until the Black Freedom Struggle of the mid-twentieth century. In this chapter's overview of that historical relationship and attendant controversies, African American Language is conceptualized as the language and discourse patterns of African slave descendants in the United States, which reflect the survival of African languages in the English used by these descendants. We may thus think of African American Language—hereinafter AAL or Black Language (BL)—as "Africanized English."

The relationship between AAL and education can be characterized in terms of three language ideologies, each creating controversy in the educational community and spreading to the broader national and international professional community and the lay public:

(1) AAL is viewed as illustrative of Blacks' cognitive and/or sociocultural deficiencies, thus mandating the need for specialized language education programs and "dialect readers" for Black students;

(2) AAL is viewed as indicative of learning disabilities and communication disorders in Black students. This language ideology was highlighted in the widely discussed,

public controversy surrounding *King v. Ann Arbor* (the "Black English" federal court case, 1977–79); and

(3) the US variety, labeled as "Ebonics," is viewed as one of several "relatives" of the African languages family found in postcolonial and post-enslavement communities. This language ideology was highlighted in the public controversy revolving around the Oakland School Board's Resolution on Ebonics issued in December 1996.

29.2 "LANGUAGE PROGRAMS FOR THE DISADVANTAGED" AND COGNITIVE DEFICIT THEORISTS (1959–1980)

AAL emerged as an issue in the education of Black people with the game-changing 1954 Supreme Court decision in *Brown v. Board of Education*, which declared "separate but equal" schooling unconstitutional. The media and lay public tend to locate the beginning of the Civil Rights Movement at Mrs. Rosa Parks's refusal to surrender her bus seat to a White passenger and the subsequent boycott led by a young Reverend Dr. Martin Luther King Jr. However, historians and legal scholars tend to agree that the movement actually began the year before Parks's historic action—on May 17, 1954, the date of the *Brown* decision mandating desegregation of the nation's K–12 schools. Going forward, conversations about "Negro English" and "speaking Negro" (as it was referred to for centuries), which had occurred primarily among academic language historians and folklorists, began to take center stage. School integration put Blacks and Whites in the same classrooms, drawing broad-based public attention to linguistic (as well as cultural and social) differences between Blacks and Whites. At the same historical moment, the broader based Black Freedom Struggle—the centuries-old resistance by African Americans to oppression and racial subordination—was evolving to a new level. The mass movement of US slave descendants, who united in disruption of the status quo with marches, sit-ins, boycotts, protests, civil disobedience, and urban rebellions, was shining the national spotlight on Blacks beyond K–12 schools. Revealed and showcased were dimensions of Black Language and Black Culture that for centuries had been hidden from White public view.

In anticipation of racially desegregated school systems across the nation, centuries of educational neglect of African slave descendants were addressed with massive federal, state, and local funding of programs and research projects dedicated to the advancement and improvement of the education of Black people. It was this motion of history that ushered in a broad range of instructional and research programs under the general rubric of "language programs for the disadvantaged."[1]

A major challenge facing these programs was the mindset that AAL was reflective of cognitive deficiency in Blacks. While this belief was subliminal and/or implied among some educators and laypersons, it was explicitly and actively promoted by a school of psychologists who came to be known as the "linguistic-cognitive deficit theorists." Psychologists such as Bereiter and Engelmann (1966), as well as Deutsch (1963), argued that AAL was "not merely an underdeveloped version of standard English," it was also "a non-logical mode of expressive behavior ... lacking the formal properties necessary for formulating cognitive concepts" (Bereiter and Engelmann 1966, 112–13). Widely quoted psychologist Arthur Jensen (1968), referring to "language in the lower class" (118), contended that it "consists ... of a relatively small repertoire of stereotyped phrases and expressions ... used rather loosely without much effort.... Much of lower-class language consists of a kind of incidental 'emotional' accompaniment to action here and now" (118–19).

Historical imperatives require that we recognize that this racialized language ideology did not emerge full-blown in the mid-twentieth century. Rather, it is rooted in the long history of scientific racism and social pathology whereby African peoples were deemed biologically un/underdeveloped and intellectually inferior to Whites. Further, over the centuries, African slave descendants came to be perceived as a critical social problem for White America. A crucial issue in the Civil War era and beyond was what to do about the "Negro problem" in the United States. (One proposal was for the country to return the Negroes to Africa.)

Scientific theories of racial superiority and inferiority located differences between members of the human species in genetic factors. African physiognomy and other racial characteristics were used to establish Black inferiority. For example, Tillinghast (1902) argues that "the convolutions in the negro [sic] brain are less numerous and more massive than in the European.... In whatever aspect ... we consider the physiological basis of mental power, whether as to size of brain, or its inner structure, or the length of its plastic period, the natives of Guinea are at a grave disadvantage in comparison with the Caucasian" (93, 95).

In this sociohistorical context, James A. Harrison produced, in 1884, what is believed to be the first linguistic study of "Negro English." Although Harrison acknowledges that AAL is unique and African-derived, he perceives its Africanness as pathological.

> The humor and naivete of the Negro are features which must not be overlooked in gauging his intellectual caliber and timbre; much of his talk is baby-talk ... the slang which is an ingrained part of his being as deep-dyed as his skin ... the African, from the absence of books and teaching, had no principle of *analepsy* in his intellectual furnishing by which a word ... can be repaired, amended, or restored to its original form.... Negro speech-organs are becoming slowly and with difficulty accustomed to the sound *th*. (1884, 233)

In this same historical moment, American linguistics was undergoing a paradigm shift to a descriptive linguistics based on objective observation rather than preconceived norms. English language pedagogy was being shaped by descriptive linguistics, grounded in the organic grammar of English. Beryl Loftman Bailey (the first Black female linguist) applauded this "more scientific view of the structure of the language" rather than the "rules of an earlier era" and called for the use of linguistics to "help both inside and outside the classroom" (1968). Thus was born the "linguistic method" applied to language pedagogy for AAL speakers.

The application of this method took the form of oral drills and exercises contrasting the forms of AAL with those of the Language of Wider Communication (LWC). In the United States, LWC may loosely be equated with "standard English." However, "Language of Wider Communication" is a more precise label, denoting the language or language variety used in any nation that helps citizens communicate across borders of race/ethnicity, region, gender, education, generation, and class. Importantly, also, "Language of Wider Communication" avoids the judgmental nuance of "standard–nonstandard." (For AAL speakers, it is important to emphasize that the term is "wider," not "Whiter" communication.)

Since AAL and LWC do not differ in every feature of English, "linguistic method" instruction allowed English teachers to call Black students' attention only to those points of difference between their speech and LWC. (This contrastive analysis strategy was also commonly used in the teaching of foreign languages.) For example, to give students practice in using the morpheme –s with third person singular present tense verbs, which is not used in these verb forms in AAL, teachers would have their students contrast "Home Talk" and "School Talk" (see Feigenbaum 1970 for more):

Home Talk	School Talk
John *work* every day.	John *works* every day.
She *see* her friend over there.	She *sees* her friend over there.
Mary *don't* like it here.	Mary *doesn't* like it here.

The first documented language intervention study of AAL-speaking students was Ruth Golden's (1962) study at Central High School in Detroit, Michigan. Her research consisted of a control group of students who followed the traditional Latinate-based grammar instructional program and an experimental group who used contrastive analysis. Students participated in thirteen half-hour speech and listening drills on tape, based on patterns of AAL that "deviated" from "standard English." All students took a pre- and post-oral test. Although Golden (1962) claims that the experimental group's post-test score was almost twice as high as that of the control group, there was no measurement of the students' oral speech in natural, unstructured, non-test speaking situations, nor was there any follow-up to assess whether or not their acquisition of LWC patterns was retained after the experiment.

Another major language experiment of this era was conducted in 1965 by Charles G. Hurst, a high school dropout who later earned a doctorate and became a college president. Using 1,209 AAL-speaking college students in their first year at historically Black Howard University (where he was speech department chair), Hurst performed a battery of oral and written tests to divide the population into three proficiency groups: high, moderate, and low. He then randomly selected 140 students from the low group, creating experimental and control groups that focused on treatments for what he termed "dialectolalia," a speech condition that Hurst (1965) believed to interfere with communication and cause maladjustment.

Hurst divided the students into seven groups, ranging from those who received no special instruction or treatment to those who had varying degrees of involvement in Howard University's speech clinic, remedial language/speech classes, and counseling sessions. All students were administered pre-and post-tests of pronunciation, a reading passage, and a one-minute impromptu speech. A panel of judges rated the students' language proficiency levels.

Hurst's results were far less dramatic than predicted. One of the most damaging results was the performance of the student group whose treatment had incorporated all elements of a complete remedial speech/language program. Despite such efforts, these students increased their LWC proficiency by a mere 0.03 points. His study did confirm that ignorance is not bliss: students in the control group—who received no special language treatment and no information about their performance on the battery of language tests they had all taken—showed a 0.34 *drop* in LWC proficiency. At the time, Hurst still maintained that such a remedial language program could "cure" all students of "Negro Dialect." However, by 1968, he was repudiating this work.

Close examination of language education programs of this period reveal mixed results. On the one hand, such programs commendably sought to address the language and literacy challenges of AAL-speaking students in a desegregating school and society. On the other, the programs reflect research design problems, mixed results, and a questionable pedagogical philosophy. The goal of many—if not most—programs was linguistic eradication of the students' AAL and its replacement with LWC. Yet the students' home, church, peers, social life—all were immersed in AAL. So there was little reinforcement of the LWC they heard and practiced in the classroom. Equally critical was that such programs were ideologically out of step with the widespread use of AAL by Blacks in speeches, at community events, and in public rallies. Reflecting the "I'm Black and I'm proud" ideology of the 1960s and 1970s, renowned poet Don L. Lee (now Haki Madhubuti) spoke on the Black Language imperative: "[B]lack poets [will] deal in ... [B]lack language or Afro-American language in contrast to standard English ... will talk of kingdoms of Africa, will speak in Zulu and Swahili, will talk in muthafuckas and 'can you dig it'" (Lee 1969, as quoted in Smitherman 1977, 180; see also Smitherman 1968, 1973; Smith 1969; Sledd 1969).

More effective and realistic applications of the "linguistic method" to the complex language-learning process facing AAL speakers were those programs that encompassed both speech and writing, used language patterns and examples from real world Black and LWC linguistic-cultural sources, and structured the instruction in the broader context of communication as opposed to simply phrases and sentences in pattern practice drills.

San-Su C. Lin's (1965) pedagogical research program was conducted at historically Black Claflin University in South Carolina. Lin recorded language from literary selections, humorous stories and anecdotes, and informative readings on a variety of general interest topics. Students developed essay topics from these recordings and read their essays aloud for discussion and feedback from their peers. They practiced natural, extemporaneous speaking in small groups, using role-playing that called for use of language patterns they had practiced in the language lab. Lin reports that there was some success in giving students control over LWC patterns, but she cautions that this control was in "delicate balance" and that a different mood or speech situation could trigger the use of the students' community speech.

Beryl Loftman Bailey's (1968) pedagogical research took the form of a summer research program at historically Black Tougaloo College in Mississippi. Her work was among the first to investigate the relationship between AAL-speaking students' speech and writing. She hypothesized that the writing was influenced by the students' speech. For example, in the speech she heard such patterns as AAL's existential "it," as in: "It was about fifteen girls participating in this," and "It's not enough room for one thing." And in the writing, she observed the same pattern: "It's one thing about the building that makes it really unique" and "It isn't but two ways to spend a vacation." One clear exception to the similarity of speech and writing in Bailey's Tougaloo students was the very low written frequency of the pattern that Stanford University linguistics professor John Rickford (1999) dubbed the "showcase variable"—invariant *be*, as in *He be slow*. Widely and frequently used in speech, this form of *be* is clearly a feature of the spoken, not written, language of AAL speakers.

Working with students at City University of New York (CUNY), Carol Reed, Milton Baxter, and Sylvia Lowenthal established the Language Curriculum Research Group (LCRG) in 1969 (Language Curriculum Research Group 1973). It grew out of their experience teaching composition in SEEK (Search for Education, Elevation, and Knowledge), an academic support program for open admissions students. The LCRG espoused a bilingual philosophy, used contrastive analysis, and sought to teach students about the history and systematic principles of their home language, while simultaneously teaching "standard English writing." The instructional materials incorporated language from everyday life in the real world, such as folk and popular song lyrics, mass media excerpts, Black Arts poetry, disc jockeys' and entertainers' raps, and short stories in several English varieties, including "Guyanese Creole" and "White nonstandard English." The program also conducted teacher training workshops for composition instructors at Brooklyn College and other colleges in the CUNY system. Course evaluations from students as well as teachers using the LCRG materials were highly positive. However, the LCRG was not only unsuccessful in getting their materials published, they also lost their Ford Foundation funding—due primarily to objections from the Black middle and leadership class.[2]

Opposition from the African American middle class and elite leadership to such language education programs can be read as a master narrative of class conflict in the Black community. Class contradictions in the previously unified, segregated Black Nation began to form in the desegregating social order of the 1960s and 1970s. This era saw the rise of a historically unparalleled middle-class formation of US slave descendants made possible by the social, economic, and political fruit of the Black Liberation Struggle. For example, over 80 percent of all Black PhDs in the 400-year existence of Blacks on the North American continent were produced between 1960 and 1980 (Blackwell 1981). The class divide on language matters reflects a psycho-cultural, linguistic "double consciousness," as DuBois put it in his book *Souls of Black Folk*, a "twoness—an American, a Negro: two souls, two warring ideals in one dark body" (1903, 3). This racial—and increasingly, class—insecurity and anxiety within many members of the Black middle class and elite leadership surfaced in several language controversies in the twentieth century and continues today to be a challenge to progressive, effective pedagogy for AAL-speaking students.

29.3 READING PROGRAMS AND AAL (1960S–1970S)

Baratz and Shuy titled their 1969 book *Teaching Black Children to Read*. The topic of "Black English" and reading was also investigated in the early research of William Labov (1972) and Kenneth Goodman and Catherine Buck (1973). There were serious—and often furious—debates about BL and reading, particularly about what were called "dialect readers." One school of thought contended that the problem of Black children's reading failures should be addressed by changing teacher attitudes toward AAL and training teachers in the systematic patterns of AAL. This training would enable teachers to differentiate between a child's actual mistakes in decoding and understanding the meaning of words in a reading text and the child's mere variation in the pronunciation of those words. The opposing school of thought was that the mismatch between the child's AAL and the language of school reading materials was a significant factor in "reading retardation" among Black youth. To reduce this mismatch, some educators and language scholars proposed the development of dual reading materials, one version in AAL and a companion version in LWC. An example was the *Ollie* reading series of Joan Baratz and William Stewart, at the Education Study Center in Washington, DC, which consisted of parallel versions in "home" and "school" talk (Baratz and Stewart quoted in Cullinan, 1974):

Home Talk	School Talk
Here go Ollie.	*This is* Ollie.
Ollie *have* a big family.	Ollie *has* a big family.
He *have* three sisters.	He *has* three sisters.
A sister *name* Brenda. . .	A sister *named* Brenda.

Such readers—and there were many others around the country—were problematic for a number of reasons. Not only did they lack cultural depth but also the language used was often stilted and unnatural. Additionally, there were slippages in the printed representations of AAL, and they displayed content and characterization bordering on racial stereotype. Further, some of the reading programs had no systematic evaluation; others lacked controls or had very small sample sizes.

A critical exception to the "dialect readers" of this era was the visionary, culturally rooted *Bridge* reading series, created by the late clinical psychologist Gary Simpkins and his collaborators, the late linguist Grace Holt and elementary school administrator Charlesetta Simpkins (Simpkins, Holt, and Simpkins 1975). Grounded in the Associative Bridging technique—which proceeded from the known to the unknown—some *Bridge* stories were written by Gary Simpkins himself; others were taken from Black Folk Tradition (e.g., "Shine," "Stagolee," "Signifyin Monkey"), with the street language sanitized for classroom use. The target student was an AAL-speaking adolescent who was several grades behind in reading level but who was too sophisticated and streetwise for the typical "See Spot run" beginning reader. The *Bridge* series began with stories in AAL and ended with those in LWC, with booklets in between containing stories written in a transitional language variety, a combination of AAL and LWC.

Simpkins conducted a national field test of *Bridge* in five locations across the country, with experimental (*Bridge*) classes and control (traditional reading material) classes. To measure results, pre and post, he administered the Iowa Test of Basic Skills in Reading Comprehension (Level 12). *Bridge* students had a mean gain of 6.2 months in reading level in the four months of instruction, compared to students in the control group who only had a mean gain of 1.6 months in the four months of the project. The fact that the control group did not even make at least a four-month gain in four months of reading instruction lends credence to the tragic axiom that the longer Black kids stay in school, the further behind they get, by comparison to their White counterparts (see, e.g., Steele 1992). Despite its proven effectiveness in the pilot studies and especially in the national field test, and despite a favorable article in *Newsweek* Magazine (Sheils and Manning 1976), opposition to the series, mainly from Black school administrators and other members of the Black leadership elite, caused the publisher to initially delay the release of *Bridge* and then to eventually cancel its publication altogether.

Even though the end goal of *Bridge* was literacy in LWC, its conceptualization and instruction implicitly celebrated Black folk and community heroes using AAL. Simpkins argued that this was fundamental to motivating students to buy into the program and to address their linguistic insecurity. His and his team's experience with Black community people, working-class parents, activists and inner-city teachers was highly positive, and these groups embraced *Bridge*'s bilingual/bicultural philosophy. However, among African American professionals, it was a different story. They objected to the use of AAL in the texts and to its use as an instructional aid. And they strongly attacked the program's "failure" to condemn AAL and promote a linguistic eradicationist message.

29.4 *KING V. ANN ARBOR*, AKA "THE BLACK ENGLISH CASE" (1977–1979)

The *King* case, formally, *Martin Luther King Junior Elementary School Children et al. v. Ann Arbor School District Board*, was filed in federal court in 1977 and went to trial in 1979.[3] In brief, the "Black English Case" was about the struggles of single African American mothers for quality education for their children.

There was extensive press, television, and radio coverage of the case, locally, nationally, and internationally, beginning July 1977 and continuing through the four weeks of the trial in 1979. In *Black English and the Education of Black Children and Youth* (1981), the published collection of papers, speeches, policy recommendations, and other material from the 1980 National Invitational Symposium on *King*, which was convened by Geneva Smitherman, the late Professor Richard Bailey's chapter listed some three-hundred articles in press coverage alone (Bailey 1981), including late writer James Baldwin's widely read and cited "If Black English Isn't a Language, then Tell Me, What Is?" which had been published in the *New York Times* on July 29, 1979. In much of the coverage, the children's AAL and that of their mothers was held up to ridicule and harsh critique, and the mothers' morals (or lack of such, according to the critics) were attacked. One Black journalist, June Brown, wrote that "mothers whose children can't read should get the boyfriends out and get the books in" (Brown 1979). Her commentary was characteristic of the media sensationalism and persistent attempts to discredit the mothers and their children and exonerate the school district.

Though popularly known as the "Black English Case," *King* was as much about mislabeling Black children "intellectually handicapped," finding them guilty of communication disorders, and failing to teach them to read as it was about "Black English." As presiding judge of the case, Charles W. Joiner wrote:

> It is a straightforward effort to require the court to intervene on the children's behalf to require the defendant School District Board to take appropriate action to teach them to read in the standard English of the school, the commercial world, the arts, science, and professions. This action is a cry for judicial help in opening the doors to the establishment.... It is an action to keep another generation from becoming functionally illiterate. (Joiner 1979, 1373)

The fifteen children in *King* were economically disadvantaged residents of the Green Road housing project in Ann Arbor, Michigan. They attended the Martin Luther King Junior Elementary School, a K–8 school where Black children comprised 13 percent of the school population of predominantly White middle- and upper-class children. Aside from the housing project children, Black students at King School were middle and upper class. Ann Arbor itself is an upscale, liberal college community, home of one of the country's elite public universities, the University of Michigan. The community prides itself on its enlightenment as exemplified by its housing plan. In the 1960s, Ann Arbor sought to promote racial, educational, and economic integration by locating low-income housing for poor Blacks in the same neighborhoods as affluent Whites and Blacks.

By the time the case came to trial, one family with four children had moved out of the district, leaving eleven children in the case. And by the time the court-mandated remedy was implemented during the 1979–80 school year, only five children were still at King School, the others having either moved out of the district or gone on to high school.

The initial claims in the legal complaint were that King School, the Ann Arbor School District, and the State of Michigan had inaccurately placed the children in learning disability and speech pathology classes; had suspended, disciplined, and repeatedly retained the children at the same grade level without taking into account their social, economic, and cultural differences; and had failed to overcome language barriers, thus preventing the children from learning to read and learning "standard English." During the pretrial stage of *King*, Judge Joiner ordered the children's lawyers to amend and revise the complaint several times, eventually dismissing the economic, social, and cultural factors, thus narrowing the case to section 1703(f) of the 1974 Equal Educational Opportunity Act (EEOA): "No state shall deny equal educational opportunity to an individual on account of his or her race, color, sex, or national origin, by … the failure to overcome language barriers that impede equal participation by its students in its instructional programs." *King* thus became the first test of the applicability of the EEOA's section 1703(f) to AAL speakers.

The school district filed a motion to dismiss the case on the grounds that the language provision only applied to those with foreign language backgrounds. Judge Joiner denied this motion, contending that there were no

> limitations on the character or source of the language barrier [other than that it has to be] serious enough to impede equal participation by … students in … instructional programs … [Thus] 1703 (f) applies to language barriers of appropriate severity encountered by students who speak "Black English" as well as to language barriers encountered by students who speak German. (Joiner, 1978)

Attorneys Gabe Kaimowitz and Kenneth Lewis (then of Michigan Legal Services) argued that there were both structural/linguistic as well as attitudinal barriers involved. However, they were unsuccessful in convincing Judge Joiner that the structural/linguistic differences posed a barrier. Instead, his ruling in the children's favor focused on the teachers' language attitudes as the barrier to the children's access to equal educational opportunity. Joiner stated:

> The court cannot find that the defendant School Board had taken steps (1) to help the teachers understand the problem; (2) to help provide them with knowledge about the children's use of a "Black English" language system; and (3) to suggest ways and means of using that knowledge in teaching the students to read. (as cited in Smitherman 1981b, 52)

The racial connection of the language issue exists in the negative attitudes directed toward the "Blackness" of Black Language. These language attitudes are rooted in the historical operations of racism in the United States. Ann Arbor failed to take "appropriate action" to address these attitudes, which constitute racialized language barriers. Hence, it was found in violation of the EEOA.

During the trial the biracial expert witness team of nationally known academics (assembled by Geneva Smitherman)—linguists, educators, reading specialists—testified on behalf of the children, presenting findings from sociolinguistic research, language education intervention programs, and sociopsychological scholarship on race, racism, and culture. Judge Joiner's ruling found the Ann Arbor School District in violation of the rights of these BL-speaking children to equal educational opportunity because of the district's inadequate institutional response to BL. The judge accepted and in his *Memorandum Opinion and Order* cited the research and evidence from linguists on Africanized English as a systematic, rule-governed variety developed by Black Americans as they struggled to combine the cultures of Africa and America.

The district's educational plan was a teacher-training project, implemented in 1979–80, for which the teachers were paid. It consisted of twenty hours of instruction, with reading teachers taking additional training. The training was designed to convey the research on African American Language and issues involved in assessing the language proficiency of AAL-speaking children. The district indicated that the training would continue to be offered in subsequent years to any teachers requesting it. Although the training program imparted knowledge about AAL, there was no follow-up on the impact, if any, of this knowledge on classroom teaching, nor on the reading and oral language skills of the AAL-speaking students. Anecdotal evidence from one of the mothers in the lawsuit indicated that her children seemed to like school more, and a claim was made that the children's attendance improved during the 1979–80 school year (Fiske 1981).

The plan was a disappointment to attorneys Kaimowitz and Lewis as well as the "Friends of King" (as Smitherman and her colleagues dubbed their advocacy team). Lewis (1980) noted that the district plan amounted to "no more than yet another shot in the arm of teacher inservice programs." While teacher training in language is desirable, it is only one component of a more comprehensive educational plan of parental involvement, community support, and especially follow-up assessment of the language and reading skills of the students whose teachers have undergone the training. However, parents were not consulted in the development and implementation of the district's plan, and neither was the community, not even Ann Arbor's Student Advocacy Center, then under the direction of Ruth Zweifler, who had been working with and providing support to the mothers over several years. Attorneys Kaimowitz and Lewis were also excluded, as well as the linguists and other scholars who had testified on the children's behalf.

While the district's remedy in *King* was insufficient (Glazer 1981), the case is significant to the language education of AAL-speaking youth for two reasons. First, it set a sociolinguistic precedent; for the first time, research and scholarship on AAL was inscribed in legal history. Second, it established a resource that other parents and communities can use for their children. As Smitherman noted in her analysis of *King*, "the ruling … established that Black English falls within the parameters of the statutory language of 1703(f) … [rendering it] a tool now available to other communities for manipulating the legal system to obtain a measure of redress from our continuing oppression" (Smitherman 1981b, 58).

29.5 THE 1996 OAKLAND SCHOOL BOARD RESOLUTION

On December 18, 1996, the Oakland Unified School District issued its "Resolution on Ebonics." It was the district's response to the report and recommendations of the African American Task Force, which had devoted significant time and effort to the issue of the low educational achievement of Black students in Oakland, California. These students had the lowest grade point average of any race/ethnic group in the district. They were 53 percent of the student population but 80 percent of the suspensions and 71 percent of the "special needs" students. The resolution, grounded in the voluminous body of linguistic scholarship on AAL, mandated the Oakland superintendent to:

> implement the best possible academic program for imparting instruction to African American students in their primary language for the combined purposes of maintaining the legitimacy and richness of such language whether it is known as "Ebonics," "African Language Systems," "Pan African Communication Behaviors" or other description, and to facilitate their acquisition and mastery of English language skills. (Oakland Unified School District 2005, 230)

The media widely reported on the resolution, locally and nationally, with the coverage extending from December 1996 until at least 2003 (Wright 2005). Again, as had been the case with the LCRG and *King v. Ann Arbor*, middle-class Black leadership led the charge against the resolution. Economist Thomas Sowell, of the Hoover Institute, asked, "From what African language did 'ain't' come?" and went on to exclaim: "You would think the Oakland School Board's program about 'black English'—'ebonics' they call it—would have died of ridicule after so many saw it for the nonsense that it is" (Sowell 1997, 13). Even those middle-class Blacks who were skillful speakers and writers of AAL themselves, such as poet Maya Angelou and Reverend Jesse Jackson, were against the resolution. Angelou, who creatively and skillfully employed AAL in such works as her 1971 collection, *Just Give Me a Cool Drink of Water 'fore I Diiie*, was "incensed" because "the idea that African Americans speak something other than English is very threatening. It could say to our young people that they don't have to learn to speak properly" (Angelou 1996). Reverend Jackson, a powerful orator in the AAL rhetorical tradition, denounced Oakland's plan in these words: "This proposal is unacceptable surrender, borderlining on disgrace" (Jackson 1996).

The Ebonics Resolution called for the recognition of Ebonics as a legitimate, rule-governed language system spoken by the majority of Oakland's Black students, and for Oakland teachers to use the students' home language as a bridge to teach them "standard English." The resolution was based on the success of students at Oakland's Prescott Elementary School, the only school in the district where the teachers were participants in California's "Standard English Proficiency Program," in which Ebonics was recognized as legitimate and systematic and used to teach literacy skills in "School English." Citing support for this approach from around the globe, Rickford (2005) makes a strong case for using the vernacular to teach the standard.

During the controversy, media pundits and the lay public derided the term *Ebonics*, which unbeknownst to most, dates to 1973 and is the label coined by clinical psychologist Dr. Robert Williams at the "Language and the Urban Child" conference he convened as then-head of the Institute of Black Studies in St. Louis, Missouri. Detailing this history in his 1975 book (reprinted in 1997), *Ebonics: The True Language of Black Folks*, which comprises his edited collection of the conference papers, Williams states that Ebonics is the language of "Black people, especially those who have been forced to adapt to colonial circumstances" (vi). *Ebonics* is not to be subsumed under English; it was conceptualized as a superordinate term, covering all Africanized language mixtures developed in the various African and non-African language contact situations throughout the world.

Oakland's position and its resolution were supported by linguists and professional organizations, among them Teaching English to Speakers of Other Languages (TESOL); American Association for Applied Linguistics (AAAL); Conference on College Composition and Communication (CCCC); Center for Applied Linguistics (CAL); and California Association for Bilingual Education (CABE). At its convention in Chicago in January 1997, the Linguistic Society of America (LSA) convened a special session on the Oakland Ebonics Resolution and unanimously passed a resolution supporting Oakland. The LSA resolution (January 3, 1997) addressed several issues:

(a) The variety known as "Ebonics, African-American Vernacular English" (AAVE), and "Vernacular Black English" and by other names is systematic and rule-governed like all natural speech varieties … Characterizations of Ebonics as "slang," "mutant," "lazy," "defective," ungrammatical," or "broken English" are incorrect and demeaning.

(b) The distinction between "languages" and "dialects" is usually made more on social and political grounds than on purely linguistic ones.… What is important from a linguistic and educational point of view is not whether AAVE is called a "language" or a "dialect," but rather that its systematicity be recognized.

(c) As affirmed in the LSA Statement of Language Rights (June 1996), there are individual and group benefits to maintaining vernacular speech varieties and there are scientific and human advantages to linguistic diversity. For those living in the United States there are also benefits in acquiring Standard English, and resources should be made available to all who aspire to mastery of Standard English. The Oakland school board's commitment to helping students master Standard English is commendable.

(LSA 1997)

Demonstrating the political significance of the Oakland controversy for elected officials, Senator Arlen Specter, Chairman of the US Senate Committee on Appropriations Subcommittee on Labor, Health and Human Services and Education, convened a hearing on Ebonics, on January 23, 1997. Linguists Orland L. Taylor (1997) and William Labov (1997) testified at the hearing.

Much to the dismay of Oakland school officials, resistance to its resolution continued. In October 1998, an anti-Ebonics ad was placed in the *New York Times*. The ad, which was posted by the National Head Start Association, featured a silhouette suggesting the figure of Dr. Martin Luther King Jr., with "I has a dream" across the body in big letters. The caption to the ad included such statements as

> Does this bother you? It should…. By now, you've probably heard about Ebonics (aka, black English). And if you think it's become a controversy because white America doesn't want us messing with their precious language, don't. White America couldn't care less what we do to segregate ourselves.

The ad ends with these words in big letters: "Speak out against EBONICS." A group of some two hundred linguists and educators, national and international, mounted a national campaign in opposition to the ad. The major action of this group, "Concerned Linguists and Educators," was a written appeal to the *New York Times* for equal time to publish their rebuttal. After several exchanges of correspondence, each signed by all members of the group, over a two- month period, the *New York Times* denied the appeal.[4]

Oakland's Black children—some of them, at least—benefited from the acrimonious debate and controversy surrounding the Oakland School Board's Ebonics Resolution. Teachers at the Phyllis Wheatley Elementary School (a pseudonym), a "large, urban school district in California," described as a "low-performing, high-poverty" school, were involved in the African American Literacy and Culture Research Project, a three-year collaborative study between a local university and the school district. A major aspect of the project was a two-year professional development program to help Wheatley teachers develop "habits of mind" in thinking about their teaching practices with urban children. That thinking included teacher attitudes toward the children's linguistic-cultural backgrounds, their parents, their home environment, and their community. The research team was under the leadership of Professor Etta R. Hollins, now Kauffman Endowed Chair for Urban Teacher Education at the University of Missouri-Kansas City (see Hollins et al. 2004).

Changes in the teachers' attitudinal and cognitive mindset were achieved through the development of a learning community in which structured dialogue and exchange of ideas and instructional strategies occurred in study groups. By the end of the two-year study, "the conversations … at the study-group changed … to be more positive about the children … to make linkages between themselves and the culture the children bring to school … to show enthusiasm for sharing strategies … and collaborating in developing new instructional approaches" (260–61). Thus, the teachers' "habits of mind" developed in a more progressive, pedagogically productive direction.

The impact of the teachers' professional development on Phyllis Wheatley students was assessed using the Stanford Achievement Test (9th edition) as mandated by the district. When Hollins's team analyzed student performance data, with 1998 results serving as pretest data and results from 1999 and 2000 as post-test data, second- and third-grade students showed significant gains in reading. Interestingly, "the poorest readers" in those grades showed the greatest gains. Hollins et al. (2004) noted that the test scores of the second- and third-grade students at Wheatley School were not typical of the district average. Rather, the research team concluded that the students' gains were clearly attributable to teachers' growth and change as a result of their participation in the development program.

29.6 CONCLUSION: "HISTORY DOESN'T REPEAT ITSELF, BUT IT DOES RHYME"

This overview locates the historical origin of AAL in the education of US slave descendants in the US Supreme Court's 1954 ruling in *Brown v. Board*. The historical account spans the latter half of the twentieth century and implicitly recalls the old axiom that those who do not learn from history are doomed to repeat it.

The overarching lesson learned from this half-century of language intervention is the power of language ideologies to impact—and derail—these interventions. Ideas about language, subliminal but ever-present, are rooted in race, class, gender, culture, and history. These social formations must be taken into account in designing and implementing "language programs for the disadvantaged."

Paramount among the social formations is class, which brings up another historical lesson. While race remains a significant factor within Black–White socio-political-economic relations, the past half-century has been witness to the "declining significance of race" within the African American population. Language and literacy intervention programs that were primed for pedagogical success—e.g., *Bridge*, the LCRG—were derailed by Black elites. By contrast, the contemporary offspring of *Bridge* and the LCRG, Dr. Noma LeMoine's *Academic English Mastery Program* (AEMP), now in dozens of schools in the Los Angeles Unified School District, manages (miraculously?) to subvert this class conflict.

Notwithstanding the crucial importance of institutional programs of language intervention, the individual teacher in her/his individual classroom plays a critical role in the language education of AAL-speaking students. Which leads to this lesson from those twentieth-century AAL language programs: it is imperative that there be consistent, ongoing, highly resourced support for teacher training and development. The occasional lecture, the one-off training workshop, the three-day conference, the one-week retreat—such activities are insufficient for achieving the language attitude change and developing the AAL knowledge base necessary for teacher—and student—success. The depth and quality of the evidence-based outcomes from the three-year African American Literacy and Culture Research Project in the Oakland School District conducted by Hollins et al. (2004) stands in stark contrast to the twenty hours of language training, with minimal empirical evidence, for teachers at Ann Arbor's King School.

In terms of the specifics of instructional strategies in language intervention pedagogy for AAL-speaking students, the lesson from twentieth-century history is that pattern practice drills, grammar and pronunciation exercises, and other forms of contrastive analysis are insufficient for meeting the higher order demands of oral and written communication. The language pedagogy has to be holistic, encompassing analysis and teaching of discourse, cultural-communication styles, and rhetorical strategies.

While history does not repeat itself, it does rhyme. The jangling, discordant language education rhythms of the twentieth century can be heard in today's secondary school teachers who admonish their students to "check your language at the door"; in elementary school initial reading classrooms, where teachers, lacking knowledge of AAL patterns, make incorrect changes to their children's language experience stories; in the movement for Common Core Standards, which do not allow for language diversity; in the Black–White achievement gap in national reading and writing scores; in the school-to-prison pipeline for young, AAL-speaking males. The fundamental lesson for progressive teachers and researchers is that they must maintain their watch and be ever vigilant as the language struggle continues.

NOTES

1. See, for instance, *Language Programs for the Disadvantaged*, an edited collection by Corbin and Crosby published by the National Council of Teachers of English in 1965.
2. For example, in 1971, the National Association for the Advancement of Colored People (NAACP) published an editorial essay in its magazine, *The Crisis*, attacking the LCRG project. Roy Wilkins, then-head of the NAACP, and other members of elite Black leadership were widely quoted in the media denouncing "Black English" as "black nonsense."
3. For Judge Joiner's Memorandum Opinion and Order, analyses and recommendations from linguists and other scholars, and James Baldwin's *New York Times* article "If Black English Isn't a Language, then Tell Me, What Is?" see Smitherman (1981a).
4. The Appeal to the New York Times publisher at the time, Mr. Arthur Sulzberger, requested publication of the Linguistic Society of America's resolution supporting the Oakland School Board and publication of the Appeal's prepared text, which concluded: "Such positive approaches [as using AAL in the teaching of literacy] have already proven successful [and] will help African-American-Language-speaking students to use language with the power and versatility of Dr. Martin Luther King, Jr." This national and international campaign was coordinated by Smitherman's African American Language and Literacy Program at Michigan State University, East Lansing, Michigan.

REFERENCES

Angelou, Maya. 1971. *Just Give Me a Cool Drink of Water 'fore I Diiie*. New York: Random House.
———. 1996. Interview. *Talk Back Live*, December 20.

Bailey, Beryl Loftman. 1968. "Some Aspects of the Impact of Linguistics on Language Teaching in Disadvantaged Communities." In *On the Dialects of Children*, edited by Alva Leroy Davis, 15–24. Urbana, IL: National Council of Teachers of English.

Bailey, Richard W. 1981. "Education and the Law: The *King* Case in Ann Arbor." In *Black English and the Education of Black Children and Youth: Proceedings of the National Invitational Symposium on the King Decision*, edited by Geneva Smitherman, 94–129. Detroit, MI: Wayne State University Center for Black Studies.

Baldwin, James. 1981. "If Black English Isn't a Language, then Tell Me, What Is?" Rpt. in *Black English and the Education of Black Children and Youth: Proceedings of the National Invitational Symposium on the King Decision*, edited by Geneva Smitherman, 390–92. Detroit, MI: Wayne State University Center for Black Studies. Originally in *The New York Times*, July 29, 1979.

Baratz, Joan C., and Roger Shuy, eds. 1969. *Teaching Black Children to Read*. Washington, DC: Center for Applied Linguistics.

Baratz, Joan C., and William Stewart, quoted in Bernice Cullinan, ed., *Black Dialects and Reading*. Urbana, IL: National Council of Teachers of English, 1974.

Bereiter, Carl, and Siegfried Engelmann. 1966. *Teaching Disadvantaged Children in Pre-School*. Englewood Cliffs, NJ: Prentice Hall.

Blackwell, James E. 1981. *Mainstreaming Outsiders: The Production of Black Professionals*. Bayside, NY: General Hall.

Brown, June. 1979. "Don't Segregate Kids for 'Black English.'" *Detroit News*, June 22.

Corbin, Richard, and Muriel Crosby. 1965. *Language Programs for the Disadvantaged*. Champaign, IL: National Council of Teachers of English.

Deutsch, Martin. 1963. "The Disadvantaged Child and the Learning Process." In *Education in Depressed Areas*, edited by A. Harry Passow, 163–80. New York: Columbia University.

DuBois, W. E. B. 1903. *The Souls of Black Folk*. New York: Fawcett.

Feigenbaum, Irwin. 1970. "The Use of Nonstandard English in Teaching Standard: Contrast and Comparison." *Teaching Standard English in the Inner City*, edited by Ralph Fasold and Roger Shuy, 87–104. Washington, DC: Center for Applied Linguistics.

Fiske, Edward B. 1981. "Black English Debate Fades in Ann Arbor Where It Began." *New York Times*, May 5.

Glazer, Nathan. 1981. "Black English and Reluctant Judges." *Public Interest Winter* 62: 40-54.

Golden, Ruth I. 1962. *The Effectiveness of Instructional Tapes for Changing Regional Speech Patterns*. Detroit: Detroit Public Schools.

Goodman, Kenneth, and Catherine Buck. 1973. "Dialect Barriers to Reading Comprehension Revisited." *Reading Teacher* 27: 6–12.

Harrison, James A. 1884. "Negro English." *Anglia-Zeitschrift für englische Philologie* 1884 (7): 232–79.

Hollins, Etta R., Linda R. McIntyre, Charles DeBose, Kimberly S. Hollins, and Arthurlene Towner. 2004. "Promoting a Self-Sustaining Learning Community: Investigating an Internal Model for Teacher Development." *International Journal of Qualitative Studies in Education* 17 (2): 247–64.

Hurst, Charles G. 1965. *Psychological Correlates in Dialectolalia*. Washington, DC: Communication Sciences Research Center, Cooperative Research Project No. 2610.

Jackson, Jesse. 1996. Interview. *Meet the* Press, December.

Jensen, Arthur. 1968. "Social Class and Verbal Learning." *Social Class, Race, and Psychological Development*, edited by Martin Deutsch, 115–74. New York City: Holt, Rinehart, and Winston.

Joiner, Charles. 1978. 451 F. Supp. 1332 (E.D. Mich.).

———. 1979. *Memorandum Opinion and Order on Civil Action 7-71861, Martin Luther King Junior Elementary School Children, et al., v. Ann Arbor School District Board*. Detroit, Michigan. July 12.

Labov, William. 1972. *The Study of Non-Standard English*. Urbana, IL: National Council of Teachers of English.

———. 1997. Congressional Testimony, January 23. In *Ebonics: The Urban Education Debate*, 2nd ed., edited by J. David Ramirez, 180–82. Clevedon, UK: Multilingual Matters, 2005.

Language Curriculum Research Group. 1973. "Teaching Standard English Writing to Speakers Showing Black English Influences in Their Writing." Unpublished teachers manual. Brooklyn, NY: Department of Educational Services, Brooklyn College.

Lee, Don L. [aka Haki Madhubuti]. 1969. "Directions for Black Writers." *Black Scholar* 1: 53–57.

Lewis, Kenneth. 1980. "Analysis of the *King* Case." Unpublished ms.

Lin, San-Su C. 1965. *Pattern Practices in the Teaching of Standard English to Students with a Nonstandard Dialect*. Washington, DC: US Office of Education Project 1339.

LSA (Linguistic Society of America). 1997. *Resolution on Ebonics*. January 3, 1997. Reprinted in *The Real Ebonics Debate: Power, Language, and the Education of African-American Children*, edited by Theresa Perry and Lisa Delpit, 160–61. Boston: Beacon, 1998.

Oakland Unified School District. 1996. *Resolution on Ebonics*. December 18, 1996. Reprinted in *Ebonics: The Urban Education Debate*, 2nd ed., edited by J. David Ramirez, Terrence G. Wiley, Gerda de Klerk, Enid Lee, and Wayne E. Wright, 15–17. Clevedon, UK: Multilingual Matters.

Rickford, John R. 1999. *African American Vernacular English: Features, Evolution, Educational Implications*. Malden, MA: Blackwell.

———. 2005. "Using the Vernacular to Teach the Standard." In *Ebonics: The Urban Education Debate*, 2nd ed., edited by J. David Ramirez, Terrence G. Wiley, Gerda de Klerk, Enid Lee, and Wayne E. Wright, 18–40. Clevedon, UK: Multilingual Matters.

Sheils, Merrill, and Richard Manning. 1976. "Bridge Talk." *Newsweek*. December 20.

Simpkins, Gary, Grace Holt, and Charlesetta Simpkins. 1975. *Bridge: A Cross-Culture Reading Program*. Experimental ed. Boston: Houghton Mifflin.

Sledd, James. 1969. "Bi-Dialectalism: The Linguistics of White Supremacy." *The English Journal* 58 (9): 1307–29.

Smith, Arthur L. [aka Molefi Kete Asante]. 1969. *Rhetoric of Black Revolution*. Boston: Allyn and Bacon.

Smitherman, Geneva. 1968. "Black Language is Black Power." Speech at Black Power Rally. 1968. Revised version published as "Black Power is Black Language," in *Black Culture: Reading and Writing Black*, edited by Gloria M. Simmons and Helene D. Hutchinson, 85–91. New York: Holt, Rinehart, Winston, 1972.

———. 1973. "White English in Blackface or Who Do I Be?" *Black Scholar* 4 (8/9): 3–15.

———. 1977. *Talkin and Testifyin: The Language of Black America*. Boston: Houghton Mifflin.

————, ed. 1981a. *Black English and the Education of Black Children and Youth: Proceedings of the National Invitational Symposium on the King Decision.* Detroit, MI: Wayne State University Center for Black Studies.

————. 1981b. " 'What go round come round': *King* in Perspective." *Harvard Educational Review* 51 (1): 40–56.

Sowell, Thomas. 1997. "Ebonics Is Still in Place Despite Obvious Failings." *Toledo Blade.* January 22, 13.

Steele, Claude. 1992. "Race and the Schooling of Black Americans." *The Atlantic Monthly* 269 (4): 68–78. April.

Taylor, Orlando L. 1997. Congressional Testimony, January 23. In *Making the Connection: Language and Academic Achievement Among African American Students,* edited by Carolyn Temple Adger, Donna Christian, and Orlando Taylor, 169–75. Washington, DC: Center for Applied Linguistics and Delta Systems Inc., 1999.

Tillinghast, Joseph Alexander. 1902. "The Negro in Africa and America." *Publications of the American Economic Association* 3 (2): 1–231.

Williams, Robert, ed. 1997. *Ebonics: The True Language of Black Folks.* St. Louis: Institute of Black Studies.

Wright, Wayne E. 2005. "Compilation of Press Articles and Other Media Coverage of Ebonics." In *Ebonics: The Urban Education Debate,* 2nd ed., edited by J. David Ramirez, Terrence G. Wiley, Gerda de Klerk, Enid Lee, and Wayne E. Wright, 199–207. Clevedon, UK: Multilingual Matters.

CHAPTER 30

MANAGING TWO VARIETIES

Code-Switching in the Educational Context

MONIQUE T. MILLS AND JULIE A. WASHINGTON

30.1 INTRODUCTION

OVER the last five decades, interest in the nature of language variation has burgeoned with studies of code-switching by individuals who are acquiring more than one language system, including bilingual (Cantone 2007; Lindholm and Padilla 1978; Zabrodskaja 2011) and bidialectal (Baratz 1967; Cook-Gumperz and Gumperz 1982; DeBose 1992; Renn and Terry 2009) speakers. *Code-switching*, defined broadly, is the systematic, alternative use of two or more linguistic codes (Swann et al. 2004). Linguistic codes include different *languages* (*bi-* or *multilingual*) and different *language varieties* (*bi-* or *multidialectal*). Efficient code-switching, bilingual and bidialectal, is necessary for academic achievement because of the predominant use of a single code in the written and spoken contexts of schooling (Levine 2010; Wheeler and Swords 2006; Yiakoumetti 2007).

Research on code-switching has been undertaken across numerous fields of study. In particular, scholars in the fields of sociolinguistics, communication sciences and disorders (CSD), psycholinguistics, and education have contributed to our understanding of code-switching. The vantage point from which code-switching has been discussed is unique within each discipline. However, each discipline can boast a positive evolution over time that has improved our understanding of the competencies and benefits inherent in the ability to successfully code-switch. For example, early sociolinguistic accounts considered code-switching within and across languages to be an irregular mixing of two linguistic codes (Labov 1971). Contemporary sociolinguistic accounts, on the other hand, consider code-switching to be a sign of communicative competence (Cantone 2007). Similarly, in CSD, a much younger field than linguistics, views of code-switching have evolved from deficit- to strength-based. Qualitative and quantitative indicators of differences in code-switching have been identified for individuals with and without language impairment (Muñoz, Copeland, and Marquardt 1997).

In terms of bidialectal code-switching, research in the field of CSD has focused primarily on African American English (AAE), the most studied dialect of American English (Wolfram and Thomas 2002). AAE is a systematic, rule-governed variety of English spoken by many, but not all, people who are reared in or reside in AAE-speaking speech communities (Green 2002; Labov 1972). These investigations have identified gender-, age-, and socioeconomic status (SES)-related differences in code-switching among young AAE speakers (Craig and Washington 2004; Terry and Connor 2012; Washington and Craig 1998b). In addition, these studies have revealed variation in the use of dialects using quantitative measures, including *dialect density*—the extent to which non-Mainstream American English (NMAE) varieties such as AAE and Southern White English (SWE) are produced (Craig and Washington 2006; Oetting and Garrity 2006). In studies examining children's use of AAE or other varieties of NMAE, dialect use often has been quantified using measures of dialect density (DDM) and dialect diversity (DVAR). These studies have demonstrated that children tend to decrease their use of AAE as they age and gain exposure to Mainstream American English (MAE)—a language variety of American English spoken across ethnic groups in commerce, government, and academic dimensions of society (Charity 2008; Wolfram and Schilling-Estes 2006).

Broadly, dialect measures, such as DDM and DVAR, are designed to represent the extent to which a child uses AAE feature tokens and AAE feature types in a conversation or narrative sample (Craig and Washington 2006; Terry 2012). These measures attempt to quantify use of AAE along a continuum from low and infrequent use, to usage that can be characterized as high (or heavy) and frequent. As such, dialect measures provide a rough estimate of NMAE production in group studies. These quantifiable distinctions have proven to be critical for characterizing performance of African American children on a variety of tasks. However, dialect measures only reveal *code-shifting* away from AAE toward MAE rather than AAE/MAE code-switching. While the CSD studies reviewed in the following sections are descriptive and have a great deal of ecological validity, they are not designed to inform our understanding of bidialectal code-switching. Thus, there remains a need for psycholinguistic studies that can provide information about how AAE-speaking children perform when processing AAE and MAE in real time. Yet, the extant literature does contribute to our understanding of code-shifting, which may be a proxy for code-switching. In the following sections, we draw on psycholinguistic studies (which focus largely on bilingualism rather than bidialectalism) in our review of cognitive factors underlying code-switching and on CSD- and sociolinguistic studies in our review of social factors influencing code-shifting.

30.2 Language Variation and Academic Success

AAE is spoken by many, but not all African Americans across the SES spectrum and across regions of the United States, as well as by non-African American members who reside in the same speech communities (Green 2002; Scanlon and Wassink 2010). When these students enter schools they encounter a second language variety, MAE. Both AAE and MAE have systematic rules governing the use of features that are *structural* (phonology, morphology, and syntax) and the use of features that are *social* (pragmatics and discourse). Although they share many of the same rules, AAE and MAE differ systematically in the application of some structural and social features. It is critical to academic success that AAE-speaking children identify the similarities and bridge the differences that these two language varieties present.

MAE—also referred to as *Mainstream Classroom English* (Washington and Mills 2011) or as *School English* (Charity 2008)—is the language variety through which lessons in literacy, mathematics, science, and social studies are delivered to students. MAE is spoken by teachers and other school professionals during classroom instruction and is predominant in textbooks and other official learning material (Washington and Mills 2011). Thus, MAE is used in academic contexts and has been discussed as the "language of literacy" (Craig and Washington 2006). Students may experience little difficulty learning MAE when they enter school if they have previously been exposed to MAE. Although AAE-speaking children are certainly passively exposed to MAE through television and radio, the classroom setting provides an opportunity to actively engage with MAE, as many African American children enter school with much more exposure listening to and speaking AAE rather than MAE. Craig and Washington (2006) found that 90 percent of the African American children in their ten-year line of studies spoke AAE upon school entry, suggesting more systematic exposure to AAE than to MAE. Production of AAE features at the time of school entry was positively associated with greater syntactic skills (Craig and Washington 1994, 1995). However, children who do not make the switch from AAE to MAE face well-documented challenges to academic achievement in areas such as reading (Craig et al. 2004).

Given the important relationship between code-switching and academic success, the sections that follow focus on a variety of factors that may underlie children's ability to code-switch between AAE and MAE; these include cognitive and social variables.

30.3 Factors Affecting Code-Switching

Code-switching is affected by both internal and external factors. Internal factors include a child's cognitive profile and age, and external factors include the child's home and language environment. In this section, we review briefly extant findings on the impact of selected internal (cognitive, age) and external (SES, communicative context) factors on both bilingual and bidialectal code-switching.

30.3.1 Internal Influence 1: Cognition

Basic cognitive processes have been identified as having important influences on an individual's code-switching abilities. In particular, studies of code-switching in bilingual speakers have identified *executive functions* as important processes to consider. Executive functions are broadly defined as an interrelated set of cognitive control mechanisms that allow planning for goal-oriented behavior (Miyake et al. 2000; Zelazo et al. 1997). At its most basic level, the executive control system regulates the ability to *inhibit* responses to irrelevant information, to *update* working memory, and to *shift* attention between cognitive tasks (Miyake et al. 2000). These combined skills are thought to be important for successful code-switching.

Aspects of executive functioning, such as inhibition (Bialystok and Viswanathan 2009) and cognitive flexibility (Bialystok and Viswanathan 2009; Carlson and Meltzoff 2008), are reportedly facilitated by bilingualism. The presence of a "bilingual advantage," in both inhibitory control and overall cognitive flexibility, is apparently a result of the bilingual child's consistent need to either suppress or activate one language based on the demands and requirements of the social context (Bialystok and Viswanathan 2009; Carlson and Meltzoff 2008). According to Bialystok (2011) and others (Carlson and Meltzoff 2008; Kovács and Mehler 2009), this repeated practice with activation and inhibition of language results in changes in brain organization and cognitive ability that manifests as heightened flexibility compared to monolingual speakers. Cognitive flexibility in young children has been demonstrated by studies in which children learn to switch rapidly and easily from one rule (e.g., sort by color) to another (e.g., sort by shape) on tasks such as the Dimensional Change Card Sort[1] (Zelazo et al. 1996) and the Faces task[2] (Bialystok, Craik, and Ryan 2006).

Although bilingualism presents numerous cognitive benefits, it is also associated with cognitive costs. Specifically, the *inhibition theory* of bilingual code-switching suggests that code-switching requires a speaker to inhibit one language so that the other language can be produced with no or minimal interference (Meuter and Allport 1999). The speed at which bilingual adults are able to inhibit depends, in part, on whether they are inhibiting a dominant, first language (L1) or a less dominant language (L2 or L3). Studies supporting the inhibition theory in bilingual adults have demonstrated the asymmetrical nature of the switch cost: that is, more inhibition, as evidenced by longer reaction-time, is needed to suppress L1 on L2-switch trials than to suppress L2 on L1-switch trials (Meuter and Allport 1999). In other words, bilingual adults reportedly expend more cognitive resources to inhibit the language that is most dominant and accessible (L1) than to suppress the language that is less dominant (L2 or L3).

However, the inhibition theory has been rejected by those who assert that the bilingual language system keeps both, or multiple, languages accessible simultaneously to allow for rapid switching between them (Grosjean 2008; Grosjean, Li, and Bialystok 2013). For example, Grosjean (2008) and Grosjean et al. (2013) claim that, during code-switching, one language is *deactivated*, rather than inhibited. This is a subtle, but important, difference from other accounts of code-switching in that code-switching is described as a dynamic process requiring the speaker to engage in active decision-making, rather than a static one in which the speaker must suppress one language in order to produce the other. Empirical evidence from one study of bidialectalism supports the idea that dominant language varieties are more difficult to deactivate than non-dominant language varieties. In a study of bidialectal code-switching in African American and European American third and fifth graders from lower-middle-SES backgrounds, Baratz (1969, 889) found that both groups of children were better able to accurately repeat sentences that were presented in their dominant language variety. That is, children experienced interference from their dominant dialect when repeating sentences in their second dialect, suggesting that these school-age children were not bidialectal because they did not have a command of both MAE and AAE. However, both groups of children—MAE speakers and AAE speakers—made repetition "errors" consistent with the systematic rules of their primary language variety.

Despite some of the costs associated with bilingualism, bilingual children overall appear to have more cognitive resources to expend relative to their monolingual peers (Bialystok and Viswanathan 2009; Carlson and Meltzoff 2008). Currently there is no parallel evidence for a similar advantage bestowed upon children who are bidialectal. Technically, children who speak two dialects can be regarded as monolingual because both varieties derive from the same language. However, code-switching has been identified as a critical skill that AAE speakers must master, and this is particularly true in educational (Crotteau 2007; Terry 2012) and employment contexts (Robbins 1988). Thus, bidialectal speakers, like bilingual speakers, must broaden their linguistic repertoires to include knowledge and use of forms that are governed largely by the spoken (or written) context. Based on research findings from bilingual children, children with more expansive language repertoires should have better developed cognition than children who only speak one language, and this should be true for language varieties as well. However, studies of cognitive processing in children who are bidialectal are critically limited (Terry et al. 2010). In one of the few published studies examining dialect density and cognitive ability, Terry et al. (2010) explored the impact of dissimilarities in morphosyntactic representation between AAE and MAE (e.g., past tense copula *was/were*) in spoken instructions on the mathematical reasoning performance of AAE-speaking second graders. Findings indicated that mismatches between AAE and MAE weakened performance on mathematical reasoning tests, posing a cognitive load on working memory. There remains a great need to fill the gap in our understanding of the underlying cognitive mechanisms that influence code-switching in bidialectal speakers.

30.3.2 Internal Influence 2: Age

A second internal factor that affects code-switching is age. In school-aged children, age is frequently presented as differences in grade-based performance. Studies of age- or grade-related changes in CSD address a need to distinguish normal language variation from language impairment, which has been acknowledged as a potential confound in understanding relationships between dialect use and academic achievement in AAE-speaking children. To this end, a body of literature focused solely on characterizing language development in children from culturally and linguistically diverse backgrounds, including AAE speakers, has emerged (Craig and Washington 2006; Horton-Ikard and Pittman 2010; Ivy and Masterson 2011; Terry and Connor 2010; Washington and Craig 2001; Washington and Mills 2011).

In an investigation examining reading performance that included children from varied dialect communities, Terry and Connor (2012) determined that dialect diversity (using DVAR) decreases from kindergarten to first grade but that this shift was not associated with changes in reading or phonological awareness skills. That work also indicated that NMAE production in kindergarten predicted reading achievement in first grade above and beyond that predicted based on children's phonological awareness skills. Thus, children's dialect use may have a greater impact than pre-reading skills on children's reading achievement in first grade. In an earlier investigation, Craig and Washington (2004) examined age-related differences in dialect density in African American children who completed a picture description task. Results indicated that dialect density decreased between kindergarten and first grade and then plateaued between first and fifth grade. Children who showed a decrease in dialect density in second grade outperformed children who did not show a decrease in dialect density on standardized tests of reading achievement and vocabulary reception. Craig et al. (2009) assessed dialect density (using DDM) in the spoken and written narratives of African American children, grades one through five. Results indicated an inverse relationship between dialect density and reading achievement.

Isaacs (1996) examined dialect density differences between African American and White children in grades three, five, and seven who were from North Carolina. Five features of nonstandard dialect were examined: presence of *be*, subject-verb agreement, possession absence, copula absence, and multiple negation. Results indicated that older students were better able to distinguish "school talk" from "not school talk" in contrasting pairs of sentences than were younger children, suggesting a more advanced ability to discriminate standard dialect from nonstandard dialect. Further, Isaacs demonstrated that semantic comprehension of standard dialect improved with age but syntax comprehension of standard dialect did not. Specifically, third graders produced more nonstandard dialect than did fifth or seventh graders. *Multiple negation* persisted across grade level, while the following nonstandard dialect features declined across grade levels: *presence of be, subject-verb disagreement, absences of possession, and absence of copula*. White and Black students did not differ in dialect density across age.

More recently, dialect density (DDM, type-based vernacular index, and frequency-based variation analysis) was examined in children, ages 4 to 13 years, from low-SES backgrounds in North Carolina (Van Hofwegen and Wolfram 2010). Results indicated a decrease in dialect density from 48 months to grade one followed by a dialect plateauing between grades one and four before an increase in dialect density from grade six to grade eight. Between grades eight and ten, there was another decline in dialect density. This study also found that dialect density was strongly related to some social variables (grade and mother's education) but not to others (gender, Afro-centrality, African American social contacts, White social contacts, and percent of African Americans in school). These data are difficult to interpret because children in different age groups were engaged in different activities (e.g., preschoolers were playing, children in the first through fourth grades were interacting with their mother, and children in grades six through ten were interacting with a peer of their choosing). The most frequently occurring AAE features in order were: nasal fronting, copula absence, auxiliary absence, third person singular –s absence, invariant *be*, negative concord, and *ain't* for 'is not.'

While the previous studies focused on age differences in the dialect density of morphosyntactic features of AAE, Harris and Moran (2006) examined phonological features of AAE in a sample of children from working-class, rural Alabama and found similarities in phonological features of AAE exhibited at preschool, elementary school, and middle school (Harris and Moran 2006). From preschool to middle school, on average, AAE-speaking children exhibited persistent use of final consonant deletion (FCD), substitution of /n/ for /ŋ/, substitution of /d/ for /ð/, deletion of /r/, and final cluster reduction (FCR) in connected speech. Three of these features—FCD, deletion of /r/, and FCR—alter the syllabic structure of the MAE form of words, which may impact children's ability to establish phonological awareness of MAE. Also, FCD and FCR may result in morphophonemic differences that affect reading as well as spelling, placing AAE-speaking children at risk for underachievement in reading and writing in MAE. However, the morphophonemic level is but one level for appraising language and literacy. Smitherman (1972) highlights the importance of analyzing text, whether spoken or written, for its content and use, as opposed to its form, where AAE and MAE differences are at their greatest.

In summary, while some morphosyntactic features (e.g., multiple negation) and phonological features (e.g., final consonant deletion) are likely to persist across age, dialect density tends to decrease over time as MAE becomes the dominant, more active, and more accessible language. The decrease in AAE production over time is not surprising in light of accounts of language dominance in bilingual individuals which hold that the language with which an individual primarily communicates becomes her or his dominant language (Heredia 1997). Heredia (1997) documented a bilingual language shifting—when the second language becomes more accessible than the first language—which occurs as a result of extensive exposure to a second language. Grosjean et al. (2013) also asserted the importance of language exposure in bilingual code-switching, suggesting that bilinguals communicate on a continuum from monolingual (e.g., French only) to bilingual (e.g., French/English), depending on the language use in their speech communities and in their everyday activities. During code-switching, the bilingual individual deactivates one language to communicate in the other (Grosjean et al. 2013). Thus, it is plausible that bidialectal (AAE/MAE) children experience a similar language shifting as they progress through their school-age years, encountering and being reinforced for speaking and writing in MAE in the classroom.

30.3.3 External Influence 1: SES

External influences on language variation and on academic outcomes include key sociodemographic variables, such as SES, and sociocultural variables, such as the communicative context within which African American children learn and use language. SES, in particular, is critical to understand because differences in dialect density and diversity are confounded somewhat by SES; heavy dialect users are most often from working-class or low-SES backgrounds. In this section, we present current findings for the influence of SES and communicative context on children's dialect use.

Children from lower SES backgrounds tend to produce AAE to a greater extent than children from higher SES backgrounds (Craig and Washington 2006; Washington and Craig 1998a, 618). For example, Washington and Craig (1998a) found that kindergartners from low-SES homes produced greater dialect density than did kindergartners from middle-SES homes during spontaneous free play. Similarly, 5- and 6-year-old AAE-speaking children in the low-SES group marked passive participles (e.g., The cat *was chased* by the dog) at lower rates than their middle-SES age- and language-matched controls (Pruitt, Oetting, and Hegarty 2011). Conversely, in an experimental study examining past tense marking, Pruitt and Oetting (2009) found no SES differences in rates of regular marking (e.g., *bounce/ed*); irregular marking (e.g., *flew*); or over-regularizations (e.g., *fly/ed*) between 5- and 6-year-old AAE-speaking participants from low- and middle-SES backgrounds.

Although much of the work on AAE has focused on low-income children who are more likely to be heavy dialect users, a small number of studies have established that AAE-speakers are also from middle-SES homes. For example, Horton-Ikard and Miller (2004) examined dialect density of middle-SES, school-aged AAE-speaking children, ages 6 to 11 years, across narrative and conversational discourse. Findings indicated a gender by discourse sampling context interaction such that boys produced a higher rate of dialect density and more diversity in the type of dialect features in narrative samples than in conversational samples compared to the girls in the study. In addition, older girls produced greater dialect densities than older boys. The following features decreased with age: invariant/habitual *be*, multiple negation, and hypercorrection. Of the morphosyntactic features of AAE that decrease over time, hypercorrection may be an index of code-switching acquisition as children experiment with MAE forms. Given that MAE is the language variety of prestige in academic settings, the authors speculated that children reduced dialect density to align their language with classroom expectations.

In summary, young African American children from low-SES backgrounds tend to produce more dialect density than children from middle-SES backgrounds (Washington and Craig 1998a, 618). AAE-speaking children from low-SES backgrounds tend to mark some aspects of past tense (regular, irregular) at rates that are typical (Pruitt and Oetting 2009) and other aspects of past tense (passive participle) at rates that are atypical (Pruitt et al. 2011) for their age. By school-age, AAE-speaking children from low-SES backgrounds demonstrate interference from AAE in a MAE repetition task, indicating that AAE was children's dominant, more active and accessible dialect (Baratz 1969). However, the dialect density of school-aged AAE-speaking children from middle-SES backgrounds varies across discourse type, demonstrating dialect shifting (Horton-Ikard and Miller 2004). Taken together, these outcomes demonstrate that the role of SES in dialect production is great and must be considered in investigations with AAE-speaking children.

30.3.4 External Influence 2: Communicative Context

While dialect density measures are useful for quantifying AAE usage in a given speech context, they do not address the underlying explanations for what features are chosen for use in any given context (Van Hofwegen and Wolfram 2010). For example, code-switching may be used as a strategy to communicate appropriately within a given context (Grosjean 2010), such as a classroom. Thus, bidialectal children who speak MAE in the classroom setting are not only demonstrating cognitive flexibility but also communicative competence.

In the classroom, children must demonstrate communicative competence by drawing upon their receptive and expressive language skills to communicate across discourse types such as: conversation, narration, oral or choral reading, and writing in MAE. Dialect density has been examined across language sampling elicitation contexts, such as free play and picture description (Washington and Craig 1998b, 1115). Results indicated that children produced higher rates of AAE types and tokens in a semi-structured picture description task than in the unstructured free play context. In an older group of third-grade children, the impact of language sampling elicitation contexts on dialect density was further examined (Thompson, Craig, and Washington 2004). The language sampling contexts included both oral (picture description) and literacy (oral reading of SAE text, writing) tasks. Results revealed that children's dialect density was greater in picture description than in either oral reading or writing contexts, suggesting that, by third grade, AAE-speaking children are aware of the need to shift from AAE to MAE across oral and literacy contexts. Not only was there a quantitative shift in dialect density, there were also qualitative differences in how AAE was represented across communicative contexts. That is, children produced morphosyntactic and phonological features of AAE in picture description whereas children produced mostly phonological features in the oral reading task and mostly morphosyntactic features in the writing task.

A similar oral to literacy context effect on dialect use has been found in other studies of school-aged AAE-speaking children in which the oral context is a spoken narrative or conversation and the literacy context is a written narrative (Craig et al. 2009; Ivy and Masterson 2011). For example, Craig et al. (2009) examined dialect density in spoken and written narratives of children, grades one through five. Results indicated that children produced greater dialect density in spoken than in written narratives. Importantly, children displaying a dialect density decrease in written narratives outperformed children who did not display such a downward shift in reading achievement. Eighty-five percent of the school-age AAE-speakers in Craig et al. (2009) shifted toward MAE on the narrative writing task, demonstrating sensitivity to context differences.

A similar downward shift in dialect density between oral and written language among eighth graders was found in another study; however, third graders showed comparable amounts of dialect use across spoken and written modalities (Ivy and Masterson 2011). This finding is different than that of Craig et al. (2009) and may stem from elicitation procedure differences. Craig et al. (2009) elicited a spoken and a written narrative. Ivy and Masterson (2011) elicited two spoken samples and two written samples that included both a narrative and a conversation (interview). Future research is needed to establish the point at which children shift from AAE to MAE in spoken language relative to written language and which elicitation contexts will be most informative for helping children maintain AAE and attain MAE.

Narratives provide an ecologically valid context within which to examine dialect use. A growing body of research demonstrates that children's oral language abilities, generally, and early oral narrative ability in particular, are predictive of later academic outcomes, including reading and writing (Griffin et al. 2004; Roth, Speece, and Cooper 1996; Tabors, Snow, and Dickinson 2001), and mathematical ability (O'Neill, Pearce, and Pick 2004). Although researchers have studied the narrative skills of African American children, as well as the relationship between children's academic achievement and AAE use, few have investigated the relationship between children's AAE use, narrative skills, and academic achievement.

Narrative skills have been described in terms of how well children organize past events. Narratives are organized on at least two levels: macrostructure and microstructure. Narrative *macrostructure* refers to the way story events are sequenced and evaluated to build a coherent story (Hughes, McGillivray, and Schmidek 1997). Narrative *microstructure* refers to the way that words and sentences come together to build a cohesive story (Hughes et al. 1997). One study of 4- and 6-year-old AAE speakers found that children who used greater dialect density also produced more complete narrative macrostructure than those with lower levels of AAE (Ross, Oetting, and Stapleton 2004). Another study of school-age children investigated the type and adequacy of cohesive devices, such as pronouns and conjunctions, used by thirty-three AAE-speaking children, aged 7, 9, and 11 years, while telling a story (Horton-Ikard 2009). Analyses revealed that proficient use of cohesive devices increased with age and that participants used cohesive devices similar to those that have been reported among child MAE speakers. Children also produced morphosyntactic AAE features that function as referential cohesive devices: undifferentiated pronoun case and pronoun extension. Taken together, these studies suggest that children draw upon AAE as a linguistic resource to support narrative performance at both macrostructural (Ross, Oetting, and Stapleton 2004) and microstructural (Horton-Ikard 2009) levels.

More recently, studies have examined whether children's dialect density is related to their performance at the two levels of narrative structure. For example, a recent study showed a negative, moderate correlation between dialect diversity (using DVAR) and narrative macrostructure (using High Point Analysis) at the end of pre-kindergarten, indicating that NMAE use may be related to narrative macrostructure ability and less so to narrative microstructure ability, which was not correlated with DVAR (Terry et al. 2013). Although a negative correlation between dialect production and narrative macrostructure was found, others have found a positive relationship between AAE and narrative macrostructure during the preschool years (Ross et al. 2004). Unlike the Ross et al. (2004) study, which only focused on one aspect of AAE, namely preterite *had + V–ed* (e.g., He *had climbed* the tree to look for his frog), Terry et al. (2013) considered a wider range of NMAE features. Additional research is necessary to clarify these relationships.

In contrast to studies of preschoolers, a study of school-age AAE-speaking children, grades two to five, indicated that dialect density (using DDM) was neither correlated with narrative macrostructure (expressive elaboration) nor microstructure (number of different word rate, clause density) (Mills, Watkins, and Washington 2013). This finding is incongruent with those of Terry et al. (2013) and may stem from differences in dialect measurement. That is, Terry et al. (2013) used DVAR, which derives from the Diagnostic Evaluation of Language Variation Screening Test (DELV-ST) (Seymour et al. 2003). Mills et al. (2013) used DDM, which is calculated from the narratives themselves. Interestingly, one measure of narrative macrostructure in Terry et al. (2013), narrative scoring scheme, was not correlated with dialect density, a finding that is consistent with Mills et al. (2013). Thus, research on the relationships between code-switching, as measured by dialect density, and literacy skills is inconclusive, requiring further investigation.

30.4 EDUCATIONAL IMPLICATIONS

The development of code-switching skills is especially important as African American children make the transition from their home communities to the school environment because of their purported relationship with reading attainment. It has been hypothesized that AAE-speaking children may be at an academic disadvantage in relation to their MAE-speaking counterparts as they matriculate through school because of the differences between their home and school language varieties. To begin, structural differences between AAE and MAE may place children at risk for underachievement in reading, decoding in particular. Although structural rules of AAE and MAE overlap in many ways, they also differ in important ways that may present a significant cognitive load that has an impact on working memory (Terry et al. 2010). Further, these differences may make it more difficult for AAE speakers to establish a relationship between spoken language and reading (Kahmi and Catts 2005; Snow, Burns, and Griffin 1998). This difficulty may, in part, explain the Black–White achievement gap in reading (Vanneman et al. 2009). Children who shift toward speaking MAE in school settings by the end of third grade are likely to be one or more grade levels ahead of their peers in reading by the end of fourth grade (Craig et al. 2004). Thus, AAE speakers may find it advantageous to shift to MAE dominance in the classroom for academic success.

Given that teachers tend to expect MAE in the classroom and may hold negative language ideologies about language varieties such as AAE (Blake and Cutler 2003), code-shifting may bridge linguistic isolation. Equally, dialect awareness programs for teachers that inform them of the well-ordered, systematic nature of AAE may also attenuate the deleterious effects of mismatches in language expectations. Indeed, studies show that dynamic assessment improves the AAE knowledge and dialect attitudes of teachers (Fogel and Ehri 2006) and pre-service speech-language pathologists (Blackburn 2012).

30.5 Conclusion

This chapter has presented our current understandings of the internal and external factors that affect language variation in African American children. While studies have discussed the issue of AAE/MAE code-shifting as it relates to academic performance, many studies have not been designed to examine this relationship directly. In the future, psycholinguistic studies will be necessary to determine the relationships between dialect production and cognitive processing and to identify African American children who are bidialectal.

Notes

1. Dimensional Change Card Sort involves sorting cards along one dimension (e.g., color) and then by another (e.g., shape). Two boxes are placed before the child, and the child is told, "Let's play the color game." In this game, the child places cards of the same dimension in the same box (e.g., "The yellow ones go in this box. The green ones go there."). Then the task switches so that the child sorts along the second dimension. The child is told, "Let's play the shape game. The cars go here. The flowers go there." Children who have sufficient executive control are able to align their card sorting with the rule given (e.g., color, shape).

2. Faces Task involves a central fixation and a stimulus that appears next to it. To be successful on the Faces task, individuals must direct their eyes to the opposite direction of a stimulus, overriding the reflexive response to look toward the stimulus. Success on the Faces task is related to greater inhibition skills.

References

Baratz, Joan C. 1967. "Language and Speech Deficits in Culturally Disadvantaged Children: Implications for the Speech Clinician." *Journal of Speech and Hearing Disorders* 32: 203–14.

———. 1969. "A Bi-Dialectal Task for Determining Language Proficiency in Economically Disadvantaged Negro Children." *Child Development* 40 (3): 889–901.

Bialystok, Ellen. 2011. "Reshaping the Mind: The Benefits of Bilingualism." *Canadian Journal of Experimental Psychology/Revue canadienne de psychologie expérimentale* 65 (4): 229–35.

Bialystok, E., Fergus I. M. Craik, and Jennifer Ryan. 2006. "Executive Control in a Modified Antisaccade Task." *Journal of Experimental Psychology: Learning, Memory, and Cognition* 32 (6): 1341–54.

Bialystok, E., and M. Viswanathan. 2009. "Components of Executive Control with Advantages for Bilingual Children in Two Cultures." *Cognition* 112 (3): 494–500.

Blackburn, Judith F. 2012. "The Effect of Dialect Instruction on Student Knowledge of and Attitudes toward African American English." *Communication Disorders Quarterly* 33 (4): 220–29.

Blake, Renée, and Cecilia Cutler. 2003. "AAE and Variation in Teachers Attitudes: A Question of School Philosophy?" *L&E Linguistics and Education: An International Research Journal* 14 (2): 163–94.

Cantone, Katja Francesca. 2007. *Code-Switching in Bilingual Children*. Dordrecht: Springer.

Carlson, Stephanie M., and Andrew N. Meltzoff. 2008. "Bilingual Experience and Executive Functioning in Young Children." *Developmental Science* 11 (2): 282–98.

Charity, Anne H. 2008. "African American English: An Overview." *Perspectives on Culturally and Linguistically Diverse Populations* 15 (2): 33–42.

Cook-Gumperz, Jenny, and John Joseph Gumperz. 1982. "Communicative Competence in Educational Perspective." In *Communicating in the Classroom: Language, Thought, and Culture*, edited by Louise Cherry Wilkinson, 13–24. New York: Academic Press.

Craig, Holly K., Connie A. Thompson, Julie A. Washington, and S. L. Potter. 2004. "Performance of Elementary-Grade African American Students on the Gray Oral Reading Tests." *Language, Speech, and Hearing Services in Schools* 35 (2): 141–54.

Craig, Holly K., and Julie A. Washington. 1994. "The Complex Syntax Skills of Poor, Urban, African-American Preschoolers at School Entry." *Language, Speech, and Hearing Services in Schools* 25 (3): 181–90.

———. 1995. "African-American English and Linguistic Complexity in Preschool Discourse: A Second Look." *Language, Speech, and Hearing Services in Schools* 26 (1): 87–93.

———. 2004. "Grade-Related Changes in the Production of African American English." *Journal of Speech Language and Hearing Research* 47 (2): 450–63.

———. 2006. *Malik Goes to School: Examining the Language Skills of African American Students from Preschool-5th Grade*. Mahwah, NJ: Lawrence Erlbaum.

Craig, Holly K., Lingling Zhang, Stephanie L. Hensel, and Erin J. Quinn. 2009. "African American English-Speaking Students: An Examination of the Relationship between Dialect Shifting and Reading Outcomes." *Journal of Speech, Language, and Hearing Research* 52 (4): 839–55.

Crotteau, Michelle. 2007. "Honoring Dialect and Culture: Pathways to Student Success on High-Stakes Writing Assessments." *English Journal* 96 (4): 27–32.

DeBose, Charles E. 1992. "Codeswitching: Black English and Standard English in the African-American Linguistic Repertoire." *JMMD Journal of Multilingual and Multicultural Development* 13 (1–2): 157–67.

Fogel, Howard, and Linnea C. Ehri. 2006. "Teaching African American English Forms to Standard American English-Speaking Teachers: Effects on Acquisition, Attitudes, and Responses to Student Use." *Journal of Teacher Education Journal of Teacher Education* 57 (5): 464–80.

Green, Lisa. 2002. *African American English: A Linguistic Introduction*. New York: Cambridge University Press.

Griffin, Terri M., Lowry Hemphill, Linda Camp, and Dennis Palmer Wolf. 2004. "Oral Discourse in the Preschool Years and Later Literacy Skills." *First Language* 24 (71): 123–47.

Grosjean, François. 2008. *Studying Bilinguals*. Oxford: Oxford University Press.

———. 2010. *Bilingual Life and Reality.* Accessed in Harvard University Press Database Online. Cambridge, MA.

Grosjean, François, Ping Li, and Ellen Bialystok. 2013. *The Psycholinguistics of Bilingualism.* Accessed in Wiley-Blackwell [database online]. Chichester, West Sussex; Malden, MA.

Harris, Kandis L., and Michael J. Moran. 2006. "Phonological Features Exhibited by Children Speaking African American English at Three Grade Levels." *Communication Disorders Quarterly* 27 (4): 195–205.

Heredia, Roberto R. 1997. "Bilingual Memory and Hierarchical Models: A Case for Language Dominance." *Current Directions in Psychological Science* 6 (2): 34–39.

Horton-Ikard, RaMonda. 2009. "Cohesive Adequacy in the Narrative Samples of School-Age Children Who Use African American English." *Language, Speech, and Hearing Services in Schools* 40 (4): 393–402.

Horton-Ikard R., and J. F. Miller. 2004. "It Is not Just the Poor Kids: The Use of AAE Forms by African-American School-Aged Children from Middle SES Communities." *Journal of Communication Disorders* 37 (6): 467–87.

Horton-Ikard, RaMonda, and Ramona T. Pittman. 2010. "Examining the Writing of Adolescent African American English Speakers: Suggestions for Assessment and Intervention." *Topics in Language Disorders* 30 (3): 189–204.

Hughes, Diana L., LaRae McGillivray, and Mark Schmidek. 1997. *Guide to Narrative Language: Procedures for Assessment.* Eau Claire, WI: Thinking Publications.

Isaacs, Gale J. 1996. "Persistence of Non-Standard Dialect in School-Age Children." *Journal of Speech, Language, and Hearing Research* 39 (2): 434–41.

Ivy, Lennette Johnson, and Julie Masterson. 2011. "A Comparison of Oral and Written English Styles in African American Students at Different Stages of Writing Development." *Language, Speech, and Hearing Services in Schools* 42: 31–40.

Kahmi, A. G., and Hugh W. Catts. 2005. "Language and Reading: Convergences and Divergences." In *Language and Reading Disabilities*, 2nd ed., edited by A. G. Kahmi and Hugh W. Catts, 1–25. Boston: Allyn and Bacon.

Kovacs, A. M., and J. Mehler. 2009. "Cognitive Gains in 7-Month-Old Bilingual Infants." *Proceedings of the National Academy of Sciences Proceedings of the National Academy of Sciences* 106 (16): 6556–60.

Labov, William. 1971. "The Notion of 'System' in Creole Languages." In *Pidginization and Creolization of Languages*, edited by Dell Hymes, 447–72. Cambridge: Cambridge University Press.

———. 1972. "The Effect of Social Mobility on Linguistic Behavior." In *A Various Language: Perspectives on American Dialects*, edited by Juanita V. Williamson and Virginia M. Burke, 640–62. New York: Holt, Rinehart, and Winston.

Levine, Glenn S. 2010. *Code Choice in the Language Classroom.* Bristol: Multilingual Matters.

Lindholm, K. J., and A. M. Padilla. 1978. "Child Bilingualism: Report on Language Mixing, Switching, and Translations." *Linguistics* 16 (211): 23–44.

Meuter, R. F. I., and A. Allport. 1999. "Bilingual Language Switching in Naming: Asymmetrical Costs of Language Selection." *Journal of Memory and Language* 40 (1): 25–40.

Mills, Monique T., Ruth V. Watkins, and Julie A. Washington. 2013. "Structural and Dialectal Characteristics of the Fictional and Personal Narratives of School-Age African American Children." *Language, Speech, and Hearing Services in Schools* 44 (2): 211–23.

Miyake, Akira, Naomi Friedman, Michael Emerson, Alexander Witzki, Amy Howerter, and Tor Wager. 2000. "The Unity and Diversity of Executive Functions and their Contributions to Complex 'Frontal Lobe' Tasks: A Latent Variable Analysis." *Cognitive Psychology* 41 (1): 49–100.

Muñoz, Maria L., G. Copeland, and T. Marquardt. 1997. "A Comparison of the Code-Switching Abilities of Aphasic and Neurologically Intact Bilinguals." *Perspectives on Culturally and Linguistically Diverse Populations* 3 (2): 10–11.

O'Neill, Daniela K., Michelle J. Pearce, and Jennifer L. Pick. 2004. "Preschool Children's Narratives and Performance on the Peabody Individualized Achievement Test—Revised: Evidence of a Relation between Early Narrative and Later Mathematical Ability." *First Language* 24 (2): 149–84.

Oetting, Janna B., and April Garrity. 2006. "Variation within Dialects: A Case of Cajun/Creole Influence within Child SAAE and SWE." *Journal of Speech, Language, and Hearing Research* 49: 16–26.

Pruitt, Sonja, and Janna B. Oetting. 2009. "Past Tense Marking by African American English-Speaking Children Reared in Poverty." *Journal of Speech, Language, and Hearing Research* 52 (1): 2–15.

Pruitt, Sonja L., Janna B. Oetting, and Michael Hegarty. 2011. "Passive Participle Marking by African American English-Speaking Children Reared in Poverty." *Journal of Speech, Language, and Hearing Research* 54 (2): 598–607.

Renn, Jennifer, and J. Michael Terry. 2009. "Operationalizing Style: Quantifying the Use of Style Shift in the Speech of African American Adolescents." *American Speech:* 84 (4): 367–90.

Robbins, Judy Floyd. 1988. "Employers' Language Expectations and Nonstandard Dialect Speakers." *The English Journal* 77 (6): 22–24.

Ross, S. H., Janna B. Oetting, and B. Stapleton. 2004. "Preterite *Had* + V-ed: A Developmental Narrative Structure of African American English." *American Speech* 79 (2): 167–93.

Roth, Froma P., Deborah L. Speece, and David H. Cooper. 1996. "Unresolved Mysteries: How Do Metalinguistic and Narrative Skills Connect with Early Reading?" *Journal of Special Education* 30 (3): 257–77.

Scanlon, Michael, and Alicia Beckford Wassink. 2010. "African American English in Urban Seattle: Accommodation and Intraspeaker Variation in the Pacific Northwest." *American Speech* 85 (2): 205–24.

Seymour, Harry N., Thomas W. Roeper, Jill de Villiers, and Peter de Villiers A. 2003. *Diagnostic Evaluation of Language Variation-Screening Test.* San Antonio, TX: Pearson.

Smitherman, Geneva. 1972. "English Teacher, Why You Be Doing the Thangs You Don't Do?" *English Journal* 96 (1): 59–65.

Snow, Catherine E., M. Susan Burns, and Peg Griffin, eds. 1998. *Preventing Reading Difficulties in Young Children.* Washington, DC: National Academies Press.

Swann, Joan, Ana Deumert, Theresa Lillis, and Rajend Mesthrie. 2004. *A Dictionary of Sociolinguistics.* Tuscaloosa: University of Alabama Press.

Tabors, Patton O., Catherine E. Snow, and David K. Dickinson. 2001. "Homes and Schools Together: Supporting Language and Literacy Development." In *Beginning Literacy with Language: Young Children Learning at Home and School,* edited by David K. Dickinson, Patton O. Tabors, David K. Dickinson, and Patton O. Tabors, 313–34. Baltimore, MD: Paul H Brookes.

Terry, J. Michael, R. Hendrick, E. Evangelou, R. L. Smith. 2010. "Variable Dialect Switching among African American Children: Inferences about Working Memory." *Lingua* 120 (10): 2463–75.

Terry, Nicole P., and Carol McDonald Connor. 2010. "African American English and Spelling: How Do Second Graders Spell Dialect-Sensitive Features of Words?" *Learning Disability Quarterly* 33 (3): 199–210.

————. 2012. "Changing Nonmainstream American English Use and Early Reading Achievement from Kindergarten to First Grade." *American Journal of Speech-Language Pathology* 21 (1): 78–86.

Terry, Nicole Patten, Monique T. Mills, Gary E. Bingham, Souraya Mansour, and Nancy Marencin. 2013. "Oral Narrative Performance of African American Prekindergartners Who Speak Nonmainstream American English." *Language, Speech, and Hearing Services in Schools* 44 (3): 291–305.

Thompson, Connie A., Holly K. Craig, and Julie A. Washington. 2004. "Variable Production of African American English across Oracy and Literacy Contexts." *Language, Speech, and Hearing Services in Schools* 35 (3): 269–82.

Van Hofwegen, Janneke, and Walt Wolfram. 2010. "Coming of Age in African American English: A Longitudinal Study." *Journal of Sociolinguistics* 14 (4): 427–55.

Vanneman, Alan, Linda Hamilton, Janet Baldwin Anderson, and Taslima Rahman. 2009. *Achievement Gaps: How Black and White Students in Public Schools Perform in Mathematics and Reading for the National Assessment of Educational Progress.* Washington, DC: US Department of Education, NCES 2009–455.

Washington, Julie A., and Holly K. Craig. 1998a. "Socioeconomic Status and Gender Influences on Children's Dialectal Variations." *Journal of Speech, Language & Hearing Research* 41 (3): 618–26.

————. 1998b. "Variable Use of African American English across Two Language Sampling Contexts." *Journal of Speech, Language & Hearing Research* 41 (5): 1115–24.

————. 2001. "Reading Performance and Dialectal Variation." In *Literacy in African American Communities*, edited by Joyce L. Harris, A. G. Kahmi, and Karen E. Pollock, 147–68. Mahwah, NJ: Lawrence Erlbaum Associates.

Washington, Julie A., and Monique T. Mills. 2011. "African American English in the Classroom." In *Language Development: Understanding Language Diversity in the Classroom*, edited by S. Levey and S. Polirstok, 227–43. Thousand Oaks, CA: Sage.

Wheeler, Rebecca S., and Rachel Swords. 2006. *Code-Switching: Teaching Standard English in Urban Classrooms.* Urbana, IL: National Council of Teachers of English.

Wolfram, Walt, and Natalie Schilling-Estes. 2006. *American English: Dialects and Variation*, 2nd ed. Malden, MA: Blackwell.

Wolfram, Walt, and Erik Thomas. 2002. *Development of African American English.* New York: John Wiley & Sons.

Yiakoumetti, Androula. 2007. "Choice of Classroom Language in Bidialectal Communities: To Include or to Exclude the Dialect?" *CJE Cambridge Journal of Education* 37 (1): 51–66.

Zabrodskaja, Anastassia. 2011. "Multidisciplinary Approaches to Code Switching." *International Journal of Bilingual Education & Bilingualism* 14 (1): 115–20.

Zelazo, Philip David, Alice Carter, J. Steven Reznick, and Douglas Frye. 1997. "Early Development of Executive Function: A Problem-Solving Framework." *Review of General Psychology Review of General Psychology* 1 (2): 198–226.

Zelazo, Philip David, Douglas Frye, and Tanja Rapus. 1996. "An Age-Related Dissociation between Knowing Rules and Using Them." *Cognitive Development* 11 (1): 37–63.

CHAPTER 31

BALANCING PEDAGOGY WITH THEORY

The Infusion of African American Language Research into Everyday Pre-K–12 Teaching Practices

SHARROKY HOLLIE, TAMARA BUTLER, AND JAMILA GILLENWATERS

31.1 INTRODUCTION

As pre-K–12 practitioners and teacher educators working toward culturally and linguistically responsive pedagogy, a fair question to ask is: To what extent has linguistic research resulted in changes in how teachers think about African American Language (AAL), teach literacy practices and language, and, most importantly, influence academic achievement? In this chapter, we explore how the study and teaching of AAL can create more culturally and linguistically responsive classrooms. In reviewing literature from linguistics, literacy studies, and teacher education, we address the praxis of infusing AAL research into teaching practices, which includes: (1) creating Culturally and Linguistically Responsive Pedagogies (CLRP), or ways of discovering the hows and whys of affirming AAL in the classroom while simultaneously teaching Academic Language (AL) (see Baker-Bell 2013; Baugh 2004; Gay 2000); (2) building a professional development model for training teachers in the linguistic research on AAL (see Delpit and Dowdy 2002; Delpit and Perry 1998; Ladson-Billings 1994); and (3) starting a laboratory school solely devoted to implementing an affirmative linguistic approach (see Hollie 2011).

The purpose of this chapter is to provide a description of these three evolutions that, when combined, offer a systemic, comprehensive, and sustainable method for building teachers' knowledge bases, developing pedagogical skills, and creating exemplary schools and classrooms. Each has attempted to expand the linguistic research on AAL by simplifying it in ways that are palatable to practicing teachers and doing so in such a way as to lead to further learning and investigation.

The body of the chapter is divided into four sections. First, we present a historical account of pedagogical approaches to teaching through AAL. In the second section, we discuss a professional development model, Language Development Program for Academic American Students (LDPAAS), now known as the Academic English Mastery Program (AEMP), created by Dr. Noma LeMoine, to whom this chapter is dedicated.[1] LDPAAS, in 1989, was one of the few urban district-supported programs dedicated to affirming the linguistic backgrounds of African American students and illustrating how teachers should be educated and how students should be taught with respect to the issue, long before the so-called "Ebonics controversy" attracted national attention. In the third section, we explore what occurs in the classroom when a teacher is "trained" to use culturally relevant and responsive pedagogies. Lastly, a school-wide model is presented as a way of bookending what could be accomplished on a national scale.

Before moving on, below are working definitions for the linguistic terms we use in this chapter, notwithstanding any definitions that have been defined in this volume by other contributors and their recommended use in discussions about linguistically responsive education:

- *Language*: a legitimate linguistic entity defined around the parameters of phonics, markers, grammar, vocabulary, nonverbal uses, and discourse styles with a heritage and purpose tied to a people as a community or citizenry;
- *Home Language* (HL): the nonstandard language utilized by family members in the home and by others in the community as opposed to the expected variety of use and instruction in schools;
- *School Language* (SL): the language utilized in the context of school, commonly associated with Standard English (SE);
- *Mainstream American English* (MAE): the accepted linguistic entity of the dominant or mainstream culture in the United States;
- *African American Language* (AAL): The systematic, rule-governed language that represents an infusion of the grammatical substratum of West African languages and the vocabulary of English. This term is not the opposite of *standard language* and will be only used in the context of the term *language*. For example, it will not be used in the context of English. There will be no use of the term *Nonstandard English*. The term *nonstandard* speaks to the *non-acceptance* of these languages, not to their lack of legitimacy;
- *Academic Language* (AL): the language used in textbooks, in classrooms, and on tests;
- *Standard English Learner* (SEL): any student for whom MAE is not spoken as the home language;
- *Validation*: the intentional and purposeful legitimatization of the home culture and language of the student who has been traditionally delegitimized by historical institutional and structural racism, stereotypes, and generalizations primarily carried forth through mainstream media and institutional knowledge sources;
- *Affirmation*: the intentional and purposeful making positive of the negative stereotypes of nonmainstream cultures and languages, again looking at the portrayals from a historical perspective.

31.2 AAL in Schools and Classrooms: Pedagogical Approaches

Over the past six decades, there have been concerted efforts to instructionally address the linguistic and cultural needs of African American students. These efforts, such as dialect readers and artful teaching, have concentrated on the dynamics of AAL, how it can influence African American student literacy, and lead to powerful and successful outcomes for students (see Braddock 1995; Darling-Hammond 1998, 78–91; Fine 1995; Foster 1995, 129–50).

31.2.1 Dialect Readers

Reading materials written in various dialects have been used instructionally to transition students into School Language. According to Rickford and Rickford (1995), studies by Tore Osterberg (1961) and Tove Bull (1990) showed success in Sweden and Norway, respectively, demonstrating in each case that dialect speakers taught by this method read better in the standard variety than dialect speakers taught through the standard variety alone. In 1974, Gary and Charlesetta Simpkins reported on their results from using *Bridge* readers, transitional readers, and AL readers. The *Bridge* materials were tested over a four-month period with 417 students in an experimental group and 123 students in the control group. On the Iowa Test of Basic Skills, the students taught by the *Bridge* method showed an average gain of 6.2 months for 4 months of instruction, compared to only an average gain of 1.6 months for students in their regularly scheduled classroom reading activities (Simpkins and Simpkins 1981).

31.2.2 Artful Teaching

Ann Piestrup (1973) found a relationship between children's reading scores and the teachers' responses to vernacular in the classroom. She distinguished what she called the *Black Artful Approach* from the *Interrupting Approach*. The *Black Artful Approach* used rhythmic play in instruction and encouraged students to participate by listening to each other's responses. Teachers attended to vocabulary differences and prevented structural conflict by teaching children to listen to the AL sound distinctions. The *Interrupting Approach* asked children to repeat words that were pronounced in dialect many times and interpreted dialect pronunciation "errors." Students tediously worked alone decoding without reading as if they understood. Piestrup (1973) found that the students taught by the Black Artful Approach had overall higher reading scores than the children taught by the Interrupting Approach. Furthermore, students with high dialect scores (i.e., those whose language differed most from AL), when taught by the Black

Artful Approach, read at similar levels as the students with the lowest dialect scores who were taught by the Interrupting Approach. Her conclusion was that the way that teachers respond to and build on the students' home and community language (i.e., vernacular) could have a powerful effect on the level of success in reading for African American students.

Despite numerous attempts to create, implement, and sustain linguistic policies that are affirmative to the recognition of AAL as a legitimate variety, it remains legally unrecognized in US language policy, which is why Hollie (2011) termed it the "unaccepted" language and why it remains of interest to educators. The professional development model and instructional methodologies presented here are not new but are a continuation toward acceptance, implementation, and institutionalization.

31.2.3 DeKalb County Schools

The DeKalb County School System in Georgia had a nonstandard language program for more than ten years. Its main tenet was to teach AL and school communication skills without devaluing the language skills that students learn at home. According to the tenets of this program, "Students are given unpressured and uninterrupted opportunities to listen to the sounds and patterns of AL. These activities occur in environments that do not require AAL speakers to shed their identities as a prerequisite for learning AL." Based on normal equivalent scores (NEC) on the Iowa Tests of Basic Skills, Title I[2] students in this program showed higher gains compared to students who were not in the program (Harris-Wright 1999, 55).

31.2.4 Use of Contrastive Analysis

Contrastive Analysis is a second language learning technique that points out predictable contrasts between SL and HL. Pointing out such contrasts so that students can identify and negotiate differences between SL and HL is precisely the goal of contrastive analysis, which has been advocated for SELs for more than thirty years. Rickford and Rickford (1995) give three rationales for using contrastive analysis:

1. SELs are typically not aware of the systematic differences between SAE and, say, AAL.
2. It allows for increased efficiency in the classroom, as teachers can concentrate on the systematic areas of contrast with SAE that cause difficulties for vernacular speakers rather than taking on the more daunting task of teaching all of English grammar.
3. It improves the teaching of SAE when compared to traditional methods (e.g., the Interrupting Approach). Taylor (1989) used contrastive analysis in a study out of Chicago, where she divided her students into two groups to explore the impact

of the AAL (i.e., HL) of the speakers. With the control group, she taught SL using conventional techniques and made no reference to the students' use of AAL. With the experimental group, Taylor used contrastive analysis, specifically drawing on their attention to the points on which their AAL and the SL differed. What she found was that the students who were using traditional techniques showed an 8.5 percent increase in their use of AAL in their writing, while the students who had contrastive analysis showed a 59 percent decrease in their use of AAL in their writing. Her conclusion was that this process of comparing the two varieties seems to lead to a much greater metalinguistic awareness of similarities and differences between AAL and SL (Taylor 1989, 107–28).

Given the above, educators should engage students in activities that help them analyze language use in order to determine if oral or written samples demonstrate AAL or SE. These kinds of activities, which are informed by critical language pedagogy (Baker-Bell 2013), help students understand language difference and validate both HL and SL. Contrastive analysis benefits student learning, understanding, and agency (see DeBose, this volume) because it: (1) increases students' ability to recognize the differences between SE and AAL; (2) develops their proficiency in editing the grammar and vocabulary of their; and (3) provides greater facility in the use of SE.

31.2.5 Summary

Despite numerous attempts to create, implement, and sustain linguistic policies that are favorable and affirmative to the recognition of AAL as a legitimate variety, it remains legally unrecognized in US language policy, which is why it is termed the "unaccepted" language, and why it remains of interest to educators (Hollie 2011). The professional development model and instructional methodologies presented here are not new—they are classroom practices dating back over forty years—but they represent a continuation in the struggle for acceptance, implementation, and institutionalization.

31.3 THE ACADEMIC ENGLISH MASTERY PROGRAM: A PROFESSIONAL DEVELOPMENT MODEL

The *Academic English Mastery Program* (AEMP) is a comprehensive, research-based professional development model designed to address the language, literacy, and learning needs of African American, Mexican American, Hawaiian American, and Native American SELs. AEMP was developed in response to three Los Angeles Unified School

District initiatives: (1) *The Action Plan for a Culturally Relevant Education that Benefits African American Students and All Other Students*; (2) *The Children Can No Longer Wait: An Action Plan to End Low Achievement and Establish Educational Excellence*; and (3) *Priorities for Education, A Design for Excellence*, each of which call for instruction relevant to the language and learning needs of AAL speakers and other SELs and for professional development based on the needs of students and teachers that addresses the process of teaching. The primary objective of the AEMP is to train teachers to incorporate research-based instructional strategies that increase the access of speakers of AAL and other SELs to rigorous standards-based curricula and improve academic achievement by facilitating their acquisition of SL in its oral and written forms without devaluing the HL and culture of the students (LeMoine 1998). The primary goal of the model for students is the use of SL proficiently and the experience of greater academic achievement. A basic premise of the AEMP intervention model is that SELs who speak languages that are at variance with the structure of SL are competent communicators within the context of their culture and HL. Although AAL and other HLs are effective means of communication both within and outside of students' communities, HL is not accepted in American educational institutions as an appropriate medium for demonstrating school learning and understanding.

A second premise of the AEMP model is that language is fundamental to learning, and mastery of AL is requisite for accessing core academic curricula. African American and other SELs must become literate in the forms of English that appear in textbooks, on standardized achievement tests, and in consumer contracts if they are to effectively negotiate learning environments and apprentice as authors, scientists, historians, and scholars. Therefore, the AEMP model provides comprehensive professional development for all stakeholders at school and supports the integration of culturally and linguistically responsive (CLR) pedagogy into all content areas. AEMP addresses the language acquisition, literacy, and learning needs of African American and other SEL populations by changing instructional practices in ways that will increase access to core standards-based curricula, improve academic achievement, and close proficiency gaps.

The AEMP model seeks to transform educational practice and improve academic achievement for SELs. The above goals are achieved through: (1) prescribing innovative instructional techniques for addressing the language acquisition and learning needs of SELs; (2) providing trained instructional leaders to support AEMP implementation; (3) conducting ongoing professional development for educators, administrators, and student support service providers; and (4) supporting parents-as-partners in education through parent engagement and education opportunities. Since the 1990s, approximately 5,000 teachers in the Los Angeles Unified School District have actively participated each year in AEMP's professional development model to the benefit of more than 25,000 students per year.

Teacher quality is an important factor in student achievement. How teachers perceive their students and define them impacts the educational experiences of students (Raible and Irizarry 2007; Rogers, Marshall, and Tyson 2006). The AEMP incorporates three components designed to ensure stakeholders are knowledgeable of current research and instructional praxis for creating CLR learning environments: (1) ongoing growth opportunities for all stakeholders—administrators, teachers, coaches, parents, and paraprofessionals; (2) school site-based learning collaborations; and (3) parent education and instructional support seminars.

31.3.1 Summer Training Academy for AEMP School Leaders and Teachers

A week-long summer institute provides AEMP facilitators and principals with the tools required to effectively move their school's instructional agenda toward positive outcomes for SELs. During the institute, teachers work in small groups, develop lessons and observe "demonstration lessons" that utilize best practices for instructing SELs. AEMP demonstration lessons provide a greater level of praxis through the integration of theory and classroom application in a professional context. These lessons provide educators with specific instructional approaches, practices, and activities that build on the language and learning strengths that SELs bring to the classroom to bolster SE proficiency and literacy acquisition. AEMP teacher facilitators receive training to increase their effectiveness as leaders, thereby fostering greater implementation of AEMP goals at individual school sites.

31.3.2 Fall Educational Seminars and Application Workshops for New Teachers

AEMP's Fall Educational Seminar Series was designed for teachers new to AEMP schools and implemented in response to the program's influx of new teachers to the district (sometimes 500 to 600 a year). The primary objective was to enhance teachers' and para-educators' knowledge, awareness, and understanding of issues of language variation in SEL populations, and develop relevant methodologies for fostering SE acquisition, literacy, and learning. The seminars include hands-on workshops designed to assist educators in identifying practical classroom application of seminar content.

31.3.3 AEMP Weekend Professional Development Conference and Demonstration Lessons

AEMP's Annual Weekend Professional Development Conference hosts over 2,300 teachers, parents, para-educators, and administrators each year. The AEMP conference offers over seventy idea-filled workshops and seminars conducted by scholars in the fields of education and linguistics as well as instructional specialists and teacher leaders in the Program. Conference attendees earn salary points and credit toward the professional development requirements for renewing their teaching credential.

AEMP demonstration lessons provide a greater level of praxis through the integration of theory and classroom application in a collegial and professional context. Teachers can watch AEMP strategies come alive in authentic classroom settings. These demonstration lessons provide educators with specific instructional approaches, practices, and activities that build on the HLs that SELs bring to the classroom to bolster SE proficiency and literacy acquisition and development.

31.3.4 Collaborations: Parents as Partners with Schools

Consistent with the philosophy that expertise emerges from dialogue and collaboration, AEMP assists schools with developing vast partnerships to impact student achievement. The Grade Level Collaborative (GLC) is centered on specific AEMP instructional focal areas and encourages grade-level colleagues to engage in relevant discussions regarding effective instructional approaches for SELs.

In addition to GLCs, the AEMP advocates for the development of school partnerships with the children's first teachers: their parents. A core aspect of the AEMP intervention is the establishment of an AEMP Parent Information/Involvement Center at each school, staffed by trained Parent-Community Representatives. The Parent-Community Representative promotes partnerships with teachers to foster a "pro-education" climate and a college-going culture in the homes to empower SELs to do well in school.

African American SELs need to acquire proficiency in the language and literacy of school in order to more effectively access core academic curricula. Historically, educational institutions in the United States have had great difficulty meeting the language acquisition and learning needs of SEL populations and, in particular, African American SEL populations. SELs have the dubious distinction of having some of the lowest standardized achievement test scores in language and literacy, high dropout and failure rates, and difficulty accessing core academic curricula. In order to increase academic achievement among SELs, educators must be able to accept and affirm language diversity, facilitate second-language and literacy acquisition, and make spaces for the rich language, cultural experiences, and funds of knowledge that SEL students possess.

31.4 CULTURALLY AND LINGUISTICALLY RESPONSIVE PEDAGOGY: INSTRUCTIONAL MODEL

CLRP focuses on classroom management, academic vocabulary, academic language, and academic literacy. Without expanding academic vocabulary and increased reading and writing skills, students will not succeed in educational institutions. Therefore, educators have to use instruction methods that are responsive, validating, and affirming (Hollie 2011).

For the purpose of this chapter, we are focusing only on the area of responsive AL, which generally means the teacher views the language of many, but not all, African American students as systematic and rule-governed and the acquisition of that language as natural, complex, and meaningful. Specifically, teachers have to build an understanding of how language works in general, how language develops and changes, and form a respect for AAL as a linguistic system (Baker-Bell 2013). According to Lisa Delpit (2006), it is important for children to feel they are bringing something from home to the school. To deny the student's language is to deny the student, for language is a major part of one's total self. She offers a summation for language diversity and literacy learning in the classroom for African American students and other SELs. Delpit (2006) and Kelley (1997) reiterate that teachers should recognize that the linguistic form a student brings to the classroom is inextricably tied to community and personal identity.

31.4.1 Validation and Affirmation in the Classroom

The key to developing a positive attitude about AAL requires three steps that we have used with teachers in professional development workshops across the country for the past fifteen years (Hollie 2011).

Step One: Belief in three linguistic absolutes. Educators have to subscribe to three absolutes as their first steps for being able to validate and affirm their students' HLs:

1. All languages are good. Conceptually and linguistically speaking, there is no such thing as a bad language per se. Languages are not inherently bad, improper, wrong, or incorrect. In CLR, these terms are considered deficit in nature and useless with an affirmative position on language.
2. All linguistic forms are rule-governed and patterned. They are not haphazard, made-up, randomized, or created by rappers. The range of these rules covers all the language dimensions—phonics, morphemes, syntax, semantics, pragmatics, and discourse. Indeed, the fact that there are rules in each of these dimensions speaks to the veracity of the linguistic entity.
3. We acquire the language that is spoken by the primary caregivers at home beginning at pre-birth to pre-kindergarten. In fact, the language that is spoken at home will be the language at school. The child comes to school with all the rules of that language intact and, most importantly, with a positive view of that language. Unfortunately, the beginning of school chips away at that positive view as all of sudden students are told that the way their grandparents, uncles, siblings, and parents speak is wrong.

Step Two: Familiarity with the linguistic system of AAL. The linguistic system that governs AAL needs to be made clear in order for educators to validate and affirm it and its speakers. For example, teachers who understand the need to validate and affirm their students' use of HL must understand that AAL does not equal slang, which is fleeting vocabulary rather than a linguistic system or grammar, or profanity (see Spears 2001), and it is not happenstance. In order to be able to accurately assess their AAL speakers' use of language in oral and written forms and employ effective pedagogical strategies that help students master SE, educators need an awareness of the research-based linguistic system of AAL. (See table 31.1 for an abbreviated survey of salient linguistic features of AAL commonly discussed in our professional development workshops with teachers.)

In our workshops, familiarity with the system of AAL and the ability to validate and affirm students' HL of AAL is based on the need for educators to grasp three directives: (1) *lose the hegemonic view of SE*; (2) *understand the derivation of the home language system in the context of the indigenous language*; and (3) *code-switch appropriate to the context*.

For the first directive, educators need to understand that the grammar of SE is not the exemplar of all language varieties. A rule or feature in SE does not mean that all varieties have that same rule or apply that rule in the same way—or that they should. Adopting this broader perspective of language can help educators to stop equating language

Table 31.1 Salient Linguistic Rules of AAL

Categories	Examples
Sounds	
"th" sounds (digraphs)	*Dis* is my *mouf.*
Consonant Clusters	I put my *tes'* on your *des'.*
	Can I *ax* you something?
Short "e"/Short "i" Vowels	I am *tin* years old.
Reflexive	*Yo sista* is *Ca'ol.*
"r" or "er" sound	Did you *caw* me?
Markers (Morphemes)	
Past Tense Marker *–ed*	He *visit* us yesterday.
Possessive Marker	That is my *sister* bike.
Plural Marker	I have 25 *cent.*
Markers (Syntax)	
Multiple Negation	He *don't* have *none.*
Habitual Be	She *be* mean.
Topicalization	That *boy he* funny.
Present Tense Copula Verb	She *pretty.*
Regularized Patterns	
Reflexive Pronoun	He hurt *hisself.*
Present Tense Singular Verb	He *run* fast.
Past Tense Singular Verb	We *was* here.

Source: Adapted from Rickford 1999, tables 1.1 and 1.2, 4–9.

variation and difference with language deficit. For example, understanding that possession is expressed with –'s/–s' inflections in SE, word order and the proposition *de* in both French and Spanish, and word order and linguistic context in AAL helps educators respect, validate, and affirm linguistic variance in the classroom.

For the second directive, educators need to become familiar with how the HL system came into existence, especially in comparison to the SE system. Educators need to be trained to understand that AAL linguistic rules demonstrated in students' speaking, writing, and oral reading (ways they pronounce the words they read) do not represent random mistakes by students or something to "correct" by the swipe of a pen or "restating." For instance, AAL speakers avoid clustering homogeneously voiced consonants at the ends of words (Rickford and Rickford 2000). Therefore, while *last* may be pronounced /læst/ in SE and /læs/ in AAL, both are simply different realizations of the same word.

By accepting the first and second directives, educators can better address cross-cultural misunderstandings. When students' linguistic variation is treated as linguistic deficiency, everyone loses. When linguistic differences reveal themselves to educators who are not knowledgeable about the system of AAL, it can appear that students who speak and write in alignment with their HL need "correction" to align with the SE system. For example, it can appear as if students who speak or write both *a zebra* and *a elephant* is "correctly" using the indefinite article *a* in the first example but "incorrectly" using the indefinite article in the second instance. Educators unaware of the linguistic variation might "correct" students' written work, or restate "Do you mean *an elephant?*" to students who do not hear the difference. Neither approach supports students' acquisition of the SE target. Educators who understand that the indefinite article is regularized as *a* in AAL but is expressed as *a/an* in SE depending on the following sound can use contrastive analysis to help students understand the system of their language use and variation. Although comprised predominantly of English vocabulary/lexicon, AAL has maintained in its substratum some grammatical, phonological, and pragmatic linguistic features that can be traced to indigenous West African languages (LeMoine 2007; Smitherman 1977; Williams 1990). As is the case with most language users, use of language does not mean the understanding of how it works or how to describe it. In other words, *knowing* one's language does not constitute one *knowing about* language. As is the case in foreign language teaching, students need to be taught explicitly the rules of SE, AAL, or any other language (e.g., learning a second language in a classroom often leads to a better understanding about grammar in both the second language and the native language).

In addition to belief in the three linguistic absolutes discussed above (Step One) and familiarity with the linguistic system of AAL (Step Two), developing a positive attitude about AAL requires a final step, namely, *Step Three: Pointing toward Instruction*. After developing a familiarity with common language rules, educators then know how to validate and affirm by not "fixing" or "correcting" AAL. These and similar terms are considered deficit terminology and should not be used in an affirming classroom, where students learn how to switch between HL and AL. It is important to consider if students have the foundational understanding of why and how to code-switch. Although some students, particularly older ones, may gauge when it is appropriate to code-switch, that does not mean they will be able (or desire) to code-switch.

CLR educators use linguistic knowledge in their pedagogy to help students understand language diversity and build bidialectalism and biliteracy in SE and AAL through instructional activities designed to help students (1) understand how to identify the subject of a sentence and apply this knowledge to determine whether that subject is singular or plural; (2) compare and contrast how the base form of the corresponding verb is regularized following both singular and plural subjects and how subject-verb agreement is accomplished following singular or plural subjects in SE; (3) analyze oral and written language samples and have the ability to explain why they represent AAL or SE; (4) identify the subjects for which the verb is not regularized and practice using the SE subject/verb pair in oral and written form; and (5) practice applying the subject/verb agreement concept to oral and written forms.

31.4.2 Using Contrastive Analysis while Teaching Students How to Code-Switch

Educators do not have to teach AAL speakers how to use their HL, as AAL speakers arrive at school having already learned their HL. However, CLR educators want to equip their students with the skills needed to move between HL and AL in ways that will promote affirmation and academic achievement. In order to develop classroom activities that promote code-switching, CLR educators should pre-assess students' use of targeted AAL systems. In doing so, educators should listen to students speak and read their writing and other texts. Students' use of AAL in school contexts (i.e., classroom discussions, presentations, or academic writing) provides examples of the HL for teachers to assess how to instruct students to code-switch.

31.4.2.1 *Pre-assess Students' Use of Targeted AAL Linguistic Features*

Listen to students speak in discussions and conversations, read their writing, and listen to them read aloud. In her work on critical language pedagogy, April Baker-Bell (2013) discusses how she worked alongside an AP English Language Arts teacher to develop a unit to explore AAL. In the five-week unit, students engaged in several written activities to "understand the complex nature of language systems" (360), and in discussions to "recognize who is privileged and ... marginalized by language use" (360). Therefore, teachers can collect writing samples or guide students through some of the activities (see Baker-Bell 2013, 360–63) to assess students' perceptions and uses of AAL.

31.4.2.2 *Conduct a Language Development Lesson about an AAL Language Rule*

Teachers do not have to teach AAL speakers how to use an HL rule since AAL speakers arrive at school having mastered the use of the HL rule. The AAL speaker may not be consciously aware of this language use, however. Therefore, teachers should:

- Introduce the HL rule in a way students will understand.
- Explain to students why the rule exists in AAL.
- Teach students how the AAL rule is implemented in SE.

31.4.2.3 *Use Contrastive Analysis to Help Students Distinguish between AAL and SE*

Engage students in activities that help them analyze language use in order to determine if oral or written samples demonstrate AAL or SE. For example, the students can read and respond to language samples of AAL and SE, create visual representations of who speaks which language form, and then engage in small-group and large-class discussions (Baker-Bell 2013, 360). Similar kinds of activities help students understand language difference and help to validate both language forms.

31.4.2.4 *Teach Students a Strategy to Help Them Identify the Use of the AAL Language Rule in Oral and Written Samples*

Teach students strategies to help them accurately translate AAL into SE and vice versa. Table 31.2 provides a sample instructional sequence for teaching multiple negation.

There are three ways teachers can have students practice language switching. Many of the instructional activities are based in contrastive analysis and vary by the content that is being taught and/or the grade level of the students. This means that the content areas of reading/language arts and social studies will have more opportunities for sentence lifting and retellings, while other content areas, including math and science, are more geared toward role-playing and teachable moments. Teachers can collect writing samples and use formative assessment data to have students practice language switching across content areas and grade levels through: (1) sentence lifting, (2) retellings, and (3) role-playing.

Sentence lifting refers to the use of literature, poetry, songs, plays, student elicited sentences, or prepared story scripts that incorporate specific contrasts in HL and SL rule forms. The student performs the contrastive analysis translation to determine the underlying rules that distinguish the two language forms.

Retellings are contrastive analysis activities in which students are told a story or text that is heavily embedded with SL. Students are then required to retell the story or text in the HL. The story retelling is taped and compared and contrasted with the language of the text.

Table 31.2 Instructional Sequence

Sample CLR instruction	Example using Multiple Negation
Pre-Assess students' use of targeted AAL Linguistic Feature	Teacher observes that students' oral and written language samples provide evidence of students' use of HL Rule Multiple Negation in contexts in which SE is situationally appropriate.
Introduce the "Home Language" Rule in a way students will understand	Teacher conducts a read-aloud of "Harriet Tubman" by Eloise Greenfield, a poem that demonstrates the use of Multiple Negation. • After the read-aloud, the teacher engages the class in a discussion of the language variation demonstrated in the poem. • This classroom conversation highlights the fact that the author used HL in a way that is used in many homes and communities, and helps students understand why this use of the HL rule is valid. Teacher tells the students they are going to learn more about this AAL language rule. • Multiple Negation is the use of multiple negative words in a sentence. The more negative intensifiers in a sentence, the greater the negative sentiment being expressed. • This is not to be confused with the SE rule "Double Negatives" in which two negative words cancel each other out, expressing a positive sentiment.
Teach strategy to help students identify the use of the linguistic feature in oral and written samples	Strategy: Teaching students to highlight the negative words they see, or hear, in a sentence can help them determine whether a language sample is an example of HL or SL. 1. SE Rule: Only allows for the use of one negative word in a sentence. 2. AAL Rule: Allows for the use of more than one negative word in a sentence. Sample: "We *don't never* have *no* homework on Friday." • This sentence is written in HL because it has more than one negative word in a sentence. It's an example of Multiple Negation.
Distinguish between Home Language and School Language	Provide students with opportunities to analyze language samples to determine whether they examples of AAL or SE. In AAL samples, students will be able to highlight more than one negative word; while SE samples will only contain one negative word. • Students can classify sentences, and are able to prove a sentence is an example of HL or SL based on the language rules demonstrated in the sentences.
Code-Switch Teach students strategies to code-switch.	The teacher explains that while both AAL and SE are valid language forms, students should be able to code-switch in order to use either form when situationally appropriate. • Help students understand that code-switching Multiple Negation will require them to either replace one of the negative words with a SE intensifier or change some of the vocabulary words used in the sentence in order to accurately translate the HL sentiment being expressed. Samples: *We don't never have no homework on Fridays* becomes: *We never have homework on Fridays*, or *We don't ever have any homework on Fridays*.
Assess	The teacher used lines from the poem (sentence lifting contrastive analysis) to assess students' ability to identify the use of the linguistic feature, as well as their ability to code-switch the feature. • After code-switching the poem, the class discussed why they believed the author included HL in the poem in the first place and discussed how the use of HL can affect the impact of the poem.

Role-playing is to give students opportunities to practice situations through acting and writing with SL. Students have to discuss how they determined which was the most appropriate language, HL or SL, depending on the environment, audience, purpose, and function.

Examples of each activity are provided in table 31.3.

Table 31.3 Contrastive Analysis Examples

Type of contrastive analysis	Examples of classroom activities
Sentence Lifting	**Poetry Analysis:** Present students with a poem containing the AAL linguistic features being studied in class. Prompt students to think about why the author chose AAL for the poem. Have students use strategies provided to code-switch the poem into SE. Students should recite both the SE and AAL versions of the poem aloud. Discuss the author's purpose for writing the poem, and the message being conveyed in the literature. Have students determine whether the use of AAL helped the author convey this message.
Retellings	Conduct a read-aloud of a story. Select a SEL to retell the story while being taped. Allow students to hear the recorded version of the retelling, identifying instances in which the student retells story elements, heard in SE, using AAL linguistic features. Script these oral samples, if desired, to have students code-switch them in written form.
Role–Playing	"I had a great time with my friends today! We was playin video games at the arcade, and I was the race car champion! The new race car games was awesome! They was way better than the games at the old arcade. Marco was trying to beat my time, but he couldn't. The prizes at the new arcade was better than the ones at the other arcade. My friends and I was all having a good time, but we had to go home. Marco said, "You was on point today, man!" I was good today, and I can't wait to go back!"
	The above "script" is written in AAL. Students can work in partnerships to determine one situation in which the script would be appropriate to recite as is, and one situation in which it would be appropriate to recite in SE. Partners can work together to code-switch the script. Students should "act out" the script with their partners, and in front of the class, using the AAL version in its situationally appropriate scene, and the SE version its situationally appropriate scene.
Teachable Moments	TEACHER: "What observations have we made about the isopods?" STUDENT: "The isopods be diggin' in the dirt." TEACHER: "Great observation, they do spend a lot of time digging in the dirt. Now, can you code-switch your sentence, 'The isopods be diggin' in the dirt?' We're speaking like entomologists at work, right now! STUDENT: "The isopods are usually digging in the dirt." TEACHER: Thank you.

31.4.3 Teachable Moments: Infuse Writing into Daily Instruction

CLR educators understand they are teachers of language in all content areas, engaging students in rigorous, standards-based content lessons throughout the curricular day. Teachable moments are examples of code-switching opportunities that occur in authentic, natural classroom contexts. A teachable moment can occur when a teacher elicits spontaneous verbal or written responses from students about material read or presented and creates on the spot opportunities for situational appropriateness in the classroom. (Table 31.3 provides examples of contrastive analysis activities used successfully in CLR classrooms across the country.) Daily writing activities can include those suggested in the following subsection.

31.4.3.1 *Conducting Writer's Workshops*

During writer's workshops, the teacher can meet with individual students or small groups of students to help them effectively use AAL in writing for which HL proficiency is desired (e.g., poems, narratives, dialogue) or code-switch their use of HL in writing for which SE proficiency is the language expectation required for the type of writing being produced (e.g., expository text, writing being produced for a rubric).

31.4.3.2 *Journal Writing*

Allow students time to write in their journals daily, responding to various writing prompts. Journal writing allows students to practice using the writing strategies they are learning in class in authentic ways. As such, teachers can use view students' journal writing as artifacts that provide insight into a student's: spelling abilities, ability to write on topic, ability to organize ideas, and vocabulary use. A student's journal writing, viewed as a writing artifact, provides evidence of an AAL speaker's proficiency in the use of the HL and SE writing conventions.

31.4.3.3 *Proofreading Sponge Activities*

Literacy research consistently shows that student writing is improved through a process of writing, feedback, and revision. Guiding students through those stages of writing development are important—at any age. Provide students with three to five sentences containing spelling, punctuation, or capitalization errors. The sentences used for this kind of activity should reflect the kinds of spelling, capitalization, and punctuation errors that are frequently appearing in students' writing at a given time. The sentences provided for students to edit *should not* contain samples of their home language.

31.4.3.4 *Code-Switching Sponge Activities*

Provide students with three to five sentences containing samples of students' home language collected from: student work samples, oral samples you have overheard and scripted, or from literature. Be careful when attempting to create your own samples of students' home languages if it is one you are not fluent in, as this could result in inauthentic language samples that are not rule governed and may not accurately represent the HL you are trying to demonstrate. This kind of exercise allows students to practice revising writing for specific SE writing conventions being studied in class. The goal of code-switching the work of others during the revision stage of the writing process encourages students to be able to revise their own work when the use of SE is situationally appropriate. In addition, this kind of activity promotes metalinguistic awareness in students as they begin to think about their language use when writing.

The following is an example of a code-switching sponge activity that was observed and recorded in a third grade classroom in South Central Los Angeles (2005). It demonstrates students effectively using strategies that they were taught to help them code-switch between their use of multiple negation in the HL into equivalent SE forms. The following was written on the board:

> Code-Switching
> 1. My sister don't never share with me.
> 2. I don't have no pencil.
> 3. Grace is bold because she don't take nothing from nobody!

The dialog between the teacher and the class went something like this:

TEACHER: Who can explain what multiple negation is? (Several students raise their hands to answer the question.)
SELECTED STUDENT: Multiple negation is when we use more than one negative word in a sentence.
TEACHER: When we use more than one negative word in a sentence, are we using school language or home language?
CLASS: Home language!
TEACHER: Today, we are code-switching, instead of proofreading. Can someone tell me the difference between code-switching and proofreading? (Several students raise their hands to answer the question.)
SELECTED STUDENT: Proofreading is to correct mistakes, but code-switching doesn't have any mistakes because it's our home language.
TEACHER: That's right, it's not mistakes. The sentences you see on the board are examples of sentences that we can use in our home language. There's nothing wrong with our home language at all. We just have to make sure we know how to code-switch our home language when are speaking and writing in situations that call for school language.
TEACHER: Before we code-switch these sentences, let's read them. (The class chorally reads each sentence, using correct HL prosody and intonation.)

Students were then given time to code-switch the sentences on the board. Students' code-switching translations of the sentences included the following:

> 1. My sister never shares with me./My sister never shares anything with me./My sister doesn't ever share anything with me.
> 2. I don't have a pencil.
> 3. Grace is bold because she doesn't take anything from anybody!

The students participated in the activity as a class. For each sentence, students volunteered to go to the board and share their code-switching strategy with the class. In one exchange, the class helped a student who had not successfully code-switched the first sentence.

STUDENT: I put, my sister doesn't never share with me.
TEACHER TO CLASS: Doesn't, never. What's going on with *doesn't never*?
ANOTHER STUDENT THROWS HIS HAND INTO THE AIR AND ANSWERS: It's still multiple negation!
TEACHER: It's still multiple negation because the sentence has how many negative words?
CLASS: Two!
TEACHER: And how many negative words do we use with school language?
CLASS: One!

For the third sentence, the following exchange occurred:

TEACHER: Grace is bold because she doesn't take anything from anybody! Now, what does this mean? (Students are instructed to talk to their partners about the character they were writing about in class.)
SELECTED STUDENT: Grace is bold because she didn't let the kids in her class tell her she couldn't be Peter Pan because she was Black.

31.4.4 Implications for Explicit AAL Instruction

Since AAL speakers, like speakers of other varieties, may not be consciously aware of language rules, it is important to introduce AAL and SE rules in ways that students will understand. Teaching students how the AAL rule is realized in SE will provide students with strategies to help them identify the use of the AAL rule in oral and written samples. Such strategies can help students answer this important question, asked by a third grader, "How do I know when I'm using Home Language?" By developing an understanding of why they need to acquire the SE rule, both students and teachers begin to move toward educational experiences that affirm students' home languages and identities in ways that promote academic achievement and positive self-awareness.

31.5 THE PRAXIS OF AAL: THE CULTURE AND LANGUAGE ACADEMY OF SUCCESS

In 2003, Hollie and two colleagues founded a charter school in Los Angeles called the Culture and Language Academy of Success (CLAS). CLAS is a kindergarten through eighth-grade laboratory school that espouses culturally and linguistically responsive pedagogy as its primary approach. In its nine years of existence, CLAS has become a national model for culturally and linguistically responsive teaching and for having success with African American students. At CLAS, we validate and affirm AAL starting at kindergarten, where students learn about their linguistic heritage as Africans in America. Students then learn the dimensions of SE through the lens of their home languages. Contrastive analysis is a primary teaching strategy as well.

CLAS has maintained high achievement data according to the California Standards Test and the Academic Performance Index (API), specifically in English Language Arts, when compared to the local district and the state. According to the California state report card on schools, known as the API, CLAS scored 822 for its elementary school and 728 for its middle school in 2010. Nearly 60 percent of the students at CLAS are advanced or proficient in reading/English language arts, according to the Adequate Yearly Progress or the Federal report card (Hollie 2011).

CLAS's classroom practices centralize language. The common themes of these classroom practices are as follows. First, they recognize that any linguistic entity brought to the classroom setting is a natural occurrence. Educators in these schools and classrooms have confronted stereotypes and misconceptions about dialects through professional development and pre-service training (Wolfram 1999, 53). Second, linguistic entities are regular in patterns that can be used as a teaching tool for increased proficiency in the target language. According to Wolfram (1999), "It is essential for dialect awareness programs to combat the stereotype that vernacular varieties are nothing more than imperfect attempts to speak the standard variety" (53). Language varieties are systematic, rule-governed linguistic systems that demand instructional validation and affirmation.

31.6 CONCLUSION

In order to propel students who speak AAL toward proficiency in SE and AL, the home language of these students must be validated and affirmed through culturally and linguistically responsive pedagogy. Ideally, sustaining policies that influence schools at the district and/or state levels could mandate the processes of validation and affirmation. What we have offered here are practical pedagogical approaches and activities that move toward culturally and linguistically responsive classrooms. In the absence of policies guiding how to teach and co-construct knowledge with students who speak AAL, we advocate for educational spaces that promote validation, affirmation, and building through dialogue.

NOTES

1. See LeMoine (1996, 1998, 1999).
2. Title I, formerly known as Chapter 1, is part of the Elementary and Secondary Education Act of 1965 and is the foundation of the federal commitment to closing the achievement gap between low-income and other students. Nearly 14,000 of the 15,000 school districts

in the nation conduct Title I programs. The original purpose of Title I was to allocate additional resources to states and localities for remedial education for children in poverty. The 1994 reauthorization of Title I shifted the program's emphasis from remedial education to helping all disadvantaged children reach rigorous state academic standards expected of all children. Title I funds can be used for instructional activities, counseling, parental involvement, and program improvement. In return, school districts and states must meet accountability requirements for raising student performance (NAEYC, National Association for the Education of Young Children, website, http://www.naeyc.org/policy/federal/title1).

References

Baker-Bell, April. 2013. "'I Never Really Knew the History behind African American Language': Critical Language Pedagogy in an Advanced Placement English Language Arts Class." *Equity and Excellence in Education* 46 (3): 355–70.

Baugh, John. 2004. "Standard English and Academic English (Dialect) Learners in the African Diaspora." *Journal of English Linguistics* 32 (3): 198–209.

Braddock, Jomills Henry. 1995. "Tracking and School Achievement: Implications for Literacy Development." In *Literacy among African-American Youth: Issues in Learning, Teaching, and Schooling*, edited by Vivian L. Gadsen and Daniel A. Wagner, 153–76. Cresskill, NJ: Hampton.

Bull, Tove. 1990. "Teaching School Beginners to Read and Write in the Vernacular." *Tromso Linguistics in the Eighties* 11: 69–84. Oslo: Novus.

Darling-Hammond, Linda. 1998. "Education for Democracy." In *A Light in Dark Times: Maxine Greene and the Unfinished Conversation*, edited by William C. Ayers and Janet L. Miller, 78–91. New York: Teachers College Press.

Delpit, Lisa. 2006. *Other People's Children: Cultural Conflict in the Classroom.* New York: New Press.

Delpit, Lisa, and Joanne Kilgour Dowdy. 2002. *The Skin That We Speak.* New York: New Press.

Delpit, Lisa, and Theresa Perry. 1998. *The Real Ebonics Debate: Power, Language, and the Education of African American Children.* Boston: Beacon.

Fine, Michelle. 1995. "Silencing and Literacy." In *Literacy among African-American Youth: Issues in Learning, Teaching, and Schooling*, edited by Vivian L. Gadsen and Daniel A. Wagner, 201–22. Cresskill, NJ: Hampton.

Foster, Michele. 1995. "Talking that Talk: The Language of Control, Curriculum, and Critique." *Linguistics and Education* 7 (2): 129–50.

Gay, Geneva. 2000. *Culturally Responsive Teaching.* New York: Teachers College Press.

Harris-Wright, Kelli. 1999. "Enhancing Bidialectalism in Urban African American Students." In *Making the Connection: Language and Academic Achievement among African American Students*, edited by Donna Christian and Orlando Taylor, 52–59. Urbana, IL: NCTE.

Hollie, Sharroky. 2011. *Culturally and Linguistically Responsive Teaching and Learning: Classroom Practices for Student Success.* Huntington Beach, CA: Shell Education.

Kelley, Robin D. G. 1997. *Yo Mama's Dysfunktional!: Fighting Culture Wars in Urban America.* Boston: Beacon.

Ladson-Billings, Gloria. 1994. *The Dreamkeepers: Successful Teachers of African American Children.* San Francisco: Jossey-Bass.

LeMoine, Noma. 1996. *Linguistic Research and Educating African Americans.* Los Angeles: Los Angeles Unified School District.

————. 1998. *English for Your Success*. Maywood: People's Publishing.

————. 1999. *Language Variation and Literacy Acquisition in African American Students*. Los Angeles: Los Angeles Unified School District.

————. 2007. *Teachers' Guide to Supporting African-American Standard English Learners*. Los Angeles: Los Angeles Unified School District.

Osterberg, Tore. 1961. *Bilingualism and the First School Language—An Educational Problem Illustrated by Results from a Swedish Dialect Area*. Umeå: Väster-bottens Tryckeri.

Piestrup, Ann McCormick. 1973. *Black Dialect Interference and Accommodations of Reading Instruction in First Grade*. Monograph of the Language Behavior Research Laboratory 4. Berkeley: University of California.

Raible, John W., and Jason G. Irizarry. 2007. "Transracialized Selves and the Emergence of Post-White Teacher Identities." *Race Ethnicity and Education* 10 (2): 177–98.

Rickford, John R. 1999. "Phonological and Grammatical Features of African American Vernacular English." In *African American English*, by John R. Rickford, 3–14. Malden, MA, and Oxford, UK: Blackwell.

Rickford, John, and Angela Rickford. 1995. "Dialect Readers Revisited." *Linguistics and Education* 7 (2): 107–28.

Rickford, John R., and Russell J. Rickford. 2000. *Spoken Soul: The Story of Black English*. New York: Wiley.

Rogers, Theresa, Elizabeth Marshall, and Cynthia Tyson. 2006. "Dialogic Narratives of Literacy, Teaching, and Schooling: Preparing Literacy Teachers for Diverse Settings." *Reading Research Quarterly* 41 (2): 202–24.

Simpkins, Gary, and Charlesetta Simpkins. 1981. "Cross Cultural Approach to Curriculum Development." In *Black English and the Education of Black Children and Youth: Proceedings of the National Invitational Symposium on the King Decision*, edited by Geneva Smitherman, 221–40. Detroit: Wayne State University.

Smitherman, Geneva. 1977. *Talkin and Testifyin: The Language of Black America*. Detroit, MI: Wayne State University Press.

Spears, Arthur K. 2001. "Directness in the Use of African American English." *Sociocultural and Historical Contexts of African American English* 27: 239–59.

Taylor, Hanni U. 1989. *Standard English, Black English, and Bidialectalism*. New York: Peter Lang.

Williams, James Dale and Grace Capizzi Snipper. 1990. *Literacy and Bilingualism*. New York: Longman.

Wolfram, Walt. 1999. "Dialect Awareness Programs in the School and Community." In *Language Alive in the Classroom*, edited by Rebecca Wheeler, 47–66. Westport, CT: Praeger.

CHAPTER 32

HISTORY OF RESEARCH ON MULTILITERACIES AND HIP HOP PEDAGOGY

A Critical Review

K. C. NAT TURNER AND TYSON L. ROSE

> There is a difference between history and origins; you can't have a real history without a comprehension of an *ORIGIN*. Not *how* did something come about, which is history; this happened, this happened, but *why* did something happen. We are never going to have true history until we get this origin right. The origin of Hip Hop has less to do with "A" happened, then "B" happened, then "C" happened then "D" happened. The origin has to do with what were the causes, what were the events in nature that caused Hip Hop to be.
>
> (KRS-ONE, n.d.; emphasis added)

EDUCATORS around the world are using Hip Hop as a way to create a bridge between students' interests and educators' learning objectives. In numerous cases, the primary focus has tended to utilize Hip Hop culture solely as a pedagogical strategy to spur students' increased engagement and act as an entry point to teach traditional subject matters. While these educators demonstrate significant gains in student success utilizing these methodologies, these strategies may not fully acknowledge the larger contextual *ORIGINS* of Hip Hop as defined above by Hip Hop artist and scholar KRS-ONE. These *ORIGINS* are rooted in Afro-Diasporic ways of knowing, as embodied through Hip Hop language, literacy and cultural practices, production, and performance. In this chapter we will frame the history of research on multiliteracies and Hip Hop pedagogy by connecting the multiple ciphas[1] of Hip Hop–based educational practices including: African aesthetics, African American Language and Literacy practices, African American and Latino cultures, Hip Hop culture, social justice education, critical pedagogy, culturally relevant pedagogy, and multiliteracies. Finally, the chapter builds on the impetus and value of this research to chart future directions that center on multimodal media production in the development of critical media literacies toward a Critical Social Justice Hip Hop Pedagogy.

32.1 INTRODUCTION: CURRENT HIP HOP–BASED EDUCATIONAL PRACTICES

Today, more than ever, Hip Hop is being used as a way to get students interested in academics during the formal school day in math and science education, SAT vocabulary preparation, English as a Second Language (ESL) curriculum, current events, and, most commonly, English language arts. In addition to this widespread practitioner use, researchers in multiple disciplines, including education and linguistics, have studied how Hip Hop culture is being used for language and literacy learning around the globe (Alim, Ibrahim, and Pennycook 2009). These studies typically have looked at how what has been termed *Hip Hop–based education* (HHBE) can be used to develop critical literacy, academic skills, language acquisition, citizenship, self-esteem, and other transferable skills in students (Hill 2009). Other examples of HHBE practices range from its usage as a culturally relevant teaching methodology, the use of Hip Hop to teach canonical literary texts, the utilization of Hip Hop aesthetics and creative practices as a way to analyze educational processes, and/or as the object of study (Akom 2009; Alim 2007; Duncan-Andrade and Morrell 2008; Fisher 2007; Mahiri 2004).

Surprisingly, there has been relatively little discussion of how the production of Hip Hop texts themselves can be used to develop critical media literacies with historically marginalized youth populations (Pirbhai-Illich, Turner, and Austin 2009; Turner, 2012). Like other forms of *multimodal media production* (MMP), the production of multimodal Hip Hop texts must be seen as a literate practice that necessitates an exploration of how the texts arise, an account for audience, as well as aesthetic and other features that make them coherent versus disjointed.

The proliferation of Hip Hop in higher education is further evidenced by the multiple Hip Hop conferences held each year on university campuses and the operation of institutionally funded educational think tanks and research centers dedicated to exploring Hip Hop in education. Notably, Cornell University established the Hip Hop Collection in 2008 and most recently in May 2012, New York University's Hip-Hop Education Center (HHEC) announced a partnership with Columbia University's Institute for Urban and Minority Education (IUME) to continue conducting research on Hip Hop education and expand its use in New York City schools and across the nation (Diaz, Fergus, and Noguera 2011).

Hip Hop culture is being used as a culturally relevant pedagogical strategy to increase student motivation; however, Delpit (2001) and Rickford (1998) argue that African American Language (AAL), which is also referred to as *Ebonics, African American Vernacular English*, and *Black English Vernacular*, and which we extend to Hip Hop Nation Language (HHNL) (Alim, Ibrahim, and Pennycook 2009), must also be used to master the dominant discourse as well. From the perspectives of these scholars, students' awareness of their own histories and language is critical to their success in learning, but engagement alone can leave students in limbo if it is not linked to the promotion of academic literacy development, civic engagement, and college access. Along these lines, Morrell and Duncan-Andrade (2004) were among the first to document their use of Hip Hop as a pedagogical strategy to bridge students' engagement with their culture and the canonical texts they were responsible for teaching as part of the California state standards. In their landmark piece, the authors explore "how teaching [H]ip [H]op as a literary genre could help scaffold and develop the academic literacies of youth who have often been labeled as 'non-academic' or 'semi-literate'" (247). Morrell and Duncan-Andrade's (2004) decision to include Hip Hop pedagogy in their classroom reflects their understanding that it was their responsibility as teachers to reach all of their students and one way they could accomplish this goal was by building on the culture, language, knowledge, and literacy practices their students brought with them to school every day. Significant scholarship suggests that if teachers take what are already legitimate youth interests and relate them to the standards and larger issues of righteousness and social justice, youth will want to learn (Duncan-Andrade 2004; Jocson 2008; Morrell 2004).

32.2 AFRO-DIASPORIC ROOTS OF HIP HOP

While it is clear that many of the educational researchers engaging in this work are aware of the Afro-Diasporic roots of Hip Hop, what is less clear is their communication of these roots in their scholarship to the practitioners who take up these practices. For instance, the connection of Alim, Ibrahim, and Pennycook's (2009) HHNL (and literacy practices) and AAL (and its literacy practices) is rarely explicated. Smitherman (1997) and Alim (2002) among others have made this connection explicit, explaining the similarities between the Hip Hop MC and the traditional African griot as well as the linkages between the Niger-Congo Bantu roots of the grammatical structure of AAL with HHNL, but a gap in the literature remains. This gap directly translates to how teachers and, by extension, students view Hip Hop as a relatively new cultural phenomenon with minimal reference to its historical and cultural roots. When students are left without a clear understanding of how Hip Hop culture—which has clear Afro-Diasporic roots, or what Osumare (2007) explains as the cultural aesthetic and traditional practices from the African continent and the Caribbean—is linked to their own familial histories, they are unable to make the deep connections related to their knowledge of self and self-image.

32.3 THE CRITICAL MULTILITERACIES

Although not all Hip Hop practices are explicitly critical, they do have the potential to serve as a site for the development of an ever-expanding set of literacies (Hill 2009; Stovall 2006) that are increasingly necessary to critique what Rose (2008) terms the "gangsta-pimp-ho trinity" promoted by commercial Hip Hop. The necessity for these new literacies have developed in the past thirty years alongside an explosion of devices used for communicating and have been termed multiliteracies (New London Group 1996). The New London Group (1996) and others have since defined (multi)literacies as varied and relative to the social context or discourse involved but inextricably linked with issues of ideology and power (Delpit 2001; Gee 2001; Kramsch 2004; Street 1984). New Literacy theorists have articulated a praxis that includes media production as a process that can link ways of thinking about critical literacy with the ability to decipher and produce empowering forms of media (Hull and Shultz 2002; Lemke 1998; Mahiri 2004; Morrell and Duncan-Andrade 2004; Sholle and Denski 1993).

This expansion of the definition of literacy is particularly significant for teachers who must now, in light of Hip Hop's global commercial success and the corporate marketing of the gangsta-pimp-ho trinity, teach students how to critique media as text, change patterns of interactions with media, and, finally, produce counter-hegemonic media. Increasingly, the ability to evaluate the credibility of media sources by deconstructing multilayered (e.g., clothing, facial gestures, body art, sound, and dance) content involves a vital set of literacy skills that students can ultimately use to raise questions about the politics of representation for people of color in our hyper-mediated society (S. Hall 1997). Namely, what are the intentions of media producers, and how do they or do they not reinforce the racial, economic, sexual, and gender hierarchies that Hill-Collins (1990) calls a "matrix of domination"?

32.4 AFRO-DIASPORIC ORIGINS OF HIP HOP: A LESSON FROM THE TEACHER

> Yo, 'cause I'm a teacher
> Boogie Down Productions is made up of teachers
> Teachers teach and do the world good
>   KRS-ONE—My Philosophy (http://www.ohhla.com/)

32.4.1 African Aesthetics of Hip Hop

As established in the introduction to this chapter, Hip Hop culture and cultural practices offer a unique way to conceptualize language and literacy practices. Many scholars have focused their attention on the sociolinguistic practices that are embodied through Hip Hop culture. By firmly establishing that the origins of Hip Hop lie in West African oral traditions, an important link has been made to the historical development of Hip Hop in context of its Afro-Diasporic roots (Osumare 2007). An important development in the scholarship has been in expanding the scope to include not only African oral traditions but other aesthetic and performative practices that have also been transmitted through the "transcultural flow" of African cultures in the Americas (Osumare 2007). These "African aesthetics" provide a link that allows for "similar aesthetic principles [to be recreated] in new sociopolitical contexts [which] became absolutely crucial to the survival of people of African descent" (25). At the heart of Hip Hop culture lies this "African aesthetic" connecting Hip Hop culture firmly to these West African traditions and providing the context for re-imagining self in these new locations (Osumare 2007).

32.4.2 Hip Hop *ORIGINS*

Hip Hop culture is acknowledged by Hip Hop insiders to have originated in the South Bronx, New York, during the post–Black Power movement of the 1960s (Chang 2005; Reeves 2008; Rose 1994). Hip Hop emerged in America during the tumultuous years of the 1970s and solidified its presence during Ronald Reagan's presidency in the 1980s. Over this time period, New York and the South Bronx, in particular, had come, in many ways, to epitomize postindustrial urban decay and was recognized nationally as synonymous with crime and poverty (Price 2006). This environment was the symptomatic expression of exclusionary urban planning, redlining practices, corporate divestment, reduction in resources to urban centers, and White flight. This was the legacy of the policies of post–World War II America (Chang 2005; Forman and Neal 2004; Price 2006; Reeves 2008). Hip Hop originated in this environment, its origins in constant communication with its Afro-Diasporic and Black Power roots, manifesting what Reeves (2008) describes as a "revolutionary youth culture" (M. R. Hall 2011; Osumare 2007; Rose 1994). Hip Hop culture and practices can only be understood in the relational context of the conditions that existed in the communities from which it emerged. These conditions signify what Osumare (2007) terms "connective marginalities: various social and historical realms that form the context for youth participating in [H]ip [H]op" (69). These realms are defined, both domestically and globally, as the sites where many forms of marginalities are expressed: Afro-Diasporic cultures, the global poor, peoples who have experienced historic oppression, and youth culture in general (Osumare 2007). These connective marginalities help to explain why Hip Hop has become one of the most important vehicles for youth and oppressed peoples to express their humanity and resistance from Africa to China, and everywhere in between (Akom 2009; Alim et al. 2009).

32.4.3 AAL: Marginalized Variety of English

AAL is neither inherently superior nor inferior to any other language in terms of logic or functional utility among native speakers (Baugh 1983), yet it has been historically marginalized as a variety of English and its speakers shunned. Baugh (1983) explains,

> Most of the early educational programs to help [B]lacks learn standard English began with the objective of eliminating street speech; this was seen as a dialect that

should not be tolerated. This practice reinforced the negative impression of [B]lack speech that was already held by the dominant culture. (8)

Likewise, Morgan (1994) argues persuasively that crude, overly general descriptions of the African American speech community that ignore changing class dynamics, exclude women, and stereotype sexual attitudes in presenting linguistic data, reinforce the image of AAL as a sign of poverty and oppression and only help marginalize its speakers.

32.4.4 Language as Resistance

In one of the first academic publications presenting research on communicative practices within the Hip Hop Nation, Smitherman (1997) explores the link of these practices to AAL and demonstrates how HHNL serves as a language of resistance and cultural connection. Smitherman's sociolinguistic analysis of the lyrics of several Hip Hop artists demonstrates several distinct AAL syntax and phonological features in the genre. Although her analysis is restricted to only one element of Hip Hop culture, rapping, Smitherman's (1997) contention is that, because rap lyrics accurately portray "the pathologies, and resistance against White America's racism and Eurocentric cultural dominance" (7), it makes an excellent vehicle for bringing conversations about these subjects into the classroom.

32.4.5 Linking HHNL to Education

In addition to Africanist aesthetics derived from Hip Hop's Afro-Diasporic roots, Hip Hop is a multimodal form of cultural expression that has been at the forefront of technological innovation since the late 1970s, when youth of color breathed life into older technologies to invent artistic forms of participating in an entirely new transnational, hybrid culture. Therefore, Hip Hop "generationers," as labeled by Kitwana (2002), are necessarily what Mahiri et al. (2007) call "digital natives." The importance of the link between Hip Hop, the largest cultural phenomena in the world today, and the digital tools students are accustomed to using for composing multimodally cannot be understated and must be explored within the context of skills they will need in future social, civic, academic, and professional contexts. As Finnegan (2002) notes, youth today can instantly transmit MMPs throughout the world (sometimes in real time)—a capability that has never existed before but one that is becoming increasingly important as society continues the push to digitize (i.e., translate into numerical data accessible through computers) many of the operations previously done in person or with print copies (Manovich 2001). For an extensive treatment of how multimodal Hip Hop production can be used to develop these important information and communication technology (ICT) literacies, see Turner (2011).

Barely forty years old, Hip Hop is one form of MMP that youth continue to use to define, entertain, and defend themselves. Of course some of their styles may be appropriated and reproduced from what they see in the mass media, but it is important not to think of all media as unidirectional or something that youth do not interpret but merely receive passively (Buckingham 2003). Instead, it is important to hear and read how the production of multimodal media transforms youth, who, in turn, have transformed the very definition of being a media producer. Willis et al. (1990) call this transformation "symbolic creativity," a process in which new meaning is inscribed on already commonly understood symbols—a fundamental practice in Hip Hop called *sampling*. Wu-Tang Clan's sampling of dialogue from Kung-Fu movies and Das EFX's references to cartoons in their lyrics (RZA 2005) are examples of this hybridized practice of producing situated new meanings. Bakhtinian (1981) concepts of discourse, heteroglossia, and dialogism are all relevant in Hip Hop because, by its very nature, it is intertextual, including references to other songs, artists, and spaces (e.g., *hoods*). The significance that Hip Hop is multimodal means its message is conveyed through many different stylistic elements (explained below), modalities, and with great illocutionary force to the audience.

32.5 Expanding the Cipha: Connecting the Multiple Elements of Hip Hop–Based Education

32.5.1 Multiple Elements and Ciphas of Hip Hop–Based Educational Practices

In his comprehensive review of Hip Hop–based education studies, Petchauer (2009) defines three major strands of work in the field of HHBE: (1) using rap lyrics as curricular and pedagogical resources; (2) interpreting Hip Hop meanings and identities, particularly how youth construct their identities through Hip Hop; and (3) analyzing Hip Hop aesthetic forms, which refers to studies that conceptualize the learning produced by participation in the culture. Although these categories form a useful heuristic for conceptualizing the different types of scholarship in the field of Hip Hop education, it is less clear how this scholarship can be meaningfully integrated into a coherent pedagogical strategy. What are Hip Hop–based pedagogy strategies that educators can apply to their practice that will develop greater knowledge of self among students and increased engagement in actions to transform current inequalities they face? For example, what are the connections between the areas of Hip Hop scholarship that can be leveraged to create a Hip Hop pedagogy that is critical and based on social justice? In this section we explore the connections between Petchauer's (2009) three strands of Hip Hop scholarship with the aim of identifying which elements can inform future directions for a coherent whole. To do this, we explore the connections first between: (1) Hip Hop identities and HHBE; (2) Hip Hop identities and Hip Hop aesthetic forms; and, finally, (3) Hip Hop aesthetic forms and HHBE.

32.5.2 Hip Hop Identities and Hip Hop–Based Education

The relationship between Hip Hop and how African American, Latino, and certain Asian youth identify themselves is best explained by Osumare's (2007) concept of connective marginalities (explained above). Connective marginalities are helpful in understanding why Hip Hop serves as the primary lens through which many youth view themselves and their world. The African aesthetic that Osumare refers to is predominantly found in African American and Latino culture, exerts an influence on everything from fashion to music choice, and is being mediated through Hip Hop culture. At every level of her connective marginality heuristic (culture, class, historic oppression, youth), both youth and adults connect with Hip Hop culture's African aesthetic. Because HHNL is a primary language that students bring with them to school, and that sometimes emerges in the classroom, it is critical for educators to be aware of the centrality of Hip Hop culture to their students. This is why developing an understanding or having familiarity with HHNL is useful for educators looking to connect with students and/or parents and inform their own culturally relevant and responsive pedagogy.

32.5.3 Hip Hop Identities and Aesthetic Forms and HHBE

Although new words are created daily, some of the key features of HHNL such as signifying (creating new meanings for old words and signs) are based on African traditions that will not change (Rose 1994). These ways of being and participating in the cultural production of Hip Hop's aesthetic forms follows Willis's (1990) concept of symbolic creativity (the necessary work people do appropriating old meanings and making new meanings). For example, in a song written as part of a youth extended day program, a student named Gina starts off the verse to a song using the stylized lexicon of the "Hyphy Movement"[2] such as "go stuwie uwie" and "ridin the yellow bus" but then moves into a critique of President George W. Bush centered on his (mis)handling of Hurricane Katrina within a larger context of Black death. This cultural work cannot be meaningfully separated from the identities of many of the youth and adults who educators work with in schools today.

In line with the literature that states that youth are engaging in literacy practices in out-of-school contexts that involve learning (Hull and Shultz 2002), the production of Hip Hop multimodal texts also has affordances for individual and community development. Hip Hop culture is produced by youth every day in the streets (and other historically marginalized spaces). From the language to the dances, Hip Hop culture is constantly shifting, variable, and morphing, and is generally how youth express themselves. Even Hip Hop artists go to watch the practitioners of the culture and then reflect their culture back to them in the music as a type of street ethnographer (Forman 2002). So it is in this context that engaging Hip Hop culture and the artifacts it produces as a curricular or pedagogical resource is so useful. As a pedagogical strategy, it builds on culturally relevant (Ladson-Billings 1994); critical pedagogy (Freire 1970; Giroux

1987); and cultural modeling (Lee and Majors 2003) approaches that argue education must begin by taking the students from where they are and utilize generative concepts to advance their thinking. Collectively, these educational theories have their roots in Vygotskyian ([1935] 1978) sociocultural theories of education that likewise argue for beginning the curriculum with the needs of the students and not the parameters of the discipline. Today, students are in desperate need of knowledge of self, which is why an understanding of Hip Hop culture and history can forge powerful conversations with students. This represents a pedagogical shift of meeting students where they are. It is important for teachers to have in-depth knowledge about the students they are teaching and the subject matter being presented (Ladson-Billings 1994). Educators are often not understood because their language is not attuned to the concrete situation of their students (Freire 1970). To ignore the existence of these problems in communication is a failure to provide equal education under the law (Morgan 1994).

32.5.4 Social Justice Education

Social justice education (SJE) offers additional resources to support educators in conceptualizing HHNL as a language of resistance (Akom 2009; Reeves 2008) and valuable literacy practices. By providing a pedagogical framework that theorizes oppression at the individual, interpersonal, and societal levels, SJE provides a framework that can appreciate and acknowledge the historical development of HHNL in the context of oppression and resistance to these conditions (Adams, Bell, and Griffin 2007). This process opens the possibility for educators to understand HHNL as a literacy practice that embodies the experience of marginalized communities (see discussions of Osumare above) and provides educators with skills that value reflection and an attention to the social relations of power in classroom spaces. The goal of SJE also enables the intentional "develop[ment] [of] critical analytic skills necessary to understand oppression and socialization within oppressive systems, and to develop a sense of agency and a capacity to interrupt and change oppressive patterns and behaviors" (Adams 2007, 2). This intentional focus on the development of resistance and agency is analogous to the development of Hip Hop culture and its practices (including HHNL) in the aftermath of the Black Power and civil rights movements. Among the other goals of SJE, the particular focus on power, resistance, and agency lays the foundation for a conceptual understanding of HHNL as a literacy of liberation, not a deficiency or pathology of the communities that engage in it. In other words, HHNL as a literacy of liberation can be what Alim (2011) terms an "ill literacy" where the "ill" represents a positive evaluation of "creative and/or counterhegemonic practices" (121).

32.5.5 Critical Pedagogy

The connections between Hip Hop and critical pedagogy have recently become a focus of those scholars who wish to emphasize Hip Hop culture as a location that supports a critical engagement with power, agency, identity, and in particular to conceptualize schools as a site for the reproduction of oppressive social relations (Akom 2009; Alim 2007; Hill 2009). Darder, Baltodano, and Torres (2009) explain that critical pedagogy has developed out of a tradition of educators who wished to continue the transformative works of Paulo Freire, Myles Horton, and others whose "radical principles, beliefs, and practices contributed to an emancipatory ideal of democratic schooling" (2). This tradition draws on a theoretical foundation that: values multiple perspectives, critiques power in the classroom, is dedicated to the development of individual and collective agency, intentionally works to create avenues for social transformation, and recognizes schools as sites for social and cultural reproduction of existing relations of power and privilege. Hip Hop culture, as described above, relies on a critique of the conditions that precipitated its own creation. These racialized and class-based oppressive social structures continue to exist in the communities that many students live in. These conditions continue to limit the life chances and opportunities available to youth from these communities. Hip Hop therefore offers the ability to engage the process of "textual analysis" (Hill 2009) of these existing conditions but also represents a "liberatory practice [that] is rooted in the long history of the Black freedom struggle and the quest for self-determinism for oppressed communities around the world" (Akom 2009, 53). If HHNL is indeed acknowledged as the dominant language of youth culture, then educators need some familiarity with the language. It is important to recognize these practices for their agentic and liberatory capacities. It is equally important to recognize the need for educators to reflect on their own power and capacity to either involve or marginalize HHNL users in their classrooms. Engaging with Hip Hop as a discursive practice in and of itself represents a critical pedagogy. Through a critical engagement with Hip Hop, educators can learn much about the critiques of schooling, classroom practices, desires and wants of students who utilize HHNL. Valuing the outside literacy practices of HHNL users provides multiple entry points to understand the critical capacities embodied through Hip Hop culture and cultural practices.

32.6 CONCLUSION: FUTURE DIRECTIONS FOR HIP HOP–BASED EDUCATION: TOWARD A CRITICAL SOCIAL JUSTICE HIP HOP PEDAGOGY

The literature is clear and has been for some time. High achieving students typically have high levels of self-esteem often originating from knowledge of self as in the case of students studying in the Chicano Studies program in Tucson, Arizona, featured in the film *Precious Knowledge* and recent research on Black high achievers who demonstrated a critical race achievement ideology (Carter 2008). The need for programs that can lead to these outcomes and then move students to action is evident, and Hip Hop culture is just one means for accomplishing this. Hip Hop culture can be utilized to create a classroom space where students feel they can bring up and address issues, such as: (1) inequality in urban education, (2) racial justice, (3) traumatic life experiences, and (4) popular culture as resistance. The production of Hip Hop multimodal texts can be used to involve students in critically thinking about their lives and expressing themselves using social and literacy practices that demand reading and writing. Inherent in students' production of multimodal media artifacts are literacy practices they already engage in outside of school as well as others that help them cultivate a productive future for themselves and challenge injustice in their communities. Short of having voting rights for under-age youth, MMP provides an opportunity for them to represent their perspective on the most pressing issues in our world today.

Hip Hop culture and practices, viewed in the manner that has been described in this chapter, are grounded in and reflect the social and cultural *origins* as well as forty years of global expansion. Hip Hop has supported an active and experiential process that supports the creation of possibilities for critical meaning-making, that is, as a way for people to not only understand the world around them but to discover ways of changing these conditions. Freire and Macedo (1987) define their conception of literacy as "learning how to write the world, that is having the experience of changing the world and touching the world" (49). With the increased emergence of HHBE programs, it is of increasing importance to look critically at the ways in which these programs are being envisioned, designed, and implemented. Hip Hop culture is complex; it is by no means a panacea—it cannot be everything for everybody. Hip Hop cultural practices and representations are both an expression of society and resistance to asymmetrical relations of power; these practices and representations likewise embody both the potential to reify oppression and to manifest liberation. This understanding is a key element that should drive the successful integration of Hip Hop into education. It is imperative that educational programs that purport to be Hip Hop or utilize Hip Hop practices and modes of meaning-making endeavor to embody the critical capacities of Hip Hop culture to work towards transformation and a more socially just society.

NOTES

1. *Cipha*: Originally represented the physical arrangement (a 360-degree circle) in which Hip Hop cultural practices were engaged, e.g., emceeing (rappin') or breakdancing. In the context of this scholarship, the meaning has been expanded to include what Alim (2009) defines as the "fundamental unit of analysis" in Hip Hop. It does not only signify a physical formation but is representative of multiple ways of knowing and doing that are manifested globally through interaction, communication, and localization.
2. *Hyphy*: "Goin dumb," "sideshows," and "gettin hyphy" are all practices linked to the hyphy style of music and dance associated with San Francisco Bay Area Hip Hop culture. The terms were created by Bay Area rapper Keak da Sneak and have come to represent a style of music and dance associated with San Francisco Bay Area Hip Hop culture.

REFERENCES

Adams, Maurianne, Lee Anne Bell, and Pat Griffin, eds. 2007. *Teaching for Diversity and Social Justice*. 2nd ed. New York: Routledge.

Akom, A. Antwi. 2009. "Critical Hip Hop Pedagogy as a Form of Liberatory Praxis." *Equity and Excellence in Education* 42 (1): 52–66.

Alim, H. Samy. 2002. "Street-Conscious Copula Variation in the Hip Hop Nation." *American Speech* 77 (3): 288–304.

———. 2007. "Critical Hip-Hop Language Pedagogies: Combat, Consciousness, and the Cultural Politics of Communication." *Journal of Language, Identity, and Education* 6 (2): 161–76.

———. 2011. "Global Ill-Literacies: Hip Hop Cultures, Youth Identities, and the Politics of Literacy." *Review of Research in Education* 35 (1): 120–46.

Alim, H. Samy, Awad Ibrahim, and Alastair Pennycook, eds. 2009. *Global Linguistic Flows: Hip Hop Cultures, Youth Identities, and the Politics of Language*. New York: Taylor and Francis.

Bakhtin, Mikhail M. 1981. *The Dialogic Imagination: Four Essays by M. M. Bakhtin*. Translated by C. Emerson and M. Holquist. Austin: University of Texas.

Baugh, John. 1983. *Black Street Speech: It's History, Structure, and Survival*. Austin: University of Texas.

Buckingham, David. 2003. *Media Education: Literacy, Learning and Contemporary Culture*. Cambridge, UK: Polity.

Carter, Dorinda. 2008. "Achievement as Resistance: The Development of a Critical Race Achievement Ideology among Black Achievers." *Harvard Educational Review* 78 (3): 466–97.

Chang, Jeff. 2005. *Can't Stop Won't Stop: A History of the Hip-Hop Generation*. New York: St. Martin's.

Darder, Antonia, Martha P. Baltodano, and Rodolfo D. Torres, eds. 2009. *The Critical Pedagogy Reader*. Vol. 2. New York: Routledge.

Delpit, Lisa. 2001. "The Politics of Teaching Literate Discourse." In *Literacy: A Critical Sourcebook*, edited by Ellen Cushman, Eugene R. Kintgen, Barry M. Kroll, and Mike Rose, 545–54. Boston: Bedford/St. Martin's.

Diaz, Martha, Edward Fergus, and Pedro Noguera. 2011. *Re-Imagining Teaching and Learning: A Snapshot of Hip-Hop Education*. http://steinhardt.nyu.edu/metrocenter/hiphopeducation/snapshot-of-hiphop-education.

Duncan-Andrade, Jeff. 2004. "Your Best Friend or your Worst Enemy: Youth Popular Culture, Pedagogy, and Curriculum in Urban Classrooms." *Review of Education, Pedagogy, and Cultural Studies* 26: 313–37.

Duncan-Andrade, Jeff, and Ernest Morrell. 2008. *The Art of Critical Pedagogy: Possibilities for Moving from Theory to Practice in Urban Schools*. New York: Peter Lang.

Finnegan, Ruth. 2002. *Communicating: The Multiple Modes of Human Interconnection*. London: Routledge.

Fisher, Maisha T. 2007. *Writing in Rhythm: Spoken Word Poetry in Urban Classrooms*. New York: Teachers College.

Forman, Murray. 2002. "Space Matters: Hip-Hop and the Spatial Perspective." In *The 'hood comes first': Race, Space, and Place in Rap and Hip-Hop*. Middletown, CT: Wesleyan University.

Forman, Murray, and M. A. Neal. 2004. *That's the Joint!: The Hip-Hop Studies Reader*. New York: Routledge.

Freire, Paulo. 1970. *Pedagogy of the Oppressed*. New York: Seabury.

Freire, Paulo, and Donaldo Macedo. 1987. *Literacy: Reading the Word and the World*. South Hadley, MA: Bergin & Garvey.

Gee, James Paul. 2001. "Literacy, Discourse, and Linguistics: Introduction and What Is Literacy?" Chap. 30. In *Literacy: A Critical Sourcebook*, edited by Ellen Cushman, Eugene R. Kintgen, Barry M. Kroll, and Mike Rose, 525–44. Boston: Bedford/St. Martin's.

Giroux, H. 1987. "Introduction." In *Literacy: Reading the Word and the World*, edited by Paulo Freire and Donald Macedo, 1–27. Westport, CT: Bergin & Garvey.

Hall, Marcella Runell. 2011. "Education in a Hip Hop Nation: Our Identity, Politics & Pedagogy." PhD diss., University of Massachusetts.

Hall, Stuart. 1997. *Representation: Cultural Representations and Signifying Practices*. London: Sage/Open University.

Hill, Marc Lamont. 2009. *Beats, Rhymes, and Classroom Life: Hip-Hop Pedagogy and the Politics of Identity*. New York: Teachers College.

Hill-Collins, Patricia. 1990. *Black Feminist Thought: Knowledge, Consciousness, and the Politics of Empowerment*. Boston: Unwin Hyman.

Hull, Glynda A., and Katherine Shultz, eds. 2002. *School's Out! Bridging Out-of-School Literacies with Classroom Practice*. New York: Teachers College.

Jocson, Korina M. 2008. *Youth Poets: Empowering Literacies In and Out of Schools*. New York: Peter Lang.

Kitwana, Bakari. 2002. *The Hip-Hop Generation: Young Blacks and the Crisis in African American Culture*. New York: Basic Civitas Books.

Kramsch, Claire. 2004. "Language, Thought, and Culture." In *The Handbook of Applied Linguistics*, edited by A. Davies and C. Elder, 235–62. Malden, MA: Blackwell.

Ladson-Billings, Gloria. (1994). *The Dreamkeepers: Successful Teaching of African American Children*. San Francisco: Jossey-Bass.

Lee, Carol D., and Yolanda Majors. 2003. " 'Heading up the street': Localised Opportunities for Shared Constructions of Knowledge." *Pedagogy, Culture and Society* 11 (1): 49–67.

Lemke, Jay L. 1998. "Metamedia Literacy: Transforming Meanings and Media." In *Handbook of Literacy and Technology: Transformations in a Post-Typographic World*, edited by David Reinking, Michael McKenna, Linda D. Labbo, and Ronald D. Kieffer, 283–301. Hillsdale, NJ: Lawrence Erlbaum.

Mahiri, Jabari. 2004. "Street Scripts: African American Youth Writing about Crime and Violence." In *What They Don't Learn in School*, edited by Jabari Mahiri, 19–42. New York: Peter Lang.

Mahiri, Jabari, Malik Ali, Allison Lindsay Scott, Bolota Asmerom, and Rick Ayers. 2007. "Both Sides of the Mic: Community Literacies in the Age of Hip-Hop." In *The Handbook of Research on Teaching Literacy through the Communicative, Visual and Performing Arts*, Vol. 2, edited by James Flood, Diane Lapp, and Shirley Brice Heath, 279–87. The International Reading Association. Mahwah, NJ: Lawrence Erlbaum.

Manovich, Lev. 2001. *The Language of New Media*. Cambridge, MA: MIT.

Morgan, Marcyliena. 1994. "The African-American Speech Community: Reality and Sociolinguistics." In *Language and the Social Construction of Identity in Creole Situations*, edited by Marcyliena Morgan. Los Angeles: The Center for Afro-American Studies, UCLA. (Reprinted by permission of the author.)

Morrell, Ernest. 2004. *Linking Literacy and Popular Culture*. Norwood, MA: Christopher-Gordon.

Morrell, Ernest, and Jeff Duncan-Andrade. 2004. "What They Do Learn in School: Hip-Hop as a Bridge to Canonical Poetry." In *What They Don't Learn in School: Literacy in the Lives of Urban Youth*, edited by Jabari Mahiri, 247–68. New York: Peter Lang.

New London Group. 1996. "A Pedagogy of Multiliteracies: Designing Social Futures." *Harvard Educational Review* 66 (1): 60–92.

Osumare, Halifu. 2007. *The Africanist Aesthetic in Global Hip-Hop: Power Moves*. New York: Palgrave Macmillan.

Petchauer, Emery. 2009. "Framing and Reviewing Hip-Hop Educational Research." *Review of Educational Research* 79 (2): 946–78.

Pirbhai-Illich, Fatima, K. C. N. Turner, and Theresa Y. Austin. 2009. "Using Digital Technologies to Address Aboriginal Adolescents' Education: An Alternative School Intervention." *Multicultural Education and Technology Journal* 3 (2): 144–62.

Price, Emmett G. 2006. *Hip Hop Culture*. Santa Barbara, CA: ABC-CLIO.

Reeves, Marcus. 2008. *Somebody Scream!: Rap Music's Rise to Prominence in the Aftermath of Black Power*. New York: Faber and Faber.

Rickford, John. 1998. "Using the Vernacular to Teach the Standard." http://www.stanford.edu/~rickford/papers/VernacularToTeachStandard.html.

Rose, Tricia. 1994. *Black Noise: Rap Music and Black Culture in Contemporary America*. Hanover, NH: Wesleyan University.

———. 2008. *The Hip Hop Wars: What We Talk about When We Talk about Hip Hop*. New York: Basic Civitas.

RZA. 2005. *The Wu-Tang Manual: Enter the 36 Chambers*. Vol. 1. New York: Penguin.

Sholle, David, and Stan Denski. 1993. "Reading and Writing the Media: Critical Media Literacy and Postmodernism." In *Critical Literacy: Politics, Praxis, and the Postmodern*, edited by Colin Lankshear and Peter McLaren, 297–321. New York: State University of New York.

Smitherman, Geneva. 1997. "'The Chain Remain the Same': Communicative Practices in the Hip Hop Nation." *Journal of Black Studies* 28 (1): 3–25.

Stovall, David. 2006. "We Can Relate: Hip-Hop Culture, Critical Pedagogy, and the Secondary Classroom." *Urban Education* 41 (6): 585–602.

Street, Brian V. 1984. *Literacy in Theory and Practice*. Cambridge: Cambridge University.

Turner, K. C. Nat. 2011. "Rap Universal: Using Multimodal Media Production to Develop ICT Literacies." *Journal of Adolescent and Adult Literacy* 54 (8): 613–23.

———. 2012. "Multimodal Hip Hop Productions as Media Literacies." Themed Issue: *The Educational Forum* 76 (4): 497–509.

Vygotsky, L. [1935] 1978. *Mind in Society*. Translated by Michael Cole, Vera John-Steiner, Sylvia Scribner, and Ellen Souberman. Reprint, Cambridge, MA: Harvard University.

Willis, Paul E., Simon Jones, Joyce Canaan, and Geoff Hurd. 1990. *Common Culture: Symbolic Work at Play in the Everyday Culture of the Young*. Boulder, CO: Westview.

CHAPTER 33

AFRICAN AMERICAN VERNACULAR ENGLISH AND READING

WILLIAM LABOV AND BETTINA BAKER

33.1 INTRODUCTION

IT is well known that the inequitable outcomes in reading achievement between African American and White students have been a persistent problem in the United States.[1] Figure 33.1 summarizes the problem, showing the results of National Assessment of Educational Progress (NAEP) reading assessments, disaggregated by race. Although there is a significant improvement in the scores of African American students over time, the difference remains substantial and reflects the underlying condition: that large numbers of African American children do not adequately demonstrate their use of reading as a tool for educational success.

Although reading is only one of three linguistic skills important for educational success, we consider it more fundamental than writing or speaking in Standard Classroom English (hereinafter SCE), defined negatively as a dialect without any marked regional, local, social class, or ethnic features that may be stigmatized by classroom teachers. We define *reading* as the decoding and comprehension of information encoded on the printed page, the prerequisite for most other forms of learning in the school system.

Research findings on the impact of African American Vernacular English (AAVE) language patterns on reading acquisition rates fall into the following three main categories:

(1) *Correlations between the overall use of AAVE features and standardized test scores.* Craig et al. (2009) found an inverse relationship between AAVE speech patterns and performance on standardized reading achievement tests. They also found that AAVE speech production rates predicted outcomes on oral reading fluency, but not comprehension, on the GORT-3[2] (Thompson, Craig, and Washington 2004). Champion et al. (2010) found a statistically significant correlation between second- and fourth-grade

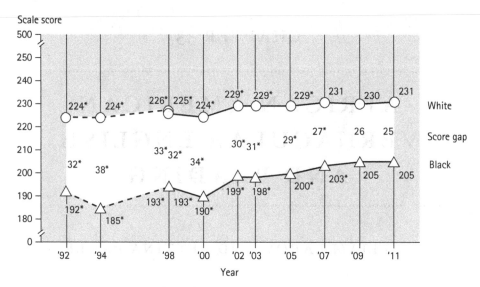

FIGURE 33.1 Fourth-grade NAEP reading scores, by race, 1992–2011.

* = significantly different from 2011.

Source: NAEP 2011.

African American students' Diagnostic Evaluation of Language Variation-Screening Test (DELV-ST) scores and their performance on the GORT-4 comprehension subtest. AAVE speakers who possessed the least SCE speech patterns scored lower on the GORT-4 comprehension subtest. Thompson et al. (2004) found that while African American children's production of both phonological and morphosyntactic features of AAVE were reduced between oral and reading tasks, students still produced phonological features of AAVE while reading out loud. Finally, Charity, Scarborough, and Griffin (2004) found a correlation between familiarity with SCE and increased standardized reading test scores. As important as these research results are, they do not bear directly on the problem of raising reading levels.

(2) *The effect of attitudes toward dialect differences on the part of teachers and students learning to read.* Considerable research has shown that children's nonstandard dialect has more influence on teachers' expectation of their performance than their writing skills, drawing skills, or appearance (Charity Hudley 2009; Rosenthal and Jacobson 1968; Seligman, Tucker, and Lambert 1972). Additional research found that teachers have limited knowledge of AAVE and are unsure of teaching SE to AAVE speakers (Gupta 2010). There is no doubt that negative attitudes toward nonstandard English can alienate AAVE speakers from the schooling process. But the report of the National Reading Conference Committee on the Prevention of Reading Difficulties among Young Children concluded that improving attitudes toward reading did not in itself raise reading levels (Snow et al. 1998). Improved methods of instruction are required.

(3) *Findings on the need for greater metalinguistic awareness in AAVE speakers and its impact on literacy acquisition rates.* Snow et al. (1998) and several other researchers

concluded that phonemic awareness was a major—perhaps the biggest—factor in the acquisition of literacy (Liberman et al. 1974; Liberman, Shankweiler, and Liberman 1989; Blachman 1997). Since that time research has found that phonological awareness patterns of AAVE speakers differ from those of SE speakers (Craig et al. 2009; Terry and Scarborough 2011). Poe, Burchinal, and Roberts (2004) found that both language and phonological skills are significant predictors of African American children's success in reading. A study of the effects of AAVE features on phonological awareness tests revealed significant differences between AAVE- and SE-speaking first graders, and concluded that children's success in reading could be predicted with 96.7 percent accuracy (Harris 2008). While Connor and Craig (2006) found a nonlinear relationship between AAVE use and phonological awareness and early literacy skills, their research gave leeway to the view that metalinguistic awareness is utilized by more successful readers who speak AAVE. J. Terry et al. (2010) have interpreted their studies of math word problems, to be summarized below, supporting the theory that promoting metalinguistic competencies in AAVE speakers will increase their proficiency in reading SE texts.

The focus of this chapter is on the ways in which the reading skills of African American children for whom AAVE is their native and primary language are affected by specific structural features of AAVE, as opposed to correlations of reading skills with race or with combined indices of the use of AAVE features. This chapter examines the evidence on how differences in the American English varieties spoken by African American and White students contribute to the difference in reading achievement shown in figure 33.1.

Through our engagement with efforts to raise reading levels throughout the United States, we have become alerted to the fact that linguistic issues are only one of the major causes of reading failure, and it is important to see how linguistic contributions to the problem interact with other causes. In our practical efforts to apply linguistic thinking to raising reading levels, we recognize the effects of malnutrition, lead poisoning, and lack of routine health care in low-income areas, which too often lead to cognitive problems. We recognize the effects of inadequate school resources as shown by the absence of current textbooks, inadequate or nonexistent libraries, and insufficient technology resources. The negative attitudes toward AAVE and those who speak it as their native and primary language that are the focus of (2) above have a profound effect upon learning and must be countered in any successful program. It is in this larger setting that linguistic research on methods of improving reading must be found useful and effective in spite of all other obstacles.

33.2 African American Vernacular English

The dialect we will focus on will be referred to as *African American Vernacular English* (AAVE). It is the everyday variety of African American Language (AAL) that is consistently used in low-income urban areas.[3] Although many differences in pronunciation reflect the influence of the surrounding mainstream communities, no regional differences have been reported in the overall grammatical structure of the variety we will be dealing with. We will base our description of AAVE on a "Summary Statement on African American English" representing the unanimous views of nine researchers who have contributed to our current knowledge of this variety (Labov et al. 2012). Our discussion of the effects of AAVE on reading will be drawn from the results of a large-scale testing of the Reading Road[4] tutorial program in Philadelphia elementary schools. Although there are no qualitative difference in the use of AAVE features from our results in Atlanta and Southern California, there are quantitative differences;[5] hence, focusing on the Philadelphia sample will better control the study of the effects on reading.

In this chapter, we will be comparing AAVE with SCE. The domains of agreement between AAVE and SCE are very large; here we will be dealing with differences. Table 33.1 is a schema of the major types of grammatical differences.

Column D in table 33.1 provides a sampling of the many unique semantic developments in the tense, mood, and aspect system of AAVE that are not present in SCE (see DeBose, this volume). It has not been shown that the presence of these variations in the home language of AAVE speakers has consequences for the reading of SCE texts, and they will not be discussed further in this chapter.[6] Column A in table 33.1 lists variable phonological features that are deleted more frequently in SCE than in other varieties. Columns B and C in table 33.1 are the morphosyntactic features of AAVE whose implications for reading are the main focus of this chapter. In column B of table 33.1, we list two areas in which variable processes in the phonology lead to substantial percentages of absence of morphological elements: the clitic /z/ representing the auxiliary and copula *is,* and absence of the suffix /t/ or /d/ representing past tense *−ed* as a result of the reduction of complex codas listed in column A in table 33.1.

Table 33.1 Major Features Differentiating AAVE from Other Varieties

Phonological reduction leading to			
Variable phonology A	Variable morphology B	Morphological absence C	Presence of unique semantic features D
Complex codas	Copula {is/are}	Possessive {s}	Habitual BE
Tautosyllabic liquids	Past {ed}	Verbal {s}	Preterit HAD
			Resultative BE DONE
			Remote perfect BIN
			Perseverative STEADY
			Indignative COME.

Column C in table 33.1 lists two items of the morphosyntax of other American English varieties that are absent from AAVE, qualitatively different from the items in column B on the basis of three properties:

(1) much higher rate of absence, close to 100 percent for many speakers
(2) no phonological conditioning of the segmental environment
(3) hypercorrection: insertion in environments not found in other varieties.

Figure 33.2 shows property (1) in the speech of struggling African American and White readers in Philadelphia. The gulf between the two groups of speakers is far greater for the items of column C than column B in table 33.1.

Figure 33.3 shows the results of a logistic regression analysis of the absence of verbal –s in the speech of fifty-eight African American children in elementary schools in Atlanta, Philadelphia, and California. The black symbols indicate the proportion of absence registered, and the white symbols indicate the factor groups found to be significant. The proportional differences are shown to be significant for only two groups: (1) Noun phrase subjects showed greater degree of absence than pronoun subjects, and (2) the three geographic regions are ordered as Atlanta, Philadelphia, and California. But no significant effects were produced by the preceding and following segments, as well as the type of verb, grade, or gender. This is in sharp contrast to many studies of AAVE that show final consonant clusters and copula variation with strong and consistent conditioning of the preceding and following segments (see Labov 1972; Wolfram 1969; Rickford et al. 1991).

Property (3) is illustrated by frequent occurrence of verbal –s in persons other than third singular.

He can goes out.
         —T-Birds, 13 (Labov et al. 1968, 166)

In contrast, no one has recorded hypercorrect examples of past tense –ed; that is, its use in present tense environments. Verbal –s and possessive –s differ markedly in

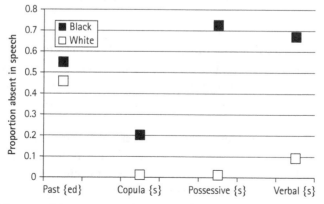

FIGURE 33.2 Absence of four morphological elements in the speech of African American and White struggling readers in low-income Philadelphia schools (N = 25 for each).

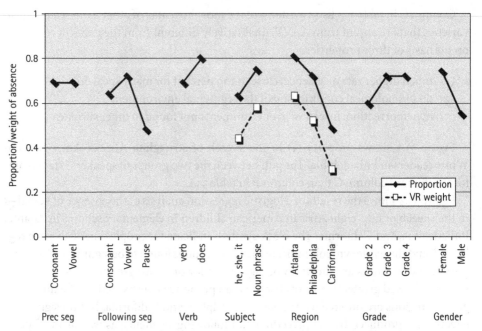

FIGURE 33.3 Conditioning factors for absence of verbal {s} in the spontaneous speech of fifty-eight African American struggling readers, Philadelphia.

the generality of the grammatical environments involved. The absence of verbal –s is accompanied by a general absence of subject-verb agreement, including irregular verbs *have, was,* and *do.*[7] But the grammatical function of possessive –s is maintained rigorously in absolute position (e.g., *This is hers, yours, John's, mines*).

33.3 AAVE Speakers' Knowledge of SCE Inflections

In 1967, Torrey conducted an experiment in a South Harlem second-grade classroom in connection with studies of AAVE in South Harlem (Labov et al. 1968). Second graders were interviewed, tested for their knowledge of the information conveyed by the SCE inflections, given grammatical instruction on the same inflections, and then re-tested. In the test for the meaning of possessive -s, children heard either *The duck nurse* or *The duck's nurse,* and then had to draw a line pointing to either a picture of a duck dressed as a nurse or a duck in bed with a nurse standing by. The test for the meaning of verbal -s took two forms: its use to distinguish singular from plural used the utterances *The cat splashes* or *The cats splash.* Since the marker of the plural was phonetically neutralized, only the presence or absence of verbal -s was available to identify plurality. A second test examined the subjects' ability to use verbal -s to distinguish present versus past tense. The two utterances

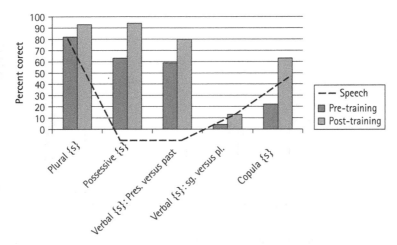

FIGURE 33.4 Percentage of realization in speech and correct identifications of meanings of inflections by African American second graders in New York City, before and after training.

Source: Torrey 1983.

were *The man hits the dog* and *The man hit the dog*, and the pictures showed a man in the act of hitting a dog with a stick or the man waving the stick and the dog running away.

Figure 33.4 shows Torrey's (1983) results for the percent of the presence of English inflections in spontaneous speech (dashed line) and the percent of correct responses by AAVE speakers before and after training in SCE. The plural showed very little deletion and a corresponding high rate of success in identifying its meaning. The possessive *-s* showed more presence than in the studies of Harlem adolescents and moderate recognition rates. The biggest effect was shown for the ability to recognize the singular with verbal *-s*. The 5 percent correct rate before training indicates that the second graders consistently associated verbal *-s* with the plural, with very little effect of training.

Torrey's (1983) results show that verbal *-s* was being used with a frequency similar to that of possessive *-s* but that it carried far less information and might in fact be a source of confusion in texts that depended on singular/plural distinctions for full comprehension.

Ball (1995) replicated Torrey's (1983) experiments in a Detroit area school and found a much higher correct rate of verbal *-s* in the picture meaning test (71 percent versus Torrey 13 percent) but also found that verbal *-s* showed no improvement on training as opposed to 84 percent -> 91 percent for possessive *-s*.[8]

33.4 The Effect of SCE Inflections on Other Cognitive Tasks

Efforts to determine the cognitive status of inflections in AAVE were stimulated by the remarkable results of J. Terry et al. (2010) in their analysis of the effect of grammatical

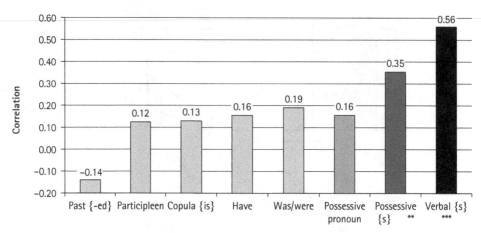

FIGURE 33.5 Correlations of influence of grammatical form on African American second graders with inhibition of scores on WJ-R Applied Math problems.

Light grey: n.s.; dark grey: *p* < .001; black: *p* < .00001.

Source: Based on J. Terry et al. 2010.

forms on the ability to solve word problems. The subjects were seventy-five African American second graders, part of the longitudinal study at the Frank Porter Graham Center of UNC.[9] The authors constructed a complex measure of the influence of a given linguistic feature on a student, which took into account the student's ability, the difficulty of the problem, and the student's score on the overall Dialect Density Measure (Craig 2004). Figure 33.5 shows the correlation of this measure with the students' W scores on the Woodcock-Johnson-R (WJ-R) Applied Math Test[10] for eight of the linguistic features in the text of the word problems. In other words, the more often that third singular –s occurred in the wording of the problem, the worse students did—taking into account the other factors built into the measure. Only two of these were significant: verbal –s and possessive –s, the items whose morphological status in AAVE has been questioned in figures 33.2, 33.3, and 33.4. Furthermore, the effect for verbal –s is considerably greater than for possessive –s. It may also be noteworthy that these second graders show a bimodal distribution in their response to verbal –s: it is only half the population that shows this negative effect, and for them it is quite strong (Terry et al. 2009).

Terry et al. (2009) considered a number of explanations for this effect, all mediated by the strain on working memory produced by linguistic differences. They consider the possibility that the problem lies in the strength or weaknesses of the representations—that it is the consistency with which children hear the SCE inflections at home. But the lack of such effects with the variable features of AAVE leads Terry et al. (2009) to conclude that the major problem lies in the categorical character of the differences associated with verbal –*s* and possessive –*s*:

> it is not the mismatches between [AAVE] and [SCE] generally that pose a cognitive burden for the children in our study. Instead the penalty results from the type of mismatch involved, specifically whether the two dialects have mismatched representations. (Terry et al. 2009, 15)

For further results and interpretation, see Terry et al. (this volume).

33.5 THE IDENTIFICATION OF ERRORS IN ORAL READING

We now turn to some of the results derived from a national test of a tutorial program, *The Reading Road Program* (RRP), designed to raise reading levels in low-income schools (Labov and Baker 2000). The RRP is an intrinsically motivated approach that takes into account a child's cultural and linguistic backgrounds in the presentation of its materials. The target population includes White, Latino/a, and African American struggling readers in Philadelphia, Atlanta, and California, but here we will be focusing only on African American and White children in Philadelphia.

We also turn to the main interaction in which children's reading abilities are assessed and developed: the correction of oral reading by the classroom teacher or tutor. It is here where knowledge of children's home language becomes crucial. The central question for the teacher is to decide whether or not the reader has succeeded in the task of decoding and comprehending the information in the text. If so, it is annoying and confusing for the teacher to repeat his or her own version of the text. If not, correction is in order so that wrong patterns will not be reinforced and learning will take place. We proceed on the maxim that efficient instruction will correct only those productions of the learner that need correction, and use our linguistic analysis to make instruction more efficient in this respect. The practical guide can be formulated as the golden rule of oral reading (Goodman 1965; Labov 1965):

> Correct the production of the wrong word, but ignore
> differences in pronunciation of the right word.

But as we will see, a good proportion of children's productions are ambiguous in this respect and linguistic analysis has little to say. Consider the following text from *Ray and His Bad Cat*, the initial diagnostic reading used in RRP.

Text: The cat spit out the chips and jumped in Ray's coat

The following are errors noted by tutors for the oral reading of African American second graders:

(a) The cat *spot* out the chips and jumped in Ray's *coal.*
(b) The cat spit out the chips and *jump* in Ray's coat.
(c) The cat spit out the chips and jumped in *Ray* coat.
(d) The cat spit out the chips and *junk* in Ray's coat.

In (a), there is no doubt that *spot* and *coal* are *true errors*, since they select the wrong words. But in (b), *jump* is only a *potential error*, as it is impossible to determine whether the reader failed to recognize the past tense in the original "jumped" or whether s/he did but simplified the final cluster /pt/ in the pronunciation. In (c), *Ray* is also a potential error, since one does not know whether the reader failed to recognize that *Ray* was the possessor of the object that followed. But in (d), the absence of the past tense is accompanied by the selection of the wrong consonant and the wrong word, so that there is no doubt that this is a true reading error. Though it is not possible to know how much the final cluster contributed to the error, one can compare the frequency of true errors in words containing past tense clusters with the total frequency of this feature in the text. One strategy then for estimating the effect of a given linguistic feature on decoding is to ignore the potential errors that might be the effect of AAVE phonology or morphology on production, and perform such a calculation feature by feature. Figure 33.6 compares this error rate with its frequency of absence in the speech of struggling African American and White readers for the items in columns B and C of figure 33.2.

It can be seen that there is only a small quantitative difference in the treatment of past tense *–ed* by AAVE speakers in speech and reading, with African Americans some 10 percent higher. This conforms to the view that both AAVE and SCE grammars share the same intact *–ed* morphology and the same variable rule of *–t,d* deletion (Labov et al. 1968; Guy 1980). The effect on reading of *–ed* is also similar: for both groups, it is the orthographic accumulation of symbols at the ends of words that is responsible for the frequency of true errors. The situation is quite different for possessive *–s* and verbal *–s*. As already seen in figure 33.3, there are radical differences in the frequencies of absence in speech for African American and White struggling readers.

But figure 33.6 shows no differences by race in the rates of true reading errors. We have to bear in mind that these true reading errors combine the absence of the linguistic variable with other deviations from a correct reading. It appears that the presence or absence of the inflection is a relatively minor part of the decoding problem that depends

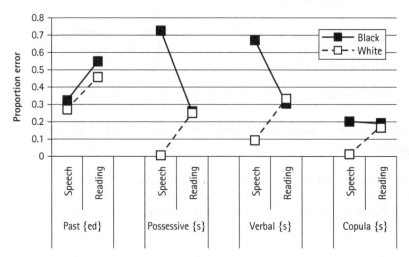

FIGURE 33.6 Absence of element in speech compared to clear error rates in reading for four linguistic variables for White and Black struggling readers in Philadelphia (N = 25 for each group).

on phonemic/graphemic relations of a more general sort. To estimate the actual influence of the reader's grammar on reading, we need to isolate the grammatical effect from these more general orthographic effects. This requires returning to the analysis of potential errors that represent just such an isolation. Unlike the data for clear errors, there are significant differences by race in the proportion of such potential errors. Figure 33.7 shows that number for the four morphosyntactic features we have been examining. There is no difference in the frequency for past –*ed*, but the values of possessive –*s* and verbal –*s* for African American struggling readers are twice that for White struggling readers. As in other data presented, this difference is less for copula –*s*.

The number of such potential errors is not great, but they are valuable indicators of the reading process if we can differentiate them by whether or not the semantic content of the inflection is retained. A comparison of error type (c) with type (e) below shows how this can be done.

(c) The cat spit out the chips and jumped in *Ray* coat.
(e) The cat spit out the chips and jumped in *Ray coal.*

In type (c), we have no way of knowing whether the reader has absorbed the semantic information intended in the text *Ray's coat:* that the cat jumped into some object belonging to Ray. But in (e) the reading *coal* is not consistent with this information, and the whole sentence fails to make sense. It is a product of a default reading procedure that selects any common word that starts with the printed first consonant and vowel. This makes it more probable that the reader correctly interpreted the *'s* in *Ray's* in (c) than in (e). The analysis presumes that even non-fluent SCE readers, reading well below a basic level, use syntactic and semantic context in decoding simple text, although their prosody gives the impression that they are reading one word at a time.

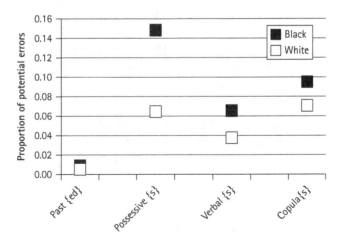

FIGURE 33.7 Number of potential errors, by race, for four morphosyntactic features for struggling readers in Philadelphia in pre-test diagnostic reading, *Ray and His Bad Cat* (N[Black] = 112, N[White] = 62).

We therefore argue that any given reading error casts a *semantic shadow* over the following text and that potential errors can be disambiguated by the presence or absence of errors following in the same sentence. We are of course only dealing with the probability that a given potential error is a true error or a correct reading, but applied over a given data base, we can determine those probabilities relative to the AAVE features of interest. The basic data for this study is the initial reading of the diagnostic text *Ray and His Bad Cat*. For each grammatical category, we identify and sum the clear errors, potential errors, and correct readings for all subjects in the group. We then sum for each category the number of words following in the same sentence for each type of reading error, sum the errors (of whatever type) occurring in the reading of those following words, and calculate the proportion of errors in following words for that type of error in that category.

Table 33.2 below shows the data for the four morphosyntactic categories of figure 33.2 in the readings of 112 African American children in Philadelphia. The diagnostic text contains fifteen tokens of past *–ed*, five possessive *–s*, three verbal *–s*, and eight copula *–s*. The numbers of potential errors are small compared to correct readings and clear errors, ranging from 1 percent for past *–ed* to 15 percent for possessive *–s*. For White children, the numbers of potential errors is only one-twentieth that of the African American children, but there is still sufficient data to show the proportion of following errors for each category.

Figure 33.8 displays that proportion of following errors for 112 African American struggling readers in Philadelphia as compared with the 62 Philadelphia White students with the same range of reading difficulties. In all categories, the proportion for clear errors is roughly twice that for correct readings, a result that gives weight to the semantic shadow hypothesis. For the crucial type of potential error, we find that values vary from one end to the other of this range. For the past tense *–ed*, potential errors group with correct readings, which means that the absence of the inflection does not indicate a loss of meaningful information. In this respect, White struggling readers behave in just the same way as Black struggling readers, as the preceding data in figures 33.2, 33.3, 33.5, and 33.6 predict that they would.

The other three morphosyntactic forms display a radically different picture, and show identical patterns. For White struggling readers, there is no significant difference between potential errors and clear errors. This means that the absence of the inflection is a failure in decoding equivalent to any other failure in decoding. For African American struggling readers, potential errors are intermediate—significantly different

Table 33.2 Woodcock–Johnson III WA Percentile Scores, by Race, After Forty Hours of RRP Instruction, 2001–2003

	Pre-test	Post-test	Gains	N
Black	32.3	41.7	9.4***	124
White	27.6	36.5	8.9***	103

N = 227. *** = statistically significant at the $p < .001$ level.

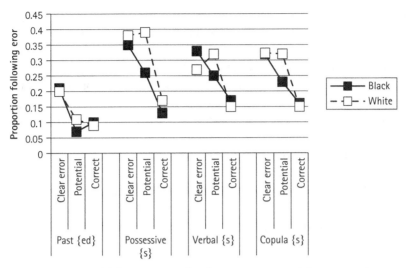

FIGURE 33.8 Frequency of following error for clear errors, potential errors, and correct readings for four AAVE features in the pre-training reading text, *Ray and His Bad Cat.*

from both clear errors and correct readings. This indicates that in a good number of cases the reader identified the stem form accurately and read the rest of the sentence in a form consistent with AAVE grammar with zero realization of the inflection. Again, these results are consistent with the findings of Torrey (1983) and N. Terry et al. (2010) in figures 33.4 and 33.5. They strengthen the argument for differentiating the status of past tense *-ed* as categorically present in AAVE grammar as opposed to a less certain status for verbal *-s* and possessive *-s*. These data do not, however, differentiate the copula *-s* from the others in the way that the results of figures 33.6 and 33.7 do.

33.6 IMPLICATIONS FOR READING

These results confirm arguments from linguistic analyses on the status of morphosyntactic inflections in AAVE. They apply less directly to efforts to raise reading levels. In this section, we will compare the general reading performance of African American and White students and see how this relates to the four morphosyntactic variables that have been under review. All students in this study were selected by the same criteria: the low-income school had to have 65 percent eligible for the federal free or reduced lunch program, and the student had to be in the 35th percentile or below on the WJ III Word Attack or Word ID scores.[11] Using these criteria we selected 124 African American students and 103 White students for the test of the RRP in Philadelphia, Atlanta, and Southern California. The initial mean Word Attack scores showed an advantage for African Americans (32nd percentile as against 27th for Whites). After completing the RRP in six weeks, the scores for both groups were almost ten percentile points higher (significance of the gain: $p < .0001$ for both).

The WJ III Word Attack test does not test decoding skills for the full range of phonemic/graphemic variables covered in a linguistic approach to reading instruction. Figure 33.9 shows error rates for twenty such variables in the reading of the diagnostic passage *Ray and His Bad Cat*, before and after the RRP. The most difficult are shown at the left, beginning with coda –*gh* (i.e., the "ghost letters") in *right, tough, cough*, etc. and the maximally complex onsets CCC-, as in *scratch* and *string*. The easiest items for decoding appear at extreme right—single initial consonants and single vowels. Both groups follow the same progression of reading difficulty, but African American students show a consistent advantage.

Figure 33.10 shows the corresponding reading error rates for the variables that have been the main focus of this chapter: the morphemes that have been identified as variably present in the grammar of AAVE along with the past tense –*ed*, which is considered more firmly established. Here one might have expected higher error rates for verbal –*s* and possessive –*s*, but the overall picture is that African American and White readers

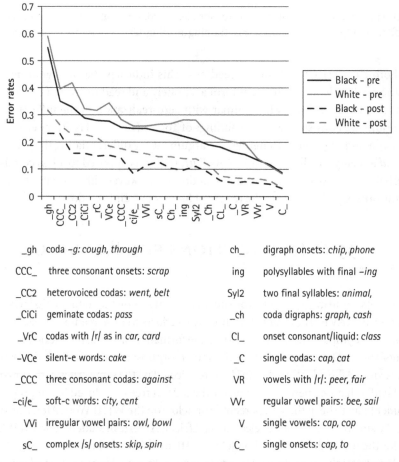

_gh	coda –*g: cough, through*		ch_	digraph onsets: *chip, phone*
CCC_	three consonant onsets: *scrap*		ing	polysyllables with final –*ing*
_CC2	heterovoiced codas: *went, belt*		Syl2	two final syllables: *animal,*
_CiCi	geminate codas: *pass*		_ch	coda digraphs: *graph, cash*
_VrC	codas with /r/ as in *car, card*		Cl_	onset consonant/liquid: *class*
-VCe	silent-e words: *cake*		_C	single codas: *cap, cat*
_CCC	three consonant codas: *against*		VR	vowels with /r/: *peer, fair*
-ci/e_	soft-c words: *city, cent*		Wr	regular vowel pairs: *bee, sail*
Wi	irregular vowel pairs: *owl, bowl*		V	single vowels: *cap, cop*
sC_	complex /s/ onsets: *skip, spin*		C_	single onsets: *cap, to*

FIGURE 33.9 Error rates for twenty phonemic/graphemic variables in reading the diagnostic, *Ray and His Bad Cat*, before and after the Reading Road program for 124 African American and 103 White students in Philadelphia, Atlanta, and Southern California, 2001–2003.

show the same rates of clear errors and the same rates of improvement with instruction. The interference of these grammatical differences with SCE is not shown in a higher error rate as compared to Whites who do not share the grammatical features of AAVE. It is realized in the elimination of the consistent advantage in decoding skills that African American readers exhibited in figure 33.9.

We can obtain further insight into this situation by comparing different types of standardized test scores. Figure 33.11 adds the percentile scores for WJ III Word ID and Passage Comprehension to the scores from WJ III Word Attack already provided in table 33.2, by race before and after the RRP. For all three measures, gains are significant. Since WJ III Word Attack and Word ID both have to do with decoding individual words,

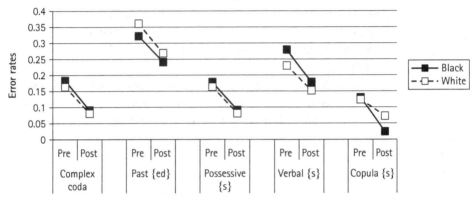

FIGURE 33.10 Pre- and post-test clear error rates in words including five features of AAVE in the Reading Road program in Philadelphia, 2001–2003 (N[Black] = 124, N[White] = 103).

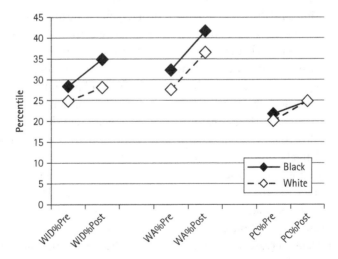

FIGURE 33.11 Pre- and post-test percentile scores on Woodcock-Johnson III Word ID, Word Attack, and Passage Comprehension in Philadelphia, 2001–2003 (N[Black] = 124, N[White] = 103).

the simple view of reading (Hoover and Gough 1990) leads us to expect greater gains in this domain. For both measures, African American students are again superior to White students (all differences by race are significant at the .02 level). But this advantage disappears when it comes to passage comprehension, where African American and White students' scores are equivalent and gains are more limited.

33.7 CONCLUSION

All of our efforts to understand the linguistic status of the –s inflections in AAVE are aimed at the question that heads this concluding section. Our first efforts in this direction were concentrated on the effects of phonological reduction with consequent increase in homonymy (Labov 1995). The results summarized here indicate that this is not as great a problem as the effects of unrecognized grammatical elements exemplified by possessive and verbal –s.

The repeated pattern is that, when African American students are identified as struggling readers, they do relatively well on the phonemic/graphic relations involved in decoding individual words and relatively worse (1) when passage comprehension is being tested, and (2) when possessive –s and verbal –s are involved in a given word. This is consistent with the linguistic analysis that these elements are morphemes variably inserted in the course of speech production without a regular basis in the underlying grammar. It is also consistent with findings that the recognition of these –s inflections involve processing problems above the word level, as shown by the work of Torrey (1983), Ball (1995), and J. Terry and colleagues (2009, 2010). Throughout these studies, there is a repeated contrast between the reading of –ed in final clusters, sensitive to phonological reduction, and the reading of the morphosyntactic features, which are not.

J. Terry et al. (2009, 2010) account for the interference of the –s inflections with math problems through an extra load on working memory. But Torrey's (1983) findings indicate a more substantial mismatch: that her second graders are more likely to interpret a verbal –s as a sign of the plural than as a sign of the singular. To the extent that is true, verbal –s is like throwing a monkey-wrench into the reading machinery and we can expect the interference with the reading of the following text that we found. Yet it is important to realize that these potential errors—absence of the inflection with no other change—are relatively rare. Most of the errors involving the –s inflections are "clear" errors, where the presence of the alien element interferes with the decoding of the rest of the word, and the interference with comprehension is triggered by that initial error.

The reading lesson we take from this is that careful instruction on the function of verbal –s and possessive –s will raise reading levels. Not by a large amount, but enough to achieve a significant increase in accuracy and comprehension. This is not an easy matter, since verbal –s is an instrument of subject-verb agreement, which has three properties most difficult for struggling readers to deal with: (1) it is abstract, (2) discontinuous, and (3) without any semantic interpretation in all but a few cases. It is not accidental that in most of these results, verbal –*s* has a more negative impact on reading than possessive –*s*. Nevertheless, the time spent on subject-verb agreement will have more benefit for the reader than time spent on plural –*s*, which is hardly necessary, or time spent on past tense –*ed*, which reflects knowledge that is already in the reader's mind.

We are satisfied that a partial reversal of reading failure can contribute to that larger reversal that is still known as "Adequate Yearly Progress." The RRP has been effective in achieving that level with efforts in Chester, Pennsylvania, where the program was implemented with hundreds of low-income, African American students. The present focus of the RRP is on grammatical inflections. *Portals to Reading* (Labov et al. 2010) is a Language Arts intervention program for grades four to eight, which incorporates the basic approach of the RRP. We have not yet had the opportunity of looking over teachers' shoulders to see how they respond, but this is clearly only a first step. We have every reason to think that more time and ingenuity devoted to this instructional area informed by the knowledge of the features of AAVE will have a significant result in our efforts to reduce inequity in reading achievement.

NOTES

1. Middle-class, as well as low-income, African American students continue to fall below their White peers on standardized reading achievement tests (Singham 1998; Bub et al. 2005), providing a case for the exploration and identification of variables beyond poverty that are responsible for this unacceptable discrepancy in American students' literacy rates.
2. The Gray Oral Reading Test, or GORT, is one of the most widely used measures of oral reading fluency and comprehension. GORT is a norm-referenced, reliable, and valid test of oral reading rate, accuracy, fluency, and comprehension.
3. Baugh (1983) defines AAVE as the language system used by African Americans who talk with, live with, and work with other African Americans, primarily.
4. See the web site http://pri.sas.upenn.edu/.
5. Struggling readers in Atlanta show a higher concentration of AAVE features than in Philadelphia, and those in Southern California lower, an effect that appears to be caused by a lower degree of racial segregation in the schools studied.
6. One possible effect stems from the fact that the auxiliary-like markers of AAVE shown in caps do not participate in the obligatory inversion, tag formation, or adverb placement rules of SCE, and thus make it more difficult to identify the location of the INFL node in the verb phrase.
7. But maintaining agreement in the finite forms of to be: am, is, are.
8. Ball concludes from her data that Detroit AAVE does have verbal {s} in its underlying forms.
9. See Van Hofwegen and Wolfram 2010.
10. The Woodcock-Johnson Tests of Cognitive Abilities is a set of intelligence tests first developed in 1977 by Richard Woodcock and Mary Johnson and subsequently revised in 1989 and 2001. The last version is often referred to as the WJ-III.
11. The Word Attack test involves the reading of nonsense words of increasing length and complexity of phonemic/graphemic relations. The Word ID test involves the reading of extant English words of increasing orthographic complexity.

References

Ball, Arnetha F. 1995. "Language, Learning and Linguistic Competence of African American Children: Torrey Revisited." *Linguistics and Education* 7: 23–46.

Baugh, John. 1983. *Black Street Speech: Its History, Structure, and Survival.* Austin: University of Texas Press.

Blachman, Benita. 1997. "Early Intervention and Phonological Awareness: A Cautionary Tale." In *Foundations of Reading Acquisition and Dyslexia*, edited by Benita Benita Blachman, 409–30. Mahwah, NJ: Lawrence Erlbaum.

Bub, Kristen L., Richard J. Murnane, John B. Willett, and Kathleen McCartney. 2005. "Explaining Puzzling Patterns in Black–White Achievement Gaps." Paper presented at the Twenty-Seventh Annual APPAM [Association for Public Policy Analysis and Management] Research Conference: Understanding and Informing Policy Design, Washington, DC, November 3–5.

Champion, Tempii B., Linda I. Rosa-Lugo, Kenyatta O. Rivers, and Allyssa McCabe. 2010. "A Preliminary Investigation of Second- and Fourth-Grade African American Students' Performance on the Gray Oral Reading Test—Fourth Edition." *Topics in Language Disorders* 30 (2): 145–53.

Charity Hudley, Anne. 2009. "African American English." In *Handbook of African American Psychology*, edited by Helen A. Neville, Brendesha M. Tynes, and Shawn O. Utsey, 199–210. Thousand Oaks, CA: Sage.

Charity, Anne H., Hollis S. Scarborough, and Darion M. Griffin. 2004. "Familiarity with School English in African American Children and Its Relation to Early Reading Achievement." *Child Development* 75 (5): 1340–56.

Connor, Carol McDonald, and Holly K. Craig. 2006. "African American Preschoolers' Language, Emergent Literacy Skills, and Use of African American English: A Complex Relation." *Journal of Speech, Language, and Hearing Research* 49: 771–92.

Craig, Holly K., and Julie A. Washington. 2004. "Grade-Related Changes in the Production of African American English." *Journal of Speech, Language, and Hearing Research* 47 (2): 450–63.

Craig, Holly K., Lingling Zhang, Stephanie L. Hensel, and Erin J. Quinn. 2009. "African American English–Speaking Students: An Examination of the Relationship between Dialect Shifting and Reading Outcomes." *Journal of Speech, Language, and Hearing Research* 52: 839–55.

Goodman, Kenneth S. 1965. "Dialect Barriers to Reading Comprehension." *Elementary English* 42: 853–60.

Gupta, Abha. 2010. "African-American English: Teacher Beliefs, Teacher Needs and Teacher Preparation Programs." *Reading Matrix: An International Online Journal* 10 (2): 152–64.

Guy, Gregory R. 1980. "Variation in the Group and the Individual: The Case of Final Stop Deletion." In *Locating Language in Time and Space*, edited by William Labov, 1–36. New York: Academic.

Harris, Amy Weddington. 2008. "The Effect of Dialect Produced by Typically Developing African American Elementary Students on Phonological Awareness and its Implications for Reading." *Dissertation Abstracts International Section A: Humanities and Social Sciences* 68(10-A):4241.

Hoover, Wesley A., and Philip B. Gough. 1990. "The Simple View of Reading." *Reading and Writing: An Interdisciplinary Journal* 2: 127–60. Houghton Mifflin Harcourt. 2010. PORTALS to Reading. Boston.

Labov, William. 1972. *Language in the Inner City*. Philadelphia: University of Pennsylvania.

———. 1995. "Can Reading Failure be Reversed: A Linguistic Approach to the Question." In *Literacy among African-American Youth: Issues in Learning, Teaching and Schooling*, edited by V. Gadsden and D. Wagner, 39–68 Cresskill, NJ: Hampton.

Labov, William, H. Samy Alim, Guy Bailey, John Baugh, Anne H. Charity, Lisa J. Green, John Rickford, Tracy Weldon, and Walt Wolfram. 2012. "Summary Statement on African American English." In *Dialect Diversity in America*, edited by William Labov, 1–8. Charlottesville: University of Virginia.

Labov, William, and Bettina Baker. 2010. "What is a Reading Error?" *Applied Psycholinguistics* 31: 735–57.

Labov, William, Paul Cohen, Clarence Robins, and John Lewis. 1968. *A Study of the Non-Standard English of Negro and Puerto Rican Speakers in New York City*. 2 vols. Philadelphia: U.S. Regional Survey.

Labov, William, I. Soto-Hinman, S. Dickson, Anne Charity Hudley, and B. Thorsnes. 2010. *Portals to Reading: Intensive Intervention*. Boston: Houghton Mifflin Harcourt.

Liberman, Isabelle Y., Donald Shankweiler, F. William Fischer, and Bonnie Carter. 1974. "Explicit Syllable and Phoneme Segmentation in the Young Child." *Journal of Experimental Child Psychology* 18 (2): 201–12.

Liberman, Isabelle, Donald Shankweiler, and Alvin M. Liberman. 1989. "The Alphabetic Principle and Learning to Read." *Haskins Laboratories Status Report on Speech Research*, SR-101/102, 1–13.

NAEP. 2011. *Reading 2011: National Assessment of Educational Progress at Grades 4 and 8*. Washington, DC: US Department of Education, National Center for Educational Statistics, Institute of Education Sciences.

Poe, Michelle D., Margaret R. Burchinal, and Joanne E. Roberts. 2004. "Early Language and the Development of Children's Reading Skills. *Journal of School Psychology* 42 (4): 315–32.

Rickford, John R., Arnetha Ball, Renée Blake, Raina Jackson, and Nomi Martin. 1991. "Rappin on the Copula Coffin: Theoretical and Methodological Issues in the Analysis of Copula Variation in African-American Vernacular English." *Language Variation and Change* 3 (1): 103–32.

Rosenthal, Robert, and Lenore Jacobson. 1968. *Pygmalion in the Classroom*. New York: Holt, Rinehart and Winston.

Seligman, Clive R., G. Richard Tucker, and Wallace E. Lambert. 1972. "The Effects of Speech Style and Other Attributes on Teachers' Attitudes towards Pupils." *Language in Society* 1 (1): 131–42.

Singham, Mango. 1998. "The Canary in the Mine." *Phi Delta Kappan* 80 (1): 8–15.

Snow, Catherine E., M. Susan Burns, and Peg Griffin, eds. 1998. *Preventing Reading Difficulties in Young Children*. Washington, DC: National Academies.

Terry, J. Michael, Evangelos Evangelou, Richard L. Smith, J. E. Roberts, and S. L. Zeisel. 2009. "Dialect Switching and Mathematical Reasoning Tests: Implications for Early Educational Achievement." Manuscript.

Terry, J. Michael, Randall Hendrick, Evangelos Evangelou, and Richard L. Smith. 2010. "Variable Dialect Switching among African American Children: Inferences about Working Memory." *Lingua* 120: 2463–75.

Terry, Nicole Patton, Carol McDonald Connor, Shurita Thomas-Tate, and Michael Love. 2010. "Examining Relationships among Dialect Variation, Literacy Skills, and School Context in First Grade." *Journal of Speech, Language, and Hearing Research* 53 (1): 126–45.

Terry, Nicole Patton, and H. S. Scarborough. 2011. "The Phonological Hypothesis as a Valuable Framework for Studying the Relation of Dialect Variation to Early Reading Skills." In *Explaining Individual Differences in Reading: Theory and Evidence*, edited by S. Brady, D. Braze, and C. A. Fowler, 97–120. New York: Psychology.

Thompson, Connie, Holly Craig, and Julie Washington. 2004. "Variable Production of African American English across Oracy and Literacy Contexts." *Language, Speech and Hearing Services in Schools* 35: 269–82.

Torrey, Jane. 1983. "Black Children's Knowledge of Standard English." *American Educational Research Journal* 20: 627–43.

Van Hofwegen, Janneke, and Walt Wolfram. 2010. "Coming of Age in African-American English: A Longitudinal Study." *Journal of Sociolinguistics* 14: 427–55.

Wolfram, Walt. 1969. *A Sociolinguistic Description of Detroit Negro Speech*. Arlington, VA: Center for Applied Linguistics.

CHAPTER 34

DIALECT SWITCHING AND MATHEMATICAL REASONING TESTS

Implications for Early Educational Achievement

J. MICHAEL TERRY, RANDALL HENDRICK, EVANGELOS EVANGELOU, AND RICHARD L. SMITH

34.1 INTRODUCTION

IN the application of linguistic research to education, a chief focus has been the role that language—more specifically, phonological and grammatical differences between African American English (AAE)[1] and Standard Classroom English (SCE)—may (or may not) play in the academic performance of those African American students who are speakers of AAE. The primary goal of this chapter is to contribute to this growing literature by advancing understanding of the mechanisms by which language affects academic achievement. We identify specific structural features of AAE, whose divergences from SCE, we contend, pose problems by creating a significant additional cognitive load for young AAE speakers who are taught and tested in SCE. We trace and quantify the effect of this load on the scores of AAE-speaking second-grade students on the Woodcock-Johnson-R (hereinafter, WJ-R) Test of Applied Problems (Woodcock and Johnson 1989; for more information, see http://www.fasttrackproject.org/techrept/w/wjr/), and we argue that the need to bear its weight may play an important part in preventing a significant number of these students from reaching their full educational potential.

That high levels of AAE use and poor academic performance are correlated has been documented and is widely accepted (Craig, Connor, and Washington 2003; Craig and Washington 2006; Charity, Scarborough, and Griffin 2004; Labov and Baker, this volume); structural explanations for the correlation, such as the one we advance here, however, are less widely embraced. Since the earliest work on the impact of dialectal differences on learning to read carried out in the 1960s and 1970s, researchers, with some notable exceptions (see Charity et al. 2004; Poe, Burchinal, and Roberts 2004; Labov and Baker, this volume), have generally shifted their thinking from seeking primarily structural explanations for the general relationship between dialect use and academic achievement to more social accounts. William Labov remains one among a few whose work continues to uncover both the social and structural mechanisms that account for the correlation. As he related at a 2011 meeting of the National Research Council, however, even his original research on AAE in South Harlem argued that the main way in which the dialect interferes with school success is its social symbolism as a predictor of academic failure and disciplinary problems. In the wake of such studies, structural accounts tend to be dismissed. For example, highly critical of the view that any structural differences between AAE and SCE are significant enough to explain poor academic performance, sociologist John Ogbu, in his influential article "Beyond Language: Ebonics, Proper English, and Identity in a Black-American Speech Community" (1999), draws warranted attention to the effect that different cultural rules governing dialect use, as opposed to different grammatical rules governing language structure, may have on students mastery of SCE and general academic success. His view is that a major part of current racial disparities in achievement results from many African American students seeing speaking SCE as "talking White," success in academics as "acting White," and both the former and the latter as being in conflict with their Black identities (Fordham and Ogbu 1986). Other researchers, for example, Tyson, Darity, and Castellino (2005), argue that in the main, Black students, like their White peers, are achievement oriented, and that the stigma of success in school is generalizable beyond any one group. Their work suggests that school structure, rather than home culture, offers a better explanation for any racialized peer pressure against academic achievement that might exist. Further, they argue that recognizing the similarity between the stigma of "acting White" for Black students and that of "acting high and mighty" for low-income Whites is critical in understanding the issues concerning Black students' academic success (Tyson, Darity, and Castellino 2005).

No matter the specific mechanisms at work, students' relationships to their language and other issues of identity undoubtedly affect their acquisition of SCE, and, as a result, their test scores on language-related tasks and academic performance in general. Still, the extent to which differences in the structural features of AAE and SCE themselves may help explain why AAE-speaking children tend to fare poorly in school remains an open question. We believe that finding an answer to this question will require the sorting out of the relative roles that language structure and culture (both at home and at school) play in the process, but that structural mismatches cannot be ignored. In this account, we outline a structural hypothesis aimed at helping explain the correlation between high levels of AAE usage and low levels of academic achievement. The hypothesis, as suggested, is based on the needs of AAE-speaking students to maintain, as well as switch between, grammatical structures from two different dialects, thereby adding a cognitive load to the language processing task. While broad in their potential impact on education, the structural differences we identify as problematic are specific enough to lend themselves to the consideration of practical intervention strategies.

34.2 A Structural Hypothesis

34.2.1 Beyond Reading

Students who read well are most apt to experience success in other academic areas, and those who do not usually face wide-ranging academic problems. Because of this, research aimed at determining the role of dialectal variation in the inequitable educational outcomes of African American and White students has, to a great extent, focused on the disparity between the reading abilities of AAE-speaking African American children and their White SCE-speaking peers. The chief hypothesis guiding much of the work in this area has been that differences in AAE and SCE phonology result in a basic sound to written-letter decoding problem for many AAE speakers (see Labov and Baker 2010; Labov and Baker, this volume). Other studies have suggested that the purely phonological differences that exist between the two dialects have far less effect on children's learning to read than is often argued (Harber 1977; Hart, Guthrie, and Winfield 1980; Gemake 1981).

There is mounting evidence that differences in AAE and SCE morphology and syntax may have a greater effect on the process of children's learning to read than differences in phonology (Bartel and Axelrod 1973; Steffensen et al. 1982; Craig and Washington 2004; Van Hofwegen and Stob 2011). Still, the mechanisms by which morphosyntactic differences influence children's reading proficiency remain unclear. No reading-specific cause-effect relation has been discovered, and there is no guarantee that one exists.

Complementing the important body of work that documents the influences AAE has on literacy (Bartel and Axelrod 1973; Steffensen et al. 1982, Purcell-Gates 1996; Gutman, Sameroff, and Eccles 2002; Charity, Scarborough, and Griffin 2004; Craig and Washington 2006; Labov and Baker 2010; Labov and Baker, this volume; Mills and Washington, this volume), we seek to broaden the scope of the discussion on dialect and achievement beyond reading to other critical areas of early education. We test the hypothesis that the morphosyntactic organization of AAE, to the extent that it contrasts with SCE, has significant effects on the performance of AAE-speaking African American second-grade students on the WJ-R Applied Problems subtest, a test of mathematical reasoning. Even though students taking this test are provided with written copy, the test questions are read aloud by the test administrator and repeated as often as a student might require in order to lessen the role that reading likely plays in the process, especially for such young readers. The task, then, raises the question of processing grammatical differences rather than phonological decoding per se.

34.2.2 The Search for a Mechanism

We analyze the performance of young students because we believe it offers the earliest and clearest venue for assessing the differing causal explanations for understanding the correlation between AAE and low academic achievement. One line of explanation views AAE as principally a series of linguistic markers correlated with social conditions extrinsic to the dialect that negatively impact achievement. For example, Craig and Washington's (2006) analysis holds that AAE's correlation with socioeconomic status, race, teacher expertise, and home literacy habits results from its speakers' limited experience with SCE used in educational settings. Students with this limited experience, it is suggested, face a disadvantage in comparison to students who have more extensive experience with SCE. This general picture is made somewhat more complex by the recognition that some students have linguistic skills that allow them to exploit even limited experience with SCE more efficiently than others. Other extrinsic explanations, as discussed earlier, suggest a determining role for broader cultural practices and styles of interaction in the home (Heath 1983; Fordham and Ogbu 1986; Roberts, Burchinal, and Durham 1999).

A second strategy of explanation attributes the effect to the intrinsic linguistic difference between AAE and SCE. On this view, a mismatch between the organization of the grammars of AAE and SCE poses a burden for children either because they need to switch between the two dialects (Green 1995) or because semantic differences systematically lead them astray (Torrey 1983). Here, too, differences in students' linguistic abilities, whether due to differences in familiarity with SCE or other cognitive skills, complicate the picture. Of course, these two broad approaches are not mutually exclusive, and each likely has a role in a full explanation of the effect AAE has on academic achievement. We believe that understanding in this area will most likely be advanced by greater attention to the relative weight of various explanatory factors, and by greater specificity about the causal mechanisms that could yield observed results.

Factors extrinsic to language can be expected to exert broad influence within a domain of achievement. In contrast, intrinsic factors concerning mismatches between AAE and SCE should have effects that closely track the distribution of those mismatches. Therefore, we test our hypothesis that the morphosyntactic organization of AAE has an effect on AAE-speaking African American students' performance on the WJ-R Applied Problems subtest by determining whether performance on that test correlates with specific structural mismatches between AAE and SCE. We hypothesize that morphemic divergences, in particular, will be the most likely locus for observing the effects of such mismatches. In the end, we find support for an explanation based on the need for children to maintain separate systems and switch between different morphological representations rather than differences in the content carried by those representations.

34.3 THE MATHEMATICAL REASONING DATA

Eighty-seven African American students were recruited from North Carolina community-based childcare centers to participate in a longitudinal study of children's health and development (Roberts et al. 1995). As a part of this study, at regular intervals, language samples were taken from the students, and they were administered a series of diagnostic tests to assess their linguistic and other cognitive abilities. Of central importance here, these tests included both the Calculation and Applied Problems subtests from the WJ-R Psycho-Educational Battery. Applied Problems is a subtest that assesses skill in analyzing and solving verbal math problems, or "word problems," as distinct from the Calculation subtest, which tests accuracy of calculation procedures. For example, the question, "If you have eight pennies and you spend two of them, how many pennies would you have left?" has the form of a typical Applied Problems question. In addition to the Applied Problems and Calculation subtests of the WJ-R, other diagnostic tests included the WJ-R Letter-Word Identification subtest, which assesses skills in identifying isolated letters in words, and the Clinical Evaluation of Language Fundamentals (CELF-3) (Semel, Wiig, and Secord 1995), an instrument designed to measure overall receptive and expressive language ability. In addition to these tests, conversational language samples were collected from each of the study participants. Each sample was transcribed using Systematic Analysis of Language Transcripts (SALT) (Miller and Chapman 2000). Study participants were also screened to identify any hearing loss. All tests were administered by one of seven trained examiners with expertise in speech and language assessment. All tests were given at the Frank Porter Graham Child Development Center, a university research facility at the University of North Carolina.

The WJ-R subtests were given at kindergarten entry and at the end of each grade year beginning with first grade. The data analyzed here include the individual responses of seventy-five of the original study participants at second grade. The mean age of the students at the time of testing was 8.32 years. Standard scores, called W scores, were calculated from the students' results. W scores are based on the Rasch ability scale (see http://www.rasch-analysis.com/rasch-analysis.htm for more explanation) and are centered on a value of 500, which is the approximate average performance of a beginning fifth grader. The sixty questions on the Applied Problems subtest increase in difficulty and are divided into pages. Students were "ceiling tested" by complete pages until the six highest-numbered items were failed, or until the last test item was answered.

In addition to data concerning individual students' performance on each test question, three members of our team coded each test question for a range of linguistic properties. Reliability between coders was established over the last ten questions, as linguistically speaking, the last questions are the most complex, and therefore most likely to reveal any coding inconsistencies. Subsequently six morphological features were chosen for further statistical analysis. The first five—past tense –ed, past participle –en, past tense copula was/were, auxiliary have, and third person singular –s—were all chosen because they have been identified as points of divergence between AAE and SCE (Green 2002; Craig and Washington 2006; Wolfram and Shilling-Estes 2006). They may, however, represent different types of divergences (Green 2011). The final feature, counterfactual conditional if + –ed, was selected because of its importance to reasoning tasks and the possibility of interaction with –ed. All six features are listed along with SCE and AAE examples in table 34.1.

We seek, then, to determine whether the African American students in this study's performance on the WJ-R Applied Problems subtest correlates with those mismatches

Table 34.1 The Six Morphosyntactic Features Analyzed

Morpheme or Morpheme Combination Coded	Examples	
	Standard Classroom English (SCE)	African American English (AAE)
Past tense –*ed*	Jill walked Jack to school.	Jill walked Jack to school. OR Jill walk Jack to school.
Participle –*en*	Jill has written a letter.	Jill have wrote a letter.
Past tense copula ("was," "were")	Jack and Jill were late for school.	Jack and Jill was late for school.
Auxiliary "have"	Jill has written a letter.	Jill have wrote a letter.
Third person singular –*s*	Jill eats a lot of ice-cream.	Jill eat a lot of ice-cream.
Counterfactual conditional (*if* + –*ed*)	If Jill walked Jack to school, he would get there earlier.	If Jill walk Jack to school, he would get there earlier. OR If Jill walk Jack to school, he would get there earlier.

between AAE and SCE that are represented by the linguistic features in table 34.1. Simply being African American, however, does not guarantee that one is a speaker of AAE. Further, there is substantial variation among AAE speakers in the use of those AAE features that contrast with SCE. To measure the variation in students' use of AAE, we calculated dialect density measures (DDMs) from unscripted language samples for the students, using the list of AAE features given in Craig and Washington (2004). A DDM is a measure of the rate of dialect feature production calculated as a ratio of number of dialect features to number of words or utterances (Oetting and McDonald 2002; Craig and Washington 2004; Renn and Terry 2009). The mean DDM score for the students in the study is 0.168 with a standard deviation of 0.124. As our interest here is in quantifying the amount of AAE a student uses rather than labeling him or her as an AAE speaker or SCE speaker, we do not employ a "cut off" score for AAE speaker status. In interpreting these numbers, it is important to recognize that the vast majority of AAE speech overlaps with SCE and other dialects of English.[2]

34.3.1 Establishing a Linguistic Effect

As previously outlined, our initial data set comprised the individual responses of seventy-five students to the portion of the sixty WJ-R Applied Problems subtest questions that each of them answered. These data were further complemented by counts of the number of times that each of the six linguistic features summarized in table 34.1 appear in each of the WJ-R Applied Problems subtest questions, and DDMs of each student's AAE production. Our goal here is to determine whether the features in table 34.1 influence students' performance on the WJ-R Applied Problems subtest. To this end, we model whether or not a student answers a given problem correctly as a function of that student's general mathematical ability, the level of difficulty of the problem itself, and the presence or non-presence of any of the linguistic features in table 34.1. We employ a Bayesian Markov Chain Monte Carlo Method (MCMC) to estimate the unknown parameters, including the effect of the features on a student.[3] Full details of the model including estimates of model's goodness of fit are given in Appendix A.

We hypothesized that morphemic mismatches between AAE and SCE would affect student performance in learning and testing situations. For each linguistic feature we examined, table 34.2 provides the correlation between a student's total score on the WJ-R Applied Problems subtest and the measure of the influence of that feature on a given student provided by the model. If there is no correlation between a student's score and the linguistic feature, we expect the correlation to be near zero. A high positive or negative value indicates that the effect of the feature is strong.

In the case of a positive correlation, a high negative feature effect on a student indicates that student has worse than average scores on questions in which the feature appears; a high positive feature effect, on the other hand, indicates the student has higher than average scores in which the feature appears. The reverse is true in the case of a negative correlation. Table 34.2 also provides the *p*-value for the null hypothesis—that there is no correlation between a student's score and the linguistic feature—as well as the lower and upper bounds for the 95 percent confidence interval for the correlation.

The results in tables 34.2 and 34.3 suggest that the linguistic features we examined do influence students' overall scores, although the effect of some seems to be negligible.

Table 34.2 Test Score and Feature Effect Correlations

Linguistic feature	Correlation with score	Feature effect statistics		P-value
		95% Confidence interval		
		Lower bound	Upper bound	
Past tense –*ed*	−0.14	−0.09	0.36	0.23
Participle –*en*	0.12	−0.11	0.34	0.29
Past tense copula ("was," "were")	0.19	−0.04	0.40	0.10
Auxiliary "have"	0.16	−0.07	0.37	0.18
Counterfactual conditional (*if* + –*ed*)	0.43	0.23	0.60	<0.01
Present third singular –*s*	0.56	0.38	0.70	<0.01

Table 34.3 Feature Effects Averaged across Students

	Feature effect statistics		
Linguistic feature	Correlation with score	Standard deviation	Coefficient of variation
Past tense –ed	−0.03	0.05	−1.66
Participle –en	−0.07	0.29	−3.92
Past tense copula ("was," "were")	−0.08	0.03	−0.45
Auxiliary "have"	−0.10	0.03	−0.03
Counterfactual conditional (if + –ed)	0.12	0.05	0.41
Present 3rd singular –s	0.50	0.68	−1.36

Third person singular –s appears to have the greatest effect; in contrast, the past tense copula *was/were* and counterfactual conditional *if* + –*ed* appear to have the least effect. Although the counterfactual conditional *if* + –*ed* is estimated to have a small effect, it is noteworthy that the effect it has is facilitative; its presence increases the likelihood that a student will answer a question correctly. As this feature was included in our coding because of the possibility of interaction with –*ed*, a feature whose effect was not facilitative, and not because counterfactuals appear to work differently in AAE than in SCE, this positive effect is likely due to the counterfactual's ability to make transparent the logic of questions in which it is found.

Turning to table 34.3, for each linguistic feature, this table shows the value of the model's measure of the effect of that feature on a student averaged across students, its standard deviation, and coefficient of variation.

While table 34.2 shows that, according to the model, third person singular –s has the greatest effect on students' overall scores, in table 34.2 we are able to see that it also exhibits a high degree of variation. This indicates that there are some students who are highly affected by the presence of this particular feature and others who are not. This finding is consistent with those of Johnson, de Villiers, and Seymour (2005) and de Villiers and Johnson (2007).

The data in table 34.2 can also be represented as histograms of the effect of each linguistic feature on the model's measure of the influence of that feature on a given student.[4] Such histograms are given in figure 34.1. The histograms show clearly the influence of each linguistic feature on the students' scores.

These histograms visually demonstrate that third person singular –s has the widest variation with multiple major groups of students, some highly affected by the feature, others moderately, and still others little at all. Past tense copula *was/were* and participle

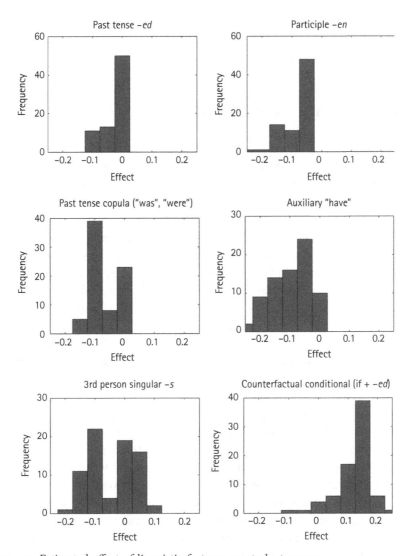

FIGURE 34.1 Estimated effect of linguistic features on student scores.

–en also show at least two groups, although the variation is smaller than that shown by third person singular *–s*. Past tense *–ed* exhibits the least variation.

34.3.2 The Size of the Effect

Our model allows us to estimate the size of a feature's effect on the average student in each of the groups identified. For third person singular *–s*, the most important feature lowering the overall score, the results are as follows. In the highly affected group, roughly

15 percent of the students, the average student would answer 9 percent more questions correctly if the effect of this feature were removed. The size of this effect, then, appears to be educationally significant.

34.3.3 Variation in the Effect on Students

Of the morphemes considered in our study, third person singular *–s* not only had the strongest effect on students, but it also showed the widest variation, splitting the students into three distinct groups: those highly affected by the presence of the feature, those moderately affected, and those who showed little effect. To aid in both theoretical and practical concerns, we would like to know why any morphological feature would affect different AAE speakers as differently as third person singular *–s*.

Two possible reasons unrelated to dialect are available for consideration. One could argue that although this and the other effects we have identified track specific morphological features, the grouping is, in fact, driven by the students' general intelligence rather than the organization or use of their individual grammars. The case for general intelligence has been made based largely on the fact that there is a correlation between scores on tests of demonstrably distinct domains of cognition. For example, while a great deal of evidence shows that verbal memory (and ability) is distinct from spatial memory (and ability), research shows a correlation between subjects' scores on tests of the two (Gardner, Kornhaber, and Wake 1996). If general intelligence or access to general working memory is the hidden driver behind the linguistic effects and groupings that we have identified, we would expect that introducing a measure of spatial reasoning ability—an ability distinct from linguistic abilities but presumably driven by general intelligence—into our MCMC algorithm should lessen the apparent effect of the linguistic features. Using the Block Design subtest from the third edition of the Wechsler Intelligence Scale for Children (Wechsler 1991), as such a measure, we re-ran our MCMC algorithm. This subtest involves copying small geometric designs with four or nine larger plastic cubes. Our re-run of the algorithm showed no significant difference in the size of the effects identified or the groupings of students affected. The independence of spatial reasoning abilities from the linguistic effects is strong evidence that they and the groupings are driven by more linguistically specific factors than general intelligence.

One possible language-based explanation unrelated to dialect might be that the students most affected by the linguistic features are either linguistically delayed or disordered. As the students in this study are beyond the age when problems with morphosyntax typically suggest delay, disorder is the more plausible of these two options. However, it too is unlikely as the student's scores on the Clinical Evaluation of Language Fundamentals (CELF-3) (Semel, Wiig, and Secord 1995), a test commonly used by speech-language pathologists to identify language disorder, do not indicate disorder within the group of students most affected by the linguistic features. Thus, it seems as though a linguistic cause other than delay or disorder is at the root of the variation in the effect of the linguistic features on students' test performance. Before proposing a plausible cause for this variation, we consider the variation in the effects of the linguistic features themselves.

34.3.4 Variation in the Effects of Features

In explaining why any of the linguistic features we tested would have an effect on test performance, and why some, like third person singular −s, have a greater effect than others, our leading hypothesis is that morphosyntactic features whose semantic content is phonologically null in one dialect but not the other pose the greatest difficulty. In this case, SCE third singular −s carries present tense meaning while that found in AAE sentences like "John eat" is not phonologically expressed by them.[5] (See Terry et al. [2010] for further discussion of this perspective and Green [2011] for arguments that third person singular −s in not a part of child AAE grammar.)

An additional strength of the general hypothesis is that it may also allow us to explain the variation in the effect this feature has on student performance by drawing a connection to an otherwise anomalous finding noted in Craig and Washington (2004). They report that dialect switching between AAE and SCE is typically accompanied by reduced sentence complexity on the part of the speaker. This suggests to us that dialect switching is purchased at the cost of linguistic complexity. Viewed in this light, the results of our MCMC analysis might suggest that children who must switch between AAE and SCE during mathematical testing sacrifice cognitive resources that would otherwise be available for actual problem solving had they not needed to switch. Although we hypothesize that some morphemes are cognitively taxing in dialect switching, we distinguish ours from the view that the chief source of AAE speakers' problems with third person singular −s is a confusion with the meaning of the homophonous plural morpheme (Torrey 1969). Likewise, we distinguish our dialect-shifting hypothesis from the highly contested view that the semantic organization of AAE is such that it does not allow for the efficient representation of key mathematical concepts (Orr 1987; cf. O'Neil 1990 and Baugh 1999).

34.3.5 Dialect Switching

Without a direct measure of the dialect switching abilities of the students in this study, we are unable to completely confirm our suspicion that it is precisely those students who find it most difficult to switch from AAE to SCE who, in turn, are the most affected by dialect mismatches such as the presence of third person singular −s in test questions. We expect, however, that there is considerable overlap between those students who struggle to switch dialects and those students who have the greatest need to do so. Put another way, although all AAE speakers dialect shift to some degree, we expect that the more monodialectal AAE speakers in our sample will, for the most part, be the "heavier" dialect speakers and vice versa. Given this reasoning, we predict that introducing the students' DDMs into our MCMC algorithm will change the average student value of our measure to the extent to which a given linguistic feature affects a student, its correlation with test scores, and the coefficient of variation for each of the features we considered. The values for these statistics after re-running our algorithm with the DDMs included are given in tables 34.4 and 34.5.

Table 34.4 Feature Effects Averaged across Students (AAE Production Included in Model)

	Feature effect statistics		
Linguistic feature	Mean	Standard deviation	Coefficient of variation
Past tense –ed	−0.03	0.05	−1.40
Participle –en	−0.14	0.32	−0.23
Past tense copula ("was," "were")	−0.20	0.04	−0.19
Auxiliary "have"	−0.16	0.37	−0.23
Counterfactual conditional (if + –ed)	0.11	0.05	0.44
Present third singular –s	0.06	0.07	−1.16

Table 34.5 Test Score and Feature Effect Correlations (AAE Production Included in Model)

	Feature effect statistics			
	Correlation with score	95% Confidence interval		P-value
Linguistic feature		Lower bound	Upper bound	
Past tense –ed	0.14	−0.09	0.36	0.24
Participle –en	0.11	−0.12	0.33	0.35
Past tense copula ("was," "were")	0.18	−0.05	0.39	0.13
Auxiliary "have"	0.14	−0.09	0.36	0.23
Counterfactual conditional (if + –ed)	0.42	0.21	0.59	<0.01
Present third singular –s	0.72	0.59	0.81	<0.01

Across students there is variation in the effect of each of the linguistic features we examined, variation in how well they performed on the test, and variation in their AAE production. With the addition of a DDM term into our model, the correlation between the model's measure of the influence of a given feature on a given student and student test scores, as shown in table 34.4, can be viewed as a measure of the extent to which the variation on those three dimensions overlaps. The strong correlation and high coefficient of variation reported in table 34.4 suggest that the linguistic effects that we have identified are, in fact, effects of dialect and that the stronger the dialect, the stronger the effect. Thus, these numbers are supportive of our dialect-switching hypothesis.

On the other hand, a potential criticism of the dialect-switching hypothesis is that a similar pattern of results might be achieved simply by looking for a correlation between the length of a question (in terms of the number of sentences it contains), its difficulty and students' performance. From this perspective, the number of times third person singular −s occurs in a test question might be thought of as a stand in for the number of sentences in that question. While this alternative seems plausible enough on the surface, it does not fit well with the data in our study. This is because it is only narrowly consistent with the information about third singular −s; other features, such as the past tense marker −ed, or the counterfactual conditional if + −ed pattern with multiple sentences in the WJ-R Applied Problems subtest, yet they do not show nearly as strong correlation with students' performance. And in the case of the counterfactual conditional if + −ed, the correlation runs in the opposite direction: the more instances of third person singular −s there are in a question the worse students do; the more instances of the counterfactual conditional there are, the better. Patterns such as these show the value of an analysis that is more finely grained than simply counting sentences, one that focuses instead on the particular morphemes that mismatch in AAE and SCE within multiple sentences.

Our dialect-switching hypothesis explains the apparent negative effect of AAE on WJ-R Applied Problems subtest that we have identified in cognitive processing terms as it places the source of the effect in AAE-speaking students' need to switch between two dialects with dissimilar morphosyntactic systems. While this is our leading hypothesis, a non-processing reading of the data is, however, still possible. One might argue that lack of familiarity with the narrative style used in the test questions is the source of the difficulty for AAE-speaking students. In order to explore the viability of this line of causal explanation, we investigated the distribution of third person singular −s and conditional counterfactual if + −ed clauses in the WJ-R test questions. Neither feature appeared to occupy an especially salient position that might affect test performance directly or connect to any known differences in AAE and SCE narrative styles (Champion 2003; Champion and McCabe, this volume). While we cannot rule out the possibility of a successful narrative-based account of the data, before such an explanation can be tested, the narrative features thought to be responsible of the patterns in the data would need to be characterized and the way in which they could interact with question difficulty would need to be made precise. Until such an account is proposed, in our view, the dialect-switching hypothesis remains the clearest explanation with the greatest empirical support.

34.4 CONCLUSION

The results of our analysis show that linguistic features in general, and linguistic features associated with structural differences between AAE and SCE, in particular, can have a significant impact on young AAE-speaking students' performance on tests of mathematical reasoning that are given in SCE. That impact can be facilitative, as in the case of the counterfactual conditional *if + −ed*, a feature associated with reasoning tasks, but not dialectal difference, or it can be inhibitory, as in the case of third person singular *−s*, a point of divergence between the two dialects. Importantly, the inhibitory impact we identify is independent of individuals' abilities in spatial reasoning and, therefore, appears not to be a matter of general intelligence. Nor does it appear to be associated with any language delay or disorder. Instead, the impact that we have documented provides support for our initial hypothesis that some dialectal differences pose problems for some AAE-speaking students on verbally mediated reasoning tasks such as the WJ-R Applied Problems subtest due to the demands of switching between different linguistic representations.

The significance of this line of inquiry is quite broad, having strong implications for both linguistic theory and educational practice. With respect to linguistic theory, we see an important hypothesis that follows from trying to understand why dialect switching poses a cognitive load. Our finding that third person singular *−s* has a significant impact on performance on mathematical reasoning tasks makes the most sense if we tie this impact to differences in whether a linguistic feature has an overt morphemic representation in one or both dialects that must be managed.

With respect to educational practice, the features we identify as inhibiting student performance—third person singular *−s* chief among them—are specific enough to lend themselves to very focused intervention strategies. The ability to arm teachers with the knowledge of which dialectal differences are likely to pose significant problems for learners and which are not holds with it the promise of more targeted strategies for helping AAE-speaking students to navigate the dialects that are used at home and at school, and for reducing any negative effects that differences between them might cause. Targeting, however, is only half of the issue. Understanding what makes a feature like third person singular *−s* more problematic than other features is important in determining what type of targeted intervention will be most effective. Thus, the practical issue of intervention is very much connected to the more theoretical issues outlined above.

There is no simple answer to the question of how dialectal difference affects educational achievement. No doubt a variety of complex social and structural factors have roles they play and the results of our analysis argue that differences in the morphosyntactic inventories of dialects and the need to manage them deserve attention as one of those factors.

APPENDIX A

A.1 The Model

Let z_{ij} denote the score of student i on question j; z_{ij} takes the value 1 for a correct answer and the value 0 for an incorrect answer. Students in this study were ceiling tested, and no student was asked every question. We treat unasked questions as missing values and ignore them. Define y_{ij} as a measure of how well the student i knows the answer to question j and treat it as an unobserved random variable such that y_{ij} is an unobserved random variable such that $z_{ij} = 1$ if $y_{ij} > 0$ and $z_{ij} = 0$ if $y_{ij} \leq 0$. Our principal interest lies in the effect that each feature k has on a student i, represented as α_{ik}. We let x_{jk} represent the number of times the linguistic feature k appears in a question j and use it as a measure of the influence of k on the question. In addition to the six features we study, we expect a student's answer to be affected by that student's overall mathematical ability and the difficulty of the question being asked. We represent these effects as η_i and β_j, respectively.

The model we use is:

$$y_{ij} = \eta_i + \beta_j + \sum_{k=1}^{6} \alpha_{ik} x_{jk} + \epsilon_{ij} \tag{1}$$

for $i = 1, \ldots, 75$ and $j = 1, \ldots, 60$.

The term ϵ_{ij} represents the error of the model. This error is assumed to be introduced by other factors we have not taken into account (e.g., socioeconomic status and properties of the student's home environment). It is taken to be independent of the other variables.

A.2 Assumptions

Because the students and the questions were chosen randomly from a larger group of students and questions, it is logical to treat all η_i, β_j, and α_{ik} as random effects.

We assume that random effects have a normal distribution and that they are independent of each other:

$$\eta_i \sim N\left(\mu_\eta, \sigma_\eta^2\right), \quad i = 1, \ldots, 7$$

$$\beta_j \sim N\left(\mu_\beta, \sigma_\beta^2\right), \quad j = 1, \ldots, 60,$$

$$\epsilon_{ij} \sim N\left(0, \sigma_\epsilon^2\right), \quad i = 1, \ldots, 75, \quad j = 1, \ldots, 60,$$

$$\alpha_{ik} \sim N\left(v_k, \tau_k^2\right), \quad i = 1, \ldots, 75, \quad k = 1, \ldots, 6.$$

The parameters $\mu_\eta, \mu_\beta, v_k, \sigma_\eta^2, \sigma_\beta^2, \sigma_\epsilon^2$, and τ_k^2 are unknown and, together with η_i, β_j, and α_{ik}, must be estimated from the data.

A.3 Approach

We apply a Bayesian Markov Chain Monte Carlo (MCMC) method (Young and Smith 2005, 22–48) to estimate the unknown parameters.

A.3.1 Simplification of the Model

Given the initial assumptions we can simplify the model:

- The model is only affected by the difference between μ_η and μ_β and not by their individual values. So we set $\mu_\beta = 0$.
- If we multiply all the y_{ij}'s by the same positive constant, the values of z_{ij} do not change, so we can set $\sigma_\epsilon^2 = 1$.

The model becomes:

$$\eta_i \sim N\left(\mu, \kappa_\eta^{-1}\right),$$

$$\beta_j \sim N\left(0, \kappa_\beta^{-1}\right),$$

$$\epsilon_{ij} \sim N(0,1),$$

$$\alpha_{ik} \sim N\left(\nu_k, \lambda_k^{-1}\right),$$

$$y_{ij} = \eta_i + \beta_j + \sum_{k=1}^{6} \alpha_{ik} x_{jk} + \epsilon_{ij},$$

$$z_{ij} = \begin{cases} 1 \text{ if } y_{ij} > 0, \\ 0 \text{ if } y_{ij} \leq 0. \end{cases}$$

Note that we now write the variances as κ_η^{-1}, κ_β^{-1}, and λ_k^{-1} instead of σ_η^2 σ_β^2, and τ_k^2 to simplify calculations.[6]

A.3.2 Priors for the Hyperparameters

The parameters μ, ν_k, κ_η, κ_β, and λ_k are called hyperparameters.
We used:

$$\mu \sim U\left(-\infty, \infty\right),$$

$$\nu_k \sim U\left(-\infty, \infty\right),$$

$$\kappa_\eta \sim Gamma(a,b),$$

$$\kappa_\beta \sim Gamma(a,b),$$

$$\lambda_k \sim Gamma(a,b),$$

where U denotes the uniform distribution and Gamma[7] the gamma distribution and $a = b = 0.01$.[8]

We assume that the hyperparameters are independent from each other and also they are independent from the effects α, β, and η and from the error ϵ.

A.4 The MCMC Algorithm

Let I represent the number of students ($I = 75$). J is the number of questions ($J = 60$), and K is the number of linguistic factors ($K = 6$). The joint density of (κ_η, λ_k, μ, v_k, η_i, β_j, α_{ik}, y_{ij}, z_{ij}) is proportional to

$$\kappa_\eta^{a-1}e^{-b\kappa_\eta} \cdot \kappa_\beta^{a-1}e^{-b\kappa_\beta} \cdot \prod_{k=1}^{K}\left\{\lambda_k^{a-1}e^{-b\lambda_k}\right\} \cdot \prod_{i=1}^{I}\kappa_\eta^{\frac{1}{2}}e^{-\frac{1}{2}\kappa_\eta(\eta_i-\mu)^2} \cdot \prod_{j=1}^{J}\kappa_\beta^{\frac{1}{2}}e^{-\frac{1}{2}\kappa_\beta\beta_j^2} \cdot$$

$$\prod_{i=1}^{I}\prod_{k=1}^{K}\lambda_k^{\frac{1}{2}}e^{-\frac{1}{2}\lambda_k(\alpha_{ik}-v_k)^2} \cdot \prod_{i=1}^{I}\prod_{j=1}^{J}e^{-\frac{1}{2}\left(y_{ij}-\eta_i-\beta_j-\sum_{k=1}^{K}\alpha_{ik}x_{jk}\right)^2} \cdot Q\left(y_{ij}, z_{ij}\right) \qquad (2)$$

where

$$Q(y,z) = \begin{cases} 1 \text{ if } y > 0 \text{ and } z = 1, \\ 1 \text{ if } y \leq 0 \text{ and } z = 0 \\ 0 \text{ otherwise.} \end{cases}$$

With the exception of z_{ij}, all the variables in (2) are unknown. The Bayesian solution to this problem is to construct the conditional density of (κ_η, κ_β, λ_k, μ, v_k, η_i, β_j, α_{ik}, y_{ij}) given all the z_{ij}. The basic idea of MCMC sampling is to construct a Monte Carlo sample from the joint density (2) by successively updating each of the unknown random variables.

A.5 Updating Scale Parameters

The scale parameters are κ_η, κ_β, and λ_k, $k = 1, \ldots, K$. Updating the scale parameters consists of a random sample of one observation from the $Gamma(a', b')$ distribution where:

- for κ_η, $a' = a + \frac{1}{2}I$ and $b' = b + \frac{1}{2}\sum_i(\eta_i - \mu)^2$
- for κ_β, $a' = a + \frac{1}{2}J$ and $b' = b + \frac{1}{2}\sum_j\beta_j^2$
- for λ_k, $a' = a + \frac{1}{2}I$ and $b' = b + \frac{1}{2}\sum_i(\alpha_{ik} - v_k)^2$

A.6 Updating Location Parameters

The location parameters are μ, v_k, η_i, β_j, and α_{ik}. Updating the location parameters consists of a random sample of one observation from the $N\left(\dfrac{B}{A}, \dfrac{1}{A}\right)$, where:

- for μ, $A = I\kappa_\eta$, $B = \kappa_\eta\sum_i\eta_i$
- for v_k, $A = I\lambda_k$, $B = \lambda_k\sum_i\alpha_{ik}$

- for η_i, $A = \kappa_\eta + J$, $B = \mu\kappa_\eta + \sum_j\left(y_{ij} - \beta_j - \sum_k \alpha_{ik}x_{jk}\right)$
- for β_j, $A = \kappa_\beta + I$, $B = \sum_i\left(y_{ij} - \eta_i - \sum_k \alpha_{ik}x_{jk}\right)$
- for α_{ik}, $A = \lambda_k \sum_j x_{jk}^2$, $B = \lambda_k v_k \sum_j x_{jk}\left(y_{ij} - \eta_i - \sum_{k'} \alpha_{ik'}x_{jk'}\right)$

A.7 Updating y_{ij}

The conditional distribution of y_{ij} given all the other unknowns is $N\left(\eta_i + \beta_j + \sum_k \alpha_{ik}x_{jk}, 1\right)$ (including the condition $Q(y_{ij},z_{ij}) = 1$). Rejection sampling to sample y: consecutive values were generated from the conditional distribution until the condition $Q(y_{ij},z_{ij}) = 1$ is satisfied.

A.8 Implementation

For starting values, we set $y_{ij} = 1$ when $z_{ij} = 1$ and $y_{ij} = -1$ when $z_{ij} = 0$. We set all the location parameters equal to 0 and all the scale parameters equal to 1. We then ran 10,000 iterations as "burn in" updating all the unknowns. The results were discarded. This is done so that the starting values that we chose for the first step would not affect the results. 100,000 more iterations were then carried out, and the results of each 100th step were preserved to compile a sample size of 1,000 from the posterior distributions of the unknown variables. We use the superscript (n) to refer to the nth observation in the sample so that $\alpha_{3,10}^{(45)}$ means the 45th observation in the sample of the parameter $\alpha_{3,10}$.

A.9 Checking the Fit of the Model

We can use at least two different methods to check how well our model explains the data.

A.9.1 Using the Estimated Values, $\hat{z}_{ij}$ Compared to the Original Values of z_{ij}

Using the simulated data, we calculated the values $\hat{z}_{ij}^{(n)}$, where $\hat{z}_{ij}^{(n)}$ is the estimated value of z_{ij} for the nth observation.

First, we calculate $\hat{y}_{ij}^{(n)}$ by:

$$\hat{y}_{ij}^{(n)} = \eta_i^{(n)} + \beta_j^{(n)} + \sum_{k=1}^{6} \alpha_{ik}^{(n)} x_{jk}$$

where $\eta_i^{(n)}$, $\beta_j^{(n)}$ and $\alpha_{ik}^{(n)}$ refer to the nth observation in the sample. Then, we set $\hat{z}_{ij}^{(n)} = 1$ if $\hat{y}_{ij}^{(n)} > 0$ and $\hat{z}_{ij}^{(n)} = 0$ if $\hat{y}_{ij}^{(n)} \leq 0$. This is done for each n. Then for each pair (i, j) we calculate the sample mean $\hat{z}_{ij}$ of $\hat{z}_{ij}^{(n)}$, $\hat{z}_{ij} = \dfrac{1}{1000}\sum_n \hat{z}_{ij}^{(n)}$. This is a number between 0 and 1. We then divide the interval $[0, 1]$ into $L = 10$ equally spaced subintervals: $[0.0, 0.1), [0.1, 0.2), \ldots, [0.9, 1.0]$ and I take the average $\hat{\bar{z}}_{ij}^{[l]}$ of the $\hat{z}_{ij}$'s that belong to the subinterval l, $l = 1, \ldots, L$. This defines a set of pairs (i, j). We also take the average $\hat{\bar{z}}_{ij}^{[l]}$, of the observed z_{ij}'s, for those (i, j) 's.

We expect that if we plot the $\hat{\bar{z}}_{ij}^{[l]}$'s against the $\hat{\bar{z}}_{ij}^{[l]}$'s, then we will get a straight line. The plot is shown in figure A.1. The correlation is 0.8702.

A.9.2 Plots of the Median of β_j's against the Proportion of Correct Answers for Question j

The overall difficulty of question j is estimated by β_j. We expect an increasing pattern between the median of β_j's and the average number of correct answers for each question.

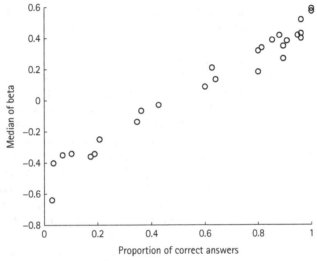

FIGURE A.1   Plot of $\hat{\bar{z}}_{ij}^{[l]}$'s against $\hat{\bar{z}}_{ij}^{[l]}$'s.

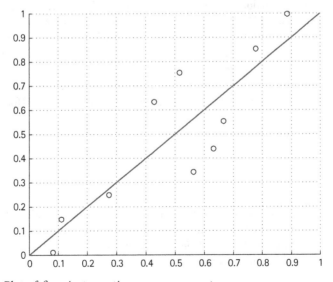

FIGURE A.2   Plot of β against question average correct answers.

The plot is shown in figure A.2. The increasing relationship is more obvious here. The correlation is 0.9818.

NOTES

1. By African American English, we mean the relatively uniform variety spoken by many but not all African Americans throughout the United States. Defined by its grammar and use, we are most concerned with those features of the variety that are common to many of its regional sub-varieties.
2. This overlap highlights a potential problem with the use of DDMs and similar token-based measures of dialect use. Such measures typically count as features of the dialect only those features that contrast with those of more mainstream dialects. See Green (2011) for further discussion of this issue.
3. We treat the model parameters (the student's general mathematical ability, the overall difficulty of the question, and the extent to which the student is affected by a given linguistic feature) as random effects. The Bayesian-MCMC approach to fitting the model is to define prior distributions for these parameters and use Gibbs and Metropolis sampling to construct posterior distributions for all the unknowns. The posterior distributions are then used to determine which, if any, linguistic features influence students' scores. If one treats the influence of the linguistic features as fixed rather than random effects (i.e., if one assumes the influence of a particular linguistic feature is the same for all students), it is possible to estimate the model by standard logistic regression. However, not only is the number of unknown parameters too large to assume fixed effects, but doing so prevents testing whether the amount of AAE a student uses correlates with the effect AAE features have on test performance, an important hypothesis pursued here.
4. One observation of the first linguistic feature, past tense –ed, was omitted as an outlier. The value was –0.4.
5. At first blush, this might appear to apply equally well to past tense –ed, a feature that showed little effect, as it does to third person singular –s, the feature that showed the greatest effect; past tense –ed is often omitted in AAE. However, following Green (2011), we assume such omission is due to the presence of a variable rule within AAE grammar as opposed to the overt marking of the feature not being a part of the grammar as we believe is the case with third person singular –s.
6. Because using a *Gamma* distribution for the prior of κ_η, κ_β, and λ_k gives a *Gamma* posterior distribution for those variables so I will get a distribution in a closed form.
7. The density for the *Gamma(a, b)* distribution is $f(x) = \dfrac{1}{r(a)} b^a x^{a-1} e^{-bx}$.
8. This is a typical choice for the MCMC.

REFERENCES

Bartel, N. R., and J. Axelrod. 1973. "Nonstandard English Usage and Reading Ability in Black Junior High Students." *Exceptional Children* 38: 653–55.

Baugh, John. 1999. *Out of the Mouths of Slaves: African American Language and Educational Malpractice.* Austin, TX: University of Texas.

Champion, Tempii B. 2003. *Understanding Storytelling among African American Children: A Journey from Africa to America*. Mahwah, NJ: Lawrence Erlbaum.

Charity, Anne H., Hollis S. Scarborough, and Darion M. Griffin. 2004. "Familiarity with 'School English' in African American Children and Its Relation to Early Reading Achievement." *Child Development* 75: 1340–56.

Craig, Holly K., Carol M. Connor, and Julie A. Washington. 2003. "Early Positive Predictors of Later Reading Comprehension for African American Students: A Preliminary Investigation." *Language, Speech, and Hearing Services in the Schools* 34: 31–43.

Craig, Holly K., and Julie A. Washington. 2004. "Grade-Related Changes in the Production of African American English." *Journal of Speech, Language and Hearing Research* 47: 450–63.

———. 2006. *Malik Goes to School: Examining the Language Skills of African American Students from Preschool–5th Grade*. Mahwah, NJ: Lawrence Erlbaum.

de Villiers, Jill G., and Valerie E. Johnson. 2007. "The Information in Third-Person /s/: Acquisition across Dialects of American English." *Journal of Child Language* 34: 113–58.

Fordham, Signithia, and John Ogbu. 1986. "Black Students' School Success: Coping with the 'Burden of Acting White.'" *Urban Review* 18: 176–206.

Gardner, Howard, Mindy L. Kornhaber, and Warren K. Wake. 1996. *Intelligence: Multiple Perspectives*. Fort Worth, TX: Harcourt Brace College Publishers.

Gemake, Josephine S. 1981. "Interference of Certain Dialect Elements with Reading." *Reading Improvement* 18: 183–99.

Green, Lisa J. 1995. "Study of Verb Classes: Implications for Education." *Linguistics in Education* 7: 65–81.

———. 2002. *African American English: A Linguistic Introduction*. Cambridge: Cambridge University.

———. 2011. *Language and the African American Child*. Cambridge: Cambridge University.

Gutman, Leslie M., Arnold J. Sameroff, and Jacqulynne S. Eccles. 2002. "The Academic Achievement of African American Students during Early Adolescence: An Examination of Multiple Risk, Promotive, and Protective Factors." *American Journal of Community Psychology* 30: 367–99.

Harber, Jean R. 1977. "Influence of Presentation Dialect and Orthographic Form on Reading Performance of Black Inner-City Children." *Educational Research Quarterly* 2: 9–16.

Hart, Jane T., John T. Guthrie, and Linda Winfield. 1980. "Black English Phonology and Learning to Read." *Journal of Educational Psychology* 72: 636–46.

Heath, Shirley Brice. 1983. *Ways with Words: Language, Life, and Work in Communities and Classrooms*. Cambridge: Cambridge University.

Johnson, Valerie E., Jill G. de Villiers, and Harry N. Seymour. 2005. "Agreement without Understanding? The Case of Third Person Singular /s/." *First Language* 25: 317–30.

Labov, William, and Bettina Baker. 2010. "What is a Reading Error?" *Applied Psycholinguistics* 31: 735–57.

Miller, Jon F., and Chapman, Robin. 2000. "SALT: Systematic Analysis of Language Transcripts (Version 9.0)." Madison: Language Analysis Laboratory, Waisman Center, University of Wisconsin.

O'Neil, Wayne. 1990. "Dealing with Bad Ideas: Twice Is Less." *English Journal* 79: 80–88.

Oetting, Janna B., and Janet L. McDonald. 2002. "Methods for Characterizing Participants' Nonmainstream Dialect Use in Child Language Research." *Journal of Speech, Language, and Hearing Research* 45: 505–18.

Ogbu, John. 1999. "Beyond Language: Ebonics, Proper English, and Identity in a Black-American Speech Community." *American Educational Research Journal* 36: 147–84.

Orr, Eleanor Wilson. 1987. *Twice as Less: Black English and the Performance of Black Students in Mathematics and Science.* New York: Norton.

Poe, Michele D., Margaret R. Burchinal, and Joanne E. Roberts. 2004. "Early Language and the Development of Children's Reading Skills." *Journal of School Psychology* 42: 315–32.

Purcell-Gates, Victoria. 1996. "Stories, Coupons, and the TV Guide: Relationships between Home Literacy Experiences and Emergent Literacy Knowledge." *Reading Research Quarterly* 31: 406–28.

Renn, Jennifer, and J. Michael Terry. 2009. "Operationalizing Style: Quantifying Style Shift in the Speech of African American Adolescents." *American Speech* 84: 367–90.

Roberts, Joanne E., Margaret R. Burchinal, and Meghan Durham. 1999. "Parents' Report of Vocabulary and Grammatical Development of African American Preschoolers: Child and Environmental Associations." *Child Development* 70: 92–106.

Roberts, Joanne E., Margaret R. Burchinal, Lynn P. Medley, Susan A. Zeisel, Martha Mundy, Jackson Roush, Stephen Hooper, Donna Bryant, and Frederick W. Henderson. 1995. "Otitis Media, Hearing Sensitivity, and Maternal Responsiveness in Relation to Language during Infancy." *Journal of Pediatrics* 126: 481–89.

Semel, Elenor, Elisabeth H. Wiig, and Wayne A. Secord. 1995. *Clinical Evaluation of Language Fundamentals 3 (CELF3).* San Antonio, TX: The Psychological Corporation.

Steffensen, Margaret S., Ralph E. Reynolds, Erica McClure, and Larry F. Guthrie. 1982. "Black English Vernacular and Reading Comprehension: A Cloze Study of Third, Sixth, and Ninth Graders." *Journal of Reading Behavior* 14: 285–98.

Terry, J. Michael, Randall Hendrick, Evangelos Evangelou, and Richard L. Smith. 2010. "Variable Dialect Switching among African American Children: Inferences about Working Memory." *Lingua* 120: 2463–75.

Torrey, Jane. 1983. "Black Children's Knowledge of Standard English." *American Educational Research Journal* 20: 627–43.

Tyson, Karolyn, William Darity Jr., and Domini R. Castellino. 2005. "It's Not a Black Thing: Understanding the Burden of Acting White and Other Dilemmas of High Achievement." *American Sociological Review* 70: 582–605.

Van Hofwegen, Janneke, and Reuben Stob. 2011. "A Longitudinal Analysis of the Relationship between Reading and AAE Vernacularity." Paper presented at New Ways of Analyzing Variation 40, Washington, DC, October 27–30.

Washington, Julie A., and Holly K. Craig. 2001. "Reading Performance and Dialectal Variation." In *Literacy in African American communities*, edited by Joyce L. Harris, Alan G. Kamhi, and Karen E. Pollock, 147–68. Mahwah, NJ: Lawrence Erlbaum.

Wechsler, David. 1991. *The Wechsler Intelligence Scale for Children—Third Edition.* San Antonio, TX: The Psychological Corporation.

Wolfram, Walt, and Natalie Schilling-Estes. 2006. *American English: Dialects and Variation.* Malden, MA: Blackwell.

Woodcock, Richard W., and Mary Bonner Johnson. 1989. *Woodcock-Johnson Psycho-Educational Battery—Revised.* Allen, TX: DLM Teaching Resources.

Young, G. A., and Richard L. Smith. 2005. *Essentials of Statistics Inference,* 22–48. Cambridge: Cambridge University.

CHAPTER 35

....

BEYOND BIDIALECTALISM

Language Planning and Policies for African American Students

....

JOHN BAUGH

35.1 INTRODUCTION

....

BEFORE turning our attention to linguistic matters, it is important to place African American *bidialectal education* within its historical context. Readers of this chapter know well that the US Supreme Court ruled to abolish racially segregated public schools in their landmark *Brown v. Board of Education* (*BOE*) unanimous decision in 1954. The legacy of educational segregation is racist at its core, and the academic dislocation of slave descendants still resonates in educational achievement gaps that reflect vast differences based on race and socioeconomic status. Our focus is devoted to Black students who are US slave descendants (USSD); that is, not merely "Black students," per se. This distinction is vital, especially so in the wake of *Brown v. BOE*, which is cast in explicit racial terms.

> We come then to the question presented: Does segregation of children in public schools solely on the basis of race, even though the physical facilities and other "tangible" factors may be equal, deprive the children of the minority group of equal educational opportunities? We believe that it does. *Brown v. BOE*, 347 U.S. 483 (1954)

The Supreme Court's legal emphasis on race, rather than slave decadency, is quite understandable in historical context, because the vast majority of the Black population in America in 1954 retraced their ancestry to Africans who had once been enslaved. Ensuing efforts to close educational achievement gaps between Black and White students have not kept pace with changing demographic trends that have diversified America's Black population. Ogbu's (1978) distinguished study of caste-like groupings in America is illustrative in this regard, because he makes a crucial distinction between

Americans whose ancestors immigrated to the United States voluntarily, and those whose American ancestors were forced to come to this land against their free will (e.g., African slaves); Ogbu classifies these citizens as "involuntary immigrants," thereby avoiding attempts to lump all Blacks into the same educational category. By this distinction, we see that many African Americans, like President Obama, are descendants of voluntary immigrants, whereas the vast majority of African Americans, like Michelle Obama, are descendants of slaves who were involuntary immigrants. President Obama is biracial; Michelle Obama is not biracial. President Obama grew up in Hawaii, dislocated from African American culture, which he himself describes:

> I can't even hold up my experience as being somehow representative of the Black American Experience (after all, you don't come from an underprivileged background: a Manhattan publisher helpfully pointed out to me); indeed, learning to accept that particular truth—that I can embrace my Black brothers and sisters, whether in this country or in Africa, and affirm a common destiny without pretending to speak to, or for, all of our various struggles. (Obama 1995, xvi)

Michelle Obama grew up in Chicago, deeply integrated into African American culture and intimately familiar with the civil rights movement, the NAACP, Dr. Martin Luther King Jr., Malcolm X, SNCC (Student Nonviolent Coordinating Committee), and the Black Panthers, who had a very strong presence in Chicago during her early childhood. In short, the African American population today is far more diverse, owing to the fact that, since 1954, the Black population has grown to include many more voluntary immigrants, some of whom are also slave descendants, although their ancestors were enslaved outside of the United States (e.g., Brazil, Haiti). A significant number of other African Americans are voluntary immigrants from elsewhere throughout the entire African Diaspora. The linguistic and educational consequences of these trends are the object of this discussion, which, again, devotes primary emphasis to students who are not merely Black, but who are USSD. These are the students who are the object of *Brown v. BOE*, and they are among the African American students who suffer the greatest educational disadvantages. Alas, due to considerable ignorance, many uninformed people believe that racial educational achievement differences are fundamentally attributable to *African American Vernacular English* (AAVE).[1]

35.2 DIFFERENT OR DEFICIENT?

Labov's classic 1969 article, titled "The Logic of Nonstandard English," exposed racial bias against students who spoke the *Black English Vernacular*; indeed, at that time Labov referred to their speech as "Nonstandard Negro English." Changing linguistic nomenclature notwithstanding, African American Language (AAL)[2] has been the object of considerable educational misinformation. Orr (1987) claimed that students who speak "Black English" cannot conceive of mathematical concepts in ways that are comparable to students who speak *Standard American English* (SAE).[3] She conducted experiments with students from Washington, DC, who attended an affluent private high school—a school where she served as principal—and reached out to less affluent African American students by providing free tuition. Despite very good intentions, Ms. Orr insisted that all mathematical problems be converted into English prose prior to completion, and she also utilized other innovations, such as utilizing base-6 rather than the traditional base-10 model as a means of determining if students, from all backgrounds, were grasping various mathematical concepts. As a result of these procedures, many of the less affluent Black students who attended the school were forced to employ a combination of literacy skills with new mathematical procedures with which they were quite unfamiliar, and as a result they tended to fail most of their mathematical assignments.

Under completely different circumstances, Farrell (1983) claimed that Black students were incapable of abstract thought because of copula absence; his hypothesis was that copula verbs (e.g., *is* and *are*) are essential for abstract thought, including writing systems that represent vowels. Both Orr and Farrell overstated their respective cases, but their independent analyses are illustrative of the *deficit hypothesis*, namely, that USSD who speak AAVE are at an educational and cognitive disadvantage when compared to students who are native speakers of SAE.

Farrell (1983) called for the reinstatement of the McGuffy readers that European immigrants used during the 1920s and 1930s. He argued that African American students would be exposed to SAE as well as to the traditional American cultural values that are endemic throughout the homespun McGuffy readers, which depict an ideal life for anyone who aspires to live "the American dream." Although Farrell does not advocate bidialectal education, per se, his explicit hypothesis that SAE proficiency is necessary for academic achievement is echoed in the efforts by Baratz and Shuy (1969) to use second language education techniques to help African American students learn SAE. Maintaining Labov's *difference* (not deficit) orientation, Baratz and Shuy (1969) offered support for bidialectal education by which Black students proficient in their native AAVE could be introduced to SAE as a second dialects using techniques from bilingual education, thereby enhancing their prospects for achieving greater academic success.

35.3 Elaborated or Restricted Codes?

Farrell's (1983) hypothesis found sympathy with Bernstein's (1972) early formulation of *elaborated codes* and *restricted codes*. Whereas he dismissed Jensen's (1969) genetic argument that Blacks were intellectually inferior to Whites, Farrell (1983) believed that literacy and proficiency in SAE were essential if Blacks who spoke non-dominant dialects were ever going to engage in abstract thought, which is essential for academic success. In England, Bernstein (1972) studied class differences in language usage among White students, concluding that upper-class speakers of the elaborated code had cognitive access to universalistic concepts, while working-class speakers of the restricted code displayed linguistic content that was highly particularistic, lacking in abstraction. Bernstein (1972) also observed that children in England who spoke the elaborated code were raised in families that were highly individualistic, that is, where opinions were prized and encouraged regardless of age or sex; working-class families by contrast were highly positional, with male paternal leadership being dominant whenever possible, followed by fairly rigid family rankings based on age. Although Bernstein never studied African American students, his research from England proved to be influential among educators and sociolinguists within the United States as they considered whether AAVE was a restricted code. Those who considered AAL to be linguistically deficient could easily consider nonstandard AAVE to be a restricted code. The best linguistic evidence, embodied in the works of Baugh (1983, 1999), Labov (1972), Fasold (1972), Wolfram (1969, 1991), Rickford (1999), Green (2002, 2011), Mufwene et al. (1998), Smitherman (1977), and others, confirms that AAVE is linguistically distinctive and therefore different from SAE; that is, due to a combination of linguistic and sociohistorical circumstances, AAVE is unique to America's African slave descendants.

35.4 THE POLITICS OF BIDIALECTAL EDUCATION FOR BLACK STUDENTS

Although linguists have been in long-standing agreement that AAVE is different from SAE, and it is not linguistically or cognitively deficient, educators have often concluded that students who speak Nonstandard English (NSE) lack sufficient intellectual capacity to achieve and maintain academic excellence. In the worst cases, educators have openly denigrated students for speaking AAVE, claiming, as Shelby Steele (1990) observed, that those who speak AAVE should be ashamed of themselves and adopt SAE with utmost dispatch in order to fully participate in mainstream American culture, that is, with its (potential) promise of full employment and the economic benefits that accrue to those who employ spoken and written forms of SAE with fluency.

The birth of bidialectal education grew from a pragmatic integration of educational and linguistic research. Baratz and Shuy (1969) were first to recognize that second language education techniques could be used to help introduce Black students to SAE. Labov (1972), Wolfram (1969), and Smitherman (1977) spoke of the special educational and linguistic circumstances that impacted Black students throughout the United States; they collectively recognized a combination of social, linguistic, legal, and educational impediments to America's Black students, who at that time were largely composed of USSD.

In support of efforts to help students who are native speakers of NSE, the Teachers of English to Speakers of Other Languages (TESOL) included the teaching of SAE as a second dialect within its early mission. This recognition, although devoted primarily to African American and Hawaiian students, differed from TESOL's larger mission to teach English to students for whom English was not their mother tongue. In the cases of AAVE and Hawaiian Pidgin English (HPE), children spoke and learned NSE vernaculars natively in their home communities, thereby facing different linguistic and educational challenges than is the case for students who are not native English speakers. This discussion would also be incomplete should we ignore the economic dislocation and disparities that exist for the majority of native speakers of AAVE and HPE; they tend to be poorer than their affluent counterparts who are native speakers of SAE. Thanks substantially to the leadership of Professor Charlane Sato, the state of Hawaii was able to implement a highly successful bidialectal education program for native Hawaiians, which was the Kamehameha Early Education Program (KEEP) (see Romaine and Rickford 1999). Due to the relative isolation of the Hawaiian Islands from the rest of the United States, the federal educational funding that was used for many years to support KEEP was not well known on the mainland, nor did it serve as a model for educators who were trying to teach SAE as a second dialect to African American students who were native speakers of AAVE.

Smitherman (1977) describes the circumstances she faced when speech pathologists misdiagnosed her speech as abnormal linguistic development. Craig and Washington (2004, 2006), Wyatt (1995), Seymour (2004), Vaughn-Cooke (2007), Stockman (2010), and others proved that African American children who are native speakers of AAVE are not suffering from pathological speech disorders; their linguistic development is perfectly normal for children who are the descendants of Africans who were once enslaved in America. Smitherman (1981) brought the linguistic and educational plight of African American students to its legal apex as a result of the 1979 "Black English trial" in Ann Arbor, Michigan. Similar to Smitherman herself many years before, eleven African American students who attended the Martin Luther King Jr. Elementary school had been evaluated by a speech pathologist who placed all of the plaintiffs in special education (i.e., remedial) classes because they were diagnosed as having abnormal linguistic development. For example, these children routinely said the name *Ruth* with the same pronunciation as SAE *roof* and consistently substituted the /Vf#/ phonemes for their SAE equivalent /Vth#/ in other words as well. According to the best pathological diagnostics that were available at that time, which were developed for children who were native speakers of SAE, any normally developing native speaker of SAE would not be expected to produce these "mistakes." In short, the linguistic and historical evidence emphatically confirmed that AAVE pronunciations such as *toof* (/tuf/) for *tooth*, *boof* (/buf/) for *booth*, or *roof* (/ruf/) for *Ruth* is—in reality—quite normal for children who grow up speaking AAVE natively.

Judge Charles Joiner ultimately ruled in favor of the African American plaintiffs, indicating that the Ann Arbor school district had an obligation to develop programs for their teachers that would better inform the teachers on how best to educate students who are native speakers of AAVE. As a result of that ruling, educators in California took notice and created a new program in Sacramento in 1981 titled the "Standard English Proficiency Program for Speakers of Black Language," which became known as California's SEP program. Although California educators were influenced by Judge Joiner's ruling, the Ann Arbor School district did not appeal his ruling; as a result, Judge

Joiner's ruling was relevant to the Midwest, but it did not have the same national impact as did *Lau v. Nichols* (1974), which was the result of a landmark Supreme Court ruling. Nevertheless, Judge Joiner's ruling set the stage for the 1996 Ebonics controversy that evolved, at least in part, as a result of California's efforts to promote SAE acquisition by African American students.

Before turning to Ebonics, the politics of bidialectal education for African American students was lambasted by Sledd (1973). Whereas the vast majority of linguists and educators promoted some form of bidialectal education, in which AAVE would be treated with respect as a student's home language and SAE would be introduced as a second dialect for academic purposes, Sledd (1973) took considerable exception. He advocated an alternative position—one that called upon all students to learn a second dialect, not merely speakers of AAVE. Sledd's contention was that a disproportionate educational burden rested solely at the feet of AAVE-speaking students, because they were being asked to learn a second dialect, while no such educational program existed for students who were native speakers of SAE. Sledd argued that SAE-speaking students should learn AAVE as a second dialect; the result would not only provide educational exposure to the grammatical rules and systematic nature of AAVE, it could also instill linguistic empathy, while simultaneously defusing some of the linguistic stereotypes pervasive among Americans who denigrate AAVE. Sledd's (1973) observations were highly controversial; his detractors felt that efforts to promote the teaching of AAVE were misplaced because it had no academic or professional value (see Farrell 1983).

Since then a number of scholars have abandoned simplistic bidialectal educational ventures in favor of more comprehensive efforts to promote academic English proficiency among all students, regardless of background. LeMoine and Hollie (2007) are highly illustrative in this regard; their efforts grew from early work within California's SEP programs, resulting initially in the Language Development Program for African American Students (LDPAAS), which was implemented through the Los Angeles Unified School District. A combination of intensive teacher preparation, curriculum development, and carefully crafted programmatic implementation were central to their efforts, which expanded to include other students for whom SAE was not native. As a result, LeMoine (2003) developed educational programs specifically for SAE learners, which is far more expansive than the population of USSD who were the object of *Brown v. BOE* and Judge Joiner's ruling in favor of the African American plaintiffs in the Black English trial (see Smitherman 1981).

35.5 EBONICS GENESIS AND GLOBAL DISSEMINATION

Prior to 1973, the term *Ebonics* had never been heard. Robert Williams (1975) coined the term by combining the words *ebony* and *phonics*. Whereas linguists who studied

Black language usage in America did so under different labels, including *Nonstandard Negro English* during the 1960s, *Black English* and *Black English Vernacular* during the 1970s, and *African American Vernacular English* in the 1980s. This changing terminology was not the result of political correctness; rather, linguists were seeking to pinpoint culturally relevant terminology, growing from ethnographic linguistic changes within Black communities across the nation. Elsewhere (Baugh 1991), I explore changing terms of self-reference among American slave descendants, and throughout American history the ways in which Black people have been portrayed is ever changing. For example, the NAACP (National American Association of Colored People) maintains its historical name despite the fact that few African Americans refer to themselves as *Colored People* or *Negroes* (e.g., United Negro College Fund). During my childhood, referring to another African American as *Black* was considered to be highly offensive, so much so that it evoked formal backlash, but later it became popular to exclaim that "Black is beautiful," and, inspired by the late James Brown, African American youth during the 1960s echoed his call to "Say it loud; I'm Black and I'm proud."

It was more than a rising spirit of Black pride and the birth of Black Studies departments that prompted Williams (1975) and his colleagues to coin the term *Ebonics*. In much the same manner that Chomsky (1965) formulated the concept of Universal Grammar, Williams and his colleagues created linguistic terminology that exceeded English, by linking its relevance to the African slave trade, that is, rather than to English exclusively.

> I am talking about an ebony language. We know that ebony means black and that phonics refers to speech sounds or the science of sounds. Thus, we are really talking about the science of [B]lack speech sounds or language. (Williams 1975, 14)

Based on this definition, Ebonics in the United States was in contact with English, whereas Ebonics in Brazil was in contact with Portuguese, and Haitian Ebonics was in contact with French. Linguists who studied AAL usage did so with emphasis on English (see Green 2002, 2011; Labov 1972; Mufwene et al. 1998; Rickford 1999; Wolfram 1969, 1991). Due to a complex set of circumstances, combined with serendipity, California's SEP program adopted Ebonics as their preferred terminology to describe the language of African American students in that state. One of the relevant considerations regarding the educational plight of bidialectal education programs for Black students has to do with federal educational classifications of students who are eligible for funds to help them gain English proficiency. As federal laws are currently written, USSD are excluded from funds used to teach English as a second language. Educators in Oakland recognized that students who were enrolled in SEP programs in that city could benefit from additional educational attention; however, by the spring of 1996 Oakland's school board was trying to sort out new and innovative educational strategies to overcome disproportionate school failure by the majority of African American students who were enrolled in that district. In an effort to tackle these problems head-on the Oakland school board created an African American Educational Task Force, which included the late Professor John Ogbu, who was well known for his innovative studies of caste-like groups in the United States (1978). Based on his advice and that of other scholarly and educational experts, the Oakland African American Educational Task Force encouraged the adoption of a resolution to declare Ebonics to be the native language of Oakland's 28,000 Black students. Moreover, their preliminary resolution did so by exclaiming, quite controversially, that Ebonics was not genetically related to English. Given the racial specificity embodied in Williams's (1975) original definition of Ebonics, Oakland's choice of the phrase "genetically related" was most unfortunate, because the ensuing firestorm was stoked, at least in part, by the resurrection of Jensen's (1969) volatile claim that Blacks are genetically and cognitively inferior to Whites, based on genetic differences and standardized test scores. Linguists routinely speak of languages in terms of familial relationships, as in French, Italian, and Spanish being part of the Romance language family, or English and German part of the Germanic language family; linguists speak of such groupings as being genetically related, but those linguistic connections are in no way connected with human biology or corresponding racial classifications.

Why, then, did the Ebonics controversy that began in Oakland capture global attention, particularly throughout the African Diaspora? Briefly, many Black people throughout the world are linguistically dislocated from sources of linguistic power; such is the case in South Africa, the United States, and France, among others, where the vast majority of Black people are considered to be part of a linguistically disempowered group. The linguistic, racial, and educational events that transpired in Oakland resonated with many Black people, especially so if they lacked fluency in the dominant language(s) where they resided. Secretary of Education Richard Riley weighed in by exclaiming that bilingual education funding would not be provided to speakers of Black English. His rationale, quite simply, was that any student who was a speaker of English, be it *standard* or *nonstandard*, should not be eligible for funding reserved for students for whom English is not native. In addition, I would be remiss to neglect the obvious budgetary impact that would accrue from the expansion of federal funding for "bilingual education," that is, if it also included AAVE-speaking students.

35.6 SOME MISSING ELEMENTS: EDUCATIONAL REFORMS AND LANGUAGE DEVELOPMENT

We will turn our attention momentarily to some unfinished objectives regarding the education of students who lack SAE fluency, but before doing so it is useful to recognize that the US federal government has attempted to instill educational reforms that claim to offer some assistance in this regard. However, the educational plight of students who are USSD is systematically overlooked through these efforts, including No Child Left Behind (NCLB) and new efforts to promote Common Core Standards (CCS), which are intended to alter the ways in which students are taught, tested, and evaluated.

A significant amount of this effort has been devoted, quite understandably, to students who are not native speakers of English. Both NCLB and CCS offer a combination of funding and incentives to help local schools promote English acquisition among children, and, in some cases, to extend that language development to adults and other family members who may also lack (standard) English proficiency.

For many reasons, some of which have already been described, Black students who speak AAVE tend to be disregarded by both NCLB and CCS, particularly regarding any provisions that specifically address their unique linguistic or educational circumstances. Moreover, when these reforms do address traditional English language learners, that is, students for whom English is not their mother tongue, the vast majority of attention is devoted to native speakers of Spanish, which, again, is somewhat understandable given the vast numbers of native Spanish speakers that reside throughout the United States.

Although some private foundations have tried to provide limited funding to advance literacy for African American students who speak AAVE, the federal government and the vast majority of state governments have stepped away from this linguistic mission in the wake of the Oakland Ebonics controversy. Federal funding for language arts education for USSD is nearly nonexistent, and while the CCS take pains to identify the goals educators must strive to achieve for all students pertaining to reading, writing, speaking, and listening, these goals are espoused in ways that either downplay or ignore the fact that students who are not raised in homes where SAE is the norm will confront considerable educational disadvantages and will require alternative forms of instruction if they ever hope to meet the laudable comprehensive educational goals set forth in the CCS.

The CCS, while worthwhile, do not formally acknowledge that less fortunate children are likely to attend underfunded schools with inexperienced teachers who are ill-equipped to offer the kind of accelerated instruction that is necessary if poor students ever hope to demonstrate academic skills comparable to those of their more affluent peers who attend better funded schools and whose parents already possess the linguistic advantages that NCLB and CCS promote for all students. This is despite the fact that we know well that many American students are raised in homes and communities where SAE is rare, if not nonexistent.

35.7 Conclusion: Unfinished Objectives: Eliminating Educational Achievement Gaps for Students Who Lack Fluency in Standard American English

Because the Ebonics controversy was never truly resolved, there are no legal statutes, such as *Brown v. BOE* or *Lau v. Nichols*, that are nationally applicable to AAVE-speaking students. In the wake of the hostile reception that greeted Oakland's Ebonics resolution, school districts throughout the nation have been loath to follow in their footsteps, and, as previously mentioned, educational programs have been sporadic or nonexistent in many schools that serve significant numbers of African American students. Due substantially to differences in local educational circumstances, educational needs vary substantially, since populations of AAVE-speaking students shift from school-to-school.

California implemented several efforts to increase SAE fluency for Black students through the Standard English Proficiency Program for Speakers of Black Language (i.e., SEP). Moreover, several of the programs that grew from that effort were inspired by Williams's (1975) formulation of Ebonics. Language arts education for Black students in Oakland and Los Angeles, among other cities, was informed and inspired by Ebonics scholarship, which, while innovative, differed substantially from the prevailing linguistic research that explicitly confirmed that USSD are native speakers of English. Any linguistic suggestion that slave descendants, as a group, are not speakers of English is misplaced. However, in much the same manner that White speakers of Appalachian English speak a non-dominant (i.e., nonstandard) dialect, AAVE by virtue of its historical, social, linguistic, educational, and racial dislocation from SAE, is also a non-dominant dialect that was once characterized as *substandard English* (see Bloomfield 1933). Racism against Blacks in America accounts, in part, for some of the lingering linguistic stigma and misconceptions that many uninformed people harbor about AAVE (Baugh 1999; Steele 1990). Although some affirmative action programs were developed to help overcome historical disadvantages owing to slavery, most—if not all—of them that have been based on race have been highly controversial, especially so in the wake of the Obama presidency, since America's First Family also happens to be an African American family. For many people it is more than symbolic that a Black man has obtained the most powerful and influential position in the world; many people therefore conclude that this could not have transpired if anti-Black racism were still strongly embraced.

Despite the obvious progress in race relations that the Obama presidency affirms, the educational and employment prospects for Blacks in America still suffer from disproportionate economic disparities. Linguists who study AAVE, along with many of their educational colleagues, have developed and devised programs and strategies to improve the educational prospects for Black students regardless of their heritage status; that is, some Black students may be USSD, while others—like President Obama—are African Americans who do not retrace their family or linguistic ancestry to anyone who was ever enslaved. It is noteworthy that President Obama is also biracial, and his family history is one that is steeped in middle-class White American culture from the heartland of Kansas. Due, at least in part, to the considerable cultural and linguistic diversity among African Americans, our focus on USSD is intentional.

Because many of the educational programs that have been designed to overcome discrimination are based on racial classification, they remain highly controversial, especially to those who no longer feel that race is a legitimate barrier to employment and educational opportunities. Indeed, voters in California passed Proposition 209, which made it illegal for the state to maintain educational programs or preferences based on race. As a direct result of Proposition 209, the Language Development

Program for African American Students (LDPAAS), which was created in the wake of the Ann Arbor ruling with the help of California's SEP program, evolved into the Academic English Mastery Program (AEMP), which is a comprehensive educational program that serves students from diverse backgrounds. LeMoine (2003) implemented expanded programs for "Standard English learners," that is, students for whom SAE is not native. In some instances, these students may be learning English as a second language; in other instances, they may be learning SAE as a second dialect. Regardless of the student's linguistic heritage, AEMP expands fluency in the dominant linguistic norms for speaking and writing for Standard English learners. In addition, LeMoine's efforts are consistent with the CCS goals, and they advance literacy for those who are English language learners as well as those who may be native speakers of nonstandard English dialects.

A wonderful constellation of research in the fields of anthropology, education, and linguistics has provided a plethora of superb suggestions to advance academic achievement for Black students, including those who are native speakers of AAVE. Morgan (2009) and Alim (2007) offer anthropological and ethnographic insights into the lives and language of Black Hip Hop devotees; their scholarship offers insight into the home language, linguistic battles, and cultural pressures that impact the lives of urban youth. Ball (1995), Lee (1993), Rickford (2007), Lanehart (2001), Foster (1997) Smitherman (1977), LeMoine and Hollie (2007), and Paris (2009, 2012) all explore the educational circumstances pertaining to language arts education for Black students. In addition, every entry contained within Part V of this edition of the *Oxford Handbook for African American Language* provides a wealth of relevant educational, linguistic, and historical information that are central to the academic well-being of Black students across America. All of these scholars are highly sensitive to the cultural contexts in which AAVE or academic usage of SAE is appropriate. Their insights are balanced between enhancing literacy, that is, reading and writing (see Ball 1995; Rickford 2007), and information that is vital to teachers who may or may not be familiar with AAVE or other aspects of African American cultures (see Foster 1997; Lanehart 2001; LeMoine and Hollie 2007). Of equal significance, Lee (1993), Labov (2006), and Paris (2012) build cultural and educational bridges between schools and the home language usage of students. Rickford and Rickford (2000) provide one of the most vivid portrayals of *Spoken Soul*, and the full life of Black language usage in America. That work is highly complementary to some highly technical linguistic analyses by Wolfram and Thomas (2002), Yeager-Dror and Thomas (2010), Green (2002, 2011), Rickford (1999), Mufwene et al. (1998), Labov (1972), Baugh (1983, 1999), and Spears (2007). The vast majority of these linguists have offered a broad array of suggestions for the educational advancement of Black students, and Green's (2011) most recent contributions in this regard are worthy of recognition because they are intentionally designed to complement alternative educational strategies and programs. She notes, "From my vantage point, the goal is not to 'wipe out' [African American English], it is to offer a linguistic alternative that happens to be acceptable in academic settings" (Green 2011, 221).

Paris (2012, 96) offers fresh insights, observing that "the long struggle against dehumanizing deficit approaches to education and toward humanizing resource approaches has never been easy." He advocates a comprehensive approach, which he characterizes as "the stance," which builds upon "the practice of culturally sustaining pedagogy." His observations exceed the narrower educational orientation that is the locus of these remarks, namely, educational suggestions devoted to students who were once eligible for the LDPAAS program, which is to say, prior to the highly politicized implementation of California's proposition 209. In the spirit of social justice and educational equity that has always been embodied within our collective American national ethos, there are undeniable linguistic considerations that grow from *Brown v. BOE*, but they are not truly relevant to all African Americans based on race. The vast majority of USSD have, as involuntary immigrants, suffered greater linguistic, political, judicial, economic, residential, and educational dislocation from more affluent Americans (Ogbu 2003). Their educational plight and circumstances may differ greatly from biracial African Americans whose ancestors are not slave descendants, or whose ancestors are more recent voluntary immigrants from other parts of the African Diaspora. Elsewhere these accounts are described in terms of historical hardships (Baugh 2006) that do not conflate easily with race. In order to move beyond deficit models of education, or simplistic bidialectal efforts that fall short of Paris's (2012) formulation of "the stance," we are unlikely to overcome the shameful legacy of slavery upon which the birth of the nation owes its very existence unless we embrace Green's (2011, 220) proposal to make students "aware of systematic AAE patterns and constructions, give corresponding MAE [Mainstream American English] patterns, and teaching them to identify distinctions independently."

NOTES

1. African American vernacular English (AAVE) refers specifically to the colloquial speech of US slave descendants (USSD) who infrequently employ mainstream Standard American English.

2. All references to African American Language (AAL) are intended to be applicable to all African Americans regardless of their linguistic background or heritage. This could include naturalized citizens who were born outside of the United States, as well as those people of African descent whose ancestors were once enslaved in the United States or elsewhere, such as Haiti or Brazil.

3. Standard American English (SAE) is sometimes described as "Mainstream United States English" and it refers to the dominant linguistic norm within the United States that is promoted in academic, legal, governmental, and other highly professional contexts. Although linguistically inaccurate, many American citizens characterize SAE as "proper English" or "correct English," that is, despite the fact that such assertions have no linguistic basis and reflect political circumstances where the speech of the middle and upper classes has come to be equated with linguistic norms that are perceived by many to be error free.

REFERENCES

Alim, H. Samy. 2007. "'The Whig Party don't exist in my hood': Knowledge, Reality, and Education in the Hip Hop Nation." In *Talkin Black Talk: Language, Education, and Social Change*, edited by H. Samy Alim and John Baugh, 15–29. New York: Teachers College Press.

Ball, Arnetha F. 1995. "Text Design Patterns in the Writing of Urban African American Students: Teaching to the Cultural Strengths of Students in Multicultural Settings." *Urban Education* 30: 253–89.

Baratz, Joan C., and Roger Shuy, eds. 1969. *Teaching Black Children to Read*. Washington, DC: Center for Applied Linguistics.

Baugh, John. 1983. *Black Street Speech: Its History, Structure, and Survival*. Austin: University of Texas Press.

———. 1991. "Changing Terms of Self Reference among American Slave Descendants." *American Speech* 66: 133–46.

———. 1999. *Out of the Mouths of Slaves: African American Language and Educational Malpractice*. Austin: University of Texas Press.

———. 2006. "It Ain't about Race: Some Lingering (Linguistic) Consequences of the African Slave Trade and Their Relevance to Your Personal Historical Hardship Index." *Du Bois Review* 3: 145–59.

Bernstein, Basil. 1972. "Social Class, Language, and Socialization." In *Language and Social Context*, edited by Pier Paolo Giglioli, 157–78. New York: Harmondsworth.

Bloomfield, Leonard. 1933. *Language*. New York: Holt and Company.

Brown v. Board of Education, 347 U.S. 483 (1954).

Chomsky, Noam. 1965. *Aspects of a Theory of Syntax*. Cambridge, MA: MIT Press.

Craig, Holly, and Julie Washington. 2004. "Grade-Related Changes in the Production of African American English." *Journal of Speech, Language, and Hearing Research* 47: 450–63.

———. 2006. *Malik Goes to School: Examining the Language Skills of African American Students from Preschool–5th Grade*. Mahwah, NJ: Lawrence Erlbaum.

Farrell, Thomas J. 1983. "IQ and Standard English." *College Composition and Communication* 34: 470–84.

Fasold, Ralph. 1972. *Tense Marking in Black English: A Linguistic and Social Analysis*. Urban Language Series 8. Washington, DC: Center for Applied Linguistics.

Foster, Michele. 1997. *Black Teachers on Teaching*. New York: New Press.

Green, Lisa. 2002. *African American English: A Linguistic Introduction*. Cambridge: Cambridge University Press.

———. 2011. *Language and the African American Child*. Cambridge: Cambridge University Press.

Jensen, Arthur R. 1969. "How Much Can We Boost IQ and Scholastic Achievement?" *Harvard Educational Review* 39: 1–123.

Labov, William. 1969. "The Logic of Nonstandard English." Linguistic-Cultural Differences and American Education: Special edition of the *Florida Foreign Language Reporter* 7: 60–74, 169.

———. 1972. *Language in the Inner City: Studies in the Black English Vernacular*. Philadelphia: University of Pennsylvania Press.

———. 2006. "Reducing the Achievement Gap for African American Children." Presentation at the Fourth Annual Reading First Superintendents Summit Meeting in San Francisco, California, November 2.

Lanehart, Sonja, ed. 2001. *Sociocultural and Historical Contexts of African American English.* Philadelphia: John Benjamins.

Lau v. Nichols, 414 U.S. 563 (1974).

Lee, Carol D. 1993. *Signifying as a Scaffold for Literary Interpretation: The Pedagogical Implications of an African American Discourse Genre.* Champaign-Urbana, IL: National Council of Teachers of English.

LeMoine, Noma. 2003. "The Impact of Linguistic Knowledge about African American Language/Ebonics on Teacher Attitude toward the Language and the Students who Speak It." PhD diss., University of Southern California.

LeMoine, Noma, and Sharroky Hollie. 2007. "Developing Academic English for Standard English Learners." In *Talkin Black Talk: Language, Education, and Social Change*, edited by H. Samy Alim and John Baugh, 43–55. New York: Teachers College Press.

Morgan, Marcyliena. 2009. *The Real Hiphop: Battling for Knowledge, Power, and Respect in the LA Underground.* Durham, NC: Duke University Press.

Mufwene, Salikoko, John Rickford, John Baugh, and Guy Bailey, eds. 1998. *African-American English: Structure, History, and Usage.* New York: Routledge.

Obama, Barack. 1995. *Dreams from My Father.* New York: Three Rivers Press.

Ogbu, John U. 1978. *Minority Education and Caste: The American System in Cross-Cultural Perspective.* New York: Academic.

———. 2003. *Black American Students in an Affluent Suburb: A Study of Academic Disengagement.* Mahwah, NJ: Lawrence Erlbaum.

Orr, Eleanor Wilson. 1987. *Twice as Less: The Performance of Black Students in Mathematics and Science.* New York: Norton.

Paris, Django. 2009. "'They're in My Culture, They Speak the Same Way': African American Language in Multiethnic High Schools." *Harvard Educational Review* 79: 428–47.

———. 2012. "Culturally Sustaining Pedagogy: A Needed Change in Stance, Terminology, and Practice." *Educational Researcher* 41: 93–97.

Rickford, Angela. 2007. "The Art and Science of Teaching Narrative Reading Comprehension: An Innovative Approach." In *Talkin Black Talk: Language, Education, and Social Change*, edited by H. Samy Alim and John Baugh, 56–76. New York: Teachers College Press.

Rickford, John. 1999. *African American Vernacular English: Features, Evolution, Educational Implications.* Malden, MA: Blackwell.

Rickford, John, and Russell Rickford. 2000. *Spoken Soul: The Story of Black English.* New York: John Wiley and Sons.

Romaine, Suzanne, and John Rickford, eds. 1999. *Creole Genesis, Attitudes, and Discourse.* Philadelphia: John Benjamins.

Seymour, Harry N. 2004. "The Challenge of Language Assessment for African American English-Speaking Children: A Historical Perspective." *Seminars in Speech and Language* 25: 1–12.

Sledd, James. 1973. "Bidialectalism: The Linguistics of White Supremacy." In *The Varieties of Present-Day English*, edited by Richard W. Bailey and Jay L. Robinson, 319–30. New York: Macmillan.

Smitherman, Geneva. 1977. *Talkin and Testifyin: The Language of Black America.* Boston: Houghton Mifflin.

———, ed. 1981. *Black English and the Education of Black Children and Youth: Proceedings of the National Invitational Symposium on the King Decision.* Detroit, MI: Wayne State University Center for Black Studies.

Spears, Arthur. 2007. "African American Communicative Practices: Improvisation, Semantic License, and Augmentation." In *Talkin Black Talk: Language, Education, and Social Change*, edited by H. Samy Alim and John Baugh, 100–14. New York: Teachers College Press.

Steele, Shelby. 1990. *The Content of Our Character: A New Vision of Race in America*. New York: St. Martin's.

Stockman, Ida J. 2010. "A Review of Developmental and Applied Language Research on African American Children: From a Deficit to Difference Perspective on Dialect Differences." *Language Speech and Hearing Services in Schools* 41: 23–38.

Vaughn-Cooke, Fay. 2007. "Lessons Learned from the Ebonics Controversy: Implications for Language Assessment." In *Sociolinguistic Variation: Theories, Methods, and Applications*, edited by Robert Bayley and Ceil Lucas, 254–75. Cambridge: Cambridge University Press.

Williams, Robert Lewis, ed. 1975. *Ebonics: The True Language of Black Folks*. St. Louis, MO: Robert Williams and Associates.

Wolfram, Walt. 1969. *A Sociolinguistic Description of Detroit Negro Speech*. Washington, DC: Center for Applied Linguistics.

———. 1991. *Dialects and American English*. Englewood Cliffs, NJ: Prentice-Hall.

Wolfram, Walt, and Erik Thomas. 2002. *The Development of African American English*. London: Blackwell.

Wyatt, Toya. 1995. "Language Development in African American Child Speech." *Linguistics and Education* 7: 7–22.

Yeager-Dror, Malcah, and Erik R. Thomas. 2010. *African American English Speakers and Their Participation in Local Sound Changes: A Comparative Study*. Publications of the American Dialect Society, #94. Raleigh: Duke University Press.

PART VI

·······································

LANGUAGE IN SOCIETY

·······································

CHAPTER 36

AFRICAN AMERICAN CHURCH LANGUAGE

CHARLES E. DEBOSE

Caint nobody do me like Jesus
Caint nobody do me like the Lord
Caint nobody do me like Jesus
He's my friend

36.1 INTRODUCTION

As used in this chapter, African American Church Language (AACL) refers to a distinctive sub-variety of African American Language (AAL) used in markedly sacred contexts. For present purposes, the term *AAL* is used with reference to distinctive words, expressions, and ways of speaking used by members of the African American speech community to index their cultural identity (DeBose 2009). Instances of AAL, thusly defined, may contain dialect features identified in empirical samples of African American English (AAE) such as copula absence and final consonant cluster simplification. It may also contain other features, referred to here as *identity markers* (DeBose 2005, 131), the selection of which indexes a particular social identity claimed by the speaker. The selection of *caint*, in the above-quoted lyrics of the African American praise song "Caint Nobody Do Me Like Jesus" is a case in point.

In isolation, the negative marker *caint* might be considered a feature of Southern dialect. It is one of several features that frequently occur in the language of Black speakers or singers whether or not they speak Southern English. The lyrics of the song in which it occurs contain features of pronunciation and grammar that are stigmatized as bad language in the public domain but not in the domains of African American home, community and church life, or the lyrics of sacred songs, to the extent that they artfully engage intended audiences.

Ethnographic studies of African American discourse describe African American verbal culture in a way that highlights its artistic quality. Mitchell-Kernan (1972) calls attention to an "artistic component of Black language" (164) found not only in music and dance but also in everyday acts of speaking. The opening lines of a casual conversation between her and three young men in their early twenties whom she encounters in a public park is a good example of the artful quality of AAL. In that anecdote, one of the young men initiates the conversation in this way (I = informant; R = researcher):

> I: Mama you sho is fine.
> R: That ain' no way to talk to your mother. (164)

The ability to communicate artfully and well is highly valued in African American culture, so much so that distinctive ways of speaking known by such names as *signifyin, markin, woofin/sellin wolf tickets*, and *playin the dozens* are cultivated (see Smitherman 1994). In the domain of Black church life, distinctive ways of speaking bear such names as *preachin, prayin, testifyin, moanin/groanin*, and the *Amen Corner* (see Smitherman 1994). All of them involve artistic performance as a key ingredient. As DeBose (2005) notes, "It may be surprising to an outsider the extent to which mundane aspects of the everyday experience of African Americans involve performance" (137).

The account of AACL developed in the following pages is done with the understanding that the performance of Black culture takes place on a continuum ranging from everyday life to more formal settings—from the stage, the pulpit, and the podium, to the street corner. It includes world-renowned musical genres, which have common performance features referred to as "African continuities" (Smitherman 1977) that manifest themselves in secular genres such as jazz, rhythm and blues, and rap as well as in markedly sacred genres such as gospel, and what are traditionally known as "Negro spirituals."

One of the most pervasive African continuities in the Black experience is referred to as *call and response*. It is a common feature of a variety of church-related ways of speaking and musical genres, including the Amen Corner (see Smitherman 1994), which is discussed further below. Call and response is a common feature of Negro spirituals, as well as gospel music and contemporary praise songs.

Improvisation is a key feature of African American performance in general and church life in particular. It is discussed further below as it relates to the genres of prayin, testifyin, preachin, and other aspects of the domain of African American church life known as "havin church."

A key point developed in the following pages is that creative energy, and artistic expression permeates the Black experience. *It is not art for art's sake, however, but art for the sake of empowerment* (DeBose 2010). A pervasive theme—alluded to above with reference to the song "Caint Nobody Do Me Like Jesus"—is the use of lexical items and grammatical structures that are generally stigmatized but are distinctive features of AAL. DeBose (2005) alludes to this point in discussing a "proposed diglossia model" of the language situation in the African American speech community, saying that it "is difficult to conceptualize, partly because of the way that it often uses vernacular forms and features, but for different functions than those fulfilled by the local vernacular" (136); he further notes,

> It is the language of the Negro spirituals highlighted in lyrics such as "Josh'a fit de battle ob Jericho" and "Steal away to Jesus, I aint got long to stay here;" … Rhythm and Blues lines like "Lawdy, Lawdy, Lawdy Miss Claudie, you sho look good to me;" and of memorable Jazz songs like "Is you is or is you ain't my baby." (DeBose 2005, 136)

The proposed diglossia model posits the coexistence of two divergent varieties of AAL in a complementary functional relationship, one labeled L and used in normal everyday interaction, the other labeled H and reserved for use in performance: whether on the stage or in the streets, as long as it qualifies as talking Black as a marked choice in any of the genres of performance listed above. A testable hypothesis of the diglossia model is that, normally, stigmatized linguistic features occur more frequently in the performance language of speakers than in their everyday vernacular.

An analysis of the frequency of occurrence of selected AAE features reported by Pitts (1993) and cited in Green (2002) supports the claim that markedly Black features occur more frequently in performance: "The climactic sermons were marked by increased use of vernacular speech, in which the variable he considered occurred with greater frequency" (Green 2002, 147).

DeBose (2005) cites evidence presented by Alim (2002) of variation in the frequency of typical AAL features in performances by Hip Hop artists, noting that it is "consistent with an emerging diglossia in the African American speech community, in which the vernacular of everyday communication of former generations is threatened with extinction. Because of an established tradition, however, of artful use of language based on traditional Black vernacular forms it continues to evolve into new forms, the most recent of which is Hip-Hop" (DeBose 2005, 138).

A key to understanding the exemption of AAL as a language of performance from the stigma that would affect it in other contexts is the sociohistorical context of struggle against oppression in which it evolved to its present form, as well as its role as a tool of empowerment for the struggle, which is discussed in the next section with reference to the concept of agency.

36.2 AGENCY AND EMPOWERMENT

For present purposes, *agency* may be defined as acting from a critical perspective that does not take for granted the rightness or inevitability of established social rules, principles, and values (DeBose 2010). When members of a marginalized group achieve a sufficient level of critical awareness of their plight to identify and speak out against embedded evils and injustices, the act of doing so is tantamount to self-affirmation and solidarity with those who share their plight. A good example of such critical aware- ness is the post–Civil War African American freedom song "Oh Freedom" (year of song unknown), which is thought to have originated at a place in the Sea Islands known as Ibo Landing (Goss and Barnes 1984), where a slave ship docked carrying Africans who had boarded under the false impression of going to work as free persons. When the Africans disembarked and found out that they were destined for involuntary servitude, they are said to have responded by backing into the water and drowning themselves, singing:

> Oh Freedom
> Oh Freedom over me
> And before I be a slave I'd be buried in my grave
> And go home to my Lord and be free.

Theologian Cheryl Sanders (1995) traces the journey of African American Christians "from slavery to liberation, and from victimization to moral agency." Citing examples of "testimony" in a collection of slave narratives compiled in the 1930s by the WPA Federal Writers Project, Sanders makes the key point that "Christian slaves who spoke with elo- quence of their conversion experiences often testified against the evil of slavery" (1995, 10). She also alludes to the fact that African slaves in the United States developed a dis- tinctive "folk religion" referred to by scholars as the "invisible institution," which com- bined elements of mainstream Protestant religions "with African religious values and practices" and was practiced in secret in "clandestine prayer meetings, held late at night in the slave quarters and hush harbors" (12). The singing of sacred songs undoubtedly was also a part of such worship.

James Cone (2003) examines Black spirituals from a theological perspective and underscores a pervasive theme of God's involvement in the Africans' struggle against slavery: "making right what Whites have made wrong." Cone contends that the slaves "rejected white distortions of the gospel, which emphasized the obedience of slaves to their masters" (780). He further contends that a strong sense of identity with Old Testament stories of deliverance from slavery and resistance to oppression is unmis- takable in common spiritual lyrics: "Black people sang about Joshua and the Battle of Jericho, Moses leading the Israelites from bondage, Daniel in the lion's den, and the Hebrew children in the fiery furnace" (ibid.).

Morgan (2002) alludes to conditions of slavery and White Supremacy in the south- ern United States prior to the 1960s that were fertile ground for the survival of a "counter-language ... based on African norms of interaction" that uses indirectness, and "an exacting sense of speaker agency" with Black audiences to "camouflage the content and intent of speakers." Morgan further notes that "it may not have survived and been adapted were it not for dominant Southern society's relentless monitoring of African American's communication and language" (2002, 24–25).

An interesting example of indirection that may qualify as counter language is the refrain to the spiritual "All God's Chillun Got Shoes," the first verse of which says

> *I got shoes, you got shoes, all a God's chillun got shoes*
> *When I git ta Heaven gonna put on my shoes gonna walk all over God's Heaven*

Subsequent verses substitute such items as a robe, a crown, a harp, wings, etc. for the "shoes" in the first verse, and each verse is followed by the refrain

> *Everybody talkin bout Heaven aint goin there*

The song is said to have originated in a conversation in which a slave woman was explaining to her child that although he had no shoes on Earth, all of God's children would have shoes when they got to Heaven, which prompted the son to ask his mother whether she thought the slave master would go to Heaven. The mother's response, "Everybody talkin bout Heaven aint goin there," reflects critical awareness of the immorality of slavery (Warren 1998, 24). The indirectness of the reply, in not mentioning the slave master, allowed slaves to sing the song in his presence without his being aware of the implied judgment of him and Christian slaveholders in general as hypocrites.

The concept of speaker agency is used in recent studies of language and social identity with reference to the extent to which speakers' choices to speak one way or another involve critical awareness of the consequences. Lanehart (2002, 161-65) calls attention to the extent to which the Black female participants in her study exercise linguistic agency in choosing to use either SAE or AAL. The next section calls attention to some of the AAL identity markers alluded to above that might be selected by members of the African American speech community who can and normally do speak SAE but find it in their interest to talk Black as a marked choice.

36.3 IDENTITY MARKERS

Scholars of Black preaching contend that highly educated Black clergy find it necessary to use markedly Black speech in sermons if they want to be positively received by Black congregations (Mitchell 1990, 80). Fluent speakers of SAE can also be observed in African American church services producing markedly Black speech in Amen Corner responses (e.g., Sho nuff! You know you right!). In such a context, features like the pronunciation of sure as sho, and the absence of the contracted copula /r/ in you right, are best treated, not as dialect features, but as instances of talking in a way that identifies the speaker as an incumbent of the Amen Corner role. A number of other common words: such as *floor, store*, and *your* have r-less pronunciation in AAL (i.e., flo 'floor', sto 'store', and yo 'your').

It was noted above that the negation marker *caint* is, ambiguously, a feature of Southern dialect as well as an AAL identity marker. The same is true of the pronunciation of the pronouns *I* and *my* as /a/ and /ma/, respectively. African American church leaders who normally say /ai/ 'I' and /mai/ 'my' may select the monophthongal forms of such words in an effort to communicate effectively with a Black audience. A preacher, for example, when telling what is on the menu for an upcoming meal, might make a point of pronouncing *pie* as /pa/:

"Yall be sho ta check out Susta Jones sweet potato *pa*."

Other AACL lexical items pronounced in a distinctive manner include the word *choir*, pronounced /kwa/; *church*, pronounced to rhyme with *much*; and the Amen Corner response *Well* pronounced with a low front vowel (i.e., /wæl/).

The word *sister* pronounced as *susta* is a feature, not only of AACL, but more generally of Black in-group communication, where the word *susta*, as well as *brotha*, can mean more than the dictionary definition of 'sibling.' In Black culture, they may also convey the special meaning of 'African American (male or female)' in a context in which a speaker aims to communicate to an addressee that a person under discussion is Black. The words also have special meaning in the domain of church life, where they serve as forms of address and courtesy titles when speaking to or about fellow church members. So does the word *mother*. In Black church life, it is used in reference to senior female lay leaders of a congregation, who are sometimes referred to as *church mothers*.

The identity markers discussed in this section support a generalization about AAL identity markers: there is a tendency for the more archaic member of a set of words like *can't* and *caint* to be selected when talking Black as a marked choice; further, the more archaic choice may also be a feature of Southern dialect. Two other words that support this generalization are the second person plural pronoun *yall* and the future marker *gon* 'going to.' The r -less pronunciation of words like *flo* 'floor' is not a general Southern feature but is a feature of Black Southern dialect.

The prevalence of Southern features in the language of Black performance can be traced to the Great Migration (see Morgan 2002), in which much of the African American population moved from places in the rural South to urban centers in the North and West. Many descendants of the original migrants have shifted from the southern Black Belt language of their ancestors to the vernaculars of their present homes. On Sunday mornings, however, and other occasions when they might happen to be having church, they are likely to do so in AACL.

36.4 Havin Church

The use of a verb *havin church* to denote a traditional African American worship service aptly connotes the extent to which it is a focal point for the kind of artful and engaging performance that is the hallmark of Black verbal culture. The music, prayers, testimonies and preaching are all energized by enthusiastic audience involvement. Green (2002) offers a succinct overview of the typical Black church service as consisting of "musical devotions, ritual programs and celebrations, dedications, sermons, prayers, testimonials, and weekly announcements" (146). She further notes that participants in such worship "may engage in nonverbal communication such as head-nodding, feet-patting, hand-waving and clapping, body-swaying, and standing" (146).

The focus of this section on typical features of the Black worship experience is an opportunity to examine the viability of the proposed diglossia model of the language situation in the African American speech community based on what is known about the language varieties typically spoken by members of African American congregations as their everyday vernacular, and the extent to which they use AAL in the performance of rituals such as singing, praying, testifying, and preaching. In congregations with which this author is familiar, senior members (in age) are most likely to have participated in the Great Migration and retained a Southern Black dialect spoken in their ancestral community; while younger members speak an urban variety of AAL or a regional variety of General American English. Those who do not normally speak AAL are most likely to perform in AAL when singing songs with markedly Black lyrics such as the praise song cited at the beginning of this chapter or a spiritual such as "All of God's Chillun got Shoes," or to describe the goal of their experience in such words as *to have a good time in the Lord*, or with such words as, *I want to get my praise on* (Smitherman 1977; Green 2002). Smitherman (1977) offers a list of "traditional terms and concepts" from the Black church that includes: *Lord ham mercy* or *Lord a mercy* 'popular idiomatic interjection to indicate surprise or agreement,' and the Amen Corner responses *Tell the truth!* and *Well, all right!*

The ritual of *prayin*, as corporal prayer is referred to in Black worship, involves improvisation as well as call and response. In a similar manner to long narrative poems, *toasts* (see Smitherman 1977, 1994) such as the heroic urban narratives *The Signifyin Monkey*; and *Shine and the Titanic* (see Abrahams 1964, 1970; Anonymous 1970); certain prayers are maintained across generations through an oral tradition. They are learned through the experience of seeing them performed by others and performing them from memory. The quality of improvisation makes each performance, whether a toast or a prayer, unique for all of its similarity to other performances of the same piece.

Pinn (2002) gives the following example of a prayer frequently heard in Black worship services in a very similar form, stating, "Whether the date is 1928 or 1998 ... one might hear words similar to these."

> *Almighty and all wise God*
> *It is once more and again that a few of your hand made children*
> *Are gathered here together to call upon your holy name*
> *We bow at your footstool Master thanking you for our spared lives*
> *We thank you that we were able*
> *To get up this morning clothed in our right minds*
> *For Master, since we met here*
> *Many have been snatched away from the land of the living*
> *And hurled into eternity*
> *But through Your goodness and mercy we have been spared*
> *To assemble ourselves together one more time*
> *To call upon a captain who has never lost a battle.* (69)

In the Black church experience, praying is typically performed by ordained clergy, or by experienced lay leaders. The main qualification is the ability to engage a congregation in a moving experience of connection with the Divine. Pinn claims that "the prayer leader is usually selected because of a special talent for effective praying" (69) and that such praying is accomplished through the recitation of "images and phrases—religious clichés of sorts—commonly found in public prayers" (69). He does not mention language choice as a factor in the effectiveness of engaging a Black church audience by using AAL identity markers. Nor does he comment on the advisability of taking advantage of opportunities to do so.

While there are few markedly AAL features in the written form of the above prayer, a skilled performer has many opportunities to say it with markedly Black pronunciation. The words in the line "We bow at your footstool Master thanking you for our spared lives," for instance, offer several opportunities for markedly Black pronunciation, e.g., pronouncing *your* and *for* as /yo/ and /fo/, respectively, and pronouncing *thanking* as "thankin."

The genre of testifyin is performed under similar conditions to those of praying to the extent that it qualifies as what Smitherman (1977) refers to as "a ritualized form of Black communication." The following example includes a number of "religious clichés" that have been used in a similar manner in testimonies performed at different times and places over a number of years.

> *First giving honor to God*
> *I want to thank and praise the Lord*
> *For his goodness and mercy*
> *For being clothed in my right mind*
> *He didn't have to do it*
> *But He woke me up this morning*
> *and started me on my way*

Notwithstanding the fact that it is laden with clichés, the above testimony can be delivered in a manner that gets the Amen Corner going, simply by saying each line deliberately with AAL pronunciation, and pausing long enough after each line for a response to the call. Smitherman further defines testimony in a manner that highlights its similarity to preaching insofar as it involves giving "verbal witness to the efficacy, truth, and power of some experience in which all Blacks have shared" (58). In fact, one of the frequently cited qualities of an effective sermon is inclusion of a personal testimony about something that the preacher has faced and overcome with God's help, which encourages those in the audience facing similar issues to keep the faith.

Effective preaching is enhanced by the qualities of effective prayer and testimony just discussed that may be summarized as *audience engagement*. One gets immediate feedback on how well a prayer or testimony is engaging a congregation through Amen Corner responses, and if the responses are not frequent or enthusiastic it might be due to the speaker's failure to take advantage of opportunities to use AAL identity markers. The next section of this chapter includes an extended example of a typical Black sermon.

36.5 THE PREACHED WORD

A number of distinctive features of AACL occur in the context of the *Preached Word*. At the top of the list is the above-mentioned audience participation: the so-called Amen Corner. A preacher is highly conscious of the importance of audience involvement and works on getting it going from the moment of getting off his or her feet, and approaching the *sacred desk*, as the pulpit is sometimes called. The sermon often follows a musical selection, which offers the preacher an opportunity to start engaging the congregation. At the close of a hymn, such as "God is a Good God," the preacher might make a traditional opening call like "Let the Church say Amen." After getting the requested response, s/he has the option of shifting to the topic of the hymn, for example:

PREACHER: Church! Aren't you glad!
CONGREGATION: Yes!
PREACHER: Ain't you glad the God we serve is a good God!
CONGREGATION: Yes He is!/Oh yes!/So glad!/etc.

Alternately the preacher might follow the first request for an Amen with variations such as,

PREACHER: Let the Church say hallelujah!
CONGREGATION: Hallelujah!
PREACHER: Let the Church say praise God!
CONGREGATION: Praise God!

After attaining the sought after audience engagement, as well as a brief silence, the minister proceeds to make appropriate salutations to dignitaries in attendance, continuously striving to keep the audience engaged. This writer remembers one particular preacher who liked to end salutations to named dignitaries by saying, "and Lottie, Dottie and Everybody."

Even when reading a scripture text to support the sermon message, the preacher will not miss the opportunity to engage the congregation. A scripture frequently read at Easter services narrates the story of Mary going to the tomb where Jesus was buried to discover that it is empty. The scripture begins with the phrase *Early Sunday morning* and is frequently read in a way that pauses after the first word. Then after several repeats of *Early*, the preacher may continue with the rest of the phrase, *Sunday morning,* and then continue to read the rest of the scripture, pausing for amen responses at every opportunity. For example:

PREACHER: Early
CONGREGATION: Early
(Repeat)
PREACHER: Early Sunday morning!
CONGREGATION: Yes!

The body of the sermon continues to be delivered in a call-and-response format, with the preacher constantly checking for signs that the congregation is getting the message, especially if the point challenges believers in some way, and taking every occasion to use markedly Black language. If the challenge is for believers to grow spiritually in their personal relationship with God, for instance, the preacher might—after making the general assertion—elaborate with "down home" examples:

PREACHER: You might have heard yo mamma say God is real
CONGREGATION: Waal!
PREACHER: You might have heard your Auntie Mamie say the same thang.
CONGREGATION: Preach the Word
PREACHER: You might have heard the preacher say
God is real
CONGREGATION: Say it, say it, say it!
PREACHER: But Church!
I'm here to tell you
Like it's a natural fact
You got to know God for yourself
CONGREGATION: [silence]
PREACHER: I don' thank yall hear me!
You got to know God fo yoself.

To drive the point home a preacher might resort to body language, saying:

Touch yo neighbor on the right and tell em
God is real.
CONGREGATION: God is real.
PREACHER: Touch yo neighbor on the lef and tell em
You got to know God fo yoself.
CONGREGATION: You got to know God fo yoself.

Another distinctive characteristic of Black preaching is in the area of voice quality, where rising and falling intonation patterns correspond to high points of message delivery and reach a peak at the end of a sermon, referred to in the jargon of homiletics as the *celebration* and in Black church jargon as *whooping*. Pinn (2002) describes "whooping" in the following quote. He notes that it is also known as "sing-song" or "chanting."

This is a rhythmically stylized presentation ... in which the preacher, with creative illustrations, bodily movement, changes in voice (intonations), and dramatic appeal ... makes the point. . . . [T]he minister begins in a mild tone and gradually increases the strength and excitement of the voice until reaching a climax marked by exaggerated gestures and booming voice. . . . The congregation speaks its approval of the message through shouts of "Amen!" (63)

Pinn further explains how preachers sometimes "will call for a response from the congregation with expressions such as, 'Can I get a witness!' or 'I wish you would pray with me!' or simply, 'Somebody say Amen!'" (63–64)

In present-day Black preaching circles, the term *whoop* can be a complimentary reference to a celebratory wrap-up of a sermon with the above-described features of rhythm, tempo, intonation, and call and audience response. The ability to whoop well would be listed on a minister's résumé of admirable traits. The term is derived, however, from "whooping and hollering," traditionally used in a derogatory sense to characterize a minister's preaching as consisting of more style than substance. Pinn (2002) calls attention to an ongoing debate among scholars of Black preaching on the merits of whooping (64).

A form of sermon delivery that used to be common in Black churches, but may be dying out, is literally sung in tune with notes of a pentatonic scale. Studies claim that it is a continuity of an African form of worship. Spencer (1987) refers to this style as a "Chanted Sermon" and alternatively as "homiletical musicality": "One who observes the Black Church from within the context of its life as a worshipping community is soon struck by the degree to which the preaching is musical" (ix). Spencer further notes that in the culture of the Black church, a sermon that lacks a substantial amount of such musicality tends to be judged critically and treated as a different form of address than a sermon (i.e., "a speech, address, or lecture"). He further notes that in the vernacular of the culture, preaching of this type must "start low, go slow, climb higher, and strike fire" (ix).

Spencer's comment calls attention to the role of improvisation in Black preaching and in Black performance in general. Improvisation, mentioned above as an African continuity, is a recognized prime ingredient of jazz. It is also a major feature of whooping and reaches a high point in the closing celebratory phase of a sermon. Many preachers move fully into the traditional musical chant form in coordinated artful improvisation with church musicians. The preacher might start chanting the lyrics to a traditional hymn, in a call-and-response pattern, deviating from the melody and rhythm of the song, and improvising on the lyrics:

PREACHER: I was sinking deep in sin
CONGREGATION: Well!
PREACHER: Down in the miry clay.
CONGREGATION: Oh my!
PREACHER: And then the Lord saw me, and he pulled me out
CONGREGATION: Hallelujah!
PREACHER: God picked me up! Oh yes he did!
CONGREGATION: Tell the truth now!
PREACHER: Pick me up and turn me roun.
CONGREGATION: Praise God!
PREACHER: And planted ma feet on higher ground!
Can I git a witness?
CONGREGATION: Amen

In the celebration phase of the sermon, the preacher uses body language, frequently moving away from behind the podium, turning around when saying a phrase like "He pick me up and turn me roun." The congregation rises to its feet and joins in with hand-clapping and other forms of body language. As the musician senses that the celebration is winding down, the accompaniment changes from freestyle rifting along with the call and response to introducing the actual tune of the hymn, as the congregation joins in singing.

It should be clear from the above examples that the language of Black preaching, like other varieties of AACL, frequently contains markedly Black features. The above noted ways in which preachers use such language as a means of audience engagement clearly involve speaker agency. Consequently, the linguistic features of such speech are not dialect features but identity markers produced in acts of talking Black as a marked choice.

The case for treating AAL as the H variety in a diglossia model of the AA language situation, suggested by the above example of Hip Hop language, is complicated by the fact that with the exception of Black spirituals, the language of Black performance does not fit the category of classical language (Stewart 1968). A strong case can be made, however, on other grounds.

Evidence that elements of Black preaching such as the above-mentioned musicality, audience participation, and improvisation are continuities of the same traditions that produced spirituals and other distinctive ways of speaking associated with Black church life strengthens the case for describing the AAL language situation as a case of diglossia (Ferguson 1959). When AACL is spoken in the pulpit as a vehicle of the Word of God, it derives prestige befitting an H variety from its function.

36.6 Conclusion

Several issues raised in this discussion could benefit from future research on the distinction made here between dialect features and identity markers. The word *caint*, for instance, as in the title of the song "Caint Nobody Do Me Like Jesus," which was quoted in the introduction, might be characterized by a linguistically knowledgeable observer as a dialect feature in isolation of its discourse context of musical performance. Unless AAL were the native language of the singer, however, it would be an instance of talking (singing) Black as a marked choice.

Future studies could collect and analyze adequate samples of the language of various modes of performance, including Blues, Spirituals, Gospel, Hip Hop, testifyin, prayin, signifyin, and trash talking, to make more definitive conclusions than are presently possible about the extent to which the same and/or different features occur in dialect speech and the language of Black performance, and their relative frequencies.

Another promising area of research would involve interdisciplinary collaboration at a higher level than presently exists between AAL scholars and theologians, such as the ones cited as experts on Black theology and Black preaching, as well as other areas of expertise that complement linguistic knowledge of AAL.

REFERENCES

Abrahams, Roger D. 1964. *Deep Down in the Jungle: Negro Narrative Folklore from the Streets of Philadelphia*. Hatboro, PA: Aldine Transaction.

———. 1970. *Positively Black*. Englewood Cliffs, NJ: Prentice-Hall.

Alim, H. Samy. 2002. "Street Conscious Copula Variation in the Hip Hop Nation." *American Speech* 77: 288–304.

Anonymous. 1970. *Shine and the Titanic, The Signifying Monkey, Stackolee, and Other Stories from Down Home*. San Francisco, CA: More Publishing Company.

Cone, James H. 2003. "Black Spirituals: A Theological Interpretation." In *African American Religious Thought: An Anthology*, edited by Cornel West and Eddie S. Glaude Jr., 775–89. Louisville, KY: John Knox Westminster.

DeBose, Charles E. 2005. *The Sociology of African American Language: A Language Planning Perspective*. Hampshire, UK: Palgrave Macmillan.

———. 2009. "Church Lady Talk." In *African American Women's Language: Discourse, Education, and Identity*, edited by Sonja Lanehart, 276–90. Newcastle, UK: Cambridge Scholars.

———. 2010. "Sacred to Secular Crossover: The Case of Sam Cooke." Paper presented at the Conference on African American Linguistics, San Antonio, Texas, November 2–3.

Ferguson, Charles A. 1959. "Diglossia." *WORD-Journal of the International Linguistic Association* 15 (2): 325–40.

Goss, Linda, and Marian E. Barnes. 1989. *Talk that Talk: An Anthology of African-American Storytelling*. New York: Simon and Shuster.

Green, Lisa. 2002. *African American English: A Linguistic Introduction*. Cambridge: Cambridge University Press.

Lanehart, Sonja L. 2002. *Sista, Speak! Black Women Kinfolk Talk about Language and Literacy*. Austin: University of Texas Press.

Mitchell, Henry H. 1990. *Black Preaching: The Recovery of a Powerful Art*. Nashville, TN: Abingdon.

Mitchell-Kernan, Claudia. 1972. "Signifying and Marking: Two Afro-American Speech Acts." In *Directions in Sociolinguistics: The Ethnography of Communication*, edited by John Gumperz and Dell Hymes, 161–79. New York: Holt, Rinehart, and Winston.

Morgan, Marcyliena. 2002. *Language, Discourse, and Power in African American Culture*. Cambridge: Cambridge University Press.

Pinn, Anthony B. 2002. *The Black Church in the Post–Civil Rights Era*. New York: Orbis Books.

Pitts, Walter F., Jr. 1993. *Old Ship of Zion: The Afro-Baptist Ritual in the African Diaspora*. New York City: Oxford University Press.

Sanders, Cheryl J. 1995. *Empowerment Ethics for a Liberated People*. Minneapolis, MN: Fortress.

Smitherman, Geneva. 1977. *Talkin and Testifyin: The Language of Black America*. Boston: Houghton Mifflin.

———. 1994. *Black Talk: Words and Phrases from the Hood to the Amen Corner*. Boston: Houghton Mifflin.

Spencer, Jon Michael. 1987. *Sacred Symphony: The Chanted Sermon of the Black Preacher.* New York: Greenwood.

Stewart, William. 1968. "Continuity and Change in American Negro Dialects." *Florida FL Reporter* 6: 3-4, 14–16, 18.

Warren, Gwendolyn Sims. 1998. *Ev'ry Time I Feel the Spirit: 101 Best-Loved Psalms, Gospel Hymns, and Spiritual Songs of the African-American Church.* New York: Henry Holt and Co.

CHAPTER 37

THE (RE)TURN TO REMUS ORTHOGRAPHY

The Voices of African American Language in American Literature

JAMES BRAXTON PETERSON

37.1 INTRODUCTION

MACAULAY (2006) argues that perhaps the most important advantage of English orthography "is that because the normal orthography does not indicate phonetic quality [i.e., pronunciation] directly, the same spelling system can be used by people who speak very different dialects" (79). While the nuances of literary dialect and the deployment of it for the purposes of indexing, defining, and sometimes overdetermining African American identity in American literature are beyond the scope of Macaulay's discussion, his claim unveils a persistent issue: the problem of representing the speech of characters in American literature who do not use some variety of Standard American English (SAE) and/or whose presence is marked as "Other." This is often the case with African American characters but also with characters whose speech is not considered part of mainstream society and culture, such as southerners or Chicano Americans or Bostonians.

Throughout most of American literary history, however, authors who attempt to craft the language of African American characters have not in fact used "the same spelling system." No orthographic system has ever been developed or agreed upon for how to represent different dialects of American English because "the same spelling system" masks pronunciation differences that exist regionally, socially, and otherwise. As a result, various authors have constructed their own way to address this issue: the use of *eye dialect*. However, a significant problem with the use of eye dialect is that it tries to relay information about pronunciation in ways that look deviant but are not. The system is used for what an author considers to be ethnic or dialectal characterizations without taking into consideration its use in African American speech communities, where oftentimes the pronunciation is the same. For example, *was* and *is* are spelled in eye dialect—for only certain characters in the story, of course—as *wuz* or *waz/iz,* even though this is also the predominant pronunciation among SAE speakers. This problem with the orthography used to represent African American characters, both within literature and beyond, has been chronically understudied. No complete history of orthographic representations of the speech of African American characters in literature exists, and (sadly) this chapter will not be sufficient to fill that gaping space in the scholarship with respect to African American literature or linguistics.

In this chapter, I interrogate how and why authors represent language use in the African American community in the ways they do on the printed page. This endeavor, in my opinion, cannot exist in either a linguistic or literary vacuum. I follow Lanehart (2001) who argues that "we cannot talk about a language without considering and trying to understand the people in and of their sociocultural and historical contexts. In other words, the language and the people are inextricably linked" (1). My central claim is that throughout American literary history, writers return to a form of eye dialect referred to as *Remus orthography.* And they have continued to do so well beyond the historic linguistic analyses of this phenomenon, even though its usage retains its historically revealed pitfalls. Ultimately the presence of Remus orthography in American literature reflects and represents racial tensions, policies, and ideologies in American society.

For the most part, I employ the term *African American* in this chapter to refer to and/or describe the people, culture, and language spoken by Black folks who are descended from enslaved Africans in America. However, as a result of some of the scholarship glossed and quoted in this chapter and because the term *Black* can often capture cultural, ethnic, linguistic, and diasporic nuances that *African American* simply cannot, I will occasionally use *African American* and *Black* interchangeably—noting well the complexities and complications inherent in such use. For some of the scholars briefly engaged in this chapter, *Black* was (at the time) the appropriate term of self-identification for African Americans; for others, the term *Black* better captures the syncretic cultural milieu within which African diasporic culture, language, literature, and so on might more appropriately be discussed.

I will also use the term the editors of this volume use to refer to language use in the African American community, *African American Language* (hereinafter AAL). Lanehart (2001) defines AAL as encompassing "the whole of language uses in the African American community and not just what may appear as peculiarities or the most striking features. The entire system should not be segmented based on what seems 'authentic' or peculiarly non-standard, but, instead, on what actually describes the language of a people" (7).

37.2 EYE DIALECT AND REMUS ORTHOGRAPHY

According to Minnick (2004), "there is an abundance of skepticism about the linguistic value of literary dialect—which is defined here as written attempts at representing

social, regional, or other types of spoken linguistic variation—still the analysis of literary dialect can be as important to linguistic study as it is to literary study" (xvi). In this
chapter, I use the term *African American literary dialect* (hereinafter AALD) to mean
the broad or generalized ways in which American authors represent language use in
the African American community on the printed page. AALD that relies too heavily
on orthographic approximations of so-called peculiarities in the speech of African
Americans is often referred to as *eye dialect*.

There have been a number of developments in how orthography is deployed to represent AAL on the printed page since the earliest incarnations of AALD in American
literature. Moreover, and more recently, authors have used certain orthographic representations of AALD that revert to what Hadler (1998) refers to as *Remus orthography*, "a
written language riddled with apostrophes, misspellings, and omitted letters and words"
(108). The term *Remus orthography* is appropriately taken from the name of the narrator
in several of Joel Chandler Harris's African American folktales. Uncle Remus is a kindly
old former slave who would be described as "A Good Negro," and who Chandler uses to
represent what he believes is the language of the Old South and Gullah (see Harris 1881).
Please note that aside from Hadler (1998), I am not aware of any other scholar using the
term *Remus orthography* to refer to orthography used to represent AAL on the printed
page. I have chosen to adopt this term because it captures some of the "sociocultural
and historical contexts" to which Lanehart (2001) refers and thereby serves as a distinct
form of eye dialect that finds its context in racial attitudes that historically informed
orthographic representations of AAL in American literature. The use of Remus orthography for the specific purpose of representing African American identity and place in
American literature has been both strategic and tragic in a way that is often framed as
nostalgic. The use of Remus orthography also exploits and suffers from the *politics of
orthography* inherent in many attempts to visibly represent African American voices on
the printed page (Peterson 2004).

37.3 THE POLITICS AND IDEOLOGIES OF ORTHOGRAPHY

Peterson (2004) offers a schema with four modes for interpreting and reading linguistic
identity in multi-ethnic American literature: (1) *author's identity* (e.g., insider-outsider)
(431); (2) *stereotypes*, propagated tools of oppression and reflections of ignorance that
operate on many linguistic and discursive levels (431-32); (3) *situational contexts*, which
form the pragmatic milieu for sociolinguistic variation and provide certain situations in
literature that readers are meant to discern from the nuances of identity inferred from
linguistic contextual information (e.g., a text set during slavery will likely have main
characters who are Black) (432); and (4) *the politics of orthography*, which will be the
focus of my comments here.

Sociolinguistic representations in literature reveal the hegemonic relationship between standard English spellings and the vernaculars that have distinct linguistic systems but must conform to standard orthography for standard American English. Politics also underscores the narrative interface between social biases like racism or sexism and the plot, with its characters and their ways of speaking. When speech is represented in literature through misspellings and the use of apostrophes and other diacritical marks (consider *dey be chillin'*), the vernacular is always visually incorrect. This style of presenting sociolinguistic variation is a kind of eye dialect—a term linguists have traditionally used to describe techniques for representing in print the speech of characters who speak vernaculars of American English. This is often the most subtle, but probably the most linguistically productive, approach for analyzing the literary representation of identity. Vernaculars of American English are as systematic and rule-governed as standard American English. In order to portray these vernaculars, authors regularly scramble standard spelling into what appears to be gibberish and looks and reads like a form of language derived from standard American English and subordinate to it (Peterson 2004).

This critique is provided for non-African American writers as well as African American writers who use eye dialect, even when they do so subversively. However, African American writers such as Zora Neale Hurston and Sapphire rely on their insider knowledge of sociolinguistic conventions of AAL and often demonstrate a working knowledge of the more subtle, less visible features of AAL such as zero copula, regularization of verb patterns, and distinct vocabulary (432–33).

Hadler's (1998) history and overview of AALD is instructive as it informs the ways in which nationalism and important developments in religion work together with racism and representation in the earliest moments of American literary and orthographic history. Hadler turns to the seminal work of Levine (1977) because it relies so heavily on the transcriptions of AALD in its investigations of Black culture. Levine opens with "A Note on Black Dialect," a fairly lengthy disclaimer through which he tries to account for the limitations of Remus orthography.

> The language I have been forced to rely upon is a mélange of accuracy and fantasy, of sensitivity and stereotype, of empathy and racism. The distortions, where they exist, were not always conscious; people often hear what they expect to hear, what stereotype and predisposition have prepared them to hear. Thus the variety and subtlety of Negro [sic] speech was frequently reduced to what the auditor thought Negroes [sic] spoke like. Even when the pronunciation of a given word was precisely the same as that of the collectors, their desire to indicate the exotic qualities of [B]lack speech led them to utilize such misleading and superfluous spellings as wen for "when," fo'ks or fokes for "folks," w'ite or wite for "white," wuz for "was," bizness for "business," ... wurst for "worst," frum for "from," reel for "real," cullered for "colored," ... and so on and on. (xxix)

Levine (1977) ultimately concludes that to impose an orthographic system on transcribed Black speech would further convolute the already complicated matter of representing Black voices on the printed page.

Hadler (1998) laments that "[t]he use of non-standard language to represent the speech of African American characters is now standard practice in scholarship. Remus orthography is so pervasive it has become invisible and is read unchallenged" (100). For Hadler, these complicated orthographic matters are informed by the earliest developments in American letters—especially as those developments sought to identify a particularly Eurocentric sense of American identity in literature and culture. According to Wolfram and Thomas (2002), who trace the early developments of AAL, "[a]ccounts that aim to capture 'literal words' of African Americans are certainly subject to a kind of stereotyping that seizes selectively on particular structures—and in some cases structures not characteristic of the normative population—that exaggerate differences, resulting in caricatures that are not faithful to actual spoken language" (16).

In 1865, William Frances Allen published "The Negro Dialect" in *The Nation* (Hadler 1998). Allen would go on to also work on *Slave Songs of the United States* (Allen, Ware, and Garrison 1867). According to Hadler (1998), Allen studied Gullah, and "it would have been almost impossible for Allen not to conclude that the dialect was a curiosity warped by isolation and would soon 'vanish'" (102). This perception of AAL as fleeting was coupled with sustained efforts to deny any of the African cultural traits passed on in AAL that might provide it with some semblance of legitimacy. "Possible Africanisms are often explicitly dismissed; the language and the culture that these scholars described is always a degenerate variant of English" (Hadler 1998, 102). Thus, in addition to orthographically diminishing the cultural capacity of Black speech, early White American writers and scholars also deliberately dismissed inherent cultural features in the speech that they were portraying and transcribing.

Undermining AAL was an effective tool in the more comprehensive effort to undermine the humanity of Black people in America. Pseudoscience contributed to this effort as well. "While much of American race science did not explicitly concern itself with 'voice,' the theories did locate the African American physical body on the low end of a long continuum" (Hadler 1998, 112). Black voice and the faces central to the articulation of that voice were linchpins for Black humanity. "Through mechanisms of power and control, Euro-Americans tried to control the content of African American speech ... [O]ne instrument of that control—the orthographies and transcriptive systems that shaped the parameters for the *written* representation of the voice—was very successful" (Hadler 1998, 115).

Remus orthography was successful at overdetermining the representations of AAL in the earliest recorded histories of African Americans and the ways in which various written media depicted Black identity on the page. Since early philologists insisted that AAL had only English roots, Remus orthography had the dual impact of visually reflecting the "diminished nature" of African American speech and also abnegating any possibility that the distinctiveness of AAL could be rooted in a specifically African cultural tradition. Missionaries, historians, and even members of the abolitionist movement who were ideologically invested in ending human bondage in America, all used Remus orthography to represent African American voices in literature. Considering the literary and linguistic legacies of Remus orthography, Hadler's call for a more in-depth examination of African American identity and orthographic representation continues to be compelling.

Remus orthography came into vogue in the immediate aftermath of the Civil War, a moment in which the possibility of African American citizenship and sociopolitical participation in the American public sphere became a plausible reality. Certain systematic attempts (e.g., racist policies, mob violence) to oppress African Americans beyond the long history of institutional slavery were best served via racialized orthographic representations like Remus orthography that re-inscribed the tenets of White supremacy—that is, representations that dehumanized African Americans by denying them cultural legitimacy and linguistic intelligence.

37.4 LINGUISTIC POSSIBILITIES FOR LITERARY DIALECT

Dillard (1977) focuses on lexical developments, but he also asks what has continued to be an important and often ignored question in language and linguistics studies: Can we trust literary sources? The "we" here refers to scholars in the fields of philology, (socio) linguistics, and/or language variation—who at the time were mostly White men. The answer to this question is complicated but it, essentially, amounts to a "no," not just for Dillard but for many language variationists whose data most often rely on live recordings of conversational speech.

Dillard (1977) effectively captures some of the tensions and racial conflicts at issue with respect to the use of lexicon and orthography in order to represent African American identity in American fiction. Dillard parses Mark Twain's critique of James Fenimore Cooper in "Fenimore Cooper's Literary Offenses" (1895), an essay aimed at taking Cooper to task for dialectal orthographic inconsistencies in one speaker. Dillard debunks Twain's critique by asserting the basis for code-switching in "multidialectal societies," the now conventional notion that speakers shift registers depending on the context of a particular speaking situation. He goes on to argue that the challenge with AALD is that it is always rendered in some form of Remus orthography (Dillard does not use this term), while non-Black characters who speak in some other variety of American English (i.e., not AAL) are often represented using SAE orthography. This separate but unequal orthography reflects the segregationist policies that ultimately became law. The fact that linguistic and orthographic ideology manifested in Remus orthography for African American speakers and SAE orthography for White speakers in most of early American literature should deepen our understanding of the limitations of Remus orthography as a linguistic tool for representing AAL.

Another interesting point that Dillard (1977) makes here is that:

> It is easy to see why some members of the Black community have been angered by White writers' use of Black English [i.e., AAL]: The fact that most skilled practitioners ... learned it from the slaves they owned and sold is enough to motivate anger. Even after

the difficult task of factoring out slavery and its consequences, another objection easily arises: White writers of Negro dialect may write it for purposes of ridicule. (147)

Note here that these points are made by a White scholar who in this very same text suggests that the "super-SAE" with which many slave narratives were written is proof that they were edited or written by White abolitionists too eager to validate the humanity of their fugitive subjects. Dillard's arguments about lexicon and the limitations of the use of Remus orthography are fraught with the racial tensions that undergird both the origins of White scholars transcribing AAL (i.e., White writers attempting to represent AAL through Remus orthography) and the continued complexities that Black writers wrestle with when confronting similar and distinct challenges in their own attempts to represent the Black voice on the printed page.

Of course, slavery and racial ideologies are at the root of these matters. If the separate but unequal paradigm for racialized orthographic representations presaged the actual Jim Crow policies that made "separate but equal" a debilitating reality for Black America, then it would seem to be logical—if not simplistic—that Remus orthography harkened back to and reminded Black readers of the immediately preceding historical moment where the "Peculiar Institution" was the dominant mode of existence for Black folk in America. "White-produced dialect literature did shift to the false nostalgia of plantation evocations in an effort to reconstitute the most outwardly paternalistic of master-slave relations" (Hadler 1998, 117). More to the point here is that authorship—especially the race of the author—affects the ways in which orthographic representation is received and perceived. I posit that this begins to make the case for both authorship and situational contexts (Peterson 2004) to be considered whenever debates about the politics of orthography and/or the use of Remus orthography arise.

What Dillard's work similarly underscores is the extension of these racial and racially inflected issues (with respect to the use of Remus orthography) back into the scholarship itself. How are African American scholars in linguistics (and other disciplines) to take the ways in which Dillard casually refers to slave ownership being at the root of representational controversies or the cavalier ways in which he posits the lexicon as the distinctive feature of AAL? Ultimately Dillard concludes that scholars should use "literary works as a means to a general overview—not to make confident decisions about either lexical items or grammatical structures solely on the evidence provided by any writer of fiction" (152). For Dillard, White writers who were exposed to AAL "insofar as orthography will permit" have done a good job of representing Black speech on the page (155). He also gives kudos to William Wells Brown and Charles Chesnutt for mastering AAL. But he reserves his highest "prize" for Richard Wright and his deft deployment of AAL lexical items: "the accuracy of his contemporary Black speech is impressive. Finding a word or expression in Wright's works is perhaps the best possible corroboration of the hunch that it was genuinely Black" (Dillard 1977, 155). Dillard's argument about Wright underscores the ways in which orthography alone, especially Remus orthography, must be "read" in the context of other attributes of the reading experience—most especially authorship and the situational contexts within the narrative itself.

37.5 A Closer Look at (African) American Writers and Literary Dialect

As mentioned above, Minnick (2004) concedes that "there is an abundance of skepticism about the linguistic value of literary dialect"; however, she also argues that "the analysis of literary dialect can be as important to linguistic study as it is to literary study" (xvi). Minnick (2004) suggests that the use of AALD, especially when it takes eye dialect or Remus orthography forms, is a powerful reflection of racial attitudes in America; in some cases the rendering of Remus orthography serves the sociopolitical purpose of establishing national American identity in and through American literature. For example, Minnick (2010) claims that "the popularity of literary dialect in realistic fiction after the Civil War coincided with renewed attention to the idea of a distinctly American language, motivated now by … concerns about the possibility of corruption of American English by non-mainstream regional, racial, social, and immigrant influences" (183).

Minnick (2010) combines literary, historical, and cultural studies analyses with sociolinguistic metrics—designed to quantify AAL features represented in the AALD of specific characters in American literature. When she applies these methods to one of the most popular texts in American literature, Mark Twain's *Huckleberry Finn* (1884), she finds that one of Twain's most criticized and politicized characters—Jim—actually reflects the fact that the author was a "mostly conscientious observer and reporter of common features of African American English" (184). But the effect of Twain's use of Remus orthography to depict Jim's character still serves to stigmatize him and through very subtle sociolinguistic manipulations (e.g., frequencies for /n/ articulation, i.e., the use of *-in* instead of *-ing* as a word ending, in the literary dialect of Jim versus Huck), Twain effectively "Others" Jim in the text (Minnick 2010).

Minnick (2010) is also adept at configuring the social bind that many early African American writers found themselves in when they employed Remus orthography to represent AALD. For some, like Paul Laurence Dunbar, the use of Remus orthography presented professional conundrums from which he never fully emerged. For others, specifically Charles Chesnutt, using the Remus orthography was one way to signify on the racial and social justice issues of the time period. "Chesnutt … privately expressed a deep ambivalence toward African American vernacular speech, believing that it was a legacy of nearly universal forced illiteracy under slavery, yet he used it to create some of the most linguistically and artistically important literary representations of African American English in U.S. literary history" (Minnick 2010, 188).

Minnick (2010) and Baker (1987) argue that Chesnutt's use of Remus orthography, especially in the stories collected in *The Conjure Woman* (1899), was infused with subtle sustained critiques of White supremacy and the unchecked violence of racism during American slavery and in the Reconstruction-era South. "[I]n the guise of the plantation tradition, and especially in the camouflage of dialect, Chesnutt was free to critique the cruelest realities of slavery, including families torn apart, violence, and forced illiteracy, and thus subvert the racist agenda of the genre" (Minnick 2010, 189). Minnick's suggestion that Remus orthography can obscure the sociopolitical themes of Chesnutt's best work helps to elucidate the potential for AALD to function in the service of important social justice issues with respect to race and racism in the United States.

Rickford and Rickford (2000) pose a fundamental question with respect to literary dialectal representations of AAL: "Does it limit or liberate?" (38) The answer has been and continues to be that AALD has the potential to produce brilliant depictions of Black life on the page, but when AAL is rendered exclusively in eye dialect or Remus orthography, then the limitations of SAE orthography and the historical biases and prejudices associated with representations of AAL on the printed page can present themselves.

According to Wolfram and Thomas (2002), in their analysis of the earliest written texts featuring African American speech, "[t]he comparison of the amanuensis and the literary dialect samples strongly suggests that an emerging literary convention for AAVE [African American Vernacular English] may have influenced transcribers attempting to represent the 'literal voice' of African Americans" (18). Wolfram and Thomas (2002) establish the written representational history of Remus orthography that later informs one of Minnick's (2010) central arguments: that "[l]iterary dialect served well into the twentieth century as part of an infrastructure of ideologies that privilege standard American English" (191).

Literary critics have not shown much interest in critiquing or systematizing eye dialect. For some time now the area of literary studies has focused on theories of authorship, thematics, narrative, culture, and other macro-units or attributes that for the most part do not delve into the idiosyncrasies of grammar and grammatical representation using orthography—or the representation of linguistic elements in print, new media, and digital/electronic texts. There is also the fundamental irony of SAE orthography and its relationship to Remus orthography and other iterations of eye dialect. Generally speaking, "literature accepts the paradox of eye dialect: a misspelling which actually approximates the standard pronunciation of a word represents ignorance, while a correct spelling which is phonetically incomprehensible represents normality" (Walpole 1974, 193).

37.6 LITERARY DIALECT IN THE CLASSROOM

The concept of eye dialect comes up often in the scholarship of pedagogues who are interested in the challenges faced by students when reading eye dialect in American fiction. Garrigues (2003) challenges her students to "tune their ears" to Hurston's "written oral art" in *Their Eyes Were Watching God* (1937), hereinafter *Their Eyes*. "As with other texts thick with dialect, it is easier for students to begin by hearing the natural cadence of the spoken language than by struggling to decipher the invented spellings of the written word" (Garrigues 2003, 23). Garrigues uses a range of techniques to acclimate her students to character voices represented using eye dialect in *Their Eyes*. Students read aloud and do plenty of group-related work, but Garrigues begins the unit by playing the audiobook version of *Their Eyes*, featuring Ruby Dee. Garrigues's success in teaching students to wrestle with eye dialect and to, in effect, teach them how to become more literate, relies on hearing the African American voice in order to best understand it.

Hearing African American speech from a native speaker may be one way of "cheating" the overdeterminant limitations of Remus orthography, but Hurston's *Their Eyes* works over and against the traditional nineteenth-century framing of AAL in other ways on the page and within the orthographic context of the novel itself. Dillard (1977) and Peterson (2004) argue that Hurston's representation of early mid-twentieth century AAL benefits greatly from her use of AAL lexicon, and other less orthographically ostensible features of AAL. Minnick (2010) claims that "[t]he direct speech of the characters and the free indirect discourse that distinguishes the dialectally represented narration … are as striking for their lyrical and poetic expressions as for their reliance on distinctly dialectal grammatical and phonological features" (121). Wideman (1976) suggests that Hurston's limited use of Remus orthography is additionally offset by the situational contexts of an African American speech community. "Hurston returns dialect to its roots in Black folk speech, elaborating the context in which Black speech is the independent expression of a speech community rather than a shorthand for indicating Negro inferiority" (36).

37.7 CASE STUDIES OF REMUS ORTHOGRAPHY

Paul Laurence Dunbar's career is an important case study both because he used both Remus and SAE orthography and he publicly lamented the ways in which expectations that he would write in "Negro dialect" as well as the responses to when he did or did not had a negative impact on his sense of himself as a writer. In a short story titled "Anner 'Lizer's Stumblin' Block," published in a collection of stories titled *Folks from Dixie* (Dunbar [1898] 2008), Dunbar's sophisticated approach to navigating the politics of orthography is on full display. "Anner 'Lizer's Stumblin' Block" is about a plantation community in Kentucky at a time when enslaved Black folk are becoming more and more religious. Dunbar opens the narrative by articulating the vast visual contrast of the white and gray wintery landscape with the dark slave cabins that are foregrounded in the opening scene. The story's main character, Anner 'Lizer, is the most attractive woman in the community. The story chronicles her Christian conversion narrative, a process that is stymied over the course of several days because of her preoccupation with the fact that her love interest, Sam Merritt, does not seem to have any interest in the church, the daily revivals, or religion itself.

The use of orthography in the short story mirrors the stark contrast of the narrative's opening scene. Dunbar's narrator delivers the story in formal SAE prose: "[a]t a distance from the house the cabins of Negroes stretched away in a long, broken black line that stood out in bold relief against the extreme whiteness of their surroundings" (3). The speech of all of his Black characters, however, is portrayed using Remus orthography. Near the narrative's conclusion, Anner 'Lizer says the following to Sam: "Sam, you's my stumblin' block in de high-road to salvation; I's be'n tryin' to git 'ligion fu' fou' nights, an' I cain't do it jes' on yo' 'count; I prays an' I prays, an' jes' as I's a'mos' got it, jes' as I begin to heah de cha'iot wheels a-rollin', yo' face comes right in" (14). These "broken black lines" on the white printed page construct an inferior frame around Black subjectivity and pander to Dunbar's White audience's senses of Black intellectual and linguistic capabilities even as readers are forced to acknowledge Dunbar's felicity with SAE. The ironic juxtaposition here is, I believe, deliberate and ingenious: the powerful analogy of "broken black lines" against a white backdrop as the archetypal symbolic image of Remus orthography—broken black lines representing African American Language on the white printed page.

Dunbar's shifting orthography performs his own internal tensions as a nineteenth-century Black writer, limited by the expectations of the (White) literary market and the conventional sense of Black humanity, yet, in his work he is able to work through some of these tensions. AALD represented by Remus orthography in "Anner 'Lizer's Stumblin' Block" functions much like the mask "that grins and lies" from Dunbar's perennially anthologized poem, "We Wear the Mask" (1896). One aspect of the story subtly unveils the ways in which Dunbar uses Remus orthography and the quaint nature of his characters as a mask that ultimately subverts those readers who may miss some of the nuances of narration. The narrator describes the intensity of a religious meeting as follows: "[t]he weirdness of the scene and the touch of mysticism in the services—though of course she did not *analyse* it thus—reached her emotional nature and stirred her being to its depths" (5; emphasis added). Dunbar works within the narrative to establish the situational context for the religious themes of the story. He uses terms like "mourner" and "seekin" to refer to congregants on the verge of conversion and the process by which "mourners" find God, respectively. This moment where he analyzes the mystic aspect of the religious rituals that he narrates is an important one—the use of AAL, even in the form of Remus orthography has established the narrator's credibility. No need to belabor this here, but one pervasive stereotype applied to Black folk in the nineteenth century are the histrionic ways in which religious rituals were carried out. What Dunbar does here, is establish the narrator's rationality over and against the less rational, less enlightened Anner 'Lizer, and in so doing he re-inscribes the effects of Remus orthography's framing of Black subjectivity as inferior to his White readers. But the mask, as it were, rests on the face of the nearly homophonous "analyse" and the protagonists' name—Anner 'Lizer—rendered in Remus orthography throughout the narrative. Anner 'Lizer, is actually able to discern the mystic qualities of these religious ceremonies—evidenced in her patience with her own delayed conversion and her willingness to accept (and rationalize) the mysterious appeal of a light that draws her into the forest/wood for the conclusion of the short story. Dunbar's use of a homophonic mask deepens the complexity of what it means for Black writers to write in Remus orthography and for readers to parse the narratological implications inherent in this usage. Dunbar is not alone in his strategic use of Remus orthography. Tricomi (2006) provides excellent insight and analysis into how Harriet Ann Jacobs deployed Remus orthography and varied her use of it for sociopolitical reasons. He describes Jacob's use of dialect in *Incidents of the Life of a Slave Girl* (1861) as "supple ... [responding] to a range of artistic—sometimes even poetic—and ethical purposes" (625).

Wideman's (1976) assessment of the effects of AAL in American literature marks a counter-hegemonic response to the tyranny of Remus orthography by Black writers in the latter half of the twentieth century. "In the 1960s a reaction against this prison house of language led Black poets to obscenity, to experiments with sounds and screams, street talk, to an alienation from the text so that written language was replaced by oral performance, the shout, chant, the weaving of musical instruments with the human voice" (35). Considering the works of Amiri Baraka, Toni Morrison, Ralph Ellison, and others, Wideman might agree that the interpolation of AAL into literature was yet another response to the hegemonic force of Remus orthography.

Wideman's (1976) listing of the counter-hegemonic forcefulness of oral forms of AAL highlights the ways in which an author's return to Remus orthography can be offset in a variety of performance milieus. Wideman takes his own analysis into account in *Philadelphia Fire* (1990), a surreal retelling of the 1985 firebombing of a residential neighborhood in west Philadelphia. In it, Wideman abandons the conventions of Remus orthography by minimizing the use of apostrophes as diacritics that highlight phonetic absence. For example, he uses *youall* for *y'all* and *-in* instead of *in'* for words ending in *–ing* to indicate "g-dropping." This amounts to a fundamental adjustment away from the limitations of Remus orthography and the overemphasis on the visual that eye dialect requires.

According to Wideman (1976), racism in America, especially in the publishing industry, promoted the use of Remus orthography as yet another way to uphold White supremacy. Wideman singles out Paul Laurence Dunbar, James Weldon Johnson, and Charles Chesnutt as writers who, working within the limitations established by the market for Remus orthography, wrestle with the ways in which SAE orthography works to contain the Black voice. All three of these writers were "expected" to write in AAL and all three of them resisted the orthographic strictures of the Black speaking subject generated via the nineteenth-century White imagination.

Notwithstanding Wideman's comments and criticisms, the use of Remus orthography by contemporary Black writers remains a contested issue. Walpole (1974) argues that "in the common miracle of transcribing conversation, eye dialect can be linguistically illogical, socially offensive, and yet dramatically indispensable" (191). Consider the following excerpt from Sapphire's (1996) novel, *Push*, which was made into a popular film titled *Precious* (2009):

(1) This the biggest thing to happen to Precious P. Jones in her life.
(2) I got the AIDS virus.
(3) Thas what tess say.
(4) We sitting in circle thas when I tell class.
(5) Jus' like it's cornflakes for breakfast (93).

The deleted copulas in lines (1) and (4) as well as the consonant cluster reduction in line (3) are linguistically ungrammatical in SAE and its orthography, but these features are grammatical in AAL. The scene, like so many in *Push* (and *Precious*), can be interpreted as socially offensive not just because of Precious's blunt blurting out of her health condition but because readers and viewers know that she contracted the virus from an incestuous rape (i.e., she was raped by her father) sanctioned by her own mother. Readers are also aware of the fact that Precious's language issues result at least in part as a consequence of her inadequate education. The dramatic indispensability of the language and literacy issues for the novel is difficult to debate considering the ways in which Sapphire commits to dramatizing Precious's illiteracy via Remus orthography, and, generally speaking, the author's deliberate crafting of an idiolect for her main character that puts into bold relief the systematic underpinnings of AAL more broadly speaking.

37.8 CONCLUSION

The long history of AALD in American literature suggests that the racial background of the author, the historic period, and the sociohistorical context of the narrative all work to determine the sensibility of and the rationale behind literary dialectal usage. That said, there are significant orthographic, racial, and sociopolitical distinctions between what Joel Chandler Harris does with Remus orthography versus what Zora Neale Hurston does with it.

For Wideman (1976), early uses of Remus orthography reflect the confrontation between African orality and European (or Eurocentric) literacy. "The literary frame in which dialect appeared was a natural extension of the colonial relationship assuring that the interface would be rendered in the terms of the literate culture" (35). Wideman is particularly concerned with how Black speech might evolve in Black voice, in terms of the Black speaking subject, wrestling with questions as to how Black speech will ultimately realize itself as literary language. The tradition of AALD that dominated nineteenth-century American literature (i.e., Remus orthography) and what scholars like Dillard (1977) consider to be an essential representation of Black subjectivity was, according to Wideman (1976), a systematic, calculated effort to re-establish White supremacy in language just as Black writers were mastering the formal properties of the English language and its attendant orthography.

The aural and oral tokens of AAL underscore the literal limitations of Remus orthography. This is why teachers will find success when their students hear Ruby Dee on the audiobook for *Their Eyes* before they read it. It is also why *Precious*, the film version of Sapphire's *Push*, can enjoy some critical insulation from the kinds of analysis that Wideman levies at Remus orthography in African American literature. Ultimately the rules for Remus orthography are quite simple. Black voices are best represented by actual Black voices, orally and orthographically. SAE orthography was not designed (or developed) to reflect or represent Black linguistic subjectivity and thus AAL enjoys its evolution into AALD most effectively in those contexts where the aural is not overde-termined by the literal. SAE orthography has the benefit of allowing various pronun-ciations for a single spelling, but if readers/writers want to hear a nonstandard variety the orthography must be adjusted in some way, hence the need for AALD in American literature.

African American authors will likely continue to use Remus orthography strategi-cally. Many of them, including Wideman, Toni Morrison, and Colson Whitehead, among others, will opt to distance their works from Remus orthography by minimiz-ing diacritics and focus on less orthographically visible ways to represent AAL on the printed page; while others, like Sapphire, will choose to embrace Remus orthography for important artistic reasons. But without a systematic way of representing AAL in lit-erature, the reasons why authors make these decisions is where the issues with AALD will remain for the foreseeable future.

REFERENCES

Allen, William Frances. 1865. "The Negro Dialect." *The Nation* 1: 744–45.

Allen, William Frances, Charles Pickard Ware, and Lucy McKim Garrison. 1967. *Slave Songs of the United States*. New York: Simpson.

Baker, Houston A., Jr. 1987. *Modernism and the Harlem Renaissance*. Chicago: University of Chicago.

Chesnutt, Charles W. 1899. *The Conjure Woman*. New York: Houghton, Mifflin and Company.

Dillard, J. L. 1977. *Lexicon of Black English*. New York: Seabury Press.

Dunbar, Paul Laurence. 1896. "We Wear the Mask." *Lyrics of Lowly Life*. New York: Dodd, Mead, and Company.

———. [1898] 2008. *Folks from Dixie*. Reprint, New York: Barnes & Noble.

Garrigues, Lisa. 2003. "Porch Talk: Reading Their Eyes Were Watching God." *English Journal* 93(1): 21–28.

Hadler, Jeffrey. 1998. "Remus Orthography: The History of the Representation of the African American Voice." *Journal of Folklore Research* 35 (2): 99–126.

Harris, Joel Chandler. 1881. *Uncle Remus, His Songs and His Sayings: The Folk-Lore of the Old Plantation*. New York: D. Appleton and Company.

Hurston, Zora Neale. 1937. *Their Eyes Were Watching God*. Philadelphia: J. B. Lippincott.

Jacobs, Harriet Ann. 1861. *Incidents in the Life of a Slave Girl*. Boston: Thayer & Eldridge.

Lanehart, Sonja L., ed. 2001. *Sociocultural and Historical Contexts of African American English*. Amsterdam: John Benjamins.

Levine, Lawrence W. 1977. *Black Culture and Black Consciousness: Afro-American Folk Thought from Slavery to Freedom*. New York: Oxford University.

Macaulay, Ronald. 2006. *The Social Art: Language and Its Uses*. New York: Oxford University.

Minnick, Lisa Cohen. 2004. *Dialect and Dichotomy: Literary Representations of African American Speech*. Tuscaloosa: University of Alabama.

———. 2010. "Dialect Literature and English in the USA: Standardization and National Linguistic Identity." In *Varieties of English in Writing: The Written Word as Linguistic Evidence*, edited by Raymond Hickey, 163–96. Amsterdam: John Benjamins.

Peterson, James. 2004. "Linguistic Identity and Community in American Literature." In *Language in the USA: Themes for the Twenty-First Century*, edited by Edward Finegan and John R. Rickford, 430–44. Cambridge: Cambridge University.

Precious: Based on the Novel Push by Sapphire. 2009. Produced and directed by Lee Daniels. Santa Monica, CA: Lionsgate. Film.

Rickford, John Russell, and Rickford, Russell John. *Spoken Soul: The Story of Black English*. New York: Wiley, 2000.

Sapphire. 1996. *Push*. New York: Vintage Contemporaries/Vintage Books.

Tricomi, Albert H. 2006. "Dialect and Identity in Harriet Jacobs's Autobiography and Other Slave Narratives." *Callaloo* 29 (2): 619–33.

Twain, Mark. 1884. *The Adventures of Huckleberry Finn*. London: Chatto & Windus.

———. 1895. "Fenimore Cooper's Literary Offenses." *North American Review* 161: 1–13.

Walpole, Jane Raymond. 1974. "Eye Dialect in Fictional Dialogue." *College Composition and Communication* 25 (2): 191–96.

Wideman, John Edgar. 1976. "Frame and Dialect: The Evolution of the Black Voice in American Literature." *American Poetry Review* 5 (5): 34–37.

———. 1990. *Philadelphia Fire*. New York: Vintage Contemporaries/Vintage Books.

Wolfram, Walt, and Erik R. Thomas. 2002. *The Development of African American English*. Malden, MA: Blackwell.

CHAPTER 38

···

AFRICAN AMERICAN
LANGUAGE AND
BLACK POETRY

···

HOWARD RAMBSY II AND
BRIANA WHITESIDE

38.1 INTRODUCTION

···

WE offer a discussion of Black poetry and how the art form corresponds to African American linguistic practices. We discuss how Black poets utilize the African American lexicon, proper nouns and historical figures, and verbal practices in order to present ideas. In addition, we point out the ways that African Americans express themselves by drawing on the poetic inspiration of Black poets. We also describe how Black poetry has influenced the development of Spoken Word Poetry and rap. Overall, we demonstrate, by using examples from a wide range of poems, that Black poetry serves as a repository of African American Language (AAL) and, conversely, that AAL serves as a vital storehouse of expressions and ideas for Black poets.

For the purposes of this essay, we use *Black* and *African American* interchangeably to refer to people of African descent in the United States. We refer to poems by African Americans as *Black poetry*. As such, Black poetry constitutes an expansive, interrelated body of works that are typically lineated artistic expressions presented in stanzas and with the use of various poetic devices. We define African American Language as the broad, diverse set of linguistic practices employed by Black people. As Geneva Smitherman has noted, "Black Language is Euro-American speech with an Afro-American meaning, nuance, tone, and gesture" (1977, 2).

38.2 The Lexicon/Vocabulary of AAL in Black Poetry

African American poets have collectively adopted, adapted, and repurposed literally millions of words and phrasings based on varieties of American English and African American Language (AAL) in order to communicate a range of ideas in their works. Poets have used distinct language to express Black pride, pay tribute to revered historical figures, document significant events, and articulate grievances. Therefore, their poems absorb and display the full system of AAL. According to Stephen Henderson in his well-known book, *Understanding the New Black Poetry: Black Speech and Black Music as Poetic References* (1973), African Americans use *mascon words*, or words that resonate in powerful and psychic ways for insiders while seeming neutral for outsiders (44). Mascon words, including general cultural terms, proper nouns, and place names, as well as culturally derived syntax and metaphors, signal the abundant interconnections between AAL and Black poetry.

In efforts to convincingly present AAL practices on the page, poets enact several different approaches. They adopt the personas of notable historical figures, project militant tones and rhetoric, and display Black pride. Their poems approximate AAL patterns, and they routinely signify and utilize metaphors that might resonate with African Americans. In addition, Black poets incorporate street speech in their works as a way of highlighting connections to urban or vernacular Black folks. Accordingly, a considerable amount of Black poetry resembles or showcases African American speech and speaking patterns.

Many of the most popular and historically significant poems by Black poets contain words frequently used in multiple Black discourses. Black poets have regularly employed terms signaling community or kinship, including *sister, brother, mama, our, us*, and *we* in their works. They have also utilized racial identifiers, including *Negro, Black, White*, and *darker brother*, as well as terms such as *slave, cool*, and *hip*. Further, terminology associated with Black musical discourses like *jazz, blues, funky, groovin*, and *rap* have repeatedly appeared in Black poetry. Black poets have collectively echoed and re-presented a truly massive amount of words uttered in multiple African American communities. The sheer number of Black-inflected words presented in poems by Maya Angelou, Amiri Baraka, Gwendolyn Brooks, Lucille Clifton, Paul Laurence Dunbar, Nikki Giovanni, Robert Hayden, Langston Hughes, Larry Neal, Sonia Sanchez, Margaret Walker, and dozens more—not to mention the frequency in which poems by the writers showcasing such words are reprinted—gave shape and definition to the genre formerly known as "Negro American poetry" and what we now refer to interchangeably as *Black poetry* and *African American poetry*.

The recurring words that appear in Black poetry, in fact, signify the multiplicity of African American linguistic practices. Dunbar and Hughes channel the vernacular language use of the African American community. The figures who appear in Margaret Walker's poems such as Molly Means, Kissie Lee, Stagolee, and Poppa Chicken reflect her links to Black folk speech, that is, informal ways of talking among African Americans, and culture, while Melvin B. Tolson's references in *Libretto for the Republic of Liberia* (1953) to Diogenes of Sinope, Banquo from Shakespeare's *Macbeth*, Gaea, and Oedipus, among others, reflect the ability of a Black poet to infuse Latin, Greek, and English ideas and terminology into verse. The discourse of militancy that permeates poems by Haki Madhubuti, Sonia Sanchez, Askia Toure, and several others associated with the Black Arts Movement of the 1960s and 1970s indicates a capability among Black poets of adapting Black Power rhetoric. In addition, Tracie Morris's discussions in her poem "Project Princess" (2000) of "weaved hair," "shrimp earrings," and teeth with "gold initials" and Saul Williams's mentions of breakbeats, basslines, and niggaz in his poem "Ohm" (2000) reveal that poets have been interested in speaking contemporary languages of Black style and Hip Hop. Taken together, even Black poetry in English comprises an incredible range and diversity.

The words poets use also correspond to the many ways that we describe one another and our cultural practices. In her poem "Raised by Women" (2003), Kelly Norman Ellis mentions "high yellow" and "mocha brown" women, references to popular skin tone labels that we use, and she also references well-known cuisines such as chitlins and cornbread; a Black dance, the Boogaloo; and a hairstyle, the afro (5). The lead female protagonist in Kevin Young's volume *Black Maria* (2007) goes by the name Delilah *Redbone*—her last name also referring to a popular term that Black people use to refer to Black women with a type of light skin tone. In their poems, countless Black poets refer to themselves and companions as "black" or "Black" and thus highlight a preferred racial identity marker for large numbers of people. The presence of popular African American cultural signifiers throughout Black poetry reveals the extents to which Black poets wish to link to AAL and idioms.

38.3 AFRICAN AMERICAN PROPER NOUNS IN BLACK POETRY: HISTORICAL FIGURES

Over the last fifty years, in particular, poets have collectively taken proper nouns and nicknames in AAL and made those words central to Black poetry. The names of revered historical figures such as Frederick Douglass, Harriet Tubman, Nat Turner, Malcolm X, Rosa Parks, Sojourner Truth, and Angela Davis appear in volume and poem titles as well as in the body of individual works. Hughes's "Frederick Douglass: 1817-1895" (1966); Dudley Randall's "Frederick Douglass and the Slave Breaker" (1972); Vivee Francis's "Frederick Douglass Speaks before the Anti-Mexican War Abolitionists" (2006); Tim Seibles's "Douglass, a Last Letter" (2006); and Evie Shockley's "From the Lost Letters of Frederick Douglass" (2011b) and "(Mis)takes One to Know One" (2011a) all reference the venerable ex-slave, Frederick Douglass. Poets also regularly namecheck musicians, presenting James Brown, Miles Davis, Charlie Parker, and Aretha Franklin in poems. Dozens of poets have also mentioned saxophonist John Coltrane, often referred to by his nickname, Trane. In her poem "How Long has Trane Been Gone" (2002), Jayne Cortez, for instance, mourns the admired jazz musician while maximizing the pun on his name as a locomotive. At intervals in the poem, she writes, "How long how long has that Trane been gone" (Cortez 2002, 13-15). The regular and widespread appearances of names and proper nouns throughout the body of Black poetry constitute one of the genre's most indelible direct ties to AAL. Generally, Black speakers and poets apparently display cultural knowledge and pay tribute to revered figures by frequently uttering their names.

38.3.1 Historical Markers and Place Names

Historical markers and place names are important referents in African American discourses. Canonical poems have referenced Africa, the American South, New York City, and Chicago to track migration patterns as well as the popularity of those sites in conversations about Black history and culture. Langston Hughes's "The Negro Speaks of Rivers" (1921) is one of the most widely anthologized poems documenting several sites, including the Euphrates, the Nile, the Congo, Mississippi, and New Orleans, that reverberate with Black cultural heritage, that is, geographic locations where peoples of African descent have resided. Hughes's reference to "rivers ancient" acknowledges a Black past, and his observations that "my soul has grown deep like the rivers" highlight a long-running intellectual and spiritual heritage (1921, 71). Hughes maps the migration patterns of a people across time and space through geographically specific and culturally distinct place names. His words signal the locations where Black peoples have been or imagined themselves.

38.4 AAL Syntax and Semantics in Black Poetry

The copula, or variants of the verb *to be*, constitutes one of the most salient aspects of AAL grammar. According to Geneva Smitherman, "*be* is omitted when the statement applies only to the present or when it has the effect of communicating an all-time truth" (1977, 264). The omission of the copula in AAL allows speakers to highlight direct relationships between what they are describing. For instance, the speakers in Gwendolyn Brooks' "We Real Cool" (1960) adhere to the AAL practice by omitting the copula "are" between "we" and "real cool" (i.e., "we Ø real cool"), thus indicating the timelessness of their style (73). The speakers are not merely "like" someone cool or "as" cool as someone else; instead, they are the very embodiment of coolness. The exclusion of *like* and *as* in Brooks's famous phrasing "we real cool" corresponds directly to popular Black syntax.

Black poets have long deployed word phrasings that echo or channel AAL practices. Word pairings like *Black man, Black woman, bad man, bad woman, the blues,* and *Hip Hop* in poetry reflect long-standing engagements by Black poets with phrases often spoken in African American communities. Margaret Walker's poem "For My People" (1942) remains so popular, in part, because of the extended and ongoing histories of Black folks referring to members of common racial or ethnic groups as "my people." Walker's celebration of and offering "for" her people rests on a subtle yet resonant word pairing that signifies kinship among diverse groups of people "in the clay and dust and sand of Alabama" and "thronging 47th Street in Chicago and Lenox / Avenue in New York and Rampart Street in New / Orleans" (1942, 6–7). Walker's "people" comprise a vast network of citizens in diverse geographic spaces across the country, and by referring to African Americans as simply "my people," she displays senses of familiarity and spiritual kinship.

Walker's warm tribute to "my people" stands out and contrasts the popular utterance "my people, my people" often spoken, as Zora Neale Hurston among others has explained, when Black people are embarrassed or ashamed of public actions by other Black people (1942, 216). When and if a group of Black people exhibits problematic behavior that seems to confirm negative stereotypes, other, ostensibly more refined, Black people might look on, shake their heads in disapproval, and quietly say in frustration, "my people, my people." Walker's recurring "my people" resonates so strongly with some readers because of their awareness of the gloomy "my people, my people." Many of the more creative or attentive Black poets demonstrate and utilize familiar African American word pairings in their works. According to Baraka in his poem "Jungle Jim Flunks His Screen Test," African Americans involved in verbal rituals such as the dozens sometimes added a word in front of "ugly" to intensify insults, referring to rivals as "dirty ugly, sick ugly, devil ugly, death ugly" (2004, 24). Baraka's "ugly" additions and Walker's "my people" signal the range of possibilities for word pairings based on AAL that poets have employed.

In an effort to speak to "the people," Black poets often speak like the people. They infuse mascon words and commonly used African American phrases and proper nouns in their poems and, thus, connect to multiple Black American linguistic discourses. Their poems preset culturally distinct descriptors and adaptation of AAL practices such as the omission of the copula. As a result, the words and wording of many Black poems reflect and display dimensions of AAL. Furthermore, Black poetry represents a deep and long engagement among large numbers of poets with AAL in its manifold permutations.

38.5 AFRICAN AMERICAN LANGUAGE AS BLACK POETIC INSPIRATION

The language patterns and practices of African Americans have long inspired the compositions of Black poets. The prevalence of persona poems, for instance, where poets assume the first-person perspectives of a range of historical figures and African American characters, reflects the degrees to which writers have sought to emulate a variety of Black speakers. Brooks emulates the street talk of boys in "We Real Cool" (1959). Hughes adopts the point of view of a woman passing on advice to her child in his poem "Mother to Son" (1922), and Hughes takes on the voice of the outspoken Madam Alberta K. Johnson. As Hughes biographer Arnold Rampersad has noted, the Johnson character was "an assertive, brassy Harlem heroine" (2002, 78). In one poem, Hughes's character states that "the Madam stands for business" (Rampersad 1994, 301). In another poem, Hughes's character says,

> I don't
> give a damn!
> Leave me and my name
> Just like I am! (1994, 356)

The Madam Alberta K. Johnson poems allow Hughes to explore and project a representative or stereotypical forceful Black woman character, one whose speech is candid, authoritative, and sassy.

Modern and contemporary poets have often assumed the voices of ex-slaves in their poems and participated in the African American verbal art of talking back. Cultural critic bell hooks noted that in African American communities " 'back talk' and 'talking back' meant speaking as an equal to an authority figure" (1989, 5). Talking back, noted hooks, "meant daring to disagree and sometimes it just meant having an opinion" (1989, 5). Elizabeth Alexander's poem "The Venus Hottentot" (1990), where she takes on the perspective of indentured servant Saartjie Baartman, may have resonated with so many readers because they appreciated the extent to which her sentiments corresponded to the back talk of African American linguistic discourse. With confidence, like Hughes's Madam Alberta K. Johnson, Alexander's Baartman says,

> I speak
> English. I speak Dutch. I speak
> a little French as well, and
> languages Monsieur Cuvier [the scientist observing her body]
>   will never know have names (2010, 6)

When Opal Palmer Adisa adopts the persona of the insurrectionist Nat Turner, she announces that

> i would do it again
> plot and plan
> and kill too (2006, 14)

Apparently, speaking in the voices of Baartman and Turner inspired Alexander and Adisa, respectively, and large numbers of other poets as well, to exhibit the defiant choices of words and tone that they imagined emanating from the mouths or at least the minds of back-talking Black folks.

Malcolm X was arguably the single most influential speaker for Black poets during the 1960s and 1970s. As a charismatic Black Nationalist figure whose speeches were infused with militancy, intellectualism, Black pride, and humor, Malcolm served as a powerful muse for countless Black poets during the 1960s and 1970s. In fact, shortly after Malcolm's assassination in February 1965, groups of Black poets, including Amiri Baraka and Larry Neal, began organizing in Harlem what would become known as the Black Arts Movement, a wide-ranging African American literary and cultural enterprise that placed Malcolm's Black Nationalist ideas at its core. "If you want to grasp the importance of Malcolm X," observed editor and Black Arts contributor Joe Goncalves in 1966, "compare the late writings of Sonia Sanchez or Imamu [Amiri] Baraka with their early, pre-Malcolm works" (quoted in Johnson and Johnson 1979, 185). Evidently, Malcolm's philosophies, public persona, and dynamic speaking style inspired dozens of Black poets to take similar approaches in the composition and performance of their works. Malcolm X's (1963) interest in talking "right down to earth in a language that everybody here can easily understand" and his capabilities of merging street talk and professorial discourses emerge from and link to multiple African American linguistic practices.

Sonia Sanchez's question in her poem "blk/rhetoric" about

> . . . who's gonna
> take all the young/long/haired/
> natural/brothers and sisters
> and let them
>
> grow. . .

assist them in recognizing their self-importance, and prepare them to move in "revolutionary/lines/toward the enemy" sounds like a phrasing out of a Malcolm X or Black Power speech (1969, 64). Baraka's poem "SOS" also corresponds to nationalist discourse as the poet offers the dispatch:

> Black People, come in, wherever you are, urgent, calling
> You, calling all Black people
> calling all Black people, come in, Black people, come
> on in (1971, 181)

In his poem "Notes from a Guerilla Diary" (1972), Askia Toure notes that "I wanted to be an artist"; however, that was "before revolution turned me/towards/Islam and Malcolm's eyes glowing with compassion" (220). Not coincidentally, a rather large number of poems expressing Black militancy appeared during the Black Arts Movement, which Larry Neal referred to as the "aesthetic and spiritual sister of the Black Power concept" (1968, 29). Poets clearly found inspiration in the language of Black Power and the discourses of Black Nationalist activism.

The strong senses of Black pride that pervade AAL also emerge in the poetry. Poets frequently highlight the aesthetic and cultural splendor of African Americans. Helene Johnson's (1927, 1353) description of a "disdainful and magnificent" African American in "Sonnet to a Negro in Harlem" and the portrayal of a cypress-like and impervious sister in "I am a Black Woman" (2003, 1851) by Mari Evans reflect how poets routinely utilize words to celebrate and praise African Americans. In a celebration of distinctive, culturally prominent body features, Patricia Smith's "Hip-Hop Ghazal" (2007) gives love to "us brown girls," "swinging blue hips," and "ringing true hips," and Lucille Clifton's "Homage to my Hips" (2012) offers tribute to "mighty hips" that "have never been enslaved" (198). Sterling Brown's "Ma Rainey" (1932); Tyehimba Jess's volume *Leadbelly* (2005), devoted to the legendary folk singer; Mitchell L. H. Douglass's *Cooling Board: A Long-Playing Poem* (2009); and Monica Hand's *Me and Nina* (2012), which pays tribute to Nina Simone, are indicative of the tendency of poets to celebrate African American musicians. A substantial number of Black people have long spoken with tremendous "race pride" or cultural affirmation, and poets have clearly taken note, collectively producing expansive bodies of work projecting and preserving that sense of pride.

38.5.1 Signifying in Black Poetry

Signifying constitutes a time-honored and playful art form in African American communities, and not surprisingly, poets interested in the vibrancy and power of AAL regularly incorporate such verbal practices of slyly and creatively communicating ideas to outwit a rival and entertain audiences. "Signifying poetry holds special fascination for me," noted poet Carolyn Rodgers. "Signifying is a way of saying the truth that hurts with a laugh, a way of capping on (shutting up) someone" (1969, 14). In addition, signifying allows speakers to illustrate linguistic and intellectual dexterity by showcasing abilities to reference multiple people, events, and experiences with minimal word use. Phillis Wheatley's remarks in her poem "On Being Brought from Africa to America" (1773) can be read as a sly critique of her primarily White audience. She observes that although "Some view our sable race with scornful eye," they should remember that "*Christians, Negros,* black as *Cain,* / May be refin'd, and join th' angelic train" (Wheatley 2003, 219–20). That an enslaved woman is covertly reminding her White audience how to be better Christians could definitely be read as her signifying. The speaker of Ishmael Reed's ([1976] 1989) poem "Flight to Canada" cleverly signifies throughout a letter to his former master. At one point, he informs Massa Swille that he stole the owner's money but says,

> Don't worry
> Your employees won't miss
> It & I accept it as a
> Down payment on my back
> Wages (5)

Of course, those "employees" are slaves, and "back wages" refers to funds owed as well as the crushing weight of slave labor.

Hurston's anthropological studies led her to conclude in her essay "Characteristics of Negro Expression" (1934, 1042–43), that African Americans use visual language and analogies as tools for expressing ideas in evocative ways. Metaphorical speech and phrasings permeate African American linguistic practices, allowing Black people to draw culturally distinct parallels, evoke emotional responses, and display racial and ethnic awareness of multiple experiences. Black poets, inspired by such illustrative and reference-rich language usage, have effectively infused their works with words and phrases that draw on and correspond to popular African American metaphors. Jordan writes in her "Poem about My Rights":

> I am the history of rape
> I am the history of the rejection of who I am
> I am the history of the terrorized incarceration of
> myself (2005)

Her presentation of herself as the histories or embodiments of multiple troubling circumstances illustrates how a poet utilizes metaphors to intensify an idea.

Since the time that they were separated from their ethnic groups, chained together on slave ships, and had their communities destroyed, Black people have been inclined to establish imagined communities, referring to themselves as *us, we, brothers, sisters,* and *family.* In his book *The Slave Ship* (2007), Marcus Rediker notes that captives on ships "inaugurated a 'fictive' but very real kinship to replace what had been destroyed by their abduction and enslavement in Africa" (8). The communal language or rhetoric of kinship that permeates African American linguistic discourses, consequently, saturates Black poetry. Dunbar's "We Wear the Mask" (1895), Claude McKay's "If We Must Die" (1919), and Margaret Walker's "We Have Been Believers" (1937) all rely on the plural pronoun "we" or a sense of African American community to convey meaning. The implied Black audiences of Haki Madhubuti's "A Poem to Compliment Other Poems" (1969), Etheridge Knight's "I Sing of Shine" (1971), Saul Williams's "Ohm" (2000), and several other poems are suggestive of a communal impulse running through the language of Black poetry. The references to Africa as actual and ancestral homeland in Phillis Wheatley's "On Being Brought from Africa to America" (1773),

Countee Cullen's poem "Heritage" (1925), Langston Hughes's "The Negro Speaks of Rivers" (1921), and Tyehimba Jess's "When I Speak of Blues Be Clear" (1997) are indicative of the attention to the Black diaspora that African American poets often express. In addition, the multiple presentations of "us" in several of Baraka's poems, including "A Poem for Black Hearts" (1965), "Dope" (1979), and "In Walked Bud" (1987) indicate a familial spirit. Well versed in the art of celebrating and displaying kinship, Black poets demonstrate their interest in links among diverse groups of Black people through repeated usage and valuation of terms that evoke racial and cultural interconnectivity.

Smitherman (1977) has noted that African Americans regularly delete the final orthographic <g> in the free morpheme in words and thus end up with terms like *singin*, *hangin*, *chillin*, and *groovin*. AAL speakers forgo standard pronunciations in favor of vernacular modes of expression and thus demonstrate a mutual tone with their interlocutors. Poets interested in approximating the sound of Black speech and in the unity of communal interaction with their audiences often participate in "g-dropping" in their poems. The speaker in Langston Hughes's "Mother to Son" (1922), for example, notes that she has

> been a-climbin' on,
>
> And reachin' landin's,
>
> And turnin' corners,
>
> And sometimes goin' in the dark (87)

The tough speaker in Tyehimba Jess's "1912: blind lemon jefferson explaining to leadbelly" (2005) discusses "thieves schemin' a blind man's cash" and a rival came "back three times for a ass whuppin' only a fool could want again" (18). The "g-dropping" present in these and other poems clarify the veracity of the speakers' links to Black vernacular discourses.

John Baugh explains in *Black Street Speech: Its History, Structure, and Survival* (1983) that "street speech is the nonstandard dialect that thrives within the Black street culture" (6). Often mistakenly referred to by the public as "street slang" or "slang," vernacular varieties of AAL allow speakers to interchange personal needs and ideas comfortably, and create coded language to fit their daily lives. Baugh demonstrates that African American vernacular speech is characterized by cultural identity, flexible dialect, a sense of stylistic variations, and references to Black survival (1983, 1, 6–7). Poets interested in appealing to or displaying the features of Black life and culture in urban contexts often utilize course vernacular speech in their works. Phrases like "Hard Rock was 'known not to take no shit / From nobody,'" and "man, that's one crazy nigger" from Etheridge Knight's "Hard Rock Returns to Prison from the Hospital for the Criminal Insane" (2003, 1909–10) signal the coarse language employed by some poets in order to represent the tough and bad (as in cool) talk of Black men. The speaker in Gary Copeland Lilley's poem "Report from Marcus, the Hearse Driver for Wilson's Funeral

Home" (2004) also displays fluency in the language of the streets. "Yall know we buried Stinky today," he says.

> Some fool
>
> sprayed across the street from the church
>
> you ain't dead dawg (67)

The nickname "Stink," the awareness graffiti rituals after someone's death, and phrasings like "yall," "ain't," and "dawg" verify the speaker's and Lilley's connections to the knowledge and language of the streets.

38.6 BLACK POETRY AS INSPIRATION AND REPOSITORY FOR AFRICAN AMERICAN LINGUISTIC PRACTICE

On January 20, 2009, even causal African American observers were likely aware what Reverend Joseph Lowery was invoking during his benediction at President Barack Obama's first inauguration. "God of our weary years. God of our silent tears," he said. "Thou who hast brought us thus far along the way." He went on to quote what was for millions of us easily recognized as the final verse of the Black national anthem, which for more than 100 years now has been sung by African American school children and attendees at cultural events all across the country. "Lift Every Voice and Sing" (1899) by James Weldon Johnson is widely experienced and performed as a song; however, the anthem began as merely a poem. The journeys from poem to song to national anthem to the opening words of a benediction for the nation's first Black president suggest something about the moving and inspiring power of African American verse. In addition, the attention to history, the display of a communal tone, and the summoning of cultural pride in "Lift Every Voice and Sing" reveal how poetic words and wording can serve as a celebration and repository of AAL.

Although poets have long found considerable inspiration in AAL, speakers and performers have in turn been inspired by Black poetry. Consider that Paul Laurence Dunbar, Langston Hughes, Maya Angelou, and Nikki Giovanni, for example, are more than simply poets. They are beloved cultural figures who initially gained wide attention because of their perceived achievements as poets and writers. Commentators routinely refer to Hughes as the "Poet Laureate of Black America," and the existence of dozens of middle schools and high schools named after Dunbar in Black-populated areas across the country testify to how highly he is regarded among African Americans. The proper nouns *Dunbar, Wheatley, Hughes, Baraka,*

Maya, and *Angelou* signify the names of prominent Black poets, and those names also serve as mascon words that evoke figures or even brands that carry value well beyond discourses of poetry.

38.7 BLACK WOMEN IN BLACK POETRY

Angelou's poetry is rarely, if ever, a focal point of scholarly inquiry, and she is almost never mentioned as a significant influence among contemporary formal poets. Nevertheless, Angelou was arguably one of the most well-known and adored poets in the world. Two of her poems, "Phenomenal Woman" (1978a) and "Still I Rise" (1978b), have been, for decades, recited and read at African American cultural programs such as pageants and talent competitions. Black girls and young Black women aspire to become the confident woman described in Angelou's "Phenomenal Woman" by assuming her persona and uttering her words. The poem is widely performed because the speaker projects an audacious sense of confidence that showcases Black pride and a celebration of a woman's agency and grandeur. Angelou's "Still I Rise" presents a speaker who has been maligned "in history / With your bitter, twisted lies" and trampled on "in the very dirt (1994, 163). Despite these and a series of other degradations, she remains resilient and rises. When readers perform the poems for audiences, they convey Angelou's self-assured tones and project themselves as powerfully ascendant.

Similar to Angelou's two poems, Giovanni's "Ego-Tripping" (1973) has also been a mainstay among young Black women participants in cultural programs, as they have proudly taken on the persona of the braggadocios speaker in the poem. Giovanni first recorded a reading of "Ego-Tripping" in 1971 with the New York Community Choir at Canaan Baptist Church in Harlem for her album *Truth Is on Its Way* (1971). In 1973, the poem was printed in her book *ego-tripping and other poems*, with illustrations by George Ford. For Black people, especially young Black women, to take on the persona of Giovanni's speaker means embodying an eternal, bold, and shape-shifter who was "born in the congo," "built the sphinx," created the Nile River, "sowed diamonds in my back yard" (2–3) turned herself into Jesus, and sailed around the world. Giovanni's speaker is far more than a strong Black woman. She is a supernatural force with an incredible yet delightful ego. For decades now, African American reader-performers have found "Ego-tripping" empowering, while audiences have viewed those performing the piece as phenomenal women. The popularity of Giovanni's and Angelou's poems among Black women and general audiences over the years are a testament to the notion that poems possessing a richness of culturally distinct metaphors and displaying empowering and resilient tones can inspire the language practices that African Americans choose to continually perform.

38.8 Spoken Word and Rap or Reader-Performers

The imperatives articulated among Black Arts poets of the 1960s and 1970s to perform and not simply read poems served as blueprints for the linguistic acts and verbal routines that form the basis of rap music and spoken word poetry. Audiences find the art form's signature styles, such as militant rhetoric, Hip Hop-inflected cadences and terminology, and various rhyme patterns, entertaining, culturally affirming, and useful for consciousness building. Accordingly, spoken word poetry is a prominent medium through which many Black artists choose to articulate their ideas. Jessica Care Moore earned multiple wins for her performance of "The Black Statue of Liberty" (1995) at Show Time at the Apollo competitions. Her emphatic deliveries of lines like "I wear a crown of knowledge cause i'm a conscious queen," "Taking all my people back home and breaking them mentally free," and "Go strong Black woman" were in the traditions of Malcolm's militant oratory, Giovanni's and Angelou's popular empowering poems, and Black pride rhetoric, all of which circulate in African American linguistic communities. Saul Williams's incorporation of beatboxing in his poem "Ohm" (2000) and Tracie Morris's vocal emulation of turntablism in performances of her poem "Project Princess" (2000) signal the extents to which performers adapt Hip Hop aesthetics into their works. Spoken word and its talented practitioners offer countless inspiring models for what people can do with AAL.

In addition to displaying the capabilities of reader-performers with astounding oratorical skills, Black poetry serves as a repository of AAL practices. The poems of Paul Laurence Dunbar, Langston Hughes, and Gwendolyn Brooks retain the words and phrasings of those poets as well as the speech patterns—real and imagined—of the many different characters who popularize their works. In his amusing poem "Bling Bling Blues" (2008a), Kevin Young presents a blues man turned Hip Hop star who recalls when hunger was once a major problem but that was in the days before "diamond shoes / hurting my feet" and "my wallet won't / fit my 50s" had become more pressing issues (71). "Bling Bling Blues" simultaneously records the humor of the blues, the megalomania of Hip Hop, and Young's interest in highlighting the convergence of different musical forms. More broadly, as one of our most densely populated genres, African American poetry charts the artistic language practices of hundreds of poets, many of whom have produced and performed poems that seek to capture the resonance of Black speech.

The view of Black poetry as a repository and poets as archivists or cultural historians is quite evident among the many contemporary poets who choose to produce full-length volumes documenting the lives and perspectives of enslaved people and runaways. Thylias Moss's *slave moth* (2004), Quraysh Ali Lansana's *They Shall Run: Harriet Tubman Poems* (2004), Frank X. Walker's *Buffalo Dance: The Journey of York* (2004), Natasha Trethewey's "Native Guard" from *Native Guard* (2006), Walker's *When Winter*

Come: The Ascension of York (2008), and Young's *Ardency: A Chronicle of the Amistad Rebels* (2011) represent some of the extended treatments of slavery. Those works and dozens of individual poems about slavery produced by writers over the last decade alone reflect what literary scholar Herman Beavers (2003) describes as "an impulse" by poets "to enter the archives and use its contents as sources of creativity" (182). The hundreds of contemporary poems devoted to the writings and inner thoughts of African Americans who lived over 150 years ago reveal an interest among several poets in the art and politics of retrieval as well as the representation of the past in verse. This widespread undertaking constitutes a notable series of instances where poets utilize distinct words and wording, historical figures and characters types, and treatments of history and archival sources to advance African American interests.

38.9 Conclusion

Black poets have long served as figures of inspiration in African American communities. Some of their poems are used in pageants, speech competitions, spoken word shows, scholarship essays, Black history assemblies, movies, and, as previously noted, during the benediction at the inauguration of the first Black president. Poets serve as cultural archivists who preserve and allow voices from the past to speak to present and future generations. At the same time, poets have regularly adapted and presented AAL in their works and showcased fundamental elements of African American linguistic discourse such as Black pride, culturally distinct people and place names, and significant historical events. As a result, the dynamics of AAL have become integral to the production of Black poetry while Black poetry has simultaneously been a defining muse for the practice of AAL.

References

Adisa, Opal Palmer. 2006. "Peeling Off the Skin." In *Gathering Ground: A Reader Celebrating Cave Canem's First Decade*, edited by Toi Derricotte and Cornelius Eady, 14–16. Ann Arbor: University of Michigan.

Alexander, Elizabeth. 1990. "The Venus Hottentot (1825)." In *Crave Radiance: New and Selected Poems 1990-2010*, 3–7. Minneapolis: Graywolf.

Angelou, Maya. 1978a. "Phenomenal Woman." In *And Still I Rise*. New York: Random House.

———. 1978b. "Still I Rise." In *And Still I Rise*. New York: Random House.

———. 1994. *The Collected Poems of Maya Angelou*. New York: Random House.

Baraka, Amiri. 1965. "A Poem for Black Hearts." *Negro Digest* 14 (11): 8.

———. 1971. "SOS." In *The Black Poets: An Anthology*, edited by Dudley Randall, 181. New York: Bantam Books.

———. 1979. "Dope." In *Poetry for the Advanced*. New York: Morrow.

———. 1987. "In Walked Bud." In *The Music: Reflections on Jazz and Blues*. New York: Morrow.

————. 2004. "Jungle Jim Flunks His Screen Test." Rpt. in *Somebody Blew Up America & Other Poems*, 24–27. Philipsburg, St. Martin: House of Nehesi, 2007.

Baugh, John. 1983. *Black Street Speech: Its History, Structure, and Survival*. Austin: University of Texas Press.

Beavers, Herman. 2003. "The Archival Impulse in African American Poetry; Playing in the Past." In *Rainbow Darkness: An Anthology of African American Poetry*, edited by Keith Tuma, 173–83. Oxford: Miami University.

Brooks, Gwendolyn. 1959. "We Real Cool." *Poetry* 94 (6): 373.

Brown, Sterling. 1932. "Ma Rainey." In *The Collected Poems of Sterling Brown*, edited by M. Harper, 62–63. New York: Harcourt.

Clifton, Lucile. 2012. "Homage to My Hips." In *The Collected Poems of Lucille Clifton 1965–2010*, edited by Kevin Young and Michael S. Glaser, 198. Rochester: BOA Editions.

Cortez, Jayne. 2002. *Jazz Fan Looks Back*. Brooklyn, NY: Hanging Loose.

Cullen, Countee. 1925. "Heritage." *Survey*, March 1.

Douglass, Mitchell L. H. 2009. *Cooling Board: A Long-Playing Poem*. Pasadena, CA: Red Hen Press.

Dunbar. Paul Lawrence. 1895. "We Wear the Mask." In *Majors and Minors: Poems*, by Paul Lawrence Dunbar. Toledo, OH: Hadley and Hadley.

Ellis, Kelly Norman. 2003. *Tougaloo Blues*. Chicago: Third World.

Evans, Mari. 2003. "I Am a Black Woman." In *The Norton Anthology of African American Literature*, edited by Henry Louis Gates Jr. and Nellie Y. McKay, 1851–52. New York: Norton.

Francis, Vivee. 2006. "Frederick Douglass Speaks before the Anti-Mexican War Abolitionists." In *Blue-Tail Fly*, 15. Detroit: Wayne State University Press.

Giovanni, Nikki. 1971. *Truth Is on Its Way*. New York: Right-On Records. Album.

————. 1973. *Ego-Tripping and Other Poems for Young People*. New York: Lawrence Hill.

Hand, Monica. 2012. *Me and Nina*. Farmington, MA: Alice James Books.

Henderson, Stephen, ed. 1973. *Understanding the New Black Poetry: Black Speech and Black Music as Poetic References*. New York: Morrow Quill Paperbacks.

hooks, bell. 1989. *Talking Back: Thinking Feminist, Thinking Black*. Boston: South End.

Hughes, Langston. 1921. "The Negro Speaks of Rivers." *The Crisis* 22 (2): 71.

————. 1922. "Mother to Son." *The Crisis* 25 (2): 87.

————. 1966. "Frederick Douglass: 1817–1895." *Liberator*.

Hurston, Zora Neale. 1934. "Characteristics of Negro Expression." Rpt. in *The Norton Anthology of African American Literature*, edited by Henry Louis Gates Jr. and Nellie Y. McKay, 1041–53. New York: Norton, 2003.

————. 1942. "My People, My People." *Dust Tracks on the Road*. Urbana: University of Illinois.

Jess, Tyehimba. 1997. "When I Speak of Blues Be Clear." *Cave Canem*.

————. 2005. *Leadbelly: Poems*. Seattle, WA: Wave Books.

Johnson, Abby Arthur, and Ronald Maberry Johnson. 1979. *Propaganda and Aesthetics: The Literary Politics of Afro-American Magazines*. Amherst: University of Massachusetts.

Johnson, Helene. 2003. "Sonnet to a Negro in Harlem." In *The Norton Anthology of African American Literature*, edited by Henry Louis Gates Jr. and Nellie Y. McKay, 1353. New York: Norton.

Johnson, James Weldon. 2004. "Lift Every Voice and Sing." In *James Weldon Johnson: Writings*, 874–75. New York: Library of America.

Jordan, June. 2005. "Poem about My Rights." *Poetry Foundation*. http://www.poetryfoundation.org/poem/178526.

Knight, Etheridge. 2003. "Hard Rock Returns to Prison from the Hospital for the Criminal Insane." In *The Norton Anthology of African American Literature*, edited by Henry Louis Gates Jr. and Nellie Y. McKay, 1909–910. New York: Norton.

Lansana, Quraysh Ali. 2004. *They Shall Run: Harriet Tubman Poems*. Chicago, IL: Third World Press.

Lilley, Gary Copeland. 2004. *The Subsequent Blues*. New York: Four Way Books.

Madhubuti, Haki. 1969. "A Poem to Compliment Other Poems." In *Don't Cry, Scream*. Chicago: Third World Press.

Malcolm X. 1963. "Message to the Grassroots." Speech. Detroit, Michigan, November 10.

Moore, Jessica Care. 1995. "The Black Statue of Liberty." In *Listen Up! Spoken Word Poetry*, edited by Zoe Anglesey, 59–60. New York: One World.

Morris, Tracie. 2000. "Project Princess." *Our Souls Have Grown Deep like the Rivers*. RHINO. CD.

Moss, Thylias. 2004. *Slave Moth*. New York: Persea Books.

Neal, Larry. 1968. "The Black Arts Movement." *Drama Review* 12 (Summer): 29–39.

Rampersad, Arnold. 2002. *The Life of Langston Hughes*: Volume II: *1914–1967, I Dream a World*. New York: Oxford University.

———, ed. 1994. *The Collected Poems of Langston Hughes*. New York: Vintage.

Randall, Dudley. 1972. "Frederick Douglass and the Slave Breaker." *Black World* 21 (11): 64.

Rediker, Marcus. 2007. *The Slave Ship: A Human History*. New York: Viking.

Reed, Ishmael. (1976) 1989. *Flight to Canada*. Reprint, New York: Atheneum.

Rodgers, Carolyn. 1969. "Black Poetry: Where It's at." *Negro Digest* 18 (11): 7–16.

Sanchez, Sonia. 1969. "blk/rhetoric." *Negro Digest* 18 (11): 64.

Seibles, Tim. 2006. "Douglass, a Last Letter." *Manthology: Poems on the Male Experience*, edited by Craig Crist-Evans, Roger Weingarten, and Kate Fetherston. Iowa City: University of Iowa Press.

Shockley, Evie. 2011a. "(Mis)takes One to Know One." In *The New Black*. Middletown, CT: Wesleyan.

———. 2011b. "The Lost Letters of Frederick Douglass." In *The New Black*. Middletown, CT: Wesleyan.

Smith, Patricia. 2007. "Hip-Hop Ghazal." *Poetry Foundation*. Last Modified July/August 2007.

Smitherman, Geneva. 1977. *Talkin and Testifyin*. Boston: Houghton Mifflin.

Tolson, Melvin B. 1953. *Libretto for the Republic of Liberia*. New York: Twayne.

Toure, Askia Muhammad. 1972. "Notes from a Guerilla Diary." In *Black Spirits: A Festival of New Black Poets in America*, edited by Woodie King, 220–22. New York: Vintage.

Tretheway, Natasha. 2006. "Native Guard." In *Native Guard*. Boston: Houghton Mifflin.

Walker, Frank X. 2004. *Buffalo Dance: The Journey of York*. Lexington: University Press of Kentucky.

———. 2008. *When Winter Come: The Ascension of York*. Lexington: University Press of Kentucky.

Walker, Margaret. 1937. "We Have Been Believers." In Walker 1989, 9–10.

———. 1942. "For My People." In Walker 1989, 6–7.

———. 1989. *This is My Century: New and Collected Poems*. Athens: University of Georgia.

Wheatley, Phillis. 1773. "On Being Brought from Africa to America." Reprint in *The Norton Anthology of African American Literature*, edited by Henry Louis Gates Jr. and Nellie Y. McKay, 219–20. New York: Norton, 2003.

Williams, Saul. 2000. "Ohm." *Our Souls Have Grown Deep like the Rivers*. RHINO. CD.

Young, Kevin. 2005. *Black Maria: Being the Adventures of Delilah Redbone & A.K.A. Jones*. New York: Knopf.

———. 2008a. "Bling Bling Blues." In *Dear Darkness*, 71–72. New York: Knopf.

———. 2008b. *Dear Darkness*. New York: Knopf.

———. 2011. *Ardency: A Chronicle of the Amistad Rebels*. New York: Knopf.

CHAPTER 39

....

AFRICAN AMERICAN DIVAS OF COMEDY

Staking a Claim in Public Space

....

JACQUELYN RAHMAN

39.1 INTRODUCTION

....

THE language of African American stand-up comedians is often a gauge of attitudes and beliefs that exist in the African American community as opposed to mainstream society. In the well-planned performances of socially conscious comedians, there is a distillation of semiotically powerful features that convey predetermined messages that are heavily laden with cultural knowledge and understandings (Rahman 2007, 2011). The linguistic choices that comedians make reflect a metapragmatic awareness of the social meanings that inhere in the resources available to them and their audiences, making their performances a mirror by which the community sees itself.

This chapter examines comedic narratives by Loni Love, Adele Givens, and Sherry Singleton, three socially conscious comedians who are among the few women who have become successful in performances before mixed-gender, primarily African American, audiences. The chapter shows how, working in the male-dominated field of stand-up comedy, the women boldly claim a gendered style of community language onstage as a symbol of survival (Rahman 2007) and strong female identity, using it as a resource in their strategies to overcome the unique challenges they face.

Jacobs-Huey (2006) sees African American comedic performance as a genre that both reflects and shapes the cultural understandings that African Americans have of the world and their place in it. She notes the in-group aspect of African American comedy, seeing performances of African American comedy as communal events where "audiences mark their participation in joke telling through such responses as laughter, silence, heckling, and applause" (72). African American audiences can be strongly supportive of comedic excellence, but they do not hesitate to offer negative assessments when they find a performance lacking (Rahman 2007), which is why Richard Pryor often commented that African American audiences are very difficult to please (Watkins 1999). Still, where comic performance is concerned, African American men have historically received more favorable treatment from the Black community than African American women have.

To highlight discussion of the special problems that African American women comics may face onstage, I first discuss the relatively advantaged position that African American male comic performers have traditionally occupied in the African American community. Following that, I explain the challenges that women have faced in this area before I analyze the narratives of three African American women comic performers.

39.2 Male Advantage in Public Humor

Because of the extreme vulnerability of being onstage, a comedian must begin to build solidarity and comic authority with an audience from the start of a performance (Greenbaum 1999; Rahman 2007). Solidarity is based on a perception of shared knowledge and experiences (Schilling-Estes 1998). Schilling-Estes (1998) notes that solidarity can occur when the language of a public performer evokes cultural images that the audience and performer share. Establishing solidarity allows a comedian to connect emotionally and intellectually with an audience, working to bridge the gap that normally exists between a public speaker and an audience. If a comedian is unable to build solidarity, an audience will not respond favorably no matter how clever the material may be (Greenbaum 1999; Rahman 2007). Comic authority evolves from the same African American cultural knowledge that produces solidarity. It is related to the credibility of a comedian. To project comic authority, a comedian must demonstrate knowledge of African American culture through performance content and then convey that knowledge through linguistic virtuosity and cleverness that shows understanding of the verbal traditions, values, lifestyle, culture, and concerns of the African American community.

Unlike African American women, African American men have a long tradition of performing comedy publicly in the community (Watkins 1999; Littleton 2006). This tradition provides the knowledge base for building solidarity and comic authority needed for dealing with heckling and harassment in the interactive environment of African American comedy. Going back to slavery, men created humor for slave communities, often at the expense of their masters (Cowan 2001). African American men frequently engaged in public practices such as *toasting*, which involves telling humorous long tales filled with braggadocio, and *playing the dozens*, which is a form of ritual insult similar to certain verbal practices found in West Africa (for more discussion of these terms, see Smitherman's dictionary on language use in the African American community, *Black Talk* [1994] 2000). In recent decades, features of playing the dozens have emerged in Hip Hop culture (Wald 2012), where men have also dominated.

With a centuries-old tradition of public performance, African American men in comedy have access and license to deploy a range of linguistic tools to build solidarity and comic authority. In the small, but growing, body of literature on comedy, Rickford and Rickford (2000) note that successful African American comedians call on a rich repertoire of African American discourse practices at all linguistic levels (for phonological and syntactic characteristics of language use in the African American community, see DeBose, this volume; Green and Sistrunk, this volume; Thomas, this volume; Thomas and Bailey, this volume; and Walker, this volume) in creating and practicing their craft.

Rickford and Rickford (2000) observe that men such as Red Foxx "have talked frankly about the critical role the vernacular has played in their comedy" (57). Male comedians employ grammatical and discursive features of vernacular varieties of African American Language[1] (AAL) profusely in their performances, and their use of these varieties onstage includes lexical and discourse items associated almost exclusively with men in conversation, such as *bro* and *dog/dawg* (Rahman 2012; Smitherman [1994] 2000). Aside from helping them to build solidarity, the profanity that male comedians use helps them to build solidarity and semiotically casts them as possessing a degree of toughness and street knowledge (Edwards 1996) that is helpful for establishing a simultaneously approachable persona who is street-smart and down-to-earth, yet in control.

39.3 FEMALE DISADVANTAGE IN PUBLIC HUMOR

Because they are often viewed differently from men, African American women comedians have been particularly vulnerable to heckling and harassment (Watkins 1999; Littleton 2006). As Watkins (1999) observes, historically, women of any race who have attempted a career in comedy have often experienced severe public censure, but African American women who have pursued careers in stand-up comedy have faced an intersectional mix of gender and race-related challenges. The extreme gender-based difficulties they have faced from male audience members, as well as fellow male comedians, have caused a number of African American women to avoid or leave stand-up comedy (Littleton 2006). Bertice Berry, a Ph.D. who left academia to become a stand-up comedian, describes the sexism and harassment she experienced, which contributed her decision to leave the comedy circuit (personal communication, March 9, 2002). Television personality, Sherri Shepherd, cites the thick skin required for success as a stand-up comic as a significant factor in her decision to leave the circuit and enter an area of entertainment other than stand-up comedy: "I wasn't a very confrontational person and I noticed that women on the road had to be very confrontational … so I didn't want to go on the road" (Littleton 2006, 292).

One reason for the difficulties African American women face in performing comedy is that, unlike men, they are not licensed by African American cultural traditions of respectability to make public use of vernacular, community language, and certainly not with humor. Thus, unless they are willing to flout or suspend the social norms of propriety and respectability assigned to women by the African American community and by mainstream society, African American women are deprived of access to a valuable resource for establishing the all-important solidarity and authority with any audience. Another problem African American women encounter is an African American community norm that forbids women from joke-telling and being funny in mixed gender situations, private or public. Daryl Dance (1998) notes that African American women have a rich tradition of creating humor but that they have generally felt compelled to limit their jokes and humor to single-gender gatherings. "African American women have always had to contend with [W]hite America's derogatory image of them as laughing clowns, incapable of serious and tragic concerns" (Dance 1998, xxiii). Influenced by this and the New Negro Movement (see the discussion in section 39.4 below), "African American women's humor has been an *in-house* affair ... it was not considered ladylike to tell jokes or even to laugh too loud publicly" (Dance 1998, xxii–xxiii).

While there are some men who accept and appreciate women's comedy performance, there are many who hold sexist views that regard humor as a male profession. African American women who appear in comedy venues may be essentialized, with their gender used as a deterministic feature that makes them unfit for comedic performance. Because she often performed immediately after male acts, Bertice Berry reports that she had to devote a part of her act to "undoing" the sexist damage done by the act preceding hers (personal communication, March 9, 2002).

39.3.1 The Exception to the Rule: Jackie "Moms" Mabley (March 19, 1894–May 23, 1975)

An example of the effect of attitudes and beliefs historically facing African American women in comedy is the work of the late Jackie "Moms" Mabley, a female comedian who primarily performed on African American comedy circuits (i.e., the "Chitlin" Circuit, the Apollo), but also in mainstream society venues (e.g., The Merv Griffin Show, The Smothers Brothers Comedy Hour, and Rowan & Martin's Laugh-In) through much of the twentieth century. Watkins (1999) notes that "perhaps more than any of the other early Apollo comics, Moms Mabley foreshadowed the shift to direct social commentary and stand-up comic techniques" (393). As Littleton (2006) observes, Moms Mabley presented "some of the most insightful material of her day" (79). Below is an example of Mabley's work from the Civil Rights Era, in which she highlights the hypocrisy of segregation.

> I was on my way down to Miami ... I mean "*They*"-ami. I was ridin' along ... goin' through one of them little towns in South Carolina. Pass through a red light. One of them big cops come runnin' over to me, say, 'Hey woman, don't you know you went through a red light.' I say, 'Yeah, I know I went through a red light.' 'Well, what did you do that for?' I said, 'Cause I seen all you White folks goin' on the green light ... I thought the red light was for us!' (Watkins 1999, 392)

As a woman, Mabley encountered negative reactions to her gender-blind efforts to perform in an arena reserved almost exclusively for men. Though part of the problem Mabley experienced stemmed from the previously discussed long-standing African American ideological view that women should not be funny in public or in mixed company, part of the problem also stemmed from community norms that deprived women of the right to public use of vernacular varieties of AAL.

Early in her career, Mabley chose a radical strategy to counter the extreme sexism she experienced in attempting to perform. To detract from her gender and deflect sexist reactions, Mabley created a stage identity as a "sage, down-to-earth, elder woman" (Watkins 1999, 390), despite being in her twenties when she began her career. With the asexual persona of a community elder dressed like a bag lady in her iconic floppy hat and flower dress, she was able to co-opt linguistic resources that men employed onstage and engage in biting social commentary with impunity (Littleton 2006). Mabley displayed a social consciousness throughout her career, with her insistence on participating in a male-dominated field and her willingness to openly confront issues related to the hypocrisy of a racist system. Her self-presentation stood in contrast to the "Mammy" persona that Bloomquist (this volume) describes as being foisted on African American women who chose to perform in other arenas (e.g., Butterfly McQueen as an Academy Award-winning actress). Mabley acquired an "unrestrained mystique, a self-issued license to say whatever she pleased, however she pleased to say it" (Rickford and Rickford 2000, 65). Mabley's attitudes and behavior, both onstage and off—she was a bisexual woman who often had a good-looking woman on her arm and dressed in men's clothing in her daily life (see the HBO documentary *Whoopi Goldberg Presents Moms Mabley*)—stood in opposition to the values of the New Negro Movement, which influence the African American community to this day.

39.4 THE LASTING EFFECT OF THE NEW NEGRO MOVEMENT

Historically, the African American community has seen a public presentation of a prim, demure identity mediated by Standard American English (SAE) as part of a special role assigned to women in "the work of uplifting the race" (Gates 1988, 136). As Gates notes, "to speak proper was to *be* proper" and this "would ensure one's rights" (1988, 136) and eliminate racist beliefs—or so it was believed. This attitude was related to the New Negro Movement that developed in the late 1800s and early 1900s among the emerging African American intellectual class. A goal here was to destroy the then rampant negative stereotypes of African Americans and replace them with an image that conformed as closely as possible to the European ideal (Gates 1988). Adams (1904) places the Black woman, as Gates notes, "at the center of the movement to gain respectability for African Americans" (1988). "Black women promoted a politics of respectability that emphasized sexual propriety, polite manners, and modest attire among other social practices to reform negative ideas about [B]lack women" (Richardson 2009, 292). The idea among African American intellectuals was to promote the values of the New Negro Movement among the masses of African American women and construct a narrowly conservative identity for all African American women.

Research suggests that thinking from the New Negro Movement continues in the African American community, particularly where women are concerned; women are judged more harshly than men for public use of vernacular varieties of AAL (Rahman 2008). Use of "proper" language by women is, in the minds of some community members, still tied to Black respectability, as seen in the recent case of Rachel Jeantel. Jeantel, a 19-year-old witness in the 2013 trial for the murder of Trayvon Martin, received severe criticism as a Black woman for her public use of nonstandard American English and her mix of AAL and Haitian Creole. According to Baugh, "Anyone who lacks fluency in mainstream … English may be at a considerable disadvantage: educationally, economically, occupationally, and, at times, legally" (Baugh, this volume). If the speaker is female, "she might be subjected to even higher scrutiny by African Americans … because she is expected to be representing the [B]lack community. And speaking 'proper' English is bound up with [B]lack respectability" (Muhammad 2013). So, for a Black woman to use a vernacular variety of AAL publicly is still an act of audacity—or worse—that may subject her to public excoriation from not only mainstream society but also her own community. Barring the radical strategy of Moms Mabley, African American women who want to work in stand-up comedy, unlike men, have virtually no models and no legitimate access to the linguistic tools available to Black men. So, what do African American women comics do?

39.5 WHAT AFRICAN AMERICAN FEMALE COMEDIANS DO

This chapter illustrates a practice common among African American female comedians: use of vernacular varieties of AAL in public spaces. The comedians discussed in this chapter: (1) employ a broadly vernacular AAL, as illustrated in tables 39.1 and 39.2; and (2) totally usurp community norms of propriety for public presentation by Black women while ostensibly overlooking male audience members. But within their AAL, they draw on discursive features specifically associated with African American women to create a women's style. This African American Women's Language (AAWL) is a variety of AAL that contains a range of lexical, discursive, prosodic, and other grammatical features associated with African American women, particularly when conversing with close friends (Rahman 2011; Lanehart 2009; Troutman 2002; Morgan 2002, this volume). As Troutman (2001, 224) notes, "lighter-toned conversations" between African American female friends involve "talking that talk" and displaying verbal acuity that

Table 39.1 Some Phonological Features of AAL

Feature	Example
Monophthongization of /ai/	*my* [ma]
Deletion or vocalization of post-vocalic /r/	*sister* [sɪstə]
Realization of initial /ð/ as [d]	*this* [dis]
Reduction of word-final consonant clusters	*just* [dʒus]
Deletion of unstressed initial syllables	*about* [baʊt]
Deletion or vocalization of post-vocalic /l/	*toll* [tow]
Realization of final /ŋ/ as [n]	*smiling* [smallin]

Table 39.2 Some Grammatical Features of AAL

Feature	Example
Existential *it*	I believe it's a man in this place right now.
Multiple negation	He can't hardly see nothin'.
Leveling	They was tellin' y'all.
Zero Copula	She Ø not here.
Habitual *be*	John be at the store.
Ø third person singular –*s*	He thinkØ he goin' to work now. . .

calls on the multidimensional array of discursive features of AAWL. Men watching African American women perform find themselves listening in on sometimes outrageous and subversive exaggerations of "woman talk." The style the female comedians create builds a "friendship" and solidarity with women in audiences and discourages the occurrence of sexist heckling and harassment by men.

39.5.1 African American Female Comedians' AAL Varieties

While their performances are framed in African American discourse and culture, as Troutman (2001) observes, there are features that African American women share with women outside the community. Availing themselves of their solidarity-building potential, the women bring to the stage topics, features, and practices that mirror those that research indicates are common among female close friends. Research shows that discussion of personal relationships is frequent among African American women and is a way of creating closeness between them (Mitchell-Kernan 1972; Morgan 2002; Troutman 2002). Johnson and Aries (1998) note that women talk about all the "significant relationships in their lives: their children, their husbands, their families of origin, and their in-laws. They talk of their relationships with co-workers, with other friends and each other. Beyond that, they talk to each other about their work and daily lives" (219). Reid (2009) observes that African American women in conversation with close friends engage in secret-sharing. According to Johnson and Aries (1998), women discuss very intimate topics, "sharing their deepest feelings, problems, and concerns" (217). The comedians intertwine their talk of relationships with attention to topics such as food, cooking, appearance, and family and childrearing, which are associated with traditional roles of women.

In AAWL, conversational talk among friends is collaborative (Reid 2009; Troutman 2002) and tag questions (i.e., questions appended to the end of a statement) serve to encourage collaboration. In one instance, AAWL may consist of a yes/no question having a pronominal subject whose antecedent is the subject of the sentence to which it is appended. The polarity of a tag is often the reverse of the polarity of the main clause so that a positive main clause takes a negative tag and vice versa. Tag questions may also occur as invariant forms, such as "Right?" and "OK?" Examples from Love (2002) include: "And White people love potlucks in a office, don't they?" and "Amy'll get a attitude, OK?"

African American women in comedy may use tag questions to promote closeness and solidarity among women friends by fostering the perception of an egalitarian relationship, where collaborators in conversation share in seeking answers, rather than having one speaker dominate. When a group of African American women shares a history and worldview, tag questions may also serve as a cue for backchanneling as a way to show support for what a speaker is saying.

The African American comedians discussed here make frequent use of tag questions, sometimes intensively soliciting responses from women. So when Adele Givens tells her audience, "Quit trippin' about little bitty flaws, all right?" women in the audience receive this as an invitation to respond. They reply with backchanneling interjections like "That's right!" and "I hear you!" In all of the narratives, questions from the comedians elicit responses from female audience members, resulting in an event containing elements of call-and-response, which DeBose (this volume) describes as "[o]ne of the most pervasive continuities of the Black Experience."

As part of their gendered presentation, the comedians presented here also compliment women in their audiences. Holmes (1998) describes a *compliment* as a speech act that "attributes credit to someone other than the speaker for some 'good' (possession, characteristic, skill, etc.) which is positively valued by the speaker and the hearer. ... Furthermore, women offer compliments routinely as a way of building solidarity with other women. ... Compliments are 'social lubricants' that serve to increase or 'consolidate' solidarity between the speaker and addressee" (101).

The comedians employ a range of gendered terms of address and reference. Among African American women, *girl* as a term of address is a *culturally toned diminutive* that allows women to express solidarity (Troutman 2002) and, as Spears (2009) notes, "to perform or present identity" (86). "If they view themselves as peers, one African American female can and will call another African American female *girl* ... this usage is ... devoid of belittling or degrading denotations or connotations" (Troutman 2001, 17).

Shared knowledge of the African American verbal practice of *indirectness* (Morgan 1998, 2002; Spears 2001; Jacobs-Huey 2006) also contributes toward creating a connection between the comedians and their women audience members; rather, it evokes memories of witnessing or participating in similar experiences, and contributes to humor through its incongruity by demonstrating a comedian's cultural knowledge and verbal agility while using the vernacular. According to Morgan (1996, 1998), *pointed indirectness* occurs when a speaker makes a statement to an addressee that is actually meant for another person who is present (i.e., the intended target) to hear. "This type of indirectness is only successful if recognized by hearers who share prior knowledge about events, or where the context has been established in such a way that the addressed target and those around can determine the identity of the intended target" (Morgan 1998, 258). *Baited indirectness* differs from *pointed indirectness* in that it occurs "when a speaker attributes a feature to a general target and audience that may be true for a segment" (Morgan 2002, 47).

39.6 THE NARRATIVES OF THREE AFRICAN AMERICAN WOMEN IN COMEDY

39.6.1 Adele Givens in *Queens of Comedy* (2001)

Completely overlooking men in the audience, Adele Givens opens her act by complimenting women, referring to them as *queens* and addressing them as *ladies*:

(1) I am so glad y'all decided to join the Queens of Comedy tonight!
So glad to see so many *queens* in the house with me tonight!
Now, *ladies* ...

Givens continues to speak directly to women in her audience, occasionally using gendered forms of address. She points to the media as the culprit in perpetuating an ideology of beauty that devalues the natural physical attributes that most African American women possess, causing them to aspire to unattainable standards of beauty. She warns women not to be deceived by media presentations that can be damaging to their self-esteem: "We start getting tricked—by these magazines and these televisions."

Taking the stance of friend-as-advisor in her evaluative comments, Givens counsels women, telling them not to be deceived by fantasy beauties in the media:

(2) I want you to quit disrespectin' yourselves, ladies ...
I don't give a damn what—understan' that ...
A flaw ain't shit but an identifying mark.

After appealing to the women's self-esteem, Givens's comedy routine asks them to accept and triumph over the realities of life. Acknowledging the importance of romantic relationships, she draws on comedic incongruity to say,

> (3) If you Ø cockeyed, find a man who had a stroke, goddamn it.
>   That's right.
>   You Ø cockeyed, he Ø sideways.
>   Y'all Ø the perfect couple.

Givens strengthens her alignment with women by critiquing the empty lifestyles of Hollywood fantasy beauties. "You read about 'em—goin' to the hospital" for complaints like "exhaustion and dehydration. . ." Givens then further aligns herself with her female listeners by reciting a list of responsibilities associated with "real women," who do not have the luxury of hospitalization for exhaustion.

> (4) I know some women got two jobs, six kids, no man … You hear me?
>   She gotta go to PTA meetings, after school programs, football practice, Riverboat Casino . . .
>   In the real world, when you get exhausted, you take a fuckin' nap, doncha?

Drawing on lexicon with meanings related to activities historically associated with African American women, Givens involves women in her audience by using questions intensively. She packs three tag questions and three direct questions into her three-minute narrative. Each question elicits vigorous responses from the African American woman-dominated audience. Including "Riverboat Casino" in the list of serious responsibilities of "real women" is a humorous instance of baited indirectness since recreational time at a Riverboat Casino is hardly a requirement for single mothers who have obligations such as PTA and after-school programs. Audience members appear to recognize that adding "Riverboat Casino" to the list is a humorous dig at any woman present who may be expending her limited time and money gambling.

The Givens narrative also addresses issues of childrearing and the relationships that African American women have with their children. Givens first portrays a middle-class White establishment woman whose child criticizes her with "Mommy, you're fat." The mother accepts the child's criticism, responding with an immediate phone call to Jenny Craig. Givens then compares the middle-class mother's hyperbolically ineffectual response to her own reaction when her child criticizes her weight. Not willing to accept what she perceives as smart-mouthing, Givens gives an outrageously exaggerated account of disciplining her own child where she uses the phone for a purpose other than calling Jenny Craig. In a supposed instance of woman-to-woman self-disclosure, Givens critiques the stereotype of the abusive African American mother:

> (5) I picked up that phone and I knocked that little bitch down a flight of stairs.
>   I told her, "You Ø the reason why mama's so fat." . . .
>   I beat her so long I lost fifteen pounds, and now I feel great!

39.6.2 Loni Love on *Comic View* (June 21, 2002)

Loni Love projects feelings related to the alienation that lower-ranking workers may experience in the workplace where they see no opportunity for advancement (Kantor 1993; Rahman 2007), as she constructs the persona of a low-salaried office employee revealing her secret misgivings about office potluck dinners.

In a performance before a seemingly African American audience, Love opens with humorous lines that express both baited and pointed indirectness as she takes a stance meant to align her with her African American audience:

> (6) I'd like to say hello to all the White people in the audience.
>   (She then goes on to suggest that nosey White people are hiding in the audience.)
>   You know they Ø up in here. They Ø nosey. Ain't they nosey?

The entire comedic rant against potlucks becomes an instance of pseudo pointed indirectness, in which Love speaks to African American women about potlucks for the benefit of nosey White people who are supposedly eavesdropping. Assuming that African American women share her views on potlucks, she attempts to align with them by asking, "What's up with them [White people] and these damn potlucks?"

The worker character hesitates to tell her supervisor of her reluctance to participate lest it affect her employment.

> (7) I can't tell Amy, "Amy, I just don't want to be in a potluck this month."
>   Amy'll get a' attitude and [say], "You're not bein' a team player."

In delivering this line, Love produces a highly constricted [r] in *player* and *you're*, imitating perceived mainstream middle-class White speech (Rahman 2008).

The employee character copiously employs a cooking lexicon to relate that while ethnic workers spend hours preparing colorful heritage dishes for potlucks, Whites invariably bring "them nasty-ass salads. . . . The one with the marshmallows, mayonnaise and apples in it." In a critique of her supervisor's bland culinary contribution to potlucks, the employee complains,

> (8) The purpose of a potluck, y'all—is for everybody to bring one dish, right?
>   (Pause while audience responds)Black people, we Ø gon bring what?
>   (Pause while audience begins to name items of soul food)
>   The greens, the candied yams, the chicken . . .
>   Hispanic people Ø gon bring the tacos, the burritos . . .
>   Chinese people Ø gon bring the rice, the egg rolls . . .

Finally, the worker character switches from a stance of frustration to one of defiance:

> (9a) I spoke up one day. . .
>   I said, "Listen, Amy, listen. Look at Felipe!
>   He's been cooking tamales since four-thirty this morning.
>   I've been cooking chicken and collard greens.
>   Wu Sung is still on the egg rolls . . .
>   And you bring a damn marshmallow and mayonnaise salad?

She then reverses the commonly used corporate "team player" metaphor that Amy employs. Rather than speaking in a mainstream American English variety, she uses her own vernacular to say accusingly to her supervisor,

(9b) You Ø not a team playa!"

Here, post-vocalic /r/ is absent in *you're* and *player*, respectively. Love ends her narrative by making amends to the imaginary White audience members:

(10) But we love you, White people, so keep coming.

39.6.3 Sherry Sinclair on *Comic View* (April 3, 2002)

Sherry Sinclair begins her performance by complimenting and questioning women in the audience:

(11) All the independent women in the house, make some noise!
      Women, we do got it goin' on!

She then asks the women a question that evokes responses:

(12a) Anybody ever work in corporate America?

As narrator, Sinclair takes a self-disclosing stance as she confides her feelings of fragmentation as the only African American at her corporate American job:

(12b) I was like four different parts of people.
       (She humorously adds)
       They should've paid my ass more cause they was gettin' four for the price of one.

"Sherry" is the persona that Sinclair presents at work, a cheerful, "non-threatening, conforming African American" who is seemingly well integrated into the corporate environment. Sherry shows a comedic acquiescence to what the comedian portrays as the normative linguistic and social behaviors of the corporation. In her few lines as Sherry, Sinclair uses linguistic features and discursive content that point to a stance representing alignment with the establishment. Below is an excerpt that contains the fluffy, "water cooler" conversation of Sherry.

(13) Sinclair as Sherry:
      Hi. Good morning. Hi. How're you? How was your weekend?
      Oh, I love your outfit!
      (14) Sinclair as narrator:
      They loved Sherry.
      But you gotta watch out for Sherry cause Sherry will tell on you.

Like not directly but indirectly—for people takin' long lunches.
Sherry wait right good 'til the boss is standin' right there—an' be like. . .
(15) Sinclair as Sherry:
WOW! I didn't know we had hour-and-a-half lunches!
How long do you have to be here to get THAT?!

Sherry makes small talk, which includes the perceived gendered topic of appearance. There is also a suggestion of pointed indirectness. So, when Sherry innocently exclaims to her co-worker about taking long lunch breaks, she actually intends for the boss to hear, since she waits until the boss is present to raise the subject. Her deployment of features of SAE occurs within a "Valley Girl" suprasegmental frame characterized by sharply rising intonation and a glottalized final /t/ in *outfit*. The incongruity of Sherry as an African American Valley Girl contributes to the humor.

Making allowances for comedic exaggeration, the style-shifting that Sinclair displays is consistent with linguistic changes that often occur when African American women negotiate the workplace (Rahman 2008). Jones and Shorter-Gooden (2003) observe that shifting language and behavior style is a survival strategy that African American women regularly employ in the workplace to respond to challenges posed by "racial and gender stereotypes, bias, and mistreatment" (150):

> the daily migration from home to office can contain all the fears, doubts, and challenges of leaving one's country for a foreign land. The workplace is where Black women feel they must shift most often, engaging in a grown-up game of pretend as they change their voices, attitudes, and postures to meet the cultural codes of workaday America. … Many women testify to spending several hours a day feeling profoundly disconnected from who they truly are. (Jones and Shorter-Gooden 2003, 150)

39.7 Discussion of Linguistic Resources

As a rule, linguistic features only indirectly index social categories; *stances* may indicate attitudes or behaviors and these may in turn be associated with a particular category (Ochs 1992). Except when imitating other groups (e.g., example 7), comedians in this research call on community language at all linguistic levels in displaying stances that bond them with the African American women in their audiences (e.g., examples 1, 2, and 11). They make use of various features of AAL (e.g., examples 3, 5, 6, 8, 9b); within that variety they make extensive use of AAWL (e.g., examples 4 and 8).

A characteristic of stand-up comedy is that comedians generally deploy a small set of features that are particularly salient in constructing their acts (Rahman 2007). With only a few minutes to accomplish their goals, these comedians distill some of the most significant gendered topics from general female parlance so that these pervade their narratives. Table 39.3 shows six major topics in the comedians' narratives. Each narrative addresses at least four of the six major topics. Relationships and self-disclosure

Table 39.3 Major Narrative Topics of African American Women Comedians

Comedian	Narrative length (minutes)	Appearance	Food	Relationships	Job	Child-rearing	Self-disclosure
Givens	3.0	X		X		X	X
Love	2.5		X	X	X		X
Sinclair	4.5	X		X	X		X

Table 39.4 Frequency of AAWL Discourse Features in Comedy Narratives

Comedian	Narrative length (minutes)	Questions (including tag questions)	Compliments	Gendered terms of address	Indirectness
Givens	3.0	6	4	5	1
Love	2.5	10	0	0	3
Sinclair	4.5	1	3	2	1

are particularly prominent topics, suggesting that the comedians are sharing their innermost secrets with the audience. The women do not employ a wide range of discourse features associated with African American women, but drawing on the style of African American women in conversation, they make use of questions (example 8), compliments (example 11), gendered terms of address (example 1), and indirectness (example 15). They employ these salient discourse features extensively, emphasizing them through use of prosodic features such as timing, stress, and amplitude. The comedians' creation of a style that appears to mirror that of African American women in conversation evokes enthusiastic responses from female audience members.

A comedian's unique style leads to emphasis of particular features to construct a gendered "friend" identity. Questions appear particularly frequently in some of the narratives (examples 4, 6, 8). They serve the function of drawing women in the audience into active participation in the performance, loosely analogous to when close African American friends use questions to draw each other into a conversation. Love does not use compliments or gendered terms of address, but in her two-and-a-half-minute narrative, she asks ten questions, which is more than any of the other comedians in a single narrative. Table 39.4 shows the intensity of questions, compliments, gendered terms of address, and instances of indirectness that occur in the discursive style of the narratives.

39.8 CONCLUSION

Examining the work of these African American female comedians affords an opportunity to observe a crystallization of linguistic practices of African American women.

Lacking a strong tradition of public comic performance, the women in this research display an innovative strategy that allows them to overcome sexist harassment. Highlighting salient features of AAWL, a subvariety of AAL, they build "friendship" with African American women in the audience.

Along with friendship, their audacious and masterful, yet unlicensed, use of a variety of AAL onstage allows them to project toughness and authority. Their bold and irreverent public use of profanity (akin to male comedians) contributes to this. In the strong solidarity-laden environment the female comedians create, sexist harassment is unlikely to occur.

This chapter focuses on African American women in comedy, but further research is needed on the work of all African American comedians as they devise strategies to deal with their unique situations as Black bodies in a White world and to address social and political issues that are relevant to the African American community. Moving deeper into the twenty-first century, concerns within the African American community continue to emerge and change, leading to new types of social commentary and activism from comedians. For example, it is no longer possible for a comedian to create humor based on the implausibility of an African American becoming president—though there can be jokes about the unlikelihood of a second African American becoming president—but that creates space for the introduction of new topics by African American comedians that provide social commentary and activism.

AAWL is just one subtype of AAL. With the increasing diversity of the African American community, African American women in comedy will need to construct characters from various varieties of the African diaspora. A question is how comedians will employ linguistic features to portray the many varieties of AAL now spoken. Looking to the broader community, there is need for increased study of the structure and function of culturally and ethnically based varieties of AAL (see Smitherman, this volume).

The African American community has a strong tradition of comedy. Even though African Americans have been stereotyped as simple-minded buffoons (see Bloomquist, this volume), the creation of humor involves complex cognitive processes and, as Rahman notes (2007), humor has historically been a key factor in allowing African Americans to survive and retain a sense of self-worth. Added to that, laughter provides untold benefits to physical health and resistance (see Morgan, this volume). In the future, socially conscious African American comedians will continue to create and push the envelope, humorously bringing important issues to the fore. Hopefully, there will be increased numbers of African American women among them to express a broader point of view of the Black community.

NOTE

1. For the purposes of this chapter, the term *African American Language* (AAL) covers a range of speech styles associated with the African American community. While the speech styles themselves have identifying features based on factors such as region and gender, speakers of AAL overall employ, in varying degrees, distinctive features of grammar, phonology, and discourse.

REFERENCES

Adams, John H., Jr. 1904. "A Study of the Features of the New Negro Woman." *Voice of the Negro* 1: 323–25.

Cowan, William Tynes. 2001. "Plantation Comic Modes." *Humor* 14: 1–24.

Dance, Daryl Cumber. 1998. Introduction to *Honey, Hush: An Anthology of African American Women's Humor*, edited by Daryl Cumber Dance, xxi–xxxv. New York: Norton.

Edwards, Walter F. 1996. "Sex-Based Differences in Language Choice in an African American Neighborhood in Detroit." In *Focus on the USA*, edited by Edgar W. Schneider, 183–93. Philadelphia: John Benjamins.

Gates, Henry Louis, Jr. 1988. "The Trope of a New Negro and the Reconstruction of the Image of the Black." *Representations* 24: 129–49.

Greenbaum, Andrea. 1999. "Stand-Up Comedy as Rhetorical Argument: An Investigation of Comic Culture." *Humor: The International Journal of Humor Research.* 12: 33–46.

Holmes, Janet. 1998. "Complimenting—A Positive Politeness Strategy." In *Language and Gender: A Reader*, edited by Jennifer Coates, 71–88. Malden, MA: Blackwell.

Jacobs-Huey, Lanita. 2006. *From the Kitchen to the Parlor: Language and African American Women's Hair Care.* Oxford: Oxford University.

Johnson, Fern L., and Elizabeth J. Aries. 1983. "The Talk of Women Friends." *Women's Studies International Forum* 6: 353–61.

Jones, Charisse, and Kumea Shorter-Gooden. 2003. *Shifting: The Double Lives of Black Women in America.* New York: HarperCollins.

Kantor, Rosabeth. 1993. *Men and Women of the Corporation.* New York: Basic Books.

Lanehart, Sonja L., ed. 2009. *African American Women's Language: Discourse, Education, and Identity.* Newcastle upon Tyne: Cambridge Scholars.

Littleton, Darryl. 2006. *Black Comedians on Black Comedy: How African Americans Taught us to Laugh.* New York: Applause Theater and Cinema Books.

Mitchell-Kernan, Claudia. 1972. "Signifying, Loud-Talking, and Marking." In *Rappin and Stylin' Out: Communication in Urban Black America*, edited by Thomas Kochman, 315–35. Champaign: University of Illinois.

Morgan, Marcyliena. 1996. "Conversational Signifying: Grammar and Indirectness among African American Women." In *Grammar and Interaction*, edited by Elinor Ochs, Emanuel Schegloff, and Sandra Thompson, 405–34. Cambridge: Cambridge University.

———. 1998. "More than a Mood or an Attitude: Discourse and Verbal Genres in African American Culture." In *African American English: History, Structure and Use*, edited by Salikoko Mufwene, John R. Rickford, Guy Bailey, and John Baugh, 251–81. New York: Routledge.

———. 2002. *Language, Discourse, and Power in African American Culture.* Cambridge: Cambridge University.

Ochs, Elinor. 1992. "Indexing Gender." In *Rethinking Context: Language as an Interactive Phenomenon*, edited by Alessandro Duranti and Charles Goodwin, 335–58. Cambridge: Cambridge University.

Rahman, Jacquelyn. 2007. "An *ay* for an *ah*: Language of Survival in African American Narrative Comedy." *American Speech* 82: 65–96.

———. 2008. "Middle-Class African Americans: Reactions and Attitudes toward African American English." *American Speech* 83: 141–76.

———. 2011. "Woman to Woman: Building Solidarity in African American Female Comedy." *English World-Wide* 32: 309–37.

———. 2012. "The N Word: Its History and Use in the African American Community." *Journal of English Linguistics* 40: 137–71.

Reid, Calaya. 2009. "Struggles Creating African American Women's Language and Character: Dialogues in *Take Her Man*." In *African American Women's Language: Discourse. Education, and Identity*, edited by Sonja L. Lanehart, 228–44. Newcastle upon Tyne: Cambridge Scholars.

Richardson, Elaine. 2009. "Gender Ideologies in Hip Hop Feminism and Performances of Black Womanhood." In *African American Women's Language: Discourse, Education, and Identity*, edited by Sonja L. Lanehart, 291–304. Newcastle upon Tyne: Cambridge Scholars.

Rickford, John R., and Russell J. Rickford. 2000. *Spoken Soul: The Story of Black English*. New York: John Wiley & Sons.

Schilling-Estes, Natalie. 1998. "Investigating Self-Conscious Speech: The Performance Register in Ocracoke English." *Language in Society* 27: 53–83.

Smitherman, Geneva. [1994] 2000. *Black Talk: Words and Phrases from the Hood to the Amen Corner*. New York: Houghton Mifflin.

Spears, Arthur K. 2001. "Directness in the Use of African American English." In *Sociocultural and Historical Contexts of African American English*, edited by Sonja L. Lanehart, 239–59. Philadelphia: John Benjamins.

———. 2009. "Theorizing African American Women's Language: GIRL as a Discourse Marker." In *African American Women's Language: Discourse, Education and Identity*, edited by Sonja L. Lanehart, 76–90. Newcastle upon Tyne: Cambridge Scholars.

Troutman, Denise. 2001. "African American Women: Talking that Talk." In *Sociocultural and Historical Contexts of African American English*, edited by Sonja L. Lanehart, 211–37. Philadelphia: John Benjamins.

———. 2002. "We Be Strong Women": A Womanist Analysis of Black Women's Sociolinguistic Behavior." In *Centering Ourselves: African American Feminist and Womanist Studies of Discourse*, edited by Marsha Houston and Olga Idriss Davis, 99–122. Cresskill, NJ: Hampton.

Wald, Elijah. 2012. *The Dozens: A History of Rap's Mama*. New York: Oxford University.

Watkins, Mel. 1999. *On the Real Side: A History of African American Comedy*. Chicago: Lawrence Hill.

Media Sources

Givens, Adele. 2001. *Queens of Comedy*. Paramount Pictures and Latham Entertainment, DVD.

Goldberg, Whoopie, dir. 2013. *Whoopie Goldberg Presents Moms Mabley*. HBO Documentary Films, November 18, 2013.

Love, Loni. 2002. "Comic View." Black Entertainment Television. June 21, 2002.

Muhammad, Khalil Gibran. 2013. Language on Trial: Rachel Jeantel. *Here and Now*. http://hereandnow.wbur.org/2013/06/28/n-word-language June 28, 2013.

Sinclair, Sherry. 2002. Comic View. Black Entertainment Television. April 3, 2002.

CHAPTER 40

....

THE CONSTRUCTION OF ETHNICITY VIA VOICING

African American English in Children's Animated Film

....

JENNIFER BLOOMQUIST

40.1 INTRODUCTION

....

THIS chapter provides a brief outline of the history of African Americans[1] in the entertainment industry from minstrel shows to present-day films. Included is a discussion of stock character types (e.g., the mammy, buck, and coon). While much of the criticism of such characters is historical in scope, I contend that these caricatures are alive and well and completely uncontested in contemporary animation, unlike those that we find in non-animated films. Hence, in some respects, animated films have not evolved in the same way traditional films have in providing a more well-rounded view of social and cultural life in a global society. The bulk of the chapter will focus on documenting the parallels between images of African Americans in traditional films and those found in animation. I am particularly interested in looking at the distortion of African American English[2] (AAE) since this seems to be a more necessary feature of the construction of animated Black characters than it is for similar roles in live-action film. While the focus of this project is the linguistic representation of African Americans in animated film, we still see vestiges of these early physical grotesques in contemporary animation. When these physical cues, even when they are intended to be subtle (enlarged lips, for example), are paired with dialogue that is clearly meant as an imitation of AAE, the result is a construction of an ethnic stereotype that serves as a historical reflection of European American attitudes regarding African Americans. As a result, such depictions provide non-Black acculturated people with a perception of Blackness that is inaccurate but portrayed as authentic and open to mimicry.

Although Blacks were used to provide amusement for White audiences on plantations throughout the enslavement period, national White fascination with African American life as popular entertainment began with the proliferation of minstrel shows in the late 1820s.

These traveling variety shows, mostly featuring music and comedy, dominated American entertainment until well into the 1880s and featured so-called "Ethiopian delineators," who were all-White, all-male casts in blackface. Their comedy hinged on gross misrepresentations of what the actors determined to be (southern) Black culture, including singing, dancing, and delivering comedic speeches. In the early days of minstrelsy, more often than not, the actors had little or no real contact with African Americans, so their version of Black culture was almost entirely grounded in racist stereotypes and was used as a tool to further malign Blacks and to promote justifications for slavery. Some of the most influential minstrels, such as Dan Emmett, the performer best known for composing "Dixie" and "Turkey in the Straw," claimed to have listened to the songs of slaves, and Tomas "Daddy" Rice, who is credited with being one of the originators of minstrelsy, reportedly imitated the dances of a crippled Black hostler named Jim Cuff (fictionalized as Jim Crow) (Comer 2005). Even when African American actors began participating in minstrelsy in the 1840s (also in black-face), the caricatures of blackness persisted. These depictions of Black life were particularly damaging since, at the height of their popularity, minstrel shows played small towns and large cities alike, in every region of the country. Common both in the North and the South, their reach also extended as far west as the frontier towns of Cincinnati and Louisville, and they were enormously popular in Europe and the British Isles as well. The performances drew large and enthusiastic White audiences, many of whom had never seen an African American in person—and even those Whites who were familiar with Black culture accepted these comedic distortions of Black life as valuable entertainment. For example, in his *Autobiography*, Mark Twain famously recalls the minstrel show writing, "To my mind it was a thoroughly delightful thing and a most competent laughter-compeller and I am sorry it is gone" (as quoted in Strausbaugh 2006, 108).

Other ethnic and immigrant groups such as Italians, Irish, Jews, Germans, and even poor country Whites (portrayed as rubes) were lampooned in minstrel shows, but Black characters were arguably more frequent and more popular, and the acceptance of comedic, exaggerated Black life became more powerful over time. Eventually, as minstrelsy became more widespread, it created its own frame of reference such that it no longer mattered that the performances had little to do with genuine Black music, dance, or speech patterns. Even after the traveling shows faded into obscurity by the turn of the twentieth century, the farcical and damaging construction of Black ethnicity in minstrelsy was co-opted by vaudeville shows and early film. The comic archetypes developed in minstrel shows, Uncle Tom, the Mammy, (Zip) Coon, pickaninnies, and Sambo provided the architecture for the Black comic roles that are shockingly prevalent even today in both traditional and, perhaps to an even greater degree, animated films.

A number of critics have maintained that even though uninformed (and sometimes ill-intended) Whites created them, Black stock characters began with at least some foundation in reality. It has also been argued that with the contributions of African American actors and writers in vaudeville and early film, such as Bert Williams, Mantan Moreland, Step 'n Fetchit, and Hattie McDaniels, many of the stock characters developed in minstrel shows were reclaimed by Blacks and elevated so that they eventually became more humane and realistic versions of Black culture (Strausbaugh 2006, 140). However, when we look at Black language[3] use in the early history of the entertainment industry, particularly at the heavy-handed distortion and exaggeration of AAE, the ignorant dialogue written for Black roles, and the types of topics scripted for Black characters, I am not sure we can feel reassured by Black participation in helping to craft these images. The subtleties of Black interpretations, when they were there for general audiences, were often too few and far between, and the linguistic construction of ethnicity too shaped by the racist ideology of the time to afford these roles much dignity in the White imagination.

Black language has long been a fascination of Whites in entertainment, and the language of minstrel shows and the comedic dialogues crafted for the "Black" actors in them was constructed in such a way as to depict Blacks as shiftless, lazy, ignorant buffoons, at turns docile then emotive and always sexually preoccupied. The language was written in broad "Negro dialect" so that the often-stigmatized phonological and syntactic features of AAE were particularly exaggerated in an attempt to underscore widely held White beliefs regarding Black intelligence, integrity, and morality. On one hand, the language of characters such as Uncle Tom, Jim Crow, and the Mammy was simplified to construct one-dimensional meek, loyal Black servants who blissfully served White masters and longed nostalgically for the comfort and ease of plantation life. On the other, stump speeches delivered by slick, "citified dandies" such as Zip Coon (a northern, urban Black man trying to live above his station) were characterized by language that poorly approximated White, upper-class speech and that was usually rife with nonsense, malapropisms, and puns. Stump speech topics varied from pure nonsense to parodies of politics, science, and social issues. Both the topic itself and the coon's inability to comprehend it served as sources of comedy. As Robert Toll points out in *Blacking Up*, "education was minstrelsy's most popular professional target. With great pomposity and empty heads, 'edjumakated' Blacks felt they could explain anything," including, for example, transcendentalism:

> Transcendentalism is dat spiritual cognoscence ob psychological infrsgibility, connected wid conscientient ademption ob incolumbient spirituality and etherialized connection—which is deribed from a profound contemplation of the irregability ob dose incessimable divisions ob de more minute portions ob subdivided particles ob inwisible atoms dat become ana-tom-catically tattalable in de circumbulatin commotion ob ambiloquous voluminiousness. (as quoted in Toll 1974, 70)

With the use of nearly indecipherable dialogue such as this, audiences were invited to see Blacks who aspired to education and intelligence as ridiculous. Unfortunately, once African Americans established themselves in minstrelsy (many claiming to be ex-slaves to appear even more authentic), the humiliating mischaracterizations of Blacks became even more potent. Because Black actors "inherited the White-created stereotypes and could make only minor modifications in them, Black minstrels in effect added credibility to these images by making it seem that Negroes [*sic*] actually behaved like minstrelsy's Black caricatures" (Toll 1974, 196). In the remainder of this chapter, I will outline the most prominent and persistent of these character types and will demonstrate the ways in which they have been featured prominently in animated films.

40.2 UNCLE TOM

Uncle Tom was the first Black stock character to appear in early film and was based on the title character in Harriet Beecher Stowe's novel *Uncle Tom's Cabin* (1852). Unlike the novel, the film and theater versions of the character were created in defense of slavery; Uncle Tom was crafted as perpetually happy in slavery—content, loving and loyal to his master. He was faithful, meek, and subservient and also was cast as old, physically weak, and dependent on Whites, which further demonstrated that, in the post-emancipation fear of free Black men, he was not a threat to the White establishment. In Edwin Porter's (1903) twelve-minute film adaptation of *Uncle Tom's Cabin*, a blackfaced White actor plays Tom as generous, selfless, and happy to be on the plantation—he is the acceptable (i.e., "good") Negro. In 1927, Harry Pollard remade the film, and his version featured the first Black actor to play Uncle Tom: James B. Lowe. Over time, "Tom" was further expanded to become a popular stock character in films and included a range of African American men supposedly happy to serve Whites such as: Uncle Daniel, who dies for the sake of his former master in *Confederate Spy* (1909) and a freed slave who returns to bondage in order to help his master overcome financial difficulties in *For Massa's Sake* (1911), *Birth of a Nation* (1915), and *Hearts in Dixie* (1929), and Uncle Remus in *Song of the South*. The Tom character was played by a number of notable Black actors including: Bill "Bojangles" Robinson in *The Little Colonel* with Shirley Temple (1935); Clarence Muse in *Show Boat* (1936), *Follow Your Heart* (1936), *Zanzibar* (1940), *Heaven Can Wait* (1943), *Joe Palooka in The Knockout* (1947), and *Riding High* (1950); and Sidney Poitier in *Edge of the City* (1957), *The Defiant Ones* (1958), *Lilies of the Field* (1963), *The Slender Thread* (1965), *A Patch of Blue* (1965), and *To Sir With Love* (1967). Stephen Railton suggests that, in more recent films, Morgan Freeman played the role of Tom in his portrayal of Hoke Colburn in *Driving Miss Daisy* (1989) as did Michael Clark Duncan in his role as James Coffey in *The Green Mile* (1998).

In animated films, Uncle Tom made his debut in such shorts as *Uncle Tom and Little Eva* (1932), *The Old Plantation* (1935), *Uncle Tom's Bungalow* (1937), and *Uncle Tom's Cabana* (1947), but he emerges in feature-length animated films as well, most notably in the live-action (i.e., unanimated) character of Uncle Remus in *The Song of the South* (1946), but also as the crows in *Dumbo* (1941) and as Baloo the Bear in *The Jungle Book* (1967). In his earliest incarnation, animated Tom is not particularly memorable—he is obviously decrepit and worn, but he is not as recognizable in *Uncle Tom and Little Eva* as he is in later shorts where he is visually codified as the iconic tom with a heavy white beard, bald head, ragged clothes, glasses (usually), and a body that is clearly stooped and physically weak. In *Uncle Tom's Bungalow*, the narrator introduces Tom with, "And here comes Old Uncle Tom now. Gettin' kinda feeble. Just look at those knees shaking." Tom is almost always situated in these shorts in scenarios that demonstrate his satisfaction with plantation life—he is often depicted at ease, singing, dancing, or otherwise relaxing. In one remarkable scene from *Uncle Tom and Little Eva*, he is even shown polishing the outsized ball and chain attached to his ankle—an obvious indicator by the animators that he cherishes enslavement. An exception to this version of Tom is in *Uncle Tom's Cabana*, which departs from several established characterizations (e.g., it is staged in an otherwise urban setting, not the countryside; Eva is a highly sexualized, adult nightclub singer rather than a little girl) and situates Tom as a heavy-set, cigar-smoking (eventual) nightclub owner. Later, when animals replace humans as the central characters in animated films, Tom's usual physical particulars are either non-existent (e.g., the crows are not drawn in any way that invokes typical Tom imagery) or are at least secondary to the clearly scripted behavioral characteristics, broadening the role so that acting like a tom is possible even without looking like one.

In addition to the distortions of his physical features that underscore his weakness and servitude, the animated character of Uncle Tom is further so defined linguistically, in the type of language he uses, the content of his dialogue, and in his manner of speaking. Tom's scripts are heavily influenced by the perception of Black language inherited from minstrelsy, and his language is a simplistic misrepresentation of AAE. Outside of "yassuh's" and "yessum's," his dialogue has very little content, and when he does have something to say, it is usually marked by ignorance and superstition. Finally, Tom's voice is often either high-pitched and wavering (to demonstrate his advanced age and timidity), or deep and slow to underscore his simplemindedness. For example, in *The Old Plantation* (1935), a slowly tottering Tom sings "Ahm 'a comin', though my head is bending low";[4] in *Uncle Tom's Bungalow*, he says to a whip-cracking Simon Legree, "muh body might b'long to you, but muh soul b'longs to Warner Brothers!"; and finally, in *Uncle Tom's Cabana*, where Tom promises, "Wahl now chil'ren, ol' Uncle Tom's gon' tell you the real true story about Uncle Tom's Cabin," a child asks him, "Is you sho' all you been tellin' us is da true?" and Tom replies, "Wahl now, wait a minnit boy. If'n it ain't da truth, Ah hope dat lightnin' come down an' strike me dead!" And, of course, lightning does strike, revealing the story to be one of Tom's childlike imaginations.

Finally, in all of the early cartoon shorts that feature Tom, music plays an important role in the construction of the character as well. The musical score emphasizes Tom's passive acceptance of (and sometimes even enthusiastic participation in) plantation life. Typically, nostalgic songs such as "Swanee River," "Dixie," "Carry me back to Old Virginny," or "Old Kentucky Home"—all of which wistfully yearn for the tranquility of pre-emancipation days—accompany Tom's introduction to audiences. In fact, in *Uncle Tom and Little Eva*, even after Tom hurls his ball and chain at Simon Legree, thereby simultaneously defeating the villain and symbolically casting off slavery, Tom, Topsy, and Liza all sing happily to the strains of "Dixie" as the cartoon ends, leaving the audience to believe that, given the choice between freedom and enslavement, Tom and other "good Negroes" prefer the latter.

40.3 THE MAMMY

Another character that makes her debut early in both traditional and animated plantation genre films as a "good Negro" is the Mammy. She was originally the female version of Uncle Tom and is typically a heavy-set, dark-skinned domestic servant, always dressed in an apron and a bandana, and is usually shown happily doing housework (i.e., cooking, cleaning, hanging laundry out to dry, etc.) or doting on her White charges. As she develops over the history of entertainment, she remains desexualized, devoted, subservient, and fiercely loyal to Whites, but over time, and through the talents of several African American actresses who played iconic mammies, she also became a more complex character who was consistently sassy, sharp-tongued, and sharp-witted. While Tom is rarely cast as directly oppositional (he could challenge his masters in nonconfrontational ways, as we will later see in the discussion of *Song of the South*), the Mammy evolves in a way that lays the foundation for what eventually becomes the mythical "strong Black woman" in entertainment. Unlike Tom, her gender and her intimacy with the families that she serves allows her certain opportunities to stand her ground with Whites (usually for their own good), and so the Mammy is cast as the earthy maternal character who dispenses tough love and common sense to the Whites she loves and protects.

Since, at one point, this was the only role open to them, mammies were played by almost every notable Black actress, including Gertrude Howard, who was one of the first Black actresses to appear onscreen in *Uncle Tom's Cabin* (1927), and who was later cast as the mammy figure in *Show Boat* (1929), *Hearts in Dixie* (1929), and *I'm no Angel* (1933), and Madame Sun-te-Wan, who appeared in roles such as "Black cook" in *Imitation of Life* (1934), "scrubwoman" in *Island in the Sky* (1937), and "Eve, a Black servant," in *The Toy Wife* (1938). Other mammies included Libby Taylor (who played maids in over sixty films); Marietta Canty, known for her roles in *The Lady is Willing* (1942) and *Father of the Bride* (1950); Ethel Waters, *The Member of the Wedding* (1952); and most famously, Louise Beavers (who appeared in over 150 films as a housekeeper, cook, or maid) and Hattie McDaniel, who is credited with bringing humanity and dignity to the mammy characters she played, especially those in *Judge Priest* (1934), *The Little Colonel* (1935), and *Gone With the Wind* (1939).

In animation, Mammy appears in some of the same early shorts that feature Tom, such as *The Old Plantation* (1935), and is included in films like *The Adventures of Little Black Sambo* (1935), *Three Orphan Kittens* (1935), *More Kittens* (1936), *The Bookworm* (1939), *Scrub Me Mama, With a Boogie Beat* (1941), and *Coal Black and De Sebben Dwarfs* (1943). She also figures prominently as the faceless "Mammy Two Shoes" in the *Tom and Jerry* series where she is voiced by Lillian Randolph, known for her mammy roles on radio shows like *The Great Guildersleeve* (1942) and *Amos 'n' Andy*. Like Uncle Tom, the mammy has changed shape and costume over time; as we will see later in the discussion of contemporary animated films, even if she is not dressed in an apron and a bandana with children on her knee or washing at her feet, the mammy is still recognizable as a Black, self-sacrificing (but feisty) caretaker. For example, in *Song of the South*, the Mammy is live-action Aunt Tempy and, like Uncle Remus, the film's Tom, she is a prototypical example of the character type; however, the mammy has more recently been animated as a hippo (Gloria in *Madagascar I* and *II*), a muse (Thalia in *Hercules*), a 1950s show car (Flo in *Cars*), a woolly mammoth (Ellie in *Ice Age*), a skunk (*Over the*

Hedge's Wanda), and a one-hundred-year-old voodoo priestess (Mama Odie in *Princess and the Frog*).

Like Uncle Tom and all the other Black stock characters in early animated films, the mammy's caricature is deliberately constructed on what is intended to be comedic physical, behavioral, and linguistic misperceptions of African America. In *The Old Plantation* (1935), Mammy sings and dances around the plantation while picking cotton happily to "de rhythm o' de cotton pickin' song," and even after she's worked all day in the fields (with eyes half closed, she wipes her brow and her arms lie limp with exhaustion), she brightens up at the sight of Little Eva, exclaiming with delight, "Well, well if dere ain't Mammy's honey chile!" and rushes to the crib to cuddle and rock the sleeping child. She introduces *Coal Black and de Sebben Dwarves* (1943) as a fairytale while holding a child by the firelight, saying "heh, heh, heh, oh honey chile! And what story would you like Mammy to tell you tonight?" In *Scrub Me Mama, With a Boogie Beat* (1941), Mammy, like the other lethargic Black inhabitants of Lazytown, is confronted by the curvy and urbane light-skinned newcomer who chides her, "Listen, Mammy, that ain't no way to wash clothes! What you all need is rhythm," to which Mammy (voiced by White actor, Danny Webb) replies, "Wuh-wuh-uh-wuh-whut you all mean, rhythm?" All the townspeople, including several mammies, then become inspired by the singing and suggestive dancing of the visitor and finish out the film by happily performing stereotypical rural Black activities (washing, shining shoes, and eating watermelon) to the "boogie-woogie beat." In *Little Black Sambo* (1935), after washing her child, Sambo, in a tub and with a washboard (as she would clothes), Mammy (named "Mumbo" in this short) tells her son, "Now run along play, honey chile, but watch out for dat baaad ol' tiger. Dat ol' tiger sho' do like dark meat!" and sends him out to play in the jungle. Mammy in *Little Ol' Bosko and the Cannibals* (1937) is perhaps the forerunner of *Tom and Jerry's* Mammy Two Shoes as her face is never shown, but she is recognized by her slouching stockings, slippers, and broom and dustpan as well as by her domestic tasks. Again, her dialogue is an exaggerated form of AAE. When looking for Bosko, she calls, frustrated, "Bosko! lan' sakes! I wonder where dat chile done got to now ... now don't dat beat the very all get out!" A similar mammy character appears in Disney's *Pantry Pirate* (1940) where she chastises Pluto with "c'mon git outta here. Doggone you lazy good fo' nuthin' no account hound! You let me ketch you messin' round mah kitchen again I'm gonna bus' all da hide offa you!" and later, after Pluto's antics result in a loud crash in the kitchen, "Wha's goin' on down dere? What in da name a' goodness is dat yellah devil up to?"

Between 1940 and 1952, the animated mammy figure still most familiar to contemporary audiences, Mammy Two Shoes, appeared in over twenty *Tom and Jerry* cartoons. While audiences rarely see her from the waist up, what we do see of her tells us that, like other mammies in animation, she is heavy-set and wears an apron and housedress, and her slovenliness is signaled in her slouching patched socks and floppy slippers. Since she has an incomplete physical presence, her characterization necessarily hinges on her dialogue, which is written and delivered in the style of other mammies. She ceaselessly berates Tom for misbehavior (regardless of his guilt or innocence) in an exaggerated form of Southern AAE:

Mm, mm. Dat good fo' nuthin' cat. Jus' a minnit you good fo' nuthin; cheap fur coat
… if you breaks one mo' thing, you is goin; out! O-W-T, out. Thomas, if you is a
mouse catcher, I is Lana Turner, which I ain't. The trouble wit' you is you is getting
too old to catch mice. (*Old Rocking Chair Tom* 1948)

The Original Mammy Two Shoes, reportedly inspired by Hattie McDaniel, was later
replaced in Tom and Jerry cartoons (the updated *Tom and Jerry Tales*, which aired from
2005 to 2008) with a more politically correct White version. Although the White character is still heavy, feisty, and speaks with a southern accent, she differs from her Black
predecessor in that she is named "Mrs. Two Shoes" and has a husband and a son.

40.4 SAMBO

Another Black male character prominently featured alongside the Mammy in both
traditional and animated American film is the Sambo. Although critics differ in their
descriptions of such characters according to age (e.g., Lehman defines the Sambo as a
child [2009, 54], but other sources cast him as an adult), the caricature of the Sambo is
consistently marked by his naiveté—he is always shown to be gullible, superstitious, and
fearful. In his adult incarnation, the Sambo is a loyal and childlike companion to Whites
and is often cast as a domestic servant. His role, as such, positions him in film as a con-
fidant to White men (similar to the part the mammy plays with her White mistresses);
consequently, we most often see adult Sambo in uniform and in servitude to Whites.
Although the mammy character expands over time so that Black women are imagined
to have a certain strength and "attitude," the same does not occur with Sambo. His access
to White male culture is narrowly constructed so that the Sambo is never cast as a threat
to White male dominance. His unequal status (employee) and his exaggerated artless-
ness allow White audiences to remain secure in their expectation that "good" Black men
lack the guile necessary to usurp White authority; not only does he accept his subordinate role, Sambo embraces servitude and the protection of Whites because, due to his
mental and emotional immaturity, he is completely unable to fend for himself.

Sambo makes his debut in early silent films: George Reed plays "Nigger Jim" in
Huckleberry Finn (1920) and in D. W. Griffiths's *One Exciting Night* (1922), and Porter
Strong plays the role of Romeo Washington; however, one of America's best known
Sambos is the character Rochester van Jones played by Eddie Anderson on TV and
radio in *The Jack Benny Show* (his first appearance was on the radio show in 1937, and
the television program ran from 1950 to 1965) and in the films *Jezebel* (1938), *You Can't
Cheat an Honest Man* (1939), *Love Thy Neighbor* (1940), and *The Meanest Man in the
World* (1943). As Jack Benny's valet, Anderson was the first African American to have a
regular role on a national radio show and became an iconic Sambo who was characterized not only as a devoted servant, but as a lazy, shiftless, drinking gambler as well, and
much of his dialogue revolves around such topics. Rochester's dialogue is also written to

highlight his subservience to the White characters on the show. For example, while he is addressed as "Rochester," he uses Mr. and Miss to refer to Whites. Anderson's popularity was such that he appeared outside of *The Jack Benny Show*. He is referenced on *Amos 'n' Andy* and was in episodes of the *Milton Berle Show* and *Bachelor Father*—but always as Rochester, the butler/valet. The entire cast of *The Jack Benny Show* voiced their respective characters in Warner Brothers' 1959 cartoon *The Mouse that Jack Built*, where all of the actors were animated as rodents. Rochester becomes such an identifiable stock character, and a symbol of a particular (and problematized) type of Black male success that in the animated short *The Goose Goes South* (1941), a mammy picking cotton has a pack of infant Sambos on her back, all of whom are saying, "Hello Mr. Benny," loudly into toy telephones. The mammy complains in exasperation to her fellow slaves, "They all wants to grow up to be Rochesters!"

In fact, most of the animated representations of Sambo are children. This is undoubtedly due to the influence of Helen Bannerman's 1899 illustrated story entitled *Little Black Sambo*, which was the tale of a clever and well-dressed Black boy who outsmarts a succession of tigers. While critics have argued that Bannerman never intended for her original story to be a racist depiction of Black children, the book's popularity launched a number of re-illustrated versions. Similar to the fate of *Uncle Tom's Cabin*, *Little Black Sambo* was reproduced with more explicit anti-Black themes and illustrations with crudely distorted Black caricatures, and often positioned the title character stereotypically on southern plantations or in the jungles of Africa. In addition to Bannerman's story, there were also adaptations of Pat Sullivan's *Sammy Johnsin* cartoon series, a newspaper comic strip that first appeared in 1916 and featured a Black boy living on a plantation with his mammy mother. Later, an animated Sambo stars in animated shorts such as *Little Black Sambo* (1935) and in the Happy Harmonies[5] *Little Ol' Bosko* series, including *Little Ol' Bosko and the Cannibals* (1937), *Bosko in Baghdad* (1938), and *Little Ol' Bosko and the Pirates* (1937). Sambo is also cast as Eightball in *A-Haunting We Will Go* (1939) and *Silly Superstition* (1939) and as Jasper in puppetoon shorts like *Jasper and the Watermelons* (1942) and *Jasper and the Haunted House* (1942). Sambo has no dialogue in *Little Black Sambo*, but in all of the other films in which he is featured (like other Black characters of the time), he speaks an overblown and inaccurate form of AAE. For example, in *Bosko's Easter Eggs* (1937), he sings to himself:

"Now Easta tahm is de tahm fuh eggs, and de tahm fuh eggs is da Easta tahm, / an' ah praise da lawd as ah clahm da fence dat ah ain' gonna teah muh Sunday pants" and later, when attempting to steal eggs from a hen, Bosko says, "well hello dere miz chicken. You sho' is lookin' mighty scrumptious t'day. Well jus' lookit alla dem eggs. You sho is powerful uncomfta'bul sittin on all dem eggs."

Bosko then proceeds to trick the hen into leaving her nest and steals her eggs—perhaps foreshadowing a future in chicken stealing, a habit that characterizes stereotypical adult Black male behavior in early entertainment history.

40.5 THE COON

Black *children* are seldom lampooned in contemporary films; we really only see them featured prominently in films like *Bebe's Kids* (1992) and *Fat Albert* (1972–84). Modern versions of animated Sambo have returned to the adult version. There is a bit of ambiguity here though, since the adult Sambo is similar to another stereotypical Black male character created in minstrelsy that endures in traditional and animated films: the Coon. As David Pilgrim (2000) explains, in his discussion of racist caricatures at Ferris State University's Jim Crow Museum:

> The coon caricature is one of the most insulting of all anti-Black caricatures. The name itself, an abbreviation of raccoon, is dehumanizing. As with Sambo, the coon was portrayed as a lazy, easily frightened, chronically idle, inarticulate, buffoon. The coon differed from the Sambo in subtle but important ways. Sambo was depicted as a perpetual child, not capable of living as an independent adult. The coon acted childish, but he was an adult; albeit a good-for-little adult. Sambo was portrayed as a loyal and contented servant. Indeed, Sambo was offered as a defense for slavery and segregation. How bad could these institutions have been, asked the racialists, if Blacks were contented, even happy, being servants? The coon, although he often worked as a servant, was not happy with his status. He was, simply, too lazy or too cynical to attempt to change his lowly position. Also, by the 1900s, Sambo was identified with older, docile Blacks who accepted Jim Crow laws and etiquette; whereas coons were increasingly identified with young, urban Blacks who disrespected Whites. Stated differently, the coon was a Sambo gone bad. (http://www.ferris.edu/jimcrow/coon/)

The coon has historically been used for comic relief in television and movies, and of all the actors who played the coon, Steppin Fetchit (born Lincoln Perry) became most closely identified with the character in his recurrent role as "The Laziest Man in the World" in films such as *The County Chairman* (1935), *Judge Priest* (1934), and *Steamboat Round the Bend* (1935). Famous imitators in traditional film include Mantan Moreland (who was featured in over seventy "race movies" but is best known for his role as "Birmingham Brown," the chauffeur in the *Charlie Chan* series); Willie Best (billed as "Sleep n' Eat"); Sam "Deacon" McDaniel (brother to the more famous Hattie); Dudley Dickerson (master of the "scared reaction"); Fred "Snowflake" Toones (typecast as a porter in nearly fifty films); and Nicodemus Stewart, who voiced Br'er Rabbit in *Song of the South*. More recently, comedians like Richard Pryor, Martin Lawrence, and Tracy Morgan have filled the role.

In animation, the coon makes his appearance as a cartoon version of Steppin Fetchit as a reluctant frog-groom in *Clean Pastures* (1937) and a blackbird who testifies in *Who Killed Cock Robin* (1935). In *The Goose Goes South* (1941), Hanna and Barbera explicitly define a southern tobacco worker as " 'a lazy Steppin' Fetchit type worker (who) listens in a stupid lazy manner.' The script also describes the character's speech as 'very slow' and contains unintelligible dialogue for actors to voice for African American characters, reflecting the identification of the characters as rural laborers" (Lehman 2009, 44). There are also several coon characters in *Scrub Me Mama with a Boogie Beat* (1941), a short in which Black men make up most of the town's lazy inhabitants—the opening scenes show sleeping Black men who are too tired to even participate in stereotypical "Black" activities such as fishing and picking cotton; one pair is initially shown too lazy to even fight, slowly slapping one another while saying "take dat/You take dat/Ah bus' yo' head." A number of other shorts show Black male characters defined by typical coon characteristics established in minstrelsy such as drinking, gambling, eating watermelon, and stealing chickens.

Contemporary cooning is evident in the animated characters voiced by today's Black comedians, notably Eddie Murphy, as Donkey in the *Shrek* series, and as Mushu in *Mulan*; Chris Rock as Marty in *Madagascar* (2005) and *Madagascar: Escape 2 Africa* (2008); Tracy Morgan in *Rio* (2011); and Will Smith in *Shark Tale* (2004).As did their historical counterparts, these actors play secondary roles in characters that are lazy, superstitious, childlike, and comical. They are still marked by the use of exaggerated AAE and are often thuggish as well. For example, in the *Transformers* sequel, *Revenge of the Fallen*, twin brothers Skids (Tom Kenny) and Mudflap (Reno Wilson) are not only distortions of what is assumed to be African American behavior but are also characterized by their cowardice and stupidity in contrast to the other heroic autobots. Although the film is not animated in the traditional sense, their faces in robot mode look like early twentieth-century portrayals of Blacks with buckteeth, bulging eyes, and large ears; one of them even has a gold tooth. They admit to not knowing how to read, reference "ass-kickin'" and "booty-calls," and even threaten to "pop a cap in someone's ass."

40.6 CONCLUSION

The Tom, Mammy, Sambo, and Coon characters that were established in minstrelsy are still the easiest to spot in contemporary media, especially in traditional and animated film. Certainly some of these characters are more nuanced than their predecessors in some ways; in others, they are as underdeveloped, insulting, and static as they were when they were developed by blackface performers. Other lesser characters have also emerged over time, such as the Black buck, the tragic mulatto (or jezebel), and the mystic Negro, but these roles tend to feature less prominently overall in feature-length animated films intended largely for child audiences. Perhaps it is because these secondary Black character types are more "adult" in that they necessarily invoke notions of obvious violence and sexuality; hence, they only make cameo appearances in animated films rated PG. Not only is it disappointing that so many other negative stereotypes remain completely intact for child audiences today, but it is equally troubling that despite the gains African American actors have made in traditional films, even with the creation of Disney's first Black princess in *The Princess and the Frog* (2009), we have yet to see the development of positive new Black character types in animated film.

When African American mothers who took their daughters to see Disney's *The Princess and the Frog* were asked for reactions to the film, their responses were overwhelmingly positive. Many thought the story was well crafted, that there was a strong feminist message (unlike most Disney princesses, Tiana is not rescued by her prince and does not end up living in a palace, but owns her own restaurant instead), and that race was less important than the message of hard work and triumph over adversity. It was left to the critics to point out that Disney's first Black princess spent 70 percent of her time on screen as a frog, that her voice, for most audiences, was not "identifiably Black" (and so it was easy to forget her human ethnicity), and that the setting of 1920s New Orleans might have done more to perpetuate racial stereotypes than dispel them. Without a doubt, there are positive messages in animated films; we often look to animated films to introduce children to social or developmental situations and to teach moral and ethical lessons, and children are shown a variety of familial relationships, gender roles, and conflicts between good and evil through animated characters; it is upon these characters and situations that they begin to build their own belief systems. Children, in part, form their expectations for a variety of behaviors and social roles by watching animated films. According to Michael Baran, "most people think that children don't attend to subtle messages about race and gender in movies, but it's really the opposite" (Barnes 2009). Animated films offer children intricate teachings about race by guiding them through the complexities of highly racialized scenarios, and they teach children how to maneuver within the general terrain of "race" by highlighting quite specific differences. These films provide children with the necessary tools to reinforce expectations about normalized racial dynamics. The way in which ethnicity is constructed by animators—linguistically, physically, behaviorally, and otherwise—warrants scrutiny because of animated films' outsized impact on children.

NOTES

1. In this chapter, I am using *Black* and *African American* to mean the racial/ethnic category that includes people who have total or partial ancestry from any of the regions in sub-Saharan Africa. Similarly, I use *White* and *European American* interchangeably to mean the ethnic categories that include people who have ancestry in Europe. I understand that these two groups are not homogeneous and also often overlap, but for the purposes of this chapter, I am using both as general categories that rely on a set of shared historical and cultural practices.

2. I am using *African American English* (AAE) to refer to a subsystem of English spoken largely (but not exclusively) by African Americans. I intend my use of the term to refer to the distinct set of phonological and syntactic rules that are now aligned in many ways with the rules of other dialects, and which have influenced and been influenced by southern varieties as well.

3. I do not use *AAE* and *Black language* interchangeably in this chapter as I consider the two to be different ideologically. When I use *Black language*, I am referring to a language type which is broader than AAE, and which includes the misrepresentations and

misunderstandings of the language spoken by Black people. *Black language* in this chapter not only refers to AAE as a linguistic system but also to the distortion and misappropriation of AAE, often when used by Whites who attempt to imitate AAE.

4. Unless otherwise noted, I have transcribed all of the dialogue quoted in this chapter.

5. The Bosko who appeared in MGM's *Happy Harmonies* (1934–38) is distinct from the earlier Looney Tunes Bosko who, based in appearance on Fritz the Cat, appears to be a forerunner of Mickey Mouse. While that Bosko is simian in appearance, except for his very earliest incarnation, he is relatively unmarked in terms of race; that is, he is not shown in any of the stereotypical "Black" environments (e.g., plantation, jungle) popular in the animation of Blacks in that era, and he is accompanied by show standards, not minstrel tunes. Notably, In *Bosko, the Talk-Ink Kid* (1929), he is voiced (by White actor Carman Maxwell) with an exaggerated and unconvincing AAE, and performs similar to other minstrel characters, but by 1931, Johnny Murray, who gives him a Mickey-Mouse-like falsetto, voices him, and the character is stripped of racial connotations.

REFERENCES

A Haunting We Will Go. 1939. Directed by Burt Gillet. Los Angeles, CA: Twentieth Century Fox.

A Patch of Blue. 1969. Directed by Guy Green. Beverly Hills, CA: Metro-Goldwyn-Mayer.

Bannerman, Helen. 1899. *Little Black Sambo.* London: Grant Richards.

Barnes, Brooks. 2009. "Her Prince Has Come. Critics too." *The New York Times*, May 31. http://www.nytimes.com/2009/05/31/fashion.

Bebe's Kids. 1992. Directed by Bruce Smith. Hollywood, CA: Paramount.

Bosko's Easter Eggs. 1937. Directed by Hugh Harman. Beverly Hills, CA: Metro-Goldwyn-Mayer.

Bosko, the Talk-Ink Kid. 1929. Directed by Hugh Harman and Rudolf Ising. Burbank, CA: Warner Bros.

Cars. 2006. Directed by John Lasseter and Joe Ranft. Burbank, CA: Buena Vista.

Clean Pastures. 1937. Directed by Friz Freleng. Burbank, CA: Warner Bros.

Coal Black and de Sebben Dwarfs. 1943. Directed by Robert Clampett. Burbank, CA: Warner Bros.

Comer, Jim. 2005. "Every Time I Turn around: Rite, Reversal, and the End of Blackface Minstrelsy." Ferris State University. n.d. http://www.ferris.edu/news/jimcrow/links/comer/.

Confederate Spy. 1910. Directed by Sidney Olocott. New York: Kalem.

Driving Miss Daisy. 1989. Directed by Bruce Beresford. Burbank, CA: Warner Bros.

Dumbo. 1941. Directed by Samuel Armstrong, Norman Ferguson, Wilfred Jackson, Jack Kinney, Bill Roberts, Ben Sharpsteen, and John Elliotte. New York: RKO.

Edge of the City. 1957. Directed by Martin Ritt. Beverly Hills, CA: Metro-Goldwyn-Mayer.

Father of the Bride. 1950. Directed by Vincente Minnelli. Beverly Hills, CA: Metro-Goldwyn-Mayer.

Follow Your Heart. 1936. Directed by Aubrey Scotto. Hollywood, CA: Republic Pictures.

For Massa's Sake. 1911. Directed by Joseph A. Golden. New York: General Film Company.

Gone With the Wind. 1939. Directed by Victor Fleming and George Cukor. Burbank, CA: Warner Bros.

Hearts in Dixie. 1929. Directed by Paul Sloane. Los Angeles, CA: Twentieth Century Fox Film Corporation.

Heaven Can Wait. 1943. Directed by Ernst Lubitsch. Los Angeles, CA: Twentieth Century Fox Film Corporation.

Hercules. 1997. Directed by Ron Clements and John Musker. Burbank, CA: Buena Vista Pictures.

Huckleberry Finn. 1920. Directed by William Desmond Taylor. Hollywood, CA: Paramount.

I'm No Angel. 1933. Directed by Wesley Ruggles. Hollywood, CA: Paramount.

Ice Age. 2002. Directed by Chris Wedge and Carlos Saldanha. Los Angeles, CA: Twentieth Century Fox.

Imitation of Life. 1934. Directed by John M. Stahl. Universal City, CA: Universal.

Island in the Sky. 1937. Directed by Herbert I. Leeds. Los Angeles, CA: Twentieth Century Fox.

Jasper and the Haunted House. 1942. Directed by George Pal. Hollywood, CA: Paramount.

Jasper and the Watermelon. 1942. Directed by George Pal. Hollywood, CA: Paramount.

Jezebel. 1938. Directed by William Wyler. Burbank, CA: Warner Bros.

Joe Palooka in the Knockout. 1947. Directed by Reginald Le Borg. Hollywood, CA: Monogram.

Judge Priest. 1934. Directed by John Ford. Los Angeles, CA: Twentieth Century Fox.

Lehman, Christopher P. 2009. *The Colored Cartoon: Black Representation in American Animated Short Films, 1907–1954.* Amherst: University of Massachusetts.

Lilies of the Field. 1963. Directed by Ralph Nelson. Beverly Hills, CA: United Artists.

Little Black Sambo. 1935. Directed by Ub Iwerks. Burbank, CA: Celebrity Productions.

Little Ol' Bosko and the Cannibals. 1937. Directed by Hugh Harman. Beverly Hills, CA: Metro-Goldwyn-Mayer.

Little Ol' Bosko and the Pirates. 1937. Directed by Hugh Harman. Beverly Hills, CA: Metro-Goldwyn-Mayer.

Little Ol' Bosko in Bagdad. 1938. Directed by Hugh Harman. Beverly Hills, CA: Metro-Goldwyn-Mayer.

Love Thy Neighbor. 1940. Directed by Mark Sandrich. Hollywood, CA: Paramount.

Madagascar. 2005. Directed by Eric Darnell and Tom McGrath. Glendon, CA: DreamWorks Distribution.

Madagascar: Escape 2 Africa. 2008. Directed by Eric Darnell and Tom McGrath. Hollywood, CA: Paramount.

More Kittens. 1936. Directed by David Hand and Wilfred Jackson. Beverly Hills, CA: United Artists.

Mulan. 1998. Directed by Tony Bancroft and Barry Cook. Burbank, CA: Buena Vista Pictures.

Old Rockin' Chair Tom. 1948. Directed by Joseph Barbera and William Hanna. Beverly Hills, CA: Metro-Goldwyn-Mayer.

One Exciting Night. 1922. Directed by D.W. Griffiths. Beverly Hills, CA: United Artists.

Over the Hedge. 2006. Directed by Tim Johnson and Karey Kirkpatrick. Hollywood, CA: Paramount.

Pantry Pirate. 1940. Directed by Clyde Geronimi. New York: RKO.

Pilgrim, David. "The Coon Caricature." The Jim Crow Museum of Racist Memorabilia Website. http://www.ferris.edu/jimcrow/coon/(accessed 2/12/2013).

Riding High. 1950. Directed by Frank Capra. Hollywood, CA: Paramount.

Rio. 2011. Directed by Carlos Saldanha. Los Angeles, CA: Twentieth Century Fox.

Scrub Me Mama with a Boogie Beat. 1941. Directed by Walter Lantz. Universal City, CA: Universal.

Shark Tale. 2004. Directed by Bibo Bergeron, Vicky Jenson and Rob Letterman. Glendon, CA: DreamWorks.

Show Boat. 1929. Directed by Harry A. Pollard and Arch Heath. Universal City, CA: Universal.

Show Boat. 1936. Directed by James Whale. Universal City, CA: Universal.

Shrek. 2001. Directed by Andrew Adamson and Vicky Jenson. Glendon, CA: DreamWorks Distribution.

Silly Superstition. 1939. Directed by Burt Gillet. Universal City, CA: Universal.

Song of the South. 1946. Directed by Wilfred Jackson and Harve Foster. New York, NY: RKO.

Steamboat Round the Bend. 1935. Directed by John Ford. Los Angeles, CA: Twentieth Century Fox.

Stowe, Harriet Beecher. 1852. *Uncle Tom's Cabin; or, Life among the Lowly*. Boston: Jewett.

Strausbaugh, John. 2006. *Black Like You; Blackface, Whiteface, Insult and Imitation in American Popular Culture*. New York: Penguin.

The Amos 'n' Andy Show. 1951-53. Directed by Charles Barton. Los Angeles, CA: CBS.

The Birth of a Nation. 1915. Directed by D. W. Griffith. Hollywood, CA: Epoch.

The Bookworm. 1939. Directed by Friz Freleng and Hugh Harman. Beverly Hills, CA: Metro-Goldwyn-Mayer.

The County Chairman. 1935. Directed by John G. Blystone. Los Angeles, CA: Twentieth Century Fox.

The Defiant Ones. 1958. Directed by Stanley Kramer. Beverly Hills, CA: United Artists.

The Goose Goes South. 1941. Directed by Joseph Barbera and William Hanna. Beverly Hills, CA: Metro-Goldwyn-Mayer.

The Green Mile. 1999. Directed by Frank Darabont. Burbank, CA: Warner Bros.

The Jungle Book. 1967. Directed by Wolfgang Reitherman. Burbank, CA: Buena Vista.

The Lady is Willing. 1942. Directed by Mitchell Leisen. Culver City, CA: Columbia.

The Little Colonel. 1935. Directed by David Butler. Los Angeles, CA: Twentieth Century Fox Film Corporation.

The Meanest Man in the World. 1943. Directed by Sidney Lanfield. Los Angeles, CA: Twentieth Century Fox Film Corporation.

The Member of the Wedding. 1952. Directed by Fred Zinnemann. Culver City, CA: Columbia.

The Mouse the Jack Built. 1959. Directed by Robert McKimson. Burbank, CA: Warner Bros.

The Old Plantation. 1935. Directed by Rudolf Ising. Beverly Hills, CA: Metro-Goldwyn-Mayer.

The Princess and the Frog. 2009. Directed by Ron Clements and John Musker. Burbank, CA: Walt Disney.

The Slender Thread. 1965. Directed by Sydney Pollack. Hollywood, CA: Paramount.

The Toy Wife. 1938. Directed by Richard Thorpe. Beverly Hills, CA: Metro-Goldwyn-Mayer.

Three Orphan Kittens. 1936. Directed by David Hand. Beverly Hills, CA: United Artists.

To Sir, With Love. 1967. Directed by James Clavell. Culver City, CA: Columbia Pictures.

Toll, Robert C. 1974. Blacking Up: The Minstrel Show in Nineteenth-Century America. New York: Oxford University.

Transformers: Revenge of the Fallen. 2009. Directed by Michael Bay. Hollywood, CA: Paramount.

Uncle Tom and Little Eva. 1932. Directed by Amadee J. Van Buren. New York, NY: RKO.

Uncle Tom's Bungalow. 1937. Directed by Tex Avery. Burbank, CA: Warner Bros.

Uncle Tom's Cabana. 1947. Directed by Tex Avery. Beverly Hills, CA: Metro-Goldwyn-Mayer.

Uncle Tom's Cabin. 1927. Directed by Harry A. Pollard. Universal City, CA: Universal.

Uncle Tom's Cabin. 1903. Directed by Edwin Porter. Edison.

Who Killed Cock Robin? 1935. Directed by David Hand. Beverly Hills, CA: United Artists.

You Can't Cheat an Honest Man. 1939. Directed by George Marshall and Edward F. Cline. Universal City, CA: Universal Studios.

Zanzibar. 1940. Directed by Harold D. Schuster. Universal City, CA: Universal.

CHAPTER 41

....

SWB (SPEAKING WHILE BLACK)

Linguistic Profiling and Discrimination Based on Speech as a Surrogate for Race against Speakers of African American Vernacular English

....

JOHN BAUGH

41.1 INTRODUCTION

....

WHY SWB? Why not TWB: "Talking while Black"?[1] Frankly, either formulation serves to convey forms of linguistic discrimination that are the result of racial stereotypes about Black speakers who live in different parts of the world. This chapter is devoted primarily to a review of linguistic circumstances in the United States that are most relevant to Black Americans, through criticism of Ebonics, and as a result of limited educational opportunities. The 1996-1997 Oakland Ebonics controversy has strong educational relevance, calling language education policies into question. Additional evidence of linguistic bias against African Americans was on display during the George Zimmerman murder trial, where many who disparaged Rachel Jeantel's speech and inability to read cursive writing vilified her.

Racial disparities in the workplace, education, housing, health, law, and other social institutions in the United States were reinforced by linguistic differences that are the product of slavery due substantially to involuntary immigration (see Ogbu 1978). We will present some experimental findings that are the result of collaboration with fair housing agencies across the country that have observed differential treatment of fair housing testers who request appointments to see properties by phone. That is to say, those who receive their telephone inquiries do not see them. Non-White callers are far less likely to be granted appointments in affluent communities than are White callers, and linguistic profiling appears to restrict access to housing for those who lack fluency in Mainstream American Standard English (MASE).[2]

The discussion also describes instances of linguistic harassment on the job, where English language learners, all of whom were born in Africa, were depicted by racist insults that resulted in a hostile work environment. The collective episodes of linguistic discrimination that are described will be examined in terms of their legal relevance prior to some educational suggestions that precede concluding remarks.

41.2 LINGUISTIC BIGOTRY: EBONICS AND THE DENIGRATION OF AAVE

Linguistic bigotry exists in various forms throughout the world. Within the United States, where European colonization and slavery resulted in the social stratification of MASE, language usage by slave descendants remains controversial. Anyone who lacks fluency in MASE may be at a considerable disadvantage: educationally, economically, occupationally, and, at times, legally, in various regions of the United States. The year 1996 witnessed the global introduction of Ebonics,[3] when the Oakland school district in California's Bay area declared it to be the native language of 28,000 Black students who were enrolled in that district. Outcries against Ebonics were vitriolic and extensive from both Blacks and Whites who challenged its very existence. In actual fact, Robert Williams (1975) coined the term *Ebonics* during a conference in 1973 that explored the psychological development of Black children. Although no linguists participated in that conference, Williams and his colleagues introduced the idea that African slavery had international linguistic consequences that exceeded English usage by Blacks in the United States.

The vast majority of the original contributions that are contained within the *Oxford Handbook on African American Language* serve to illustrate and clarify many of the long-standing misconceptions that are associated with African American Vernacular English (AAVE)[4] and its speakers. Smitherman's (this volume) historical observations are keenly relevant, as are Spears's (this volume) depictions of standard renditions of African American Language.[5] Anderson (this volume) describes corresponding linguistic attitudes and ideologies that help to understand the motivation behind those middle-class African Americans whose speech is evaluated by Britt and Weldon (this volume). When these chapters are viewed collectively, it becomes clear that speakers of AAVE have been the objects of linguistic discrimination, which has inescapable racial relevance.

41.3 LINGUISTIC PROFILING AND UNEQUAL ACCESS TO HOUSING: EXPERIMENTAL RESULTS

Evidence of racial discrimination in housing against African Americans exists and results—at least, in part—from linguistic stereotypes. To investigate this claim, housing testers across the United States made telephone calls to rental and sales offices in large urban communities in Pennsylvania, Missouri, Ohio, and California. Serendipity plays a role in these results because they are the product of collaboration with fair housing agencies in different communities that tracked the results of telephone inquiries by testers who were adult men and women from diverse racial and linguistic backgrounds. Our results are not merely the product of racial classification; rather, we also identify the linguistic heritage of a speaker, in addition to other demographic traits, such as age, sex, education, and the region of the United States where the person may have been raised.

The National Fair Housing Alliance (NFHA) is devoted to the elimination of housing discrimination and their organization was the first to alert me to the fact that many of their African American testers were being denied appointments to see housing based on telephone calls. That is, although the recipients of these calls never saw the caller (i.e., housing tester), NFHA noted that Black and Latin@ testers were frequently being denied appointments while White testers were granted appointments. Massey and Lundy (2001) conducted experiments in Philadelphia where they noted that female speakers of vernacular Black English[6] were least successful in obtaining appointments to view housing. In light of the significant number of female-headed African American households, NFHA's findings were potentially discriminatory, if not indicative of illegal housing restrictions. The challenge: how do you prove racial discrimination has taken place, sight unseen? We chose to conduct experiments, and the results presented herein are illustrative of racial bias that has been documented based on race and linguistic background.

In short, racial classification alone is insufficient for adequate policies to overcome housing discrimination, educational disparities, or many other social maladies that have heretofore been garnered by race alone (e.g., *Brown v. Board of Education*). Thus, by exploring linguistic stereotypes, we extend some of the research methods employed by Lambert and Tucker (1972) and Preston (1989) to identify demographic perceptions that were conveyed by various housing testers across the United States. Prior to conducting any telephone requests for appointments, housing testers made high-quality recordings of three things: (a) the alphabet, (b) counting to twenty, and (c) reciting or reading the nursery rhyme "Mary had a little lamb." Various listeners, all of whom were adults who grew up in the United States and were native speakers of American English, listened to the entire recording before guessing the speaker's sex, age, education, race, the region of the country where they might have been raised, and an assessment of their native language (i.e., is it English or not English?). In some cases, such as the speaker's sex or native language, it was fairly common to obtain categorical agreement about a speaker; that is, everyone recognized the sex of the speaker upon hearing the voice, or everyone could detect that the speaker's native language was English, or not. However, traits such as age, education, race, or regional background were less reliable; nonetheless, their variability proved to be important because linguistic profiling takes many forms that frequently exceed racial background alone. Strong evidence reflects another of Massey and Lundy's (2001) findings; namely, Blacks who are proficient speakers of MASE are often granted appointments, or their telephone messages receive positive replies. Our findings indicate that Blacks who speak MASE are frequently perceived to be White, but rarely is this perception universal. Black people frequently detect the race of fellow African Americans, despite fluency or not in MASE (see Spears, this volume; Britt and Weldon, this volume). Although some judges who are not African American correctly identify the race of Blacks who employ MASE, the majority of non-African American judges conclude that these rare speakers are White. Results presented in tables 41.1 and 41.2 are significant because they reflect different racial impressions of a single bidialectal speaker who can switch freely between MASE and African American Vernacular English (AAVE), this assessment being based primarily on phonological and prosodic characteristics that have nothing whatsoever to do with syntactic, morphological, or morphophonemic variability.

In this instance, the female speaker depicted in table 41.1 was clearly perceived to be White by the vast majority of those who heard her voice. When the very same speaker produced a speech rendition using her AAVE variety, she was routinely identified as a Black speaker. Few housing testers shared this linguistic dexterity, which is particularly noteworthy in this context because it demonstrates that many speakers of American English strongly associate speech with race.

Table 41.1 Judges' Perception of Speaker 1 guise (N = 29)

Speaker 1			
Sex	Male (0)	Female (29)	
Age	18–29 (0)	30–39 (8)	40–49 (15) 50+ (6)
Education	High School (12)	College (14)	Professional School (3)
Race	White (27)	Black (0)	Jewish (2)
Region	Northeast (11) Southwest (0)	Southeast (2) West (0)	Midwest (12) National Standard (4)
Native Language	English (29)	Not English (0)	

Table 41.2 Judges' Perceptions of Speaker 2 guise (N = 29)

Speaker 2			
Sex	Male (1)	Female (28)	
Age	18–29 (13)	30–39 (10)	40–49 (6) 50+ (0)
Education	High School (17)	College (12)	Professional School (0)
Race	White (0)	Black (27)	African (2)
Region	Northeast (2) Southwest (2)	Southeast (9) West (0)	Midwest (10) National Standard (4)
Native Language	English (27)	Not English (2)	

The title of this chapter is drawn in part from the perceptions of race that differ for these rare, but fluent, bidialectal speakers of diverse African American dialects. Their cultural and linguistic heritage can, like a chameleon, be revealed or concealed depending upon the speech event at hand. Face-to-face discussion cannot conceal the race or sex of an interlocutor, but whenever telephone conversations between strangers occur, perceptions of race may "color" the ways in which callers are treated, especially if they seek to purchase goods or services through telephone calls—sight unseen.

41.4 Insights from Preliminary Evaluations

A great deal of the research related to linguistic profiling began with analyses by Purnell, Idsardi, and Baugh (1999), at which time they observed that many speakers of American English, regardless of dialect background, were able to accurately identify the racial background of a speaker based on brief comments. The vast majority of listeners were capable of racial recognition upon hearing a single word: *hello*. The experiments of Purnell et al. also maintained strict control over grammatical structure, indicating that listeners were tuning into subtle differences in pronunciation. More precisely, the differences that listeners heard between MASE, AAVE, and Chicano English were concentrated on intonation, prosody, and phonetic properties associated with an identical grammatical sentence. They maintained the same sentence structure to insure that listeners would not base their judgments on specific lexical or unique dialect features.

Many of those who listened to different speakers would often comment on the fact that some people "sounded Black" or others "sounded White," where it was apparent that these listeners were making close associations between the speech of an individual and their corresponding racial background. Indeed, it is because many people come to make these associations (i.e., they associate particular speech styles with members of a given racial group) that some people have fallen prey to linguistic discrimination as a surrogate for racial discrimination.

Massey and Lundy (2001) did not confine their experiments to utilization of the same grammatical utterance. They employed MASE, as well as two varieties of Black speech, including a more standardized rendition, similar to the speech described by Spears (this volume) and Britt and Weldon (this volume), as well as AAVE. In their case, dialect features associated with AAVE were utilized, and recipients of phone calls were exposed to greater linguistic variability than was first employed by Purnell, Idsardi, and Baugh (1999).

As a result of these experimental studies, we know well that unscrupulous business practices that deny goods or services to potential clients or customers who are perceived to be less than desirable, based entirely on the sound of their voice over the telephone, may become unwitting victims of linguistic profiling. Ironically, during the economic downturn that resulted in the escalation of housing prices before the national collapse of the real estate market, some disreputable lenders would use linguistic profiling to ensnare potential victims. In several instances, scam artists would use random-digit dialing associated with working-class communities and would initiate calls in the hope of convincing homeowners to refinance their homes. Not only were many of the victims of these scams members of minority groups, they were often older. As a result, these examples of linguistic profiling discriminated on the basis of race and age, not to deny goods or services, but to entrap elderly minority homeowners into entering contracts they could not sustain. Thus, during the course of our research on linguistic profiling we have seen it used on some occasions to exclude potential customers, while under other circumstances (typically during difficult economic circumstances) the same techniques have been used to identify unwitting victims.

41.5 ILLUSTRATIONS IN THE COURTROOM: THE LINGUISTIC DEVALUATION OF RACHEL JEANTEL

Although many of the linguistic profiling studies have occurred in social settings where either housing or employment was denied to a person who did not speak MASE, the United States witnessed a clear case of linguistic discrimination during the George Zimmerman murder trial regarding his actions leading to the death of 17-year-old, Trayvon Martin, a young African American whom Mr. Zimmerman suspected of being a burglar. Readers who are unfamiliar with the case may be unaware that the last person to speak with Trayvon Martin was his friend Rachel Jeantel, who was talking to him during a cell phone conversation at the very moment that Mr. Martin realized Mr. Zimmerman was following him.

Ms. Jeantel was called upon to testify in the case, and because her testimony was televised nationally, she became the object of close scrutiny by the public and members of the media who were transfixed by the trial during its deliberations. Ms. Jeantel was on the witness stand for several hours that spanned a two-day period. Prior to her testimony in court, Don West, an attorney who defended Mr. Zimmerman throughout the case, had deposed her. Although the public was not privy to observing Ms. Jeantel's deposition with Mr. West, it was obvious from the outset that their exchanges in the courtroom were contentious, occasionally confrontational, and, at times, hostile. Mr. West did his best to discredit Ms. Jeantel whenever possible because she was one of the most important witnesses for the prosecution. Mr. West was clearly mindful of the fact that her remarks—and her obvious sense of loss—could result in a murder conviction for his client. Whereas Ms. Jeantel was a young African American woman with limited education, Mr. West knew well that he needed to cast doubt about Ms. Jeantel's recollections and actions related to events that ultimately resulted in Trayvon Martin's death.

The first day of Ms. Jeantel's testimony was not only heated, it evoked a huge amount of commentary by pundits and through social media, including many overtly racist comments about her appearance and her speech. A brief sampling of the commentary related to her testimony serves to illustrate the point at hand:

(1) "Rachel Jeantel looked so irritated during the cross-examination that I burned it on DVD and I'm going to sell it as media goes to court."
(2) "Rachel Jeantel has absolutely no respect for this country's judicial system. Humanity as a whole would be embarrassed."
(3) "It's no excuse to use age for Rachel Jeantel's demeanor. Her attitude & grammar is playing right into stereotypes about Black women."
(4) "This Rachel Jeantel witness is dumber than a box of rocks. Zimmerman might get off."
(5) "Guess why all the Black animals think Rachel Jeantel is a Rhodes scholar with veracity who offered credible testimony."[7]

Personal and racist insults notwithstanding, Rachel Jeantel's testimony was notably different during her second day on the witness stand. Whereas her first day of testimony was often combative and confrontational, her second day of testimony was laconic and subdued. Mr. West made explicit reference to her change in demeanor during questioning about who introduced the specter of race into the encounter between Mr. Zimmerman and Mr. Martin.

Testimony Excerpt A:

MR. WEST: Describing the person is what made you think it was racial?
MS. JEANTEL: Yes.
MR. WEST: And that's because he [Trayvon Martin] described him as "A creepy-ass cracker?"
MS. JEANTEL: Yes.
MR. WEST: So it was racial, but it was because Trayvon Martin put race in this.
MS. JEANTEL: No.
MR. WEST: You don't think that's a racial comment?
MS. JEANTEL: No.
MR. WEST: You don't think that "creepy-ass cracker" is a racial comment?
MS. JEANTEL: No.
MR. WEST: Are you O.K. this morning?
MS. JEANTEL: Yeah.
MR. WEST: You seem so different than yesterday. Just checking.
JUDGE: Is that a question?
MR. WEST: Did someone talk with you last night about your demeanor in court yesterday?
MS. JEANTEL: No, I went to sleep.

Mr. West's observation that "You seem so different than yesterday" reflects the fact that he detected an unmistakable contrast in the way in which Ms. Jeantel responded to his questions during her second day on the witness stand. Moreover, he questioned whether or not someone discussed her demeanor during her first day of testimony, which, again, was quite contentious and confrontational. Ms. Jeantel's testimony, cited above, is striking by virtue of its laconicity; moreover, her responses were delivered in a quiet—non-confrontational—tone of voice on the second day. She attributed this difference in style to the fact that she had been able to "sleep" and that it was not the result of someone telling her she needed to modify the way in which she presented herself in court.

Mr. West also drew attention to a note that Ms. Jeantel shared with Trayvon Martin's mother. At first blush, it might have appeared that Ms. Jeantel wrote the note herself; however, when Mr. West provided Ms. Jeantel with a copy of the note to read from the witness stand, she balked, as illustrated in the following exchange.

Testimony Excerpt B:

MR. WEST: Ms. Jeantel would you take a look at that copy of the letter, and let me ask you a couple of questions about it? Do you recognize that letter as being one that you said earlier was prepared to be given to Ms. Fulton (i.e., Trayvon Martin's mother)?

MS. JEANTEL: Yes.

MR. WEST: And, that letter was prepared with the assistance of a friend of yours named Francine Serve?

MS. JEANTEL: Yes.

MR. WEST: And you and Ms. Serve talked about what you wanted to be in the letter, and then she helped write it in a way that was legible; correct?

MS. JEANTEL: Yes.

MR. WEST: But, the contents of the letter are yours.

MS. JEANTEL: Yes.

MR. WEST: Are you able to read that copy well enough that you can tell us if it's, in fact, the same letter?

MS. JEANTEL: No.

MR. WEST: Are you unable to read that at all?

MS. JEANTEL: Some, I do not. . .

MR. WEST: Can you read any of the words on it?

MS. JEANTEL: I don't honestly … um … cursive, I don't read cursive.

Mr. West then read the letter, asking Ms. Jeantel if his rendering was accurate, to which she responded affirmatively. Although the public was not privy to the deposition that Mr. West conducted with Ms. Jeantel, it is difficult to imagine that they did not discuss this letter, or the fact that Ms. Jeantel needed the assistance of her friend Francine in order to write it. In this instance, linguistic profiling has more to do with literacy, or a lack thereof, than with speech. It is clear from Mr. West's questions that he knew very well that Ms. Jeantel did not write the letter herself. Clearly, if Rachel Jeantel's writing abilities were sufficiently adequate, she would not have needed the help of her friend to write to Trayvon's mother. Thus, by first acknowledging that the letter under consideration was one that Rachel Jeantel prepared with the help of a friend, Mr. West was able to convey, albeit indirectly, that Ms. Jeantel needed assistance in order to send a letter to Trayvon's mother about the episode she overheard on the phone.

It would, of course, be wrong to speculate about Mr. West's intentions or motives during this line of questioning. However, once he had established that Ms. Jeantel prepared the letter with the assistance of her friend, to then ask if she not only recognized the letter, but to then confirm that it accurately reflected her (i.e., Ms. Jeantel's) dictation demanded that she either confirm that she could read the letter—under oath—or admit that she was incapable of reading. Rather than confirm that she (i.e., Ms. Jeantel) could not read at all, she stated under oath that she had difficulty reading writing that was in a cursive format. Although Mr. West could have provided her with a typed transcript of the letter, previously written in cursive, which might have further exposed Ms. Jeantel's reading difficulties, he chose instead to read the letter in a manner that called explicit attention to some of its nonstandard content.

By asking Ms. Jeantel to read a letter that she had asked her friend to prepare, Mr. West was able to draw attention to Ms. Jeantel's literacy limitations, and, in so doing, he (perhaps inadvertently) reinforced many of the linguistic stereotypes about African Americans that were more vividly on display during Ms. Jeantel's first day of testimony when she produced much of her narrative using AAVE.

The Zimmerman trial is quite significant for many reasons, but from a linguistic point of view, Rachel Jeantel's testimony illustrates that linguistic profiling need not only result from negative reactions to a person's speech. Rather, it is quite possible that a person may be the object of linguistic discrimination based on their ability, or inability, to read and write fluently. It is evident from many of the tweets through social media that Ms. Jeantel evoked considerable racial and linguistic animosity throughout her testimony. While it is also true that many people were sympathetic to her plight, and agonized over the way she was negatively depicted through various hostile comments about her appearance and language, for the purpose of this discussion it is important to know that a great deal of the adverse commentary directed toward her is the result of linguistic profiling.

Mr. West knew well that Rachel Jeantel's testimony could have been very damaging to his client, and, without explicitly asking her about her education, he was able to expose the fact that she had difficulty writing. She also used AAVE during her testimony. Having known that Ms. Jeantel needed help writing a letter provided an opportunity for Mr. West to further damage Ms. Jeantel's appearance during the trial, and by doing so Mr. West was attempting to diminish any negative impact that her remarks might have on Mr. Zimmerman.

In response to Mr. West's assertion that Mr. Martin attacked Mr. Zimmerman, Ms. Jeantel responded, "You ain't get that from me." In addition, there were occasions where Ms. Jeantel recounted Mr. Martin's use of the word *Nigga* as he was trying to describe Mr. Zimmerman's actions while following him. Although John McWhorter attempted to explain many of the reasons that Ms. Jeantel used AAVE during an interview on CNN, the fact that Mr. West set the stage for this linguistic ridicule is further evidence of the potential negative reactions that many people may have to someone who is "Speaking while Black."

41.6 SOUTH AFRICAN (DIS)SIMILARITIES

Although the main focus of this discussion is devoted to linguistic circumstances in the United States, Black English usage in other parts of the world have resulted in some discriminatory circumstances, and they are worthy of brief commentary despite the fact that they do not pertain directly to African Americans. Echoes of linguistic dislocation exist in South Africa, for example, which is another nation with a history of overt racial discrimination that was maintained through apartheid. Blacks were not only excluded from economic and educational opportunities, the indigenous languages of Black South Africans were not deemed official until apartheid fell and Nelson Mandela became the first democratically elected Black South African president. Neville Alexander (2000, 2002) is the architect of South Africa's new language policies, which now embrace eleven official languages, although recent history has demonstrated that English and Afrikaans retain the greatest econolinguistic clout (Baugh 1996).

Whereas European colonization of the United States resulted in the massive dislocation and deaths of Native Americans, White settlement of South Africa did not replicate the slaughter and dislocation of Native Black South Africans to the same degree that is embodied in the iconic "Trail of Tears" that is associated with the reduction and elimination of American Indians. Blacks remain the majority in South Africa; they were not imported as slaves through an Atlantic crossing. South African apartheid maintained three racial classifications: Black, Colored, and White. By contrast, racial classifications for Blacks in the United States adhered to the *one drop rule*; namely, anyone who had the slightest trace of African ancestry in their blood was designated as *Black* or *Negro* or *Mulatto* or by some offensive derogatory reference. The anti-Black racism that existed under *Jim Crow* in the United States and under *apartheid* in South Africa reinforced linguistic segregation as well, giving birth to instances of linguistic profiling against Black people in both countries.

In South Africa, forms of linguistic discrimination were reinforced by the Bantu educational policies that restricted access to either English or Afrikaans. By advocating that all children be taught in their mother tongue, the educational polices born of the Bantu education programs perpetuated the status quo, where the native languages of Whites had institutional econolinguistic value in ways that were simply not afforded to indigenous Black South African languages. This lack of linguistic fairness lies behind Alexander's (2000, 2002) efforts to embrace eleven official languages. Thus far, these efforts are more symbolic than egalitarian due to the pragmatic reality that English is the only official South African language with global utility outside of that country.

41.7 LINGUISTIC HARASSMENT ON THE JOB

Linguistic stereotypes about Blacks in the United States tend to reinforce racial stereotypes. Although there are many Blacks (and Latin@s) who are fluent speakers of MASE, the significant majorities maintain nonstandard English varieties that can become surrogate targets for racial discrimination. In some instances insensitive employers, or worse—racist employers, have used language in the work place that is highly offensive to Black people. Cases are ongoing that pertain to allegations that employers or supervisors of non-White employees used derogatory terms, such as "coons" or "apes" or "monkeys" or worse, in ways that create hostile work environments.

Occasionally, workers are the objects of linguistic discrimination that reinforces racial discrimination. For example, many African immigrants who have learned English as a second language are not merely "Black," but they are also "English language learners." Blacks who are native speakers of AAVE may or may not suffer (dis)similar discrimination that could differ depending upon linguistic usage and situational circumstance. For example, a group of men—all of whom were born in Africa—claim that one of their White supervisors routinely referred to them in derogatory ways, comparing them in unflattering ways with animals commonly found in Africa. They further claimed that this linguistic harassment extended to disparaging comments about their food, which often consisted of traditional African stews that were prepared by their wives. They took great umbrage at these pejorative comments and subsequently filed formal grievances against their employer resulting from their perceptions of linguistic harassment in their workplace.

Linguistic harassment on the job is difficult to detect, and therefore often overlooked as a potential barrier to success. The United States is composed of citizens and residents who are connected to most of the world's languages and speech communities. As such, most Americans are aware of linguistic discrimination because their ancestors who first learned English may have been objects of linguistic ridicule and discrimination because speakers "from the old country" may have been perceived to be "un-American." Through the acquisition and use of MASE, many descendants of immigrants who have moved to America from nearly everywhere on earth have hoped to improve their social station while overcoming some of the historical linguistic hardships that were suffered by their ancestors who first immigrated to the United States.

41.8 LEGAL RELEVANCE

The evidence is clear; linguistic discrimination exists and takes different forms in different circumstances. For many years, unscrupulous people have been able to exclude prospective tenants, clients, patients, students, and others on the bases of their linguistic (in)abilities. Heretofore, the most common defense against linguistic profiling derives from the absence of face-to-face interaction. Those accused of linguistic profiling via telephone calls often claim they had no idea about the race or sex or age or national origin of unknown callers who may seek their goods or services. Massey and Lundy (2001) confirm that telephone messages are often used for screening purposes, with racial bias and significance for (un)equal access to housing, especially for Black women who speak AAVE.

The quest for equal opportunities and justice remain, despite the clear civil rights advances and progress that have witnessed the elections of Black presidents in South Africa and the United States. The South African "Truth and Reconciliation Commission" is illustrative of the combined linguistic and racial considerations that are relevant to maintaining or dismantling the historical political and economic scaffolds that perpetuate racial dislocation (Gibson 2004). Briefly, courts throughout the world will need to be enlisted and enlightened to potential sources of linguistic profiling and linguistic harassment that may exist nationally, or which may need to be brought before international tribunals in support of human rights because people of African descent are not the only ones who are victims of unwelcome linguistic profiling.

41.9 POTENTIAL EDUCATIONAL ASSISTANCE

The controversy over Ebonics that erupted in Oakland, California, in 1996 created an awkward educational climate for educators seeking to find ways to improve the educational plight of students who speak AAVE. Some educators tackled the issue directly, which was the case in Los Angeles with the "Language Development Program for African American Students" that was created by Noma LeMoine. However, California voters passed a law that made it illegal to provide educational assistance based on race, and LeMoine expanded her educational efforts to promote greater proficiency through the "Academic English Mastery Program," which was not confined to African American students specifically.

LeMoine and Hollie (2007) offer many suggestions that teachers may find useful when working with students who are native speakers of AAVE, as well as others striving to increase their MASE fluency. They are mindful of the culture and living conditions that impact many African American students, as well as ideas about ways to motivate learning without demeaning the heritage of the students they teach.

Long before the Ebonics controversy briefly captured global attention, putting a spotlight on the language and education of African American students, alternative educational programs had been developed in Hawaii that shared similar educational goals for poor Hawaiian children, many of whom were native speakers of Hawaiian Pidgin English. The Kamehameha Early Education Program (KEEP) was created during the 1970s in an attempt to uplift the educational prospects for disadvantaged Hawaiian students, and because the program was implemented on an island state in the middle of the Pacific Ocean, it was not well known on the mainland. In 1981, a team of educational researchers, led by Courtney Cazden of Harvard University, conducted an evaluation of the KEEP program that is highly informative, and which holds many lessons that can potentially be applied to many less fortunate African American students attending urban and rural schools throughout the mainland.

One of the problems that emerged during the Ebonics controversy resulted from claims that African American students did not speak English, which was inaccurate.

AAVE has many unique linguistic characteristics that do not exist in MASE, but AAVE is unmistakably English, and educational proposals that argue for bilingual education were somewhat overstated. Those who created Hawaii's Kamehameha Early Education Program recognized that a combination of cultural and linguistic considerations, along with specific teaching strategies (rather than prescriptive dictates) could be of greater educational benefit to many less fortunate Hawaiian students.

Because students who speak AAVE are educated under very different circumstances (i.e., some attend schools with diverse populations, while others attend schools that lack racial diversity), flexible solutions are most likely to succeed. Educators working in schools where most students speak AAVE will need different teaching strategies than will teachers who have fewer AAVE-speaking students, particularly if those students are bused to schools away from their home community. Because alternative solutions are likely to be necessary, educators may benefit from considering some of the lessons that were learned in Hawaii long ago.[8] For example, KEEP evaluated the language that children used in their home setting in comparison to the similarities and dissimilarities with MASE. KEEP also included specific guidance for teachers, helping to dispel myths that Hawaiian students lacked the will or ability to devote concentrated effort toward their academic work. Instruction expanded to include more topics that were focused on Hawaiian culture and other topics of local concern to enhance student motivation and interests. While KEEP cannot merely be replicated in schools on the mainland, lessons learned long ago in Hawaii could be adapted in ways that might enhance educational prospects for students who speak AAVE.

41.10 CONCLUSION

Alternative forms of linguistic discrimination exist throughout the world. Here we have devoted attention to Black speakers of non-dominant languages or dialects in the United States and South Africa. In each nation, we find individuals who have considerable linguistic dexterity, and who adapt their speech to meet the immediate conversational needs of the speech event at hand. In some instances the speaker may be bidialectal, with the linguistic competence to communicate in both MASE and their home language.

Bidialectal or multidialectal speakers differ considerably from those who possess linguistic competence of two or more mutually unintelligible languages (i.e., bi- or multilingual). Those who have the ability to speak more than one dialect of a single language (i.e., bi- or multidialectal) do so with greatest emphasis on phonological and phonetic properties of a given language, that is, along with skilled manipulation of intonation, prosody, and pitch, among other morphological and lexical variability that is specific to the dialects in question.

Shibboleths have been documented since the beginning of recorded human history. We all know well who talks "like us" and those who "don't talk like us." The present discussion explores the educational, economic, and legal consequences of linguistic profiling and linguistic harassment in different speech communities, especially if they appear to reinforce documented racial discrimination against groups that may have unique and identifiable linguistic characteristics. Because this type of "ear-witness" discrimination is difficult to detect, identify, and prove in a court of law, it is important that those who speak non-dominant dialects or non-dominant languages are aware of their linguistic circumstances, but also the constraints they may face from those who are fluent speakers of surrounding dominant languages and dialects. In many instances, the forms of linguistic discrimination that we have observed can exceed race. It is my hope that a combination of linguistic and legal vigilance may result in greater racial and judicial equity in the future for unwitting victims of linguistic profiling whose only crime is SWB: namely, "Speaking while Black."

Notes

1. I would like to thank Sonja Lanehart, Ayesha Malik, and an anonymous reviewer for their close reading of this chapter, as well as their helpful suggestions. The National Science Foundation and the Ford Foundation have provided funding related to my research on this topic, and I would not have been able to complete this chapter had it not been for their support. Any limitations in this chapter are entirely my responsibility.
2. Mainstream American Standard English (MASE) is the dominant influential dialect spoken by well-educated Americans in different parts of the country. Other terms, such as Standard American English are used synonymously.
3. Ebonics was coined by combining the words Ebony and Phonics to refer to the linguistic consequences of the African slave trade, that is, wherever slaves were sold after the Atlantic crossing.
4. African American Vernacular English (AAVE) has been characterized by different labels since the 1960s, initially being called Nonstandard Negro English. During the 1970s, the terms Black English and Black English Vernacular (BEV) were used by many linguists until AAVE was adopted during the 1980s. All of these labels refer to the colloquial vernacular dialects spoken by many US slave descendants in urban and rural communities throughout the nation.
5. African American Language (AAL) has broader reference than the vernacular dialects specified by AAVE. Today African Americans include Black people from various parts of the world, some of whom, like President Obama, are not slave descendants nor are they native speakers of AAVE.
6. Vernacular Black English is synonymous with African American vernacular English (AAVE) and differences in terminological reference do not imply differences in the colloquial speech patterns of United States slave descendants who utilize these styles of speaking.
7. Sherri Williams reported these quotes, which can be found at https://storify.com/SherriWrites/good-bad-and-ugly-tweets-about-rachel-jeantel.
8. A full report on the Kamehameha Early Education Program can be found at http://files.eric.ed.gov/fulltext/ED215039.pdf.

References

Alexander, Neville. 2000. "English Unassailable and Unattainable: The Dilemma of Language Policy in South African Education." Rondebosch, *South Africa: Project for the Study of Alternative Education in South Africa* (PRAESA).

———. 2002. "Linguistic Rights, Language Planning and Democracy in Post Apartheid South Africa." In *Language Policy: Lessons from Global Models*, edited by Steven J. Baker. Monterey, CA: Monterey Institute of International Studies.

Baugh, John. 1996. "Dimensions of a Theory of Econolinguistics." In *Towards a Social Science of Language: Papers in Honor of William Labov*, Vol. 127, edited by Greg Guy and William Labov, 297–419. Philadelphia: John Benjamins.

Gibson, James L. 2004. *Overcoming Apartheid: Can Truth Reconcile a Divided Nation?* New York: Russell Sage Foundation.

Lambert, Wallace E., and G. Richard Tucker. 1972. *Bilingual Education of Children: The St. Lambert Experiment*. Rowley, MA: Newbury House.

LeMoine, Noma, and Sharroky Hollie. 2007. "Developing Academic English for Standard English Learners." In *Talkin Black Talk: Language, Education, and Social Change*, edited by H. Samy Alim and John Baugh, 43–55. New York: Teachers College.

Massey, Douglas S., and Garvey Lundy. 2001. "Use of Black English and Racial Discrimination in Urban Housing Markets: New Methods and Findings." *Urban Affairs Review* 36 (4): 452–69.

Ogbu, John. 1978. *Minority Education and Caste: The American System in Cross-Cultural Perspective*. New York: Academic.

Preston, Dennis. 1989. *Perceptual Dialectology*. Dordrecht: Foris.

Purnell, Thomas, William Idsardi, and John Baugh. 1999. "Perceptual and Phonetic Experiments on American English Dialect Identification." *Journal of Language and Social Psychology* 18 (1): 10–30.

Williams, Robert. 1975. *Ebonics: The True Language of Black Folks*. St. Louis, MO: Robert Williams and Associates.

PART VII

LANGUAGE AND IDENTITY

CHAPTER 42

RACIALIZING LANGUAGE

Unpacking Linguistic Approaches to Attitudes about Race and Speech

KATE T. ANDERSON

42.1 INTRODUCTION

Is race a legitimate category of linguistic differentiation? In other words, can someone's race shape how they speak or how they sound to others? If so, how does this come to be? In which contexts and according to whom do links between race and speech style become assumed as real or meaningful? In this chapter, I explore various ways that linguists have attempted to answer these questions, framing the larger issue of attitudes about African American Language (AAL) and the construction of research on them.

Although linguists have been writing about a speech style associated with African American communities for quite some time, this work was done almost entirely by White linguists until the 1970s. Since then, an abundance of linguistic research on AAL has been conducted both from within and outside of AAL speech communities. Detailed linguistic studies have examined structural, cultural, and historical descriptions of AAL (see Green 2002; Morgan 2002; Mufwene 2001; Rickford 1999; Smitherman 1977; Wolfram and Thomas 2002). Given the proliferation of linguistic research on AAL, including sizable bodies of research that explore the linguistic features associated with AAL, the development of identities at various scales of social life relating to the African American community, and the documentation of listeners' abilities to accurately identify race based on speech cues, it is easy to presume the existence and relevance of AAL as a variety. This chapter aims to complexify the naturalized assumption that named language varieties have certain qualities and are spoken by certain people by unpacking three different linguistic approaches to understanding how speech is heard to be, constructed as, or performed as indicative of a speaker's race. As such, I consider the theoretical assumptions and methodologies that guide the quite different research foci and implications of these approaches—sociophonetic, ethnographic, and discursive.

In their work on race, language, and identity, Le Page and Tabouret-Keller (1985) forecast the foci of these approaches in their framing of language as dependent upon at least three social components: (1) scholars' descriptions of a speech style, (2) conceptions disseminated within communities, and (3) individuals' perceptions of a speech style. Taking these three vantage points into consideration, speech or a speech style is no more measurable or discrete than the discourses that various sources, both authorized (scholarly) and not (folk), make meaningful.

The three linguistic approaches to studying links between race and speech that I discuss below include: (1) the *Sociophonetic Approach*, which examines listeners' identification of race based on speech stimuli in order to identify the linguistic features present in speech that is racially identifiable by listeners; (2) the *Ethnographic Approach*, which considers the linguistic practices of communities from insiders' perspectives; and (3) the *Discursive Approach*, which analyzes individuals' commentary about links between race and speech in order to identify ideological bases for beliefs about those links.

While the aim of this chapter is not to argue for the greater usefulness of one of these approaches over the others, I do aim to highlight the strengths of each because an understanding of what this complementary set of approaches allows us to ask and conclude broadens the avenues for future study. Each approach, while certainly not monolithic in its focus (and not mutually exclusive either, as some scholars blend these approaches), constructs a different way to define attitudes about race and speech, and each tells us something different about the implications of such links in the larger social arena. As such, different views of "what counts" as legitimate foci of linguistic inquiry take precedence in each of these approaches.

In the sections that follow, I discuss each of the three approaches, including their basic theoretical assumptions and prominent methodologies. I also provide illustrative examples from three representative studies. The closing discussion then teases apart the different ways that listeners', speakers', and linguists' attitudes and beliefs function in each approach, which I argue constructs distinct definitions of the links between race and speech.

42.2 Sketching the Three Approaches

Researchers can take different starting points in understanding how speech comes to be associated with a speech style that is then linked to race. For example, one can begin with the features of a speech style that is supposedly racially marked or spoken by someone who is racially identified/affiliated (linguistic behavior), as with the Sociophonetic Approach. Or, how people actually use speech in agentive ways (linguistic repertoires) can serve as a starting point, as with the Ethnographic Approach. Lastly, research can start with how listeners make sense of a speech style (i.e., accurately identify it or not, characterize it, evaluate it), as with the Discursive Approach. These three starting points implicitly prioritize the perspectives of three distinct stakeholders in the race-speech linking process: linguists, speakers, and listeners. Asking questions of each group allows us to reach different conclusions about links between race and speech.

42.2.1 The Sociophonetic Approach

Studies spanning six decades have documented claims that listeners can often accurately label a speaker's race with little difficulty (see Baugh 1996; Buck 1968; Dickens and Sawyer 1952; Graff, Labov, and Harris 1986; Purnell, Idsardi, and Baugh 1999; Shuy, Baratz, and Wolfram 1969; Tarone 1973; Thomas and Reaser 2004; Tucker and Lambert 1969; Walton and Orlikoff 1994). This body of research primarily addresses response accuracy and correlations between social variables and listeners' judgments of race, or which acoustic features of the speech stimuli correlate with individuals' ability to identify race from vocal cues.

Sociophonetic studies begin with a speech signal—a recording of someone speaking (e.g., a word, a passage), sometimes acoustically altered to control for variables such as pitch or duration. Based on how listeners identify the race of the speaker, linguists then interpret the salience and presence of phonetic/phonological features in that speech signal, extrapolating outward to make claims about characteristics of a variety. This approach assumes language can reflect, or be emblematic of, racial identity. The analytic foci in sociophonetic studies are linguistic features and their relationship to predetermined social categories. Speech is thus seen as a signal, and the attitudes considered implicit to a judgment of speaker's race (based on speech stimuli) are then used to describe aspects of the variety.

In terms of underlying assumptions, this approach presupposes that reactions to speech reflect underlying saliencies that exist in the speech signal itself (a priori perceptions of it). These assumptions afford certain types of questions and preclude others. A large part of how we process difference in speech lies just below the level of awareness. In other words, we make distinctions between voices that we hear as "different" (e.g., *I can tell she's not from here, but I'm not exactly sure why*) but are oftentimes unable to call upon the linguistic or prosodic features that lead to our noticing. Yet, some of the microphonetic features of speech such as voice quality, segment duration, coarticulation, vowel quality, and voice onset time contribute to our sense of a speaker's racial identity without knowing exactly why. As such, certain research methods and techniques are employed to uncover salient features present in speech signals. Sociophonetic studies do not claim that race and linguistic behavior form an immutable connection, but their analytic focus trains on macroracial categories and microphonetic details of speech. Therefore, when a speaker sounds African American to listeners, it is explained in this approach by certain linguistic features present in signals of speakers that are identified as African American with high incidence by listeners. How these features got there is sometimes speculated on in the sociohistorical background to the study, but this often is not the main focus of sociophonetic studies.

Types of data used in sociophonetic studies include recorded voices (i.e., speech stimuli presented as tokens, usually at the word, phrase, or sentence level), some of which may be acoustically altered. Analytic methods include acoustic analysis of phonetic, phonological, and prosodic features of speech using specialized software programs (e.g., Praat) and statistical analysis of correlation between different types of features and racial categorizations of voices (e.g., ANOVA—multi-regression analysis). The Sociophonetic

Approach allows researchers to ask such questions as, "Which linguistic features are present in speech that listeners determine to sound African American?" and "What are the most salient features in a signal, without which race cannot be determined?"

Thomas and Reaser's (2004) study, "Delimiting Perceptual Cues Used for the Ethnic Labeling of African American and European American Voices," serves as the example of a Sociophonetic Approach to the study of attitudes about AAL. Based on a review of the literature on listeners' abilities to identify race based on speech cues alone, the authors claimed that little consensus had been reached in delimiting the types of cues (and their relative importance) that allow listeners to distinguish European American and African American voices. They then conducted a speech identification experiment whereby 117 university students identified 45 tokens of speech as either African American or European American. These forty-five tokens were culled from eighteen speakers (European American and African American from a linguistically distinct area known as Hyde County, North Carolina, and the nearby mainland area).

Their study draws on the "atypical" features of the African American speech community in Hyde County to determine the relative importance of two types of cues used to compare African American and European American voices: intonation and vowel quality. The main assumption underlying the study is that there are "prototypical African American characteristics" (beyond morphosyntax and lexicon) that listeners "strongly associate with African American speech" and which are phonetic/phonological in nature (Thomas and Reaser 2004, 55).

The results of their analysis suggested that when the atypical vowel quality of Hyde County African American speakers (which sounds much more like local, vernacular European American vowels from the same area) was eliminated from the samples, listeners did not misidentify this group nearly as often. Examples of these vowel qualities that are common to the speech of many African American and European American residents of Hyde County include: fronting of /aʊ/ glides (*how*/haʊ/ sounds more like *hahye*/haə/) and /o/ fronting (*hoe*/ho/ sounds like *hey*/hei/). Also, the Hyde County African American speakers were misidentified less in low-pass filter than other treatments (unaltered and monotonized) when subject pronouns were prominent in the sample, suggesting that the preservation of stress- or pitch-related subject pronoun pronunciation (in the absence of vowel quality to confound it) resulted in a less atypical sounding speaker profile for these listeners. The authors' claims stemming from this study are that acoustic modification cannot prove that a cue is important for identification, only whether it is possible without it. Importantly, Thomas and Reaser (2004) concluded that delimiting perceptual cues, as their study begins to do, is an arduous process with confounding methodological choices often requiring painstaking acoustic analysis.

42.2.2 The Ethnographic Approach

While the Sociophonetic Approach to understanding racialized attitudes toward speech focuses on the perception of speech as a signal, the Ethnographic Approach looks at how people talk, align themselves, and forge identity and community through their language use (Baugh 1983; Lanehart 2002; Morgan 1991; Smitherman 1977). I refer to this as the Ethnographic Approach because most of the methods used in this method draw from ethnographic traditions in anthropology whereby researchers engage in extended data collection/construction in partnership with the individuals and communities being studied (see Bucholtz and Hall 2007).

The Ethnographic Approach to studying race and speech began when African American scholars gained a presence in the field of linguistics in the 1970s and 1980s. Coinciding with the years after the American Civil Rights Era and the social turn in linguistics and similar social sciences, linguists began exploring cultural contexts of language use and symbolic meanings related to identity and speech style. Many of these African American linguists engaged in ethnographic studies of AAL (see Baugh 1979, 1983; Mitchell-Kernan 1972; Smitherman 1977), which explored features, uses, and symbolic meaning of AAL situated amidst community norms and values.

At the heart of the ethnographic movement in linguistic accounts of AAL is a concern with representing an emic (insider) perspective to counter the studies that came before, which focused on more mechanical aspects of AAE (sometimes misinterpreting or misrepresenting its varied use among speakers). Morgan (2001) aptly points out that essentializations of what constitutes AAL and its speakers predominated in early sociolinguistic research. The focus she cites in the work I describe here as ethnographic illuminates the contrast between conceptions of AAL as a form of creative resistance to mainstream, dominant language practices and beliefs, and AAE as the product of a historicized "Otherness" imposed upon African American, ex-slave communities. The cultural positioning of AAL as a choice, a stance, and a form of identity are thus central to the Ethnographic Approach.

Unlike the Sociophonetic Approach, the Ethnographic Approach locates AAL in individual and community practices rather than in voices. As such, studies using the Ethnographic Approach often describe and explain language use and characteristics at a larger granularity than those using the Sociophonetic Approach, or the more general descriptive sociolinguistic studies that follow from the tradition begun in the 1960s. So while language use comprises part of the analytic focus of the Ethnographic Approach, that use is always explained amidst cultural values in order to understand how attitudes within and outside of the African American speech community continue to shape what it means to speak AAL (and what AAL sounds and feels like). One of the main aspects that set the Ethnographic (and Discursive) Approach apart from the Sociophonetic Approach described above is a concern with ideology and explicit commentary on the subjective nature of sociolinguistic research.

The underlying philosophical assumption here is that language is a practice that is socially enacted and recognized, relational, and political. Theorizing links between race and speech in this way necessitates a reformulation of how the study of language practices and perceptions arise and how knowledge about them is generated. Three main assumptions underlie the Ethnographic Approach: (1) speech communities are fluid and comprised of agentive individuals; (2) individuals enact linguistic practices agentively, in part based on stylization with respect to various communities, identities, and experiences; and (3) examining linguistic repertoires and practices complements data highlighting how speakers regard their own speech and speech communities.

Data in studies using the Ethnographic Approach include extended observations, interviews, auto-ethnography, and case study. Sometimes ethnographic studies incorporate acoustic analysis of linguistic features but then situate such micro-analysis amidst other contextual data and complementary types of analysis. Methods for analysis often include interpretive qualitative analyses, discourse analysis, and narrative analysis.

H. Samy Alim's (2004) monograph, *You Know My Steez: An Ethnographic and Sociolinguistic Study of Styleshifting in a Black American Speech Community*, serves as the illustrative example for the Ethnographic Approach to studying attitudes about AAL. Alim's study examines the linguistic practices of African American students at a diverse alternative high school serving a low-income community (Sunnyside) in California. Alim spent over two years as a teacher-researcher in the community of Sunnyside and taught a course there on Hiphopography, which used Hip Hop to teach theory and methods related to sociolinguistics and ethnography of communication.

The analytic focus of Alim's study is on interactional style (both that of the speakers and researchers) as a methodological construct for understanding speech style and variation in light of community contexts. This focus centrally locates speech style in interactions, which are always socially, politically, and historically motivated. Alim's main claim is that speech style is inclusive of its features, uses, and the identities it shapes and is shaped by and, as such, can only be understood when studied in varied contexts of use by immersed and reflexive researchers who become or are part of the community. Drawing on conversations, interviews, and observations of students in and out of the school over his two-year involvement as teacher-researcher, Alim analyzed features of the students' and his own speech style and discursive strategies, framed by an anthropological and sociological examination of the socio-politico-historical context of the youths' lives. The speech events that he analyzed included not only peer-peer talk but also Stanford University researchers' talk with youth, as well as his own varied interactions with them across contexts in the roles of teacher and researcher-mentor.

The following research questions guided his analysis: (1) How and when do interlocutors co-construct speech styles? (2) How and when do race and gender matter interactionally? and (3) What causes the youth to style shift and how do interlocutors invite the use of Black language? The main assumptions underlying the study include that: style-shifting is a form of cultural practice; speech style and meaning are co-constructed through interaction; rigorous and sensitive analysis requires attention to values and orientations within the community; and speech not only reflects but also constitutes realities.

In this study, Alim (2004) examined the students' and his own speech style through roles, identity characteristics, discourse strategies, and style-shifting across varied communicative contexts. He makes connections between language and life by reflecting on the youths' conversational "street sessions," classroom participation, and other contexts (including what they have to say about their own speech). This close look at sociolinguistic style, with particular attention to copula variation, plural and third-person singular –s absence, and invariant *be*, highlights connections between style, race, gender, and Hip Hop community familiarity. He then examined these features together with discourse strategies (e.g., Black American falsetto, suck-teeth, battling mode) to see what students were responding to interactionally when they style-shifted (e.g., content, interlocutor style or role, context), as well as the context for his own style-shifting differences (street conversations as researcher and classroom talk as teacher).

Alim's study stresses the importance of interactional style (both that of speakers and researchers) as a methodological construct for understanding speech style and variation in light of the "educational, historical, and community contexts students are in" (2004, 80). As such, Alim claims that an Ethnographic Approach is consonant with and mutually beneficial in tandem with a more traditional sociolinguistic approach (in which linguistic variables are explored in relation to more static macrosocial demographic variables). While not all scholars have at their disposal the necessary methodological toolkits (i.e., theoretical perspectives and analytic methods) to do this type of cross-cutting work, scholars in dialogue across disciplinary boundaries can accomplish more in concert with each other than in a paradigm vacuum.

42.2.3 The Discursive Approach

The attitudes that individuals articulate toward speech and the racialization to which they contribute constitute the focus of the Discursive Approach. According to this view, varieties and the attitudes surrounding them reflect social values attributed to supposed speech style differences and the racial differences they then come to represent for listeners (see Alim, Lee, and Mason Carris 2011; Anderson 2007, 2008; Bucholtz 2011; Chun 2011). The Discursive Approach considers how differences in speech style are talked about as socially significant, in context, by listeners, including the implications stemming from such evaluations.

Clearly, not everyone who identifies as African American also identifies as a speaker of AAL or even agrees with the legitimacy of that label. Yet, some of these individuals might still be said by others to sound African American; conversely, speakers who do not identify as African American might be thought to sound African American. As such, the links between race and speech style become more complex when known labels are introduced into the mix, be they of a linguistic nature (e.g., AAL) or reinforced by popular media (e.g., slang). While the Sociophonetic Approach looks to the features of a canonized dialect or speech style to locate a speaker within a typology, and the Ethnographic Approach examines the practices of communities and how they identify (or not) with a specific racial group, the Discursive Approach analyzes how people characterize speech, speakers, and values attached to these in terms of race.

Studies of attitudes about race and language using the Discursive Approach begin with listeners' talk about race and speech (i.e., *race talk*) and draw conclusions about circulating discourses that allow individuals to make or justify links between racial categories and ways of talking. This approach assumes that language constitutes the primary resource that listeners use to frame their characterizations of speech in light of race and vice versa. As such, race is seen as a linguistically mediated construct. Discursive studies often draw on data from interviews or other types of conversations in which race is made a topic (either by the researcher or the participants themselves). Interactional and discourse analysis of individuals' metacommentary on why speech is racially identifiable predominate methodologically. In such studies, participants often react to and discuss speech stimuli or recount experiences and beliefs they hold.

The epistemological grounding of the Discursive Approach lies in the social meanings that listeners attribute to speech, which hinge on the theoretical assumption that reactions to speech are not neutral or purely linguistic. How people identify and justify reactions to ways of speaking or speaker groups (e.g., AAL, African Americans) depends upon their experiences, what they hear, what they think they hear, with whom they are talking, and the available categories with which to make sense of all that is at their disposal. An important component to how experience and perceptions gain value and recognizability is that of language ideologies—strongly held, underlying assumptions, beliefs, and expectations about the intersection of language style and social attributes that usually remain tacit (Irvine 2001; Lippi-Green 2011). These beliefs or assumptions are often transparent in that they are unquestioned and circulate in public discourses as "the ways things are" (e.g., "African Americans just sound *that way*"). Ideological assumptions guide perceptions of and reactions to others' social characteristics based on what they sound like.

Three broad assumptions guide the Discursive Approach: (1) language is a social act, not a mental entity or system; (2) speech styles, or dialects, only exist in that people conceive of, name, and categorize them and their speakers; and (3) appropriate sites for analyzing the ways that speech is identified racially are the discourses that circulate and explicate such identifications. This focus is on the interactional and social nature of racialized linguistic significance and how discursive resources operate along with ideological resources to enable speech styles to become imbued with significance that has socially recognized, indexical meaning. This approach can further explicate how what scholars have labeled AAL and its speakers are social constructs that shape how speech style and race have become linked in public discourses.

The types of questions linguists taking this approach ask include: "How do ways of speaking and types of speakers become socially significant constructs that are linked?" and "How do listeners attribute differential status and power to speakers by implicitly or explicitly orienting to racial categories of speech or speaker?" According to the discursive view, speech styles are thus mobile, ideological labels and not facts or entities—either social or linguistic.

My own work on race talk and the ways listeners construct and draw upon language ideologies in order to imbue speech with racial meaning serves as the example for the Discursive Approach. In "Justifying Race Talk: Indexicality and the Social Construction of Race and Linguistic Value" (2008), Anderson examines interviews with ten women who are asked to describe the people they imagine behind the recordings of voices they hear. The focus of analysis in this study was on the ways these listeners justified their racial identifications of the voices as connected with perceived linguistic habits or speech style. Thus, the Discursive Approach locates the link between race and speech in everyday talk and the ideologies surrounding it. No one instance of race talk solidifies a link between hearing a certain type of speech and assuming it comes from a person of a certain race. Rather, over time such connections circulate in conversations, media, scholarship, and so on. All of us consume and produce the idea of race and language as inherently linked.

The main research question driving this study asks how the ideological, social construction of race connects to interviewees' different ways of linking speech style and race. An underlying assumption is that how individuals talk about and justify their talk about racial identification of speakers informs our understanding of how these links come to be. In Anderson (2008), I claimed that such race talk (and the interdiscursive resources we all draw upon to make it make sense to ourselves and others in the day to day) creates and maintains realities. Thus, how individuals talk about race has implications for the creation and maintenance of acceptable ways of reacting to and talking about race and speech in the broader arena.

Findings from Anderson (2008) include two main types of evaluative messages that framed listeners' justifications for hearing voices as racially identifiable: (1) explicit links, which posit that experience with noticeable, specific linguistic behavior allowed listeners to identify certain voices racially (e.g., "And I KNOW what my sister's talking about, she has that rhythmic sound that she's talking about. So I would say she's Black."); and (2) implicit links, which gloss over actual linguistic behavior and, instead, name speaker groups and the supposedly stereotypic characteristics of members (e.g., "It's the different sound that comes through the vocal chords of Blacks and Whites"). In the first instance, listeners first notice speech and, based on experience, then forge a link to a racial group. In the second, implicit justifications presume the ubiquity of a speech style that necessarily follows from the supposed obviousness of someone's noticeable race (based on a general belief in "the way things are"). Explicit justifications are less ideologically loaded, whereas implicit justifications contribute to (and draw on) beliefs that there are essentializing qualities to the speech of African Americans and other racial groups. These beliefs shape how speakers are heard and the meanings made about their speech style when compared to how they actually sound. As such, the implications of Anderson (2008) lie in the connections between normative evaluative race talk and its role in the discursive reproduction of language ideologies.

42.3 Where Attitudes and Beliefs Are Located

The role of beliefs centrally frames each of the linguistic approaches to studying links between race and speech discussed here. The Sociophonetic Approach looks to speech stimuli as data from which to draw conclusions about reasons for racial identification located in racially recognized voices. Here, belief is folded into reactions to speech. Linguistic interest is trained on the apprehension of language and labeling of race based on an auditory reaction. Thus, belief is agnostic for the sake of research, and ideology, performativity, and agency on the part of listener or speaker are bracketed off. The Sociophonetic Approach focuses epistemologically on what is heard.

In the Ethnographic Approach, linguistic practices (as performed or discussed) serve as the data upon which claims about links between embodied racial identity and linguistic choices and habits are based. In other words, groups and what they do are seen as historically and socially shaped. As such, beliefs about the links between race and speech mediate between personal experience and widely available ways to perform linguistic identity. Belief in this sense is therefore subjective but collectively reified and constructed. The ethnographic approach thus focuses epistemologically on what is enacted.

Lastly, in the Discursive Approach data include individuals' articulated beliefs about the links between race and speech, which are seen as constructing links that traverse micro- and macro-levels. In this way, beliefs are what end up creating the linkages, whether or not the beliefs are grounded in actual linguistic habits or not and whether the believer has any legitimate right to shape such linkages (either by group membership or "scientific" merit). Thus, the discursive approach focuses epistemologically on what is talked about.

Researchers can examine the relationship between race and speech as: (1) one given a priori via a speech signal and racial ascription; (2) performed over the flows of an individual's life relative to communities, contexts, and identities; or (3) understood through circulating, ideological discourses that are available when individuals, groups, or media characterize and evaluate speech and speech style. Methodological choices for data and analyses in each of the three approaches depend upon what counts to the researcher as relevant, which shapes research questions and implications accordingly. Epistemologically, proponents of interdisciplinary linguistic research on race, perception, and ideology (e.g., Eckert and Rickford 2001; Mendoza-Denton 2002; Schilling-Estes 2004; Wolfram 1998) have made a clear case for the need to include such concerns in linguistic study. In this chapter, I have highlighted the sources of knowledge that each major linguistic approach to studying the links between race and speech prioritizes and the types of understanding we can gain from each. Table 42.1 outlines the main distinctions between these three approaches—Sociophonetic, Ethnographic, and Discursive.

Microphonetic features of speech, macrosocial categories of race, and mesolinguistic ideologies of language garner different weight and attention across these three approaches to attitudes shaping what we understand as racialized speech. As such, this chapter offers a synthesis of three types of linguistic research on racialized accounts of speech in order to foster a cross-paradigmatic dialogue that informs linguistic theory and method, but also, real-life issues surrounding discrimination and language ideologies in social constructions of race and speech style.

Table 42.1 Distinctions Between the Three Approaches to Studying Attitudes about Race and Speech Style

	Epistemological unit	Privileged perspective	Site of linkage between speech and race
Sociophonetic	Salient linguistic features present in voices, correlated with race	Linguist	Speech (microsocial practice) reflects macrosocial identity
Ethnographic	Styles and repertoires that afford identity construction, affiliation, agency	Speaker/speech community member	Speech is agentive stance taking/ orientation/belonging vis-a-vis available macrosocial identities
Discursive	Ideological links between ideas of person and ideas of speech style	Listener	Speech comes to be emblematic for macrosocial identity via mediating mesosocial ideologies

42.4 CONCLUSION

I hope to have moved far beyond simple contrasts between these three approaches. Each allows us to see part of the larger picture, and each is more complete in light of the others. While a single study likely cannot unify all three approaches because assumptions about reality and knowledge and the attendant foci differ, a mutual respect and awareness of these different views of the same phenomenon in each other's findings can promote applicability of how we understand linkages between race and speech—including linguistic profiling (Baugh, this volume), art forms (Rambsy, this volume), media (Bloomquist, this volume), and raising awareness of linguistic pluralism.

REFERENCES

Alim, H. Samy. 2004. *You Know My Steez: An Ethnographic and Sociolinguistic Study of Styleshifting in a Black American Speech Community*. Durham, NC: Duke University Press for the American Dialect Society.

Alim, H. Samy, Jooyoung Lee, and Lauren Mason Carris. 2011. "Moving the Crowd, 'Crowding' the Emcee: The Coproduction and Contestation of Black Normativity in Freestyle Rap Battles." *Discourse and Society* 22: 422–39.

Anderson, Kate T. 2007. "Constructing 'Otherness': Ideologies and Differentiating Speech Style." *International Journal of Applied Linguistics* 17: 178–97.

———. 2008. "Justifying Race Talk: Indexicality and the Social Construction of Race and Linguistic Value." *Journal of Linguistic Anthropology* 18: 108–29.

Baugh, John. 1979. "Linguistic Style Shifting in Black English." PhD diss., University of Pennsylvania.

————. 1983. *Black Street Speech: Its Structure, History, and Survival.* Austin: University of Texas.

————. 1996. "Perceptions within a Variable Paradigm: Black and White Racial Detection Based on Speech." In *Focus on the USA*, edited by Edgar Schneider, 169–82. Philadelphia: John Benjamins.

Bucholtz, Mary. 2011. "'It's Different for Guys': Gendered Narratives of Racial Conflict among White California Youth." *Discourse and Society* 22: 385–402.

Bucholtz, Mary, and Kira Hall. 2007. "Ethnographic Methods in Sociolinguistics." Panel presented at the annual meeting of the Linguistic Society of America, Anaheim, California, January 4–7.

Buck, Joyce. 1968. "The Effects of Negro and White Dialectal Variations upon Attitudes of College Students." *Speech Monographs* 35: 181–86.

Chun, Elaine. 2011. "Reading Race beyond Black and White." *Discourse and Society* 22: 403–21.

Dickens, Milton, and Graham Sawyer. 1952. "An Experimental Comparison of Vocal Quality among Mixed Groups of Whites and Negros." *Southern Speech Journal* 17: 178–85.

Eckert, Penelope, and John Rickford, eds. 2001. *Style and Sociolinguistic Variation.* New York: Cambridge.

Graff, David, William Labov, and Wendell Harris. 1986. "Testing Listeners' Reactions to Phonological Markers of Ethnic Identity: A New Method for Sociolinguistic Research." In *Diversity and Diachrony*, edited by David Sankoff, 45–58. Philadelphia: John Benjamins.

Green, Lisa. 2002. *African American English: A Linguistic Introduction.* New York: Cambridge University.

Irvine, Judith T. 2001. "Style as Distinctiveness: The Culture and Ideology of Linguistic Differentiation." In *Style and Sociolinguistic Variation*, edited by Penelope Eckert and John Rickford, 21–43. New York: Cambridge University.

Lanehart, Sonja L. 2002. *Sista Speak!: Black Women Kinfolk Talk about Language and Literacy.* Austin: University of Texas.

Le Page, Robert, and Andrée Tabouret-Keller. 1985. *Acts of Identity: Creole-Based Approaches to Language and Ethnicity.* New York: Cambridge University.

Lippi-Green, Rosina. 2011. *English with an Accent: Language, Ideology, and Discrimination in the United States.* 2nd ed. New York: Routledge.

Mendoza-Denton, Norma. 2002. "Language and Identity." In *The Handbook of Language Variation and Change*, edited by John Chambers, Peter Trudgill, and Natalie Schilling-Estes, 475–99. Malden, MA: Blackwell.

Mitchell-Kernan, Claudia. 1972. "Signifying and Marking: Two Afro-American Speech Acts." In *Directions in Sociolinguistics*, edited by John Gumperz and Dell Hymes, 161–79. Malden, MA: Blackwell.

Morgan, Marcyliena. 1991. "Indirectness and Interpretation in African American Women's Discourse." *Pragmatics* 1: 421–51.

————. 2001. "The African American Speech Community: Reality and Sociolinguistics." In *Linguistic Anthropology: A Reader*, edited by Alessandro Duranti, 74–94. Malden, MA: Blackwell.

————. 2002. *Language, Discourse and Power in African American Culture.* New York: Cambridge University.

Mufwene, Salikoko S. 2001. "What is African American English?" In *Sociocultural and Historical Contexts of African American English*, edited by Sonja Lanehart, 21–51. Philadelphia: John Benjamins.

Purnell, Thomas, William Idsardi, and John Baugh. 1999. "Perceptual and Phonetic Experiments on American English Dialect Identification." *Journal of Language and Social Psychology* 18: 10–30.

Rickford, John R. 1999. *African American Vernacular English*. Malden, MA: Blackwell.

Schilling-Estes, Natalie. 2004. "Constructing Ethnicity in Interaction." *Journal of Sociolinguistics* 8: 163–95.

Shuy, Roger, Joan C. Baratz, and Walt Wolfram. 1969. "Sociolinguistic Factors in Speech Identification." Washington, DC: Center for Applied Linguistics. National Institute of Mental Health Research Project No. MH-15048-01.

Smitherman, Geneva. 1977. *Talkin' and Testifyin': The Language of Black America*. Boston: Houghton-Mifflin.

Tarone, Elaine. 1973. "Aspects of Intonation in Black English." *American Speech* 48: 29–36.

Thomas, Erik, and Jeffery Reaser. 2004. "Delimiting Perceptual Cues Used for the Ethnic Labeling of African American and European American Voices." *Journal of Sociolinguistics* 8: 54–70.

Tucker, G. Richard, and Wallace E. Lambert. 1969. "White and Negro Listeners' Reactions to Various American-English Dialects." *Social Forces* 47: 463–68.

Walton, Julie H., and Robert F. Orlikoff. 1994. "Speaker Race Identification from Acoustic Cues in the Vocal Signal." *Journal of Speech and Hearing Research* 37: 738–45.

Wolfram, Walt. 1998. "Language Ideology and Dialect: Understanding the Oakland Ebonics Controversy." *Journal of English Linguistics* 26: 108–21.

Wolfram, Walt, and Erik Thomas. 2002. *The Development of African American English*. Malden, MA: Blackwell.

CHAPTER 43

AFRICAN AMERICAN STANDARD ENGLISH

ARTHUR K. SPEARS

43.1 INTRODUCTION

IT is essential to draw attention to the existence of African American Standard English (AASE) since many linguists, other scholars, and laypersons typically make a distinction between African American English (AAE) and Standard American English (SAE), erroneously implying that all AAE is vernacular (i.e., nonstandard). Taylor (1983) made this point, and it still holds. Earlier, for example in the 1950s to 1960s, AAE was sometimes referred to as "Black[1] dialect," as opposed to SAE. This use of *dialect* implied that a dialect is somehow less than a standard language variety. Among linguists, *dialect* is used non-judgmentally. It refers merely to a different way of speaking the "same" language. Thus, AAE is a dialect of American English (composed of many subdialects), just as what Queen Elizabeth II of Great Britain speaks is also a dialect of English. The term *language variety*, or just *variety*, is sometimes used instead of *dialect* to avoid any suspicion of evaluation, particularly among lay audiences.

AASE can be defined for introductory purposes as a standard variety (composed of many subvarieties) of American English that has distinctively Black (i.e., African American) grammatical features, hereinafter DBGFs.[2] DBGFs are found uniquely, or nearly so,[3] in AAE varieties. An example of a DBGF is what linguists term *stressed BIN*, written with capital letters in AAE studies to indicate stress and spelled in this manner to emphasize that it is the AAE form (e.g., *She BIN married*, "She has been married a long time and still is married"). Overwhelmingly, the speakers of AAE are African American,[4] though there are exceptions.

AASE is a group of varieties of AAE. AASE is a type of AAE: it has DBGFs, but none that are stigmatized or considered nonstandard (e.g., the use of *ain't*). For the most part, no one but an AAE specialist could detect the DBGFs in AASE because they are grammatically camouflaged, as explained below.

Pointing out the existence of AASE is not the only reason for writing about it. AASE is an excellent site for the study of language in society and culture. First, it contributes greatly to our understanding of linguistic accommodation (Coupland 2010), since within its grammar we see clearly the push-pull of the "two-ness" of African American culture (DuBois [1903] 1961), the simultaneous existence in the Black psyche of Eurocentric and African American-centric norms, often in conflict with each other. AASE provides accommodation research, in particular, a site for enriching its understanding of long-term accommodation processes, those involving *enregisterment*—the formation and maintenance of language varieties. Particularly useful in this regard is the notion of *grammatical camouflage* (Spears 1982, 2007, 2008; Spears and Hinton 2010) and especially camouflage as linked to *grammatical incommensurability* (Spears 2009), grammatical features in one language having no counterparts in certain other languages or dialects. Camouflage is a macro-pattern in AASE grammar, one making it difficult to detect DBGFs in AASE—and African American Vernacular English (AAVE) as well. The disapproval marker and semi-auxiliary *come* is one example: *He came[5] coming in my room, didn't even knock* "He had the nerve to come in my room. . . ." The first *come* is the disapproval marker, expressing the speaker's strong disapproval; and the second, the familiar motion verb *come* (Spears 1982, 2008).

Second, and directly related to the first point, AASE provides insight into language contact (more importantly, dialect contact), in revealing how ethno-racially linked grammar features are retained but often modified in order for speakers to walk with equilibrium the fine line between community-external linguistic pressures and community-internal ones (Spears 2007, 2008).

Third, AASE is an endangered dialect (Spears and Hinton 2010). Two factors explain the endangerment: (1) the advanced age of the bulk of its speakers, over 60 with their formative years occurring during the last chapters of the US Reign of Terror[6] against Blacks and other people of color (a.k.a. the Jim Crow Era) and (2) the end of the social conditions that fed this variety's genesis and maintenance.

Fourth, AASE speech provides a window into language use, notably how DBGFs are deployed stylistically and situationally in ways shaped by Eurocentric versus African American-centric rules for the display of affect. Apposite here is the observation that some DBGFs have grammaticalized conversational stances and affect that are important in African American culture (Abrahams 1970, 1976; Spears 2001, 2009).

Fifth, in characterizing AASE speakers and their formative milieu, we also gain a much needed elaboration of our view of the African American community that is not attached in the main to the parade of Black images in the US popular imagination that prioritizes poverty and degradation.

There are many reasons for positing that there are standard varieties of AAE, especially once one realizes that there are many varieties of Standard English (SE), which vary according to region and social factors. Consider recent US presidents—Presidents Obama, George W. Bush, Clinton, and George H. W. Bush. Most people would agree they speak SE—and agree they all speak differently from one another. Furthermore, none of them speaks like Queen Elizabeth II, of Great Britain; yet, she clearly speaks

SE also. We might go on to clarify that she speaks Standard British English, while the presidents speak SAE. Already we have two types of SE. President Clinton speaks SAE differently from each of the other presidents. The claim giving rise to this chapter is that some varieties of AAE are standard, in the same sense that the presidents' varieties are all standard—and different from one another. Those differences are clearly based on, minimally, regional differences in terms of where the presidents have spent portions of their lives and what their socioeconomic status is.

Since the notion of standard is critical for this chapter, I will begin with a discussion of it. Afterwards, I will discuss some scholars' previous views on standard African American English, which I label SAAE, in contradistinction to AASE, the focus of this chapter. Then I turn to how we characterize subvarieties of AAE such as AASE and AAVE. Next are observations on the social locus of AASE, followed by a grammatical characterization of AASE, in which the critical notion of camouflage is discussed.

The data used in this chapter are based on my native speaker knowledge of AAE, including AASE, which is a product of my lifelong experience living in multiclass African American communities. In some cases, I have drawn on information gained from notes and recordings.

In this chapter, I look at AASE from a structural (i.e., grammatical) standpoint, and I will engage the sociocultural context and variables affecting it. Since, as noted below, AASE is really a collection of very closely related language varieties, when I discuss it, I am really discussing a cluster of dialects (i.e., AASE), within which can be found varieties reflecting particulars relating to region, speakers' social position (especially their education), speech setting details, situational footings, language ideologies, and other factors.

43.2 THE NOTION OF STANDARD LANGUAGE OR DIALECT

SE is one dialect of English (Bex and Watts 1999; Trudgill 1999). More precisely, it is one collection of dialects that is distinguished from vernacular (or nonstandard) dialects (Trudgill 1999). For convenience, I will sometimes speak of it as if it were one dialect.

The most serviceable and brief characterization of SAE (and other Standard Englishes around the world) is that it is primarily identified by stigmatized grammatical features that it does not have. This is the view that I have presented in the past (e.g., Spears 1988, 2008; Spears and Hinton 2010) because it zeroes in on the crux of the matter in terms of grammar. Most of the features that are not standard are stigmatized: for example, the use of *ain't* and multiple negatives (as in "They *ain't never* here"; the italicized items are negatives). In other words, the description or attempted definition (see below) of SE ends up being a list of grammatical features SAE does not have, but which vernaculars to varying degrees do. Wolfram and Schilling-Estes make a similar point in stating that

"Standard American English seems to be determined more by what it is *not* than by what it is" (2006, 12). They continue with an empirical observation: "To a large extent, American English speech samples rated as standard English by a cross-section of listeners exhibit a range of regional variation in pronunciation and vocabulary items, but they do *not* contain grammatical structures that are socially stigmatized" (Wolfram and Schilling-Estes 2006, 12).

Wolfram and Schilling-Estes address the question of who speaks SAE and what social context it is used in by stating that *standard[7] dialect* is the "dialect associated with those socially favored in society; the dialect considered acceptable for mainstream, institutional purposes" (2006, 406). However, as they also stress in the same writing, the matter of what a standard is, more specifically SAE, is actually a difficult one. Thus, they usefully stress the distinction between formal SAE and informal SAE. The former is based on writing and is reflected in books on grammar and usage, dictionaries, and kindred works. Such reference works are prescriptive in that they assert what their authors believe people should write and say rather than describing how "standard" speakers actually speak. "[T]here are virtually no speakers who consistently speak formal standard English as prescribed in the grammar books. . . [and] it is not unusual for the same person who prescribes a formal standard English form to violate standard usage in ordinary conversation" (Wolfram and Schilling-Estes 2006, 10-11). I cite the example of many middle-class, college-educated speakers, including some professors of English (Black, White, and other), who most hearers would label as speaking SAE but who use subjective case pronouns after prepositions (e.g., "between you and *I*") instead of the objective case pronouns (e.g., "between you and *me*") prescribed by grammar books and prescriptive authorities on SAE.

We can get much further in attempting to define grammatically formal SE than informal SE because the former is codified in grammatical reference works. Nevertheless, as linguists often remind non-specialists, there exists no complete grammatical description of SE or any other dialect or language. Hence, ultimately we cannot provide a full grammatical definition of SE. The spoken, informal SE exists in the ears of hearers; and, as we might expect, those hearers judge differently depending on their regional and social origin, and the regional and social origin of the speakers.

Wolfram and Schilling-Estes's (2006) definition of standard dialect is unremarkable in terms of where they state the standard is spoken. The thorny issue concerns who speaks the standard and whether they are only "socially favored" people in society since, indeed, African Americans have not historically been socially favored. Moreover, in spite of remarkable improvements in the social status of the African American population in the last forty years, today they cannot reasonably be labeled as "socially favored" by any means. Yet, it is clear that historically and today there are some African Americans who hearers judge as speaking the standard. In spite of this, as Wolfram and Schilling-Estes (2006, 11–12) helpfully underline, the judgments of hearers as to who is speaking the standard on a given occasion are subjective and are obviously influenced by the race of the speaker. Thus, we can read Wolfram's and Schilling-Estes's (2006) statement as being on target about standard speakers being relatively socially favored, in general as compared to other members of their social group, and, in the case of African Americans, other members of their ethno-racial group.

I define AASE in an essentially negative way (in terms of what it does not have), as I would grammatically define standards generally. The definition applies to all varieties of AASE, since AASE is itself a cluster of regional varieties. AASE is a cluster of AAE dialects having some DBGFs, but no stigmatized grammatical features that appear on lists of nonstandard grammatical features presented by prescriptive grammarians, educators, and others.

DBGFs are uniquely found, or nearly so, in dialects of AAE. However, AASE has none of the AAE grammatical features that are stigmatized, whether they are DBGFs or not. However, AAVE does have them (though not every variety of AAVE has all of the stigmatized DBGFs). Habitual *be* (e.g., "Ellen *be* studyin all the time") is one of the stigmatized DBGFs obviously absent from AASE.

In AASE, DBGFs are found in all components of grammar (including phonology and lexicon, in the sense that I use *grammar*, in addition to morphology and syntax-semantics), but my focus below in remarks on AASE grammar will be on function word examples. It is important to clarify that the DBGFs in AASE are ones that have often passed under the radar of traditional grammarians, educators, prescriptivists of all kinds, and others who tend strongly to stigmatize features of Black languages, and Black culture more broadly, owing to their stigmatizing generally of (racial) blackness itself. The DBGFs of AASE are largely camouflaged (Spears 1982, 2008; Spears and Hinton 2010): their true grammatical nature as forms distinctive to AAE is usually not noticed by persons not specializing in AAE. (See more on grammatical camouflage below.) When such DBGFs occur in AASE, they appear to the non-AAE specialist to be no different from items found in non-African American dialects, and they are not stigmatized. One might conjecture that, if these grammarians and others knew about the DBGFs in AASE, they would put them on the nonstandard list. In this connection, I should observe that the stigma that US society has historically attached to most things African American, and black in general, is nowadays changing noticeably. Features of African American language and culture generally are now more often accepted without stigma in at least some social contexts. Examples of this come from AAE vocabulary associated with, for example, Hip Hop, jazz, rhythm and blues, and fashion.

43.3 PREVIOUS RESEARCH: STANDARD AFRICAN AMERICAN ENGLISH

Some conceptualizations of what I label as SAAE, in contradistinction to AASE, are in circulation, positing that SAAE differs from the SE of Whites and other non-African Americans in regard to certain aspects of use (i.e., communicative practices) and grammar—mainly phonology (and prosody in particular) and lexicon, with few if any vernacular (i.e., nonstandard) features tied to morphology, syntax, and semantics. This variety, though conceptualized by some Black linguists along with non-linguists interested in language, has not been discussed at any length in the literature, except by Hoover (1978), but warrants mention and study. However, I should stress that SAAE cannot be precisely compared to AASE because the notion of DBGF was not conceptualized in writings dealing with SAAE.

Hoover (1978) states that the Black standard (what I label as SAAE) contains very few if any vernacular grammatical features (i.e., features relating to morphology and syntax-semantics, following the American Structuralist, pre-Chomskyan sense, in which she uses *grammar*). In Taylor's writings, at least two views of Standard Black English are presented. Taylor (1971) sees Standard Black English as including even such a feature as invariant, habitual *be* (e.g., *He always be studying after dinner* "He habitually studies after dinner"). It is not clear whether Taylor actually means to state that habitual *be* occurs in the speech of Standard Black English speakers after they have switched to a vernacular Black English variety. However, Taylor (1983) sees Standard Black English as spoken by "Black speakers who use Standard English phonology and grammar when speaking informally, while simultaneously using Black rhetorical style, prosodic features, and idioms" (135). Taylor's (1971) view does not fit within what I term SAAE, if indeed he actually wished to include habitual *be* in Standard Black English; Taylor's (1983) view does, however, fit into what I term SAAE.

Varieties fitting Taylor's (1983) characterization of (what I call) SAAE are, in my experience, those of younger (roughly under 60) Blacks from solidly middle-class backgrounds. This group controls an SAAE variety with no vernacular features, though on certain occasions they may use a variety with vernacular features. I believe that Hoover's (1978) description of a Black standard was more person-based than language variety-based. That is, she probably conflated varieties of middle-class speakers, "light" vernacular and standard varieties, where the standard was autonomous in the sense that it was sometimes spoken with no admixture of vernacular features.

As noted, the term *AASE* explicitly references a variety including DBGFs, which Hoover (1978) and Taylor (1983) did not label. Keep in mind that some grammatical features associated with AAE (particularly AAVE) occur also in non-AAE varieties, e.g., *ain't* and multiple negation. AASE is also a variety with no vernacular features, as noted above. The use of the term *AASE* is important since it makes explicit claims that Hoover (1978) and Taylor (1983) did not make.

In sum, SAAE is the cover term for the varieties characterized by Hoover (1978) and Taylor (1983). SAAE varieties, stated differently, are those that have no vernacular features (Taylor 1983) or have only a few—if any (Hoover 1978). Hoover (1978) and Taylor (1983) did not explicitly characterize the notion DBGF, so the varieties that they describe cannot be fully distinguished from AASE, which is claimed to have DBGFs. AASE is a different conceptualization of a Black standard in that it explicitly includes a number of DBGFs in the Black standard. This view of AASE is in most details in accord with my earlier statements on the Black standard (Spears 1982, 1988, 2007; Spears and Hinton 2010, inter alia), though I have used terms other than AASE.

43.4 AFRICAN AMERICAN STANDARD ENGLISH

To the extent that we can actually define language varieties, standard or vernacular, we do so based on their speakers and/or their grammatical traits. Sometimes we use socio-historical information (e.g., in defining pidgin and creole languages as language categories and specific pidgin and creole languages). Defining on the basis of grammar, we normally use a collection of grammatical features whose co-occurrence defines the variety, whether or not those traits are unique to that variety. In the case of AAE, a definition can be usefully fashioned by a list of selected features unique to AAE, or what I labeled above as DBGFs.

AASE is a variety of AAE (and also SAE) that has no grammatical features usually considered nonstandard and no stigmatized ones but, nevertheless, has DBGFs. Among the nonstandard (or vernacular) features absent from it are the use of *ain't* and multiple negatives, as in He *don't never* bring none (negatives underscored). As noted, DBGFs are those uniquely found, or nearly so, in dialects of AAE. Definitions could take into account non-DBGFs, but definitions restricted to DBGFs are certainly adequate for a grammar-based definition that accurately identifies this language variety.

As noted, DBGFs are found in the lexicon, phonology, and other parts of grammar. It is important to stress again that the DBGFs in AASE are ones that have escaped the attention of prescriptivists because they are largely camouflaged (Spears 1982, 2008, 2009; Spears and Hinton 2010). They are typically heard without attracting attention.

43.5 THE SOCIAL LOCUS OF AASE

AASE is very closely associated with a delimitable group of African American speakers: generally over 60; raised in all-Black, multiclass communities, under segregation and roughly twenty years thereafter; and members of the contemporary Black elite (for lack of a better term).[8] This elite, which existed in all sizable cities, included the most educated, highest income, and wealthiest members of Black communities. Though they were overwhelmingly middle class,[9] it would be misleading to state that all were. In analyzing Black communities, the notion of middle class, and class notions generally, have limited utility because they do not allow us to capture adequately the social strata and dynamics of such communities. The Black elite, thus, included members who in White communities might have been classified as working, middle, and upper class. The Black elite, however labeled, is a necessary notion for understanding many social patterns, even something as simple as who could appropriately eat in or even enter whose home.[10]

Based on income, wealth, and occupation alone, some were upper class. Some, not many, were working class in terms of wealth, education, and occupation. It is important to point out, however, that, as the term is typically used, there was no Black upper class, per se. That is to say, that there was no such class as classes are normally conceived: there was no largely endogamous upper class that, in terms of subculture—mores, tastes, attitudes, social life, lifestyle, usual dwelling type, and so on—was distinct from the more affluent sectors of the Black middle class. The Black elite was far and away the most highly educated group, though some (e.g., wealthy businessmen) had no more than a grade-school education. With regard to skin color, this group was mostly light skinned (though certainly not all were), and the wives of this group's men, who were often darker skinned, were for the most part (1) very light skinned or able to pass for White (*high yellow* in AAE); or (2) "looked like an Indian [Native American]," the AAE locution for those who were brown-skinned, but—the saving grace in colorist thinking (Spears 1999; Walker 1998; Whylie 1999)—had *good hair* (i.e., straight or loosely wavy hair), often thinner lips and narrower noses—in other words, they looked like the Indian of the community's stereotype.

The terms "Black Bourgeoisie" (Frazier [1957] 1962) and "Black Anglo-Saxons" (Hare [1965] 1992) attempt to describe the social behavior and psychological outlook of only one segment of what I refer to as the Black elite. The group they describe is primarily the subgroup referred to by Blacks of the era as "Colored Society" or "Negro Society." Some members of the Black elite participated minimally in "society," some of them, no doubt, sharing some of Frazier's ([1957] 1962) and Hare's ([1965] 1992) unbalanced and socioculturally unsophisticated views of them as self-absorbed, pretentious, largely not wealthy, non-civically minded, dysfunctional mimics of wealthy Whites. Hare's (1992) work is properly taken as a parody, with certain biting truths. Frazier's ([1957] 1962) book shows little if any understanding of Black entrepreneurship (Walker 1998) in its sociocultural and historical context and, more particularly, of Black behavior, events, tropes, and language, often having similar forms to White ones, though frequently quite different in terms of meaning, function, and significance. Just as Black language is full of camouflage, in terms of grammar and use, so also is Black culture full of cultural camouflage, which Herskovits (1941) called "masking." Frazier's charge of dysfunction is actually an artifact of his Eurocentric lens, gained during his graduate training at the University of Chicago, which he never outgrew. Not surprisingly, Frazier exaggerated dysfunction in this group (Kilson 2002). Moreover, Frazier and Hare ignore the crucial fact that most key figures in the African American struggle for civil rights, before and after the civil rights movement (1950s–1970s) came from the Black elite (Bennett 1973), which subsumed "Negro society." Perhaps most importantly, in criticizing the Black elite for its insignificant capital accumulation, Frazier seemed unaware that no capitalist class can develop in despotic regimes, in which significant accumulation of capital is confiscated by the despotic ruling group, thus preventing a capitalist class from forming.[11] The United States was such a despotic regime for Blacks, and most, if not all, who accumulated any wealth at all and kept it had White patrons (often kin) who protected them from confiscation.

43.6 Grammatical Camouflage

As I observed above, the DBGFs that appear in AASE are camouflaged. It is practically impossible for anyone not a specialist in AAE grammar to detect them. Since most AASE speakers are sensitive to the stigma still attached to things Black, they would probably try to rid their speech of these features if they knew what they were. AAE specialists, for their part, are sometimes reluctant to discuss camouflaged, distinctively Black grammatical features for fear that speakers' knowledge of them might inadvertently promote the attrition and perhaps eventual disappearance of these features and AASE itself. Because every language variety is precious in that it carries the history and culture of a people, linguists often act to preserve language varieties, trying not to do anything that might hasten their demise.

Note also that this chapter focuses on only one AASE DBGF, one that is easy to explain to non-linguists: stressed *BIN*. *BIN* is pronounced with more emphasis (stress) and, in most varieties, always with high pitch. Consider the following sentences, which most hearers would assume to be the same sentence:

(1) They've *BIN* living in Chicago. (AASE)
    'They've been living in Chicago a long time and still are living there.'
(2) They've been living in Chicago. (other non-African American dialects, henceforth OAD)
    'They've been living in Chicago (no length of time implied) and still are.'[12]

The two sentences are grammatically different, however. BIN is a type of auxiliary that occurs only in AAE. It is distinct from the past participle of *be* (*been*), which occurs in all American English dialects and has a different meaning, as indicated by the glosses. (This, as other AAE features, has spread outside Black communities and outside of AAE into some other communities and language varieties, for example, Puerto Rican and Dominican English in many parts of New York City.) This feature has never been classified as nonstandard by prescriptivist grammarians, as noted above, probably because they did not know of its existence.

Note the following AAVE sentence:

(3) They *BIN* living in Chicago. (AAVE)

This sentence has a nonstandard grammatical feature: the absence of any form, contracted (*'ve*) or not, of the auxiliary verb *have*. These examples are useful because they offer a good example of how AAVE, AASE, and other varieties of American English differ.

Remember that some nonstandard grammatical features that occur in AAVE also occur in vernacular varieties of American English, for example, Appalachian English, Ozark English, and indeed in varieties spoken by the great majority of the

English-speaking American population. (Many Americans erroneously believe that the great majority of American English speakers speak standard varieties.) For example,

(4) She done ate all of it. VERNACULAR (NONSTANDARD)
     'She has eaten all of it' = 'She's eaten all of it' STANDARD

This example has the nonstandard auxiliary verb *done* and a nonstandard past participle of *eat*. The standard past participle is *eaten*.

The foregoing treatment of stressed *BIN* demonstrates, with the example of one grammatical feature, how camouflage works. Before concluding, it should be pointed out that camouflage is an artifact of a more fundamental process in AASE grammar, what we might term a *macrogrammatical principle*. The principle is segmental conformity: an AASE utterance must segmentally conform, basically, to non-Black varieties of SAE. Again note that the AASE sentence in (2) includes the auxiliary (*–ve* < *have*), while the AAVE counterpart does not. Stated differently, the AASE sentence segmentally conforms to other SAE dialects, while the AAVE sentence does not. (*Segmental* refers to vowel and consonant quality, without taking into consideration prosody, (i.e., intonation, pitch, tempo, rhythm, stress, and so on). In transcriptions of speech, segmentals are written on the line, while suprasegmentals, prosodic indicators, are written above consonant and vowel symbols. *Segment* is the cover term for consonants, vowels—and, of course, glides.)

Segmental conformity is opposed to suprasegmental, or prosodic, conformity. Prosody includes stress. The AASE sentence, then, segmentally conforms but does not suprasegmentally conform to its counterpart sentence in non-AASE. The AAVE sentence does not conform in both ways, neither segmentally (e.g., having no auxiliary as in the example) nor suprasegmentally. Segmental conformity is one of a few wide-ranging processes that produce grammatical camouflage, the grammatical result of historical assimilationist pressures on African Americans, pressures that constrain AASE grammar. There remains a great deal to state concerning details of how segmental conformity works in AASE; however, this discussion explains the basic idea and, most important, demonstrates how AASE can retain DBGFs by making them essentially undetectable. In cases of DBGFs that cannot be camouflaged (e.g., habitual *be*) those features are excluded.

43.7 Conclusion

We can understand clearly that AASE is the result of a social regime of racial subordination in which what were fundamentally White-controlled language norms regimented Black speech but did not stamp out language behavior—with respect to use or grammatical structure—that gave Black language and culture its distinctiveness. Grammatical camouflage is most easily seen with morphology and syntax, but it is also manifest in other areas of grammar. In vocabulary, "evil" serves as an example, often taking the meaning of grouchy, cantankerous, and/or difficult to get along with, instead of the meaning assigned by non-AAE dialects: "wicked, depraved, sinful."

We cannot leave this subject without stressing that language regimentation has not been due solely to the imposition of external norms imposed on the Black community, primarily via the educational system and mainstream media. The externally imposed language (and general cultural) norms were infused with Blackness, so to speak, with the result that Black community-internal norms emerged. These norms were in turn hierarchically imposed by Blacks in the higher echelons of the Black world upon those in the lower ones. Thus, members of the Black elite, many of whom were educators, strictly imposed the standard language ideology and grammatical norms specifically of the elite on lower status members of the elite and those outside the elite. We have to keep in mind that education generally in the pre-1970s was more oriented toward grammar instruction and the policing of students' language and the language of community members. The same occurred outside of schools, for example, in churches and other sites where norm-upholding adults were present.

In the all-Black schools I attended, for example, stigmatized vernacular language features elicited reprimand and sometimes punitive measures. Even students, during all-student gatherings, regimented the language of other students to conform to the student "standard," which tolerated a small set of vernacular forms (e.g., *ain't* and multiple negatives). Even students, who today might be labeled thugs or gang members,[13] participated in language policing, upbraiding or ridiculing peers for using habitual *be, aks* (cp. *ask*), or pronunciations considered to diverge too far from the standard norm.

Educators in my family and their friendship circles never used vernacular forms, not even during their stays at vacation resorts or at lively parties and other informal occasions. The adults in my extended family (mostly teachers, ministers, school administrators, and business owners) and their social peers used AASE even when they were furious. Occasionally, they said something that was clearly AAVE but for a particular effect or, as was typical, to mock someone else's speech. However, I would assume that those in my relatives' friendship circles who came from backgrounds where AAVE was normally used, did indeed switch to AAVE on social occasions that were not in the social repertoire of those who were raised in elite families.

It would not be incorrect to state that standard language was a key focus in the regimentation of behavior in the AASE-speaking milieu and that its role as an extreme object of desire—indeed, its fetishization and the sometimes extreme grammatical hypercorrection that it caused[14]—was due to its serving as an index of social status. AASE was intimately tied to being a "college man" or a woman college graduate.[15] In the absence of wealth or affluence, which was usually the case with individuals and families in the Black community, AASE and what it indexed became all the more important in securing social status. With wealth and affluence, fluency in AASE was still required for significant participation in elite institutions. Lack of fluency in AASE was (and is) also a notable, but not publicly discussed and sometimes not even privately admitted, deal breaker for marriages. AASE was a form of cultural capital unhinged from financial capital and thus almost served as a substitute for it, in a zone where capital accumulation was systematically repressed by community-external forces.

Notes

1. *Black* and other forms of this word (e.g., *Blackness*) are capitalized when referring specifically to African Americans. Lower case *black* refers to those who are labeled black as a racial classification.

2. See Spears (2007, 2008, 2009) for discussions of additional DBGFs.

3. Some of these features we know are not 100 percent exclusive to AAE, but they are much more robust in the speech of African Americans and have a vastly wider geographical distribution, e.g., habitual, invariant *be* (Bailey and Bassett 1986). Also, it can reasonably be supposed that this form was diffused from AAE to English dialects of southern Whites, pace Bailey and Bassett.

4. See Spears and Hinton (2010) for an extended discussion of who African American refers to.

5. Most AAE speakers would use *come*, but one certainly hears *came*.

6. It was indeed a reign of terror. For a useful overview, see Blackmon (2008). For an update on the post–civil rights movement period, see Alexander (2010).

7. There is not agreement on whether *standard* in *Standard English* should be capitalized. In this chapter, it is capitalized.

8. Tracey Weldon's research on middle-class AAE (in this volume) and my conversations with her have helped me clarify the social locus of AASE. My extended family (that I had contact with growing up) belonged to the group I describe. I still have difficulty talking about it because we were trained not to say anything indicating that we belonged to it to anyone who was not clearly also a member—even though most other Blacks already knew or found out quickly. Knowledge of one's membership in the group was not infrequently inconvenient. This inconvenience was perhaps greater for darker-skinned members like me, who, once uncovered, were often seen as willful deceivers, having used dark-skin to "infiltrate" another group. (Both of my parents were light skinned, my mother more so; my father appeared brown skinned clothed, having been permanently tanned by the southern sun of his youth. My grandmothers were dark skinned. My grandfathers had White fathers, and, as was not uncommon for rural men like them of that era, the second half of the nineteenth century, they married dark-skinned women, seemingly to remove the stigma of their parentage and reinforce their connection to the Black community.

9. This is in regard to income and wealth, but not at all education. Some earned middle-class level salaries from, strictly speaking, working-class jobs. Some persons, who did not meet all the normal criteria for membership in the elite, were nevertheless accepted as "full" members because of their look (*high yellow*, or "light-skinned enough or almost to pass for White") and their style (e.g., clothes, cars, homes, social circuit, demeanor). Landry (1987) and Frazier ([1957] 1962) approach some of the social differences I discuss by using the notions of Old Black Middle Class and New Black Middle Class. Landry makes much clearer that the former were incorporated into the latter. "Working-class" members of what I call the Black elite were overwhelming like the Old Black Middle Class with regard to manners, lifestyle, demeanor, skin color, and so on.

10. All of the neighbors on our side of the short block I grew up on had similar salaries, though there were significant wealth differences. The parents in the elite households were quite friendly with all the neighbors, and some of the neighbors (non-elite and elite) belonged to the same church (the "yella" church, with the largest concentration of elite members and "yellow" ones). However, non-elite parents never entered elite homes and vice-versa.

11. The confiscation of Black assets by Whites was rampant during the Reign of Terror and before. All of my parents' close friends who came from elite families had tales of asset confiscation, sometimes called "whitecapping" by historians. There was also asset infringement, the illegal exploitation by Whites of Black assets. For example, Whites would farm Black farmland and log Black-owned timberland without permission and with impunity. These historical currents are hardly discussed in US histories, thereby fueling blame-the-victim discourses, which seek to trivialize, if not to nullify, Black grievances. All groups of color (e.g., Latino/as, Asians) have suffered the same fate. In regard to Latina/os, perhaps the best known cases are those involving Tejanos and Californianos in the nineteenth century.

12. Observe that there are other, rare readings of this sentence that I do not include here, but none of them are equivalent to the readings of the AASE example here.

13. Those students did indeed belong to gangs, but they styled themselves as members of "social clubs" and reasonably so. The social clubs, if you will, did not engage in any really illegal or violent behavior, although their behavior sometimes may have skirted the boundaries of such. For example, the clubs did organize fights, one group against another, but I know of no cases where anyone was seriously hurt. These fights were mainly occasions for members and prospective members to demonstrate toughness, courage, and masculinity. In addition, as the gangs of today (e.g., the Crips, the Bloods), they were involved in charitable activities for the benefit of specific individuals or the community.

14. This grammatical hypercorrection occurred in the speech of both those fluent in AASE (e.g., teachers) (normally phonology only) and those not.

15. The term *college woman* was seldom used.

REFERENCES

Abrahams, Roger D. 1970. *Positively Black*. Englewood Cliffs, NJ: Prentice-Hall.

———. 1976. *Talking Black*. Rowley, MA: Newbury House.

Alexander, Michele. 2010. *The New Jim Crow: Incarceration in the Age of Colorblindness*. New York: New Press.

Bailey, Guy, and Marvin Bassett. 1986. "Invariant *be* in the Lower South." In *Language Variety in the South: Perspectives in Black and White*, edited by Michael B. Montgomery and Guy Bailey, 158–79. Tuscaloosa: University of Alabama.

Bennett, Lerone, Jr. 1973. "Black Bourgeoisie Revisited." *Ebony* 28 (10): 50–55.

Bex, Tony, and Richard J. Watt, eds. 1999. *Standard English: The Widening Debate*. London: Routledge.

Blackmon, Douglas A. 2008. *Slavery by another Name: The Re-Enslavement of Black Americans from the Civil War to World War II*. New York: Doubleday.

Coupland, Nikolas. 2010. "Accommodation Theory." In *Society and Language Use*, edited by Jürgen Jaspers, Jan-Ola Östman, and Jef Verschueren, 21–27. Amsterdam: John Benjamins.

DuBois, W. E. B. [1903] 1961. *The Souls of Black Folk*. Reprint, Greenwich, CT: Fawcett.

Frazier, E. Franklin [1957] 1962. *Black Bourgeoisie: The Rise of a New Middle Class in the United States*. Reprint, New York: Collier Books.

Hare, Nathan. [1965] 1992. *The Black Anglo-Saxons*. 2nd ed. Reprint, Chicago: Third World.

Herskovits, M. 1941. *The Myth of the Negro Past*. New York: Harper and Brothers.

Hoover, Mary Rhodes. 1978. "Community Attitudes toward African American English." *Language in Society* 7: 65–87.

Kilson, Martin. 2002. "E. Franklin Frazier's Black Bourgeoisie Reconsidered: Frazier's Analytical Perspective." In *E. Franklin Frazier and Black Bourgeoisie*, edited by James E. Teele, 118–36. Columbia: University of Missouri.

Landry, Bart. 1987. *The New Black Middle Class*. Berkeley: University of California.

Spears, Arthur K. 1982. "The Black English Semi-Auxiliary *come*." *Language* 58 (4): 850–72.

———. 1988. "Black American English." In *Anthropology for the Nineties*, edited by Johnnetta B. Cole, 96–113. New York: Free Press.

———. 1999. "Race and Ideology: An Introduction." In *Race and Ideology: Language, Symbolism, and Popular Culture*, edited by Arthur K. Spears, 11–58. Detroit: Wayne State University.

———. 2007. "Bare Nouns in African American English (AAE)." In *Noun Phrases in Creole Languages*, edited by Marlyse Baptista and Jacqueline Guéron, 421–34. Philadelphia: John Benjamins.

———. 2008. "Pidgins/Creoles and African-American English." In *The Handbook of Pidgins and Creoles*, edited by Silvia Kouwenberg and John Victor Singler, 512–42. Blackwell.

———. 2009. "On Shallow Grammar: African American English and the Critique of Exceptionalism." In *The Languages of Africa and the Diaspora: Educating for Language Awareness*, edited by Jo Anne Kleifgen and George C. Bond, 231–48. Bristol, UK: Multilingual Matters.

Spears, Arthur K., and Leanne Hinton. 2010. "Language and Speakers: An Introduction to African American English and Native American Languages." In *Language, Inequality, and Endangerment: African Americans and Native Americans*, edited by Arthur K. Spears. Special Issue of *Transforming Anthropology* 18 (1): 3–14.

Taylor, Orlando. 1971. "Response to Social Dialects and the Field of Speech" (ERIC Document Services No. ED 130 500). In *Sociolinguistics: A Cross-Disciplinary Perspective*, edited by Roger W. Shuy, 13–20. Arlington, VA: Center for Applied Linguistics.

———. 1983. "Black English: An Agenda for the 1980s." In *Black English: Educational Equity and the Law*, edited by John Chamber, Jr., 133–43. Ann Arbor, MI: Karoma.

Trudgill, Peter. 1999. "Standard English: What It Isn't." In *Standard English: The Widening Debate*, edited by Tony Bex and Richard J. Watts, 117–28. London: Routledge.

Walker, Juliet E. K. 1998. *The History of Black Business in America*. New York: Macmillan.

Whylie, Donovan. 1999. "Colorstruck at the Movies: *New Jack City*." In *Race and Ideology: Language, Symbolism, and Popular Culture*, edited by Arthur K. Spears, 181–95. Detroit, MI: Wayne State University.

Wolfram, Walt, and Natalie Schilling-Estes. 2006. *American English: Dialects and variation*. 2nd ed. Malden, MA: Blackwell.

CHAPTER 44

......

AFRICAN AMERICAN ENGLISH IN THE MIDDLE CLASS

......

ERICA BRITT AND TRACEY L. WELDON

44.1 INTRODUCTION

WHILE a number of scholars have pointed out that African American English[1] (AAE) falls on a continuum of social dialect features that reflect a speaker's socioeconomic status, among other factors (see Labov 1972; Baugh 1983; Taylor 1983; Spears 1988; McWhorter 1998), the use of AAE by middle-class speakers has often been over-looked in favor of the idealized, vernacular speech patterns of working-class African Americans and urban African American youths. Yet, an emerging body of research provides evidence that the use of AAE by middle-class African Americans is rich and dynamic, reflecting the complex social, economic, and professional domains that shape middle-class African American life and linguistic behavior. This chapter provides an overview of important themes, discoveries, and directions for future research on middle-class African American English (MCAAE).

44.2 DEFINING THE AAE CONTINUUM

Despite over forty years of sociolinguistic research on AAE, linguistic attention to the variety has remained fairly narrowly focused on working-class vernacular speech. Labov (1972) directed attention to the Black English Vernacular (BEV) as "that relatively uniform grammar found in its most consistent form in the speech of Black youth from 8 to 19 years old[2] who participate fully in the street culture of the inner cities" (1972, xiii). Middle-class African American speakers, falling outside the limits of this "street" or "vernacular" culture, were dismissed as linguistic "lames" and systematically excluded from consideration in AAE research. In fact, with the exception of Wolfram's (1969) social stratification study in Detroit, Michigan, almost none of the seminal studies on AAE gave any serious consideration to middle-class speakers.

Bucholtz (2003) attributes this phenomenon to a practice of "strategic essentialism" by which linguists focused on the most marginalized and stigmatized members of the African American speech community in an effort to highlight the legitimacy of the vernacular. She also argues, however, that such tendencies reflect a type of "sociolinguistic nostalgia" by which the most "exotic" linguistic practices have been treated as the most "authentic." This sociolinguistic practice has, thus, resulted in a conflation of AAE with nonstandard, or vernacular, language usage. As observed by Marcyliena Morgan (1994):

> because vernacular AAE has been defined as hip, male, adolescent, street, or gang-related speech, nonvernacular speech is described as weak, lame, or White (Labov 1972). Those who do not fit the model of the vernacular-idealized speaker... are therefore, according to this sociolinguistic paradigm, not African American or, to put it in modern terms, not the "authentic Other." (135)

Despite these tendencies, broader linguistic definitions of AAE have actually been in circulation since the earliest days of research on the variety. While Labov's early definition of the vernacular set the standard for decades of research to follow, he actually proposed at the outset that a distinction be made between the terms *Black English Vernacular* and *Black English* (BE), with the latter being used as a more general cover term to refer to:

> the whole range of language forms used by Black people in the United States: a very large range indeed, extending from the Creole grammar of Gullah spoken in the Sea Islands of South Carolina *to the most formal and accomplished literary style.* (1972, xiii; emphasis added)

Along these lines, studies such as Hoover (1978), Taylor (1983), and Spears (1998) have called for increased attention to the more standard end of the continuum, where standard grammatical constructions are used in combination with more ethnically marked and/or vernacular lexical, rhetorical, phonological, and prosodic features (see also Spears, this volume.) As observed in Mufwene (2001), broader definitions such as these are not only more inclusive but also more consistent with community notions of "talking Black."

Given these acknowledgments of the breadth and diversity of the African American speech community, it is surprising that sociolinguists have not directed more attention to middle-class speakers. In recent years, a small number of studies have begun to address these gaps in the sociolinguistic literature, with examinations of *social stratification, intra-speaker variation, identity and public performance,* and *language ideologies and attitudes.* Before discussing this emerging line of research, however, we will consider the African American middle class itself, and the social and historical context that defines it.

44.3 DEFINING THE AFRICAN AMERICAN MIDDLE CLASS

Scholars have used a number of factors (taken alone or in combination) to determine a person's membership in the middle class. Landry (1987) uses *occupation*, with white-collar workers (e.g., those with jobs in management, sales, and clerical positions), small businessmen, and individuals in trained service positions (e.g., firemen, policemen, and dental assistants) making up this class segment. Others use *income relative to the poverty limit*, in some cases defining the middle class as earning between twice and four times the federally defined poverty level (Massey and Fischer 1999; Adelman 2004), or *median income* levels as a threshold (Haynes 2001; Lacy 2007). Others, such as Marsh et al. (2007) have created a Black middle-class index (BMCi) that assigns points based on the *educational attainment* (four years or more of college); *wealth* (i.e., home ownership); *per-person income* (a measure that allows for the comparison of incomes of families of different sizes); and *occupational prestige* of individuals in a household to determine whether the household has attained middle-class status. Families receiving a score of four (i.e., one point for each of the four measures) are considered middle class.

Despite these differences in approaches, scholars have long discussed the growth and distribution of an elite or upwardly mobile segment of the African American community.[3] A small elite that, prior to the Civil War, served the White upper class eventually shifted to a budding middle class that was primarily dedicated to the service of the African American community (Frazier 1957; Wilson 1978; Landry 1987). In 1915, a steady flow of African Americans to the North to fill wartime industrial positions created a new opportunity for the growth of an African American middle class and a greater diversity of occupations within the African American community (Frazier 1957). In fact, the elite that emerged around 1915 consisted of entrepreneurs and professionals (such as doctors, dentists, and lawyers) that, due to discrimination, were highly dependent on fellow African Americans for support and patronage (Landry 1987; Lacy 2007). Although members of the White middle class in the early 1900s had access to "clean" clerical and sales positions, African Americans were still excluded from expanding into this occupational tier. However, a major shift driven by Civil Rights Era legislation occurred between 1960 and 1970, such that the African American middle class doubled and one in every four African American workers was middle class (Landry 1987, 70). Despite these gains, Oliver and Shapiro (1995) point out that, at the time of their study, African American families needed two incomes to maintain middle-class status; African American wage earners made one-fifth less than their White counterparts; African American families had a net worth that was one-fifth that of Whites; and young African American families often lacked substantial assets (96).

Furthermore, although African Americans have shown some gains in attaining middle-class status since the 1980s, they still lag behind Whites in noticeable ways. For example, Pattillo-McCoy (1999) points out that by 1995 half of all African American workers had attained middle-class jobs (compared to 60 percent of Whites). And while middle-class Whites traditionally occupy upper-middle-class occupations (including professionals and executives), middle-class African Americans tend to occupy lower-middle-class professions (including sales and clerical positions) (22). In addition, as a result of the Great Recession ending in 2009, the overall wealth gap between African Americans and Whites has widened significantly. A 2011 Pew Research Center report finds that African American households in 2009 had a median net worth (defined as the sum of all assets minus debts) of $5,677, while White households had a median net worth of $113,149 (Taylor et al. 2011, 1). Furthermore, a Pew Research Center report (2012) defines middle-income households as "those with a size-adjusted household income that is two-thirds to double the overall median size-adjusted income" (64). For example, for a three-person household in the year 2010, the middle-income range was from $39,418 to $118,255 (64). As of 2011, 70 percent of White adults were classified as middle income compared to 11 percent of Black adults (67).

Alongside wealth and income gaps, the growth of the African American middle class has been hampered by discriminatory practices that serve to delimit and constrain the geographic expansion of the African American community. For example, African Americans have historically lived in "Black Belts," or concentrated areas of settlement whose boundaries are strictly enforced by discriminatory housing policies and violence (Patillo 2005). According to Massey and Denton (1993):

> well-educated, middle-class Blacks of the old elite found themselves increasingly lumped together with poorly educated, impoverished migrants from the rural south; and well-to-do African Americans were progressively less able to find housing commensurate with their social status. (30)

Thus, African Americans are more likely than other ethnic groups to live in highly segregated communities (Massey and Fischer 1999). Furthermore, in a study of three metropolitan areas (Chicago, Detroit, and Cleveland) in 1990, Alba, Logan, and Stults (2000) find that White residents live in neighborhoods that are twice as affluent as African Americans. And in an investigation of segregation patterns for middle-class African Americans in fifty large metropolitan areas of the United States in 1970, 1980, and 1990, Adelman (2004) finds that middle-class African Americans are more likely to live in moderate to highly segregated communities and in neighborhoods that are more disadvantaged or have more negative neighborhood characteristics than their White counterparts.

While the studies described above indicate that middle-class African Americans tend to experience urban blight and high rates of segregation, Lacy (2004) provides a critique of this generalization by suggesting that many of these studies are in fact, characterizing the experiences of lower-middle-class African Americans (i.e., those who make less than $50,000 per year, lack college degrees, and occupy clerical and sales positions) (2).

Lacy (2004, 2007) details the experiences of a small but growing segment of the middle-class African American community that lives in suburban settings in Black and White middle-class enclaves that are not in close proximity to urban blight. For example, African American residents of middle-class enclaves in Fairfax County, Virginia, and Prince George's County, Maryland, enjoy similar lifestyle choices to their middle-class White counterparts (Lacy 2007). In addition, Lacy (2004) argues that while members of the African American middle class may work and operate in predominantly White contexts, some are engaged in a type of *strategic assimilation* where their interactions in African American spaces (including the African American church, African American fraternities and sororities, and other African American social institutions) provide them with a continual connection to the African American social world and cultural practices.

Overall, these studies suggest that researchers must be careful when choosing the factors that signal an individual's or family's class status. Furthermore, the data suggest that, while middle-class African Americans have historically lived in close proximity to other class segments of the African American community and have experienced unpleasant living conditions that often align with the experiences of the working class and poor, further differentiation of the middle class based on income, profession, and residential location (i.e., urban versus suburban) is necessary to tease apart the nuances of the middle-class African American experience.

44.4 The Study of African American English in the Middle Class

44.4.1 Social Stratification

Since Labov's seminal research in the 1960s and 1970s, social stratification studies have played a central role in the language variationist tradition, revealing interesting patterns of behavior among lower-middle-class speakers, in particular, who have been described as "linguistically insecure" and prone to hypercorrection[4] in the direction of mainstream prestige norms (see Labov 1966, 1972).[5] Few researchers, however, have examined the ways in which phonological and grammatical variables are distributed across social class categories in African American communities. The earliest study, and one of the few studies to date, to provide this type of investigation is Wolfram (1969). In this study, Wolfram examines the social stratification of four phonological and four grammatical variables (see table 44.1) in the speech of forty-eight African American speakers, evenly distributed across four social class categories (lower working, upper working, lower middle, and upper middle), in Detroit, Michigan.

Table 44.1 Phonological and Grammatical Features Analyzed in Wolfram (1969)

Phonological	Examples[a]
1. Variable reduction of word-final consonant clusters	1. *test* [st]/[s] *laughed* [ft]/[f]
2. Variable realization of morpheme medial and final /Θ/ as [Θ], [f], [t], or Ø (i.e., zero realization)	2. *tooth* [Θ]/[f] *nothing* [Θ]/[f]/[t]/Ø *with* [Θ]/[f]/[t]/Ø
3. Variable realization of syllable final /d/ as [d], [tʼ], [ʔ], or Ø	3. *good* [d]/[tʼ]/[ʔ]/Ø
4. Variable absence of post-vocalic /r/	4. *work, car, brother* [r]/Ø

Grammatical	Examples[a]
1. Variable copula absence	1. *Dolores_ the vice-president.* *We_ going Friday night.*
2. Invariant *be* in habitual or future contexts	2. *Sometime she be fighting in school. (hab.)* *I be twelve February seven. (future)*
3. Variable realization of suffixal /–z/ in third person singular present tense, possessive, and plural environments	3. *He stand_ on his hind legs. (third sing. pres.)* *He was really my grandfather_ dog. (poss.)* *I wish I had a million dollar_. (plural)*
4. Multiple negation	4. *I couldn't hardly pick him up.* *I don't bother nobody.* *They didn't have no gym.*

[a] All examples are drawn from Wolfram (1969).

Among his findings, Wolfram observes relatively consistent use of Standard American English (SAE) features among middle-class speakers, though younger speakers exhibit some individual variation, and women across all social class categories show greater tendencies toward SAE forms. He also observes that the grammatical variables exhibit sharp stratification across social classes (suggesting a greater linguistic salience), whereas three of the four phonological variables are gradiently stratified.[6] While these results seem to support the perception of middle-class speakers as "lames" relative to their working-class peers, they also draw attention to the complicating effects of sex, age, and linguistic salience (among other factors) on the social stratification of the observed variables.

Nguyen (2006) extends the focus on the social stratification of phonological variables, using data from the 1966 corpus on which Wolfram (1969) was based and contemporary interviews that she and others conducted between 1999 and 2004 in Detroit, Michigan. In her examination of syllable-final /d/ (see table 44.1), Nguyen finds that both "high status" and "low status" speakers exhibit a preference for the "AAE variants" [ʔ] and Ø over the "non-AAE variant" [d],[7] which both groups reportedly use with low, but relatively equal frequency. Upper-class speakers use [ʔ] more frequently, while lower-class speakers prefer Ø. Furthermore, Nguyen observes higher status speakers *leading* in a change toward a context-dependent pattern of [ʊ] fronting (e.g., in *could* or *look*),[8] suggesting that middle-class speakers are not categorically disconnected from vernacular culture but are, instead, speakers who "can and do introduce new features into AAE that may be adopted by speakers of all social status backgrounds" (2006, 178).

Jones and Preston (2011) revisit the question of linguistic salience in an investigation of the vowel systems of working- and middle-class African Americans in Lansing, Michigan. In this study, Jones and Preston observe upper-middle-class speakers, young women in particular, making use of a "divided vocalic system" that is "at once reflective of on-going local changes in the front vowel system (in this case, the Northern Cities Chain Shift[9]), but at the same time reflective of older African American norms in the back vowel system" (6–1). Upper-middle-class speakers participate in the local pattern of /ae/-raising (e.g., *cad* [kæd] as *ked* [kɛd] or *kid* [kɪd])—"a regional but not ethnic characteristic," which is gradiently stratified across social classes (6–10). However, they resist the local pattern of /a/-fronting (e.g., *cod* [kɑd] as *cad*[kæd]), which, according to Jones and Preston, is resisted by almost all of the African American speakers in their study, resulting in a sharp stratification across *ethnic* (rather than social class) boundaries. Jones and Preston conclude that /a/-fronting is "a phonological marker of ethnic identity, and perhaps… even an avoided White sound" (6–10). More significantly, they suggest that this behavior may be reflective of a "push-pull" effect (Smitherman 1977), by which African Americans, and perhaps middle-class African Americans in particular, avoid highly stigmatized grammatical features, while retaining a symbolic African American identity through the manipulation of certain finely tuned phonological features (see Spears, this volume).

While the social stratification studies discussed here, all of which are based in Michigan, suggest that middle-class African American speakers are more likely to draw on (ethnically marked, but perhaps less overtly stigmatized) phonological resources as opposed to grammatical ones in their AAE usage, the paucity of research in this area leaves much to be explored. The findings by Jones and Preston, as well as Nguyen, challenge previously held assumptions about middle-class African American speakers as "lames" who simply assimilate into White middle-class norms of behavior at the expense of their African American identities. While the speakers in these studies show tendencies toward standard (or *overt*) prestige norms, particularly with regard to salient grammatical features, they also draw on the *covert* prestige (see Baugh 1999) of certain vernacular and/or ethnically marked phonological features, for the purpose of racial/ethnic identity and solidarity building.[10] More such studies are needed, and in a variety of regional and social contexts, to get a fuller understanding of this phenomenon.

44.4.2 Intra-Speaker Variation

Research on the linguistic repertoire and communicative practices of individual speakers has yielded considerable debate over the question of whether observed patterns of variation represent dialect mixture, by which speakers draw from two separate linguistic systems, or whether the variation is inherent to a single system.[11]

DeBose (1992) contends that the lack of attention in the early literature to intra-speaker variation in AAE is reflective of an inherent variability bias, which "presupposes a monolingual language situation in the African American speech community" (158). DeBose, instead, adopts a code-switching framework in his analysis of the conversational strategies of a middle-class African American woman, whom he describes as a "balanced bilingual speaker of [Black English] and [Standard English]." A similar model is used in Linnes (1998), in a comparison of standard-vernacular variation among middle-class African American speakers and middle-class German–English bilinguals. Linnes argues that alternations in the African American speech community represent a broad diglossic relationship, by which ethnic themes are linked to the vernacular, while more mainstream themes are tied to the standard. And Stanback (1984) uses a code-switching model to describe the individual variation that she observes in her examination of two middle-class African American women, whose patterns of vernacular usage shift according to the gender and race of their conversational partners.

However, Scanlon and Wassink (2010) take issue with the code-switching approaches described above, noting that:

> there is a danger in equating categorical or frequent use of core AAE features with expression of African American identity, because it implies that higher-status speakers who display variable use of core AAE forms or limited use of only a subset of forms are less 'Black' than speakers who deploy a full range of core AAE features. (206)

Instead, they use an approach that takes into account the multidimensionality of intra-speaker variation and recognizes the potential for African American identities to be expressed by a range of stylized features, not limited to the vernacular core. In their analysis of interview data from a middle-class African American woman 65 years of age, Scanlon and Wassink (2010) find that *pin-pen* merging and (ay) monophthongization or reduction (e.g., in *hide, height, high*) show signs of shift according to interlocutor ethnicity and familiarity, as well as some accommodation to interlocutor speech.

Studies of style-shifting or code-switching among MCAAE speakers represent an important complement to social stratification studies in that they help to shed light on individual aspects of AAE usage and the varied and multidimensional contexts in which such uses emerge. This continuum, or bidialectal ability, may be a reflex of the middle-class experience of crossing the boundaries of multiple speech communities and the need to communicate with both African American and White neighbors, friends, and colleagues (Garner and Rubin 1986; Lacy 2004; Moore 2008; Rahman 2008). For example, in Moore (2008), a woman prides herself for her abilities to cross social and ethnic boundaries: "When I'm with them [her professional status-seeking peers], I talk like them, eat like them, dress like them. But I prefer to think of myself as classless" (505). Furthermore, Garner and Rubin (1986) find that among Southern African American attorneys, code-switching may even surface as a rhetorical strategy depending on the audience, the level of rapport that they want to build, and the social risks of speaking either a standard or vernacular variety.

44.4.3 Identity and Public Performance

For the African American professional, language is an important tool for expressing ethnic identity and navigating the demands of a multiethnic personal and professional environment. While not all African American public figures fall squarely in the middle class in terms of income, there are some elements of their experiences that also cause them to use language as a tool for bridging African American and White worlds. For example, Hay, Jannedy, and Mendoza-Denton (1999) find that the use of /ay/ monophthongization significantly increased in the speech of African American talk show host Oprah Winfrey in the presence of an African American referee.[12] Weldon's (2004) examination of the speech of African American leaders speaking at the 2004 "State of the Black Union" symposium reveals variation in the distribution of AAE features ranging from speakers who made very little use of vernacular features to speakers, such as the host Tavis Smiley, who used a wide range of features. As Weldon observes, the types of variation seen at this symposium, which took place in front of a predominately African American audience while being simultaneously aired live on CSPAN, may relate to situational constraints, such as the host's need to appeal to audience members from both standard- and vernacular-speaking communities. Overall, Weldon reveals the flexibility of African American professional language, including the use of African American rhetorical strategies such as signifying, call-response, and African American preaching register.

As observed by Geneva Smitherman, African American public figures often tap into the sacred-secular continuum of African American speech (see Smitherman 1977, 2000). This continuum, with its emphasis on verbal performance and its foundation in a spiritual worldview, is the thread that unifies the speech styles of a wide array of African American public speakers from poets, disc-jockeys, and rappers, to politicians, academicians, and preachers. Drawing from this understanding of the sacred-secular continuum, Britt (2011a, b) finds that African American public speakers at the 2008 "State of the Black Union" symposium made limited use of hallmark vernacular features of AAE (such as copula deletion and invariant *be*), yet consistently utilized elements from African American preaching style, allowing them to take controversial political stances as they expressed their ethnic, religious, and philosophical affiliation with members of the African American community.

Similarly, Kendall and Wolfram's (2009) study of style-shifting patterns in the speech of three African American leaders of two southern African American communities showed that the leaders demonstrated a range of standard and vernacular features. However, the speakers also lacked significant style-shifting between formal, public speaking, and broadcast events and informal interview contexts. Kendall and Wolfram attributed this unexpected result, in part, to the demographic makeup of the communities themselves, which may have placed different pressures on the leaders that determined which dialect features surfaced in their speech.

Language may also serve a *creative,* rhetorical function for African American public speakers, as observed by Ervin-Tripp (2001), in an examination of the speech of Stokely Carmichael, Chair of the Student Non-violent Coordinating Committee (SNCC), and comedian and political activist Dick Gregory. In this study, Ervin-Tripp finds that AAVE surfaced strategically in the punch line for Carmichael when he intended to make a point to African American audience members, and contrasted with his standard speaking style, which he directed at members of the media and the television audience. On the other hand, Gregory moved back and forth between AAVE and more standard speech as a rhetorical tool to give voice to the various "characters" in his narrative.

44.4.4 Language Ideologies and Attitudes

The range of middle-class African American language practices described above may reflect deeper ideologies and attitudes about language. Wassink and Curzan (2004) define language ideology as "a system of collectively held beliefs or dispositions toward language" that governs how speakers "interpret and understand the language variation they encounter" (175). Borrowing from W. E. B. DuBois's notion of "double consciousness," Smitherman (2006) uses the term "linguistic push-pull" to describe the practice of "Black folk loving, embracing, using Black Talk, while simultaneously rejecting and hatin on it" (i.e., covert prestige) (6).[13] A discussion of middle-class African American language ideology is critical here, since members of the middle class are often "pushed and pulled" between positive and negative evaluations of AAE and more mainstream varieties. For example, broader, mainstream discourses tend to devalue and subordinate non-mainstream varieties like AAE, and speakers of AAE may internalize these norms and even reject any view that AAE has internal structure and regularity (Lippi-Green 1997). Yet, Smitherman (2000) points out that African Americans may be divided generationally on their views on AAE such that older, more established leaders may reject AAE while younger African Americans may be more accepting (153). Morgan (1994, 2001, 2002) has also observed that African Americans vary widely in their language attitudes, ranging from the view that AAE is a useful expressive tool and a symbol of resistance (e.g., Toni Morrison) to the belief that it is a symbol of slave mentality (e.g., Bill Cosby). As a result, a speaker's use of AAE may send signals about their age, class, ethnic orientation, and level of integration into the mainstream, as well as their own personal language ideologies.

In a study of the correlations between parents' economic and education levels and perceptions of the appropriate contexts for AAE use, Hoover (1975) found that parents who were highly educated and who had high positive ethnicity tended to support the use of AAE in the classroom (101). Thus, Hoover observed that "Africanized English is valued for solidarity purposes, for logic, and as a preserver of Black culture" (102) and that "their most salient reasons for keeping both were 'survival' and 'communications'" (102). Hoover (1978) also found that educated professionals did not oppose AAE in schools because "the standard level can be learned from them at home" (81). However, African American parents with low preference for AAE in schools (including those who spoke AAE at home) felt that "their children would learn vernacular Black English with friends and that the school's job was to teach the 'other kind'—the kind they didn't know" (81). Hoover concluded that "Black consciousness, political involvement, cultural behavior and general attitudes to Black English. . . were significantly related to parent's attitudes toward vernacular English" (83).

Rahman (2008) also investigated middle-class African American attitudes toward speech that "sounds Black" and found that speech lacking ethnically or regionally marked features is seen as more standard and more appropriate for professional contexts, reflecting both higher education and higher class status. Yet this result does not suggest that the participants viewed AAE negatively. As Rahman puts it, "they see SE [standard English] as appropriate for advancing in mainstream environments" (167). For these speakers, AAE is valued as a tool that keeps them connected to their African American heritage. Interestingly, African American Standard English (see Spears, this volume) was viewed by listeners in Rahman's study as suitable for all contexts. This intermediary variety is seen as an important tool for meeting both the need for professionalism as well as the need to identify with the African American community.

Others have investigated perceptions of standard and vernacular language use in college students revealing that African American students also tend to rate standard varieties more favorably in formal contexts, tend to give higher ratings to "appropriate" code-switching (i.e., using standard varieties in formal contexts and vernacular varieties in informal contexts, and not vice versa), and tend to see standard speakers as more competent and likeable (Larimer, Beatty, and Broadus 1988; Doss and Gross 1992; White et al. 1998; Koch, Gross, and Kolts 2001). However, White et al. (1998) also found that African American students may not internalize discrimination against the language of lower-status African Americans as much as Whites. Furthermore, White et al. suggest that an understanding of the student's ethnic affiliation is important since students without a strong African American identity rated vernacular varieties much lower than standard varieties when compared to students who scored higher on an African Self Consciousness scale.[14]

While these studies may suggest that there is a higher value for standard over vernacular varieties, there is still evidence that both standard and vernacular ways of speaking have value for middle-class African Americans, depending on the contexts of use and the speaker's ethnic (and even class) orientations. For example, Moore (2008) conducted ethnographic fieldwork in a low-income neighborhood near downtown Philadelphia and identified six distinct class identities—ghetto, poor, working-class, multi-class, middle-class-minded, rich/upper-class. Within this continuum, multi-class and middle-class individuals share professional and income similarities. However, multi-class individuals are distinguished by the fact that they have moved through several class layers between childhood and adulthood, and the ways that they intentionally remain connected, both personally and in terms of their residential choices, to low-income African Americans. On the other hand, middle-class African Americans are seen as individuals who gravitate toward White standards and status symbols, who live in predominantly middle-class neighborhoods, and who are more inclined to adopt an integrationist ideology.

These class structures have interesting implications for language. Multi-class individuals value code-switching patterns as a sign of their ability to move comfortably across class and cultural boundaries. On the other hand, some middle-class-minded individuals may be redefining traditionally White middle-class habits (including speaking SAE) as authentically African American. For example, one middle-class-minded participant, Valerie, was often criticized for her insistence that her children use SAE in all contexts. In fact, this was "her way of claiming cultural space, in this case language, as authentically Black, that had previously been identified only with White people" (Moore 2008, 502).

Valerie's experiences are not uncommon among middle-class-minded or upwardly mobile African Americans who grapple with the view of SAE varieties as "White" language. For example, Fordham and Ogbu (1986) examine the conflicting messages sent to African American students about the ways that academic achievement is associated with "acting White" and the ways that "certain forms of behavior and certain activities or events, symbols, and meanings are *not appropriate* for them because those behaviors, events, symbols, and meanings are characteristic of White Americans" (181). Smitherman (1977) also argues that members of the African American community may view the use of what is considered "White English" as suspect.

Similarly, Baugh (2000) gives a personal account of his own chameleon-like abilities to navigate this social minefield by using nonstandard speech with friends while embracing standard language with his family and at church (6). These examples suggest that while an individual may have fairly positive views of both mainstream varieties and AAE, they still may be pushed and pulled between external, competing discourses that require competence in mainstream varieties and the need to be fluent in AAE (or to avoid "talking proper") as a sign of ethnic solidarity.

44.5 CONCLUSION

Contrary to early research, which portrayed middle-class African Americans as "lames" relative to African American vernacular language and culture, the studies reviewed here show that the African American middle class is not a monolithic group but has internal variations and nuances that are linked to a wide variety of linguistic behaviors. For example, middle-class African Americans who live in distinctly middle-class enclaves, who are second generation members of the middle class, and who may be more middle-class-minded, may have a different set of attitudes and linguistic practices from middle-class African Americans who are first generation members of the middle class or who live in close proximity to the working class. Furthermore, middle-class individuals' linguistic practices may also be responsive to external pressures such as audience composition, the need to express their ethnic orientation linguistically, or the need for creative and rhetorical moves during professional or public speaking engagements. Overall, the middle class provides an exciting site of sociolinguistic research given that middle-class African Americans often fall on the boundary between speech communities and display the nuances and tensions of that experience in their linguistic choices.[15]

Overall, the research previously conducted on the linguistic practices of middle-class African Americans, whether first generation or second generation, strongly demonstrates that AAE is complex. Furthermore, research on AAE needs to be more inclusive of all members of the African American community, regardless of age/generation, class, gender, region, education, and sexuality.

NOTES

1. With the exception of direct quotes or references to other studies, we use the label African American English (AAE) in accordance with the most common practice in the current literature, though we recognize that African American Language (AAL) is also becoming a popular choice among linguists. Our decision to use the AAE label is also driven by the observation made by Mufwene (2001) that most speakers of the variety see themselves, first and foremost, as speakers of English.

2. In this same text, Labov later described the age range as that of 9 to 18 (1972, 257).

3. See also Spears (this volume) for a discussion of the "Black elite" as it pertains to the "social locus" of African American Standard English (AASE).

4. The term *hypercorrection* is used here to refer to the observed tendency for lower-middle-class (LMC) speakers to exhibit more extreme style-shifting than their upper-middle-class (UMC) counterparts, resulting in a *crossover pattern* in more formal styles, by which LMC speakers exhibit higher frequencies of the prestige variant than UMC speakers (see Labov 1972, 244–45).

5. Later, alternative approaches to style and sociolinguistic variation have challenged the unidimensional nature of this approach and, consequently, the findings associated with it. See Eckert and Rickford (2001) for a discussion of various approaches to style and sociolinguistic variation.

6. The /θ/ variable (e.g., in *tooth* or *nothing*) is the exception here, where "14 of the 24 middle class informants exhibit categorical absence of the [f] variant" (Wolfram 1969, 85).

7. Nguyen uses the notation [alv] in the study itself to refer to the non-AAE variant, which includes any alveolar stop closure on the coda, voiced or voiceless (2006, 75). However, given the relative infrequency of [t] in her study, we refer to the non-AAE variant here simply as [d].

8. Specifically, Nguyen observes here a pattern by which [ʊ] is fronted more in pre-alveolar contexts (e.g., *put*) than in pre-velar ones (e.g., *look*).

9. For more on the Northern Cities Chain Shift (NCCS), see Labov, Yeager, and Steiner (1973).

10. The terms *overt* and *covert* are used in sociolinguistics to draw a distinction between the prestige norms of mainstream society and those of smaller social groups, respectively (Labov 1966).

11. For overviews of this debate, see Labov (1982); Bailey (1993); Dayton (1996); Labov (1998); Mufwene (1992); Benor (2010).

12. In the tradition of Bell (1984), the term *referee* is used here to refer to people who are not part of the present audience, but who, nonetheless, have the potential to influence the speaker's language through the speaker's mere reference to them.

13. See also Smitherman (1977, 2000); Morgan (1994); Lippi-Green (1997).

14. The African American Consciousness scale is a forty-two-item questionnaire that assesses the individual's recognition of, value for, and respect for Black/African identity, African survival, and African development and their level of resistance toward "anti-Black" elements in society. See White et al. (1998) for more details.

15. Weldon (forthcoming) provides a fuller treatment of many of the issues discussed in this chapter.

References

Adelman, Robert. 2004. "Neighborhood Opportunities, Race, and Class: The Black Middle Class and Residential Segregation." *City & Community* 3 (1): 43–63.

Alba, Richard, John Logan, and Brian Stults. 2000. "How Segregated are Middle-Class African Americans?" *Social Problems* 47 (4): 543–58.

Bailey, Guy. 1993. "A Perspective on African American English." In *American Dialect Research*, edited by Dennis Preston, 287–318. Philadelphia: John Benjamins.

Baugh, John. 1983. *Black Street Speech: Its History, Structure, and Survival.* Austin: University of Texas.

———. 1999. *Out of the Mouths of Slaves: African American Language and Educational Malpractice.* Austin: University of Texas.

———. 2000. *Beyond Ebonics: Linguistic Pride and Racial Prejudice.* New York: Oxford University.

Bell, Allan. 1984. "Language Style as Audience Design." *Language in Society* 13 (2): 145–204.

Benor, Sara Bunin. 2010. "Ethnolinguistic Repertoire: Shifting the Analytic Focus in Language and Ethnicity." *Journal of Sociolinguistics* 14 (2): 159–83.

Britt, Erica. 2011a. "'Can the Church Say Amen': Strategic Uses of Black Preaching Style at the State of the Black Union." *Language in Society* 40 (2): 211–33.

———. 2011b. "Talking Black in Public Spaces: An Investigation of the Identity and the Use of Preaching Style in Black Public Speech." PhD diss., University of Illinois at Urbana-Champaign.

Bucholtz, Mary. 2003. "Sociolinguistic Nostalgia and the Authentication of Identity." *Journal of Sociolinguistics* 7: 398–416.

Dayton, Elizabeth. 1996. "Grammatical Categories of the Verb in African-American Vernacular English." PhD diss., University of Pennsylvania.

DeBose, Charles. 1992. "Codeswitching: Black English and Standard English in the African-American Linguistic Repertoire." *Journal of Multilingual and Multicultural Development* 13: 157–67.

Doss, Richard, and Alan Gross. 1992. "The Effects of Black English on Stereotyping in Intraracial Perceptions." *Journal of Black Psychology* 18 (2): 47–58.

Eckert, Penelope, and John R. Rickford, eds. 2001. *Style and Sociolinguistic Variation*. Cambridge: Cambridge University Press.

Ervin-Tripp, Susan. 2001. "Variety, Style-Shifting, and Ideology." In *Style and Sociolinguistic Variation*, edited by Penelope Eckert and John R. Rickford, 44–56. Cambridge: Cambridge University.

Fordham, Signithia, and John Ogbu. 1986. "Black Students' School Success: Coping with the 'Burden of "Acting White."'" *The Urban Review* 18 (3): 176–206.

Frazier, E. Franklin. 1957. *Black Bourgeoisie: The Rise of the New Middle Class in the United States*. London: Collier Books.

Garner, T., and D. L. Rubin. 1986. "Middle Class Black's Perceptions of Dialect and Style Shifting: The Case of Southern Attorneys." *Journal of Language and Social Psychology* 5 (1): 33–48.

Hay, Jennifer, Stefanie Jannedy, and Norma Mendoza-Denton. 1999. "Oprah and /ay/: Lexical Frequency, Referee Design and Style." In *Proceedings of the 14th International Congress of Phonetic Sciences*. San Francisco: n.p. CD-ROM.

Haynes, Bruce. 2001. *Red Lines, Black Spaces: The Politics of Race and Space in a Black Middle-Class Suburb*. New Haven: Yale University Press.

Hoover, Mary Rhodes. 1975. "Appropriate Use of Black English by Black Children as Rated by Parents." PhD diss., Stanford University.

———. 1978. "Community Attitudes toward Black English." *Language in Society* 7 (1): 65–87.

Jones, Jamila, and Dennis R. Preston. 2011. "AAE & Identity: Constructing & Deploying Linguistic Resources." In *The Joy of Language: Proceedings of a Symposium Honoring the Colleagues of David Dwyer on the Occasion of his Retirement*, edited by David Dwyer. http://www.msu.edu/%7Edwyer/JOLIndex.htm.

Kendall, Tyler, and Walt Wolfram. 2009. "Local and External Language Standards in African American English." *Journal of English Linguistics* 37: 5–30.

Koch, Lisa, Alan Gross, and Russell Kolts. 2001. "Attitudes toward Black English and Code Switching." *Journal of Black Psychology* 27 (1): 29–42.

Labov, William. 1966. *The Social Stratification of English in New York City*. Washington, DC: Center for Applied Linguistics.

———. 1972. *Language in the Inner City: Studies in the Black English Vernacular*. Oxford: Blackwell.

———. 1982. "Objectivity and Commitment in Linguistic Science: The Case of the Black English Trial in Ann Arbor." *Language in Society* 11: 165–201.

———. 1998. "Coexistent Systems in African-American Vernacular English." In *African American English: Structure, History, and Use*, edited by Salikoko S. Mufwene, John R. Rickford, Guy Bailey, and John Baugh, 110–53. London: Routledge.

Labov, William, Malcah Yaeger, and Richard Steiner. 1973. *The Quantitative Study of Sound Change in Progress*. Philadelphia: US Regional Survey.

Lacy, Karyn R. 2004. "Black Spaces, Black Places: Strategic Assimilation and Identity Construction in Middle-Class Suburbia." *Ethnic and Racial Studies* 27 (6): 908–30.

———. 2007. *Blue-Chip Black: Race, Class, and Status in the New Black Middle Class*. Berkeley: University of California.

Landry, Bart. 1986. *The New Black Middle Class*. Los Angeles: University of California.

Larimer, George, David Beatty, and Alfonso Broadus. 1988. "Indirect Assessment of Interracial Prejudices." *Journal of Black Psychology* 14 (2): 47–56.

Linnes, Kathleen. 1998. "Middle-Class AAVE versus Middle-Class Bilingualism: Contrasting Speech Communities." *American Speech* 73: 339–67.

Lippi-Green, Rosina. 1997. *English with an Accent: Language, Ideology, and Discrimination in the United States.* New York: Routledge.

Marsh, Kris, William Darity, Philip Cohen, Lynne Casper, and Danielle Salters. 2007. "The Emerging Black Middle Class: Single and Living Alone." *Social Forces* 86 (2): 735–62.

Massey, Douglas S., and Nancy Denton. 1993. *American Apartheid: Segregation and the Making of the Underclass.* Cambridge, MA: Harvard University.

Massey, Douglas S., and Mary J. Fischer. 1999. "Does Rising Income Bring Integration? New Results for Blacks, Hispanics, and Asians in 1990." *Social Science Research* 28: 316–26.

McWhorter, John. 1998. *Word on the Street: Fact and Fable about American English.* New York: Plenum Trade.

Mendoza-Denton, Norma, Jennifer Hay, and Stefanie Jannedy. 2003. "Probabilistic Sociolinguistics: Beyond Variable Rules." In *Probabilistic Linguistics*, edited by Rens Bod, Jennifer Hay, and Stefanie Jannedy, 97–138. Cambridge, MA: MIT.

Moore, Kesha. 2008. "Class Formations: Competing Forms of Black Middle-Class Identity." *Ethnicities* 8 (4): 492–517.

Morgan, Marcyliena. 1994. "The African American Speech Community: Reality and Sociolinguistics." In *Language and the Social Construction of Identity in Creole Situations*, edited by Marcyliena Morgan, 121–48. Center for African American Studies.

———. 2001. "The African-American Speech Community: Reality and Sociolinguistics." In *Linguistic Anthropology: A Reader*, edited by Alessandro Duranti, 74–94. Cambridge, MA: African Americanwell.

———. 2002. *Language, Discourse, and Power in African American Culture.* Cambridge: Cambridge University.

Mufwene, Salikoko. 1992. "Why Grammars are Not Monolithic. In *The Joy of Grammar: A Festschrift in Honor of James D. McCawley*, edited by Diane Brentari, Gary N. Larson, and Lynn A. MacLeod, 225–50. Amsterdam: John Benjamins.

———. 2001. "What is African American English?" In *Sociocultural and Historical Contexts of African American English*, edited by Sonja Lanehart, 21–51. Amsterdam: John Benjamins.

Nguyen, Jennifer. 2006. "The Changing Social and Linguistic Orientation of the African American Middle Class." PhD diss., University of Michigan.

Oliver, Melvin, and Thomas Shapiro. 1995. *Black Wealth, White Wealth: A New Perspective on Racial Inequality.* New York: Routledge.

Pattillo, Mary. 2005. "Black Middle-Class Neighborhoods." *Annual Review of Sociology* 31: 305–29.

Pattillo-McCoy, Mary. 1999. *Black Picket Fences: Privilege and Peril among the Black Middle Class.* Chicago: University of Illinois.

Pew Research Center, Washington, DC. 2012. "Fewer, Poorer, Gloomier: The Lost Decade of the Middle Class." http://www.pewsocialtrends.org/files/2012/08/pew-social-trends-lost-decade-of-the-middle-class.pdf.

Rahman, Jacquelyn. 2008. "Middle Class African Americans: Reactions and Attitudes toward African American English." *American Speech* 83 (2): 141–76.

Scanlon, Michael, and Alicia Beckford Wassink. 2010. "African American English in Urban Seattle: Accommodation and Intraspeaker Variation in the Pacific Northwest." *American Speech* 85 (2): 205–24.

Smitherman, Geneva. 1977. *Talkin and Testifyin: The Language of Black America*. Detroit, MI: Wayne State University.

——. 2000. *Talkin that Talk: Language, Culture, and Education in African America*. New York: Routledge.

——. 2006. *Word from the Mother: Language and African Americans*. New York: Routledge.

Spears, Arthur. 1998. "African-American Language Use: Ideology and So-Called Obscenity." In *African-American English: Structure, History, and Use*, edited by Salikoko Mufwene, John R. Rickford, Guy Bailey, and John Baugh, 226–50. London: Routledge.

Stanback, Marsha Houston. 1984. "Code-Switching in Black Women's Speech." PhD diss., University of Massachusetts, Amherst.

Taylor, Orlando. 1983. "Black English: An Agenda for the 1980's." In *Black English: Educational Equity and the Law*, edited by John Chambers, Jr., 133–43. Ann Arbor, MI: Karoma.

Taylor, Paul, Rakesh Kochhar, Richard Fry, Gabriel Velasco, and Seth Motel. 2011. "Twenty-to-One: Wealth Gaps Rise to Record Highs between Whites, Blacks and Hispanics." Pew Research Center, Washington, DC. http://www.pewsocialtrends.org/files/2011/07/SDT-Wealth-Report_7-26-11_FINAL.pdf.

Wassink, Alicia Beckford, and Anne Curzan. 2004. "Addressing Ideologies around African American English." *Journal of English Linguistics* 32 (3): 171–85.

Weldon, Tracey. 2004. "African American English in the Middle Classes: Exploring the Other End of the Continuum." Paper presented at annual meeting of New Ways of Analyzing Variation, Ann Arbor, Michigan, September 30–October 3.

——. Forthcoming. *Middle Class African American English*. Cambridge: Cambridge University Press.

White, Michael, Beverly Vandiver, Mariah Becker, Belinda Overstreet, Linda Temple, Kelly Hagan, and Emily Mandelbaum. 1998. "African American Evaluations of Black English and Standard American English." *Journal of Black Psychology* 24 (1): 60–75.

Wilson, William. 1987. *The Truly Disadvantaged: The Inner City, the Underclass, and Public Policy*. Chicago: University of Chicago.

Wolfram, Walt. 1969. *A Sociolinguistic Description of Detroit Negro Speech*. Washington, DC: Center for Applied Linguistics.

CHAPTER 45

....

AFRICAN AMERICAN WOMEN'S LANGUAGE

Mother Tongues Untied

....

MARCYLIENA MORGAN

45.1 INTRODUCTION

....

A *mother tongue* refers to the first language learned as an infant, child, and youth.[1] Mothers teach their children their language as they nurture and socialize them to understand and participate in the social world. Though her position as the first source to impart knowledge and insight about language and culture may be unrecognized due to gender stereotypes, in a mother's arms is where a child's involvement in family, culture, community, and nation begins. A mother's fundamental role in building and sustaining society is often framed within discourses that belie and minimize her powerful and indispensable position. Like many women of the world, African American women recognize that their responsibilities as mother are viewed as instinctive and natural. Although African American women also share the need of most women to consistently defend their worth, they have additional responsibilities to unravel the realities and ideologies around gender in relation to race and social class in the United States. In many instances, African American women are all too aware of the stereotypes of Black mothers—where they are described as loving too much or too little, but never as the 'good' woman/mother.[2]

While this chapter is about the linguistic research that has emerged concerning African American Women's Language (AAWL), it should be noted that it is deeply rooted in African American women's roles and representations in society as well as in issues of gender and racial justice. This is partly because the early stages of the linguistic research coincided with the political and social movements of the 1960s and 1970s. It is also because Black women regularly comment that they believe they are often stereotyped and viewed as problematic in society while also viewed as lacking social and feminine respectability.

African American women's speech styles are important in the African American community, though in linguistic studies women's language use has mainly been viewed as indistinguishable from men's usage.[3] Nancy Henley (1995) explores this widespread view in early anthropological work and writes that "anthropologists identified sex differentiation in far-off tribal societies, but not their own. Women's forms were often viewed as 'women's language' because the language spoken by the men of these societies was seen by these mostly male anthropologists as 'the' language" (1995, 362). Considering this proclivity, it is predictable that research on AAWL has focused on males and tended to ignore the presence of female data in the overall description of the African American speech community. This invisibility makes the analysis of AAWL especially challenging since, in general, African American women are: (1) absent from the debate on how Western societies identify women's roles and language; (2) absent in discussions of ways that women's language is unique, similar, and different from men in general; and (3) affected by societal attitudes and negative stereotypes toward their speech and use of varieties of African American Language (AAL) in ways that Black men are not.

In order to further address the issues described above, this chapter critically analyzes the relevant theories and research on AAWL, and reviews and critiques the ideological, cultural, and social arguments that helped shape them. As indicated above, while this chapter reviews and critiques previous research on AAWL, it also reflects how AAWL is deeply rooted in African American women's roles and representation in society as well as issues of gender and racial justice. The African American speech community is one that relies on women's input and ideology. Consequently, women's subordinate status in linguistic descriptions impedes our understanding of language in the African American speech community, in general, and women's language, in particular.

45.2 RECOGNIZING WOMEN'S INFLUENCE IN THE AFRICAN AMERICAN SPEECH COMMUNITY

In the United States, the untangling of perspectives on women's roles in language and discourse began in earnest in the 1970s, amidst the political struggles of the Black Power movement and the growing women's movement. In response to questions raised about society's implicit and explicit lack of support for women's rights, Robin Lakoff (1975) published *Language and Woman's Place* (*LWP*). The text began as an article in 1973 and quickly became the most influential and provocative treatise on language and gender.

In *LWP*, Lakoff argued that women and men talk differently and that women's speech reflected male dominance in society. Lakoff suggested that male speech styles were so dominant and different from women's styles that women's speech actually contributed to the perpetuation of stereotypes as well as women's secondary role in society. Her argument was based on observations and intuitions about middle-class White women and focused on what she considered to be the two main forms of discrimination in women's language: that women are taught a weaker form of language than men (e.g., tag questions), and an inherent sexism in the structure and usage of language itself (e.g., euphemisms for women). Lakoff's work was also influenced by the social and political definitions of feminism of the era that considered males and females in opposition to each other. This perspective of feminism is referred to as the *difference* and *dominance* perspective (see Eckert and McConnell-Ginet 2003; Talbot 2010; Wolfram and Schilling-Estes 1998). Research and theories about this dichotomy represent the first period of systemic investigation into the relationship of gender and language. However, as the study of gender and language grew, preoccupation with identifying direct contrasts between the speech of men and women was regularly criticized. As Jennifer Coates (1998) explains, "In the early years... research into the interaction of language and gender relied on a predominantly essentialist paradigm which categorized speakers primarily according to biological sex, and used mainly quantitative methods" (3).

In many respects, Lakoff's (1975) argument that women's speech both reflected and supported the perpetuation of stereotypes of women's secondary role in society was analogous to the argument put forth in a 1960 essay on racism and language written by Ossie Davis (1967) titled, "The English Language Is My Enemy." Davis, an acclaimed actor and civil rights activist, examined the significance of words that include *dark* and *black* as morphemes in English. He argued that racism is so embedded in American ideology that one cannot speak and learn English without also learning negative views of Blackness and participating in the stereotyping of African Americans.

> If you consider the fact that thinking itself is sub-vocal speech—in other words, one must use words in order to think at all—you will appreciate the enormous heritage of racial prejudgment that lies in wait for any child born into the English Language. Any teacher good or bad, [W]hite or [B]lack, Jew or Gentile, who uses the English Language as a medium of communication is forced, willy-nilly, to teach the Negro child 60 ways to despise himself, and the [W]hite child 60 ways to aid and abet him in the crime. (1967, 11–12)

With the exception of Davis's (1967) argument, early discussions of race, social class, and racial dominance (as compared to male dominance) were largely absent from the linguistic discourse and analysis during the late 1960s and the 1970s. Much of the linguistic work on dialectology focused on regional variation, and sociolinguistic studies and were mainly of the White working class.

Considering the marginal inclusion of African American women in discussions of feminism and language and gender, it is not surprising that the study of AAWL did not appear as central to sociolinguistic studies of the African American speech community. Rebecca Walker (2005) explains the dilemma faced by working-class women, women of color, and Black women, in particular, whose speech communities did not represent the ideologies of middle-class White women.

> For many of us it seems that to be a feminist in the way that we have seen or understood feminism is to conform to an identity and way of living that doesn't allow for individuality, complexity, or less than perfect personal histories. We fear that the

identity will dictate and regulate our lives, instantaneously pitting us against someone, forcing us to choose inflexible and unchanging sides, female against male,
[B]lack against [W]hite, oppressed against oppressor, good against bad. This way of
ordering the world is especially difficult for a generation that has grown up transgender, bisexual, interracial, and knowing and loving people who are racist, sexist, and
otherwise afflicted. (Walker 2005, 22)

The battles that emerged during the larger women's movement over the demand that
women of different races and classes be included were also reflected in the research
on AAWL. The groundbreaking linguistic argument of the late 1970s—that AAL is a
systematic dialect and should be respected as such—was founded on the assumption
that it is men who create and speak African American vernacular speech, since "it was
assumed at the time that vernacular dialects were maintained and transmitted primarily
by adolescent males" (Wolfram and Schilling-Estes 1998, 187). Comprehensive review
of ethnicity and gender research in linguistics critiqued this problem and argued that
the language of working-class women and women of color has been on the periphery
as a unique, marginal, or special case, rather than as one among many examples of language (see Henley 1995). Cameron and Coates (1988) addressed these issues by integrating women's diversity, especially in terms of social class and culture, in their critique
of arguments regarding generalizations made concerning women's prestige usage. They
argue that what is considered conservative for middle-class women may not be seen as
conservative for working-class women for whom it can be innovative instead. This creates a superficial contradiction about what formal and informal styles of language use
among women means when compared to men's usage. Cameron and Coates consider
this view part of the folklore about women (as mysterious creatures) and argue that it
is actually based on the notion that "male behaviour and male norms are prototypical"
(1988, 24).

The truth is that the African American speech community, with its array of ideologies and practices, was developed within a social history that included a mandatory
language style that was publicly and enforcedly marked as subservient. During US slavery and until the 1960s in the South, Blacks could not exhibit linguistic agency nor
could they initiate verbal interactions with Whites without being under the threat of
death (see Morgan 2002). Control and surveillance were relentless and occurred within
all aspects of Black life, especially in terms of day-to-day interactions. Interaction styles
included nearly every conservative, overly polite verbal and non-verbal expectation of
women's speech framed within a racial prejudice: (a) use formal address when speaking to a White person, (b) do not speak unless spoken to, (c) do not speak assuredly
(use hedges), and (d) do not make statements (overuse tag questions), and so on. The
discursive requirements also included non-verbal rules such as stepping aside when
a White person approaches, keeping one's head lowered and not looking at someone
directly in the eye. Thus, linguistic and conversational cues of subservience and depen-
dence were necessary as performatives to corroborate the defense for slavery, and later
segregation.

Since the struggle against racial bigotry and injustice was the main civil rights concern for the Black community, African American women essentially represented both racial and gender issues. Unlike the White women in language and gender studies, African American women were not considered significantly different from Black men in terms of AAL usage. This representation at the height of the feminist movement did not result in African American women being considered feminist and assertive in terms of women's rights and participation in society. In fact it placed them further outside the language and gender discussion in that the scholarship on AAWL was not aligned with feminist arguments that did not recognize racial discrimination and focused on comparison and difference exclusively in terms of middle-class White males and females.

45.3 AAWL VISIBILITY IN SOCIOLINGUISTICS: CONSERVATIVE AND INNOVATIVE

Though theorizing about women's language relies heavily on the understanding of interaction and the social context in which it occurs, early sociolinguistic studies of vernacular usage among African American women adopted the assumptions of general linguistics: that all women's language is more conservative than men's and that women adopt innovative features more quickly than men (Jespersen [1922] 1964). However, what is referred to as conservative and innovative use of language can at times refer to the same interaction, depending on speech community norms and social context (see Cameron and Coates above). Since women's designation as conservative speakers is based on the speech of middle-class White women, when in contrast with Black women's speech it is treated as the unmarked and "normal and good" speech. Several important AAL research projects of the late 1960s and 1970s included observations and, in some cases, data about Black women's language use that revealed this fact. For instance, in the Detroit studies of 1969, Walter Wolfram found that African American women used more standard forms when compared to African American men. Wolfram (1969) reported that lower-working-class men deleted copulas (e.g., "She Ø smart") 66 percent of the time, while women did so 48 percent of the time (178). In contrast, in research conducted in Washington, DC, Ralph Fasold (1972) reported that his team found little to no difference among African American men and women.

Some linguists turned to social and psychological explanations for the contradictory findings by suggesting that women are insecure, mysterious, status seeking, and so on. While these explanations reflected the stereotypes that Lakoff (above) decried, they also expose the traps of the linguistic terrain that women navigate in general. When these traps are combined with the racial terrain, Black women often must consider how they are viewed as a result of being Black women and what their language use contributes to that assessment. As Patricia Nichols suggests, variation may be based on "both culture-specific and crosscultural" factors (1982, 55). As the social context shifts, language ideology concerning attitudes toward dialect usage, linguistic accommodation, intentionality, and so on, shifts as well.

In her study of Black women's language in rural coastal South Carolina from 1974-1975, Nichols ([1982] 1998, 1983, 2009) compared linguistic usage between the mainland and islands. She was concerned with community norms and differences in those norms. While many Blacks in the region had been Gullah speakers, Nichols reported that at the time of her study, "The language now used by [B]lacks . . . constitutes a post-creole continuum . . . which encompasses creole, non-standard, and standard varieties of English" (1998, 57). She focused on the use of three syntactic variables:

(1) the *for-to* complementizer
     "I come *for* get my coat."
(2) the static-locative preposition *at*
     "Can we stay *to* the table?"
(3) the third person singular pronoun *it*
     "Well, *ee* was a fun to me."
     "Over there they call *um* over the island." Nichols ([1982] 1998, 57)

Nichols found that older African American women from the mainland showed more conservative linguistic behavior than the African American men, while African American women from the island were actually more innovative than the African American men. The contrasts continued for other age groups as well, though at times African American men used more standard forms and vice versa (1998, 60). She found a correlation between the linguistic variables used by the African American women and the variety of social relations and the type of jobs the women worked. She reports that "all island women work outside the home at some time during their lives, as do most [B]lack women in the area" (60). Thus, women who had stable jobs that did not include outsiders were more linguistically conservative than those who had more mobility. She concluded that how social class was defined and an understanding of the types of jobs available to African American women influenced the language variety that occurred across generations and communities.

Jennifer Bloomquist (2009) was also interested in whether women would adhere to mainstream language standards more consistently than do men (cf. Trudgill 1972) or whether they were more likely to take the lead in adopting linguistic innovations (Labov, Yaeger, and Steiner 1972). She examined women's language in an isolated African American community in rural Pennsylvania's Lower Susquehanna Valley (LSV). When Bloomquist compared urban and rural African American women's use and knowledge of words and expressions common in the LSV lexicon, she found some notable differences. These linguistic differences were, with respect to location, shaped by social history, contact, and identity. She found that African American women did not change and alter their variety to accommodate outsiders and varieties spoken by Whites in the area, though they incorporated linguistic features and styles typical of the region. She argued that these data contradict earlier claims about the relative uniformity, and to some extent, the supraregionality of AAL. However, she worried that while the African American women represented a stable speech community that is part of the region, sociolinguistic studies often excluded their communities in regional studies as though the women did not use local language. Bloomquist issues a warning to linguists who have this tendency that "excluding African American data in regional language variation research, and then comparing AAL. . . to 'White' regional language norms. . . furthers the assumption that the varieties are necessarily and fundamentally distinct" (2009, 181).

Research on young children's acquisition of AAL may also provide insight on language development and change, as well as the role of gender in the development of conservative and innovative usage in African American speech communities. This information may also offer insight on language socialization, in general, and regarding gendered speech and language use, in particular. As Green and Conner (2009) explain, children have to learn the phonology, morphology, and syntax of their native languages as well as the discourse styles and pragmatic and rhetorical uses of the words and phrases. They provide evidence of this from a 5-year-old girl who has learned the pragmatic use of *all* in AAL.

(4) . . . like they was playing dress up. Looking *all* cute.

Green and Conner write, "Given the context *all* is used in [4] to underscore the very "cute" appearance of the characters. . . . While it is true that *all* is a quantifier, in this context the word does not just have the meaning of 'totally'" (2009, 91-92).

Green and Conner (2009) also examined African American girl's rhetorical uses of past time preverbal markers in data from the language of developing, AAL-speaking girls. They found that when they considered simplex forms in which single verbs are marked with past tense morphology (e.g., *worked*) or unmarked (e.g., *work*), the girls employed what might be called conservative practices. In contrast, when they used complex sequences (*had* + verb or *BIN* + verb) they not only represented the past perfect but also regularly referred to events that were accomplished and/or achieved in the past. Thus, early stage AAL-speaking girls use forms both to indicate events in past contexts and as rhetorical markers in oral discourse. In fact, Green and Conner argue that at four years, some of the children "talk about and/or comprehend past events in at least three contexts: simple past, remote past, and preverbal *had* event marking" (2009, 106). They also found that the girls could use stressed *BIN* beyond that of a tense-aspect marker and in aggrandizement contexts.

These findings on the language development of young African American girls suggest that they are learning discourse and language norms that identify them as AAL speakers who also learn the importance of stress, vowel length, and pragmatic forms that may be most associated with AAWL. The question of acquisition is not only concerned with when a child acquires a feature but also when it is used with competence according to speech community standards and expectations. When these questions are examined in women's language, they are also focused on race, language competence, and performance and gender. To answer the question of what is AAWL and who speaks it requires the examination of the complexity of African American speech communities from the perspective of the full range of linguistic analysis as well as language ideology.

45.4 "What Had Happened Was...": Mars and Venus Meet the Middle Passage

The study of the vernacular, the ordinary language of a people, implies analytical focus on language use in everyday activities and among all social actors living in a speech community. As discussed above, the Black "subjects" of the sociolinguistic research were predominantly male (see Jackson [1974] 2004; Abrahams 1970, 1976; Folb 1980), and as Smitherman reveals: "the content of their speech data primarily sexual" (1977, 162). The content of the verbal genres collected often focused on the denigration of African American women and were, therefore, misogynistic and sexual. However, research on women revealed that the content of the genres was not what defined them. Rather, verbal genres are defined by their structure, function in linguistic and social contexts, and as part of speech community norms. African American women's verbal genres, narratives, and conversation styles are characterized by an elaborate system of indirectness and contrast with Standard English verbal styles (Morgan 2002; Spears 2009). The discourse styles and genres also reveal a gendered language ideology in which conservative and innovative styles represent the inequalities between men and women, Blacks and Whites, social classes, and Black women and White women. Much of the research on verbal genres of African American women has focused on indirectness like he-said/she-said routines, signifying, and reading.

Signifying or playing the dozens has been described as a form of play, especially among African American males (see Kochman 1974). However, research on African American women and girls reveals that the dozens is actually one example of an elaborate system of indirection (cf. Goodwin 1990; Morgan 2002; Smitherman 1977). Indirection is not simply a lack of straightforwardness. It is an intentional lack of straightforwardness. It is through the exploration of intentionality that indirection can be deciphered and understood. The object of signifying is determined by possible motives of the speaker, how meaning is conveyed, and how the targeted person and other hearers interpret the meaning of what is said. Mitchell-Kernan (1972) argues that it is a powerful form of communication for women because it can convey meaning without directly confronting the person targeted. For instance, Mitchell-Kernan (1972) describes signifying as "the recognition and attribution of some implicit content or function which is obscured by the surface content or function" (317–18). Her 1971 study of African American Language and culture in Oakland, California, demonstrates that women participate in conversational signifying (Mitchell-Kernan 1971, 65–106) and employ linguistic practices similar to those of men. In this case, the socially accepted message serves as a metaphor for the intended message. What a sentence means is a combination of what is intended and the significance of how it is framed within a sentence and discourse.

Unlike her male peers who mainly "play" signifying games, girls are much more invested in what is actually said, who says it, hears it, and if the person who said it actually means it. Marjorie Goodwin's (1990) analysis of he-said/she-said disputes among African American girls details the elaborate lengths to which participants are willing to go in order to determine who said what behind someone's back. African American girls learn that who talks about another girl behind her back risks being labeled an instigator. The entire ritual involves investigation, evidence, confession, and resolution in the form of apology or confrontation. Goodwin (2003, 2006) has also found that contrary to Carol Gilligan's (1982) claim that conflict is disruptive to middle-class White girls, they also "premise their moral decision making on context-specific principles based on social relationships" (2006, 246). Thus, rather than learning to "play nice," all girls participate in a range of interactions.

As African American girls grow into women, their expression and defense of social face appear in everyday conversations rather than ritualized routines. Morgan (2002) found that signifying and instigating also occur in adult conversations, though through the use of more indirect reference and indexicality. She also reports that for teenagers, he-said/she-said events include discourse strategies that not only introduce potential conflict but also use strategies that reestablish the social order as well. These include investigating and clearing the messenger (instigator); investigating, interrogating, and clearing so-called friends; investigating, interrogating, and clearing the voice of the offending parties; and, finally, resolution.

Another discourse feature found in AAWL research is *reading dialect*. Reading dialect occurs when features from AAL and Mainstream American English (MAE) are contrasted. Members incorporate distinct dialect forms and functions, and contrast them with their possible linguistic counterparts in the other dialect and constantly make use of the possible meanings implied by the particular forms and functions chosen. Thus, in some interactions formal usage may signify that racism, sexism, or other forms of inequality are in play. Another verbal feature found in African American women's discourse is what Morgan (2002, 2003) calls "the Black woman's laugh." It is similar to Irving Goffman's (1978, 1981) response cries in that it indexes the thoughts of the speaker. In the case of AAWL, Morgan argues that it is often called the *fool's laugh* and suggests that what is occurring or being talked about is considered foolish and not in any way funny.

In her analysis of a radio panel discussion convened in 1992 following civil unrest in response to the Rodney King verdict, Mary Bucholtz (1996) found that the Black women participants used several of the discursive strategies described above to construct social identities in terms of gender, social class, and race. These included reading dialect and signifying. Of the six panelists, five were African American, including two women and three men, and there was one White male. Bucholtz reports that at times the women interjected distinctive phonological features and vernacular lexical items that served to establish the solidarity of the speakers as African American. In other instances, the women panelists used questions and deixis in a way that weakened the role of the moderator to direct the interview. She argues, "The panelists' use of the vernacular as an emblem, rather than as the primary linguistic code, demonstrates that the social meaning of the language is retained, or even enhanced, within an institutional context" (279).

In her research on African American women teachers, Michele Foster (1995) was interested in whether teachers used more conservative and formal styles in the classroom. By using the framework of performance theory and discourse analysis, Foster argues that the African American women in her study intentionally and systematically used features of African American discourse style, such as code-switching, in order to express their identity and solidarity with students. Her data contests the notion that middle-class African American speech patterns align more closely with Standard American English than those of working-class African Americans (Labov 1969). Thus, not only did the middle-class women retain their ability to communicate in the African American vernacular, but they also used African American discourse to index a social identity and communicate a particular stance or point of view (see Stanback 1986). She concludes: "African American English enables these women to communicate cognitive, affective content not available in the standard form of the language, to create and maintain social relationships and express solidarity with listeners" (Foster 1995, 347).

The significance of indirectness and signifying and reading in interaction is magnified in African American women's narrative practices. There are several narrative styles identified in African American folklore, writing, and art. For example, Gwendolyn Etter-Lewis (1996) finds that African American women routinely use three narrative styles—unified, segmented, and conversational—within interactions and narratives (178). These styles appear in a non-contiguous yet complimentary fashion as they shift according to topic, imagined audience, local knowledge, and so on. These narratives are co-authored and include issues of changing values and culture, especially regarding what it means to be a woman, and morality, personal responsibility, and sophistication.

Sonja Lanehart (2002) interviewed intergenerational female family members to determine attitudes toward language, literacy, identity, ideologies, education, and sociolinguistic contexts. She found that both societal standards and notions of identity influence the women's attitudes toward standardization and the vernacular. Lanita Jacobs-Huey (2006) examined women's discourse practices in the cultural setting of a beauty salon. She found that interactions between Black women relied on knowledge of indirection as well as discourse markers representing the attitude of the speaker. She also found that symbols of African American culture, race, and gender regarding hair types, styles, and care as well as authority and respect were common themes in any interaction. Her work revealed a complex interaction of cultural negotiation, discourse, and norms.

Spears (2009) examined the function of the word *GIRL* to highlight the importance of intonation as discourse markers in African American women's interactions (see Smitherman 1977). He analyzed the occurrence of the word *girl* in interactions (see Troutman 2001; Scott 2002; Morgan 1996) and argues that though the word retains its dictionary meanings, it is also what he calls *metadiscursive* in that it is a cultural marker that indexes language ideology and discourse styles and accounts for the "flavor" of Black speech (Spears 2009, 77). Spears focuses on *GIRL* in clause-initial position when it is said with a long, stretched, rising intonation. He argues that with *GIRL*, AAWL speakers are able to perform or present solidarity and identity. "In using *GIRL*, they also mark their discourse as AAWL, i.e., as African American women talking in AAWL" (2009, 86).

45.5 Gender and
R-E-S-P-E-C-T: Conservative
and Innovative

African American women contribute to the language patterns and ideology of their speech community. That is, the language choices cannot be simply understood within dichotomies of conservative/innovative, dominance/difference, and so on. Rather, it is embedded in how women are considered in society and in the social and cultural contexts where it matters and where it does not. As Mercer famously argued, "One thing at least is clear—identity only becomes an issue when it is in crisis; when something assumed to be fixed, coherent, and stable is displaced by the experience of doubt and uncertainty" (1994, 259).

AAWL reflects the range of AAL usage found throughout the community. But it is more than that. It is also, as Mitchell-Kernan (1972) suggests, a metaphor and symbol of injustice and inequality between social classes, men and women, Blacks and Whites in general—and Black women and White women, in particular. The combination of respectability, citizenship, and womanhood is a consistent theme in works directly pertaining to AAWL as well. As Evelyn Higginbotham (1993) argues, the only recourse that women had to oppose the social structures and symbolic representations of White supremacy was a discourse based on middle-class White women's language. She argues that was the response to the time when

> crude stereotypes of [B]lacks permeated popular culture and when 'scientific' racism in the form of Social Darwinism prevailed among professional scholars and other thinking people... can be characterized by the concept of the 'politics of respectability'... the discourse of respectability in an era when African Americans' claims to respectability invariably held subversive implications. (186–88)

When introducing the linguistic and discourse systems and strategies of women of color in the United States, and from non-European cultures as well, AAWL is regularly considered a subsection of White women's speech. However, as early debates in feminist studies revealed, while race and gender may be relevant to Black women, race may not trouble many White women.[4] This is especially true in a system where the notion of the "'good/normal' woman is constructed against working class women and women of color" (Higginbotham 1992, 8). It is because of this difference that the examination of the language use and strategies of African American women provide significant examples of how gender is constructed for both Black and White women. The attempt to control Black women's speech is evidence that the very speech style that Lakoff (above) critiqued was also considered ideal White women's speech and socially marked as good and proper. A major problem is the belief that Black women should use White women's speech and do not use it. Many women and linguistic researchers resist this description of White women's speech and have provided valuable data and analysis that proves that it is indeed mostly part of the folklore about women.

Since the conservative standard is often associated with power and prestige, in general when women's language is compared to men's, it is a question of whether women deviate more or less from the male prestige standard. In contrast, the African American standard is based on Black male vernacular usage rather than middle-class male usage. Black male usage is not associated with White male economic, political, and social power in society. Rather, it is associated with male dominance and masculinity. Because Black women's language usage has been viewed as the same as Black men's vernacular speech, Black women's speech has been placed in a peculiar position of being judged in terms of Black male dialect variation, Black male style, and White middle-class women's speech. Consequently, Black women's speech is severely evaluated when considered as women's speech and is often depicted as harsh, inappropriate, and domineering language rather than strong and direct. This reality played out tragically in the legal trial regarding the 2012 murder of Trayvon Martin.

In the summer of 2013, many were riveted to the broadcast of the racially charged trial of George Zimmerman for the killing of the 17-year-old African American Trayvon Martin, who was returning home after purchasing candy from a neighborhood store. An important part of the prosecution against Zimmerman was testimony from Martin's female friend, Rachel Jeantel, who was on the phone with Martin as Zimmerman followed him—and later shot him dead. Jeantel's testimony was central to the assertion that Zimmerman was not in a life-threatening situation when he shot his victim and was, therefore, guilty of murder. However, the defense strategy was to attack the character of Rachel Jeantel. Her testimony was met with contemptuous commentary from the media and online outlets that ridiculed her appearance, speech, and discourse style by referring to her as an animal, fat, and so on. Britney Cooper (2013), a columnist for Salon.com writes:

> These kinds of terms—combat, aggression, anger—stalk [B]lack women, especially [B]lack women who are dark-skinned and plus-sized like Rachel, at every turn seeking to discredit the validity of our experiences and render invisible our traumas. By painting Rachel Jeantel as the aggressor, as the one prone to telling lies and spreading untruths, it became easy. . . to treat this 19-year-old, working-class [B]lack girl, a witness to the murder of her friend, as hostile, as a threat, as the one who needed to be regulated and contained and put in her place.

According to John Rickford (2014), Jeantel's discourse style included indirection and signifying and her linguistic features included the following: stressed *BIN*, as in "I was *BIN* paying attention, sir" meaning, "I've been paying attention for a long time, and am still paying attention"; *preterit HAD*; *ask* as *ax*; *inverted did* in embedded sentences, as in "He had aks me *did* I go to the hospital" ('He asked me whether I had gone to the hospital'); absence of *auxiliary IS* ("He ø trying to get home, sir."); and absence of possessive *–s* and third present *–s*, as in "He a momma ø boy" and "He love ø his family" Rickford (2014).

That Jeantel was aware of the stereotyping during her interrogation was discussed on many Black-themed blogs that concluded that the way the defense attorney spoke to her was designed not only to discredit her but also to condescend to and humiliate her. Britney Cooper provided a theory of the significance of Jeantel's speech in relation to her identity by stating that "Rachel Jeantel has her own particular, idiosyncratic Black girl idiom, a mashup of her Haitian and Dominican working-class background, her southern U.S. upbringing, and the three languages—Haitian Kreyol (or Creole), Spanish, and English—that she speaks." There was also consensus that Rachel Jeantel acknowledged as much by her repeated use of dialect reading with her clear pronunciation of "Yes, Sir."

Rachel Jeantel's attitude on the witness stand did not represent dialect accommodation, but rather pride in her Black women's speech and cultural background. Once she seemed to realize that the defense attorney was ridiculing her speech, she continued to use vernacular forms of expressions. She was called ignorant, ghetto, fat, arrogant, and worse. Had she been a vernacular-speaking Black male, it is not clear that her speech would have been associated with ignorance, deception, and so on. It might have been viewed as the norm for a teenager in the African American vernacular speech community. Instead, she was compared to middle-class White woman physically and in terms of language. In the end, her statements were presented as unintelligible, inaccurate, and untrue.

45.6 Conclusion

One of the paradoxes of women's history is that as social progress occurs, many issues are reframed rather than resolved. This is especially true for African American women who are still judged by a standard of unachievable respectability. Political Scientist Melissa Harris-Perry begins her (2011) book, *Sister Citizen: Shame, Stereotypes and Black Women in America*, with an analysis of one of the most heartbreaking and powerful stories of Black women: *Their Eyes Were Watching God*. Harris-Perry places this Zora Neale Hurston novel, written in 1937, at the heart of her political analysis of today's America in terms of race, social class, and the role of Black women, in particular. The main character of the novel, Jamie Mae Crawford, lives in rural Florida after World War II and must survive gender and racial roles that not only constrain her sense of self but also attempts to destroy and bury any remnants. Harris-Perry argues that this novel remains relevant because Black women are inherently political. She writes, "They are political because [B]lack women have always had to deal with derogatory assumptions about their character and identity" (2011, 15).

This chapter has argued that AAWL is political. The research on African American women represents a feminist perspective on the role of women in society and how women's voices can be powerful in situations of dominance and bigotry. AAWL studies conducted within the sociolinguistic tradition include research on all aspects of vernacular features as well as standard features. Research on discourse, narratives, and verbal genres represent how women express their lives, ideas, and roles in interaction in particular and society in general. African American women's issues include race and justice for all members of the community. AAWL is conservative and innovative. It is creative and ordinary. It is varied and complex, as a women's language must be. It often appears as a defiant voice out of sync with other women. In fact African American women's speech is a metaphor for women's voices everywhere. It exposes the silencing of women's voices and the politics of language and discourse norms and standards for all women. It is the mother tongue.

NOTES

1. The title of this chapter refers to Marlon Riggs's pioneering (1989) documentary on homosexuality in the Black community entitled *Tongues Untied*.
2. The 1965 Moynihan Report, "The Negro Family: The Case for National Action," blamed the Black family and mothers, in particular, for poverty, crime, and so on. Hortense Spillers (1987), in her critique of Moynihan (1965), offers this quote from his report: "In essence the Negro community has been forced into a matriarchal structure which, because it is so far out of line with the rest of American society, seriously retards the progress of the group as a whole" (Moynihan 1965, 75).
3. This is also true in the social sciences and humanities in general.
4. It is this particular problem, along with issues of sexism in the civil rights and Black Power movements that led to the Black Feminist Movement (see Roth 2004).

REFERENCES

Abrahams, Roger. 1970. *Deep Down in the Jungle*. Chicago: Aldine.
———. 1976. *Talking Black*. Rowley, MA: Newbury.
Bloomquist, Jennifer. 2009. " 'People Say I Speak Proper, but Girl, I'm Ghetto!' Regional Dialect Use and Adaptation by African American Women in Pennsylvania's Lower Susquehanna Valley." In *African American Women's Language: Discourse, Education, and Identity*, edited by Sonja Lanehart, 165–83. Newcastle: Cambridge Scholars.
Bucholtz, Mary. 1996. "Black Feminist Theory and African American Women's Linguistic Practice." In *Rethinking Language and Gender Research: Theory and Practice*, edited by Victoria L. Bergvall, Janet M. Bing, and Alice F. Freed, 267–90. London: Longman.
Cameron, Deborah, and Jennifer Coates. 1989. "Some Problems in the Sociolinguistic Explanation of Sex Differences." In *Women in Their Speech Communities*, edited by Jennifer Coates and Deborah Cameron, 13–26. London: Longman.
Coates, Jennifer, ed. 1998. *Language and Gender: A Reader*. Malden, MA: Blackwell.
Cooper, Brittney. 2013. "Dark-Skinned and Plus-Size: The Real Rachel Jeantel Story." *Salon*. http://www.salon.com/2013/06/28/did_anyone_really_hear_rachel_jeantel/.

Davis, Ossie. 1967. "The English Language Is My Enemy." Reprint in *Life Lit by Some Large Vision: Selected Speeches and Writings by Ossie Davis (Foreword by Ruby Dee)*, edited by Ossie Davis and Ruby Dee, 11–12. New York: Aria, 2006.

Eckert, Penelope, and Sally McConnell-Ginet. 2003. *Language and Gender*. Cambridge: Cambridge University.

Etter-Lewis, G., and Michele Foster. 1996. *Unrelated Kin: Race and Gender in Women's Personal Narratives*. New York: Routledge.

Fasold, Ralph. 1972. *Tense Marking in Black English: A Linguistic and Social Analysis*. Arlington, VA: Center of Applied Linguistics.

Folb, Edith. 1980. *Runnin' Down Some Lines: The Language and Culture of Black Teenagers*. Cambridge, MA: Harvard University.

Foster, Michele. 1995. "'Are you with me?' Power and Solidarity in the Discourse of African American Women." In *Gender Articulated: Language and the Socially Constructed Self*, edited by Kira Hall and Mary Bucholtz, 329–50. New York: Routledge.

Gilligan, Carol. 1982. *In a Different Voice: Psychological Theory and Women's Development*. Cambridge, MA: Harvard University.

Goodwin, Marjorie H. 1990. *He-Said-She-Said: Talk as Social Organization among Black Children*. Bloomington: Indiana University.

———. 2003. "The Relevance of Ethnicity, Class, and Gender in Children's Peer Negotiations." In *The Handbook of Language and Gender*, edited by Janet Holmes and Miriam Meyerhoff, 29–31. Oxford: Blackwell.

———. 2006. *The Hidden Life of Girls: Games of Stance, Status, and Exclusion*. Oxford: Blackwell.

Green, Lisa, and Tracy Conner. 2009. "Rhetorical Markers in Girls' Developing African American Language Use." In *African American Women's Language: Discourse, Education, and Identity*, edited by Sonja Lanehart, 91–109. Newcastle upon Tyne: Cambridge Scholars.

Harris-Perry, Melissa. 2011. *Sister Citizen: Shame, Stereotypes, and Black Women in America*. Cambridge, MA: Harvard University.

Henley, Nancy. 1995. "Ethnicity and Gender Issues in Language." In *Bringing Cultural Diversity to Feminist Psychology: Theory, Research and Practice*, edited by Hope Ladrine, 361–96. Washington, DC: American Psychological Association.

Higginbotham, Evelyn B. 1992. "African-American Women's History and the Metalanguage of Race." *Signs* 17: 251–74.

———. 1993. *Righteous Discontent: The Women's Movement in the Black Baptist Church, 1880–1920*. Cambridge, MA: Harvard University.

Hurston, Zora Neal. 1937. *Their Eyes Were Watching God*. New York: Harper Collins.

Jackson, Bruce. [1974] 2004. *Get Your Ass in the Water and Swim like Me: African-American Narrative Poetry from the Oral Tradition*. Reprint, London: Routledge.

Jacobs-Huey, Lanita. 2006. *From the Kitchen to the Parlor: Language and African American Women's Hair Care*. Oxford: Oxford University.

Jespersen, Otto. [1922] 1964. *Language: Its Nature, Development and Origin*. Reprint, London: Allen and Unwin.

Kochman, Thomas, ed. 1972. *Rappin' and Stylin' out: Communication in Urban Black America*. Urbana: University of Illinois Press.

Labov, William. 1969. "Contraction and Deletion and Inherent Variability of the English Copula." *Language* 45: 715–62.

Labov, William, Malcah Yaeger, and Richard Steiner. 1972. *A Quantitative Study of Sound Change in Progress*. Philadelphia: US Regional Survey.

Lakoff, Robin. 1975. *Language and Woman's Place*. New York: Harper and Row.

Lanehart, Sonja. 2002. *Sista, Speak! Black Women Kinfolk Talk about Language and Literacy*. Austin: University of Texas.

Mercer, Kobena. 1994. *Welcome to the Jungle: New Positions in Black Cultural Studies*. New York: Routledge.

Mitchell-Kernan, Claudia. 1971. *Language Behavior in a Black Urban Community*. Berkeley, CA: Language Behavior Research Laboratory.

———. 1972. "Signifying, Loud-Talking, and Marking." In *Rappin' and Stylin' out: Communication in Urban Black America*, edited by Thomas Kochman, 315–35. Urbana: University of Illinois Press.

Morgan, Marcyliena. 1996. "Conversational Signifying: Grammar and Indirectness among African American Women." In *Interaction and Grammar*, edited by Elinor Ochs, Emanuel Schegloff, and Sandra Thompson, 405–33. Cambridge: Cambridge University.

———. 2002. *Language, Discourse and Power in African American Culture*. Cambridge: Cambridge University.

———. 2003. "Signifying Laughter and the Subtleties of Loud-Talking: Memory and Meaning in African American Women's Discourse." In *Ethnolinguistic Chicago: Language and Literacy in Chicago's Neighborhoods*, edited by Marcia Farr, 51–76. Mahwah, NJ: Lawrence Erlbaum.

Moynihan, Patrick. 1965. "The Negro Family: The Case for National Action." (Moynihan Report) Washington, DC: Office of Policy Planning and Research, US Department of Labor.

Nichols, Patricia C. 1982. "Black Women in the Rural South: Conservative and Innovative." Reprint in *Language and Gender: A Reader*, edited by Jennifer Coates, 55–63. Malden, MA: Blackwell, 1998.

———. 1983. "Linguistic Options and Choices for Black Women in the Rural South." In *Language, Gender and Society*, 54–68. Rowley, MA: Newbury House.

Nichols, Patricia Causey, ed. 2009. *Voices of Our Ancestors: Language Contact in Early South Carolina*. Columbia: University of South Carolina Press.

Rickford, John. 2014. "Rachel Jeantel's Language in the Zimmerman Trial." Language Log. http://languagelog.ldc.upenn.edu/nll/?p=5161.

Riggs, Marlon. 1989. *Tongues Untied*. Frameline and California Newsreel. DVD.

Roth, Benita. 2004. *Separate Roads to Feminism: Black, Chicana, and White Feminist Movements in American's Second Wave*. Cambridge: Cambridge University.

Scott, Karla. 2002. "Black Women's Everyday Talk." In *Centering Ourselves: African American Feminist and Womanist Studies of Discourse*, edited by Marsha Houston and Olga I. Davis, 53–73. Cresskill, NJ: Hampton.

Smitherman, Geneva. 1977. *Talkin and Testifyin: The Language of Black America*. Boston: Houghton Mifflin.

Spears, Arthur. 2009. "Theorizing African American Women's Language: *Girl* as a Discourse Marker." In *African American Women's Language: Discourse, Education and Identity*, edited by Sonja Lanehart, 76–90. Newcastle: Cambridge Scholars.

Spillers, Hortense J. 1987. "Mama's Baby, Papa's Maybe: An American Grammar Book." *Diacritics* 17 (2): 64. doi:10.2307/464747.

Stanback, Marsha H. 1986. "Language and Black Woman's Place: Evidence from the Black Middle Class." In *For Alma Mater: Theory and Practice in Feminist Scholarship*, edited by Paula A. Treichlet, Cheris Kramare, and Beth Stafford, 177–96. Urbana: University of Illinois.

Talbot, Mary M. 2010. *Language and Gender*. Cambridge: Polity.

Troutman, Denise. 2001. "African American Women: Talking that Talk." In *Sociocultural and Historical Contexts of African American English*, edited by Sonja Lanehart, 211–38. Amsterdam: John Benjamins.

Trudgill, Peter. 1972. "Sex, Covert Prestige, and Linguistic Change in the Urban British English of Norwich." *Language in Society* 1: 179–95.

Walker, Rebecca. 2006. "Being Real: An Introduction." In *The Women's Movement Today: An Encyclopedia of Third-Wave Feminism*, edited by Leslie Heywood, 19–23. Westport, CT: Greenwood.

Wolfram, Walter. 1969. *A Sociolinguistic Description of Detroit Negro Speech*. Washington, DC: Center for Applied Linguistics.

Wolfram, Walt, and Natalie Schilling-Estes. 1998. *American English*. Oxford: Blackwell.

CHAPTER 46

BLACK MASCULINE LANGUAGE

DAVID E. KIRKLAND

46.1 INTRODUCTION

As soon as they hear Black males, they either shrink or scowl (or do both) because the particular dark-shaded phallic rhythms that rise from our bellies make many people uncomfortable (see Kirkland 2013). They hear our Father Tongue through the same veiled deficit prisms through which they see us. In fact, the deficit prisms guiding their (mis)conceptions of Black males are so pervasive, so entrenched, and so unbelievably fastened to our most egregious associations of human behavior that we (all of us) rarely recognize these unconscious and negative associations with Black Masculine Language (BML) as a problem (Noguera 2008).

Beneath this deficit veil, too many of us (Black males included) have been conditioned to understand BML as a kind of sociolinguistic deformation—something to loathe instead of something to value and affirm. In this vein, BML has been pathologized, associated loosely with slang and street talk, violence and hypersexualization, ignorance and aggression (Alim 2005; Baugh 1995, 1999; Labov 1972, 2010; Rickford and Rickford 2000; Smitherman 2006, 1977). However, in spite of prejudicial public perceptions, BML does important work in the Black community, specifically (Craig 2010; Haddix 2009; Smitherman 2006), and throughout the globe, more generally (Alim 2006; Alim, Lee, and Mason Carris 2011; Baker-Kimmons and McFarland 2011; Paris 2009).

As such, scholars of Black Language (BL)[1] have vehemently warned against the mistake of dismissing BML as a linguistic deficiency (Ball and Farr 2003; Baugh 2000, 2009; Smitherman 1999). Hence, anyone familiar with the prevailing ideologies surrounding it knows that BML enjoys a peculiar and sometimes special place in the American linguistic imagination. That is, it enjoys male privilege in relation to AAWL (see Lanehart 2009; Morgan, this volume), and the psychology surrounding it is often as complex as it is contradictory. Perhaps one problem with writing this chapter is the idea that much of what we know about language is gendered knowledge based on male usage (see Labov 1972; Lanehart 2009; Morgan, this volume). Hence, for some, any commentary on BML underwrites a long-standing hegemonic contract that further privileges a configuration of language that embodies a particular (though raced) patriarchy that guarantees the dominant (sup)position of men over the subordination of women.

Notwithstanding, in many public contexts, BML is scorned and finds itself at odds with the status quo. What is likely to conjure envy and desire also and simultaneously invokes fear and loathing. Both social exigencies exist side by side, producing phobias and fetishes in non-linguistic discussions of BML. However, understanding the language—how it performs legitimate communicative work (Gilyard 1991), and how narrow notions obscure its importance in American linguistic heritage and reify deficit ideas of Black males (Kirkland 2013)—is a key part of freeing Black people from the tangles of linguistic racism and the traps of deficit logics. In this chapter, I describe the indistinguishable purposes and patterns of usage, which behave according to fixed sets of rules, and code and govern BML.

46.2 Understanding Black Masculine Language

By BML, I do not mean languages used by only Black men. It is vital that those of us who study BLs move beyond essentializing descriptions of how Black people use language and toward more nuanced interpretations of the textured and pluralistic forms and flows that comprise the multi-sensual, multi-accentuated repertoire of languages that Black people, regardless of gender,[2] use. In this light, I theorize BML as a communicative practice associated more or less with Black male identities (Smitherman 2006; Young 2004). This understanding of BML sees it as a particular yet unstable *sociolect* of BL, or what is sometimes called a *genderlect* (i.e., a language variety associated with a specific gender; though, I use the term loosely here to refer to sets of linguistic performances and associations that are mainly reflective of maleness). This particular description of BML locates the linguistic scripts we typically ascribe to Black masculinity on a fluid plane of socially coded expectations of linguistic behavior that can be grouped and understood by patterns of racial (Black) and gendered (male) boundaries of practice that are tied to one's social and cultural identities.

Given this definition, there is not much difference between BML and BL, BML's umbrella category (see Spears, this volume). Like BL, BML has an ability to shape shift, to alter cadences of (mainstream) languages to fulfill a variety of functions tied to counterhegemonic articulations of Black identity (see Lanehart, this volume). In BML, terms such as *nigga* transgress and transform the meaning of associated and sometimes pejorative terms in ways that reinterpret the Black self and begin to erase or interrupt some of the prejudices maintained by hegemonic systems of language. As in the case of nigga, this transformation sometimes takes place by transfixing word parts (-*er*) and (-*a*) to image contrasting words with not only inverted meanings but also with varying proximities to agency for users. We see this at work in the contrast of *nigger* (which denotes racial inferiority) and *nigga* (which in BML, as in BL, can sometimes denote endearment). As Campbell (1997) notes, Blacks sometimes use "the standard English pejorative label '*niggers*,' by replacing '-*ers*' with 'the Black vernacular -*az* to affirm' their identity and community 'in the face of anyone or anything that poses a threat to Blackness'" (68). Here, *nigga* works to not only interrupt racist discourses that seek to code Black inferiority, the term also reinvents Black identity linguistically, affirming a meaning that is both human and desirable (see Alim, this volume).

Another example is *brother*, which denotes a male sibling. However, *brotha* (like *nigga*) transforms the idea of the term to specifically code/capture Black masculinity, connoting close friendships and/or male-to-male nonsexual relationships that might be defined as closer than friendship. Both *nigga* and *brotha*, by contrasting the -*er* and -*a* endings, signal their transformations/transgressions of the hegemonic meanings of mainstream words. In this transformation, BML users gain a certain kind of agency over terms and self and, through the act of counter-labeling, gain a particular kind of freedom over themselves and their language.

These figurations of BML are not without complication. Such uses of BML have been policed as much as they have been celebrated and exoticized by a public too willing to dismiss BML as slang, street talk, or sybaritic. Moreover, because it transgresses the social role assigned to language by the dominant culture (as in the case of *nigga*) and is criticized as primordial and primitive because it embodies and expresses a tone that explicitly rejects the reigning codes of propriety and place (as in the case of *brotha*), BML has seen its rejection early in American linguistic history. Scholars such as Labov (1972) have noted how mainstream attitudes toward various elements of BML have associated it with laziness and stupidity (see Kirkland, Jackson, and Smitherman 2001; Rickford and Rickford 2000).

In his study on the perceptions of Black males, Foster (1995) provided an empirical context for this peculiar, prejudicial gaze policing BL. He cited a number of studies that found Black males "disproportionately identified as behaviorally disordered or emotionally disturbed" (39). More specifically, he found that of the "Whites [surveyed]: (a) 53.2 percent rated Blacks as less intelligent, (b) 56.1 percent rated Blacks as more violence prone, (c) 77.7 percent rated Blacks as likely to prefer living on welfare, and (d) 62.2 percent saw Blacks as being lazier" (42). In spite of these (mis)conceptions, Foster suggested that so-called "street corner language of Black males" did valuable work in Black male lives. According to Foster:

> Most often, the street corner [Black] male student used his street corner language and behavior—survival and coping techniques—that were appropriate for his survival on the street corner, but caused him problems in school. Some of these street corner coping and survival techniques included, *playin' the dozens, ribbin', signifyin', woofin',* and non-verbal kinesic behaviors. (38)

The linguistic dissonance between the Black world, where BML gained incredible purchase, and the wider world, where it caused its users incredible trepidation, should not be overlooked. Much of this dissonance, according to educational researchers and sociolinguists (Alim 2005; Kinloch 2005; Paris 2009), is rooted in a misunderstanding or dismissal of the important work that BL does in Black social life and beyond.

We now hold a treasure trove of scholarship in Black linguistics that details the remarkable utility of BML in Black social life (see Makoni et al. 2003). Perhaps chief among this work is Labov's (1972) foundational study of BL, which sought to affirm the product of Black lungs by describing the deep contents of BML and its concern with countercultural themes (some of which is indeed problematic): drugs, sexism, pleasure, excess, nihilism, defiance, pride, and the cool pose of disengagement. For Labov, these items were all a part of the style, personality, vision, and countercultural practice of BML, which could not be confined within the dominant cultural logics surrounding language. In his work, Labov painstakingly illustrated how BML challenged dominant linguistic orthodoxy between the races; however, with respect to women, he maintained this same powerful and defiant linguistic performance of Black manhood while overlooking unequal relations of power between the sexes.

Notwithstanding, Labov's (1972) early research into what he termed "Black English Vernacular" described the remarkable linguistic dexterity that BML users flexed. For Labov, this verbal flexing amounted to particular political disturbances and cultural rearticulations of the ever-emerging Black self. That is, BML enabled and ultimately manufactured an alternative cultural experience for its users. Hence, early on, Labov and others (Baugh 1999; Smitherman 1977; Wolfram 1969; Wolfram and Christian 1989) were charting the usefulness of BML, documenting its subversive (though stigmatized) nature. Moreover, because it operated differently than mainstream hegemonic codes, BML required new contextualizations and different frames for social and linguistic assessment. Yet, in a stubborn and highly racialized public, old frames that privileged the primacy of elite White language practices continued to dominate. In this context, BML continued to be figured in the public imagination as the basis of legitimate linguistic prejudice—critiqued or celebrated, as in the case of rappers (see Alim, this volume); viewed as naturalized and commodified speech, as in the case of athletes (see Smitherman 2006); as symbols of menace and threat, as in the case of Black gang members (see Baugh 1999); and as noble warriors, as in the case of Black nationalist groups such as the Black Panthers and the Fruit of Islam (see Alim 2006; Kynard and Eddy 2009).

46.3 THE EVOLUTION OF BML IN BLACK SOCIAL LIFE

As much as one might experience it daily through ads, music, television, situation comedy, sports, and so forth, the utility of BML in Black social life seemed historically structured by and against dominant (and dominating) discourses of masculinity and race, specifically (Whiteness). For example, Baker-Kimmons and McFarland (2011) write about "the Black jazz men" of the 1950s and 1960s. In so doing, they describe, notably, how the language use and style of musicians such as Miles Davis and John Coltrane became emblematic of "the complex social relations (race, class, sexual) and cultural politics surrounding the self-construction and representation of the Black masculine in the public sphere" (337). In the mouths of Black men, or at least through Black masculine strategies for subverting power through linguistic play, BL gained a kind of swag. In this "cool" space, BML scripts and proverbs began patterning the dialectal dispositions of the Black masculine communicator in desirable and stylish ways. Take, for example, the statement:

(1) *"Yo, homie! Don't hate the playa; hate the game"* (Kirkland 2006).

From a purely descriptive standpoint, the statement reveals BML as patterning certain scripts of the Black self. These scripts, what Lanehart (this volume) calls "Acts of Identity" (from Le Page 1986; Le Page and Tabouret-Keller 1985) and "Possible Selves" (from Markus and Nurius 1986), illuminate features of Blackness disposed through language that are rife with the wisdom and experience of Black "socioculture," "sociohistory," and "sociopyschology." In this use, the language makes intimate the strange, necessarily disarming or disrupting (as in fully *signifyin*[3]) by naming the world in ironic, witty, and, sometimes, humorous terms.

In example (1), *homie* not only acts as an accepted (and acceptable) term of Black masculine endearment signaling casual friendship (cf. *nigga* and *brotha*, as discussed earlier in this chapter), but also offers a conceptual metaphor (Lakoff and Johnson 2003) that explains sociocultural nature and human sociopsychology. If used in this latter way to signify (or signal) the natural equalities of person (we are all equally *playas* in some unjust game), then the informal personal label *homie* expresses more than familiarity; it suggests equanimity in that one can't judge or be seen or see themselves as superior to another *homie/playa*. Hence, judgment (or indictment of social inequity) expresses a macro consciousness that is critically aware of inequity in society (i.e., *the game*).

In many accounts, our "language selves" (see Lanehart, this volume) are more than cultural, historical, or psychological. They, too, are gendered (see Morgan, this volume). In her discussion of the term *playa*, Smitherman (2006) speaks to the gendering of BL when she writes:

> Although the term and the concept of 'playa' predates the Blackploitation films of the late 1960s and 1970s, it was during that era that 'playa' became synonymous with Pimp or Mack, who was characterized as a shrewd manipulator of women or a scam artist with dazzling rhetorical skills. (69)

She further describes how the term *playa* has been picked up by either male rappers to describe the heights of their exploits or used to describe *B-Ball playaz* and other men who are at the top of their games. While it might be said that *playa* occupies gender-neutral space (in the sense that anyone can play and be played), one must note how the term, as Smitherman discusses it, is typically gendered as male. While this seems to be the case, I do acknowledge exceptions. Smitherman explains that "increasingly, in twenty-first-century Black America, playaz are women" too (69). However, in spite of its use, BML terminology such as *playa* often reinvents/inverts the Black (male or female) self, disassociating it with mainstream proclivities and reconfiguring it as something human and almost certainly as something cool.

This coolness—which I describe as subversive though stylized linguistics acts of "our hoped for possible selves" (see Lanehart, this volume)—has had a long-standing cultural history in the Black community, and among Black males, in particular. According to Majors and Billson (1993), Black men employed coolness during slavery:

> To say the least, slavery hindered the Black man's ability to control his role. Thus, the Black male has had to read the world from his perspective and devise ways to meet the needs of himself and his family in slavery and its aftermath of racism and oppression. One of the ways of knowing and acting exploited by Black males is being cool. (681)

My own research on Black males and language has also pointed to the significance of "cool" in the innovation of a subversive, though liberatory Black (masculine) communication style (Kirkland 2011c; Kirkland and Jackson 2009). In a study of Black masculine literacy practices, Kirkland and Jackson (2009) described the inversion of words like "dog," frequently used among young "cool" Black men, to signify acceptance, loyalty, and camaraderie (see Smitherman 2000). We found that though many words and expressions such as *dog* used in the lexical corpus of BML have passed from the mainstream lexicon (see Morgan 2005), the flavor of the word and the style of its saying adopted new meaning in the crafty mouths of "cool" BML users. It is within this larger backdrop of invention complemented by acts of inversion and innovation that BML gets its characteristic forms. Hence, its utility in Black social life (among other things) can be understood as functioning as a sort of linguistic trickster act (see Gates 1988)—one that conceals uncharacteristic things such as meanings and ideas, faces and otherwise legible but less acceptable social functions (e.g., fear, vulnerability, discomfort) (Neal 2013).

In this light, Baker-Kimmons and McFarland (2011) suggested that through strategic acts of cool, Black males, particularly Black jazz musicians (though not exclusively), innovated BML in the process of constructing cool poses. As innovators of BML, these men, Baker-Kimmons and McFarland argued, challenged dominant cultural assumptions about masculinity and race. Through their music and style, these (largely heterosexual) Black men defined themselves linguistically and on terms of their own against a hegemonic White social order that sought to devalue them and their cultural-linguistic practices. Hence, their creative, cool uses of language did important counterhegemonic work in helping to articulate a different way of knowing the Black self, a knowledge that would further seed other, *hoped for* articulations of (revolutionary) Blackness. In this way, BML also gave Black people, particularly certain Black men, a lens for seeing the world through the very structures of feeling they assumed, articulated, and enacted (see Smitherman 1999)—from the defiant cool pose of Black jazz men to the new cosmopolitan appetite that jazz and the new Black social life craved.

46.4 BML IN CONTEMPORARY CONTEXTS

In addition to helping to construct Black subversive selves, BML offered itself to users as a language of resistance. Discussing a young Black research participant who knowingly rejected mainstream written codes, Fecho (2003) illustrated the suspicion some BML users express in relation to the monolingual hegemony of "mainstream codes":

> Robert grasped that many codes were within his reach, but also grasped that these codes brought advantages and costs. He came to realize that it was difficult at best to operate and sound natural in a language code with which one had little practice using or had mixed feeling about acquiring. . . . What I learned was that, for these students and others like them, it was a matter of if they were able to speak and write in the mainstream codes. . . but was more a matter of figuring out why they would feel disposed to do so. (67)

Robert's suspicion of mainstream codes is not surprising. Citing Labov's (1972) research "in male linguistic dominance," Smith et al. (2000) wrote: "It was discovered that in urban settings, standard pronunciation is associated with women more than men, making formal English a gender marker for women" (431). For students such as Robert, appropriating mainstream codes is not a politically or culturally innocent act. Rather, it carries "advantages and costs," as well as raising questions that center on uncomfortable topics within gender, race, and sexuality. Anticipating such questions, Fecho suggested that had Robert appropriated mainstream codes he would have also accommodated the litany of "feared possible selves" associated with it because any code (as in language) is very much about the politics of identity and the tensions corresponding to it (see Lanehart, this volume).

For contemporary examples, some of the linguistic scholarship on Hip Hop[4] helps explain the situation of BML (see Alim, this volume). In his foundational analyses of what he calls "Hip Hop Linguistics" and "Hip Hop Nation Language," Alim (2006) alludes to a grammar structure for BML, describing how it differs from canonical grammars and hegemonic Englishes (and even from BL, as it is more traditionally/or narrowly understood). For example, in Hip Hop as in BML, Alim sees a "new equative copula" (i.e., the verb *to be*) employed in the masculine to brag or to place emphasis not on doing (i.e., a verb phrase) but on naming one's being (i.e., a noun phrase). He describes how rappers (cf. BML users) use the copula with noun phrases to construct ideas and images of the self even though previous literature on invariant *be*[5] (Fasold 1972; Labov et al. 1968; Wolfram 1969) deemed sentences like (2)-(4) as ungrammatical:

(2) "I be the king supreme."
(3) "He be my father."
(4) "I be the head nurse."

Smitherman (2006) explains this more "contemporary" linguistic innovation the following way:

> For more than four decades in Black America, you would hear statements like "This my pastor," not "This be my pastor." However, today's Black Hip Hop youth have expanded (or perhaps resurrected) the domain of the Black Language icon, *be*. Today in Hip Hop Music, we hear: "Dr. Dre be the name" (from the producer and co-founder of NWA): "I be the insane nigga from the psycho ward" (from Method Man); "My grammar bees Ebonics" (Nelly)... (102)

When examined closely, Smitherman's (2006) examples suggest that BML users (in this case, rappers) do much more than simply innovate the copula construct; they reconfigure the language with brazenly masculine undertones that operate within forms of Black (masculine) discourse, such as machismo and braggadocio (see Kirkland 2011c). Moreover, if we take, for instance, example (2) in relation to examples (3) and (4), a clear discourse of braggadocio can be observed. This form of Black discourse earmarks gender-specific linguistic results not unlike the associated forms of masculinity found in other languages. With this said, I have noticed at least three common patterns of grammar significant (though not exclusive) to BML users:

- Use of invariant *be* for emphatic present as opposed to future tense—what I call the God tense for boasting and constructing exaggerated figurations of the self (see Smitherman 1999)

(5) "I *be* the king supreme." (i.e., I *am* [presently] *the* [highest-ranking] king.)

- Use of alliteratives in grammatically inverted structures

(6) "*Real* recognize *real*." (N.B.: contextual signals for tense)
(7) "*O*nly *n*iggas *k*now *n*iggas."

- Implied or deleted elements (usually *like* or *as*) in simile or simile-like structures (often used in rapping, toasting, and boasting)

(8) "I gotta put that patch over my third eye, [deleted *like*] Slick Rick." (from Lil' Wayne's "My Homies Still")
(9) "Give you that iPhone 4, [deleted *like*] FaceTime" (from Fabolous's "You Be Killin Em")

Hip Hop, as it embraces BL, has also afforded its typically male interlocutors a rich, dynamic, and unique phonetic repertoire. Hip Hop Nation Language, like BML, pronounces –*ing* (/ɪŋ/) as –*in* (/ɪn/), as in *chillin, feelin, hatin,* and so on:

(10)   "He be *controllin* the mic"

This phonetic element promotes what could be called a *cool effect*, or natural smoothness of sound concerned with cadence and flow, which also evokes rhythm and confidence (i.e., key elements in BML, which in some ways exist as linguistic performances that disrupt dominant linguistic scripts) (Rickford and Rickford 2000; Smitherman 1977, 1999). Like BL, BML use is also typified by unique consonant constructs, significantly the comparative difference between its initial, middle, and final consonant sounds and that of mainstream Englishes:

(11)   Variation in pronunciation of /θ/ and /ð/
        (a) *the* pronounced /də/ in BL (i.e., /ð/ as /d/)
        (b) *father* pronounced /fɑdə/ in BL (i.e., /ð/ as /d/)
        (c) *with* pronounced /wɪf/ or /wɪd/ in BL (i.e., /θ/ as /f/ or /d/)
(12)   Post-vocalic -/r/ variation
        (a) *cypher* pronounced /saifə/ in BL and usually spelled *cypha*
        (b) *nigger* pronounced /nɪgə/ in BL and categorically spelled *nigga*

In the context of BML, these linguistic comparatives point out two things with which this chapter has been concerned: a linguistic utility primed at various aspects to transgress hegemonic modes of mainstream languages and script deep dimensions of Black (male) identity. In this way, there is important overlap between Hip Hop Linguistics and BML, when the two entities work in mutually representative ways to resist cultural hegemony while languaging Black masculine being. Thus, in the shift from jazz to Hip Hop, the myriad purposes associated with subversion, resistance, and the varied practices that codify, for example, coolness have remained relatively stable from Hip Hop to BML. That is, rappers today, like the Black jazz musicians of yesterday, invent and invite language as a resource to invert power in acts of being and in the processes of negotiating otherwise socially and politically hostile environments. Hence, the linguistic forms of resistance that the jazz men of the 1950s and the 1960s practiced continued to play, in part, on the cool and cutting Black masculine linguistics of Hip Hop today (see Alim, this volume; Smitherman 2006).

The contemporary forms of BML found in Hip Hop also invite new raw and real associated content that wear the chiseled face of a kind of reclaimed but hypermasculine Blackness, which itself has been subject to public scrutiny, spectacle, and open attack (see Alim, this volume). In the global assault on Hip Hop, even newer forms of BML have surfaced, facing familiar kinds of surveillance, scrutiny, and discrimination as its predecessor forms. These new forms have now become so widely known and studied that they work as an explicit sign(ifying) and smoldering example of the everyday existence of discrimination that BML and its users continue to endure (Alim 2006; Miner 2009; Petchauer 2009; Richardson 2006). According to Morgan and Bennett (2011):

> Among African hip-hop artists in particular, there is a sustained critique of hard-core Hip Hop. Commercial gangsta rap lyrics have been central to hardcore Hip Hop culture, and have historically represented, (in some cases) analyzed, and (in too many others) glamorized the intersection of masculinity, dominance, and violence. As a result, hardcore Hip Hop culture has been the historical target of global and American communities; and it has produced a contested relationship with local hip-hop cultures in the United States and elsewhere. (189)

Usually searching for reasons to vilify it, the public has limited BML to the image or sound of an imagined and offensive Hip Hop (Neal 2013), particularly as filtered through the linguistics lenses of gangsta rap (see Smitherman 2006). As the public associates it more-and-more with what it imagines to be a hardcore Hip Hop culture, BML becomes limited to extreme tropes of hegemonic masculinity. Hence, BML, like gangster rap, becomes an easy target of sustained critique—vilified as violent, misogynistic, profane, materialistic, and so on in spite of its incredible complexity and the important work that it does in Black social life.

For many young Black males, however, the utility of this language has never been limited to the hood or the gangster set. Researchers of Black male literacy development have been ardent in their descriptions of how Black males use BML as a rich resource to mediate their literacy development (Haddix 2009; Kinloch 2008; Kirkland 2010, 2011a, b, c, 2013; Kirkland and Jackson 2009). In their study of literacy practices of a group of inner-city youth, Mahiri and Sablo (1996) described the intricate communicative work of BML (in Hip Hop culture). Moving away from a deficit model and toward a profit one, they productively analyzed a rap from a Black male student (Troy) who attended an afterschool program in California. In so doing, they illustrated the complex role that BML plays in Black male development—in this case, how it helped Troy to structure and frame his thoughts and experiences. They found:

> The structure of his [Troy] rap... reveals his mastery of other rhetorical devices reflective of African American language styles along with an expert knowledge of contemporary African American slang terminology and its use. As Troy explained, "skrill" was a combination of the terms "scratch"—a somewhat dated slang term for money—and "mill" or million; the term could also refer to a meal ticket, he indicated. For example, he uses the slang term "doe" (for "though") to emphasize his points in a way that simulates elements of African American preaching style ("you don't feel me doe," "I got two families that love me doe"). In effect, "doe" redirects readers' (or listeners') attention to and intensifies the importance of the thematic points made in the preceding lines of their respective stanzas. Additionally, Troy's use of a second-person reference ("you") in these two lines is reflective of the dialogicality, or multivoicedness... [which] is an essential part of African American youth discourse. This technique drives home the meaning of Troy's words to persons

outside of the two families who feel for and love him—persons who may not know or understand the particular "family values" of these two groups. (2004, 173-74)

Campbell (1997) similarly described the role that BML plays in the development of its users. He studied a group of "Black inner city male students," whom he saw as natural "code meshers" because of the ways they mixed elements of BML with academic discourse in their essays. For Campbell, these male students' "Hip Hop" language practices were an inseparable part of who they were, as BML gave them the linguistic platform to articulate and embody charismatic, heterosexual, Black male identities. Young (2004) troubled Campbell's heteronormative view of masculinity as the prime basis for languaging an authentic Black male self. For Young, as much as it might be a language of identity and utility in and out of school contexts for young Black males, BML could also be a mask for young Black males who are subject to a particular kind of scrutiny reserved for those who perform non-dominant sexualities. In discussing this particular tension, Young, a Black male himself, wrote:

> They were words I had often used to mask the fear and pain that I experienced while growing up as a rather bookish boy with a high-pitched voice in the ghetto—a boy often teased, called sissy and fag, because I liked performing in school plays instead of playing sports. It didn't help that I had no "raunchy macho," or couldn't develop that "special [pimp] walk," or that I was no good at the "distinctive handshakes and slang" that early childhood education researcher Janice E. Hale-Benson describes as the "common manhood rites" for black boys (170). Because of this, my gender performance was incompatible with what was required of black boys. So for psychological protection, I convinced myself that I didn't give a fuck about the ghetto and longed only to get out. (2004, 11)

While Young's experience masking himself with BML to escape social scrutiny within the Black community presents a needed example of the complexity of BML use, scholars such as Craig (2010) have viewed BML use as less a mask and more like a strategic choice. According to Craig, BML gives users, particularly Black male users, a set of rhetorical choices with language and other modalities to help them constitute their Black masculine identities in situations and environments hostile to it. Craig, for example, maintains that Black male use of and association with BML (and, increasingly, Hip Hop) helps users to define what it means to be Black and male in homogeneous and hostile public contexts. The Black males in his study learn how to adapt to such situations using BML in ways that implicate the meaning and importance of race-and-gender-accented language as a survival strategy, as a means of making adjustments, and as a way of publically identifying themselves (i.e., demasking). Understanding BML from this vantage point helps BL researchers begin to see the linkages between language and the negotiated/constructed Black self, or "how young people actually use these texts to construct their identities, their unique subjectivities, and the social networks in which they are embedded" (Dimitriadis 2001, 29).

46.5 CONCLUSION

The relationship between BML and Black (male) identity(ies) is complicated. From its origins until now, BML has done important but complex work in Black communities, helping to shape Black social life and the Black self on terms that are uniquely ours (see Lanehart, this volume) while at the same time providing users a powerful tool to subvert and resist cultural domination and other dimensions of injustice perched against Black social realities. In this light, the language has never been deficit or substandard as compared to ruling, mainstream linguistic codes. Rather, it was invented through necessity and evolved based on utility. Over time, the language has come to do important work for its users, who often critically employ it as a:

1. Strategy for navigating the world
2. System for expressing Black manhood/masculine being
3. Form of resilience/resistance
4. Posture of aggression, strength, and power

These functions of BML have not developed in isolation, but in collaboration with popular shifts in Black subcultures, such as music (e.g., jazz and Hip Hop) and sports (e.g., B-Ball). And at times, they are promulgated through poverty and educational neglect. In spite of how it emanated and continues to evolve, BML has emerged as an option for all its users, but particularly young Black males in the Hip Hop sector, with a desperate need for guidelines concerning maturity and meaning. This is perhaps why acts of (Black) masculinity such as coolness continue to define the angles on which BML slides.

Even still, this chapter merely scratches the surface with respect to how Black masculine ways work (with)in BL. Deep levels of comparative and inductive investigations are still needed to map the totality of BML and the rules governing its use in Black communities and beyond. What happens when BML—and not just the words that flow out of the mouths of young Black men (as a gender performance)—is adopted by non-Black masculine beings? What happens to that person's gender performance and the expression(s) of BML itself? BML, among other things, is subversive and demonized, but also readily adopted across racial and gender lines. Thus, in this chapter, I have sought to theorize BML critically by exploring issues of power, desire, hybridity, and pluralism as well as the fluidity and splintering of the masculine impulses that reside in Black whispers. In this light, we do know some things about BML. We know that BML includes many languages, in particular the languages of the many people who clothe themselves in Black masculine bodies, cultural struggles, and political upheavals that leave articulations of Black masculinity displaced or obsolete and the social derisions and lineages of oppression that foment twisted tongues beyond and through chattel spaces. This language, fitted with its own sounds, rules, and vocabularies has emerged as the Black masculine vocal chord—broken and collected, creatively carved and socially strained out of a stew of many delicate voices all folded into one.

If BML boasts such elegance, how can hegemonic sentiments concerning BL—and, by association, Black people—persist, subjecting BML and its users to fierce public spectacles and ongoing demonization? Key elements of this sociolinguistic tangle—Black people's seeming love for BML beset against the severe hatred it receives in public, including by Black people (i.e., via covert prestige)—are reinforced by contradiction, which is itself further complicated by minstrelized representations of BML and its users in mainstream society (Kirkland, Jackson, and Smitherman 2001; Rickford and Rickford 2000). In viewing BML from the margins of this gaze, two sites representing seemingly opposite ends of the spectrum of contemporary racism reveal the continuing significance of the historical obsession with controlling and "taming" Black (male) bodies and tongues. And though I only hint at it in this chapter, four common themes permeate the public construction of BML and work to justify, even beyond deficit perspectives, linguistic racism. These include a continued emphasis on BML as: (1) inherently aggressive, hypersexual, and violent; (2) wild, unruly communicative practices needing taming; (3) a product of a deficient Black culture; and (4) a corruption of "naturalized" (therefore inherently "superior") codes of communication.

In spite of how the public perceives them, the languages of Black people, and particularly of Black males, are firmly rooted in the linguistic ecologies of Black America: in neighborhoods and schools, play spaces and work sites, and anywhere else we might socially find Black men and boys communicating. Hence, BML is not confined to the gendered space that is the Black male body; rather, it is a continuance of African languages inflected by subversive derivatives of mainstream, colonial, hegemonic dialects. Further, BML is a form of BL forged between the bonds of brothers (and sisters) who share not only patterns of communication but also deep and abiding histories of performance and oppression where the still emerging subjectivities of Black men and boys (and dare we include women, girls, the genderedly different, and the genderless) are subject to sociolectal (re)shaping. These new insights, if considered seriously, have the potential to liberate Black bodies from the shackles of prejudice and extend conversations about race, gender, language, and literacy in ways that might ultimately expand frameworks for how we understand the life of language in the Black (masculine) world.

Notes

1. In this chapter, I refer to Black Language (BL) as an umbrella category that contains beneath it gendered, classed, regional, and subcultural variations. Many of these varieties, as they intersect and overlap with BL, also intersect and overlap with one another. Hence, BML explains internal variation within BL by gender (for a discussion of AAWL, see Morgan, this volume). Further, I have chosen not to contrast variants of BL (e.g., BML versus Hip Hop Nation Language [see Alim, this volume] or BML versus AAWL [see Morgan, this volume] to avoid the less than useful impulse and counterproductive or dysconscious practice of pitting Black subgroups against one another). Therefore, in this chapter, I do my best to explain BML as a gendered variant of BL and only refer to other variations of BL when they become useful for helping to illuminate BML and its many aspects.

2. By gender, I am referring to the range of behaviors characteristic of and differentiating seemingly opposing acts of masculine and feminine socializations. In this sense, gender is distinguished from sex. Sex refers to biological makeup and, by contrast, gender refers to the social construction of maleness and femaleness (as in gender roles). Hence, a female can be masculine or use masculine language just as a male can be feminine or use feminine language. Though many of the examples of BML offered in this chapter feature men and boys, I do attempt to be careful about how and when I use "male/female," "woman/man," and "masculine/feminine."

3. According to Smitherman (2006), "signifyin is a style of verbal play that focuses humorous statements of double meaning on an individual, an event, a situation, or even a government" (68).

4. Hip Hop Linguistics is replete with examples of Black male language usages. Much like jazz before it, Hip Hop and its artists, who are predominately Black and male, have done interesting things with BL (Alim 2006), not only marking it as masculine but also helping us understand the various kinds of work the language achieves in Black (male) life.

5. The use of the unconjugated to be verb to mark habitual or extended actions. In BL, the invariant *be* is used to mark things such as tense and aspect instead of the inflected forms of *be*, such as present tense is/are and the past tense was/were.

REFERENCES

Alim, H. Samy. 2005. "Critical Language Awareness in the United States: Revisiting Issues and Revising Pedagogies in a Resegregated Society." *Educational Researcher* 34 (7): 24–31.

———. 2006. *Roc the Mic Right: The Language of Hip Hop Culture.* New York: Routledge.

Alim, H. Samy, Jooyoung Lee, and Lauren Mason Carris. 2011. "Moving the Crowd, 'Crowding' the Emcee: The Coproduction and Contestation of Black Normativity in Freestyle Rap Battles." *Discourse & Society* 22 (4): 422–39. doi: http://dx.doi.org/10.1177/0957926510395828.

Baker-Kimmons, Leslie, and Pancho McFarland. 2011. "The Rap on Chicano and Black Masculinity: A Content Analysis of Gender Images in Rap Lyrics." *Race, Gender & Class* 18 (1/2): 331–44.

Ball, Arnetha F., and Marcia Farr. 2003. "Language Varieties, Culture, and Teaching the English Language Arts." In *Handbook of Research on Teaching the English Language Arts*, edited by James Flood, Diane Lapp, James R. Squire, and Julie M. Jensen, 435–45. Mahwah, NJ: Lawrence Erlbaum.

Baugh, John. 1995. "The Law, Linguistics, and Education: Educational Reform for African American Language Minority Students." *Linguistics and Education* 7: 87–105.

———. 1999. *Out of the Mouths of Slaves: African American Language and Educational Malpractice.* Austin: University of Texas Press.

———. 2000. *Beyond Ebonics: Linguistic Pride and Racial Prejudice.* New York: Oxford University Press.

———. 2009. "Linguistic Diversity, Access, and Risk." *Review of Research in Education* 33 (1): 272–82. doi: 10.3102/0091732X08327188.

Campbell, Kermit. 1997. "'Real niggaz's don't die': African American Students Speaking Themselves into Their Writing." In *Writing in Multicultural Settings*, edited by Carol Severino, Juan C. Guerra, and Johnella E. Butler, 67–78. New York: MLA.

Craig, Collin. 2010. "Da' Art of Story Tellin': Black Masculine Literacies and a Rhetoric of Self-Making." PhD diss. Michigan State University.

Dimitriadis, Greg. 2001. "'In the Clique': Popular Culture, Constructions of Place, and the Everyday Lives of Urban Youth." *Anthropology & Education Quarterly* 1: 29–51.

Fasold, Ralph W. 1972. *Tense Marking in Black English: A Linguistic and Social Analysis*. Washington, DC: Center for Applied Linguistics.

Fecho, Bob. 2003. *"Is This English?" Race, Language, and Culture in the Classroom Practitioner Inquiry Series*. New York: Teachers College Press.

Foster, Herbert L. 1995. "Educators' and Non-Educators' Perceptions of Black Males: A Survey." *Journal of African American Men* 1 (2): 37–70.

Gates, Henry Louis, Jr. 1988. *The Signifyin(g) Monkey: A Theory of African-American Literary Criticism*. Cambridge, MA: Harvard University Press.

Gilyard, Keith. 1991. *Voices of the Self: A Study of Language Competence*. Detroit, MI: Wayne State University Press.

Haddix, Marcelle. 2009. "Black Boys Can Write: Challenging Dominant Framings of African American Adolescent Males in Literacy Research." *Journal of Adolescent & Adult Literacy* 53 (4): 341–43.

Kinloch, Valerie. 2005. "Revisiting the Promises of *Students' Right to Their Own Language*: Pedagogical Strategies." *CCC* 51 (1): 83–113.

———. 2008. "Writing in the Midst of Change." *English Journal* 98 (1): 85–89.

Kirkland, David E. 2006. "The Boys in the Hood: Exploring Literacy in the Lives of Six Urban Adolescent Black Males." PhD diss., Michigan State University.

———. 2010. "English(es) in Urban Contexts: Politics, Pluralism, and Possibilities." *English Education* 42 (3): 293–306.

———. 2011a. "Books like Clothes: Engaging Young Black Men with Reading." *Journal of Adolescent & Adult Literacy* 55 (3): 199–208.

———. 2011b. "Listening to Echoes: Black Men, Literacy, and the Issue of ELA Standards." *Language Arts* 88 (5): 373–80.

———. 2011c. "'Something to Brag about': Black Males, Literacy, and Teacher Education." In *Studying Diversity in Teaching and Teacher Education*, edited by Arnetha Ball, 183–200. Washington, DC: AERA.

———. 2013. *A Search Past Silence: The Literacy of Young Black Men. Language and Literacy*. New York: Teachers College Press.

Kirkland, David E., and Austin Jackson. 2009. "'We Real Cool': Toward a Theory of Black Masculine Literacies." *Reading Research Quarterly* 44 (3): 278–97.

Kirkland, David E., Austin Jackson, and Geneva Smitherman. 2001. "Leroy, Big D, and Big Daddy Speakin Ebonics on the Internet." *American Language Review* 5 (2): 22–26.

Kynard, Carmen, and R. Eddy. 2009. "Toward a New Critical Framework: Color-Conscious Political Morality and Pedagogy at Historically Black and Historically White Colleges and Universities." *College Composition and Communication* 61 (1): W24–W44.

Labov, William. 1972. *Language in the Inner City: Studies in the Black English Vernacular*. Philadelphia: University of Pennsylvania Press.

———. 2010. "Unendangered Dialect, Endangered People: The Case of African American Vernacular English." *Transforming Anthropology* 18 (1): 15–27.

Labov, William, Paul Cohen, Clarence Robins, and John Lewis. 1968. *A Study of the Non-Standard English of Negro and Puerto Rican Speakers in New York City*. Report on Cooperative Research Project 3288. New York: Columbia University.

Lakoff, George, and Mark Johnson. 2003. *Metaphors We Live by*. 2nd ed. Chicago: University of Chicago Press.

Lanehart, Sonja L., ed. 2009. *African American Women's Language: Discourse, Education, and Society*. Newcastle upon Tyne: Cambridge Scholars.

Le Page, Robert B. 1986. "Acts of Identity." *English Today* 8: 21–24.

Le Page, Robert B., and Andrée Tabouret-Keller. 1985. *Acts of Identity: Creole-Based Approaches to Language and Ethnicity*. Cambridge: Cambridge University Press.

Mahiri, Jabari, and Soraya Sablo. 1996. "Writing for their Lives: The Non-School Literacy of California's Urban African American Youth." *Journal of Negro Education* 65 (2): 164–80.

Majors, Richard, and Janet Mancini Billson. 1993. *Cool Pose: The Dilemmas of Black Manhood in America*. New York: Lexington Books.

Makoni, Sinfree, Geneva Smitherman, Arnetha F. Ball, and Arthur K. Spears. 2003. *Black Linguistics: Language, Society, and Politics in Africa and the Americas*. London: Routledge.

Markus, Hazel, and Paula Nurius. 1986. "Possible Selves." *American Psychologist* 41: 954–69.

Miner, Dylan A. T. 2009. "Provocations on Sneakers: The Multiple Significations of Athletic Shoes, Sport, Race, and Masculinity." *CR: the New Centennial Review* 9 (2): 73–107, 272.

Morgan, Marcyliena. 2005. "Hip-Hop Women Shredding the Veil: Race and Class in Popular Feminist Identity." *South Atlantic Quarterly* 104 (3): 425–44.

Morgan, Marcyliena, and Dionne Bennett. 2011. "Hip-Hop and the Global Imprint of a Black Cultural Form." *Daedalus* 140 (2): 176–96.

Neal, Mark Anthony. 2013. *Looking for Leroy: Illegible Black Masculinities, Postmillennial Pop*. New York: New York University Press.

Noguera, Pedro A. 2008. *The Trouble with Black boys: And Other Reflections on Race, Equity, and the Future of Public Education*. New York: Jossey-Bass.

Paris, Django. 2009. "'They're in My Culture, They Speak the Same Way': African American Language in Multiethnic High Schools." *Harvard Educational Review* 79 (3): 428–48.

Petchauer, Emery. 2009. "Framing and Reviewing Hip-Hop Educational Research." *Review of Educational Research* 79 (2): 946.

Richardson, Elaine. 2006. *Hip Hop Literacies*. New York: Routledge.

Rickford, John Russell, and Russell John Rickford. 2000. *Spoken Soul: The Story of Black English*. New York: John Wiley.

Smith, Erec, Jennifer Cohen, Paula Mathieu, James Sosnoski, Bridget Harris Tsemo, and Vershawn Ashanti Young. 2000. "CultureWise: Narrative as Research, Research as Narrative." *Works and Days* 33/34, 35/36 (17 and 18): 425–43.

Smitherman, Geneva. 1977. *Talkin and Testifyin: The Language of Black America*. Detroit, MI: Wayne State University Press.

——. 1999. *Talkin that Talk: African American Language and Culture*. New York: Routledge.

——. 2000. *Black Talk: Words and Phrases from the Hood to the Amen Corner*. New York: Mariner Books.

——. 2006. *Word from the Mother: Language and African Americans*. New York: Routledge.

Wolfram, Walt. 1969. *A Sociolinguistic Description of Detroit Negro Speech*. Washington, DC: Center for Applied Linguistics.

Wolfram, Walt, and Donna Christian. 1989. *Dialects and Education: Issues and Answers*. Englewood Cliffs, NJ: Prentice Hall.

Young, Vershawn Ashanti. 2004. "Your Average Nigga." *College Composition and Communication* 55 (4): 693–715.

CHAPTER 47

HIP HOP NATION LANGUAGE

Localization and Globalization

H. SAMY ALIM

47.1 INTRODUCTION

THE use of the term *Hip Hop Nation Language* (HHNL) in the United States has generally referred to language and language use within the Hip Hop Nation (HHN), a diverse, imagined community whose members (known as *heads*) practice and/or appreciate Hip Hop's expressive culture. Specifically, the use of HHNL has been tied to the linguistic systems and cultural modes of discourse that both derive from and reinvent the African American Oral Tradition. From the very beginning, the concept of HHNL was framed by two related groups of theorists: (1) Youth artists involved in Hip Hop cultural and lyrical production—many of them Hip Hop icons, from Afrika Bambaataa to Kurupt, from Scarface to Eve; and (2) writers and scholars of African American literature, from James G. Spady to Geneva Smitherman, from Kamau Brathwaite to John Edgar Wideman.

Caribbean historian, poet, and literary and music critic Kamau Brathwaite (1984, 13) described the "nation language" of Anglophone Caribbean poetry in these terms: "Nation language is the language which is influenced very strongly by the African model, the African aspect of our New World/Caribbean heritage. English it may be in terms of some of its lexical features. But in its contours, its rhythm and timbre, its sound explosions, it is not English." Brathwaite went on to consider "nation language" as both English and African at the same time, but an English which is like a "howl, or a shout, or a machine-gun or the wind or a wave." While many sociolinguists would describe *nation language* as merely a variety born out of processes of creolization, Brathwaite's emphasis on the literary and creative impulses of Black speakers foregrounds the expressive uses of the variety. In contemporary Hip Hop, artists often go beyond a *wind* or a *wave* and come through with the force of a tsunami. Just check Nicki Minaj's *monster* verse on "Monster" (2010), where many critics claim that she outshined other top emcees on the same track, including Jay-Z, Kanye West, and Rick

Ross. Switching between at least three different personas, each accompanied by different voices, Nicki also flexes a mix of African American Language (AAL) and rapid-fire, staccato Caribbean Creole varieties, while elongating vowels and producing guttural growls—all the while multiply encoding her rhymes with HHNL slang and hidden allusions that span everything from popular culture to high fashion. This *nation language* is what the Wu-Tang Clan's Raekwon theorized, in very similar terms as Brathwaite, as "machine-gun-rap" in the now classic Hip Hop album *Wu-Tang Forever* (1997).

Importantly, when Hip Hop artists speak of *language*, they do not narrowly define it in terms of its morphosyntactic or phonological features. In the "linguistic culture" (Schiffman 1996) of Hip Hop, language is understood in broad semiotic terms, or as Philly artist Beanie Sigel explains, "85 percent of communication is non-verbal." Language is a field from which everything communicates—clothes, facial expressions, gesture, and bodily comportment along with graffiti and other forms of visual art. Artists' definitions of language often include aesthetic and stylistic choices (creative use of silence and syllabic stress, for example); language ideologies and processes of identification (how language indexes cultural politics and identities); the sociopolitical contexts of language use in Hip Hop (from police surveillance to political discourse); and various cultural modes of discourse (from call and response, signifyin, or entering the cipher, among others).

For this chapter, I acknowledge this complexity, while outlining HHNL for the field of linguistics. In previous research (Alim 2004a, 2006), I have described HHNL as characterized by ten tenets:

1. HHNL in the United States is rooted in AAL and communicative practices (Spady 1991; Smitherman 1997; Yasin 1999). Linguistically, it is "the newest chapter in the African American book of folklore" (Rickford and Rickford 2000). Thus, HHNL both reflects and expands the African American Oral Tradition.
2. HHNL is just one of the many language varieties used by African Americans.
3. HHNL is widely spoken across the country and is adapted and transformed by various racial and ethnic groups inside and outside of the United States.
4. HHNL is a language with its own grammar, lexicon, and phonology as well as a unique communicative style and discursive modes. When an early Hip Hop group called The Treacherous Three rhymed about a "New Rap Language" in 1980, they were well aware of the uniqueness of the language they were rappin in.
5. HHNL is best viewed as the synergistic combination of speech, music, and literature. Yancy (1991) speaks of rap as "musical literature (or rhythmic-praxis discourse)." HHNL is simultaneously the spoken, poetic, lyrical, and musical expression of the HHN.
6. HHNL includes ideologies about language and language use.
7. HHNL is the central locus of identification for those seeking recognition and ratification as *Hip Hop heads*, members of the imagined community known as the HHN.
8. HHNL exhibits regional variation (Morgan 2001; Blake and Shousterman 2010). For example, most members of the HHN recognize the *urr* variable—pronouncing *here* or *hair* as *hurr*—as a feature of a Southern/Midwestern variety of HHNL. Even within regions, HHNL exhibits individual variation based on life experiences.

9. The fundamental aspect of HHNL—and perhaps the most astonishing to some of its more uninformed critics—is that it is central to the lifeworlds of the members of the HHN and suitable and functional for all of their communicative needs.

10. HHNL is inextricably linked with the sociopolitical circumstances that engulf the HHN. How does systemic police brutality and racial abuse—such as the NYPD-style *stop and frisk* policies or Florida-style *stand your ground* laws, for example, shift the discourse of the HHN? How do the sweeping forces of urban gentrification impact language and language use? Like Rose (1994) first argued, Hip Hop continues to articulate the shifting terms of Black marginality in the United States—and, I would add, language shifts to reflect and constitute those terms.

47.2 "Word Candy, S-L-A-N-G": The Politics and Pleasure of Slang

HHNL is language and language use within the HHN, particularly during Hip Hop-centered cultural activities, but also during other artistic, creative, playful, and intimate contexts. The linguistic landscape of Hip Hop includes concert performances, conversational discourse, interviews, and the language of Rap lyrics and album interludes. In this section, I will discuss how HHNL both reflects and expands AAL and language use, beginning with its hallmark, slang. In the following excerpt from my interview with San Francisco Bay Area Hip Hop legend, JT the Bigga Figga (November 2000), he breaks down some of the local Hip Hop slang—particularly the language of icon E-40—and situates it within the "language of the streets" (J = JT the Bigga Figga; A = Alim):

J: The language of the streets, I would say, is words that we. . . . Hip Hop and the streets damn near is one, you might as well say that. I could use E-40 as a example. He's someone who's real good at taking words, taking a regular word that we use, but he apply it to something else. A pager to E-40 is called a *locker*. A cell phone to E-40 is a *communicator*. A gun or a pistol is his *Pillsbury*. . . . Marijuana to him is called *broccoli*. Gin or Hennessey or alcohol or drink would be called *firewater*. . .

A: How does he come up with all this different stuff, man?

J: Just hangin out and just different people talkin. And, you know, "fo sheezy, off da heezy!" [*fo sheezy* derives from *for sure*, meaning 'definitely'; *off da heezy* derives from *off the hook*, a form of emphatic positive evaluation]. Me and you, what we doin right now, to him, it's called *marinating*. Marinating. We marinatin right now. . . . [*Marinating* means to be in deep conversation about something]. That's just *his* way of describing stuff from a different perspective and somebody somewhere else might not understand it, you know, unless you hang. . . . because you get the language by hangin around. The language, the language in the streets, man. . . . straight from the streets.

E-40 is often credited with developing a highly individualized and innovative repertoire of slang. According to 40, he doesn't necessarily "get the language" by hangin in the streets, but he *is* the streets. He has not only embarked on authoring his own *E-40's Dictionary of Slang*, but he recently (half?)-joked on a record that:

> Anything you got I can sell it to hustlas, think I cain't?/
>
> Gift of gab, sell the White House black paint/
>
> Word candy, S-L-A-N-G/
>
> Thinkin about takin a million dollar insurance policy out on my mouthpiece!

[E-40 uses "mouthpiece" not to mean "lawyer," but rather as his ability to make others do what they might not otherwise do through his clever use of language] ("Function," *The Block Brochure: Welcome to the Soil 2*, 2012).

But slang in Hip Hop is about more than just the pleasure derived from inventing new ways of saying things or bolstering one's social status in the streets. It is also about developing local identities for youth within a national Hip Hop Culture that is paying much more attention to regional distinctions within the form. As I have written elsewhere (Alim 2004b), young bloods in the Bay Area sometimes use highly localized lexicon to mark not only the San Francisco Bay Area but also smaller areas within the region. Youth in Sunnyside, for example, have documented their use of the word *rogue* to refer to each other. In addition to gendered and generational social meanings, the broader sociopolitical significance of the term is evident when one considers the semantic inversion involved in its usage. Rather than the negative meaning proscribed by the dominant group (think of a *rogue state* in US foreign policy, for example), youth have long been referring to themselves as *rogues* precisely because it represents a nonconformist attitude toward authority. (Of course, it has been more than interesting hearing these youth comment on Sarah Palin's 2009 book title, *Going Rogue: An American Life!*) Youth in this area and around the country have also been using the terms *savage* and *gangsta* in similar ways, semantically expanding inverting their meanings.

The unabated drive for stylistic distinction does other kinds of sociopolitical identity work as well. Hip Hop cultural practices are embedded within a cultural matrix of locally relevant, and always evolving, social meanings and discourses. In a political climate where youth programs are all but non-existent, Black youth in the Bay Area—led by E-40, Keak the Sneak, Dem Hoodstarz, The Federation, Mistah F.A.B., and other "Hyphy Movement" /ˈhaɪfiː/ artists—have carved out a place for themselves, creating a world that privileges their sensibilities, styles, and street language, while simultaneously writing themselves into history. In the process of refusing to be the next *untold story*, they have created a lexicon of "Yay Area" life to describe the "shifting terms of their marginality" (Rose 1994).

When popular discourses associate the Hyphy Movement (for definition, see Turner and Rose, this volume; Alim 2006a) with "ignorant slang" or "sideshows"—spontaneous street, block party-like gatherings where participants perform stunts with their cars—there is no effort to contextualize sideshows as part of the Bay Area's car culture at least since the 1980s. When they speak of the "social chaos" and the "rampant drug culture" involved in "gettin hyphy," there is no attempt to address Oakland's deteriorating public schools (not to mention the school shutdowns) and the thriving, underground drug economy, both of which fuel record-setting homicide rates in the area. Rather, youth involved in the Hyphy Movement are blamed for the social deterioration of their city, while the racism of neglect that leads to such urban decay goes unchallenged. The artist who coined the phrase "ridin' the yellow bus" (meaning 'to get hyper'), Oakland's Mistah F.A.B., represents the Hyphy Movement's potential for youth empowerment and involvement in the political process. As a participant in a voter registration drive (Vote Fo Sheezy), F.A.B. got *hella* people to come out and vote for 2006 mayoral candidate Ron Dellums. A *Los Angeles Times* interview with an executive assistant for the Dellums campaign confirmed the Hyphy Movement's ability to swing not just asses, but votes, too: "Hyphy brought in a new demographic that I hadn't seen in my last seven years working in politics. . . . These rappers were in folks' ears, planting seeds. For this generation, it's such a powerful movement. It gave us a visible push" (Lee 2006). In the context of rife state and cultural politics, Hip Hop youth use language to make sense of their existence and to help shape their future—and as Rickford and Rickford (2000, 86) note, "to tell America about herself in a language" that she barely understands.

47.3   "I Like the Way You Do that Right Thurr (Right Thurr)": Hip Hop's Localization and Linguistic Consciousness

Youth who participate in Hip Hop Culture are known for their conscious use of language to construct particular identities. In writing about AAL's divergence from "standard" English, Smitherman and Baugh (2002, 20) noted this conscious manipulation of language in relation to identity work:

> Graffiti writers of Hip Hop Culture were probably the coiners of the term "phat" (meaning excellent, great, superb). . . although "phat" is spelled in obvious contrast to "fat," the former confirms that those who use it know that "ph" is pronounced like "f." In other words, those who first wrote "phat" diverged from standard English as a direct result of their awareness of standard English: the divergence was not by chance linguistic error. There is no singular explanation to account for linguistic divergence, but Hip Hop Culture suggests that matters of personal identity play a significant role.

This conscious linguistic manipulation deals with matters of spelling and phonemic awareness (see Morgan 2001 and Olivo 2001 on "spelling ideology"). One particular case—perhaps the most controversial use of language in Hip Hop Culture—is the term *nigga*. The HHN realized that this word had various positive in-group meanings and pejorative out-group meanings, and thus felt the need to reflect the culturally specific meanings with a new spelling (*nigger* becomes *nigga*). A *nigga* is your main man, or one of your close companions, your homie. Recently, the term has been generalized to refer to any male (one may even hear something like, "No, I was talkin about Jimmy, you know, the Asian nigga with the glasses," though it usually refers to Black men). Tupac Shakur, showing Hip Hop's affinity for acronyms, transformed the racial slur into the ultimate positive ideal for young Black men—"Never Ignorant Getting Goals Accomplished."

Recently, rapper Nas has continued to lead the "N-word" controversy. Alim and Smitherman (2012) detail Nas's heated debates with Reverend Jesse Jackson in 2007 after Jackson was caught privately using the very term that he vehemently criticized Hip Hop for publicly. Nas had planned to release his ninth studio album under the title "Nigger." And while most Hip Hop artists supported his decision, the NAACP put out an official statement denouncing Nas's album title and Jesse Jackson appeared on Fox News (or as Nas calls it, "Fix News") to condemn the artist. Speaking to MTV News, Nas insisted that he and other Hip Hop heads were "taking power away from the word." Reverend Al Sharpton went so far as to say that Nas, rather than taking the power away from White folks, was actually "helping out the racists." Nas went on to produce "N.I.G.G.E.R.," a song that highlighted the racist spelling of the term in order to underscore the shift from the old racism of the past to the new racism of the twenty-first century (" 'Cause anytime we mention our condition, our history or existence, they callin' it 'reverse racism' "). Even more recently, at the time of this writing (May 2014), the National Football League is considering banning the word and has sparked the most recent round of mania around Black speech.

In addition to spelling and phonemic manipulation, HHNL speakers also intentionally highlight regional differences in pronunciation by processes such as vowel lengthening and syllabic stress (Morgan 2001). When Bay Area rappers JT the Bigga Figga and Mac Mall announced the resurgence of the Bay Area to the national Hip Hop scene with "Game Recognize Game" (1993), they did so using a distinctive feature of Bay Area pronunciation. The Bay Area anthem's chorus repeated this line three times: "Game recognize game in the Bay, man." "Man" was pronounced "mane" [men]/"mang" to accentuate the nasalization that had come to be associated with the Bay Area. Also, when fellow Bay Area rapper B-Legit boasted about his slang, he did so using the same feature to stress his Bay Area linguistic origins: "You can tell from my slang I'm from the Bay, mane" (2000).

Meanwhile in St. Louis, Missouri, rappers Nelly and the St. Lunatics were among the first rappers to represent their city on a national scale. Language was an essential part of establishing their identity in the fiercely competitive world of Hip Hop Culture. For example, in one of their first singles they emphasized every word that rhymed with "urr" to highlight a well-known (and often stigmatized) aspect of Southern/Midwestern pronunciation (here as "hurr" [hʌr:]; care as "curr" [kʌr:]; air as "urr" [ʌr:], and so on). By intentionally highlighting linguistic features associated with St. Louis (and other southern cities), they established their tenacity through language while eschewing dominant perspectives of their speech.

This variable—which Blake and Shousterman (2010) refer to as the "urr" variable—has come to take on national (and perhaps international) significance in Hip Hop. In Alim (2007, 161), we see how some San Francisco Bay Area youth have begun using the "urr" variable to forge local identities as Hip Hop heads. The following is an excerpt of a recorded conversation with these youth about their multiple linguistic styles (L = Latasha; A = Alim):

L: Yeah, like the way I talk to my teacher ain't the same way I talk with the 3L Click.
A: 3L Click? What's that?
L: All of our names begin with "L", so we named our click after that, the 3L Click. It's me, LaToya and Lamar...
A: And how is the way y'all talk different from the way you talk to the teacher?
L: Well, it's like, you know that rapper, Nelly?
A: Yeah, yeah.
L: How he say everything like "urrrr", like for "here" he'll be like "hurrrr"?
A: Yeah! [Laughing] "I ain't from round hurrrr!"
L: [Laughing] That's how we try to talk!
A: Why, though?!
L: Cuz we like it!

In a prime example of what I have referred to as *Hip Hop Linguistics* (Alim 2006), Blake and Shousterman (2010) provide a diachronic analysis of the "urr variable" (vowel centralization before /r/) in St. Louis and consider the impact of Hip Hop's dramatic use of this variable on AAL. They demonstrate brilliantly the interplay between the historic use of the "urr variable" in St. Louis (providing evidence for sound change, with a clear rise in contemporary usage) and what one might refer to as the *hyper-use* of this feature by Hip Hop artists in "the Lou." Further, they theorize that this generous use by Hip Hop artists supports the rise in local usage of this feature, and that artists' linguistic choices are reflective of their desire to represent their local hoods. Importantly, for the study of AAL, and language in general, Blake and Shousterman (2010, 242) conclude that "there is a co-construction of identity between community members and rappers from the area, which indicates that mass communication is affecting the language of local communities, in this case via the music of hip-hop artists, and vice versa."

Hip Hop youth not only manipulate AAL phonology, but they are also conscious of its syntactic structure as well. On his platinum single "Country Grammar" (2000), Nelly proclaims, "My gramma bees Ebonics." Clearly, HHNL speakers vary their grammar consciously. An analysis of copula variation in the speech and the lyrics of Hip Hop artists concluded that higher levels of copula absence in the artists' lyrics represented the construction of a street conscious identity—where the speaker makes a linguistic-cultural connection to the streets (Alim 2006). Much of the scholarship on HHNL has concluded that the syntax of HHNL is essentially the same as that of AAL

(Remes 1991; Smitherman 1997, 2000; Yasin 1999; Rickford and Rickford 2000; Morgan 2001). This is true. But we can and must also raise an important question: How does HHNL both confirm and challenge our knowledge of AAL syntax?

Probably the most oft-studied feature of AAL is habitual or invariant *be*. Early studies of AAL syntax (Labov et al. 1968; Fasold 1972) noted the uniqueness of this feature and were in agreement that it was used for recurring actions ("She be watching TV every day after school") and could not be used in finite contexts ("She be the boss"). Building upon this research, we see that HHNL provides numerous examples of what I have called be_3, or the *equative copula*, in AAL (Alim 2004b, 180–90). Some examples of this construction (Noun Phrase # be # Noun Phrase) from Hip Hop lyrics follow:

> "I be the truth."—Philadelphia's Beanie Sigel
> "Dr. Dre be the name."—Compton's Dr. Dre
> "Brooklyn be the place where I served them thangs."—New York's Jay-Z
> "My squad be the official click in this rap shit."—New York's Spliff Star

These are but a few of countless examples in the corpus of Hip Hop lyrics, but I have also noted the equative copula construction in everyday conversation as well, as in the following examples:

1. In a conversation between a Black journalist and a Black Hip Hop artist, who was approximately 30 years old, the journalist commented with amazement about how the Bay Area managed to produce dozens of successful, independent Hip Hop artists. The journalist asked, "How y'all do that shit, man?" And the artist answered, with obvious hometown pride, "We *be* them Bay boys."
2. A Black scholar in his 30s was talking to me about his numerous accomplishments and those of other successful Black scholars. In a moment of boasting, he said, "You know we *be* some baaad brothas."
3. A Sista in her early 20s and a group of friends were on their way home from hearing a speech in San Francisco. Somebody mentioned how some folks at the venue were opposed to the speaker's strong, political message. The Sista, noticeably upset, responded, "They *be* some *weak*-minded muthafuckas!"

It is possible that speakers of AAL have begun using this form only recently and that it signals an evolution in AAL's verbal system. Alternatively, the form may have always been present in AAL but simply not noted by linguists. The form has been cited in at least two earlier studies of AAL: (1) in Henrie (1969), cited in Fasold (1972), "She *be* a rich lady and (2) in Baugh (1983), "They *be* the real troublemakers"; "The Clovers *be* the baddest ones around here." The form is also present in the writings of Black Arts Movement poets of the 1960s and 1970s (see Rambsy and Whiteside, this volume), most notably in Sonia Sanchez's *We Be Word Sorcerers*. As with the "urr variable" in St. Louis, it is possible that Black poets and members of the HHN, with their extraordinary linguistic consciousness and their emphasis on pushing the linguistic envelope, have supported the use of this form in everyday conversation. More ethnographic research needs to be done on the relationship between language use in Hip Hop and the development of local varieties of AAL.

47.4 CONCLUSION: "SHOW ME RESPECT, J'SUIS LA TRUE *ILL* NANA": FROM LOCALIZATION TO GLOBALIZATION OF HIP HOP AND AAL

While the national Hip Hop scene continues to become more and more localized, these local features, such as the "urr" variable, have also simultaneously spread nationally. As we read above, Alim (2007, 161) provides evidence of the "urr" variable being explicitly discussed and used by youth in the San Francisco Bay Area, for example, while Blake et al. (2008) provide evidence from New York City and Ohio, as well as its use in Hip Hop lyrics by artists from New Orleans, Detroit, Atlanta, Chicago, Brooklyn, and Memphis. As first noted by Morgan (2001), since Hip Hop heads claim urban, working-class AAL as the prestige variety, we have seen a greater emphasis on phonology as a cultural, class-based, regional identifier within Black America. In the case of the *urr* variable, it has not only moved from regional to supraregional, but the feature has also been, to some extent, globalized (Blake et al. [2008] cite London's Lady Sovereign, a White female emcee and among the first mainstream queer Hip Hop artists, as using it in her 2006 rap "Random").

At the beginning of this chapter, I noted that HHNL in the United States has generally referred to linguistic systems and cultural modes of discourse that both derive from and reinvent the African American Oral Tradition. Due to Hip Hop's globalization, we can now start thinking beyond a normative *Hip Hop Nation Language* and move toward *Hip Hop Nation Language Varieties (HHNLVs)*, including those that borrow from but are not necessarily derived from African American Language and Culture. An emerging body of work demonstrates that Hip Hop youth from North America to North Africa use varieties of HHNL to challenge dominant arrangements of languages, identities, and power (Pennycook 2007; Alim et al. 2009; Terkourafi 2010; Ibrahim 2014).

Sarkar and Allen's (2007) and Sarkar's (2009) work on "the transformative power of Hip Hop language mixing" provides one example of these HHNLVs in Montréal, Quebec, which has experienced sweeping demographic changes in the last two to three decades. The increasing racial, religious, and linguistic diversity since the 1970s has been followed by the concomitant influx of Hip Hop cultural practices, which youths have employed to help describe and transform their realities. Afro-diasporic youth, dealing with often tumultuous immigration experiences and their subsequent subjugation due to skin color, draw on their knowledge of Black ideologies of race and nationalism, partly through the role of Malcolm X as a Hip Hop icon (Sarkar and Allen 2007), to introduce local narratives of racism in order to critique a global system of racialized oppression. Symbolically, many of them have engaged in the process of semantic inversion by reclaiming *nègs* in the same way that many Black American Hip Hop youth have reclaimed *nigga* (i.e., as a term of camaraderie or endearment), as we saw above, and as we see in J.Kyll's lyrics below.

Within this broad context, young women like the Haitian-origin J.Kyll also critique the sexism they experience at dance clubs and parties, where young men feel entitled not just to gaze at women's bodies, but to put their hands on them. In this example, Standard Quebec French is unmarked; **European French** is bold and underlined; <u>Standard North American English</u> is underlined; *AAL* is italicized; <u>*HHNL slang*</u> is italicized and underlined; and ***Haitian Creole*** is bold and italicized. J.Kyll writes (incidentally using the inverted "ill" in the first line):

> <u>Show me respect</u>, j'suis la <u>true</u> <u>*ill*</u> **nana**
> Pourquoi t'es venu, si tu *front* **sou kote**?
> Fais pas ton <u>mean</u>, j'vois ton **bounda** sauter
> Si tu sais pas danser, qu'est-ce que t'as à te moquer?
> Dis-le, t'aimes mes <u>moves</u>, pas vrai, t'es choqué?
> Hey! Mais qu'est-ce ta main fait là? <u>Go away</u>!
> ***Nèg pa lave, pafume*** . . . <u>No way</u>!
> *You tha man*, toutes les femmes te veulent. . . oh! ouais!
> <u>You wanna get down, you go down</u>! <u>O.K.</u>

The following is the English gloss:

> Show me respect, I'm a woman to reckon with
> Why did you come, if you're going to sneak around?
> Don't be nasty, I saw your ass jumpin'
> If you can't dance, quit making fun of me
> C'mon, you like my moves, admit you're pissed off
> Hey! What's your hand doing there? Go away!
> Black who'd rather wear perfume than wash.. . . No way!
> You tha man, all the girls are after you. . . yeah, right!
> You wanna get down, you go down! O.K.
> (J.Kyll of Muzion, 1999, "Lounge with Us," Mentalité moune morne)

As they work to make sense of shifting terrains of race and gender, the HHNLVs of Montreal youth like J.Kyll are marked by mixing and shifting between nine different language varieties and styles, including several varieties of French, English, AAL, Haitian and Jamaican Creole, and Spanish. Through interviews and analyses of their linguistic practices, Sarkar (2009) demonstrates how these youth consciously contribute to the creation of the cultural and linguistic diversity around them, rather than merely reflecting it. For these Hip Hop heads, HHNLVs operate as a positive, unifying social force, even as they disregard staunch efforts by state institutions to maintain a "rigidly normative, prescriptive French-language dominance" (154).

Related social, political, and linguistic processes occur throughout Africa, as documented in the work of Perullo and Fenn (2003), Omoniyi (2006, 2009), and Higgins

(2009). Higgins situates her study of Tanzanian youth's HHNLVs within the historical, linguistic context of Tanzania's move from an explicit anti-English language policy to one of Swahili-English bilingualism. These language policy shifts were never seen as on-the-ground realities, and today, Tanzanian youth are redefining themselves and their local environments through HHNLVs that rely on a combination of "African American English," specifically HHNL in the United States, a local street code known as *Kihuni*, and kiSwahili. In doing so, they are performing new, local forms of indignity that recast their marginalization as an empowered transnational form of identification (Higgins 2009, 109).

Similarly, Omoniyi (2009) posits HHNLVs in Nigeria as a new site for the articulation and contestation of multiple identities. These identities are articulated, in large part, through the use of multiple language varieties, including a complicated mix of local languages (some being varieties other than their mother tongues). Youth often code-switch, for example, between Yoruba, Igbo, and AAL, while using Nigerian Pidgin as a new sort of *lingua franca*. These HHNLVs not only put Nigeria on the Hip Hop map, but they also undermine official language policies that are based on the dominant view of English as the *lingua franca* of Nigeria (Omoniyi 2009, 125).

As Hip Hop continues to expand its global reach, AAL will be used in increasingly dynamic ways across an increasingly diverse array of contexts. HHNL's globalization, coupled with Hip Hop youth's love affair with language, will undoubtedly continue to produce new and remarkable instances of the local and global uses of AAL.

REFERENCES

Alim, H. Samy. 2004a. "Hip Hop Nation Language." In *Language in the U.S.A.: Themes for the Twenty-First Century*, edited by Edward Finegan and John R. Rickford, 387–409. Cambridge: Cambridge University.

———. 2004b. *You Know My Steez: An Ethnographic and Sociolinguistic Study of Styleshifting in a Black American Speech Community*. Durham, NC: Duke University Press.

———. 2006. *Roc the Mic Right: The Language of Hip Hop Culture*. London: Routledge.

———. 2007. "Critical Hip Hop Language Pedagogies: Combat, Consciousness, and the Cultural Politics of Communication." *Journal of Language, Identity, and Education* 6 (2): 161–76.

Alim, H. Samy, Awad Ibrahim, and Alastair Pennycook, eds. 2009. *Global Linguistic Flows: Hip Hop Cultures, Youth Identities, and the Politics of Language*. New York: Routledge.

Alim, H. Samy, and Geneva Smitherman. 2012. *Articulate while Black: Barack Obama, Language, and Race in the United States*. New York: Oxford University.

Baugh, John. 1983. *Black Street Speech: Its History, Structure, and Survival*. Austin: University of Texas.

Blake, Renée, Sonya Fix, Cara Shousterman, and Simanique Moody. 2008. "'Y'all ain't from around Hurr': Hip Hop and a Case of Regional Variation in AAE." Unpublished ms.

Blake, Renée, and Cara Shousterman. 2010. "Diachrony and AAE: St. Louis, Hip-Hop, and Sound Change Outside of the Main stream." *Journal of English Linguistics* 38 (3): 230–47.

Brathwaite, Kamau. 1984. *History of the Voice: The Development of Nation Language in Anglophone Caribbean Poetry*. London: New Beacon Books.

Fasold, Ralph. 1972. *Tense Marking in Black English: A Linguistic and Social Analysis*. Washington, DC: Center for Applied Linguistics.

Henrie, Samuel N. 1969. "A Study of Verb Phrases Used by Five-Year-Old Nonstandard Negro English Speaking Children." PhD diss., University of California, Berkeley.

Higgins, C. 2009. "From da Bomb to *Bomba*: Global Hip Hop Nation Language in Tanzania." In *Global Linguistic Flows*, edited by H. Samy Alim, Awad Ibrahim, and Alastair Pennycook, 95–112. New York: Routledge.

Ibrahim, Awad. 2014. *The Rhizome of Blackness: A Critical Ethnography of Hip Hop Culture, Language, Identity, and the Politics of Becoming*. New York: Peter Lang.

Labov, William, Paul Cohen, Clarence Robins, and John Lewis. 1968. *A Study of the Non-standard English of Negro and Puerto Rican Speakers in New York City*. Report on Co-operative Research Project 3288. New York: Columbia University.

Lee, C. 2006. "Up from the Underground." *Los Angeles Times*. July 23. http://articles.latimes.com/2006/jul/23/entertainment/ca-hyphy23.

Morgan, Marcyliena. 2001. "'Nuthin' but a G thang': Grammar and Language Ideology in Hip Hop Identity." In *Sociocultural and Historical Contexts of African American Vernacular English*, edited by Sonja Lanehart, 185–207. Athens: University of Georgia Press.

Olivo, W. 2001. "Phat Lines: Spelling Conventions in Rap Music." *Written Language and Literacy* 4 (1): 67–85.

Omoniyi, T. 2009. "'So I Choose to da am Naija Style': Hip Hop, Language, and Postcolonial Identities." In *Global Linguistic Flows*, edited by H. Samy Alim, Awad Ibrahim, and Alastair Pennycook, 113–35. New York: Routledge.

Pennycook, Alastair. 2007. *Global Englishes and Transcultural Flows*. London: Routledge.

Perullo, Alex, and John Fenn. 2003. "Language Ideologies, Choices, and Practices in Eastern African Hip Hop." In *Global Pop, Local Language*, edited by Harris M. Berger and Michael T. Carroll, 19–52. Oxford: University of Mississippi.

Remes, Pieter. 1991. "Rapping: A Sociolinguistic Study of Oral Tradition in Black Urban Communities in the United States." *Journal of the Anthropological Society of Oxford* 22 (2): 129–49.

Rickford, John R., and Russell J. Rickford. 2000. *Spoken Soul: The Story of Black English*. New York: John Wiley.

Rose, Tricia. 1994. *Black Noise: Rap Music and Black Culture in Contemporary America*. Middletown, CT: Wesleyan University.

Sarkar, M. 2009. "'Still Reppin *por mi Gente*': The Transformative Power of Language Mixing in Quebec Hip Hop." In *Global Linguistic Flows*, edited by H. Samy Alim, Awad Ibrahim, and Alastair Pennycook, 139–58. New York: Routledge.

Sarkar, Mela, and Dawn Allen. 2007. "Hybrid Identities in Quebec Hip-Hop: Language, Territory, and Ethnicity in the Mix." *Journal of Language, Identity, and Education* 6 (2): 117–30.

Schiffman, Harold F. 1996. *Linguistic Culture and Language Policy*. London: Routledge.

Smitherman, Geneva. 1997. "'The Chain Remain the Same': Communicative Practices in the Hip Hop Nation." *Journal of Black Studies* 28 (1): 3–25.

———. 2000. *Talkin that Talk: Language, Culture, and Education in African America*. New York: Routledge.

Smitherman, Geneva, and John Baugh. 2002. "The Shot Heard from Ann Arbor: Language Research and Public Policy in African America." *Howard Journal of Communication* 13 (1): 5–24.

Terkourafi, Marina. 2010. *The Languages of Global Hip Hop*. London: Continuum.

Wideman, John Edgar. 1976. "Frame and Dialect: The Evolution of the Black Voice in American Literature." *American Poetry Review* 5 (5): 34–37.

Yancy, George. 1991. "Rapese." Cited in James G. Spady, *Nation Conscious Rap: the Hip Hop Vision*. Philadelphia: Black History Museum.

Yasin, Jon A. 1999. "Rap in the African-American Music Tradition: Cultural Assertion and Continuity." In *Race and Ideology: Language, Symbolism, and Popular Culture*, edited by Arthur K. Spears, 197–224. Detroit, MI: Wayne State University.

CHAPTER 48

··

AFRICAN AMERICAN LANGUAGE AND IDENTITY

Contradictions and Conundrums

··

SONJA LANEHART

People create their linguistic systems (and we all have more than one) so as to resemble those of the groups with which from time to time they wish to identify. Both the groups, and their linguistic attributes, exist solely in the mind of each individual. When we talk we project the universe as we see it on to others as on to a cinema screen in our own images, *expressed in the language we consider appropriate at that moment,* and we invite others by these acts to share our universe. *This does not necessarily mean that we accommodate our behaviour to resemble that of our audience,* though we may do so. *Rather, we behave in the way that—unconsciously or consciously—we think appropriate to the group with which at that moment we wish to identify.*

Robert Le Page, *Acts of Identity* (1986, 23; emphasis added)

48.1 INTRODUCTION

I have lived with Robert Le Page and Andrée Tabouret-Keller's (1985) research on creole communities and identity since I was an undergraduate student meditating on the weight of language and identity. I am forever drawn to Le Page's (1986) words because, as I chose to emphasize in his words above, people create their ever-evolving linguistic repertoires and express them, sometimes consciously and sometimes unconsciously, as an act of identity, which can be for accommodation, solidarity, disidentification, or even defiance. It is often purposeful. It is performance/performed. It is something we do; we do language (Morrison 1993), and our identity is part of that action.

I remember when I was an emerging scholar presenting my research at the 1995 annual meeting of the Modern Language Association (MLA) about standard language ideology—I stated that standard language was a myth. A senior scholar challenged me at the end of my presentation because I had presented speaking mainstream language while espousing the legitimacy of varieties that are discriminated against and looked down upon, such as African American Language (AAL) and Southern White Vernacular English. The senior, White, male scholar (did I really need to specify?) wanted to know why I did not make my presentation using AAL if I thought so highly of it. I responded that, though AAL is systematic and rule-governed and is quite capable of being used for such a purpose, what made him think I felt that he or the audience was worthy of such access to that aspect of my identity? What do I have to prove through performance that suits "the master" and not myself when I choose and how I choose? My language was and is my power: you see/hear the "me" I choose to reveal and through that revelation you see your place (see Paul Laurence Dunbar's "We Wear the Mask"). The language we choose to use at any given moment with any given audience is ours and ours alone. And though linguistics is business, language is personal. AAL is very personal to me. Those MLA days helped me to understand the hegemony inherent in the "language line" (Hopson 2003, 228), which is the intersection of language and the color line (see DuBois [1903] 1994 in *The Souls of Black Folk*) as manifested in the role of language in the social and cultural reproduction of group and class positions. While that MLA experience was meant to dress me down, I was able to stand on the shoulders of Black giants who had been cultivating my language prowess long before I even realized it. I have come to realize that the language line, and my response and growth from it, has shaped me more than I ever realized. Though the MLA interrogator meant to undermine my authority and authenticity in my identity by not performing AAL for him, he ignited my voice to move from trying to prove myself through the language I used to instead performing the identity I allow to be accessible and effective for my purposes. In addition to Le Page, I have a shero whose words resonate with me and also have influenced why I use the term *African American Language* as opposed to the variety of other names for language use in African American communities:

> For those of us who live and work in the Black community, the study of African American Language is not just an academic exercise, *it is our life.*
>
> Geneva Smitherman, "Foreword," Sociocultural and Historical Contexts of
> African American English (2001, ix; emphasis added)

Again, for me, this is personal.

My goals for this chapter are to define and discuss difficult terms related to language and identity in African American communities. In doing so, it is important to discuss the contradictions we find in studying the languages and identities of people in African American communities that arise from within and without, as well as conundrums resulting from these contradictions. In examining these contradictions and conundrums, I discuss identity and communities of African Americans through their language attitudes, beliefs, practices, and ideologies via linguistic pride and acceptance, linguistic prejudice, and linguistic shame and denial.

48.2 ACTS OF IDENTITY: THERE IS
POWER IN THE WORD

Our language and culture reflect our past, our present, and our future possibilities. Though the crux of this chapter stands on Le Page's (1986) and Smitherman's (2001) words above, James Baldwin's words nearly four decades ago in reference to the case of *Martin Luther King Junior Elementary School Children et al. v. Ann Arbor School District* (1979), aka the "Black English Trial" or the "Ann Arbor Decision" (see Smitherman, this volume; Baugh, this volume; Hollie, Butler, and Gillenwaters, this volume) are as true today as they were nearly forty years ago:

> The brutal truth is that the bulk of White people in America never had any interest in educating Black people, except as this could serve White purposes. *It is not the Black child's language that is despised. It is his experience.* A child cannot be taught by anyone who despises him, and a child cannot afford to be fooled. *A child cannot be taught by anyone whose demand, essentially, is that the child repudiate his experience, and all that gives him sustenance, and enter a limbo in which he will no longer be Black, and in which he knows he can never become White.* Black people have lost too many Black children that way. (1979, 19E; emphasis added)

Baldwin's words must have been in the mind of author and activist Alice Walker when she penned the words below for Celie in *The Color Purple* (1982, 216) that I began my writing career with:

> Darlene trying to teach me how to talk. She say us not so hot. A dead country give-away. You say us where most folks say we, she say, and peoples think you dumb. Colored peoples think you a hick and white folks be amuse. What I care? I ast. I'm happy. But she say I feel more happier talking like she talk. . . . Every time I say something the way I say it, she correct me until I say it some other way. Pretty soon it feel like I can't think. My mind run up on a thought, git confuse, run back and sort of lay down. You sure this worth it? I ast. She say Yeah. Bring me a bunch of books. Whitefolks all over them, talking bout apples and dogs. What I care bout dogs? I think. Darlene keep trying. Think how much better Shug feel with you educated, she say. She won't be shame to take you anywhere. Shug not shame no how, I say. But she don't believe this the truth. Sugar, she say one day when Shug home, don't you think it be nice if Celie could talk proper. Shug say, She can talk in sign language for all I care. . . . But I let Darlene worry on. Sometimes I think bout the apples and the dogs, sometimes I don't. *Look like to me only a fool would want you to talk in a way that feel peculiar to your mind.* (emphasis added)

(I wanted to title my first book *Peculiar to Your Mind*, but some viewed that title as evoking mental illness. In the context of this chapter on AAL and identity, that is ironic.) What is more peculiar to your mind than being something or someone you are not?

Baldwin's and Celie's points are powerful and true in my life and experience—and in the literature (see "The Whig Party Don't Exist in My Hood" in Alim and Baugh 2007; Banks 2011; Delpit and Dowdy 2008; Fisher 2007; Gilyard 1991, 2011; Kinloch 2011; Kirkland 2013; Lanehart 1996, 1998, 2002, 2007, 2009; Paris 2011; Smitherman 1977, 2000, 2006). And although Baldwin did not capitalize "Black" and "White," I did so for him and do so throughout because it is important to realize that these are not colors—they are concepts and social constructions; they are identities. In reality, people who represent these names are not actually these colors.

In the documentary *Dark Girls* (2011), there is a little girl who is darker than her brothers and mother, and she is pained by that fact. She refuses to be called "black" because she says she is not. In reality, her skin is not black—but she is a Black body. The distinction is important. Though her brothers and mother are of a lighter complexion, they are Black bodies as well. That is why the *one-drop rule* and names like *octoroon, mulatto, quadroon, good hair* do not let one escape the marginalization of the Black body and what goes with the narrative that has been constructed; you are still Black even if you are not black/Black or have one drop of black/Black blood so long as society says you are (e.g., Barack Obama is called our first Black president even though he is biracial; see comedian Donald Glover on how our identity is often constructed for us in the skit titled "We Get It" on the website http://www.cc.com/video-clips/11diik/comedy-central-presents-we-get-it). So, I use "Black" and "White" because they are so much more than colors, just like hair in the Black community is not just hair (see Jacobs-Huey 2006 and Chris Rock's 2009 documentary film *Good Hair*). As James Sledd noted forty years ago, even "compassionate, liberal educators, knowing the ways of society (i.e., the narrative society has constructed about blackness/Blackness), will change the color of a student's vowels because they cannot change the color of their students' skins" (1972, 325). Sounds like Baldwin, doesn't it?

As a Texan and a graduate of the University of Texas at Austin, I was exposed to James Sledd's "Bi-dialectalism: The Linguistics of White Supremacy" (1972) and "Doublespeak: Dialectology in the Service of Big Brother" (1984). Sledd, as a southern White male, spoke about language and identity rights for African Americans (and southerners) in a way they could not (Freed 1995) because, as is still the case, African Americans were seen as too close to the situation. I have always found it troubling/problematic/ironic that, with the inclusion of African Americans and other people of color into the academy, aka the Ivory Tower, we have often been discouraged from studying our own people because we are accused of being too close to the situation and therefore unable to be objective, whereas Whites have freely studied everyone for centuries and seemingly without reproach or prejudice or subjectivities in the eyes of the research community or the ever-nebulous "they" (see, for example, Jackson 2004). That is why Tim Wise (2010, 2011, 2012) can talk about racism—and be heard—in a way Black people cannot. Whose statement, though essentially saying the same thing, has more gravitas for you: Baldwin's or Sledd's?

Since I have delineated "Black" and "White," it is time to do so for AAL. Here, I simply define *African American Language* as language spoken by or among African Americans (see Mufwene 2001). That is not to say non-Blacks cannot speak it or use it, just as those who are not Japanese can still learn or acquire and use Japanese (e.g., my son is learning Japanese and wants to live there someday). Likewise, it does not mean that *all* African Americans speak AAL because not all African Americans, just like not all people of Japanese descent or Mexican descent, speak their heritage languages. AAL, like any variety, is part of a community and socioculture and history; it is inextricably linked with American slave descendants, forged from pain, hardship, family, NOMMO (the Afrocentric concept meaning "the power of the Word"), tradition, memory, community, spirituality, perseverance, and strength. It is not slang or street language spoken only by adolescent and young adult, low-income males in urban areas (i.e., AAL speakers are not the White dialectology research equivalent of NORMs[1]). It is Spoken Soul (Rickford and Rickford 2000); R&B and Jazz; Gospel and Spirituals; Hip Hop Nation Language (see Alim, this volume); Gullah (see Weldon and Moody, this volume); and, most of all, it is rule-governed and systematic (hence Parts II and IV of this volume; see also Green 2002), just as any and every other language variety. It encapsulates time (hence Part I of this volume), space (hence Parts V, VI, and VII of this volume), and place (hence Part II). It can be learned just like Japanese or French or Swahili. However, what makes AAL different from any of those other varieties is its sociocultural and historical contexts (see Baugh 1999, 2000; Ogbu 1978), which are unique to the involuntary immigration of the American slave experience through the Middle Passage.

Language indexes our identities (Lanehart 2007; Paris 2011); our cultures (Morgan 2002); our communities (Kirkland 2013; Richardson 2013; Spears 1988, 2001); our experiences (Jacobs-Huey 2006; Lanehart 2001; Morgan 2003); our ethnicities (Benor 2010); and our sociocultures (Wolfram and Thomas 2008). Language is our homeland (Marshall 1983). Despite the contested origin and development of AAL that can never be proven for lack of necessary data and evidence (Lanehart 2007), what is certain is the people who created it out of necessity were in a place involuntarily (Ogbu 1978); therefore, the birth of a language such as AAL, just like the birth of a nation such as the United States, was forged by fire and pain and in shame.

48.3 PECULIAR TO THE MIND: IDENTITY IN MOTION—CONTRADICTIONS AND ALL

48.3.1 Linguistic Prejudice

The paraphrasing below of James Gee's (1990) "literacy myth" is where we still are today despite all the research in linguistics and cognate fields that tells us otherwise.

The claims that have been made for standard English in the traditional sense of "the correct or proper way to speak" are nearly limitless. Such standard English is claimed to lead to logical, analytic, critical and rational thinking, general and abstract uses of language, the recognition of the importance in clearly and precisely distinguishing time and space, political democracy and greater social equity, and wealth and productivity. It is also supposed to represent people who are innovative, achievement oriented, productive, cosmopolitan, media and politically aware, more globally (nationally and internationally) and less locally oriented, less likely to be perceived as having committed a crime, and more likely to take education and the rights and duties of citizenship seriously. The common popular and scholarly conception that standard English has such powerful effects as these constitutes what this researcher calls the "myth of standard English."

Despite the research, the people who use what are called nonstandard varieties of English (or any language), as AAL is often called, believe this as much as those who think they use this mythical standard English. We should not be surprised. In his *Pedagogy of the Oppressed* (1989), Paulo Freire rightly explicates how, after the revolution, the oppressed become the oppressors. How many African Americans have excoriated other African Americans for using AAL? How many children—like those who are left-handed or speak Spanish or Louisiana French Creole or Gullah or...—have been told not only by "those with the army and the navy" but their own people, that they are less than for being who they are, for living their sociocultural and historical contexts? Baldwin was right; however, what he failed to see was that the enemy was within as well as without.

African American communities self-hate because that is what society and history teaches. Being Black is not being White and not being White is, well, a problem. As DuBois said more than a hundred years ago in *The Souls of Black Folk* ([1903] 1994), "The problem of the Twentieth Century is the problem of the color-line (v)... How does it feel to be a problem? I answer seldom a word. And yet, being a problem is a strange experience,—peculiar even for one who has never been anything else" (1). Our hair is kinky/nappy/not good (see the comments about gymnast Gabby Douglas after winning a gold medal at the Olympics); our skin is ashy or dark (see the comments about Lupita Nyong'o being cast in the 2013 film adaptation of *Twelve Years a Slave* or, to the contrary, Zoe Saldana being cast as Nina Simone); our noses are big/broad; our butts are too big (see the endless comments about First Lady Michelle Obama); our language is undeveloped (see the comments about AAL being viewed as baby talk); our minds are feeble and our culture deficient (see for yourself the countless examples since I refuse to cite them); and so on. The "scholarship" on how American slave descendants and Blacks in general are less than, including with respect to their language, overwhelms anything to the contrary.

As a result, we have employers—Black and non-Black—who say they will not hire someone who pronounces *ask* as "aks" (a common pronunciation in AAL) or uses "double negatives" (*multiple negation*) because it represents faulty thinking (as if language were math) or who pronounces *four* as "foe" (again, common in AAL) or who just plain does not use "good" English (i.e., "bad" English is a synonym for AAL). Witness the testimony by Rachel Jeantel in the 2013 trial of George Zimmerman for the murder of teenager Trayvon Martin or the backlash against Richard Sherman of the Seattle Seahawks after his remarks following the 2013 NFC Championship game against the San Francisco

49ers. The social media comments linking language and intelligence, sanity, cleanliness, integrity, and just about anything else were swift, daunting, and shocking.

Smitherman's *Talkin and Testifyin* (1977) provides examples of how diminishing a child's language diminishes and ultimately silences the child (see, for example, 201-41). Hollie, Butler, and Gillenwaters (this volume) provide examples of how AAL has been handled in the classroom and how it can be changed. Baugh's *Out of the Mouths of Slaves* (1999) provides a long history of the miscarriages of justice against AAL in schools (i.e., malpractice) and society. And, despite its eloquence and authority, William Labov's "The Logic of Nonstandard English" (1972), a seminal article written more than forty years ago, still has not made enough impact to quash the illogic behind this linguistic prejudice. Ideologies and beliefs run deep, but, at some point, one has to ask, "Is it really about the language?"

> The person who talks right, as we do, is one of us. The person who talks wrong is an outsider, strange and suspicious, and we must make him feel inferior if we can. That is one purpose of education. In a school system run like ours by [W]hite businessmen, instruction in the mother tongue includes formal initiation into the linguistic prejudices of the middle class. (Sledd 1972, 320)

Mission accomplished.

Predictably, we maintain our own linguistic prejudice and self-indictment. We tell ourselves (and allow others to do the same) that African Americans who want an education, who want to learn, and who want to achieve more than who or what they are that they are "acting White" (see Fordham and Ogbu 1986, 1996). There are many ways I can think of for such a term, but to derogatorily identify African American who want something? If that is "acting White," what is acting Black?

48.3.2 Covert Prestige in the Midst of Linguistic Shame and Denial

In response to the Oakland school board's December 18, 1996, resolution to recognize "Ebonics" as the primary language of African American students in that California district, poet Maya Angelou told the *Wichita Eagle* that she was "incensed" and found the idea "very threatening." NAACP president Kweisi Mfume denounced the measure as "a cruel joke," and although he later adopted a friendlier stance, the Reverend Jesse Jackson on national television initially called it "an unacceptable surrender, borderlining on disgrace" (Rickford and Rickford 2000, 5).

This protest against AAL was not new. Benjamin Alexander (1979) said the following in response to the verdict by Judge Charles W. Joiner in the Black English Trial:

> I will not accept the legitimacy of Black English or any other kind of non-prescribed English. . . . If people cannot communicate in Standard English and have not developed their talents and skills—then who wants them? . . . I consider it a cheap insult

to see educational standards lowered in Ann Arbor schools—solely for [B]lack students. How can we justify recognition of their non-prescribed broken English and then ask teachers to learn it? (437–38)

As can be seen, the Oakland controversy was not new. It was a repeat of history that we are sure to see again because the issue has not been ethically, morally, equitably nor educationally, legally, or politically resolved. These differing opinions among African Americans represent a history of contradictions.

Well, you might ask, "Where were regular Black folk during these crises?" They too were denying the legitimacy of their language, culture, and history. Some of the very people who speak AAL everyday are some of its most vehement and vocal critics (see Hollie, Butler, and Gillenwaters, this volume, for the discontinuance of the Simpkins and Simpkins dialect readers through efforts of the African American community despite the success of the readers, all because of linguistic shame and denial). In "What Is African American English?" (2001), Mufwene relates the following incident during the Ebonics Controversy that exemplifies the contradiction:

> A young man in a congregation to which I was explaining the situation said in reference to Ebonics, perceived as the speech of "the ignorant" and gang members, "Ain't nobody here talk like that." His focus may not have been so much on those features in his own statement that make it obvious to a linguist that he speaks AAVE [African American Vernacular English] but on the kinds of words and communicative exchanges which are contained in several examples that linguists and the media have provided of what AAVE or Ebonics is. (35)

In a separate incident and as further evidence, the following conversation occurred primarily between an African American mother (G) and her oldest daughter (D) while her youngest daughter (S) tried to intervene. Both G and D strongly identify with the language and culture of the African American community and both use AAL:

G: I see they took Patti LaBelle's show off.
D: I know. I *likeded* that show.
G: Now what ø you sayinø that fuh?
S: It's supposed to be on next week.
G: That's <indecipherable> talking bout I "likeded" that show.
D: I say I *likeded* that show.
G: I liked. L-I-K-E-D.
S: It's coming on today.
G: Don't you go down there changing—acting—changing yo uh speech. That's two things—cause something else you said. "Those *tesses*." Better be trying to tell them. (Lanehart 2002, 178)

D's use of AAL seems to be offensive to G while, at the same time, G, like the speaker Mufwene (2001) refers to above, has no problem with her own use of AAL. G corrects D and tells her to be an example to others in the African American community when she returns to her hometown, which G clearly sees as less linguistically capable than where D currently lives.

There are many examples of linguistic shame and denial. For example, during the "Ebonics Controversy" when prominent members of the African American community such as Bill Cosby, Maya Angelou, Kweisi Mfume, and Jesse Jackson spoke against what the Oakland Unified School District Board was trying to accomplish for the well-being of African American children because they did not care about the educational benefit or outcomes amidst their blind denial of the—their—language under fire. They disregarded AAL with a passion as well as its politicization and racialization. They apparently apologetically, or maybe covertly, value AAL since they use it in their livelihoods and in their speech (e.g., Cosby in *Uptown Saturday Night, Let's Do It Again*, and *Fat Albert*; Angelou in every one of her poems; and Jackson in his rhetorical style that is right out of the Black church). Linguistic shame is powerful.

An irony in this contradiction of practice and belief is the fact that the language of African Americans has existed for hundreds of years. While AAL speakers deny the efficacy of AAL, they continue to use it—at home with family and friends, at church, at beauty and barber shops, in literature and song eloquently and without excuse, and, yes, at school—but most will not publicly accept it as legitimate expression outside their community other than to refer to it as colloquial or substandard or bad English. Clearly, there is an issue of covert prestige[2] involved because no matter how much some African Americans denigrate AAL and say that it is "bad" English, they continue to acquire and use it and pass it on within the African American community. For some African Americans, it is the only language they know (Ogbu 1999). This contradictory stance presents a conundrum in a day and time when salient characteristics (Rickford 1999) as opposed to the actual features (Green 2002) of the language and discourse practices (Mitchell-Kernan 1972; Morgan 1996, 2002) of the people are appropriated by non-African Americans for the purpose of making money, selling African American culture to the highest bidders and the hungriest consumers of our culture (e.g., Miley Cyrus twerking at the 2013 Video Music Awards and just about every Nike ad). The message seems to be that it is OK to act Black or mimic Blackness, but it is not OK to actually be Black and talk Black (see Smitherman 1994). It may be cool to show your swagger in certain places and spaces—when it is being appropriated and profited on by "Others"—but it is certainly not FUBU appropriate (i.e., For Us By Us, or if you are actually Black and a real-life, authentic AAL speaker).

I have provided several classic examples of how covert prestige works: love it behind closed doors or in the dark; hate it in the plain light of day or the bright white rays of light. If the African American community cannot and will not accept its own language variety and variation without hierarchy and prejudice, then who else will or should? To paraphrase Napoleon's revised commandment in George Orwell's *Animal Farm* (1945), "all language varieties are equal, but some are more equal than others" in the eyes of AAL speakers and (over)hearers.

48.3.3 Linguistic Pride and Acceptance

However, other African Americans say very different things about their language. Some realize the language and the people are inextricably linked, as evidenced in the work of Geneva Smitherman (see Smitherman 2000) and attested by Toni Morrison during an interview in response to the question, "What do you think is distinctive about your fiction? What makes it good?"

> *The language, only the language. . . .* It is the thing that [B]lack people love so much. . . . The worst of all possible things that could happen would be to lose that language. There are certain things I cannot say without recourse to my language. It's terrible to think that a child with five different present tenses comes to school to be faced with those books that are less than his own language. And then to be told things about his language, which is him, that are sometimes permanently damaging. (Morrison 1981, 27; emphasis added)

Toni Morrison is one of the few African American writers who unabashedly loves on her language, the language of African Americans, born out of necessity. While many past and present writers and artists use AAL as part of their creativity, Morrison is exceptional in the rhythm and expression of AAL. Langston Hughes and Zora Neal Hurston love AAL, but few do AAL like Morrison. The richness of AAL is described in Alim (this volume); DeBose (this volume); Kinloch (2011); Kirkland (2013, this volume); Paris (2011); Paris and Winn (2013); Rambsy and Whiteside (this volume); and Young et al. (2014); and, as noted earlier, anything done by Geneva Smitherman, "Dr. G." We see it in the creativity of youth, especially those immersed in Hip Hop and the evolution of Hip Hop in the classroom (see, for example, Jabari Mahiri's scholarship in addition to Alim's).

Gloria Anzaldúa's "How to Tame a Wild Tongue" ([1987] 2007) powerfully articulates where we stand—and have stood for so—on language differences, language identities, and language reclamation:

> Until I can take pride in my language, I cannot take pride in myself. Until I can accept as legitimate Chicano Texas Spanish, Tex-Mex and all the other languages I speak, I cannot accept the legitimacy of myself. Until I am free to write bilingually and to switch codes without having always to translate, while I still have to speak English or Spanish when I would rather speak Spanglish, and as long as I have to accommodate the English speakers rather than having them accommodate me, my tongue will be illegitimate. I will no longer be made to feel ashamed of existing. I will have my voice: Indian, Spanish, white. I will have my serpent's tongue—my woman's voice, my sexual voice, my poet's voice. I will overcome the tradition of silence. (81)

In spite of a love-hate relationship enmeshed in a history of degradation and covert prestige, we do language well.

48.4 Our Language Selves

I have discussed various aspects of the language perspectives of African Americans: Linguistic Prejudice; Linguistic Shame and Denial; and Linguistic Pride and Acceptance. Now I want to provide a process for identity self-deconstruction among the language reality we live every day. Mura (1992) provides a basis for the need for self-deconstruction:

> What I am trying to do in both my writing and my life is to replace self-hatred and self-negation with anger and grief over my lost selves, over *the ways my cultural heritage has been denied to me*, over the ways that people in America would assume either that I am not American, or conversely, that I am just like them; over *the ways my education and the values of European culture have denied that other cultures exist*. I know more about Europe at the time when my grandfather came to America than I know about Meiji Japan. I know Shakespeare and Donne, Sophocles and Homer better than I know Zeami, Basho or Lady Murasaki. *This is not to say I regret what I know, but I do regret what I don't know.* (17; emphasis added)

Many people who speak a variety of language that is not valued or held in esteem share Mura's sentiment of denial, regret, and loss. For example, in addition to AAL, Louisiana French Creole and Cajun, Spanish, and Native American language speakers have historically been asked to deny or hide their native languages while embracing and valuing American English and culture over all else—as if it were exceptional. Such students have historically been asked to not speak their language in school—or risk punishment (physical, emotional, and psychological). Parents hid their native languages from their children, so they would not speak English with an accent, and teachers tried to beat it out of them (see Lippi-Green 2012). And, yet, those languages and people persist.

We are taught to hold linguistic prejudice, self-denial, and hatred as part of our ongoing post-traumatic slave syndrome[3] (DeGruy 2005). It is one of the few things dispersed equitably among the population through schools and communities and policies. As African Americans (or Mexicans or Latin@s or any "foreigner"), the person not like "US," regardless if "they" have actually lived in and been in these lands for centuries, we come to realize very early that we are not part of the "some." That privilege belongs to those who have the army and the navy. We (i.e., those not born into the "US" and not easily accepted into it and told to go back to whence we came—even if that actually is right here in the good ole "US" of A) have been told that if we speak like the "US," we will be OK. However, research has already shown that "underlying grammatical patterns of standard English are apparently learned through 'meaning' and intensive interaction with those who already use standard English grammar, not simply by exposure in the mass media or in schools" (Labov and Harris 1983, 22). Consequently, "[B]lacks who move in [W]hite circles show a major shift in their grammar in the direction of the [W]hite norm, but the same is not true for [W]hites who move in [B]lack circles" (Ash and Myhill 1983, 16). You can't just catch it; you have to live it.

Tabouret-Keller's (1997, 323) discussion about identity better explains this situation:

An individual's ability to get into focus with those with whom he wishes to identify is constrained. One can only behave according to the behavioral patterns of groups one finds it desirable to identify with to the extent that:

(a) one can identify the groups (see Le Page 1986; Markus and Nurius 1986);
(b) one has both adequate access to the groups and ability to analyze their behavioral patterns (see Labov and Harris 1983; Ash and Myhill 1983);
(c) the motivation for joining the group is sufficiently powerful, and is either reinforced or lessened by feedback from the group (see Le Page 1986; Markus and Nurius 1986);
(d) we have the ability to modify our behavior (see Ogbu 1999).

Hence, there is a sense of community at the same time there is otherness. We choose to be part of groups, groups choose us, and others say we are part of some other group and not theirs. Why? I suggest there are two language realities for this situation: Le Page's "Acts of Identity" (see above) and Hazel Markus's "Possible Selves."

> Possible selves represent individuals' ideas of what they might become, what they would like to become, and what they are afraid of becoming, and thus provide a conceptual link between cognition and motivation. . . . *An individual is free to create any variety of possible selves, yet the pool of possible selves derives from the categories made salient by the individual's particular sociocultural and historical context and from the models, images, and symbols provided by the media and by the individual's immediate social experiences.* Possible selves thus have the potential to reveal the inventive and constructive nature of the self but they also reflect the extent to which the self is socially determined and constrained. (Markus and Nurius 1986, 954; emphasis added)

Acts of Identity and *Possible Selves* together represent our language identity and our language selves (Lanehart 1996, 1998; see Lanehart 2002 for more details). As African Americans, we hold a certain socioculture and sociohistory that is uniquely ours. While this relates to double consciousness (DuBois [1903] 1994; Smitherman 1977) or multiple consciousness and multiple jeopardy (King 1988), we can also think about this in sociopsychological terms: We have ways of speaking and communicating that are derived from our experiences. How that language manifests itself depends more on our degree of identity with particular aspects of our language selves and how we see ourselves in micro and macro ways than it does with the person we may be speaking to at a given moment. How we present ourselves linguistically stems from our identity, but that identity is composed of our past, current, and future possible selves as well as space (i.e., where we are and where we want to be) and place (who we are and who we want to be—or don't want to be since our feared possible selves are as important as our hoped for possible selves). We "act" as we see fit; but it is based on a more holistic perspective of how we see ourselves and the world around us (for a keen description of Barack Obama's deftness in doing language, see Alim and Smitherman 2012).

48.5 Conclusions

Continued research in AAL and identity has expanded over the last few decades and become more inclusive by expanding its understanding and definition of AAL, such that there is now research on women (Lanehart 2009; Morgan, this volume); children (Champion and McCabe, this volume; Green 2011; Green and White-Sustaíta, this volume; Newkirk-Turner, Horton, and Stockman, this volume; Oetting, this volume; Van Hofwegen, this volume; Wyatt, this volume); rural areas (Cukor-Avila and Bailey, this volume); different classes (Britt and Weldon, this volume); and different repertoires (Spears 1988, this volume). I hope to see identity research expand more into gender and sexuality (there is a paucity of research on African American lesbian or gay identified speakers) and religion (we know not all AAL speakers are Christians or part of the traditional Black church).

Nevertheless, based on past and current research, I can draw some conclusions about language and identity in the African American community.

1. The conflict between the language of identity and education and society is evident with many African Americans, especially those with access to or immersion in higher education. We are convincingly told that who we are—African American Language speakers—is not who we should want to be. Some conform to this ideology and some do not—none should have to.

2. African Americans will continue to speak the language of their community despite antagonistic pressures socially, economically, educationally, and otherwise. We can continue to produce generations of African Americans who have a love-hate relationship with the very essence of who they are because they are made to believe that, though they cannot change the color of their skin, things will be better for them if they can just change the color of their language—benefiting no one—or we can encourage a people who have been only discouraged and scorned to accept who they are and demand that others do the same—benefiting all.

We share our language of identity with those we choose, and we keep it from those who are not worthy of our community or who are just simply not part of our community. We do not have anything to prove, but we have everything to gain. We have a community that has stood the test of time, torment, and terror—and still we rise (Angelou 1978):

> Out of the huts of history's shame
> I rise
> Up from a past that's rooted in pain
> I rise
> I'm a black ocean, leaping and wide....
> Bringing the gifts that my ancestors gave,
> I am the dream and the hope of the slave.
> I rise.

NOTES

1. NORM is an acronym that stands for "non-mobile older rural male." Dialectologists usually selected NORMs because their goal was to select uneducated, untraveled participants who were "unspoiled" speakers of the region. That meant no women, Blacks, people of color, and so on.

2. Baugh (1999, 131) describes covert prestige as the belief by AAVE speakers, or any devalued variety, that their language is "bad" even though they tacitly value it as seen in their continued use of it in their speech and their appreciation of it in their music (e.g., jazz, blues, and rap), literature, and other verbal art forms.

3. *Post-Traumatic Slave Syndrome* <http://joydegruy.com/resources-2/post-traumatic-slave-syndrome/> is a theory that explains the etiology of many of the adaptive survival behaviors in African American communities throughout the United States and the Diaspora. It is a condition that exists as a consequence of multigenerational oppression of Africans and their descendants resulting from centuries of chattel slavery, a form of slavery that was predicated on the belief that African Americans were inherently/genetically inferior to whites. This was then followed by institutionalized racism that continues to perpetuate injury. Thus, resulting in M.A.P.:

   M: Multigenerational trauma together with continued oppression;
   A: Absence of opportunity to heal or access the benefits available in the society; leads to
   P: Post Traumatic Slave Syndrome

   Under such circumstances, these are some of the predictable patterns of behavior that tend to occur: vacant esteem, literacy deprivation, distorted self-concept, antipathy or aversion for the following:
   - the members of one's own identified cultural/ethnic group;
   - the mores and customs associated with one's own identified cultural/ethnic heritage;
   - the physical characteristics of one's own identified cultural/ethnic group.

REFERENCES

Alexander, Benjamin H. 1979. "Standard English: To Hell with Anything Else." South Bend: Fellows, American Council on Education, 437–40.

Alim, H. Samy, and John Baugh. 2007. *Talkin' Black Talk: Language, Education, and Social Change*. New York: Teachers College Press.

Alim, H. Samy, and Geneva Smitherman. 2012. *Articulate While Black: Barack Obama, Language, and Race in the U.S.* Oxford: Oxford University Press.

Angelou, Maya. 1978. "Still I Rise." In *And Still I Rise: A Book of Poems*, by Maya Angelou. New York: Random House.

Anzaldúa, Gloria. [1987] 2007. "How to Tame a Wild Tongue." In *Borderlands/La Frontera: The New Mestiza*, 3rd ed., edited by Joan Pinkvoss, 75–86. San Francisco: Aunt Lute Books.

Ash, Sharon, and John Myhill. 1983. "Linguistic Correlates of Interethnic Contact." Paper presented at the Twelfth Annual Conference of New Ways of Analyzing Variation, Montreal, Canada, October 27–29.

Baldwin, James. 1979. "If Black English Isn't a Language, then Tell Me, What Is?" *New York Times*, July 29, 19E.

Banks, Adam J. 2011. *Digital Griots: African American Rhetoric in a Multimedia Age*. Carbondale: Southern Illinois University Press.

Baugh, John. 1999. *Out of the Mouths of Slaves: African American Language and Educational Malpractice*. Austin: University of Texas.

———. 2000. *Beyond Ebonics*. New York: Oxford University.

Benor, Sarah B. 2010. "Ethnolinguistic Repertoire: Shifting the Analytic Focus in Language and Ethnicity." *Journal of Sociolinguistics* 14 (3): 159–83.

Dark Girls. 2011. Directed/produced by D. Channsin Berry and Bill Duke. Documentary film. Chatsworth, CA: Image Entertainment. http://officialdarkgirlsmovie.com/.

DeGruy, Joy. 2005. *Post-Traumatic Slave Syndrome: America's Legacy of Enduring Injury and Healing*. Joy DeGruy.

Delpit, Lisa, and Joanne Kilgour Dowdy, eds. 2008. *The Skin that We Speak: Thoughts on Language and Culture in the Classroom*. New York: New Press.

DuBois, W. E. B. [1903] 1994. *The Souls of Black Folk*. Mineola, NY: Dover.

Dunbar, Paul Laurence. 1895. "We Wear the Mask." In *Majors and Minors: Poems*, by Paul Laurence Dunbar, 21. Toledo, OH: Hadley and Hadley.

Fat Albert and the Cosby Kids. 1972-1984. Created by Bill Cosby and Ken Mundie. Animated television series. New York: CBS Television.

Fisher, Maisha T. 2007. *Writing in Rhythm: Spoken Word Poetry in Urban Classrooms*. New York: Teachers College.

Fordham, Signithia, and John U. Ogbu. 1986. "Black Students' School Success: Coping with the 'Burden of "Acting White." ' " *The Urban Review* 18 (3): 176–206.

———. 1996. *Blacked out: Dilemmas of Race, Identity, and Success at Capital High*. Chicago: University of Chicago Press.

Freed, Richard D., ed. 1995. *Eloquent Dissent: The Writings of James Sledd*. Portsmouth, NH: Heinemann.

Freire, Paolo. 1989. *Pedagogy of the Oppressed*. Translated by Myra Bergman Ramos. New York: Continuum.

Gee, James. 1990. *Social Linguistics and Literacies: Ideology in Discourse*. London: Falmer.

Gilyard, Keith. 1991. *Voices of the Self: A Study of Language Competence*. Detroit, MI: Wayne State University.

———. 2011. *True to the Language Game: African American Discourse, Cultural Politics, and Pedagogy*. New York: Routledge.

Good Hair. 2008. Directed by Jeff Stilson. Produced by Chris Rock. Documentary film. Santa Monica, CA: Lionsgate. DVD.

Green, Lisa J. 2002. *African American English: A Linguistic Introduction*. Cambridge: Cambridge University.

———. 2011. *Language and the African American Child*. Cambridge: Cambridge University.

Hopson, Rodney. 2003. "The Problem of the Language Line: Cultural and Social Reproduction of Hegemonic Linguistic Structures for Learners of African Descent in the United States." *Race, Ethnicity, and Education* 6 (3): 227–45.

Jackson, Ronald L., II, ed. 2004. *African American Communication and Identities: Essential Readings*. Thousand Oaks, CA: Sage.

Jacobs-Huey, Lanita. 2006. *From the Kitchen to the Parlor: Language and Becoming in African American Women's Hair Care*. Oxford: Oxford University.

King, Deborah K. 1988. "Multiple Jeopardy, Multiple Consciousness: The Context of a Black Feminist Ideology." *Signs* 14 (1): 42–72.

Kinloch, Valerie. 2011. *Urban Literacies: Critical Perspectives on Language, Learning, and Communities*. New York: Teachers College.

Kirkland, David. 2013. *A Search Past Silence: The Literacy of Young Black Men*. New York: Teachers College.

Labov, William. 1972. "The Logic of Nonstandard English." In *Language in the Inner City: Studies in the Black English Vernacular*, by William Labov, 201–40. Philadelphia: University of Pennsylvania Press.

Labov, William, and Wendell Harris. 1983. "DeFacto Segregation of Black and White Vernaculars." Paper presented at the Twelfth Annual Conference of New Ways of Analyzing Variation, Montreal, Canada, October 27–29.

Lanehart, Sonja L. 1996. "The Language of Identity." *Journal of English Linguistics* 24 (4): 322–31.

———. 1998. "Our Language, Our Selves." *Journal of Commonwealth and Postcolonial Studies* 4 (1): 24–36.

———, ed. 2001. *Sociocultural and Historical Contexts of African American English*. Amsterdam: John Benjamins.

———. 2002. *Sista, Speak! Black Women Kinfolk Talk about Language and Literacy*. Austin: University of Texas.

———. 2007. "If Our Children Are Our Future, Why Are We Stuck in the Past? Beyond the Anglicists and the Creolists, and toward Social Change." In *Talkin' Black Talk: Language, Education, and Social Change*, edited by H. Samy Alim and John Baugh, 132–41. New York: Teachers College.

———, ed. 2009. *African American Women's Language: Discourse, Education, and Identity*. Newcastle-Upon-Tyne: Cambridge Scholars.

Le Page, Robert B. 1986. "Acts of Identity." *English Today* 8: 21–24.

Le Page, Robert B., and Andrée Tabouret-Keller. 1985. *Acts of Identity: Creole-Based Approaches to Language and Ethnicity*. Cambridge: Cambridge University.

Let's Do It Again. 1975. Film. Directed by Sidney Poitier. Burbank, CA: Warner Bros.

Lippi-Green, Rosina. 2012. *English with an Accent: Language, Ideology, and Discrimination in the United States*. 2nd ed. New York: Routledge.

Markus, Hazel, and Paula Nurius. 1986. "Possible Selves." *American Psychologist* 41: 954–69.

Marshall, Paule. 1983. *Reena and Other Stories*. New York: Feminist Press.

Martin Luther King Junior Elementary School Children v. The Michigan Board of Education, the Michigan Superintendent of Public Instruction and the Ann Arbor School District Board, 1979. Civil Action No. 77–71861 U.S. District Court Eastern District of Michigan Southern Division.

Mitchell-Kernan, Claudia. 1972. "Signifyin, Loud-Talking, and Marking." In *Rappin' and Stylin' out: Communication in Urban Black America*, edited by Thomas Kochman, 315–35. Urbana: University of Illinois.

Morgan, Marcyliena. 1996. "Conversational Signifying: Grammar and Indirectness among African American Women." In *Interaction and Grammar*, edited by Elinor Ochs, Emanuel Schegloff, and Sandra A. Thompson, 405–33. Cambridge: Cambridge University.

———. 2002. *Language, Discourse and Power in African American Culture*. Cambridge: Cambridge University.

———. 2003. "Signifying Laughter and the Subtleties of Loud-Talking: Memory and Meaning in African American Women's Discourse." In *Ethnolinguistic Chicago: Language and Literacy in Chicago's Neighborhoods*, edited by Marcia Farr, 51–76. Mahwah, NJ: Lawrence Erlbaum.

Morrison, Toni. 1981. "A Conversation with Toni Morrison. 'The Language Must Not Sweat.'" Interview by Thomas LeClair. *New Republic*, March 21, 25–29.

———. 1993. *The Nobel Lecture in Literature*. New York: Random House.

Mufwene, Salikoko. 2001. "What is African American English?" In *Sociocultural and Historical Contexts of African American English*, edited by Sonja L. Lanehart, 21–51. Amsterdam: John Benjamins.

Mura, David. 1992. "Strangers in the Village." In *Race, Class, and Gender: An Anthology*, edited by Margaret L. Andersen and Patricia Hill Collins, 11–20. Belmont, CA: Wadsworth.

Ogbu, John U. 1978. *Minority Education and Caste: The American System in Cross-Cultural Perspective*. New York: Academic.

———. 1999. "Beyond Language: Ebonics, Proper English, and Identity in a Black-American Speech Community." *American Educational Research Journal* 36 (2): 147–84.

Orwell, George. 1945. *Animal Farm: A Fairy Story*. London: Secker and Warburg.

Paris, Django. 2011. *Language across Difference: Ethnicity, Communication, and Youth Identities in Changing Urban Schools*. Cambridge: Cambridge University.

Paris, Django, and Maisha T. Winn, eds. 2013. *Humanizing Research: Decolonizing Qualitative Inquiry with Youth and Communities*. Thousand Oaks, CA: Sage.

Richardson, Elaine. 2013. *PHD (Po H# on Dope) to Ph.D.: How Education Saved My Life*. New York: New City Community.

Rickford, John R. 1999. *African American Vernacular English: Features, Evolution, Educational Implications*. Oxford: Basil Blackwell.

Rickford, John R., and Russell J. Rickford. 2000. *Spoken Soul: The Story of Black English*. New York: John Wiley & Sons.

Sledd, James. 1972. "Bi-Dialectalism: The Linguistics of White Supremacy." In *Contemporary English*, edited by David Shores, 319–30. Philadelphia: Lippincott.

———. 1984. "Doublespeak: Dialectology in the Service of Big Brother." *College English* 33 (4): 439–56.

Smitherman, Geneva. 1977. *Talkin and Testifyin: The Language of Black America*. Detroit, MI: Wayne State University.

———. 1994. *Black Talk: Words and Phrases from the Hood to the Amen Corner*. New York: Houghton Mifflin.

———. 2000. *Talkin that Talk: Language, Culture and Education in African America*. New York: Routledge.

———. 2001. "Foreword." In *Sociocultural and Historical Contexts of African American English*, edited by Sonja L. Lanehart, ix. Amsterdam: John Benjamins.

———. 2006. *Word from the Mother: Language and African Americans*. New York: Routledge.

Spears, Arthur K. 1988. "Black American English." In *Anthropology for the Nineties*, edited by Johnnetta B. Cole, 96–113. New York: Free Press.

———. 2001. "Directness in the Use of African American English." In *Sociocultural and Historical Contexts of African American English*, edited by Sonja L. Lanehart, 239–60. Amsterdam: John Benjamins.

Tabouret-Keller, Andrée. 1997. "Language and Identity." In *The Handbook of Sociolinguistics*, edited by Florian Coulmas, 315–26. Oxford: Blackwell.

Twelve Years a Slave. 2013. Directed by Steve McQueen. Century City, CA: Fox Searchlight Pictures.

Uptown Saturday Night. 1974. Directed by Sidney Poitier. Burbank, CA: Warner Bros.

Walker, Alice. 1982. *The Color Purple*. New York: Harcourt Brace Jovanovich.

Wise, Tim. 2010. *Colorblind: The Rise of Post-Racial Politics and the Retreat from Racial Equity*. San Francisco: City Lights Books.

———. 2011. *White like Me: Reflections on Race from a Privileged Son*. Berkeley, CA: Soft Skull.

———. 2012. *Dear, White America: Letter to a New Minority*. San Francisco: City Lights Books.

Wolfram, Walt, and Erik R. Thomas. 2008. *The Development of African American English*. Oxford: Blackwell.

Young, Vershawn Ashanti, Rusty Barrett, Y'Shanda Young-Rivera, and Kim Brian Lovejoy. 2014. *Other People's English: Code-Meshing, Code-Switching, and African American Literacy*. New York City: Teachers College Press.

AUTHOR INDEX

Subject Index